REVENUE

The author and publisher acknowledge with gratitude the permission granted by Butterworths to use material published in the UK Tax Guide in the preparation of this book. The copyright in such material is held by Butterworths.

The publisher also acknowledges the permission granted by the Stationery office and the OECD to reproduce materials which appear in Chapter 6.

Revenue Law

JOHN TILEY

Professor of Taxation Law
and Fellow of Queens' College
University of Cambridge

• HART •
PUBLISHING
OXFORD – PORTLAND, OREGON
2000

Hart Publishing
Oxford and Portland, Oregon

Published in North America (US and Canada) by
Hart Publishing c/o
International Specialized Book Services
5804 NE Hassalo Street
Portland, Oregon
97213-3644
USA

Distributed in the Netherlands, Belgium and Luxembourg by
Intersentia, Churchillaan 108
B2900 Schoten
Antwerpen
Belgium

First published 2000, Reprinted 2001, 2004

Hart Publishing Ltd is a specialist legal publisher based in Oxford, England.
To order further copies of this book or to request a list of other publications please write to:

Hart Publishing Ltd, Salter's Boatyard, Folly Bridge,
Abingdon Road, Oxford OX1 4LB
Telephone: +44 (0)1865 245533 or Fax: +44 (0)1865 794882
e-mail: mail@hartpub.co.uk
www.hartpub.co.uk

British Library Cataloguing in Publication Data
Data Available
ISBN 1 84113–152–0 (cloth)

Typeset by Hope Services (Abingdon) Ltd.
Printed in Great Britain by Lightning Source Ltd.

Preface

The appearance of a fourth edition of a book 19 years after the appearance of the third calls for some explanation. That it appears at all is due first and pre-eminently to the magnificent and disinterested generosity of Butterworths who have given me a free hand to reproduce material which has already appeared both in Revenue Law and in the UK Tax Guide and which is their copyright. I have taken full advantage of this permission so that the text of the Tax Guide has been lightly pruned rather than butchered. Thanks are due also to the bold spirit which is Hart Publishing who have speculated that this book is worth a new edition. As some may be able to recall, the first edition of Revenue Law was published, by Butterworths, in 1976 and the third in 1981. Since 1981 the technical part of the text has appeared, with annual updatings, sometimes by me and sometimes by others, as part of Butterworths UK Tax Guide (and more recently as Tiley and Collison's UK Tax Guide). However the historical, comparative and policy settings were all discarded and although bleeding chunks of that material were published as a separate almost 100 page Policy Supplement (until 1995-96) which Butterworths generously distributed without charge, this was generally agreed to be no substitute.

The immediate objective of those early editions was to produce a textbook designed for university law students to learn the subject in the way I thought was the right one. A more remote objective was to try to raise the status and standing of tax law in law faculties. As the new millennium breaks and tax is seen to be trying to make a more substantial presence in law curricula it seems right to me to make one more—and probably last—effort.

My view of the way in which students should study tax law remains a broad and demanding one. First and foremost there must be technical competence with a good grasp of the primary sources. That competence can be tested in many ways ranging from elementary computation to planning transactions. However the tax student must demonstrate more than technical competence in the current materials. Our subject moves so fast that a failure to understand why things change or have changed or may change in the future will produce someone who has been trained rather than educated, a monkey rather than a Socrates—with due apologies to the monkey. It is for this reason that this book contains much citation of secondary material which in turn ranges from articles in the British Tax Review to the policy discussions in the publications of the Institute for Fiscal Studies. However the material also hints at the riches available to a study of comparative taxation (whether or not strictly up to date), much is to be learnt from the experience of others. And yet I finish this book aware that the footnotes can only hint at the literature available out there. I am conscious that I have not cited much from the accounting literature available in the UK and that I have preferred to use the footnotes to cite American law review articles rather than domestic accounting ones. This has been a deliberate choice – the book is long enough already.

Naturally tax studied to this depth requires a one year's masters course of its own, which will soon become more common, but I hope that parts of the book can be used to provide material for a one year introduction to tax course for undergraduates. Experience shows that while Part III on Capital Gains Tax, Part IV on Corporation Tax and Part IX on Inheritance Tax can all be studied in detail there is much of use in the first two or three chapters of each part. I am all too aware that there is nothing on VAT, Stamp Duty or NICs – but fortunately there is much material on these in Tiley and Collison's UK Tax Guide.

Looking back on these efforts of the last three years I am aware of many changes since 1976 and that first edition. First, there has been the appearance of several students books, some very good such as Whitehouse (edited by a team of five) and Shipwright and Keeling (edited by a team of two). This book is longer, more detailed, more policy based and tries to refer to the legal literature in a traditional, not to say old fashioned, way.

Secondly, there have been changes which have driven this book to its present terrible length. These changes start with the deluge of primary legislative material which can be chronicled/tracked in the ever-rising number of pages in Butterworths Yellow Tax Handbook. Likewise there has been an increase in the provision of official information, notably the Inland Revenue Manuals. This book mentions some of these sources but does not try to be exhaustive in such matters – which can be tracked in the notes to the sections in Butterworths Tax Handbooks – since its purpose is to enable the reader to discover what the statute says and neither what the Revenue says the statute says nor how the Revenue proposes to soften the words which they have persuaded Parliament to enact.

Thirdly, there has been the development of the computer and word processing packages. A boon to authors and a curse to publishers and readers, these developments make it too easy to write at length. I have not listed websites and yet these are now probably used at least as much as books. Tax law students may be lucky enough to have access to a commercial website such as Butterworths Tax Service for UK tax law but they can also look at the website for the Institute for Fiscal Studies www.ifs.org, from which there are links to many other sites, including all official UK ones. Finance Departments of other countries have their own websites such as the Canadian Ministry of National Revenue and Australia where the ATAX site is also particularly helpful, as do international organisations, whether official such as the OECD in Paris (www.oecd.org) or charitable such as the IBFD in Amsterdam (www.ibfd.nl). From this point on one can spend far too much time browsing instead of thinking but that does not stop it being fun.

Fourthly, there has been the developing influence of European Community Law and the more recent incursion of Human Rights Law. This has meant not only deep structural challenges such as those posed by Vanistendael (below p. 762) but also the constant threat of challenge to our legislation by the courts (chapter 2).

Fifthly, there has been the effort of our own courts to control avoidance (chapter 5). This story is a long way from being done but is nonetheless fascinating. Unfortunately it can distract attention from other and no less important areas.

Finally, perhaps the most intriguing changes have been political. Returning to 1981 has been like visiting a half forgotten world in which tax was based on perceptions or misperceptions of equity rather than neutrality and where high marginal tax rates of income tax (just reduced from 98% and 83% to 75% and 60%) and of Capital Transfer Tax (with a top rate of 75% so that tax could be three times the value of the net benefit received) were the norm—and the fact of trade union power a matter for democratic concern and social fact. We had accepted such things either because they were part of the postwar consensus which Mrs Thatcher was about to dismantle or because the system had so many loopholes that the fierceness was false. There are also social changes and especially those which lie behind the rules on the taxation of the family; here the changes have been in the direction of making marriage less important and concentrating either on the state of living together or the presence of children. To what extent these changes are responses to the values of a younger political elite and to what extent to the fear of challenge under non-discrimination rules is a tale waiting to be told when the Revenue files are opened or, less plausibly, when the politicians write their memoirs. I have tried to rewrite the text by reference to today's obsessions, economic and social, but were another edition to be written in twenty year's time it will no doubt have just as much change to record.

There never is a right time to stop writing a book on tax law. Since the draft of this text was completed, the OECD has produced a new commentary to its double tax treaty, we have been promised a new Capital Allowances Bill based on the work of the Tax Law Rewrite committee, there have been decisions of the courts (I have taken account only of two or three important ones since May). Reference is also made to the Limited Liability Partnerships Act 2000 which is to come into force from a date to be announced. The publishers have worked very hard to take account of these changes. We even have a provision in this year's Finance Act which does not come into force until 2002–03. This relates to the rules on car benefit (p. 294) It will be seen that the current rules encourage high business mileages; indeed the notes to the Finance Bill 1999 suggested that as many as 300million extra business miles were driven. Under the new rules (FA 2000 Sch 11) which are to apply as from April 2002, based on a mixture of the price of the car and a level of CO_2 emissions. In 2002-03 the lowest charge is set at 165gms per kilometre but this to be lowered in later years. The CO2 figure is then used to find a percentage on a table (minimum 15%); the taxable benefit is that percentage of the price of the car. An expensive car with high CO_2 emissions and high business mileage will have a higher tax charge than now; an expensive car with low emissions and a low business mileage may well be cheaper than now. A cheap car with low CO2 emissions will certainly be cheaper than now. Mondeo man driving an average business mileage may well find little difference. Special rules apply to diesels (a surcharge applies) and to other special types of car such as bi-fuel and electric cars. One waits to see what will happen in 2002. Other changes made in FA 2000 e.g. on Enterprise Management Incentives and on Mixer companies are likely to be amended next year.

One of the author's more pleasant tasks is that of thanking those who have helped to get this book before the public. Apart from giving thanks to Butterworths for their support and permissions and to Richard Hart himself for his unending care and encouragement, I must thank Richard's staff and especially Hannah Young who probably now knows more tax law than she ever hopes to need. Thanks are also due to my colleagues here in Cambridge, principally for their forbearance, to the staff of the Squire Library especially David Wills and Peter Zawada and to those computer specialists who have coped with me and my requests especially Sarah Kitching and Andrew Gerrard. Thanks are due to the University of Cambridge, especially for its enlightened policy on sabbatical leave, to the Law School of Case Western Reserve University, Cleveland, Ohio and the Research School of Social Science at the Australian National University, Canberra, where I spent sabbatical terms, and to the University of Michigan where I was able to try out some of my ideas in a comparative tax law seminar during a short visit. Thanks are due also to the Institute for Fiscal Studies for countless lectures and seminars.

Thanks are due also to my many tax friends in the United Kingdom and elsewhere who in one way or another have assisted me, whether indirectly by their writings, seminar participations and conference addresses or directly by conversations and discussion. Their names are recorded in the footnotes but I must make special mention of John Avery Jones, David Oliver and Malcolm Gammie who have shown, like Ash Wheatcroft before them, that the boundary between the academic and the practical does not have to exist in this area. David Oliver kindly read Part VIII but the mistakes, deliberate or accidental, remain my own.

It is customary to dedicate a book. It was tempting to dedicate it to those apparently tireless Inland Revenue officers who work so hard to make our tax system work, or to those taxpayers who have managed not only to complete their tax forms correctly, i.e. without Revenue corrections, but also to calculate their tax correctly using the Revenue's own calculation forms, But these might have seemed sycophantic or frivolous. Instead this book is dedicated, as it should be, to my family and so with thanks to my wife, Jillinda, and our three children, Nicholas, Christopher and Mary, with special apologies to Mary in that, while her (elder) brothers chose the colours for the second and third editions, she should have been deprived for so long of her right to choose the colour for this the fourth.

JT
Cambridge
5 November 2000

Contents

PART III CAPITAL GAINS TAX

PART IV CORPORATION TAX

PART V CHARITIES

PART VI SAVINGS

PART VII ANTI-AVOIDANCE

PART VIII INTERNATIONAL

List of Abbreviations

AAP	annuity and annual payment
ACE	allowance for capital equity
ACT	advanced corporation tax
AESS 2000	all-employee share scheme
APSS	approved profit-sharing scheme
BES	business expansion scheme
CAA 1990	Capital Allowances Act 1990
CBA	chargeable business assets
CDT	capital disposal tax
CEN	capital export neutrality
CFC	contolled foreign company
CGT	capital gains tax
CGTA 1979	Capital Gains Taxes Act 1979
CIN	capital import neutrality
CIT	comprehensive income tax
CPM	comparable profits method
CTT	capital transfer tax
CUP	comparable uncontrolled price
DLT	development land tax
DLTA 1976	Development Land Tax Act 1976
DTR	Department for Transport and the Regions
ECJ	European Court of Justice
EIS	enterprise investment scheme
EMI	enterprise management incentive
EMU	European Monetary Union
ESC	Extra Statutory Concession
ESOP	employee share ownership plan
ET	expenditure tax
F(No. 2)A	Finance (No. 2) Act
FA	Finance Act
FII	franked investment income
FOREX	foreign exchange
FRS	financial reporting standard
GDP	Gross domestic product
GNP	gross national product
GWR	gift with reservation
ICAEW	Institute of chartered Accountants in England and Wales
IFS	Institute of Fiscal Studies
IHT	inheritance tax
IHTA 1994	Inheritance Tax Act 1984
ISA	interest savings account
MPS	money purchase scheme
NAFTA	North American Free Trade Agreement
NICs	National Insurance Contributions

NR	non resident
OECD	Organisation for Economic Co-operation and Development
OEIC	open-ended investment company
PA 1989	Pensions Act 1989
PAYE	pay as you earn
PCTA 1968	Provisional Collection of Taxes Act 1968
PEP	personal equity plan
PET	potentially exempt transfer
PRP	profit-related pay
PRs	personal representatives
QCB	qualifying corporate bonds
QUEST	qualifying employee share trust
RDS	relevant discounted security
SIS	share incentive scheme
SP	Statement of Practice
SSAP	Statement of Standard Accounting Practice
TA 1988	Taxes Act 1988
TCGA 1992	Taxation of Capital Gains Act 1992
TEC	Training and Enterprise Council
TMA 1970	Taxes Management Act 1970
TSS	terminal salary scheme
UET	universal expenditure tax
UnASOS	unapproved share option scheme
USM	Unlisted Stock Market
VAT	value added tax
VATA 1984	Value Added Tax Act 1984
VCT	venture capital trust
WFTC	working families tax credit

Table of Cases

Table of Legislation

The old numberings are in brackets.

1. INTERNATIONAL

2. COUNCIL OF EUROPE

3. EUROPEAN COMMUNITIES

4. UNITED KINGDOM

Secondary legislation

5. OTHER JURISDICTIONS

PART I

Introduction

1

Definitions and Theories

1.1 A Tax

1.1.1 Definitions

With the advent of devolution of taxing powers within the UK in 1999 and the UK's membership of the European Community since 1973 it may one day become necessary for UK courts to define what they mean by a tax, something already attempted in other countries.[1] The *Oxford English Dictionary* defines a tax as "a compulsory contribution to the support of government levied on persons, property, income, commodities, transactions etc, now at a fixed rate mostly proportionate to the amount on which the contribution is levied". This, when stripped of its limited view as to the purpose of taxation, its irrelevant description of the tax base and its undue stress on proportionate as opposed to progressive taxation, tells

[1] The matter may have arisen in some contexts already, e.g. the rule that a foreign revenue law will not be enforced by the UK courts, but the analysis so far is rudimentary (see chapter 59 below). The Scotland Act 1998 gives the Assembly powers to vary the income tax rate for Scottish taxpayers (see ss 73–80) but gives no other taxing power; for financial provision, see ss 64–72. On the "Tartan Tax", see Heald and Geaughan [1997] *BTR* 337; in the 1970s the Kilbrandon Report had rejected financial devolution: Cmnd 5460, ch. 15.

us very little, beyond the fact that taxes are compulsory. To this criterion one may add that taxes are imposed under the authority of the legislature levied by a public body and that they are intended for public purposes.[2]

1.1.2 Charging for services

These criteria become clearer when distinguishing a tax from a charge for a government service.[3] First, some service must be provided directly to the individual if the payment is to be a charge for a government service.[4] There is a substantial difference between paying a road toll and paying a tax to be used for the defence of one's country. Secondly, the charge must be related to the service given, and not varied according to the person's ability to pay or to some other criterion such as the value of that person's property.[5] Therefore, the Canadian courts have held that provincial probate fees which varied with the size of the estate were taxes; they were intended to raise money for the court administration in general, not just to offset the actual costs of probate.[6] The Supreme Court of Canada underlined this point by suspending the declaration of invalidity for six months to prevent the immediate deprivation of an important source of revenue; invoking principles of restitution the court allowed the litigant personal representative to recover the fee, which had been paid under protest. Thirdly, it is no objection that a charge may result in a profit, provided only that the profit is a reasonable one.[7] On this basis a steep increase in charges for services provided by the Government, as used to be the case in pre-privatisation days with water rates, energy prices or in Post Office charges, had some of the characteristics of a tax when intended as a fiscal device to restrain domestic consumption.[8] In the Government's own statistics items treated as taxes include not only vehicle excise duty but also Mrs Thatcher's famous community charge; however, the television licence is not included.[9] If the Government decided to deal with pollution by means of a finite number of permits which could initially be bought from the Government and later sold to anyone, it is not clear whether the cost of the permits would be a tax or a charge.[10] In the UK we have the phenomenon of local councils imposing conditions on the grant of planning permission, e.g. that the developer will provide a swimming pool for the residents. This form of extortion is thought not to be a tax but it is not really a payment for services either.[11]

[2] Major J., in *Re Eurig's Estate* (1998) 165 DLR (4th) 1, 10; citing Duff J. in *Lawson* v. *Interior Tree, Fruit and Vegetable Committee of Direction* [1931] SCR 357 (Can.). See also Latham C.J. in *Matthews* v. *Chicory Marketing Board* (1938) 60 CLR 263, 276 (Vic.).

[3] *Air Caledonie* v. *Commonwealth* (1988) 165 CLR 462. esp. 467: immigration legislation including airport passenger fee for immigration clearance charged on all passengers arriving in Australia on an overseas flight; fee held to be a tax and so Act invalid.

[4] Duff C.J., in *Re Tax on Foreign Legations and High Comrs' Residence* [1943] SCR 208 (Can.). Note the refusal of Lord Cairns to use the presumption of a strict interpretation of tax law when considering tolls: *Pryce* v. *Monmouthshire Canal and Rly Companies* (1879) 4 App Cas 197, 202.

[5] Montgomery J. in *Societe Centrale D'Hypothesques* v.*Cite de Quebec* [1961] QLR 661; see also water rates and *Daymond* v. *South West Water Authority* [1976] AC 609, [1976] 1 All ER 39.

[6] *Re Eurig's Estate* (1998) 165 DLR (4th) 1, 11; see Bowman (1998) 46 *Can. Tax Jo.* 1278.

[7] *Minister of Justice for Dominion of Canada* v. *Levis City* [1919] AC 505, PC.

[8] See Sabine, *British Budgets in Peace and War*, 163, and R.C. Canada (1966), Study 24, 1–10.

[9] On TV licences, see *Congreve* v. *Home Office* [1976] QB 629, [1976] 1 All ER 697.

[10] Marchetti ((1980) 33 *Natl Tax Jo.* 233) argues that it would be a charge.

[11] They, are however, "exactions"; for a general discussion from the US perspective, see *Law and Contemporary Problems*, Vol. 50.

1.1.3 Other issues

A number of more subtle points have arisen in Australia.

(1) The fact that raising money is not the Government's primary purpose in imposing a levy, does not prevent it from being a tax.[12]
(2) The element that the collection be compulsory was held to be satisfied where the state compulsorily acquired an asset (flour) and then allowed the former owner to reacquire it at a higher price, requiring him to store it at his own risk in the meantime.[13] The difference between the two prices was held to be an excise tax even though there was no legal obligation, as opposed to commercial necessity, to buy the flour back.
(3) An arbitrary exaction is not a tax; it must be possible to point to the criteria by reference to which the liability to pay the tax is imposed and to show that the way in which the criteria are applied does not involve the imposition of a liability in an arbitrary or capricious manner.[14] The Australian High Court upheld a provision under which tax was to apply unless the Commissioner was "of the opinion that it was unreasonable that the section should apply".[15] In this vein some judges have also stated that compulsory acquisition by the Government cannot be a tax.[16]
(4) The requirement that the money should be paid to the Government was called into question when a levy was imposed on blank recording tapes, the levy to be paid to a body set up by the music industry to compensate artistes. This was held to be a tax even though it was not levied by a public authority; what mattered was that there was a compulsory acquisition of money under statutory powers which was not a payment for services.[17]
(5) There is considerable Australian unease about the status of franchise fees.[18] All the Australian material has now to be seen against a background of shifts of judicial thinking and the move away from legalism.[19]

1.1.4 EC law

Article 25 (ex Article 12) of the EC Treaty directs Member States to refrain from introducing between themselves any new customs duties on imports or exports or any charges having equivalent effect. In applying this provision the European Court of Justice looks at the effect of the tax and not its purpose. It struck down an Italian tax on the export of art treasures [20] so getting around the Italian Government's argument that the purpose of the levy

[12] *Northern Suburbs Cemetery Reserve Trust* v. *Commonwealth* (1993) 24 ATR 1, 7 (primary purpose to encourage employers to provide training); see also *Osborne* v. *Commonwealth* (1911) 12 CLR; and the discussion in Zines, *The High Court and the Constitution* (4th ed. 1997), 29–31.

[13] *A.-G. (NSW)* v. *Homebush Flour Mills Ltd.* (1937) 56 CLR 390.

[14] *DFC of T* v. *Brown* (1958) 100 CLR 32, 40; discussed in *MacCormick* v. *FCT* (1984) 15 ATR 437; "bottom-of-the-harbour" scheme legislation imposing liability on shareholders who had ceased to hold shares in the company held not to be arbitrary.

[15] *Giris Pty Lt* v. *FCT* (1969) 1 ATR 3; however the reasoning is confused—Zines p. 159

[16] *MacCormick* v. *FCT* (1984) 158 CLR 622, 640.

[17] *Australian Tape Manufacturers Assocn* v. *Commonwealth* (1993) 176 CLR 480 (Copyright Act including levy on blank tapes with proceeds paid to copyright owners whose works might be copied; Act held invalid because the levy was a tax.

[18] Complicated by the uncertainty over the meaning of the term "excise duty". For an example of the confusion, see the 4–3 decision in *Capital Duplicators Pty Ltd.* v. *ACT* (1993) 27 ATR 1.

[19] Zines, above at n. 12, ch. 17.

[20] Case 7/68 *Commission* v. *Italy* [1968] ECR 423, [1969] CMLR 1.

was to keep national art treasures within Italy. It also held that a country could not invoke Article 36 (now Article 30) of the Treaty to justify a tax; Article 30 could only be used to justify non-fiscal barriers falling within Article 30 (now Article 28).[21]

Article 25 does not apply to charges for services. The European Court, like the Canadian courts before it, has insisted that for a charge to escape Article 25 on this basis the trader must receive a separate identifiable benefit in return for the sum paid and that the sum must be proportionate to the benefit. As such, a charge levied at a frontier as part of a general system of quality control has been struck down.[22] A charge for warehousing facilities at a frontier may escape Article 25; presumably the state must show some specific benefit beyond the standard procedure for clearing customs.[23] A fee for an inspection where the inspection is mandatory under EC law can be justified and so escape Article 25; however, perhaps surprisingly, a different conclusion was reached where the inspection was merely authorised by Community law.

1.1.5 Social security contributions

Provided these could be regarded simply as compulsory insurance payments, they may be considered as the price of a benefit purchased directly but compulsorily from the state, although the compulsory element might have turned such payments into taxes.[24] However, now that payments are graduated in a way which does not relate directly to the graduation in benefit, they ought to be treated as taxes.[25] This is particularly true when the payer has earned enough to be entitled to maximum benefits and so can derive no benefit from the exactions which still have to be paid,[26] or, conversely, is entitled to a benefit without having to contribute.[27] Despite this, the UK government machine clings lovingly to the principle that social security levies are a contribution not a tax. It is not clear to what extent this is simply because they were administered by the Department of Social Security.[28] Recent reform suggestions include giving deductions against National Insurance Contributions (NICs) for certain expenditure which have previously been relieved only against corporation tax or income tax.[29]

1.1.6 Fines

A more subtle problem is the difference between a fine and a tax, particularly when government motives on such matters as cigarette smoking are, to say the least, ambiguous.[30] At first

[21] See discussion by Weatherill and Beaumont, *EC Law* (Penguin, 3rd ed.), ch. 13.

[22] Case 63/74 *W. Cadsky SpA* v. *Instituto nazionale per il Commercio Estero* [1975] ECR 281; see also Case 170/88 *Ford Espana SA* v. *Spain* [1989] ECR 2305, esp. on proportionality.

[23] Weatherill and Beaumont, above at n. 21, 463–464.

[24] However, the mere fact that they are both taxes does not mean that they are the same for all purposes; thus EC Regulation No. 1408/71 governs the national insurance treatment of non-residents whereas there is no equivalent for income tax, as the case-law of the ECJ in chapter 2 below shows.

[25] They are not taxes for parliamentary purposes: McKintosh, in *Taxation Policy*, 138. *Metal Industries (Salvage) Ltd.* v. *S. T. Harle (Owners)* 1962 SLT 114 held employer's contribution to be taxes.

[26] For example, continuing to pay NICs having already earned the maximum retirement pension.

[27] See Johnson and Stears (1996) 17(1) *Fiscal Studies* 105 discussing the basic state retirement pension.

[28] For an (ultimately unsuccesful) example of the Department's wish to keep its own territory see [1998] *BTR* 209.

[29] *Financial Times*, 15 June 1998.

[30] For sustained denunciation of such taxes, see the essays collected in Shugart (1997). For a comparison of regulatory fines and taxation as ways of encouraging behaviour, see Ogus (1998) 61 *MLR* 767. See also Poddar, in *Taxation to 2000 and Beyond*, Canadian Tax Foundation Paper No. 93, ch. 3. *The Economist*, 27 July 1996, 19–21, cites Hopkins of Rochester Institute of Technology (US); and see R. Hahn (ed.), *Risks Costs and Lives Saved* (OUP, 1996); Viscusi of Duke University is quoted as reporting a cost-benefit analysis showing that a regulation saved 13 lives at a cost of $4 m a piece.

sight it might appear that there is no difference between a fixed rate of fine and a tax, but the power of the court to vary the normal fine and to enjoin against continued breach[31] marks off the breach of the criminal law from the carrying-on of a taxable activity. Fines or penalties imposed to regulate an activity are more complex; penalties imposed to encourage prompt compliance with filing or other requirements are really more in the nature of late filing charges or interest charges than fines.[32] The distinction matters because traders may not deduct fines in computing their taxable profits,[33] but may be able to deduct taxes.

1.2 Objectives and Functions of Tax

Much of the material which follows is economic in formulation. However, this is because there has been too little participation by UK legal scholars in the debates. The tax system expresses many political and social values; critics and defenders of those values will therefore have much to say about aspects of current and proposed tax rules, just as they have about any other aspects of legal rules. One can find much of interest in the contributions from critical legal theory and from feminist jurisprudence.[34]

1.2.1 Raising revenue

The classical function of the tax system is to raise revenue to meet government expenditure. As an alternative to taxation the Government might commandeer resources or print money or even borrow it, but taxation is either more efficient or more just than each of these.[35] The government expenditure that requires to be met is either the provision of services which the free market cannot provide, such as defence, law and order and parks, or the provision of services which the state feels are better provided by itself, such as health services and education—often called public goods.[36] Views as to which services should be provided by the state have changed over the years—as privatisation shows. Whether, in practice, taxes were raised to meet expenditure, or vice versa, was a question which caused great worries in the 1970s.[37]

As Levi shows in her classic study,[38] while rulers maximise revenue to the state they cannot do just as they please; they are subject to the constraints of relative bargaining power *vis à vis* constituents, their transaction costs and discount rates. These constraints determine the choice of revenue system.

[31] *A.-G.* v. *Harris* [1961] 1 QB 74, [1960] 3 All ER 207; but see also Menzies J. in *Fairfax* v. *FCT* (1965) 114 CLR 1, 17.

[32] US Senate Report No. 92–437, 92 Cong. 1st Sess. 74 (1971).

[33] *McKnight* v. *Sheppard* [1999] STC 669.

[34] A valuable starting point is the sceptical article by Zelanak (1998) 76 *North Carolina LR* 1521, and the footnote-laden responses at 1581–1888. For a brief introduction to feminist issues and a valuable bibliography, see Young, "Taxing Times for Women", in Krever (ed.), *Tax Conversations* (Kluwer, 1997), 261–92; see also (1999) *Sydney LR* 487.

[35] RC Canada (1966), Vol. 2, 2–7.

[36] On user charges as alternatives for certain goods, see Bird in Krever (ed.), above at n. 34, 513–46.

[37] See Diamond, *Public Expenditure in Practice* (Allen and Unwin, 1975), 66; cited by Morgan, *Over Taxation by Inflation* (IEA, 1977), 59.

[38] Levi, *Of Rule and Revenue* (University of California Press, 1988); in addition to Levi's own examples, see those from 1688 to 1783 in John Brewer, *The Sinews of Power* (Unwin, 1989).

1.2.2 Redistribution

In the past, great emphasis was placed on the objective of redistribution of wealth. This had two quite distinct forms. The first was the doctrine that taxation should be based on ability to pay; it could also be based on the idea that the tax system should correct the outcome of pure market forces. The second form presupposed that the existing distribution[39] was unjust and concluded that this should therefore be undone. This second principle sees confiscation as a legitimate objective of taxation. These views were very influential from 1945 until the election of Mrs Thatcher in 1979.

From 1979 to 1997 wealth became socially acceptable and it was seen that productive wealth, providing, for example, increased employment, was positively desirable. During this period the poor were helped by welfare payments rather than by the tax system. Important changes to the structure helping the poor were made but were general in nature—lowering the rate of tax, including NICs, and raising the tax threshold.

The election of the Blair Government in 1997 has kept to this creed but, having committed itself not to raise the basic or higher rates of income tax, uses the language of fairness rather than redistribution. There are various forms of redistribution; for example, any change in the tax burden is a redistribution. The 1999 working families tax credit costs £5 bn, the same as the amount raised by the abolition in 1997 of pension funds' right to the repayment of a dividend tax credit—few saw this as a redistribution from tomorrow's pensioners to today's working families.[39a] The new child tax credit will cost the same as the old married couples' allowance, making a redistribution from married couples to families with children. The new credits are paid regardless of the parents' marital status. It remains to be seen whether these worthy measures will be effective given the scale of the problem; some do not regard them as worthy at all (see below at §§9.4 and 11.5).

Methods of redistribution through the tax system include not only increasing the rate of tax but also abolishing allowances or reducing their value—perhaps to be replaced by tax credits. One can also look to the tax transfer system whereby progressive taxes on income are used to fund subsidies to low-income households and the use of progressive taxes to fund public services which particularly benefit the poor, e.g. public housing. One might also consider, subject to the realities of the EC's VAT system,[40] adjusting indirect taxes so that taxes on goods purchased largely by high-income consumers are combined with subsidies to other services which are used chiefly by low-income consumers.[41]

1.2.3 Management of the economy

The role of tax changes in altering the level of demand is now accepted, although mechanisms such as credit control and the raising of welfare payments are other useful devices in stabilising the economy.[42] Governments let their borrowings rise as economies slow down,

[39] For a Labour view on the present distribution while in opposition, see *Social Justice: A Report of The commission on Social Justice* (1994); but see also the critique by The Adam Smith Institute. In the 1970s the Royal Commission on Distribution of Income and Wealth published much data. For up-to-date figures, see *Inland Revenue Statistics* (1999), chs 2 (income) and 13 (wealth).

[39a] Perhaps because some of the money was used to finance an immediate cut in corporation tax rate.

[40] See *R. v. Customs and Excise Commrs, ex parte Lunn Poly Ltd.* [1998] STC 649.

[41] Musgrave and Musgrave, *Public Finance in Theory and Practice* (McGraw-Hill, 1989), 11.

[42] On use of tax to cope with financial volatility, see Haq Kaul and Grunberg (eds), *The Tobin Tax Essays* (OUP, 1996).

provided this reflects the cyclical effects of automatic stabilisers, lower tax revenue and higher unemployment pay, and not a sudden rush into long-term commitments for extra spending or reduced tax rates. At present, greater emphasis is placed on monetary measures such as interest rates and exchange rates.[43] If the UK joins EMU it will lose its right to set interest and exchange rates; one may then expect fiscal policy to become more prominent (unless that is also pooled). Management of particular sectors, as opposed to "the economy," can also be achieved by regulation. Current fashion suggests help for small and medium-sized enterprises[44]—usually to undo the damage done to them by other changes affecting companies generally.

1.2.4 Affecting behaviour

The tax system is more than a matter of economics. It can be used for specific purposes, such as discouraging the use of alcohol or cigarettes and so trench on individual forms of pleasure. Where subsidies are provided, short term ones may be more effective than long term.[45]

1.2.5 The power of tax

It is misleading to regard taxes simply as a means of obtaining revenue. Tax is the most pervasive and privileged exercise of the police power of the state. It determines the directions in which people may become wealthy by determining the directions in which they may not.[46] By using its taxing power, a government may make some people rich and other people poor without falling foul of charges of corruption or favouritism unless,of course, their reliefs are too narrowly targeted.

1.3 Criteria used in Tax Design[47]

1.3.1 List

According to the Meade Committee Report (1978),[48] a good tax structure must take into account many factors: the effects on economic incentives; its fairness as between persons of similar taxable capacity; its effects upon distribution between rich and poor; whether it is compatible with desirable international economic relations; and its simplicity, ease of understanding and absence of excessive administration costs. This list is of great importance since it shows how matters have developed since Adam Smith listed his famous "canons of taxation", 200 years ago in *The Wealth of Nations*,[49] i.e. that tax should be charged in proportion to ability, that it should be certain not arbitrary, that it should be charged at

[43] See Sandford, *Public Finance* (4th ed. Pergamon, 1992), ch. 12. Other useful sources include Dell, *The Chancellors* (Harper Collins, 1997) and G. Davies, *A History of Money* (Univ. of Wales Press, 1996), esp. ch. 8.

[44] On business incentives see Rushton (1992) 40 *Can. Tax Jo.* 639.

[45] Goldberg (1994) 49 *Tax Law Review* 305; see also Ogus, above at n. 30.

[46] Groves (1948) 1 *National Tax Jo.* 23; on tax system as legal maid of all work, see Fuller, *Morality of Law* (revised ed., Yale Univ. Press, 1969), 166.

[47] For tax design itself see, Thuronyi *et al.*, *Tax Law Design and Drafting* (IMF, 1996), Vol. 1 and (1997) Vol. 2. On the balance between *ad valorem* and specific taxation, an issue in indirect design, see Keen (1998) 19 *Fiscal Studies* 1.

[48] Meade, *The Structure and Reform of Direct Taxation* (Allen and Unwin, London 1978) I.F.S. at p. 20.

[49] OUP, 1976, Book 5, ch. 2, 825–8; for some necessary correctives, see Lynn (1976) 29 *National Tax Jo.*369.

a time which was most convenient to the taxpayer and that the costs of collection should be as low as possible. The Meade Committee list, with its emphasis on matters of efficiency and international relations, reflects the influence of what economists know as the optimal theory of taxation.[50] An altogether different approach uses benefit theory; tax should be charged payers pay because they receive benefits from the state. This is an old and generally unfashionable approach and is not considered further here.[51]

Whichever list is chosen, some way must be found of overcoming the conflict between these different criteria. The extent and nature of that conflict depend opon which school of economic thought one belongs—reconciliation is more difficult for older views of economics than for the optimal tax theory. A third school of economic thought, public choice theory, must also be considered. We first consider the criteria in the light of the older approach which has dominated both Royal Commissions and so much government thinking and rhetoric.

1.3.2 Equity

Equity is traditionally divided into two types: horizontal equity, which means that those in equal circumstances should pay an equal amount of tax; and vertical equity, which means that those in unequal circumstances should pay different amounts of tax. The reason why equity is regarded as important is partly the moral view that it is right and proper, in the same way that equality before the law is right and proper, and partly a pragmatic view that, if a system is believed to be fair and equal, taxpayers will be more willing to co-operate with it. However, the statement that equity is important does nothing to help one determine which circumstances are equal and which are unequal.[52] Equity may be satisfied by a proportional system of taxation, just as much as by a progressive system of taxation. In assessing how equitable a system is, attention must be paid to the whole range of taxes and benefits. Setting the top rate of income tax to 40% in 1988 recognised that equity does not demand confiscation; the present administration has pledged not to raise the basic or higher rates of income tax for the life of this Parliament; freezing the nominal rates of tax has not stopped governments from raising money by other means.[53]

Equity issues can also arise between countries (see below at §58.1) and between generations.[54]

1.3.3 Neutrality[55]

This has been the most important canon in the 1980s and early 1990s. A tax is neutral if it avoids distortions of the market. A selective tax, such as the now defunct motor vehicle tax,

[50] Among other books, see Atkinson and Stiglitz, *Lectures on Public Economics* (1980); Prest and Barr, *Public Finance* (7th ed., Weidenfeld, 1985); Sandford, *Public Finance* (4th ed, Pergamon, 1992), Shoup, *Public Finance* (Weidenfeld and Nicolson, 1969); Musgrave Public Finance in *Theory and Practice*, supra n. 41; Rosen, *Public Finance* (5th ed., McGraw-Hill, 1999); and Stiglitz, *Economics of the Public Sector* (2nd ed., Norton, 1988).

[51] For a good account, see Cooper, *Australian Tax Forum*, Vol, 11, 397.

[52] "Vertical equity means graduated or disproportional taxation . . . and the moment you abandon . . . the cardinal principle of exacting from all individuals the same proportion of their income or their property, you are at sea without rudder or compass, and there is no amount of injustice or folly you may not commit": McCulloch, *A Treatise on the Principles and Practical Influence of Taxation and the Funding System* (1863), 145.

[53] For the view that this straitjacket has had unfortunate effects, see [1998] *BTR* 317.

[54] See Robinson (1998) 19 *Fiscal Studies* 447.

[55] Groves (1948) 1 *Nat. Tax Jo.*, 18; and Bracewell Milnes [1976] *BTR* 110.

is not neutral, since it encourages consumers to spend their money on another item rather than on a car. A tax such as insurance premium duty or airport passenger duty may, however, be seen as neutral because it strives to impose a duty on something which is outside the VAT net and so reduces the disparity. Other areas where neutrality is much invoked are the taxation of a company as compared with that of a partnership, and the taxation of profits earned within, compared with those earned outside the UK. The UK tax system has many rules which break the principle of neutrality. Worse, there are many technical rules which make significant tax differences according to which of two or more methods is adopted to achieve a given result. The effect is harmful since it encourages the expenditure of money on expert tax advice (expenditure which is, in economic terms, unproductive), and on schemes which may make a trade less efficient. The assimilation of tax rates, both in the corporate and personal sectors, so far as they apply to income and capital gains, was a major advance in the direction of neutrality; the retreat from this in 1998 in favour of the tapering relief, even if only for non-corporate taxpayers, is regrettable.

Of course, a system may consciously choose to distort the market. Thus, the oft-mooted tax on those who drive their cars into city centres is an attempt to keep many such users off the road, so clearing the way for improved public transport—and less congestion. The principle of neutrality simply asserts that all distortions should be conscious and so subject to justification through the political process.

1.3.4 Certainty

Certainty means first that the scope of the tax should be clear. Penumbral areas cause resentment among taxpayers cast into the darkness and undermine the principle of equity, besides increasing the cost of the system. The canon of certainty entails both that the tax can be enforced and that enforcement will actually occur. A tax that is easily evaded causes resentment and often a decline in taxpayer morality. Certainty means also that the Treasury will be able correctly to predict how much tax is gathered in [56]and, perhaps, the effects of the tax.

1.3.5 Administrative efficiency

Only those who regard the duty of the tax system as being to confiscate wealth in order to provide employment would be happy with a tax whose administration costs exceeded the tax yield. Capital gains tax is a prime example of a tax where, because of the grant of exemptions, the yield from the tax may decline while the costs of collection as a percentage of the tax collected may increase sharply. In 1998–1999 the cost yield ratio was 1.33% for all taxes. The figure for income tax, assuming that NICs are included, was 1.64%; corporation tax, 0.71%; stamp duties, 0.13%; CGT, 1.61%; and IHT and related taxes, 1.57%.[57] The direct yield to the Revenue of tackling non-compliance was £4 bn; equivalent to the yield from an increase in the basic rate of income tax of between 1 pence and 2 pence.[58]

[56] However see Nigel Lawson on the risks of "seduction by apparently precise fine tuning" in his memoirs, *The View from No. 11* (Bantam Press, 1992), 376.

[57] Board of Inland Revenue Report for year ended 31 March 1999, Cm. 4477 (1999), 33, 60. These figures tend to rise when economic activity is slack.

[58] Board of Inland Revenue Report, Cm. 4477, 66, Table 10.

These figures take no account of compliance costs, which comprise: money costs, such as fees paid to legal advisers; time costs, such as time spent on preparing tax returns; and psychological costs, such as the stress and anxiety often caused by incomprehension of tax returns and obligations. A recent survey showed that even by ignoring the psychological elements, the costs of compliance were several times the administrative costs.[59] A commitment to reducing these costs formed part of the Taxpayers Charter; proposals for changes to business tax included compliance cost assessments.[60] However, criticisms of such proposals are that they are large, they are particularly inequitable in their incidence and they create resentment. Reduction of such costs should therefore be, and continue to be, an object of tax policy. A recent Australian study confirms these lines of thought, showing that compliance costs are regressive and fall with particular severity on the smallest business taxpayers.[61] UK compliance costs have tended to be lower than the average for OECD countries. This is partly because of the absence (until 1997) of a self-assessment system, and partly because of the presence of what is believed to be an efficient PAYE system. However, a recent UK study showed that for 1995–1996 compliance costs came to £1 bn with smaller businesses the hardest hit since they were unable to enjoy economies of scale or cash flow advantages of deducting sums from employees' pay before paying the Government.[62] Where these conditions do not apply, for example in relation to CGT, compliance costs can be very high. Of course, statistics can prove anything—if one employs an accountant to prove to the Revenue that no CGT is due, should one be glad to have a nil tax liability, or cross because one has had to pay to establish it?

1.3.6 Symmetry

Although this is not an economic criterion it has been much in demand in the 1980s and 1990s. In essence, symmetry demands that when a transaction is entered into by two taxpayers the tax treatment of the two should, in certain circumstances, be symmetrical. An absence of symmetry can create arbitrage opportunities. Symmetry is not a natural state of affairs. If A sells an asset to B there may be many tax factors governing A which are quite irrelevant to B. Thus, the transaction may be on capital account by A and on revenue account by B; A may have to pay tax on the proceeds in one year and B entitled to a deduction in another; or the UK tax system may govern A, but a foreign tax system may govern B. Symmetry has been a feature of recent tax reform in quite distinct ways. There have been effort to stops A and B from exploiting differences of timing where they are closely related, while leaving the situation as it is for unrelated taxpayers. Equally, for example in the corporation tax rules for loan relationships, there have been efforts to ensure the same treatment for A and B regardless of whether they are related—in that area, therefore, the legislation has got rid of the distinction between capital and income and differences of timing. See chapter 48 below.

[59] The principal UK scholar here is Sandford. For an introduction, see *More Key Issues in Tax Reform* (Fiscal Publications, 1995), ch. 6; Sandford (ed.), *Tax Compliance Costs Measurement and Policy* (Fiscal Publications 1995); and Sandford, Godwin and Hardwick, *Administrative and Compliance Costs of Taxation* (Fiscal Publications, 1989). On particular difficulties, e.g. those experienced by widows and divorced women, see James, Lewis and Allison, *The Comprehensibility of Taxation* (Avebury, 1987).

[60] DTI, *Checking the Cost to Business* (1992). Good examples of Regulatory Impact Statements are attached to the proposals discussed below at §§16.7 and 16.10.

[61] Evans, Ritchie, Tran-Nam and Walpole, *A Report into Taxpayer Costs of Compliance—Australian Taxation Office* (1997); see also the Report of the Third TAX Conference, *Tax Administration* (Prospect, 1998).

[62] Collar and Godwin (1999) 20 *Fiscal Studies* 423.

1.4 The Three Schools of Economic Thought

When the first edition of this book was written the prevailing school was the "equity" school. Since then, two other views—the optimal theory of tax and public choice theory—have joined equity in the foreground of the debate over tax policy. The views are well summarised by Hettich and Winer in a 1985 article on which the following text draws heavily.[63] They conclude that a new synthesis is needed since the three schools clash sharply.

1.4.1 The comprehensive income or equity school

This is associated with Simons[63a] and Haig; its objective was to create an equitable tax system to be achieved by having a comprehensive tax base as best representing a person's ability to pay (see below at §1.6.1). Normally this was achieved by an income tax but it could also be achieved by an expenditure tax or a mixture of the two. Simons considered that other taxes should be abolished except property tax and petrol tax. This approach naturally gave rise to much debate on the ideal tax base. It rejected special provisions or "preferences". It is the approach most favoured by law students because it is relatively easy to understand and has been worked out most fully by the Canadian Royal Commission in 1966.[64]

Its theoretical strength—the single idea of equity—was also its weakness. A single idea could not accommodate ideas such as economic efficiency as part of its base. Strong on horizontal equity, it could, of itself, provide no structure for vertical equity.

1.4.2 The optimal taxation school[65]

Whereas Haig Simons' scholars want a tax base which is broad, optimal tax theorists want a base which is inelastic;[66] they favour utilitarianism over equity.[67] This school goes back to sacrifice theory, and stresses that all taxpayers should suffer an equal sacrifice while also saying that the least sacrifice should be occasioned to the whole. Sacrifice can also be explained in terms of loss of utility or loss of social welfare as a whole. Stripped of this intimidating terminology the doctrine is utilitarian in nature. Tax designers must take account of the effects of the tax rules so as to achieve the best trade-off between the inevitable costs of the tax and the goals of equity; this is done by looking for and at the effects of changes on the welfare of households. This means that one must be able to model the effects of tax. Tax A will be better than tax B if it produces the same amount of revenue for the Government but involves less loss of satisfaction to the taxpayer. As an example of this approach one may look at the deduction of expenses. The equity school looks on these as matters which are deductible because they are part of the costs of earning income; the optimal theory looks at the consequences both distributional and economic, invites one to decide which consequences one wants and then shapes the tax system accordingly.[68] Since governments rarely

[63] Hettich and Winer 38 *National Tax Jo.* 423–45.

[63a] Henry Simons *Personal Income Taxation* (Univ. of Chicago 1938).

[64] See below at n. 111, 30.

[65] For a tough introduction, see Heady, 14 *Fiscal Studies* 15; see also Palsgrave, *Dictionary of Economics*. The seminal article is Ramsey (1927) 37 *Economic Journal* 47. For examples of optimal tax theory, see Cooper (1994) *Federal Tax LR* 414, and Zolt (1996) 16 *Virgina Tax Review* 39.

[66] Head, in Head and Krever (1996), 210.

[67] Kaplow (1995) 48 *National Tax Jo.* 497.

[68] Griffith (1994) 41 *UCLA LR* 1769; discussed by Edgar, in Krever (ed.), *Tax Conversations* (Kluwer, 1997).

seem to do anything optimally these findings have not been fully exploited; the findings have been much better exploited by insurance companies.[69] The theory has no formal counterpart to the Canadian 1966 Royal Commission, but Hettich and Winer point out that the Meade Committee Report in 1978 placed great emphasis on the role of economic efficiency; the Committee also stated that it is an important guide for tax design rather than a practical basis for tax reform.

Optimal taxation differs from equity in several ways. Perhaps most significantly it does not claim universality, but claims simply to be a useful way of looking at things. It provides a basis on which the degree of vertical equity in the tax can be determined; that basis is the trade-off. It is also open to persuasion on the question whether the marginal tax rate should rise progressively, accepting, for example, that there might be much to be said for having low marginal rates of tax at the bottom and top of the income scale. It also has no problem with the idea of many taxes rather than one—as long as each is optimal. Optimal tax is a highly sophisticated approach which depends on the quality of the information it gets on what people do.

While equity taxation tends to disregard such matters as the imputed income arising from household services (when considering family taxation), or leisure as an alternative to income (usually on the ground that these are unmeasurable), optimal taxation regards these as important. Optimal tax accepts that it may not be possible to tax such items, since they are hard to quantify, but insists that they be taken into account as part of the assessment of the efficiency of the tax.[70]

The point is well made by Apps in language typical of this school:[71]

> "Modern public finance theory recognizes that information asymmetries constrain the government to taxing indicators of what it would like to tax. Observed money income is such an indicator and gives rise to complications because among other things, it omits the value of non-market time. Ideally the government would like to impose lump sum taxes of varying amounts on given characteristics of individuals, such as endowments and tastes, that determine their opportunity sets and levels of well being, but these cannot be observed. The consequent constraint on the choice of tax base gives rise to two important problems (i) horizontal and vertical inequities due to "errors"; the indicators are not perfectly correlated with the opportunities and well being of the individual and (ii) efficiency losses due to incentive effects; the indicators are usually under the control of the individual and so taxing them is distortionary."

1.4.3. Public choice theory

This school, associated with the names of Brennan and Buchanan,[72] rejects the assumption made by other schools that government is inherently benevolent. Its insight is that while everyone accepts that businessmen act in their own interest rather than the public good, the same is also true of government officials who will be concerned to provide advice which appeals to their superiors and so enhances their chances of promotion.[73] Government is

[69] *The Economist*, 12 October 1996, 120, celebrating the award of the Nobel Prize for Economics to Vickrey and Mirrlees.

[70] For example, Apps, in Head and Krever (1996), ch. 3; and Jones and Savage, ibid., ch. 4.

[71] Apps, ibid., 83.

[72] *The Power to Tax* (1980); see also Brennan, in Krever (ed.), above at n. 68, 87–106; Buchanan (1976) 6 *Journal of Public Economics* 17; and Brennan and Buchanan 8 *Journal of Public Economics* 255. See also Symposium (1998) 51 *National Tax Jo.* 359. Among critics, see Shaviro 139 *University of Pennsylvania LR* 1, esp. 64.

[73] See Tullock, *The New Palgrave Dictionary of Economics* (MacMillan), Vol. 3, 1040.

capable of malevolence or, at least, is at risk of being taken over by malevolent interest groups. Public affairs should be analysed on the basis that the voter is the consumer and the officials are the company. A top official cannot always know what every junior official does—hence the unbreakable coffee pot.[74] Moreover, a bureaucracy can be a budget maximiser.[75] It follows that taxpayers need constitutional protection against taxation. Ideally, taxes should be imposed (and designed) by a special convention of taxpayers. If it has to be imposed by existing political institutions they should operate behind a Rawlsian "veil of ignorance".[76] Naturally, such an approach, with its emphasis on the acceptability of the process rather than the result, tells us relatively little about the ideal tax structure; loopholes are acceptable if the process is acceptable.

Whereas the Haig Simons school wants a base which is broad and optimal theorists want one which is inelastic, public choice theorists compromise by wanting a base which is narrower than that of the first group and more elastic than that of the second; the object is always to reduce revenue potential and to control the size of the public sector. They tend to favour proportional rather than progressive taxation[77] and quite like earmarked taxes.[78]

1.4.4 Partial tax reform

While these ideas may be used as the basis of complete redesign of a tax system, as in the Canadian Royal Commission of 1966, they are also of importance as arguments used in the course of partial tax reform.[79] Four lessons must, however, be learned. First, any fundamental reform of the tax law over a brief period will generate windfall gains and losses on a wide scale and in a capricious and inequitable pattern.[80] Secondly, the period of transition may be difficult politically. Undoing a piece of economic folly can be difficult (Vickrey chooses the classical system of corporate taxation and points to the high nominal rates of tax during a transition to an integration model.) Thirdly, as a survey of the voter reaction to the Canadian goods and services tax shows, "political parties would do well to avoid a detailed programme of tax reform as a platform to contest elections. Voter misconceptions and ignorance combined with scare tactics from other parties, can be a recipe for disaster".[81] The fourth lesson comes from the Meade Committee Report in 1978 which not only stressed the problem of transition, but also underlined the point that tax systems have to operate in an international world; one's own dreams may be impractical if not implemented by trading partners.[82]

[74] The US Department of Defense is supposed to have designed a coffee pot which was so strong that it would not break up in a crash which would kill all the crew members and destroy the plane itself.

[75] On the famous proposition 13 designed to curb budget maximisers in California, see Conference Supplement to (1979) *National Tax Jo.*

[76] Rawls, *A Theory of Justice* (OUP, 1972). For a starting point, see Solomon and Murphy (eds), *What is Justice?* (OUP, 1990), Pt. 2.

[77] (1993) 46 *National Tax Jo.* 401.

[78] Buchanan (1963) 71 *Journal of Political Economy* 457.

[79] On partial tax reform, see Feldstein (1976) 6 *Journal of Public Economics* 71; on reform more generally, see Sandford (ed.), *Succesful Tax Reform* (1993).

[80] See Vickrey, "The Problem of Progression" (1968) *University of Florida LR* 437, reprinted in (1996) *Public Economcs* 171, 179.

[81] Wallschutsky and Lewis *More Key Issues in Tax Reform* (1995), ch. 10; see also Steinmo in Sandford (ed.), above at n. 79, ch. 11.

[82] Meade Report chapter 21.

1.5 Classification of Taxes[83]

1.5.1 *Proportional, progressive and regressive (and degressive)*

A proportional or neutral tax is one which takes a constant proportion of income; a progressive tax takes an increasing proportion as income rises;[84] a regressive tax takes a declining proportion of income as income rises. A progressive tax system may be more or less steep; the UK income tax system has become much less steep since 1979, culminating in the two-rate structure (25% and 40%) introduced in 1988, since greatly deformed to the present 10%, 22% and 40% for non-savings income. However, 1988 also saw capital gains tax being made more progressive by the assimilation of the tax rates with those for income tax.

The case for a progressive tax system rests on vertical equity and, perhaps more basically, on assumptions about the obligation of citizens to the community in which they live, assumptions which raise issues much wider than mere economic analysis. Feminist theory suggests that women may be more supportive of redistribution than men.[85] If state expenditure is to be financed, it is thought proper that those with the most should contribute the most, i.e. that they should pay not just more (which would be the case under a proportional tax) but "more more". At one time this was explained in terms of benefit, i.e. that those with the most got the most benefit from the protection of their wealth which the state afforded;[86] but this reasoning was plainly insufficient once the state entered the field of social security. Modern optimal explanation tends to be in terms of sacrifice theory or of marginal or discretionary income,[87] the point here being that the provision of the essentials of life takes a certain amount of income, and that above this level individuals have a discretion over how they will spend it. It is more legitimate to tax the discretionary income than the essential income. Economic advantages are also claimed in that a progressive tax system diminishes oscillations in the trade cycle (by taking money out of the economy as incomes rise) and assists demand management (by shifting money into the hands of those liable to spend it).

The argument against a progressive tax turns largely on incentives. It is thought that high rates of tax discourage that spirit of enterprise which ought to be a mainspring of human activity. A high marginal tax rate, on one view, should encourage individuals to work even harder to achieve an increase in net income—the income effect—or to take more leisure instead of working—the substitution effect.[88] Surveys provide little cogent support for either view. A study by Brown and Sandford on the effect of the 1988 income tax rate changes on 300 accountants concluded that there was a negligible effect on work effort and enterprise and no discernible effect on emigration or immigration and no increase in rev-

[83] On fluidity of terminology, see Hicks (1946) *Economic Journal* 38.

[84] If there is a flat rate of tax, but an initial exemption or threshold, there will, as income above that threshold rises, be a constant rate of tax but a higher average tax rate. This is a mutation of progressive tax and is sometimes called a degressive tax.

[85] See Kornhauser 86 *Mich. LR* 465. See also Kornhauser 76 *North Carolina LR* 1609–28 and 47 *American University LR* 151, maintaining her view by criticising certain empirical research.

[86] See Blum and Kalven, *The Uneasy Case for Progressive Taxation* (Univ. of Chicago Press, 1953); and Galvin and Bittker, *Income Tax: How Progressive Should It Be?*

[87] See Fagan (1938) 46 *Jo. of Pol. & Econ.* 457; and Canada, above at n. 8, Vol. 2.

[88] Break [1957] *BTR* 101; Working Group on Migration Cmnd 3417 (1967); and *Taxation and Incentives* (IFS, 1976). See also R. C. Canada, (1966), Study No. 4; and Chatterjee and Robinson (1969) 17 *Can. Tax Jo.* 211–20. Bracewell-Milnes has pointed out that a comparison of a real with a hypothetical situation is something which cannot be done empirically; however, he also points out that incentives are none the less real for being empirically immeasurable: *Is Capital Taxation Fair?* (Institute of Directors, 1974), 9.

enue.[89] This is in line with earlier experience which suggested that at rates of 40% or less, income tax has a slight incentive effect and, at 70%, a net disincentive effect.[90] The same survey, however, suggested one possible and, if so, very significant benefit—the rates may have reduced tax avoidance and improved the quality of investment. A variant of these views suggests that if the rich are taxed less they will invest more, so generating wealth for others—the so-called trickle-down effect. J. K. Galbraith is supposed to have described this theory as being that if the horse is fed enough oats some will pass through to the road for the sparrows.[91]

The problem of progression must also be examined in the light of deductions. A high marginal rate of tax may be to spend more money on an item of deductible expense, e.g. to decide to fly across the Atlantic by Concorde rather than economy class. If I have a marginal rate of 80%, then 80% of the fare is paid by the government. If I choose to fly Concorde because I will be paying only 20% of the fare, the tax system encourages inefficiency.

Another factor against progressive taxation is that it can lead to a separation of political power from financial responsibility; this view also lay behind the replacement of domestic rates with the community charge, or poll tax as it came to be known.[92] A further problem is that while there may be little elasticity about working for a wage, there may be a much greater elasticity when one comes to the effect of taxes on capital.[93]

These various points must, however, be judged from the general viewpoint and not merely from that of income tax. First, if proportional taxation is accepted as preferable to regressive taxation, then some taxes, of which income tax is a prime example, must be made progressive in order to offset the regressive effects of other taxes—always assuming that social security benefits are not sufficient to offset these taxes.[94] Secondly, society must decide how much of its social expenditure is to be financed out of taxes and how much by direct payment, for example the provision of retirement benefits and education; if these are to be financed by direct payment, the case for a progressive tax becomes stronger since the level at which income becomes discretionary is raised. Thirdly, a tax system with a tax base which fails to catch many types of income must, given a certain sum of government expenditure, have a higher rate than one which catches all. Finally, it by no means follows that a progressive tax need be a penal tax.

1.5.2 Direct and indirect taxes[95]

This distinction is not important for UK tax law, but is for some Commonwealth and European countries with federal structures. According to Mill:[96]

> "A direct tax is one which is demanded from the very persons who, it is intended or desired, should pay it. Indirect taxes are those which are demanded from one person in the expectation and intention that he shall indemnify himself at the expense of the other: such as the excise or customs. The producer or importer of a commodity is called upon to pay a tax on it, not with the intention to

[89] Brown and Sandford [1991] *BTR* 414; also in *Key Issues in Tax Reform* (1993), ch. 9.

[90] See Sandford, *Economics of Public Finance* (1992), 158–60.

[91] Cited by Molloy (1994) *National Business Review* (New Zealand).

[92] On the story of this tax, see Butler, Adonis and Travers, *Failure in British Government: The Politics of the Poll Tax* (OUP, 1994). On Scottish experience, see Scobbir, Reid and Barker [1990] *BTR* 343.

[93] McLure (1980) 33 *National Tax Jo.*; and Boskin (1978) *Journal of Political Economy.*

[94] The argument is disputed by Bracewell-Milnes [1974] *BTR* 378.

[95] Hicks (1946) *Economic Journal* 38.

[96] *Principles of Political Economy*, Book V, ch. 3.

levy a peculiar contribution upon him, but to tax through him the consumers of the commodity, from whom it is supposed that he will recover the amount by means of an advance in price."

On this definition certain taxes on expenditure, e.g. motor vehicle licence duty, are direct taxes. The distinction has become less clear as the real incidence of taxation has been explored by economists. Thus, some research suggests that the taxation of profits of companies results in the shifting of that tax on to consumers or employees of the company.[97] Such a tax has, however, been classified as direct because courts, such as the Privy Council on appeals from Canada, have paid attention to that part of Mill's formulation which emphasised the intention and expectation that the tax would be shifted. There is thus a fundamental distinction between the economic recoupment of a direct tax and the simple passing on (often in the form of a straight percentage of the price) which is the hallmark of an indirect tax, i.e. between the recovery of a direct tax by a more-or-less circuitous operation of economic forces and the passing on of a tax in recognisable form. In applying this distinction the courts will treat a tax as direct notwithstanding that actual payment may be enforced against some intermediary so that income tax on employment income is not less direct because the employer must deduct tax. Canadian provincial probate fees were held to be direct taxes because although the personal representatives were liable for the tax they were liable only in their representative capacity, and not liable personally. The tax was thus a direct tax on the estate, not an indirect tax levied on the personal representatives.[98]

In Canada direct taxes may be levied by the federal or provincial governments; indirect taxes are imposed by the Federal Government alone. The courts have classified as direct taxes not only such taxes as income tax, and capital duty,[99] but also a tax on department store catalogues distributed without charge.[100] On the other hand, they have classified as indirect taxes not only such obvious items as customs and excise duties and sales tax, but also stamp duty,[101] a succession duty which could be collected from someone other than the beneficiary (e.g. a personal representative),[102] and gross revenue taxes.[103] Every tax must be judged on its own. By rejecting—inevitably—the test of economic incidence which would mean that almost every tax was at risk of being classified as indirect,[104] the courts have been forced back on to a test of whether or not the general tendency of a tax can be passed on, and this must lead to borderline cases. This has, in turn, led to the use of direct taxes only marginally different from indirect taxes, for example the use of consumer taxes rather than excise taxes and of succession duty rather than estate duty. Combining tax reductions with pay restraint—as attempted in the UK the mid 1970s[105]—threatened to turn employment income tax into a charge on the employer as a form of grossing-up the net wage.

The balance between direct and indirect taxation has long been a problem in the UK owing to the contrasting philosophies of different governments which, believing that direct

97 See below at §44.3.2.

98 *Re Eurig's Estate* (1998) 165 DLR (4th) 1, 12–13.

99 *Bank of Toronto* v. *Lambe* (1887) 12 App Cas 575; Lord Greene in *A-G for British Columbia* v. *Esquimault and Nanaimo Rly Co.* [1950] AC 87, 113. See La Forest, *Allocation of Taxing Power under the Canadian Constitution* (2nd ed. 1981), ch. 4.

100 *Minister of Finance of New Brunswick* v. *Simpson Sears Ltd.* (1982) 130 DLR (3rd) 385.

101 *A-G for Quebec* v. *Reed* (1884) 10 App Cas 141.

102 *Cotton* v. *R* [1914] AC 176; distinguishing *R.* v. *Lovitt* [1912] AC 212.

103 *R.* v. *Caledonian Colleries Ltd.* [1928] AC 358.

104 La Forest, above at n. 99, 74.

105 See Healey, *The Time of My Life*, 397.

taxation was progressive and indirect taxation regressive,[106] acted accordingly. In 1979 Geoffrey Howe reduced the rate of income tax, paying for it by increasing VAT. Despite the contemporary uproar, he was merely restoring the balance to what it had been earlier (see below p. 111)—a point he himself never made. The divide between the two types of tax is not absolute. Indirect taxes may affect the cost of living and so be taken into account when fixing tax threshold and social security levels. A state may, when introducing a sales or value added tax, also introduce credits against income taxes for the an amount of the new tax—with refunds made to those who did not pay income taxes.[107]

Indirect taxes are also of interest for the light they shed on social attitudes. It has been observed that it is generally a feature of the civilised world that the most unacceptable vices are punished by imprisonment, or worse, the somewhat less serious vices punished by fines and the most venial by heavy taxes. It is impossible to dismiss the idea that an Erewhon-like reversal of attitudes might take place, so that, for example, sales of tobacco and alcohol will render the vendor liable to imprisonment, whilst excise will be imposed on soft drugs and the use of brothels—as well as income tax on the proceeds of both.[108]

1.6 Tax Base and Income: Theory

The UK tax system contains a series of separate but sometimes overlapping direct taxes. Of these, traditionally the most important has been income tax.[109] Such a tax has many advantages. The evidence suggests that, at least in the absence of very high rates, it has a smaller disincentive effect than other taxes, that it is the most effective tax in redistributing income, that it serves as a strong, built-in stabiliser by collecting more money as incomes rise and that through it the Government can influence the savings ratio and so the growth rate.[110] There are two principal theoretical models for direct taxation. The first is the comprehensive income tax (CIT) or net accretion principle; the second is the expenditure tax (ET).

1.6.1 Comprehensive income tax (CIT): Haig-Simons

Under this principle income is:[111]

> "(T)he algebraic sum of (1) the market value of rights exercised in consumption and (2) the change in the value of the store of property rights between the beginning and end of the period in

[106] E.g. Snowden, cited in Mallet and George, *British Budgets 1913–1921* (London, 1933), 10: "These taxes violate every canon of taxation, because they tax a man not in proportion to his ability to pay nor according to those benefits he receives but according to his personal tastes".

[107] Pechman, IFS Lecture (1973), 8.

[108] Messere, IFS Lecture Series No. 2 (1974), 18. Note also Menzies J. in *Fairfax* v. *FCT* (1965) 114 CLR 1, 17 suggesting that a special prohibitive tax on income derived from the sale of heroin may not be a law "with respect to taxation" but rather a law made for the suppression of the trade by imposing penalties described as tax for participation in it.

[109] For a survey of different views of income, see (1990) 53 *Wueller Political Science Quarterly* 83, 557, and (1990) 54 *Political Science Quarterly* 555.

[110] Due and Friedlander, *Government Finance*, 251; Jay [1957] *BTR* 16.

[111] Simons, *Personal Income Taxation* (1938), 50. A famous attempt to build a system on this principle was made by the Canadian Royal Commission in 1966: see esp. Vol. 3, 22–5, 39–53, 461–531, and resulting literature, esp. Bittker 80 *HLR* 925, 81 *HLR* 1032; Musgrove 81 *HLR* 44; Pechman 81 *HLR* 63; Galvin 81 *HLR* 1016. For reflections after 20 years, see Sandford [1987] *BTR* 148; Brooks *et al.*, *The Quest for Tax Reform* (Carswell, 1988); and Osgoode Hall L.J., Vol. 26.

question. In other words, it is merely the result obtained by adding consumption during the period to 'wealth' at the end of the period and then subtracting 'wealth' at the beginning."

For those frightened by the word "alegbraic", the concept means simply that income is the net sum of consumption and saving.[112] On this definition income would include not merely income as conventionally defined but also all capital gains[113] and even gifts, inheritances and lottery winnings. Moreover, because assets would be valued at the end of each year all increases in wealth would be brought in—whether or not realised. The principle would apply equally to losses.

1.6.2 *The imputed income problem*

Few ideas cause law students from common law countries more difficulty than this; grasping the idea gives a view of life akin to that gained by Alice going down the rabbit hole. Imputed income arises where "an individual who owns productive assets, or who supplies production services, uses them directly to produce goods or services that he consumes himself".[114] For example, if farmer Alf supplies himself with his own produce he is, in effect, bartering his time and the use of his capital for the food he eats. Although he does not turn his goods or services into cash income, he should be taxed on the value of the profits from the goods or services he receives. Few would doubt that if Alf exchanges his produce with produce from farmer Ben, each has income—even though it is received in kind. Self-sufficiency and exchange should, in economic theory, be treated alike.[115] Under present UK law the exchange situation is clearly taxable (if not often reported) and self-sufficiency will arise if it comes within *Sharkey* v. *Wernher* (see below at §23.5.1.3).

Students have even more difficulty with the next example—the imputed rent that arises from owner occupation of property. Yet in 1989 this basis of taxation was used in 12 of the 23 OECD countries;[116] it had been in force in the UK as the original Schedule A until 1963[117] and was the basis of the rating system of local taxation until 1989.[118] The rating system was replaced by the community charge, to be replaced, in turn, by the council tax.[119] There is much to be said for a property tax as a proxy for imputed income.[120]

Under the old Schedule A, occupiers of property were charged on the annual value of the property, in theory the amount of rent that could be charged. If they were the owners this value was added to their income from other sources to compute total income. If they were not the owners, but paid rent to someone else, they were entitled, when paying that rent, to deduct income tax and set that off against their own liability.[121]

112 Bradford, *Untangling the Income Tax* (1986), 17.

113 Simons, above at n. 111, 81 was not worried that tax might be deferred until realisation but his followers were: *Surrey Pathways to Tax Reform*, 120.

114 R. C. Canada, (1966), Vol. 3, 47. For discussion of the theory, see Marsh (1943) 58 *Political Science Quarterly* 514–36, Goode (1960) 15 *Jo. of Finance* 504; and Merz (1977) 30 *National Tax Jo.* No. 4.

115 For discussion, see (1988) 43 *Tax Law Review* 447. However, see Goode, *The Individual Income Tax* (Brookings, 1976), 150–1, arguing that the performance of these services competes with leisure which is another form of consumption which escapes tax, so that imputed income should not be taxed.

116 Messere (1993), 281, Table 10.13; for earlier survey, see Merz (1977) 30 *National Tax Jo.* 435–8. For distributional consequences of alternative solutions in the UK, see Callan (1992) 13(1) *Fiscal Studies* 58.

117 e.g. ITA 1952, ss 82–116, repealed by FA 1993, s. 14.

118 See *Local Government Finance*, Cmnd. 6543 (1976), 169–71.

119 For review of the community charge, see Butler, Adonis and Travers, *Failure in British Government: The Politics of the Poll Tax* (OUP, 1994). On Scottish experience, see Scobbir, Reid and Barker [1990] *BTR* 343.

120 See Bradley [1996] *BTR* 168.

121 *Royal Commission Final Report*, Cmd. 9474 (1955), §§811–15.

The theory of this charge to tax was upheld by the Royal Commission in 1955[122] on grounds of equity. Suppose Alf and Beryl each have a capital sum. Alf invests the money in income-producing assets and has to pay rent for his living accommodation; Beryl buys a house. Alf will pay income tax on investment income but is not allowed to deduct the rent paid; Beryl will pay no tax since she receives no taxable benefit under current UK law. This is inequitable; their taxable capacities are the same, but their tax liabilities differ.

This argument has often proved misleading for lawyers. First, equity may equally be satisfied by proving that rent should be deductible in computing income rather than that the owner-occupier should be taxed on the value of the notional benefit. However, few would wish to see such an erosion of the tax base and the problems of housing finance are far too deep to be treated in such a way.[123] Secondly, using the rent foregone as the measure of liability suggests that the basis of liability is income foregone, e.g. that a person would be taxed who deliberately chooses to invest in shares with a lower than average return. However, this is to misunderstand the doctrine—the owner occupier is being taxed on a benefit received, not one foregone.

A critic of imputed income may also try to kill it off by pointing to its potential application. The classic nineteenth century example concerned the drastic tax changes which occurred when a man married his housekeeper, so that she no longer received a taxable salary for her services. Further, if the tax system decides to tax those who, for example, grow their own vegetables as a hobby, it must then decide whether to allow them deduct the costs incurred in that and, perhaps, other, less-productive hobbies. Most tax systems reject any idea that personal expenditure should be deductible. The housekeeper problem can be put in a form more acceptable to some twenty-first century readers in the form of the proposal that housework should be regarded as taxable income; this could be accompanied by a refundable tax credit for low-income individuals.[124]

The UK system of taxing owner-occupiers fell into disrepute and complexity because of the difficulty of carrying out the five-yearly valuation and the many restrictions on housing after the Second World War. There was also constant pressure for deductions for repairs in computing taxable income, which came close to making the tax voluntary; today, an insistence that such deductions would be allowed only against a valid receipt bearing the relevant VAT registration would have interesting effects on the black economy. Further, when the overdue valuation was carried out it was realised that this would lead to a sudden jump in tax liabilities, and so be deflationary. The ultimate decision to abolish the charge rested just as much on a political desire to help owner-occupiers and others, as on any doctrinal view.

1.6.3 Expenditure tax (ET)

Dissatisfaction with the income tax base (CIT) has led to the periodic revival of interest in a direct tax based on expenditure (ET), in the UK most recently in the Meade Committee Report published in 1978.[125] Similar schemes have been put forward in Australia,[126]

122 Ibid., §§824–35; see also Schreibe (1978) 31 *National Tax Jo.* 10.

123 For a model of how to write a book on housing finance, see Hills, *Unravelling Housing Finance* (OUP, 1992).

124 Staudt (1996) 84 *Georgetown LR* 1571–647.

125 See also Kaldor, *An Expenditure Tax* (1955).

126 Parsons (1986) 3 *Australian Tax Forum* 233.

Ireland, Sweden[127] and the United States[128] It is fair to say that in the UK the idea took much of it strength from the very high rate structure then prevalent and the effect of those rates on the costs of capital to business. The reduction in rates has reduced—but not removed—these objections, enabling one to see things more calmly.

Although this idea has gone underground in recent years, it is still very much alive and will be due for resurrection as economies develop an increasing thirst for investment and so seek ways of encouraging savings. This idea is distinct from the familiar indirect taxes on expenditure; it would apply progressive rates of tax to a taxpayer's total expenditure over the year.

Ideal

In its purest form, such a tax would start with something close to a comprehensive income tax by requiring a composite return of a person's receipts during the year. From this would be deducted sums spent on saving and to the resulting figure would be added sums spent from capital on consumption-dissaving. There would thus be two key differences from the present tax base: it would not tax income saved but would tax capital dissaved. The chances of such a tax being achieved in its purest form are as remote as achieving a pure comprehensive income tax.

Half-way houses

Some of the objectives of an expenditure tax could be achieved in less pure forms by: (a) not taxing income from saving; (b) giving remission from tax on sums spent on savings during the year; or (c) replacing basic rate income tax with a VAT and then having a pure expenditure tax for higher rate taxpayers— the extra sums gathered by the VAT presumably being used to increase welfare payments for those below the present tax threshold. Of these, (a) does not tax dissaving from capital, (b) does so only erratically, and (c) would preserve the present divide between basic and higher rate taxpayers and between proportionate and progressive taxes, and has become more difficult to apply in light of the new income tax rate structure and the increase in VAT rates from 8% in 1978 to 17.5% today.

Arguments for ET

The first argument for an ET is that while, like a CIT, it claims to be based on ability to pay, ET claims also to be based on a moral principle that one should be taxed on what one takes out of the common pool of production. The disadvantage of this, apart from doubts over the notion of a common pool, is that it completely ignores contributions made to society otherwise than through saving. Moreover, Keynesian economics suggests that there can be a moral virtue in spending on consumption when the economy is slack.

Secondly, some arguments are based on those things which an ET tries to do but which a CIT does not: in particular, that an ET will encourage saving by providing a higher rate of return than would be the case under a CIT. This arises because in calculating the total return one would take account of the fact that one puts into the investment an amount which has

[127] First Report of the Commission on Taxation Dublin (July 1982) and S. O. Lodin, *Progressive Expenditure Tax: An Alternative* (Stockholm).

[128] There is useful survey by Toder, in Krever (ed.), *Tax Conversations*, above at n. 68, 159; *US Treasury Blueprints for Basic Tax Reform* (1st ed. 1979, 2nd ed. 1984); see also Bradford, *Untangling the Income Tax* (1986); Andrews 87 *HLR* 1113, Warren 88 *HLR* 947; Andrews 88 *HLR* at 981; and Pechman (ed.), *What Should Be Taxed* (Brookings Institution, 1980). For criticism, see Gunn (1979) 46 *University of Chicago LR* 370; and Musgrave, *Canadian Tax Foundation Paper No, 66*, 20.

not been taxed. To this there are a number of counter arguments. If there is a constant total demand for saving within the economy, the effect may be a fall in interest rates, so that the true net yield will be as before. Moreover, what would be the effect of the tax on dissaving? Would it diminish the incentive to save? Further, while the tax seems to encourage a person who can save—for example an entrepreneur building up his business—it says nothing about a person who inherits wealthThere may be a distinction between the two in that the latter will be subject to a heavy capital accessions tax; yet will not such a tax also have a strong effect on the initial incentive to save? Finally, is it really desirable to allow the accumulation of wealth through saving without limit? In other words, would an ET really be a miser's charter? [129]

Thirdly, a negative argument is that an ET will avoid some of the complexities of the conventional income tax. In 1978 the list of rules to be abolished was: (a) the distinction between income receipts and capital receipts; (b) close company apportionment rules; (c) special rules for trusts; (d) averaging rules; and (e) inflation relief for capital gains. Of these, (a) is also aimed at by a CIT and appears unattainable, although assimilation of rates and various anti-avoidance rules have helped; (b) has been achieved; (c) may be conceded, but (d) and (e) are more controversial. Point (d) has been made less acute by the reductions in rates. As to (e) one should note that while a CIT may accept the desirability of indexing capital gains which an ET does not, ET does this only at the price of taxing all such gains whether or not due to inflation; the only question for an ET is whether the proceeds are spent or saved. In the event, indexation relief for capital gains was introduced in 1982 and has been replaced by tapering relief in 1998 for future gains only, and not for corporation tax.

Fourthly, problems arose from the distortions of the capital market which distortions would not arise under an ET since all investment would be tax free. Distortions arose because different tax rates meant different tax returns for different individuals; moreover, these distortions were compounded by the fact that some assets received capital allowances while others did not. There was therefore a substantial lack of fiscal neutrality in the capital market, which was illustrated dramatically by the Meade Committee. Added irrationality arose from the different systems of taxation applied to incorporated and unincorporated businesses, and by the different treatment accorded as a business uses loan capital or equity capital and, whether a company retains or distributes its profits. After 1978 some of the distortions were reduced—particularly by the 1984 changes to capital allowances and the 1987 and 1988 assimilation of capital gains and income tax rates. If distortions persist, those change still show an alternative way of dealing with them—remove the incentives to invest and reduce general tax rates, i.e. a full-blown CIT combined with a flat-rate tax.

Problems with a pure ET[130]

Most problems were raised in 1978; the intervening 22 years have not solved them. First, some old problems will remain, for example how one determines the income to be adjusted for saving and dissaving, and what the distinction is between a business expense incurred in producing income (and so deductible) and a (chargeable) consumption expense. Secondly, there are problems common to both a CIT and an ET, such as the selection of the

[129] See O'Kelley (1981) 16 *Georgia LR* 1.

[130] This section draws heavily on the principal response to the Meade Report: Prest [1978] *BTR* 176. For a defence, see Kay (1980) 1(3) *Fiscal Studies* 47. On criticism of proposals for taxation of capital, see Bracewell-Milnes [1979] *BTR* 25, 42 (Kay), 43. On use of direct consumption taxes in developing countries, see Zodrow and McClure (1990) 46 *Tax Law Review* 405.

appropriate tax unit. Thirdly, there is the central problem of defining expenditure, particularly problems of loans, gifts, housing and education, the last being tied up with the appropriate treatment of human capital.[131] Again, what of contributions to charities? A good argument can be made that consumption should be confined to divisible private goods and services whose consumption by one household precludes enjoyment by others; it follows that this would not cover collective goods whose enjoyment is not preclusive. Whether to accept this, and, if so, where to draw the line, are matters of policy and judgment choice rather than logical demonstration.

Some problems can be resolved by having a scheme of registered assets (saving) and unregistered assets (consumption). This enables taxpayers to invest their money in order to be taxed immediately or subsequently. However, this solution is questionable; acute problems of theory underlying a tax based on both moral and economic principles should not be resolved by taxpayer choice based on treasury fiat. Further, such a scheme causes problems. First, it presupposes a nation of avid readers who will know, at the end of each tax year, just what their expenditure is to date and who will therefore spend the last Sunday of the tax year arranging purchases of registered or unregistered assets to determine their final tax liabilities to their best advantage. Secondly, an ET bears harshly on a person who faces a heavy and unexpected item of expense, unless he has had the foresight to build up a stock of unregistered assets which can be realised without tax liability and the good fortune to ensure that their value has not been ravaged by inflation. Thirdly, the scheme may bear harshly on the elderly since it is usual for a person to retire on a pension and with some capital. Such people use capital in retirement; at present they pay tax only on their income, whereas under an ET they would have a greater tax liability. It is true that they may have been able to save more thanks to an ET, but they are still left with a higher final liability at a time when they cannot increase income.

Finally, three other areas of difficulty can be noted. The first concerns the rate of tax, which will clearly have to be higher than the current rates of income tax in force to pay for the relief of savings and which, as just seen, will cause particular problems for the old since they tend to dissave. The second difficulty is transitional: how could the system deal with assets acquired before an ET was introduced?[132] The third difficulty is one of scope: how would such a system work internationally,[133] particularly in countries which retained an income tax base; and how would one deal with an individual who saved up money in the UK, but who then spends it overseas?

The Meade Committee Report produced solutions to all these problems. It may be concluded that a system of ET is indeed workable, but that the adjustments needed to make the scheme workable also reduce its attractions.

The current UK income tax

Income tax in its present form can be seen, like many around the world, as a compromise between the two principles,[134] except that the term compromise suggests a degree of "conscious" thought. Something close to an ET applies to pension arrangements under which there is full deduction for payments into a scheme, non-taxability while the assets are held

[131] On which, see Zelanak (1996) 50 *Tax Law Review* 1; and Kaplow, 35

[132] See Zodrow, in Krever (ed.), above at n. 68, 187.

[133] See Peggy Musgrave, in Krever (ed.), above at n. 68, 447–69.

[134] Thus the final note of Gunn's article in (1979) 46 *University of Chicago LR* 370, referring to the Meade Committee Report, states that the UK has so many special rules for savings that it employs an ET in any case.

in the fund and eventual tax liability on the pension. Yet this favours the person who can plan long term—it suits the savings patterns of civil servants rather than entrepreneurs. Some degree of compromise (or inconsistency) may actually be justifiable.[135] The reliefs for savings are considered below.

The current UK income tax law is limited by four principal factors. First, for income tax there is the Schedular system which makes no attempt to tax matters not falling within the various Schedules. Secondly, in applying the terms used in the various Schedules the courts have adopted a view that capital gain should and can be distinguished from income—a view reinforced by the doctrine that income must have a source. Although the UK has had a CGT since 1965, it is a limited and unsatisfactory tax. Thirdly, there are numerous exceptions to the bases for the various taxes, based on a mixture of practicality and expediency. This problem is not unique to the UK tax system and it has become common to refer to many of the reliefs and exemptions as shelters or tax expenditures[136] (see below at §1.7). The virtue of this analysis is that by dramatising the cost of a relief, it may cause the relief to be re-examined not least to see whether the same objective could be achieved another way. There are, however, difficulties, particularly over definition. Tax shelters have been succeeded by other problems stemming from the financial world, with its development of new financial instruments[137] undermining traditional principles of the tax system, such as the distinction between capital and income, or rules about timing, and by the real or virtual world of electronics where the principles most at risk are those relating to the location of income. Finally, there is the problem of the attitude of the courts towards avoidance schemes, a story in its own right and with its own chapter (see chapter 5 below). In 1978, when the Meade Committee reported, it was fair to say that UK courts had not yet shown much willingness to protect the tax base against flagrantly artificial schemes.

1.7 Tax Expenditures[138]

A tax expenditure is a concept radically distinct from an expenditure tax. It has been defined as "an exemption or relief which is not part of the essential structure of the tax in question but has been introduced into the tax code for extraneous reason".[139] An example is mortgage interest relief from income tax; this is thought to be a tax expenditure because it is not an essential feature of an income tax and because the Government has foregone tax on the amount of the interest paid. Such a relief is the functional equivalent of a public expenditure. The concept is useful in that it dramatises the cost of reliefs and so may cause a re-examination of the reliefs. If the relief can be justified as a public expense it may still have

135 For example, McCaffery 70 *Texas Law Review* 1145.

136 The United States has experienced special problems which were settled temporarily in the Tax Reform Act 1986 (TRA 1986): see Birnbaum and Murray, "Showdown at Gucci Gulch" (1987); and Chirelstein [1986] *Florida State LR* 207. On the TRA 1986, see comment by Auerbach and Slemrod (1997) 35 *Journal of Economic Literature* 589, 628. "A decade of analysis had not taught us much about whether the TRA 1986 was a good idea (which is not the same as saying that it was not a good idea)."

137 See Schenk, in "Foreword to Colloquium on Financial Instruments" (1995) 50 *Tax Law Review* 487; on UK rules, see further, chapter 48 below.

138 See chapter 6 below, table 4.

139 Willis and Hardwick, *Tax Expenditure in the United Kingdom* (Heinemann, 1978), 1. The concept was developed by Stanley Surrey: see, generally, Surrey and McDaniel, *Tax Expenditures* (Harvard University Press, 1985); Bradford, above at n. 112, ch. 11; and summary by Brooks (1986) 34 *Can. Tax Jo.* 681.

to be justified in terms of efficiency, i.e. that the tax system is the most appropriate way of providing the expenditure. A list of the current UK reliefs is set out in chapter 6.

The concept is not, however, without difficulties. First, there is the problem of determining what reliefs are part of "the essential structure" of the tax.[140] This problem is more acute in the UK where there seems to be little agreement on what the essential structure is. Thus, a revenue expense incurred by a businessman in generating profit, e.g. paying employees a proper wage, is an expense incurred in achieving what is to be taxed and so a part of the essential structure. However, one may have more difficulty with the proper treatment of losses and their relief against either general income or trading income from the current or later years. Another example is mortgage interest (finally repealed in 2000). In 1799 relief was available for all types of interest since these payments were regarded as charges on income and so part of the essential structure of the tax; viewed in this light mortgage interest relief could be considered one of the last embodiments of true principle rather than an anomaly. One might try to avoid these difficulties by reducing the object of the exercise to that of indicating "the cost of special tax provisions which can be considered as alternatives to direct expenditure and loan programmes".[141] However, this not only reduces an important exercise in theory to the level of a political game over departmental budgets, but begs the question of how costs are estimated.[142] Supporters of an expenditure or consumption tax have to face similar problems in distinguishing what is an essential part of the tax, i.e. an item which should be deductible as an item of saving or investment, from what is an item of consumption and so not deductible; consumption is not a self-defining term.

[140] See Bittker (1969) 22 *National Tax Jo.* 244; and Bittker, *Taxation of Income, Estates and Gifts*, §3.6. Bittker also asks why a tax expenditure budget is not mirrored by an "expenditure tax budget" based on the theory that excluding a group of citizens from a subsidy granted to other similarly situated citizens is equivalent to taxing the excluded persons: see ibid., 368, §3.6.

[141] Surrey and Hellmuth 22 *National Tax Jo.* 530.

[142] The process usually assumes that the taxpayer would spend his money in exactly the same way and be subject to his marginal rate of tax; it thus ignores the effect of taxing the income.

2

Jurisdiction: The Taxing Power

2.1 The Power to Tax: the UK, the Tax Year and the Annual Tax

The power to levy taxes is only one manifestation of the sovereignty of Parliament. The Bill of Rights provides that no charge on the subject shall be levied by pretence of prerogative without the consent of Parliament.[1] The Bill of Rights is not pure history; in the 1992 decision in *Woolwich Building Society* Case it was invoked by Lord Goff as one reason for granting restitution.[2] There is a presumption that express statutory authority is needed before a tax can be imposed;[3] however, this does not apply to a charge levied for services.[4] Taxation bills begin in the House of Commons, the powers of the House of Lords being limited.[5] Each year a Finance Bill begins in March or April; currently this is preceded by a pre-Budget report in November of the previous year announcing proposed changes in the tax system, when spending decisions are also announced.[6]

[1] 2 Will. and Mar. (c. 2), art. 4; on tax provisions of the Bill of Rights, see Williams [1989] *BTR* 370.

[2] [1992] STC 657, 677j.

[3] *A-G* v. *Wiltshire United Dairies* (1921) 37 TLR 884. Cf. Emergency Powers (Defence) Act 1939, ss 1(3) and 2. On (non-)limitation by international law, see *Cheney* v. *Conn* [1968] 1 All ER 779, 44 TC 217. The same presumption applies to requisitioning a person's property without paying for it: *A-G* v. *De Keyser's Royal Hotel* [1920] AC 508; on which, see Scott and Hildesley, *The Case of Requisition* (OUP, 1920).

[4] *China Navigation Co. Ltd.* v. *A-G* [1932] 2 KB 197.

[5] Parliament Act 1911, s. 1. See, generally, Bradley and Ewing *Constitutional Law* (12th ed.), ch. 17; and Erskine May, *Parliamentary Practice* (Butterworths, 22nd ed. (1997), chs 30–33.

[6] A unified Budget (i.e. one covering both spending and taxing) was tried from November 1993 to November 1996. It had been proposed in *Budgetary Reform*, Cm. 1867 (March 1992); it was criticised in *The Economist*, 27 November 1993, but supported by many worthies including the Armstrong Report for IFS (1980) and Treasury and Civil Service Committee of HC 1982. See also Symposium *Fiscal Studies*, Vol, 14, No. 1, 77.

2.1.1 *The United Kingdom*

The legislation applies to the United Kingdom, i.e.England, Wales, Scotland and Northern Ireland, and the Scilly Isles,[7] but not the Channel Islands nor the Isle of Man.

2.1.2 *Tax year*

For income tax and CGT, the tax year runs from 6 April to 5 April, so that the year from 6 April 2001 to 5 April 2002 is known as the tax year 2001–02. Different rules apply to corporation tax.[8] The reason for these dates is that the financial year originally began on Lady Day, 25 March; this was changed in 1752 when the calendars were altered.[9] Almost any dating is arbitrary and change now would, if we still lived in a world in which Britain traded with its imperial (date-sharing) partners, merely substitute the apparently rational for the attractively picturesque. Today there may well be compliance-cost advantages in moving to a year beginning on 1st January, this being the most common in other trading partner countries.[10]

2.1.3 *Annual taxes*

Income tax (and corporation tax, but not CGT, VAT or Stamp Duties) is an annual tax, and the charge is reimposed by Parliament each year in the Finance Bill.[11] The result is that the Tax Acts are really in the nature of an Income Tax Clauses Act and apply whenever any Act imposes an income tax.[12] The Finance Bill also amends the rules for the other taxes.[13] The resulting combination of measures of great economic importance and matters of great technical subtlety discussed against the background of the hurly burly of Parliamentary procedure is, not surprisingly, capable of error.

The notion of income tax as an annual tax is rooted in history, with the need to ensure that the Crown did not try to tax its subjects without having to recall Parliament. It is also an optimistic reminder that income tax was originally a temporary tax; the tax has remained in force every year since 1842. The notion of an annual tax is, however, more modern. Parliament granted the tax for three years in 1842, 1845 and 1848, and for seven years in 1853. New Zealand has moved away from an annual tax, but an official report in 1998 recommended its return to symbolise the relationship between Crown and Parliament.[14]

[7] TA 1988, Sch. 30, paras 6(2)(b), 21. See also FA 1986, s. 108 on the definition of the UK relating to oil taxation.

[8] And, before its abolition, to DLT: see DLTA 1976, s. 13.

[9] Royal Commission (1920), App. 7(o).

[10] The case for the change was argued 20 years ago by Johnson (1980) *Fiscal Studies*, Vol. 1, No 3, 29.

[11] The term Finance Bill was first used in 1894: see Jeffrey Cook [1994] *BTR* 365.

[12] *Per* Atkin L.J. in *Martin* v. *Lowry* (1926) 11 TC 297, 317.

[13] The practice of having a single bill dealing with all taxes stems from Gladstone's battles with the House of Lords: see Magnus, *Gladstone* (John Murray, 1954), 151. There is nothing inevitable about this; the Australian constitution s. 55 requires law imposing tax to deal with one subject of taxation only; this is to prevent earmarking of unrelated matters which the Senate cannot amend because of s. 53.

[14] *Tax Compliance: Report to the Treasurer by a Committee of Experts* (Wellington, December 1998), para. 2.200.

2.1.4 Qualifications

These simple statements must now be qualified in four ways. First, since 1913 there has been statutory authority for collecting taxes on the authority of a resolution of the House of Commons notwithstanding that the Finance Bill itself has not yet been passed. Secondly, the legislation passed by the UK Parliament will be of no effect to the extent that it breaches European Community law; legislation which breaches discrimination rules will have no effect against a citizen of another Member State, and an appropriate directive not enacted by the UK Parliament will be of direct effect and so can be used by a qualifying taxpayer. Thirdly, we have the European Convention on Human Rights incorporated into UK domestic law to some extent by the Human Rights Act 1998. Fourthly, we now have a limited delegation of the taxing power to the Scottish Assembly. These are discussed at 2.2–2.5.

2.2 Qualification (1): The Provisional Collection of Taxes

Since income tax is an annual tax[15] and is imposed by a charge in each year's Finance Act, difficulties have arisen where the Finance Act has not become law by the start of the tax year (6 April). Until 1913 tax could not lawfully be collected simply on the basis of a resolution of the House of Commons.[16] The Provisional Collection of Taxes Act 1913 (now PCTA 1968) gave temporary statutory effect to resolutions of the House of Commons.[17] Resolutions, if passed in March or April, expire on 5 August next and, if passed in any other month, expire after four months.[18] New taxes are expressly excluded. In the days of the unified budget, Royal Assent was required by 5 May.[19]

2.3 Qualification (2): The European Community[20]

2.3.1 EC's own resources

Since 1975 the financial basis of the Community is provided entirely out of the revenues of the Community. It consists of agricultural levies, customs duties and proportion of VAT; which proportion is now equivalent to a percentage which has varied between 1% and 1.4% applied to a VAT base limited to 55% of GNP.[21] It is not correct to say that when the VAT rate in the UK is increased (or decreased) there is a change in the UK's contribution to the European Community. This basis was settled by the European Council Meetings of February 1988 and December 1992, which also agreed a ceiling of 1.277% of Community GNP and added a further resource based on GNP.

[15] See above n. 8.

[16] *Bowles* v. *Bank of England* [1913] 1 Ch 57. The Finance Acts of 1909, 1910 and 1911 reached the statute book 13, seven and seven months respectively after the start of the financial year. Mr Bowles was an opposition backbencher; the dilatory Chancellor of the Exchequer was Lloyd George.

[17] On temporary effect of resolution for stamp duty, see FA 1973, s. 50.

[18] PCTA 1968, s. 1. The background is explained in the Government White Paper, *Budgetary Reform*, Cm. 1867 and, more specifically in HM Treasury press release, 31 December 1992, (1993) *Simon's Tax Intelligence* 160.

[19] FA 1993, s. 205.

[20] The broadest, technical, overall account of EC tax harmonisation policy is Terra and Wattel, *European Tax Law* 2nd ed 1997, Fed Deventer (1997). See also Williams *EC Tax Law*, (Longmans 1998) Farmer and Lyal *EC Tax Law* (OUP, 1994) and Radaelli, *The Politics of Corporate Taxation in the European Union* Routledge (1997), esp. chs 5 and 6.

[21] Bainbridge and Teasdale, *Penguin Guide to the EU* (1996) p. 358.

2.3.2 Restraints on fiscal sovereignty: the basic position

EC law limits the rights of member governments to levy taxes by taking precedence over Acts of Parliament.[22] This supremacy does not apply to those areas in which sovereignty has not been ceded.

Supremacy issues first arise in connection with UK legislation. The UK Parliament may find that its legislation conflicts with principles of the EC law[23] or that it has not followed the proper procedure, e.g. by not consulting the Commission,[24] so that in either case its legislation is of no effect. However, issues also arise when an individual taxpayer is accorded rights under EC law through the doctrine of direct effect.[25] Provisions of EC law having direct effect include rights under the EC Treaty or other EC law. The provision must be clear and concise; it must be unconditional and unqualified and not subject to the taking of any further measures on the part of a Community or national authority and must leave no substantial discretion in its implementation to a Community or national authority.[26] Several Treaty provisions have been given direct effect in taxation. The European Court has asserted a pre-emptive jurisdiction to forestall divergent interpretations of a directive by allowing a reference by a national court on a domestic tax issue.[27]

A failure to implement directives properly and in time will enable a taxpayer to assert the rights set out in the directive against the Member State,[28] if the conditions for direct effect apply. In addition, the citizen may be able to recover damages from the state under the principle in *Francovitch*[29] for failure to implement the directive—this right may arise even though the principle required for direct effect is not satisfied.[30]

State aids[31]

Some of the provisions, e.g. Article 87 (ex Article 92) of the EC Treaty concern state aid and case-law, and establish clearly that tax provisions which are in substance state aid fall foul of these provisions unless clearance has been obtained from the Commission under Article 88 (ex Article 93). A recent example arose when the UK Parliament increased the rate of insurance premium tax for certain types of insurance sold through travel agents without obtaining clearance from the Commission; the English court held that this differential taxation would distort competition and intra-Community trade, and so breached Article 87.[32]

Indirect taxes and similar charges

Article 90 (ex 95) of the EC Treaty prohibits discrimination against imports from other Member States by the levy of charges higher than those on domestic products. Article 91 (ex 96) prohibits refunds on exports exceeding the actual taxation imposed on the goods. The Treaty Article 93 (ex 99) also required the Commission to consider how the legislation of turnover

22 *Stoke-on-Trent City Council* v. *B and Q plc* [1991] 4 All ER 221, 223.
23 As in the famous *Factortame* case: *R* v. *Secretary of State for Transport. ex parte Factortame* [1991] 1 AC 603.
24 As in *R.* v. *Customs and Excise Commrs, ex parte Lunn Poly Ltd.* [1999] STC 350.
25 Case 26/62 *Van Gend en Loos* v. *Nederlandse Tariefcomissie* [1963] ECR 1.
26 Edward and Lane, *European Community Law*, para. 133.
27 Case C–28/95 *Leur Bloem* [1997] STC 1205; see Betten [1999] *CMLR* 165.
28 The so-called "vertical" direct effect of directives allows the enforcement of rights against the member state but not against other citizens: Edward and Lane, above at n. 26, para. 148.
29 Ibid., para. 141.
30 Case C–91/9 *Faccinni Dori* v. *Recreb* [1994] ECR I–3325.
31 See Evans, *State Aid* (OUP 1998); Schon (1999) 36 *CMLR* 911; and Monti (1998) *EC Tax Review* 200.
32 *R.* v. *Customs and Excise Commrs, ex parte Lunn Poly Ltd.* [1999] STC 350.

taxes could be harmonised, a process which has given us the famous Sixth Directive imposing a common tax base to VAT throughout the Community, and enacted in the UK as the VATA 1984, now consolidated as the VATA 1994. This surrender of sovereignty in relation to turnover taxes does not extend to taxes which are not turnover taxes, e.g. insurance premium tax.[33]

Direct taxes—no compensation for effects on trade

Article 92 (ex Article 98) of the EC Treaty extends the principle of Article 91 (ex Article 96) to direct taxation and prohibits Member States from operating systems of compensation for the effects of direct taxation on intra-Community trade. However, this is subject to a right of derogation, provided the Government obtains authorisation from the Commission.

Harmonisation

Article 94 (ex Article 100) of the EC Treaty provides for the approximation of laws by directives, and it is on this basis that the Commission has tried to achieve harmonisation of company taxes. No article requires harmonisation as Article 93 (ex 99) does for indirect tax. Directives under Article 94 require unanimity in the Council. There has been regular UK legislation to implement directives, as in 1990 when the Revenue was placed under a duty to provide information about liabilities to tax in another Member State.[34] The Single Market programme provided its own impetus leading to the Ruding Committee's 1992 report on the distortions caused by different corporation tax systems, the extent to which those could be removed by market forces and the desirability of legislation towards harmonisation should those forces not be enough.[35] Two Directives were enacted in 1990, the Parent-Subsidiary Directive and the Mergers and Acquisitions Directive, designed to grant to cross-border transactions the same favourable treatment as is provided for equivalent purely domestic transactions. The UK introduced the appropriate implementing legislation,[36] but the Revenue conceded that the Directives would probably have had direct effect anyway.[37] In addition, a multilateral convention on transfer pricing is now in force, along with a Council regulation on administrative co-operation in the field of indirect taxation.[38]

The ever-closer operation of the European single market is undermining many traditional assumptions and techniques of international tax. This should cause no surprise to students of history of the United States, Germany or Italy. The UK is developing a halfway house between international tax and domestic tax to encompass the European Community. Recent areas of work include avoiding discrimination in the treatment of withholding taxes on royalties, interest and the consolidation of cross-border losses,[39] the co-ordination of treaties,[40] and the problems of small and medium-sized enterprises.[41] However, the

[33] Ibid.

[34] FA 1990, s. 125.

[35] See below at §44.3.

[36] Dir 90/435 (OJ 1990 L 225/6) and Dir 90/434 (OJ 1990 L 225/1) respectively.

[37] *EC Direct Tax Measures: A Consultative Document* (December 1991), para. 2.13.

[38] (1992) *Simon's Tax Intelligence* 161.

[39] On 2000 negotiations at Feira see Weiner, 20 (26) *Tax Notes International*, 26 June 2731–2734. COM/90/595; see comments by CFE, 22 April 1992; (1992) *Simon's Tax Intelligence* 490, and text printed in (1992) *Intertax* 27.

[40] (1993) *Simon's Tax Intelligence* 350. For comment, see, e.g. Hinnekens (1994) *EC Tax Law Review* 146 suggesting that the Commission should not interfere in what are essentially bilateral negotiations but may have a role in major matters such as limitation of benefit clauses. For a consideration of how treaties beween the North American Free Trade Agreement (NAFTA) countries might be changed to eliminate tax barriers to cross-border investment see Arnold and Harris (1994) 49 *Tax Law Review* 529; on differences between the European Community and NAFTA, note Gammie 49 ibid., 647–8.

[41] See 94/C187/04, reprinted in (1994) *Simon's Tax Intelligence* 862; see also Written Answer, 7 December 1995, Qn E–2158/94 (OJ 1995 C36/95), reported in (1995) *Simon's Weekly Tax Intelligence* 361.

bigger—and even more intractable—issue is how profits can satisfactorily be attributed to one country rather than another as the old assumptions become more unreal.[42] At present, this is masked by other disagreements over the nature and purpose of corporate tax itself.[43] Into this confused area the European Court of Justice makes its own occasional contributions on the basis of the non-discrimination principles, which tax lawyers tend to find unsettling.

Non-discrimination principles[44]

Non-discrimination is at the heart of the EC Treaty and the law, including case-law, which has followed from it. Although direct tax law has not been harmonised, the tax laws of the Member States must not infringe these principles.[45] Sometimes EC law is concerned with discrimination on grounds of sex,[46] but in the tax context it is usually on grounds of nationality. Moreover, while EC Treaty articles concern nationals and non-nationals, case-law often concerns non-residents. This is because the most frequent example of the non-national is the non-resident. It should be understood that when passages in cases talk about non-residents they are actually concerned only with nationals of the European Community.

The concept of discrimination is not straightforward. The case-law of the ECJ distinguishes direct discrimination from indirect or covert discrimination. The language used by the European Court is not always precise, but the distinction seems to be between those measures which break the non-discrimination principle on their face, e.g. rules applying only to nationals of a certain state, and those which simply have that effect. The importance of the difference is that if a measure falls within the direct category then justification must be sought within the words of the Treaty itself.[47] Not only are there few such justifications,[47a] but the Court interprets them strictly. However, most tax discrimination problems arise in the context of residence rather than nationality, and so normally belong in the covert or indirect discrimination category. Covert discrimination may be justified if the discriminatory measure pursues a legitimate objective compatible with the Treaty, and the national rules are appropriate to attain that objective, going no further what is necessary for that purpose.[48] Article 48 ex 58 makes it clear that when one is dealing with the right of establishment of enterprises, i.e. companies or firms as opposed to individuals, those with a registered office or central administration within the community are to be treated the same way as natural persons who are nationals of Member States. This means that what may be covert discrimination for an individual may be overt discrimination for an enterprise. The picture is further muddied by another line of jurisprudence suggesting that the Court can review national measures which, although not actually discriminatory, are liable to hinder or make less attractive the exercise of the fundamental freedoms guaranteed by the Treaty.[49]

[42] For a solution, see Gammie's views, cited in House of Lords Select Committee on the European Union HL-92, 15th Report, 1998–1999 session, para. 227.

[43] Ibid., para. 225.

[44] Good starting points are Lyons [1994] *BTR* 554; Woutters (1999) 8 *EC Tax Review* 98; and van Raad (1995) 4 *EC Tax Review* 190.

[45] Case 270/83 *Commission* v. *France* [1986] ECR 273, para. 24.

[46] Inland Revenue Press Release, 9 February 1995; (1995) *Simon's Weekly Tax Intelligence* 248.

[47] *Bond van Adverteerders* v. *Netherlands* [1988] ECR 2805, para. 34.

[47a] e.g. Art 46 (ex 56) lists public order, public safety and public health.

[48] Case C-19/92 *Kraus* v. *Land Baden-Wurtemburg* [1993] ECR I–1663, para. 32.

[49] Case C–55 /94 *Gebhard* [1996] ECR I–1416, para. 37; discussed by Richardson [1998] *BTR* 302, who also cites the opinion of the Advocate-General in Case C–80/94 *Wielockx* [1995] ECR I–2493, para. 17.

The European Court, not content simply with creating two or more categories of discrimination of uncertain content, also had difficulties in deciding when discrimination arises. This is because of a lack of clarity over what has to be compared with what to see if there is discrimination. The usual comparison is between a resident and a non-resident, but the Court might be asked to compare the position of two non-residents.[50] In the tax context a comparison between the tax position of a resident with that of a non-resident will almost always result in discrimination since the whole nature of international tax as developed by the OECD is to separate taxation of those resident in state A from the rules taxing those who are resident in state B but who have a source of income in state A. Both are liable to pay tax in state A, but the bases on which they pay are usually different. State A, as the state of residence, is presumed to be the person's tax home or base, and so it is entitled to tax all the income wherever it arises, making adjustments according the taxpayer's overall position; state B, as the state of source, is expected to charge only on income arising within its borders, leaving overall adjustments of the tax burden to state A. A tax treaty between state A and state B will usually contain a non-discrimination clause of it own under which state A is not allowed to discriminate against residents of state B.[51] This non-discrimination is separate from, and usually more specific than, that created by EC law.

The non-discrimination principle is embodied for tax purposes in four freedoms: the free cross-border movement of employees (Article 39; ex Article 48); freedom of establishment for businesses (Article 43; ex Article 52); freedom to provide services (Article 49; ex Article 59); and free movement of capital (Article 56; ex Article 73B). Tax provisions which break, or may break, these provisions may be challenged in court action, but are more frequently the subject of investigation by the Commission. These may range widely: in 1992 there were suggestions that certain anti-treaty shopping clauses in treaties with countries such as the United States might be in conflict with Community law.[52] It is thought that these specific powers prevent the court from relying on the more general anti-discrimination rule in Article 12 (ex Article 6).[53]

UK Parliament's pre-emptive or corrective legislation

The 1995 legislation extending the benefits of share schemes to part-time employees[54] and of TESSAs to relevant European institutions should be seen as moves to head off investigation by the Commission.[55] In 1992 the Commissioner in charge of taxation indicated that the restriction of the qualifying maintenance deduction to orders made by UK courts may infringe Community law;[56] amending legislation was accordingly passed.[57] In the 1980s capital duty was abolished.[58] FA 2000 continues this process, see p. 37.

50 See discussion by Richardson [1998] *BTR* 283, 292–5 (concluding that this comparison is not appropriate).
51 See below at §65.5.
52 Written Question No .2046/90 (OJ 1991 C79/28); (1991) *Simon's Tax Intelligence* 366.
53 See Richardson [1998] *BTR* 281, 291, citing Case C–112/91 *Werner* 1993 ECR I–429, para. 20.
54 FA 1995, s. 137.
55 TA 1988, s. 326A, as amended by FA 1995, s. 63.
56 (OJ 1992 C89); (1992) *Simon's Tax Intelligence* 479.
57 F (No. 2) A 1992, s. 61.
58 On capital duty, see Farmer (1999) 8 *EC Tax Review* 45.

2.3.3 Restraints on fiscal sovereignty: the non-discrimination case-law of the European Court[59]

The general approach

The European Court has usually taken a broad approach to the non-discrimination principle, as is illustrated by one of the earliest cases. In the *French Tax Credits* case[60] an Italian insurance company had set up a branch in France. The branch received dividend income from French sources. Under French tax law, companies could reclaim the tax credit accompanying the dividend from the French revenue; however, repayment was refused if the company was not resident in France. The refusal was held to breach Article 43 (ex Article 52). Even if the disadvantage to the Italian company under the present rule was compensated for by other advantages, they could not justify this breach of the duty under Article 43, which was to accord foreign companies the same treatment as was accorded to French companies. The extent of the disadvantage could not be in issue since Article 43 prohibits all discrimination even if only of a limited nature. Moreover, the fact that the Italian company could have got the benefit of the credit if it had established a French subsidiary (rather than a branch) was irrelevant since this interfered with the freedom to trade in another Member State in a vehicle of its own choice—whether branch or subsidiary.

Article 39 cases

Article 39 (ex Article 48) guarantees freedom of movement and bans any discrimination based on nationality between workers of the Member States as regards employment remuneration and other conditions of work and employment. The article has been extended by case-law to ban covert forms of discrimination which, by the application of criteria of differentiation other than nationality, lead to the same result. In *Biehl* v. *Administration des Contributions du Grand-Duche de Luxembourg*[61] a provision of the Luxembourg tax code denying a PAYE repayment to persons ceasing to be resident was struck down because it operated against taxpayers who were nationals of other states.[62] This was so even though there was an administrative procedure which gave much the same result—an administrative discretion was no substitute for rights.

Cross-frontier workers: employed (Article 39) and self-employed (Article 43)

Case-law since *Biehl*, has generally concerned the problem of cross-frontier workers—where X, a person resident in state A is employed in state B. State B will usually tax non-residents on a basis less favourable than its own residents refusing, for example, personal allowances or deductions for pension contributions, leaving all those deductions and adjustments to state A, the country of residence. State B's attitude, while conforming to established international tax norms, may have unfortunate effects if X's only income arises in state B. If, as is common in continental Europe, state A does not tax foreign income at all, X will have a tax liability in state B but not in state A, while receiving deductions in state A but not in state B. The problem is that while the European Court agrees that state B may tax

[59] See Lyons [1994] *BTR* 554; Stanley (1997) *CMLR* 713.

[60] Case 270/83 *Commission* v. *French Republic* [1986] ECR 273, ECJ.

[61] Case C–175/88 [1991] STC 575, ECJ. The principle of equal treatment with regard to remuneration would be rendered ineffective if it could be undermined by discriminatory national provisions on income tax; hence EC Regulation No. 1612/68, Art. 7.

[62] [1991] STC 575, paras 11–14.

non-residents differently from residents, the effect is sometimes to deprive X of the economic value of the right to work across the border. One solution is to define those circumstances in which the economic disadvantage to X is so severe as to amount to a breach of Article 39 (ex Article 43). However, the cases put the matter the other way round. Given that state B is not taxing the same way as its residents, can it justify the different treatment on objective differences? The difference is that under the second approach the rule will be struck down whenever it is unjustified, not when the the problem is severe. The difference is shown in the *Asscher* case (see below).

Deductions and aggregation

In *Finanzamt Köln–Altstadt* v. *Schumacker*[63] state B was compelled to grant X aggregation of spousal income and relief for certain losses and for certain insurance payments (old age, sickness and invalidity) where X derived his income entirely or almost entirely from state B; here, X derived 90% of his income from state B and that sufficed. State B could not justify the difference simply on the basis of non-residence. In the analogous case of *Wielockx* v. *Inspecteur der Directe Belastingen*[64] a self-employed person working in state B but resident in state A was allowed to use state B's rules permitting deduction of a pension contribution; the precise percentage of income earned in state B was not clear, but was probably more than 90%.

These decisions may be seen as a sensible development of international tax norms in that the country of source, is in economic terms, preponderant and so can be treated as if it were the country of residence. This approach is reinforced by the decision in *Gschwindt* v. *Finanzamt Aachen–Ausenstadt*.[65] Here the worker derived only 58% of total income from state B, which was therefore entitled to withhold the benefit of income-splitting, leaving such matters to state A, the country of residence.

Tax rates

In *Asscher* v *Staatssecretaris*[66] the issue concerned not the availability of deductions, but the rate of tax. Under the laws of state B, if X had been resident in state B or 90% of his income had been taxable in state B, the rate would have been the normal progressive rate (13%); instead, it was a flat rate of 25%. The Court held that X was entitled to the lower rate in state B. Two points were underlined. First, although residents and non-residents could be taxed differently, the fact that the income earned in state B, while not taxed in state A, was taken into account in determining total income for progression in state A, made it reasonable for X to be able to use the progressive rate scale in state B. Secondly, the fact that the 13% rate would have applied under state B's law if X had paid social security contributions, so making the 13% rate compensation for paying those contributions, was no justification.

Four points may be made. First, while this decision makes sense in a country like the Netherlands, which exempts foreign income but takes it into account for progression, it makes less sense where the foreign income is not exempt or is fully exempt. Secondly, the decision encourages free riders who can split their incomes between countries so as to attain

[63] Case C–279/93: [1995] STC 306, ECJ. For survey of practices in different countries, see 35 *European Taxation* 347.

[64] Case C–80/94 [1995] STC 876.

[65] Unreported, 14 September 1999, ECJ.

[66] Case C–107/94 [1996] STC 1025; see Stanley (1997) *CMLR* 713; Lyons [1996] *BTR* 641; and Williams (1997) 6 *EC Tax Review* 4, 6.

the most advantageous overall position.[67] Thirdly, the court's understanding of the Dutch system was incomplete and the basis of the decision was therefore flawed.[68] It is clear that the *Asscher* decision, in its rejection of the conventional understanding of the roles of source taxation and residence taxation, take us way beyond the limits of *Schumacker*; what is not clear is whether further facts will persuade the Court to retreat. Finally, one should note the curious fact that the Court took a distinction based on residence and treated it as covert discrimination based on nationality, even though the two cases compared involved nationals of the same Member State.[69] It may therefore be that the Court is trying to find a way of allowing a person resident in one Member State the right to set up establishments in more than one Member State.[70]

Article 43 cases

Article 43 (ex Article 52) of the EC Treaty guarantees freedom of establishment and expressly bans restrictions on the setting-up of agencies, branches or subsidiaries by nationals of any Member State in the territory of any other Member State. This is extended to companies and firms by Article 48 (ex Article 58). It has been interpreted broadly so as to ban not only overt discrimination by reason of nationality or, in the case of a company, its seat, but all covert forms of discrimination which, by the application of other criteria of differentiation, lead to the same result.[71] Its wide scope has already been seen in the *French Tax Credits* case. The taxpayer also won in *R.* v. *IRC, ex p Commerzbank AG*.[72] Here, a German bank with a UK branch had successfully argued that it was entitled to exemption from UK tax on interest received from US corporations;[73] its claim to repayment supplement was succesful even though the UK domestic legislation clearly did not allow repayment supplement to a non-resident. The UK had argued that it was entitled to withhold the repayment supplement since Commerzbank, unlike resident companies, was exempt on the income originally in issue. This was swept aside. "The argument cannot be upheld. The fact that the exemption in question was available only to non-resident companies cannot justify a rule of a general nature withholding the benefit. That rule is therefore discriminatory".[74] This seems to leave it open to the UK to introduce a rule barring repayment supplement where the repayment claim arises in respect of income which is exempt from tax only by reason of non-residence; however, the UK statute was amended more generously, by removing the restriction altogether.[75] Meanwhile, it should be noted that the ban on repayment supplement remains effective for individuals, etc., not entitled to invoke Community rules, e.g. persons not resident in a Member State. The decision may be seen as the forerunner of the *Asscher* case.

In *Halliburton Services BV* v. *Staatssecretaris van Financiën*,[76] the Court required an exemption from a Dutch transaction tax which was given to corporate reorganisation

[67] Williams (1997) 1 *EC Tax Review* 4, 8

[68] van Raad [1996] *Tax Notes International* 471, 473.

[69] Stanley, above at n. 66, 718.

[70] Ibid., 721.

[71] Judgment of the European Court in *Commerzbank* (below, para. 4, citing Case 152/73 *Sotgiu* v. *Deutsche Bundespost* [1974] ECR 153, para. 11. *R.* v. *IRC, ex parte Commerzbank AG* [1993] STC 605, 621, para. 14, ECJ.

[72] [1993] STC 605, ECJ. For subsequent action, see (1993) *Simon's Tax Intelligence* 1091, 1264. For speculation about ambit, see Sandler [1993] *BTR* 517.

[73] *IRC* v. *Commerzbank AG* [1990] STC 285.

[74] [1993] STC 605, 622, ECJ.

[75] FA 1994, Sch. 19, amending TA 1988, s. 824 (income tax) and TA 1988, s. 826 superseding s. 825 for corporation tax as from start of pay and file (1993).

[76] Case C–1/93 [1994] STC 655.

involving two Dutch companies where the transfer of property involved a Dutch and a German company. This matter is of importance to the UK by reason of the number of corporate reorganisation provisions which are similarly expressed to be confined to situations in which both companies are resident in the UK.[77] These anxieties are strengthened as a result of the decision in *ICI plc* v. *Colmer*.[78] The case concerned the UK rule that consortium relief for losses, now in TA 1988, ss 402 and 413, could be claimed only where the holding company's 90% subsidiary trading companies were also companies resident in the UK. The challenge was made under Article 52. The main point made by the Court was that the restriction was not justifiable under EC law as it stood. The restriction to UK resident companies was an obvious breach of Article 43 and therefore would have to be struck down unless the UK could justify it, which it could not. In response FA 2000 s. 97 contains a rule extending consortium and group relief to all non-resident companies while s. 75 contains rules regulating the way in which capital allowances for machinery and plant are given to non-residents.

In the *St Gobain*[79] case the German branch of a French company sought to take advantage of certain clauses in treaties made by Germany with other states (i.e. not France). The court held that the French branch was entitled to do so. While the language is typically expansive the issue only arises because of a provision of German domestic law which gave relief by reference to the treaties. Despite this narrow point the UK legislature, perhaps wisely, took it as its cue to extend various double taxation reliefs to UK branches of foreign companies; see FA 2000 s. 103, and see below at §65.1.

Article 56 Freedom of movement of capital

The first case to be decided solely on the basis of freedom of movement of capital is *Secretaris van Financien* v *Verkooijen* Case C-35/98 (decided 6 June 2000). This freedom is set out in art 73 (1)(d) now 56 (1)(a) of the Treaty and was implemented by Directive 88/361/EEC of 24 June 1988 (OJ 1988 L 178 p.5) In this case V, a Dutch resident, received dividend income from as Belgian company which was subject to 25% withholding in Belgium in the usual way. If the dividends had been from a company with its seat in the Netherlands V would have been entitled to an exemption on the first NLG 1,000 of dividend income. V appealed on the basis that EC law did not allow Dutch tax law to restrict the exemption to companies resident in the Netherlands but should apply to companies resident in all member states. On a reference from the Hoge Raad under art 234 (ex 177) the ECJ agreed with V.

The purpose of the exemption (para 11) was partly to increase interest in equity shareholdings—and so the amount of capital subscribed to Dutch companies and the second was to compensate in some small way for the effect of the Dutch classical system of corporate taxation which meant that no part of the corporate was imputed through to the shareholder. This was treated by the court as a clear breach of EC law since it constituted an obstacle to a Belgian company raising capital in the Netherlands.

[77] See Keeling and Shipwright [1995] *European Law Review* 580, esp. 595–6.

[78] Case C–264/96 [1998] All ER EC 585, [1998] STC 874; on treatment of outstanding cases, see Inland Revenue Press Release, 26 February 1999; (1999) *Simons Weekly Tax Intelligence* 312. For later discussion of the House of Lords see [1999] STC 1089.

[79] *Compagnie de Saint-Gobain* v. *Finanzamt Aachen-Innenstadt* (Case C–307/97) see (1999) *Simons Weekly Tax Intelligence* 1856. See Oliver [2000] *BTR* 174.

Taxpayer defeats

The above cases show that it is open to any Member State to justify its discriminatory provision either in accordance with Article 56 or, if the discrimination is covert rather than overt, on more general grounds. We now turn to the justifications which have succeeded (1)–(4) and (6) and an important but problematic limitation ((5)).

(1) Community law insufficiently developed: Daily Mail. Taxpayers do not always succeed in invoking these articles. In the *Daily Mail* case[80] a UK resident company failed to circumvent the then UK rule requiring the company to obtain Treasury consent before emigrating because the UK consents could insist on the settlement of tax liabilities prior to departure. However, this was partly because of the undeveloped nature of European company law rules on freedom of movement, e.g by the diversity of rules in different Member States on matters such as whether the company's personality could continue in the new country.[81]

(2) Need to protect cohesion of B's tax system: Bachmann. Of more interest is the famous decision in *Bachmann* v. *Belgium State*[82] allowing B to maintain rules necessary to the "cohesion" of its system. Here B allowed X to deduct sickness and invalidity insurance contributions only if paid to a company recognised by the authorities in B. B established an objective reason for the refusal; under B's law any income eventually paid out under the policies would be taxed in B[83] and this could be monitored by restricting the deduction to contributions made to a Belgian company. Moreover, where contributions had not been deducted the sums paid out were not subject to tax. The restriction of the right to deduct to payments made in B was therefore justified in the interests of the cohesion of its tax system. No less crucially B had established that there was no other way of protecting that cohesion and that the provisions met the EC principle of proportionality; where, in a later case, double tax treaty provisions were in place, the court said that those provisions were sufficient to protect the cohesion of B's system.[84]

The *Bachmann* case was also raised—and distinguished—in the *Verkooijen* case (above). the ECJ said that in *Bachmann* there had been a direct link in the case of one and the same taxpayer between the grant of the tax advantage and the offsetting of that tax advantage by a fiscal levy both of which related to the same tax. This narrow but entirely sensible analysis of the *Bachmann* case shows that the tax authorities in the Member States will have to be careful in their use of *Bachmann.*

(3) Treaty-making powers. These articles do not prevent states from making tax treaties which allocate tax jurisdiction on the basis of nationality, at least where they are in accordance with international norms. Therefore, the taxpayer lost in *Gilly* v. *Directeur des Services Fiscaux Bas Rhin.*[85] The case concerned the French–German double tax treaty, and frontier workers. Mr and Mrs G lived in France, but while Mr G, a French national, worked in France, Mrs G, a German national, worked in Germany. Mrs G, who had acquired French nationality on marriage and so was a dual national, paid tax in Germany at a rate higher

[80] *R* v. *HM Treasury and IRC, ex parte Daily Mail and General Trust plc* [1988] STC 787.

[81] Ibid., 807, para. 21.

[82] Case C–204/90 [1994] STC 855.

[83] The Court assumed that tax was paid by the company; this was not correct: see Lyons (1995/96) *EC Tax Journal* 27, 47.

[84] Case C–80/94 *Wielockx* [1995] STC 876; however, it has been pointed out that the particular article of the OECD Model Treaty on which the Court relied did not apply to pensions from self-employment: see Richardson [1998] *BTR* 283, 284.

[85] Case C–336/96 [1998] All ER EC 826, [1998] STC 1014; see comments in (1998) *IBFD Journal* 328.

than she would have had to pay under French law because the German system was more steeply progressive and the family quotient system applicable in France, the state of residence, did not apply in Germany, the state of source. The tax treaty provided her with a credit in France for the tax paid in Germany, but only up to the rate applicable in France. This left some German tax still unrelieved. Could Mrs G reclaim it from France under EC law? The answer was "no". The Court first held that the duty on Member States imposed by Article 293 (now Article 220) to eliminate double taxation within the Community was not capable of having direct effect. It then held that in the absence of harmonisation, it was open to Member States to define the criteria for allocating taxing powers between themselves with a view to eliminating double taxation; there was nothing objectionable in a tax treaty making distinctions on the basis of nationality, i.e no breach of Article 39 (ex Article 48). This conclusion owed much to the fact that the treaty was based on international practice as represented by the OECD Model Treaty. It would seem to follow that it is open to a Member State to sign a treaty with another Member State conferring a benefit on their residents or nationals without being forced to provide equivalent treatment to people from other Member States. This decision challenges the belief held in some other countries that where Member State A grants a treaty benefit to residents of Member State B it can be made to extend the same tax treatment to residents of all other Member States; however, see further below at §65.1. The Court also held that since the object of the tax treaty was to prevent double taxation, not to ensure that the tax paid in one state was no higher than would have been paid in the other, there was nothing contrary to Article 39 in these arrangements.

Unfortunately, the boundary between *Gilly*, on the one hand, and *Schumacker* and *Wielockx*, on the other, is very hard to determine.[86] The view taken here is that the Court quite deliberately, and, some might say, wisely, backed off from a decision which could have been used to unpick the tax treaty network. However the result is intellectually indefensible, and has been even harder as a result of the St Gobain case—see below at §65.1.

(4) Interpretation of national law still a matter for national court. In *ICI plc* v. *Colmer*[87] the House of Lords was faced with two ways of interpreting UK tax law. The first would have prevented a breach of EC law; the second would not. The European Court ruled that there was no EC law obligation on a national court to prefer the first construction to the second.

(5) Nationals. The purpose of this case-law is to protect nationals of other Member States; residence has been equated with nationality because most non-residents will be nationals of other Member States, so that covert discrimination is revealed. Nationals of states outside the European Community are not entitled to protection under these rules. Therefore, a US company with a branch in the UK cannot complain about being discriminated under, say, French law. However, some care is needed where subsidiaries involved. If a US company establishes a UK subsidiary it will be open to the subsidiary to complain of discrimination under French law since, as a company established under UK law, it has UK nationality. However, it may be that it will not be entitled to complain of the discrimination if the reason for the French rule is to discriminate against companies owned by US parents rather

[86] See, generally, Hedemann-Robinson [1999] *BTR* 128, 135–8; see also JFAJ [1999] *BTR* 11 suggesting that if *Gilly* is right, and the Schumackers had been resident in France, the *Schumacker* decision would have been different for the year in which Mrs Schumacker had some earned income, but the same for the year in which she had none. On failure of the court to clarify matters in *Eshurind* Case C–391/97 see *JGFAJ* [2000] *BTR* 195.

[87] Case C–264/96 [1998] All ER (EC) 585, [1998] STC 874; on treatment of outstanding cases, see Inland Revenue Press Release, 26 February (1999) *Simons Weekly Tax Intelligence* 312.

than against companies resident in the UK. There is, as yet, no case-law in the tax area to justify these speculations.

(6) Administration. In *Future Participations SA and Singer* v. *Luxembourg*[88] the taxpayer was the Luxembourg branch of a French company. In such circumstances Luxembourg only taxed the profits attributable to the branch (or permanent establishment) and did not insist that accounts be kept in Luxembourg. Stricter rules applied however when the branch sought to use trading losses from a previous year. Here Luxembourg insisted that (1) the loss had to be economically related to the income and (2) accounts had to be kept in Luxembourg. The court held that (1) did not breach Article 43 as the Luxembourg position was completely reasonable but went on to say that (2) did. (2) was a breach because it was not necessary to achieve the legitimate purpose advanced by the tax authorities. It did not however follow that Luxembourg had to accept a simple apportionment basis.

2.3.4 Other aspects of Community law

Interpretation

In EC law the courts adopt a purposive interpretation and treat VAT law as a matter of principle and purpose.[89] The court states the principle and then works down to the facts. Moreover, literal interpretations are rejected in favour of the purpose of the directive;[90] only if all else fails do the courts proceed to a literal approach.[91] This approach comes naturally when UK courts face problems of interpreting EC law as such, or UK rules based on EC directives. However, the schizophrenic state under which tax matters are tested on a literal basis in a domestic context and on a purposive basis in a European context may become unstable, especially as the volume of EC material expands. The idea of English courts finding themselves championing a minority tradition in a sea of other ideas is particularly piquant for Scots lawyers, who have had to suffer this since the Act of Union. A related phenomenon is the practice already seen in UK legislation implementing the Mergers Directive to ensure that cross-border transactions are not favoured at the expense of purely domestic ones.[92]

The role of the Commission—and its views

Since the Commission has enforcement powers under the EC Treaty one must pay particular attention to its views. One view is that current EC law does not oblige a Member State to grant the withholding tax rate of its most favourable bilateral agreement automatically to taxpayers of another state which is not covered by the agreement.[93] However, the Commission was largely instrumental in pressing the *French Tax Credits* case and the refusal to allow the Court to weigh the advantages and disadvantages of doing business as a branch rather than as a subsidiary; many see this as the false start of the Court's adventures into this area.

[88] [1997] STC 1301 Case C–250/95.

[89] See Avery Jones (1996) 17 *Fiscal Studies* 63; see further below §3.1.2.

[90] For example, Case 154/80 *Staatssecretaris van Financiën* v. *Coöperatieve Vereniging "Coöperatieve Aardappelenbe-waarplaats GA"* [1981] 3 CMLR 337 (the *Dutch Potato* case) and Case 89/91 *Staatssecretaris van Financiën* v. Hong Kong Trade Development Council: [1983] 1 CMLR 73, ECJ.

[91] Case 139/84 *Van Dijk's Boekhuis BV* v. *Staatssecretaris van Financiën* [1986] 2 CMLR 575, ECJ, distinguishing the creation of a new article from the thorough repair of an old article.

[92] Inland Revenue, *EC Direct Measures—A Consultative Document* (1991) paras 2.4, 2.5, 2.10.

[93] Written Answer, 9 November 1992, Qn 647/92 (OJ 1992 C40/93); reported in *Simon's Tax Intelligence* 302.

Tax competition

The case-law so far considered has been concerned to make sure that a non-national is treated at least as favourably as a national. Attention is now being paid (but not yet by the Court) to the opposite problem—where the non-resident is treated more favourably, and the Member States compete unfairly for business. The European Community has an (unenforceable) code of conduct for Member States in such matters (see below at §64.1).

Mutual assistance

An EC directive[94] provides for mutual assistance in recovery of unpaid taxes. This may soon be expanded to make a major exception to the general principle of the conflict of laws that the UK will not enforce a revenue law of another country to allow the enforcement of taxes on income and capital, i.e. foreign equivalents of income tax, corporation tax and CGT (but not inheritance tax).[95]

2.4 Qualification (3): Human Rights Law[96]

There is the possibility of challenge under the law relating to human rights—a matter one can test with regard to retroactive legislation. Retroactive legislation does not conform easily to human rights doctrines but has been a standard feature of a system, such as that in the UK, which is still dominated by Diceyan views of parliamentary sovereignty. Thus, what is now TA 1988, s. 399 banning loss relief for commodity was introduced in 1978 but was retroactive to 6 April 1976. Another problem arises from the practice of reversing court decisions with retroactive effect save for those litigants who had actually won their cases *vis à vis* the Revenue: the reversal of *IRC* v. *Padmore* and the famous *Woolwich Building Society* cases are examples here. However, it has to be noted that no challenge to retroactive legislation has yet been successful in Strasbourg.[96a]

Human rights may become relevant to tax law in three ways. First, although the UK signed the European Convention on Human Right in 1950, it saw no need to incorporate it into domestic law—no doubt because it was thought that rights were sufficiently well protected through existing judicial and political procedures. Finally, in 1998 the Convention was given some effect in domestic law by the Human Rights Act 1998. As from 2nd October 2000[96b] the UK courts must interpret legislation so as to give effect to Convention rights and, if this is impossible, have a power to declare that legislation is incompatible with the Convention.

The fact that the court (High Court and above) has the power to make this declaration explains how Convention rights are reconciled with the sovereignty of Parliament. If Parliament decides it does not want to amend the law, even by the fast track process suggested in the Act, there is nothing the litigant can do but follow the familiar path to Strasbourg. Equally there is nothing to stop the Westminster Parliament from repealing the Act itself or withdrawing from the Convention altogether.

[94] Directive 76/308/EC.

[95] Baker [1999] *BTR* 14.

[96] See, generally, Baker [2000] *BTR* 211; also printed in [2000] *European Taxation.*

[96a] See Baker [2000] *BTR* at 225.

[96b] Certain Scottish matters concerning the Scottish Parliament and Executive were already subject to the Act and the Scottish courts

In addition, s. 6 of the Act makes it unlawful for a public authority, an expression covering a court or tribunal and a person whose functions are, even in part, of a public nature e.g. revenue departments, to act in way which is incompatible with convention rights; judicial remedies are governed by s. 8. The court or tribunal must have regard to, but is not bound by the jurisprudence of the 'Strasbourg Organs'[96c].

In *National Provincial Building Society* v. *UK* [97] the European Court of Human Rights declined to interfere with the UK legislature's reversal of the *Woolwich* case with retroactive effect in relation to building societies other than the Woolwich. However, while at first sight it appears to leave a high "margin of appreciation" to the signatory states in fiscal matters, the decision is narrow in scope. First, it proceeds on an interpretation of the facts distinctly favourable to the Revenue. Secondly, it deals with a situation in which Parliament had tried to amend the law, and the subordinate law-making process had got it wrong first time; as such, the UK system was allowed a second chance to do by primary legislation what it had certainly wanted to do the first time because this was obviously consistent with the legislature's intent (one cannot pretend that the building societies had much in the way of legitimate expectations). Thirdly, the case tells us nothing about the attitude of the court if the UK legislation had tried to remove the fruits of victory from the Woolwich Building Society itself.

The second way in which the Convention is important is the influence it has had on the development of UK law, especially in administrative law matters.[98] With the incorporation of the Convention into UK law one may expect the process to continue and even accelerate, although the form in which it has been incorporated may discourage the courts from challenging parliamentary sovereignty too directly.

Finally, the Convention is influential in the development of fundamental principles of EC law, principles said to emerge in part from the common traditions of the Member States.[99] The importance here is that these fundamental principles are capable of direct effect, and therefore, thanks to the supremacy of EC law, will override Diceyan parliamentary sovereignty.[100] In this connection one should note that the German constitution specifically prohibits retroactive legislation.

The question whether tax legislation can be declared incompatible with the European Convention is an open one. The Commission on Human Rights and the Court of Human Rights have indicated a willingness in principle to use Article 1 of the First Protocol in an appropriate case (of which there has been none). The Convention bans confiscation and there must come a point at which excessive taxation becomes confiscation.[101] Similarly, the 1997 privatisation windfall tax charged on the difference between the flotation price and a multiple of average profits for the first four years was a tax on shareholders who had not necessarily benefited from these profits in those years and was clearly vulnerable to

[96c] See Baker [2000] *BTR* pp. 216–9.

[97] [1997] STC 1466 see Baker at p. 225.

[98] See, e.g. Klug and Starmer [1997] *Public Law* 223.

[99] Hartley, *Foundations of European Community Law*, ch. 5 and essays by Jacobs, Ellis and Usher in *Droits sans Frontieres: Essays in Honour of L. Neville Brown* (1991) 235–42, 265–76 and 277–93 respectively; see also Weiler, in Winter (ed.) *Reforming the Treaty of the European Union* (Kluwer, 1996), 78.

[100] See, for example, *Hodgson* v. *Commrs of Customs and Excise* (1996): right of appeal conferred when none available under domestic law.

[101] *Svenska Managementgruppen AB* v. *Sweden* (1985) Application No 11036/84 45 DR 211, Commission.

challenge; but no challenge was mounted.[102] Both the Commission and Court of Human Rights have also indicated a willingness to use Articles 1 and 14, the non-discrimination articles. A complaint was made that a UK rule in TA 1988, s. 259, which, *inter alia*, gave a relief to a married man whose wife was incapacitated but not to a married woman whose husband was incapacitated broke the Convention. This was ruled admissible but a friendly settlement was reached.[103] S. 259 was immediately changed.[104] The UK widow's bereavement allowance under s. 262 has also given rise to a friendly settlement but the Revenue have refused to grant relief to other litigants.[105] However, discrimination may be cured by withdrawing relief from those previously entitled to it just as much as by extending it to the applicant, and this duly happened. The Convention may also become relevant when considering procedures adopted by the Revenue in administering tax law (see chapter 4 below).

These issues of discrimination on grounds of gender and through lack of respect for family life a combination of pleas based on Art. 14 (linked to Art. 1 of the First Protocol) and Art. 8, are likely to be particularly difficult. Thus a case is pending in which a tax privilege available only to married couples, has been withheld from one party in a couple who have cohabited for 30 years. If this is held to breach the Convention one can see quickly that there will be similar pleas by other couples, heterosexual or homosexual, who have cohabited for lesser periods. However, there will be other problems. Just as cohabitees will be demanding privileges given to married couples, so married couples will be wondering whether assessments made under anti-avoidance rules applicable to spouses should be overturned because they do not apply also to cohabitees. Thus while cohabitees might seek the protection of the exemption for interspousal transfers in IHTA 1984 s. 18, a married woman might wonder why she has to suffer from TCGA 1988 s. 77 because her husband is a beneficiary under a settlement she has created—or from IHTA s. 203 which makes her liable for certain IHT when a cohabitee is not liable. If such'counter-claims' by spouses succeed, many provisions of the tax code will have to be revisited; if they fail we shall end with a pick and mix approach in which cohabitee can pick which rules they want, scarcely a dignified conclusion to arguments alleged to be based on respect for family life. One half way house would be to allow the cohabitee to have the protection of the rule for spouses but on condition that they abide by all other tax rules relating to spouses; however such a mealy mouthed approach has been rejected by the ECJ in its anti-discrimination jurisprudence. The question whether the Strasbourg organs and now the UK courts will adopt broad or narrow stances on these issues is one for the answer to which we are all waiting eagerly.

2.5 Qualification (4): Federalism

The UK Parliament at Westminster, as the sovereign body in tax matters, has allowed other organs of government to levy taxes. The Council Tax is levied by local authorities under the Local Government Finance Act 1992. The Scottish Parliament has a limited tax varying

[102] On this windfall tax, see Chennells (1997) 18 *Fiscal Studies* 279. *The Economist*, 5 July 1997 speculated that the costs of a lengthy legal battle were thought to be too high; it is more likely that the companies did not wish to challenge a government with such a large popular mandate so soon after the election, especially since companies subject to greater competitive pressure would, under the formula, pay less tax than other companies. On earlier windfall taxes, see Unwin [1984] *BTR* 343. A complaint about a Swedish windfall tax was ruled inadmissible in *Wasa Liv* v *Sweden*, Application 13013/87.

[103] *McGregor* v. *UK*. Application 30548/96.

[104] FA 1998, s. 26.

[105] Application No. 13120/97.

power under the terms of the Scotland Act 1998 (see above §1.1). However, both these are Acts of the Westminster Parliament and so may be amended or repealed by that Parliament. If federalism is to develop within the UK, financial matters will have to be addressed since the taxing power is central to any division of powers in a federal system—just as it was the key power in the struggle between the Crown and the English Parliament in the seventeenth century. One judicial observer has gone so far as to assert that the importance of tax in a federal system is that more than any other power it has the capacity to destroy federalism.[106] No doubt this is one of the many reasons why member states are so reluctant to transfer significant revenue-raising powers to the institutions of the European Union.

[106] See the discussion in Zines (1997) pp. 34–6 citing for this belief Latham CJ in the *Banks Nationalisation* case (1948) 76 CLR 1, 183–4 (Zines goes on to express some scepticism).

3

Sources

3.1 Statutes[1]

3.1.1 The shape of the statute book: consolidation

Statute law for a particular tax can be found in the statute which introduced that tax, as amended subsequently. Amendments may be made to the text of the original Act, or a new provision may be introduced to exist alongside the original Act. The result could be described as a "patchwork", were it not for the overtones of antique cosiness that word implies; it is better described as a shambles. The text relating to a particular tax may be consolidated, e.g. income tax in 1918, 1952, 1970 and 1988, corporation tax in 1970 and 1988, CGT in 1979 and 1992, corporation tax on capital gains in 1970 and 1992, VAT in 1983 and 1994 and CTT (now IHT) in 1984.[2] The perfection of consolidation, however, is often marred within weeks.[3] The quite distinct concept of codification is regarded as an impossible task; but an invaluable attempt was made in 1936.[4]

A tax Bill is usually certified as a Money Bill, which means that although the House of Lords may amend it, the House of Commons is not bound by the amendment and the Bill may take effect in its unamended form within one month of being sent from the Commons to the Lords.[5] If, however, a Bill contains an exemption for a specific person or entity, it is a hybrid bill which has its own very long procedure (enabling other entities to object).[6] It has therefore been known for certain, apparently general alterations to be drawn in such a way as to have the specific effect sought. As Nigel Lawson put in relation to one such clause,

[1] For an excellent general introduction to legislation, see Miers and Page, *Legislation* (Sweet and Maxwell, 1990).

[2] On parliamentary procedures for consolidation, see TLRC (November 1996), Part 2.

[3] e.g. FA 1988 removing TA 1988, s. 16.

[4] Cmd 5123.

[5] A Money Bill is defined under Parliament Act 1911, s. 1(2) as one dealing only with matters of national (as opposed to local) taxation, public money or loans or their management; the Speaker's certificate is conclusive. See Erskine May, *Parliamentary Practice* (22nd ed.), 806–8.

[6] Ibid., 483–4.

"Fortunately in this context, the language in which Finance Bills are drafted is so arcane as to bear little resemblance to the English language and no-one spotted what this particular clause was really about".[7]

3.1.2 Reform

Dissatisfaction with the state of tax statute law is nothing new, but has become more intense;[8] nor is it confined to the UK. In Australia complaints have been grouped under three heads. First, the quantity of legislation is too great: Vann claims that Australia has the longest tax statute in the world.[9] Secondly, the quality is poor: again, Vann claims that Australia the most unreadable tax statute in the world. This generates a desire to make statutes more intelligible and so more accessible. Thirdly, judges, faced with a mass of complexity, play safe and give a literal interpretation.[10] This causes draftsmen also to play safe, enacting yet more detailed and, therefore, over-long and incomprehensible provisions. Draftsmen also take great care over transitional matters.[11]

Such complaints are also made in the UK. The apparent solution is to cut this circle at all available points. Incomprehensibility is being addressed by the UK's Tax Law Rewrite project, an Inland Revenue project stemming from a backbench amendment to the Finance Bill in 1995,[12] but with an Australian precursor.[13] If this were successful, it might make not for a shorter statute book, but one which takes less time to read—and so shorter in a different sense. Another idea is the more extensive use of algebraic formulae rather than words.[14] However, an alternative proposal might address all three problems—to move to a more explicitly principle-based tax system. A statement of principles would make it easier for judges (and others) to interpret the statutes and may also make for a shorter statute book. Judges would have to interpret such statutes purposively. In New Zealand the traditional approaches to interpretation have been abolished in favour of an Acts Interpretation Act under which judges are to accord to every Act and statutory provision such fair, large and literal interpretation as will best ensure the attainment of the object of the legislation according to it true intent, meaning and spirit.[15]

Another hope is that tax law can be made more purposive in form, and the Tax Law Rewrite Project has produced some essays in this direction,[16] purposive legislation, purposively construed is the goal. The boundary between principle and purpose is obscure.

[7] *Memoirs*, 354–5.

[8] For example Tax Law Review Committee, *Final Report on Legislation* (IFS, 1996); for important earlier work, see Special Committee of Tax Law Consultative Bodies)September 1993 and 15 March 1990); and Gammie, "The Process of Tax Reform in the UK" Law Society (15 March 1990).

[9] Ault *et al.*, 10.

[10] For example Deane J. in *Hepples* v. *FCT* (1991) 91 ATC, esp. 4818–19.

[11] There is much interesting US debate on transitional rules: see Logue (1996) 94 *Michigan LR* 1129; Graetz (1977) 126 *University of Pennsylvania LR* 47; and Kaplow (1986) 99 *HLR* 506.

[12] FA 1995, s. 160; the Revenue report and background paper written under s. 160 is entitled "The Path to Tax Simplification" (1995); for reservations, see Beighton [1996] *BTR* 1.

[13] The Tax Law Improvement Project (TULIP); for empirical evidence of degree of enhanced readability, see Smith and Richardson (1999) 20 *Fiscal Studies* 321. See also James, Sawyer and Wallschutzky, in *Tax Administration* (Prospect 1998), 333.

[14] For example Robson [1989] *BTR* 361.

[15] Richardson (1986) 12 *Monash Law Review* 35, 36.

[16] For example *The Relief for Trading Losses of Companies* (February 1998).

Without going down any of these routes it may be better to insist that tax legislation should be recognised as having a structure and ensuring that the structure is adhered to.[17]

One model for a principle-based approach can be seen in EC law, whether through the EC Treaty itself or through directives, as with VAT.[18] Another model is the Dutch Tax Code. Van Raad, after noting that in the 1960s the Dutch code for personal income tax covered less than 20 pages in print, complained that by 1996 it had grown to more than four times its original size and that three decade of additions (often dealing with avoidance) had obfuscated the Act's original, well-balanced structure. He also noted that tax Acts and decrees now amounted to some 350 pages of print.[19] In comparison, the number of pages of UK legislation on income and corporation tax and CGT (and statutory instruments) amounted to 3,936.[20]

One must not try to build too great hopes on new approaches to statutory drafting. Simpler words mean little without a simpler policy behind them. Principles and purposes clearly have a role but there seems little escape from highly detailed information at some stage in the process.[21] In the common law world this may take the form of regulations, as in the United States, statutory instruments or binding rulings, as in Australia, New Zealand and Canada, or Revenue practice, as in the UK. It may also take the form of "safe harbour" provisions in the statute itself. Prebble suggests that one reason why continental systems may have less detailed legislation is the possibly chauvinistic view that they have not yet reached the levels of sophistication of Anglophone systems and tolerate more breaches of neutrality in their tax bases.[22] Whether sophistication is a good or bad thing is not explored.

Prebble's other argument is more fundamental and goes to the nature of tax law. "Income tax law", he writes:[23]

> "is different in kind from law in general and from tax laws (such as VAT) which depend on transactions or states of fact. Unlike other laws, income tax law does not relate to its subject matter, which is the facts and legal relations in business activity. Income tax law ignores some facts and transactions and it recharacterises others. In other words it is dislocated from its subject matter."

The use of the word "dislocated" suggests a degree of unnaturalness and difficulty. An easier way of making the point is to say that the facts with which the income tax system has to wrestle include not only the raw primary facts (including legal facts) but also the characterisation of those primary facts established by other branches of law—a process entirely familiar to students of the conflict of laws.[24] Tax law must frequently draw lines between activities which are legally distinct but economically similar; legislators can drawn these lines where they wish but efficiency arguments suggest that lines should be drawn so that a transaction or item is taxed in the same way as its closest substitutes.[25]

[17] Pagan (1993) 4 *Fiscal Studies* 90.

[18] Avery Jones (1996) 17(3) *Fiscal Studies* 63 ; for comments, see Prebble [1998] *BTR* 112.

[19] Ault *et al.*, 84. The same lament was made by the UK's 1936 Codification Committee comparing the Acts of 1842 and 1853 with the law in 1936.

[20] *Butterworths Yellow* and *Orange Tax Handbooks* (1999–2000) omitting EC law; in 1968–1969 there were 998 pages in the *Butterworths Yellow Tax Handbook.* The 1997–1998 figures do not include Revenue material such as concessions or statements of practice.

[21] See also McCaffery (1990) *Wisconsin Law Review* 1267.

[22] [1998] *BTR* 112, 123.

[23] [1998] *BTR* 112 (see comment on VAT at 123); and [1994] *BTR* 380.

[24] [1997] *BTR* 180, 191.

[25] Weisbach (2000) (29)1) *Journal of Legal Studies*, Pt 1; arguing that the benefits of keeping the substitutes together outweighs the negative effects of raising an inefficient tax.

There are also parliamentary problems. If new statutes are to be made more purposive in nature, what happens to the old? If the suggestions of the Tax Law Rewrite Project were to be enacted, how would parliamentary time be found? A long bill requires a streamlined procedure but, since it would make substantive changes, it would not be a consolidation Bill and so could not enjoy the procedural advantages of the consolidation process; it would raise other issues such as the role of the House of Lords in fiscal matters.[26]

3.1.3 Current rules of interpretation: approaches and rules[27]

UK tax law recognises several approaches to issues of construction. The best traditional summary was set out by Lord Donovan in *IRC* v. *Mangin*:[28]

"(1) The words are to be given their ordinary meaning. They are not to be given some other meaning simply because their object is to frustrate legitimate tax avoidance devices . . . [m]oral precepts are not applicable to the interpretation of revenue statutes.
(2) . . . one has to look merely at what is clearly said. There is no room for any intendment. There is no equity about a tax. There is no presumption as to tax. Nothing is to be read in, nothing is to be implied. One can only look fairly at the language used.
(3) [T]he object of the construction of a statute being to ascertain the will of the legislature it may be presumed that neither injustice nor absurdity was intended. If therefore a literal interpretation would produce such a result, and the language admits of an interpretation which would avoid it, then such an interpretation may be adopted.
(4) [T]he history of an enactment and the reasons which led to its being passed may be used as an aid to construction."

Today, the ordinary meaning has to be weighed more explicitly against context and purpose. As usual the more variables there are the more difficult it is to tell what weight to place on one variable rather than another. In the past judges have had to wrestle with legislation of great complexity, and from time to time have warned that it is possible that the obscurity of an enactment or the uncontrollable width of its language—or of the discretion needed to implement it—may compel a court to find that no reasonable construction is available and that the taxpayer is therefore not to be charged.[29] The House of Lords has shown itself capable, on the one hand, of depriving a provision of any effect[30] and, on the other, of imposing double taxation.[31] Whether the same results would be achieved today is unclear.

At one time it was thought that clear words were needed to impose a charge to tax so that ambiguities might be resolved in favour of the taxpayer. It is still the case that clear words are needed, but taxpayers must distinguish a situation in which there are two competing interpretations of the statute from one in which the clear interpretation goes against the taxpayer but the taxpayer wishes to complain on grounds of fairness. The clear words doctrine may have a role in the first situation; it has none in the second.[32]

[26] See IFS Tax Law Review Committee, *Parliamentary Procedures for the Enactment of Rewritten Tax Law* (November 1996).

[27] For a good theoretical introduction, see Freeman, "Positivism and Statutory Construction", in Guest (ed.), *Positivism Today* (Dartmouth, 1996). For an interesting exercise (involving now repealed legislation), see Bennion [1983] *BTR* 74.

[28] [1971] AC 739, 746, [1971] 1 All ER 179, 182. However see Robertson, *Judicial Discretion in the House of Lords* (OUP, 1999) Chapter 3.

[29] *Customs and Excise Commrs* v. *Top Ten Promotions Ltd.* [1969] 3 All ER 39, 93, HL, *per* Lord Donovan, and 95 *per* Lord Wilberforce; *Vestey* v. *IRC* [1980] AC 1148, [1980] STC 10.

[30] *IRC* v. *Ayrshire Employers Mutual Insurance Association Ltd.* [1946] 1 All ER 637, 27 TC 331, HL.

[31] *Cleary* v. *IRC* [1967] 2 All ER 48, 44 TC 399; see below at §57.6.3.

[32] *Leedale* v. *Lewis* [1982] STC 835, 844, 56 TC 501, 540, *per* Lord Wilberforce.

Establishing parliamentary purpose—*Pepper* v. *Hart*

The court may look at the purpose and history of the relevant legislation and, to this end, reference may be made to the state of the law, and the material facts and events with which it is apparent that Parliament was dealing.[33] In *Pepper* v. *Hart*[34] the House of Lords, reversing centuries of case-law, held that the court could consult *Hansard* in order to interpret the words of the legislation where that legislation was ambiguous or obscure, or led to an absurdity. The courts would rely on statements made by ministers or other promoters of the Bill and any other parliamentary material needed to understand those statements and their effects—provided the statements relied on were clear.[35] In this case the House concluded that a reading of *Hansard* showed that in 1976 a particular statement by the minister in charge of the Bill was that in determining the measure of cost incurred by an employer in providing an in-house benefit in kind it was necessary to look at marginal cost not overall cost. It followed that that was how the provision should be construed. This interpretation is controversial,[36] and one authoritative source suggests that its main beneficiary will be the executive.[37]

Hansard has been cited to the court in subsequent cases, but with no decisive effect.[38] Usually, judges either refer to *Hansard* under this rule, or state that it does not meet the criteria (referring to it in any case and stating that it makes no difference). Unsurprisingly, there has been no case in which judges have said that the provision is clear and so no reference may be made, but that if they had looked *Hansard* it would have made a difference.

Other UK statutory interpretation rules

While the courts will try to avoid highly inequitable or manifestly unfair results,[39] where the words are wholly unambiguous the court is bound by its literal interpretation, however unreasonable.[40] Arguments based on competing anomalies do not find favour.[41] Where a statutory provision is enacted but is based upon a misconception of what the law then was, the law remains as it was and does not share the misconception of the legislature.[42]

There is a presumption that provisions dealing with the machinery of taxation do not impose a charge.[43] The courts will not construe a machinery provision so as to defeat the charge;[44] however, the absence of machinery has been used to qualify a charge.[45]

[33] See Lord Macdermott in *IRC* v. *Rennell* [1964] AC 173, 198 and Lord Macdermott in *Madras Electric Supply Corpn Ltd.* v. *Boarland* [1955] AC 667, 686, 35 TC 612, 640, [1955] 1 All ER 753, 760.

[34] [1992] STC 898.

[35] [1992] STC 898, 922, 923.

[36] For criticism, see Baker [1993] *CLJ* 353; and Bennion [1995] *BTR* 325. For history and comparisons, see Rawlinson [1983] *BTR* 274; articles cited by Arnold in (1984) 32 *Can. Tax Jo.* 400; and Bale (1995) 74 *Canadian Bar Rev.* 1. For a case which should have been decided differently, see *Leedale* v. *Lewis* [1982] BTR 835 as discussed at [1983] *BTR* 70 *JFAJ*. See also Robertson *op cit.* above n. 28, Chapter 5.

[37] Denzil Davies [1993] *BTR* 172.

[38] For example *Massmould Holdings Ltd.* v. *Payne* [1993] STC 62.

[39] *Coutts & Co.* v. *IRC* [1953] AC 267, 281, [1953] 1 All ER 418, 421, *per* Lord Reid.

[40] *Plumbly* v. *Spencer* [1999] STC 677, 684c, *per* Robert Walker L.J.; see also Lord Reid in *IRC* v. *Hinchy* [1960] 1 All ER 505, 512, 38 TC 625, 652.

[41] *Dale* v. *IRC* [1953] 2 All ER 671, 676, 34 TC 468, 488, HL, *per* Lord Normand.

[42] *Davies, Jenkins & Co. Ltd.* v. *Davies* [1967] 1 All ER 913, 915, 922, 44 TC 273, 287, HL.

[43] *Straits Settlements Commr of Stamps* v. *Oei Tjong Swan* [1933] AC 378, 389, *per* Lord Macmillan.

[44] *IRC* v. *Longmans Green & Co. Ltd.* (1932) 17 TC 272, 282.

[45] *Colquhoun* v. *Brooks* (1889) 14 App Cas 493, 506, 2 TC 490, 500.

There is a presumption that words used in the same contexts in different statutes are used in the same sense.[46]

Where a particular interpretation would give the Revenue the power to distribute the burden of tax between taxpayers, the courts will reject it.[47] The courts may lean against a construction which the Revenue is unwilling to apply in its full rigour.[48]

When interpreting a consolidated enactment, the court should not, in general, refer to the earlier Acts. However, the court is entitled to have regard to the fact that a subsection was later added to the original section.[49]

The Taxes Acts[50] are equally applicable in England and Wales, Scotland[51] and, for most of them, Northern Ireland. It follows that the language they employ should be construed so as to have, as far as possible, uniform effect in all four countries alike.[52] Some provisions speak the language of the English lawyer, perhaps with some Scots legal phrases casually thrown in; here, the courts must take the meanings of the legal expression from the law of the country to which they properly belong and must then apply that meaning by analogy, even if such a construction does violence to some of the best-established doctrines of Scots law.[53]

When provisions are ambiguous, the court may consider the effect of subsequent legislation only when the two views of the original statute are equally tenable and there are no indications favouring one rather than the other. The argument advanced in favour of this rule is that the new provision could only have been required if one view was held by Parliament rather than the other.[54]

Where statutes deem certain things to be as they are not, the court must consider for what purposes and between what persons the statutory fiction is to be resorted to.[55]However, this does not require the court to abandon the golden rule of construction, i.e. that the grammatical and ordinary sense of the words should be adhered to unless that would lead to absurdity or inconsistency, in which case the grammatical and ordinary sense of the words may be modified to avoid that absurdity and inconsistency but no further.[56]

3.1.4 The literal versus purposive debate

The blend of approaches in Lord Donovan's words is not only about the most coherent explanation of what judges actually do, but also avoids "schools" of thought.[57] For completeness, however, mention should be made of two of these schools or approaches.

[46] *Gartside* v. *IRC* [1968] AC 553, 602, [1968] 1 All ER 121, 131, *per* Lord Reid. But this is only a presumption: see Atkin L.J. in *Martin* v. *Lowry* [1926] 1 KB 550, 561, 11 TC 297, 315.

[47] *Vestey* v. *IRC* [1980] AC 1148, [1980] STC 10, 54 TC 503.

[48] *Wicks* v. *Firth* [1983] 2 AC 214,t 231, [1983] STC 25, 29, *per* Lord Bridge; quoted by Chadwick L.J. in *Dunlop International* v. *Pardoe* [1999] STC 909, 916.

[49] *IRC* v. *Joiner* [1975] 3 All ER 1050, [1975] STC 657, 50 TC 449, but note the more restrictive approach of Lord Diplock and see the discussion by Baxter in (1976) *Conveyancer* 336, 343. See also Bramwell [1992] *BTR* 69.

[50] Defined in TA 1988, ss 831, 832.

[51] On construction and Scots law, see the positive suggestions by Jones [1986] *BTR* 75; as far as one can see, these suggestions have been completely ignored.

[52] Viscount Simon in *I T Commrs for General Purposes (City of London)* v. *Gibbs* [1942] 1 All ER 415, 422, 24 TC 221, 236, 244, HL. Hence, English courts will follow Scottish decisions: *Wiseburgh* v. *Domville* [1956] 1 All ER 754, 758, 36 TC 527, 538–9, CA, *per* Lord Evershed MR.

[53] *Lord Advocate* v. *Countess of Moray* [1905] AC 531, 540, HL, *per* Lord Macnaghten.

[54] *Finch* v. *IRC* [1985] Ch 1, 15, [1984] STC 261, 272, CA, *per* Oliver L.J.; and *Westcott* v. *Woolcombers Ltd.* [1986] STC 182, 191, 60 TC 575, 586, *per* Hoffman J.

[55] *RC* v. *Metrolands (Property Finance) Ltd.* [1981] STC 193, 208, 54 TC 679, 697, *per* Nourse J.

[56] Peter Gibson J. in *Marshall* v. *Kerr* [1993] STC 360, 365, 67 TC 56, 79 CA, Unfortunately the application of these words in this case was reversed by the House of Lords.

[57] The well known antipathy between Lord Simonds and Lord Denning on these issues is a warning precedent.

(a) The literal approach

The literal approach was, for a long time, the favoured UK approach to tax interpretation. Citizens are not to be taxed unless they are designated in clear terms by the taxing Act as taxpayers and the amount of their liability is clearly defined.[58] One reason for this is that apart from statute there is no liability to pay any tax and no antecedent relationship between the taxing authority so that no reasoning founded on any such *a priori* liability or relationship can be used in the construction of the Act.[59] Other reasons may include the need to protect the individual from the state, the analogy of criminal offences and some sort of *contra proferentem* rule, but these do not explain the strictness with which other tax provisions are construed against the taxpayer.

This approach has several consequences. First, it is for the Crown to establish that the subject falls within the charge.[60] This means that if the words are ambiguous the subject is entitled to the benefit of the doubt. But the principle is not that the subject is to have the benefit if, on any argument that ingenuity can suggest, the Act does not appear perfectly accurate but only if, after careful examination of all the clauses, a judicial mind still entertains reasonable doubts as to what the legislature intended:[61] if there is no ambiguity the words must take their natural meaning.

Secondly, strict interpretation applies to the taxpayer just as much as to the Revenue. If a literal interpretation produces a construction whereby hardship falls on innocent beneficiaries by the rights, monstrous or otherwise, conferred on the Revenue, that interpretation must be adhered to and the hardship produced is not a relevant consideration unless, now, s. 3 of the Human Rights Act 1998 could apply.[62] Further, where an exception from taxation is provided by a statute, that exception is to be construed strictly and any ambiguity construed against the taxpayer.[63] It is as well to recall here that support of the very highest authority can be found for general and apparently irreconcilable propositions.[64]

Thirdly, the literal approach led to ever-more-complex statutory forms as the draftsmen tried to cover all angles. It also encouraged a belief among some practitioners that judges were at best neutral to matters of aggressive tax planning.

Strict interpretation does not necessarily apply to anti-avoidance provisions phrased in broad language which deliberately eschews legal terms of art.[65]

(b) The purposive approach

The purposive approach is intended to stand in complete contrast to the literal approach. Such contrasts are usually unfair. Literalists accuse purposivists of wanting to ignore the plain words of the statute; purposivists accuse literalists of "legalism" and of wanting to be bound by the plain words of a statute even though the purpose of the statue is clear. However, as Sir Owen Dixon said on becoming Chief Justice of Australia speaking,

[58] *Vestey* v. *IRC* [1980] STC 10, 18, 54 TC 503, 581, *per* Lord Wilberforce; but contrast *Floor* v. *Davis* [1979] 2 All ER 677, [1979] STC 379 (in which Lord Wilberforce dissented).

[59] *Pryce* v. *Monmouthshire Canal and Railway Companies* (1879) 4 App Cas 197, 202, 203, *per* Lord Cairns L.C.

[60] *Re Micklethwaite* (1855) 11 Exch 452, 456, *per* Parke B.; approved by Lord Halsbury L.C. in *Tennant* v. *Smith* [1892] AC 150, 154.

[61] *Wilcox* v. *Smith* (1857) 4 Drew 40, 49, *per* Kindersley V.-C.

[62] *Re Joynson's WTs* [1954] Ch 567, 573 *per* Danckwerts J.; and see *IRC* v. *Hinchy* [1960] 1 All ER 505, 38 TC 625.

[63] *Littman* v. *Barron* [1951] 2 All ER 393, 398, 33 TC 373, 380, *per* Cohen L.J.

[64] *A.-G.* v. *Prince Ernest Augustus of Hanover* [1957] AC 436, 464, *per* Viscount Simonds.

[65] *Greenberg* v. *IRC* [1972] AC 109, 137, 47 TC 240, 272, *per* Lord Reid.

admittedly, of constitutional matters, "There is no other safe guide to judicial decisions in great conflicts than a strict and complete legalism".[66] This, of course, ignores the problems of what is meant by "legalism".

The first modern tax case where a majority of the House of Lords came out in favour of the purposive approach was *McGuckian* v. *IRC* in 1997[67] For Lord Steyn the 1981 decision in *Ramsay* marked an intellectual breakthrough in that tax law could catch up with the rest of the legal system and move from a literal interpretation to one based on context and designed to identify the purpose of a statute and give effect to it.[68] The effects of adopting this approach are uncertain. It can certainly make a change to the ways in which cases are argued and judgments written; it may also make a difference to the ways in which statutes are drafted. What is unclear is whether it will make any difference to the results of cases—at least outside the avoidance area. Courts must have a clear idea as to the purpose to be achieved, which raises the issue of which extrinsic aids may be used.[69]

3.1.5 US developments

The UK's legal history has been marked by a tendency for American ideas to filter into the system many years after they have become current in the United States; often the period is related to the gap between a judge being a student in the United States and becoming a judge in the UK. The purposive approach was promulgated with particular vigour by Hart and Sacks in their seminal but cyclostyled work *The Legal Process.*[70] However, just as the UK courts may be[70a] moving towards purpose, some US courts are re-emphasising the role of textual formalism in the interpretation of statutes, a move associated especially with Justice Scalia. This school of thought goes beyond the search for the intention of congress (intentionalism) or for the purpose or objective of the statute (purposivism) and finds its basis in what Eskridge calls "holistic textualism".[71] The approach was set out by Justice Scalia in the following terms in *Green* v. *Bock Laundry Machine Co.*:[72]

> "The meaning of terms in statute books ought to be determined, not on the basis of which meaning can be shown to have been understood by a larger handful of the members of Congress; but rather on the basis of which meaning is (1) most in accord with context and ordinary usage, and thus most likely to have been understood by the *whole* Congress which voted on the words of the statute (not to mention the citizens subject to it), and (2) most compatible with the surrounding body of law into which the provision must be integrated—a compatibility which, by a benign fiction, we assume Congress always has in mind."

[66] (1952) 85 *CLR* xiv. For reaction against formalism (as opposed to legalism), see Zines 444–9.

[67] [1997] STC 918. Canadian courts have apparently reverted from purposive to plain meaning: see *Corporation Notre Dame de Bon Secours* (1995) 95 DTC 5017 and *Friesen* 95 DTC 5551.

[68] For an example of tax law being regarded as different, see Evans L.J. in *Ingram* v. *IRC* [1997] STC 1234, 1251, where, after outlining the argument, he says, "I would be prepared to hold in any other context that this produces a result which is so clearly at variance with the apparent object of [the section] that it cannot be regarded as a proper interpretation of the section".

[69] On (lax) Canadian practice, see Bowman T.C.C.J. in *Glaxo Wellcome Inc.* v. *The Queen*, 96 DTC 1159 (1996); and Bowman (1995) 43 *Can. Tax Jo.* 1167, 1186.

[70] Finally published by Foundation Press in 1995.

[70a] A purposive construction was rejected in *Clarke* v *British Telecom Pension Scheme Trustees* [2000] STC 228 CA on which see Kerridge [2000] *BTR* 397 esp. at 400.

[71] 37 *UCLA Law Review* 621; see also Eskridge, *Dynamic Statutory Interpretation* (Harvard UP, 1994), ch. 1, n. 64 for some later literature. For a discussion of US tax law in the light of the new approaches, see Popkin, (1988) 61 *Southern California Law Review* 541 and Livingston (1996) 51 *Tax Law Review* 677.

[72] 490 US 504, 528.

The issue is, like every other issue in the United States, very controversial. A great weight of US scholarship has devoted itself to the study of legislation over the last 20 years; there has been relatively little counterpart in the UK law schools.[73]

There are many reasons why it may be inappropriate for the UK to model its approach to interpretation on that of the United States. The systems are too dissimilar for an instinctive adoption of US practices and these differences show themselves not only in words used when approaching legislation but, more fundamentally, in the role of the court, the drafting of legislation and the attitude to rule-formality.[74]

3.2 Cases

Cases are authorities in the usual way according to the rule of precedent, save that tax is a UK law and so English courts will accept Scottish decisions as binding, and vice versa. However, in assessing the value of a precedent in tax law special complications arise from the fact that the appeal structure in the UK allows the courts to reverse a decision of the Commissioners only for error of law or because it cannot be supported on the evidence. Decisions of the Special Commissioners have been published since 1996.[75] Where the hearing has been held in private the case may have to be published in such a way as to preserve the anonymity of the taxpayer.[76]

3.3 Revenue Practice—Information

Although not directly binding, statements of Revenue practice are of great importance in the practical administration of the system. Major changes of policy in recent years have led to a great increase in the amount of information being made available. These informal arrangements sometimes defer a charge. Naturally, the Revenue assumes that taxpayers taking the benefit of the deferral will pay the deferred tax in due course; however, the fact that the basis was concessionary meant that there was no legal obligation to do so. Such an obligation was imposed in 1999;[77] it is a reserve power in that it is imposed only if the taxpayer fails to observe the terms of the concession. The charge cannot be for less than the amount deferred by way of concession.

3.3.1 Extra-statutory concessions

Extra-statutory concessions (ESCs) are few, tightly written and almost legislative in form. A booklet gathering these concessions together (IR 1) is published periodically. One crucial

[73] See, generally, Eskridge, above at n. 71, esp. 41–7 and 225–37. For UK comments, see Freeman, above at n. 27; Cross, *Statutory Interpretation*, 3rd ed., Bell and Engle (eds.) (Butterworths, 1995). See also MacCormick and Summers, *Interpreting Statutes* (Dartmouth, 1991).

[74] See, generally, Atiyah and Summers, *Form and Substance in Anglo-American Law* (OUP, 1987), chs 1, 4, 11; there is a summary of some of the points by Popkin at [1991] *BTR* 284–6.

[75] Special Commissioners (Jurisdiction and Procedure) Regulations 1994 (SI 1994/1811), para. 20.

[76] See (1996) *Simon's Weekly Tax Intelligence* 863.

[77] FA 1999, s. 76. The notes to the Finance Bill 1999 refer specifically to concessions D15, D16 and D22. See also Revenue Interpretation, *Tax Bulletin No, 43*, October 1999 and Revenue *CGT Manual*, paras 13650–62.

difference between an ESC and a statutory provision is that the Revenue can withhold the benefit of the concession if it is so minded without direct legal—as distinct from political or administrative—consequences. However, the development of administrative law remedies[78] suggests that an assessment made on the basis of withholding a concession could be quashed on the basis of breach of the duty to act fairly as between different taxpayers.[79] Such a situation would arise only where the taxpayers could bring themselves within the scope of the concession; in this connection, it is important to note that the list of concessions is prefaced with a general statement that a concession will not be given where an attempt is made to use it for tax avoidance.[80] In a note to a new concession the Revenue stated that concessions are used "to deal with what are, on the whole, minor or transitory anomalies . . . and to reduce cases of hardship at the margins of the code when a statutory remedy would be difficult to devise or would run to a length out of proportion to the intrinsic importance of the matter".[81] Concessions may not be concessions at all.[82] New ESCs have become much less common in recent years.

3.3.2 Statements of practice

Sstatments of practice (SPs) are now published on a regular basis; these are only slightly less formal than the concessions.

3.3.3 Revenue interpretations and decisions

SPs are now supplemented by published Revenue interpretations; these interpretations are heavily qualified and the Revenue will not necessarily regard itself as bound by them. Revenue Decisions are notes of decisions in individual cases. No new decisions have been released since 1994.

3.3.4 Manuals

The most interesting source of information (from an academic point of view) is the internal manuals which have now been published. Certain passages are held back for operational reasons. Some of the contents are essays of the highest quality and interest. Until recently these were confidential to the Revenue although, of course, their contents were well known to those highly trained inspectors who left the service for private practice. In proceedings for judicial review a court ordered discovery of such documents but only because the taxpayer's argument relied on having been informed that there was a Revenue view of the correct construction of a provision and that that construction was in his favour.[83]

[78] Rowland [1995] *BTR* 115 argues that these judicial review remedies are not enough.

[79] For example the unsuccessful application in *R.* v. *IRC, ex parte J. Rothschild Holdings* [1987] STC 163; *R.* v. *Inspector of Taxes, ex parte Brumfield* [1989] STC 151; *R.* v. *IRC, ex parte Kaye* [1992] STC 581.

[80] This general anti-avoidance statement was used by the Revenue to defeat a move to quash an assessment for breach of natural justice in *R.* v. *IRC, ex parte Fulford-Dobson* [1987] STC 344.

[81] Inland Revenue Press Release, 16 February 1989, (1989) *Simon's Tax Intelligence* 74. Despite this there have been periodic calls for them to be made statutory—e.g. Treasury Minute of 31 December 1897, and Fifth Report of Public Accounts Committee 1966–67, 601. On legality, see Williams [1979] *BTR* 137; and *Vestey* v. *IRC* [1980] AC 1148, [1980] STC 10, 54 TC 503.

[82] In *Steibelt* v. *Paling* [1999] STC 594, 604 Sir Richard Scott V.-C. refused to regard ESC D 24 as a concession so much as an interpretation.

[83] *R.* v. *IRC, ex parte J. Rothschild Holdings plc* [1986] STC 410; upheld [1987] STC 163, 61 TC 178, CA.

3.3.5 *Rulings*[84]

There is no general scheme whereby taxpayers can obtain advance rulings on the tax consequences of a particular transaction. However, in practice advice is often available provided there is a detailed scheme; the Revenue usually insists on knowing the identity of the taxpayer concerned.[85] The Revenue is not there to provide a free legal aid clinic, but it is in the Revenue's interests to be helpful. Where an application for judicial review is made on the basis of a ruling, the Revenue will be bound by its advance ruling only in if the taxpayer gave full details of the specific transaction on which he sought the Revenue's ruling, indicated the ruling sought and made it plain that a fully considered ruling was sought, and indicated the use he intended to make of any ruling given, and the ruling or statement made was clear, unambiguous and devoid of qualification.[86] A breach of a representation by the Revenue will not amount to an abuse of power if the taxpayer knows that clearance at local level is not to be treated as binding on the Revenue or he has not fully disclosed all relevant material to the inspectors.[87] Full disclosure is not necessarily made merely because sufficient information has been disclosed to enable inferences to be drawn. In principle a clearance can be withdrawn; however, the consequent transaction may have gone too far for the Revenue to do this without administrative law consequences.[88] It is not yet clear whether obtaining a ruling on the status of a taxpayer will necessarily protect the taxpayer from assessment to tax on a transaction if that transaction was not disclosed.[89] In certain circumstances the legislation will prescribe a clearance procedure, usually as part of broad anti-avoidance legislation.[90] A right of appeal against a refusal of clearance is not always available; whether the refusal to give a right of appeal breaches human rights legislation is one of those issues awaiting resolution.[91]

3.3.6 *Miscellaneous*

In addition Revenue also publishes its views on some points of interpretation, e.g. in correspondence with professional bodies and, increasingly, in its quarterly Bulletins. In the past, information has also been gleaned from the reports of the Parliamentary Commissioner for Administration and the Revenue's own Adjudicator.

84 The Revenue issued a consultative document on pre-transaction rulings in 1994 (see James [1996] *BTR* 6) but this was not proceeded with; for criticism see Chan (1997) 18 *Fiscal Studies* 189. On advance rulings, see the still valuable work by Prebble, *Advance Rulings on Tax Liability* (Victoria University Press, Wellington, 1986).

85 The terms on which advice is available are set out in ICAEW Memorandum TR 818: see (1990) *Simon's Tax Intelligence* 893; see also later correspondence in ICAEW Memorandum TR 830, reproduced in (1991) *Simon's Tax Intelligence* 404.

86 *R.* v. *IRC, ex parte MFK Underwriting Agencies Ltd.* [1989] STC 873, 62 TC 607; see also *R* v. *IRC, ex p Camacq Corpn* [1989] STC 785, 62 TC 651; e Tidball [1991] BTR 48; and, more generally, Hinds [1991] *BTR* 191.

87 *Matrix-Securities Ltd.* v. *IRC* [1994] STC 272, 66 TC 587, HL. For a full account of the facts, see *Matrix Securities Ltd.* v. *Theodore Goddard* [1998] STC 1 See also text of letter from the Inland Revenue dated 3 June 1994 and reprinted in (1994) *Simon's Tax Intelligence* 729. Among notes on this case, see Eden [1994] *BTR* 254; and Sandler [1994] *CLJ* 273.

88 *Matrix-Securities Ltd.* v. *IRC* [1994] STC 272, 66 TC 587, HL; the taxpayer may have a claim for damages: [1992] STC 272, 284, *per* Lord Griffiths; see below at §4.2.

89 *R.* v. *IRC ex p Howmet Corp* [1994] STC 413, QBD.

90 For example TA 1988, s. 707, but not TCGA 1992, s. 30. For an example of difficulties that arise in practice, see ICAEW memorandum TR 657, reprinted in (1987) *Simon's Tax Intelligence* 321.

91 See views of professional bodies reported in (1991) *Simon's Tax Intelligence* 453, para. 19.

4

The Setting of the Tax System

4.1 Introduction

Making the fiscal system work is, said the two Musgraves, a large part of making democracy function.[1] The setting of the UK tax system is important for a variety of reasons. Clearly, one has to know the basic rules governing the reporting of income, the calculation of tax and the enforcement of liability to tax. Secondly, one ought to be aware of Revenue powers to ensure that the basic structure works, including the imposition of interest or penalties under the tax legislation or the criminal law and the role of other agencies where tax fraud and other fraud overlap. However, it is also important to put this structure into a wider context. One part of that wider context is concerned with the balance of power between taxpayers and the executive.[2] Tax is, after all, probably the branch of law through which most

[1] Musgrave and Musgrave, *Public Finance in Theory and Practice* (1st ed.), preface. Reprinted in 5th ed. (McGraw-Hill 1989), xvii.

[2] See, e.g. Goldberg [1996] *BTR* 9.

citizens come into contact with the state, especially if one includes indirect contact through the PAYE system. Another part of that context is the need to be able to assess the efficacy of the rules in the same way as a criminologist looks at the efficacy of the criminal law. In the administration of the tax system one has to ask what the rules are for. Research in many areas of government regulation suggest that a flexible approach to enforcement may be much better than a top down, legalistic, going-by-the-book version.[3] However, this assumes that the regulator's purpose is to try to educate and to secure co-operation. Whether this is the right model for the tax system is precisely the question at issue. One needs to know when the demands of equity may have to reduced in the name of effective compliance. One has to know about the extent to which the professions are to be seen as enforcers of the system through codes of ethics imposed on qualified practitioners (and the extent to which a knowledge of the code forms part of the qualification process). In order to form some assessment of the system it is also desirable to know how efficient the services provided by tax professionals are. However, the tax system should also be seen as a system which has to work. Finality is an important virtue and yet this can mean that Revenue practice is upheld even though it is not consistent with the law. Administrative efficiency is a value greatly prized by the Inland Revenue, but many recent changes suggest that the Government is anxious to use the Revenue to carry out non-tax programmes, such as the repayment of student loans and the working families tax credit;[4] even the change to self-assessment, which was clearly a tax matter, was not handled satisfactorily. These—and many other—reasons suggest that the material to be sketched in this chapter is important; however, there is much room for more research.

4.2 The Board of Inland Revenue

Responsibility for the administration[5] of income tax, CGT, corporation tax, inheritance tax and stamp duty is entrusted to the Board of Inland Revenue. Although the legislation talks of inspectors and collectors,[6] recent legislation, especially in relation to self-assessment, consistently refers to an "*officer* of the Board" rather than "an Inspector".

4.2.1 The department

The Board is one of the four departments—the Treasury, the Inland Revenue, Customs and Excise and the Bank of England (now independent in some matters)—which report to the Chancellor of the Exchequer. Denis Healey wrote that the last three departments considered themselves to be at least as independent of the Treasury as the three armed services were of the Ministry of Defence.[7] He also said that the Inland Revenue considered itself as laying down the law to a nation of natural tax dodgers, while Customs and Excise were more down to earth, believing that human frailty is often rooted in a lack of understanding rather than

[3] For example Bardach and Kagan, *Going by the Book: The Problem of Regulatory Unreasonableness* (Temple University Press, Philadelphia, 1982); Braithwaite, *To Punish or Persuade: The Enforcement of Coal Mining Laws* (SUNY, Albany, 1985).

[4] For comments of CIOT Low Incomes Tax Reform Group, see CIOT Press Release, 4 October 1999.

[5] On the role of tax policy during the 1980s, see Beighton (1987) *Fiscal Studies* 1.

[6] TMA 1970, s. 1, as amended by FA 1990, s. 104.

[7] *The Time of My Life*, 373.

in deliberate dishonesty. VAT and other indirect taxes are administered by the Customs and Excise Commissioners.

At one time the Inland Revenue worked in local offices at which taxpayers could discuss their tax affairs with the relevant officer. The 1980s saw a change of practice, with business dispersed to regional offices;[8] the trend has continued with self-assessment and the change in social practices in greater willingness to use the telephone and electronic communication.

4.2.2 Scrutiny

The Board is scrutinised by various persons or bodies, including the Parliamentary Commissioner for Administration and the Inland Revenue's own Adjudicator.[9] Within Parliament it is scrutinised by the Select Committee on the Treasury and the Civil Service.[10] The Revenue makes an Annual Report to the Treasury which is laid before Parliament.

4.2.3 Commuting liability

The Board is under a duty to collect taxes but is not guilty of an abuse of power in entering into special arrangements absolving taxpayers from liability to tax. One taxpayer has no sufficient interest to ask a court to investigate the tax affairs of another;[11] however, this must be distinguished from a situation in which the Revenue's approach to a question of interpretation of law is wrong.[12] In carrying out the duty laid on it the Board must act with administrative common sense.[13] However, this discretion does not justify a court in construing a section of an Act so as to give the Board a discretion over how to allocate a tax liability between different taxpayers, nor does it provide a legal basis for the practice of extra-statutory concessions.[14] Unlike the Revenue, Customs and Excise has statutory authority to grant reliefs by order.[15] This means that many rules are made by Custons and Excise which would have to go into primary legislation if introduced by the Inland Revenue. It is typical of the way the UK tax system is run—as a club whose members are the professions and the department—that there has been no pressure from club members to put concessions on a proper legal basis. However, judges remain critical.[16] One day the court may have to decide whether it is theoretically possible to order the department to give the taxpayer the benefit of a concession, i.e. to make an assessment which is not in accordance with the law.

[8] See the interesting letter by Battishall [1988] *BTR* 155.

[9] See Beighton 16 *Tax Notes International* 1439–45. For a comparison of the UK Adjudicator with the US taxpayer advocate (to the advantage of the the UK), see Kornhauser (1998) 16 *Tax Notes International* 537. See also Stebbings [1993] *BTR* 301 and comments on the First Report [1994] *BTR* 545.

[10] See e.g. Select Committee, *Sixth Report 1998–99*. On the early work of this Committee, see Robinson, in *The New Select Committees* (1989); and, on Treasury response, see Hills (1981) 4(1) *Fiscal Studies* 1.

[11] *IRC* v. *National Federation of Self-Employed and Small Businesses Ltd.* [1981] 2 All ER 93, [1981] STC 260 (Fleet Street amnesty not illegal).

[12] *R.* v. *A.-G. ex parte ICI* (1986) 60 TC 1, [1987] 1 CMLR 72.

[13] *Vestey* v. *IRC* [1980] STC 10, 19, 54 TC 503, 582, *per* Lord Wilberforce. The Board remits tax in certain cases when the failure to collect was due to official error; the extent of this practice is governed by the circumstances of the taxpayer: ESC A19.

[14] *Vestey* v. *IRC* [1980] STC 10, 35, 54 TC 503, 599,*per* Lord Edmund Davies, citing Williams [1979] *BTR* 137.

[15] Customs and Excise (General Reliefs) Act 1979, s. 9.

[16] See also Wade and Forsyth, *Administrative Law* (8th ed. OUP, 1994), 407.

4.2.4 *Confidentiality/secrecy*

Information received in the execution of duty may not be disclosed to other bodies, including other government departments, without statutory authority.[17] Release of information relating to the tax affairs of "an identifiable person" without such authority or consent may be a criminal offence.[18] There is no statutory authority for releasing information to the police (or the CPS). The modern mantra that we need "joined-up government" can undermine this confidentiality; thus, the Revenue practice of releasing to the Department of Trade and Industry information about penalties charged on directors for tax fraud may well be unlawful—unless, of course, the taxpayer agrees.[19] Release to the Revenue departments of other countries may be authorised under treaty provisions [20] or under EC law.[21]

4.2.5 *Reliance on Revenue statements*

Conventional wisdom is that there is no estoppel against the Crown; hence, no legal reliance may generally be placed on statements by officers of the Board so as to make the court determine a tax appeal in the way stated by those officers.[22] However, compensation has been obtained through the Parliamentary Commissioners for Administration and may be obtainable in tort;[23] in addition, such statements may furnish the very basis for an application for judicial review of a Revenue decision.[24]

4.2.6 *Citizens' Charter*

Like other government departments, the Inland Revenue was party to the (now superseded) Citizens' Charter.[25] A taxpayer has relied on it in court to argue that no reasonable inspector who had the Charter in mind would have issued a notice seeking information from the taxpayer in such terms; the taxpayer failed on the facts.[26]

[17] TMA 1970, s. 6 and FA 1989 ss 182, 182A. On release to Social Security Department, see Social Security Administration Act 1992, s. 122, and to Charity Commissioners, see Charities Act 1993, s. 10. See also public interest immunity in *Lonrho* v. *Fayed (No. 4)* [1994] STC 153.

[18] FA 1989, s. 182, replacing the Official Secrets Act 1911, s. 2.

[19] The information is used by the DTI in considering whether a person should be disqualified.

[20] See chapter 59 below.

[21] FA 1990, s. 125.

[22] *Southend on Sea Corpn* v. *Hodgson (Wickford) Ltd.* [1962] 1 QB 416, [1961] 2 All ER 46; see, however *R.* v. *IRC, ex parte J. Rothschild Holdings plc* [1987] STC 163, 61 TC 178 where an estoppel issue was raised in judicial review proceedings but failed on the facts.

[23] Wade and Forsyth, above at n. 16, 339–344; see also comments of Lord Griffiths in *Matrix Securities Ltd.* v. *IRC* [1994] STC 272, 284, HL, on possible compensation claim if the Revenue withdraws clearance after expense incurred in reliance on the clearance; see also Eden [1994] *BTR* 263. On wider issues, see the fascinating book by Farnsworth, *Changing Your Mind: The Law of Regretted Decisions* (Yale, 1999).

[24] See chapter 3 below; see also Hinds [1991] *BTR* 191.

[25] Inland Revenue Press Release, 13 August 1991, (1991) *Simon's Tax Intelligence* 771; see also Inland Revenue Press Release, 11 February 1992, (1992) *Simon's Tax Intelligence* 178. The Citizens' Charter has been superseded; on which see Brodie, *Taxation*, 13 April 2000, 40.

[26] *Kempton* v. *Special Commirs and IRC* [1992] STC 823, 66 TC 249.

4.3 Establishing Liability to Tax—Self-Assessment and Revenue Assessment

A liability to tax arises when taxpayers are assessed to tax; today, the assessment will usually be made by the taxpayers themselves (self-assessment) but may sometimes be made by the Revenue, i.e. where the self assessment provisions do not apply. Where T, a taxpayer, falls within the self-assessment regime, but the Revenue makes an assessment, e.g. because T has not made a return, the theoretical position is that the assessment is indeed made on T's behalf and so is a self-assessment which remains valid until vacated by the delivery of the proper return.[27] Penalties, interest and surcharges may also be due; the role of the surcharge is confined to self-assessment. The rules for assessment outside self-assessment are not discussed here. If T has not received a return there is an obligation to give notice of any liability to tax within six months of the end of the year.[28]

4.3.1 Self-assessment

The self-assessment regime applies whenever T is sent a notice by an officer of the Board.[29] At present the Revenue sends these forms only to individual taxpayers who are self-employed or whose tax affairs are complicated; there is no legislative reason (as opposed to practical reason) for them to stop there. The regime applies to income tax, CGT and class 4 NICs. It applies to partnerships[30]—even though the primary liability is on the partners to make their own returns—and to trustees[31] and estates. For corporation tax see §45.6.2.

Filing date

The return must be delivered by the filing date—31 January following the year of assessment, i.e. 31 January 2002 for the year ending 5 April 2001; if later, the return is due three months after the notice was given. The taxpayer, T, must file the return[32] and calculate and pay the tax.[33] Failure to make the assessment means that the Revenue may do this for T.[34]

For many taxpayers a more significant date is 30 September. If T delivers the return by 30 September (or, if later, within two months of the notice being given), the Revenue must do the arithmetic on the basis of the figures supplied and calculate the tax due.[35] This is not the same as Revenue assessment—it is self-assessment with the aid of revenue calculation. Tax is due on the same date—31 January. There are penalties for late and incorrect[36] returns; which may be fixed or tax-related and may be reduced or waived by the Revenue. [37] On receiving the form the Revenue check it for arithmetical errors before making the assessment on the basis of these figures. Questions of substance are left till later.

27 TMA 1970, s. 9(3). See Collison, *Income Tax Under Self Assessment* (Accountancy Books, 1998).
28 Ibid., s. 7(1).
29 Ibid., s. 8.
30 Ibid., ss 12AA, 12AB—see chapter 19 below.
31 Ibid., s. 8A—see chapter 29 below.
32 Ibid., s. 8.
33 Ibid., s. 9.
34 Ibid., s. 9(3).
35 Ibid., s. 9(2).
36 On self-assessment and status of incomplete returns and use or provisional figures, see RI 191.
37 TMA 1970, ss 93, 102.

Underpayment: surcharges

Surcharges apply where the tax is not paid at all or is underpaid. A surcharge of 5% of the unpaid tax due applies after 28 days, and a similar amount after a further six months.[38] Again, the Revenue may waive or reduce the surcharge.[39] A right of appeal to the Commissioners exists on the basis of a reasonable excuse for not paying the tax;[40] inability to pay the tax is not a reasonable excuse.[41] Surcharges will not be imposed if a taxpayer finds a bona fide mistake and volunteers the information to the Revenue at once and pays the tax.[42] The taxpayer may amend the return within 12 months of the filing date and the Revenue may revise the assessment to correct "obvious" errors or mistakes within nine months.[43]

If a return has been made negligently or fraudulently and the return is then amended the amendment does not prevent the Revenue taking action, including penalties in respect of the earlier error.[44]

The 12-month enquiry window

Under TMA 1970, s. 9A, the Revenue may investigate the return within 12 months after the filing date—the "enquiry window";[45] this is to recover tax underpaid under the self-assesment process. Thereafter, tax may only be recovered under the discovery powers in TMA 1970, s. 29. This is begun by a formal written notice; no reason need be either held or given. There is no need to complete the enquiry within the 12-month period. The notice of enquiry triggers various information powers[46] which may only be used to get information reasonably required for the purpose, a matter on which an appeal may be made to the Commissioners.[47] Documents not in the taxpayer's power or possession may not be called for under this power. These enquiry powers are separate from other information powers. There are parallel provisions where an officer investigates a claim made outside a tax return.[48] The taxpayer must be told when the enquiries are completed;[49] this prevents any further enquiry under this rule,[50] but not under the discovery power in s. 29.

When will an enquiry be made?

It is likely that certain criteria will be evolved by the Revenue in selecting returns for attention.[51] As in the United States, a taxpayer's request for an advance ruling is followed by an investigation to make sure that the terms of the ruling have been adhered to. There is also a random selection process of about 1 in 1,000 taxpayers.[52]

[38] Ibid., s. 59C.
[39] Ibid., s. 59C(11).
[40] Ibid., s. 59C (7)–(9).
[41] Ibid., s. 59C(10).
[42] Collison, above at n. 27, para. 22.1.
[43] TMA 1970, s. 9(4).
[44] RI 196.
[45] TMA 1970, s. 9A; on similar provisions for partnership returns, see s. 12AC. On late returns see s. 9A(2).
[46] Ibid., s. 19A; penalties for non-compliance may be due under s. 97AA.
[47] Ibid., s. 19A (6)–(9).
[48] Ibid., Sch. 1A, para. 5.
[49] Ibid., s. 28A(5).
[50] Ibid., s. 9A(3).
[51] See e.g. Collison, above at n. 27, 25.3 and 25.4 citing Revenue Enquiry Handbook EH 1025–6 and other paras.
[52] See Collison *op. cit*, 25.2 citing Enquiry Handbook para 370.

4.3.2 Discovery assessments

If an officer discovers that income or capital gains which should have been assessed have not been or that an assessment is or has become insufficient or that any relief is or has become excessive, that officer may make an assessment to recover the loss of tax. The notion of discovery is interpreted widely in relation to Revenue assessments[53] but the circumstances in which they can be made is narrowed for self-assessment.

The self-assessment rules restrict the power to make a discovery assessment. T is safe if the return was made in accordance with normally accepted practice at the time the return was made.[54] Secondly, if the return was not in accordance with such practice, the discovery assessment may only be made if either the taxpayer or agent has been guilty of fraud or negligence,[55] or the officer could not reasonably be expected to be aware, on the basis of the information then available to him, that additional tax was due under TMA 1970, s. 29.[56] Information is made available if it is contained in the taxpayer's return, or other forms, e.g. a claim, or is produced in the course of the enquiry. It is also treated as made available if it can reasonably be expected to be inferred by the officer—or is notified in writing by T.[57] Particular problems may be anticipated in complex cases where much information is provided.[58]

Continuing meaning of discover

In the old assessment rules the word "discover" covered a variety of circumstances; the word is apt to cover any case in which, for any reason, it newly appears that the taxpayer has been undercharged.[59] Therefore, an assessment may be made where the Revenue decides that a company should be treated as a dealing company rather than an investment company,[60] where a new inspector takes a different view of the law from his predecessor,[61] or to correct an arithmetical error in the computation. Where the self-assessment form has been returned, the rules discussed above may protect the taxpayer; if no return has been made, they will not (so the cases cited remain good law).

Barred by agreement

Under the pre-1996 law it was held that a new assessment may not be made under s. 29 if there has been an agreement between the Inspector and T on the point within TMA 1970, s. 54.[62] The effect of settling the appeal is to create a contract; it follows that if the document recording the contract does not do so accurately it may be rectified.[63] Where a taxpayer made a claim which was erroneously agreed by an inspector, a later inspector is not entitled

[53] See below at n. 59.
[54] TMA 1970, s. 29(2)—the concept is borrowed from TMA 1970, s. 33 for claims by the taxpayer.
[55] Ibid., s. 29(4).
[56] Ibid., s. 29(5).
[57] Ibid., s. 29 (6).
[58] See Inland Revenue Bulletin (1996), 313–15.
[59] *Cenlon Finance Co. Ltd.* v. *Ellwood* [1962] 1 All ER 854, 859, 40 TC 176, 204, *per* Viscount Simonds.
[60] *Jones* v. *Mason Investments (Luton) Ltd.* (1966) 43 TC 570, [1967] BTR 75 JGM.
[61] *Parkin* v. *Cattell* (1971) 48 TC 462.
[62] The taxpayer is protected only on the particular point agreed: *Kidston* v. *Aspinall* (1963) 41 TC 371.
[63] *R.* v. *Inspector of Taxes, ex parte Bass Holdings Ltd.* [1993] STC 122, 65 TC 495 (group relief to be allowed once, not twice). Silence in face of an offer does not make an agreement: *Schuldenfrei* v. *Hilton* [1999] STC 821, CA, eschewing language of offer and acceptance.

to make a "discovery" assessment on finding the error.[64] The test is whether a reasonable man would conclude that the inspector had agreed the claim. Since the agreement rule remains in place this must still be good law.

Time limits

The normal time limit for a s. 29 assessment is five years from 31 January following the end of the year of assessment.[65] However, this is extended to 20 years for fraudulent or negligent conduct[66] and reduced to three years for personal representatives settling a deceased's liability.[67]

4.3.3 Payments

Payment on account[68]

A central part of the self-assessment system requires T to make payments on account in advance of 31 January following the end of the year. These are due, in two equal instalments, by 31 January in the year of assessment and 31 July following that year. Normally these are calculated on the income for the previous year.[69] There is a *de minimis* limit for this obligation: no payment is due if the sum is less than £500. Likewise no payment is due if more than 80% of the preceding year's liability will be collected by deduction at source.[70]

The payment on account settles the liability to pay on account. There is no liability to pay either interest or any surcharge if the year's income turns out to be higher than estimated. However, if the year's income is lower, taxpayers will receive interest (although this usually deducted from their eventual overall liability to tax).[71]

The liability to pay on account can be avoided if the liability will be covered by deduction at source[72] or there will be no liability to tax at all; claims may be made at any time before 31 January following the year of assessment.[73] A Revenue officer may waive the liability by notice.[74] Penalties arise if a claim to reduce the liability is made fraudulently or negligently.[75]

When and how are payments made?

A payment by cheque is treated as received when the cheque is received by the Revenue—provided it is paid on first presentation.[76] At one time certificates of tax deposit[77] could be used to settle tax liabilities.[78] However this has been discontinued as being inconsistent with self-assessment.

64 *Scorer* v. *Olin Energy Systems Ltd.* [1985] STC 218, 58 TC 592, HL; see Williams [1992] *BTR* 323; on Revenue practice, see Statement of Practice SP 8/91.
65 TMA 1970, s. 34; special rules apply to emoluments because of the subtleties of their timing rules: s. 35
66 TMA 1970, s. 36.
67 Ibid., s. 40.
68 See Inland Revenue Bulletin (1996), 353–6 and Collison *op. cit.* 4.2.
69 Special rules apply if the assessment is late or is amended, etc.: TMA 1970, s. 59A, esp. subs (4)–(4B)
70 Ibid., s. 59A(1)(d); on deduction at source, see s. 59A(8).
71 Ibid., s. 30(1).
72 Elaborately defined in ibid., s. 59A(8).
73 Ibid., s. 59A(3).
74 Ibid., s. 59A(9).
75 Ibid., s. 59A(6).
76 Ibid., s. 70A.
77 Issued under the National Loans Act 1968.
78 See *Simons Direct Tax Service* A.3, 1327. On compensation for certificate surrendered see FA 1995, s. 157.

Record keeping and penalties

If the taxpayer is carrying on a trade, profession or business (including the letting of property) all necessary records must be kept until the fifth anniversary of the due date for payment.[79] Therefore, records for 1998–1999 must be kept until 31 January 2005. There are also rules as to the form in which records of a business must be kept.[80] A shorter period applies if there is no trading, etc., income.

4.3.4 Subsequent events

Once an assessment has been made it cannot be changed except under the TMA 1970 rules,[81] which broadly means Revenue enquiry (s. 29), appeal (see below at §4.4)[82] and agreement (above §4.3.2).[83] It may be open to the Revenue to issue a second (additional) assessment rather than to seek an increase in the first on appeal.[84] Provided the assessment is not to make good a loss due to fraudulent or negligent conduct, a taxpayer may also reopen matters by making a claim for any further relief for that year within one year from the end of the chargeable period in which an assessment is made.[85]

Validity of the assessment

This is unlikely to arise under self-assessment but may do so in the few remaining cases of Revenue assessment. An assessment is valid even though it refers to an incorrect provision.[86] An assessment may be saved from invalidity by TMA 1970, s. 114[87] which lists various errors which may not invalidate the assessment. However, an assessment issued for the wrong year cannot be saved by s. 114 even though the taxpayer was not and could not have been misled.[88] See also below §4.4.3.

Claims

Error mistake claims. Taxpayers may claim that too much tax has been paid by reason of their own error or mistake, in which case the Revenue will grant relief.[89] The overpayment may arise under the self-assessment regime or otherwise. No relief can be given where the assessment was made on the basis of the practice generally prevailing when the return was made,[90] a rule which sensibly prevents the Revenue from having to reopen matters following some decided case or change or view.

[79] TMA 1970, s. 12B(1), (6).

[80] Ibid., s. 12B(3); on penalties see ibid., s. 12B(5).

[81] Ibid., s. 30A.

[82] Ibid., s. 50(6) ff.; the right of appeal is given by s. 31.

[83] Ibid., s. 54.

[84] *Duchy Maternity Ltd.* v. *Hodgson* [1985] STC 764.

[85] TMA 1970, ss 43A, 43B, added by FA 1989, s.150: it appears that this does not apply when the assessment is an original (but late) assessment, as distinct from an additional assessment.

[86] *Vickerman* v. *Personal Representatives of Mason* [1984] STC 231.

[87] On s. 114, see *Fleming* v. *London Produce Co. Ltd.* [1968] 2 All ER 975, 44 TC 582.

[88] *Baylis* v. *Gregory* [1987] STC 297, 62 TC 1, CA. See also *IRC* v. *McGuckian* [1994] STC 888, 69 TC 1 (CA NI) where the court refused to allow the alteration of an assessment where the inspector had been under a misapprehension but had not made a mistake, since he had intended to do what he had done.

[89] TMA 1970, s. 33(1); however see Stopforth [1989] *BTR* 151 for limitations on this relief.

[90] Ibid., s.33(2A).

Other claims. Tax legislation includes many reliefs, elections, etc., which have to be claimed by the taxpayer.[91] Frequently this will now be done in the course of the self-assessment process.[92] A taxpayer who has forgotten to make a claim may be able to amend the self-assessment return—the residual error mistake claim applies to all assessments, including self-assessments. Amendments of claims are also allowed.[93] Where an assessment is made under s. 29, and is not to make good a loss due to fraudulent or negligent conduct, the taxpayer may make any claim for further relief for that year within one year from the end of the chargeable period in which an assessment is made.[94]

Time limits

Unless statute prescribes otherwise, claims must be made by the end of five years following 31 January after the fiscal year to which it relates.[95] If an assessment is made late the consequential claim can be made up to any time after the end of the fiscal year following that in which the assessment is made.[96] There are further rules for appeals following the refusal of a claim. Certain claims are reserved to the Special Commissioners.[97]

4.3.5 Assessment of self-assessment[98]

At first sight the shift of costs from the Inland Revenue to the general taxpayer seems a rather perverse form of privatisation. There is, however, more to the problem than that. Clearly, a desire to reduce government expenditure is one of the aims of the change; another is a sincere wish to reduce some taxpayers' compliance costs. Under the old system of assessment, the Revenue had to make assessments within a certain, and often quite unrealistic, time limit, not least because only when the assessment had been made could a liability to pay tax actually arise. If, often for very good reasons, accounts were not ready, the Inspector would make an estimated or provisional assessment. This would be followed by amended or additional assessments, which represented a very real compliance cost to major taxpayers. The new system avoids such unnecessary "ping-pong" by making the taxpayer submit his return by 31 January, and ensures government cashflow by the system of payment of accounts. There are, however, others, e.g. older taxpayers,[99] for whom the change represents a new and significant expense—and a great opportunity for tax advisers. It may be that the real world with which the tax system has to grapple can no longer be adequately policed without this shift in practice and that older people's interests have to be sacrificed.

Another major benefit has been a reform of some of the less-intelligible substantive rules, notably the abolition of the preceding year of assessment and the rewriting of the Schedule A rules. Forms have had to be rewritten to enable taxpayers to calculate their own tax, instead of supplying information required by the Revenue. The rule under which the Revenue can be required to do the calculations is also beneficial and bridges the old system

[91] The procedure is laid down in TMA 1970, s. 42. It applies also to elections: s. 42(10).

[92] Ibid., s. 43(2) subject to subs. (3) which refers to PAYE computations.

[93] Ibid., s. 42(9).

[94] Ibid., ss 43A, 43B. It appears that this does not apply when the assessment is an original (but late) assessment as distinct from an additional assessment.

[95] Ibid., s 43(1).

[96] Ibid., s, 43(2); for further assessments, see ss 43A, 43B.

[97] Ibid., s. 46C.

[98] See *BTR Self-Assessment* Issue [1999] No. 4 and literature there cited. On possible extension to PAYE, see James [1994] *BTR* 204 (for the extension) and Sandford [1994] *BTR* 674 (against).

[99] For special problems, see CIOT Low income Tax Reform Group.

with the new. There are also philosophical (or even constitutional) aspects in the rights of citizens to take charge of their part in the process. Rights, however, also come with obligations. Under the old regime taxpayers could disclose the nature of any transaction without being obliged to indicate to the Revenue that certain anti-avoidance provisions might apply. Under self-assessment taxpayers must apply the relevant provision to themselves; failure to do so may lead to interest, surcharges and, of course, penalties. They cannot rely, as in the old days, on the Revenue deciding not to apply the provision.

Overall, the change has been completed successfully in that the new system is in place and delivering tax payments.[100] Apart from some teething troubles,[101] notably over the boundary between partnership tax and individual partner tax, and between PAYE and self-assessment, some concern remains. First, when will the Revenue get a reasonable proportion of the assessments correct? Figures released in early 2000 suggested that the Revenue was processing, even if most of these errors were trivial, only 72% of assessments correctly first time, i.e. two million were incorrect. Secondly, one waits to see how the Revenue will strike the balance between deterrence and forgiveness in administering the system and how willing it will be to use the reasonable excuse provisions. American experience, which the Chancellor invoked as a good precedent when introducing the system in 1993, has turned very sour, with Revenue agents confessing to malpractices used to terrorise or mislead taxpayers.[102] This has led to a new structure for the US Internal Revenue Service, with a board of management on which independent members are in the majority, and a reversal of the burden of proof. It is unlikely that the best traditions of the Revenue will be abandoned unless it feels that it is losing the war against the tax evader—due to too few resources. The dreadful modern mania for setting measurable performance targets will not help either. The threat of reform along US lines may be the taxpayer's best hope should the existing scrutiny arrangements fail. Thirdly, in their anxiety to assist taxpayers Revenue "help offices" give much advice, some of which is simply wrong. Taxpayers will feel very aggrieved if the advice they are given is wrong and the Revenue refuses to stand by it for lack of written evidence. Finally, how will the nation divide between those who think they can cheat on a system which has so relatively few checks and those honest or even fearful people who will not claim all the reliefs to which they might be entitled? In this connection the very well-meaning explanations of the current law (as understood by the Revenue) which appear on the information notices should really be written by an outside body and not by the Revenue. These explanations are creating safe harbours of interpretation (a law within the law), to be put alongside the existing interpretation provisions.

[100] *See Sixth Report of the House of Commons Select Committee on the Treasury 1998–99*; and comments by Chamberlain [1999] *BTR* 445.

[101] See ICAEW comments, available at tdtf@icaew.co.uk; and see [1998] *Simons Weekly Tax Intelligence*, 58, 741.

[102] On US legislative response, see Mumford [1997] *BTR* 481; see also the experience of Professor Graetz in Graetz (1997), 92.

4.4 Appeals

4.4.1 Appeals to Commissioners against assessment[103]

The right of appeal

A taxpayer, T, may wish to appeal against an officer's amendment to T's self-assessment[104] or against the refusal of a claim or election.[105] Similarly, T, aggrieved with an assessment which is not a self-assessment, may want to appeal. T must give notice in writing to the Revenue within 30 days of its issue.[106] By contrast, notice of a VAT appeal is sent to the tribunal itself.[107] Other methods of appeal include seeking the opinion of the court[108] and an originating summons,[109] but not arbitration.[110]

The tribunal

The appeal will be made either to the General Commissioners, a body of lay persons assisted by a qualified clerk,[111] or the Special Commissioners, who are highly qualified persons. Today the Commissioners' role is to adjudicate rather than to assess.[112] The current rules on Special Commissioners restrict eligibility for future appointments to persons who are legally qualified and make it usual for a commissioner to sit on his own. Legislation may reserve particular appeals to one or other body; otherwise the choice is with the taxpayer. Appeal may also lie to the Lands Tribunal and to the special tribunal appointed under TA 1988, s. 706.

The choice of tribunal as between the two sets of Commissioners is governed by factors: for example, the General Commissioners sit locally[113] and are cheaper and quicker; however, the Special Commissioners are a more professional body with more time to give to a complex case and, perhaps, have a reputation for insisting on more proof from the Revenue in cases of alleged omitted profits. Costs may be awarded by the Special Commissioners against a party who has behaved "wholly unreasonably" and has so behaved "in connection with the hearing".[114] Merely adhering to an untenable argument is not such behaviour unless the argument is know to be untenable.[115] The question whether reasonableness is to be determined objectively or subjectively awaits decision.[116] The Special Commissioners

[103] The whole topic of appeals in tax matters is under review following a report by the IFS Tax Law Review Committee in 1998. The Lord Chancellor's Department issues a Consultative Document in April 2000. For a consideration of the appeals system in the light of the Keith Committee Report, see Bartlett [1988] *BTR* 371, 408. See also Walton [1980] *BTR* 282.

[104] I.e. under TMA 1970, s. 28A(2) or (4); on partnerships, see ss 28B(3) and 30B(1).

[105] I.e. under ibid., s. 28(4A).

[106] TMA 1970, s. 31.

[107] See, generally, Avery Jones, "First Philip Hardman Memorial Lecture" [1994] *BTR* 3.

[108] As in *A.-G.* v. *National Provincial Bank Ltd.* (1928) 14 TC 111.

[109] As in *Buxton* v. *Public Trustee* (1962) 41 TC 235 (charitable nature of trusts), but not in *Argosam Finance Co. Ltd.* v. *Oxby* [1964] 3 All ER 561, 42 TC 86 (vexatious).

[110] See Sheridan [1978] *BTR* 243. The US Tax Court (rule 124) allows binding arbitration on questions of fact; usually, these are questions of valuation: see Sansing (1997) 50 *National Tax Jo.* 279.

[111] On clerks see Stebbings [1994] *BTR* 61; on history, see Stebbings [1992] *BTR* 398.

[112] *Wicker* v. *Fraser* [1983] STC 505; see also Stebbings [1993] *BTR* 52.

[113] On choice, see TMA 1970, s. 44(2) *et seq.*

[114] Special Commissioners (Jurisdiction and Procedure) Regulations 1994 (SI 1994/1811), para. 21.

[115] *Carter* v. *Hunt* [2000] STC (SCD) 17.

[116] In *Salt* v. *Young* [1999] STC (SCD) 249 the Commissioner suggested that the test may be subjective.

may now sit in public.[117] Legal aid is not available in either tribunal but there is no reason why a taxpayer should not use a McKenzie friend in appropriate circumstances.[118] The taxpayer may elect which body to appeal to, but this election may be overridden by a direction of the General Commissioners.[119] General Commissioners, however, are empowered to transfer a case to the Special Commissioners if the latter body consents and the case involves either complex matters or will take too much time.[120]

Each party is allowed to produce evidence.[121] The onus is on the taxpayer to disprove the assessment,[122] a rule which may be rationalised on the basis that he knows all the facts and therefore should have to prove them. Once an appeal is launched it can be withdrawn only with the consent of the Revenue.[123]

Procedure at hearings is governed by regulations which took effect in 1994.[124] Both sets of Commissioners may review their decisions on an application by a party or of their own motion,[125] but only for administrative error, the failure of one party to appear (for good and sufficient reason) or the failure of accounts to reach the tribunal even though they had been delivered to the Revenue.

The procedures are different from VAT appeals. *Inter alia*, the Commissioners normally sit in private; whereas the VAT tribunal sits in public. Appeal lies from the Commissioners to the Chancery Division and, in the case of the General Commissioners, by case stated; an appeal from the Tribunal goes to the Queen's Bench Division. Rationalisation seems desirable.

4.4.2 *Further appeals*

In England and Wales a further appeal lies to the High Court from a decision of the General Commissioners by the ancient (and now procedurally improved) process of case stated.[126] In Scotland appeal lies to the Court of Session and in Northern Ireland to the Court of Appeal (Northern Ireland). Appeals lie only on questions of law.[127] A party must apply within 30 days after the Commissioners have made their determination, declare dissatisfaction with that determination and ask for a case to be stated for the opinion of the High Court.[128] The clerk has 56 days in which to do this and there are procedures for commenting on the case.[129] The Commissioners have the power to require the would-be

117 Special Commissioners (Jurisdiction and Procedure) Regulations 1994, para. 15. On human rights problems see Baker [2000] *BTR* 211 at 243.

118 On McKenzie friends, see *McKenzie* v. *McKenzie* [1970] Ch 33. However, *R.* v. *Leicester City Justices* [1991] 3 All ER 935 shows that there is no right to such a friend; on use in proceedings not held in public, see *R.* v. *Bow County, Court ex parte Pelling*, (1999) *NLJ* 1369.

119 TMA 1970, s. 31(5A)–(5E).

120 Ibid., s. 44(3A).

121 See Regulations for Special and General Commissioners 1994 (SIs 1994/1711 and 1994/1812) paras 17 and 15, respectively; on expert evidence, see paras 12 and 9 respectively.

122 *Norman v. Golder* [1945] 1 All ER 352, 26 TC 293.

123 TMA 1970, s. 54.

124 Made under TMA 1970, ss 56B, 56C; on information powers of Special Commissioners, see SI 1994/1811, regs 4, 9, 18.

125 SIs 1994/1811 and 1994/1812, paras 17, 17; see, generally, Stebbings [1995] *BTR* 395.

126 Chancery Division Civil Procedure Rules Order 29. A case stated does not "disclose a cause of action" and so proceedings to strike out a case stated under the old RSC Ord. 18 were inappropriate; *Petch* v. *Gurney* [1994] STC 689, CA.

127 TMA 1970, s. 56.

128 See SI 1994/1812, paras 20–23.

129 For an example of problems facing the parties, see *Fitzpatrick* v. *IRC* [1991] STC 34.

appellant to identify the question of law to be addressed in the case stated.[130] The case-stated procedure is enduring rather than endearing.[131]

Appeals may go from the Special Commissioners by simple appeal[132]—without the complexity of the case stated. However, the appeal still lies only on questions of law and, moreover, any tax found by the Special Commissioners to be due must be paid.[133] It is also provided that appeals may go from the Special Commissioners direct to the Court of Appeal,[134] but only on questions of law.

When can the court reverse the Commissioners?

Lord Radcliffe's test(s). The court can reverse a decision of the Commissioners only for error of law, and so not simply on the basis that the judge would have reached a different conclusion. The facts may be such that the court assumes there has been some error of law. In *Edwards* v. *Bairstow and Harrison*[135] Lord Radcliffe said it did not much matter whether this state of affairs was described as one in which there was no evidence to support the determination, the evidence was inconsistent with and contradictory of the determination, or the true and only reasonable conclusion contradicted the determination. Rightly understood, each phrase propounded the same test. He preferred the last of the three.

The question whether an issue is one of fact or law is not always easy.[136] Dickinson wrote memorably of "matters of law which grow downwards into the roots of fact while matters of fact reached upwards without a break into matters of law".[137] Some see the whole exercise as legalism rather than realism and treat the distinction between law and fact as a legal fiction on the basis of which judges determine jurisdiction.[138] Nevertheless, some matters, like the construction of documents or statutes, are clearly questions of law; others, such as whether a document was executed on a particular date, are clearly questions of fact. Difficulties arise where the Commissioners, having decided the true meaning of the statute in issue, have to apply that meaning to the facts. The difficulties are of two sorts.

The first difficulty is the familiar problem of finding the right approach[139] to primary and secondary facts, the latter being inferences drawn from the former. In general such inferences are matters of fact and the courts are reluctant to substitute their own views, the more so since the Commissioners, unlike the court, have seen the witnesses. These secondary facts are still findings of fact.[140] Thus the question whether a trade is being carried on is one of fact. The Commissioners must not only decide the primary facts, such as what transactions were carried on and when, but also form their own conclusion as to whether or not these activities amounted to a trade, a conclusion which must depend on a whole range of cir-

130 SI 1994/1812, reg. 20(3).

131 For criticism, see Potter [1970] *BTR* 38, 41; for history and criticism, see Stebbings [1996] *BTR* 611.

132 TMA 1970, s. 56A.

133 Ibid., s.56A(8), (9).

134 TMA 1970, s. 56A(2); see also Civil Procedure Rules 1999, r. 52.

135 [1955] 3 All ER 48, 57, 36 TC 20, 229; see application by Megarry J. in *Redditch Electro-Plating Co. Ltd.* v. *Ferrebe* (1973) 48 TC 635, 645; and qualification by Lord Diplock in *CCSU* v. *Minister for Civil Service* [1985] AC 384, 410.

136 See Lord Simon in *Ransom* v. *Higgs* [1974] STC 539, 561. Among much literature, see Endicott (1998) 114 *LQR* 292.

137 *Administrative Justice and the Supremacy of Law* (1927), 51; quoted by Beatson (1984) 4 *OJLS* 22, 31.

138 Laws [1999] *BTR* 159.

139 See, e.g. Beatson (1984) 4 *OJLS* 22, 39–45.

140 Lord Brightman in *Furniss* v. *Dawson* [1984] STC 153, 167.

cumstances and impressions.[141] However, the question of the meaning of trade is one of law. Therefore, the question whether an isolated transaction can come within the meaning of trade is one of law; whether the particular transaction comes within the meaning of trade is one of fact. The legal system ought to accept that if a particular issue is one of fact, cases on almost identical facts may fall either side of the line. Some judges may be tempted to say in such circumstances that the two sets of Commissioners cannot both be right and extricate themselves from the mess by characterising the issue as one which is of mixed law and fact.[142] Such judges are incorrect in their premise and so in their conclusion. Other judges show greater humility.[143]

The second difficulty is that the law can be formulated in such a way as to leave it more or less to the Commissioners to decide the case, depending on the level of abstraction employed. Thus, in employment cases the issue may be: is payment a reward for services or, more simply, is it an emolument? Clearly, the latter leaves more to the Commissioners and reduces the court's power to intervene.

Outcome. When the court has heard an appeal by way of case stated it may make such order as it may see fit.[144] This has been interpreted widely so as to enable the court to uphold an assessment as if it had been made under a different section, or to remit the matter to the Commissioners with a direction to uphold it as if it had been made under a different section. The court is confined by the facts determined and the issues raised by the case stated and is neither expected nor permitted to wander further afield.[145]

Reference back. The court may sometimes remit the case to the Commissioners for additional findings of fact. However, this will be done only if such findings are material to some tenable argument, at least reasonable upon the evidence adduced and not inconsistent with findings already made.[146]

Appeal lies from the High Court to the Court of Appeal (or their Scottish and Northern Ireland equivalents) and the House of Lords in the usual way, but still only on questions of law.[146a]

4.4.3 Public law and other challenges to the Commissioners' or officers' decisions

Judicial review[147]

This remedy is equally applicable to the decision of the Commissioners or to the original assessment; it is also applicable quite separately from the assessment process to any situation in which officers of the Revenue exercise a power committed to them by the state. An application may be made only if the court has granted leave. It is subject to a time limit of three months from the date the ground first arose (although the court may extend the limit) and requires an applicant to have sufficient interest or *locus standi*.[148]

[141] Lord Sands in *IRC* v. *Hyndland Investment Co. Ltd.* (1929) 14 TC 694, 700.

[142] Lord Templeman in *Fitzpatrick* v. *IRC (No. 2)* [1994] STC 237, 242e, 246g, HL. See Olowofoyeku [1996] *BTR* 28.

[143] Lord Jauncey and Lord Mustill in *Fitzpatrick* v. *IRC (No. 2)* [1994] STC 237, 248, 255, HL.

[144] TMA 1970, s. 56(6).

[145] *McKnight* v. *Sheppard* [1997] STC 846, CA; reproving Lightman J. for his approach in [1996] STC 627.

[146] *Consolidated Goldfields plc* v. *IRC* [1990] STC 357, 361, Scott J.; applied in *Carvill* v. *IRC* [1996] STC 126; but distinguished in *Bradley* v. *London Electricity plc* [1996] STC 231.

[146a] On appeal to CA see Civil Procedure Rules r. 52.

[147] See generally Saunders, *Judicial Review in Tax Disputes* (Wiley, 1996) and Bartlett [1987] *BTR* 10.

[148] RSC Ord. 53, rr. 3, 4.

The court will not allow an applicant to use judicial review where the point should be dealt with by appeal.[149] Conversely, allegations of unfairness in the conduct of the appeal by the General Commissioners[150] are matters for judicial review and not for appeal. When judicial review is sought applicants must ensure that they do not act too early or too late.[151]

The grounds for judicial review are, of course, the same as in other areas of law, and were set out in 1985 by Lord Diplock[152] as comprising illegality, irrationality and procedural impropriety. Illegality covers errors of law; irrationality covers *Wednesbury* unreasonableness, i.e. a decision which is so outrageous in its defiance of logic or accepted moral standards that no sensible persons who applied their minds to the question could have arrived at it; procedural impropriety covers not only the failure to observe the rules of natural justice but also errors in the tribunal's own procedures. Today this formulation must also be interpreted to embrace the emerging doctrines of legitimate expectations and proportionality.

Public law defence

The second remedy is to establish a public law defence to a Revenue enforcement action,[153] e.g. by arguing that the original assessment is *ultra vires* and therefore void. In *IRC* v. *Aken*[154] this line of argument was used—unsuccessfully—to argue that the profits of prostitution could not be taxable since, as a matter of law, the profits of an illegal activity cannot be subject to tax. The Court of Appeal rejected this argument. Judges will no doubt keep this use of the *ultra vires* doctrine under very tight control to prevent it from becoming another avenue of appeal. Inspectors do not act *ultra vires* merely by making a mistake of law. Since *IRC* v. *Aken* was decided the courts have developed the law on collateral challenge. The House of Lords has held that it is open to citizens charged with a criminal offence to argue that the law under which they are charged is invalid.[155] That case concerned a prosecution for breach of a byelaw against smoking. The House had to distinguish a recent case[156] which had not allowed a person to challenge the validity of an enforcement notice in the planning notice enforcement proceedings and did so by treating the matter as one of statutory construction. In planning law Parliament had provided a complex system of appeal and the decision was addressed to the defendant; the exercise of the right of appeal and judicial review was enough. These might have had weight in tax matters but were swept aside by the Court of Appeal in *Pawlowski* v. *Dunnington*.[157]

Damages?

The third remedy is the altogether more ingenious suggestion that a cause of action lies against the Crown for damages, perhaps even exemplary damages, on the unlawful collec-

[149] See discussion by Dyson J. in *R.* v. *IRC, ex parte Bishopp* [1999] STC 531.

[150] *Mellor* v. *Gurney* [1994] STC 1025.

[151] See. e.g. *R.* v. *IRC, ex parte Ulster Bank* [1997] STC 832, CA (too early); *R.* v. *IRC, ex parte Allen* [1997] STC 1141 (too late).

[152] *Council of Civil Service Union* v. *Minister for Civil Service* [1985] AC 374, 410

[153] *Pawlowski* v. *Dunnington* [1999] STC 550 (taxpayer allowed to argue legality of condition for Revenue action under PAYE regulations allowing action against employee for recovery of tax following deduction by employer). On differences between public law defence and judicial review, see ibid., 557, *per* Simon Brown L.J.

[154] *IRC* v. *Aken* [1990] STC 497, CA.

[155] *Boddington* v. *British Transport Police* [1999] 2 AC 143; see Elliott 3 *Judicial Review* 144, Forsyth (1998) *Public Law* 364 and Hare [1998] *CLJ* 429.

[156] *R.* v. *Wicks* [1998] AC 92.

[157] See above at n. 155.

tion of or demand for tax.[158] This argument may gain credibility as a result of the incorporation of the Human Rights Convention in October 2000. However, a credible argument is not necessarily a successful one.

4.5 Encouraging Payment of Tax[159]

Pity the poor tax collectors: in Russia, in 1996, 26 collectors were killed and 74 injured in the course of their work; six were kidnapped and 41 had their homes burned down.[160]

4.5.1 Late payment—problems of interest

Interest runs from the date on which tax is payable, to the date of actual payment.[161] This applies to tax due on an assessment, payments on account, the balancing charge to tax, an amendment to a self-assessment, unpaid PAYE and any surcharge. Interest is now calculated on a compound basis.[162] Concessionary relief is available if the taxpayer dies before the payment date.[163] If an enquiry results in an increase in tax liability the taxpayer will be liable for the increase in the amount due under a balancing payment and the following year's payment on account, as well as interest on the increased balancing payment and on any extra payments on account. Payment of the following year's balance in full and at the right time will prevent interest liability arising on the payments on account for that year.[164] Although the taxpayer may agree with the Revenue to postpone the payment of tax where a liability is in dispute[165] this will have no effect on the remorseless application of the rules where tax is eventually held to be due

Interest is charged under a formula which sets the rate at reference rate, plus 2.5% reduced by basic rate income tax;[166] it is not deductible in computing income.[167]

Delaying payment—amounts in dispute

Taxpayers intending to appeal against the amendment or assessment may apply to postpone the payment of tax in dispute; any tax not in dispute is due at the normal time. If the taxpayer (T) and the Revenue cannot agree (in writing) on the amount in dispute. the Commissioners may determine the matter.[168] If the T pays the tax but later wins the appeal, the tax will be refunded together with repayment supplement; if the appeal is lost, tax is due as from the original proper date with any interest consequences.

[158] Wilde [1995] *BTR* 137, relating Art. 4 of the Bill of Rights to the Crown Proceedings Act 1947. The argument may be weakened (but not destroyed) by the decision of the House of Lords in *O'Rourke* v. *Camden B.C.* [1998] AC 188; on which see Carnwarth [1998] *Public Law* 407.

[159] Much of the modern law derives from the work of the Keith Committee, *Enforcement Powers of Revenue Departments*, Cmnd 8822 (1983) and Cmnd 9120 (1984); for a contemporary view, see White [1983] *BTR* 332 and [1984] *BTR* 74; for a retrospective review, see Ivison [1989] *BTR* 217. For results of current compliance work, see Inland Revenue 141st Annual Report, Cm. 4477 (1999) App. 2.

[160] *The Economist*, 31 May 1997, 19.

[161] TMA 1970, s. 86—the due date is set out in the self-assessment process.

[162] On interest see Collison, op. cit. §§22.6–22.10.

[163] ESC A17.

[164] Collison. op. cit. §22.6.

[165] Under TMA 1970, s. 55.

[166] Ibid., s. 89; FA 1989, s. 178; and SI 1989/1297, reg. 3AA, as amended.

[167] TMA 1970, s. 90.

[168] Ibid., s. 55; on time limit see s. 55(3).

Interest on tax overpaid—repayment supplement

Where tax has been overpaid, repayments will carry interest as from 31 January following the end of the fiscal year.[169] The payments are tax free.[170] This mirrors the liability to pay interest on unpaid tax. Repayment supplement can arise if payments on account of tax or balancing liability are found to be excessive, there is a reduction in any surcharge or penalty, or there is a repayment on any other income tax paid by or on behalf of the taxpayer. The rate of interest is less than that used for interest due to the Revenue, being reference rate minus 1%.[171]

4.5.2 Court action

The Revenue has a formidable battery of powers to collect tax.[172] It may sue in the magistrates' court (for amounts up to £2,000),[173] the county court (without limit) or the High Court.[174] There is no limit on the jurisdiction of the sheriff court in Scotland.[175] The Crown's status as preferential creditor on insolvency has been abolished; however, it remains for taxes for which the taxpayer acts as agent for the Revenue, notably in respect of PAYE, NICs, withholding taxes on payments to subcontractors and VAT for six months.[176] The Revenue may also levy distraint on the goods and chattels (but not perishable food)[177] of the person liable and may obtain a warrant to enter premises during the day time.[178]

4.5.3 Penalties and criminal offences[179]

In addition to interest (and the payment of the tax due), incorrect returns may attract a penalty of 100% of the tax lost.[180] This applies if the return was made fraudulently or negligently. If the return was not made fraudulently or negligently, but an error comes to the taxpayer's notice, it must be remedied without unreasonable delay—or negligence will be assumed.[181] Since the penalty is geared to the tax lost no penalty can arise if any tax would be time-barred.[182] Total penalties are reduced if two or more tax-geared penalties arise in respect of the same tax.[183] Anyone who assists in preparing the return or account may be fined up to £3,000.[184] In most cases the Revenue will, if given reasonable co-operation by the taxpayer and his advisors, accept a penalty of about 25% of the tax lost in cases of pure

169 TA 1988, s. 824.
170 TA 1988, s. 824(8).
171 SI 1989/1297, reg. 3AB, added by SI 1996/3187.
172 It also has many powers to direct withholding tax at source, e.g. from visiting entertainers and sportsmen.
173 Summary Proceedings (Financial Limits) Order 1991 (SI 1991/1625).
174 See the County Courts Act 1984, ss 40(2), 41(1) for power to transfer proceedings, and SI 1991/724 amending TMA 1970, s. 66.
175 Ibid., s. 67.
176 Insolvency Act 1986, Sch. 6.
177 *Morley* v. *Pincombe* (1848) 2 Exch 101.
178 TMA 1970, s. 61.
179 See Keith report, above at n. 159, chs 17, 19, 21; for a dated, but still interesting comparison of UK practice with that in India, see Kumar Jain [1987] *BTR* 353.
180 TMA 1970, s. 95; for partnerships see s. 95A and for corporation tax s. 96.
181 Ibid., s. 98.
182 For years following 1982–1983 a simple 20-year period applies: TMA 1970, s. 36; for earlier years, see s. 36 (original version).
183 Ibid., s. 97A, added by FA 1988, s. 129.
184 TMA 1970, s. 99.

negligence, and between 50% and 75% for fraud; in the absence of co-operation the Revenue will press for maximum penalties.[185]

In severe cases the Revenue may opt to press criminal charges in the criminal courts;[186] a criminal prosecution does not exclude penalties.[187] For the number of recent prosecutions, see below at p. 78 the Revenue prefers the penalty procedure over criminal prosecution since prosecution is a drastic step which ought to be reserved for really serious cases, and because of the practical difficulties involved in preparing criminal cases.[188] The decision to prosecute in a particular case is amenable to judicial review.[189] If, however, a criminal prosecution succeeds, the imposition of a custodial sentence of up to three years is very likely; short-term prison sentences are often accompanied by a swingeing fine.[190] Whether this private prosecution cum plea bargaining service is consistent with the proper goals of the criminal law (as opposed to the convenience of tax administrators) is another matter.[191]

The peculiar nature of these penalty powers may be illustrated by a number of special rules.

(1) Proceedings may be before the Commissioners—and so heard in private.
(2) The death of the taxpayer does not end the proceedings.[192]
(3) The Board has power to mitigate penalties even after the courts have pronounced.[193]
(4) There are time limits for the recovery of penalties.[194]
(5) There is an important rule of evidence which applies to any criminal or civil proceedings as well as those for penalties under which the Revenue may inform the taxpayer that it has the power to accept a pecuniary settlement and that the Board has a practice of being influenced by a full confession. Any statements made by the taxpayer are admissible despite the inducement;[195] the settlement gives rise to a contractual debt[196] and is not illegal.[197] There is a special right of appeal to the courts against the summary award of penalties by Commissioners.[198]

A decision by the Revenue to offer immunity from prosecution as part of a settlement involving the payment of tax, interest and penalties in respect of tax offences, normally prevents criminal prosecution by the Revenue. However, where there are offences other than offences under the tax legislation, the Crown Prosecution Service (CPS) may still launch a prosecution of its own; the doctrine of the indivisibility of the Crown does not prevent this.[199] It may be that the CPS will be allowed to do this only where the taxpayer did not

185 Moores and Rowland, *Yellow Tax Guide 1999–2000*, under TMA 1970, s. 95.

186 For example, Theft Act 1968, s. 32(1)(a); *R.* v. *Hudson* [1956] 1 All ER 814, 36 TC 561; see also Keith report, above at n. 159, chs 9, 13, 22.

187 Statement of Practice SP 2/88.

188 Evidence submitted to the Royal Commission on Criminal Procedure.

189 *R.* v. *IRC, ex parte Mead and Cook* [1992] STC 482, 65 TC 1.

190 See Ahmad and Hingun [1995] *BTR* 581 who suggest that sentencing guidelines from the Court of Appeal are more flexible than in the 1960s.

191 See Roording [1996] *Crim LR* 240. For an early article contrasting the treatment of social security fraud and tax fraud, see McEwan [1981] *Conveyancer* 114.

192 TMA 1970, s. 100A.

193 Ibid., s. 102.

194 Ibid., s. 103.

195 Ibid., s. 105.

196 *A.-G.* v. *Midland Bank Executor and Trustee Co. Ltd.* (1934) 19 TC 136; *IRC* v. *Nuttall* [1990] STC 194, CA.

197 "A beneficial and merciful practice", *per* Rowlatt J. in *A.-G.* v. *Johnstone* (1926) 10 TC 758.

198 TMA 1970, s. 53

199 *R.* v. *W* [1998] STC 550; for criticism, see Elwes and Clutterbuck [1999] *Crim LR* 138.

expect the settlement to terminate the CPS prosecution;[200] if the case is not so confined the decision will seriously have weakened the Revenue's negotiating hand. As already seen, in the converse case where a criminal prosecution has been brought for fraud, the Revenue may still seek to exact penalties under the tax legislation.[201]

The Revenue may begin these back duty cases following a tip-off about a likely suspect (ex-spouses and ex-employees are common sources) or it may simply disbelieve the taxpayer's return.[202] Once alerted the Revenue may require a complete statement of means and a satisfactory explanation of all sums appearing in bank accounts or supporting a luxurious lifestyle. To this end the Revenue is reported to keep records of all horse racing results. An exhaustive back duty inquiry may lead to the exoneration of the taxpayer, in which case the Revenue may reimburse the taxpayer's costs but only if there was a serious error on its part.

Tax law and criminal law

There is something of a cultural gap between the precise technical world of the tax lawyer and the broad brush of the criminal lawyer; however over-confidence about an avoidance scheme can become evasion and lead to a prison sentence,[203] for the taxpayer and adviser alike. The common law offence of cheating the public revenue still exists, being expressly preserved by the Theft Act 1968,[204] with no maximum penalty and with uncertain and wide ambit.[205] As A. T. H. Smith writes, "Like many of the ill defined common law offences, cheating is one whose boundaries are indistinct, and the courts have not resisted the temptation recently to extend the law (or take an extensive view of its scope) when the issue has arisen".[206] Ormerod suggests that the *actus reus* of the offence has become so wide that it can best be stated in negative terms.

> "There is no need for a dishonest act; an omission will suffice.[207] The act or omission must be intended to prejudice the Inland Revenue, Customs and Excise or the DSS—and not a local authority. There is no requirement of operative deception, nor of a need to prove actual loss to the revenue or to any other. It is not necessary to prove that the conduct resulted in any gain to himself. The type of behaviour caught includes failing to account for VAT, withholding PAYE and national insurance contributions, failing to register for VAT and simply failing to disclose income."

Self-assessment has imposed new obligations on taxpayers to report and assess their liabilities accurately. The breadth of the offence means that the only live issue at the trial will be dishonesty.[208]

Criminal lawyers dislike the width of the common law offence, particularly as expressed in *R.* v. *Mavji*[209]—the fact that the decision creates a liability for omissions as opposed to

[200] Rhodes *et al.* (1998) 148 *NLJ* 747; the article contains a useful explanation of the different modes of Revenue investigation and suggests that it was important in this case that the Revenue proceeded in the "neutral" mode. The authors were involved as counsel on the case—is it desirable for them to be allowed to comment in this way?

[201] On practice, see Statement of Practice SP 2/88 and IR 131.

[202] Other sources include government contracts, a customer being suspicious when asked for a bearer cheque (*Rosette Franks (King Street) Ltd.* v. *Dick* (1955) 36 TC 100), and even a reported robbery (*Crole* v. *Lloyd* (1950) 31 TC 338); informers may be rewarded.

[203] A court may also make a confiscation order under the Criminal Justice Act 1988, s. 71.

[204] Theft Act 1968, s. 32(1)(a).

[205] For criticism (and references to relevant literature), see Ormerod [1998] *Crim LR* 624; and A. T. H. Smith, *Property Offences* (Sweet and Maxwell, 1994), paras 20.106 *et seq.*

[206] Smith, ibid., para 20–106.

[207] The appellant's submission (that there was no duty to disclose) would, if accepted, "provide nothing but a licence for cynical and deliberate tax evasion": *R.* v. *Dimsey* [1999] STC 846, 859, *per* Laws LJ.

[208] Ormerod, above at n. 205, 626–7.

[209] [1987] 1 WLR 1388.

acts and that it removes any requirement of deception[210] (making something akin to fraud suffice). There are also wider objections to the role of criminal law and judicial activism, and unease over the central element of dishonesty.[211] The test used asks whether D's act was dishonest by the standards of reasonable and honest people and whether D realised that his act would be regarded as dishonest by such people. The former question is really one of law and not appropriate to a jury.[212] This, of course, leads to another and more fundamental question, i.e. whether it is appropriate to have trial by jury at all where the facts are complex.[213] FA 2000 s. 144 creates a new offence of being knowingly concerned in the fraudulent evasion of income tax. This applies to acts or omissions on or after 1 January 2001.

Criminal law and tax avoidance

Recent case-law has examined the question of when tax avoidance becomes cheating the public revenue. First, it may be assumed that if the scheme is successful at the technical tax level, there can be no criminal offence; the public revenue cannot be cheated if it has lost no tax.[214] This means that the transactions must be genuine (as opposed to shams—on which distinction see below at §5.6.3). If the scheme succeeds as technical tax law, it does not matter that there was no initial full disclosure of all the facts provided the Revenue eventually agrees, or a court eventually holds, that no tax has been lost, a prosecution for *attempting* to cheat the public revenue should also fail.[215] The practical problem for the defence in such cases is to establish that the scheme works; the device of a trial within a trial without the jury, however appropriate, is unavailable since the issues are often of mixed fact and law. The theoretically correct solution would be to adjourn the criminal case until the tax answer has been reached by the tax tribunal.

Secondly, it may be assumed that in the converse situation where the scheme is a sham, there is potential criminal liability, especially if there has been suppression of relevant facts. This leaves the third (and middle) situation where the scheme is not a sham but still fails at the technical level so that a tax liability does arise but the taxpayer fails to report it. In *R.* v. *Dimsey*[216] the Court of Appeal had no hesitation in upholding a conviction. It was held that an individual who had de facto control of a company and so arranged its affairs that the company made profits but did not declare them to the Revenue was cheating the Revenue; the position would be even stronger if the company was set up to operate in such a way. The case also shows that the words used in a judge's summing-up, like some cases stated, must be viewed in context; errors of tax law will not, of themselves, invalidate the conviction. There is something wrong here; simply leaving such matters to the jury seems perverse, the more so when one reads statements of judges who have no experience of tax law trying to explain some of the doctrines in terms a jury is meant to understand. At least this decision is an improvement on the earlier and most unsatisfactory[217] case of *R.* v. *Charlton*,[218] even

[210] Smith, above at n. 205, para. 20–111.

[211] Griew [1985] *Crim LR* 341; and other literature cited by Ormerod, above at n. 205.

[212] See Ormerod, above at n. 205, 632 *et seq.*

[213] See, in a different context, Wright, *Complex Trials and Financial Regulation*, LSE Financial Markets Group Special Paper No. 104 (August 1998). Rosalind Wright, Director of the Serious Fraud Office, drew attention to the decision of the Court of Appeal quashing the conviction in the County Natwest trial because the trial took too long and the issues were too complex.

[214] It is not, however, necessary for the prosecution to prove a loss to the Revenue: see *R.* v. *Hunt* [1994] STC 819, 827.

[215] Smith and Hogan, *Criminal Law* (9th ed., Butterworths, 1999), 327–34.

[216] [1999] STC 846.

[217] Thus, at no point did the judges in charge of the case address (or, apparently, understand) the distinction between a sham transaction and a transaction entered into for tax avoidance purposes: see generally Venables 7 *Offshore Taxation Review* 1; and Brandon 8 *Offshore Taxation Review* 9.

[218] [1996] STC 1417; for comment by one of those convicted, see Cunningham, *Taxation*, 4 January 1996, 329.

if it does nothing for those convicted in that case. Tax lawyers find this "robust" attitude inappropriate and wonder whether criminal law will find it possible to cope with the concept of innocent evasion.[219] In 1997–1998, 14 people were prosecuted by the Board of Inland Revenue for false returns of income; of these, three were acquitted and no evidence was offered against four.[220]

New Offence. FA 2000 s. 144 creates a new offence where a person is "knowingly concerned in the fraudulent evasion of income tax" and the thing is done or omitted on or after 1 January 2001.

4.5.4 *Compliance—effectiveness of sanctions?*[221]

Work has been carried out in the United States to investigate the effects of sanctions under tax law on taxpayer behaviour. Although the conclusions reached are tentative they do not make encouraging reading for the Revenue. By looking at the extent to which taxpayers think they will be audited (perceived certainty) and the severity of any sanction imposed (perceived severity), Long and Schwartz,[222] after looking at later returns by people who had been audited, concluded that audits appeared to be marginally effective in reducing the frequency of reporting errors but not their size, and that there were almost as many people who were initially compliant who became non-compliant, as taxpayers who had been non-compliant but who became compliant. The conclusion that the presence of audits did not decrease non-compliance naturally raises the question why this should be so. Answers tend to focus on the negative effects of the blanket enforcement of complex laws. These included the IRS tendency to treat violators the same whether they acted inadvertently or intentionally, the lack of relative risk to the determined violator who would usually get away with paying tax and interest, and the lack of judicial review. Needless to say, other surveys suggest different results.[223] The UK rules normally include penalties as well as interest, and also provide for appeals against penalties. However, while it is a matter for debate whether the Inland Revenue is able to distinguish sufficiently between deliberate and inadvertent loss, there can be no doubting that the UK tax rules are now about as complex as the US rules were then. Another study suggests that audit may be better at deterring the overstatement of deductions as opposed to the under-reporting of income.[224] As a fascinating footnote one should record the (again US) survey on the effects of status in income tax audits. Using occupational status as a measure of status, Kinsey and Stalans conclude that taxpayers of higher status tended to get more advantageous settlements than those of lower income status—but only as long as they represented themselves. Once tax practitioners were involved, status advantages disappeared: "tax practitioners level the playing field by disrupting social influence and deference processes".[225] An altogether different line of work suggests ways in

[219] On problems of scope of evasion, etc., see Sawyer [1996] *BTR* 483

[220] 141st Report, for year ending 31 March 1999, Cm. 4477, 79.

[221] On US compliance literature, see survey article by Andreoni, Eraud, and Feinstein (1998) 36(2) *Journal of Economic Literature* 818–60. See also Slemrod (ed.), *Why People Pay Taxes* (University of Michigan Press), reviewed by Wetzler (1993) 46 *National Tax Jo.* 255. On corporate tax evasion, see Cooper 50 *Tax Law Review* 3. For explanations of US aggression in self-assessment see Rosenberg (1996) 16 *Virgina Tax Review* 155. On myths that evasion can be reduced by having a simpler tax system or lower rates of tax, see Graetz and Wilde (1985) 38 *National Tax Jo.* 355.

[222] Long and Schwartz paper presented to Annual Meeting of Law and Society Association Washington, DC, June 1987 on work carried out in 1986.

[223] For example Witte and Woodbury (1985) 38 *National Tax Jo.* 1.

[224] Kinsey, *Theories and Models of Tax Cheating Criminal Justice Abstracts*, September 1986, 403–25.

[225] Kinsey and Stalans, September 1996, looking at state as opposed to federal audits.

which one should behave when being audited, in order to get the best result. The provision of "soft lighting, alcohol, videos and more" is not recommended since this suggests that the company has something to hide.[226]

4.6 Revenue Information Powers

4.6.1 Gathering information from third parties

TMA 1970 gives the Revenue power to issue notices to gather various details,including the names of "lodgers and inmates" resident in a person's dwelling house,[227] any interest payments made by banks or other persons without deducting tax,[228] and payments from lessees, etc.,in relation to Schedule A.[229] Broadly, these powers go back only three years. In addition, but still subject to the three-year limit, there is a rule requiring persons in receipt of taxable income belonging to another to provide information;[230] these words were interpreted by the court at face value and so could be used to require an auctioneer to provide details of the sums paid to a seller.[231] There is a separate power not restricted to three years for stock jobbers transactions[232] and certain information about securities.[233] There are also separate rules for capital gains.[234]

4.6.2 Documents and information[235]

The Revenue has wide information powers which may be grouped under four heads:

(a) powers to require a taxpayer[236] to deliver documents in that person's possession or power [237] or furnish other particulars[238] containing information relevant to the tax liability of that person;
(b) power to require equivalent documents or information from any other person;[239]
(c) power requiring the person to make documents relating to another person available for inspection;[240] and
(d) power to call for the papers of a tax accountant.[241]

[226] See (1998) 46 *Can. Tax Jo.* at 733 describing some of the advice given in a piece under review as "somewhat Machievellian and borderline unethical".

[227] TMA 1970, s. 14; see also s. 15 (employers), s. 16 (fees, etc., paid to traders, etc.) and 16A (agency workers).

[228] Ibid., s. 17 (banks, etc.) and 19 (others); if tax is deducted, other reporting provisions apply which do not depend on notice.

[229] Ibid., s. 19.

[230] Ibid., s. 13.

[231] *Fawcett* v. *Special Commissioners and Lancaster Farmers Auction Mart Co. Ltd.* [1997] STC 171, 69 TC 279, CA; reversing Rattee J. at [1995] STC 61. For criticism of the decision of Rattee J. see [1995] *BTR* 181.

[232] TMA 1970, s. 21.

[233] Ibid., ss 23,d 24.

[234] Ibid., ss 25–28.

[235] On Revenue powers during the self-assessment enquiry window, see above at §0.00.

[236] TMA 1970, s. 20(1). Documents include computer records. The reasonable assistance of the computer's operators may be required (FA 1988, s. 127). Taxpayer includes a deceased taxpayer TMA 1970 s. 20(6).

[237] TMA 1970, s. 20(1)(a).

[238] Ibid., s. 20(1)(b).

[239] Ibid., s.20(2).

[240] Ibid., s. 20(3).

[241] Ibid., s. 20A.

The falsification of documents which have been called for is a criminal offence.[242] Information gathered from a citizen by the state for one purpose should not be used by the state for another purpose; public interest immunity may prevent the disclosure in civil proceedings of documents in the hands of the Inland Revenue relating to a taxpayer's tax affairs.[243] These information-gathering powers now apply for the purpose of a liability to tax under the law of another member state of the European Community.[244]

These powers are limited in various ways. The inspector's opinion in (a) and (c) above that the documents or information are needed must be reasonable[245] and a written summary of reasons, must be given.[246] In (a) and (c) the consent of a General or Special Commissioner is required—who must be satisfied that the Revenue is justified in using the powers.[247] (b) may be exercised only by the Board itself and the Board's opinion must be reasonable; the Board must have reasonable grounds for believing not only that there has been or may be a failure to comply with the Act but also a consequential serious prejudice to the proper assessment or collection of tax.[248] A notice under (c) must name the taxpayer unless a Special Commissioner has allowed otherwise.[249] The documents must be specified with some particularity[250] and the Revenue must behave fairly.[251] In addition, certain documents are excluded—personal (e.g. medical) records and journalistic material.[252]

The power under (d) relates to the papers of a tax accountant who has been convicted of a tax-related offence; the officer seeking the order must act with the authorisation of a member of the Board given in relation to the particular case,[253] Again, personal records and journalistic material are excluded.[254] This power is separate from the power of the court to order discovery of documents in the course of litigation.

All these powers are subject to further rules, some of which are procedural, but others substantive. The powers cannot be used to get documents or information relating to the conduct of an appeal.[255] There is a general limitation period of six years, except in cases of fraud.[256] There is also protection for the professional privilege of a barrister, advocate or solicitor[257] with equivalent, but disappliable, protection for auditors and tax advisers.[258]

242 Ibid., s. 20BB, added by FA 1989, s. 145.

243 *Lonrho v. Fayed (No. 4)* [1994] STC 153, CA.

244 FA 1990, s. 125; see also Directive 77/799/EEC; (1989) *Simon's Tax Intelligence* 481, 484, 714.

245 An objective test was applied in *IRC v. Rossminster* [1980] STC 42.

246 TMA 1970, s. 20(8E); for an illustration see saga of *R. v. IRC, ex parte Continental Shipping SA* [1996] STC 813, and its successor *R. v. IRC, ex parte Archon Shipping* [1998] STC 1151, §20(8E) is subject to s. 20B(1B), which imposes a duty to give reasons, but with protection for sources (s. 20(8G)); and to a Commissioner's power to waive this rule (s. 20(8G)).

247 TMA 1970 s. 20(7A)(b). The person from whom the documents are sought has no right to see this summary (*R. v. IRC, ex parte Taylor* [1988] STC 832).

248 TMA 1970, s. 20(7A)(a).

249 Ibid., s. 20(8B).

250 *R. v. IRC, ex parte Ulster Bank* [1997] STC 823.

251 *R. v. IRC, and MacDonald ex parte Hutchinson* [1998] STC 680, where the judge expressed doubts about whether the Revenue had behaved fairly.

252 TMA 1970, s. 20(8C)—defined by reference to the Police and Criminal Evidence Act 1984, ss 12, 13.

253 TMA 1970, s. 20A (subject to s. 20B).

254 Ibid., s. 20A(1A), added by FA 1989, s. 143.

255 TMA 1970, s. 20B.

256 Ibid., s. 20B(5), (6).

257 Ibid., s. 20B(8). On the scope of professional privilege of barristers, see *Dubai Bank Ltd. v. Galadari* [1989] 3 All ER 769, CA, doubting *R. v. Board of Inland Revenue, ex parte Goldberg* [1988] STC 524, 61 TC 403. Professional privilege does not extend to the solicitor's own tax affairs (*R. v. IRC, ex parte Taylor (No. 2)* [1990] STC 379, 62 TC 578). See also the Keith report, above at n. 159, ch. 26.

258 TMA 1970, s. 20B(9), (10); on disapplication see s. 20B(11)–(14).

The scope of professional privilege has, however, been restricted to the particular powers mentioned in the statute. Privilege cannot be invoked if the Revenue can use some other power, such as the basic power in TMA 1970, s. 20(1).[259] This decision is highly controversial and may be challenged in due course.[260]

4.6.3 *Serious tax fraud (1): powers of entry and search*[261]

There is a power to enter and search premises for information relating to a serious offence relating to tax, provided a warrant is obtained from a sheriff (in Scotland) a Circuit judge (in England and Wales) and a county court judge (in Northern Ireland).[262] This has long been controversial. Unfortunately, there is at least one recent example where the Revenue exercised its powers under the warrant in an improper way. Fortunately a timely application for judicial review led to the grant of an interim injunction to stop the search.[263]

The application may be (and usually is) made *ex parte*, i.e. without giving notice to the person whose premises are to be searched. The Revenue officer applying for the warrant must have reasonable grounds for suspecting that an offence has been committed and, more significantly, must have the approval of the Board itself. This power is confined to cases of serious fraud.[264] The Revenue must specify details, e.g. as to number of officers who are to exercise the warrant (although they may take helpers with them), the times of day during which the power is to be exercisable and whether or not a constable in uniform is required.[265] There are many ancillary rules, such as the duty to retain and inspect warrants and procedures for listing and recording documents removed.[266] Officers may remove only documents which they have reasonable cause to believe may be required in evidence for the offence which triggered the application for the warrant.[267] They must not seize or remove any document to which a claim of legal professional privilege could successfully be made.[268] In the *Rossminster* case in 1980,[269] the House of Lords, in proceedings for judicial review[270] to quash a warrant, held that a warrant under a much earlier version of the legislation was valid so far as the power to enter and remove papers was concerned. It held that the taxpayers had not established that the Revenue had acted outside the scope of the warrant, leaving open the question whether the owners of the premises could succeed in trespass.

[259] Ibid., s. 20B(8) refers to s. 20(3), (8A) and 20A(1); the major power in s. 20(1) not covered.

[260] *An Applicant* v. *An Inspector of Taxes* [1999] STC (SCD) 189; for critical comment, see Ferguson (1999) 501 *Tax Journal* and (1999) 502 *Tax Journal*; for a defence of the decision as a matter of law, see Passmore (1999) 505 *Tax Journal*, who ends by suggesting that the decision may be different once the Human Rights Act 1998 comes into force.

[261] For review, see Walters [1998] *BTR* 213; see also the Keith Report, above at n. 159, ch. 9.

[262] TMA 1970, ss 20C (1), 20D.

[263] *R*, v. *IRC, ex parte Kingston Smith* [1996] STC 1210, 1214–15.

[264] TMA 1970, ss 20C(1), 20D(3).

[265] Ibid., s. 20C(1A), (3); helpers may include independent legal advisers (*R.*v. *IRC, ex parte Tamosius* [1999] STC 1077).

[266] TMA 1970, ss 20C(5)–(7) and 20CC.

[267] However, public interest immunity may protect the officer from further questioning on this, at least at the judicial review stage: see Walters [1998] *BTR* 213, 214.

[268] *R.* v. *IRC, ex parte Tamosius* [1999] STC 1077.

[269] [1980] STC 42, 52 TC 160, HL.

[270] Walters, above at n. 267, 215 describes judicial review in this context as "an illusory rather than a real protection for citizens" because of the public interest immunity.

4.6.4 Serious tax fraud: (2) judicial order for documents

FA 2000 adds a new Revenue power, TMA 1970, s. 20BA, in cases of serious tax fraud.[271] As we have just seen the Revenue had one power (under s. 20) to call on a third party to produce documents relating to the affairs of a taxpayer. In addition they had, under s. 20C, the power to enter the premises of a third party connected with the taxpayer and seize relevant documents. The new power sits between the two. The person must hand over the documents within ten working days from delivery of the order; the order may specify a later date.[272] The documents must be evidence of the offence under investigation. Notice of the application for the order must be given unless the judicial authority is satisfied that this would seriously prejudice the investivation.[273] Like s. 20C s. 20BA is concerned with serious tax fraud and so has procedural safeguards similar to those in s. 20C. Unlike 20C it simply instructs the third party to comply with the notice and deliver up the documents; neither entry onto the premises nor seizing and taking away are required. Like s. 20C judicial authorisation is needed (and at the same level); the officer making the application must have been authorised by the Board of Inland Revenue for the purposes of this section—as opposed to this application. Professional privilege is also preserved and the act contains procedures for resolving disputes as to the extent of the privilege.[274] The Revenue may make rules to determine how a person complies with the order.[275] The sanction for failure to comply is the general sanction for contempt of court.[276]

4.7 The Professional's Role: Ethics

The role of the tax adviser has emerged in a typically English, pragmatic way. Work is carried out not only by lawyers (whether barristers or solicitors) and accountants (in one or other professional body of accountants), but also by the increasingly influential Chartered Institute of Taxation (CIOT) which attained chartered status in 1994. There are also advisors who have no professional qualification as such, ranging from retired and highly skilled members of the Inland Revenue to complete freelancers with less impressive achievements.

Professional tax advisers face a range of problems concerning professional ethics.[277] Clearly, they are under a duty to their client, but they also owe a duty to observe the profession's standards. They must not make a tax return they know to be false (or they will face not only disciplinary procedures but also criminal prosecution). The CIOT suggests that the client's position should be presented in a way which is factually correct and is not intended to mislead an ordinarily competent inspector. If the Revenue makes an error in calculating tax which favours the taxpayer, tax advisers are under a professional obligation to advise the

[271] TMA 1970, s. 20BA and Sch 1AA added by FA 2000 Sch 39; see Inland Revenue Press Release 7 April 2000, (2000) *Simons Weekly Tax Intelligence* 572. For original proposals see Inland Revenue press release, 25 November 1999, (1999) *Simons Weekly Tax Intelligence* 1881.

[272] TMA 1970, s. 20BA(2).

[273] Ibid., Sch 1AA, para. 3.

[274] Ibid., paras 5, 6.

[275] Ibid., paras 7, 8

[276] Ibid., para. 9.

[277] See *CIOT Professional Conduct in Relation to Taxation: Rules and Guidelines*, issued October 1997; see also New Zealand guidelines, printed at [1996] *BTR* 502–4 and Ross, *Ethics for Tax Practitioners* (Australian Tax Research Foundation, Study No. 18).

client to inform the Revenue, and to refuse to act further for that client if the client does not follow that advice. However, there are many more difficult or grey areas where professionals may disagree on whether the Revenue should be informed of something, e.g. where the client takes a particular view which is different from the published Revenue view (here, the decision whether or not to inform must rest with the client). While there is no need to provide the Revenue with gratuitous information, relevant facts should never be concealed from the Revenue. This area of professional ethics is much studied in the United States and awaits proper study in the UK.[278] Some members of the profession consider that the CIOT guidelines provide too much co-operation with the Revenue. It is unfortunate that these members are reluctant to engage in public debate.

4.8 Administration and Human Rights

Although the European Convention on Human Rights says little directly on tax matters, the courts and the Commission have begun to use the Convention indirectly.[279] The Convention gives various procedural rights in civil cases, including a fair trial and appeal to an independent tribunal (Article 6(1)) and, in criminal cases, more substantial rights such as a presumption of innocence, a right to be informed promptly of the nature and cause of the accusation, adequate and reasonable time and facilities to prepare the defence, a right to legal aid if insufficient means are available, and a right to examine prosecution witnesses (Article 6 (2)). Although a tax dispute is not at present regarded as giving rise to a civil obligation—and so will not be within Article 6 (1)—the Strasbourg Court of Human Rights has held that a civil claim which originates in tax, e.g. an action in restitution for wrongly paid tax, can be a civil right or obligation.[280] Similarly, although tax law is not the same as criminal law, the court has held that the concept of crime under Article 6 (2) is autonomous, and so has held that an action for a tax penalty can be a "criminal charge" within Article 6 (2).[281] Other issues which have been held to be capable of coming within Article 6(2) include a 100% tax penalty,[282] an unjustifiably prolonged Revenue investigation[283] and a penalty imposed for fraud committed by someone else.[284] The classification of an automatic, tax-geared penalty in *Bendenoun* v. *France*[285] as a criminal matter depended on the co-existence of several features: that the surcharge covered all citizen as taxpayers, that it was intended to deter, that it was substantial and that imprisonment could be imposed if it were not paid. How a penalty would be regarded if it lacked some of these features is unclear.[286] Article 8, guaranteeing respect for privacy and family life, has also been invoked to counter Revenue searches without a warrant,[287] and, at Commission level only, a Revenue request for information about detailed personal expenditure.[288]

[278] See papers given at the ABA Conference (London) July 1985, including one on UK aspects by Avery Jones.
[279] See Baker [2000] *BTR* 211.
[280] *National and Provincial Building Society* v. *UK* [1997] STC 1466.
[281] *Bendenoun* v. *France* (1994) 18 EHRR 54 (tax geared penalty); *A.P., M.P. and T.P.* v. *Switzerland* (1997) 26 EHRR 541.
[282] *J.J.* v. *Netherlands* (1998). Application 21351/93 28 EHRR 168.
[283] *Hozee* v. *Netherlands* (1998)—much would depend on the degree of co-operation of the taxpayer.
[284] *A.P., M.P. and T.P.* v. *Switzerland* (1997) 26 EHRR 541.
[285] (1994) 18 EHRR 544.
[286] See Persson-Osterman, *Cambridge Yearbook of European Legal Studies* (Hart, Oxford, 1999).
[287] *Funke* v. *France* (1993) 16 EHRR 297, 332, 357 (no warrant was needed under French law at that time).
[288] *X. (Hardy-Spirlet)* v. *Belgium* (1982) 31 DR 231.

Matters which may be looked at in future include[289]: the scope of professional privilege; whether the Commissioners are an "independent" tribunal (especially where deputies are used); whether the Commissioners may continue to sit in private; whether points may be taken to the Commissioners by the Revenue when the taxpayer has no equivalent rights; the highly selective number of cases chosen for criminal prosecution; the right of the Crown to prosecute after a tax settlement has been reached; whether a taxpayer is given an effective right of appeal if the only remedy in a case is judicial review; the rule that any disputed VAT must be paid before an appeal can be begun and the refusal of a court to allow a taxpayer accused of fraud to summon and cross-examine the informer. It is clear that there are many human rights issues which can be raised; how far they will succeed is a very different matter.

[289] See Oliver [2000] *BTR* 199 and Peacock and Fitzpatrick [2000] *BTR* 202. For lessons from Canadian experience see Lacey [2000] *BTR* 378.

5

The Control of Avoidance

5.1 Language—Avoidance, Evasion, Mitigation and Planning

Politicians, tax officials and practitioners spend a lot of time and energy on the problem of tax avoidance. No one seems to have a very precise idea of what is meant by the term,[1] but it is to be distinguished from evasion, which is illegal. If two people marry in order to reduce their tax burden they are practising tax avoidance; if they tell the Revenue that they are married when they are not, they are guilty of tax evasion, and may well be prosecuted. There is also an important distinction between a scheme under which no liability to tax arises (tax avoidance) and one under which a charge arises but the tax cannot be collected.[2] The latter may be evasion and subject to penalty. Other terms used in discussion—and in case-law—are tax mitigation and tax planning, which may be seen as subsets of tax avoidance or as independent categories, depending on the context in which one finds oneself; they are all, however to be distinguished from tax evasion.

Unfortunately, tax evasion itself has developed a number of "frayed edges". Thus, it is sometimes used to cover all case of non-compliance even though non-compliance[3] may be

[1] See IFS Tax Law Review Committee (TLRC), *Report on Avoidance* (November 1997), 2.

[2] See comments of Brightman J. in *Roome* v. *Edwards* [1979] STC 546, 561–5 (removed from bound volume—see [1979] *BTR* 261). See also the comments of Templeman L.J. in *IRC* v. *Stype Investments Ltd.* [1982] STC 625, 637.

[3] On causes of non-compliance, see Cooper (1994) 50 *Tax Law Review* 35.

deliberate or accidental and may give rise to penalties under tax legislation, prosecution under criminal law, or both. Evasion may even result from taking a position on tax legislation which is later shown to be incorrect.[4] If these are all examples of evasion, its greatest cause may be not fraud or greed, but the complexity of the tax legislation; the category, instead of being one of undoubted opprobrium, can become a matter of judicial hindsight. It is such considerations which encourage those who believe in a low rate, broad-based tax system, with few opportunities for tax saving.

Tax mitigation[5] is distinguished from tax avoidance because judges, when dealing with a provision turning on the presence of tax avoidance, invented the term "mitigation" in order to mark off transactions which would not be caught by the provision.[6] In this context therefore tax mitigation and tax avoidance are mutually exclusive. Today, tax avoidance arises where the taxpayer reduces a liability to tax without incurring the economic consequences that Parliament intended to be suffered by any taxpayer qualifying for such reduction in that liability.[7] Tax mitigation arises where the taxpayer takes advantage of a fiscally attractive option afforded by the tax legislation, and genuinely suffers the economic consequences that Parliament intended to be suffered by those taking advantage of the option. There are therefore two elements: economic consequences and parliamentary intent. The first element asserts that there should be some genuine economic consequences, while the second enables the court, on a case-by-case basis, to control which consequences will qualify. Today, a couple marrying to reduce tax would be treated as examples of tax mitigation.

The problem with tax mitigation is that while it provides a coherent reason for saying, in a particular case, that the facts do not amount to avoidance, and so do not trigger the application of some rule, it does not provide a clear way of telling whether those particular facts fall one side of the line or the other—it can be a conclusion, not a test, and so restates the problem rather than solves it.[8] Thus, why is it that there were no "genuine economic consequences" in the leading avoidance case of *Furniss* v. *Dawson*?[9]

Tax planning is what all sensible people do in order to reduce their tax liabilities. The boundary between tax avoidance and tax planning is shadowy at best; what matters is the boundary between successful and unsuccessful tax planning. On the question whether tax planning can come within the common law offence of cheating the public revenue see above at §4.5.3.

Tax planning is best understood by reference to the words "who", "what", "when" and "where".[10]

- "*Who*": tax planning may involve the careful selection of the particular taxpayer who will, for example, receive the income or realise a loss; thus, it may be another member of the family with little other income or relief, or a subsidiary of a company.

[4] E.g. the scope of TA 1988, s. 145 in relation to shadow directors in *R.* v. *Allen* [1999] STC 846.

[5] See, e.g. Lord Templeman in *Ensign Tankers (Leasing) Ltd.* v. *Stokes (Inspector of Taxes)* [1992] 1 AC 655, 676–7, [1992] STC 226, 240–1 64, TC 617, 741–2 and Lord Goff at 681, 244–5 and 746–7 respectively.

[6] e.g. Lord Templeman in *Commr of Inland Revenue* v. *Challenge Corporation* [1987] AC 155, 167–8, [1986] STC 548, 554–5, PC (New Zealand).

[7] *IRC* v. *Willoughby* [1997] STC 995, 1003–1004 below at 60.6.1.

[8] For a rare attempt to take matters further, see Rosenberg (1988) 87 *Michigan LR* 365–497, arguing that avoidance arises because the tax system uses a transactional rather than economic basis to determine income. As such, avoidance arises if a taxpayer's tax return understates income when computed on an economic basis, unless the taxpayer's behaviour corresponds with statutory policy goals of statutory provision underlying that understatement.

[9] See below at §5.6.4.

[10] For a more sophisticated (US) account, see Stiglitz, *Economics of the Public Sector* (3nd edn., Norton, 1988), ch. 24; see also Cooper's analysis of tax shelters in (1985) 85 *Columbia LR* 657.

- "*What*": with care, it may also be possible to influence the type of receipt, whether capital or income, or one type of income rather than another, e.g. employment income or business income.
- "*When*": timing is also important; and paying attention to timing may enable the taxpayer to postpone a liability to tax, for example by taking advantage of a deferral rule, or to avoid being caught by an artificial tax rule which forbids, for example, the carrying back of an unused capital loss.
- "*Where*": location is important since placing income or assets outside the taxing jurisdiction may mean no liability to UK tax, or no liability until income is remitted to the UK. The downside of this is that liability may be incurred under the foreign tax system. However, the foreign tax system may be different to the UK system, and the exploitation of gaps between tax systems is the forte of the international tax specialist.

Before leaving this topic one should note that while there has been much legislative (and occasional judicial) activity to prevent a person from converting income into capital, there has been none to stop conversion in the opposite direction.

5.2 Importance

The importance of tax avoidance for present purposes is threefold. First, from the wider perspective it is not possible to assess the effectiveness of a tax system unless it can be seen what degree of avoidance is practised and permitted by the system. Thus, to have a rule that trading profits of charities are not exempt from tax is one thing; to learn that this is routinely avoided by having a separate trading company which assigns its profits to its charitable owners makes the rule look less fierce. Secondly, while legislation to counter avoidance can be among the most complex in our tax code, it can also be among the simplest. The question of a general anti-avoidance provision remains a live one. Thirdly, from the law student's perspective, the case-law on avoidance tell us much about the problems posed by legislation and statutory purpose.

5.3 Ten Methods of Legislative Control—Plus One

No legislature can allow taxpayers to continue to arrange their affairs in such a way that the tax system becomes voluntary (pay the Revenue or pay an adviser),[11] or that government revenue fall short of what is needed. Various solutions have been suggested or adopted. Of the list which follows the 1966 Canadian Royal Commission gave us (1)–(3) and (5);[12] it is not pretended that the boundaries are always precise. A recurring issue is the appropriate mental element.[13]

(1) The "sniper approach" contemplates the enactment of specific provisions identifying, with precision, the type of transaction to be dealt with and prescribing, with precision,

[11] For contrasting views of the 1970s and the *Rossminster* saga, see Gillard, *In the Name of Charity* (1985) and Tutt, *The Tax Raiders* (1987), reviewed by Davies [1988] *BTR* 311.

[12] Carter Report, Vol. 3, App. A, 552.

[13] On which, see Avery Jones [1983] *BTR* 9, 113.

the tax consequences of such a transaction. This has been the traditional pattern of UK legislation. One example is the rule for business entertainment expenses.[14]

(2) The "shotgun approach" contemplates the enactment of some general provision imposing tax on transactions which are defined in a general way. The difference between this and the sniper approach lies in its conscious rejection of certainty. Of this, TA 1988, s. 703 probably represents the most obvious example, but others include TA 1988, ss 775 and 776. All these sections create penumbral areas although such areas are circumscribed.

(3) The "transaction not at arm's length approach" provides that the tax consequences will be different from what they would normally be, by treating the transaction as if it had taken place between parties at arm's length.[15] Typical examples are the rules substituting market value for the price, if any, actually received for disposal of capital assets, and sales between associated persons for capital allowance and profits purposes for income tax. Technically, this is a means of carrying out one of the other approaches, rather being than a separate approach, since the circumstances in which the technique is applied can be described with more or less precision.

(4) The "specific administrative threshold approach" grants wide powers to an official in order to counteract specified tax avoidance transactions and states what is to happen if the official wishes to invoke the rule. An example is the Australian legislation dealing with "bottom of the harbour" schemes.[16] UK examples are TA 1988, s. 766AA, TCGA 1992, ss 30–33 and 137.

(5) The "general administrative control approach" contemplates the grant of wide powers to an official or administrative tribunal in order to counteract tax avoidance transactions in general. There is no such provision in UK law at present.[17]

(6) The general anti-avoidance rule. This is close to (5) but the difference is that it purports to have justiciable boundaries determined by court process rather than by administrative discretion. It is not currently part of UK law, but examples can be found in Australia and New Zealand where similar words are interpreted very differently.[18]

(7) Retroactive legislation. In some ways the easiest and most effective method, retroactive legislation was used famously in 1978 to stop relief for losses arising from commodity straddles.[19] Today, the possibility of challenge under the human rights legislation may be a restraint on such legislation. There is also the more immediate political problem of getting a provision through Parliament. It is, however, common for an announcement to be made in Parliament that a particular scheme will be dealt in the next Finance Bill and that the legislation will be retroactive to the date of the announcement; this is unlikely to attract human rights problems and has encountered no parliamentary problems.

(8) Penalties.[20] At present, tax avoidance is lawful whether or not it is successful. This means that if an avoidance scheme is attempted, but fails, the taxpayer must simply

[14] TA 1988, s. 577.

[15] There is almost no UK authority on when people are dealing at arms length—see a discussion of Canadian material in Owen (1992) 40 *Can. Tax Jo.* 829.

[16] Constitutionality was considered in *MacCormick* (1984) 15 ATR 437.

[17] On excess profits tax during the Second World War, see below at §5.5

[18] Richardson (1986) 12 *Monash LR* 35.

[19] FA 1978, s. 31; now TA 1988, s. 399. For details of the scheme see Gillard, above at n. 11, 182–92.

[20] See TLRC report, above at n. 1, ch. 6.

pay the tax with any interest or surcharges. By contrast, in New Zealand a special tax penalty of 100% of the shortfall is incurred where "abusive tax avoidance" leads to a shortfall of NZ $10,000 or more in the self-assessment system. The penalty is reduced to 25% if there is adequate disclosure when the return is filed—a very important practical matter since so much turns on whether the Revenue can discover what was going on.[21] There are also penalties of 20% for taking an incorrect tax position. These have been criticised for blurring the distinction between evasion and avoidance.[22]

(9) Criminal law. The principal differences between this approach and (8) above are that penalties may include imprisonment and disqualification from offices. Criminal law also exposes the advisers to liability (to imprisonment, see above at §4.5.3).

(10) The alternative minimum tax on gross income. This is attractive to government because much planning involves using deductions. Such a tax is in force in Canada and the United States.[23]

(11) Finally, legal rule may be abandoned in favour of social pressure. If one considers how drinking and driving has become socially unacceptable, the same could be achieved in relation to tax avoidance, by proclaiming the virtues of the honest taxpayer.[24] Perhaps the nebulous nature of such pressure will match the nebulous nature of the concept. One should not hope for too much—it is easy to see whether a person has been drinking alcohol but much less easy to tell when a person has indulged in tax avoidance.

5.4 Is Avoidance a Problem?[25]

The case for legislation to outlaw avoidance can be put in a number of ways.

(1) The result would be a simplification of the tax laws. However, simplification in the code would simply produce uncertainty at the administration level and thus destroy the real advantage of simplification.

(2) It would act as a deterrent to other tax avoidance projects.[26] This would be an advantage since prevention is better than the resentment that arises when taxpayers, who are unable to take advantage of these schemes, see others using them until such time as the legislature catches up. However, deterrence must not impede genuine business transactions. The general solution to this problem is the clearance procedure, but only if this is implemented with sufficient resources.

(3) It would prevent so much skill and human resources being devoted to rather dubious activities.[27] Ignoring the mere rhetoric in the word "dubious", and not pausing to question the premise of the criticism that those possessing these skills could be put to more productive uses, it may be concluded that such skills would be used simply in

[21] See Keith Committee, *Enforcement Powers of Revenue Departments*, Cmnd 8822 (1983), ch. 7; and the facts of *IRC* v. *McGuckian* [1997] STC 908.

[22] On the New Zealand experience, see Sawyer [1996] *BTR* 483 and, more broadly, *Tax Compliance, Report to the Treasurer by a Committee of Experts* (Wellington, NZ, December 1998), esp. ch. 6.

[23] ITA, s. 127.5–127.55 (Canada) and IRC §55 (US). On US, see Bittker §111.4. The tax receives characteristically trenchant criticism by Bittker (1966) 21 *Tax Law Review* 1.

[24] See Schiemann L.J. in *Schuldenfrei* v. *Hilton* [1999] STC 821, 832.

[25] For an invigorating and rigorous analysis, see Shenfield *The Political Economy of Tax Avoidance* (IEA Occasional Paper No. 24, 1968).

[26] The present tax code has *in terrorem* provisions, e.g. TA 1988, ss 770A, 775 and TCGA 1992, s. 30.

[27] The price of legal expertise is high.

corresponding with the Revenue to determine whether a scheme would fall within the discretion, instead of challenging such a scheme in court. Being able to express an argument is not as important as understanding how the Revenue exercises a particular discretion and so having the information which governs the argument. The best way of lowering the costs of tax advice lies in the publication of information; the Inland Revenue manuals tend to fall silent when avoidance looms.

(4) If recent judicial attempts to develop doctrines to counter tax avoidance have passed their zenith, a statutory anti-avoidance device may be needed to maintain the integrity of the tax base. Moreover, a statutory provision can run from a certain date and include provision for a clearance procedure, neither of which is true for judicial doctrine.[28]

Other arguments are more questionable. Thus, it is not known how much tax is lost by "artificial" as opposed to "legitimate" tax avoidance schemes.[29] There is little direct evidence that avoidance leads to evasion, although the resentment that comes from watching others save tax may cause a decline in taxpayer morality—a proposition which leads to an examination of the tax base and of those items of income which escape tax altogether, just as much as those which escape tax through artificial devices. Finally, there is no evidence that artificial devices cause any increase in the burden on other taxpayers.

If the case for a general anti-avoidance provision is rejected, and the case for a sniper as distinct from the shotgun approach is accepted, it is necessary also to accept all the consequences of that approach. If the argument is based on the rule of law, the concept of certainty and the rejection of official discretion, then one must also reject any discretion of the Revenue to soften the application of a particular rule in hard circumstances. All too often critics of the Revenue really want the best of both worlds—a Revenue bound hand and foot by red tape in its efforts to get taxes, but with unfettered power to waive tax due.

It would be unwise to leave this problem without noting the comment of the 1955 Royal Commission that the existence of widespread tax avoidance is evidence that the system, not the taxpayer, is in need of radical reform.[30]

5.5 Precedents, Proposals and Other Countries

A general anti-avoidance provision was included in the UK's excess profits tax during the Second World War.[31] However, that scheme was less than fully effective: (a) because the Revenue needed to have access to information, and parliamentary feeling on this was extremely sensitive and unwilling; and (b) because the test of counter-avoidance was a motive of avoiding tax and the Revenue found it extremely difficult to provide evidence to rebut alleged motives.[32] It is largely due to the experience of that tax that later anti-avoidance provisions have tended to refer to matters such as the main benefit rather than motive;

[28] For criticisms of judicial solution, see TLRC report, above at n. 1, ch. 4.

[29] See Sandford, *Hidden Costs*, ch. 8.

[30] Cmd 9474 (1955) §33; cited by Kay [1979] *BTR* 354, 365.

[31] FA 1941, s. 35; for an example of its application, see *Crown Bedding Co. Ltd.* v. *IRC* [1946] 1 All ER 452, 34 TC 107, CA.

[32] Sir Leonard Barford, IFS Conference, 22; see also Sabine, *British Budgets in Peace and War (1936–1945)*, 197, 200, 260.

this change was made in the excess profits tax in 1944.[33] Similar powers were part of profits tax[34] and the special charge in 1967.[35]

Examples of the administrative control approach can be found in Germany,[36] the Netherlands,[37] Canada,[38] Australia[39] and New Zealand.[40] The United States has no such provision, but the situation there is different from that in the UK.[41] Many continental countries have a doctrine of abuse of rights—in addition to, or in place of, a general anti-avoidance provision.[42] Tax authorities in the Netherlands have suspended the application of their special rules and left all to the doctrine of abuse of rights.[43] No country seems to be at ease with its system, but this is largely because of the elusive nature of the distinction between acceptable and unacceptable tax avoidance and shifts in judicial perceptions, which are every bit as difficult as those in the UK. Thus, in Australia the first general provision was subsequently replaced because it had suffered too much at the hands of the judges. Later case-law not only weakened the new provision but reinvigorated the old.[44]

The choice between these various approaches is not an easy one since equity and certainty are in conflict. Tax equity demands that artificial tax avoidance schemes should be of no effect, yet certainty demands that the tax laws should be such that an individual can arrange his affairs in the expectation that he will or will not have to pay tax.

5.5.1 IFS Tax Law Review Committee's proposal 1997[45]

The IFS' Tax Law Review Committee (TLRC) produced a report with a number of conclusions. First, specific avoidance provisions should continue to be used. Secondly, without actually recommending a General Anti Avoidance Rule (or GAAR) it suggests that a GAAR with proper safeguards may well be preferable to the present uncertain state of case-law. The report goes on to recommend safeguards which it regards as proper.

The TLRC GAAR has several elements.

(a) A purpose clause to deter or counteract transactions which are designed to avoid tax in a way which conflicts with or defeats the evident intention of Parliament
(b) The basic rule which contrasts a "tax-driven" transaction with a normal transaction; a person is to be taxed in accordance with the normal transaction. Where, because the tax-driven transaction does not have a non-tax objective and so there is no normal transaction, tax is to be charged as if it had not taken place.
(c) Protected transactions. The rule is not apply to a protected transaction. If there is a multiple step transaction the rule will not apply if the transaction, taken as a whole, is entirely or mainly a protected transaction.

[33] FA 1944, s. 33.
[34] FA 1951, s. 32; see [1964] *BTR* 129.
[35] FA 1968, s. 50.
[36] See TLRC report, above at n. 1, 29.
[37] See Van der Stok [1998] *BTR* 150.
[38] See Arnold [1995] *BTR* 541; Roxan [1998] *BTR* 140; and TLRC report, above at n. 1, 17–21. For an early detailed analysis, see Arnold and Wilson (1988) *Can. Tax Jo.* 829, 1123, 1369.
[39] See Harris [1998] *BTR* 124, and TLRC report, above at n. 1, 21–4; on the *Spotless* case, see also Krever (1997) 45 *Can. Tax Jo.* 122.
[40] See TLRC report, above at n. 1, 24–6.
[41] See Tiley and Jensen [1998] *BTR* 161; and TLRC report, above at n. 1, 26–8.
[42] See Ward *et al.* [1985] *BTR* 68; and Ward and Cullity (1981) *Can. Tax Jo.* 451; see also Frommel (1991) *Intertax* 54 (France).
[43] TLRC report, above at n. 1, 29.
[44] See Harris [1998] *BTR* 124; see also [1996] *BTR* 453, 656. On old Australian law, see Lehmann, in Krever (ed.), *Australian Taxation Principles and Practice* (Longman, Melbourne, 1987).
[45] For a very different but earlier view, see Masters [1994] *BTR* 647.

(d) Burden of proof. It is to be assumed that a transaction is not a tax-driven transaction but, equally, it is to be assumed that it is not a protected transaction.
(e) The procedure to be followed by the tax authority would be spelt out. The authority would issue written notice specifying the tax-driven transaction and the normal transaction, stating that it was not a protected transaction and giving details of every other person to whom it had given written notice relating to the same transaction.
(f) The taxpayer could invite the authority to review its decision, giving reasons why it should do so.
(g) Appeal would then lie to the Special Commissioners or VAT Tribunal.
(h) All this would be backed up by a prior clearance procedure with provision being made for publication of advance rulings.
(i) Finally, an annual report would be made to Parliament giving full details of the operation of the rule.

UK tax authorities flirted with the idea of a general anti-avoidance rule in 1998, building on, but departing from, the TLRC model. The TLRC was severely critical of the Revenue's proposal.[46] The truth is probably that the scheme would have worked only with a proper system of rulings. The government was not willing to pay the financial costs of such a system, nor was it willing to pay the political cost of trying to force such a system onto taxpayers. A cynic might say that the Inland Revenue proposal was designed to be so bad that it was bound to be rejected.

5.6 UK Judicial Doctrines with Regard to Tax Avoidance

It is not—and probably never will be—possible to state the true doctrine of tax avoidance conclusively. This is partly because of the changing membership of the judiciary and partly because of the nature of the judicial process. It may be a strength of the judicial process that it makes it possible to obtain agreement where this is necessary, but makes it unnecessary to obtain agreement where this is impossible;[47] however, this results in many loose ends. Moreover, this process has certain features which make a general anti-avoidance rule (GAAR) more attractive to some. Proponents of a GAAR find the case-law approach, especially the composite transaction rule (see §5.6.4 below) objectionable in that it is: insufficiently targeted (as compared with a GAAR and the GAAR's notion of protected transactions); restrictive (in its insistence on having a preordained transaction and a tightly drawn sense of "preordained"); arbitrary (in that when it applies it simply knocks out a step; hypocritical) or unprincipled (by falsely presenting itself as a matter of simple interpretation when it is actually a matter of complex application[48]); retrospective and uncontrolled (through the lack of any clearance procedure). So in *Moodie* v *IRC* the House of Lords decision reversed its own earlier decision in *Plummer* v *IRC*.[49] There is also a strand of criticism which regards the whole line of cases as unconstitutional.[50]

[46] TLRC Response to IR's Consultative Document (IFS, February 1999).
[47] Sunstein, *Legal Reasoning and Political Conflict* (1996).
[48] For example, Whitehouse (1994) *Private Client Business* 71, 82.
[49] [1993] STC 188 reversing [1980] AC 896 [1978] STC 793; see Gillard op. cit. chapter 3.
[50] See e.g. Bartlett [1985] *BTR* 338.

5.6.1 Respect for legal facts created by the parties (Westminster)

That the courts must have respect for the legal facts created by the parties was laid down by Lord Tomlin in *IRC* v. *Duke of Westminster*[51] when he said:

> "Every man is entitled if he can to arrange his affairs so that the tax attaching under the appropriate Acts is less than it otherwise would be. If he succeeds in ordering them so as to secure that result, then, however unappreciative the Commissioners of Inland Revenue or his fellow taxpayers may be of his ingenuity, he cannot be compelled to pay an increased tax."

It followed that a transaction which, on its true construction, was of a kind that would escape tax, was not taxable on the ground that the same result could have been achieved by a transaction in another form which would have attracted tax.

In *IRC* v. *Westminster* the Duke of Westminster covenanted to pay an employee a sum of £1.90 per week; the covenant was to last seven years whether or not the employee remained in the Duke's service. The employee already had a wage of £3 a week and he was told that while he would be legally entitled to the full £3, it was expected that, in practice, he would take only the balance of £1.10 to bring his total up to £3. The purpose of the scheme was to enable the Duke to deduct the payment in computing his total income for surtax.[52] The scheme succeeded; the true construction of the document showed that these sums were not income of an employee under Schedule E but income from an annuity under Schedule D, Case III. As Lord Tomlin said, there could be no collateral contract to serve the Duke, i.e collateral to the bond. Even if there had been, it could not have affected the nature of the rights arising under the bond.[53]

In reaching this conclusion the court was entitled to look at all the circumstances of the case, including the fact that the taxpayer had received a letter containing the expectations of the Duke already referred to. However, the court was also entitled to look at the fact that the legal right to payment would continue even though the employment ceased. In this connection the Commissioners' conclusion that the payments would start as employment income but would cease to be such income if he ceased to be employed by the Duke looks very odd.

This decision is a shibboleth for modern judicial attitudes. Lord Atkin, dissenting, thought that the covenant was a term of the contract of employment and not just an expectation.[54] Today, Lord Templeman would agree.[55] Other judges have also wondered about the decision in *Westminster*, but for different reasons. Some expressly or implicitly take the simple contractual line expressed by Lord Atkin; others take a more apocalyptic line.[56] The *Westminster* starting point was accepted by Lord Wilberforce in *Ramsay* (see below at §5.6.4). Today, one might consider that in *Westminster* the scheme of allowing the assignment of income by covenant was a permitted option (and so tax mitigation) or a protected transaction (under a GAAR).

The doctrine emerging from the *Westminster* case is that taxpayers and the Revenue are bound by the legal results which the parties have achieved—even though this may be inconvenient for the Revenue. The court cannot disregard those facts just because of the tax

[51] [1936] AC 1, 1919 TC 490, 520.
[52] The scheme was stopped in 1936. See now TA 1988, s. 347A.
[53] [1936] AC 1, 18–19, 19 TC 490, 519–20.
[54] [1936] AC 1, 14–15, 19 TC 490, 516–17.
[55] See *Ensign Tankers (Leasing) Ltd.* v. *Stokes* [1992] 1 AC 655, 669, [1992] STC 226, 235, 64 TC 617, 735, HL.
[56] Lord Steyn in *IRC* v. *McGuckian* [1997] STC 907, 69 TC 1.

avoidance purpose which may have led the parties to create those facts in the first place. A more recent example is *Reed* v. *Young*[57] in which the House of Lords held that since the parties had created a limited partnership the court was bound to give effect to a tax saving scheme based upon that legal structure. The *Westminster* doctrine was highly regarded by the Inland Revenue, not least because it was applied in its favour when the taxpayer had carried out a transaction in a manner less than wholly tax-efficient.[58]

One should distinguish the *Westminster* doctrine outlined above from a *Westminster* approach which tended to look kindly on attempts to avoid tax. This approach has wavered since 1980 as the courts have been presented with highly artificial schemes—with mixed results.

Finally, although the courts have long recognised that tax avoidance is lawful, it is not yet a virtue. In *Re Weston's Settlement*[59] the Court of Appeal declined to approve a variation of trust where the only advantages accruing to the beneficiaries on whose behalf they were being asked to approve the variation were financial, stemming almost exclusively from the saving of tax. Similarly, in *Sherdley* v. *Sherdley*[60] the Court of Appeal declined to make an order for financial provision of a child when the only reason for that order would have been the tax saving; this was reversed by the House of Lords, but is an indication of a general attitude.

5.6.2 Court looks to facts not labels

The *Westminster* doctrine was sometimes expressed in the form that the court must look to the form of the transaction and not its substance. This formulation is, however, misleading in that it tends to suggest that the form of a transaction, a matter which may be within the control of the taxpayer, will be conclusive for tax purposes. Often, however, the legal form used by the parties is not conclusive and here it is accepted that the court must look at the substance of the matter in order to determine the true tax consequences of the transaction in the legal form adopted by the parties. Thus, by looking at the substance the court could conclude that this form attracted tax just as much as another. In these instances the court is not putting upon the transaction a legal character which it did not possess, but is trying to discover the true character in tax law of the transaction entered into.[61] As such, the court may hold that a trade is carried on by a partnership even though the only document states that there was none,[62] that a trader is still trading even though he says he is not,[63] or that the person claiming to trade is simply the means through which the trade is carried on by someone else.[64] In such contexts the documents cannot be used to deny proven facts. Where, however, both the facts and the legal arrangements point in the same direction, the court may not disregard them.[65] It follows that the name given to a transaction by the parties concerned does not necessarily decide the nature of the transaction.[66] A description of

57 [1986] STC 285, 59 TC 196.

58 For example, *IRC* v. *Fleming & Co. (Machinery) Ltd.* (1951) 33 TC 57, 62.

59 [1969] 1 Ch 223, [1968] 1 All ER 720. For critical comment, see Bretten [1968] *Conveyancer* 194; Harris [1969] *Conveyancer* 183, 191 *et seq.*

60 [1987] STC 217; see [1987] *BTR* 337.

61 *IRC* v. *Mallaby-Deeley* [1938] 4 All ER 818, 825; 23 TC 153, 167, *per* Sir Wilfrid Greene M.R.

62 *Fenston* v. *Johnstone* (1940) 23 TC 29.

63 *J. and R. O'Kane & Co. Ltd.* v. *IRC* (1922) 12 TC 303.

64 *Firestone Tyre and Rubber Co. Ltd.* v. *Lewellin* [1957] 1 All ER 561, 37 TC 111.

65 *Ransom* v. *Higgs* [1974] 3 All ER 949, [1974] STC 539.

66 *Secretary of State in Council of India* v. *Scoble* [1903] AC 299, 4 TC 618.

a series of payments as an annuity or a rentcharge does not determine its character.[67] It goes without saying that this rule applies whether it is invoked by the taxpayer or by the Revenue. As the US 9th Circuit once put it, "One should not be garrotted by the tax collector for calling one's agreement by the wrong name".[68]

All the cases in which the Revenue have succeeded under the *Ramsay* composite transaction rule (see below at §5.6.4) can be seen as examples of this rule.

5.6.3 *The court is not bound to respect sham transactions*

This is because the sham nature of the transaction prevents the parties from creating the legal facts hoped for. A transaction is a sham if the acts done were intended to give the appearance of creating legal rights different from those which were actually created.[69] Such schemes fail for the simple reason that the tax falls to be levied on the basis of the actual legal rights created. This argument, although frequently advanced by the Revenue, does not meet with great success. The new approach based on the decision of the House of Lords in *Furniss* v. *Dawson*[70] encouraged the courts to give the Revenue occasional glimpses of success. In *Sherdley* v. *Sherdley*[71] Sir John Donaldson MR thought that an order to pay school fees to a school on behalf of a child, and made at the suit of the parent against whom the order would have been made, would be a sham. This use of the sham argument is highly questionable and probably erroneous. The decision was later reversed by the House of Lords, but without discussion of this point.[72] Since then the orthodox narrow definition of a sham transaction has prevailed.[73] In *Hitch* v. *Stone*[74] the court reversed a finding by the Commissioners that a transaction was a sham. The judge said that that finding was made in the teeth of the parties' own evidence and that the other evidence was largely circumstantial. The mere fact that the parties had tried to implement a complex avoidance scheme did not make the documents a sham. Artificiality did not make a transaction a sham; indeed the more artificial it was the less likely it was to be a sham. The judge also held the facts might well show that the rule in 5.6.4 might have applied but the Revenue had not presented the case that way and it was too late to do so then.

5.6.4 *Composite transactions: courts will look at end results whether transaction is a) circular and self-cancelling (*Ramsay*) or b) linear (*Furniss v. Dawson*)*

W. T. Ramsay Ltd. v. *IRC*[75] concerned CGT. A company (R) had a large gain (£187,977) and wished to create an allowable loss which could be set against the gain and so remove its liability for tax. Under the scheme, R bought shares in a company and proceeded to make it

[67] *IRC* v. *Land Securities Investment Trust* [1969] 2 All ER 430, 45 TC 495.

[68] *Pacific Rock and Gravel Co.* v. *US* 297 F 2d 122, 125 (9th Cir. 1961).

[69] See Diplock L.J. in *Snook* v. *London and West Riding Investments Ltd.* [1967] 1 All ER 518, 520l; [1967] 2 QB 686, 702; and Lord Devlin in *Campbell Discount Ltd.* v. *Bridge* [1962] 1 All ER 385, 402. See also Lee [1997] *NILQR*; and McCutcheon [1978] *BTR* 196 on Revenue arguments in *Frost* v. *Newstead* [1978] STC 239, 53 TC 525.

[70] [1984] STC 153, [1984] 1 All ER 530.

[71] [1986] STC 266, 273. Balcombe, L.J. disagreed (at 278) and Neill L.J. made no comment.

[72] [1987] STC 217.

[73] See, e.g. Lord Goff in *Ensign Tankers (Leasing) Ltd.* v. *Stokes* [1992] 1 AC 655, 681, [1992] STC 226, 244–5, 64 TC 617, 746–7.

[74] [1999] STC 431.

[75] [1982] AC 300, [1981] STC 174, 54 TC 101. The scheme was countered (in 1978) by what is now TCGA 1992, s. 30.

two loans each of £218,750 at 11%; the loans were made with the aid of the funds borrowed from a bank associated with the vendors of the scheme. R had the right to decrease the rate of interest on one loan, on one occasion only, provided there was a corresponding increase on the other loan. R caused the rate on one loan to drop to nil and on the other to rise to 22%; it sold the latter loan for £391,481, a gain of £172,731. The other loan was repaid at par by the company, but the shares in the company were sold at a large consequential loss (£175,731). The narrow *ratio* of the House of Lords' decision was that the gain on the sale of the debt was a chargeable gain because the debt was a debt on a security (a chargeable asset) and not a simple debt (a non-chargeable asset) (see below at §34.4). However, the wider and more important *ratio* was that the court was entitled to look at the whole transaction and so to conclude that the taxpayer had suffered a loss of only some £3,000. As Lord Wilberforce said:[76]

> "[The approach for which the Crown contends] does not introduce a new principle; it would apply to new and sophisticated legal devices, the undoubted power and duty of the courts to determine their nature in law and to relate them to existing legislation. While the techniques of tax avoidance progress are technically improved, the courts are not obliged to stand still."

Following *Ramsay* v. *IRC* it was possible to argue that the decision affected simply circular, self-cancelling transactions,[77] leaving the *Westminster* principle intact for other transactions. However, this was hard to sustain following the decision of the House of Lords in *IRC* v. *Burmah Oil Co Ltd.*[78] In this case the company, B, had transferred property to a subsidiary, S, but had left the money outstanding. As the property had declined in value and was the only substantial asset held by S, it was clear that the debt was worthless. By means of a loan from a fellow subsidiary bank, SB, S was enabled to repay the original loan to B and, by means of a rights issue, attracted further money from B with which to pay off SB. S was then liquidated. The effect was to substitute equity (a chargeable asset) for simple debt (a non-chargeable asset).[79] The scheme failed. The House of Lords, applying the *Ramsay* doctrine, refused to allow B to deduct the payments made under the rights issue in computing its loss on the shares of S when S was liquidated. There were superficial differences between the facts in this case and those in *Ramsay* in that the scheme was designated only for B, instead of being bought "off the shelf", and that B used its own money in making the various payments instead of borrowing it—but these differences were of no real importance. In the course of their speeches, both Lord Diplock and Lord Scarman went out of their way to emphasise "that *Ramsay*'s case marks 'a significant change in the approach adopted by this House in its judicial role' towards tax avoidance schemes".[80]

Any remaining doubts were blown away by the decision of the House of Lords in *Furniss* v. *Dawson.*[81] Here, a shareholder wished to sell his stake in company A to company C (Wood Bastow). He followed what Lord Brightman called "a simple and honest scheme which merely seeks to defer payment of tax until the taxpayer has received into his hands the gain which he has made". The shares in company A were exchanged for shares in company B (Greenjacket) and company B then sold the shares in company A to company C. The House

[76] [1982] AC 300, 326, 54 TC 101, 187.

[77] As had been argued in the case itself (54 TC 101, 182); see Berg [1984] *BTR* 128.

[78] [1982] STC 30, 54 TC 200. See Goldberg [1982] BTR 13; and Ashton [1983] *BTR* 221.

[79] The Commissioners had found that the steps would, almost inevitably, have been carried through.

[80] [1982] STC 30, 39, 54 TC 200, 222. It is hard to see why this decision was not applied in *Macniven* v. *Westmoreland Investments Ltd.* [1998] STC 1131, CA.

[81] [1984] AC 474, [1984] STC 153, 55 TC 324.

of Lords held that, although there was an express finding that all the steps were genuine, nonetheless the effect of the transactions for tax purposes was that the shareholder had disposed of his shares in company A to company C in return for consideration paid to company B.

Lord Brightman, after stressing that no distinction was to be drawn in fact (because none existed in reality) between a series of steps carried through under a non-binding arrangement and those carried through under a contract, stated that the preconditions for the applicability of the *Ramsay* principle were:[82]

> "First, there must be a pre-ordained series of transactions; or, if one likes, a single composite transaction. This composite transaction may or may not include the achievement of a legitimate commercial (i.e. business) end . . . Secondly, there must be steps inserted which have no commercial (business) purpose apart from the avoidance of a liability to tax—not 'no business effect'. If those two ingredients exist, the inserted steps are to be disregarded for fiscal purposes."

Therefore, the preordained series of transactions began with the sale by the taxpayer to company B and ended with the sale by company B to company C. This led to the excision of the intervening steps and therefore the whole scheme fell to be treated as a sale by the taxpayer direct to company C in return for money paid to company B, thereby excising company B from this affair until the very end. This case must be treated with caution since if company B or is merely ignored, the result is nonsensical in that the taxpayers end up holding shares in company B, the very existence of which, it seems, should be ignored.

Lord Bridge took a wider approach. Whether this will prove correct in the long run remains to be seen; it has not proved correct in the short run:[83]

> "When one moves from a single transaction to a series of interdependent transactions designed to produce a given result, it is, in my opinion, perfectly legitimate to draw a distinction between the substance and the form of the composite transaction without in any way suggesting that any of the single transactions which make up the whole are other than genuine . . ."

The importance of this approach is, first, that it enables one to explain the existence of company B and, secondly, that it is much wider and more flexible than the simple—almost mechanistic—excision approach of Lord Brightman. The consequences of Lord Bridge's approach would be extremely wide. Even the US tax system, which Lord Bridge mentions, although not with unqualified enthusiasm, and which accepts the doctrine that the court must tax by reference to substance rather than form, finds it extremely hard to determine when the legal form of a transaction is to prevail.[84]

Following *Furniss* v. *Dawson* it was possible to argue that the law was in a highly malleable state and that the position was analogous to that of the law of negligence following *Donoghue* v. *Stevenson*, or the rule against perpetuities immediately after the *Duke of Norfolk*'s case in 1681. The analogy of the rule against perpetuities became highly apposite after the decision of the House of Lords in *Craven* v. *White*[85] which, with its insistence on following the approach of Lord Brightman, can be made to look like the developed rule

[82] [1984] AC 474, 527, [1984] STC 153, 166g, 55 TC 324, 401.

[83] [1984] AC 474, 517, [1984] STC 153, 158, 55 TC 324, 392.

[84] For a general account of US doctrine, see Bittker, *Federal Taxation of Income Estates and Gifts*, esp. ch. 4. For an example of scepticism, see Rice, 51 *Michigan LR* 1021. See also Millett [1986] *BTR* 327; and Tiley [1987] *BTR* 180, 220, [1988] *BTR* 63, 108. For examinations of the UK cases from a US perspective, see Popkin [1991] *BTR* 283; and Brown, 15 *Hastings International and Comparative Law Review* 169.

[85] [1989] AC 398, [1988] STC 476, 62 TC 1. See Ashton [1988] *BTR* 482; Mansfield [1989] *BTR* 5; and Tiley [1989] *BTR* 20.

against perpetuities with reasonably clear, if not translucent, guidance as to when one is straying into dangerous territory. This analogy is less strong after *McGuckian* in 1997 (see below §5.6.5).

The composite transaction doctrine has attracted a number of decisions and propositions.

(**a**) In determining whether there is a composite transaction the court asks whether, at the time of the first transaction it was "practically certain" that the second would follow.

In *Craven* v. *White* (and associated appeals)[86] the House of Lords had to consider the status of *Furniss* v. *Dawson* and its application to three sets of facts. In *IRC* v. *Bowater Property Developments Ltd.* the court was dealing with a development land tax (DLT) fragmentation scheme. A sister company to the taxpayer company was contemplating a sale to X. The sale did not materialise and the land was sold to the taxpayer for 97½% of its market value. Subsequently, in order to take advantage of the rule that allowed each disponer, for DLT purposes, to claim an exemption on the first slice of realised development value (at that time £50,000), the taxpayer transferred the land in question to five companies in the same group. This transfer had corporation tax consequences for the taxpayer company. A year later X reopened negotiations and, 19 months after the disposal by the taxpayer to the five companies, contracts were exchanged between the five companies and X. This was for a different price and on different terms from the original deal. Could this be treated as a single disposal by the taxpayer company to X, thus giving the companies only one exemption rather than five? A unanimous House of Lords said "no".

In *Baylis* v. *Gregory* the taxpayer was contemplating the sale of his company to Y. He went through a *Furniss* v. *Dawson* operation and transferred the shares in his company to an Isle of Man company in exchange for shares in that company. However, Y, unlike Wood Bastow in *Furniss* v. *Dawson*, did not complete the sale. A year or so later a new and independent purchaser, Z, appeared and, after a further eight months, the sale to Z went through. Since the taxpayer had an intention to use the same provision as that which the taxpayers were trying to use in a *Furniss* v. *Dawson* scheme, did it follow that the eventual sale to Z was by the taxpayer rather than by the Isle of Man company? A unanimous House of Lords said "no" and the taxpayer got his deferral.

In *Craven* v. *White* the taxpayer owned all the shares in company Q and was advised that it should seek either a merger or a sale. As a first step the taxpayers carried through a *Furniss* v. *Dawson* style share for share exchange with an Isle of Man company. At that time there was the prospect of either a merger with company C or a sale to company O. If the merger had gone through there would have been a deferral of liability under the reorganisation provisions in any case. If, however, the sale to O took place, the facts were close to *Furniss* v. *Dawson*. At the time of the share exchange (11 July) the prospects for the sale to O did not look promising, but on the same day O asked for a further meeting. Following further negotiations, including one "stormy meeting", the sale to O finally went through on 9 August of the same year. The Commissioners rejected the taxpayer's evidence that its sole intention in carrying through the exchange was to merge with C and said that the primary objective was the sale to O and that the taxpayer was keeping its options open. This time the House of Lords said "no", but by a bare majority. It held that the taxpayer was not to be taxed as if it had sold its shares direct to O; the entity making the disposal to O was the Isle of Man company.

[86] I.e. *IRC* v. *Bowater Property Developments Ltd.* and *Baylis* v. *Gregory*.

Having quickly and decisively rejected the view that *Furniss* v. *Dawson* should be taken as the beginning of the development of a general anti-tax avoidance jurisprudence,[87] the House of Lords considered the degree of certainty that had to exist before the steps could be said, to use Lord Brightman's word, to be "preordained". Lord Oliver, with whom the other members of the majority agreed, said that the question was whether the intermediate transfer was, at the time it was effected, so closely interconnected with the ultimate disposition that it was properly to be described as not in itself a real transaction at all, but merely an element in some different and larger whole without independent effect. This was a question of fact which had to be approached within the bounds of what was logically defensibl. *Furniss* v. *Dawson* applied only where there was no practical likelihood that the pre-planned events would not take place in the order ordained; in this sense the intermediate transaction was not even contemplated practically as having an independent life. Lord Keith said that steps could be said to be preordained if, and only if, at the time the first step was entered into the taxpayer was in a position, for all practical purposes, to secure that the second step was also entered into. Lord Jauncey was tempted by a formulation in terms of whether there was no real likelihood that the second step would not go through but felt that this might be too rigid; the temptation to be a parliamentary draftsman was resisted.

Lord Oliver's full formulation was:[88]

> "(1) that the series of transactions was, at the time when the intermediate transaction was entered into, preordained in order to produce a given result; (2) that that transaction had no other purpose than tax mitigation; (3) that there was at that time no practical likelihood that the preplanned events would not take place in the order ordained, so that the intermediate transaction was not even contemplated practically as having an independent life; and (4) that the preordained events did in fact take place. In these circumstances the court can be justified in linking the beginning with the end so as to make a single composite whole to which the fiscal results of the single composite whole are to be applied."

The two dissentients were Lord Templeman and Lord Goff—but only in *Craven* v. *White.* Lord Goff considered that the matter could not be dealt with on the practical certainty test. While the interruption in *Bowater* and the unformed plan in *Baylis* v. *Gregory* obviously dictated the conclusion in those cases, *Craven* v. *White* was different since the sale to O was a primary purpose of the share exchange. Lord Templeman felt that the three majority speeches went too far in narrowing *Furniss* v. *Dawson* and would revive a surprised tax avoidance industry. He said that *Craven* v. *White* was indistinguishable from *Furniss* v. *Dawson.*[89] He protested that the House had not laboured in *Furniss* v. *Dawson* to bring forth a mouse and that the limitations placed upon that case by the majority were based neither on principle nor on the speeches in that case.

Just how certain does it have to be that the second step will follow the first? This was, of course, the key issue in *Craven* v. *White.* Cases since then have reiterated the test there laid down.[90] In *Hatton* v. *IRC*[91] Chadwick J. said that a preordained series of transactions meant

[87] Among many matters which troubled the House, as they had troubled the Court of Appeal, was what the legal status of the first transaction would be while one waited to see what might ensue, and, in particular, the status of any assessments to tax which might have been made on the basis of that first transaction (as might have occurred in the *Bowater* case).

[88] At 514, 507, 203.

[89] However, his test is very close to that of Lord Oliver at n. 88 above.

[90] For example, *Fitzwilliam* v. *IRC* [1993] STC 502, 67 TC 614, HL and *Hatton* v. *IRC* [1992] STC 140, 67 TC 759, both dealing with IHT; and *Shepherd* v. *Lyntress* [1989] STC 617, 62 TC 495.

[91] [1992] STC 140, 67 TC 759.

nothing more than a series of transactions which had been pre-planned to take place in a specific order in circumstances in which there was, at the time the first transaction was entered into, no practical likelihood that the remaining transactions would not take place in that order. There was, he said, no requirement of control over the decision to take the subsequent steps. Similarly, in *Fitzwilliam* v. *IRC*[92] there was a preordained scheme despite the fact that the clients were kept in the dark as to the totality of the scheme—and that one of them was separately advised after the half way point.

There is no mechanistic time period after which transactions cannot be linked. In *Pigott* v. *Staines Investments Co. Ltd.*[93] steps taken 10 months apart were treated as one by the Commissioners, and Knox J. held that they had made no error of law in reaching that decision. The brevity of the period between the two steps is, therefore, a relevant but not conclusive factor. In *News International plc* v. *Shepherd*,[94] where A sold quoted shares to B, a subsidiary, and B sold them on the Stock Exchange, the court held that B was the seller of the shares and that A was not. This was because there was no evidence of an arrangement that B would inevitably make the sale. However, it was suggested that a different result might have been reached if the shares had been in an unlisted company so that everything (including the purchaser from B and the price to be paid) would have been cut and dried before the sale by A to B.

(**b**) Where the composite transaction is commercial in nature the end result must reflect the commercial reality *Ensign Tankers.*

Lord Templeman delivered the unanimous opinion of the House of Lords in *Ensigh Tankers (Leasing) Ltd* v. *Stokes*,[95] the correct approach is to look at the commercial reality of the situation. What may matter just as much is the emphasis placed by Lord Templeman on the obligation of the courts to ensure that the taxpayer does not pay too much tax, not just too little. Neither the taxpayer nor the Crown should be deprived of the fiscal consequences of the taxpayers' activities properly analysed.

In the *Ensign* case the question was whether the taxpayer was entitled to capital allowances for expenditure incurred on the production of a film. The taxpayer company, E, which, as may be surmised from its full name, had little to do with the world of films, formed a limited partnership, V, with some other companies to provide finance for a film to be directed by John Huston and starring Michael Caine. The film was also to feature such soccer legends as Bobby Moore and Pele and was called "Escape to Victory". V put up 25% of the estimated cost of the film ($3.25 m out of $13 m) the balance being provided by a non-recourse loan made to the general partner by the film company, L, a part of the Lorimar group with whom the partnership had no other connection. The partners, including E, had no personal liability. The film company was also to be responsible (on similar terms) for any cost overrun. The receipts from the film would be divided 25% to the limited partnership and 75% to the film company until the loan was paid off and then to paying off the loan to cover the costs of the overrun of costs ($1 m) and any interest on such loans.

What V, and therefore E, hoped to achieve was that in return for putting up less than[96] 25% of the cost, they would be able to receive capital allowances on the total cost of production; this was because the rate of corporation tax rate was then 50% and the rate of the

92 [1993] STC 502, 536 67 TC, 757, HL, *per* Lord Browne-Wilkinson.
93 [1995] STC 114, 68 TC 342.
94 [1989] STC 617, 619.
95 [1992] 1 AC 655, 671, [1992] STC 226, 236, 64 TC 617, 736; see Shrubsall [1992] *BTR* 279.
96 After taking account of the cost overrun which was also financed by non-recourse loan.

relevant allowances 100% of the expenditure. The Crown's attack was no less extreme; this was not a trading transaction and therefore E was not entitled to any allowance at all, not even the expenditure of $3.25 m which had been incurred.

The Commissioners held that this was not a trading transaction since V's paramount object of the transaction was to obtain a fiscal advantage. This was reversed by Millett J. who held, *inter alia*, that the taxpayer was trading and that the correct test was an objective one; the full allowance was therefore due.[97] The Court of Appeal reversed Millett J.[98]

The House of Lords, reversing the Court of Appeal, produced a new solution. This was a trading transaction. V, and therefore E, was entitled to capital allowance on the expenditure actually incurred. However, the expenditure incurred was $3.25 m not $14 m. This conclusion involved a close analysis of the facts to determine their true legal effect. The scheme would not be allowed to have the apparently magical effect of creating expenditure for tax purposes of $14 m while incurring real expenditure of only $3.25 m. The expenditure of the remaining $10.75 m was really incurred by L.[99] The House of Lords proceeded to penalise the taxpayers, for attempting a scheme which "brought no credit" on their advisers,[100] by making them pay all the costs of the appeal.[101]

(**c**) The result of the application of the composite transaction doctrine must be intellectually sustainable; the court's job is to identify the composite transaction; it may not alter the character of the transaction or pick bits out of it (*Fitzwilliam*).[102]

The decision of the House of Lords in *Fitzwilliam* v. *IRC*[103] establishes that if the Crown wishes to use the new approach to create a charge to tax, the mere fact that a scheme is preordained is not, of itself, sufficient. The court must consider whether it is possible, realistically and intellectually, to treat the scheme as a whole. If the Crown's case requires the court to pick and choose different bits of the scheme and treat them in different ways, the court cannot realistically or intellectually treat the scheme as a whole and therefore will not do so.[104] This case also underlines the gulf between Lord Templeman and some of his colleagues. The details are set out below at §67.7.

(**d**) The composite transaction doctrine is best seen as a rule of statutory application rather than simple interpretation. This proposition contradicts some of the words of members of the House of Lords but is consistent with what they do.[105]

(**e**) The characterisation of a composite transaction is a question of fact, not law.

In *Furniss* v. *Dawson* Lord Brightman said that:[106]

> "the correct approach in this type of case, where inferences have to be drawn, is for the commissioners to determine (infer) from their findings of primary fact, the further fact whether there was a single composite transaction in the sense in which I have used that expression, and whether that transaction contains steps which were inserted without any commercial or business purpose apart

[97] [1989] STC 705, 64 TC 617.

[98] [1991] STC 136, 64 TC 617.

[99] On present Revenue treatment of "security" arrangements in relation to films, see Statement of Practice SP 1/98, paras 66–68, continuing pre-*McGuckian* practice.

[100] [1992] 1AC 655, 667, [1992] STC 226, 244, 64 TC 617, 733.

[101] [1992] 1 AC 655, 686, STC 226, 234 64 TC 617, 751.

[102] *Fitzwilliam* v. *IRC* below n. 103; see also *Renaud* v. *IRC* [1999] STC (SCD) Sp. Com.

[103] [1993] STC 502, 67 TC 614, HL; see Whitehouse 1994 Private Client Business 72.

[104] See also *Young* v. *Phillips* [1984] STC 520, 58 TC 232.

[105] The authority for it is Nourse L.J. in *Fitzwilliam* v. *IRC* [1992] STC 185, 198j, CA, 67 TC 614, 702c.

[106] [1984] AC 474, [1984] STC 153, 55 TC 324.

from a tax advantage; and for the appellate court to interfere with that inference of fact only in a case where it is insupportable on the basis of the primary facts so found".

However, in *Fitzwilliam* v. *IRC* Lord Keith said that the question was essentially one of law.[107]

(**f**) The composite transaction doctrine applies where steps are inserted which have no business purpose other than the avoidance of tax. It not, however, necessary that the attempt to save tax would have succeeded.[108]

(**g**) Where a particular step has been inserted in the composite transaction the composite transaction doctrine will not apply if the taxpayer can show that there is a commercial purpose, however slight, behind the inserted step.

This is part of Lord Brightman's formulation in *Furniss* v. *Dawson* and has not yet been questioned, for example, by suggesting that the commercial motive should be the main (as opposed to the only) motive. In *Craven* v. *White* it was held in the Chancery Division[109] that where two courses of action were genuinely open to the taxpayer and actively being considered by him, one of which would have entitled him to use the deferral under what is now TCGA 1992, s. 136 despite *Furniss* v. *Dawson*, and the other which would not, the Revenue could not use *Furniss* v. *Dawson* to deprive him of the deferral since there was a sufficient commercial motive at the time of the disposal. This aspect of the case was not discussed in the House of Lords.[110] In *Ensign Tankers (Leasing) Ltd.* v. *Stokes* Millett J. held in the Chancery Division that the court could not disregard the existence of a limited partnership where it was commercially essential to have some structure to regulate the relationship of the parties.[111]

(**h**) The composite transaction doctrine is not confined to income or capital gains tax; whether it applies to another tax depends on the nature of that tax.

So far, the cases have involved CGT, income tax (or their corporate equivalent), VAT and stamp duties. The doctrine has even made a surprise appearance in landlord and tenant law.[112] It has been held that IHT is affected despite having its own anti-avoidance provision in the associated operations rule.[113] The doctrine has not been applied to VAT,[114] perhaps because VAT is a European tax on individual supplies which cannot be looked through.[115] It could be argued that stamp duties are not affected since those are taxes on instruments not transactions; however, it can be countered that the new rule is ideally designed to counter avoidance schemes because it requires a broad view of the transaction which is being carried out by the instrument. This approach was adopted by Vinelott J. in *Ingram* v. *IRC*.[116] If the doctrine is simply one of characterisation of the facts all taxes are open to its application.

107 [1993] STC 502, 515, 67 TC 614, 731, HL.

108 *IRC* v. *McGuckian* [1997] STC 907, 914, 69 TC 1, 77, *per* Lord Browne Wilkinson.

109 [1985] STC 531.

110 However, Lord Oliver said that there was a bona fide commercial purpose: [1988] STC 476, 510.

111 [1989] STC 705, 770, 64 TC 617, 705. Millett J. also stated that it was logically impossible to conclude both that the partnership was trading and that the transaction entered into had no commercial purpose (at 771, 706). The Revenue did not appeal against this part of the judgment: [1991] STC 136, 149.

112 *Gisborne* v. *Burton* [1988] 3 All ER 760, CA; see comment by Martin (1988) *NLJ* 792.

113 *Fitzwilliam* v. *IRC* [1993] STC 502, 67 TC 614, HL.

114 *Customs and Excise Commrs* v. *Faith Construction Ltd.* [1989] STC 539, upholding [1988] STC 35; for a note on the 1988 decision see Sinfield [1988] *BTR* 200.

115 See TLRC report, above at n. 1, para. 2.28.

116 [1985] STC 835.

(**i**) Both the taxpayer and the Revenue may invoke the composite transaction doctrine.

If the doctrine is truly a matter of applying the tax legislation to the facts before the court then there is no logical reason why the taxpayer should not seek to characterise the facts in issue as one composite transaction.[117] The obstacle is the decision of the Court of Appeal in *Whittles* v. *Uniholdings Ltd. (No. 3)*[118] where the court rejected an invitation to treat the two parts of a foreign currency arrangement as one. The taxpayer had borrowed the dollar equivalent of £14 m, rather than sterling itself, because the rate of interest was lower. The taxpayer accepted the offer of dollars on condition that the exchange risk was eliminated by a forward purchase of dollars to repay the loan. The bank would not have entered into the contract without such a forward contract and would have insisted on it if the taxpayer had not done so. The facts occurred before the FA 1993 rules on foreign exchange came into force so that, if the two transactions had been carried through entirely separately, the gain realised on the disposal of the rights under the forward contract would have been taxable, but the loss on the dollar loan would not have been an allowable loss (being incurred in respect of a capital liability, not an asset). In the Chancery Division Sir John Vinleott held that it was a single composite transaction so that the company had neither a profit on the forward purchase nor a sterling loss on the repayment of the loan.[119] On appeal Aldous L.J. agreed with Sir John Vinelott,[120] but Nourse L.J. and Sir John Balcombe[121] did not. For the majority of the Court of Appeal the taxpayer would not have been able to argue the point before the emergence of the *Ramsay* principle, which was described as the "fiscal nullity" doctrine, and certainly could not do so now. For them the new approach applied when there was no contractual arrangement. The taxpayers would have lost even if there had been a contractual tie between them and the bank and so could not use the new approach to get them home on the basis that there was a practical certainty that the second step would follow the first. The majority assertion that the *Ramsay* case is a doctrine of fiscal nullity and, by inference, not available at the suit of the taxpayer begs the very point at issue; US experience is very different.[122]

(**j**) Where the taxpayer can bring itself clearly within (the purpose of) a specific relieving provision of the tax legislation the court will not withhold that relief.

This issue is at the heart of the distinction between tax avoidance and tax mitigation; these rules do not apply to tax mitigation. Following precedents in other countries which have had to wrestle with general anti-avoidance provisions, it can be argued that the courts should not allow the use of the *Ramsay* principle if the taxpayer has simply carried out a straightforward transaction falling exactly within the purpose and ambit of a provision of the tax legislation.[123] In *Shepherd* v. *Lyntress Ltd.* Vinelott J. rejected a "frontal assault on the ability of a group to hive down losses into a subsidiary and to sell the subsidiary to another group willing to purchase it so that it can set its own gains against the losses".[124] The problem is how to mark this off from the use of the share-for-share exchange rule in *Furniss* v.

[117] There are early but conflicting *dicta* in *Pattison* v. *Marine Midland Ltd.* allowing the taxpayer to invoke the argument against the Crown's effort to "invent an artificial accounting scheme which serves no purpose and is designed solely to create a liability to tax": [1983] STC 269, 276, CA. In *Ewart* v. *Taylor* [1983] STC 721 Vinelott J. gave the taxpayer "only very limited chances of success". See also Vinelott J. in *Bird* v. *IRC* [1985] STC 584, 647.

[118] [1996] STC 914, 68 TC 528, 594.

[119] [1995] STC 185, 68 TC 528.

[120] [1996] STC 914, 931g, 68 TC 528, 594.

[121] [1996] STC 914, 924f, 932, 68 TC 528, 585, 595.

[122] See [1998] *BTR* 161, 178.

[123] As was stated by Walton J. in *Reed* v. *Nova Securities Ltd.* [1982] STC 724 at first instance.

[124] [1989] STC 617, 650, 62 TC, 543.

Dawson itself. Presumably, what marks *Furniss* v. *Dawson* off from this scenario is the fact that the share exchange was followed immediately by the sale.

The inclusion of the words "the purpose of" in brackets above would make the test more restrictive by contemplating the need for a person to show that he comes within the purpose and spirit of the relief. This is envisaged in the TLRC formulation of the protected transaction but it may not be correct to state it as current UK case law—unless perhaps the approach of Lord Steyn (below §5.6.5) is accepted.

(**k**) Where a specific anti-avoidance rules apparently applies to a transaction the court should use the new approach to determine the facts to see whether and how the specific anti-avoidance rule applies.

In *Bird* v. *IRC*[125] Vinelott J. suggested that the Revenue could not rely both on TA 1988, s. 703 and the new approach against the same taxpayer in respect of the same transaction—so leaving open the question whether the taxpayer can rely on the new approach instead of s. 703. In that case, however, it was said that the Revenue could choose whether to assess under some other provision (which would become applicable as a result of applying the new approach), or under s. 703.[126] Similar problems have arisen over the relationship between the general associated operations provision in IHT and the new approach. Here, too, the availability of the express provision may not exclude the new approach and the point has been expressly left open by one member of the House of Lords[127] in a case in which the other judges have decided in the sense of proposition (k).

This assumes that the composite transaction rule is used for determining the true facts to which the tax law must be applied. If, however, it is a fiscal nullity rule then a different approach may be taken. It may be open to the Revenue to tax on the basis either of the specific anti-avoidance rule on one set of facts or under the new approach if this would justify a different characterisation of the facts to which that or some other tax provision may become applicable.

(**l**) The new approach can change the time and place of a transaction.

The courts have determined what the facts are, but have given little guidance as to when or where they take place.[128] Thus, suppose that I am about to emigrate (1 April) and wish to postpone a CGT disposal until after I cease to be resident in the UK—so avoiding CGT—and yet require the certainty of the sale. I therefore agree that my purchaser shall have an option to buy on any day in May and I have the right to insist on a sale during June. This agreement is made in January but the CGT timing rule will make the date of the disposal the date when the contract become unconditional.

(**m**) The composite transaction doctrine may apply to a double tax treaty.

The writer's preferred view is that the tax treaty must apply to the facts as they are determined by the courts of the signatory states. Where the two states determine the facts differently the mutual agreement procedure will have to be invoked. The composite transaction doctrine is simply one way in which the UK courts determine the facts.

[125] [1985] STC 584, 647.

[126] Lord Keith in *Bird* v. *IRC* [1988] STC 312, 318 (in that case the other provision was s. 419 but the only possible Revenue assessment would be out of time).

[127] Lord Browne-Wilkinson in *Fitzwilliam* v. *IRC* [1993] STC 502, 536, 67 TC 614, 75, HL;8 and see also below at §38.31.

[128] See the discussion by Gammie, *Strategic Tax Planning Part D* (Sweet and Maxwell, 1990), D35.

(**n**) The doctrine can be repealed only with great difficulty.

This depends on the nature of the doctrine. If it is rule of interpretation then Parliament can simply change the rule. However if it is a rule of application it is hard to see how Parliament can change it.

5.6.5 Avoidance outside §5.6.4; traditional judicial functions

The composite transaction doctrine is only one of the techniques used by the courts to control avoidance; it does not supersede the application of other, and usually more traditional, methods of applying tax law. An avoidance transaction which escapes the composite transaction doctrine may still fail.

Lord Hoffmann put this clearly in a non-tax case, when he said

> "[I]f the question is whether a given transaction is such as to attract a statutory benefit . . . or burden, such as income tax, I do not think it promotes clarity of thought to use terms like stratagem or device. The question is simply whether upon its true construction the statute applies to the transaction. Tax avoidance schemes are perhaps the best example. They either work . . . or they do not work . If they do not work, the reason is simply that, upon the true construction of the statute, the transaction which was designed to avoid the charge to tax actually comes within it. It is not that the statute has a penumbral spirit which strikes down devices or stratagems designed to avoid its terms or exploit its loopholes. There is no need for such spooky jurisprudence."[129]

There is much that is attractive in Lord Hoffmann's back-to-basics approach, especially the notion of simplicity and the rejection of any suggestion that tax law is an arcane mystery; it is also welcome in stressing the importance of application as well as interpretation. However, the statement begs many questions about the intellectual processes used by the judges in deciding how the facts are to be characterised in the first place and how they set about interpreting the tax statutes.[130] Thus some judges seem to think that they have the power to strike down avoidance schemes in the name of purposive statutory interpretation—others do not. This rather provocative proposition rests on the statements of Lords Steyn and Cooke in *IRC* v. *McGuckian.*[131] One could easily hold such wide ranging views after the speech of Lord Bridge in *Furniss* v. *Dawson* and no doubt it was for this very reason that the new approach was rejected in Ireland,[132] Canada[133] and Australia.[134]

In *IRC* v. *McGuckian*[135] the facts of the case were relatively simple. The taxpayer (M) wanted to avoid exposure to wealth tax and so implemented a scheme to reduce the value of shares in an Irish company (B) which he owned with his wife. The scheme involved (i) the payment of large sums by way of dividend by B, (ii) the establishment of a non-resident trust of which B and his wife would be beneficiaries, although only his wife was an income beneficiary, and (iii) the sale by the trust of the rights to the dividends—the sale was to a company resident in the UK (MA). If the scheme succeeded it would not only avoid wealth tax but also extract the profits from the company in tax-free form as far as M was concerned. Although all five speeches in the House of Lords concur in the result, there are in fact two

[129] *Norglen Ltd* v. *Reeds Rains Prudential Ltd* [1997] 3 WLR 1177 at 1186.
[130] [1987] *BTR* 180 at 190–5 suggesting the different levels of reasoning involved in a tax avoidance case.
[131] [1997] STC 908 at 916 and 920, 69 TC 1 at 81 and 84.
[132] *McGrath* v. *McDermott* [1988] IR 258.
[133] *Stubart Investments Ltd.* v. *The Queen* [1984] CTC 294, 84 DTC 6305.
[134] *John* v. *FCT* (1989) 166 CLR 417 at 435; see Harris [1998] *BTR* 124 at 127.
[135] [1997] STC 908.

strands of thought. The speeches of Lord Browne-Wilkinson and Lord Clyde are highly analytical and straightforward applications of the composite transaction doctrine; those of Lord Steyn and Lord Cooke are more wide-ranging; Lord Lloyd agreed with all of them and gave no reasons of his own. It is interesting to note that the decision in *McGuckian* was given four weeks before that in *IRC* v. *Willoughby* (see above at §5.1.1) and that of the five judges who sat in *McGuckian*, not one sat in *Willoughby*. The importance of the *McGuckian* decision in 1997 is that while it reiterates the emerging rule, it also provides a juristic basis for many other changes and developments; in many ways we are now back to the uncertain days following *Furniss* v. *Dawson*.

In *McGuckian* the inspector made the assessment two weeks before the six-year deadline[136] not under s. 730 (a bond washing rule) but under s. 739, a provision dealing with transfers of assets abroad by virtue of which M had power to enjoy the income of a non-resident (the trust). M's counsel argued that the assessment was wrong in law because what M could enjoy from the trust was not income but capital. The House held that the effect of applying the composite transaction doctrine was that the trust was treated as receiving not capital but income, i.e. not the proceeds of sale of the right to the dividend but the dividend itself. The only reason for the assignment of the right of the dividend was to gain a tax advantage. It was then necessary to apply the tax legislation by disregarding the assignment and applying s. 739 to the real transaction.

However, both Lord Steyn and Lord Cooke would have held the payment to the trust for the right to the dividend to be income not capital without reference to the *Ramsay* principle at all.[137] If the remarks of these two judges are to be taken at face value then the new approach is not just the rule at set out at §5.6.4 above, but is part of a wider formulation in which the courts will develop a purposive approach to questions of interpretation. Foremost among the issues of purpose will be whether this sort of transaction was one which Parliament would have wished to bless, so that transactions which come within the words of a section will not be taxed under its provisions. If this is right, we will have moved towards a US-style, business-purpose test and, perhaps other tests as well. Lord Cooke indicated unease not only over the *Westminster* case[138] but also *Craven* v. *White*.[139]

Older case-law made it reasonably clear that the new approach in §5.6.4 did not apply to single step transactions. Following *Craven* v. *White* it appears clear that the new approach is concerned simply with the question of whether two or more steps are to be taxed as one. Single step transactions are thus outside its scope.[140]

[136] On subsequent litigation on whether the inspector had a duty to make an assessment within the time allowed rather than seeking leave to make it outside, see *Re McGuckian* [1999] STC 578.

[137] This implicit repudiation of the decision in *IRC* v. *Paget* (1938) 21 TC 667 is in accordance with a decision of the Australian High Court (*FCT* v. *Myer Emporium Ltd.* (1987) 18 ATR 693) a case not cited in *McGuckian* but undoubtedly well known to Lord Cooke). On *Myer*, see Wainemeyer (1994) 19 *Melbourne University LR* 977. *Paget* was the reason for the introduction of what is now s. 730; if Lords Steyn and Cooke are right, s. 730 is redundant. Once again, Lord Lloyd agreed with all the reasoned speeches so we may take it that this proposition had the backing of a majority of the House of Lords.

[138] *McGuckian*[1997] STC 908, 921b, 69 TC 1, 84.

[139] "A difficult case": [1997] STC 908, 920g, 69 TC 1, 85. The author confesses that he finds the dissenting speeches in *Craven* v. *White* more convincing than the majority; see also [1989] *BTR* 20.

[140] *Customs and Excise Comrs* v. *Faith Construction Ltd.* [1988] STC 35, upheld, on different grounds, at [1989] STC 539, CA.

5.6.6 *Three examples from the lower courts*

The Sark Lark; Young v. *Phillips*[141] stands as authority, even if only *obiter*, for the importance of the end result, and for two consequential rules: (1) that the end result, as determined by the courts after disregarding the inserted steps, cannot itself be disregarded; and (2) that it is the end result that must be subjected to the application of the tax legislation and not any of the inserted steps. This analytical approach is fully in line with that of the House of Lords in *Craven* v. *White.*

This case involved a plan by taxpayers who were resident in the UK but not domiciled here to relocate assets outside the UK so that the disposal of those assets would take place outside the UK with the result that they would be taxed only if the proceeds were remitted to the UK. The taxpayers held shares in an English company. A Jersey company was established in which the taxpayers had no interest. The English company resolved to issue preferred ordinary shares, to be paid for by capitalising accumulated profits. Renounceable letters of allotment were issued in respect of the new shares. The Jersey company then agreed to issue shares to the taxpayers for £1,364,216. The taxpayers went to Sark, another of the Channel Islands, and disposed of their rights under the letters of allotment to the Jersey company for £1,364,216. The taxpayers then became registered shareholders of the Jersey company.

The Revenue assessed the taxpayers to CGT on the basis that the disposal of shares comprised in the letter of allotment was the disposal of assets located in the UK; this argument succeeded. However, the judge went on to consider what would have happened if the assets had been situated in the Channel Islands at the time of the disposal. Here the Revenue's argument was that under TCGA 1992, s. 30 the taxpayers had exercised control over the company causing a loss in value and therefore there was a deemed disposal. The court held, however, that this was a share-for-share exchange and therefore TCGA 1992, s. 127 directed that there should be no disposal (see below at §41.5). The Revenue tried to get around s. 127 in two ways. First, it argued generally that once a scheme to avoid tax had been proved it was enough for the Revenue to show that the substance of the matter was that value had passed out of the shares held in the English company. Nicholls J. rejected this argument. The end result of the transaction after removing the inserted steps was that shares were issued by the English company to the Jersey company. That was the relevant transaction to which the tax legislation had to be applied; the relevant transaction could not be disregarded. However, the judge went on to say that the protection of s. 127 would be denied the taxpayer because of TCGA 1992, s. 137.

The Revenue also argued that since there was a composite transaction having a number of steps spread over a period of time, the disposal of the letters of allotment had to be treated as taking place over a similar period of time and, since that period began before the taxpayers went to Sark, the disposal took place in England. This too was rejected. The argument assumed that the shares were issued to the taxpayers; this was not so because the end result of the scheme was that the shares were issued not to the taxpayers but to the Jersey companies.

Pigott v. *Staines Investments Co. Ltd.*[142] takes its lead from the point established in *Fitzwilliam* that while the effect of the doctrine being applied is to make the whole matter one transaction for tax purposes, that does not mean that the Revenue will defeat it. The

[141] [1984] STC 520, 58 TC 232.

[142] [1995] STC 114; see McGowan [1995] *BTR* 411.

court must still assess whether the Crown's position is "realistic" and "intellectually defensible". However, the case shows some signs of going back to the "enduring effect" argument used in the early stages in *Furniss* v. *Dawson*;[143] the courts will not disregard the enduring effects of what the parties have done when applying the new approach.

The case concerned a surplus ACT scheme. BAT, the parent company, had a subsidiary, BATCo. ATCo and other subsidiaries made large profits but paid little corporation tax presumably because much of that liability was offset by foreign tax credits. This meant that when BAT paid dividends to its shareholders, and so paid ACT, it was unable to set that ACT off against any mainstream corporation tax. To solve this problem the group bought in a company, immediately renamed Staines Investments Co. Ltd. (S), with a history of a steady stream of UK profits and corporation tax, and inserted it between BATCo and BAT; this was effected by BAT selling its holding in BATCo to S in return for shares in S, a share-for-share exchange. Ten months later BATCo paid its dividend to S and elected to pay it under a group dividend election so that no ACT fell due from BATCo; this dividend was paid out of profits earned by BATCo after S had joined the group. S then paid a dividend of a similar amount to BAT but did not make the group election and so paid ACT. S then sought to carry the ACT back to the maximum of six years permitted by TA 1988, s. 239(3), so entitling it to prepayment of the corporation tax paid in those years and now covered by the ACT. The Revenue refused repayment invoking the *Ramsay* principle. Knox J. found that the Commissioners, who had decided against the Revenue, had committed no error of law.

Counsel for the Revenue put the case narrowly; it was not argued that payment of a dividend had been made by BATCo directly to BATsince counsel accepted that the status of S as a subsidiary of BAT and as the holding company of BATCo had both to be taken as enduring features of the structure created by the parties. (One may wonder why this was not also the case for Greenjacket in *Furniss* v. *Dawson*.) Nor did the Crown argue, as it had before the Commissioner, that the payment by BATCo to S was not a distribution. Rather, counsel viewed the matter as a quadripartite contract under which the dividend would be paid on up the chain. Knox J. rejected the Crown's argument. He stressed that if a parent company (P) had a subsidiary (S) which had a subsidiary (SS) and SS paid a dividend to S which S was contractually bound to pay on to P, it was natural that S should pay it up to P by way of dividend. Such a contractual arrangement would not deprive the dividends received by S of their status as distributable profits in the hands of S. The Revenue's argument would recharacterise a perfectly normal and straightforward commercial transaction as a thoroughly abnormal and unusual transaction, the only merit of which was that it attracted a tax disadvantage. That went beyond disregarding steps taken only for a tax advantage.

Given the points conceded by the Crown the decision is probably correct. In reviewing it, two matters should be noted. The first is that the decision shows the complexity into which courts all too rapidly fall when they come to apply the new approach; the more complex the reconstruction of the transaction, the less likely it is that the courts will recharacterise it. The second is the need to avoid an over-simplified version of the *ratio* of the decision. The case does not decide that normal and reasonable transactions are safe; after all, the transaction in *Furniss* v. *Dawson* itself was normal and reasonable.

The third decision is *Macniven* v. *Westmoreland Investments Ltd.*[144] Here, trustees of a pension scheme lent £20 m to a would-be investment company to enable it to repay £20 m

[143] [1982] STC 267 (Vinelott J). Monroe described Vinelott J.'s analysis as "penetrating, careful and much to be valued": [1998] STC 1131 reversing [1982] *BTR* 200 at 209; Monroe died before the House of Lords decided the appeal.

[144] [1997] STC 1103.

in interest due to the scheme. What seems to have weighed with the Court of Appeal was that in *Burmah* the taxpayer company began with a non-allowable loss on a loan investment whereas in *Westmoreland* the company began with an interest charge which was clearly allowable but the company had no money with which to pay it; the scheme provided the company with funds to make that payment.[144a]

5.6.7 Conclusions

The period 1979 to 1988 saw some sharp variations in judicial attitudes, particularly in the House of Lords. The period began with two decisions upholding avoidance schemes and adopting a strict construction: *IRC* v. *Plummer*[145] and *Vestey* v. *IRC*.[146] There followed a more radical era beginning with *Ramsay* v. *IRC* in 1981 and culminating in *Furniss* v. *Dawson* in 1984. That more radical approach was restricted by the 1988 decision in *Craven* v. *White*, but restriction is not abolition and did not prevent the House from overruling *IRC* v. *Plummer* as being inconsistent with the later decisions of *Moodie* v. *IRC*.[147] Since then, the narrowing of the possibilities for the Revenue in *Fitzwilliam* v. *IRC*[148] has been followed by their reopening in *McGuckian*. One may also note, perhaps a little cynically, that *Donoghue* v. *Stevenson* was followed by a period of narrowing judicial decisions before being allowed to develop into the principle tort that lawyers recognise today. It seems unlikely that either the Revenue or the tax reformers can wait that long. A general anti-avoidance might seem more likely but the effect of *McGuckian* is that the Revenue can challenge a wide variety of schemes without having to put in place the expensive procedural safeguards designed by the TLRC.

This leaves one task: to try to make sense of the case-law using the distinction between tax avoidance and tax mitigation.[198] *Ramsay*, *Burmah* and *Ensign Tankers* can be seen to be cases of avoidance, as can *Moodie* v. *IRC*.[150] *Coates* v. *Arndale*[151] is a case on the scope of trading and falls the wrong side of that line. *Magnavox Electronics* v. *Hall*[152] is a case in which the taxpayer failed to alter date of a transaction by a preordained series of transaction.

Cases in which the taxpayer was held to be entitled to take advantage of a particular provision—and so are examples of mitigation—include: *Reed* v. *Nova Securities*[153] where the House of Lords declined to alter the Commissioners' finding that there was enough of a trading feel to the transaction to come within what is now TCGA 1992, s. 173; *Shepherd* v. *Lyntress*[154] where Vinelott J. held that a transaction was able to take advantage of what is now TCGA 1992, s. 171 (intra-group transfer of capital asset), *Reed* v. *Young* [155] where the House of Lords held that taxpayers were entitled to the fiscal consequence of limited partnerships; *Cooke* v. *Blacklaws*[156] (use of foreign company to employ taxpayer); *Reed* v.

[144a] [1998] STC at 1143–1144.
[145] [1979] STC 793, 54 TC 1.
[146] [1980] STC 10, 54 TC 503.
[147] [1993] STC 188, 65 TC 610, HL.
[148] [1993] STC 502, 67 TC 614, HL.
[149] See above at §2.1; and especially Lord Nolan in *IRC* v. *Willoughby* [1997] STC 995, 1003–1004.
[150] [1993] STC 188, 65 TC 610.
[151] [1984] STC 637, 59 TC 516.
[152] [1985] STC 260, 59 TC 610; see [1985] *BTR* 313 criticising the case for its treatment of *Edwards* v. *Bairstow*.
[153] [1985] STC 131, 59 TC 516.
[154] [1989] STC 617, 62 TC 495.
[155] [1986] STC 285, 59 TC 196.
[156] [1985] STC 1, 58 TC 255.

Clark[157] ("dropping out"); and *Pigott* v. *Staines Investments Co. Ltd.*[158] (ACT transfer scheme).

Other cases cannot so easily be classified. For example, how would *IRC* v. *Bowater Property Developments*[159] be classified? By contrast with DLT the corporation tax rules for small profits (see below at §45.5) dilute the relief by reference to the number of associated companies. By contrast, for the now repealed DLT which had a threshold (eventually) of £75,000, there was no dilution by reference to the numbers of associated companies. Does this mean that Parliament was approving schemes whereby a company faced with a large DLT bill would create nine subsidiary companies and divide 9/10ths of the land between them so that the threshold became £750,000? In *Bowater* the scheme was upheld by the House of Lords, although not on this ground: if this was tax mitigation rather than avoidance it looks odd; if it was avoidance it looks to be wrongly decided.

Is *Furniss* v. *Dawson* a case in which the taxpayers did just too little to bring themselves within the provision which Parliament had made for the deferral of tax, whereas in *Craven* v. *White* they had done just enough? These cases show that the distinction between tax mitigation and tax avoidance is in the end one of degree rather than kind, and this is reinforced by the frequency with which the Court of Appeal or House of Lords reverse the High Court or Court of Appeal respectively.

In the early summer of 2000 two major judicial issues present themselves: the immediate issue is whether the House of Lords will reverse the Court of Appeal in *MacNiven* v. *Westmoreland Investments*;[160] the other issue is whether the courts will recognise the implication of *McGuickian* that the new approach is to be used whether it hinders or helps the taxpayer.

If the House of Lords decide to uphold the Court of Appeal it is to be hoped that they will take the opportunity to revisit all the case law since *Ramsay*. While the *Ramsay* decision itself seems safe as a case on circular self-cancelling transactions, others do not. In particular one hopes that the distinction between mitigation and avoidance will be scrutinised to see if it can provide a rigorous intellectual basis for this important area of law and, if it can, to see how far it can be used to explain those cases decided before its emergence, principally *IRC* v. *Burmah Oil Co* and *Furniss* v. *Dawson* itself. If the distinction cannot provide this intellectual basis it should be discarded and another basis found. Whether that will be found in the approach of Lord Hoffmann outlined above at §5.6.5 may well depend on the accident of whether or not Lord Hoffmann is sitting.

157 [1985] STC 323, 58 TC 528.
158 [1995] STC 114, 68 TC 342.
159 [1988] STC 476, 62 TC 1.
160 [1998] STC 1131.

6

Tax Systems and Figures

This brief chapter looks at some statistics to do with tax systems. The usual sources for these are the annual volumes produced by the OECD the UK's Inland Revenue and the UK's Customs and Excise departments. There is material of more general interest in the United Kingdom National Accounts produced annually by the Office for National Statistics.

The tax information here presented is a fraction of what is available.

6.1 The Tax Burden

This is usually presented in terms of the burden of tax as a percentage of Gross Domestic Product.

Table 6.1 contains detailed information over a long period. It is taken from Table 5 of the OECD 1997 Statistics and shows the total tax revenue as a percentage of GDP on a three year moving average.

6.2 The Tax Mix

Table 6.2 is taken from Table 131 of the OECD Revenue Statistics and shows the main central government taxes as percentages of total tax revenues of central government. The OECD produces separate tables for local government and federal systems. The numbers and categories of taxes at the head of each column use the standard OECD classification of taxes; this classification is also used in, and so will become much clearer after studying, Table 6.3 which gives the yield from the different taxes in the United Kingdom over the last 35 years. The OECD classification scheme is explained in Annex I to the Report.

Before making some points on Table 6.3 it is necessary to say something about the balance between direct and indirect taxation in the UK.

The UK Inland Revenue Statistics begin with a table showing the amounts of UK central government tax collected by that department as compared with Customs and Excise, Vehicle Excise Duties, Selective Employment tax and National Insurance Surcharge. The figures take no account of National Insurance Contributions which are paid direct to the National Insurance Fund. On this basis the estimate for 1999–2000 is 56.6%. Figures for other years

TABLE 6.1 Total tax revenue as percentage of GDP—three year moving average

	1966	1970	1975	1980	1985	1990	1993	1994	1995	1996	
Canada	27.0	31.2	33.1	32.3	33.4	36.0	35.5	35.3	35.4	36.0	Canada
Mexico				16.0	16.9	17.3	17.5	17.2	16.9	16.7	Mexique
United States	25.5	27.7	27.3	27.6	26.6	27.8	28.0	28.3	28.82	29.2	Etats-Unis
Australia	22.1	23.1	26.6	27.2	29.4	28.9	27.7	28.5	29.4	29.8	Australie
Japan	18.1	19.5	21.9	25.3	27.7	30.7	28.4	28.3	28.1	28.5	Japon
Korea			15.1	17.4	16.8	18.6	19.9	20.3	20.8	21.1	Corée
New Zealand	25.2	26.7	31.0	33.2	31.9	37.7	36.5	36.9	36.7	36.6	Nouvelle-Zélande
Austria	34.3	35.1	37.5	40.5	42.1	41.1	43.3	43.0	43.3	43.6	Autriche
Belgium	32.8	35.8	40.8	44.3	46.6	43.4	44.9	45.4	45.7	45.7	Belgique
Czech Republic							42.5	41.7	40.2	39.3	République tchèque
Denmark	31.8	39.9	42.4	45.0	49.1	47.8	48.7	49.4	49.7	49.5	Danemark
Finland	31.4	32.7	38.0	37.5	40.8	44.6	45.7	45.5	46.3	46.3	Finlande
France	34.5	35.1	37.0	41.3	44.3	43.0	43.4	43.7	44.3	44.7	France
Germany	32.0	33.4	36.4	37.9	37.8	37.3	38.2	38.3	38.2	37.8	Allemagne
Greece	19.4	21.0	21.5	24.5	29.4	28.9	31.3	31.7	31.9	32.6	Grèce
Hungary						46.1	46.1	45.0	42.9	41.0	Hongrie
Iceland	26.2	27.0	29.6	29.7	28.9	31.7	31.4	31.1	31.4	31.9	Islande
Ireland	26.4	29.8	31.3	32.1	37.1	34.3	34.9	34.4	34.0	33.1	Irlande
Italy	25.7	26.5	26.4	29.6	35.2	38.7	42.2	42.0	41.8	42.8	Italie
Luxembourg	27.7	29.2	37.6	43.2	46.1	43.2	44.0	44.6	45.2	45.8	Luxembourg
Netherlands	34.0	37.4	42.5	44.7	44.5	45.5	46.3	44.7	42.8	41.8	Pays-Bas
Norway	31.0	35.8	40.3	42.7	43.5	41.6	40.8	41.0	41.4	41.9	Norvège
Poland						37.2	41.3	42.7	42.5	41.9	Pologne
Portugal	16.4	19.0	21.2	24.4	27.9	30.5	32.7	32.6	33.0	33.6	Portugal
Spain	15.1	16.8	19.1	24.1	29.3	34.6	35.3	34.2	33.5	33.0	Espagne
Sweden	35.8	40.1	44.5	49.3	50.7	54.9	49.5	48.5	49.0	49.9	Suède
Switzerland	20.1	22.4	27.7	29.0	30.9	30.9	32.1	32.9	33.6	33.9	Suisse
Turkey	10.9	13.0	15.5	17.6	15.8	19.9	22.4	22.5	23.4	25.3	Turquie
United Kingdom	31.6	36.0	35.0	34.6	37.6	36.2	34.5	34.5	34.9	35.2	Royaume-Uni
Unweighted average:											*Moyenne non pondérée:*
OECD Total	26.5	28.9	31.2	32.7	34.6	36.0	36.7	36.7	36.7	36.8	OCDE Total
OECD America	26.3	29.4	30.2	25.3	25.6	27.0	27.0	26.9	27.0	27.3	OCDE Amérique
OECD Pacific	21.8	23.1	23.7	25.8	26.4	29.0	28.1	28.5	28.8	29.0	OCDE Pacifique
OECD Europe	27.2	29.8	32.9	35.4	37.8	38.6	39.6	39.5	39.5	39.6	OCDE Europe
EU 15	28.6	31.2	34.1	36.9	39.9	40.3	41.0	40.8	40.9	41.0	UE 15

range from 0.0% (1908–1909) to 79.3% (1918–1919). By 1948–1949 the figure had settled at 56.1% and for most years since then the figures has remained in the 50–60% range with a high of 58.8% in 1978–1979 and a low of 52.2% in 1993–1994. The figure went over 60% for each year from 1973–1974 to 1978–1978 but this was largely due to the fact that indirect taxes were not increased in line with inflation during the first of those years. This was because while inflation was severe the government was conducting a wages freeze and did not wish to increase prices. While this seems very strange today it should not be overlooked that governments have always—and necessarily—conducted a wages policy in relation to the public sector.

6.3 The UK System—Receipts

Table 6.3 is informative but daunting. It was originally Table 69 of the OECD Revenue Statistics. . . . It is one of a series of tables in common form for all OECD countries which is why it includes taxes not in force in the UK, such as wealth taxes. These tables include amounts collected at or for local government level (4100 *et seq*).

In looking at Table 6.3 it is necessary to bear a number of points in mind. First, it refers to payments received not payments due and so may contain entries for taxes which were repealed some years earlier; these payments do not necessarily indicate fault on the part of taxpayers as the rules of those taxes may allow payment to be made by instalments or deferred until some later event. Secondly, it only includes figures required by the OECD. More information on some of the questions is available in the Annual Reports of the Revenue or the National Statistics already referred to. Thirdly, the earlier years are covered only at five year intervals. A tax which did not generate payments in one of the years will not appear. Entry 1300 covers payment by companies which cannot be allocated between the corporate and the private sector; this is because most of these refer to withholding taxes and it was not known how the payments were allocated. Finally, ACT payments etc. are treated as paid by the company even though they may give rise indirectly to tax credits which can be used by certain shareholders.

On substantive matters in Table 6.3 it is interesting to note 5122 (Profits of Fiscal Monopolies). These refer to items such as the profits of liquor stores where the government runs these outlets as a monopoly. These are treated as taxes and are to be distinguished from profits of nationalised undertakings, like transport systems, which are primarily payments for services (see above at §1.1). Further, under heading 3000, it is interesting to note that the national insurance surcharge is treated as a tax and not as a social security contribution. Also on heading 3000, it is probably correct to repeat the figures 850 (1970) and 1 (1975) in the following line as receipts from Selective Employment Tax.

6.4 The UK Tax System—Reliefs

The preceding Table, 6.4, taken from Table 5.1 of the Inland Revenue Statistics for 1999 shows the estimated cost of "structural reliefs" for 1998–1999 and 1999–2000. Readers are also referred to the long list of tax allowance and reliefs in force but for which costs cannot even be estimated; the list is in Appendix B.2 and comprises 46 items for income tax and corporation tax, 45 for CGT and 33 for inheritance tax.

The equivalent table of the Inland Revenue Statistics for 1991 shows some striking differences. The 1991 figures, at 1991 levels and not adjusted for inflation, show the married couple's allowance, then available generally to all married couples living together, cost 5,400 m and mortgage interest 7,700 m. Life assurance premium relief cost 340 m. The cost of the personal allowance was 24,400. In 1990–1991 the basic rate of tax was 25%, there was neither a starting rate of 10% nor a savings rate of 20%.

Table 6.2 The main central government taxes as percentage of total tax revenues of central government[1]

	1000 Income & Profits / Revenu & Bénéfice			1000 Individuals / Personnes physiques			1200 Corporate / Des sociétés			2000 + 3000 Soc. Security & Payroll[2] / Séc. Sociale & Salaires[2]			4000 Property / Patrimoine			5100 General taxes / Impôts généraux			5120 Specific goods & services / Biens et services déterminés			Other taxes / Autres impôts			
	1975	1985	1997	1975	1985	1997	1975	1985	1997	1975	1985	1997	1975	1985	1997	1975	1985	1997	1975	1985	1997	1975	1985	1997	
Federal countries																									**Pays fédéraux**
Australia	69.9	67.0	72.8	54.5	55.5	54.0	15.5	11.5	18.8	0.3	0.1	2.5	0.6	0.4	0.0	8.3	9.7	10.8	20.8	22.4	13.6	0.1	0.3	0.4	Australie
Austria	32.2	31.2	38.8	25.0	26.1	28.4	6.9	5.0	8.1	16.5	16.2	19.2	3.0	2.5	0.5	26.7	30.0	26.4	20.9	16.6	12.4	0.7	3.6	2.7	Autriche
Belgium	56.6	60.0	61.8	45.9	51.8	43.0	10.5	7.9	18.5	1.6	1.9	2.8	3.7	3.0	4.6	25.1	23.3	8.7	11.4	10.1	18.0	1.5	1.7	4.2	Belgique
Canada	69.4	67.9	74.2	46.7	52.5	56.4	20.9	13.9	16.4	—	—	—	0.0	—	—	12.8	14.2	16.6	17.0	17.9	9.2	0.7	0.0	0.0	Canada
Germany	42.3	43.6	41.6	37.0	36.0	36.2	5.2	7.6	5.5	—	—	—	1.9	0.7	0.1	29.1	32.7	30.7	26.7	22.9	27.6	0.0	0.0	0.0	Allemagne
Mexico		25.3	32.1								0.7	—		—	—		18.2	21.7		55.3	42.9		0.6	3.3	Mexique
Switzerland	30.2	31.2	33.0	24.0	25.5	23.9	6.3	5.7	9.1	—	—	—	4.1	9.0	7.2	28.3	32.4	35.7	37.3	27.5	24.1	0.0	0.01	—	Suisse
United States	86.5	87.9	90.7	64.9	74.3	72.7	21.6	13.6	18.0	—	—	—	2.4	1.4	2.0	—	—	—	10.8	10.5	7.2	0.2	0.1	0.1	Etats-Unis
Unweighted average	55.3	51.8	55.6	42.6	45.9	44.9	12.4	9.3	13.5	2.6	2.4	3.1	2.3	2.1	1.8	18.6	20.1	18.8	20.7	22.9	19.4	0.5	0.8	1.3	*Moyenne non pondérée*
Unitary countries																									**Pays unitaires**
Czech Republic			26.2			11.5			14.7			0.1			1.7			40.9			27.5			3.6	République tchèque
Denmark	48.6	44.8	47.2	44.8	36.1	36.5	3.9	6.0	7.1	0.2	2.8	0.9	2.8	3.5	2.0	24.7	29.4	30.3	20.5	17.8	17.4	3.1	1.6	2.2	Danemark
Finland	35.0	33.4	33.6	31.6	30.5	25.2	3.4	2.9	8.4	4.1	0.9	4.0	3.4	4.5	2.8	29.7	35.1	35.7	27.0	25.1	22.1	0.7	1.1	1.7	Finlande
France	31.0	33.8	32.3	20.7	24.2	18.7	10.1	9.4	13.6	3.8	4.4	6.1	3.2	3.5	4.7	45.1	41.7	38.6	15.5	15.7	16.4	1.4	1.0	1.9	France

Greece	18.9	27.8	33.6	12.7	22.0	19.3	5.0	4.4	9.3	0.3	1.9	2.3	14.1	4.1	5.6	26.9	27.4	33.5	33.9	31.5	21.8	5.9	7.3	3.2	Grèce
Hungary			34.6			26.7			7.8			6.1			0.9			32.2			25.1			1.2	Hongrie
Iceland	13.1	13.4	22.6	10.6	11.4	18.9	2.5	2.0	3.7	8.5	7.4	11.4	2.8	5.5	6.2	35.1	40.6	38.5	39.5	31.3	17.3	1.0	1.9	4.1	Islande
Ireland	38.8	42.0	48.6	32.5	38.1	36.8	6.2	3.9	11.7	0.9	4.2	2.9	3.2	2.1	3.3	19.0	25.1	25.6	35.4	24.3	17.6	2.8	2.2	2.1	Irlande
Italy	39.0	56.6	56.8	27.7	42.3	41.8	11.3	14.4	15.6	—	0.9	0.2	5.9	4.0	5.1	26.9	23.3	20.9	26.2	13.2	15.0	2.0	2.0	2.0	Italie
Japan	67.2	70.1	58.7	37.8	39.4	34.5	29.4	30.7	24.2	—	—	—	6.0	8.1	8.4	—	—	16.7	24.7	20.2	14.1	2.1	1.6	2.0	Japon
Korea	24.7		35.3	9.6		21.5	10.0		13.5				4.7		3.7			27.9			27.9			5.3	Corée
Luxembourg	59.8	57.2	49.8	42.7	38.3	30.4	17.1	18.9	19.4	—	—	—	6.9	7.5	11.0	18.4	16.1	18.4	11.2	16.1	18.3	3.7	3.1	2.4	Luxembourg
Netherlands	58.7	50.8	47.6	45.6	37.4	28.5	13.1	13.4	19.1	—	—	—	3.0	3.2	5.0	24.4	31.2	29.3	11.1	11.0	14.7	2.8	3.7	3.4	Pays-Bas
New Zealand	72.1	73.5	62.4	58.8	64.0	45.6	12.8	8.9	11.2	—	0.7	1.0	2.6	1.5	0.6	9.8	11.1	25.5	14.4	12.4	8.8	1.2	0.9	1.8	Nouvelle-Zélande
Norway	19.2	33.9	35.4	16.1	7.2	17.4	3.1	26.7	18.0	4.0	2.0	2.3	2.3	1.3	1.6	40.5	30.5	34.2	31.7	30.5	25.1	2.5	1.8	1.5	Norvège
Poland			40.3			27.9			12.4			1.4			0.0			34.5			23.6			0.2	Pologne
Portugal	26.7	33.3	41.3			25.9			15.2	3.8	3.5	—	3.8	2.6	0.3	17.1	17.4	31.5	41.2	39.7	25.1	7.4	3.5	1.7	Portugal
Spain	40.6	48.6	52.5	26.3	37.7	37.1	14.3	10.3	15.1		0.8	0.8	12.3	3.4	0.4	29.0	23.2	30.0	17.8	23.5	16.4		0.5	−0.1	Espagne
Sweden	41.7	22.1	23.3	37.9	16.4	10.0	3.8	5.7	13.3	8.5	24.2	22.8	2.2	4.3	8.6	23.4	25.8	27.1	20.7	21.3	16.5	3.6	2.2	1.7	Suède
Turkey		43.3	32.3		32.4	25.6		11.0	6.7		—	—		5.3	3.2		27.4	38.4		14.7	6.2		9.3	19.9	Turquie
United Kingdom	63.5	55.9	48.1	56.8	37.6	32.3	8.8	18.2	15.8	0.0	0.0	—	2.4	2.6	9.1	13.4	20.1	23.9	19.0	18.4	17.0	1.8	3.1	2.0	Royaume-Uni
Unweighted average	41.1	43.6	41.1	32.0	32.2	27.2	9.7	11.7	13.1	2.3	3.2	3.0	4.8	4.0	4.0	23.9	25..0	30.2	24.4	21.6	18.8	2.8	2.7	3.0	*Moyenne non pondérée*

[1] Excluding social security contributions accruing to social security funds./Sont exclues les cotisations de sécurité sociale versées aux fonds de sécurité sociale.

[2] These comprise only social security contributions accruing to central government./Ne sont incluses que les cotisations de sécurité sociale versées à l'administration centrale.

TABLE 6.3 United Kingdom. Details of tax revenue, in millions of pounds sterling

	1965	1970	1975	1980	1985	1990	1994	1995	1996	1997
Total tax revenue	10,495	19,080	37,343	81,153	133,565	199,524	229,607	250,697	264,925	283,775
1000 Taxes on income, profits and capital gains	4,050	7,705	16,716	30,703	51,688	78,771	81,179	91,318	96,941	104,853
1100 Of individuals	3,618	6,016	14,936	23,868	34,820	55,633	62,700	67,727	68,694	70,382
1110 On income and profits	3,615	5,752	14,448	23,376	33,965	53,741	61,879	66,875	67,623	69,901
Income tax				23,370	33,965	53,741	61,879	66,875	67,623	69,901
Surtax				6	—	—	—	—	—	—
1120 On capital gains	3	264	488	492	855	1,892	821	852	071	481
1200 Corporate	484	1,658	2,310	6,835	16,868	23,138	18,479	23,591	28,347	34,471
1210 On profits	484	24	18	6,585	16,331	22,119	17,858	22,967	27,523	33,426
Petroleum revenue tax				1,799	7,369	942	822	834	1,362	1,467
Supplementary petroleum duty				—	—	—	—	—	—	—
Corporation tax				4,735	8,948	21,043	17,036	22,153	26,161	29,349
Corporation tax overspill relief				−1	—	—	—	—	—	—
Profits tax				—	—	—	—	—	—	—
IBA levy				52	14	134	—	—	—	—
Windfall tax				—	—	—	—	—	—	2,610
1220 On capital gains	—	—	—	250	537	1,019	621	604	824	1,045
1300 Unallocable between 1100 and 1200	−52	31	−530	—	—	—	—	—	—	—
2000 Social security contributions	1,685	2,655	6,540	13,531	23,769	34,243	41,586	43,987	46,227	48,924
2100 Employees	770	1,171	2,562	5,228	10,938	13,124	17,211	18,495	190,01	21,250
2200 Employers	831	1,354	4,068	8,210	12,245	19,984	23,260	24,184	25,454	27,198
2300 Self-employed or non-employed	75	114	195	317	745	1,177	1,469	1,541	17,71	1,840
2400 Unallocable between 2100, 2200 and 2300	9	16	−285	−224	−159	−42	−354	−233	1	−1,364
3000 Taxes on payroll and workforce		850	1	3,498	42	—	—	—	—	—
Selective employment tax				—	—	—	—	—	—	—
National insurance surcharge				3,498	42	—	—	—	—	—
4000 Taxes on property	1,591	2,378	4,746	9,774	16,061	15,899	24,587	26,748	28,456	30,686
4100 Recurrent taxes on immovable property	1,228	1,827	4,022	8,665	13,979	12,823	21,317	23,387	24,610	25,859
4110 Households	539	783	1,604	3,687	5,777	1,794	8,841	9,480	9,938	10,839
Northern Ireland rates paid to CG				37	55	113	81	100	80	83
Council tax				—	—	—	8650	9330	9793	10715
Rates				3,650	5,722	1,681	110	50	65	41
4120 Others	689	1,094	2,418	4,978	8,202	11,029	12,476	13,907	14,672	15,020
National non-domestic rates				—	—	9469	12312	13627	14424	14711

Rates paid to LA				4,925	7,972	1,403	37	108	106	144
Northern Ireland rates paid to CF				53	71	110	127	172	142	165
London Regional Transport levy				—	159	47	—	—	—	—
4200 Recurrent taxes on net wealth	—	—	—	—	—	—	—	—	—	—
4210 Individual	—	—	—	—	—	—	—	—	—	—
4220 Corporate	—	—	—	—	—	—	—	—	—	—
4300 Estate, inheritance and gift taxes	287	383	307	479	923	1,321	1,439	1,441	1,637	1,601
4310 Estate and inheritance taxes	287	383	307	479	923	1,321	1,439	1,441	1,637	1,601
Death duties				423	806	1,275	1,413	1,410	1,594	1,558
Development land tax				42	66	6	—	—	—	—
Taxes on other capital transfers				14	51	40	26	31	43	43
Special tax on bank deposits				—	—	—	—	—	—	—
Betterment duty				—	—	—	—	—	—	—
Special charges				—	—	—	—	—	—	—
Special contribution				—	—	—	—	—	—	—
4320 Gift taxes	—	—	—	—	—	—	—	—	—	—
4400 Taxes on financial and capital transactions	76	124	266	630	1,159	1,755	1,831	1,920	2,209	3,226
Stamp duties				630	1,159	1,755	1,831	1,920	2,209	3,226
4500 Non-recurrent taxes	—	26	2	—	—	—	—	—	—	—
4510 On net wealth	—	—	—	—	—	—	—	—	—	—
4520 Other non-recurrent taxes	—	26	2	—	—	—	—	—	—	—
4600 Other recurrent taxes on property	—	18	149	—	—	—	—	—	—	—
5000 Taxes on goods and services	3,619	5,492	9,342	23,647	42,005	62,127	81,853	88,401	93,146	99,216
5100 Taxes on production, sale, transfer, etc.	3,406	5,105	8,862	22,677	39,144	59,168	77,593	84,271	88,871	94,893
5110 General taxes	647	1,304	3,326	11,897	20,679	33,846	46,113	48,467	51,623	55,454
5111 Value added taxes	—	—	3,326	11,897	20,679	33,846	46,113	48,467	51,623	55,454
Value added tax				11,893	20,527	33,330	47,181	48,257	51,593	55,703
Adj. to VAT contribution				4	152	516	−1,068	210	30	−249
Purchase tax				—	—	—	—	—	—	—
5112 Sales tax	647	1304	—	—	—	—	—	—	—	—
5113 Other	—	—	—	—	—	—	—	—	—	—
5120 Taxes on specific goods and services	2,759	3,801	5,536	10,780	18,465	25,322	31,480	35,804	37,248	39,439
5121 Excises	2,383	3,424	4,725	8,616	14,867	19,740	26,342	27,923	29,937	31,567
Beer				1,029	1,943	2,220	2,560	2,585	2,625	2,714
Wines, spirits, cider and perry				1,513	2,230	2,627	3,074	2,891	3,003	3,079
Tobacco				2,735	4,378	5,541	6,839	7,331	7,651	7,716
Hydrocarbon oil				3,327	6,292	9,335	13,869	15,116	16,658	18,058
Other excise duties				12	24	17	—	—	—	—

Table 6.3 *cont.*

	1965	1970	1975	1980	1985	1990	1994	1995	1996	1997
T5122 Profits of fiscal monopolies	—	—	—	—	—	—	—	—	—	—
5123 Customs and import duties	343	250	540	1,109	1,424	1,837	2,134	2,458	2,318	2,284
Customs duties				—	—	—	—	—	—	—
Import duties				855	1,269	1,710	1,981	2,308	2,137	1,999
Agricultural levies				254	155	127	153	150	181	285
Temporary charges of import				—	—	—	—	—	—	—
5124 Taxes on exports	—	3	4	−1	—	36	—	—	—	—
Levies on exports				−1	—	36	—	—	—	—
5125 Taxes on investment goods	—	—	—	—	—	—	—	—	—	—
5126 Taxes on specific services	33	124	258	456	728	1,022	1,398	3,901	3,791	4,898
Betting				456	728	1,022	1,151	1,567	1,465	1,522
National Lottery contributions to fund				—	—	—	98	1,360	1,297	1,512
Air passenger duty				—	—	—	33	339	353	442
Insurance premium tax				—	—	—	116	635	671	1,044
Landfill tax				—	—	—	—	—	5	378
5127 Other taxes on internet, trade and transactions	—	—	—	—	—	—	—	—	—	—
5128 Other taxes	—	—	9	600	1,446	26,87	1,606	1,522	1,202	690
Fossil fuel levy				—	—	875	1,355	1,306	978	418
Sugar levy				21	49	46	98	55	26	91
European coal and steel levy				12	9	11	—	—	—	—
Gas levy				83	525	291	153	161	198	181
Car Tax				484	863	1,464	—	—	—	—
5130 Unallocable between 5110 and 5120q	—	—	—	—	—	—	—	—	—	—
5200 Taxes on use of goods and perform activities	212	446	698	1,326	2,401	3,186	4,465	4,608	4,756	4,971
5210 Recurrent taxes	212	446	698	1,326	2,401	3,186	4,465	4,608	4,756	4,971
5211 Paid by households: motor vehicles	118	237	390	729	1,485	1,841	2,555	2,651	2,793	2,982
Motor vehicle				726	1,482	1,837	2,546	2,641	2,782	2,972
Boat licences				3	3	4	9	10	11	10
5212 Paid by others: motor vehicles	74	208	304	588	906	1,134	1,302	1,313	1,367	1,362
Motor vehicle levy				588	906	1,134	1,302	1,313	1,367	1,362
5213 Paid in respect of other goods	20	1	4	9	10	211	608	644	596	627
ITC franchise payments				—	—	—	380	398	408	422
Telecommunications regulator fees				—	—	7	8	9	9	10
Gas regulator fees				—	—	2	3	5	8	12
Electricity regulator fees				—	—	5	11	8	15	16

Water regulator fees				—	—	6	9	9	12	11
Securities and investment Board fees				—	—	16	19	20	20	20
Company registration surplus fees				—	—	12	3-	21	4	—
Consumer and credit act fees				9	10	163	148	174	120	136
Fees paid to the Environment Agency				—	—	—	—	—	—	—
1936 Title Act payments				—	—	—	—	—	—	—
5220 Non-recurrent taxes	—	—	—	—	—	—	—	—	—	—
5300 Unallocable between 5100 and 5200	1	−59	−218	−356	460	−227	−205	−478	−481	−648
6000 Other taxes						8,484	402	243	155	96
6100 Paid solely by business	—	—	—	—	—	—	—	—	—	—
6200 Other	—	—	—	—	—	8,484	402	243	155	96
Community charge				—	—	8,484	402	243	155	96

Starting in 1980, tax revenues are reported following a more detailed format.
Year ending 31 December.
The community charge replaced domestic rates in Scotland in April 1989 and was extended to England and Wales in April 1990. Since the tax is a lump-sum levied on each adult in a household, it has been classified in heading 6200 (domestic rates are classified in heading 4100).
Heading 2000 includes some voluntary contributions which cannot be separately identified.
Source: National Income and Expenditure, Central Statistical Office, Annual Reports of the Inland Revenue and Customs and Excise Department.

TABLE 6.4 Tax expenditures and structural reliefs[1]

	Estimates cost for	
	1998–1999	1999–2000
Tax expenditures		
Income tax		
Relief for		
Approved pension schemes[2,3]	11,400*	12,900*
Approved profit sharing schemes[4]	190*	210*
Approved discretionary share option schemes[5]	110*	90*
Approved savings-related share option schemes	490*	420*
Personal Equity Plans[7]	1,000*	1,000*
Individual Savings Accounts[8]	0	100
Venture Capital Trusts[9]	70*	80*
Enterprise Investment Scheme[10]	80*	100*
Profit related pay	1,500*	900*
Vocational training[11]	45	55
Exemption of:		
First £30,000 of payments on termination of employment	1,100*	1,100*
Interest on National Savings Certificates including index-linked Certificates	230*	190*
Tax Exempt Savings Account interest	400*	350*
Premium Bond prizes	110*	90*
SAYE	110*	90*
Income of charities[12]	925	950*
Foreign service allowance paid to Crown Servants abroad	100*	100*
First £8,000 of reimbursed relocation packages provided by employers	300*	300*
Tax credits:		
Life assurance premiums (for contracts made prior to 14 March 1984)[11]	115	110

	Estimated cost for	
	1998–1999	1999–2000
National insurance contributions		
Contracted-out rebate occupational schemes of which:		
Occupational schemes deducted from National Insurance Contributions received	5,960	6,180
Occupational schemes (COMPS) paid by Contributions Agency direct to scheme	80	90
Reliefs with tax expenditure and structural components		
Income Tax		
Married couple's allowance[17]	2,800	2,000
Age-related allowances[18]	1,100	1,250
Additional personal allowance for one parent family[19]	220	150
Relief for maintenance payments[20]	90*	90
Exemption of:		
British government securities where owner not ordinarily resident in the United Kingdom[21]	1,000*	1,000
Child benefit (including one parent benefit)[22]	800*	850
Long-term incapacity benefit[23]	450*	400*
Industrial disablement benefits	80*	80*
Attendance allowance	275*	210*
Disability living allowance	350*	350*
War disablement benefits	110*	90*
War widows pension	80*	60*
Income tax and corporation tax		
Capital allowances[24]	19,800*	21,000*
Of which:		
Temporary first year allowances for SMEs	neg	230*
Corporation tax		

Mortgage interest[11,13]	1,900	1,600
Working Families Tax Credit	—	1,300*
Capital gains tax		
Exemption of gains arising on disposal of only or main residence[14]	1,400*	1,350*
Retirement relief	240*	190*
Inheritance tax		
Relief for:		
Agricultural property	120*	120*
Business property	110*	120*
Heritage property[15]	50*	60*
Exemption of transfers to charities on death	275*	300*
Structural reliefs		
Income tax		
Personal allowance	31,200	31,900
Income tax and corporation tax		
Double taxation relief[16]	5,500*	5,500*
Corporation tax		
Reduced rate of corporation tax on policy holders' fraction of profits	300*	300*
Small companies' reduced rate of corporation tax	1,150*	1,250*
Capital gains tax		
Indexation allowance and rebasing to March 1982[25]	1,500*	1,400*
Taper relief[26]	70	170*
Exemption of:		
Annual exempt amount (half of the individuals' exemption for trustees)[27]	1,500*	1,500*
Gains accrued but unrealised at death[28]	750*	850*
Petroleum revenue tax[29]		
Uplift on qualifying expenditure	200	170
Relief for exploration and appraisal expenditure	30	15
Oil allowance	260	190
Safeguard: a protection for return on capital cost	280	270
Tariff receipts allowance	70	80
Exemption for gas sold to British Gas under pre-July 1975 contracts	140	100
Inheritance tax		
Nil rate band for chargeable transfers not exceeding the threshold	5,600*	5,900*
Exemption of transfers on death to surviving spouses[30]	1,000*	1,100*
Stamp duties		
Exemption of transfers of land and property where the consideration does not exceed the threshold[31]	230*	240*

These figures are particularly tentative and subject to a wide margin of error.

[1] Only reliefs with an estimated cost of at least £50 m are included (see paragraph 19). Costs are on an accruals basis unless otherwise specified. The costs of the personal income tax allowances do not cover individuals who are not on Inland Revenue records because their income is below the tax threshold.

[2] Calculated using unapproved schemes as a benchmark with which to compare the present regime. The cost of tax relief on capital gains of funds is not included as lack of information on the length of time that pension funds hold various types of assets means that a reliable estimate cannot be made. The cost reflects that pension providers are no longer entitled to payment of tax credits on UK dividends paid on or after 2 July 1997.

[3] The cost of tax relief for employers' contributions is included on the basis that under present arrangements employers' contributions are not taxable as a benefit in kind of the employee.

Notes *continued over*

Notes *cont.*

[4] The costs take into account that tax relief is denied where the participants sell the shares within 3 years of the date of appropriation.

[5] The costs take into account the partial offset provided by liability to capital gains tax arising from disposals of shares acquired under the scheme.

[6] Excludes the cost of the tax-free bonus or interest received under a SAYE contract.

[7] Includes the CGT cost of capital gains within Personal Equity Plans.

[8] Individual savings accounts (ISAs) started on 6 April 1999.

[9] Includes the CGT costs of deferral reliefs and exempting gains from tax.

[10] The EIS and capital gains tax reinvestment relief were rationalised from April 1999 to create a unified scheme. The figure includes the CGT cost of deferral relief.

[11] Including the cost of deductions at source for non-taxpayers.

[12] These figures comprise:

i. the total sum paid to charities, certain heritage bodies and museums, and scientific research associations in respect of tax credits on dividends, and income tax deducted at source from other investment income; payments under deeds of covenant; and single donations by companies and individuals under the Gift Aid scheme. Information is not available about income received by these bodies without deduction of tax, and no allowance in the figures is made for this; and

ii. an estimate of the higher rate relief received by the payers of covenanted sums and single donations under Gift Aid;

[13] Covering qualifying interest on loans for the purchase (or improvement if loan prior to 6 April 1988) of the main or only residence.

[14] Calculated on the assumption that there would be no relief for gains when disposal proceeds were applied to the purchase of another house. The costs quoted do not represent the yield from abolition of the relief: consequential effects on the housing market would substantially reduce the yield.

[15] This is the cost of claims processed in the year, including the cost of conditional exemption, maintenance funds and property transferred by acceptance in lieu and private treaty sale arrangements.

[16] Based on provisional CT Pay and File data for accounting periods ending in 1997–1998 and the results of the 1997–1998 Survey of Personal Incomes.

[17] From 1993–1994 the married couple's allowance can be transferred to the wife or split equally between husband and wife regardless of income.

[18] These figures represent the cost of the aged personal and aged married couple's allowance over the corresponding allowances for non-aged taxpayers. They include £45 m in 1998–1999 and £55 m in 1999–2000 for the cost of the higher aged allowances for those aged 75 and over.

[19] Including small amounts (under £5 million) for the additional personal allowance available to a married man with children whose wife is totally incapacitated.

[20] The cost includes maintenance payments under the new rules (Finance Act 1988) as well as the old rules.

[21] Taxed at the lower rate from 1996–1997.

[22] The figures assume that child benefit is paid to the mother or lone father.

[23] Incapacity benefit replaced invalidity benefit and sickness benefit from April 1995. Benefit for new claimants after that date is taxable, except for benefit received in the first twenty-eight weeks of incapacity. Incapacity benefit paid to existing claimants at April 1995 remains exempt.

[24] The figures for capital allowances are net of balancing charges. They include writing down and other allowances. Temporary first year allowances are available to small and medium sized enterprises for expenditure incurred between 2 July 1997 and 1 July 2000 for expenditure on plant and machinery.

[25] The estimated costs relate to gains of individuals and trustees only. Company gains are not included because of estimation difficulties.

[26] In 1998–1999 and 1999–2000 taper relief is only available for those disposing of business assets.

[27] These estimates allow for windfall gains arising from the disposal of shares issued in connection with building society and insurance company de-mutualisations. The figures shown for 1998–1999 and 1999–2000 are rounded to the nearest £½ bn to reflect uncertainty due to the exceptional level of de-mutualisation activity in recent years.

[28] These estimates assume deferral relief on transfer of assets between spouses would be available.

[29] The figures are net of any consequential effect on corporation tax and represent the effect on calendar year accruals in 1998 and 1999. The cost of all types of expenditure relief (i.e. capital expenditure, including uplift, operating expenditure and exploration and appraisal expenditure) is £1,910 m in 1998–1999 and £1,790 m in 1998–1999. These figures reflect the fact that, in the case of PRT, no distinction is made between revenue and capital.

[30] These costs are in respect only of transfers for which an account is submitted to the Capital Taxes Office.

[31] The threshold does not apply to transfers of shares.

6.5 Finally

The following two tables, 6.5 and 6.6, taken from Inland Revenue Statistics (Tables 2.4 and 2.5) are of interest when considering the burden of income tax.

TABLE 6.5 Shares of total income tax liability

Quantile groups of taxpayers	1992–1993	1993 1994	1994–1995	1995–1996	1996–1997	1997–1998	1998–1999[1]	1999–2000[1]
Top 1 per cent	16	16	17	17	20	20	20	20
Top 5 per cent	33	33	34	34	37	37	37	38
Top 10 per cent	44	44	45	45	48	48	48	50
Next 40 per cent	43	43	42	42	40	40	40	39
Lower 50 per cent	13	13	13	13	12	12	12	11
All taxpayers (= 100%) (£ b)	60.7	61.4	66.3	72.0	73.7	79.5	85.0	85.6

[1] Provisional.

TABLE 6.6 Income tax liabilities, by income range, 1999–2000[1,2]

Range of total income (lower limit)	Tax liability of starting rate taxpayers[3]		Tax liability of savings rate taxpayers[4]		Tax liability of basic rate taxpayers[5]		Tax liability of higher rate taxpayers[6]		Total tax liability before tax credit[7]	Total tax liability after tax credit[7]	verage rate of tax	verage amount tax
	Number of taxpayers	Amount	Number of taxpayers	Amount	Number of taxpayers	Amount	Number of taxpayers	Amount				
£											%	£
4,335	0.7	20	—	—	—	—	—	—	20	20	1%	30
5,000	1.5	140	0.3	50	2	530	—	—	730	650	3%	200
7,500	—	20	0.2	100	3	2,290	—	—	2,400	2,200	7%	630
10,000	—	20	0.2	210	6	9,180	—	—	9,410	8,810	11%	1,400
15,000	—	20	0.1	140	4	11,200	—	—	11,400	10,900	14%	2,480
20,000	—	30	0.0	110	5	19,560	—	—	19,700	19,100	16%	3,960
30,000	—	10	0.0	20	1	5,270	1.3	11,100	16,400	16,100	19%	7,100
50,000	—	—	—	—	—	—	0.7	12,600	12,700	12,500	27%	17,700
100,000	—	—	—	—	—	—	0.2	15,300	15,300	15,300	33%	69,700
All ranges	2.3	260	0.9	630	21	48,070	2.3	39,100	88,000	85,600	17%	3,260

1 Provisional
2 Excluding MIRAS.
3 Taxpayers with a 10% marginal rate on their earnings, which for this purpose includes all taxable income other than savings or dividends.
4 Taxpayers who would be liable at the savings or dividends rate if they had an extra £1 of earnings.
5 Taxpayers with a 23% marginal rate on their earnings.
6 Taxpayers with a taxable income above the basic rate threshold limit.
7 In this context tax credits refer to allowances given at a fixed rate, for example the married couples' allowance.

PART II

Income Tax

7

Income Tax: Basic Concepts

7.1 Introduction

Under the doctrine that income tax is an annual tax, each year's Finance Act charges income tax for that year;[1] TA 1988, s. 1 then directs that income is taxable if it falls within one or other of the Schedules in that Act.[2] Income tax is charged at the rates in force for the particular year of assessment on the income attributed by the tax system to that year. The tax system therefore sets the rates of tax (which may vary according to the type of income), defines what is meant by income, and defines when and to whom it arises and, because of international rules, where it arises. These issues, so simply stated, form the subject of Part II of this book, as supplemented by Parts V–VIII. This chapter deal with the definition of income in relation to the Schedules and other rules.

7.1.1 What is income?[3]

The UK concept of income is explained below at §7.3. UK courts have not been adventurous in seeking out new types of taxable income. While the words of Lord Steyn and Lord Cooke in *IRC* v. *McGuckian*[4] can be seen as the start of a wider view, history suggest that

[1] For example, FA 2000, s. 31 for 2000–01.
[2] These rules were actually contained in Schedules to the Act until the 1952 consolidation, when they became part of the text.
[3] See Thuroni (1990) 46 *Tax Law Review* 45.
[4] [1997] STC 907, 69 TC 1.

theirs may well be lone voices. Meanwhile, Australian courts have already taken a wider view.[5]

American lawyers, with a system based on a global as opposed to Schedular view of income,[6] have been vigorous in finding many different types of income; thus state lottery winnings are taxable. In *Zarin* v. *Commissioner*[7] the taxpayer had borrowed $3.4 m of gambling chips, lost them all at the tables and then agreed to settle with the gambling house for $500,000. The court's decision that the taxpayer was not liable to tax on the $2.9 m debt forgiven is very controversial. However, the intellectual vigour with which the United States finds income is no greater than that with which they seek deductions—as the debates on the concept of "human capital" and the possible deduction of educational expenses show.[8]

7.1.2 By whom is income tax payable?

TA 1988, s. 1 makes it clear that income tax is paid by *individuals* at certain rates. However, basic rate tax is not confined to individuals which indicates, correctly, that income tax is also paid by persons or entities other than individuals. The principal other "persons" are trusts and estates in administration. Partnerships are now taxed on a transparent basis with each partner responsible for their own tax affairs. Companies resident in the UK usually pay corporation tax rather than income tax; however, non-resident companies may find themselves liable to income tax. Income tax also applies to shadowy entities called "bodies of persons". These are defined in s. 832, but the definition rarely applies; the concept should, therefore, be repealed.[9]

7.1.3 Rates of income tax

The income tax rates in force in 2000–2001[9a] are: (a) the "starting" rate (10%) applicable to taxable income between nil and £1,520; (b) the "basic" rate (22%) applicable to taxable income between £1,520 and £28,400; and (c) the "higher" rate applicable to taxable income above £28,400. This simple structure is complicated in two ways. The first is by reference to the taxpayer: as we have just seen, (a) and (c) apply only to individuals. The second is by reference to the type of income. Savings income (defined below at §7.7) is taxed at 10%, 20% (not 22%) or 40%;[10] however, dividends have their own regime and are taxed at 10% (Schedule F ordinary rate) and 32.5% (Schedule F upper rate).[11] For dividend/savings

[5] *FCT* v. *Myer Emporium Ltd.* (1987) 18 ATR 693, a case not cited in *McGuckian* but undoubtedly well known to Lord Cooke. On *Myer*, see Waincmyer (1994) 19 *Melbourne University LR* 997.

[6] See discussion by Bittker and Lokken, *Federal Taxation of Income, Estates and Gifts*, 5 vols. (Warren Gorman & Lamont, NY, 1989) op cit., §5.1; on lessons to be learned from US tax policy, see articles in (1998) 184 *Fiscal Studies*.

[7] 916 F 2d 110 (1990). This case generated much literature, among the best of which are Shaviro 45 *Tax Law Review* 215; Newman 50 *Tax Notes* 667; and Gunn 50 *Tax Notes* 893. See also Dodge, Johnson and Shaviro 45 *Tax Law Review* 677, 697, 707 respectively.

[8] On human capital, see Beer [1987] *BTR* 392; on US debate on human capital see, *inter alia*, Zelanak (1996) 51 *Tax Law Review* 1, discussing views of Kaplow (1994) 80 *Virginian Law Review* 1477; and response by Kaplow to Zelanak (1996) 51 *Tax Law Review* 35. The Kaplow-Zelanak debate is part of a wider debate over a consumption tax. See also Stephan (1984) 70 *Virginia LR* 1357. For UK work in relation to certain training costs, see Blundell, Dearden, Maghir, and Sianesi (1999) 20 *Fiscal Studies*.

[9] See Avery Jones [1991] *BTR* 453.

[9a] See TA 1988, s. 1(2) as amended by Income Tax (Indexation) Order SI 2000/806.

[10] TA 1988, s. 1A (1); on complications surrounding the 20% savings rate, see [1996] *BTR* 342.

[11] TA 1988, s. 1B.

income accruing to trusts, see chapter 29 below, and for dividends savings income accruing to estates, see chapter 30 below. This structure is an improvement on the previous structure which had become so complicated by the start of 1999–2000 that it had to be altered by FA 2000 with retroactive effect (see below at §7.7.2).[12]

7.2 The Schedular System

7.2.1 The Schedules

The UK has a Schedular system of income tax. TA 1988 listed six Schedules (A–F); but only four still exist.

Schedule A (TA 1988, s. 15) taxes the annual profits or gains arising in respect of rent and similar payments from land in the UK. "Profits" includes some premiums. The tax is calculated on the balance of receipts minus allowable deductions.[13].Receipts and expenses are recognised in accordance with normal accountancy principles. The rent charged is that attributable to the tenant's occupation during the tax year. This may mean disregarding the dates when sums fall due or are paid and dissecting payments for a period which straddles the beginning or end of a tax year. Rent from property outside the UK forms a second but separate aggregate and is taxed under Schedule D, Case V.[14]

Schedule B (TA 1988, s. 16) was repealed in 1988.[15] This Schedule taxed the occupation of certain woodlands in the UK on a special value (a form of imputed income).

Schedule C (TA 1988, s. 17) was repealed in 1996 as part of the simplification of the tax treatment of interest; interest formerly within Schedule C now comes within Schedule D, Case III.

Schedule D (TA 1988, s. 18) taxes annual profits or gains which fall into one or other of its six Cases:

—Case I taxes profits or gains arising from any trade;
—Case II taxes the profits or gains arising from a profession or vocation;
—Case III taxes interest, annuities and other annual payments together with discounts and those dividends from public revenue which previously fell within Schedule C;
—Case IV taxes residents on the profits or gains arising from securities outside the UK;
—Case V taxes residents on the profits or gains arising from possessions out of the UK;
—Case VI taxes any annual profits or gains not falling under any other Case or Schedule.

This list, set out in TA 1988 s. 18(3), has to be read in conjunction with s. 18 (1), especially when dealing with international matters. For corporation tax, Case IV was repealed and Case III rewritten in 1996.

Schedule E (TA 1988, s. 19) taxes emoluments from an office or employment; the tax is usually collected by PAYE. This Schedule has three Cases according to international factors.

Schedule F (TA 1988, s. 20) taxes distributions by companies resident in the UK, the tax is due on the dividends of the year of assessment and, for most taxpayers, is in effect, taxed at source.

[12] A 10% rate now applies to savings income under FA 2000, s. 32; previously, savings had been taxed at 20% and 40%, and the 10% rate introduced in 1999–2000 was not available for such income. On retroactivity see s. 32(4).

[13] TA 1988, ss 21, 21A, 21B.

[14] TA 1988, s. 65A, added by FA 1998.

[15] The charge to tax under this Schedule was abolished with effect from 6 April 1988 subject to transitional provisions in FA 1988, s. 65, Sch. 6.

Buried in these provisions are rules on the territorial scope of the income tax. Schedule D, Cases IV and V (and parts of Schedule E) charge residents on their worldwide income; the other parts of Schedule E as well as Schedule A and D Cases I–III and VI charge non-residents on their income arising within the UK.

7.2.2 The system

Income tax is one tax; each Schedule has its own rules for computation of income. At one time the Schedules had different dates for payment, different rates and different administrations. A Schedular system must be distinguished from a global definition of income. In recent years some global systems have adopted Schedular features.[16] Thus, the Nordic countries have moved from a global system based on progressive rates to a Schedular system with a progressive tax applying to most types of income, but with investment income and capital gains taxed at low uniform rates with restrictions on deductibility of passive losses.[16a]

Features

The Schedular system has three features which differentiate it from a pure global system:

(a) Income. If an income receipt does not fall within any Schedule it is not taxable.[17]

(b) Rules exclusive. Where income falls within a Schedule it falls to be computed in accordance with the rules in that Schedule and no other. As Lord Radcliffe has said:[18]

> "Before you can assess a profit to tax you must be sure that you have properly identified its source or other description according to the correct Schedule; but once you have done that, it is obligatory that it should be charged, if at all, under that Schedule and strictly in accordance with the Rules that are there laid down for assessments under it. It is a necessary consequence of this conception that the sources of profit in the different Schedules are mutually exclusive."

In *Fry* v. *Salisbury House Estate Ltd.*[19] a company received rents from unfurnished offices in a building. The company also provided services for the offices, such as heating and cleaning, at an additional charge. The rents were chargeable under Schedule A, although the basis of assessment at that time was not simply the rents minus costs of maintenance but the annual value of the premises, which were revalued every five years, minus a statutory allowance for running costs, an example of imputed income. The company agreed that its profits from the ancillary services fell within Schedule D, Case I, but resisted the Revenue's argument that it was liable to tax on the *actual* rent received under Schedule D, Case I rather on than the *notional* imputed rent charged under Schedule A. The Revenue conceded that it would have to make an allowance in computing tax under Schedule D, Case I for the tax due under Schedule A.[20] The House of Lords found for the company. Although the company could be said to be carrying on a trade and, therefore, fell within Schedule D, Case I, the Schedules were mutually exclusive and each Schedule was dominant over its own subject matter. The charge under Schedule A therefore excluded the charge on the excess rent under Schedule D, Case I.

[16] See Ault *et al.*,153–7, 245–8.
[16a] See below n. 108.
[17] *Graham* v. *Green* [1925] 2 KB 37, 9 TC 309.
[18] *Mitchell and Edon* v. *Ross* [1961] 3 All ER 49, 55, 40 TC 11, 61.However, see Kerridge [1980] *BTR* 233.
[19] [1930] AC 432, 15 TC 266. Decision reversed by FA 1940, ss 13–18.
[20] See *Russell* v. *Aberdeen Town and County Bank* (1888) 2 TC 321.

However, although the Schedules are mutually exclusive, the Cases within each Schedule are not; the Revenue may choose the Case. Therefore an insurance company may be taxed either under Schedule D, Case I on its profit or on its investment income minus management expenses.[21] Such choices will not often arise. The choice is reflected in the self-assessment process: taxpayers make their returns on the basis they select but the Revenue may require them to produce information to support it—and may overrule the choice.[22]

(c) Losses. Losses arising under one Schedule may not necessarily be set against a profit under another; losses attracts only such relief as each set of rules allows. Some types of loss can be set off against *general* income of the same or preceding (but not later) year(s), notably Schedule D, Cases I and II.[23] However, losses under Schedule A and Schedule D, Case VI are given relief only by being rolled forward to be set off against the income of later years taxed under the same Schedule or Case.[24] Losses under Schedule D, Cases I and II, which have not been used up by being set off against general income of the same and following year(s), may then be rolled forward indefinitely, but only against profits of that trade.

Businesses in the financial sector often had their profits taxed under Schedule D, Case I. However, as with insurance companies it was, in theory, open to the Revenue, for example, to insist on interest received being taxed under Schedule D, Case III instead. This could have significant effects if the business was trying to use trading losses from past years or a foreign tax credit, which could be set only against income of the trade and so not against Schedule D, Case III income. The segregation of interest income to Schedule D, Case III led to the loss or tax credit not being available until a later period or being lost completely. Today, these consequence do not apply for corporation tax and there are few financial businesses outside the corporate sector.

7.3 The UK Concept of Income

Apart from the Schedular system which, as already seen, excludes any receipt not coming within one or other of the Schedules, the UK has two important principles limiting the scope of the tax: "capital" and the "source".

7.3.1 Capital

Capital is not income. The Schedules include the wide phrase "annual profits" and contain, in Schedule D, Case VI, a residuary case to cover receipts not caught by the other Schedules and Cases. However, the courts have construed that phrase in a limited way—generally, profits are income only if they possess a quality of recurrence[25]—and have confined Case VI to profits similar to those caught by the other Schedule and Cases (see below at §28.1).

The courts' decision to exclude capital is entirely understandable. When income tax was first introduced in 1799, not only were various existing forms of capital already subject to other taxes, but there was also a substantial area of law, that of trusts, where a very sharp

[21] *Simpson* v. *Grange Trust Ltd.* [1935] AC 422, 427, 19 TC 231, 251, HL. *per* Lord Wright.

[22] TMA 1970 s. 28A(7A) and for corporation tax, FA 1998, Sch. 18, para. 84.

[23] TA 1988, ss 380, 381.

[24] TA 1988, ss 379A, 392.

[25] *Moss Empires Ltd.* v. *IRC* [1937] AC 785, 21 TC 264. This does not prevent single payments from being caught, e.g. the single commission paid in *Ryall* v. *Hoare* (1923) 8 TC 521 and taxed under Schedule D, Case VI.

distinction between income and capital receipts had been drawn.[26] Further, in so far as business was concerned, Adam Smith had drawn the distinction between fixed and circulating capital, and between income profits and capital gains. The fundamental nature of the distinction between income and capital does not mean that it is easy to apply.[27] Today, income tax is supplemented by a capital gains tax (on distinctions, see below at §§32.7, 47.3.1).

Although the legislature has occasionally intervened to tax capital receipts, e.g. certain premiums on leases (see below at §25.5), the proceeds of certain life assurance policies, (see below at §55.5) and golden handshakes (see below at §14.5), the basic distinction between income and capital is central to the system. The reason for this acceptance by the legislature is probably the high value placed by the legislature on the requirement of certainty in the sense of enforceability or practicality, even at the expense of equity. It also explains the great insistence on the system of deduction of tax at source, a system which has, at one time or another, covered almost all payments other than the profits of a trade or profession, and short interest. The legislature was, for a long time, reluctant to tax payments which could not conveniently be taxed at source.[28] As a consequence of these rules, non-taxable receipts include not only capital gains, but also gambling winnings,[29] instalments of capital (see below at §27.4.5), most gifts (but see below at §§14.4, 21.4), including the remission of a debt (but see below at §23.1.2) and loans.[30]

7.3.2 The source

Interpretation of the Schedules is governed by the doctrine of the source. The courts have held that every piece of income must have a source,[31] and reports abound with references to "fruit and tree".[32]

The doctrine has been applied to exempt certain types of income which clearly ought to have been taxed. These payments escaped tax because, as income tax was an annual tax, it followed that not only must the income arise within the tax year but the source must also exist in that tax year. Hence, it was decided that: (1) post-cessation receipts of a trade were not taxable (see below at §23.1); (2) where a person is taxed on a remittance basis and money is brought into this country in a year in which its source does not exist, no tax is payable; and (3) payments made after an employment has ceased but for services rendered as an employee cannot be attributed retrospectively to the years of service.[33] Of these, (1)

[26] Financial markets had not yet reached a point at which to stretch the credibility of the distinction.

[27] For example, Lord Macdonald in *California Copper Syndicate Ltd.* v. *Harris* (1904) 5 TC 159, 165

[28] See, e.g., RC 1920, §156; both graduation and differentiation were (rightly) regarded as inconsistent with deduction at source: Mallett, *British Budgets 1887–1913*, 278.

[29] *Graham* v. *Green* (1925) 9 TC 309. The gambling industry pays many taxes, but the exemption for an individual winner is a remarkable exception to the principle of taxing according to ability to pay. For treatment in some other countries, see Ault *et al.*, above at n. 16, 185. The present position was defended by the Royal Commission on Gambling, Cmnd 6643 (1976), esp. 31. On taxation of gambling more generally, see IFS Green Budget 2000, §7.3.

[30] A genuine loan is not income. It could, in theory, be treated as a receipt when received, and as a deduction when repaid, but this would be administratively burdensome and would give rise to opportunities for income averaging or splitting. Loans may be taxed if made by a close company to a participator. See also *Jacobs* v. *IRC* (1925) 10 TC 1; *Clayton* v. *Gothorp* [1971] 2 All ER 1311, 47 TC 168; *Esdaile* v. *IRC* (1936) 20 TC 700; and *Stoneleigh Products Ltd.* v. *Didd* (1948) 30 TC 1. For a conceptual analysis of below-market loans, see Hadari [1995] *BTR* 557.

[31] For example, *Brown* v. *National Provident Institution* [1921] 2 AC 222, 246, 8 TC 57, 89, *per* Lord Atkinson; and *Leeming* v. *Jones* [1930] 1 KB 279, 297, 15 TC 333, 349–50, *per* Lord Hanworth. See also, e.g., *Stainer's Executors* v. *Purchase* [1951] 2 All ER 1071, 32 TC 367; and *Carson* v. *Cheyney's Executors* [1958] 3 All ER 573, 38 TC 240.

[32] For comparative treatment, see Krever (1990) 7 *Australian Tax Forum* 191.

[33] *Bray* v. *Best* [1989] 1 All ER 969, [1989] STC 159, HL.

and (3) have been reversed by statute, and (2) has less significance because the remittance basis has been drastically reduced. However, the principle remains.

7.4 Timing[34]

7.4.1 Importance of timing

The issue of timing is important for several obvious reasons:

(1) Income tax is charged as income of a year of assessment, i.e. income from 6 April 2000 to 5 April 2001 is brought into the taxpayer's self-assessment for 2000–01. The taxpayer must therefore include all such income, omitting income attributable to other years, and will be liable to interest surcharge and penalties for incorrect submission.
(2) The law may be changed so that the tax treatment will differ according to whether the payment is income of year 1 or year 2.[35]
(3) A relief may be geared to a maximum percentage of a person's total income for that year—as with certain pension plan contributions.[36]
(4) The Revenue must generally issue any discovery assessments within six years of the end of the chargeable period to which it relates.[37]
(5) The effective rate of tax may vary according to the time it becomes chargeable. This is because the taxpayer's marginal rate of tax may vary from one year to the next (a matter of less importance after the reduction of rates in 1988) and because UK tax law still contains no general averaging provision.
(6) In general, the value at the time the income arises is relevant for tax purposes; subsequent changes in value are usually ignored.[38]
(7) Reliefs may be available against the income of a particular year.[39]

Non-receipt means no income

The issue of timing is relevant to a more subtle matter, namely the non-correlation of the rules with regard to receipts with those for expenses. One cannot be taxed on income one does not acquire; however once income has been acquired, a deduction for paying it back will be allowed only if it is permitted by the deduction rules appropriate to the Schedule. Therefore preventing the income from arising will avoid tax, whereas a receipt followed by a disposal will not. In *Way* v. *Underdown (No. 2)*[40] an insurance agent gathered in a premium and subsequently paid back to the insurer an amount equal to his commission on the premium. It was held that since there was no obligation to repay he could not deduct the

[34] See also the now dated account in [1982] *BTR* 23.
[35] As in *Strick* v. *Longsdon* (1953) 34 TC 528 (special contribution for 1947–1948).
[36] TA 1988, ss 619, 640.
[37] TMA 1970, s. 34; income tax seems to have been avoided in *Heasman* v. *Jordan* [1954] 3 All ER 101, 35 TC 518. This leads to obvious avoidance whereby a special bonus would be declared for one year, more than six years before the declaration. As a result legislation introduced what became TMA 1970, s. 35 (now superseded).
[38] This is of crucial importance when dealing with payments in kind or payments in foreign currency. For authority in the latter instance, see *Payne* v. *Deputy Federal Commr of Taxation* [1936] AC 497, [1936] 2 All ER 793; and *Greig* v. *Ashton* [1956] 3 All ER 123, 36 TC 581.
[39] As in *Parkside Leasing Ltd.* v. *Smith* [1985] STC 63, 58 TC 282.
[40] [1975] 2 All ER 1064, [1975] STC 425, 49 TC 648, CA.

sum in computing his taxable profits; he was therefore taxable on the commission. However, had he simply not collected the premium in full in the first place he may well not have been taxed.

7.4.2 General timing rules

Timing questions depend first on whether accounting principles are adopted. If they are, as in Schedule A and Schedule D, Cases I and II, then those principles must be considered. Where accounting principles are not relevant, a two-stage process is adopted. The first stage is to ask whether tax law treats the income as arising when it falls due or only when it is paid. The general answer given by UK cases is that an assessment cannot generally be made until the payment has been received. The second stage asks whether the payment, once received, may be backdated or, to use the customary terminology, "related back" and be treated as income of the period when it became due.[41] However, this backdating does not occur very often. Usually, the payment is taxable only when paid and is then treated as income of the year of receipt, summarised in the much-abused *dictum* that "receivability without receipt is nothing".[42] This has been applied to the payment of arrears of interest causing payments for six years to be treated as the taxable income of one year.[43] Precise rules cannot be stated owing to the dearth of authority. Statute now provides that there can be no relating back for remuneration falling within Schedule E;[44] the income is taxed when received or when due for payment, whichever is the earlier.[45]

Receipt?

What amounts to receipt? Where trustees or personal representatives receive income, that receipt may be treated as receipt by the beneficiaries, as may receipt of income by an agent for a principal or by one partner for the other.[46] It has been held, however, that the mere receipt of a cheque is not a receipt of income, even if drawn on the Bank of England.[47] Where a taxpayer, T, directs payment to a third party, so that T never actually receives payment, the economic control shown by the direction is still sufficient to amount to receipt.[48] The crediting of an account, which act enures to the benefit of the account-owner, will also be a receipt,[49] as will a payment made direct to a third party to discharge the taxpayer's

[41] This applies to payments falling within TA 1988, s. 835; see *Whitworth Park Coal Co. Ltd.* v. *IRC* [1959] 3 All ER 703, 38 TC 531. It used to apply to payments falling within Schedule E, but see now below at §14.2.

[42] Rowlatt J. in *Leigh* v. *IRC [*1928] 1 KB 73, 77, 11 TC 590, 595.

[43] *Leigh* v. *IRC* ibid. (Schedule D, Case IV). Concessionary relief is available for retrospective increases in such foreign pensions (ESC A55). A completely different approach is adopted for interest payments for corporation tax: see FA 1996 and below at §48.1.

[44] FA 1989, ss 36–45, see above at §6.29.

[45] TA 1988, s. 202A; FA 1989, s. 37(1).

[46] *IRC* v. *Lebus' Executors* (1946) 27 TC 136, 147.

[47] *Parkside Leasing Ltd.* v. *Smith* [1985] STC 63, 58 TC 282. By contrast, a payment in respect of tax to the Revenue is treated as occurring when the cheque was received by the Revenue provided the cheque is paid on first presentation (TMA 1970, s. 70A).

[48] Lord Hansworth M.R. in *Dewar* v. *IRC* [1935] 2 KB 351, 367, 19 TC 561, 577.

[49] *Dunmore* v. *McGowan* [1978] 2 All ER 85, [1978] STC 217; discussed at [1982] *BTR* 23, the point there taken being approved in *Macpherson* v. *Bond* [1985] STC 678. *Dunmore* v. *McGowan* was followed in *Peracha* v. *Miley* [1990] STC 512, CA (see below at §26.1.2), but distinguished in *Girvan* v. *Orange Personal Communication Services Ltd.* [1998] STC 567.

obligations to that third party.[50] Where a payer is under a duty to deduct the recipient's tax on that income, the sum withheld is treated as having been received by the taxpayer.[51]

Remittances

Certain foreign income is taxable not because it has accrued but because—and so only when—it is remitted to the UK (see below at §60.4).

Preceding year and current year

The preceding year basis of assessment, now obsolete, survived until 1996–1997. It may therefore be necessary to consider it in order to understand a case relating to those years. It did not apply to corporation tax.

Usually, the income for the year of assessment is that arising, in the sense just discussed, within the year from 6 April to 5 April next—the current year basis. Therefore income arising in 2000–01 is taxed as income of 2000–01. Under the preceding year system, however, the income for 1999–00 would have been taxable in 2000–01, while income for 2000–01 would have been taxable in 2001–02. This way of putting it is slightly inaccurate. The theory was that the source was taxed on its statutory income for the year of assessment, the preceding year's income being simply the measure of that income. As Rowlatt J. once put it, "You do not tax the years by which you measure; you tax the year in which you tax and you measure by the years to which you refer".[52]

Under the preceding year basis the income was taxed according to the rates in force in the year of assessment, and not those in the year when the income actually arose. It followed that the amount taken as income for the year of assessment might bear no relation to the income actually arising during that period; if there was a sharp drop in income from the source, the tax payable during the year might even exceed the income from that source. The system gave rise to many problems and caused many complexities in the tax legislation.[53] The biggest objection to the old system was that when it was applied to a business, the total profit taxed was not the total profit made.[54] The repeal was beneficial and overdue (but not well executed). Some may see a very faint echo of the old system in the rules directing payment of tax on account in two instalments by reference to the previous year's income.[55]

7.5 Exemptions

Certain types of payment or persons are specifically exempt from liability to income tax by legislation or concession. The following list is not exhaustive, but indicates the types of exemption made. references to sections are to those of the TA 1988.

(1) *Welfare payments.* S. 617 excludes certain social security benefits, e.g. invalidity benefit and analogous payments by foreign countries to UK residents (ESC A24). On housing

[50] *Cf. Salter* v. *Minister of National Revenue* (1947) 2 DTC 918.
[51] TA 1988, s. 349.
[52] *Fry* v. *Burma Corpn Ltd.* (1930) 15 TC 113, 120 followed most recently in *Moore* v. *Austin* [1985] STC 673.
[53] See the third edition of this book, paras 5.12 and 5.13, and *Revenue Consultation Document on a Simpler System for the Self Employed,* discussed by Shipwright [1992] *BTR* 12.
[54] This was largely because of special rules governing the beginning and ending of the business or other source.
[55] TMA 1970, s. 59A; see chapter 4 above.

grants paid by local authorities, see s. 578. Concessions apply to adoption allowances (ESC A40) and certain pensions for disabled employees (ESC A62). Interest on damages payable for personal injuries and annuities (including the assignment of such annuities) payable under structured settlements of claims for such injuries are exempt under ss 329, 329A and 329B (for foreign courts, see ESC A30). Also exempt are annuities and pensions payable to victims of National Socialist persecution under the laws of West Germany or Austria (s. 330) and New Deal payments to the over-50s, etc FA 2000 s. 84.

(2) *Employment-related payments.* Exempt under this category are redundancy payments (s. 579), the first £30,000 of compensation for loss of employment (s. 148), long service awards, luncheon vouchers, miners coal, and profit-related pay (now obsolete).

(3) *State service.* Ss 315–318 make exempt from income tax war widows, pensions, wounds and disability pensions, allowances, bounties and gratuities paid for additional service in the armed forces and annuities and additional pensions to holders of gallantry awards. Other state service exemptions are foreign service allowances for civil servants (s. 319), grants under the European Assembly (Pay and Pensions) Act 1979, s. 3 (s. 190) and certain related payments together with similar payments for Ministers and MPs, etc.

(4) *Savings.* The tax system grants special tax privileges to savings, see Part V but see also compensation for mis-sold pensions (FA 1996, s. 148), annuities under certain policies (ss 580A, 580B) and certain bonds when held by non-residents FA 1996 s. 154.

(5) *Education and training.* Scholarship income arising from a scholarship held by a person receiving full-time instruction at a university, college, school or other educational establishment is exempt from income tax (s. 331) (see also SP 4/86, revised in 1992 on sandwich courses, the need for revision arising as a result of *Walters* v. *Tickner* [1992] STC 343). Certain education allowances under the Overseas Aid Act Schemes (ESC A44) and interest attached to certain repayments of student loans to the student (s. 331A, added by FA 1999) are also exempt. See also below §§10.10 and 15.5.

(6) *Exempt persons.* Ss 505–514 provide reliefs for, among others, charities, the British Museum and Natural History Museums, scientific research organisations, agricultural societies and the Atomic Energy Authority.

(7) *Exempt people—international.* There are exemptions for various Commonwealth and foreign representatives (ss 320–322),[56] various payments to members of visiting forces (s. 323), the International Maritime Satellite Organisation (s. 515) and certain other international organisations (s. 582A). Special rules also apply to government securities held by non-resident central banks (s. 516) and the issue departments of the Reserve Bank of India and the State Bank of Pakistan (s. 517).

(8) *Government.* There are also exemption for local authorities and health service bodies (ss 519, 519A). The Crown is not liable to tax unless statute otherwise provides;[57] therefore, the private estates of the Crown are subject to tax.[58]

[56] See Morris [1991] *BTR* 207 and exchange of views by Adderley and Morris on a stamp duty point at [1992] *BTR* 122. The Government must be reocgnised by the UK: *Caglar* v. *Billingham* [1996] STC (SCD) 150.

[57] TA 1988, s. 829; on royal taxation see Pearce and Crump [1994] *BTR* 635; and Bartlett [1983] *BTR* 99.

[58] Crown Private Estates Act 1862. There is much background material in Philip Hall, *Royal Fortune* (Bloomsbury, 1992), summarised in *The Economist*, 25 January 1992, 35.

7. 6 Prohibited Deductions

The legislation may provide that certain sums are not to be deductible in computing income under various heads. There are now three such provisions. TA 1988, s. 577A provides very succinctly that in computing income for Schedule A or D no deduction shall be made for any expenditure incurred in making a payment which constitutes the commission of a criminal offence. Examples are bribes contrary to the Prevention of Corruption Acts and payments contrary to the Prevention of Terrorism Acts.[59] Perhaps oddly, s. 577A does not apply to either Schedule E or CGT. These examples are much narrower than the potential ambit of the section, which seems to encompass any act amounting to the offence of aiding and abetting the commission of an offence by another. Presumably, a criminal offence means an act or omission which is an offence under the criminal law of some relevant part of the UK rather than under some foreign jurisdiction. Expenditure incurred in making a payment induced by blackmail is also barred.[60]

Of the other two provisions the older relates to the non-deduction of war risk premiums and payments for war injuries to employees.[61] The more recent provision deals with business entertainment expenses under Schedules A, D and E (see below at §22.7). Since Schedule F allows no deduction in any case, this makes the prohibition effective for all parts of income tax.[62]

7.7 Classification of Income (I): Savings, Schedule F and Ordinary Income

7.7.1 What is savings income?

"Savings income" consists of (a) certain types of income chargeable under Schedule D, Case III (principally interest and discounts) and any equivalent foreign income[63] and (b) any income falling into Schedule F or any equivalent foreign income.[64] "Equivalent foreign income" is equivalent to a description of savings income but which arises from securities or other possessions out of the United Kingdom.

Specific exclusions

Despite the breadth of (a) above, certain types of income are specifically excluded. These are: (i) any annuity—other than a purchased life annuity; (ii) any other annual payment that is not interest; (iii) any rent received in respect of mines and quarries, which is brought into Schedule D, Case III by TA 1988, s. 119; (iv) any overseas income that is assessed on a remittance basis; and (v) income from a foreign estate charged under the terms of TA 1988, s. 695(4)(b) or 696(6).[65] In addition, it is provided that income treated as arising on a

59 Inland Revenue Press Release, 11 June 1993, (1993) *Simon's Weekly Tax Intelligence* 957.
60 TA 1988, s. 577A(1A).
61 Ibid., ss 586, 587.
62 Ibid., s. 577.
63 Ibid., s. 1A(3).
64 Ibid., s. 1A(2)(b), (5).
65 Ibid., s. 1A(2)(a).

"chargeable event" when a withdrawal is made from a non-qualifying life assurance policy[66] is not within the definition of "savings income". Rent from land charged under Schedule A and equivalent foreign income is similarly not savings income.

7.7.2 Rates for taxing savings income

Special rates have applied to savings income since 1996–1997. When this is received by a taxpayer (T) whose total income is less than the upper limit of the basic rate band,[67] savings income, other than dividend income, is taxed at the starting rate of 10% and then the lower rate of 20% only (not at the basic rate of 22%), and then at 40%. In determining whether savings income falls within the basic rate band, it is treated as the highest part of an individual's income (other than termination payments and income arising on certain chargeable events).[68]

Where T's other income exceeds the upper limit of the basic rate band, savings income is assessed at the higher rate of 40%.[69] If it has been received under deduction of tax at 20% a further 20% must be accounted for in the taxpayer's self-assessment. Suppose that T has Schedule A income equivalent to any reliefs, Schedule E income of £16,000 and interest of income of £4,000 gross (£3,200 net of tax withheld at 20%). T's interest income will be taxed at 20%. If the Schedule E income rises to £36,000 the interest income is treated as the top slice of T's income and so liable to tax at 40%; T will have to pay a further 20% (£800) so that the interest will have borne tax of £1,600 in total.

Where T's other income is less than the upper limit of the basic rate band, but the addition of savings income takes the taxpayer above that band, tax is charged at the lower rate on the amount of income required to bring the rate up to the upper limit of the basic rate band, and tax at the higher rate is charged on the excess. Thus, if T's Schedule E income were £26,400, £2,000 of the interest payment would be charged at 20% and £2,000 at 40%.

If payments are required to be made under deduction of tax, the lower rate of tax is applied where the payment is savings income in the hands of the recipient.[70] This explains why the 10% starting rate was not initially applied to savings income in 1999; it relieved the Revenue of the task of repaying tax. Although this was charged retrospectively, history suggests that very few of the 2.5 m taxpayers will actually claim back the £30 due to them.[71]

Taxation of Schedule F income. Dividends and other distributions, are also savings income. Qualifying distributions carry a tax credit at 1/9th,[72] which is not generally repayable.[73] Two rates of tax are applied to such income: the Schedule F ordinary rate of 10%,[74] and the Schedule F upper rate of 32.5%. To achieve consistency, higher rate taxpayers are taxed at 32.5%. This, numerically, gives the taxpayer the same income net of tax as a liability at 40% with a tax credit of 20% which was the basis of taxation, for earlier years.[75] This two-rate tax structure applies also to equivalent foreign income except that there will be no tax credit.

[66] Ibid., s. 540.

[67] £28,400 for 2000–01.

[68] TA 1988, s. lA(5), (6), inserted by FA 1996, s. 73.

[69] 40% for 2000–2001, TA 1988, s.1(2)(b), applied by s. 1A(1)(b).

[70] TA 1988, s. 4(1A) inserted by FA 1996, s. 73(2).

[71] IFS Green Budget, 2000, 74; on retroactivity see FA 2000, s. 32(4).

[72] F (No. 2) A 1997, s. 30(3), inserting TA 1988, s. 231(1A).

[73] See below §46.3; the exceptions are ISAs etc. and sometimes under a double taxation agreement.

[74] TA 1988, s. 1B.

[75] Ibid.; for worked example, see Inland Revenue Press Release, 2 July 1997, para. 16, (1997) *Simon's Weekly Tax Intelligence* 903.

Suppose that T has Schedule A income equivalent to any reliefs, Schedule E income of £16,000, and receives dividends of £3,600 plus credit of £400, i.e. £4,000 gross. T's Schedule F income is taxed at 10%. If the Schedule E income rises to £36,000 instead of £16,000, the dividend income is treated as the top slice of T's income and so liable to tax at 32.5%; T will have to pay a further 22.5% (£900), so that the dividend income will have borne tax of £1,300 in total.

Problems

(1) What happens if T has both ordinary savings income and Schedule F income? Here the problem arises as one nears the basic rate limit and one has to decide which is the top slice, as where T has Schedule A income equivalent to any reliefs, Schedule E income of £24,400, receives gross interest of £4,000 and gross dividend of £4,000. The dividend is treated as the top slice, and £900 extra tax must be found; if the interest income had been the top slice T would have had to find an extra £800.

(2) What happens at the bottom of the income scale?[76] This is where the absence of any repayment claim makes a substantial difference. Suppose that T has state pension income of £4,000 and £2,000 gross of other income. If that other income consists of interest, £400 will have been withheld at source and T will recover it from the Revenue; if it consists of dividends the credit will be £200 but T will be unable to reclaim it from the Revenue.

(3) Dividend or bonus; bottom slices and top slices. The question whether to pay money out by dividend or a Schedule E bonus is always complex (see below at §45.7) . However, the present rules provide one further twist. Suppose that T has savings income equal to the basic rate limit (£16,400 interest and £12,000 dividends). If no other income accrues to T in that year all the income falls below the basic rate limit and there will be no further tax to pay. The company is proposing to pay out £10,000 either as bonus or gross dividend. If the bonus is paid, tax will become due. However, the effect of these rules is that the bonus becomes the bottom slice of the income and the dividend becomes the top slice of income; this means that £10,000 of the dividend income is taxed at the special Schedule F upper rate of 32.5%, with a tax credit equivalent to 10%, while the bonus can use the starting rate of 10% for the first £1,520 and the 22% rate will be applied to the £8,480.[77]

For a (historical) explanation of how such a complex system came into existence, see §12.9.

7.8 Classification of Income (II): Earned and Investment Income

7.8.1 Importance

The distinction between earned income and investment income is important for retirement annuity and personal pension relief calculations, which are, at least until 2001, confined to earned income from certain sources (and cannot be used for investment income or capital

[76] I gratefully acknowledge the use of a paper presented by H. Wyn Jones at a CIOT conference in October 1999.
[77] Ibid.

gains)[78] and are used for identifying certain income of husband and wife.[79] The distinction is not the same as that in §7.7 above, i.e. between savings and other income for tax rate purposes; thus, income from land will be investment income, but is not savings income. The UK system has made greater use of the distinction in the past, as three examples show:

(1) Until 1984 investment income was taxed more heavily than earned income.[80] From 1973 to 1984 this was achieved by a device known as the additional rate;[81] in 1983–1984 this was charged on that part of an individual's total income wehich consisted of investment income in excess of £7,100.[82]
(2) From 1973 to 1990, when joint taxation of spouses was the rule, a wife could elect to be taxed separately from her husband in respect of her earned income, but not her investment income.
(3) For a far longer period, also ending in 1990, the distinction was also important for the wife's earned income relief.

The most common types of investment income are rent, interest and dividends. Income from furnished holiday accommodation is expressly treated as earned income.[83] Income arising under the new form of Schedule A is computed under trading profit principles but is not trading income; it remains investment income.

7.8.2 Definitions

Investment income is that which is not earned income. The question whether income is earned is one of law.[84] Earned income is defined in three main categories.[85]

Category 1 is any income arising in respect of any remuneration from any office or employment including pensions, superannuation or other allowances, deferred pay or compensation for loss of office. Income is earned within this rule if it is a reward for services. This means that any income within Schedule E will be earned. In *Dale* v. *IRC*[86] annuity payments to a trustee "so long as he acts as trustee" were held by the House of Lords to be earned income. In that case the trustee was to receive the payments; the amount and value of the work actually done was irrelevant.[87] The Revenue argued that since a trustee was not entitled to remuneration for his services as distinct from the reimbursement of expenses, the annuity was a conditional gift. However, the House of Lords held that the income was earned since the condition of the annuity was compliance with the testator's condition of serving as a trustee.

Dividends have been held to be earned income provided they are a reward for services; however, this was before the new Schedule F was introduced.[88] In *White* v. *Franklin*[89] the

[78] TA 1988, ss 623(2), 644. Technically, these sections use identical words rather than referring to s. 833(4) as such.
[79] Ibid., s, 282 A(4A) earned income cannot fall within s. 282 A.
[80] FA 1971, s. 32(1) (repealed by TA 1988, s. 844, Sch. 31); see *Ang* v. *Parrish* [1980] 2 All ER 790, [1980] STC 341 and see below at §31.1).
[81] Before 1970 the "standard rate" of income tax applied to all "income" while "earned income" attracted a special relief.
[82] F (No. 2) A 1983, s. 1.
[83] TA 1988, s. 504.
[84] *Lawrance* v. *Hayman* [1976] STC 227, 51 TC 376.
[85] TA 1988, s. 833(4); the list is supplemented in s. 833(5), (6).
[86] [1953] 2 All ER 671, 34 TC 468.
[87] 34 TC 468, 493, *per* Lord Normand.
[88] TA 1988, s. 832 does not mention Schedule F income and s. 20 prevents any Schedule F income from falling under another Schedule.
[89] [1965] 1 All ER 692, 42 TC 283, [1965] *BTR* 152.

taxpayer (T) was assistant managing director of a company. T's mother and brother settled 50% of the issued share capital to trust to pay the income to the taxpayer "so long as he shall be engaged in the management of the company", with remainder to the mother and others. It was held that his income from the trust was earned income. The Commissioners had found that the settlement had been made as an inducement to T to remain with the company, and so the income accrued to him *because*, and not simply *while*, he was an active director.[90] It was also important that the trust held a large block of shares in the employing company so that T's work would produce direct results. These, however, were matters of fact to support the inference that the purpose of the settlement was to keep T interested in the company, and were not simply an arrangement in a family settlement distributing income arising from family property to persons with certain qualifications.[91] This appears to be a borderline case.[92]

If a payment of income is not only in return for services but also for some other consideration, there can be no apportionment of the income so as to treat even a part of it as earned;[93] the question is one of the construction of the arrangement.

These allowances may be in respect of the past service of the particular individual (I), or of I's spouse or parent, or of any deceased person. An allowance paid to the child of a former employee is earned income of the child.

Category II is any income from any properly which is attached to or forms part of the employment of any office or employment of profit held by the individual. In *White* v. *Franklin* (above) an argument based on this provision was not pursued. The provision has remained unchanged since the days of the old Schedule A and its purpose may have been to treat as earned income the imputed income arising from beneficial occupation of property.[94] It may be applied to treat the benefit received by an employee for accommodation under TA 1988, s. 143 as earned income (see below at §15.3). Another example is dividend income from shares held under an employee participation scheme.[95]

Category III is any income which is charged under Schedule D and immediately derived by the individual from a trade, profession or vocation carried on by him as an individual or as a partner personally acting in the partnership.[96] The trade must have been carried on by the individual. In *Fry* v. *Shiels Trustees*[97] trustees legally owned and managed a business, the income of which was held for infant beneficiaries. It was held that the income was not earned since the profits were eared by the trustees and so by individuals who certainly did not own them. A trustee-beneficiary would, in such circumstances, presumably be allowed to treat the income as earned and would be allowed to keep the benefit. In a similar vein it has been held that income received as a name at Lloyds, i.e. as a member of a syndicate, was not "relevant earnings" for pension purposes; the taxpayers' activities, which mostly involved deciding with which syndicate he would place his money were preparatory to a trade which was, in fact, carried on by others on his behalf.[98]

[90] 42 TC 283, 284.

[91] [1965] 1 All ER 692, 699.42 TC 283, 297.

[92] See Vinelott J, in *O'Leary* v. *McKinlay* [1991] STC 42, 53.

[93] *Hale* v. *Shea* [1965] 1 All ER 155, 42 TC 260.

[94] This was introduced to protect the vicar's income from tithe rent charges on glebe land. 51st Report of Board of Inland Revenue, 1908 Cond 7572, p. 152.

[95] *Recknell* v. *IRC* [1952] 2 All ER 147, 33 TC 201.

[96] *Cf.* TA 1970, s. 122(2)(b) (repealed by FA 1974) and see the comments of Lindsay J. in *Koenigsberger* v. *Mellor* [1993] STC 408, 414.

[97] [1915] SC 159, 6 TC 583.

[98] *Koenigsberger* v. *Mellor* [1993] STC 408, 67 TC 280.

Further difficulties have arisen from the requirement that the profit must be derived immediately from the business, since this suggests that other profits equally taxable under one of these Schedules are not derived immediately, but only incidentally. An example is *Northend* v. *White, Leonard and Corbin Greener*[99] where interest accruing to a solicitor on money deposited at a bank on general deposit account was held to be investment income. The source was not the carrying-on of the profession but rather the loan deposit with the bank. This conclusion has been criticised.[100]

Today, income in the form of dividends will be earned income under this rule only if it falls outside Schedule F (because Schedule F excludes Schedule D, Case I[101]) and so cannot fall within any other Schedule. However, statute provides that where shares are held as trading assets, the dividends arising from those shares are now treated as part of the trading profits of the business and so outside Schedule F[102] and so can be earned income.

Category IV—others. Certain types of income are declared to be earned income. These include certain pensions,[103] social security benefits,[104] post-cessation receipts (see below at §23.4), income from the sale of patent rights for an invention actually devised by the taxpayer (see below at §24.11), and golden handshakes (see below at §14.5.4) and income from furnished holiday lettings (see below at §25.3.2).

Annuities to former partners or their widows or dependants are treated as earned income subject to certain limits.[105]

7.8.3 Policy: Differentiation

Differentiation, i.e. a higher tax on investment income as opposed to earned income, was abolished in 1984. This higher rate of tax had been part of the system since 1907, when it was introduced as an alternative to a wealth tax.[106] Clearly, investment income is heavily concentrated in the upper income groups,[107] but many retired people derive a substantial percentage of their income from investments. Today, the chaotic rate structure and the refusal to allow those exempt from income tax to recover the tax credit on dividends make for a very unclear picture when one tries to discover the extent to which differentiation is part of the system. In other countries, e.g. Sweden, the tax system has moved in a different direction, with normal progressive rates charged on earned income and a flat rate tax on investment income.[108]

[99] [1975] STC 317, 50 TC 121, the interest belonged to the solicitor thanks to Solicitors Act 1965, s. 8(2).

[100] The decision in *Northend* rests on a statement by Pennycuick J. in *Bucks* v. *Bowers* [1970] 2 All ER 202, 46 TC 267 which may only be a *dictum*; the decision in that case was later reversed by statute.

[101] TA 1988, s. 20; Schedule F was created in 1965. This was subject to FA 1971, s. 32(4) where such dividends earned income, but this was repealed in 1984.

[102] F (No. 2) A 1997, s. 24, which applied as from 2 July 1997.

[103] TA 1988, s. 133.

[104] Ibid., s. 617, but not for all purposes, e.g. ibid., ss 257, 287(2).

[105] TA 1988, s. 628.

[106] FA 1907, s. 19. Originally, differentiation was achieved by a special relief for earned income, but after 1973 the basic rate applied to earned income and an additional rate to investment income. See also The Meade Report 40, 317–318, Sandford, Willis and Ironside, *An Annual Wealth Tax*, esp. 17: 29.

[107] *Inland Revenue Statistics* (1999), Table 3.4; see also Royal Commission on Distribution of Income and Wealth, 7th Report, Cmnd 7595 (1979) 2: 51.

[108] Stevens (1996) EC *Tax Review* 6.

Reasons

(1) The basis on which the argument for differentiation was eventually put was the precariousness of industrial incomes. This would be more obvious at a time when family settlements were still the rule and wealth was expressed in terms of income rather than capital, as readers of novels by Jane Austen and Henry James will attest.
(2) The cost of obtaining investment income is less than the expense incurred in earning a living or even in terms of effort, irksomeness or merely sacrifice of leisure. The generous principles of deductions in computing profits under Schedule D, Cases I and II reduce the force of this argument just as the niggardly rules under Schedule E increase it.
(3) This rather more diffuse argument asserts that the possession of capital gives power and other advantages over and above those arising in the form of investment income.[109] However, the adoption of a wealth tax or, where wealth is acquired by succession, an inheritance tax may be preferable to a surcharge on income; if power is the criterion one should consider those aspects of society which give power without capital, especially through the Civil Service or political parties.
(4) A lower rate of tax on earned income offers some incentive to tax payers to stimulate personal effort. Estate duty, when introduced in 1894, was presented as a form of differentiation and a deferred income tax; the duty was not repealed when the relief for earned income was introduced.
(5) A surcharge would be a tax on leisure; this argument carries more conviction when the threshold is higher.

It may be noted that a political party (or government) wishing to charge all earned income to national insurance contributions may see little wrong in attaching a similar level of tax to investment income.

[109] The same point can be used against an expenditure tax: see, e.g. Jones 29 *St Louis LR*, 1155, 1170.

8

The Tax Unit

8.1 Introduction: The Tax Unit—Family or Individual

This topic is a battleground. As Apps points out:[1]

> "The taxation of the family is arguably the central issue in the analysis of reforms of the tax system. Families form by far the largest group of taxpayers, they earn the greatest share of income, and direct and indirect taxes on their income are the largest source of government revenue . . . All too often the debate is motivated by ideological commitment to reinforcing traditional gender roles within the family and to extending the gap between rich and poor. Much of the controversy surrounding reforms widely debated in recent years can be traced to the fact that they imply major changes of distribution of tax burden within and across families which are inconsistent with conventional equity and efficiency criteria for tax design."

It is important to note that the question whether the tax system should look to the family unit is separate from the question whether that unit should be based on the legal status of marriage.

Much of the debate has an air of grand theory about it. A different approach may be to break the debate down into different issues, some requiring an individual basis, others a family unit basis.[2] However, even this approach has problems of defining the unit, where the unit rather than the individual is to be taken into account.

The following chapter concentrates on income tax. Capital taxes still favour marriage. IHT gives exemptions for inter-spousal transfers, even when the parties are living apart. CGT directs that inter-spousal transfers shall be at such figure that neither gain nor loss accrues. However, this is confined to spouses living together and is not necessarily an advantage. Many taxes use the concept of connected or associated persons, with marriage always coming within these links of connection and association. Why different taxes should treat

[1] Apps, in Head and Krever (eds) (1996), ch. 3 at p. 81.

[2] For example Maloney (1989) 3 *Canadian Journal of Women and the Law* 182.

the family unit differently is unclear. One answer may be that pragmatism is preferred to high theory; a more likely explanation is simple muddle.

8.2 Current UK Income Tax Law

8.2.1 The tax unit

Individuals not spouses

The UK income tax for 2000–01 reflects the values of the recent age of extreme individualism tempered by a new wish to use the tax system to alleviate child poverty. The tax unit in the UK is the individual. Individual taxation took effect in 1990. From 1990 to 2000 marital status had one tax advantage—the married couple's allowance. However, that was removed with effect from 2000 as part of a shift in fiscal concern over legal status to children.

The reasons for the 1990 change to individual taxation are mostly self-evident. The changing role of women and an overdue recognition of their rights came to be combined with unease about defining the family unit to which any tax regime, whether favourable or unfavourable, should be applied.[3] The 1990 married couple's allowance was a somewhat dubious device to ensure that there were no losers as a result of the change; its value was steadily eroded by chancellors of both Conservative and Labour governments.[4] The increasing emphasis on the individual[5] and on doctrines of neutrality also played a part. Among the strands of these doctrines was the desirability of allowing spouses to act as independent persons when looking after their tax affairs, so affording a degree of privacy. Current rules allow a significant amount of income-splitting between spouses.

The introduction of the new credits for children reopened the issue of individual taxation. From the point of view of a policy geared to fairness and helping the lower paid, the needs of the family unit should have determined entitlement to credits. For reasons of expediency the eventual conclusion was a compromise. The rule governing the new children's tax credit (which begins in 2001) is that if the circumstances of one partner deprive that partner of entitlement to the credit then neither can claim it. This halfway house prevents the system from having to consider the resources of the unit as a whole. However, the working families tax credit (WFTC) takes account of family resources as a whole, establishing whether their income reaches the level at which phasing out should begin.

Children as individuals. Since the current system treats spouses as separate taxpayers it is no surprise that it treats parents and children also as separate. Permissible income-splitting between parents and minor children is much more restricted than between spouses. Today parents with children may claim the WFTC and, as from 2001, the Children's Tax Credit. Previously, tax reliefs for children were available, but these were abolished as a corollary of

[3] The change to the individual as the basis of tax was made by Nigel Lawson, who was Chancellor in Mrs Thatcher's third administration. His predecessor, Sir Geoffrey Howe, had wished to make the change (and had published a Green Paper on this in 1980—Cmnd 8093) but seems to have encountered resistance from Mrs Thatcher, perhaps because she thought that the idea came from Sir Geoffrey's wife, Elspeth: see Lawson, *The View from No. 11*, 881.

[4] On the period 1990–1997 see [1998] *BTR* 317, 339–40.

[5] Symbolic of these values is the change of terminology in certain CGT reliefs from "family" company, to "personal" company, e.g. TCGA 1992, ss 157, 163, as amended by FA 1993.

the introduction of the tax-free child benefit see §8.3.2. Now, it is government policy to try to merge the WFTC, the child tax credit and the still current child benefit into one.[6]

Child care expenses have not usually been deductible in the UK. However, they form an element of the WFTC. Relief has been available under American and Canadian law which allow deduction of actual costs on child care when a parent goes out to work. Such deductions are limited by maximum figures and by the age of the children. These limits are an attempt to distinguish the expense of going out to work from mere personal expenses—the relief is designed to meet the needs of working parents and not simply to subsidise domestic service. The precedent of the relief is important because the expense is incurred for a mixture of business and personal reasons. If the expense is allowed, why should relief not be given to handicapped persons who incur expenses in riding to work by taxi, to professional people who incur expenses in obtaining qualifications, or to wage earners who incur expenses in moving from job to job?[7]

8.2.2 Whose income is it?

UK legislation begins by assuming that an individual's income is income which accrues to that individual in accordance with the rules appropriate to each head of income (or Schedule). Income-splitting between spouses may be practised if, for example, the wife runs a business and employs her husband. The money paid to the husband will be deductible in computing the profits of the wife's business and will be taxable to the husband as employment income. Such arrangements must, of course, be genuine and are closely scrutinised by the Revenue.[8] Capital-splitting is also permitted. Since the UK knows no system of community of property, spouses may put assets into joint names or divide assets between them as they wish. There is also a system of potential community of property in that the courts have very extensive powers to reallocate the assets on divorce including pension rights, but this does not affect the spouses' right to divide their wealth as they see fit.

Joint income

Where income is joint income it is normally divided according to the spouses' interests in it.[9] For spouses living together this result is modified in two ways.

(1) Income from property in joint names—joint income. Where property is held in the names of a husband and wife who are living together, the starting point is that income from that property is divided equally between the spouses unless the spouses make a declaration[10] that they wish to be taxed according to their actual entitlements.[11] A declaration once made remains in force There is no provision for revocation of a declaration. If the spouses cease to live together, both the statutory presumption of equality and any declaration cease to apply and, thereafter, income will be attributed according to their entitlements. It is

[6] Government Pre-Budget Report 1999, 6 Budget HC 346, paras §§5.16 *et seq.*

[7] See Pechman, 8 *National Tax Jo.* 120; and Arnold (1973) *Can. Tax Jo.* 176.

[8] They must also conform to the minimum wage legislation as will usually be the case if the purpose is to use up the husband's personal reliefs.

[9] TA 1988, s. 277.

[10] The form of the declaration is governed by ibid., s. 282B. Notice of election must be given to the inspector within 60 days beginning with the date of the declaration (s. 282B(3)); declarations do not have retroactive effect, (s. 282B(2)).

[11] Ibid., s. 282A.

expressly provided that the declaration ceases to be effective automatically if the beneficial interests in the income or the property cease to accord with the declaration.[12]

These special rules directing equal division unless the spouses elect for actual entitlement apply only if the income arises from property held in the names of the husband and wife. If the property is held in the name of one spouse, but the income legally belongs to both, that income should be divided between them for tax purposes also.

These special rules are expressly excluded in certain situations. These are: (i) where the beneficial entitlements to the income are different from the beneficial shares in the underlying property itself;[13] (ii) where the income consists of earned income or partnership income;[14] (iii) where neither of the spouses is beneficially entitled,[15] e.g. because they are trustees; and (iv) where the income to which one spouse is entitled beneficially is treated as the income of the other or of a third party by some other tax provision.[16]

(2) Inter-spousal transfers; the settlement rules in TA 1988, s. 660A. Various rules may apply where income arises under a settlement. A settlement is defined as including any disposition, trust, covenant, agreement, arrangement or transfer of assets.[17] Case-law limits the scope of these rules by stating that a settlement occurs only if there is some element of bounty about the transaction.[18] In broad terms, where one spouse has carried out a transaction falling within this definition of settlement, and income later arises to the other spouse as a result of that transaction, the income is treated as that of the settlor-spouse and not of the other spouse. The actual wording of the provision covers situations wider than this. This rule therefore appears to prevent income-splitting between the spouses by the device of transferring either assets or income between them. There are four exceptions to the rule:

(a) First, there are exceptions from the term "spouse" These are (1) a person to whom the settlor is not for the time being married but may later marry, (2) a spouse from whom the settlor is separated under an order of a court, or under a separation agreement or in such circumstances that the separation is likely to be permanent, or (3) the widow or widower of the settlor.[19]

(b) The rule does not deprive an outright gift between the spouses from having that effect for tax purposes. The legislation does not wish to inhibit such generosity but is anxious to prevent the exploitation of the separate taxation of spouses. It therefore provides that an outright gift of property by one spouse to the other is to be treated as outside these settlement rules unless either (1) the gift does not carry a right to the whole of that income, or (2) the property given is wholly or substantially a right to income.[20] Point (2) was considered in *Young* v. *Pearce*[21] where Sir John Vinelott held that where two taxpayers arranged for their trading company to issue preference shares to their wives, dividends later declared in respect of the preference shares were within (2) and so fell to be

12 TA 1988, s. 282B(5).
13 Ibid., s. 282B(4).
14 Ibid., s. 282A(4).
15 Ibid., s. 282A(2).
16 Ibid., s. 282A(5).
17 Ibid., s. 660G—for a general description of these rules against "settlements", see chapter 31 below.
18 The Revenue view is that bringing a spouse into partnership is an arrangement. Therefore if a wife brings her husband into partnership and he does not truly earn his share of the profits the income accruing to him will be treated as accruing to her; bounty is shown by the fact that he did not earn his share (see below at §31.2).
19 TA 1988, s. 660A(3).
20 Ibid., s. 660A(6).
21 [1996] STC 743, 70 TC 331.

treated as income of the husbands. Although there was an outright gift of the preference shares the fact that the shares carried no rights other than a right to income, e.g. they carried no rights on a winding-up of the company, showed that they were substantially a gift of income. (3) In addition, a gift is not an outright gift if it is subject to conditions, or if the property given or any derived property is or will or may become, in any circumstances whatsoever, payable to or applicable for the benefit of the donor.[22]

(c) Also outside the rule is an irrevocable allocation of pension rights by one spouse to the other in accordance with the terms of a relevant statutory scheme. [23]

(d) Payments on family breakdown are also outside the rule (see below at §8.3).

Where people live together but do not marry the rules do not apply, although the more general parts of s. 660A, etc. may do so.

8.2.3 Children

The presence of children affects tax liability in a number of ways but, at least at present, less so than in most other systems.[24] A special provision prevents certain child care costs incurred by an employer in providing such services from being taxable benefits of the employee.[25] The 1999 working families tax credit (WFTC) includes a substantial element for child care; this is to meet 70% of eligible child care costs up to a maximum of £150 for families with more than one child (£100 for one-child families). Both the WFTC and the new children's tax credit begin in 2001 depending on there being qualifying children.

Children of whatever age are independent persons as far as the tax system is concerned. Their income is in principle therefore taxed separately from that of their parents. Their personal reliefs are available to be set against their own income only. There is no quotient system in the UK.

As with spouses, income-splitting through employment is possible for children. However, here too the taxpayer must be able to establish the genuineness of the payment. In one case a parent sought to deduct payments to a child spouse but the court concluded that they were really pocket money and so not genuine income of the child—and so not deductible.[26]

Income arising in favour of an unmarried child under 18 is treated as that of the parent if the income arises under a settlement made by the parent.[27] The term "settlement" is widely defined to includes any transfer of assets (see further chapter 13 below). Therefore if M opens a bank account in the name of her child, S, and puts £10,000 in it, the interest arising from that £10,000 will be treated as income of M and not of S.[28] There is a *de minimis* exception of £100 from all sources under s. 660B of TA 1888; [29] there is also an important exception if the money is placed in an accumulation trust and the money is not paid out to

[22] TA 1988, s. 660A(6).

[23] Ibid., s. 660A(7) but not an assignment of the state retirement pension (*Meredith-Hardy* v. *McLellan* [1995] STC (SCD) 270). s. 660A(7) is to be replaced by s. 600A(11)–(13) as from 2001–02 FA 2000 s. 61. Sch. 13, para 26.

[24] For details of tax thresholds for different family units since 1990–1991, see *Inland Revenue Statistics 1999*, para. 2.7; see earlier volumes for earlier years. For comparisons, see Messere, *Tax Policies in OECD Countries*, Tables 10.5 and 10.6, and below at §8.4.1.

[25] TA 1988, s. 155A; this exception is narrowly confined, e.g. the services must be provided on premises made available by the employer alone.

[26] *Dollar* v. *Lyon* [1981] STC 333, 54 TC 459.

[27] TA 1988, s. 660B.

[28] *Thomas* v. *Marshall* [1953] 1 All ER 1102, 34 TC 178.

[29] TA 1988, s. 660B(5).

M or used for M's benefit while a minor.[30] Such income is taxed at ordinary trust rates—and not those of the settler.

8.3 UK History[31]

8.3.1 Spouses

Before 1973

Under the law prevailing up to 1973 a wife's income was simply treated as that of her husband. This meant that her income was added to his and so taxed at the cumulative rate appropriate to their joint income. However, in practice the provision of an additional personal relief for married women (the wife's earned income relief) and the practice of having a long band of income taxed at what we now call the basic rate, reduced this financial injustice.

1973–1990

The first major change came in 1973 when spouses were allowed to elect that the wife should be taxed separately on her earned income.[32] This change was only of advantage to those whose combined incomes took them significantly into higher rate liability, since one effect of the election was to lose a right to the married man's allowance and make do with an ordinary personal allowance instead.[33] The 1973 change did not affect the wife's investment income, which was not taxed separately until the general change to separate taxation under the 1988 legislation (which came into effect in 1990).

Administration

The basic old rule of aggregation had one other effect: all the wife's tax affairs were handled by her husband, while she had no right or duty to see his. This demeaning state of affairs could be avoided only if the wife opted to be assessed separately (as very few chose to do).[34]

Background to older law

It must be recalled that the older law made some sense under the previous social and fiscal conditions to which it applied. Social conditions were based on the norm of a single earner household (in which the earner was nearly always the husband), the extreme rarity of people cohabiting unless they were married, and a tax system which had a long band of income taxed at a single rate which would be the family's marginal rate whether one or both spouses worked.

8.3.2 Children

From time to time the UK system has treated all unearned income of an unmarried child under the age of majority as that of the parents, e.g. 1968–1972. There is no such rule at

[30] TA 1988, s. 660B (2).

[31] For a fuller account of these older systems, see the third edition of this work, ch. 6. For an account of challenges under the European Convention of Human Rights see Baker [2000] *BTR* 211 at 252.

[32] On earned income, see above at §7.8.2.

[33] TA 1988, s. 287.

[34] Ibid., s. 283 (repealed as from 1990 by FA 1988).

present. Previously parental child allowances, i.e allowances claimed by parents because they had children, formed part of the UK income tax system until 1979–1980, before being abolished as a result of the introduction of the child benefit scheme. Before 1979–1980 the tax system provided child allowances, while the social security system provided family allowances. Tax allowances would be given to father in calculating his tax liability, while family allowances were usually paid in cash to the mother each week. There were also rules which phased out the benefit of the family allowances for the relatively well-off. In 1979–1980 child tax reliefs were abolished; the money saved was used to increase family allowances, which were recast as child benefit and still payable in cash each week to the mother.

8.4 Policy

The correct tax treatment of the family is one of the most contentious issues in tax policy. This section begins with a list of approaches in other systems and then outlines some of the theoretical and policy issues which make this topic so difficult.

The traditional starting point is that there are two models between which the tax system must choose. Under Model A the incomes of married couples are aggregated. Model B takes the individual as the starting point and finishing point. In designing our ideal tax system we must choose between them. However, once the choice has been made, refinements can then be introduced to the system; these refinements may be radical, e.g. by following the aggregation of incomes (Model A) with equal division of that income between the spouses.

8.4.1 Other systems[35]

Systems which direct the aggregation of all or some income within the family recognise the desirability of taxing the amount of income earned by a single person more heavily than the same amount earned by a family. From 1990 to 2000 the UK system allowed a married couple an extra deduction (the married couple's allowance) if they lived together, but gave no deduction for children as such.[36] By contrast, under the French quotient system[37] the family income—including that of the children—is first aggregated whether it comes from spouse or child, and is then divided according to the number of people in the family, a child counting as a half, save for single parent families, where the first child counts as a whole. Thus, a married couple with two children would have their income divided into three parts. The general rates of tax are then applied to each part separately and the tax due is the aggregate. The system lowers the average tax rate and, by sharply mitigating the theoretically progressive tax system, discriminates heavily against the single person.

[35] For a 1998 European survey, see Maria Teresa Soler Roch (ed.), *Family Taxation in Europe* (Kluwer, 1999). For general literature see the citations by Books, in Head and Krever (eds), ch. 2; see also Messere, above at n. 24, esp. the tables at 10.2–10.6 and, in Head and Krever (eds) (1996), the contributions by McIntyre (on the United States) and Sommerhalder (on Europe). For older analyses, see Oldman and Temple (1959) 12 *Stanford LR* 585; Bittker 27 *Stanford LR* 1389; and Royal Commission Canada, Study No. 10.

[36] Allowances or credits also form part of many other systems. Messere, above at n. 24, lists 13 OECD countries.

[37] For a comparison of the French quotient system and units of consumption, see *Impots et Reforme Fiscale* (Cahiers Francais No. 274, January 1996), 28.

Other systems may apply different schedules to families and individuals, with the premises behind the schedules varying widely.[38] Some systems apply joint income taxation with income-splitting—a form of quotient system for spouses only,[39] while other systems offer taxpayers a choice of forms.[40]

8.4.2 Rhetoric

Family unit (Model A)

The case for Model A, i.e. aggregation, was stated by the Canadian Royal Commission in 1966 which recommended aggregation with a separate rate schedule rather than splitting.[41]

> "We believe firmly that the family is today, as it has been for many centuries, the basic economic unit in society. Although few marriages are entered into for purely financial reasons, as soon as a marriage is contracted it is the continued income and financial position of the family which is ordinarily of primary concern, not the income and financial position of the individual members. Thus, the married couple itself adopts the economic concept of the family as the income unit from the outset. In Western society the wife's direct financial contribution to the family income through employment is frequently substantial. It is probably even more true that the newly formed family acts as a financial unit in making its expenditures. Family income is normally budgeted between current and capital outlays, and major decisions involving the latter are usually made jointly by the spouses."

Individual (Model B)

The case in favour of the individual (Model B) is argued with equal vigour in a paper published by the chairman of the the Australian Taxation Review Committee in 1975. After stating that the married woman enjoys identical legal status with her husband with regard to ownership and disposition of property and the enjoyment of income therefrom, and that this accords with the desire of married women to achieve equality with their husbands in all respects, a desire for which there is every moral and social justification, Mr Justice Asprey, writing in his personal capacity stated:

> "What then is the justification for the Revenue in any country compelling the aggregation of the married woman's income with her husband and exacting from her (as well as from her husband) a greater amount by way of taxation than if she were single and owned the same income producing assets and performed the same services for reward? Is it for no other reason but to obtain a greater amount of tax from a married couple than would be payable if they were taxed as individuals? Is it that it is considered more equitable that two persons, because they are married to each other, should each be more heavily taxed than if they were unmarried persons? Is the reason to be put that it is a more simple system of taxation from the point of view of the Revenue or the taxpayers? Or, is the aggregation procedure to be justified upon the ground that it provides the Revenue with some assistance in the prevention of tax evasion by income splitting? I say some assistance because I believe it to be true that no reasonable person would be bold enough to assert that aggregation would put an end completely to evasion of taxation in the marriage sphere."

[39] Messere cites Portugal.

[40] Messere, Table 10.2, cites Germany, Ireland, Norway and Spain.

[41] Vol. 3, 123. For criticism, see McIntyre, in Brooks (ed.), *The Quest for Tax Reform: The Royal Commission on Taxation 20 Years Later* (1988).

Some arguments dissected

Stripped of the language of persuasion, the first passage quoted above asserts simply that the family is the basic economic unit in society, deciding its income and expenditure patterns as a unit and, therefore, that the same unit should be taken as the basis of the tax system. Similarly reduced, the second passage begins by taking the pure form of the family unit—aggregation with neither further deductions or credits nor a separate structure (Model A)—and then asking why the family should pay more tax than if its members had remained single. As we have seen, other countries do not usually tax on the basis of aggregation without some form of relief through division, quotient or extra relief.

8.4.3 The conflicting criteria game: Meade's list

The debate sometimes leads to the listing of criteria, individual items being not only disputable but also conflicting. The following list is from the Meade Report (chapter 18):

1. The decision to marry or not to marry should not be affected by tax considerations.[42]
2. Families with the same joint resources should be taxed equally.
3. The incentive for a member of the family to earn should not be blunted by tax considerations which depend upon the economic position of other members of the family.
4. Economic and financial arrangements within the family (e.g. as regards the ownership of property) should not be dominated by sophisticated tax considerations.
5. The tax system should be fair between families which rely upon earnings and families which enjoy investment income.
6. Two persons living together and sharing household expenditures can live more cheaply and therefore have a greater taxable capacity than two single persons living separately.
7. The choice of tax unit should not be excessively costly in loss of tax revenue.
8. The arrangements involved should be reasonably simple for the taxpayer to understand and for the tax authorities to administer.

Such lists are of dubious value since the criteria are of different orders and often rest on a prejudgment of one fundamental question, i.e. whether the basic unit is to be the household or the individual. Consider, for example, criterion 3. Although presented as a truth, it is in fact a consequence, perhaps a desirable one, of taking the individual as a unit. If the family is taken as the unit, this criterion cannot be met. However, if this criterion were reshaped a different criterion would be produced which the family unit could satisfy; i.e. "if it is desirable that the family should earn more money should the tax system encourage a member to start work rather than an existing earner to earn more?"[43]

These arguments show that there is little chance of agreement over the criteria. The position is complicated, however, by the fact that even if the criteria were agreed there is an inevitable conflict between criteria 1 and 2. Suppose that H1 earns £20,000, and H2 earns £40,000. In a progressive tax system it is inevitable that the total tax paid by H2 would be more than double that paid by H1. Suppose that H1 marries W1 who also earns £20,000, so that their combined income is £40,000. Accepting criterion 1, the tax burden on H1 and W1

[42] For effects of change in tax law on timing of marriage in UK and Canada, see Gelardi (1996) 49 *National Tax Jo.* 17.

[43] For scepticism of empirical studies on how families allocate the extra tax burden when one member returns to work, see McIntyre, in Head and Krever (eds), above at n. 35, 9–11; for evidence of reluctance to return to work if tax rates high, see Gann (1980) 59 *Texas Law Review* 25.

should not alter when they marry; this means that their combined tax would be less than that paid by H2. The problem arises when H2 marries W2, who earns nothing. If one persists with criterion 1 the tax burden on H1W1 will be less than the burden on H2W2 and, thus, criterion 2 will not be met.

The variation of Model A (which introduces splitting) leads to other results. Under such a system H2W2's £40,000 would be attributed to them equally and taxed accordingly; thus producing equality with H1W1 but only at the cost of breaking criterion 2 for H2W2. Without such a system, however, it is inevitable that married couples would pay more tax than two single persons with the same total income.[44]

8.4.4 New ways of playing the game: modern fundamentalism

Benefit or Control?

The family unit debate can be taken further and deeper into the realm of tax policy.[45] Model A claims to rest on the Haig Simons' definition of income.[46] This takes as its starting point the income actually received by the taxpayer and asserts the irrelevance of the particular *source* of the sums spent on consumption or added to the store of wealth; it thus focuses on benefit. Model B focuses not on benefit but on control, it asserts that the tax system should tax the person who controls the source and/or disposition of that income. Behind these two normative propositions are two empirical propositions. Model A asserts that spouses usually share the material benefits generated by their income; Model B asserts that the person who controls the source decides the disposition.[47] Critics of Model B argue that by stressing control it looks to income potential rather than actual market outcomes, an idea which can be taken much (much) further and that, if one want to pay attention to what couples actually do, one may go against the Haig-Simons' line that the source of the consumption is immaterial.[48] The choice between benefit and control is fundamental in determining the tax base; the choice made there will determine the choice to be made on the tax unit itself.[49]

Supporters of Model B assert that Haig-Simons definition is of limited use because it ignores incentive effects and relies too much on "observed money income" as the measure of taxable capacity.[50] In their ideal fiscal world, the tax system would charge not an individual's "observed income" but the underlying characteristics such as endowments (mental

44 This form of argument is used by Munnell, in Aaron and Boskin (eds), *The Economics of Taxation* (Brookings). It has been systematically savaged by a leading scholar in optimal tax theory: see Apps, in Head and Krever (eds), above at n. 35, 82–6.

45 See, generally, Head and Krever, above at n. 35. For an utilitarian argument in favour of Model A, see Steuerle, in Penner (ed.), *Tax Treatment of Households of Different Size in Taxing the Family* (1983).

46 It is unclear which side can more convincingly claim the support of Haig Simons: see Head, in Head and Krever (eds), above at n. 35, 202–203. For an extension of the argument to other taxes, see McIntyre, in Bird and Crossen (eds), *The Personal Income Tax: Phoenix from the Ashes* 145–83.

47 UK research suggests that there is little pooling: seeLundberg, Pollok and Wales (1997) *Journal of Human Resources* 463, showing that the 1977 change from tax allowance to child benefit resulted in much more expenditure on children. For discussions of foreign family sharing practices, see McIntyre (1985) 49 *Albany Law Review* 275 and Kornhauser (1993) 45 *Hastings Law Review* 63. McCaffery 40 *UCLA LR* 983 uses the game theory to argue that actual sharing is irrelevant; Zelanak 67 *Southern California LR* 339 argues that couples share, but that the control principle is still valid.

48 McIntyre, in Head and Krever (eds), above at n. 35, 5.

49 McIntyre and Oldman (1977) 90 *Harvard LR* 1609.

50 The fullest explanation of this approach is to be found in Atkinson and Stiglitz, *Lectures on Public Economics* (1980).

or physical ability) and tastes, which determine a person's "opportunity sets" and "levels of well being".[51] A family's welfare, and therefore the true measure of what should be taxed, will not be adequately determined on the basis of observed income since this omits both household services and leisure (see quotation from Apps at p. 14 above).

Imputed income: a marriage penalty or a tax on marital advantage?

Supporters of Model B argue that much of the support for Model A with splitting comes from high-income, single-earner households and is a disguised form of asking for an (unjustified) redistribution of the tax burden.[52] Such arguments sometimes assume that these families have dependent children, and sometimes do not. They also point out that supporters of Model A could achieve their objectives under a system of independent taxation by sharing their assets so that income is evenly divided, and pointing out that husbands, as statistically the more common financially dominant partner, do not want to do this. Supporters of Model B treat the wish to avoid a "tax penalty" on marriage as misconceived; for them, marriage brings advantages which justify an extra burden of tax.[53] It as this point that one can see differences between traditional legal analysis within the legal tradition and an optimal economic approach. Traditional legal analysis treats items of imputed income as non-taxable, because they are immeasurable. Optimal analysis accepts that these items are impossible to measure, but says that it is wrong therefore simply to ignore them. Instead, they should be taken into account when designing rate structure and unit.

The advantages of marriage are shared expenses and services, such as housekeeping, lawn mowing and chauffering, which increase the amount of disposable income. On this basis marriage brings about a higher standard of living. Central to such arguments, however, is the assumption that under consideration are two people with the same combined income levels before and after marriage. Therefore, such arguments prove only that married couples should pay more tax than is paid by two single persons with the same total incomes; they say nothing about a comparison between a married couple and one single person with the same income.

Optimal tax critics of Model A argue strongly that Model A is hostile to the interests of the family's second earner. Secondary income partners are typically female, with lower earning capacities and more responsive labour supplies. Higher taxes on them would reinforce existing constraints on their choice between working at home or in the market. This could lead to a stronger division of labour on the basis of gender and increase inequality both at home and in the market.[54]

Children

The addition of children may bring other advantages to the parents if older children care for younger ones—and do so without payment.[55] However, it also raises the question why parents do or should spend money on their children. At this point some tax theorists tend to allow their arguments to range very widely. If one could imagine a world of complete

[51] Atkinson and Stiglitz 6 *Journal of Public Economics* 55, cited by Apps, in Head and Krever (eds), above at n. 35, 83.

[52] Brooks, in Head and Krever (eds), above at n. 35, 36.

[53] For an argument in favour of taking account of imputed income, see Apps, in Head and Krever (eds), above at n. 35; for arguments *against* taxing the imputed income, see McIntyre and Oldman (1977) 90 *Harvard LR* 1609 and Brooks, in Head and Krever (eds), above n. 35, 49.

[54] Apps, in Head and Krever (eds), above at n. 35, 103.

[55] For criticisms, see Apps and Reece, summarised by Apps in Head and Krever (eds), above at n. 35, 85–7.

information, a child (acting through its parent as agent) could borrow against future income. Because the world does not provide such complete information, parents spend money on their children even though they cannot recover it and even though it may not prove to be in the child's best interests. More importantly, from the point of view of its supporters, Model B argues for public provision for children either directly in the form of cash transfers or indirectly through the provision of education and care. Meanwhile, direct and indirect taxes on "observed income" are distortionary because they encourage individuals to switch to untaxed domestic activity.

Hidden deep inside this question is, of course, another—the relevance of the status of marriage. Should the discussion concern cohabiting couples or married couples and, if it is the latter, should this involve long-term settled relationships with a sexual content, or simply people who happen to share expenditures within a house? We wait to see what impact the Human Rights Act 1998 will have, especially on issues such as same-sex couples.[56]

Other questions are whether the tax system affects individual decisions to marry, a point on which the empirical evidence is inconclusive[57] and whether couples actually share, the evidence on which is uncertain.[58] Does it matter whether couples share? Some supporters of Model B argue that it does not.[59]

Public choice

What does public choice theory have to contribute? Its first point is that the political process will not produce a system which is the most equitable and efficient. A Leviathan government (i.e. legislators and bureaucracy), has its own interest to protect and is very well placed to do so. This argues for a constitutional rule that no tax discrimination should take place between single households and two-earner households, the purpose being to restrict the ability of a revenue-maximising government to impose different taxes on individuals who have identical market incomes but different demand curves.[60] However, this simply illustrates the main public choice thesis that the government can and will tax in its own interest.

8.4.5 Conclusion

One reads such literature with a shaking head. Altruism (love seems an overloaded and intrusive expression) seems to be absent from the debate. The debate goes far wider than just the taxation of the family, but that does not mean that the family issue is unimportant. The tax unit provides an important instance of another debate, i.e. the role of gender in society. As so often, tax law provides a sharp instance of what some think life is all about—money, sex and power.

[56] On Article 8 (Respect for Private and Family Life) see Baker [2000] *BTR* 211 at 253; for Canadian experience see Lacey [2000] *BTR* 378.

[57] See three articles in the *National Tax Journal*: Sjoquist and Walker 48 *National Tax Jo.* 547; Alm and Whittington *National Tax Jo.* 565; and Gelardi 49 *National Tax Jo.* 17. The first article suggests that the US tax penalty did not deter people wanting to marry; the second suggests that some may be deterred; the third is not confined to the United States.

[58] For discussions of family sharing practices see McIntyre (1985) 49 *Albany Law Review* 275 (yes and relevant); Zelanak (1993) 67 *Southern California LR* 339 (yes, but irrelevant); and Kornhauser (1993) 45 *Hastings Law Review* 63.

[59] McCaffery (1993) 40 *UCLA LR* 983 uses the game theory to argue that actual sharing is irrelevant; Zelanak, above at n. 57, argues that couples share but that the control principle is still valid.

[60] See Brennan and Brooks, in Head and Krever (eds), above at n. 35, 139; and comments by Head (ibid.), 210.

9

Taxation and Social Security

9.1 Introduction

The social security system is relevant for tax lawyers for three immediate reasons. First, some social security benefits are taxable, while others are not; secondly, the progressivity of the tax system cannot be assessed without taking account both of the effect of the reduction in benefits as income rises and of the impact of National Insurance contributions (NICs); thirdly, NICs are particularly important when considering benefits in kind. However, behind all these is an awareness that tax and social security are two systems within which an individual's rights depend on the answer to one question: what is my income? Since two systems turn on one question it is tempting for an interfering or ambitious Chancellor to think that the systems should and could be merged.

9.2 Taxation of Benefits[2]

Payments under the social security system fall into two main categories: contributory benefits, which depend on certain contribution requirements being met; and non-contributory benefits.

In general, the longer-term contributory benefits are taxable under Schedule E.[3] These include retirement pensions in Category A or Category B, widow's pension and widowed mother's allowance (the basic flat-rate allowance and any earnings-related increase), statutory maternity pay and statutory sickness pay. Incapacity benefit has been taxed since its

[1] The history of the issues can be seen in the reports and Green Budgets produced by the Institute for Fiscal Studies (IFS), e.g. *Tax Reform: Options for the Third Term* (1987), 13–29; *Tax Options for 1991* (Commentary No. 28) (1991), 69–72; *Tax Options for 1993* (Commentary No. 33), 83–8) and *Tax Options for 1997* (Commentary No. 56); and the Green Budget 1999 (Commentary No. 76).

[2] For a comprehensive list, see "Social Security", in *Tolley's Income Tax 2000–01*.

[3] TA 1988, s. 617(1); all social security benefits are taxable under Schedule E unless specifically exempted. The receipts basis for Schedule E, introduced in 1989, does not apply to the taxable social security benefits: FA 1989, s. 41(c), (e).

introduction in 1995–1996.[4] The weekly allowance for a widowed mother's children is exempt from tax.[5]

Of the short-term contributory benefits, sickness benefit and maternity allowance are exempt from tax, as is the widow's payment (a lump sum of £1,000). Unemployment benefit, including any increase for adult dependants, is taxable. Unemployment benefit is paid gross but PAYE adjustments are made on return to work. Job seekers' allowance is taxable if above a certain maximum.[6]

Non-contributory benefits are generally exempt from income tax. These include various war disablement benefits and industrial injury benefits. Others are means-tested and the system does not usually charge income tax here because the means-testing itself is regarded as a sufficient "tax". Some benefits are payable as of right without regards to means and are non-taxable, e.g. child benefit (which will exist alongside the children's tax credit as from 2001–2002).

Among the non-taxable but means-tested benefits are income support (but see below), students' grants, social fund benefits, council tax benefit and housing benefit. The non-taxable, non-means-tested benefits include attendance allowance, Christmas bonus for pensioners, fares to school, improvement grants, mobility allowance, widow's allowance and the Youth Training Scheme. Special arrangements have been made for certain fostering allowances; New Deal payments to employees by employers are taxable once the subsidy level is passed.

Although generally exempt from tax, income support is taxable in two situations.[7] The first is where the payment is made in respect of a period where the right to income support is conditional on the claimant being available for employment. The second is where the payment is for a period in which the claimant is one of a married or unmarried couple and the claimant, but not the other partner, is involved in a trade dispute as a result of which reduced income support is payable. However, in these cases tax is not charged on any income support in excess of the "taxable maximum".

9.3 Impact of NICs

NICs are important because they affect the tax burden on the employer, the employee and sometimes the self-employed. For employees, the normal rate is 10% of earnings between £76 a week (£3,952 p.a.) and £535 a week (£27,820 p.a.). The rate of employer's NICs for 2000–01 is 12.2% on all earnings over £84 a week (£4,368 p.a.). These rates are reduced for both employer and employee if the employee is contracted out of the state earnings related pension scheme. The employer's threshold is now tied to the value of the personal allowance in TA 1988, s. 257; the employee's threshold will be similarly tied as from 2001.

These rates represent a considerable rationalisation on what had previously been in force. Earlier systems had been progressive in that the tax rate rose as income rose. However, at first these applied the new rate not just to the "slice" above the critical threshold figure, but also to all earnings. This system, known as the "slab" system, meant that the marginal effects

[4] See FA 1994, s. 139, as amended by FA 1995, s. 141; see also Budget Statement, paras 81–83, (1993) *Simon's Tax Intelligence* 1453.

[5] TA 1988, s. 617(2)(aa).

[6] Ibid., s. 151A.

[7] Ibid., s. 151.

of £1 of extra income could be to cause a very severe tax burden. It is no wonder, therefore, that it was not in the interests of either employer or employee to raise wages in certain situations unless by a very great amount—hence, the bunching of wage rates at certain levels. NICs provided the last example of the UK's use of the slab system; the slab system was also used for supertax from 1911–1926 and for estate duty until 1968.

"Poverty traps", "unemployment traps" or, more generally, the "surtax on the poor", have been addressed in stages. Before the Social Security Act 1986 came into force, the reduction in benefits combined with the start of income tax and NIC to lead to the net rate of "tax" exceeding 100%. This was because the social security clawback rules were applied to gross income, i.e. before income tax or NICs. After the Social Security Act 1986 the amount of benefit was related to income net of tax and NICs.[8] Despite this, the rates remain much higher than the top rate of income tax (40%). Writing in 1993 Hills suggested that while the 1986 reforms largely removed the problem of people losing more than 100% of any extra income, and so ending up worse off, substantially more people faced rates above 70%. These figures applied to families in work; those out of work and receiving income support could still lose 100% of additional part-time earnings.[9] Further work was carried out by Nigel Lawson in 1989,[10] but it fell to Gordon Brown to complete the process by aligning the threshold for NICs with that of the personal relief for income tax, paid for by an extra charge on employer's contributions for higher paid.[11] The introduction of the working families tax credit (WFTC) has been another major reform, but the proud boast that the credit will help many relatively well-off families means a major extension of people facing high marginal effective rates of tax.[12]

The cap on the employee's NICs (at £27,820 p.a.) (it does not apply to the employer's NICs) is an important feature. When combined with income tax rates it makes for an odd marginal rate structure since the cap applies before the 40% top rate of income tax applies. Thus, while a person with £27,819 has a marginal rate of 32% (22% + 10%), a person with £27,820 has a marginal rate of 22%. This 22% rate will apply until the higher rate applies which will usually not be less than £32,785. (£28,400 + the £4,385 personal relief). The gap between the top of the basic rate band and the upper earnings limit for NICs has reduced in recent years.[13]

NICs are not charged on the same basis as ordinary income.[14] They apply to Schedule E income and, sometimes Schedule D. As from 2000–01, Class 1A rates apply to all benefits in kind taxable under Schedule E; however, this is usually a charge on the employer and not on the employee.[14a]

Governments hemmed in by political constraints and so unable to raise the explicit rate of income taxes, have sometimes regarded NICs as a useful alternative source of revenue.[15]

[8] See Cmnd 9691.

[9] Hills, *The Future of Welfare* (1993), 25, who pointed out that in 1992–9193 1.9 m unemployed non-pensioners were receiving income support and in this position.

[10] For assessment, see Dilnot and Webb (1989) 10(2) *Fiscal Studies* 38.

[11] Report No. 3, paras 2.15 *et seq.*

[12] Written Answer (see Hansard, 23 May 2000).

[13] IFS Green Budget, 2000 §5.1.

[14] See Sandler, *Harmonising the Fringes of National Insurance and Income Tax* (Commentary No. 36) and UKTG, Pt .IX.

[14a] See generally Tiley and Collison, *UK Tax Guide* Part IX. See also Redston, *Taxation* 16 March 2000, 529–531.

[15] See [1998] *BTR* 317, 334–5.

9.4 Tax Credits: Benefits Administered by the Inland Revenue

9.4.1 Working families tax credit (WFTC)[16]

The WFTC is treated here, and not with other personal reliefs and credits, for two reasons. The first is that it is a welfare right rather than a tax rule. This is shown by the fact that it does not form part of TA 1988, Part VII and so, for example, is subject to the social security rules on residence, and not the tax rules which extend the benefit of those tax reliefs to certain non-residents. The second reason is that, unlike the new children's tax credit, which is to take effect in 2001, and which forms part of TA 1988, Part VII, there is no right to the WFTC if the claimant's savings exceed £8,000. This and the DPTC (below §9.4.3) are the only tax credits which are means-tested by reference to capital.

The amount of credit depends on being in work and, for the additional credit, working at least 30 hours a week. Moreover, the WFTC lasts initially for 26 weeks and not for a tax year, and can be paid either as a tax credit through the payroll or as a welfare benefit directly from the Inland Revenue.

The credit is discussed in this book because it has tax implications for those entitled to it, and for the unfortunate employers on whom the complicated task of administering it has been placed where the claimant elects to be paid through the payroll. Like many good, simple ideas, its implementation has been extremely complicated. Cynics may note the Chancellor's insistence that the WFTC is a tax credit and so can be presented as a tax cut, whereas a similar sum spent on family benefit would be government expenditure. By so presenting it, however, the government has also opened itself up to the charge that it has introduced a higher marginal rate of tax for more people. One advantage of tax credits is that people claiming them do not suffer the stigma which attaches to welfare payments and so are more likely to claim them. Early evidence suggests, however, that the self-employed have been particularly reluctant to claim.[17] This is, in part, because of the difference between income for the purposes of the tax credit and income computed for income tax. Thus, the WFTC measure makes no allowance for capital allowances or loss relief from a previous year.[17a]

Outline of WFTC[18]

This important reform, bridging the tax and benefit systems, took effect from 5 October 1999 when it became available as payments by the Revenue direct to recipients.[19] As from 6 April 2000 the WFTC can be given effect in the wage packet via the tax system;[20] the self-employed will continue to claim direct from the Revenue. The credit has its own Employer's Guide. Couples can choose which of them is to receive the credit.

The WFTC builds on the model of the family credit, which it replaces, and so embodies social security values rather than tax values.[21] It is available to families whether or not the

[16] Tax Credits Act 1999. See also Lee, *Journal of Social Security Law* vol. 7 (2000) p. 159. Revenue Booklets.

[17] CIOT Low Income Tax Reform Group, News Release, 19 January 2000.

[17a] Even for employees there are differences e.g. only a few benefits in kind are relevant to WFTC.

[18] The credit is based on a report by Martin Taylor, *Modernisation of Britain's Tax and Benefit System (Nos 2 and 3)* (Treasury, April 1998). See also Strickland, House of Commons Research Paper 98/46, 27–30 which gathers some immediate reactions at; typically, the survey of US literature (at pp. 34–7) ignores the work published in US law journals, such as Alstott 108 *Harvard LR* 533 and Shaviro (1997) 64 *University of Chicago LR* 00.

[19] Tax Credits Act 1999, s. 5.

[20] Ibid., s. 6 and Tax Credits (Payments by Employers) Regulations, 1999 SI 1999/3219.

[21] Report No. 2 ch. 3; for a summary of the differences, see Strickland, above at n. 17, 13.

adult members are married. Like other social security benefits, it is related to income and so is phased out as income rises—the rate of phase-out is less steep than for previous benefits. It is at this point that the presence of a second parent becomes relevant. It incorporates not only an element for the sick and disabled but also an element for child care costs (a first for the tax system). There are consequential adjustments to housing benefit rules.[22] Child benefit is retained in its present form as a tax-free pay-out to all parents regardless of income—but has been increased in value.[23]

The WFTC is correctly called working families tax credit. Those out of work receive benefits from income support (IS) or job seekers' allowance (JSA). IS and JSA are not merged because the purpose of the change is to move people into the labour market, not from one form of welfare to another.[24] In 1998, 2.3 m children out of the 4.3 m living in poverty (as defined) were in families with no working parent.[25]

Some critics of the WFTC are concerned about the social values it represents.[26] Single parent families, families with two parents where only one goes out to work or where both go out to work full time or where both go out to work part time present different problems. However, it goes further. On any given income a family of four, i.e. two parents and two children, will be poorer, or, in the relevant language, will have a lower equivalised income, than a comparable one-parent family. The WFTC's concern with the single parent ignores the fact that if a lone parent is in work the family will not be in poverty, whereas families headed by a married couple will. Moreover, by assisting with paid child care costs it ignores the loss of pay by a parent wishing to stay at home. Such critics find it odd that the presence of the second parent is relevant to look at the phasing-out of the credit, but not for other aspects of the credit; conversely, they worry that insisting on taking account of joint income to this extent undermines the tax privacy achieved for taxpayers higher up the income scale. The main concern is that a policy designed to help single parent families will, of necessity, send a signal that single parenting is an acceptable, even appropriate, way for society to look after its young rather than regarding this situation as the tragic result of other circumstances.[27] While it is unlikely that those who are married will choose to separate in order to get the benefit, it just may prevent those who want to live together from doing so. Finally one may note the prediction that while some, especially single mothers, will find that WFTC makes it more attractive to go out to work, others, and especially the secondary earner in a couple may find that WFTC makes it attractive to leave the work force.[28]

Details[29]

The amount of WFTC is based on four elements:

(1) a basic credit of £53.15 (one per family);

[22] Report No. 3 para. 4.08; see Strickland, above at n. 17, 21–3.

[23] Budget 99, HC 298, para. 5.8.

[24] Report No. 2, para. 1.35.

[25] Gregg, Harkness and Machin (1999) 20 *Fiscal Studies* 163; poverty is a relative concept and is defined as income below half of mean equivalised incomes (ibid., 186).

[26] E.g. Don Draper, Tax Adviser to *CARE* (personal communication). For figures on child poverty in different family groups, see Gregg, Harkness and Machin, above at n. 25, 163.

[27] E.g. Dex and Rowthorn, *Parenting and Labour Force Participation* (ESRC Centre for Business Research, WP 74); also available in Dench (ed.), *Rewriting the Sexual Contract* (Institute of Community Studies London, 1997).

[28] Blundell, Duncan, McCrai and Meghir 21 *Fiscal Studies* 75.

[29] Social Security Contributions and Benefits Act 1992, s. 128 and Family Credit (General) Regulations 1987 as amended SI 1987/1973; for 2000–01 rates, see Inland Revenue Press Release, 9 November 1999, (1999) *Simons Weekly Tax Intelligence* 1801. A good starting point is Ogus, Barendt and Wikeley, *The Law of Social Security Law* (4th ed. 1994), ch. 12, 518–29; and the CPAG's Income Related Benefits.

(2) an additional credit of £11.25 where the main earner works for at least 30 hours a week, making a combined total of £64.40;
(3) a credit for each child related to the child's age; the credit for each child is £21.25 rising to £26.35 in the September following the child's sixteenth birthday up to the day before his nineteenth birthday;
(4) child care.[30] Certain child care costs were the subject of "disregard" rules in family credit, but these were ineffective. Eligibility for WFTC rests on being a lone parent working 16 hours a week or more, or couples where each parent works for 16 hours or more. The costs are defined as in the family credit rules. The WFTC will cover 70% of eligible costs subject to a limit of £100 a week for one child and £150 for two or more.[31] The eligible costs are for nurseries, a registered child minder, after school club and holiday plays-cheme.

To qualify for WFTC the claimant(s) may be a couple (whether or not married) or a lone parent, who have/has one or more children living with them. Claimants must be resident and entitled to work in the UK and have savings of not more than £8,000.[33] Residence is determined according to social security rules[33] and TA 1988, s. 278 below §11.1.1 does not apply.

To qualify for child care relief[34] the applicant must be entitled to WFTC, and either be a lone parent, part of couple in which both partners work at least 32 hours a week, or part of a couple where one partner is incapacitated and receiving qualifying benefit. The Childcare element in WFTC is not available to a two-parent family where only one parent works (i.e. works outside the home). The child must be of the appropriate age—the benefit runs until the September following the child's fifteenth birthday (sixteenth if disabled). The care must also meet certain conditions.

The taper

The taper will apply once the family's net income (after tax and NICs) reaches £91.45 a week; it will apply at 55% (not the 70% used for family credit). If earnings net of NIC and income tax exceed £100, 55% of the excess goes to reduce the WFTC. The Government claims that this change will mean that half-a-million families will see the return from their earnings increase by a half.[35] This taper applies to the child care element as above where the value of the credit has been increased by the inclusion of the child care element. Government figures in 1999 showed that a couple with combined gross earnings of £450 (£23,400 p.a.) could receive benefit of over £45 a week from the child care element.

Expected effects on poverty and unemployment traps

The poverty trap, described by Hills as a way of keeping down the marginal rates of tax of most earners at the expense of very high rates on a small number, is inevitable. The effect of WFTC will be to increase the number of people in the poverty trap, but substantially reduce the marginal rates. The number of people facing rates of 60% or more is put as rising from

[30] See Strickland, above at n. 17, 14–15; and see Treasury Press Release, 13 January 1999, (1999) *Simons Weekly Tax Intelligence* 158.
[31] Report No. 3, para. 3.05.
[32] Revenue Booklet, 1.
[33] Ogus, Barendt and Wikeley, above at n. 27, ch. 9, 393–401; on "living together as husband and wife", see ibid., 389–93.
[34] Revenue Booklet, above at n. 30, 4.
[35] *Red Book*, para. 3.37.

760,000 to 1,010,000; those facing rates of over 100% are expected to drop from 5,000 to nil; those facing rates of over 90% are expected to drop from 130,00 to 20,000; those facing rates of over 80% are expected to drop from 300,000 to 200,000; and those facing rates of over 70% are expected to drop from 740,000 to 260,000.[36] The unemployment trap is eased because the WFTC is more generous than family credit, which means that families will be better off, in net terms, on low wages than they were on income support.[37]

In 2000–01 the marginal rates of a married couple, each earning enough to pay 22% basic rate, are as follows. Initially there is no tax; then the 55% taper relief is met; as the 10% NIC and 10% income tax rate cuts in, the rate rises to 64%,[38] and then to 69.4% as the basic rate is met. When the taper is complete the marginal rate drops to 32% (10% NIC and 22% income tax) before dropping to 22% as the NIC ceiling is reached, and then rising to 40%.

The idea of planning seems incompatible with such a worthy device as WFTC. However, the sharp marginal rates suggest that those who are able to control their income levels might be well advised to have low incomes one year (to avoid any taper) and then very high levels another year (to avoid the 69.4% rate). This, it has been said, turns tax planning on its head.[39]

9.4.2 Other benefits and tax credits

Disabled person's tax credit (DPTC)[40]

The DPTC replaces the disability working allowance and is similar to the WFTC. Since the purpose is to help those who are disabled but in work, the person with the disability or illness must work for at least 16 hours a week, have one of a number of qualifying benefits and have savings of £16,000 or less. Unlike the WFTC, there is no need for the claimant to have any children but the amount of credit increases if there are children. The claimant must also be resident in the UK and entitled to work here.[41]

The DPTC consists of five elements:

(1) a basic credit will be £55.15, or £84.90 for a couple (whether or not married) or lone parent;
(2) an additional credit of £11.25 is payable where the claimant works for at least than 30 hours a week;
(3) a credit for each child related to the child's age; the credit being the same as for WFTC;
(4) a disabled child's tax credit of £22.25;
(5) child care.[42] The details are the same as for WFTC (see above).

Of these, (2) and (3) are the same as for WFTC, (1) and (2) differ in the amounts of credit and (4) is new. As with WFTC, the threshold for beginning the taper is £91.45 for a lone parent or couple; taper begins at £71.10 for a single person.

[36] Ibid., para. 3.37; Strickland, above at n. 17, 18–19.

[37] Strickland, above at n. 17, 19–20.

[38] Not simply 75% (i.e. 55 + 10 + 10) because the taper is applied to their income net of NIC and income tax.

[39] Maurice Fitzpatrick, Chantrey Vellacott DFK, internet communication, and Hansard above n. 12.

[40] Social Security Contributions and Benefits Act 1992, s. 129; a good starting point is Ogus, Barendt and Wikeley, above at n. 27, ch. 12, 529–34; and the CPAG's Income Related Benefits; for an exhaustive modern account, see Pollard, above at n. 27, ch. 5.

[41] Revenue Booklet, above at n. 30, 3.

[42] See Strickland, above at n. 17, 14–15.

Others

Other interactions concern the repayment of student loans and policing the minimum wage both of which fall to the Inland Revenue.[43] In 1998 the Contributions Agency was merged with the Inland Revenue.

9.5 Relationship: Other Aspects of Social Security and Tax[44]

The tax system is better at taking from people according to their ability to pay than at giving to them according to their need; the latter has been the peculiar job of the social security system.[45] The money for the social security system comes, in part, from NICs. Before 1965 these contributions were generally deductible in computing taxable income;[46] when these ceased to be deductible the personal allowance was increased by an equivalent amount but, since that time, contributions have been increased at a faster rate than personal allowances. To the extent that NICs do not provide sufficient finance, the Exchequer provides funds out of general taxation.[47]

One issue is whether NICs are a tax or a charge for services. The fact that these levies, to use a neutral word, are firmly based on the principle of contribution—a principle designed to emphasise that the contributor has a right to the benefit and is not simply the possible recipient of public charity—suggests that the levies are not simply taxes, but they are clearly more than simple charges for services (see above at §9.1).

Two other ideas for reform should be mentioned. One is the abolition of the ceiling on contributions. This could be seen as a simple measure of equity, particularly following the tax reductions for higher rates of income tax in 1988, but, of course, the effect would be to undermine the economic policy considerations behind those reductions. Another reform would be to recognise that one class of income, i.e. investment income, is not subject to NICs. This is not surprising in historical terms since no benefits could arise by virtue of such income either. However, in order to compensate for not being subject to NICs, all such income could now be subject to income tax at a rate of 40%; this would be part of a flat rate of tax on investment income.

There are always voices calling for the integration of the benefit and tax systems. This means two very different things: one is to merge the payments side, i.e. NICs and income tax; the other is to combine benefits and taxes through devices such as WFTC. Some regard such attempts to assimilate the tax and social security systems as misguided, arguing that social security benefits are necessary interventions to help individuals and families in the short term; such systems think in terms of weeks rather than a year. We wait to see what issues will arise. Similar ideas arose in the 1970s and are noted in the Appendix below.

[43] See *Taxation*, Vol. 144, No. 3729, 58.

[44] See Parker, *Instead of the Dole* (Routledge, 1989). On differences between attitudes to income tax evasion and to social security fraud see Walker (1978) 18 *British Journal of Criminology* 348; Deane 21 *British Journal of Criminology* 47; and Cook, *Rich Law Poor Law: Different Responses to Tax and Supplementary Benefit Fraud* (Open University Press, 1989).

[45] That the social security system is more significant in the reduction of inequality is clear from Hills, *The Future of Welfare* (Joseph Rowntree Foundation, 1997) ch. 1.

[46] The employer's contribution is deductible in computing business profits as part of labour costs.

[47] On governments' inconsistent approaches to the need to balance the books, see [1998] *BTR* 317, 344.

Appendix

In the 1970s much thought was given to an elaborate scheme suggested for discussion by the Conservative Government The proposal which, confusingly, was called a tax credit scheme, but which was closer to a negative income tax scheme, was set out in a Green Paper in 1972.[48] The normal tax credit scheme did nothing to provide equivalent relief to those who paid no tax. A comprehensive scheme was required for cash benefits or credits with a constant tax rate running right through the range of normal earnings. The scheme would replace the main income tax allowances and family allowances. If credit exceeded tax, the difference would be paid to the taxpayer; if tax exceeded credit, the difference would stand as a tax deduction like PAYE. Since it would be payable automatically week by week, it would become a form of additional income to the extent that it exceeded the tax which was currently due. If the credit for the whole year exceeded the tax payable for the year it would be a form of social benefit and would provide a new means of income support.

The scheme would apply only to those whose incomes fell within the present PAYE scheme and would therefore not apply to the self-employed, who would remain under the old system of personal allowances and social security payments. Problems of administration existed, but these were minor compared with those of cost. By 1986 it was estimated that it would cost £8 bn for a scheme sufficient to cover the abolition of family income supplement; if the scheme was to cover the new family credit the cost would be higher still.[49] Either extra revenue would have to be found or the real value of the benefits would have to be allowed to fall to a level where income support would still be needed. There was the further problem for those who wished to "target" the benefit less than universally that there had to be a single basic rate of "credit" for all taxpayers and it was not possible to withdraw the benefit of the "credit" steeply.

The Meade Committee[50] recommended a return to the Beveridge Scheme whereby benefits could be made at a generous level (above the poverty line) and supplementary benefit would be needed only for the few who fell through that net for some reason. Among its suggestions for financing this scheme were permitting allowances to be set only against earned income.

[48] Proposals for a Tax Credit System Cmnd 5116 (1972); see Select Committee Report (1973), 341; IFS Conference on Proposals for a Tax Credit System, March 1973; and Sandford, *Hidden Costs* (IFS), 152–6. The *Finer Report on One Parent Families* Cmnd 5629 (1974) proposed a guaranteed maintenance allowance similar to the tax credit scheme (pp. 276–314). However, on distribution of benefit, note the evidence of Professor Kaldor to the Select Committee on Tax Credit, HC 1972–1973. Supporters of a negative income tax include Friedman, *Capitalism and Freedom*, ch. 11; reprinted in *Reports on Taxation* (Duckworth, 1980), Vol. 1, 141, 12. See also Tobin, Pechman and Mieszowski 77 *Yale LJ* 1; comment in 78 *YLJ* 269; and debate between Asimov, Klein and Popkin in 8 *Harvard Journal of Legislation* 1 and vol. 9 *Harvard Journal of Legislation* 55, 63.

[49] Cmnd 9756 (1986) *The Reform of Personal Taxation*, 6.8.

[50] Chapter 13 of the Report.

10

Deductions and Credits for Taxpayer Expenditure and Losses

10.1 Introduction

The deductions discussed in this chapter are for sums spent by taxpayers or losses incurred by them; their level is therefore beyond the immediate control of the Revenue. Some are deductions from income, some are partial deductions, and some are credits. Rules for credits tend to be more complicated to draft, especially if any unused credits can be carried to another year.[1] It is sometimes suggested that the deduction by reference to actual expenditure should be replaced by standardised fixed sum deductions with or without the right to deduct actual expenditure if higher. The argument for a standardised sum is that it sacrifices equity but reduces administrative and compliance costs. The UK has not had a self-assessment system for long enough to appreciate the force of this argument, but is unlikely to sacrifice the equity element.[2]

These deductions are also important as part of the discussion of nature of income, i.e. what deductions should be allowed and why. The answers to these questions depend on the model of the relevant tax base. Advocates of tax expenditure find deductions for charitable

[1] Sunley (1977) *National Tax Jo.* 243.

[2] Kaplow 50 *Tax Law Review* 1 considers whether an individual with qualifying expenditure just below the threshold should be treated less favourably.

contributions (and, in the United States, medical expenses) objectionable. Andrews, however, defines the tax base in terms of personal consumption and accumulation of real goods and services, rather than net income, and so approves of these deductions.[3] Sections 10.2 to 10.3 below deal with allowable deductions in full, but with occasional restrictions as to the type of income against which they can be set. Sections 10.8 *et seq.* below deal with partial deductions.

10.2 Interest Payment Relief

This section deals with certain interest payments which are deductible in computing income.[4] Interest may also be deductible from a particular source falling within a particular Schedule, e.g. payments in connection with a trade falling within Schedule D, Case I.

From 1799 until 1969 the UK system took the view that interest was deductible because the tax was levied on income and, in computing income, all charges on that income, including interest should be deducted. Unfortunately, this gave rise to great complexity, not least due to the machinery by which it was implemented.

Today, interest payments are deductible only if the interest is on a loan to defray money applied for certain defined purposes.[5] The most significant deduction of interest, which was abolished as from 6 April 2000, was where money was used to purchase a private residence; this was usually given at source and so called MIRAS or mortgage interest relief at source.[6] The less common loan, to buy an annuity secured on land in which the annuitant had an interest, continues to attract limited relief but only if the loan was made before 9 March 1999.[7]

Four purposes for deducting interest are relevant today:[8] (1) for a partner or employee to buy machinery or plant; (2) to acquire an interest in a close non-investment holding company or in a co-operative or employee-controlled company; (3) to buy into a partnership; and (4) to enable personal representatives to pay certain inheritance tax.

(1)–(3) take effect as normal deductions at the taxpayer's marginal rate.[9] Since the last purpose is available only to personal representatives, it takes effect at their rate as personal representatives. Interest payments on loans to buy annuities taken out before 9 March 1999 have their own rules including relief at 23% (FA 2000 s. 83).

10.2.1 General rules

Relief is not available if the interest is incurred in overdrawing an account or debiting the holder of a credit card.[10] The interest paid must be in respect of a loan to the taxpayer; sums

[3] Andrews 86 *Harvard LR* 309; on tax expenditures, generally see above at §1.8. These and other ideas are discussed by Griffith (1980) 40 *Hastings LJ* 343.

[4] TA 1988, s. 353. The reason why these are deductible in computing "income" as opposed to "total income" is that they apply to certain entities (e.g. estate in administration) for which total income is not relevant.

[5] The purposes are set out in TA 1988, ss 354–65; there are supplementary provisions in ss 366–8. The further rules for MIRAS are contained in ss 369–79.

[6] Hence MIRAS TA 1988, s. 354.

[7] Ibid., s. 365.

[8] There must be no other purpose: s. 367(2); for an illustration, see *Cohen* v. *Petch* [1999] STC (SCD) 207.

[9] TA 1988, s. 353(1B).

[10] Ibid., s. 353(3)(a); on what is an overdraft, see *Walcot Bather* v. *Golding* [1979] STC 707, 52 TC 64.

paid in respect of a guarantee of a loan to another do not qualify.[11] Where a loan account is created by the consolidation of and transfer from overdrawn accounts nothing is actually paid to defray money applied for a particular purpose, and so no relief is due.[12] Where the rate of interest exceeds a reasonable commercial rate, no relief is given for the excess.[13]

10.2.2 Anti-avoidance

TA 1988, s. 786 is designed to prevent the conversion of non-deductible interest into a deductible annuity or other income stream; s. 786 treats the payment of such an annuity as a payment of yearly interest. Similarly, the transfer of such an income-earning asset with a duty to sell back may result in the income of the asset being treated as that of the transferor, as will the assignment, surrender or waiver of any income. This is of much less importance now that Schedule D, Case III has been reduced in scope, but it remains relevant where Case III applies, e.g. for business purposes and for corporation tax.

More broadly, s. 787 denies relief under s. 353 in respect of interest when a scheme has been created and the sole or main benefit of which is the obtaining of a reduction in tax liability by means of the relief. This was particularly designed to deal with schemes whereby an individual pays a substantial sum by way of (allowable) interest in advance and then sells the right to the capital; as a result the court looks at the scheme as a whole and not at each separate payment.[14] An example of this sort of scheme is *Cairns* v. *MacDiarmid*[15] where the Court of Appeal, applying the *Ramsay* doctrine, held that interest payable under a scheme was not interest for the purposes of s. 353.

Purpose (1): Purchase of machinery or plant eligible of capital allowances by partner or employer (s. 359)

While the partnership itself may claim the capital allowance on the plant acquired with the loan, only the individual partner can deduct the interest paid by that partner under this rule. This relief is available only in the year the advance is made and the next three years of assessment. Analogous relief is given where the capital allowance is claimed by the employer but the employee pays the interest.

Purpose (2): Acquisition of an interest in a close company (s. 360) or a co-operative or employee-controlled company (s. 361)

Relief for interest is allowable if the loan is used to acquire ordinary share capital in a close company, or is acquired by the company for use in its trade (or to repay an eligible loan). The company must not be a close investment holding company[16] and must exist wholly or mainly for the purpose of carrying on a trade.[17] Interest relief is not usually available if the business consists of the occupation of commercial woodlands.[18]

[11] *Hendy* v. *Hadley* [1980] 2 All ER 554, [1980] STC 292.

[12] *Lawson* v. *Brooks* [1992] STC 76.

[13] TA 1988, s. 353(3)(b).

[14] *Westmoreland Investments Ltd.* v. *Macniven* [1998] STC 1131, CA (s. 787 not applicable).

[15] [1983] STC 178, 56 TC 556; see Gillard, *In the Name of Charity*, 64, 264.

[16] TA 1988, s. 360(1A).

[17] See *Lord* v. *Tustain* [1993] STC 755, 65 TC 761; for discussion of the case and later amendments to s. 360, see Watson [1994] *BTR* 527.

[18] FA 1988, Sch. 6, para. 3(3),

Relief is due if the holding is a material interest or, if it is less than a material interest, the taxpayer works for the greater part of the time in the actual management or conduct of the company. Relief is still available if the company was close when the interest in the company was acquired, but is no longer close when the interest is paid. As a concession, relief will continue after shares in one company are exchanged for shares in another, provided a new loan would have satisfied all these conditions.[19] Relief is not available for shares if the person acquiring them (or that person's spouse) claims relief under the enterprise investment scheme or the now repealed business expansion scheme.[20] Similar relief is available to buy an interest in a co-operative or to lend money to such a body, and to purchase ordinary share capital of an employee-controlled company.[21]

The receipt of sums from the company may be treated as a repayment of the loan, so bringing about a reduction or extinction of the claim.[22]

Purpose (3): Buying into a partnership (s. 362)

Relief is also given on loans used to buy an interest in a partnership or to contribute capital or a premium, or to lend money to the partnership for use in its trade. The purcahser must still be a partner in the period for which the relief is claimed (and not a limited partner) and must not have recovered capital from the partnership—unless it has been taken into account.[23] The loan must still be for use in the partnership business: where A, a partnership, took out a loan for the purposes of partnership B, of which A itself was a member, A was held entitled to the relief.[24]

Purpose (4): Enabling personal representatives to pay certain IHT

See below at §30.2.

10.3 Income Losses[25]

Where a source of income generates a loss the amount of income is zero (not a negative sum). However, the legislation allows certain losses to be deducted by being set against income. As will be seen below, some losses can be set against general income, while others may be set only against income of a certain type.

10.3.1 Trading losses

A trading loss in one year can be set off against the general income of that and the previous year of assessment.[26] More formally, the relief is from tax on an amount of income for that year equal to the amount of the loss; where the income exceeds the loss the taxpayer is

19 ESC A43.

20 TA 1988, s. 360(3A); semble relief is withheld even if the claim for BES relief subsequently fails (e.g. because the trade is not a qualifying trade): ICAEW Memorandum TR 759, (1989) *Simon's Tax Intelligence* 718.

21 TA 1988, s. 361.

22 Ibid., s. 363(2); on which see Inland Revenue Interpretation RI 12.

23 As set out in s. 363.

24 *Major* v. *Brodie* [1998] STC 491.

25 For general discussion, see RC Cmd 9474 (1955), ch. 19; and for trading losses, see Cmd 8189, 77–83.

26 TA 1988, s. 380.

relieved of all liability to tax.[27] The loss can be rolled forward (indefinitely) but can only be set against later trading income of that trade.[28] See further below §20.10.

Terminal losses may be carried back.[29] A terminal loss is one sustained in the year of assessment in which the trade is permanently discontinued and in that part of the preceding year of assessment beginning 12 months before the date of discontinuance.

TA 1988, s. 381 allows a carry-back of a trading loss where the loss arises in the year of assessment in which the trade is first carried on or the next three years of assessment.[30] It applies, therefore to losses arising in the first four years of business. The loss may be carried back and set off against *general* income for the three years before that in which the loss is sustained. Income of an earlier year is taken first, so a loss incurred in 2001–02 can be carried back to 1998–99. S. 381 applies only to individuals; the other trading loss rules apply generally for income tax.

10.3.2 Other types of loss

Schedule A

The reconstruction of Schedule A for income tax has meant a new provision governing Schedule A losses.[31] The general rule is that the rents from all properties in the UK are aggregated and expenditure is deducted from the aggregate. This automatically provides loss relief for a deficit on a single property, where there is other property let to provide a surplus. Any surplus losses may be rolled forward indefinitely and set off against any profit of a Schedule A business carried on in a subsequent year.[32]

In one situation, however, the loss may be relieved against general income of the same year of assessment. Broadly, this arises where there are net capital allowances arising from plant and machinery used in an agricultural estate.[33] Special rules allow certain unused losses from before 1995–1996 to be treated as Schedule A losses: these are losses under the old Schedule A, under Schedule D, Case VI for furnished lettings, and excess interest.[34]

Furnished holiday lettings

Loss relief is available when a letting is within the definition of furnished holiday lettings (below at §25.4).[35] In *Brown* v. *Richardson*[36] the Special Commissioners considered a claim for loss relief on the basis that property had been acquired to be "let on a commercial basis and with a view to the realisation of profits".[37] An accountant and his wife had purchased a property in Cornwall, the entire purchase being funded by a mortgage secured on the couple's main residence. A partnership agreement was drawn up between the husband and wife so that profits arising on the letting of the Cornish property were split equally between

[27] Ibid., s. 380(1)(a).
[28] Ibid., s. 385.
[29] Ibid., s. 388.
[30] It is the loss that arises in the fiscal year that is relievable: see *Gascoine* v. *Wharton* [1996] STC 1481, 69 TC 147, in which a taxpayer argued unsuccessfully that reliefs should be given for a loss arising in an accounting period, part of which was not during the year of assessment.
[31] TA 1988, s. 379A, added by FA 1995, Sch. 6, para. 19.
[32] TA 1988, s. 379A(1); on calculation of loss, see s. 379A(7).
[33] Ibid., s. 379A(5).
[34] FA 1995, Sch. 6, para. 19(2), (3), referring to TA 1988, ss 392, 355(4).
[35] TA 1988, s. 503(1).
[36] [1997] STC (SCD) 233.
[37] TA 1988, s. 504.

them, but any losses were allocated wholly to the husband. Losses arose, primarily because of significant finance charges. The Special Commissioner held that account had to be taken of the deduction of charges on income in considering whether the letting was with a view to profit even though they were not technically part of the calculation of profit; "profits" meant commercial profits and not tax-adjusted profit.

Schedule E

Relief for Schedule E losses can be claimed under TA 1988, s. 380 only. However, although s. 380 refers to employments (but not to offices), the Revenue does not accept that a claim can ever arise, even when expenses exceed emoluments. This is because expenses are deductible under s. 198 only if they are defrayed out of the emoluments, and are only deductible from those emoluments.

Schedule D, Case VI

Relief for Schedule D, Case VI losses can be claimed under TA 1988,s. 392 against other Case VI income of that year and then rolled forward and set against other Case VI income of later years. However, statutes which place certain types of income in Case VI often restrict their use to absorb losses.

Schedule D, Case V

A loss arising from a trade or profession carried on wholly overseas can be entitled to relief in full under TA 1988, s. 380, 385 or 388.[38] With effect from 1998–1999, losses from the letting of foreign property are relieved in the same way as losses from the letting of property within the UK.[39] Thus, all rental income arising from overseas property is pooled, and expenses incurred in generating that income are deducted therefrom. This has the effect that loss relief is given immediately for a deficit of income on a particular property where another property has produced a surplus. An overall deficit is carried forward to a subsequent year.[40] The pool of overseas letting income assessable under Schedule D, Case V is, however, separate from the pool of UK letting income, assessable under Schedule A. There is, thus, no offset of loss from one to the other.

Schedule D, Cases III and IV and Schedule F

No relief is possible under these Schedules since the tax legislation does not permit any deductions.

10.4 Loss on Shares in Unquoted Trading Companies

Although capital losses are the province of CGT and may not be set off against income, an exception is made where the loss arises from the disposal of unquoted shares in a trading company or member of a trading group. The purpose is to allow entrepreneurs to escape the restrictive CGT rules. The loss is computed on CGT principles. The relief is available only in respect of shares for which T, the individual, or T's spouse, subscribed[41]—as distinct

[38] TA 1988, s. 391 (2).
[39] FA 1995, s. 41(8).
[40] TA 1988, s. 379A(1)(a).
[41] Ibid., s. 574(4).

from those acquired through gift, inheritance or purchase. The shares must be ordinary share capital.[42] The company must be a "qualifying trading company"; a company qualifies only if it satisfies complex criteria as to what it has been doing (e.g. trading—but not in forbidden items such as shares or land)[43] and for how long (six years if previously an investment company or a dealer in forbidden items). In addition, the company must not have its shares quoted on a recognised stock exchange and must be resident in the UK.

The disposal must be an arm's-length sale for full consideration, a distribution on winding-up, or the deemed disposal which arises when shares have become of negligible value.[44] Relief is denied even for those disposals if there is a share exchange for non-commercial reasons or value-shifting has occurred. The relief may be claimed for the year in which the loss is realised or the preceding year.[45] Any unused loss can then be set only against capital gains. Where the taxpayer also has a loss entitled to relief under TA 1988, s. 380 or 381 the present loss is absorbed first.

Further rules apply where there are mixed holdings, e.g. where some shares were acquired by subscription and others by inheritance. The rules restrict the loss to what would have been the deductible cost if mixing had not occurred. The mixing rules can be avoided by issuing different types of shares.[46] Special rules apply also to reorganisation. Legislation now affirms "beyond doubt" the Revenue view that the withdrawal of funds from share accounts with building societies or industrial and provident societies cannot give rise to this relief.[47]

10.5 Sums within TA 1988, s. 348

TA 1988, s. 348 which in effect allows the assignment of income in certain defined situations. In 2000–01 these are payments made for bona fide commercial reasons in connection with the individual's trade, profession or vocation, e.g., partnership retirement annuities, certain earn-out arrangements and payments within TA 1988, s. 125(1) (but this apparent attitude is to enable an anti-avoidance provision to operate). See further chapter 27 below.

Where these payments arise, the taxpayer (T) is allowed to deduct the gross sum in computing total income. However, T must pay basic rate tax which is then recouped by T's withholding basic rate tax when making the payment. Therefore, if T is a 40% rate taxpayer who has undertaken to pay £1,000 a year, the whole £1,000 is deductible in computing T's total income. However, T then has to pay the £220 basic rate tax which is recouped by sending a cheque for only £780 to the other party. The other party is treated as having paid £220 tax on the income. Thus, T gets full relief but in an unnecessarily complicated way.

42 Ibid., ss 576(5), 832(1).
43 Ibid., s. 576(4), (5), as amended by FA 1989, Sch. 12, para. 4.
44 Ibid., s. 575(1).
45 Ibid., s. 574(1), (2).
46 Ibid., s. 576.
47 Ibid., s. 576(5).

10.6 Qualifying Gifts to Charity under Gift Aid

An individual[48] donor (D) making a qualifying donation is treated as making a payment to charity equal to the amount of the gift grossed up at basic rate.[49] So a payment of £780 is treated as a gift of £1,000 and the charity recovers £220 tax from the Revenue.[50] If D is a higher rate taxpayer, D is entitled to total relief of £400 of which £220 is treated as having already been withheld by D; the remaining £180 of relief is given in the self assessment as a deduction in computing total income.

Where the basic rate tax treated as deducted exceeds the amount of income tax (and CGT) with which D is charged for the year D is assessable to pay tax at basic rate to make good the shortfall.[51] This rule refers to D's total liability for the year not the amount of tax charged on the £1,000 given. So if D has a taxable income of £1,860 and so a tax liability of £220 (£1,520 at 10% and £340 at 20%) for the year that will be enough to prevent any further liability under this rule; if D's taxable income had been £1,500 only £150 would have been collected from D and so D would be liable to pay the extra £72. The tax rules for different types of income mean that the tax cost to D of making a gift will vary according to its source. For a higher rate taxpayer the after tax cost of giving £780 net (£1,000 gross) will be £600 from ordinary income, £580 from interest and £555 from dividends.[52]

As a result of FA 2000 there is now no minimum sum.[53] Previously there was a minimum of £250 for qualifying gifts[54] and a £100 minimum for 'millennium gift aid' (intended for overseas low income countries and to be channelled through an appropriate UK registered charity).[55]

There must be no significant benefit to D; a saving of inheritance tax has been held to be a benefit.[56] A simple declaration by the donor has replaced the old certificate.[57]

FA 2000 s. 41 brings covenanted donations to charity within this gift aid framework. As they are also removed from TA 1988, s. 348 an express provision allows D to deduct basic rate tax.[58]

As from 6th April 2000 income tax relief may be claimed not only where the individual makes a gift of cash, as under the gift aid scheme, but also where the gift is of shares or securities. A donor making a gift of a qualifying investment defined is entitled to an income tax deduction in computing total income [59] equal to the relevant amount i.e. the market value of the investments, defined as for CGT and any associated costs of disposal.[60]

48 On the boundary between making a gift as an individual and as personal representative see *St Dunstans* v. *Major* [1997] STC (SCD) 212.

49 FA 1990, s. 25(6); the grossing up rate is tied to when the payment is due: s. 25(9).

50 Ibid., s. 25(10).

51 TA 1990, s. 25(8).

52 Lathwood Taxation vol 145 p. 118.

53 FA 1990 s. 25 amended by FA 2000 s. 39.

54 FA 1990 s. 25 (previous version).

55 FA 1925, s. 25(2)(g) as amended 1993; in 1992–93 the minimum was £600. On millennium aid see FA 1998 ss. 47 and 48; the list of countries is derived from the World Bank designation of "low income countries": Inland Revenue Press Release, 14 March 1998, (1998) *Simon's Weekly Tax Intelligence* 393.

56 Ibid. subs (5E)–(5G) so as to safeguard benefits such as free admission to National Trust properties etc. *St Dunstans* v. *Major* [1997] STC (SCD) 212. See also 31.6.2.

57 FA 1992 s. 25(1)(c).

58 FA 2000, s. 41 and 41(8).

59 TA 1988, s. 587B (2)(a)(ii); s. 83B added by FA 2000 s. 43; on timing see s. 43(3).

60 TA 1988, s. 587B (10) and subs.(6) and (7).

Investments qualify if they are quoted shares or securities, units in an authorised unit trust, shares in an OPEIC or an interest in an offshore fund.[61] The idea is to give relief where the assets are easy to value and easy to realise.[62]

The relevant amount also takes account of any consideration or benefit received, as where the benefactor sells the shares to the charity at a low price.[63] This relief is distinct from and in addition to the CGT rules exempting the donor from CGT liability. The charity's base cost of the asset is reduced by the relevant amount (or to nil if the base cost is less than the relevant amount).[64]

There are similar rules for corporation tax where it is added to the category of a charge on profits[65] s. and special rules made for insurance companies.[66]

10.7 "Full" Deduction for Certain Items Restricted as to Types of Income

Apart from losses, other sums are deductible in full but only against certain classes of income. A prime example, already seen, is loss relief under TA1988, s. 385 (see above at §10.3). However, other examples can be found in the rules for pension contributions which are available against earned income from various sources (relevant earnings) and post-cessation expenditure (see below at §23.4).

10.8 Deductions Allowed at Basic Rate

An individual resident of performing duties in the UK can claim relief for a payment in respect of a qualifying course of vocational training.[68] Relief can be set against income for the year of assessment in which the payment is made, unless it can be claimed under some other income tax rule. The payment must be in respect of allowable expenses, which are defined as fees in connection with undertaking the course, being assessed and having any resulting entry and award registered, and must be paid in connection with the individual's own training. It is also necessary that no specified public financial assistance should be received for the period. Relief is given at source at the basic rate, which means that lower rate and zero rate taxpayers may also benefit. As from 6 April 1999 higher rate taxpayers could no longer reclaim the difference between basic and higher rate.[69] The "training provider" recovers the tax from the Revenue, but must make a refund to the Revenue if there is a refund to the individual. Regulations provide for disqualification from relief, e.g. the award

[61] TA 1988, s. 587B (9) on offshore fund note subs (11).
[62] IR Notes Clause 43 para 18.
[63] TA 1988, s. 587B).
[64] TA 1988, s. 587B); among the consequential rules are references to total income for s. 550 (s. 587B (2) (b)).
[65] TA 1988, s. 587B) (a)(ii).
[66] TA 1988, s. 587B (8).
[67] For reprint of Revenue's cost-assessment see Sandford, *Tax Compliance Costs: Measurement and Policy*, 32–8.
[68] FA 1991, s. 32 and Vocational Training (Tax Relief) Regulations 1992 (SI 1992/746), as any programme or activity accredited as an NVQ or a Scottish vocational qualification other than the highest level.
[69] FA 1999, s. 59.

of a prize for completing the course.[70] The regulations do not, as yet, require successful completion of the course.

Relief was extended in 1996 to individuals aged 30 or over who attend a qualifying course of training,[71] requiring participation on a full-time (or substantially full-time) basis, provided the course lasts for a minimum of four consecutive weeks. The intention was to benefit those taking specialised courses such as MBAs.[72]

This relief is notable for three reasons. The first is as a matter of theory in that the cost of a certain type of human capital is being recognised as an allowable deduction. The second is the very large extent to which the detail of the legislation is left to subordinate legislation. The third is the mechanism by which tax can be deducted at source by the payment of lower fees. This means that the person taking the course deducts basic rate tax from the fee, whether or not he is actually liable to tax.

Payments are not deductible if the individual undertakes a course wholly or mainly for recreational purposes or as a leisure activity.[73] The boundary here will not always be easy to draw; some "Outward bound"-type courses have recreational elements but are clearly and correctly marketed as training in leadership skills—quite how far they will fit into the rest of the NVQ scheme is another matter. It was reported that in 1997–98 one-quarter of this tax relief was spent on diving courses and flying training.[74] 2000–01 is the last year in which this relief can be claimed. The relief is being superseded by Individual Learning Accounts (see below §10.10).

10.9 Deductions at 20%

Under the Enterprise Investment Scheme relief is permitted at the lower rate (not the marginal rate) by way of a reduction in tax (not a deduction in computing total income).[75] The maximum investment is £100,000 p.a.

Venture capital trust is a similar form of relief by way of tax reduction (with the same limit of £100,00 p.a.) and is permitted for contributions to collective investment schemes.[76]

10.10 Individual Learning Account

The individual learning account (ILA) is intended to provide financial and tax help with learning; for political reasons it cannot be called a "voucher". Individual learning accounts are set up under the Learning and Skills Act 2000, s. 96. People in England and Wales with an individual learning account will be eligible for 80 per cent discounts on computer liter-

[70] Vocational Training (Public Financial Assistance and Disentitlement to Tax Relief) Regulations 1992 (SI 1992/734) and Vocational Training (Public Financial Assistance and Disentitlement to Tax Relief) (Amendment) Regulations 1993 (SI 1993/1074).

[71] Defined in TA 1988, s. 589.

[72] Inland Revenue Press Releases, 28 November 1995, (1995) *Simon's Tax Intelligence* 1843.

[73] FA 1991, s. 32(1)(cb).

[74] Butterworths Annotated Finance Act 1999, s. 59.

[75] TA 1988, ss 289, 289A.

[76] TA 1988, Sch. 15B, para. 1 (added by FA 1995).

acy courses and some other specific types of learning, or 20 per cent discounts on a wide range of other eligible learning activities. (Scotland and Northern Ireland are to decide their own priorities for what will be regarded as an eligible learning activity.) The discounts will be available from 1 September 2000.

These discounts are not taxable. In addition there is no liability under Schedule E when the costs are provided an employer under qualifying fair opportunity conditions.[77]

10.11 Benefits Whether or Not Taxpayer Liable to Tax

These categories must be noted since they cause sums to be paid by the Revenue even though the person making the original payment is not subject to tax. These benefits through the tax system are:

- WFTC (see §9.4.1);
- disabled persons tax credit (see §9.4.2);
- individual learning account (see above at §10.10);

10.12 Repealed Deductions

From 1989 to 1997 an individual paying a premium under a contract of private medical insurance,[78] could claim a deduction—originally at the marginal rate and later at basic rate—but only if the person insured was an individual aged 60 or over. There was no deduction for actual medical expenditure.[79]

10.13 Obsolescent Deduction

A person making qualifying maintenance payments[80] could claim a reduction in tax in respect of those payments subject to a maximum of a sum equal to 10% of the married couple's allowance (£1,970 in 1999–00). Its repeal was a surprise, and probably an unintended casualty of the decision to abolish the married couple's allowance. It is available in 2000–01 and later years only if either the payer or the recipient was born before 6 April 1935.

[77] TA 1988, ss 200E–200H added by FA 2000, s. 58. See below §15.5.

[78] FA 1989, s. 54.

[79] For an argument in favour of such deduction on the basis of the optimal tax theory, see Boskin and Stiglitz (1997) 67 *American Economic Review* 295.

[80] TA 1988, s. 347B.

11

Personal Reliefs and Credits

11.1 General

We now turn to the rules for deductions allowed by the tax system on account of personal circumstances. Some deductions take the form of "reliefs", i.e. deductions from total income made in order to reach taxable income. Others take the form of tax "credits", i.e. a reduction in the taxpayer's liability. Since tax reliefs reduce the amount of income which is taxable they are more valuable to those paying at higher rates than to those paying at lower rate.[1] Tax credits, by contrast, are worth the same amount to all taxpayers and so can be seen as "fairer". From the introduction of the unified income tax structure in 1973 until 1994, personal allowances took only the first form. However, Conservative governments anxious to raise tax revenue without raising the tax rate began to use the second form. The new Labour administration is intent on carrying the process further in the name of fairnesss as we have seen in chapter 9. A comparative survey finds not only extensive use of both devices[2] but also some use of a zero-rated first bracket (which may or may not work out more beneficially to a high rate taxpayer depending on the way it is introduced). Rules for credits tend to be more complicated to draft especially if any unused credits can be carried to another year.[3]

Of course tax credits are of use only if one has a tax liability. Logic goes further and suggests that tax credits are replaced with a welfare benefit of value to taxpayers and non-taxpayers alike. At this point it is important to remember that the purpose of the rules is to allocate the tax burden according to ability to pay—however recent changes, notably the WFTC, lead to a blurring of these distinctions. Both reliefs and credits are to be found in TA 1988 Part VII. The Act sometimes refers to certain tax credits as tax reductions; here they will be referred to only as tax credits. The WFTC is not covered in TA 1988, Part VII, and so has been discussed above at chapter 9.

[1] For a defence of reliefs as opposed to credits, see Brannon and Morss 26 *National Tax Jo.* 599, 659; and Gottschalk 29 *National Tax Jo.* 221.

[2] Messere (1993), Tables 10.3 *et seq.*

[3] Sunley (1977) *National Tax Jo.* 243.

The allowances given in Part VII are fixed sums, either deductible from total income in calculating taxable income or credits. Being personal allowances they can be claimed only by individuals as opposed to, for example, trusts, and therefore are distinguishable from other deductions such as loss relief. Further, they may generally be claimed only by residents. Part VII allowances are available only for the year of assessment; allowances which are not used in one year cannot be rolled forward (or backwards) to another year. Some, but not all, may be assigned directly; some may be assigned indirectly if one person can provide income for another to absorb that other's allowance. The sums are index-linked but may be overriden by express legislation.[4]

11.1.1 Non-residents

Individuals who are not resident[5] are entitled to personal reliefs under Part VII only if they fall within certain categories and then only on a special basis. The categories are[6]:

(1) Commonwealth citizens or nationals of the EEA;[7]
(2) persons who are or have been employed in the service of the Crown, any missionary society or in the service of any territory under Her Majesty's protection;
(3) persons resident in the Channel Islands or the Isle of Man;
(4) persons who have previously resided within the UK but who are compelled to live abroad for reasons of health, or the health of members of their families resident with them; and
(5) widows whose late husbands (or widowers whose late wives) were in the service of the Crown.

In addition some double taxation treaties provide for relief of non-residents as if they were British subjects.[8]

These qualifying non-residents receive their allowances in full. The married couple's allowance under s. 257A is transferable by a husband to his wife if she is resident or a qualifying non-resident. However, the special transitional rules in s. 257D did not apply if the husband was not resident in the UK.[9]

11.1.2 Effect of charges

Reliefs may not be claimed for that part of the income which is needed to pay the charge.[10] Since the scheme allows for deduction of tax only at the basic rate, relief can be claimed to the extent, if any, that the relief would exceed tax at the basic rate on that income.

11.1.3 Credits/reductions

The effect of an income tax credit is the amount of that person's liability to tax for that year being reduced by an amount equal to 10% of the specified amount or the amount which

[4] TA 1988, s. 257C.
[5] On residence, see chapter 58 below.
[6] TA 1988, s. 278(2).
[7] Defined by ibid., s. 278(9).
[8] For example, Fiji (SI 1976/1342, art. 23) and France (SI 1968/1869, art. 23).
[9] TA 1988, s. 278(2A).
[10] Ibid., s. 276.

reduces the liability to nil[11]—i.e. there cannot be any repayment. In calculating the amount of tax otherwise payable, no account is to be taken of any foreign tax credit, whether under double tax treaty or unilaterally, or of any basic rate tax which is charged under TA 1988, s. 3 and which can be charged against another person.[12]

11.2 The Reliefs

11.2.1 The basic personal relief

Under TA 1988, s. 257 all individuals resident in the UK—and some non-residents—are entitled to a deduction from total income by way of personal relief. In 2000–01 the figure is £4,385 (£84 a week). So, if T has Schedule E income of £4,395, the personal relief will reduce T's total income from £4,395 to £10 and the tax bill will be £1 (since the 10% starting rate will apply). As a reduction in computing taxable income its effect is to reduce the top slice of total income—it will therefore be more valuable to a 40% taxpayer (£1,754) than to a 22% taxpayer (£964.70) or a 20% taxpayer (£877).[13] The deduction may be larger where the claimant is aged 65 or more (see below at §11.4).

11.2.2 Blind person's relief

Under TA 1988, s. 26 a registered blind person is entitled to a deduction from total income—of £1,400 for 2000–01.[14] The deduction may be claimed by a married man whose wife is blind. If they are both blind, each has the allowance. The person must be registered with a local authority for at least a part of the year; this excludes non-residents. If the eye condition develops in one year but registration is not completed until the next, the relief may, by concession be given for the first year.[15]

If the claimant is married, any unusable part of the allowance may be transferred to the other spouse. In determining the extent of the blind person's allowance which cannot be used, and so is available for transfer, no account is taken of the married couple's allowance; similarly, where the blind person is a married woman who is entitled to the whole or part of the married couple's allowance, that married couple's allowance is also ignored.

11.3 Personal Tax Credits

For 2000–01 there is one[15a] principal "tax credit" (which takes the legislative form of a tax reduction). This is the married couple's tax reduction, which is now available only if either the taxpayer or the taxpayer's spouse was over 65 on 6 April 2000 (s. 257A) (see below at §11.4.2). As from April 2001 there will be a second credit—the new children's tax credit (s. 257AA); on which, see §11.5 below. The working families tax credit and the disabled

[11] Ibid., s. 256(2).
[12] Ibid., s. 256(3)(c).
[13] £4.385 is set by Income Tax (Indexation) Order SI 2000/806. For the situation in OECD countries in 1990, see Meessere, above at n. 2, Table 10.3.
[14] On rules for calculating total income from which this relief is to be deducted, see s. 265(3).
[15] Inland Revenue Press Release, 6 October 1994, (1994) *Simon's Tax Intelligence* 1233.
[15a] See also the obsolescent widow's bereavement allowance below §11.6

person's tax credit are discussed in chapter 9 above since they are better regarded as social security benefits paid as tax credits.

11.4 Older Taxpayers

Three rules apply to older taxpayers. The basic personal relief in s. 257 is increased (see below at §11.4.1) and the married couple's allowance in s. 257A may be available (see below at §11.4.2) The increase in s. 257 is subject to being phased out as total income rises; this also applies to certain enhancements to s. 257A. While s. 257A is available only if either the taxpayer or the taxpayer's spouse was 65 or over on 6 April 2000, this date has no significance for the increase in s. 257. The problem of poverty among older people is very severe; as far as those owning their homes are concerned, releasing the value of that capital could be a significant help.[16] However, the issues presented by the very fact of an ageing population are also significant asthis leads to lower savings, slower investment growth and a reduced rate of national economic growth.[17] The *third* rule is the retention of the qualifying maintenance deduction (see above §10.11).

11.4.1 Increased level of personal allowance[18]

An individual who is aged 65 or over at any time within the fiscal year is entitled to an increased personal allowance of £5,790, instead of £4,385; the figure is £6,050 for a taxpayer who is aged 75 or over at the end of the fiscal year. If the taxpayer dies during the fiscal year, the test is applied in respect of the age that individual would have attained by the end of that fiscal year. The relief depends exclusively on the age of the claimant. However, where the individual's total income for that year exceeds a specified limit (currently £17,000) the additional allowance given on account of age (£1,405 or £1,665) is reduced by one half of the excess of total income over the £17,000. With a basic rate of tax of 22%, the effect of the restriction in age allowance is to give a marginal rate of tax of 33% when clawing back the basic personal relief. The benefit of these increases disappears altogether when income exceeds the specified limit by twice the amount of the increase age allowance (£19,810 and £20,330). Marginal rate calculations become more complex if the income consists not just of ordinary income taxed at 22% (such as a pension) but also savings income taxed at 20%.

11.4.2 Married couple's reduction

This is available to married coupled who are living together, provided either the taxpayer or the taxpayer's spouse was born before 6 April 1935, i.e. had reached 65 by 6 April 2000 (s. 257A). In 2000–01 it takes the form of a reduction in tax currently calculated at 10% by reference to a set sum. The basic sum is £5,185, but this is increased to £5,255 once the taxpayer (or spouse) reaches 75.[19] Elaborate rules are designed to ensure that claimants cannot claim this relief and the new children's tax credit in s. 257AA in the same year.

[16] See Symposium (1998) 19 *Fiscal Studies* 141; and Hancock (1998) 19 *Fiscal Studies* 249.
[17] Disney (1996) 17(2) *Fiscal Studies* 83.
[18] For history and criticism, see Morris (1981) 2(3) *Fiscal Studies* 29.
[19] TA 1988, s. 257A. Figure set by Income Tax (Indexation) Order SI 2000/806.

The maximum sums are reduced as total income rises but cannot be pulled down below the basic sum, £2000. The formula for phasing out is the same as for the relief in s. 257 and so begins at £17,000. The phasing-out of this relief follows any reduction in the s. 257 relief. So, in 2000–01 a husband of 75 or over is entitled to the £6,050 allowance which fades out at £20,030, and to the £5,255 married couple's allowance which fades out at £26,540.[20] With a basic rate of tax of 22%, the effect of the restriction in age allowance is first to give a marginal rate of tax of 33% when clawing back the basic personal relief, and then to apply a rate of 27% when clawing back the extra married couple's allowance. As before, these marginal rate calculations are more complex when savings and dividend income are included.

Allocating and sharing

The formal starting point of the legislation is still that the husband is the person entitled to this reduction.[21] The wife may then claim her half of the allowance as of right and they may jointly elect that she should get all of it; the husband can then claim his half back.[22] The outcome is that each has a right to claim half of the allowance but entitlement to the whole allowance is possible only with the consent (tacit or express) of the other. Elaborate provisions apply to notice of making such elections and terminating.[23] Where one spouse is unable to use the reduction, i.e. because he or she has no income against which to put that reduction (as distinct from not being able to use it as advantageously as the other), separate rules permit transfer and retrospection.[24]

Married and living together?

The question whether the parties are married is governed by the law of marriage and by the private international law rules for the recognition of marriages in other states. The term "wife" means "lawful wife", i.e. a woman with whom the taxpayer has entered into a relationship of marriage recognised by the civil law of the appropriate part of the UK.[25] Under the pre-1990 rules it was held that when a husband was separated from his wife, but then contracted a valid (polygamous) second marriage to a second wife, he was entitled to the allowance, as the phrase "his wife" could be construed as meaning "a person being his wife".[26] Spouses are treated as living together unless they are separated under a court order or a deed of separation or they are in fact separated in such circumstances that the separation is likely to be permanent.[27]

Transitional reliefs

The changeover to individual taxation illustrates the point that major changes result in losers as well as winners. Some situations required special rules to be made. These transitional

[20] See *Simons Direct Tax Service* E.2.304.

[21] TA 1988, s. 257A(1).

[22] Ibid., s. 257BA.

[23] Elections must be made in ibid., s. 257BA(8).

[24] Ibid., s. 257BB.

[25] *Rignell* v. *Andrews* [1990] STC 410, 63 TC 312 (an English case—had the facts arisen in Scotland the analogous question would have related to Scots law).

[26] *Nabi* v. *Heaton* [1983] STC 344, 57 TC 292, CA.

[27] TA 1988, s. 282. A spouse who is living under the same roof but not in the same household as the taxpayer is not living with that taxpayer: *Holmes* v. *Mitchell* [1991] STC 25, 63 TC 718, applying the divorce test formulated in *Hopes* v. *Hopes* [1949] P 227, [1948] 2 All ER 920, CA. On practice, see *Inland Revenue Reliefs Manual*, paras 1050–1065. If the married couple live apart and one maintains the other wholly and voluntarily, they are still taken as living apart. On social security views on living together as husband and wife, see Ogus, Barendt and Wikeley, *The Law of Social Security Law* (4th ed. 1994), ch. 9, 389–93.

rules are now obsolete.[28] These were: (1) wife as breadwinner or husband with low income (TA 1988, s. 257D); (2) the elderly couple with the husband as the younger spouse (TA 1988, s. 257E); and (3) separated spouses (TA 1988, s. 257F).

11.5 The Children's Tax Credit

Unlike the working families tax credit (WFTC) and the disabled persons tax credit (DPTC) discussed in chapter 9 above, the children's tax credit is a genuine tax credit or reduction of the familiar type and is not related to the social security system in any way. Marking a decisive shift from the old rules, which had emphasised marriage, to the new rules, which stress support for children, FA 1999 enacts the legislation for a new child tax credit.[29] It takes effect in 2001–02, one year after all the old reliefs will have been abolished.

Building on the old s. 259, FA 1999 applies where a "qualifying child" resides with the claimant during the whole or part of a year of assessment; the claimant will be entitled to a tax reduction, called the children's tax credit. A qualifying child must be under 16 and either be a child of the claimant (including a stepchild and illegitimate child) or be maintained by or at the expense of the claimant. Provisionally, FA 2000 sets the credit at £4,420 and relief given at 10%, making a maximum credit of £442.

Phasing out the credit

The credit will be reduced by £2 for every £3 by which the claimant's income is subject to higher rate tax. So, if the claimant has £32,785 (i.e. £28,400 plus £4,385) the credit is available in full. If, however, the claimant's income rises by £15 to £32,800 the figure of £4,420 drops to £4,410 and the credit is worth £441 instead of £442. The credit is based on the fact that children are living with the claimant; it differs from child benefit in that there is no increase just because more than one child resides with the claimant. Where the rules give rise to entitlement to more than one relief the claimaint's maximum entitlement is not to exceed £442.[30] Where one client is affected by this phasing out the credit cannot be transferred to the claimant's spouse or partner. By withholding the transfer of the benefit the system maintains the principle that one spouse's income should not affect the other's liability to tax.[31]

Residing with more than one claimant

A child may live with two people rather than one. Those people may be unmarried and may be same-sex couples, e.g. where one is the biological parent and the other pays for the maintenance. Further examples may also be envisaged. The parents of the child are included within the relief because although they were excluded under the old s. 259, they were entitled to the married couple's allowance. Once again, therefore, the rule shows the shifting emphasis from marriage to children. If the child lives with more than one adult at the same time during the year,[32] the relief is given once—and only once. If neither partner is a higher

[28] FA 1999, s. 32(2).

[29] Ibid., s. 30(1); backed up by TA 1988, Sch. 13A, added by FA 1999, Sch. 3 containing rules where the child resides with more than one claimant during the year. For an introduction, see Gordon 143 *Taxation* 317.

[30] TA 1988, Sch. 13A, para 6(6)(b).

[31] Inland Revenue Press Release, 9 March 1999, note 2, *Simons Weekly Tax Intelligence* 1999, 422.

[32] Ibid., para. 1.

rate taxpayer, the starting point is to give the credit to the higher earner of the two partners in the couple.[33] However, the lower earner may insist on a half share in the credit[34] or the higher earner may agree to the whole amount being transferred to the other.[35] If one earner does not have income against which to set the credit, and so is unable to use it, the surplus may be transferred to the other.[36] No other division or transfer is possible.

Where the two people with whom the child lives are not partners in this sense, e.g. the child lives half the time with each parent, the credit is to be shared between the parents as they may agree or as determined by the Commissioners.[37]

The legislation also takes account of combined cases, i.e. where the child is a relevant child of more than one pair of partners, or because he spends part of the year with one set of partners and the rest with a single parent.[38] It also makes provision for changes of circumstances during the year.[39]

11.6 "Recently" Repealed Reliefs

In 1999–2000, where a married man whose wife was living with him has died, his widow was entitled (a) for that year of assessment, and (b) for the following year of assessment (unless she married again before the beginning of it), to an income tax reduction of an amount calculated by reference to the married couple's reduction, and was restricted to 10%.[40] This relief was abolished along with the married couple's allowance. Unlike the married couple's allowance, however, it does not continue when one spouse was born before 6 April 1935. However it lingers on, for 2000–01 only, if the taxpayer became a widow in 1999–00 and has not remarried. This relief was introduced by Geoffrey Howe in 1980.[41]

The "additional relief" in s. 259 is superseded by the children's tax credit in s. 257AA. However, whereas s. 259 is repealed as from the start of 2000–01, s. 257AA does not begin until 2001–02.

TA 1988 in its original version provided for other reliefs which have now been repealed. These include the widow or widower's housekeeper relief (s. 258), the dependant relatives relief (s. 263) and relief for a claimant depending on the services of a son or daughter. All of these reliefs were repealed by Nigel Lawson in 1988 when he reduced the top rates of tax to their present level. The relief for life assurance premiums in s. 265 was restricted in 1984 to existing policies.[42]

These changes in allowances reflect a wish to abolish socially obsolete devices. However, even in 1988 some people lost out on benefits, and for them the losses were significant. In 2000 a concern for "carers" may, therefore, revive.

[33] Ibid., para. 3(1); on the situation where they are equal earners, see ibid., para. 2(3).
[34] Ibid., para 3(2).
[35] Ibid., para 3(3); the rules for the election are set out in para. 5.
[36] Ibid., para. 4; the time limits are set out in subpara. 4(4).
[37] Ibid., para 6.
[38] Ibid., para 7.
[39] Ibid., para 8.
[40] TA 1988, s. 262(l)(a), applying s. 257A(l), as amended.
[41] FA 1980, s. 23. James, Lewis and Allison, *The Comprehensibility of Taxation* (1987) point out that many widows had never dealt with tax matters while their husbands were alive.
[42] Lawson, *Memoirs*, 355. In 1999 the cost of the relief was still £110 m p.a. (Inland Revenue Statistics, Table 1.5).

12

Calculations

12.1 Introduction

This chapter draws together issues from the previous chapters with the aid of a longer example, and considers some more complicated calculation rules, before finishing on the problem of progression. The complexity of the current rate structure is addressed. In 12.2 we examine the different structures and rates which have applied at various times since the Second Word War. The Appendix at the end of this chapter will consider how the taxation of savings has changed since 1993.

12.2 Retrospective Historical Introduction: Rates and Structures

In 2000–01[1] the UK has one tax on income (income tax) and three rates of income tax: (a) the "starting" rate (10%) applicable to taxable income between nil and £1,520; (b) the "basic" rate (22%), applicable on income between from £1,520 and £28,400; and (c) the "higher" rate, applicable to taxable income above £28,400. As we have already seen (see above at §7.1) (a) and (c) apply only to individuals. Income tax applies not only to individuals but also to other bodies such as trusts and estates in administration; these bodies are concerned with (b) above, and pay basic rate income tax at 22%. Special rules may sometimes make other rates apply to such bodies.

It has also been seen that savings income is taxed at 10%, 20% (called the "lower" rate) or 40% and that special sub-rules apply for savings income consisting of dividends, etc.

[1] FA 2000, s. 31.

Savings income accruing to income taxpayers other than individuals may also attract special rates. Capital gains tax (CGT) is charged at 10%, 20% and 40% for individuals; other bodies pay at other rates.

Eleven years ago the system was much simpler. In 1989–1990[2] two rates of income tax applied to individuals—the basic rate of 25% and the higher rate of 40%—which applied to all types of income. There was no starting rate and no lower rate. Trusts might have to pay an additional rate on certain types of income. CGT was charged at the same rates as ordinary income.

Going back further to 1978–1979[3] the basic rate was 33%; with a lower rate of 25% applying to the first £750. Basic rate liability expired at £8,000, after which no fewer than nine higher rates applied, reaching the top rate of 83% at £24,000. If the taxpayer had investment income over £1,700, a surcharge or "additional rate" applied: 10% on the first £550 and 15% thereafter. Therefore, a taxpayer with over £24,000 of taxable income which included more than £2,700 of investment income had a marginal rate of 98% on such income. The normal rate for CGT was 30%; it was not tied to the income tax rate until 1988.

In 1967–1968 a "standard" rate applied, which was set at just over 41%.[4] Three lower rate bands took the form of alleviations of income tax (credits) rather than of taxable income. In addition to income tax (at 41%) a surtax[5] was charged retrospectively by FA 1968, at 10 rising rates and reaching 50% and so a top rate of 91%. The fusing of the two taxes into one occurred in 1973 as a result of FA 1971. In 1967–1968 there was no additional rate on investment income because earned income attracted a special relief—earned income relief. Personal reliefs took effect, not as deductions in computing income but as reliefs from income tax on a set sum (i.e. credits); moreover, credits might not have been available against surtax as opposed to income tax. FA 1968 had another surprise for taxpayers—a special charge of 45% on investment income over £3,000, making a theoretical top rate of 136%. This was quite deliberate; the Chancellor intended the tax to be paid out of capital as an alternative to increasing CGT or introducing a wealth tax.[6] CGT was charged at 30%.

Going back still further to 1957[7] the same basic structure of income tax with its reduced rates, surtax with its many bands, and earned income relief (extended to surtax for the first time that year) all existed, but there was one important difference: there was no CGT.

As one rehearses these snapshots, a number of features must be understood. The first is the ferocity of the income tax rates for much of this period: the present top rate of 40% was introduced in 1988.[8] The second is the non-alignment of rates of CGT (introduced in 1965) with income tax rates (this occurred in 1988). The third is the separate structure of income tax and surtax (until 1973). The fourth is the pre-1970 proliferation of lower rates of income tax below the standard rate. The fifth is the difference between having a basic rate charged on income with an additional rate charged on investment income, and a standard

[2] FA 1989, s. 30.

[3] FA 1978, s.13.

[4] FA 1967, s. 13.

[5] Introduced by FA 1926; the previous tax, super tax, which had been the subject of Lloyd George's battles with the House of Lords, was introduced in 1911. The reasons for the change from supertax to surtax can be found in the 1920 Royal Commission, 28–40, esp. para. 131; supertax was based on a slab system i.e. one in which the total income was treated as one slab and taxed at the relevant rate—e.g. 20%, 20% and 40%. Surtax was based on the familiar slice system under which each slice of the total income had its own rate; the slab system lead to anomalies when abatements ceased, allowances ended or higher brackets were reached.

[6] Butterworths, *Annotated Legislation: Finance Act 1968*, 79.

[7] FA 1957, s. 13.

[8] FA 1988, ss 23, 24.

rate on all income with earned income relief. The obvious lessons to be learned are: (1) that tax climates can change and, with the UK's electoral system, can change very quickly; (2) that there are many fiscal mechanisms for achieving what the government wants; and (3) that almost any proposal for change means reviving what has been tried before. The less obvious lesson is that one should perhaps refrain from condemning too quickly all those who, faced with such punitive rates, sought ways of reducing its burden, especially by converting income into capital gain. As Wheatcroft reportedly said, a tax system breathes through its loopholes. It is also pertinent to recall the comment of the 1955 Royal Commission that the existence of widespread tax avoidance was evidence that the system, not the taxpayer, stood in need of radical reform.[9]

12.3 Items Included in Income

Items included in income are as follows:

(i) income from each source according to the rule of each Schedule (TA 1988, s. 1). Sums deductible in computing income from each source, e.g. allowable expenses under Schedule A or Schedule D, Case I, are taken into account in computing the amount of income under that Case. If the figures show a loss, the amount to be included is nil;
(ii) income subject to deduction under the PAYE scheme—included at its gross amount;
(iii) income paid subject to deduction at basic rate (22%) at source, which must be grossed up to reflect that fact. The taxpayer is then given credit for the tax withheld. Grossing-up is carried out by multiplying the figure by the fraction 100/(100–BR) where BR is basic rate. This applies not only to annual payments and interest within Schedule D, Case III but also foreign dividends under s. 123;
(iv) bank interest and building society interest. Lower rate tax (20%) is usually deducted at source and so added back to calculate the grossed-up income;
(v) dividends under Schedule F together with the accompanying tax credit, which is now geared to the special rate of tax at 10% (TA 1988, ss 20(1), 1A);
(vi) T's share of partnership income;
(vii) income deemed to be T's under the provisions of the Act, e.g. under the anti-avoidance rules discussed below in chapter 31;
(viii) income to which T is entitled as beneficiary under a trust;
(ix) income of an unadministered residuary estate in which T has a life interest in possession or an absolute interest.
(x) any other income of T's.

Example

The following example involving X and Y, a married couple living together, will be used as the basis for the explanation which follows: facts (a)–(h) will be considered first.

In the tax year 2000–2001: (a) X is married, with children aged 19 and 15; (b) X has trading profits of £39,000 taxable under Schedule D, Case I; (c) X received £6,000 as director of a company; (d) X received payments of £4,500 by way of dividend from UK resident companies, (e) interest of £3,200 net from a building society and (f) £3,840 net interest from a

[9] Cmd 9474, §33; cited by Kay [1979] *BTR* 354, 365.

bank; (g) X also received £4,800 by way of rent and has allowable rental expenses of £650 (g). (h) Two years ago X created a revocable trust in favour of X's children; in 2000–2001, £5,500 of income arose in the trust.

Taking each fact in turn:

(a) gives no deduction. There is as yet no child credit under s. 257AA and X has too much income and too many savings to qualify for WFTC;
(b) is Schedule D, Case I income of £39,000; (c) is Schedule E income of £6,000; (d) is Schedule F income of £5,000; (e) is Schedule D, Case III income of £4,000; (f) is Schedule D, Case III income of £4,800; and (g) is Schedule A income of £4,150;
(h) is a settlement within s. 660B. Since one child is over 17 only one half of the income will be treated as X's (£2,250).

This makes X's total receipts grossed up for tax deducted £65,200.

12.4 From Income to Total Income—Deductions

An individual is liable to tax at higher or lower rates on *total* income which is defined in TA 1988, s. 835; a person's total income is also relevant to matters of reliefs.[10]

Some items (category 1) are to be "deducted from or set against" income. These sums are not deductible in computing the initial statutory income but are deductible once it has been determined; they are also deductible in computing total income (but cannot be deducted twice). So, interest on qualifying loans and loss reliefs are deductible in computing total income

Other items (category 2) are stated to be deductible in computing total income, once more making total income different from statutory income. So, annuities and annual payments still payable under deduction of tax are deductible in computing total income. For details of these devices see at §27 ff.

Also deductible in computing total income are those sums expressed to be deductible by being set only against certain classes of income. This list comprises: pension contributions—set against "relevant earnings"; and capital allowances given otherwise than as trading expenses (CAA 1990, ss 141–3).

Two types of deductions are not deductible in computing total income. The first comprises sums expressed to be deductible *from* total income, e.g. personal reliefs. Since these are to be deducted from total income in computing taxable income they cannot be deducted in computing total income. The second category comprises items expressed to be given relief by being set against a particular tax liability or tax at a certain rate; there reliefs are given separately and so are not deductible in computing total income. Therefore credits for foreign tax and contributions to Venture Capital Trusts (VCT) or Enterprise Investment Scheme (EIS) are not deductible at this point.

Example (*continued*) (facts (j)–(o))

During the year X paid: (i) mortgage interest of £3,000, (j) interest of £2,200 on a loan to acquire an interest in the close company for which X works (k), £4,000 to an ex-spouse under a court order made in 1986. (l) X was liable to pay £1,000 gross to a charity under a

[10] For example, TA 1988, ss 257(5), 257A(5), 274.

the gift aid scheme, i.e. £780 net. (m) X also paid £875 in life assurance premiums (on a contract made before 14 March 1984), (n) £3,500 under a personal pension plan and (o) £2,772 to go on a four-week, intensive, residential, full-time training course to learn about tax law.

X is unable to deduct the mortgage interest (i), the payment to the ex-spouse (k) or any element of (o); until relatively recently all three items would have been deductible. X's permitted deductions are: (j) £2,200 (loan interest), (n) £3,500 (pension—but only from relevant earnings) and (l) £1,000 to charity: a total of £6,700. X's total income is therefore £65,200 − £6,700 = £58,500.

12.5 From Total Income to Taxable Income

Personal reliefs are deductible from total income: these are the basic personal relief in s. 257 and blind person's relief in s. 265. X is entitled to the basic personal allowance of £4,385, so X's total income of £58,500 is reduced by the personal relief of £4,385, to give taxable income of £54,415.

12.6 From Taxable Income to Tax

12.6.1 Tax credits

The tax system provides a number of credits against tax. These include: credit for tax for foreign tax paid in respect of income subject to UK tax and given either under treaty or unilaterally (TA 1988, s. 790); credit for tax paid by trustees in respect of income accruing to a beneficiary under a trust; and the tax credit associated with qualifying distributions falling within Schedule F (TA 1988, s. 231). On the facts none of these apply to X. However, X is entitled to the tax credit of £500 on the dividend and to the benefit of the 20% withholding tax on the interest.

X's liability to tax on taxable income of £54,415 is as follows

£ 1,520 at 10% = £152
£26,880 at 22% = £5,913.60
£20,715 at 40% = £8,286
£ 5,000 at 32.5% = £1,760

Total tax is £16,111.60, less credit of £500 for the dividend and with credit for tax withheld on the interest and under PAYE.

X has two further tax complications. First, X is also entitled to relief on tax of £125 in respect of his life assurance premium of £1,000; this is given effect by the payment of a net premium of £875,[11] and so is ignored for present purposes. If the contract had been made after 12 March 1984, however, no relief would be given.

Secondly, there is X's £1,000 contribution to charity. So far it has been deducted from X's total income. However, X deducts basic rate tax (and only basic rate tax) in respect of this £1,000, i.e. £220. Under the gift aid rules (above §10.6), X can recoup this basic rate tax on

[11] TA 1988, s. 266(5).

£1,000 when making the payment to the charity so this is not a real tax burden. However, X must pay the tax. This is separate from X's £26,880 charged at basic rate and is simply machinery.

Y, X's spouse is a separate taxpayer. Y's income is not relevant to X's tax liability. Suppose Y simply earns £15,000 under Schedule E. Y is entitled to a single person's relief in respect of her earnings of £15,000; she will also deduct payments of £1,000 to her retirement benefits scheme.

Example

Income	£15,000	
Less pension contribution	£1,000	
Total income		£14,000
Less basic personal relief	£4,385	
Taxable income		£9,615
Tax at 10% on £1,520	£152	
Tax at 22% on £8,095	£1,780,90	£1,932.90

12.6.2 Allocation of rates and reliefs

Rules have to be provided for regulating the order in which the various tax rates are allocated and in which the various reliefs and exemption limits may be claimed.

Rates

Before self assessment it was Revenue practice to allocate tax rates so that the earliest tax due was charged at the first and lowest rates. Now that there is single combined date for reporting income and paying tax this is no longer necessary. However, it is expressly provided that interest and dividends are to be treated as the highest part of a taxpayer's income, with dividends being the highest part of that part §7.7.2.[12]

Reliefs

Deductions are allocated according to a statutory order, as follows:[13]

(1) The general rule is that deductions are to be made in the order which will result in the greatest reduction of liability to income tax. This rule is, of course, subject to express provision to the contrary.
(2) Deductions for personal reliefs, that is deductions authorised by TA 1988, Part VII, Chapter I,[14] are to be made after any other deductions.

12.7 Averaging: Spreading and Top-Slicing

There is no general averaging procedure in the UK tax system whereby income is averaged out over a number of years. Instead, the system takes the view that income tax is an annual

[12] TA 1988, s.1A(5).
[13] Ibid., s. 835(3)–(5).
[14] Including reliefs for life assurance premiums under contracts made before 14 March 1984.

tax and therefore relates only to income arising in that year. Averaging is thus allowed over the year—but not beyond it.

12.7.1 Mitigating unfairness

This is unjust in a number of ways, but less unjust now that the progressive nature of the tax system has been so drastically reduced. (1) It is inequitable for those with fluctuating incomes.[15] (2) It is inequitable for individuals whose income fluctuates around the bottom of the tax scale, since unused personal allowances may not be rolled forward to subsequent years. The arguments against allowing such rolling-forward are largely administrative; it would also make the yield from taxes more difficult to predict. (3) The absence of an averaging clause causes injustice to the individual who suddenly receives an exceptional sum which the tax system treats as income. These abnormal receipts are different from the problem of fluctuating incomes from one source, not least in that the receipt may be isolated and subjected to special treatment by the tax system.

The UK Tax system has some features which permit mitigation of the single year approach to income:

(a *Spreading*: some receipts may be spread over a number of years as follows:
- *copyright and public lending right, etc.—spreading back (ss 534 and 537)*: sums received by an author, by way of royalty (or public lending right) within the first two years of a book's life plus sums for the assignment of copyright (or public lending right) and non-returnable advances may be spread back over the period during which the author was at work on the book but with a maximum of three years.[16] This applies also to dramatic, musical and other artistic work and to payments in respect of designs (ss 537A and 537B);
- *copyright—spreading forward (s. 535)*: sums received for the assignment of a copyright more than 10 years after publication can be spread forward over six years. This does not apply to artistic works;
- *payments in respect of assignment of design rights*: these may be spread over a period of two or three years depending on how long the taxpayer was engaged in creating the design; *(s. 537A)*
- *artists' sales (s. 538)*: the price, commission or fee for a work of art can be spread over two (three) years if the work took over one (two) years;
- *patents (spreading forward) (s. 524)*: a sum received in return for patent rights is taxable as income but may be spread over the year of receipt and the next five years;
- *patents (spreading back) (s. 527)*: sums received for the use of patents over a period of at least six years may be spread back over six years.

(b) *Top-slicing*: this now applies to certain dealings with life policies.[17] The technique involves taking a certain fraction of the taxable sum and then calculating the tax payable on that slice as if it were the top slice of the income of the relevant year. That rate is then applied to the whole sum. Thus, if the sum were £15,000, the slice £1,000

[15] Royal Commission, Cmd 9474 (1955), §205. On reform, see ibid., §202; Royal Commission Canada (1966), Vol. 2, 253; Steuerle, McHugh and Sunley 31 *National Tax Jo.* 19.

[16] TA 1988, s. 534—such sums are income; *Howson* v. *Monsell* [1950] 2 All ER 1239, 31 TC 529. Public lending right was established under the Public Lending Right Act 1979.

[17] TA 1988, s. 550 (see below at §55.5.3). The rules for premiums on leases (TA 1988, s. 39(3), Sch. 2) were repealed by FA 1988, s. 73 and those for government stock (s. 52) by FA 1996.

and the rate of tax on that slice 20%, 20% would be applied to the whole £15,000. This technique differs from the first in that the payment is taxed only by reference to one year.

(c) *Farmers*: there is a system of averaging for farmers.[18] The profits of two years are compared. If the profits of either year are nil or less than 70% of the other, the profits may be equalised. Tapering relief is available where the level of profit change is between 70% and 75%. Averaging is not permitted in the first or last years of assessment.

12.7.2 Reform

Among the ideas for dealing with fluctuating incomes, two stand out. One is a tax adjustment account in which taxpayers could "park" their income but without interest until drawing it down (when tax would be paid). One problem with this is how to prevent a taxpayer from deriving benefit from the income before it is drawn down.[19] The idea was recommended by the Canadian Royal Commission, provided it was accompanied by a block averaging system.[20] The consequent Canadian legislation permitted a taxpayer to buy an income-averaging annuity.[21]

A very different solution has been proposed by Vickery.[22] The object is lifetime averaging—an attempt to build year by year what the PAYE system achieves week by week. The disadvantages of the proposal are that long run changes in the value of money would produce new inequities, and the system cannot cope with problems of family reorganisations. There would also be undesirably long lags in changing effective tax rates if the ability to pay increases (or decreases) sharply.

12.8 Excess Liability

Excess liability is a relic from the days of surtax. It is a liability to higher rate tax when there is no liability to basic (or lower) rate tax. Thus, the liability arises to the extent that the tax liability exceeds basic or lower rate liability. In its strict sense, excess liability arises when gains arise on non-qualifying life policies (TA 1988, s. 539) and when relief arises for inheritance tax on accrued income (s. 699).

There are, however, a number of other instances, for example in relation to non-qualifying distributions and stock dividends, where the expression "excess liability" is not used, and a liability to income tax arises but only to the extent that it exceeds basic or lower of ordinary rates.

[18] TA 1988, s. 96. By concession farming includes intensive livestock rearing for human consumption: see ESC A29.

[19] As with the remittance basis.

[20] Vol. 3, 261–80.

[21] Income Tax Act Canada 1972, s. 61.

[22] Vickrey, "Agenda for Progressive Taxation", 164 (also in Vickrey, *Public Economics* (CUP, 1996), 105–19); and Bird and Head, *Modern Fiscal Issues* (University of Toronto Press, 1973), 117.

12.9 Progression and the UK Tax System

The rate structure set out above represents the present UK pattern of progression.[23] In 1998–1999, of the 26.4 m taxpayers, 2.3 m had a marginal rate of 10%, 0.9 m, 20%, 21 m, 23% and 2.3 m were higher rate taxpayers.[24] In the same year, out of a total tax bill of 85 bn, 20% was attributable to the top 1% of taxpayers and 38% to the top 5%; the top 10% contributed 50%, the next 40% contributed 39% and the lower 50% contributed 11%.[25]

Certain features of the UK income tax structure call for comment. The first is the number of bands in existence. In 1978–1979 bands consisted not only of reduced and basic rates, but also nine slices taxed at higher rates—to which could be added the additional rate. From 1988–1992 the system survived with just two bands—basic rate and higher rate. The UK reduction in the number of rates is typical of many OECD countries:[26] the biggest reductions occurred in Italy which, between 1975 and 1989, cut its bands from 32 to seven, and the United States, which cut the bands from from 25 to three.

The second feature of the UK income tax structure is the long band of income taxed at basic rate. The explanation for this is largely administrative; it facilitates deduction at source and reduces the number of additional assessments the Revenue needs to make and the number of calculations taxpayers must undertake if they are subject to self-assessment. It has the further advantage of taxing entities like trusts at reasonable rates. Since, however, the changes in the bands are tied to the cost of living not average earnings, these advantages have been reduced.

The third feature of the UK income tax structure is the presence of the starting rate band. As we have seen at §12.1, lower rate bands existed until 1970, when the last was abolished in the cause of administrative simplicity. The reduced rate was revived in 1978[27] but repealed in 1980 for the administrative reasons. The reduced rate did not help the lower paid, it did not significantly increase incentives and it had little effect on the poverty trap. Research has shown that raising tax allowances is a better way of helping the poor.[28]

Despite these practical objections the idea of a reduced rate band retained a central place in the hearts of many tax reformers. Arguments based on administrative considerations are much less cogent now that we have self-assessment and computers. Personal reliefs can be seen as a form of zero-rate band for those entitled to them; the level of that personal relief is relatively high in comparative terms.[29]

It can be seen that the profile of the system is high–low–high (or not-so-high). The effect of this is to give most play to economic forces, such as incentives, in the middle of the income band. This has the advantage that it establishes a floor to poverty and a ceiling to riches. Optimal tax theory might suggest a profile that is low–high–low in terms of marginal

[23] See also Slemrod and Bakija ,*Taxing Ourselves* (MIT, 1996), ch. 3.

[24] *Inland Revenue Statistics 1999*, Table 2.5.

[25] Ibid., Table 2.4 and Tables 6.5 and 6.6 above.

[26] Dilnot, in *Key Issues* (1993), ch. 1; and Messere, *OECD* (1993), ch. 3. See also Vanistendael (1988) 5 *Australian Tax Forum* 133. On New Zealand experience, which makes the UK seem very timid, see Stephens (1993) 14(3) *Fiscal Studies* 45.

[27] It was responsible for an increase in the cost/yield ratio from 1.87% to 2%: Board of Inland Revenue, 122nd Report.

[28] Morris and Warren (1980) 3 *Fiscal Studies* 34–43. See also IFS, *Tax Options for 1991* (Commentary No. 25), 64, 65.

[29] See n. 26 above.

rates, but this would probably be opposed on distributional grounds and certainly rejected on political grounds.[30] A possible compromise is a system of constant marginal rates.[31]

Appendix: The Chaotic State of Rate on Savings—How Did We Get Here?

The legislation on taxing income from savings is a mess created by annual accretion of tax rules each of which may be acceptable in themselves but which, in combination, are not. Before 1973–1974 savings income was liable to be taxed at a higher rate than earned income because of the mechanism of the earned income relief. After the Barber reforms, the same result was achieved by means of the additional rate on investment income, which was eventually abolished by Nigel Lawson.

In 1993–1994, Norman Lamont, having reduced the tax credit accompanying a dividend to 20% of the total of the tax credit and the dividend, abolished the basic rate of tax on dividends, and introduced TA 1988, s. 207A. Subsequently, basic rate and lower rate taxpayers were liable to pay tax at 20%. This was good news only for the basic rate taxpayer—there was no real gain since the credit had been reduced. Moreover, if a covenant in favour of a charity had to be paid out of such income the taxpayer had to pay the difference between lower and basic rate. Since this extra sum was repaid to the charity, perhaps it was not so bad. Others lost out more severely. Lower rate taxpayers suffered because they could no longer reclaim the difference between the two rates, and exempt shareholders suffered because they could reclaim only lower rate instead of basic rate. These changes yielded £1 b revenue.[32] Higher rate taxpayers suffered because they had only a lower credit against their liability at 40%, yielding a further £200 m. Everyone lost out because higher contributions were needed by pension funds—even the Exchequer is rumoured to have lost because those extra contributions attracted tax relief and so reduced corporation tax receipts.

The change can also be seen in another way—as a selective revival of the additional rate on higher rate taxpayers with dividend income and as a 5% charge on part of the income of pension funds. The oddity was that this revival of the additional rate was only on higher rate taxpayers and only on dividend income. These changes meant a recasting of the rules for discretionary trusts, which were no longer charged at the sum of the basic and additional rates but at "the rate applicable to trusts".[33]

In 1996 Kenneth Clarke extended the 20% rate to interest, replacing Taxes Act 1988, s. 207A with the first version of s. 1A.[34] However, the consequences for interest payments were quite different from those for dividends because there was no associated tax credit—only a withholding tax. This time there was a real gain for basic rate taxpayers, who were now taxed at 20% instead of the new basic rate of 24%—although, as before, that gain was lost if a covenant existed in favour of charity paid for from such income. There was no change for either lower or higher rate taxpayers. There was a loss for nil or exempt shareholders who could reclaim only at 20%. One major, and possibly unintended, group of beneficiaries were non-residents living in tax havens.[35]

[30] Meade Report, ch. 14. But see Slemrod 36 *National Tax Jo.* 361–9.

[31] Meade Report, 316 "the administrative advantages would be incalculable".

[32] (1993) *Simon's Tax Intelligence* 399.

[33] FA 1993, Sch. 6.

[34] FA 1996, s. 73.

[35] [1996] *BTR* 342, 347.

The 1997 July measures made further changes.[36] TA 1988, s. 1A was joined by s. 1B, to which dividends under Schedule F and equivalent foreign income were transferred.[37] The tax credit was reduced from 20% to 10%, (i.e. from 1/4 to 1/9th of the dividend) and all repayments to pension funds, or to resident, nil-rate taxpayers, ceased. Basic and lower rate taxpayers now pay at the Schedule F rate of 10% and higher rate taxpayers will pay at a special rate of 32.5% which will ensure that, unlike Norman Lamont's 1993 change, this does not cause a real increase in their tax burden. Discretionary trusts now have their own Schedule F rates. The introduction of the 10% starting rate in 1999 caused problems because the Government did not wish to extend the benefit of this rate to savings income. This was found to contain many problems and so the 10% rate was extended to all savings income by FA 2000; the degree of error is shown by the fact that the 10% rate was then back-dated to 6 April 1999.[38]

The 1993 and 1997 raids on pension funds were handled differently as far as presentation and detail were concerned. The 1997 raid was a part of what looked like being the end of the imputation system. The reasons for the 1997 change were the same as those which drove the 1965 adoption of the classical system—the belief that retained earnings are the source of all (or most) growth and a wish to rein in the amount of money being distributed by way of dividend, an end to short term-ism. See, further, below §44.2.4.

[36] F (No. 2) A 1997 ss 30–36.

[37] Ibid., s. 31.

[38] FA 2000, s. 32(4).

13

Schedule E—Part I: Scope

13.1 Introduction

Income tax is charged under Schedule E on the emoluments from any office or employment[1] and certain pensions.[2] Liability arises under three Cases. The basic charging provision (TA 1988, s. 19(1)) taxes "emoluments from any office or employment.". A payment from an employer to an employee for some other reason than the employment will escape tax. Conversely, and less obviously, a payment from a non-employer may be taxable—if it is for services rendered under a contract of employment.[3] The test in these cases is one of causation; an emolument is a payment in return for acting as or being an employee.[4] A running

[1] TA 1988, s. 19(1) as recast, for 1989–1990 and later years by FA 1989, s. 36(2). Until 1922, Schedule E was confined to income from a public office (including the director of a company) or public employment; other employments were in Schedule D. In 1922 employments were moved to Schedule E unless they came with Schedule D, Case V; overseas remuneration from non-public office or employment remained in Schedule D, Case V until FA 1956, s. 101 when the present three-Case structure was introduced. See below at n. 12.

[2] Certain public or foreign pensions are taxable under s. 19 paras 2, 3 and 4 ; voluntary pensions are taxable under TA 1988, s. 133; occupational pensions under TA 1988, s. 597; state retirement pensions under s. 617; and personal pensions schemes under s. 648A. Pensions arising under retirement annuity contracts are taxed under Schedule D, Case III but as earned income. A pension is a taxable subject matter distinct from the office or employment (*Tilley* v. *Wales* [1943] AC 386, 392, 25 TC 136, 149, *per* Viscount Simon LC). Pensions in respect of other overseas service will come within Case IV or V if the source is foreign (see below at §34.5). A reduction of 10% is applied to pensions within s. 19, para. 4 (TA 1988, s. 196).

[3] *Blakiston* v. *Cooper* [1901] AC 104, 5 TC 347, HL; however, the fact that the payment is not by the employer may be a factor in helping a court conclude that such a payment is not an emolument (*Pritchard* v. *Arundale* [1972] Ch 229, 47 TC 680).

[4] *Shilton* v. *Wilmshurst* [1991] STC 88, 64 TC 78; see also Lord Radcliffe in *Hochstrasser* v. *Mayes* [1960] AC 376, 389, 392 who said that the test goes beyond one of simple reward for services but must still be referable to the performance of duties under the contract.

issue is the extent to which these are matters of form as opposed to substance, i.e. the question are to be answered by reference to what the parties said in their arrangements.[5] Income taxable under Schedule E is earned income.[6]

13.1.1 *Scope*

The term "emoluments" is defined to include "all salaries, fees, wages, perquisites and profits whatsoeve.."[7] This was enough to tax many benefits in kind under the general rule in s. 19. However, a payment in kind is taxable under s. 19 only if, in addition to being an emolument, it is convertible into money. For this reason a wider test (TA 1988, s. 154) applies to most employees (i.e. those earning £8,500 a year or more) and to directors. There are other special rules where either s. 19 or s. 154 are insufficient.

13.1.2 *Expenses*

By TA 1988, s. 198 expenses are deductible under Schedule E if they are incurred wholly, exclusively and necessarily in the performance of the duties of the office or employment. Travelling expenses have their own rule—they must be "qualifying travelling expenses". These are either (i) "necessarily incurred in the performance of the duties of" the office or employment, a long-established and interestingly litigated expression, or (ii) come within a new category established in 1998 relating to travel to or from a temporary workplace. The holder of the office or employment must, in either case, have been obliged to incur and have defrayed the expenses "out of" the emoluments; these words mean, in the Revenue view, that no claim for loss relief can arise under Schedule E.

Capital allowances may be claimed by the employee in respect of machinery and plant if incurred necessarily.[8]

Most emoluments paid by the employer are subject to a system of deduction of tax at source—the PAYE system.[9] Whether or not subject to that system, income is assessed on a current year basis. It is taxed on when it is received or becomes due for payment, whichever is the earlier; the old case-law rule which backdated payments to the year in which the service was performed was abolished in 1989.[10]

13.2 Office or Employment

13.2.1 *Office*

Schedule E taxes emoluments from an office or employment,[11] neither of which words is further defined. An office denotes "a subsisting, permanent, substantive position which has

[5] See Ward [1992] *BTR* 139.

[6] TA 1988, s. 833(4).

[7] Ibid., s. 131. A perquisite is merely a casual emolument additional to regular salary or wages (*Owen* v. *Pook* [1970] AC 244, 225, [1969] 2 All ER 1, 5, *per* Lord Guest).

[8] CAA 1990, s. 27.

[9] TA 1988, s. 203 (see below at §13.4).

[10] FA 1989, s. 36 see below §14.2.3.

[11] TA 1988, s. 19.

an existence independent of the person who fills it, and which is filled in succession by successive holders".[12] Examples include a director of a company,[13] even if under a contract of employment and owning all the shares, a trustee or executor,[14] a company auditor,[15] a National Health service consultant[16] and a local land charges registrar.[17]

By contrast a person appointed to act as an inspector at a public inquiry does not hold an office since the post has no existence independent of the holder; there is neither continuity nor permanence.[18] The Court of Appeal has said that an office and an employment are not mutually exclusive.[19] It is not necessary that an office should be constituted by some enactment or other instrument, nor that it should have any public relevance; however, an office is more than just a job description.[20] It thus seems that the essence of an office is the independence of its existence from the identity of the present holder.[21] It is from this element of independence that the element of continuity may be said to derive.[22]

13.2.2 Employment

An employment was once described as a post and as something "more or less analogous to an office",[23] but modern cases generally take a different tack and equate employment with a contract of service. In this way tax law uses a concept familiar in other parts of UK domestic law such as tort and employment law. In EC law the boundary between Articles 48 and 52 of the EC Treaty (now Articles 39 and 43) builds on the same foundations by characterising the essence of employment (as opposed to self employment) status as being the relationship of subordination; in the absence of subordination an activity carried out for the benefit of other economic operators or consumers is regarded as self-employment.[24] If the arrangement under which sums are paid to a taxpayer is one for services, it falls outside Schedule E.

The common law courts have used different tests at different times.[25] At one period the approach was based on control.[26] Where subjection to a person (the master) was

[12] Rowlatt J. in *Great Western Railway Co.* v. *Bater* [1920] 3 KB 266, 274, 8 TC 231, 235. See, generally Napier [1981] *Industrial Law Journal* 52; and Ward [1989] *BTR* 281, 283–95. This is not a "complete" definition (*McMillan* v. *Guest* [1942] AC 561, 564, 24 TC 190, 201 *per* Lord Atkin). When *Great Western Railway* v. *Bater* was decided Schedule E covered only public offices or employments of a public nature; other offices or employments fell within Schedule D. *Bater* concerned a railway clerk, and the House of Lords, undoing the accepted practice of decades, placed him in Schedule D. The legislative response, anticipated by the 1920 Royal Commission, was to move all the offices or employments to Schedule E (see Monroe, *Intolerable Inquisition* (Sweet and Maxwell, 1981), 25 *et seq.*).

[13] *Lee* v. *Lee's Air Farming Ltd.* [1961] AC 12, [1960] 3 All ER 420, PC. The posts of director and managing director may be separate offices (*Goodwin* v. *Brewster* (1951) 32 TC 80).

[14] *Dale* v. *IRC* [1951] 2 All ER 517, 34 TC 468; *A-G* v. *Eyres* [1909] 1 KB 723.

[15] *Ellis* v. *Lucas* [1966] 2 All ER 935, 43 TC 276.

[16] *Mitchell and Edon (Inspectors of Taxes)* v. *Ross* [1961] 3 All ER 49, 40 TC 11.

[17] *Ministry of Housing and Local Government* v. *Sharp* [1970] 2 QB 223, [1969] 3 All ER 225.

[18] *Edwards* v. *Clinch* [1981] STC 617, 56 TC 367: duties of a public nature did not necessarily make the post an office.

[19] See Buckley and Oliver L.J.J. [1980] STC 438, 445d, 455d.

[20] *McMenamin* v. *Diggles* [1991] STC 419, 430, 431, 64 TC 286, 302, *per* Scott J.

[21] Ward [1989] *BTR* 281, 287.

[22] Ibid., 294.

[23] *Davies* v. *Braithwaite* [1931] 2 KB 628, 635, *per* Rowlatt J.; see Ward, above at n. 21, 295–300.

[24] For example, the opinion of the Advocate-General in *Asscher* v. *Staatsecretarius* [1996] STC 1025, 1031 para. 28.

[25] Deakin and Morris, *Labour Law* (2nd ed. 1998), §3.4. On the Canadian enterprise control test, see Flannigan (1988) 36 *Can. Tax Jo.* 145.

[26] Deakin and Morris, ibid., §3.4.5; *Yewen* v. *Noakes* (1880) 6 QBD 530, 538, 1 TC 260, 263, *per* Bramwell L.J.

inappropriate the courts looked at subjection to the rules of an organisation—the integration test.[27] Another test was based on "economic reality" and took into account methods of payment, the freedom to hire others, whether the workers provided their own equipment, whether they had investments in their own business, arrangements for sick pay and holiday pay and how the worker was treated for income tax and National Insurance.[28] A relatively recent development has produced a test based on mutuality of obligation[29] and looks at the duration of employment, regularity of employment, whether the workers have the right to refuse work and trade custom. Under this test there is no contract of service if the worker can say no—i.e. there is no obligation on the worker to accept an offer to provide services. This last test has been used as the basis of much planning by employers anxious to get an arrangement treated as one for services and not of service. In labour law some workers rendering services under a contract for services are brought within the employment protection category by legislative redefinition.[30] Some cases have mixed all the elements in these different tests.[31]

Another test asks whether those performing the services are in business on their own account.[32] It is not possible to gain much assistance by comparing the facts of previous cases to see which facts are common, which are different and what weight was given to the common facts; the evidence must be weighed separately in each case.[33] It is open to a fact-finding tribunal to conclude that a person is in business on his own account when all that he provides are personal services.[34] It is equally open to a fact-finding tribunal to conclude that a person is in business on her own account even though there is what purports to be a written contract of employment.[35] By contrast, a person under contract to provide clerking services to a set of barristers' chambers was held to be an independent contractor on the particular facts.[36] If no services are to be performed, the contract is not one of employment.[37] North Sea divers are expressly excluded from Schedule E.[38] A person employed by a company is an employee of the company. Where a man held himself out to be an employee of a company which he controlled and created, the question whether he was such an employee or a self-employed person was treated as a question of fact.[39]

The fact that the contract is illegal cannot, of itself, convert an employee into a self-employed person. The status of contracts of employment which are illegal has not been explored in the tax context.[40]

[27] Deakin and Morris, ibid., §3.4.6; *Beloff* v. *Presdram* [1973] 1 All ER 241. 250. See also the copyright case of *Stevenson, Jordan and Harrison Ltd.* v. *Macdonald and Evans* [1952] 1 TLR 101, 111, *per* Lord Denning.

[28] Deakin and Morris, ibid., §3.4.7, citing *Hall* v. *Lorimer* [1994] STC 23, CA and *Market Investigations Ltd.* v. *Minister of Social Security* [1969] 2 QB 173.

[29] Deakin and Morris, ibid., §3.4.8, citing *O'Kelly* v. *Trusthouse Forte plc* [1984] QB 90, [1983] 3 All ER 456.

[30] For example the Employment Rights Act 1996, s. 230(3).

[31] Deakin and Morris, above at n. 25, §3.4.9; *Ready-Mixed Concrete (South East) Ltd.* v. *Ministry of Pensions* [1968] 2 QB 497, [1968] 1 All ER 433.

[32] *Andrews* v. *King* [1991] STC 481.

[33] *Walls* v. *Sinnett* [1987] STC 236, 245, *per* Vinelott J.

[34] *Hall* v. *Lorimer* [1994] STC 23, 66 TC 349, CA; followed in *Barnett* v. *Brabyn* [1996] STC 716.

[35] *McManus* v. *Griffiths* [1997] STC 1089, 70 TC 218.

[36] *McMenamin* v. *Diggles* [1991] STC 419, 64 TC 286.

[37] *Clayton* v. *Lavender* (1965) 42 TC 607.

[38] TA 1988, s. 314.

[39] *Cooke* v. *Blacklaws* [1985] STC 1 (the illegality of the arrangement was a factor, but not a conclusive one).

[40] For general problems, see Deakin and Morris, above at n. 24, §3.4.4.

Secondment

Problems may arise where an employee is seconded to work for another firm.[41] Thus, where E, the employee, earns fees from the second company but is required to account to the first company for those fees, there is authority to suggest that the payments to E should be treated as E's taxable income and so subject to PAYE; however, by concession, this is not required.[42] Where the employee is seconded to work for a charity on a temporary basis, an express provision allows the employer to deduct the costs as if the employee had remained working for the employer.[43] This provision assumes (perhaps wrongly) that the payments to the seconded employee are taxable as employment income.

13.2.3 Several employers or one profession?

A taxpayer may have more than one source of income. The existence of a daytime employment is compatible with the co-existence of a trade or profession[44] and the activity or skill used in the employment may be the same as that used in the trade or profession. Therefore, doctors may be part-time employees of a hospital trust and carry on a part-time private practice; their pay under the former source will be taxed under Schedule E, while that from the latter will be taxed under Schedule D, Case II. Similarly, a barrister with a daytime income under Schedule D, Case II may also have evening employment as a lecturer within Schedule E.[45] The premise of the case-law is that in accordance with the Schedular system of income taxation at source cannot fall into both Schedules at the same time. Kerridge has argued, challengingly, that this premise is incorrect, but the argument has not been made in any reported case since his views were published.[46]

Davies v. *Braithwaite, Fall* v. *Hitchen, Hall* v. *Lorimer*

A person may hold several offices and so be taxed under Schedule E (not Schedule D, Case II as a profession).[47] However, in relation to a series of employments, two, quite distinct approaches can be seen. In *Davies* v. *Braithwaite*[48] Lilian Braithwaite acted in the UK in a number of plays, films and wireless programmes. She had separate contracts for each play and wireless appearance. She also recorded for the gramophone and had appeared in a play on Broadway, New York. Since the performance in New York was completely outside the UK, she argued that it was an employment and, as such, that she would be taxable at that time only on such sums, if any, as she remitted to the UK. The Revenue argued that this was merely one engagement in her profession as an actress, a profession carried on inside and

[41] In *Caldicott* v. *Varty* [1976] STC 418, [1976] 3 All ER 329, 51 TC 403 a civil servant seconded to work for the Fiji Government was held to be still employed by the Crown and not by the UK Government.

[42] ESC A37. If it is E's taxable income it is hard to see how E can then deduct the sums when they are paid over to his employer since this is a disposition of income not the cost of earning it. It appears more correct to say that the obligation to account prevented the payment from having the quality of income in E's hands.

[43] TA 1988, s. 86.

[44] *Davies* v. *Braithwaite* [1931] 2 KB 628, 635, 18 TC 198, 203, *per* Rowlatt J.

[45] *Sidey* v. *Phillips* [1987] STC 87, 59 TC 458.

[46] [1980] *BTR* 233.

[47] *IRC* v. *Brander and Cruickshank* [1971] 1 All ER 36, 46 TC 574. Compare *Marsh* v. *IRC* [1943] 1 All ER 199, 29 TC 120; Nock [1973] *BTR* 260.

[48] [1931] 2 KB 628, 18 TC 198. For a slightly more modern example, see *Household* v. *Grimshaw* [1953] 2 All ER 12, 34 TC 366.

outside the UK, so that she was taxable on an arising basis under Schedule D, Case II. The Revenue won. Rowlatt J. said:[49]

> "Where one finds a method of earning a livelihood which does not contemplate the obtaining of a post and staying in it, but essentially contemplates a series of engagements and moving from one to the other . . . then each of those engagements could not be considered an employment, but is a mere engagement in the course of exercising a profession, and every profession and every trade does involve the making of successive engagements and successive contracts and, in one sense of the word, employments."

The second approach is totally different. In *Fall* v. *Hitchen*[50] a professional ballet dancer was held to be liable to tax under Schedule E in respect of a contract with one particular company because that contract, looked at in isolation, was one of service and not one for services. Pennycuick V.-C. held that this concluded the matter.[51] This is quite different from Rowlatt J. who had started with the general scheme of the taxpayer's earnings and then asked where the particular contract fitted in. In *Davies* v. *Braithwaite* no one seems to have asked whether the contract was one of service or one for services.[52]

Davies v. *Braithwaite* was resurrected in *Hall* v. *Lorimer*.[53] Here the Court of Appeal held that while the distinction between a contract of service and one for services was critical, this did not, of itself, determine whether the particular contract should be classified as one or the other. In deciding upon that classification the court may look at whether the taxpayer is in business and so see how the contract fits in with the taxpayer's overall activities. Therefore, a vision mixer who worked for 80 days over a four-year period, all on one- or two-day contracts, was held to be taxable under Schedule D, rather than Schedule E, Nolan L.J. citing both *Davies* v. *Braithwaite* and *Fall* v. *Hitchen*. Meanwhile, it should be noted the decision in *Fall* v. *Hitchen* (where the one contract in issue was for rehearsal time plus 22 weeks) is consistent with *Hall* v. *Lorimer*. It is still too early to tell what the House of Lords may do—the approach of the Court of Appeal does not sit easily with that of the House of Lords in *IRC* v. *Brander and Cruickshank* and *Mitchell and Edon* v. *Ross* (see below).

There is no infallible criterion[54] and there are many borderline cases.Aspects to be considered now are whether those involved provide their own equipment or hire their own helpers, what degree of financial risk they run, what degree of responsibility they have and how far they can profit from sound management.[55] The Revenue find the task as difficult as anyone else.[56]

Whether a contract is one of service or for services appears to be one of law, so far as the identification of the relevant criteria is concerned, but the balancing process of applying those criteria seems to be left to the Commissioners as a question of fact.[57]

[49] [1931] 2 KB 628, 635, 18 TC 198, 203.

[50] [1973] STC 66, [1973] 1 All ER 368; no appeal was made. See *Simon's Tax Intelligence* 1990, 173.

[51] [1973] 1 All ER 368, 374. The taxpayer had no other contracts at that time (unlike Miss Braithwaite); indeed, his was a full-time contract and one which prohibited him from taking on outside activities without his employer's consent.

[52] In *Mitchell and Edon* v. *Ross*, [1960] Ch 498, 521, 40 TC 11, 43, in the Court of Appeal, Lord Evershed distinguished *Davies* v. *Braithwaite* as not involving a contract of service. See also *Bennett* v. *Marshall* [1938] 1 KB 591, [1938] 1 All ER 93, 22 TC 73.

[53] [1994] STC 23, CA.

[54] See, e.g., Nolan L.J. in *Hall* v. *Lorimer* [1994] STC 23, 30e.

[55] *Ready Mixed Concrete (South East) Ltd.* v. *Minister of Pensions* [1968] 2 QB 497, [1968] 1 All ER 433; *Sidey* v. *Phillips* [1987] STC 87, 59 TC 458.

[56] See Revenue Tax Bulletin, February 2000.

[57] *O'Kelly* v. *Trusthouse Forte plc* [1984] QB 90, [1983] 3 All ER 456, CA. *Cf.* Lord Widgery C.J., in *Global Plant Ltd.* v. *Secretary of State for Social Services* [1972] 1 QB 139, 154, 155. See criticism by Pitt [1985] *LQR* 217.

Over the years, the Revenue has waged campaigns to bring many people within Schedule E by threatening to make the payer responsible for the payment of income tax under the PAYE system. The payer usually submits to this pressure since there is nothing to gain by resisting.[58] The Revenue has issued an explanatory booklet IR 56.[59] One may contrast the delegated power for the DSS to categorise workers by statutory instrument.[60]

Personal Service Companies FA 2000 rules

FA 2000, Sch. 12 enlarges the scope of Schedule E where three conditions are satisfied. (1) An individual performs services for the purposes of a business carried on by another person ("the client"). (2) The services are provided not under a contract directly between the client and the worker but under arrangements involving a third party ("the intermediary"), and (3) the circumstances are such that, if the services were provided under a contract directly between the client and the worker, the worker would be regarded for income tax purposes as an employee of the client. Where these conditions are met, payments made by the client to the intermediary not covered by payments or other benefits paid over as employment income, and taxable under Schedule E, to the worker by the end of the year or certain prior event such as dismissal, are treated as deemed Schedule E income of the worker. The new rules for NICs are set out in regulations made under powers in the Welfare Reform and Pensions Act 1999.

FA 2000, Sch. 12 is one of the most contentious items in recent tax legislation. Its target is the abuse of an intermediary personal service company (PSC). The sort of PSC that worried the government was that in which a person, E, who had been an employee of X Ltd. left X's employment and then returned to provide more or less the same services as before but as the employee of PSC with which X Ltd. made a contract for services. The worry was that the fee paid by X Ltd. to PSC would not attract PAYE or National Insurance Contributions. A payment by PSC to E would of course attract both these liabilities but what tended to happen was that PSC would simply pay E enough Schedule E income to make sure that the year would count as a contribution year for E's NICs and then pay the balance as dividend.[61]

When the government moved to counter the use of PSCs it found itself up against two problems. The first related to the central test which made these new rules apply when but for the PSC the work would have been done under a contract of employment. Test (3) above is a very uncertain and difficult area of law. The second difficulty was to decide who should be responsible for the PAYE and NICs—the original proposal would have put that burden on X, the client, but the final version chose the PSC instead. The third difficulty was that the government found itself up against not only pilots working for airlines but also a substantial sector of the computer consultancy industry, a sector with a strong North American element and so quite capable of speaking loudly.

Where the three tests are satisfied, the contracts between the PSC and X are described as "relevant engagements". Sch. 12 treats all payments made by X to the PSC as deemed Schedule E payments—and so subject to PAYE and NICs—subject to a deduction not only

[58] See HC Official Report, Vol. 45, cols 384–5, 13 July 1983, (1983) *Simon's Tax Intelligence* 309.

[59] See (1985) *Simon's Tax Intelligence* 391. See also *Simon's Direct Tax Service*, E4.211 for practice on particular occupations.

[60] Social Security (Categorisation of Earners) Regulations 1978 (SI 1978/1689).

[61] For example, Redston Taxation, Vol. 143, 667 (1999). The debate became known as the IR35 issue since this was the number of the original press release at the time of the 1999 Budget. Details of the revised proposals were contained in a press release, 23 September 1999, (1999) *Simons Weekly Tax Intelligence* 1587.

for sums actually paid as Schedule E income to E but also certain expenses such as pension contributions and a 5% general deduction.[62] The rules extend also to other benefits and not just to payments. Usually the worker must have a material interest in the company but the legislation is not confined to that situation.[63]

Among the many practical problems are the need to distinguish relevant engagements from other engagements (since PSC may well tell E to work for other people during the year) with all the apportionment problems which ensue, and the need to do so rapidly since the PSC must pay the Schedule E tax very shortly after the end of the year.[64] The Act contains rules for dealing with any distributions by the intermediary during the year; it also makes provision for multiple intermediaries.[65] Any deemed Schedule E payment is taken out of the intermediary's own income.[66]

The intermediary may be an individual or partnership as well as a company.[67] However a trust intermediary is not caught.

The rules do not apply where E works for a company which is an associated company of the client.[68] They do not affect the operation of TA 1988, s. 134 (workers supplied by agencies).[69]

Consequences

The consequences of coming within Schedule E as opposed to Schedule D, Case I or II are extensive, and rest on the doctrine that the Schedules are mutually exclusive. In *IRC* v. *Brander and Cruickshank*,[70] Lord Donovan said that this doctrine was unreal and served no useful purpose; indeed, its application in that case would cause administrative chaos.

(1) Expenses incurred for an office or employment under Schedule E will be deductible only if they conform to the strict test laid down in TA 1988, s. 198; expenses incurred for a trade or profession will be deductible on a different and less niggardly test. By concession, travelling expenses of directorships held as part of a professional practice are allowed as deductions under Schedule D.[71]

In *Mitchell and Edon* v. *Ross*[72] the taxpayer, Ross, held an appointment as a consultant radiologist under the Birmingham Regional Hospital Board, and served at a number of hospitals under that authority. He was also in private practice as a consultant radiologist, which practice he carried on at his home in Rugby. The Revenue admitted that Ross was correctly assessed under Schedule D, Case II in respect of his private practice but argued that income accruing from the hospital board should be assessed—and so calculated—under Schedule E.

At first instance and in the Court of Appeal,[73] the taxpayer argued unsuccessfully that the positions with the hospital board were not offices. He further argued that if he was

62 Paras 7–12.
63 Para. 3, esp. sub-para. (1)(b).
64 Para. 2.
65 Paras 13–16.
66 Para. 17.
67 Paras 4, 5.
68 Para. 3(1), (2).
69 Para. 24
70 [1971] 1 All ER 36, 46, 46 TC 574, 595. It seems to make Income Tax (Employments) Regulation 1993 (SI 1993/744), reg. 7(2)(b)(ii) superfluous. The concessionary relief at ESC A37 should also be noted—tax treatment of directors' fees received by partnerships and other companies.
71 ESC A4; and Inland Revenue interpretation RI 105.
72 [1961] 3 All ER 49, 40 TC 11.
73 [1959] 3 All ER 341, 40 TC 11 (first instance); and [1960] 2 All ER 218, 40 TC 11, CA.

correctly assessable under Schedule E, the employment should nonetheless also be seen as part of his profession under Schedule D, Case II so that the Schedule D rules for deduction of expenses should apply to permit the deduction of those expenses which were not deductible under Schedule E. This rested, in part, on a finding by the Commissioners that these employments were a necessary part of his profession as consultant radiologist and merely incidental to that profession.[74] Only the second point was argued in the House of Lords, and the taxpayer lost. If the employment was assessable under Schedule E, expenses in respect of that employment could be allowed only if they conformed to the requirements of the Schedule; the appointment could not be treated for tax purposes as part within and part outside the Schedule.[75]

(2) Terminal payments in connection with the ending of an office or employment may escape tax in whole or in part.[76] Compensation for the loss of a trading asset will usually be a trading receipt.[77] In *IRC* v. *Brander and Cruickshank*[78] the House of Lords held that where a firm of Scottish advocates with a substantial general legal business also acted as secretaries and/or registrars for some 30 to 40 companies, each appointment was a separate office. Therefore, thanks to the Schedule E rules, sums received on the termination of two such appointments escaped tax.[79]

The status of the earlier decision in *Blackburn* v. *Close Bros Ltd.*,[80] where sums were held to be trading receipts, is uncertain. It was doubted by Lord Guest,[81] with whom Lord Upjohn agreed, but Lord Morris regarded the facts of the earlier case as being quite different[82] and considered that the offices were not trading assets. Lord Donovan would have followed the earlier case if there had been a finding of fact that the taxpayer had sought the office as part and parcel of his trade or profession.[83] On such a finding Lord Donovan would have been prepared to hold that income payments fell within Schedule E and terminal payments within Schedule D. Lord Reid dismissed the appeal "for the reasons given by your Lordships".[84]

Given the logic of *Mitchell and Edon* v. *Ross* it is hard to understand any conclusion other than that of Lord Guest.[85] If an office falls exclusively within Schedule E it does not cease to be an office simply because it was sought; while if different payments from the same source can fall under two Schedules, as Lord Donovan suggested, the selection of the applicable rules from the range offered by the two Schedules seems arbitrary. *Hall* v. *Lorimer* can be reconciled with this on the basis either that it is still possible for a person carrying on a profession to hold an office taxable under Schedule E or, if the

[74] 40 TC 11, 32.

[75] On the concordat reached between the Revenue and the medical profession, see *Simon's Direct Tax Service* E4.211, and for treatment of retirement benefit provision, see ESC A9.

[76] Under TA 1988, ss 148, 188(4).

[77] But it may still escape tax as a gift or a capital payment and not a trading receipt (see below at §21.7).

[78] [1971] 1 All ER 36, 46 TC 574.

[79] TA 1988, s. 148 applies when the payment is not otherwise chargeable to tax. The finding that the post was an office and so within Schedule E meant that the payment was not chargeable to tax under some other Schedule, thus enabling s. 148 to operate.

[80] (1960) 39 TC 164.

[81] [1971] 1 All ER 36, 45, 46 TC 574, 593.

[82] Ibid., 42, 590.

[83] Ibid., 47, 595.

[84] Ibid., 40, 588.

[85] If the taxpayer was not carrying on a profession, the payment might have fallen within Schedule D, Case VI, but this seems to be excluded by the conclusion that the post was an office and so within Schedule E. One consequence of Lord Guest's view is that a company can hold an office and so have that income computed under Schedule E.

boundary between office and employment is too difficult to accept, that it is still possible for such a person to enter into a contract of service or an office. The matter then becomes one of fact—and one is back to the distinctions drawn by Lord Donovan.

(3) The costs of acquiring the office will not be deductible under Schedule E but will usually be deductible under Schedule D, Cases I and II.[86]

(4) Solicitor trustees receiving annuities from the trust fund for acting as trustees have traditionally been taxed on the receipt under Schedule D, Case III, with deduction at source under TA 1988, ss 348 and 349. However, as an office, the post of trustee ought to fall within Schedule E.

(5) Schedule E has operated for over 50 years under the PAYE system and on a current year basis. Until recently, Schedule D taxpayers were taxed on a preceding year basis.

(6) The capital allowance structure is much wider for trades than for employments.

Commentary

The income tax system draws a sharp distinction between the employed and self-employed. Yet income tax is not alone in doing this; the distinction is also fundamental (confining oneself to tax law) to social security contributions and benefits, and to VAT. In statistical terms the distinction is probably more significant than that between capital and income. As will be appreciated, the advantages and disadvantages of classification are mixed. However, there has been little effort until recently to quantify them. What makes matters worse is that although the distinction may be easy to state, it is not easy to apply. Moreover it has become particularly hard to apply to the many changes in work practices in the 1990s, for example casualisation and home-working. An important comparative survey shows that other countries have the same problems and that this a very fraught area, with the self-employed arguing keenly to protect their interests.[87] One solution would be to align the different tax rules so as to reduce the significance of the distinction; another would be to make status easier to determine, for example by de-linking the tax status from other rules and stating that tax classification can be different from labour law or tort. Perhaps Rowlatt J. was right after all in looking at the overall situation and not just the particular contract. Some of these issues may become clearer, but not necessarily easier, when the Contributions Agency merges with the Inland Revenue. What makes the matter more urgent is the suspicion that women are more affected by these distinctions than men; such suspicions have been known to excite the attention of the European Court.

13.3 International Aspects[88]

13.3.1 The three Cases

The three Cases of Schedule E charge tax by reference to a number of factors.

The Cases distinguish ordinary emoluments from foreign emoluments. Foreign emoluments arise if the person is not domiciled in the UK and the employer is resident outside, and not resident inside, the UK; so, ordinary emoluments arise if the person is domiciled in the UK or the employer is resident here.

[86] *Cf.* Pennycuick J. in *Blackburn* v. *Close Bros Ltd.* (1960) 39 TC 164, 173.

[87] Chamberlain and Freedman (1997) *Fiscal Studies* 87.

[88] On history of cases down to 1991, see Sheridan [1991] *BTR* 214.

If the employee is resident and ordinarily resident in the UK, Case I charges tax on the emoluments in full; special rules apply to foreign emoluments.[89] If a person is either not resident or resident but not ordinarily resident in the UK for the year, Case II charges tax on the emolument in full; again, there are special rules for foreign emoluments. Case III charges tax on a remittance basis but only when the employee is resident in the UK.

Overlap between the Cases

A charge under Case I or II excludes one under Case III.[90] Where a person has some emoluments charged under Case II and others under Case III for the same employment, emoluments received in the UK are attributed to the Case II income first.[91]

Source and timing

Case III applies to the full amount received in the UK as determined under the general remittance rules—and not the special Schedule E rules for Cases I and II.[92] However, liability under Case III arises on sums received in the UK whether or not the office or employment is still held when the emoluments are received in the UK.[93]

Place of performance of duties[94]

In determining whether duties are performed wholly outside the UK, duties performed in the UK but which are purely incidental to the performance of duties abroad are ignored.[95] Certain duties are declared to be performed in the UK, such as certain duties on board ships and aircraft and certain employments of a public nature under the Crown and payable out of public revenue.[96] These rules are varied for seafarers and their 100% reduction.[97]

13.3.2 Deductions for expenses from foreign earnings

(a) Initial and final travel expenses (s. 193)

Initial and final travel expenses are not incurred "in the performance of the duties" but to enable a person to carry them out (or return from having carried them out) as required by TA 1988, s. 198. Legislation therefore applies where the employee is resident and ordinarily resident in the UK and the emoluments are not foreign emoluments. The employee may deduct the costs of travel from any place in the UK to take up the employment, and of travel to any place in the UK on its termination. The reference to "any place in"[98] the UK is

[89] TA 1988, s. 192 infra p. 211.

[90] Ibid., s. 131(2).

[91] On allocation of earnings where duties are performed partly in the UK and partly outside, see Statement of Practice SP 5/84.

[92] TA 1988, s. 202A(3)

[93] Ibid., s. 202A(2)(b) (reversing *Bray* v. *Best* [1989] STC 159, HL). On finding the right year, see s. 19 para. 4A. When the person dies before the remittance, tax is charged on the personal representatives (TA 1988, s. 202A(3)).

[94] See *Taylor* v. *Provan* [1974] STC 168, 175, [1974] 1 All ER 1201, 1208; *Barson* v. *Airey* (1925) 10 TC 609.

[95] TA 1988, s. 132(2). *Cf.* TA 1988, s. 335; *Robson* v. *Dixon* [1972] 3 All ER 671; 48 TC 527; *Taylor* v. *Provan* [1973] 2 All ER 65, 74.

[96] TA 1988, s. 132(4); *Graham* v. *White* [1972] 1 All ER 1159, 48 TC 163. For concessionary relief for locally engaged (i.e. not UK-based) unestablished staff working abroad who are not resident in the UK and are not well paid, see ESC A25. There is also concessionary relief for the daily subsistence allowances paid to detached national experts seconded to the European Commission (Inland Revenue Press Release, 29 March 1994, *Simon's Tax Intelligence* 1994, 458.

[97] TA 1988, Sch. 12, para. 5.

[98] Added by ibid., s. 193(3).

presumably to ensure that where, for example, an employee flies from Glasgow to the United States via Heathrow, the costs of the flight from Glasgow to London are deductible and not just the costs of travel from the airport of departure from the UK.

(b) Board and lodging

Expenses of board and lodging to enable employees to carry out the duties of their employment are deductible (i) if met directly by the employer, or (ii) having been incurred by the employee are then reimbursed by the employer.[99] Therefore, no deduction is allowed where employees meet the expenses but are not reimbursed; this is presumably because in situations in which deduction is permitted the employer will claim to deduct these sums in computing his profits and so the Revenue can check the sums claimed by the employer against the sums claimed by the employee. Where the expense is incurred partly for a non-employment purpose, s. 193 permits apportionment of those costs attributable to the employee,[100] but will allow nothing for the spouse or family.

(c) Travel between multiple employments

Travel costs are also deductible where the employee has more than one employment the duties of at least one of which are performed wholly or partly outside the UK.[101] Travel from one job to another could not be said to be in the performance of the duties of either and so a special rule treats the expense as incurred in performing the duties of the employment to which he is going. This rule applies to journeys both from and to the UK but the employment[102] must not be such as to give rise to foreign emoluments. Again, apportionment is authorised if there is more than one purpose.[103]

(d) Intermediate and family travel (s. 194)

Return journeys during the performance of the duties of employment and the costs of travel by the employee's family are matters regulated separately by a different and more restrictive rule.[104] First, for the costs of family travel to qualify the employee must be absent from the UK for a continuous period of at least 60 days,[105] whether or not in the year of assessment, for the purpose of performing the duties of the employment. Secondly, the cost must be either paid or reimbursed by the employer, as in the board and lodging rule.[106] Thirdly, the rule extends only to two outwards and two inwards journeys in any year of assessment. Children must not be over 17[107] at the beginning of the outwards journey. Where the duties are performed partly in and partly out of the UK they must be such that duties being performed overseas can be performed only there and the journey must be wholly and exclusively for the purpose of performing those duties (in the case of an outward journey) or (in the case of an inbound journey) returning after performing such duties.[108] Where the duties

99 Ibid., s. 193(4)(a).

100 Apportionment is authorised by ibid., s. 193(4).

101 Ibid., s. 193(5).

102 Presumably the one to which he is going.

103 TA 1988, s. 193(6).

104 The travel may be from or to "any place in" the UK (ibid., s. 194(3)).

105 Ibid., s. 194(2). On costs of travel by a wife to accompany a director or employee in precarious health, see ESC A4(d) (the phraseology of this concession is flagrantly sexist).

106 TA 1988, s. 194(2).

107 A person reaches 18 at the start of the day which is the eighteenth birthday (Family Law Reform Act 1969, s. 9).

108 TA 1988, s. 194(3).

are of one or more employment(s) a similar rule applies. The employee can deduct the costs of travel for any journey from and to any place in the UK[109] provided the duties can be performed only outside the UK, and the absence from the UK was occasioned wholly and exclusively for the purpose of performing the duties concerned.[110] The condition that the duties can be performed only outside the UK is relaxed for seafarers.[111]

(e) Employees not domiciled in the UK (s. 195)

Employees who are not domiciled in the UK but who are paid for duties performed here are governed by a special rule.[112] Such employees must not have been resident in the UK for either of the two years preceding the year of assessment in which they arrived or must not have been in the UK for any purpose during the two years ending with the date of arrival.[113] The special rule permits the deduction of costs of travel to and from the employee's usual place of abode, i.e. where he normally lives. If he is present in the UK for a continuous period of at least 60 days for the purpose of carrying out the duties of the employment, the family travel rules are as for UK domiciled employees and it is necessary for the cost to be borne by the employer, or reimbursed separately.[114] Once here the employee is entitled to the benefit of these rules for a period of five years beginning with the date of arrival.[115]

(f) Foreign emoluments—corresponding payments (s. 192)

Foreign emoluments may attract further deductions for "corresponding payments".[116] Payments are "corresponding" if they are similar to payments which would be deductible if all the relevant elements were in the UK. Examples include alimony paid under a foreign court order, interest on a loan to purchase a sole or main residence in the employee's home country, and annual contributions to a foreign pension fund which corresponds to a UK pension fund for which relief could be given. Such payments are allowable only if they are made out of the foreign emoluments and, save for pension contributions, Revenue practice may require proof that there is not sufficient overseas income (on which UK tax is not payable) to enable the payments to be made without having recourse to the foreign emoluments.[117]

13.3.3 Double tax treaties

The effect of double tax treaties on a person who is not resident in the UK may be to grant exemption from Schedule E.

13.3.4 Note for seafarers and history

From 1974 until 1998 it was possible for an employee who had earnings for services rendered abroad (whether for a foreign or UK-based employer) to claim a 100% deduction for

[109] Ibid., s. 194(5), (6).

[110] Ibid., s. 194(4). On "wholly and exclusively" in a slightly different context, see *Mallalieu* v. *Drummond* [1983] STC 665 (below at §22.2).

[111] TA 1988, s. 194(7)–(9).

[112] Ibid., s. 195.

[113] This rule may operate harshly, for example, when an employee visits the UK with a view to seeing whether he wishes to come here to work.

[114] TA 1988, s. 195(6).

[115] Ibid., s. 195(2), (3).

[116] Ibid., s. 192(3).

[117] *Schedule E Manual*, para. 4202.

payments for those services.[118] Since 1998 this has been possible only for seafarers.[119] The rule remains of general importance for past years and for certain termination payments attributable to past years.[120] From 1974 until 1992 it was even possible to claim pension contribution deductions.[121] To qualify for the 100% deduction the earnings had to be for a "qualifying period" of at least 365 days of absence from the UK. Complicated rules related to the number of days the employee was allowed back in the UK during this period. This was repealed in 1998 because it was being "exploited" by "a few" high-earning individuals who were able to arrange their affairs so that they did not pay tax in the other country either.[122] If these words are to be taken at face value the sensible thing would have been to tie the 100% deduction to non-taxable status of the payment in the other country. It is therefore more likely that the Treasury had its eye on the £250 m it hoped to recoup. It is also likely that some of those high earning individuals will now rearrange their affairs so as to achieve non-resident status.

Before 1974 earnings from foreign employments—a different concept altogether—were taxed on a remittance basis. This meant that tax would be paid in the UK only if the money was remitted to the UK. Moreover, at that time it was taxable only if the money was remitted in a tax year in which the foreign source existed.[123]

13.4 PAYE[124]

13.4.1 Introduction

PAYE is the UK system of cumulative withholding of tax at source. It has become a mark of good manners to praise the UK's PAYE system, but there is little cogent evidence to support such an assessment in unqualified form.[124a] While the system works well it is only as good as the quality of the information supplied. A withholding system, it has been said:[125]

> "combines the expedient and the objectionable. It is a rough and ready system which virtually garnishees taxpayers' incomes, sometimes for debts they do not owe but subject in this event to refund. . . . It is surprising that this withholding system, to which strong objections may be raised on grounds of principle, has aroused so little comment. It has probably done more to increase the tax collecting power of central governments than any other one tax measure of any time in history."

The PAYE system imposes a duty on the employer[126] to account once a month (but quarterly for certain employers)[127] for the tax that he has or ought to have deducted. PAYE is distinct from provisions which direct that basic rate tax is to be deducted at source, e.g. under

[118] TA 1988, Sch. 12.
[119] Ibid., s. 192A, added by FA 1998.
[120] TA 1988, s. 188(3), Sch. 11, para. 10.
[121] Ibid., Sch. 12, para. 1A, added by F (No. 2) A 1992, s. 54.
[122] Inland Revenue Press Release, 17 March 1998 (1998) *Simons Tax Intelligence* 453.
[123] *Bray* v. *Best* [1989] STC 159; reversed by TA 1988, s. 202A.
[124] For accounts of the system, see RC (UK) 2nd Report, §§16–26, and 118th Report of the Board of Inland Revenue, Cmnd. 6302 (1976), §§93–125. See now TA 1988, ss 203, 205–207, 828, and the Income Tax (Employments) Regulations 1993 (SI 1993/744). On preparations for use of electronic transfer of data see TA 1988, s. 203(10), added by FA 1998, s. 119. For some dated comparisons with the United States, see Murray [1962] *BTR* 173.
[124a] See Brodie, *Taxation* vol. 145, 271 at 272.
[125] MacGregor [1956] 4 *Can. Tax Jo.* 171, 173; Carter, Study 16, 17.
[126] For example *Glantre Engineering Ltd.* v. *Goodhand* [1983] STC 1,[1983] 1 All ER 542, 56 TC 165.
[127] Income Tax (Employments) Regulations 1993, regs 40, 41.

the scheme for payments to sub-contractors.[128] Where the system does not apply, e.g. in the case of a non-resident employer, the employee must use the self-assessment system. In view of its effectiveness PAYE has been expanded in various ways. It also provides ample encouragement to the Revenue to argue that a contract is one of employment and not self-employment.

Construction—narrow approach

In *IRC* v. *Herd*[129] the House of Lords held that the PAYE regulations should not apply unless there was a clear direction that they should. The Revenue argued for the narrow construction, while the employee argued for a wide construction so that the burden would fall on the employer and not on himself. The charge had arisen under what became TA 1988, s. 138 on the unrealised gain on shares acquired as an employee. A specific provision now applies the PAYE rules to certain benefits from share options, etc., but did not then.[130] Lord Mackay said that the Schedule E charge was not on the amount paid but on the net gain and this involved questions of the market value of shares which are not publicly quoted and so could involve considerable calculation and, perhaps even more importantly, substantial judgments on matters of opinion.[131] He went on to emphasise that his view applied only where a particular payment is treated only in part as assessable to income tax under Schedule E; it would not prevent a payer being under an obligation to deduct tax where it was clear that there were two or more payments made together, some of which were emoluments under Schedule E while others were not.[132]

The Special Commissioners have considered, but not decided, the basic question of whether a payment means payment in money.[133] However, they have held that a payment in kind which could be converted into money was a payment for PAYE.

13.4.2 Widening the ambit by legislation

Benefits

Although PAYE was originally applied only to money payments it has since been extended to certain benefits in kind, notably tradeable assets (s. 203F),[134] but also enhancing the value of an asset (s. 203FA), share options (s. 203FB), non-cash vouchers (s. 203G), credit tokens (s. 203H) and cash vouchers (s. 203I). Apart from these extensions, PAYE applies to all income within Schedule E including, therefore, certain welfare payments; it also applies to payments of expenses and expense allowances within TA 198, s. 153. On the use of coding to collect tax on benefits outside the PAYE system see below.

Payments by others

PAYE applies to certain payments by third parties. Where an emolument is paid by a third party he may be required to deduct tax under the PAYE system.[135] PAYE may also apply to

[128] TA 1988 ss 559 *et seq* and the Income Tax (Employments) Regulations 1993.
[129] [1993] STC 436, 66 TC 29.
[130] TA 1988, s. 203FB; s. 138 was repealed before s. 203FB came into force.
[131] [1993] STC 436, 442e.
[132] Ibid., 443d.
[133] *Paul Dunstall Organisaton Ltd.* v. *Hedges* [1999] STC (SCD) 26.
[134] On which, see *DTE Financial Services Ltd.* v. *Wilson* [1999] STC (SCD) 121 for a scheme which would have avoided s. 203F but for the *Ramsay* doctrine.
[135] See also *Booth* v. *Mirror Group Newspapers plc* [1992] STC 615.

payments by an intermediary (s. 203B). The concept of a payment by an intermediary is widely defined. PAYE also applies (s. 203E) where a contractor hires employees of another person (the mobile workforce provision). This applies where the employee works for someone other than the employer and that someone, known as the relevant person, pays the employer; one or other of these will operate the PAYE system. The Revenue has the power to direct the relevant person to apply the system if it appears to the Revenue that tax will not be deducted or accounted for as usual.[136] Whenever Schedule E is extended to workers, the PAYE regulations will follow—so workers supplied by agencies are brought within Schedule E by s. 134 and so, potentially, within PAYE.[137]

International

The obligation on an employer to operate the PAYE system arises if he has a sufficient tax presence in the UK. For this purpose, a non-resident company carrying on business in the UK through a branch agency has a sufficient presence.[138] This obligation is widened by two provisions. First, where an employee works for a person based in the UK, but the actual employer is based overseas (and so outside the PAYE regulations), the person for whom the employee is working can be made to apply the PAYE system on behalf of the employer (s. 203C). The same burden falls on the person for whom the work is done where someone other than the employer makes the payment and is also outside the UK.[139] The second situation arises where an employee is not resident in the UK or, if resident, is not ordinarily resident here; the PAYE system is designed to apply only to those emoluments which are for work done in the UK, (s. 203D). The practical problem is that when the payments are actually made it may be unclear how much of the remuneration will be taxable. Employers may ask for a direction as to the proportion to be subject to PAYE; if no direction is sought, the whole payment is subject to the system.[140]

13.4.3 Liabilities under PAYE

The employer

The employer is liable to deduct PAYE in accordance with tables supplied by the Revenue and taking account of the PAYE coding of the employee, which is based on the individual reliefs for the year.[141] If the employer fails to deduct, the Revenue may demand the money from the employer.[142] If the Revenue proceeds against the employer, it was at one time held that the employer could not, in turn, recover from the employee.[143] This was because the employee was not a trustee for the employer and because the action for money had and received would not lie; the employer could only retain the sums from later payments to the employee,[144] which would be of no value if the employment had ceased. Today, the princi-

[136] TA 1988, ss 203B, 203E.

[137] On practice, see RD4 (February 1992); see also FA 1998, s. 55 for another example.

[138] *Clark* v. *Oceanic Contractors Inc.* [1983] STC 35 (where the branch was deemed to be in the UK by what is now TCGA 1992, s. 276(7)).

[139] TA 1988, s. 203C; see also Inland Revenue Press Release, 11 April 1994, *Simon's Tax Intelligence* 1994, 490.

[140] TA 1988, s. 203D; see also Inland Revenue Press Release, ibid.

[141] On coding, see the Income Tax (Employments) Regulations 1993, regs 6–13.

[142] Ibid., reg. 49.

[143] *Bernard and Shaw Ltd.* v. *Shaw* [1951] 2 All ER 267; see the discussion by Weisbard (1996) *NLJ* 1124.

[144] Note also the very special case of *Philson & Partners Ltd.* v. *Moore* (1956) 167 EG 92 where there had been an express term in a severance agreement between employer and employee that the employee should settle outstanding matters with the Revenue.

ple of restitution, which has superseded the old action for money had and received, may allow the employer to recover the payment from the employee if the employee has been unjustly enriched. However, the old rule depends not only on the scope of the action for money had and received but also on the construction of the appropriate legislation.

The employee

If there has been an under-deduction of tax by the employer the Revenue may recover the tax from the employee in two very different situations. First, the collectors may recover from the employee and not from the employer if they are satisfied that the employer took reasonable care to comply with the regulations and that the failure was due to an error made in good faith.[145] Secondly, the Board (not the collectors) may recover from the employee where it is of the opinion that the employee received the sum knowing that that the employer had wilfully failed to deduct the tax.[146] The same applies to sums which have been assessed on the employer under these rules and not paid within 30 days of the notice. Again, the Board is involved and the employee must receive the sum knowing that the employer had wilfully failed to deduct the tax.[147] It has been held that, where the Revenue seeks to use this power in county court collection proceedings, it is open to the defendant-employee to raise the public law defence that on no view of the evidence could the Board reach that conclusion.[148]

When the PAYE system has been applied to income the Crown may make an assessment as regards income in the light of the practice generally prevailing,[149] provided it does so within 12 months following the year for which the assessment was made—a rule which binds the Revenue and does not affect the taxpayer's right of appeal.[150] Separate provisions apply where an employer makes a lump sum settlement of PAYE which, it is estimated, should have been deducted on wages paid.[151]

13.4.4 The cumulative withholding system

Annual

The system is one of cumulative withholding over the year. Full account is taken of the employee's income from this source and of such personal allowances as each may be entitled to. In essence, each is allowed 1/52nd of the relevant allowances each week, or 1/12th each month. At the end of any week taxable income is calculated by subtracting the accumulated 1/52nd shares of the allowances from the taxable pay to date. If the income rises over the year the tax will rise with it; if it falls, e.g. because of a change of job or a strike, a repayment may be made by the employer, or lower tax paid for the rest of the year. In the 1970s it was realised that if an employee went on strike late in the tax year the tax repayment due would help supplement any strike pay and so prolong the strike. Repayments to people

[145] Income Tax (Employments) Regulations 1993, reg. 42(2).

[146] Ibid., reg. 42(3); as in *R.* v. *IRC, ex parte Sims* [1987] STC 211, 60 TC 398; and *R.* v. *IRC, ex parte Cook* [1987] STC 434, 60 TC 405.

[147] Income Tax (Employments) Regulations 1993, reg. 49(5); for an unsuccesful challenge by the employee, see *R.* v. *IRC, ex parte McVeigh* [1996] STC 91, 68 TC 121.

[148] *Pawlowski* v. *Dunnington* [1999] STC 551, CA.

[149] TA 1988, s. 206.

[150] *Walters* v. *Tickner* [1993] STC 624, 66 TC 174, CA.

[151] TA 1988 s. 206A and Income Tax (Employments) Regulations 1993, regs 80A–80N.

directly involved in a strike are therefore not made until the employee returns to work or finds other employment.[152]

Indirect enforcement of other liabilities by PAYE

Although the system applies to Schedule E income only, it can, in effect, be used to collect tax in respect of other sources. This is achieved by directing that the taxpayer's allowances shall be attributed to those other sources of income, thus reducing the allowances to be set against the Schedule E income and so gathering the tax from the Schedule E source. The system can also be used to collect underpayments of tax from that or a previous year, as well as to refund overpayments.

At one time, benefits in kind were not subject to PAYE directly; they could, however, be taxed indirectly by reducing the value of the reliefs which could be set against PAYE income through the coding system. Where the value of these benefits exceeded the available allowances there was provision for "negative coding" which applied whenever non-PAYE pay exceeded the allowances. Negative coding creates "additional pay" which can be taxed at source.[153] The tax to be deducted from a particular cash payment is not to exceed 50% of the payment.[154]

13.4.5 PAYE and self-assessment

In principle, the primary charge to income tax is the charge under self-assessment. PAYE is simply a method of withholding tax, which is brought into the calculation of the balancing payment. However, the Revenue does not issue self-assessment forms to those under the PAYE system. Moreover, where the underpayment in the year amounts to £1,000 or less and arises solely in respect of emoluments to which PAYE is applied, the underpayment can be collected by adjustment of the PAYE code.

A particular problem under self-assessment is that a director or employee who receives benefits in kind and to whom a self-assessment tax return is not issued, is not in a position to know whether the Revenue is proposing to collect tax on the benefits in kind through amendment of the PAYE code for the following year, or whether he should notify chargeability in order to make his own self-assessment. Penalties can be imposed if the employee does not notify chargeability.

The Revenue accepts that employees who receive such a copy of the information on a P11D can assume that any items on it which are not already taken into account for PAYE "will be" taken into account for PAYE, so that there is no need to notify chargeability because of them. This does not, however, apply where the particular employee knows that the P11D return has not, in fact, been submitted to Revenue.[155]

13.4.6 Commentary.

There are disadvantages in the PAYE system. First, there is the trouble and expense to employers of finding and paying staff to operate the system. In fact, many of these staff are ex-employees of the Revenue who leave for better pay after having been trained by the

152 Ibid., reg. 36.
153 Ibid., reg. 7(2)(b)(ii).
154 Ibid., reg. 2(1).
155 Statement of Practice SP 1/96.

Revenue. The expense of these employees will be deductible by the employer in computing his profit for the year, but this still leaves a substantial burden of the operating costs of the system to fall on the employer.[156] One wonders whether a tax credit rather than a tax deduction might not be more appropriate. Secondly, there is the fact, less pronounced in the PAYE system than in other cruder withholding systems, that tax may be withheld incorrectly and that a repayment may take some time to take effect. Thirdly, it is sometimes alleged that the PAYE system, while providing refunds if income drops, also taxes more steeply if income goes up and thus directs the taxpayer's attention to the fact that the increase is taxed at the marginal rather than the average rate. This may have a disincentive effect in that the repayments side of the PAYE system could encourage absenteeism later in the tax year when the tax refunds may be greater. A survey in 1954 found little evidence to support this.[157] A fourth disadvantage lies in the very perfection of the structure. Its complexity means that it could become something of a straitjacket in the days before computerisation.[158] As was seen above, the absence of PAYE from incentive payments meant that an employer could leave the employee to pay the tax if the employer so chose, especially if the employee had left the employment.

[156] On compliance costs, see above at §1.3.5.

[157] Royal Commission Second Report, Cmd 9105 (1954), § 130.

[158] It was regarded as responsible for such pre-1990 anomalies as a wife's earned income allowance being the same as a single person's, and not interfering with the husband's claim to the married man's allowance.

14

Schedule E—Part II: Emoluments

14.1 The Causation Test

Two House of Lords' cases provide the key to the test of a taxable emolument. The first, *Hochstrasser* v. *Mayes* (1959), talks about of rewards for services. While some refinement of some of the words used in that case may now be needed, it still represents a starting point. The second, *Shilton* v. *Wilmshurst* (1991), uses more flexible words. The precise relation between the two tests is unsettled.

14.1.1 Tests

In *Hochstrasser* v. *Mayes*,[1] a sum of money paid to compensate an employee for a loss was held not to be taxable. Upjohn J. said that the payment would be an emolument if it was made in reference to the services rendered by the employee by virtue of the office and if it was something in the nature of a reward for services past, present or future. In the House of Lords Viscount Simonds accepted this as entirely accurate, subject only to the observation that the word "past" might be open to question. In *Laidler* v. *Perry*[2] Lord Reid added that sums might be taxable even though they are not rewards, e.g. sums given to employees in

[1] [1959] Ch 22.
[2] [1966] AC 16, 30, 42 TC 351, 363. See also Browne-Wilkinson V.C. in *Shilton* v. *Wilmshurst* [1990] STC 55, 59 and 61, 64 TC 78, 95, 99, CA.

the hope that they will produce good service in the future. These comments suggest, as does the *Oxford English Dictionary*, that a reward is a recompense for something past (whether good or evil). In *Bray* v. *Best*[3] Lord Oliver could not read the expression "a reward for services" as anything more than a conventional expression of the notion that a particular payment arises from the existence of the employer–employee relationship and not from something else. In *Shilton* v. *Wilmshurst*[4] the House of Lords held that there was no reason to limit the scope of emoluments to those situations in which the payer has an interest in the performance of the duties.

Lord Reid's words in *Laidler* v. *Perry* were applied in two decisions of the House of Lords before *Shilton* v. *Wilmshurst*. In *Brumby* v. *Milner*[5] sums of money held in a profit-sharing scheme were distributed when the scheme was wound up. The House held that this payment, like the previous income payments, arose from the employment and from no other source; it was therefore taxable. In *Tyrer* v. *Smart*[6] the taxpayer applied for shares in his employing company, having preferential right of application as an employee. The House held that he was taxable on the advantage gained.

14.1.2 Hochstrasser *v.* Mayes[7]

The taxpayer worked for ICI Ltd., a large concern with factories in different parts of the UK. To encourage its employees to remain in the service of the company if asked to move to a different part of the country, the company promised to make good any loss incurred by the employee through a fall in the value of a house which the employee owned. This scheme was restricted to married employees and also to houses not exceeding £2,000 in value. On being moved from Hillhouse to Wilton, the taxpayer sold his house in Fleetwood for £1,500; it had originally cost £1,850. ICI reimbursed him this loss of £350 and the Revenue sought to assess him on the £350; it failed. The Revenue argued that all payments by employers to their employees "as such" were taxable unless they were payments in return for full consideration in money or money's worth other than for services under the employment. The House of Lords rejected this approach unanimously. It was not disputed that the company would not have made this payment if the taxpayer had not been an employee and it was clear that the company thought that it was going to benefit by having a more settled workforce if a scheme like this were in operation. Moreover, because the taxpayer had a perfectly standard wage, it could not be said that this was disguised remuneration. The House[8] held that the payment was not in respect of his services to the company but rather to compensate him for the loss which he had sustained, and was therefore not taxable. It may be noted that the company was getting the best of both worlds: the sum was not taxable in the hands of its employee but was deductible by the company in computing its profits.

What about other possible payments? As the Revenue's counsel put it, to be recouped a loss by someone else is plainly a profit. If these profits escaped tax, which profits would not?

[3] [1989] STC 159, 167.

[4] 64 TC 78 at 109 *per* Lord Templeman.

[5] [1976] STC 534, [1976] 3 All ER 636.

[6] [1979] STC 34, [1979] 1 All ER 321.

[7] [1960] AC 376, 38 TC 673. Kerridge [1982] *BTR* 272 argues that the case should have been decided on the basis that the housing arrangements were the subject of a collateral contract. On slightly different Canadian legislation, see the equivalent case of *Ransom* v. *MNR* [1967] CTC 346, discussed by Arnold and Li (1996) 44 *Can. Tax Jo.* 1; and *R.* v. *Phillips* [1994] 1 CTC 383.

[8] [1960] AC 376.

It was agreed that if the employee had suffered a bereavement and the company had seen fit to grant him something from its benevolent fund such payment would not have been taxable.[9] However, if the employee had been compensated for a loss on an investment on the Stock Exchange it is not obvious that he should would have escaped tax in respect of such a payment, although this has since been held to be so.[10] Only Lord Denning gave reasons why an indemnity of the last type would be taxable.[11] Unfortunately, this example was premised on the view that the indemnity would be by way of reward for services, a premise which automatically makes the sum taxable. Lord Denning went on to say that the sum would be taxable because the losses were "his own affair" and nothing to do with his employment, but this would be no less true of the hypothetical bereavement.

14.1.3 Shilton *v.* Wilmshurst[12]

This case concerned the transfer of Peter Shilton, then and for a long time thereafter the England football team's goalkeeper, from Nottingham Forest to Southampton in 1982. As part of the deal, Nottingham Forest paid Shilton a fee of £75,000 as an inducement to leave the club—and so go off its payroll. The Court of Appeal and Morritt J. held that the sum was not taxable. The emolument had to be referable to the performance of services by the employee under the contract of employment. The House of Lords took a different view. Lord Templeman said:[13]

> "Section [19] is not confined to 'emoluments from the employer' but embraces all 'emoluments from employment'; the section must therefore comprehend an emolument provided by a third party, a person who is not the employer. Section [19] is not limited to emoluments provided in the course of the employment; the section must therefore apply first to an emolument which is paid as a reward for past services and as an inducement to continue to perform services and, second, to an emolument which is paid as an inducement to enter into a contract of employment and to perform services in the future. The result is that an emolument 'from employment' means an emolument 'from being or becoming an employee'. The authorities are consistent with this analysis and are concerned to distinguish in each case between an emolument which is derived from being or becoming an employee on the one hand and an emolument which is attributable to something else on the other hand, for example from a desire on the part of the provider of the emolument to relieve distress or provide assistance to a home buyer. If an emolument is not paid as a reward for past services or as an inducement to enter into employment and to provide future service but is paid for some other reason, then the emolument is not received 'from the employment'".

It is not clear to what extent this formulation is meant to be a summary of existing case-law and to what extent it is meant to mark a new point of departure, but it shows how far the law had developed since 1959. This is made all the clearer by Ward's summary in 1992:[14] a sum is taxable if it is received in respect of (a) having acted as or having been an employee, (b) acting as or being an employee, (c) continuing to act as or continuing to be an employee, (d) becoming an employee or (e) undertaking to do anything within (b)–(d).

[9] Ibid., 392, *per* Lord Radcliffe.

[10] *Wilcock* v. *Eve* [1995] STC 18, 67 TC 223.

[11] [1960 AC 376, 396. *Quaere* if the loss were on shares of the employer company which he was obliged to sell on leaving the company (see above at §17.5.5).

[12] [1991] STC 88, 64 TC 78; see Kerridge [1991] *BTR* 311.

[13] [1991] STC 88, 91, 64 TC 78, 105.

[14] Ward [1992] *BTR* 139 (written before *Mairs* v. *Haughey*) [1993] STC 569; on which see [1994] *BTR* 77.

In applying these tests the courts take a realistic view of the facts. In *O'Leary* v. *McKinlay*[15] a football club made a long loan to trustees who held the money for a player. The income from the resulting investments was held to be income from the employment and so within Schedule E, and not income from a loan, which would have brought it within Schedule D, Case V.

One remaining issue concerns the question of whether a payment is an emolument: is this a question of law or of fact? In *Hochstrasser* v. *Mayes* (above) Upjohn J. took the question to be one of inference from primary fact and of legal inference, thus making the question one of law. In *Tyrer* v. *Smart*, however, the inference seems to have been treated as one of fact and so within the sole jurisdiction of the Commissioners. The position is as confused as it is unfortunate; the earlier view seems preferable.[16]

14.1.4 Consequences of causation test

Causation not consideration

Since the question is one of causation, and not consideration, the court is not confined to any expressions of consideration in any service contract. In *Pritchard* v. *Arundale*[17] a payment expressed in the contract of service to be in consideration of that service escaped tax. Conversely, in *IRC* v. *Duke of Westminster*,[18] Lord Atkin would have held the payment to be an emolument notwithstanding that the service was expressed not to be the consideration.

Condition, consideration and causation

In *Bridges* v. *Bearsley*[19] property (shares in the employer company) was transferred by other shareholders (X and Y) to an employee, B, under a deed which said that the transfer was in consideration of B remaining a director of the company. When the court looked at the circumstances surrounding the transfer it was clearly due to a wish to honour a promise made to B by the father of X and Y that the father would leave the shares to B by will and so not B's taxable emolument. Since the test was one of causation the court could look at all the circumstances.

Another cause

As seen above, a payment caused by something other than services must escape tax. Moreover the onus is on the Revenue to show that the payment is an emolument.[20]

Multiple causes

Where a payment is caused both by service and by something else, principle would suggest an apportionment of the payment, at least where this is practicable.[21] Whether there will be an apportionment if the sum is paid for two causes, neither of which can be valued, remains unclear.[22]

[15] [1991] STC 42, 63 TC 729.
[16] [1979] STC 34; Macdonald [1979] *BTR* 112.
[17] [1971] 3 All ER 1011, 47 TC 680.
[18] [1936] AC 1.
[19] (1957) 37 TC 289, CA.
[20] *Hochstrasser* v. *Mayes* [1959] Ch 22, *per* Viscount Simonds.
[21] *Mairs* v. *Haughey* [1993] STC 569; *Carter* v. *Wadman* (1946) 28 TC 41. In *Tilley* v. *Wales* [1943] AC 386, 25 TC 137 the House of Lords was relieved of the task of deciding whether an apportionment should be made since this was agreed between the parties.
[22] This was left open by the Court of Appeal in *Shilton* v. *Wilmshurst* [1990] STC 55, 64 TC 78.

Payment by non-employer

Just as a payment by an employer may not be an emolument, so a payment by someone other than the other party to the contract of employment may be an emolument.[23]

14.1.5 *Services past*

The liability to income tax of payments for services past was left open by Viscount Simonds in *Hochstrasser* v. *Mayes* but in the light of the words of Lord Templeman in *Shilton* v. *Wilmshurst* such payments will be taxable if they are also intended as an inducement to continue to perform future services. It has been held that a tip to a taxi driver is taxable even though given only at the end of the service.[24] A bonus payment to an employee[25] and a payment on completion of, say, 25 years' service with the company[26] are taxable, although in these cases, since the employment had not yet terminated, the payments may be seen as incitements to even greater service and loyalty in the future. By concession[27] an award in the form of a tangible article or shares in the employing company is tax free if the cost is reasonable, i.e. it does not exceed £20 per year of service. This limit does not appear to apply when the employee is leaving the employment.

None of these cases appears actually to turn on the question of payment for past services but the payments must have escaped tax had the point not been accepted.[28] The fact that past consideration is no consideration is irrelevant since the test is one of causation and not of consideration. The true line seems to be drawn not between services future and services past, but between a transfer caused by services and one caused by something else, e.g. a gift for personal reasons. The fact that the service is past is only one factor in enabling this line to be drawn.[29] In *Moore* v. *Griffiths*[30] the fact that the payment was not known about until after the services had been rendered tended to show that it was a testimonial, and so not taxable.

14.1.6 *Capital payments*

A few *dicta* suggest that payments can escape TA 1988, s. 19 if they are capital payments.[31] These *dicta* are unsound if they mean that a payment made in return for services can escape s. 19 because of its capital nature. In no case has the classification of a payment as capital been the prime reason for holding that the payment is not taxable; in a few cases a payment which has escaped tax because it was not made in return for services has been conveniently but irrelevantly (or even inaccurately) described as capital sum.[32] The description "capital"

[23] The person making the payment may be required to deduct tax under the PAYE system (*Booth* v. *Mirror Group Newspapers* [1992] STC 615).

[24] *Calvert* v. *Wainwright*.

[25] *Radcliffe* v. *Holt* (1927) 11 TC 621. However, will the emphasis on inducement as to future service mean that ordinary tips paid to a taxi driver, who, to the knowledge of the payer, is about to retire, escape tax?

[26] *Weston* v. *Hearn* (1943) 25 TC 425.

[27] See ESC A22.

[28] See *Henley* v. *Murray* [1950] 1 All ER 908, 31 TC 351, 366, *per* Evershed M.R.: "nor was it a reward for his past service" (not taxable); similarly, Lord Warrington in *Hunter* v. *Dewhurst* (1932) 16 TC 605, 643.

[29] As in *Cowan* v. *Seymour* [1920] 1 KB 500, 7 TC 372; *Denny* v. *Reed* (1933) 18 TC 254.

[30] [1972] 3 All ER 399, 48 TC 338.

[31] For example Lord Denning M.R. in *Jarrold* v. *Boustead* [1964] 3 All ER 76, 81; and Lord Simon in *Tilley* v. *Wales* [1943] AC 386, 393, 25 TC 136, 149.

[32] *Prendergast* v. *Cameron* (1939) 23 TC 122, 138, Finlay L.J.

is therefore best regarded simply as a convenient label for certain types of non-emoluments.[33]

14.2 Timing

14.2.1 Normal basis

Under Schedule E, Cases I and II tax is charged on the full amount of emoluments received in the year in respect of the office or employment concerned.[34] Emoluments are to be treated as received at the earlier of (a) when the payment is made of, or on account of, the emoluments, and (b) when the person becomes entitled to payment of, or on account of, emoluments.[35] The meaning of the expression "on account of" is not amplified. Where the person becomes entitled to payment but does not receive the payment, e.g. through the insolvency of the company, there is no provision giving relief.[36] These rules also apply to PAYE.[37] Since this test uses entitlement to payment as well as actual payment as tests of liability it is not really a receipts basis at all, but a mixture of receipts and earnings basis. Its importance is that it rejects decisively the old law under which the payment would be treated as income of the period during which the services were rendered, and a payment made in later year would be backdated.

14.2.2 Directors

Because directors can control how they are paid, three special rules apply:

(1) If the person is a director at any time during the year of assessment and the emoluments relate to an office or employment with that company,[38] the date on which sums on account of emoluments are credited in the company's accounts or records is used. This applies whether or not there is any fetter on the right to draw the sum.[39]

(2) If the amount to be paid for a period is determined before the period ends, the payment is treated as chargeable when that period ends, even though no payment has yet been made.

(3) Where the amount for the period is not known until later, e.g. when the bonus is finalised, the date of that determination will be taken. Where more than one of these rules, including the general rules in the previous paragraph, apply, the earliest date will be taken.

[33] For authority against such usage, see Walton J. in *Brumby* v. *Milner* [1975] STC 215, 227, 51 TC 583, 598; and Lord Coulsfield in *IRC* v. *Herd* [1992] STC 264, 286, 66 TC 29, 55; however, see Goldberg [1971] *BTR* 341, 345.

[34] TA 1988, s. 202A(1)(a); see also ICAEW Memorandum TR759, (1989) *Simon's Tax Intelligence* 716.

[35] TA 1988, s. 202B(1), added by FA 1989, s. 37(1); for origins, see Keith Committee, *Report on Enforcement of Revenue Powers*, Cmnd. 8822 (1983), 141–5.

[36] Contrast the position in Schedule D, Cases I and II (TA 1988, s. 74(j)).

[37] TA 1988, s. 203A.

[38] Ibid., s. 202B (1)(c)–(e), (2), (3) the term director is defined in s. 202B(1)(5), (6) (whether or not that office or employment is the directorship).

[39] Ibid., s. 202B(4).

14.2.3 Ceased office

It is not necessary that the office or employment should exist in the year in which the receipt arises.[40] If, in the year concerned, the office has never been held, the emoluments are to be treated as emoluments for the first year in which the office is held. Conversely if the office or employment is no longer held, emoluments are to be treated as emoluments of the last such year.[41] To this extent the legislation retains the doctrine of the source. TA 1988 does not address the problem arising where a person holds an office, resigns it and then resumes and receives a payment between the two periods of tenure. In such circumstances the answer presumably turns on the question, "which period of tenure is the payment for?".

14.2.4 Other rules

The timing rules do not override specific statutory timing rules for cash or non-cash vouchers, credit tokens and payments of compensation on retirement or removal from office.[42] They are also excluded for the beneficial occupation rules and the rules governing benefits and expenses payment for directors and employees earning £8,500 p.a. or over (see below chapter 17). Case III has its own timing rules.

14.3 Money's Worth—Discharge of Employee'sObligation: the Rule in *Nicoll* v. *Austin*

Payments applied for the benefit of the taxpayer are just as much income as moneys paid directly.[43] Where an employer discharges an existing pecuniary obligation of the employee, E, the sum paid is treated as E's income, even if it is income tax as in *Hartland* v. *Diggines.*[44] In *Hartland* v. *Diggines* a promise to pay a salary "without any deductions and taxes which will be borne by" the employer was interpreted as an agreement to pay such sums as after deduction of tax gives the net salary after deduction of tax.[45] This has been applied equally where employer and E are jointly liable.[46] The fact that the employer is under no obligation to make the payments is irrelevant.

In *Nicoll* v. *Austin*[47] the principle was applied to future obligations. The taxpayer was life director of, and had a controlling interest in, his employing company. Under his contract of service he was to continue to reside in his own house but the company would pay all outgoings in respect of his house, including rates, taxes and insurance, and the costs of gas,

[40] Ibid., s. 202A(2).
[41] Ibid., s. 19(4).
[42] Ibid., s. 202B(6).
[43] For example, *Drummond* v. *Collins* [1915] AC 1011, 6 TC 525.
[44] [1926] AC 289, 10 TC 247. See also *IRC* v. *Miller* [1930] AC 222, 15 TC 25; *IRC* v. *Leckie* (1940) 23 TC 471. An under-deduction of a director's PAYE which is accounted for to the Revenue by the employer is taxed under TA 1988, s. 164 (on which, see Revenue, *Schedule E Manual*, paras 3230 *et seq*).
[45] *Jaworski* v. *Institution of Polish Engineers in Great Britain Ltd.* [1951] 1 KB 768, [1950] 2 All ER 1191. But, *cf. Jennings* v. *Westwood Engineering Ltd.* [1975] IRLR 245. Tax-free remuneration for directors is now prohibited by Companies Act 1985, s. 311; on definition of "director", see Companies Act 1985, s. 741 and compare TA 1988, s. 168.
[46] *Richardson* v. *Worrall* [1985] STC 693, 58 TC 642 (*quaere* whether this will not be so if the primary liability and the primary benefit are the employer's).
[47] (1935) 19 TC 531.

electric ligh, telephone and of maintaining the house and gardens[48] in proper condition; however, the house remained the taxpayer's. Finlay J. held that the payments made by the company constituted money's worth to the taxpayer, who was therefore taxable.[49]

However, *Nicoll* v. *Austin* does not apply if, after leaving the employer and before being used to discharge the liability of the employee, it has become the income of someone else. In *Barclays Bank Ltd.* v. *Naylor*[50] payments were made into the bank account of a child of the employee out of a discretionary trust set up by the employer to help with employees' school fees. Cross J. held that the payments had become the income of the child, and the fact that income had been used to discharge the father's legal obligation to pay the school fees was insufficient to turn the income of the child into the income of the parent.

The payment of an expense in connection with the provision of a parking place is expressly excluded.[51]

14.4 Examples of General Principles

The question whether a particular receipt arises from the employer-employee relationship or from something else has been much explored in the case-law. Clearly, the more cogent the "something else" is, the more chance a taxpayer has of arguing that the payment falls outside s. 19.

14.4.1 General

Payments for services include not only ordinary wages and salaries but also less obvious payments, such as those to mark a period of service with the employer [52] and bonus payments whether or not contracted for[53] and even if paid at Christmas.[54] A sum paid "to preserve an employer's good name and good staff relations" was held to be taxable even though it was designed to compensate staff for the withdrawal of a benefit in kind.[55]

A payment for services may arise even if the service is not within the scope of duty. In *Mudd* v. *Collins*[56] a director who negotiated the sale of a branch of the company's business was held taxable on the sum of £1,000 granted him by the company as commission.

[48] For a doubt about the gardens, see Lord Evershed M.R., in *Wilkins* v. *Rogerson* (1961) 39 TC 344, 353.

[49] By concession this rule does not apply to the heating, lighting, cleaning and gardening costs of certain clergymen (ESC A61).

[50] [1960] 3 All ER 173, 39 TC 256. Today the scheme will not succeed if E comes within TA 1988, s. 154 ; the payment will be taxable under s. 165 and cannot be treated as exempt under s. 331 as scholarship income. See also *Constable* v. *FCT* (1952) 86 CLR 402.

[51] TA 1988, s. 197A.

[52] *Weston* v. *Hearn* [1943] 2 All ER 421, 25 TC 425.

[53] *Denny* v. *Reed* (1933) 18 TC 254. See ESC A22.

[54] *Laidler* v. *Perry* [1965] 2 All ER 121, 42 TC 351. On Christmas parties, see ESC A70; the limit of £75 per head is regarded as modest.

[55] *Bird* v. *Martland* [1982] STC 603, 56 TC 89. Payments for suggestion schemes are, in practice, governed by ESC A57.

[56] (1925) 9 TC 297, Rowlatt J. See also *Radcliffe* v. *Holt* (1927) 11 TC 621.

However, if the taxpayer can show that the payment is not for services but a testimonial, as in *Cowan* v. *Seymour*,[57] tax will not be due. Today, this decision must be considered borderline.[58]

14.4.2 Reimbursements

A payment by an employer to reimburse an expense incurred by the employee in the employment is not an emolument[59] (but this situation is not without its critics[60]). This is so even if the employee would not have been able to deduct the expense himself under TA 1988, s. 198. However, it is assumed that this applies only to expenses incurred in connection with the employment.[61] The reimbursment of an expense must be distinguished from an expense allowance, which is treated as an emolument.[62]

14.4.3 Gifts: sporting achievements

Payments which have escaped s. 19 include those made to relieve poverty,[63] as a mark of personal esteem, or to mark some particular occasion, such as the passing of an examination.[64]

Taxable gifts

The mere fact the donor is not the employer does not prevent the gift from being an emolument; the question is whether the payment is made because of the services rendered by the employee in the course of his employment. On this basis, Atkinson J. held, long ago in 1947,[65] that a tip to a taxi driver was taxable, but added that a tip of £10 would not be taxable if it was paid at Christmas or when the driver was going on holiday and was intended to acknowledge the driver's qualities and faithfulness rather than as a reward for regular service.[66] However, as always, the question is one of fact and degree. Christmas presents will be taxable if they are customary or indiscriminate.[67]

[57] [1920] 1 KB 500, 7 TC 372.

[58] *Cowan* v. *Seymour* was distinguished in *Shipway* v. *Skidmore* (1932) 16 TC 748 and in *Patrick* v. *Burrows* (1954) 35 TC 138, but was, surprisingly, followed in *IRC* v. *Morris* (1967) 44 TC 685 where the Court of Session held that there was evidence to support the Commissioners' findings. TA 1988, s. 148 applies only to payments "in consequence of the termination of the office" and so not here.

[59] *Owen* v. *Pook* [1969] 2 All ER 1, 45 TC 571; see also *Donnelly* v. *Williamson* [1982] STC 88, 54 TC 636 Reimbursement of car parking expenses when the parking space is at or near the place of work is not taxable (TA 1988, s. 197A, added by FA 1988, s. 46(4), (5)).

[60] See Lord Simon (dissenting) in *Taylor* v. *Provan* [1975] AC 194, 218, 49 TC 579, 615; and Evans [1988] *BTR* 362.

[61] Thus, in *Richardson* v. *Worrall* [1985] STC 693, 58 TC 642 a reimbursement of the cost of petrol obtained for private use was taxable; but in *Donnelly* v. *Williamson* (above at n. 59) a reimbursement of a teacher's costs for doing something outside the contract of service (attending a parents' evening) was not taxable.

[62] *Perrons* v. *Spackman* [1981] STC 739, 55 TC 403.

[63] *Turton* v. *Cooper* (1905) 5 TC 138.

[64] *Ball* v. *Johnson* (1971) 47 TC 155 (not taxable even though the bank required the employee to take A bankers examination); however, the payment is viewed by the Revenue as coming within TA 1988, s. 154 if the employee is paid at a rate of £8,500 p.a. or higher (ICAEW Memorandum TR786, *Simon's Tax Intelligence* 1990, 205.

[65] *Calvert* v. *Wainwright* [1947] 1 All ER 282, 27 TC 475; on Revenue practice, see *Simon's Tax Intelligence* 1984, 187 and *Simon's Tax Intelligence* 1985, 187.

[66] [1947] 1 ALL ER 282, 283, 27 TC 475, 478. £10 would now be worth £438 using the figures at §17.1.2.

[67] *Wright* v. *Boyce* [1958] 2 All ER 703, 38 TC 167, CA; and *Laidler* v. *Perry* [1966] AC 16, [1965] 2 All ER 121, 42 TC 351. In the latter case a company gave each of its employees a £10 voucher at Christmas, regardless of their rate of remuneration or personal circumstances; this replaced the traditional Christmas turkey which, for some reason, could not be obtained. A senior employee earning more than £2,000 a year thought the payment a charming Christmas gesture rather than as a payment for services, but this did not prevent the vouchers from being taxable under s. 19.

There is an extra-statutory concession exempting from tax gifts from third parties which are emoluments up to £150 p.a.[68]

Tests

In *Moorhouse* v. *Dooland* Jenkins L.J. stated four principles:[69]

(1) The test of liability to tax on a voluntary payment made to the holder of an office or employment is whether, from the standpoint of the person who receives it, it accrues to him by virtue of his office or employment or, in other words, by way of remuneration for his services.
(2) If the recipient's contract of employment entitled him to receive the voluntary payment that is a strong ground for holding that it accrues by virtue of the office or, in other words is a remuneration for his services.
(3) The fact that the voluntary payment is of a periodic or recurrent character affords a further, though less cogent ground for the same conclusion.
(4) On the other hand, a voluntary payment may be made in circumstances which show that it is given by way of present or testimonial on grounds personal to the recipient, as, for example, a collection made for the particular individual who is at the time vicar of a given parish because he is in straitened circumstances, or a benefit held for a professional cricketer in recognition of his long and successful career in first class cricket. In such cases the proper conclusion is likely to be that the voluntary payment is not a profit accruing to the recipient by virtue of his office or employment, but a gift to him as an individual paid and received by reason of his personal needs or by reason of his personal qualities or attainments.

These principles were stated in a case which concerned a payment by a third party. At least where the payer is the employer the intentions of the payer should also be considered.[70] The amount of the payment is also relevant.[71]

Clergy cases

It was decided early on that grants from a fund to supplement the incomes of clergy in poorly endowed parishes were emoluments.[72] Although these grants were not from the employers they were paid for services and paid to the clergy by virtue of their offices. The reason for the payments was to augment stipends—not to make grants to clergy because they were poor. In *Blakiston* v. *Cooper*[73] the House of Lords held that Easter offerings which, by custom and episcopal prompting, were given to the vicar, were also taxable.[74] The giving

[68] ESC A70.

[69] *Moorhouse* v. *Dooland* [1955] Ch 284, 304, 36 TC 1, 22.

[70] *Laidler* v. *Perry* [1966] AC 16, 35, 42 TC 351, 366, *per* Lord Hodson; and see Brightman J. in *Moore* v. *Griffiths* [1972] 3 All ER 399, 411 (employer's gift; third party's gift). If the company had, in return for their payment, used the footballer's name to advertise their products that payment would have been taxable under Schedule D, Case VI. *Quaere* whether allowing one's receipt of a gift to be used for advertisement will not also fall within Schedule D, Case VI.

[71] Hence, the difference between the wage and the benefit in *Seymour* v. *Reed* and the £10 tip in *Calvert* v. *Wainwright*. See also Lord Denning M.R. in *Laidler* v. *Perry* [1965] Ch 192, 199, 42 TC 351, 361.

[72] *Herbert* v. *McQuade* [1902] 2 KB 631, 4 TC 489.

[73] [1909] AC 104, 5 TC 347.

[74] "It may appear startling that those who on a particular Sunday—and that one of the most significant in the Christian year—contribute to the collection in their church, should be rendering unto Caesar nearly half their contributions, but so undoubtedly it is" (*per* Lord Evershed in *Moorhouse* v. *Dooland* [1955] Ch 284, 299); Whitsun gifts to the curate are also taxable (*Slaney* v. *Starkey* [1931] 2 KB 148, 16 TC 45).

may be voluntary but it is not spontaneous and there is an element of recurrence.[75] However, if the gift had been of an exceptional kind, such as a golden wedding present,[76] a testimonial or a contribution for a particular purpose (i.e. to provide a holiday or a subscription due to the personal qualities of the particular clergyman), it might be a mere present.[77] The Church of England now pools the Easter offerings for redistribution at diocesan level; one listens to episopal denunciations of the greed of tax planners with interest.

Sporting achievements—bonus or appreciation?

Seymour v. *Reed*[78] concerns the world of 1920s cricket. Seymour, the taxpayer, was a professional cricketer employed by Kent. In 1920 he was awarded a benefit season. Members of the club subscribed money to a fund for him and he was allowed to receive the gate money at one of the home matches of that season.[79] The gate money of £939.80 was held by trustees, together with the subscriptions, until Seymour had found a farm. The money was then paid over to him and used by him for the payment of the farm. The Revenue attempted to tax the £939.80 for the year when it was paid over. The attempt failed. The payment was a personal gift and not employment income. He had no right to a benefit season, the benefit would usually be towards the close of a man's career and was intended to provide an endowment on retirement; it was intended as an appreciation for services past rather than an encouragement for services to be rendered.[80]

By contrast, in *Moorhouse* v. *Dooland*[81] the Revenue succeeded. Dooland was a professional cricketer employed by East Lancashire. Under club rules he was entitled to talent money of one guinea every time he scored 50 runs or more, took six wickets or scored a hat-trick. In the 1950 and 1951 seasons Dooland qualified for talent money, and the resulting public collection, six and 11 times respectively. The Revenue successfully claimed tax in respect of the public collections. *Seymour* v. *Reed* was distinguishable on almost every point. Dooland had a contractual right to a collection; Seymour had no such right to his benefit. Dooland had a collection whenever he performed well; Seymour had only one benefit. Dooland's payments were small compared with his salary; Seymour's payment was very great. On similar reasoning footballers' benefits after only five years have been held to be taxable.[82]

It does not follow that all collections for special feats would fall within the definition of emoluments. Thus, if Dooland had no contractual right to a collection but had scored 50 runs and then taken all 10 wickets in a match so that the achievement was exceptional,[83] such a collection might not be taxable. In *Moore* v. *Griffiths*[84] payments made by the Football Association to mark England's victory in the World Cup in 1966 were held not to be taxable. The payment was intended to mark the Football Association's pride in a great achievement and it would be more in keeping with the character and function of the Association to construe the payment as a testimonial or mark of esteem. Brightman J.

[75] *Seymour* v. *Reed* [1927] AC 554, 569, 11 TC 625, 653, *per* Lord Phillimore.
[76] *Corbett* v. *Duff* [1941] 1 KB 730, 740, 23 TC 763, 779, *per* Lawrence J.
[77] *Blakiston* v. *Cooper* [1909] AC 104, 107, *per* Lord Loreburn.
[78] [1927] AC 554, 11 TC 625.
[79] For his performance see *John Wisden's Cricketer's Almanack* 1920.
[80] This is a question of fact and proof: see esp. Lord Phillimore at [1927] AC 554, 572, 11 TC 625, 655.
[81] [1955] Ch 284, [1955] 1 All ER 93, 36 TC 12.
[82] *Corbett* v. *Duff* [1941] 1 All ER 512, 23 TC 763.
[83] [1955] Ch 289, 298, *per* Lord Evershed M.R.
[84] [1972] 3 All ER 399.

added darkly, but presciently, that the payment had no foreseeable element of recurrence.[85]

14.4.4 *Compensation for surrender of advantage*

A payment by way of compensation for giving up some advantage rather than by way of reward for services is not taxable as an emolument.[86] This principle is applied even though the surrender of the advantage is a necessary consequence of taking the employment save where the advantage or right being surrendered is inseparable from, or is closely connected with, the employment. The decision whether a particular payment is for services or by way of compensation is judged according to the reality and not mere words—the tests looks at causation and not consideration.

Starting the job—Golden Hellos

Where an employer, R, makes a payment to an employee, E, at the commencement of E's service it is a question of fact whether this is a taxable payment for future services or non-taxable compensation for some loss. Remuneration for services is still remuneration for services even if it is paid in a lump sum in advance.[87] Whereas it would be very difficult to demonstrate that periodical payments are anything but taxable under Schedule E, the fact that the payment is a lump sum is a factor that can be taken into account.[88]

In *Pritchard* v. *Arundale*[89] the taxpayer, A, was in practice as a senior chartered accountant when a business friend, F, persuaded him to leave the practice and join him in business, as joint managing director of a company. A received a full salary at the commercial rate but insisted upon a stake in the business. F, who owned all but three of the 51,000 shares in the company, transferred 4,000 to A. A was held not taxable on the value of the shares transferred. Although the contract of service stated that the friend agreed to transfer the shares in consideration of A undertaking to serve the company, a contractual expression of consideration was not conclusively determinative of causation, and in any case that expression did not mean that that was the sole consideration.[90] Other factors[91] were the date of the transfer being six months before service started, the nature of the transfer, that the transferor was not technically the employer but only the principal shareholder of the employer, and that the taxpayer's surrender of his existing livelihood was expressed elsewhere in the contract. These points were emphasised by Walton J. in *Glantre Engineering Ltd.* v. *Goodhand*[92] when holding that a payment to an employee who had given up an employment elsewhere was taxable. This leaves open the question of whether the distinction is between employment and self-employment or is simply one of fact; the latter is to be preferred. Where the payment is to induce the person to leave an employment, the sum may be taxable under TA 1988, s. 148 but this must be distinguished from a payment to take up a different employment as in *Shilton* v. *Wilmshurst* (above).

[85] Ibid., 411; *quaere* whether this meant that recurrence was not foreseeable for these players.

[86] Where the payment is made in return for an undertaking the effect of which is to restrict the employee as to his conduct or activities, the payment may be taxable under TA 1988, s. 313 (see below at §14.6.5).

[87] See, e.g. Lord Greene M.R. in *Wales* v. *Tilley* (1942) 25 TC 136, 142.

[88] *Pritchard* v. *Arundale* [1971] 3 All ER 1011, 1022, 47 TC 680; followed in *Vaughan-Neil* v. *IRC* [1979] STC 644, [1979] 3 All ER 481, 54 TC 223.

[89] [1971] 3 All ER 1011, 47 TC 680.

[90] [1971] 3 All ER 1011, 1022, 47 TC 680, 687.

[91] *Quaere* how substantial these really are.

[92] [1983] STC 1, 56 TC 165; see also *Curran* v. *MNR* [1959] CTC 416.

Loss of amateur status—rugby league

At one time a person who joined a rugby league club was barred from ever again playing for, or even visiting, a rugby union club. If discovered on a rugby union ground as a spectator, he (only men were involved) would be asked to leave. If he signed as a professional he would be barred from competing as an amateur in, for example, amateur athletics.[93] Compensation for loss of these privileges was held non-taxable in *Jarrold* v. *Boustead*.[94] By contrast, in *Riley* v. *Coglan*[95] the sum involved was £500, of which £100 was to be paid on signing the professional forms and the balance on taking up residence in York. The player agreed to serve for the remainder of his playing career, or for 12 years if longer. If he failed to serve the whole stipulated period a proportionate part of the £500 was to be repaid by way of ascertained and liquidated damages. The Commissioners followed *Jarrold* v. *Boustead*, but on appeal that case was distinguished by Ungoed-Thomas J., who concluded that the £500 was to be a running payment for making the player available to serve the club when required to do so.[96] The distinction was one of fact. Coglan's contract nowhere mentioned the abandonment of amateur status, but neither did Boustead's, which provided for the payment of £3,000 on signing professional forms from which the court inferred that the payment was for loss. Coglan's £500 was coupled with the proviso that £400 was to become payable only when he took up residence in York, a factor suggesting that the payment was for services to the club. These, however, are minor differences. The principal distinction is that in Boustead's case no part of the £3,000 was returnable, whereas Coglan might have had to return some of his £500. In *Pritchard* v. *Arundale* the transfer was out and out.

Reality and the Sunday organist

It is significant that in *Jarrold* v. *Boustead* the disqualification of the player from rugby union or amateur athletics was for life. On parity of reasoning if C, a church organist, were required to give up Sunday golf as one of the conditions of employment and was paid £500 compensation, that sum would not be taxable under s. 19.[97] If, however, the condition was against playing golf at those times when C ought to be playing the organ, the payment would only be a thinly disguised remuneration. More difficult is the question whether such a sum would be taxable if the disqualification against Sunday golf or against playing rugby union were binding only so long as C was church organist or played rugby league. It may be significant that in *Pritchard* v. *Arundale*, where there was nothing to prevent the taxpayer from resuming his practice as a chartered accountant on leaving his employment, Megarry J. stressed the difficulties which a person of the taxpayer's age would find in building up his practice again.[98]

Payment as part of employer-employee relationship

A payment for loss of a right which is part of the employer–employee relationship is taxable following *Hamblett* v. *Godfrey*.[99] A payment in return for the surrender of a right which is

[93] *Jarrold* v. *Boustead* [1964] 3 All ER 76, 781, 41 TC 701, 704.
[94] [1964] 3 All ER 76, 41 TC 701.
[95] [1968] 1 All ER 314, 44 TC 481.
[96] *Cf.* the signing on payment in *Cameron* v. *Prendergast* [1940] AC 549, [1940] 2 All ER 35.
[97] Lord Denning M.R. in *Jarrold* v. *Boustead* [1964] 3 All ER 76, 80, 41 TC 701, 729.
[98] [1971] 3 All ER 1011, 1023c. Curiously, this point was not emphasised in *Glantre Engineering Ltd.* v. *Goodhand* [1983] STC 1.
[99] [1987] STC 60, [1987] 1 All ER 916, CA.

part of the employer–employee relationship, as opposed to mere social advantages, falls within s. 19. Therefore compensation for loss of the right to join a trade union was held taxable in *Hamblett* v. *Godfrey*. In *Shilton* v. *Wilmshurst*[100] Lord Templeman said that the rights lost in *Hamblett* v. *Godfrey* were not personal rights but were directly connected with the employment; it followed that the source of the payment was the employment. *Shilton* v. *Wilmshurst*[101] leaves intact the tax-free status of the payment in *Pritchard* v. *Arundale*. *Jarrold* v. *Boustead* was not cited but presumably remains in place for the same reason. The test of direct connection was used by Purchas LJ in *Hamblett* v. *Godfrey* itself.[101a]

A payment made to compensate for the loss of a contingent right (to a non-statutory redundancy payment) takes its character from the right it replaces. Since the non-statutory redundancy payment would have been tax free, compensation for its loss is also tax free.[102] In *Mairs* v. *Haughey* the Court of Appeal in Northern Ireland[103] made the point more sharply by holding that the payment was made in order to compensate for loss of those rights and not as an inducement to enter into the new contract of employment. In *Mairs* v. *Haughey* the business of the employer, R1, was being bought out by a new company, R2. E, the taxpayer employee, was offered an employment by the new employer, R2, on condition that he did not take the redundancy payments due to him from R1 under a non-statutory redundancy scheme but should, in the event of the buy-out being successful, receive an *ex gratia* sum from R1 the company, which was the sole shareholder in R2. Part of that sum was equal to a fraction of what would have been received for redundancy under the old scheme. The part which was for becoming an employee with the new company was taxable by reason of *Shilton* v. *Wilmshurst* but the other was not.[104] In *Mairs* v. *Haughey* Lord Woolf also said that prima facie a payment made after the termination of employment is not an emolument from the employment unless for example it is simply deferred remuneration.[105]

The reasoning in *Mairs* v. *Haughey* was applied in *Wilcock* v. *Eve*[106] where it was held that an *ex gratia* payment to an employee for loss of rights under a share option scheme was not taxable. The value of a grant of the right to a share option could be a taxable emolument but the value realised on its exercise could not.

Payment for giving up right already lost

If the right being compensated for no longer exists it is hard to establish that a payment is made to compensate for its loss. In *Holland* v. *Geoghegan*,[107] refuse collectors had had their right to sell salvaged property lawfully terminated; they went on strike but returned to work on payment of £450 compensation for loss of earnings due to the termination of the scheme. Foster J., reversing the Special Commissioners, held that since the right to sell salvaged property had been lawfully terminated the payment was not one of compensation for loss of a right but an inducement to return to work, and so taxable.

100 [1991] STC 88, 95, 64 TC 78, 111.
101 [1991] STC 88, 94, 64 TC 78, 108.
101a [1987] STC 60 at 69.
102 *Mairs* v. *Haughey* [1993] STC 569, 66 TC 273, 347 H.L.; for critical comment, see Ward [1994] *BTR* 77.
103 [1992] STC 495, CA NI.
104 [1993] STC 569, 66 TC 273, HL.
105 [1993] STC 569, 579j, 66 TC 273, 346.
106 [1995] STC 18, 67 TC 223.
107 [1972] 3 All ER 333, 48 TC 482.

14.4.5 Restrictive covenants

TA 1988, s. 313 was introduced[108] to reverse the decision of the House of Lords in *Beak* v. *Robson.*[109] In that case a director agreed to continue serving the company at a salary of £2,000 a year and received £7,000 in return for an agreement not to compete with the business within a radius of 50 miles for five years. The £7,000 was held not taxable.

Payment in respect of the undertaking

S. 313 applies wherever consideration is provided by the employer, whether to the employees or to others, in return for an undertaking, whether or not binding, the tenor and effect of which is to restrict employees as to their activities. The undertaking may be given before, during or after the employment. For the section to apply it must also be shown that the payment was made "in respect of" the undertaking. This requirement is not satisfied where the undertaking involves taking on the very duties inherent in and inseparable from the office or employment itself. So, in *Vaughan-Neil* v. *IRC*[110] a barrister who undertook to cease to practice at the planning bar on taking up his employment with a building contractor was held not taxable under s. 313 on the payment in return for the undertaking.

Taxation

The whole sum is subject to income tax at basic or higher rates in the usual way[111] and the income is to be treated as taxed for the purposes of TA 1988, s. 348. Before 1988 the whole was taxed in an unusual way in that it was subject only to excess liability.[112]

Deductibility

FA 1988 also makes the payment deductible by the payer—whether or not it would be deductible under normal principles and even if it is a capital payment.[113] This is achieved by directing that notwithstanding TA 1988, s. 74, any sum to which (the substituted) s. 313 applies and which is paid or treated as paid by a person carrying on a trade, profession or vocation, may be deducted as an expense. This wide authorisation apparently applies not only to payments which would otherwise be non-deductible by reason of being capital, but also payments for dual purposes or even those where the sole motivation of the payer was not for the purposes of trade.

14.5 Termination of Contracts: Compensation Payments

Payments on the termination of an office or employment are governed by an untidy mixture of statute and case-law. The case-law turns on the scope of s. 19. A payment which would fall within s. 19 may be excluded by statute. A payment which escapes s. 19 may be subject to the favourable tax regime in TA 1988, s. 148 and Schedule 11 (replacing s. 188 as

[108] FA 1950, s. 16. The purpose of backdating the section for payments within s. 34(4)(a) was to catch payments made to the managing directors of Austin and Morris Motor Companies. See Sabine, *A History of Income Tax*, 116.

[109] [1943] 1 All ER 46, 25 TC 33.

[110] [1979] STC 644, [1979] 3 All ER 481.

[111] TA 1988, s. 313(1), as substituted by FA 1988.

[112] TA 1988, s. 313(2), as originally enacted.

[113] FA 1988, s. 73. Before 1988 the payment was often non-deductible because of the decision of the Court of Appeal in *Associated Portland Cement Manufacturers Ltd.* v. *Kerr* [1946] 1 All ER 68, 27 TC 103; see below at §22.5.2.

from 1998). The following is, in part, an illustration of the principles in §14.4 above, but the case-law is best treated separately.

14.5.1 Rules

Payments will come within s. 19 only if made in return for services. If an employee owns property adjoining his employer's factory, sums paid by way of compensation under a claim for nuisance will not be taxable since they are not made in return for services. Problems arise where the claim arises out of the contract of employment. The courts might have followed the line taken under Schedule D, Cases I and II and held that sums paid in lieu of income are themselves income. However, under Schedule E a different approach prevails and sums paid to settle genuine compensation claims will escape tax under s. 19[114]—although, as has been seen, such sums will usually come within s. 148. The cases considered below are full of fine distinctions, and some important issues are still unresolved. The cases therefore turn on their own facts and, in particular, on the construction of the particular contractual arrangements.

Statutory exclusions from s. 19

Statutory redundancy payments are excluded from s. 19 (but not from s. 148) by statute.[115] Non-statutory redundancy payments are similarly excluded in practice if they are genuinely made on account of redundancy—whether the scheme is a standing one or an ad hoc arrangement to deal with a specific situation.[116]

Statutory exclusion from Schedule E: counselling

Payments incurred by an employer in providing qualifying counselling services to an employee in connection with the ending of the office or employment are excluded from Schedule E altogether.[117]

14.5.2 Case-law on compensation claims by employees against employers

In 1950 Sir Raymond Evershed M.R. memorably described the line drawn by the cases in this area as "a little wobbly".[118] Nothing much has changed. He added that the taxpayer could not make the payment one by way of compensation for loss of office simply by using a formula; that is also still good law, indicating that the matter is to be treated as one of substance and not of words or labels.[119] The following principles are relevant in this area:

(1) A sum paid by way of commutation of pension rights does not fall within TA 1988, s. 19.[120] This is not technically a matter which involves the compromise of a right arising

[114] If the compensation takes the form of annual payments it will be taxable as income under Schedule D, Case III (*Asher* v. *London Film Productions Ltd.* [1944] KB 133, [1944] 1 All ER 77). See also *Taxation Commr (Victoria)* v. *Phillips* (1937) 55 CLR 144.

[115] TA 1988, s. 579; the authority for being taken into account under s. 148 is s. 580.

[116] Statement of Practice SP 1/94.

[117] TA 1988, s. 589A; qualifying counselling services are defined in s. 589B.

[118] In *Dale* v. *de Soissons* 32 TC 118, 126.

[119] Ibid., 127.

[120] *Tilley* v. *Wales* [1943] AC 386, [1943] 1 All ER 280, 25 TC 136; see discussion in *Report of the Committee on the Taxation Treatment of Provisions for Retirement*, Cmd 9063 (1954) (the Tucker Report), paras 265–9. See also Woodhouse in *Tolley's Tax Planning 1999–2000* 1723–1748.

under the contract of employment since, while the right may have its sources in such a contract, the pension itself is a taxable entity distinct from the office or employment.[121]

(2) A payment to compensate for loss of rights under a non-statutory redundancy scheme is not taxable because it simply compensates for the loss of payments that would themselves be non-taxable.[122] Compensation for loss of rights under a voluntary redundancy scheme has escaped tax under s. 19,[123] but payments made to all employees, whether or not they were made redundant, have not.[124]

(3) A payment by way of compensation on the termination of the contract of employment, whether following judgment or by settlement, does not fall within s. 19.[125]

(4) It is unclear whether a payment will escape s. 19 if it consists of a sum stipulated in the contract as being paid by way of liquidated damages in the event of termination.[126] In theory, such payments should be treated the same as (3) since they have the same purpose. The boundary between (4) and (5–6) below would therefore be one of construction of the agreement. If this is correct, the sums will have to be a genuine pre-estimate of loss. One technical distinction is that in 5 and 6 the contract is not broken, whereas in (4) it is; however, this does not help to answer the question on which side of the line the arrangement falls. One might argue in favour of bringing (4) within s. 19 that, since they are part of the contract and therefore capable of inspiring the employee to greater effort, they must be payments for services. However, the same inspiration can be derived from knowing that in the event of breach a party can sue for unliquidated damages.

(5) A payment for continuing to work falls within s. 19.[127] Where it is agreed between employer and employee that the contract shall cease with effect from a future date, and the contract is allowed to run its natural course until that date, all sums paid under the contract come within s. 19. Payments made while serving out a period of notice remain taxable under s. 19.

(6) A payment in lieu of notice is taxable—at least where the right to make such payment is reserved to the employer in the contract of employment.[128]

(7) Where the contract of employment stipulates the sum to be paid in the event that the contract does not run its full course, the payment of that sum in accordance with the contract comes within s. 19. In *Dale* v. *De Soissons*[129] a three-year service agreement was terminable at the end of one or two years by the company; the company exercised its right to terminate the agreement after one year and paid the stipulated sum of £10,000. The payment was held to be taxable. As Lord Evershed put it:[130]

[121] *Tilley* v. *Wales* [1943] AC 386, 392, 25 TC 136, 149.

[122] *Mairs* v. *Haughey* [1993] STC 569; for critical comment, see Ward [1994] *BTR* 77.

[123] *Mairs* v. *Haughey* [1993] STC 569, HL (see above p. 232).

[124] *Allan* v. *IRC* [1994] STC 943.

[125] See *Henley* v. *Murray* [1950] 1 All ER 908, 909, 31 TC 351, 363.

[126] It is hard to find clear authority for this, but it may be implicit in *Henley* v. *Murray*; it is certainly inconsistent with the words used by Vinelott J. in *Williams* v. *Simmonds* [1981] STC 715. See also Woodhouse, supra. p. 1728, who points out that the Revenue will scrutinise the payments to see whether they are really payments in lieu of notice and so taxable.

[127] See discussion of *Hofman* v. *Wadman* (1946) 27 TC 192 in *Henley* v. *Murray* 31 TC 351; and comments by Stamp J. in *Clayton* v. *Lavender* (1965) 42 TC 607.

[128] *EMI Group Electronics Ltd.* v. *Coldicott* [1999] STC 803.

[129] [1950] 2 All ER 460, 32 TC 118, CA.

[130] [1950] 2 All ER 460, 462, 32 TC 118, 127. See also *Henry* v. *Foster* (1931) 16 TC 605.

> "The contract provided that he should serve either for three years at an annual sum or, if the company so elected, for a shorter period of two years or one year at an annual sum in respect of the two years or one year, as the case might be, plus a further sum, that is to say it was something to which he became entitled as part of the terms upon which he promised to serve."

The taxpayer was also caught in *Williams* v. *Simmonds.*[131] Here the contract was expressed to be ended in certain events and a sum then became payable under the contract. The taxpayer had the option, under the contract of treating the contract as not ended, but did not do so. Vinelott J. pointed out that had he taken that option and then reached a settlement the sum would have been outside s. 19.

If (7) is right, and especially if (4) above is determined in favour of the Revenue, a clear, but perhaps unfortunate, distinction arises between those who have the forethought to stipulate in advance what sums shall be due in the event of early termination of the contract, and those who are content to await events, between—to take a completely inappropriate analogy—the wise and the foolish virgins. Others, therefore prefer to as not what is the formal source from which the sum emerges but to ask for what the sum is designed to be paid. On this view, a genuine pre-estimate of loss should escape s. 19 even though it is stipulated for in the contract and (4) is decided in favour of the taxpayer.

(8) A payment which is not to compensate for the termination of one employment, but to encourage the start of another, will be treated as a taxable emolument under s. 19 arising from the new employment. *Shilton* v. *Wilmshurst*[132] highlights the unsatisfactory gap between payments taxable under s. 19 and compensation claims. A payment by an employer for breach of a contract of employment (a golden handshake) is not taxable under s. 19 because it is not paid under the contract, but for breach of it. Therefore, if an employer, R, breaks the contract and pays compensation, the payment will fall outside s. 19. However, if R acts as a good employer and finds a new employment for the employee before the dismissal, the payment, which is made to the employee for taking up the new employment, will be taxable under s. 19. All turns on the reason for the payment (and the evidence needed to establish it). There is much sense in the argument in *Shilton* that the payment was made to end his employment with Nottingham Forest; however, this was not so on the facts as found. There may be good sense in abolishing the special treatment for golden handshakes altogether. Lord Templeman's speech may be seen as a step towards achieving this objective by reducing the credibility of the distinctions in this area. Meanwhile, employees and their advisers know that if they want to bring the payment within s. 148 they must be extremely careful.

(9) Multiple causes—apportionment. Where a payment is made for two causes, one for future services and the other for compensation for loss of office or some other right, the courts will apportion the payment where possible.[133] Whether there will be an apportionment if the sum is paid for two causes, neither of which can be valued, remains unclear.[134]

[131] [1981] STC 715, 719, 55 TC 17, 22; for criticism, see Wosner [1982] *BTR* 121.

[132] [1991] STC 88, 64 TC 78; on the Court of Appeal decision, see Macdonald and Kerridge [1990] *BTR* 313 and 315 respectively.

[133] *Mairs* v. *Haughey* [1993] STC 569; *Carter* v. *Wadman* (1946) 28 TC 41. In *Tilley* v. *Wales* (below) the House of Lords was relieved of the task of deciding whether an apportionment should be made since this has been agreed between the parties.

[134] This was left open by the Court of Appeal in *Shiltonv Wilmshurst* [1990] STC 55, 64 TC 78.

14.5.3 Compensation for modifying contracts of employment—Hunter *v.* Dewhurst

A payment for the modification of the contract of employment ought, in principle, to be capable of escaping s. 19 in the same way as a payment for termination.[135] However, in practice, where the contract of employment continues, it is very difficult to persuade the courts that the payment is one for giving up a right under the contract as distinct from a payment for the services still to be rendered. In *Hunter* v. *Dewhurst*[136] the taxpayer wished to retire and live in Scotland, but the company wanted him to continue as a director, although undertaking less work for less pay. This rearrangement would have meant a reduction in a sum payable under a clause in the company's articles prescribing compensation of a sum equal to five years' earnings. The taxpayer agreed to continue as a director but received a lump sum of £10,000 under an agreement in which he renounced all rights to the compensation payment. The House of Lords held that this payment escaped tax, largely on the ground that it was compensation for the surrender of his contingent rights under the clause in the articles.[137] By contrast, in *Tilley* v. *Wales*[138] the taxpayer agreed to take a reduced salary of £2,000 a year in return for a payment of £20,000.[139] It was held that this was referable to the agreement to continue to serve as managing director at a reduced salary. As such, it was advance remuneration and so fell within (what is now) s. 19.

Hunter v. *Dewhurst* is a decision which has been distinguished[140] more often than it has been followed[141] and it must now be taken as confined to its special facts.[142] However, there does appear to be a clear distinction in principle between the surrender of rights under the contract, which may be taken as analogous to the surrender of pension rights in *Tilley* v. *Wales*, and a payment in consideration of refraining from resigning. In *McGregor* v. *Randall*[143] the taxpayer had been entitled to commission on profits; he received compensation in return for the loss of this right. In all other respects the employment continued. Scott J. held that s. 19 applied; he confined *Hunter* v. *Dewhurst* to its special facts and distinguished *Tilley* v. *Wales* and *Du Cros* v. *Ryall*[144] on the basis that the rights lost there would not or could not be enjoyed while the employment was current.

[135] In *Henley* v. *Murray* (above), however, Lord Evershed had distinguished the abrogation of an agreement from its modification.

[136] (1932) 16 TC 605. The Special Commissioners decided in favour of the taxpayer, as did Rowlatt J. and three members of the House of Lords; all three members of the Court of Appeal and two members of the House of Lords decided in favour of the Revenue.

[137] This is emphasised in the explanation of *Hunter* v. *Dewhurst* in *Cameron* v. *Prendergast* [1940] 2 All ER 35, 23 TC 122.

[138] [1943] 1 All ER 280, 25 TC 136.

[139] The sum paid was £40,000, but this was apportioned between the loss of pension rights and the reduction in salary.

[140] *Cameron* v. *Prendergast* [1940] 2 All ER 35, 23 TC 122; *Tilley* v. *Wales* [1943] 1 All ER 280, 25 TC 136; *Leeland* v. *Boarland* [1946] 1 All ER 13, 27 TC 71; *Bolam* v. *Muller* (1947) 28 TC 471; *Holland* v. *Geoghegan* [1972] 3 All ER 333, 48 TC 482.

[141] *Duff* v. *Barlow* (1941) 23 TC 633 and *Tilley* v. *Wales* (above) appear to be the only reported cases in which *Hunter* v. *Dewhurst* has been applied, but in the former *Cameron* v. *Prendergast* (above) was not cited. Lord Woolf refused to expres any opinion in *Mairs* v. *Haughey* 66 TC 273, 348.

[142] For example, Sir Raymond Evershed M.R. in *Henley* v. *Murray* [1950] 1 All ER 908, 911, 31 TC 351, 366.

[143] [1984] STC 223, [1984] 1 All ER 1092, 58 TC 110.

[144] (1935) 19 TC 444.

14.5.4 The special regime for payments outside s. 19[145]

Payments or benefits[146] received on retirement or removal from office or employment and which are not otherwise chargeable to tax are taxed under TA 1988, s.148 if they exceed £30,000.[147] S. 148 is a separate charging provision and can therefore apply even though the taxpayer left the UK and was neither resident nor ordinarily resident in the UK in the year in which the employment ended and the payment was made.[148] The payments or benefits must be received directly or indirectly in consideration of, or in consequence of, or otherwise in connection with the termination or change.[149]

Benefits

If the package includes a continuing benefit, such as the use of a car, the benefit is taxable in the year in which it is enjoyed. The benefit is charged at the same rate as the individual's rate for the year of enjoyment.[150]

Scope

If the payment fits the description in s. 148, it is immaterial whether or not it is paid in pursuance of a legal obligation.[151] A payment is caught even if it is made to the personal representatives of the holder or past holder of the office or employment, and even if it is paid to the spouse or any relative or dependant of his, as is a payment on his behalf or to his order.[152] The employee is also taxable even where the benefit is received by another.[153] It is immaterial whether the payment is made by the employer, a former employer or any other person.[154]

Timing

Cash receipts are treated as received when the payment is made or the recipient is entitled to call for it. A non-cash benefit is treated as received when it is actually used or enjoyed.[155]

Exclusions

Exclusions exist for payments on death, disability or injury,[156] for certain superannuation benefits or gratuities and for certain payments in relation to services for a government of an overseas territory within the Commonwealth.[157] A payment which is not a retirement benefit but is made for wrongful dismissal can come within s. 148, but Revenue practice requires a close examination of the facts to determine the genuineness or otherwise of the

[145] For 1998 reformulation, see [1998] *BTR* 420; on reporting requirements see SI 1999/70.

[146] Defined in s. 148(2) as anything that would be a taxable emolument of the employment if received for the employment or would have been chargeable but for an exemption. For pre-1988 law on provision of a car as part of the package, see *George* v. *Ward* [1995] STC (SCD) 230.

[147] TA 1988, s. 148 (1), Sch. 11, as rewritten by FA 1998 and replacing former ss 148, 188.

[148] *Nichols* v. *Gibson* [1994] STC 1029, 68 TC 611.

[149] TA 1988, Sch. 11, para. 2.

[150] Ibid., s. 148(4); previously it was tied to the year on termination. For 1996–1998 see Inland Revenue Press Release, 17 March 1997, (1997) *Simons Weekly Tax Intelligence* 381.

[151] TA 1988, s. 148(5)(b).

[152] Ibid., Sch. 11, para. 2.

[153] Ibid., Sch. 11, para. 14(1). On personal representatives of employee, see Sch. 11, para. 14(2).

[154] Ibid., s. 148 (5)(a).

[155] Ibid., s. 148(4).

[156] Ibid., Sch. 11, para. 3; see *Horner* v. *Hasted* [1995] STC 766, 67 TC 439.

[157] TA 1988, Sch. 11, paras 4–6.

claim.[158] This is in order to separate payments coming within s. 148 from those coming within s. 596A which imposes a charge in full (i.e. no £30,000 exemption) on any benefit received from an unapproved retirement benefits scheme. Certain payments in respect of foreign service are reduced by 50%,[159] but not where the emoluments were "foreign emoluments".

£30,000 threshold

In calculating the £30,000 threshold, any redundancy payment or *ex gratia* payment must be included, but not certain supplementary contributions to retirement schemes.[160] There are also valuation rules for valuing benefits (cash and non-cash).[161] Two payments for the same employment, or two payments for different employments with the same or associated employers,[162] are aggregated, but payments for distinct employments with unassociated employers are not. Where payments are aggregated, the aggregation is cumulative from year to year, the £30,000 exemption being applied to earlier payments before later ones.

[158] Statement of Practice SP 13/91, as amplified by a note from the Law Society, 7 October 1992, (1992) *Simon's Tax Intelligence* 869.

[159] TA 1988, Sch. 11, paras 9–11. On the need to define a place of service, see *Wienand* v. *Anderton* [1977] STC 12, 51 TC 570.

[160] Statement of Practice SP 2/81.

[161] TA 1988, Sch. 11, para. 12. On loans, see Sch. 11, para. 13.

[162] Ibid., Sch. 11, paras 7, 8.

15

Benefits in Kind

15.1 General

The taxation of benefits in kind raises (at least) three separate tax issues:[1] is the benefit taxable under Schedule E, is it subject to PAYE and is it liable to National Insurance Contributions (NICs)?[2] Today, many benefits in kind chargeable under Schedule E are subject to PAYE and attract Class IA NICs; formerly, PAYE and NICs would often not be payable at all. Class IA NICs differ from the normal Class I in that there is no charge on the employee but only on the employer. This may be rationalised on the basis that many of the employees concerned are well-off and above the point at which their Class 1 contributions cease. It is also likely that the Government does not want to impose further burdens on employees in light of its policy not to raise tax rates.

15.1.1 Policy

Benefits in kind also raise questions of policy. Thus, such benefits may tie employees to employers unduly, especially if the tax regime taxes such benefits lightly in comparison with a simple cash payment. In principle, all benefits in kind should be taxed, partly in order to satisfy requirements of equity and partly because failing to tax them properly leads to distortions. The Government's freezes on pay, prices and dividends in the 1970s led to the increase in benefits in kind as ways of getting round those restrictions. Benefits in kind are much loved in the UK employers as motivational devices to recruit and, perhaps more

[1] For comparative material and analayis, see *Taxation of Fringe Benefits* (OECD, 1988) and Scott, on Australia and New Zealand, in Sandford (ed.), *Key Issues in Tax Reform* (1993), 22; see also Carmody, Australian Tax Research Foundation Study No. 29 and Elmgreen, Study No. 3.

[2] See Homer and Burrows, *Tolleys Tax Planning 1999–2000*, 405–36.

importantly, to retain good staff. Incentives are used to reward high flyers or to provide incentives to improve performance. As one 1986 newspaper report put it, wives may not like husbands being pushed to reach a bonus level of £1,900, but the reward of a £1,900 video system is different.[3] One employee received a demand for £1,200 tax, plus interest and penalties, for an all-expenses paid trip to a sunshine paradise. Employers may pay the tax themselves, but they may simply fold arms and provide the Revenue with details of the benefit supplied—especially if the employee has subsequently left. In such circumstances, any exemption from PAYE and NIC was very important. The Revenue has an Incentive Valuation Unit to tax such benefits.

Current figures[4] show that cars were responsible for 53% of the total tax raised by the rules on benefits in kind. Other figures included car fuel (9%), private medical and dental insurance (8%) and transferred assets (4%). The total tax raised was £3.22 bn.

Valuation difficulties may, however, prove too great. The current rules introduced in 1988 systematically exclude any tax charge for the provision of a parking space. This was done in return for doubling the tax charge for the car itself. Valuing parking spaces had proved to be an administrative nightmare, e.g. where a company uses space in its otherwise unused basement. Fixed scales also gave rise to problems since a farmer parking in an empty field in Lanarkshire would pay as much as a city commuter.[5]

15.1.2 Tax rule choices

The general Schedule E principle that money's worth is income also applies to benefits in kind—but with difficulty. Where an employer, R, provides an employee, E, with a benefit in kind, any tax system encounters two sets of problems. The first is to define the benefits to be taxed; the second is to value them. On the first point, rules are needed to prevent a tax charge arising simply because an employer provides an office or staff support—or a better office or better support. The system, if it is of a puritanical disposition, may also have to consider at what point an office becomes so luxurious that it should be treated as a chargeable benefit. On the second point, the system provides three principal choices. (1) The most obvious choice, but also the most impractical, is to tax E on the value of the benefit to E. The impracticality arises from the subjective nature of the assessment. In Simons' famous example, how does one tax an employee who is given tickets to a Wagner opera, preferably a long one, and who hates any form of opera?[6] (2) The second choice, convertibility, taxes the employee by reference to the sums which could be derived by converting the benefit into cash. (3) The third choice is to use the cost incurred by the employer in providing the benefit.

The UK currently uses choices (2) and (3)—with extensive statutory glosses. Choice (2), convertibility, was developed by the courts and applies to all employees, subject, of course, to any statutory exclusions or modifications. Choice (3), the cost to R, was introduced by legislation in 1948 and now applies to employees earning £8,500 a year or more and to all directors (see chapter 17 below). (3) applies to a widely defined—but not universal—group of benefits. It has its own set of statutory exclusions or modifications and elaborate rules for determining the cost to the employer. The cost basis is supplementary to convertibility in that it applies only when the latter does not.

[3] *Sunday Times*, 30 November 1986.
[4] Revenue Statistics 1999, Table 4.1 (for 1997–1998).
[5] *The Economist*, 8 August 1992; the doubling of the car charge raised £1.4 bn for the Exchequer.
[6] Simons, *Personal Income Taxation* (University of Chicago, 1938), 53.

Convertibility is still important because it must be applied before the cost basis. It is not used for NIC.[7] A recent review concluded that while the advantage distorted the market, it was not right simply to value benefits in kind for NICs at least on anything like the income tax rules, given that the current NICs use a different pay period basis (i.e. weekly or monthly, not annually).[8]

PAYE is due on chargeable "payments".[9] Statute has extend PAYE to cash vouchers,[10] "tradeable assets"[11] and non-cash vouchers and credit tokens which can be exchanged for tradeable assets.[12] The Special Commissioners have considered, but not decided, the basic question whether a payment means payment in money. However, they held that a payment in kind which could be converted into money was a payment for PAYE.[13]

15.2 The Convertibility Principle—*Tennant* v. *Smith*

In *Tennant* v. *Smith*[14] the taxpayer was agent for the Bank of Scotland at Montrose. He had to occupy the bank house as custodian for the whole premises belonging to the Bank, and also to transact any special bank business after bank hours. He was not allowed to vacate the house even for a temporary period unless he had the special consent of the directors, who sanctioned the occupation of the house by another official of the bank during the agent's absence. The agent had to lock up the bank and attend to the security of the safe. There was a night bolt from the agent's bedroom to the bank's premises. The agent was not allowed to sublet the bank house nor to use it for any purpose other than the bank's business. The bank house was suitable accommodation for him but, as Lord Macnaghten observed, "his occupation is that of a servant and not the less so because the bank thinks proper to provide for gentlemen in his position in their service accommodation on a liberal scale".[15] His total income from other sources came to £375 and the value of his occupation of these premises was placed at £50. Where a taxpayer's income was below £400 he was entitled to an abatement.[16] The House of Lords held that the agent was not assessable under Schedules D or E[17] in respect of his occupation of the premises and so was entitled to the abatement. Lord Halsbury stated that the thing sought to be taxed "is not income unless it can be turned to money".[18] The agent's occupation of the premises was not capable of being converted into money since he could not let it.[19]

7 On liability to NIC see Tiley and Collison *UK Tax Guide* §§52.15 et seq. and §53.08 et seq.

8 Taylor, *The Modernisation of Britain's Tax and Benefit System Report No. 2* (1997), para. 2.16.

9 TA 1988, s. 203.

10 Ibid., s. 143.

11 Ibid., s. 203F. See the Income Tax (Employments) (Notional Payments) Regulations 1994 (SI 1994/1212), as amended by the Income Tax (Employments) (Notional Payments) Regulations 1998 (SI 1981/1891). NIC treatment is brought into line: see (1998) *Simons Weekly Tax Intelligence* 1358.

12 TA 1988, ss 203G, 203H.

13 *Paul Dunstall Organisaton Ltd.* v. *Hedges* [1999] STC (SCD) 26.

14 [1892] AC 150, 3 TC 158, HL.

15 [1892] AC 150, 162, 3 TC 158, 169.

16 5 & 6 Vict. (c. 35), s. 163.

17 Nor was he assessable under Schedule A since it was not he but the Bank which was the occupier; [1892] AC 150, 158, 3 TC 158, 166, *per* Lord Watson; ibid., 162, 169 *per* Lord Macnaghten.

18 Ibid., 156, 164; to the same effect see ibid., 159, 167, *per* Lord Watson; *per* Lord Macnaghten, at 163, 170; ibid., 164, 171, *per* Lord Field; and ibid., 165, 172 *per* Lord Hannen. Lord Morris concurred.

19 With the bank's tacit consent he used the premises for an insurance business but this was ignored. At one time it was thought that where a person was in beneficial occupation, but that occupation was not convertible (into

15.2.1 *Types of convertibility*

A benefit may be converted in ways other than simple sale. In *Abbott* v. *Philbin*[20] an option to acquire shares was non-assignable but the employee was taxable on its value because money could have been realised in other ways—by raising money on the right to call for the shares. A Special Commissioner has held that where a taxpayer received rights under a contract of employment and those rights could be converted only at a price well below their intrinsic value, the right was not taxable at all.[21]

15.2.2 *Restricting convertibility*

In *Tennant* v. *Smith* Lord Halsbury said that a thing could be treated as money's worth where the thing was capable of being turned into money "from its own nature".[22] However, in that case the only reason why the agent could not turn his occupation of the house into money was the fiat of his employer. Clearly, the loopholes in the tax net will be greatly widened if it is left to the employer to decide whether a benefit is convertible and so assessable. The courts have indicated that while restrictions imposed by employers may be treated as an effective restriction[23] this will only be so if the conditions are genuine.[24] In *Heaton* v. *Bell*[25] Lord Diplock went further and said that limitations on use arising from a contract collateral to the contract of employment into which the employee entered of his own volition would not escape tax.[26]

15.2.3 *Salary Sacrifice*

The principle[27]

A benefit can also be turned into money by being surrendered, or by not being accepted. In *Heaton* v. *Bell*[28] an employee was loaned a car by his employers and went on to what was called an amended wage basis. If the true effect had been that the employee took a lower wage and received the free use of a car, a majority of the House would have held that the employee was taxable in respect of the use of the car on the amount he would have received

money or money's worth), then if the employer paid the Schedule A tax in respect of that occupation, the employee was not taxable in respect of that payment under Schedule E (*M'Dougall* v. *Sutherland* (1894) 3 TC 261; overruled in *IRC* v. *Miller* [1930] AC 222, 15 TC 25).

[20] [1961] AC 352, 378–9, 39 TC 82, 125, *per* Lord Radcliffe.

[21] *Bootle* v. *Bye* [1996] STC (SCD) 58; it was also relevant that the event which would have made the intrinsic value realisable was outside the taxpayer's control.

[22] [1892] AC 150, 156, 3 TC 158, 164.

[23] For example, *Ede* v. *Wilson and Cornwall* [1945] 1 All ER 367, 26 TC 381 shares were issued subject to a condition that they would not be sold without employer's permission; it washeld that valuation must take account of the restriction on the effect of a term forbidding assignment of a debt. On effectiveness of a prohibition on assignment of a chose in action, see *Helstan Securities Ltd.* v. *Hertfordshire County Council* [1978] 3 All ER 262.

[24] Lord Reid in *Heaton* v. *Bell* [1969] 2 All ER 70, 79, 46 TC 211, 247.

[25] [1969] 2 All ER 70, 95, 46 TC 211, 264.

[26] *Cf.* the test that in order to be deductible, an expense must be required by the job, and not simply by the employer (see below at §18.3).

[27] See also ESC A60 (agricultural workers outside TA 1988, s. 154).

[28] [1969] 2 All ER 70, 46 TC 211.

had he surrendered that use.[29] Such statements are *obiter* since the House preferred a different construction.[30]

It has since been held that where employees could, and did, use a non-chargeable method of obtaining a benefit, the fact that they could have chosen a different method which could have resulted in a tax liability was itself enough to give rise to such a liability.[31] They used their company's credit card to pay for petrol but could instead have paid in cash and obtained a refund; by refraining from using the card they had turned the benefit to pecuniary account. Today, the fuel charge applies generally to such facts, but this does not disturb the principle.

Legislative modifications for cars and accommodation

Where a car is made available to the employee under s. 157 and an alternative to that benefit is offered, the mere fact that the alternative is offered does not make the benefit of the car chargeable to tax under these general principles.[32] The effect is that the employee will be taxed on the benefit chosen. The reason behind this apparently anodyne piece of legislation is to ensure that NICs are not avoided.[33]

On accommodation see below §15.4.1.

15.2.4 Extent of liability

Convertibility provides the test not only of liability but also of its extent. In *Weight* v. *Salmon*[34] the employee was given the right to apply for shares at less than market price and was held assessable on the difference between the market price and the price he paid. In *Wilkins* v. *Rogerson*[35] the employee was provided with a suit; he was held assessable on the second hand value of the suit, which was only one-third of the purchase price, a fact which involved "no reflection on the tailor" because "it is notorious that the value of clothing is very much reduced the moment that it can be called second hand". The value is ascertained at the date when the asset comes into charge, usually on receipt.[36] Although a special rule now applies to certain share options, other options are subject to the general rule. If an asset is received in non-convertible form but later becomes convertible, there is little reason why a charge should not arise at the later time.

[29] [1969] 2 All ER 70, 84, 46 TC 211, 263, *per* Lord Morris of Borth-y-Gest; ibid., 96, 265, *per* Lord Diplock. To the same effect, but by a different route, see Lord Reid, dissenting (at 79, 247). While Lord Morris and Lord Diplock would have quantified the benefit as the sum subtracted each week ×52 (the number of weeks in the year), Lord Reid would have taken the same sum ×50, since two weeks' notice has to be given before returning to the scheme. Therefore, while Lord Morris and Lord Diplock appear to tax the benefit foregone, Lord Reid would appear to tax the benefit that could be obtained. Lord Reid seems more correct.

[30] The correct construction of the agreement was that there was no change in the wage but the employers were entitled to deduct a sum each week in respect of the use of the car. It followed that tax was due on the gross wage each week, with no deduction for tax purposes for the sum withheld on account of the car.

[31] *Westall* v. *McDonald* [1985] STC 693, 721, 58 TC 642, 679.

[32] S. 157 is, of course, excluded if the general principles apply; on s. 157 see below §17.4.1.

[33] TA 1988, s. 157A, added by FA 1995, s. 43; see Inland Revenue press release, 21 July 1994, (1994) *Simon's Tax Intelligence* 888.

[34] (1935) 19 TC 174.

[35] [1961] 1 All ER 358, 39 TC 344.

[36] *Abbott* v. *Philbin* [1961] AC 352, [1960] 2 All ER 763, 39 TC 82. See below at §16.2.2.

15.2.5 Anomalies and distinctions

The test of convertibility gives rise to distinctions which mean significant variations in tax liability according to fiscal skill or simple luck.

(1) Whereas the provision of a benefit such as a board and lodging escapes tax, the payment of an allowance in lieu of providing that benefit does not. In *Fergusson* v. *Noble*[37] the taxpayer, a plain clothes policeman, was allowed to buy his own clothes suitable for duty and was given an allowance of £11.71. Uniformed members of the police force were provided with a uniform free of charge. It was held that the allowance was liable to tax. On similar reasoning an employee who is provided with an official house may not be taxable (but for special legislation) whereas one who is provided with an allowance is taxable,[38] a matter of great importance when the special legislation does not apply.

(2) Contrast the employee who receives a salary and, in addition, some non-convertible benefit, such as necessaries, in respect of which extra benefit there is no tax, with another employee who receives a salary and has to pay out of that salary a counter amount to secure the same necessaries.[39] The latter is assessable on the total salary and not entitled to deduct the cost of those necessaries unless they come within the strict test laid down by TA 1988, s. 198.[40]

(3) Consider the borderline between the rule in *Tennant* v. *Smith* and that in *Nicoll* v. *Austin*. If an employer buys each employee a new suit at Christmas, all the employees are taxable, but only on the second hand value of the suit[41] (*Tennant* v. *Smith*). If, however, they have already bought their suits but not yet paid for them and the employer settles the debts for them, they are taxable on the amount paid to the tailor (*Nicoll* v. *Austin*). The question of whose is the liability to be discharged, rather than what right the employees acquired, explains what remains a very technical area of law. However, its clarity leads to further anomalies. When employees drive into a garage and pump petrol into their cars they may be agents for the employer or acting on their own account.[42] If the employer is an undisclosed principal the employee is personally liable on the contract, which may be enough to make the employee liable to income tax on the full sum.[43]

[37] [1919] SC 534, 7 TC 176. See, to same effect, *Sanderson* v. *Durbridge* [1955] 3 All ER 154, 36 TC 239; *Evans* v. *Richardson* (1957) 37 TC 178.

[38] *Corry* v. *Robinson* [1934] 1 KB 240, 18 TC 411. The tax paid on a rent allowance was reimbursed by police authorities in the following financial year by means of a compensatory grant. In principle, the grant itself was taxable: see HC Written Answer, 31 January 1986, (1986) *Simons Tax Intelligence* 40; the grant was abolished in 1995 under the Police Regulations 1995 (SI 1995/215).

[39] However, see ESC A1 (flat rate allowances for clothes and tools), and the even more extraordinary ESC A6 (no tax on allowances paid to miners in lieu of their free coal).

[40] In *Cordy* v. *Gordon* [1925] 2 KB 276, 9 TC 304 the taxpayer was employed at an asylum and received a salary together with board, lodging, washing and uniform, for which he was required to pay sums which varied according to the cost of living: he was held assessable on the gross salary. See also *Machon* v. *McLoughlin* (1926) 11 TC 83; *Bruce* v. *Hatton* [1921] 2 KB 206, 8 TC 180. *Cf. Edwards* v. *Roberts* (1935) 19 TC 618.

[41] See *Wilkins* v. *Rogerson* [1961] 1 All ER 358, 39 TC 344, *per* Donovan L.J.

[42] *Richardson* v. *Worrall* [1985] STC 693, 58 TC 642.

[43] The presence of joint liability on the part of employer and employee does not necessarily mean that discharge by the employer will be a taxable emolument (see *Richardson* v. *Worrall* [1985] STC 693, 718, 58 TC 642, 675.

15.3 Vouchers and Credit Tokens; Legislation

The above anomalies have led to legislation concerning vouchers and credit tokens.

A voucher that can be exchanged for cash is taxed in full and subject to the PAYE system.[44]

A voucher, including a "cheque voucher",[45] that can be exchanged for money, goods or services—including transport— gives rise to liability on an amount equal to the cost to the person at whose cost the voucher and the money, goods or services for which it can be exchanged are provided in or in connection with that provision;[46] the value of the benefit is ignored. The liability arises when the expense is incurred[47] or, if later, when the voucher is received, although the appropriation of the voucher (e.g. by sticking it on a card held for the employee) is treated as receipt by the employee.[48] There are exemptions for certain non-cash vouchers, which include (a) travel concessions for lower paid employees of passenger transport undertakings,[49] (b) entertainment which is, broadly, provided by someone not connected with the employer, and (c) the provision of car parking at or near the place of work.[50]

Similar rules apply to credit tokens and credit cards.[51] When employees use a credit token to obtain money, goods or services they are charged to income tax on an emolument equal to the expense involved; the costs of providing the token and of any interest charges are ignored.[52]

Relief is given when the vouchers or credit token are used to meet proper business expenses or where the employee makes good the cost involved.[53] For the practice where incentive award schemes are provided by way of voucher, see Statement of Practice SP 6/85.

15.4 Living Accommodation

15.4.1 *Basic rule*

Where living accommodation is provided for X by reason of X's employment (or for X's family or household),[54] X is chargeable under TA 1988, s. 145 on the annual value of the benefit. Therefore, if X, a non-domiciled person, owns her house through a non-resident company (a favourite way of avoiding IHT), there will be a charge to income tax under this rule if she is a director, which is usually the case.[55]

[44] TA 1988, s. 143 But see ESC A2 (meal vouchers).

[45] TA 1988, s. 141.

[46] Ibid., s. 141(1).

[47] For cheque vouchers, the year is that in which the voucher is handed over in exchange for the goods, etc. (TA 1988, s. 141).

[48] FA 1988, ss 47, 48.

[49] TA 1988, s. 141(6).

[50] FA 1988, s. 46.

[51] TA 1988, s. 142. Credit token is no longer defined by reference to the Consumer Credit Act 1974, s. 14.

[52] These interest charges were originally created to give rise to liability under FA 1981, s. 71, but this was removed by FA 1982, s. 45.

[53] TA 1988, ss 141(3), (4), 142(2), (3). On vouchers for in-house sports facilities, see below at §17.3.

[54] TA 1988, s. 145(6).

[55] By reason of the definition in TA 1988, s. 168. The fact that the individual receives no other benefit or remuneration is irrelevant (*R.* v. *Allen* [1999] STC 846); on this and transfer pricing issues, see De Souza (1999) *Private Client Business* 1. For error in Court of Appeal reasoning, see McCutcheon, *Taxation 1999*, Vol, 144, 31 with regard to certain taxpayers and the scope of s. 192(2).

Otherwise chargeable

S. 145 does not apply where the accommodation is chargeable to X as income under some other provision. One way[56] in which X would be "otherwise chargeable" is by coming within the general principle of convertibility; X would be chargeable on the profit which could have been made by sub-letting the property or granting licences. However, X would also be chargeable under the general principle if the employer offered X £20 as an alternative to the accommodation, i.e. a salary sacrifice. This proved tempting for taxpayers and was stopped by legislation in 1996. TA 1988, s. 146A states that the provision of a cash alternative does not prevent s. 145[57] from applying.

Provided by reason of employment?

Whether living accommodation is provided by reason of the employment is a question of fact; however, it is deemed to be so provided if it is provided by the employer. This assumption can be avoided if it is shown that (a) the employer is an individual and provides the accommodation in the normal course of domestic, family or personal relationships, or (b) the accommodation is provided by a local authority for its employee on terms which are no more favourable than those for non-employees similarly circumstanced, a rule which means that a council house tenant cannot be charged extra rent simply because of working for the council. The rule applies only where the employer is an individual, presumably because only an individual can have domestic family or personal relationships; this leaves open the case of a family business run by a trust where, for example, the owner of the business has died and the estate has not yet been administered.

If the accommodation is provided by someone other than the employer and so escapes the deeming provision, it may still give rise to tax if it can be shown that the accommodation was in fact provided by reason of the employment (as may be the case if the accommodation is provided by an associated company or trust).

Scope of charge

S. 145 applies to living accommodation;[58] it does not apply to ancillary services, which are usually incapable of being turned into money and so will not give rise to any charge, except, perhaps, under s. 154. Such liability under s. 154 may be capped by s. 163.[59]

Exceptions from s. 145: non-beneficial occupation

If the accommodation is provided by reason of the employment, the cost will still not be chargeable if the taxpayer comes within any of the following situations which correspond broadly with the old cases of representative occupation:

(a) where it is necessary for the proper performance of the employee's duties that E should reside in the accommodation;
(b) where the employment is of a type where it is customary to provide living accommodation, and the accommodation is provided for the better performance of the duties of the employment; and

[56] X is not chargeable under s. 154 because of s. 154(2) which excludes living accommodation.
[57] S. 146A was added by FA 1996, s. 106; it also applies to s. 146.
[58] TA 1988, s. 145(7).
[59] i.e. if the occupation comes within the three categories of non-beneficial occupation, the charge under s. 154 must not exceed 10% of the total emoluments (TA 1988, s. 163); see below §17.4.6.

(c) where, there being a special threat to E's security, special security arrangements are in force and E resides in the accommodation as part of those arrangements.

Exceptions (a) and (b) are themselves excluded (so that a charge to income tax will arise under s. 145 after all) if the taxpayer is a director of the company providing the accommodation; however, this is softened by excluding a director who works full time and does not have a material interest in the company; (see below at §17.1).

Exceptions—examples

Employees coming within (a) above will include caretakers, hotel managers, and other staff who are compelled to live in hotels and the bank manager in *Tennant* v. *Smith.*[60] For this group the necessity to be in occupation must be due to the relationship between the duties and the accommodation, and not to the personal exigencies of the taxpayer.[61]

Exception (b) covers farmworkers, miners and even some university teachers; the requirement that it should be "customary" to provide the accommodation in that kind of employment is an interesting one. Customs can change and can, presumably, be satisfied even though occupation is not required by the employer. The rule that the provision must be for the better performance of the duties is presumably a question of fact and is to be determined objectively, paying attention to—but without being bound by—the terms of the employment and the views of the employer. In *Vertigan* v. *Brady*[62] the taxpayer failed to come within (b) because the provision of accommodation was not sufficiently common to be "customary". Among the issues considered by the court were (i) how many employers in this industry provided accommodation, (ii) for how long the practice had continued, and (iii) whether it had achieved general acceptance.

The charge

The charge is on the annual value to the employee of the accommodation for that period. A deduction can be made for any sum made good by X to the person at whose cost the accommodation is provided. Rent paid by the employee is therefore deductible. Benefits in kind provided in return may also, in principle, be taken into account but only if they relate clearly to the accommodation.[63] The annual value is calculated under TA 1988, s. 837. If those at whose cost the accommodation is provided pay rent which is higher than the annual value, that higher figure is to be taken.[64] In the absence of any provision directing otherwise it is to be assumed that in calculating the annual rent hypothetically payable, account is taken of all the terms of the occupation, even those imposed in connection with the office or employment. The employee may deduct from the value as ascertained any sums allowable under TA 1988, ss 198, 332 (ministers of religion).

15.4.2 Additional charge under TA 1988, s 146

If X is taxable under TA 1988, s. 145 and the accommodation costs more than £75,000 to provide, there is an additional charge under TA 1988, s. 146. X is treated as receiving a loan of the amount by which the cost exceeds £75,000 and a percentage of that loan as income in

60 [1892] AC 150, 3 TC 158, HL.
61 *Vertigan* v. *Brady* [1988] STC 91, 60 TC 624.
62 Ibid.
63 *Stones* v. *Hall* [1989] STC 138, 60 TC 738.
64 TA 1988, s. 145(2).

that year. The figure of £75,000 has not been changed since the section was introduced in 1983.[65]

Cost

The cost of providing the accommodation is the purchase price plus improvement expenditure, less any amount paid by X as reimbursement for the expenditure or as consideration for the tenancy.[66] If, when X first occupies the accommodation, the person providing the accommodation has held an estate or interest in the property for the previous six years, the market value at the date on which X first occupies the property is substituted for the purchase price.[67] Market value is defined.[68]

Employees are taxed on the additional value to them of the accommodation, which is:

(cost of providing accommodation − £75,000) × [appropriate %] − excess rent

"Excess rent" is the amount by which any rent paid by the employee exceeds the value to the employee of the accommodation.

The percentage is the official rate of interest set for the purpose of calculating the benefit of low-interest and interest-free loans to employees within s. 154 in force on 6 April beginning the year of assessment. The rate for 2000–01 is 6.25%.[69]

Example

E is an employee earning over £8,500 p.a. On 6 April 1996, E begins to occupy a house provided by X, E's employer. The house had been purchased by X on 9 November 1992[70] for £196,000; X then spent £8,000 on improvements. E reimbursed X £1,000 of the expenditure and pays a rent which exceeds the value to him of the property by £2,000. The official rate of interest on 6 April 2000 was 6.25%. The cost to the employer of providing the property is:

(£196,000 + £8,000) − £1,000 = £203,000

The additional value of the property to E is:

[(£203,000 − £75,000) × 6.25%] − £2,000 = £60,000

E is therefore taxed on an additional benefit of £6,000 in 2000–01.

15.5 Relocation Benefits And Expenses

TA 1988, Schedule 11A, introduced in 1993 to replace earlier concessionary reliefs,[71] grants relief for certain sums paid, whether to the employees, or another on their behalf (e.g. the

[65] FA 1977, s. 33A added by FA 1983.

[66] TA 1988, s. 146(4).

[67] Ibid., s. 146(6), but this does not apply if the employee's first occupation began before 31 March 1983 (s. 146(8)).

[68] Ibid., s. 146(11).

[69] Inland Revenue Press Release, 23 February 1999, *Simon's Weekly Tax Intelligence* 1999, 306.

[70] If X had purchased the property in 1987, the market value of the property on 6 April 1996 would have been substituted for the purchase price.

[71] Inland Revenue Press Release, 16 March 1993, para. 2, *Simon's Tax Intelligence* 1993, 439. The concessions superseded were A5 and A64 based on *Hochstrasser* v. *Mayes*.

removal company) in respect of "qualifying removal expenses", and exempts "qualifying removal benefits". The present ceiling of £8,000 may be increased by Treasury Order. Payments must be made or benefits provided before the end of the year following the year in which the employment is changed or moved, or a new job started.[72]

Eligible expenses[73]

Eligible removal expenses are those made on: disposal of the old residence; acquisition of the new residence; abortive acquisition; transporting belongings; travelling and subsistence; and bridging loans, including a beneficial bridging loan.[74] Also allowed are expenses incurred by the employee, as a result of the change of residence, on the purchase of domestic goods intended to replace goods used at the first residence but not suitable for use in the new one—subject to offset for sums received on the sale of the goods from the first home, which must be brought into account. The list of eligible removal benefits is similar.

Reasonable and connected

The expenses must be reasonably incurred by the employee in connection with a change of sole or main residence.[75] Therefore: (a) the change of residence must result from the employee becoming employed by an employer, or from an alteration in the employee's duties (without a change of employer) or an alteration in the place at which those duties are carried out; (b) the change must be made wholly or mainly to allow the employee to have his residence within a reasonable daily travelling distance of the place where the duties are to be performed; and (c) the employee's former home must not be within a reasonable daily travelling distance from the place where the new duties are to be performed.[76] If the claim is based on a change in the duties of the employment or the place of employment (as opposed to a change of employer), no relief is available if the former home was beyond reasonable daily travelling distance from the former place of employment.[77] There is no need actually to sell the old residence to qualify for this relief—it is sufficient that it is no longer the only or main residence, e.g. where the old house is rented out or used only at weekends. The Revenue view seems to be that the family must also use the new home as their main residence but that this is not required of employees coming to work from abroad.[78]

In determining whether the limit of £8,000 has been reached, the rules in TA 1988, s. 154 are applied to bring in the cash equivalent of the benefits. Any sums which would otherwise fall within s. 145 are also brought in—less sums made good by the employee.[79]

If the relocation package includes a beneficial loan on which tax is chargeable and the employee has not used up the £8,000 exemption on the other costs of moving house, the bridging loan, or part of it, can be included to use up the total relief available by removing days from the period for which tax is chargeable in respect of the loan.[80] In the case of foreign removals, sums allowed under other rules are not counted against the £8,000 limit.[81]

72 TA 1988, Sch. 11A para. 3(3).

73 Both eligible expenses and eligible benefits may be amended by Treasury Order (ibid., Sch. 11A, paras 15, 23).

74 Ibid., Sch. 11A, paras 7–13; and Inland Revenue Press Release, 14 April 1993, *Simons Tax Intelligence* 1993, 626.

75 Ibid., Sch. 11A, paras 3, 25.

76 Ibid., Sch. 11A, para. 5.

77 Ibid., Sch. 11A, para. 5(4).

78 Inland Revenue Press Release, 14 April 1993, *Simons Tax Intelligence* 626.

79 TA 1988, Sch. 11A, para. 24.

80 Ibid., s. 191B.

81 Ibid., Sch. 11A, paras 12(4), 21A(7), (8).

15.6 Costs and benefits of training

15.6.1 Training, scholarship and apprenticeship schemes

TA 1988, s. 588 provides an exemption in respect of expenditure incurred by an employer in connection with training schemes; the exemption allows the employer to deduct the expenditure while exempting the employee from any liability to tax under Schedule E.[82]

The exemption is given for expenditure reimbursed or incurred by the employer in connection with a qualifying course of training. The course must be attended on a full-time (or substantially full-time) basis; the employee must have been employed for two years and the opportunity to take the course must be available either generally to employees and former employees or to a particular class of such persons.[83] The course must be designed to impart or improve skills or knowledge relevant to and intended to be used in the course of gainful employment (including self-employment) of any description and the course must be entirely devoted to the teaching and/or practical application of such skills or knowledge. In addition the course must not last more than one year and all the teaching and practical application must take place in the UK.[84]

The course must be undertaken by an employee (or former employee) with a view to retraining. The course cannot be regarded as undertaken with a view to retraining unless it is begun while employed by the employer or within one year of ceasing to be so; it is also necessary that the employee should in any event cease to be so employed within two years of the end of the course.[85] This underlines the purpose of the provision—to encourage employers and employees to get retrained and they reemployed or self employed elsewhere.

Where the employee attends a full-time course at a university or technical college payments by the employer may qualify as scholarship income under TA 1988, s. 331. A statement of practice sets out the conditions to be observed.[86]

15.6.2 Work related training

TA 1988, s. 200B–200D added by FA 1998 provides a similar exemption for the expenditure incurred by the employer and the benefit received by the employee for work-related trainiang.

This differs from 15.6.1 in that the training is for an employee who is to be kept on the books of the employer. This legislation replaced a previous concession.[87] The course must be "work related" and not be within a prohibited list of activities.[88] Much of the policy and

[82] TA 1988, s. 588(1) (Schedule E), TA 1988, s. 588(3) for deduction in computing profits and TA 1988, s. 588(4) for treatment as expense of management of investment company.

[83] TA 1988, s. 589(3)—the two year employment condition means two years before he starts the course or ends the employment whichever is the earlier.

[84] TA 1988, s. 589(3).

[85] TA 1988, s. 589(4); re-employment within two years is a breach of the conditions; any breach of these conditions has to be reported within 60 days of the employer coming to know of it (TA 1988, s. 588(6)) and the normal six year time limit for assessments runs from the end of the year in which the breach occurred (s. 588(5)); there are also Revenue information-gathering powers in s. 588(7).

[86] Statement of Practice SP 4/86.

[87] Extra-statutory concession A63.

[88] TA 1988, s. 200C.

detail applies also to 15.6.3 and so is not duplicated here. Where the employee has to bear the expenses they are, by concession, deductible.[89]

15.6.3 Individual learning accounts

Where neither s. 588 nor s. 200B–200D apply, s. 200E may provide relief. These are the new individual learning accounts set up under the Skills and Learning Act 2000; the tax legislation refers to that Act for many of its definitions. The effect of s. 200E is to prevent a benefits in kind charge where the employer pays the training provider directly or the employer reimburses the costs. These rules extend also to any related costs, i.e. incidental expenses arising wholly and exclusively from undertaking the qualifying education and training.[90] The Revenue notes to the Finance Bill 2000 suggest that this test would allow additional expenses arising directly from undertaking the training, such as extra travel and additional childcare paid for or reimbursed by the employer but not preliminary or everyday expenses such as routine childcare costs. Similarly the Revenue would allow the costs of an assessment or examination and the costs of registering a qualificatiion. The cost of an award would be exempt if it were simply a recognition of achievement.

Learning from the experience of NVQs, s. 200F withholds the exemption to the extent that the education or training is actually for entertainment, recreation or reward.[91] Hence skid-pan training offered as part of the staff's annual outing (and so meeting the fair opportunity rules) would not be exempt under s. 200E. Likewise, golfing lessons offered to those sales representatives meeting sales targets would not be exempt. It will be possible to apportion such expenditure in appropriate cases.

The rules allow suitable travel and subsistence costs[92] and the costs of supplying suitable materials for the training.[93] There is even a specific exemption for things made by the trainee during training; the Revenue's example is a cake made on a catering course.

The tax exemption only applies if the employer makes those contributions available to all employees on similar terms under "fair opportunity arrangements".[94] Regulations are to be made so that different categories of Crown servants can be treated separately for these purposes; large companies are left to their own devices.

Further rules apply equivalent relief where the training is funded by third parties.[95]

[89] ESC A64 (still in force).
[90] ITA 1988, s. 200E(3) added by FA 2000, s. 58.
[91] TA 1988, s. 200F(1), (4).
[92] TA 1988, s. 200F(2).
[93] TA 1988, s. 200F(3), (5).
[94] Defined in s. 200G(2).
[95] TA 1988, s. 200J.

16

Schedule E—Part IV: Financial Benefits—Schemes to Encourage Employment Participation

16.1 Types of Scheme: General Issues

At present there are several sets of special rules relating to employee participation in schemes. Some rules concern options to acquire shares; others concern actual shares. In the order in which they appear in the legislation the rules are as follows:

(a) Profit-related pay (PRP) (TA 1988, ss 169–84). These rules give tax benefits to a certain level of pay made out of profits. They are now being phased out and cannot apply to profit periods beginning after 31 December 1999 see §16.11.

(b) Approved share option schemes (TA 1988, ss 185–7, Schedules 9 and 10). Today these schemes may be either company share option schemes see §16.5 or savings-related, approved share option schemes see §16.6; in either event they must be for employees in general (s. 185(1)(a)). FA 2000 adds a very generous share option scheme called Enterprise Management Initiative Scheme. This scheme is only available to a very few employees (see §16.7).

(c) Discretionary schemes (ExASOS) for executives (generally known as "executive" approved share option schemes). The rules grant benefits to certain types of share option scheme. Executive schemes were more popular than schemes open to all employees. From 1987–1988, 25% of companies floated on the stock exchange had SAYE schemes; in 1994–1996 it was 50%.[1] Executive schemes could be approved under ss 185–87 but no new schemes could be created after 1996.
(d) Approved profit-sharing schemes (APSSs) (ss 186–87, Schedules 9 and 10). These schemes do not involve options but the issue or transfer of actual shares to be held for employees. (See §16.8.)
(e) Share incentive schemes (SISs) (FA 1988, ss 77–88). These schemes are also for shares rather than options, but the rules consist mostly of penalties; there are no approved SISs, and so no unapproved SISs either. (See §16.4.)
(f) Employee share ownership plans (ESOPs) §16.9 (FA 1989, ss 67–74, Schedule 5). These schemes concern trusts (qualifying employee share trusts (QUESTs)) which may be used to receive money from the employer with which trustees later buy shares for employees. (See §16.9).
(g) All employee share schemes (AESS 2000) §16.10. This brand new scheme was introduced by FA 2000. It applies to all employees and has three distinct elements: free shares (maximum £3,000 p.a.), partnership shares (bought by the employee up to £1,500 p.a.) and matching shares (given on a 2 for 1 basis by the employer to match the partnership shares. Like (d) and (f) they involve the issue of shares.

The issue of shares at an under value may be treated as a loan (see below at §17.4.5).

Because these rules are often complex and restrictive, it is still common for employers to offer employees (usually only key employees) benefit schemes which fall outside the rules. Unapproved share option schemes (UnASOS) have become more popular since 1996 when approved schemes were limited to £30,000, but suffer from the rules also introduced in 1996 which make them subject not only to income tax but also National Insurance Contributions (NICs) and PAYE.[2] Any discount on the grant of non-approved options is subject to NICs.

"Phantom schemes" exist under which a tax bonus is tied to the company's share price. Neither actual shares nor options are involved here. Other, intermediate schemes can be set up in which the company buys shares for an employee but holds them in trust.

16.1.1 Factors affecting choice[3]

In studying the rules the following points must be noted which affect the willingness of the employer and employee to choose a particular benefit, bearing in mind always that their interests may not be the same:

(a) Does the employer incur an expense—if so, is it deductible in computing profits?
(b) If the employee receives a benefit, when will it be taxable?

1 Cohen [1997] *Business Law Review* 131 at 132.
2 TA 1988, s. 203FB.
3 See, generally, Scott and Savage, *Tolley Tax Planning 1999–2000* 1622–69 esp. at 1643–55; and Williams, *Taxation of Employee Share Schemes* (Butterworths), ch. 1.

(c) If the employee receives a benefit, will it be taxable to income tax under Schedule E or to CGT?
(d) If the employee receives a benefit, will it be subject to PAYE?
(e) If the employee receives a benefit, will it be subject to NICs?
(f) Will the employee incur a charge to tax if shares are sold within a certain period?
(g) What are the risks of unexpected tax charges (usually called "chargeable events")?

From a wider perspective:

(h) Must the scheme be available to all employees?
(i) Is there any limit on the amount that can be put into the scheme?
(j) What does the scheme do to the share structure of the company? Is there a risk of dilution? Does the company receive any money from the employee?
(k) Will the scheme give rise to employee participation in the company to a degree which "management" may find unacceptable?
(l) How free are employees to sell the shares and thus rid themselves of the links with the company which these schemes are meant to foster?
(m) How flexible are the schemes? Clearly, approved schemes will be less flexible than unapproved schemes since they have to conform to statutory conditions, but how flexible are they?
(n) What financial risks are inherent in the scheme (shares can go down as well as up)?
(o) From the employee's viewpoint, share options have attractions over other share plans in that no money has to be invested, there is no risk of loss since options do not have to be exercised and success can lead to a very high rate of return owing to the element of gearing involved.

The battery of sets of rules and factors makes this area complicated. In this book it is not appropriate to cover every detail; as such only the principal points will be considered in relation to each scheme. However, some other general points must be grasped.

First, this is a political minefield. Some believe in the value of share schemes as ways of encouraging better performance by executives and general loyalty of the workforce as a whole. A profit-sharer tends to take a longer-term view of company, is less inclined to leave and is probably more sympathetic to the introduction of new machinery or work practices. However, a company does not benefit if it simply uses such schemes as a way of warding off takeovers.[4] Loyalty is important not only for the company itself but also more widely, since a company with a loyal workforce is far more likely to spend money in its training and development, a matter seen as a real problem when the UK is compared with other countries. When the logic of such reward systems became too obvious, as in the case of the newly privatised companies which made substantial profits in cutting expenses by making staff redundant, the populist streak of Conservatism meant that benefits were restricted (e.g. the £30,000 limit imposed in 1996). By contrast (Old) Labour governments have traditionally been hostile to schemes attracting tax privileges, and have usually sought to impose tax penalties. Profit-sharing schemes have been anathema both to the hard left (collaborationist) and the right-to-manage right, but one can oppose them on other grounds. Some critics emphasise that options may become valueless due to a change in the general market conditions even though the company itself has been successful in comparison with other

[4] See Brookings Report 1989; in the United States a Delaware company with as little as 15% in friendly hands is difficult to take over (*The Economist*, 20 May 1989, 17).

companies in the sector in which it competes. Such critics prefer long-term incentive plans using such comparisons.[5] The Liberal Democrats[6] were responsible for the introduction of S-RSOS and APSS in the period of minority government from 1977–1979.

Secondly, much of the practical effect of the different schemes must be assessed against a changing background of the relationship between income tax and CGT. The alignment of the rates of tax in 1988 reduced the advantage of having capital gain rather than income. The question whether it is better to have capital gain or ordinary income depends on the individual taxpayer's circumstances.

Thirdly, it is open to any employer to arrange a mix of these benefits, so taking full advantage of the statutory reliefs while adding unapproved schemes on top.

16.2 Emoluments in Form of Shares and Share Options—Basic Rules

16.2.1 Remuneration in shares

Basic tax rules

If, in return for services, an employee, E, receives shares in the employing company, tax is chargeable on the value of those shares.[7] If the shares are ordinary shares, the market value on the date of receipt will be taken as the taxable amount since they could be sold at that price. If, however, they are received subject to conditions which reduce their value, that reduction will usually be reflected in a reduction in the taxable amount.[8] This was used as the basis of much planing in share incentive schemes.

Priority allocations

A charge may also arise under s. 19 if employees are given priority in a public offer and so end up with more shares than they would have got as a members of the public—assuming that the values at allocation exceeded the price paid. Special rules may exclude the charge in such cases.[9] In practice, many flotations are made by placement and not by public offer and so technically fall outside these protective rules.[10] These rules had to be modified to take account of privatisations involving two or more companies.[11] If the employee is allowed to buy at a discount, only the discount right will attract tax—provided no more than 10% of the shares are offered to the employees in priority.[12]

16.2.2 Options to acquire shares

(a) Acquisition of option

If E receives an option to buy shares, tax is due on the value of the option, i.e. the difference between the price payable under the option and the market value of the shares on the date

[5] For example, Goobey, *The Times*, 25 November 1995, Business letters.
[6] Technically, their predecessor parties.
[7] *Weight* v. *Salmon* (1935) 19 TC 174.
[8] *Ede* v. *Wilson and Cornwall* [1945] 1 All ER 367, 26 TC 381.
[9] FA 1988, s. 68; see (1987) *Simon's Tax Intelligence* 716, 866.
[10] Cohen [1997] *Business Law Review* 131.
[11] FA 1988, s. 68 (1ZA), (1ZB), added as from 16 January 1991 by FA 1991, s. 44(3).
[12] FA 1988, s. 68(1A)(a), added by FA 1989, s. 66 and FA 1991, s. 44(4); this change has effect as from 10 October 1988; see (1988) *Simon's Tax Intelligence* 748, and (1989) *Simon's Tax Intelligence* 106.

of receipt of the option.[13] If, therefore, the price payable under the option is the market value at the time of the grant, no tax is due.

(b) Exercise of option

If the shares rise in value before the exercise of the option a charge to tax will not arise under s. 19 when the option is exercised.[14] However a charge may arise under s. 135 (which does not apply, however, to approved schemes). The reason why no charge arises under s. 19 was explained by the House of Lords in *Abbott* v. *Philbin*.[15] There, E received an option to buy shares at £3.42½ p each, the market value at the date of the option, and exercised it in a subsequent tax year when the market value of the shares was £4.10. The House of Lords held that the emolument arose in the year the option was acquired, and at that time E received no benefit from it since he was merely given an option to buy at what was then full market value. The fact that the emolument subsequently increased in value did not mean that that increase in value was an emolument. Although this case has been reversed for options over shares it remains good for options over other types of property.

(c) Disposal of shares

Disposal will usually trigger a charge to CGT rather than income tax; any income tax could arise only under Schedule D, Case I. Since the asset disposed of is the shareholding, CGT will be charged on the gain realised after the acquisition of the shares.

16.3 Special Tax Rules For Share Options

16.3.1 Exercise or lapse

Share option schemes cause problems in any tax system. Most tax systems agree that the grant of an option to buy shares at a figure below the then market value is a taxable emolument, and that the gain accruing between the time of acquisition of the shares, i.e. the exercise of the option, and the date of disposal should be charged as a capital gain. Problems arise over how to tax the change in value between the date of the grant of the option and the date of its exercise.

S.135 of TA 1988 provides that where a gain is realised by the exercise of the option, income tax is to be charged on the difference between the price paid under the option, including the price of the option and the market value of the shares acquired under the option. The calculation excludes the value of employee services rendered under the option.[16] This charge excludes any liability on the grant of the option,[17] provided the option can only be exercised within 10 years.[18] The receipt of consideration in money or money's worth by an employee in return for allowing an option to lapse or granting a second option

[13] *Weight* v. *Salmon* (1935) 19 TC 173.

[14] *Abbott* v. *Philbin* see below n. 15.

[15] [1961] AC 352, [1960] 2 All ER 763, 39 TC 82.

[16] TA 1988, s. 135(3), (4) proviso.

[17] Ibid., s. 135(2), e.g. under the decision in *Weight* v. *Salmon* (1935) 19 TC 173. However, this is without prejudice to the rule for approved share option schemes in TA 1988, s. 185.

[18] This is presumable to protect the charge under ibid., s. 135(5).

or right is also treated as a taxable event.[19] The option must have been granted to E "as director or employee", a phrase which is defined as a grant by reason of the office or employment.[20] The grant may have been to that person or another, to prevent the obvious avoidance device of granting the option to the employee's spouse or nominee.

This rule doe not prevent substantial gains being made when options are given in the run-up to the flotation of a private company since the value of the share will rise following flotation as there is now a market for the shares.[21] In the light of this, companies often allow employees to have options tied to the post-flotation price.

S. 135 is an independent charging section and therefore applies whether or not the benefit of the option can be converted into cash.[22] It must be applied to the exclusion of s. 19.[23]

16.3.2 Long-term options

S. 135(5) of TA 1988 provides that if the option is capable of being exercised more than 10 years after its grant, tax is chargeable at the time of the grant on the value of the benefit granted. The purpose is to prevent the grant of options with a high value being left unexercised.[24] Any tax under charged s. 135(5) is deductible from any tax subsequently chargeable on the exercise of the option under s. 135(1).[25] To avoid any argument based on *Abbott* v. *Philbin*,[26] the value of the benefit granted is stated to be not less than the market value (at the time the right is obtained) of the shares that can be acquired, less the value of the consideration for which the shares are to be acquired. If the consideration is variable only its lowest value is taken.[27] Tax cannot be avoided by assigning the option to a person with whom the employee is connected, nor if the assignment is otherwise than by way of bargain at arm's length; in such circumstances the assignor is chargeable in respect of the gain realised by the assignee.[28]

The effect of s. 135 has been to make share option schemes unattractive in tax terms. The company receives money when the option is exercised, but not as much as on a sale to the public at that time. Although E will not normally have to pay tax until the exercise of the (not long-term) option, the gain on the exercise of the option is treated as E's income under s. 135. Moreover, E may have to sell some of the shares to raise the money to pay the tax. The scheme also involves some dilution of equity. One variant scheme addresses these issues: on the exercise of the option, the company pays money to a trust, which then buys shares for E and transfers them to E. This does not avoid s. 135 but, since only the net-of-tax sum is invested, it avoids any need to sell shares and reduces equity dilution. A better way of avoiding s. 135 is to take advantage of the statutorily approved exceptions to that section (see §§16.5–7).

[19] Ibid., s. 136(6) from 19 March 1986.

[20] Ibid., s. 140(1).

[21] Cohen [1997] *Business Law Review* 132, stating that the average discount given for option grants between six and 12 months before flotation worked out at 84.4%.

[22] *Ball* v. *Phillips* [1990] STC 675, 63 TC 529.

[23] *Wilcock* v. *Eve* [1995] STC 18, 67 TC 223.

[24] Inland Revenue Press Release, 17 March 1998, *Simon's Tax Intelligence* 1998, 459, para. 15. The 10-year period applies to options granted on or after 6 April 1998.

[25] Original version as applied in *Williamson* v. *Dalton* [1981] STC 753, 55 TC 575.

[26] [1961] AC 352, 39 TC 82.

[27] TA 1988, s. 135(5).

[28] Ibid., s. 135(6), but a special rule applies if the assignment was on bankruptcy (s. 135(7)). More devious arrangements fall within s. 135(8). Exercises of the option after the employment has ceased fall within s. 140(1).

16.4 Share Purchase Incentive Schemes

Basic Rules

Share purchase incentive schemes were introduced to avoid s. 135. Instead of being given an option to buy a share for £1—the current market value of the share which might in due course be worth £3—E would be issued with a share which ordinarily would have had a current market value of £3 but which was subject to restrictions making it was worth only £1. At a later date the restrictions would be removed. The increase in value could not be subject to tax under TA 1988, s. 135, since the employee did not realise a gain by exercising a right to acquire shares—the shares were already owned. If the company capitalised its profits to pay them up, there would be a charge under TA 1988, s. 154 on the employee on the amount so spent, but this would usually be a lot less than the gain realised.

Faced with such schemes the legislature has provided two sets of rules. Set one, §16.4.1 and 2 which was introduced in 1998, clarifies the treatment of conditional acquisitions of shares and the conversion of convertible shares. Set two, §16.4.3, which was introduced in 1988 amending earlier rules, provide a separate charge on the growth in the vale of shares in certain circumstances. Reversing the historical order, the 1998 changes are dealt with first.

16.4.1 Conditional acquisitions[29]

The schemes just described led to greater practical use of long-term share incentive schemes in which benefits accrued only if performance conditions attached to the options were satisfied. However, the assumption that there was no charge on the grant of such shares, but only when the conditions were satisfied and benefits received, rested, until 1998, on general principle rather than express provision. It could, contrary to the general assumption, be argued, on the basis of *Abbott* v. *Philbin*, that there *should* be a charge on the grant of the option based on a prediction, i.e. a guess, as to the chance that the particular employee would derive a benefit in the fullness of time thanks to the success of the company or the stock market's assessment of the company. If this were correct the charge based on guesswork at the time of the grant would exclude any charge when the conditions were removed. Therefore, in 1998 the Revenue moved to enact rules validating the general assumption. These rules apply to what are termed "conditional acquisitions of shares". The acquisition must be as a director or employee.[30]

There are elaborate rules as to when an acquisition is conditional.[31] These conditions ensure that certain pre-emption rights are not treated as conditions; also exempt are shares subject to forfeiture for misconduct or for more than one of the permitted reasons.[32]

If the condition attached to the shares must be satisfied (or not) within five years there may be no charge on the grant of the shares.[33] There will be a charge if and when the holding becomes unconditional or on any earlier sale of the shares or any interest in them.[34] The

[29] See Richards [1999] *BTR* 340.

[30] Defined in TA 1988, s. 140H; there are information powers in s. 140G. The rules apply to conditional interests in shares acquired on or after 17 March 1998 (s. 140C(4)).

[31] Ibid. s. 140C; for parallel NIC treatment, see (1998) *Simon's Tax Intelligence* 729, 1358.

[32] TA 1988, s. 140C(3A), (1A), added by FA 1999, s. 43.

[33] Ibid., s. 140A(3) is subject to s. 135 (unapproved share options) and s. 162 (deemed loan for non fully paid up shares).

[34] Ibid., s. 140A(4).

charge is on the market value of the shares (when the holding becomes unconditional or prior disposal) less allowable deductions.[35] Any liability on the grant of the shares will be taken into account to prevent a double charge.[36]

If, however, the condition could be satisfied beyond the five-year period there used to be an immediate charge when the shares were obtained, if the share were issued before 27 July 1999.[37] The charge has been abolished for shares issued on or after that date.[38]

16.4.2 Convertible shares: charge on conversion

Although the growth in value charge in FA 1988, s. 78 was effective for many purposes it did not necessarily apply where one class of shares was converted into another. TA 1988, ss 140D–140F were therefore added by FA 1998.[39] A charge arises where the person has acquired shares as a director or employee,[40] and the shares carry a right or a possible entitlement to convert the shares into shares of a different class.[41] The charge is on the market value of the new shares following conversion less any deductible amounts.[42] There is, however, an exception for the conversion of shares of one class only ("the original class") into shares of one other class only ("the new class").[43] In order to take advantage of this exception the company must be employee-controlled by virtue of these shares immediately before the conversion. Alternatively, the majority of the company's shares of the original class must at that time have been held otherwise than by or for the benefit of directors or employees of the company.

16.4.3 Growth in value charge

When special rules for share incentive schemes were introduced in 1972, they directed a special charge under Schedule E whenever the shares were disposed of or, if sooner, when a period of seven years expired.[44] There was thus a regular periodic charge on the increase in the value of the shares. At first there was an exception for approved schemes, but this was withdrawn in 1974 following a change of government.[45]

The problem with these rules was that they charged the employee on the increase in the value of the shares, whether this was due to a) the removal of the restrictions or b) to the increase in the underlying value of the shares as a result of everyone's hard work or the company's good fortune. Following a review of the legislation in 1987,[46] FA 1988 made major changes.[47] The purpose of FA 1988 s. 78 was to restrict the charge to a), where appropriate. In view of the wide changes of 1988 with a single higher rate of tax and an assimilation of

35 TA 1988, s. 140A(5); market value is defined in s. 145A(6) and allowable deductions in ss 140A(7), 140B.
36 Ibid., s. 140A(7).
37 Ibid., s. 140A(2).
38 FA 1999, s. 42(2).
39 FA 1998, s. 51; the rules apply to convertible shares acquired on or after 17 March 1998 (s. 140F(3)).
40 On which, see TA 1988, s. 140H.
41 Ibid., s. 140D(2). For parallel NIC treatment, see (1998) *Simon's Tax Intelligence* 729, 1358.
42 TA 1988, s. 140D(5); the terms are defined in the rest of s. 140D and s. 140E (which mirrors s. 140B).
43 Ibid., s. 140D(8), (9).
44 FA 1972, s. 79; later TA 1988, s. 138.
45 FA 1994 s. 20.
46 See Inland Revenue press release 26 October 1987, *Simons Tax Intelligence* p. 796.
47 Although part of FA 1988, the legislation applies to acquisitions on or after 26 October 1987; on background to legislation on treatment of earlier acquisitions which would meet the conditions for the new rules see s. 88.

the rates of income tax and CGT there were calls for the repeal of all these rules.[48] The growing gap between income tax and CGT makes action on such calls even more unlikely.

The new approach was to extend to most subsidiaries so that the employee of a subsidiary who had shares in the subsidiary could receive the same treatment. However, one type of subsidiary, called the dependent subsidiary,[49] remained subject to the old periodic charge on the general increase in the value of the shares which was enacted as FA 1988 s. 79. In addition s. 80 dealt with various benefits passing from the companies to the employee shareholders; these rules are stricter if the company is a dependent subsidiary. The Revenue view is that s. 78 contained pragmatic rules to provide the new, more generous, approach but only where the subsidiary is operating more or less independently of its group.[50] In other circumstances the Revenue feel that it is just too easy for value to be shifted around the group and so into the shares of the lucky employees or directors.

The charges apply where shares have been acquired in pursuance of a right conferred or an opportunity offered by reason of the office or employment by that or any other company.[51] They cannot apply where the shares are acquired in pursuance of an offer made to the public.[52] The frequently used terms "acquisition" and "disposition" cover increases and decreases in a person's interest in the shares.[52a]

Charge 1) chargeable events

This arises if a "chargeable event" occurs provided that the employee still owns or, technically, has any beneficial interest in, the shares.[53] The list of chargeable events covers the removal or variation of any restrictions[54] on the shares and the creation of rights or restrictions on them. It also covers the imposition of restrictions on other shares in the company since such events equally cause a shift in value between the groups of shares.[55]

The charge arises only if the person acquiring the shares or interest in them still has a beneficial interest when the relevant event occurs.[55a] Similarly there is no charge if the shareholder has not been an employee or director of that or any associated company in the last seven years.[56] There is no automatic charge at the end of seven years.[57] There is no charge if a person acquires the shares otherwise than under a bargain at arm's length with an unconnected person. Finally, there is no charge under s. 78 if the company is a "dependent subsidiary" both at the time of acquisition and of the event—here s. 79 may apply but on a quite different basis.[58]

[48] [1988] *BTR* p. 249.

[49] Defined in FA 1988, s. 86. On problems in defining dependent subsidiary see ICAEW Memorandum TR 739, 1989 *Simon's Tax Intelligence*, p. 40.

[50] 1987 *Simon's Tax Intelligence*, p. 799.

[51] If he acquires the right as a person connected with a director or employee, it is caught by s. 81(1); the term acquisition covers increases in a person's interest in the shares—FA 1988, s. 81.

[52] FA 1988, s. 77(3).

[52a] FA 1988, s. 81.

[53] FA 1988, s. 78(1).

[54] Widened by s. 78(7).

[55] FA 1988, s. 78(3).

[55a] FA 1988 s. 78(1).

[56] FA 1988, s. 78(4); if he acquired the shares as an employee of another company he must not also have been an employee of the first company at the time.

[57] FA 1988, s. 78(3).

[58] FA 1988, ss. 78(1), 79.

Various situations are excluded from this charge if various alternative conditions are satisfied.[59] The basic situation is where the shares affected are all the shares in the class. The alternative conditions are a) the directors or employees hold a minority of the shares whose value is increased;[60] b) the company is employee-controlled by virtue of the class of shares affected[60a] and c) the company is a subsidiary but not a dependent subsidiary and its shares are a single class.[61]

Charge (2) dependent subsidiary S. 79

Where the company is such a subsidiary, whether at the time of the acquisition or during his ownership of the shares, there will be a charge on the increase in value either at the end of seven years or if E ceases to own them before that time.[62] This is quite separate from the notion of chargeable events in s. 78; it will be remembered that s. 78 is excluded if the company is a dependent subsidiary both at the time of acquisition and of the event[63]—since s. 79 is sufficient. The charge is on the increase in value over this period since acquisition.[64] The charge will be reduced if E's interest is less than full beneficial ownership;[65] if E has to provide more consideration since acquisition in accordance with the terms of acquisition,[66] or if, in accordance with the terms of the acquisition, E ceases to own them by disposing of them for less than full consideration.[66a]

Charge 3) Special Benefits.[67]

This arises when the shareholder receives special benefits, the company is a dependent subsidiary and the shares are of a single class.[68] It also arises if the benefit becomes available to less than 90% of those who then hold shares of the same class as those which, or an interest in which, the person holds.[69] The charge is excluded if the shareholder has not been a director or employee of that or any associated company within the last seven years.[70]

There are a number of ancillary provisions. Thus, rules are provided for the treatment of the replacement of shares on reorganisations,[71] for the CGT consequences[72] and for the provision of information.[73]

[59] The situations are listed in subs (5) and the conditions in subs (6).

[60] FA 1988, s. 78(5), (6).

[60a] FA 1988, s. 78(5), (6)(b); employee control is defined in s. 87(2).

[61] FA 1988, s. 78(5), (6)(c).

[62] FA 1988, s. 79(2).

[63] FA 1988, s. 78(1).

[64] FA 1988, s. 79(2), (3).

[65] FA 1988, s. 79(4).

[66] FA 1988, s. 79(5).

[66a] FA 1988, s. 79(6).

[67] FA 1988, s. 80 as amended by F(No. 2)A 1992, s. 37 for benefits received on or after 12th November 1991; for explanation see Inland Revenue press release, 12th November 1991, 1991 *Simon's Tax Intelligence*, p. 1035. This rule applies where the shares have been acquired by a person connected with a director or employee: s. 83(4). The same provision carries over the rule that a person who acquires the shares otherwise than under a bargain at arm's length with an unconnected person is to be deemed to continue to hold the shares until there is a disposal of them by a bargain at arm's length to an unconnected person.

[68] FA 1988, s. 80(1A) added by F(No. 2)A 1992, s. 37(2) for benefits received.

[69] FA 1988, s. 80(2)(a) added by F(No. 2)A 1992, s. 37(2).

[70] FA 1988, s. 80(5); if he acquired the shares as an employee of another company he must also not have been an employee of that company.

[71] FA 1988, s. 82.

[72] FA 1988, s. 84.

[73] FA 1988, s. 85.

Planning

The effect of the pre-1988 rules had been to make share purchase schemes unattractive in tax terms. There was a trend away from share schemes towards performance unit schemes which allow the employee to acquire contingent rights to bonuses; these bonuses are related to the performance of the employee's unit but, being contingent, do not become taxable until the contingency is removed (as by completing a certain number of years of service). Such schemes are free of risk to the employee and avoid cash flow problems and dilution of equity.

16.5 Approved Share Option Schemes

16.5.1 Savings-related open to all and executive selective schemes

A recent survey showed that whereas in 1987, 90% of companies had approved schemes compared with 10% that had unapproved schemes, by 1996, 80% of companies had approved schemes compared with 85% unapproved.[74] Explanations included the 1988 equalisation of tax rates for CGT and income tax and the 1996 reduction in the limit for approved schemes to options over shares with a market value of £30,000. Another explanation was the 1996 rule that schemes had to be open to all employees, which applied as from 1996 and did not affect existing options. Symbolically—and accurately—the 1996 rule changes meant that schemes which had previously been called "discretionary" schemes were instead called "company" share schemes. In 1993–1994, 70,000 employees received options over shares with an initial value totalling £1,750 m; the average per employee was £25,000 and the cost of the tax relief was £70 m; in 1997–1998 the figures were 330,000, £1,070 m and £3,300 and £100 m.[75]

16.5.1 Company share schemes

Benefits of approval

No charge on exercise; CGT on disposal. Where an option is granted under an approved scheme, s. 135 is excluded. This means no charge arises on the exercise of the option provided it is exercised not less than three or more than 10 years after the grant, nor within three years of a similar exercise.[76] Instead, a charge to CGT arises on the disposal of the shares on the difference between the full cost of the option shares and the disposal proceeds.

Charge on grant. No tax charge arises on the grant of the option unless the sum of the consideration given for the option and the price payable under it is "manifestly" less than the market value of the shares at that time, in which case the difference is taxable under Schedule E as earned income.[77] The right under an option to acquire shares at a discount of up to 15% of market value was abolished by FA 1996 as part of the reaction against gains

[74] Cohen [1997] *Business Law Review* 131.

[75] *Inland Revenue Statistics*, Table 6.3 charts the information.

[76] TA 1988, s. 185(3), (5); if the second exercise occurs within three years it is no defence that the taxpayer (erroeously) thought he had no choice but to exercise the option then or abandon it: *AB* v. *BY* [1998] STC (SCD) 10.

[77] TA 1988, s. 185(4).

being made by certain executives following privatisation.[78] The amount chargeable to income tax is treated as allowable expenditure when the gain is calculated on the disposal of the shares.[79]

From 17 March 1993[80] any capital gain is calculated by reference to the actual consideration received rather than market value;[81] the value of services or past services rendered by the employee is excluded[82] so that virtually the only consideration to be brought in will be pecuniary.

Conditions for approval

Who may participate? From 1 May 1995 any full-time director or qualifying employee (whether full-time or part-time) of the company establishing the scheme (the grantor company), or of another company covered by the group scheme, are eligible to participate.[83] Anyone with a material interest in a company must be excluded, as must a part-time director.[84]

Value? As from 1996 the value of the shares (at the time the option is granted) over which each participator may hold unexercised options is restricted to £30,000. For earlier schemes the limit was the greater of (a) £100,000, and (b) four times the emoluments (for PAYE purposes, less benefits) in the year of assessment or the preceding year (or the 12 months beginning on the first day in the year of assessment for which there are such emoluments).[85] Within these limits the size of the option is at the company's discretion.

Shares. The shares must be part of the fully paid up ordinary share capital of the grantor company (or certain controlling companies)[86] and must be (a) quoted on a recognised stock exchange, or (b) shares in a company not under the control of another company unless the controlling company is quoted (and is not a close company).[87] The only special restriction permitted[88] is one imposed by the company's articles requiring the employee or director to dispose of the scheme shares at the end of the employment.[89] Conditions may also be imposed in so far as they require the shares to be pledged as security for a loan to buy them, or to be disposed of in repayment of such a loan.[90] Except in the case of a com-

[78] Ibid., s. 185(6B), added by FA 1991, s. 39(5) which also amends s. 185(6) and adds subs. (6A) on interaction with CGT and amendment of TCGA 1992, s. 120 to avoid double charge (see FA 1993, s. 105).

[79] TA 1988, s. 185(7).

[80] TCGA 1992, s. 149A, added by FA 1993, s. 104.

[81] TCGA 1992, s. 149A(1), (2), excluding TCGA 1992, s. 17(2).

[82] TCGA 1992, s. 149A(3).

[83] TA 1988, Sch. 9, para. 27, as amended by FA 1995, s. 137; previously only full-time directors and employees qualified, although they may exercise the rights after the employment ends. The right does not have to be to a particular number of shares at a particular price or at a price obtained by a set formula (*IRC* v. *Burton Group plc* [1990] STC 242, 63 TC 191).

[84] TA 1988, Sch. 9, para. 8; on definition of material interest, see ibid., s. 187(3), Sch. 9, paras 37–40; Sch. 9, para. 40 was added by FA 1989, s. 65 and excludes shares held in an employee benefit trust in the calculation of a person's holding, unless caught by Sch. 9, para. 40(3). See also FA 1989, Sch. 12, para. 9.

[85] TA 1988, Sch. 9, para. 28.

[86] Ibid., Sch. 9, paras 10–12. Sch. 9, para. 10(c)(i), relating to shares in a consortium company, was repealed by FA 1989, s. 64. The effect is to reduce the stake to be held by a member company of the consortium from 15% to 5%, making it easier for the consortium members shares to be used in this way.

[87] TA 1988, Sch. 9, paras 11, 12.

[88] Ibid., Sch. 9, paras 12, 13. On the effect of directors' discretion to refuse to register a transfer or to compel an employee to sell shares on the termination of employment, see Revenue Press Release, 11 June 1985, (1985) *Simon's Tax Intelligence* 342.

[89] TA 1988, Sch. 9, para. 12(2)–(4); such conditions are of particular benefit to family-run companies.

[90] Ibid., Sch. 9, para. 13(3), added by FA 1988, s. 66. See (1987) *Simon's Tax Intelligence* 782. This rule does not apply to savings-related share option schemes. The rule is retroactive (FA 1984, Sch. 10, para. 10(3), added by FA 1988, s. 69).

pany with only one class of share, the majority of the shares must not be beneficially held by persons who acquired the shares as a result of opportunities given them because of their employment or (if the shares are not quoted) which are held by the controlling company (or its associated company).[91] "Employee-control shares" (shares held by employees or directors of the company and which together confer control of the company) are specifically excluded from this restriction.[92]

Rights. The rights must be non-transferable. However, personal representatives of deceased participants may exercise rights within one year of death (and subject to the 10-year rule).[93]

Approval. The company establishing the scheme must apply for approval in writing. The Revenue may demand a wide range of information, and withdraw approval if the conditions cease to be met. The company may appeal to the Special Commissioners against such a decision.[94] An amendment to a scheme under which the holder of the option obtains new rights, e.g. reducing the period of time before the option becomes exercisable, cannot be made without Revenue approval.[95]

The company. The company must be, or be controlled by, a single company.[96] The scheme may contain provisions allowing for the exchange of rights following a takeover; rights to acquire shares in the new company may be acquired.[97] This has to be agreed by the new company and the value of the new option must be the same as that of the old option. The employer may now deduct the costs of introducing such schemes.[98] The rules now ensure equal treatment for men and women with regard to retirement.[99]

16.6 Approved Savings-Related Share Option Schemes

Since 1980 it has been possible to combine an approved share option scheme with an approved savings scheme so as to take advantage of the tax efficiency of the savings scheme to provide the funds to finance the exercise of the option.[100] *Inland Revenue Statistics* 1999, Table 6.2 shows that, by the end of 1997–1998, 1,834 schemes had been approved; the initial market value of shares over which options had been granted over those years totalled £19.2 bn; in 1997–1998 the average value per employee of the shares over which options had been granted was £2,500; the cost of the tax relief in those years was £450 m.

[91] TA 1988, Sch. 9, para. 14.

[92] Defined in ibid., Sch. 9, para. 14(3).

[93] Ibid., Sch. 9, para. 27(2), (3).

[94] Ibid., Sch. 9, paras 5, 6.

[95] *IRC* v. *Eurocopy plc* [1991] STC 707, 64 TC 370; and *IRC* v. *Reed International plc* [1994] STC 396, 67 TC 552.

[96] TA 1988, Sch. 9, para. 1(3); on concessionary relief for jointly owned companies, see ESC B27 (1994); *Simon's Direct Tax Service*, Division H4.2.

[97] TA 1988, Sch. 9, para. 15(7); on capital gains consequences, see TCGA 1992, s. 238.

[98] TA 1988, s. 84A, added by FA 1991, s. 42.

[99] FA 1991, s. 38.

[100] TA 1988, s. 185, Sch. 9, Pts I–III, VI. On amendments relating to the retirement age and to ensure equality of treatment for men and women, see FA 1991, s. 38.

16.1.1 Conditions of approval

The scheme

The savings scheme must be within TA 1988, s. 326 and be approved by the Revenue for this purpose.[101] The contribution must not exceed £250 a month.[102] The option is not normally exercisable for five or seven years (i.e. the period needed to attract the bonus on maturity of the savings scheme) and the price for the shares must not exceed the proceeds of the contract.

Who may participate?

The participants in the scheme, i.e. those eligible to participate, must include all UK resident and ordinarily resident employees (whether full time or part time) or full-time directors with, in each case, at least five years' service,[103] but must not include outsiders nor those with a material interest in the company if it is a close company.[104]

Shares

The shares must be ordinary share capital and must be quoted, or shares in a company not controlled by another company, or shares under the control of a non-close quoted company.[105] It follows from this that if a company is taken over, the existing scheme must be wound up (since approval will be withdrawn) and a new scheme, with its own five- or seven-year period, started in relation to the new head company. The shares must be fully paid up and not redeemable. The only restrictions permitted are those imposed by the company's articles requiring employees to dispose of their shares at the end of their employment.[106] The price at which the shares may be acquired must not be manifestly less than 80% of the market value at the time the option is acquired[107] (oddly the 80% figure was not changed in 1996). If these conditions are met, no charge arises on the grant of the option or on the exercise of the option[108] (so no TA 1988, s. 135 charge), nor is there any charge on the growth in value under FA 1988, s. 78 or 79.[109] As with §16.6 (above), special rules may apply if the company is taken over, or some similar event occurs.[110] There may be a charge under TA 1988, s. 162 if the employee is a director or higher paid employee.

The company conditions with regard to ownership and change of control are the same as for §16.5.[111] Schemes may now contain provisions allowing for the transfer of rights following a takeover so as to give rights to acquire shares in the new company.[112] This must be

[101] TA 1988, Sch. 9, para. 16.

[102] Ibid., Sch. 9, para. 24(2)(a), as amended by FA 1991, s. 40; (1991) *Simon's Tax Intelligence* 771.

[103] TA 1988, Sch. 9, para. 26, as amended by FA 1995, s. 137.

[104] TA 1988, Sch. 9, paras 8, 26. For traps where a person still has a material interest even though the company is no longer close, see Cohen [1997] *Business Law Review* 131, 132 (neither s. 415 nor non-resident status can help them in such circumstances).

[105] TA 1988, Sch. 9, para. 11.

[106] Ibid., Sch. 9, paras 12, 13.

[107] Ibid., Sch. 9, para. 25 as amended by FA 1989, s. 62(3); see also cases on Sch. 9, para. 29 above.

[108] In Statement of Practice SP 4/83, the Revenue set out the circumstances in which a participant may exercise his option when the employing company leaves a group and ceases to participate in the scheme.

[109] TA 1988, s. 185(3)(a).

[110] Ibid., Sch. 9, para. 21.

[111] Ibid., Sch. 9, para. 1(3), (4); on concessionary relief for jointly owned companies, see ESC B27. So, 51% control will suffice, 50% will not (*IRC* v. *Reed International plc* [1994] STC 396, 67 TC 552).

[112] TA 1988, Sch. 9, para. 15; on capital gains consequences, see TCGA 1992, s. 238.

agreed by the new company, and the value of the new option must be the same as that of the old option.

16.7 Enterprise Management Incentives

16.7.1 Enterprise management incentives

Enterprise management incentives (EMI) are share option schemes designed to help small companies attract and retain the key people they need and to reward employees for taking a risk by investing their time and skills in helping small companies achieve their potential. It is a mark of New Labour's striking willingness to grant great favours to small groups of people. An option only qualifies[113] if granted for commercial reasons in order to recruit or retain a key employee in a company; it must not be part of a scheme or arrangement the main purpose of which is the avoidance of tax. With limits of 15 employees and £100,000 per employee[114] the company may grant up to £1.5 m of these EMI share options. Where an employee holds options over £100,000, EMI treatment will apply to the first £100,000. The £100,000 limit applies to a three year period beginning with the date of the grant; so if an employee is given £100,000 of share options in year 1 and exercises them in year 3, no new options may be taken out until year 4 when the third anniversary of the grant comes round.

This scheme is meant to apply to small high risk companies. The company must be a qualifying compani,[115] i.e. one which is an independent[116] trading company with gross assets not exceeding £15 m.[118] The company may be listed or unlisted but must meet qualifying conditions and in particular must not be involved in certain prohibited types of trade.[119] The receipt of substantial sums by way of royalty or licence fee will disqualify a company, unless the intellectual property rights were created by the company or another group company.[120] The trade must be carried on in the UK but the company need not be resident here.[121] Only qualifying companies can form a group; only the parent can grant EMI options. Subsidiaries will prevent the parent from granting EMI options unless each subsidiary meets all these requirements.[122] The relief also applies to a company carrying on activities of research and development from which it is intended that a qualifying trade will emerge.[123]

The employee[124]

Eligible employees must work for the company for a substantial amount of their time, i.e. 25 hours or, if less, 75% of their working time;[125] they may be inventors, scientists or experts in

113 Sch. 14, para. 9.
114 Sch. 14, paras 10, 11.
115 Sch. 14, paras 12–17.
116 Sch. 14, para. 13.
117 Sch. 14, para. 17.
118 Sch. 14, para. 16.
119 Sch. 14, paras 18–26.
120 Sch. 14, para. 22.
121 Sch. 14, para. 18.
122 Sch. 14, paras 14, 15.
123 Sch. 14, para. 18(2); and see H4.
124 Sch. 14, paras 27–36.
125 Sch. 14, para. 29.

raising finance. They may offer up to £1.5 m worth of share options to help them recruit and retain the high calibre people that they need to make their company successful and grow.

There are rules on relationship between this and other share schemes.[126] The employee must not have a material interest, i.e. control of 30% or more of the ordinary share capital.[127]

The option must be capable of being exercised within ten years;[128] a charge arises if it is not exercised within the period.[129] The option may be conditional provided the condition can occur within the period. The option must be over the ordinary share capital of the company.[130]

The shares must also be fully paid up and neither redeemable nor convertible; the option must be non-assignable;[131] the terms must be agreed in writing.[132] however, there are no rules directing the conditions under which the share may be issued; so the shares may be non-voting or subject to preemption rights on the part of the company. This is to allow the company to protect its independence.[133]

16.7.2 Income tax

If the option is granted at current market value there is no income tax liability on either the grant or the exercise of the option.[134] However, if the option price is below market value there will be a Schedule E charge on the value of the discount.[135] The option may be at a nil cost; in this case a charge arises under TA 1988, s. 135 by reference to the value when the option is granted or, if lower, when it is exercised.[136] The company may grant options at a price above market value if it wishes.

Disqualifying events[137]

The precise effect of such an event depends on its nature. The events are

(a) loss of independence, i.e. becoming a 51% subsidiary of another company or otherwise coming under the control of another company;
(b) ceasing to meet the correct trading activities requirements;
(c) ceasing to meet the eligible employee requirements, e.g. the 75% working time conditions,[138]
(d) alterations in the terms of the option, the effect of which is to increase the value of the shares or to break the rules as to qualifying options;
(e) any relevant alteration in the share capital of the company;[139]

[126] Sch. 14, para. 10(6). Options under rule 10(6) count towards £100,000 limit.
[127] Sch. 14, paras 30–36.
[128] Sch. 14, para. 39.
[129] Sch. 14, para. 42(2).
[130] Sch. 14, para. 38(1)(a).
[131] Sch. 14, paras 38, 41.
[132] Sch. 14, para. 40.
[133] Inland Revenue Memorandum 4.7 and 4.9.
[134] Sch. 14, para. 45 Cl F4.
[135] Sch. 14, para. 45 Cl F4.
[136] Sch. 14, para. 46.
[137] Sch. 14, paras 47–53; on (non) effects of disqualifying event within 47(1)(a) happening to the old company following.
[138] Sch. 14, para. 52.
[139] Sch. 14, para. 49.

(f) any relevant conversion of the shares;[140]
(g) granting the employee an option under another scheme if this would take the employee over the £100,000 maximum level.[141]

The shares must be valued at the date of the disqualifying event.[142] Relief on the value down to that event continues to be available however any later increase in value is subject to a charge under TA 1988, s. 135.[143]

Other Schedule E share option rules

TA 1988, s. 162. which would otherwise deem a loan if the option price is below market value, is excluded.[144] However, various charges may arise after the shares have actually been acquired. So nothing in the new rules will prevent a charge from arising under FA 1988 on the release of rights attached to shares acquired under a qualifying option or under TA 1988, s. 140A or, if the shares are convertible, s. 140D.[145] There will also be a charge under TA 1988, s. 135 if a sum is received for the release of rights under the option itself.[146]

Capital gains tax[147] will be payable when the shares are sold but as they count as business assets they will benefit from the taper relief. The taper period will begin at the date the options are granted. When combined with the FA 2000 reduction in the taper period for business assets this means that the CGT burden will be much less than any income tax burden. Where there is a rights issue in respect of shares acquired under these options there is no amalgamation of the two holdings for CGT purposes.[148]

Further rules apply to the effect of a company reorganisation as where the company in which the employee had the relevant options is taken over and new replacement options are given by the new company.[149]

The scheme must be acceptable to the Revenue but this takes the form of notification and not approval.[150] Of course the company then runs the risk that the Revenue will argue that the qualifying conditions have not been met.

Companies will be able to grant EMIs from the time of Royal Assent, 28 July 2000.

16.8 Approved Profit-Sharing Schemes

Under approved profit-sharing schemes employees receive shares as opposed to options which are held initially in trust. The rules (TA 1988, s. 186) talk of an initial two-year period (the period of retention) and a release date (years three to five). These schemes are being phased out to make way for the scheme at §16.10. Such schemes are often used when companies are being floated in order to give every employee a small/token holding. During the period of privatisation it was common practice for a company to match purchases by

[140] Sch. 14, para. 50.
[141] Sch. 14, para. 51 referring to para. 10(6) and so to TA 1988, Sch. 9.
[142] Sch. 14, para. 53.
[143] Sch. 14, para. 55.
[144] Sch. 14, para. 54.
[145] Sch. 14, para. 55(1)(b) or (c); nots subs. (2) on valuation.
[146] Sch. 14, para. 55(1)(a).
[147] Sch. 14, paras 56–7.
[148] Sch. 14, para. 58 excluding TCGA 1992, ss 127–30.
[149] Sch. 14, paras 59–63; note also paras 42(2) and 48.
[150] Sch. 14, paras 2–71 the details required in the notice are set out in para. 2.

employees with equal number of shares in approved profit-sharing schemes.[151] By the end of 1997–1998, 1,334 schemes had been approved since they were first introduced in those years; the initial market value of share appropriated over those years totalled £5.4 bn and the cost of the tax relief was £160 m.[152]

Sums paid over by employers for such schemes are deductible for corporation tax provided the sums are spent on the acquisition of shares within the following nine months or are necessary to meet the reasonable expenses of the trustees.[153] Such sums are therefore tax-free investment funds. Approved profit-sharing schemes are also important for private companies since a member of a controlling family can sell shares to the trust and thus release capital without having to sell the business, as used to happen frequently before these schemes were introduced.

The tax treatment

Privileged tax treatment is afforded to shares appropriated to approved profit-sharing schemes. The company provides trustees with money with which they acquire shares from the company and which they then appropriate to particular individuals.[154] No income tax is paid when the shares are set aside for the employee, nor is there a charge to income tax, as opposed to CGT, on the value of the shares when they are sold provided, in general, that they are not sold for five years.

Conditions—amount

The total initial market value appropriated to any one participant should not exceed the greater of £3,000 and 10% of the employee's salary (subject to an annual maximum of £8,000).[155]

Who may participate?

As from 1 May 1995 the scheme must be open to all full-time directors and all employees whether full time or part time and who have been either a director or employed for five years or less. Those who participate must actually do so on equal terms;[156] those with material interests must be excluded.[157] Part-timers may be included.

Other

An individual cannot have further new shares in a scheme more than 18 months after leaving the job with the employer. A person with a material interest in a closed company is not eligible. Companies in a group may form a group scheme, but the company must be controlled by a single company.[158] Employee-controlled companies[159] and workers' co-operatives[160] may also set up approved profit-sharing schemes.

[151] Cohen [1997] *Business Law Review* 131, 133.
[152] *Inland Revenue Statistics*, Table 6.1.
[153] TA 1988, Sch. 10, para. 7.
[154] Ibid., s. 186, Sch. 9, Pts I, II, V, Sch. 10.
[155] Relevant amount" is defined in TA 1988, s. 187(2), as amended by FA 1991, s. 41, for 1991–1992 and later years.
[156] TA 1988, Sch. 9, paras 8, 35, 36, as amended by FA 1995, s. 137. However, the company may vary the amount received on a sliding scale depending on, for example, length of service or level of pay (ibid., Sch. 9, para. 36(2)).
[157] Ibid., Sch. 9 para. 8.
[158] Ibid., Sch. 9, para. 1(3), (4); on concessionary relief for jointly owned companies, see ESC B27.
[159] TA 1988, Sch. 9, para. 14.
[160] Defined in ibid., s. 187(10); see also Sch. 9, para. 12(2), Sch. 10, para. 2.

Chargeable disposals

When shares are appropriated to an individual, no charge arises on that appropriation whether under TA 1988, s. 19 or ss 154, 160 and 162 (see below at §§17.4.4 and 17.4.5); nor does any charge arise under FA 1988, ss 78A, 79 (see above at §16.4).[161] Dividends on scheme shares are paid over to the participants and are taxed in their hands, presumably under Schedule F. Participants are treated as absolutely entitled to the shares for CGT notwithstanding the numerous restrictions;[162] this means that they are liable to CGT at their relevant rates when disposing of the shares.

Disposal during period of retention

Participants must be bound by contract to allow the trustees to hold their shares throughout the "period of retention" and not dispose of their beneficial interests in that period.[163] The period of retention ends two years after the appropriation or earlier death or retirement by reason of injury, disability or redundancy or on reaching pensionable age. A disposal of the beneficial interest during this period gives rise to a charge as if the person disposing were a disqualified person and so chargeable.[164] Special rules allow the trust to take over new shares following a company reconstruction.[165] The trust may take qualifying corporate bonds on such a reconstruction.[166]

Later disposals

After the "period of retention", but before the "release date", the participants may, at any time direct the trustees to sell their shares and pay them the proceeds. The trustees must be directed to sell at the best price. A charge to income tax under Schedule E arises on a sale during this period; the same charge arises on any disposal of their beneficial interest.[167] The release date is either five years from the date of the appropriation, or, if earlier, on death.[168] The charge is on a reducing proportion, called "the appropriate percentage", of the "locked-in value" of the shares. The locked-in value is the initial market value of the shares or, if lower, the actual proceeds. At any time before the fourth anniversary of appropriation the whole sum is charged; after the fourth anniversary, but before the fifth, 75% is charged.

Example

Shares are allocated in year 1 with a market value of £700. The shares are sold just after the fourth anniversary for £1,000. The locked in value is £700 and the relevant percentage is 75%, so income tax is due on 75% of £700, i.e. £525; CGT may be due on £1,000 − £700, i.e. £300. If the sale had been for less than the 75% figure, e.g. £500, the income tax would have been due on 75% × that lower sum, i.e. £375.

If, during this five-year period, the employee ceases to be an employee or reaches the relevant age, the percentage is 50%. Such shares may be sold even though the two-year

161 Ibid., s. 186(2).

162 TCGA 1992, s. 238.

163 TA 1988, Sch. 9, para. 2: this is reinforced by para. 12(4) which bars any restriction requiring a person, before the release date, to dispose of his beneficial interest in shares which had not been transferred to him (this reinforcement does not apply to redeemable shares in a workers' co-operative).

164 Ibid., Sch. 10, para. 1(3).

165 Ibid., Sch. 10, para. 5.

166 TA 1988, Sch. 10, para. 5A, added by FA 1994, s. 101.

167 TA 1988, s. 186 (4).

168 Ibid., s. 187(2).

retention period has not expired. In order to remove discrimination between men and women an elaborate redefinition of the relevant age has now occurred.[169]

Adjustments

These adjustments are made if there is a capital distribution in respect of the shares. A charge arises under the rules described above where the capital distribution is received by the trustees or by the participants. Such distributions are treated as the proceeds of a percentage of the locked-in value. Where this occurs the initial market value is reduced by the amount of the capital receipt.[170] Adjustments are also made for a rights issue, the consideration paid being deducted from the proceeds of the disposal.[171]

Which shares?

Shares are treated as disposed of on a first in, first out basis. Company reconstructions, amalgamations, etc., are ignored (as they are for CGT). There is also provision for the PAYE machinery to apply where a charge to income tax arises.[172]

Other charges

Where the annual ration of £3,000 initial market value (or, if greater, 10% of salary up to a maximum of £8,000)[173] is exceeded there is a charge on 100% of the excess shares, although the charge arises on disposal and not, surprisingly, on appropriation. This provision is designed for cases where it is thought inappropriate to withdraw approval of the scheme. Death and the release date bring about a deemed disposal for this purpose. A similar rule applies to shares appropriated to unauthorised persons.[174]

These schemes are affected by FA 2000 in three ways. First, the phasing-out; no new schemes will be approved unless the application for approval is received by the Revenue before 6 April 2001; further, appropriations to such schemes will cease to have beneficial tax treatment unless completed before 6 April 2002.[175] Secondly the overlap; no benefits may be enjoyed under the new Employee Share Ownership plan in benefits also received under the s. 186 scheme in the same year; to the same end approval of the s. 186 scheme can be withdrawn if "free" shares are appropriated under the new scheme effect.[176] Thirdly, certain attempts to use s. 186 schemes to achieve effects similar to the dying profit related pay schemes are stopped; these myvolve (a) the use of certain shares in other companies where the shares carry restricted rights and (b) loans; the legislation only applies to appropriations or loans after 20 March 2000.[177]

[169] Ibid., Sch. 10, paras 3, 3A added, by FA 1994, s. 100; see Inland Revenue Press Release, 30 November 1993, (1993) *Simon's Tax Intelligence* 1518.

[170] TA 1988, s. 186(3).

[171] Ibid., s. 186(7).

[172] Ibid., Sch. 10, para. 5.

[173] Ibid., s. 187(2), as amended by FA 1991, s. 41, gives the definition of "relevant amount".

[174] Ibid., Sch. 10, para. 6.

[175] FA 2000, s. 49; on phasing out of corporation tax relief for contributions see s. 50.

[176] FA 2000, s. 50 and Sch. 8, para. 16 and s. 51.

[177] FA 2000, ss 52, 53.

16.9 Employee Share Ownership Trusts

FA 1989 contains rules (since amended) for a further incentive for employee share ownership plans. Although colloquially known as ESOPs, these schemes are termed employee share ownership trusts in the legislation. In essence these arrangements combine a share participation scheme with a trust for the benefit of the employees. The legislation ensures that the company obtains a corporation tax deduction when making its contribution to the trust and for the costs of setting it up.[178] In essence, this amounts to a two-tier structure with an employee benefit trust funded primarily by contributions by the company acquiring shares for subsequent distribution to an approved profit-sharing scheme. ESOPs have attractions for companies in that the shares can be bought in the market, and issuing new shares (which is what usually happens with share option schemes) means diluting earnings per share for existing shareholders.

An ESOP comes under these special rules if there is a qualifying employment share ownership trust. This is defined at length.[179] The trust must be established under a deed and by a company which is not controlled by any other company and is resident in the UK. The deed must appoint the first trustees and contain various rules in relation to them, e.g. as to the presence of professional and non-professional trustees and the membership of employees of the company.[180]

Certain employees *must* be included as beneficiaries (e.g. those who have been with the company or any other company within the group for at least five years, whether full time or part time), but others *may* be included. Part-time employees were included in 1995. Directors must work at least 20 hours a week, ignoring holidays and sickness; a minimum period of employment may be specified, but this may not exceed five years.[181] Those who would qualify for a SRSOS also qualify;[182] the addition of this group, which substantially overlaps the original group, was made in 1996.

The trust deed must spell out various duties of the trustees, e.g. as to their functions in receiving money from the company, investing it in the appropriate securities within the appropriate period and dealing with the securities promptly.[183] Thus, they must invest the money in ordinary shares of the founding company or spend it on some other qualifying purpose within nine months. They must not invest if the company is subsequently controlled by another company, and any acquisitions must be at a price at or below current market value. Special restrictions on the shares are not permitted, and it must be expressly stated that the trustees may not buy shares which are subject to such restrictions. The trustees are permitted to vary the basis of allocation only by reference to the basis of level of remuneration or length of service.

When the trust disposes of its shares it must do so either directly to the employees or to an approved profit-sharing scheme; any other transfer will be a chargeable event and this

[178] FA 1989, s. 67. See, generally, ICAEW Memorandum TR 759, (1989) *Simon's Tax Intelligence* 723–6. On the US counterpart, see Melton (1990) 45 *Tax Law Review* 363.

[179] FA 1989, Sch. 5.

[180] FA 1989, Sch. 5, paras 3–3C.

[181] Ibid., Sch. 5, para. 4; material interest is defined in Sch. 5, para. 16.

[182] FA 1989, Sch. 5, para. 4(2A) added by FA 1996, s. 120; there are consequence for powers (FA 1989, Sch. 5, para. 4(2B)).

[183] Ibid., Sch. 5, paras 5–10.

restriction must be spelt out in the trust.[184] Transfers "on qualifying terms" are not chargeable events.[185]

Apart from the acquisition of shares in the founding company, the purposes for which the trustees are permitted to use the money are limited to matters such as the repayment of loans taken out to acquire the shares, the payment of interest on such loans, payments to employees and payment of trust expenses. The deed must not contain features which are not essential, or reasonably incidental, to these primary purposes. A trust which ceases to satisfy some of these conditions ceases to be a qualifying ESOP—another chargeable event. There is now a clearance procedure to enable trustees to obtain confirmation that their trust satisfies these rules.[186]

On a chargeable event the relief will be clawed back from the trustees at the rate appropriate to trusts, currently 34%. The charge is made under Schedule D, Case VI. The company may be made to pay if the trustees fail to pay within six months.[187] The list of chargeable events covers: making a non-qualifying transfer (i.e. a transfer to someone other than a beneficiary or an approved profit-sharing scheme); making a transfer on non-qualifying terms or using funds for non-qualifying purposes;[188] or holding the shares for more than seven years.[189]

The amount brought into charge for expenditure on a non-qualifying purpose is the sum so spent; otherwise it is the capital gains base cost (without any allowance for indexation or tapering relief) of the security retained or transferred.[190] In computing the sum to be charged a further adjustment is made in order to achieve the legislative object of clawing back the relief rather than simply penalising the trustee. First, one adds the present sum to be charged to the total of any previous charges.[191] This is then set against the amounts deductible for corporation tax by the company (whether or not any claim for relief has actually been made). The sum to be charged is chargeable only to the extent that it exceeds the deductible amounts. Extensive information powers[192] and special rollover relief rules for the disposal of assets to such trusts also exist but only until the start of 2001–02.[193]

16.10 All Employee Share Schemes FA 2000

16.10.1

FA 2000 introduces yet another scheme, now called an all employee share plan. The plan will eventually cost around £400 m a year and it is expected that around 625,000 employees will own shares in their companies for the first time.[194] If the conditions are observed, all shares in the plan, held for five years, will be completely free of income tax and CGT while so held.

184 Ibid., Sch. 5, para 5(2)(c), (d); the chargeable events are spelt out in ibid., s. 69(1)–(3).

185 Ibid., s. 69(4), (4ZA).

186 Inland Revenue Press Release, 9 May 1990, (1990) *Simon's Tax Intelligence* 443.

187 FA 1989, s. 68.

188 Ibid., s. 69(2)–(6).

189 Ibid., s. 69(1)(c).

190 Ibid., s. 70.

191 Ibid., s. 72(3); see also s. 71 on repayment of borrowings where the amount could have been charged but for an adjustment.

192 Ibid., s. 73.

193 TCGA 1992, ss 227–35 the relief is given by s. 229, it is to be restricted by FA 2000, s. 54.

194 See Inland Revenue Press Release, 10 November 1999, (1999) *Simons Tax Intelligence* 1803.

The plan may contain three elements each with its own rules.[195] These are called free shares, partnership shares and matching shares; there is also a fourth category comprising dividend shares.

The plan may be on a group basis.[196] It needs to be approved by the Revenue.[197] It must have a purpose as defined by the legislation, to provide benefits to employees in the nature of shares which give them a continuing stake in the company; it must not have features which are neither essential nor reasonably incidental to that purpose.[198]

The plan must be available to all employees within Schedule E, Case I who meet certain conditions of eligibility.[199] There must be no preferential treatment of directors, no further conditions and no loan arrangements.[200] The employee may not also have any options held under an approved share option scheme or ESOP.[201] The employee must not have a material interest, i.e. control of more than 25% of the ordinary share capital.[202]

There are also conditions as to equal treatment to ensure that all are eligible to participarte and those who do so participate on similar terms.[203] However, this does not prevent discrimination on the basis of hours worked, remuneration or length of service; nor does it prevent plans from being performance related. Group plans must not favour directors or higher paid employees.[204]

The shares must also be fully paid up and neither redeemable nor convertible.[205] However, there are no rules directing the conditions under which the shares may be issued; so the shares may be non-voting or subject to preemption rights on the part of the company.[206] The company must either be listed or be not controlled by any other company,[207] i.e. the appropriate type of company.

For a table showing the different features see below p. 280.

16.10.2 *The free share plan*

Employers can give up to £3,000 of shares to employees. Employers do not have to treat all employees alike but may discriminate among them, e.g. for reaching performance targets and so rewarding "personal, team or divisional performance". These plans resemble approved profit sharing schemes; however, unlike those schemes, the award of free shares may be linked to performance provided the criteria are objective and are fair to all employees, i.e. the targets set are broadly comparable.[208] Comparable does not mean identical and under one variant up to 80% to be awarded on the basis of performance as long as the

[195] Sch. 8, para. 1.
[196] Sch. 8, para. 2.
[197] Sch. 8, paras 4, 5.
[198] Sch. 8, para. 7.
[199] Sch. 8, paras 7, 13–14.
[200] Sch. 8, paras 10–12.
[201] Sch. 8, para. 16; approved means approved under TA 1988, Sch. 9, so covering savings related share option schemes, other option schemes, profit sharing schemes.
[202] Sch. 8, paras 15, 17–22.
[203] Sch. 8, paras 8, 9.
[204] Sch. 8, para. 9(5).
[205] Sch. 8, paras 59–62.
[206] Sch. 8, paras 69–6.
[207] Sch. 8, para. 67.
[207] Sch. 8, paras 27–30.
[208] Sch. 8, paras 27–30.

highest reward is not more than four times greater than the award to an employee on similar terms.[209] There are also rules about the information to be given to employees.[210]

Free shares are held by trustees and appropriated to the participant.[211] The shares must remain with the trustee for a period of at least three years and not more than five. The shares must be transferred to any employee leaving the employment (even within the three year period)—and a charge may then arise; however the terms of the plan may require that the shares be forfeited when a plan is terminated.[213] The charge is on the full market value of the shares on leaving.[214] The shares may be withdrawn tax-free within the three year period if the employment ends because of redundancy or disability etc.[215] If the shares are withdrawn between years three and five there is a charge either on the value when transferred or on the value when the option was given, whichever is the lower.[216]

16.10.3 Reinvestment of cash dividends (dividend shares)

Dividends accruing on the plans shares may either by distributed in the usual (taxable) way or reinvested in "dividend shares".[217] There is a ceiling of £1,500 a year in any tax year.[218] The shares have their own three year holding period.[219] Once the three years have passed there is no income tax charge on these shares. The share may be left in the plan or transferred as the employee wishes. If the holding period rules are broken the dividend used to pay for the shares becomes taxable.[220] Certain amounts which are not reinvested may be retained by the trustees and then paid out if not used.[221]

16.10.4 CGT

A CGT liability may accrue if the employee having had the shares transferred then sells them. No liability arises on the appropriation or on withdrawal,[222] nor is there any liability on disposal of rights under a rights issue.[223] Since the base cost of the shares will be the value when they are transferred to the employee[224] little if any liability will arise if the employee sells them immediately. So long as the shares remain in the plan the employee is treated as beneficially entitled to them as against the trustee.[225] Once the shares have been withdrawn by the employee—something requires after five years anyway—they become chargeable assets and potentially liable to CGT. However the shares will be business assets for taper

[209] Sch. 8, para. 29(1)(c).
[210] Sch. 8, para. 28.
[211] On powers and duties see Sch. 8, paras 67–86.
[212] Sch. 8, para. 32; the trustees are authorised to accept certain offers in relation to the shares, para. 32.
[213] Sch. 8, para. 121.
[214] Sch. 8, para. 81(2).
[215] Sch. 8, para. 87.
[216] Sch. 8, para. 81(3).
[217] Sch. 8, paras 53–8.
[218] Sch. 8, para. 54.
[219] Sch. 8, para. 57.
[220] Sch. 8, para. 57.
[221] Sch. 8, para. 58.
[222] Sch. 8, para. 101.
[223] Sch. 8, para. 104.
[224] Sch. 8, para. 101(1).
[225] Sch. 8, para. 99.

relief; taper relief begins when the shares are withdrawn. The shares are pooled separately.[226]

CGT holdover reliefs are available not only to trustees where funds are transferred to one of these funds from a qualifying ESOP[227] but also to existing shareholders wanting to sell their shares to a new plan trust for the benefit of employees.

16.10.5 *The partnership share plan*[228]

Employees may buy shares out of their pre-tax monthly salary or weekly wages up to a maximum of £1,500 a year or £125 a month.[229] There is also a maximum limit of 10% of salary,[230] while another rule requires the employee to be informed about the possible effect of these rights on benefit entitlement.[231] The rules give the employee a tax deduction for the sums spent on the purchase of the shares. The payments must be deducted from the employee's salary.[232] The plan may allow for money to be accumulated; if it does not the sume must be invested within 30 days.[233] Sums may not be accumulated beyond 12 months.

As the employee has paid for the shares there is no minimum period during which the shares must be retained and the employee will face no charge if the shares are left in the plan for five years. If shares are removed before three years have passed the employee must pay income tax on the value of the shares when they are removed.[234] There is no deduction for the original price since it was tax free. If shares are removed between years three and five the employee must pay income tax on the sums used to buy the shares or the value when removed.[235] Charges may also arise if share money is paid over to the employee or on cancallation payments to E.[236] Sums set aside by the employee in this way are tax free yet are not deductible from salary in computing relevant earnings for pensions limits.[237] Dividend shares may arise here. The rules are the same as for free shares above.

16.10.6 *Matching (partnership) shares*

These allow employers to match "partnership" shares by giving employees up to two free shares for each partnership share they buy. They must be on the same terms and carry the same rights as the partnership shares; they must be appropriated at the same time,[238] and to all employees on the same basis. There are rules about giving employees information. The holding period rules are the same as for free shares; further rules allow the company to require forfeiture of the shares when the employee leaves employment.[239]

Income tax and CGT rules are the same as for free shares. The rules for dividend shares apply here also.

[226] Sch. 8, para. 100.
[227] Sch. 8, para. 76.
[228] Sch. 8, paras 33–48.
[229] Sch. 8, para. 36; there is also a minimum of £10 a month, para. 37.
[230] Sch. 8, para. 36(2); on salary see para. 48.
[231] Sch. 8, para. 38.
[232] Sch. 8, para. 35(1).
[233] Sch. 8, para.40; on plans with paccumulation powers see para 42(2).
[234] Sch. 8, para. 86(2).
[235] Sch. 8, para. 86(3).
[236] Sch. 8, paras 84, 86.
[237] ?? proof stage.
[238] Sch. 8, paras 49–52.
[239] Sch. 8, para. 81.

16.10.7

Employers may deduct the costs of setting up and running the plan and for the market value of any free and matching shares used in the plan.[240] The trustees are given a power to borrow money to buy the shares or subscribe for riehts issues.[241]

Inland Revenue Table
Consultative Document New Employee Share Plan November 1999, p. 8

	Free shares	*Partnership shares*	*Matching shares*	*Dividend shares*
Employment before eligibility	Up to 12 months' employment	Up to 12 months; employment	Only awarded to employees who buy partnership shares	Must be acquired with dividends from plan shares
Limits	Up to £3,000 per tax year	Up to £1,500 per tax year, capped at lower of: £125 per month and 10% of monthly salary	Up to 2 matching shares for each partnership share bought	Dividends from shares in the plan reinvested: —£500 in 1st year —£1,000 in 2nd year —£1,500 per year thereafter
Minimum amount if stated[1]		£10 per month		
Performance measures[1]	Yes	No	No	No
Holding period	At least 3 years from award[2]	None	At least 3 years from award[2]	3 years from acquisition
Forfeiture on cessation of employment[1]	Yes	No	Yes	No
Tax on award	None	None—tax relief for salary used to buy shares	None	None
Tax on removal of shares from plan within 3 years of award[3]	On market value when taken out	On market value when taken out	On market value when taken out	Original dividend taxable but in year when shares taken out of plan
Tax on removal between 3 and 5 years of award[2]	On lower of: value at award; and value on removal	On lower of: salary used to buy shares; and value on removal	On lower of: value at award; and value on removal	None
Tax on removal after 5 years	None	None	None	None
COT on removal —any time	None	None	None	None

[1] These conditions can be included at the option of the company.
[2] The holding period may be up to five years at the option of the company.
[3] PAYE and NICs will be operated in relation to any Schedule E income tax charge where the shares are readily convertible assets.

[240] Sch. 8, paras 105–13.
[241] Sch. 8, para. 69.

The impact of NICs where employees withdraw partnership shares within three years is the subject of consultation. This review has been caused by the extreme volatility of prices in the technology sector.

16.11 Profit-Related Pay[242]

Profit-related pay (PRP) was introduced by Nigel Lawson in 1987, who got the idea from a book he had read "during the longueurs of the Bonn Economic Summit".[243] In 1997 Kenneth Clarke phased the schemes out by withdrawing relief in two stages from 1998–2000.[244] FA 1998 contains rules to prevent the manipulation of profit periods.[245]

The essence of the idea was that a small fraction of pay should be tax free if coming out of a scheme funded out of profits. It is different from the various share schemes outlined above. Lawson claimed that PRP would bring pay-related performance closer to the centre of business debate. He cited an LSE study which stated that PRP led to significant reduction in volatility of employment, which, in turn, led to more and better training. PRP was replaced because succeeding chancellors had made it more attractive—until the scheme became too popular. In 1996 it was estimated that ending the scheme would save £3,100 m a year by 2001;[246] it was also said that this tax relief was never meant to be a permanent measure.

The PRP rules were important not only for the philosophy of incentives that lies behind it, but also for the burdens placed on the employer and the employer's independent accountant. Thus, the employer was responsible for ensuring that the scheme complied with the statutory requirements, for calculating the PRP profits and the amount of PRP due to each employee and then for giving tax relief through the PAYE scheme. The employer also had to certify the scheme in the first instance and its annual operation. The independent accountant acted as watchdog for the Revenue, providing a report both as to the initial registrability of the scheme and the proper operation of the scheme and tax relief thereunder.[247]

242 TA 1988, ss 164–84; and Sch. 8. See Tiley and Collison, *UK Tax Guide 1997–98*, §§6.80–85

243 Lawson *Memoirs* (1992), 439–41. The book was Martin L. Weitzman, *The Share Economy: Conquering Stagflation* (Harvard University Press, 1984); the partial tax exemption is put forward in a chapter entitled "Vaccinating Capitalism Against Stagflation". See also Luther, in *More Key Issues in Tax Reform* (1995), ch. 9 and the works there cited

244 FA 1997, s. 61; no profit period can begin on or after 1 January 2000.

245 FA 1998, s. 62, Sch. 11.

246 Inland Revenue Press Release, 26 November 1996, (1996) *Simon's Tax Intellivence* 1920.

247 TA 1988, ss 175, 181 required the independent accountant to certify that the terms of the scheme were satisfied "in his opinion".

17

Schedule E—Part IV: TA 1988, ss 153 and 154

17.1 Introduction and Definitions[1]

17.1.1 Introduction

One product of *Tennant* v. *Smith*[2] was a substantial amount of tax avoidance. What would otherwise have been remuneration was dressed up as an expense allowance or paid in the form of benefits in kind. Expense allowances were taxable in so far as they exceeded the sums actually spent by the recipient on behalf of his employer,[3] but difficult to trace, while benefits in kind, in so far as they could be traced, were taxable only if convertible into money or money's worth. However, these expenses or allowances were deductible by the employer in computing the profits of the business. To prevent such avoidance special legislation was introduced in 1948 and is now to be found in revised form in TA 1988, ss 153–68.[4] The rules also apply to payments to participators in close companies.[5] An inspector may issue a notice

[1] Inland Revenue practice is explained in Booklet IR 480 (latest edition 1999).

[2] [1892] AC 150, 3 TC 158. See above §15.2.

[3] Such sums escaped tax only if they were deductible under TA 1988, s. 198 or 201.

[4] Before 1976 certain employments were exempt, notably charities and non-trading bodies such as the civil service and trade unions. The present legislation draws no such distinctions The abolition of these exemptions had been recommended by the Royal Commission, Cmd 9474 (1955), §221; charities and non-profit making bodies are still distinct in that a director of such a body may be treated as an employee and not a director (TA 1988, s. 167(5); see above at §15.4; see also TA 1988, s. 145(5) above §15.4).

[5] Ibid., s. 418; see below at p. 284.

of nil liability or "dispensation" if satisfied that no additional tax is due;[6] this prevents the sections from applying.

17.1.2 To whom does the legislation apply?

The rules apply to directors,[7] whatever their salary (since they can fix their own income), and employees whose emoluments amount to £8,500.[8] The figure of £8,500 was set in 1978.[9] In 1989 it was decided that employees earning over £8,500 were no longer to be described as higher paid. Today, a person earning the minimum wage of £3.60 per hour has annual income of £7,488. If the figure of £2,000 used in 1948 when the provisions were first introduced had been adjusted in line with earnings it would, by 1992, have risen to £73,080, now £87,613.[10]

Director

The term "director" is not restricted to directors formally appointed as such, but extends to those in accordance with whose instructions the actual directors act—with an exception for advice in a professional capacity.[11] These shadow directors are liable whether or not they hold any office or employment.[12] However, there are exclusions for (a) full-time working directors who do not have a material interest in the company and (b) directors of non-profit-making bodies and charities provided, again, they have no material interest in the company.[13] Such persons may, however, be employees and so be caught if their emoluments amount to £8,500 or more.[14]

A directorship is full time if the director is required to devote substantially the whole of his time to the company in a managerial or technical capacity.[15] A has a material interest if A can control more than 5% of the ordinary share capital or, if the company is a close company, more than 5% of assets could be distributed to A on a notional winding-up.[16]

17.1.3 Calculating the £8,500 threshold[17]

In computing E's emoluments for the £8,500 threshold, sums treated as taxable by TA 1988, ss 153 and 154 must be included;[18] this is to prevent avoidance by means of a low salary and large expenses or benefits in kind.

6 TA 1988, s. 166.
7 TA 1988, s. 167(1). On travelling expenses note ESC A4.
8 The use of a fixed sum was criticised as arbitrary by the Royal Commission, above at n. 4, §220; however, the combination of a fixed sum and the passage of time has worked wonders for the Revenue.
9 FA 1978, s. 23, with effect from 1979–1980.
10 HC Written Answer, 10 November 1992, (1992) *Simon's Tax Intelligence* 975
11 TA 1988, s. 168(8), (9).
12 *R.* v. *Allen* [1999] STC 846.
13 TA 1988, s. 167(5).
14 Ibid., s.167(5).
15 Ibid., s. 168(10).
16 Ibid., s.168(9)–(11); shares held by associates are included. "Participator" is defined in TA 1988, s. 417(1).
17 On application where there is a car benefit under a salary sacrifice scheme, see ibid., s. 167(2B)–(2D).
18 Ibid., s. 167(2). The Revenue claims that the purpose of this last rule is to maintain equity between one who is paid a gross salary out of which deductible expenses are met and another who receives a lower salary but separate reimbursements of deductible expenses. This claim is unsound since equity could be achieved equally well by allowing both persons to deduct their expenses, and because it creates inequity between these persons and a third person who receives a lower salary but who incurs no deductible expenses because his employer meets them directly.

No deductions

Perhaps surprisingly there is no deduction in making this computation for expenses allowable under ss 198, 201 or 332(3), although an inspector may give a notice of nil liability[19] in respect of a benefit or allowance when satisfied that no extra charge to tax would arise. Such notices, however, are not issued where the effect would be to take the employee below the £8,500 threshold. An expense met directly by the employer will not be taken into account. Deduction is permitted for approved pension contributions, exempt profit-related pay and contributions under approved payroll giving schemes.[20]

Associated employments

An employer may not avoid these rules by dividing up employees' functions into different employments.[21] Similar rules apply if the second employment is with a controlled company. A director (other than a full-time working director without a material interest) of one controlled company, who is also an employee of another, is subject to these rules in respect of both situations.

17.2 Payments for Expenses and Expense Allowances[22]

Under TA 1988, s. 153 any payment[23] made by reason of the employment[24] "in respect of expenses" is, unless otherwise chargeable to tax, to be treated as income of the director or employee. The section applies not only to expense allowances but also to reimbursement of expenses actually incurred since here, too, there is payment in respect of expenses.[25] The only expenses not caught are those which the employer meets directly. The recipient may, however, deduct sums actually expended if they satisfy the tests laid down in TA 1988, ss 198, 201 or 203.[26]

S. 153 also applies to sums put at the employee's disposal and paid away by him.[27] Thus, sums are caught even though the money at no time becomes the property of the employee.[28]

The employer must report all such payments. In order to avoid too much paperwork, a notice of nil liability is often issued but these are not usually given for "round sum allowances".[29]

[19] Under ibid., s. 166.

[20] Ibid., ss. 167(1)(b), 171, 202.

[21] Ibid., s. 167(3).

[22] See ESC A61 under which the reimbursed expenses of certain living costs of members of the clergy does not apply if a member earns £8,500 p.a. or more.

[23] See *Jennings* v. *Kinder* [1958] 1 All ER 369, 38 TC 673.

[24] All sums paid by the employer are deemed to be paid by reason of the employment; other sums may be so deemed (TA 1988, s. 168(3) below p. 287).

[25] S. 153 thus sweeps in reimbursements of expenses actually incurred even though, under *Owen* v. *Pook* [1969] 2 All ER 1, 45 TC 571 (above at §14.4.2) they are not technically emoluments (see Royal Commission above at n. 4, §226).

[26] The burden of proof rests on the taxpayer to show that the expense comes within these provisions (*McLeish* v. *IRC* (1958) 38 TC 1). On reimbursement of fees for solicitors practising certificates, see a statement by the Law Society, 24 February 1993, (1993) *Simon's Tax Intelligence* 341.

[27] TA 1988, s. 153(3).

[28] Ibid., s. 153(3). The effect of this extension on s. 167(2)(b) (see above) is to make almost any employee with financial responsibility subject to these rules.

[29] Inland Revenue Booklet IR 480, §2.

17.3 Benefits in Kind

17.3.1 Outline

TA 1988, s. 154 taxes sums spent in or in connection with the provision of accommodation (other than living accommodation), entertainment, domestic or other services or other benefits or facilities of whatsoever nature. This wide-ranging provision even taxes prizes for passing examinations.[30] S. 154 is not confined to benefits in kind; it can also apply to cash.

Extent of charge

Tax is charged on the "cash equivalent" of the benefit,[31] usually the cost of the benefit to the person providing it.[32]

Making good

S. 154 does not apply if (or to the extent that) E, the employee, has "made good" the expense to R, the employer.[33] An expense may be made good by E by the payment of cash or by providing some other consideration (but not by providing services under the contract of employment).[34]

Not otherwise chargeable or exempt

S. 154 does not apply if, apart from the section, the cost would be chargeable to tax as income of the director or employee—for example under *Tennant* v. *Smith*.[35] The receipt of cash would generally fall to be taxed under the general rule in s. 19 and so not under s. 154; however, there is some authority that it can be charged under s. 154 at least if the benefit would not otherwise be taxable.[36] If the benefit could be converted into cash but only for less than its cost, it ought to follow that the cost is not "otherwise chargeable to tax on income" so that the benefit comes within s. 154.[37] If, however, the resale value is higher than cost, it appears that the Revenue can insist on the higher amount under *Tennant* v. *Smith*. S. 154 does not apply to income which is expressly excluded from tax by some other provision.[38]

[30] ICAEW Memorandum TR 786, (1990) *Simon's Tax Intelligence* 205.
[31] TA 1988, s. 156(1).
[32] Ibid., s. 154(3).
[33] If the employee pays a sum equal to the cost of providing the benefit he escapes s. 154 even though the market value is higher. *Quaere* whether a tenant paying a full market rent thereby "makes good" to the lessor any sums spent by the lessor even though those sums exceed the rent. See *Luke* v. *IRC* [1963] 1 All ER 655, 578, 40 TC 630, *per* Lord Reid but contrast Lord Guest at 586, 652.
[34] *Mairs* v. *Haughey* [1992] STC 495, 66 TC 273, CA NI.
[35] Therefore, the gift of an FA Cup Final ticket which E can sell to a ticket tout at a substantial profit is not within s. 154. However, *quaere* whether the gift of an asset which could be sold but only for a very low value would fall within s. 154—perhaps it would since in such a case what is chargeable under general principles is not "the expense".
[36] *Mairs* v. *Haughey* [1992] STC 495, 66 TC 273 (CA NI only), citing *Wicks* v. *Firth* [1983] STC 25, 56 TC 318.
[37] However, if the Revenue had believed this there would have been no need for s. 157A (see below at §17.4.1).
[38] In *Wicks* v. *Firth* [1983] STC 25, 56 TC 318 the House of Lords held that although a scholarship awarded to the taxpayer's child by his employer was a benefit provided to the taxpayer by reason of his employment, it was exempt under TA 1988, s. 331 as scholarship income. However, the effect of this decision has been reversed by TA 1988, s. 165 (see below at §17.4.8).

Provided by reason of employment

S. 154 (like s. 153) applies only where the benefit is provided "by reason of the employment". However, all provision for E, or for members of E's family or household, by the employer, R, are deemed to be made by reason of the employment—unless it can be shown that R is an individual and that the provision was made in the normal course of R's domestic, family or personal relationship.[39]

A benefit is treated as provided by the employer if it is provided at his cost. In *Wicks* v. *Firth*[40] scholarships awarded by trustees were held to be provided at the cost of the employer since the trustees used money supplied by the employer and were only performing duties imposed on them by the employer. If the benefit is provided by someone other than the employer,[41] so that the deeming provision does not apply, s. 154 will apply only if the benefit is provided "by reason of the employment". This test may be satisfied if the employment is not the sole or even the main cause but only an operative cause (i.e. a condition of benefit). The problem with this is that the test for s. 154 is then different from the general test of causation under Schedule E.[42]

17.3.2 Case-law limits on s. 154

Although s. 154 talks simply in terms of the provision of certain services, benefits or facilities, case law imposes some limits.

(1) E, the director or employee, must accept or acquiesce in the provision of the benefit. Therefore, Lord Reid in *Rendell* v. *Went*[43] considered that it was important that the director knew and accepted what was being done on his behalf even though he may not have realised how much it was costing. Lord Reid would express no opinion on the case of a company spending a large sum of money without the director's knowledge to procure an unwanted benefit.

E will usually be aware of the benefit and can avoid tax by a disclaimer.[44] However, the legislation also applies to benefits conferred on E's spouse, family, servants, dependants or guests.[45] It would seem unjustifiable to charge E with tax on sums spent in the provision of a benefit to some member of E's family of which E knew nothing, whether or not E would have been pleased if he had known, and no less unjustifiable if E had known but disapproved of it, yet E appears to be taxable.

(2) S. 154 does not require that the employee should receive the exclusive benefit. Therefore, s. 154 can apply when the service benefits both R, the employer, and E, the employee. It is immaterial that E would have spent less on the service if he had had the

[39] TA 1988, s. 168(3); *quaere* whether this can apply if the business is owned by a trust so that the trustees are the employer and a benefit is provided under the trust. This provision did not apply in *Mairs* v. *Haughey* [1992] STC 495, 66 TC 273, CA NI (where the court said that a payment which was not caused by the employment could not have been paid by reason of the employment) because the payment was not made by the employer.

[40] [1983] STC 25, 31, 56 TC 318, 363, *per* Lord Templeman; see Shipwright [1983] *BTR* 254.

[41] As in *Mairs* v. *Haughey* [1992] STC 495, 66 TC 273.

[42] [1982] STC 76, 80, 56 TC 318, 338, *per* Lord Denning M.R. This point was left open by the House of Lords: see Lord Templeman [1983] STC 25, 32, 56 TC 318, 364).

[43] [1964] 2 All ER 464, 466, 41 TC 641, 655.

[44] If E can escape tax by not using the Cup Final ticket (unless caught by convertibility), R may, of course, choose to dismiss E for such ingratitude.

[45] TA 1988, s. 168(4). E will be chargeable if the gift is to E's child.

sole choice. In *Rendell* v. *Went*[46] a company incurred expenses of £641 in the (successful) defence of one of its directors on a charge of causing death by dangerous driving. That sum was held to fall within s. 154. The expense had been incurred "in the provision of a benefit to" the director regardless of the fact that there might be good commercial reason for the expenditure and regardless of the fact that the director, left to himself, would have spent no more than £60 and no one suggested that he could have received free legal aid.

(3) The question whether there must be some benefit to the employee is a fine one. The courts have said that the receipt of a sum which was a fair valuation for loss of rights is not a benefit.[47] However it may well be that the director in *Rendell* v. *Went* would be chargeable because a service had been provided, even if he had been found guilty and given the maximum sentence so that no advantage had been gained. Similarly, where a facility is provided, it is presumably irrelevant that the employee would rather not have the benefit. Thus the cost of providing a seat in a party for the FA Cup Final would be taxable to E even though he detests football and would prefer to be at Covent Garden to attend a performance of *Götterdämmerung*—or vice versa.[48]

17.3.3 Statutory and concessionary exceptions

The following are excepted from the remit of s. 154:

(a) the provision of accommodation supplies or services used in premises occupied by the employer,[49] provided any use for non-work purposes is insignificant.[50] Thus, a director is not chargeable on sums spent on an expensive secretary or on luxurious office furniture. This test was softened in 2000 to extend the exemption to benefits used outside the workplace where they are provided solely for the purpose of the employment and used primarily for this purpose. This extension does not apply to certain expensive asset like yachts or planes;[51]
(b) meals served in canteens which are made available to the staff generally;[52]
(c) any pension, annuity, lump sum, gratuity or other like benefit to be given to the director or employee or his spouse children or dependants on his death or retirement;[53]
(d) travel warrants for HM forces;[54]
(e) medical insurance for foreign visits and medical treatment, the need for which arises while the director or employee is abroad;[55]
(f) a parking place for cars or motor cycles, or facilities for bicycles at or near the employee's place of work;[56]

46 [1964] 2 All ER 464, 41 TC 641; on apportionment, see below at §17.4.
47 *Mairs* v. *Haughey* [1992] STC 495, 66 TC 273, CA NI. This point was not argued before the House of Lords.
48 Such discrimination is ruled out by Donovan L.J. in *Butter* v. *Bennett* (1962) 40 TC 402, 414.
49 Presumably the test of occupation is that under the pre-1977 law and not that in TA 1988, s. 145 (see above at §15.3); the prime difference is category (3).
50 TA 1988, s. 155ZA added by FA 2000 Sch. 27 para 10 and superseding TA 1988, s. 155(2). Non-work use includes family use.
51 TA 1988 s. 155ZA(5).
52 TA 1988, s. 155(5). The provision of vouchers for use in a separated part of a restaurant run independently of the employer might well fall within this exception and, although vouchers for use in any restaurant would not, those for use in a particular restaurant may escape s. 154.
53 Ibid., s. 155(4).
54 Ibid., s. 197(2). But see also ESC A72 widening the list in s. 155(4) to those mentioned in s. 168(4).
55 Ibid., s. 155(6).
56 Ibid., s. 155(1A) added by FA 1988, s. 46(3); this exclusion has retroactive effect where liability was settled before 15 March 1988.

(g) entertainment by someone unconnected with E's employment;[57]
(h) benefits provided in connection with overnight absences from home;[58]
(i) living accommodation;[59]
(j) loan of computer equipment up to £500 in benefit (see below p. 290);
(k) certain child care expenses see below;
(l) loan of a bicycle or bicycle safety equipment for use on qualifying journeys;[60]
(m) a works bus service or of support for public transport bus service for use for qualifying journeys;[61]
(n) mobile phones; at one time there was a scale charge of £200 whenever a mobile telephone was provided and that phone was available for the private use of the employee or members of his family or household.[62] This was repealed in 1999 but no charge arises under the general rule in s. 154.[62a]

Legislation rendering a payment non-taxable as income may also impliedly exempt the employee from liability under s. 154, whether the payment is made to the employee or a member of his family.[63] Provisions which exclude benefits from Schedule E generally necessarily exclude any charge under s. 154 (e.g. the provision of in-house sports facilities).[64] Concessionary exemptions, such as those for miners' coal (or sums in lieu),[65] must be examined to see whether they apply to s. 154.

Child care

S. 154 does not apply to a benefit consisting of the provision of certain child care facilities.[66] This is subject to many conditions, for example: (a) the child must be one for whom the employee has parental responsibility[67] or must reside with the employee or be a child (including a step-child) of the employee and be maintained at his expense;[68] (b) the care must be provided on premises which are not domestic premises; and (c) if the premises are not made available by the employer alone, the care must be provided under arrangement made by persons who include the employer, the care must be provided on premises made available by one or more of those persons and, under the arrangement, the employer must be wholly or partly responsible for financing and managing the provision of care.[69] There is also a registration requirement for the premises.[70]

[57] Ibid., s. 155(7).
[58] Ibid., s. 155(1B), (1C); the rules in s. 200A apply.
[59] Ibid., s. 154(2).
[60] Ibid., s. 197AC, added by FA 1999, s. 50 (see below at §18.2.6).
[61] Ibid., s. 197AA, 197AB, added by FA 1999, s. 48 (see below at §18.2.6).
[62] TA 1988, s. 159A; on apportionment, see subss. (4)–(6); for definitions, see subs. (8).
[62a] s. 155A (a).
[63] See *Wicks* v. *Firth* [1983] STC 25, 56 TC 318, HL; see Shipwright [1983] *BTR* 254. The particular exemption in that case (TA 1988, s. 331) has now been the subject of special legislation (see below at §17.4.8) but the principle remains, unless the House of Lords follows its own (bad) precedent in *Thomson* v. *Moyse* (see below at §60.3).
[64] TA 1988, s. 197G.
[65] ESC A67, A6.
[66] TA 1988, s. 155A; a "child" is a person under 18, and "care" is defined as including supervised activities (s. 155A(7)). See, generally, RI 181.
[67] Defined by reference to the Children Act 1989, s. 3(1) (s. 155A(8)).
[68] Defined by TA 1988, s. 155A(3), (7).
[69] Ibid., s. 155A(2), (4), (5).
[70] Ibid., s. 155A(6).

Computer equipment

S. 154 catches an employee who has borrowed computing equipment from his employer which could be used outside the employer's premises or for non-business purposes.[71] FA 1999 makes a limited exception by excluding a charge on the first £500[72] of benefit as determined under those rules. Therefore, if R, the employer, buys a computer for £2,500 and lends it to E, the employee, the 20% charge in §17.3.5 of £500 will be exactly covered by the exception; however, if R then pays for and instals a software upgrade, a charge will apply to that excess since the threshhold will have been exceeded. Computing equipment is defined so as to include not only the computer itself (including software), but also such peripherals as modems, printers, scanners, discs and similar items designed to be connected to or inserted into the computer. Telephones are not, however, included.[73] The loan must not be confined to employees who are directors, nor may the terms offered to directors be more beneficial than those to other employees.[74] This partial exclusion rule applies only to loans.[75]

17.3.4 Extent of charge: cash equivalent

Cost

TA 1988, s. 156(2) states simply that the cost of a benefit is "the amount of any expense incurred in or in connection with its provision . . .". The practical effect is that if the cost of the benefit is £100, and the employee's, E's, marginal rate is 40%, E will acquire the benefit (£100) but pay tax of £40. However, if E had paid for the benefit out of his own pocket, the salary would have had to be increased by £167 to give £100 net of tax with which to acquire an equivalent benefit. The reason s. 154 uses this technique is to ensure consistency with s. 153; the amount charged is the same whether E receives £100 under an expense allowance which is then spent on the object, or receives the object as a benefit in kind. This example can be criticised for failing to compare like with like since the comparison is between tax of £40, leaving E with the benefit in kind, and tax of £67, leaving a benefit worth £100.

Cost—marginal or average?

In the famous case of *Pepper* v. *Hart*[76] the House of Lords held that cost meant marginal cost, not average cost. *Pepper* v. *Hart* concerned the provision of education at a private school (Malvern College) for a child of a member of the teaching staff. The member of staff paid a fee equal to one-fifth of the normal fee, which was more than enough to cover the marginal cost to the school but was substantially less than the average cost paid by other pupils. The House held that marginal cost should be used;since this had all been "made good" by the employee, no charge arose.[77]

The decision of the House was in accordance with what was thought to be general Revenue practice and, famously, what had been said to the House of Commons in 1975 (on

[71] This sentence reflects the position in 1999, i.e. when TA 1988, s. 155(2) applied; today the slightly more relaxed rules in TA 1988, s. 155ZA would apply—see above §17.3.3(a).
[72] TA 1988, s. 156A(3); s. 156A was added by FA 1999, s. 45.
[73] TA 1988, s. 156A(4), (5).
[74] Ibid., s. 156A(1)(c), (2).
[75] Ibid., s. 156A(1)(b).
[76] [1992] STC 898, 65 TC 421; criticised by Bennion [1995] *BTR* 325.
[77] On practical consequences, see Inland Revenue Press Release, 21 January 1993, (1993) *Simon's Tax Intelligence* 196.

which see chapter 3). However, the issue is not easy to resolve. Suppose that an airline provides an employee with a free seat on a flight from London to New York. One view, not canvassed in *Pepper* v. *Hart*, is that cost means opportunity cost, i.e. that if the airline could have sold the seat to an ordinary passenger at £500, it would have had an opportunity cost of £500, but it forewent the opportunity of making that sum. It is generally thought that such a cost is not "incurred". The second view, marginal cost, means the extra cost of carrying this passenger, i.e. the cost of providing another meal together with the amount of fuel needed to carry the extra weight. Of course, it might also entail a very large sum, e.g. if regulations required that another member of the cabin staff had to be hired. Matters are unclear if two employees were given the free flight but the extra member of staff was triggered by only one of them. The third view, the average cost, would mean that the airline must average the entire cost of the journey over all the passengers. However, this cost would itself be a matter of dispute since it is necessary to consider how much of the overhead cost should be included, i.e. should it be: (a) the marginal cost to the airline of running the flight, so spreading the cost over the number of passengers on the flight (a matter of some interest if, for example, the employee were the only passenger on the flight); or (b) the appropriate proportion of the cost of the entire operations of that month (or year), so treating the employee as receiving a benefit far higher than the normal fare? At present, the matter would be resolved in favour of marginal cost so that if no expense is incurred in providing the benefit, no charge can arise under s. 154.

Sale of an asset by employee to employer

Where an employee sells an asset to the employer and the cost to the employer exceeds the market value of the asset, a charge under s. 154 may arise. By concession, the Revenue does not include the transaction costs incurred, such as legal fees, in making the relevant calculations.[78] However, costs normally incurred by the vendor are not covered by this concession, nor are costs actually incurred by the employee which are reimbursed.

Asset used before transfer to employee

S. 156 (3) states that if the benefit consists of an asset, and that asset has been used or has depreciated since it was bought, the market value is to be used instead of the price.

17.3.5 Asset lent by employer

Where the asset remains the property of the employer, the employer is deemed to incur a cost equal to the sum of (a) the annual value of the asset, and (b) any other expense incurred in providing the asset other than the cost of producing or acquiring the asset.[79] The figure at (a) will be increased if the employer pays a sum by way of rent or hire which exceeds the annual value, the higher figure being taken instead.

The annual value of the asset varies according to the benefit. In the case of land, TA 1988, s. 837 applies (see above at §15.4); for other assets the figure is 20% of its market value at the time it was first applied by the employer for the employee.[80] So if an employer lends an

[78] Inland Revenue Press Release, 27 April 1994, (1994) *Simon's Tax Intelligence* 581. The rationale for the concession is to mirror TA 1988, s. 156(3) (see above at §0.00).

[79] TA 1988, s. 156(4), e.g. repair and insurance.

[80] Ibid., s.156(5); the percentage was 10% where the asset was first provided before 6 April 1980.

employee a cat, the cash equivalent will be the sum of (a) 20% of the cost of the cat plus (b) the full cost of food and any veterinary services paid for by the employer.

The costs of acquisition or production of the asset are excluded from (b) presumably because they are taken into account under (a). Acquisition and production have been construed widely. Expenditure resulting in the replacement or renewal of the asset as distinct from its maintenance is excluded; on this basis sums spent on supplying a house with a new water main were not part of (b) and so escaped tax.[81]

17.3.6 Transfer of an asset after use by employee

If an asset is subsequently transferred to the employee, E, s. 156(3) charges E on the market value of the asset when it is so transferred.[82] A different rule applies if it would give rise to a higher charge. The problem arises when an asset, e.g. a hi-fi, is lent to E and has depreciated significantly in value when the employer transfers it to E. The cash equivalent for the first two years will have been calculated on the basis of the rules already considered. Under s. 156(4) the cash equivalent on the transfer to E is the greater of (a) the asset's market value at that time less any price paid for it by the employee, and (b) the market value when it was first provided but with a deduction for amounts already taxed and any sum paid for it.[83] This alternative does not apply to cars.

Example

R provides E with a hi-fi costing £600. After two years R sells the system to E for £150, its market value being £250. E is liable on the higher of: (a) £250 − £150 = £100; and (b) £600 − (2 × 20% × £600) − £150 = £210. E is therefore liable on (b).

17.3.7 Apportionment of expenditure

If the expense is incurred by the employer partly to provide a benefit for the employee and partly for other purposes, TA 1988, s. 156(2) states that only a proper proportion of the expense so incurred will be caught by s. 154.

In *Westcott* v. *Bryan*[84] a managing director wished to live in London but the company insisted that he live in a large rambling house set in two acres of garden close to the factory in a rural area of North Staffordshire. He paid the company a rent of £140 p.a. and £500 p.a. for services and also paid the rates. In the tax year the company spent £1,017 on gas, electricity, water, insurance of contents, telephone, cleaning, window cleaning, gardener's wages and maintenance. The house was bigger than the taxpayer either needed or desired, but no specific area was set aside for the entertainment of the company's guests. The Court of Appeal held that an apportionment under TA 1988, s. 156(2) should be made even though the expenses could not clearly be severed either on a temporal or spatial basis. The method of apportionment was not canvassed in the Court of Appeal,[85] but at first instance Pennycuick J. had said that apportionment could only be calculated on a rough-and-ready

81 *Luke* v. *IRC* [1963] 1 All ER 655, 40 TC 630 (see below at p. 302).
82 TA 1988, s. 156(3); transaction costs incurred by the transferor are ignored (ibid.).
83 Ibid., s. 156(4).
84 [1969] 3 All ER 564, 45 TC 467.
85 But see ibid., Sachs L.J., 571, 493.

basis, to determine what proportion of the total expense was fairly attributable to the use or availability for use of the house by the company.[86]

Distinctions

Where a particular expense benefits both employer and employee, and no part of the expenditure is on something which benefits the employer exclusively, no apportionment can be made. In *Rendell* v. *Went*[87] (the driving case) the employer had spent a sum of money in the provision of a benefit when the employee, E, would have spent less, and no part of the sum was spent on something which did not benefit E. In *Westcott* v. *Bryan* the expenditure was made for two distinct purposes only one of which was of benefit to the director.

Set-off

Where s. 156(2) directs an apportionment, s. 156(1) limits its charge to so much of the expense as is not made good by the employee, E. Where, therefore, a sum is to be apportioned and E receives a payment for the benefit, the question arises whether the expense is apportioned first and then the payment is set off against that apportioned figure, or whether the set-off occurs first and the apportionment is then applied to that reduced figure. The former would seem more correct but the latter view appears to have been accepted in *Westcott* v. *Bryan.*

17.4 Particular Rules for Particular Benefits

17.4.1 Cars, classic cars, pooled cars and vans

In the United Kingdom company cars are much sought after. At present there are two million company car drivers and 22 m other car drivers. Tax treatment of company cars, however, has become more unfavourable. Today the taxable benefit arising from having a company car available for private use is significant. In addition, both employer's NIC (class 1A) and PAYE may be chargeable. Company cars account for over half the new car registrations in Britain, and surveys routinely show that employees would keep their company cars even if all the tax advantages were abolished.

Car available for private use: basic cash equivalent

Where a car is available for private use by reason of the employment, the employee is chargeable under s. 157 on the cash equivalent of the benefit of the car being available for private use.[88] The cash equivalent is 35% of the price of the car for that year.[89] Where two members of the same family are provided with cars by their common employer, concessionary relief ensures that each is subject to a single rather than double charge.[90] The maximum market value which can be taken for a car, whether or not it is classic, is £80,000, which may be raised by Treasury regulation. These rules make the current maximum cash

[86] 45 TC 487.
[87] [1964] 2 All ER 464, 467, 41 TC 641, 659; this distinction is criticised by Kerridge [1986] *BTR* 36.
[88] TA 1988, s. 157(1).
[89] Ibid., s. 157(2), Sch. 6, para. 1.
[90] ESC A71.

equivalent £28,000.[91] Where two or more members of a family are chargeable in respect of the same car, the benefit may, by concession, be apportioned between them.[92]

Salary sacrifice

S. 157A provides that where the employee is offered a benefit which is an alternative to the use of a car, e.g. a payment of £20 a year, the mere fact that this alternative is offered does not make the benefit chargeable under s. 19. The point is that the offer of £20 may make the benefit taxable under s. 19 and so make NIC chargeable only on £20. S. 157A prevents this avoidance of s. 157.[93]

Adjustments for business mileage; new rules from 2002–03

The 35% figures applies where the employee has no business mileage (i.e. no mileage required by the nature of his employment), or mileage is less than 2,500 miles. Where business mileage reaches 2,500 there is a reduction from 35% to 25%, with a further reduction to 15% where mileage reaches 18,000.[94] These mileage figures are proportionately reduced for periods when the car is unavailable.[95] Temporary replacements of cars and accessories of similar quality are ignored.[96] It will be seen that the current rules encourage high mileages. New rules are to apply as from April 2002, based on a mixture of the price of the car and a level of CO2 emissions.[97] In 2002–03 the lowest charge is set at 165gms per kilometre but this to be lowered in later years. The CO2 figure is then used to find a percentage on a table (minimum 15%); the taxable benefit is that percentage of the price of the car. An expensive car with high CO2 emissions and high business mileage will have a higher tax charge than now; an expensive car with low emissions and a low business mileage may well be cheaper than now. A cheap car with low CO2 emissions will certainly be cheaper than now. Mondeo man may well find little difference. Special rules apply to diesels (a surcharge applies) and to other special types of car such as bi-fuel and electric cars.

Where the car is a second (or third or higher) car, i.e. one (or more) made available to the employee concurrently with another car, the reductions for business mileage are diminished—business travel of at least 18,000 miles attracts a 25% charge.[98]

Adjustments for age of car

Chargeable amounts are reduced by one-quarter once the car is four years old at the end of the year of assessment.[99]

Offsetting payments

Sums paid by the employee to the employer for the year can be set against the cash equivalent of a company car, but only if the employee is required to pay the sums as a condition of the car being available for his private use (including use by members of his family or household).[100] Sums paid for other purposes cannot be offset. A sum paid to obtain a more

[91] TA 1988, s. 168G.

[92] ESC A71; on which, see *Taxation* (1998), Vol. 142, No. 3676.

[93] See above at §15.2.1.

[94] TA 1988, Sch. 6, para. 2, as amended by FA 1999; the pre-1999 rules reduced the charge to 22.3% and 11.67%.

[95] TA 1988, Sch. 6, para. 3; on unavailability and availability, see FA 1993, Sch.3, paras 9, 10.

[96] Income Tax (Replacement Cars) Regulations 1994 (SI 1994/778); Income Tax (Car Benefits) (Replacement Accessories) Regulations 1994 (SI 1994/777).

[97] Introduced by FA 2000 Sch 11. The notes to the Finance Bill 1999 suggested that 300 million extra business miles were driven.

[98] TA 1988, Sch. 6, para. 4, as amended by FA 1999.

[99] TA 1988, Sch. 6, para. 5, as amended by FA 1999.

[100] TA 1988, Sch. 6, para. 7.

expensive car does not reduce the benefit.[101] An insurance premium paid for a company car was held to be payable to insure the car and not for its use; since the scale charge covers the costs of insuring the vehicle this seems to be an unimaginative (and certianly non-purposive) construction of the statute.[102]

Scope

The benefits covered by the charge are all those concerned with the provision of the car, i.e. capital cost, insurance, maintenance, etc. However, the charge does not cover the costs of a chauffeur,[103] petrol[104] or car phones (unless installed and used only for business calls).[105]

Price

The relevant percentage is applied to the price of the car, a concept which is itself elaborately defined but which is basically the list price plus accessories, delivery charge, VAT and car tax.[106] Any price actually paid by the employer is ignored. An imported car is priced according to its UK list price, notwithstanding that the level of prices in the UK is notoriously high. If the car has no list price, a notional price is taken.[107]

Original accessories. The cost of standard accessories[108] included in the list price of the car will already have been brought into account. Special rules apply to other (optional) accessories, e.g. those made available as an option by the manufacturer.[109] The price of the car will have to be increased to take account of the list price of fitted accessories as set by the manufacturer or distributor where this is available—including VAT, delivery and fitting charges.[110] Where a list price is not available a notional price is used.[111] Accessories for conversion for use by a chronically sick or disabled person are ignored. [112]

Later accessories. Where an accessory is made available to E after the car is first made available,[113] the list price of accessories over £100 (including VAT, fitting and delivery) and fitted after 31 July 1993 will be included in the price of the car as regards the year in which they are fitted and all subsequent years. The removal of the accessory does not seem to have been contemplated by the legislation although the replacement of an accessory is to be covered by Treasury regulations; one wonders whether a removal can be equated with replacement by nothing. The £100 figure may be raised by Treasury regulation.

Capital contribution by E. If E makes a capital contribution to the provision of the car or accessory, the sum reduces the price of the car—not the cash equivalent. A maximum of

[101] *Brown* v. *Ware* [1995] STC (SCD) 155; E cannot deduct tax paid under s. 157 as a travelling expense under s. 198 (*Clark* v. *Bye* [1997] STC 311).

[102] *IRC* v. *Quigley* [1995] STC 931.

[103] TA 1988, s. 155.

[104] Ibid., s. 157.

[105] Statement of Practice SP 5/88.

[106] TA 1988, s. 168A(1), (2), (9); on timing of availability, see s.168A(12); on date of first registration, see s. 168(5)(d).

[107] Ibid., s. 168A(8).

[108] Ibid., s. 168A(11); see HC Official Report, Standing Committee D, cols 197–202, (1995) *Simon's Weekly Tax Intelligence* 267. Note s. 168A(11), defining accessories (but excluding a mobile phone, equipment for a disabled person to drive a car and conversion to LPG); s. 168A(10), defining qualifying accessories; and s. 168A(9)(c), (d), distinguishing standard accessories from optional accessories On timing, see s. 168A(12).

[109] TA 1988, s. 168A(9)(b), (c).

[110] Ibid., ss 168A(4), (5), 168B(2)–(4).

[111] Ibid., ss 168B(6), (7), 168B(2), (3).

[112] Ibid., s.168AA.

[113] Ibid., s. 168C.

£5,000 may be taken into account, although this sum may be raised by Treasury regulation.[114]

Classic cars. Special rules apply where the value of the car exceeds £15,000 and is higher than the manufacturer's list price when it was first registered, i.e. its price for the year. The car must be more than 15 years old at the end of the tax year.[115] In such circumstances the cash equivalent is calculated by applying the relevant percentage to the open market value of the car (and accessories) at the end of the tax year or, if different, the last day on which it was available to the employee.[116] As with other cars, contributions towards the cost of the car or accessories can be deducted up to a limit of £5,000.[117]

Exception—pooled cars

If the car is one of a pool (a concept which is elaborately defined and which broadly means that the car must be genuinely available to more than one employee and not regularly garaged at an employee's house) and any private use is purely incidental to its business use, the car is not treated as being available for the employee's use and is not a taxable emolument.[118]

Vans available for private use

A special basis of charge exists for certain commercial vehicles, statutorily referred to as vans.[119] The benefit from the private use of vans was previously exempt from the scale charge and the cash equivalent was calculated on the basis of the general rules for assets made available for the use of employees. The cash equivalent is £500 if the van is less than four years old at the end of the year concerned, or £350 if it is older.[120] The usual reductions are applicable for periods where the van is unavailable[121] or where payment is made as a condition of its being available for private use.[122]

A van is defined as a vehicle built primarily to carry goods or burdens of any description (a phrase which the Revenue clearly believes excludes the carriage of people), with a gross vehicle weight of 3.5 tonnes or less.[123] Where the gross vehicle weight exceeds this figure, any benefit from heavier vehicles is to be exempt from any charge provided the employee's use is not wholly or mainly private use.[124]

Sharing vans

Provision is made for vans which are the subject of shared use between participating employees.[125] The standard charges of £500 (or £350) for all shared vans made available by that employer are added together, and the resulting figure is divided equally between all

[114] TA 1988, s. 168D.
[115] Ibid., s. 168F(1).
[116] Ibid., s. 168F(2)–(4).
[117] Ibid., s. 168F(5)–(11).
[118] Ibid., s. 159.
[119] Ibid., s. 159AA.
[120] Ibid., Sch. 6A, para. 1.
[121] Ibid., Sch. 6A, para. 2.
[122] Ibid., Sch. 6A, para. 3.
[123] Ibid., s. 168(5A); on Revenue relief, see Inland Revenue Press Release, 16 March 1993, para. 3, (1993) *Simon's Tax Intelligence* 437.
[124] TA 1988, s. 159AC(1).
[125] Ibid., Sch. 6A, Pt II.

participating employees. Any participating employee may elect to be taxed on an alternative basis of £5 per day.[126]

17.4.2 Car fuel for company cars

Under TA 1988, s. 158 a special scale charge applies where the employer provides free petrol for private motoring in company cars: anomalously, there is no reduction in charge if the employee reimburses the employer a part of the cost. The scale charge is reduced by 50% where business mileage exceeds 18,000 miles; however, it is not increased by 50% where business mileage is less than 2,500 miles, etc.[127] This charge does not apply where an employer provides fuel for a car which is not a company car, in which case the general rules of ss 154 and 153 apply.

£8,500 threshold

A problem arises if E, an employee, has, e.g., a salary of £8,000 and potential charge of £450. E is not within the charge to tax, being below the £8,500 limit. Suppose, however, that E uses a credit card belonging to R (E's employer) to pay for £200 of repairs to the car. By TA 1988, s. 142 (see above at §14.8.3) E is taxable on £200, but on crossing the £8,500 threshold the £200 is taken out of charge again. To break this loop it is provided that car expenses which would be charged if TA 1988, s. 157 did not apply, will be taken into account in determining whether an employee is higher paid; liability will then be assessed either on the scale benefit or on the relevant expense as appropriate.[128]

Car fuel benefits for 2000–2001[129]

Petrol

Cylinder capacity of car in cubic centimetres	*Cash equivalent*
Up to 1,400 cc or less*	£1,210
1,401 to 2,000 cc*	£1,540
More than 2,000 cc*	£2,270

*Where car has no cylinder capacity the cash equivalent is £2,270.

In 1992 a lower charge for diesel was introduced. This lower charge no longer applies but the rates are still separate. For cars up to 2,000 cc the charge is £1,540; for cars above 2,000 cc the charge is £2,270.

17.4.3 Low interest loans

Under TA 1988, s. 160(1) directors and higher-paid employees are taxable on a cash equivalent of loans provided by reason of their employment.[130] A cash equivalent arises if the employee pays no interest on the loan or pays at a rate below the official rate, currently 6.25%. S. 160(2), which deals with writing off such loans, is discussed below. A loan is made

[126] Ibid., Sch. 6A, para. 8.
[127] Ibid., s. 158.
[128] Ring [1982] *BTR* 140.
[129] Income Tax (Cash Equivalents of Car Fuel Benefits) Order 1994 (SI 1994/3010).
[130] On practical problems, see ICAEW Memorandum TR 738, (1998) *Simon's Tax Intelligence* 738. On advances to meet expenses, see Statement of Practice SP 7/79. The charge arises regardless of the date of the loan (TA 1988, s. 160(7)).

when it is advanced and not when its terms are varied.[131] A loan is caught whether the employer grants or merely facilitates the loan.[132]

A loan includes any form of credit; as such, an advance of salary is caught.[133] It has been held that an interest-free equity loan, under which the borrower is to repay not the exact sum received but a proportion of the proceeds of sale of a property bought with the aid of the loan, is still a loan.[134] In *Grant* v. *Watton*[135] G, an estate agent, formed a service company to provide services to the business in return for fees from G's business. G was a director of the company. The court held that when the business failed to pay the fees to the company on time the company was providing G with a form of credit; as G was a director of the company tax was due under s. 160. In another tax context it has been held that a loan requires consensus, so that a misappropriation by a director did not give rise to a loan.[136]

The loan may be made to the employee or to his relatives. Relative is defined differently from family and means spouse, lineal ascendant or descendant, brother or sister of the employee or the spouse, and the spouses of those people.[137] It is, however, open to employees to show that they derived no benefit from the loan.[138]

Exclusions

(a) De minimis. The charge does not apply if the total of all such loans does not exceed £5,000.[139] At one time the exclusion was by reference to the amount of the cash equivalent of the loan, but this entailed all the expense of calculating the cash equivalents.

(b) Commercial terms. Loans made on commercial terms by an employer whose business includes the making of loans, where a substantial proportion of those loans are made to members of the public at large, and at arm's length, are excluded from liability to tax. The terms on which the loans are made to the employee must be comparable to the loans to the public.[140]

(c) Fixed-term loans originally at the official rate. The charge is aimed at loans below the official (market) rate of interest. If the loan is a fixed-interest loan and was not below that rate when it was made the subsequent increase in the official market rate in a later year does not cause the loan to become chargeable.[141]

(d) Death. An employee's loan ceases to be outstanding on his death[142], as such, no cash equivalents can arise for later periods.

(e) Other termination of employment. Although the legislation does not in terms address the issue of the ending of employment s. 160(1) applies only for those periods during which while the person is in employment. [143]

[131] *West* v. *Crosland* [1999] STC (SCD) 147.
[132] TA 1988, s. 160 (5)(c).
[133] *Williams* v. *Todd* [1988] STC 676, 60 TC 727.
[134] *Harvey* v. *Williams* [1995] STC (SCD) 329; and *Gold* v. *Inspector of Taxes* [1998] STC (SCD) 215 (the loan was secured on the house). The facts as reported assume that the house would go up in value; whether the lender would bear a share of any loss if the house had gone down in value is not clear.
[135] [1999] STC 330.
[136] *Stephens* v. *T. Pittas Ltd.* [1983] STC 576 (see below at §51.4).
[137] TA 1988, s. 160(6).
[138] Ibid., s. 161(4).
[139] Ibid., s. 161(1).
[140] Ibid., s. 161(1A), (1B) On Revenue practice, see Revenue interpretation RI85.
[141] Ibid., s. 161(2); on pre-1978 loans, see s. 161(3).
[142] Ibid., s. 161(6)(a).
[143] This point is the stronger because s. 160 (2) is expressly made to apply after the employment has ceased.

(f) Qualifying loans. Qualifying loans are loans in respect of which the borrower can claim deduction for the interest as a trading expense or as being for eligible for relief under s. 353.[144] Although the tax system provides relief for such interest under these rules, it first treats the cash equivalent of the benefit as arising, and then allows the deemed amount to be deducted under the other rules.[145] Qualifying loans are not taken into account in calculating the *de minimis* limit of £5,000.[146]

Relation to other tax rules

It is unclear whether an amount treated as an emolument can be a distribution under Schedule F. TA 1988, s. 20 suggests that Schedule F should prevail; what is clear is that it cannot be both.

Pre-employment loans

There is no requirement that the loan should have been made "by reason of the employment". Instead, the question is simply whether the benefit has been so obtained. Therefore, where a loan was made otherwise than by reason of employment and, on the employment beginning, the rate of interest is reduced, a charge appears to arise.[147]

Calculating the cash equivalent: the official rate

S. 160 applies whether the employee pays no interest or pays at a rate below the official rate. If the employee pays no interest, the cash equivalent will be the notional interest calculated at the official rate; if, however, he does pay interest, only the difference between what is actually paid for the year and what would be due at the official rate is brought in.[148] Loans between the same borrower and lender are aggregated; others are not—a matter of importance where different rates of interest are paid on different loans.[149]

The amount of interest due at the official rate is calculated first by taking a simple average of the loan outstanding at the beginning and end of the tax year, multiplying this by the number of months of the loan in the year and divided by 12, and then applying the official rate.[150] However, either the taxpayer or the Revenue may elect that the interest be calculated on a day-to-day basis—a matter of importance where the amount of the loan fluctuates during the year. [151] This is now fixed for a whole year in advance.[152]

Replacement loans

Further provisions deal with the calculation of the interest where an employment-related loan is replaced, directly or indirectly by a further employment-related loan, or by a non-employment-related loan which, in turn, is, in the same year of assessment or within 40 days thereafter, replaced, directly or indirectly, by a further employment-related loan. In these

[144] TA 1988 s. 160(1C).

[145] Ibid., s. 160(1A); they are treated as paid at the end of the year or trading period or, if earlier, the end of the employment.

[146] Ibid., s. 161(1)(b).

[147] *Quaere* the position of a fixed-interest loan if the interest was paid at the official rate when the loan was made but not when E becomes the employee.

[148] TA 1988, s. 160(1). The payment is "for" the year and so does not have to be paid during the year.

[149] TA 1988, Sch. 7, para. 3, as amended by FA 1991, Sch. 6, para. 3.

[150] TA 1988, Sch. 7, para. 4.

[151] Ibid., Sch. 7, para. 5; on Revenue practice, see Inland Revenue leaflet IR480, §17.25.

[152] FA 2000, s. 00.

circumstances the rules are applied as if the replacement loan or loans were the same as the first employment-related loan.[153]

Example

A has borrowed £10,000 from his employer just before the start of the year of assessment. On 30 June he repays £3,000 but on 3 September he borrows another £4,000. The amount outstanding at the end of the year of assessment is £11,000. A pays £450 in interest; assume that the official rate is 12%.

(1) Simple calculation:
Average amount outstanding during the year £11,000 + 10,000 = £10,500
Official rate at 12% would give £1,260

(2) More precise calculation:

First period 10,000 × 85/365 × 12%	£279.45
Second period 7,000 × 65/365 × 12%	£149.59
Third period 11,000 × 215/365 × 12%	£777.53
	£1,206.57

So, cash equivalent is £1,206.57 − £450 = £756.57

The official rate is determined by reference to commercial mortgage rates.[154] The official rate for 1999–2000 and 2000–2001 is 6.25%.[155]

Foreign currencies

Special rules provide for the calculation of the official rate of interest where the loan is made in the currency of a foreign country. For this rule to apply the employee must normally live in that country and have done so at some time within the period of six years ending with the year of assessment.[156] Regulations have been made for loans in Japanese yen and Swiss francs.[157]

17.4.4 Loans written off

Where the whole or part of a loan is released or written off, TA 1988, s. 160(2) imposes a charge on the amount so released or written off.[158] The release of a loan to a relative comes within this rule unless the employee can show that he derived no benefit from it.[159]

153 TA 1988, Sch. 7, para. 4(2)–(4), added by FA 1995, s. 45; a loan is employment-related if the benefit of the loan was obtained by reason of the employment; a loan is a further employment-related loan if it was obtained by reason of the same or other employment with the person who is the employer in relation to the first employment-related loan or with a person connected with that employer (on connection see TA 1988, s. 839).

154 SI 1989/1297, as amended by SI 1991/889; (1989) *Simon's Tax Intelligence* 695 and (1991) *Simon's Tax Intelligence* 434.

155 SI 1999/ 419; (1999) *Simon's Weekly Tax Intelligence* .529.

156 TA 1988, s. 160(5), words added by FA 1994, s. 88(2).

157 Taxes (Interest Rate) (Amendment) Regulations 1994 (SI 1994/1307) and Taxes (Interest Rate) (Amendment No. 2) Regulations 1994 (SI 1994/1567). The average official rates for 199? were 3.9% and 5.5% respectively (Inland Revenue Press Release, 9 April 1998, (1998) *Simon's Weekly Tax Intelligence* 604).

158 TA 1988, s. 160(2).

159 Ibid., s. 161(4).

Exceptions

(1) *Other provisions*: TA 1988, s. 160(2) does not apply if the amount written off is otherwise chargeable to tax (e.g. under s. 421);[160] however, s. 160(2) will apply if the other provision is s. 148 or 677—because the charge under those rules may be less.

(2) *Death*: no charge arises on a release which takes effect after the death of the employee.[161]

(3) *Share stop-loss rule*: where arrangements have been made with a view to protecting the holder of shares from a fall in their market value, benefits received are not caught by s. 160(2).[162] This is designed to protect those who acquired shares under incentive schemes which contained so-called stop-loss clauses; these schemes had been approved by the Revenue and it was thought wrong to alter the tax basis upon which they had been made.

Non-exceptions

S. 160(2) is quite distinct from s. 160(1) and applies whether or not the loan was chargeable under s. 160(1). The charge will therefore arise even though the loan released was used for a qualifying purpose. Similarly, the charge will arise even though the loan was released or written off after the employment ceased.[163] Where the employment later terminates or ceases to be within these rules, but the loan continues, any subsequent replacement loan will also be subject to these rules—unless it is itself under these rules regarded as having been obtained by reason of another employment.[164]

17.4.5 Share purchase schemes: deemed loans

Where (1) shares are acquired by a director or higher-paid employee as a right or opportunity offered by reason of the employment with that or any other company, and (2) the shares were issued at less than market price or in other than fully paid up form, the tax system decrees a notional loan of the difference between the amount paid for the shares and their then market value.[165] Provided the loan remains outstanding, interest at the official rate is treated as an emolument;[166] conversely, any payment of a call is treated as a repayment of the loan.[167]

When shares are acquired on a notional loan or on a real loan, and the loan is discharged or released by any arrangement involving the disposal of the shares, the aggregate amount paid for them minus any consideration received on the disposal is compared with the market value at the time of acquisition, and the amount by which the latter exceeds the former is treated as an emolument.[168] The market value at the time of the disposal is irrelevant, the purpose of this provision being to catch so-called "stop loss" arrangements under which employees would offer to accept payment at current value as satisfying the debt.

[160] Ibid., s. 161(5).
[161] Ibid., s. 161(6)(b).
[162] Ibid., s. 160(7).
[163] Ibid., s. 160(3).
[164] Ibid., s. 160(3A), added by FA 1995, s. 45(3).
[165] Ibid., s. 162. The market value ignores any restrictions other than those applying to all shares of that class.
[166] Ibid., s. 162(1).
[167] Ibid., s. 162(3)(b).
[168] Ibid., s. 162(5).

17.4.6 Living accommodation: 10% cap for certain ancillary services in certain cases

As we have seen, the provision of living accommodation is specifically excluded from TA 1988, s. 154 and is governed by s. 145 (§15.4 above). As we have also seen, the exception in s. 145(4) for the first two cases of non-beneficial occupation does not apply if the employee is a director of the company providing the accommodation, or of an associated company, unless (a) the employee has no material interest and (b) the employment is either as a full-time working director or the company is a charity or is non-profit making.[169] These rules have to be recalled when considering s. 163.

The provision of certain ancillary services is different and does fall within s. 154. However, where the occupation is excluded by s. 145(4), the taxable amount is subject to a cap. Sums in respect of (a) heating, lighting or cleaning the premises, (b) repairs (other than structural repairs)[170] maintenance or decoration, and (c) the provision of furniture or other appurtenances or effects which are normal for domestic occupation, must not exceed 10% of the emoluments of the employment. For this purpose "emoluments" include all benefits caught by s. 154 (other than the cost of these services notionally fixed at 10%—to avoid circularity) but subject to the deduction of expenses allowable under s. 198.

Subsidiary rules

Where the accommodation is provided for part of the year, but the employment is for a longer (or shorter) period, the percentage is applied to the emoluments attributable to the period of occupation. Any sums made good by the employee are deducted from the 10% cap. The 10% limit does not apply where the director has a stake of more than 5% or is a part-time director of a profit-seeking concern (because such a person cannot come within s. 145(4) in any case).

The 10% limit does not apply where the ancillary services are other than those listed; liability in respect of such services is without limit. The specific exception of structural repairs is presumably because the Revenue accepts the view expressed in *Luke* v. *IRC*[171] that these are part of the cost of acquiring or producing the asset under s. 156(5)(b).[172] Costs to the owner as owner, such as insurance and feu duty, are presumably part of the cost of providing the living accommodation and so fall within s.145.[173]

17.4.7 Tax paid by employer

If an employer fails to deduct tax from a director's emoluments under PAYE, but that tax is accounted for to the Revenue by someone other than the director, a chargeable benefit arises equal to the tax accounted for.[174] The benefit is reduced by the amount of any reimbursement made by the director. An amount accounted for after the employment ends is treated as a benefit of the last year of assessment in which the director was employed by the com-

[169] TA 1988, s. 155(3); ESC A61 does not apply to clergymen earning over £8,500 p.a.

[170] Including repairs which would be the landlord's responsibility under a lease within the Landlord and Tenant Act 1985, ss 11, 16, 36.

[171] [1963] 1 All ER 655, 40 TC 630; FA 1976, s. 62(5).

[172] This was the line taken by Lord Guest, Lord Pearce and by Lord Reid ("this is a case of any port in a storm", 665, [1963] 1 All ER 655, 40 TC 630, 646) and by Lord Dilhorne, 661, 643. The consequence of the repair will be an increase in the annual value of the premises. To hold that the expense of repair did not fall within s. 156(5) and then to increase the annual value would be a flagrant case of double taxation.

[173] See, however, *Luke* v. *IRC*, above at n. 171, on the forerunner of s. 154.

[174] TA 1988, s. 164.

pany, unless it was accounted for after the director's death.[175] The provision applies only to directors and then only if they have no material interest in the company (i.e. not more than 5% interest) and they are full-time working directors, or the company is non-profit-making or a charity.[176]

17.4.8 Scholarships

TA 1988, s. 331 provides a general exemption from income tax for scholarship income.[177] S. 165 restricts this exemption from s. 154 to the person holding the scholarship[178]—reversing the decision of the House of Lords in *Wicks* v. *Firth*.[179] Under s. 165 a director or employee earning £8,500 p.a. or more receives a taxable benefit if a scholarship is provided to a member of his family or household under arrangements made by his employer or a person connected with E.

Exception

No taxable benefit arises if the scholarship is awarded under a trust or scheme to a person receiving full-time education, and not more than 25% of the payments made under the trust in that year would have been taxable were it not for this provision[180] (i.e. the payments would have been exempt under s. 331 but for s. 165).

[175] Ibid., s. 164(3).
[176] Ibid., s. 164(2).
[177] Under ibid., s. 331.
[178] Ibid., s. 165.
[179] [1983] STC 25, 56 TC 318 (see above at §17.1).
[180] TA 1988, s. 165(3).

18

Schedule E—Part VI: Expenses

18.1 Introduction

TA 1988, s. 198, as rewritten in 1998,[1] states that "If the holder of an office or employment is obliged to incur and defray out of the emoluments (a) qualifying travelling expenses or (b) any amount, other than qualifying travelling expenses, expended wholly exclusively and necessarily in the performance of the duties of the office or employment". These words preserve most of the old concepts. The minor presentational change is the removal of a reference to the costs of keeping horse to enable employees to perform their duties.[2] The major change is in new detailed rules for travel. To be deductible, an expense must relate to an employment[3] and must have actually been incurred.[4] For the rules where a foreign element is involved, see above at §13.3.2.

18.2 Qualifying Travelling Expenses[5]

(a) Repeating the old law almost word for word, the first category of expenses consists of amounts necessarily expended on travelling in the performance of the duties of the

[1] FA 1998, s. 61, superseding an earlier effort in FA 1997, s. 62.

[2] The horse was introduced in 1853 (see 116 and 17 Vict c. 34, s. 51); on its Trojan characteristics, see Lord Reid in *Taylor* v. *Provan* [1974] STC 168, 175, [1974] 1 All ER 1201, 1206 49 TC 579, 605. For another view of the horse, see Pollock M.R. in *Ricketts* v. *Colquhoun* [1925] 1 KB 725, 732. See also *Elderkin* v. *Hindmarsh* [1988] STC 267, 60 TC 651.

[3] In *Harrop* v. *Gilroy* [1995] STC (SCD) 294 a taxpayer unsuccessfully argued for expenses to be relieved against unemployment benefit.

[4] In *Bevins* v. *McLeish* [1995] STC (SCD) 342, the taxpayer unsuccessfully argued for relief for expenditure that had not actually been made.

office or employment. TA 1998 goes on to provide expressly that expenses of travel by an employee, the holder of an office or employment, between two places at which the employee performs duties of different offices or employments under or with companies in the same group, are treated as necessarily expended in the performance of the duties which the employee is to perform at the destination and so are deductible.[6] A 51% subsidiary test is used to determine when companies are members of the same group.[7]

(b) The Act goes on to add a second category of qualifying expenses, i.e. other expenses of travelling which (i) are attributable to the necessary attendance at any place of the holder of the office or employment in the performance of the duties of the office or employment, but (ii) which are not expenses of ordinary commuting or private travel.[8] Of these, (i) is designed to clarify the law concerning the costs of travel to or from home or a temporary workplace, while (ii) is designed to prevent (i) from opening the door too wide. These changes were intended to clarify the law; the explanation of the original clarifications was rumoured to be 50 pages long.

18.2.1 Category (a): established law

Category (a) above provides much of the background to category (b). The two categories are alternatives; it is enough for the sum to come within one of them to be deductible. Under category (a) an employee may deduct amounts necessarily expended on travelling in the performance of the duties of the office or employment. This rule is very strict and concessions have been made for particularly hard cases, the most interesting being the exemption of extra travel and subsistence allowances when public transport was disrupted by strikes or other industrial action; where the employee had to work late or was severely disabled; or where car-sharing arrangements had broken down.[9] Other concessions have been superseded by category (b).[10]

In the performance of the duties of the office

To be deductible the cost must be "incurred in the performance of the duties of the office"—and necessarily so incurred. The Revenue view is that it is not necessary to take the shortest possible route provided there were good business reasons for the route chosen.[11] The costs of travelling to work from home are not, in general, deductible[12] under this head because the costs are incurred not in the course of performing the duties but in order to get to the place where the duties are to be performed. Therefore, an employee cannot deduct the extra costs of having to travel to work by car even though the car is needed for work once he gets there.[13]

6 TA 1988, s. 198(1B).

7 Ibid.; one may be a 51% subsidiary of the other, or both may be 51% subsidiaries of a third company.

8 Ordinary commuting or private travel is defined in TA 1988, Sch. 12A.

9 ESC A58, A59, A66 (revised 1999).

10 ESC A65 and RI 73.

11 RI 99.

12 *Cook* v. *Knott* (1887) 2 TC 246; *Revell* v. *Elsworthy Bros & Co. Ltd.* (1890) 3 TC 12; *Andrews* v. *Astley* (1924) 8 TC 589; *Ricketts* v. *Colquhoun* [1926] AC 1, 10 TC 118.

13 *Burton* v. *Rednall* (1954) 35 TC 435. It is interesting to compare the position in tort when the question is whether an employee is acting in the course of his employment (see *Smith* v. *Stages* [1989] AC 928, [1989] 1 All ER 833, HL).

Necessarily

In deciding whether an expense is incurred necessarily the courts began with an objective test. In *Ricketts* v. *Colquhoun*[14] Lord Blanesburgh said that the expense had to be one which each and every occupant of the particular office was necessarily obliged to incur. Thus, the necessity must emerge from the job rather than from the personal circumstances of the employee; as such, a Recorder travelling from home to court can deduct the expenses only if they would be incurred by any other person fulfilling the duties of that office which was not so.

However, this view, although making some sense in the context of a long-established statutory office with very particular duties, such as a Recorder, is inconsistent with the modern bargaining process under which the goals of an employment contract may be coloured by the interests of both employer and employee. This inevitably demands that more attention be paid to the needs of the employees, particularly when individual contracts are being negotiated with senior employees.[15] As two later decisions of the House of Lords show, in determining whether the expense would be incurred by each and every occupant of the office, it is now necessary to consider who could be appointed to hold the office. If the range of reasonable appointees is restricted, the test must be applied in relation to such potential appointees, and it is then necessary to ask whether each of these persons, if appointed, would have to incur the expense; if the answer is "yes", then the expense is deductible notwithstanding that some other person, who would not be a suitable appointee, might not have to incur it (*Owen* v. *Pook*).[16] In an extreme case it may be possible to show that the taxpayer is the only person in the world who can carry out the duties (*Taylor* v. *Provan*[17]).

18.2.2 Three House of Lords' cases

(1) *Ricketts* v. *Colquhoun*[19]

The taxpayer (R) lived in London and was a practising member of the London Bar. He was taxable under Schedule D, Case II in respect of his earnings at the Bar. He was also Recorder of Portsmouth and was taxable under Schedule E in respect of his earnings from this source. He sought to deduct the costs of travelling from his home to Portsmouth. The House of Lords rejected his appeal on two main grounds. First, when travelling to his place of work he was travelling not in the course of those duties but in order to enable him to perform them;[20] his duties only began at Portsmouth. Secondly, the expenses could not be said to have been incurred necessarily;[21] since a recorder could have lived in Portsmouth, the costs of travel from London were not necessary. A further point was that his choice of abode in London was a personal matter and the expenses consequent on that choice were therefore personal expenses.

[14] [1926] AC 1, 7, 10 TC 118, 135 (*cf.* Lord Salmon in *Taylor* v. *Provan* [1975] AC 194, 227, 49 TC 579, 622).
[15] Ward [1988] *BTR* 6.
[16] (1969) 45 TC 571.
[17] [1974] STC 168, [1974] 1 All ER 1201, 49 TC 579.
[18] See Ward [1988] *BTR* 6.
[19] [1926] AC 1, 10 TC 118.
[20] Ibid., 4, 133, *per* Lord Cave L.C.
[21] Ibid., 7, 135, *per* Lord Blanesburgh. *Cf.* Lord Salmon in *Taylor* v. *Provan* [1974] STC 168, 190, [1974] 1 All ER 1201, 1223, 49 TC 579.

(2) *Owen* v. *Pook*[22]

The taxpayer (O) was a medical practitioner who resided at Fishguard. He also held part-time appointments as obstetrician and anaesthetist at Haverfordwest 15 miles away. Under these appointments O was on "standby duty" two weekends a month and on Monday and Friday nights, at which times he was required to be accessible by telephone. If he was called at home, O would give advice by phone, sometimes set out at once and at other times await further reports. He was responsible for his patient as soon as he received the telephone call. Although he received a payment for travelling expenses this was only for the last 10 of his 15 miles. O was assessed in respect of the payments received for the 10 miles and denied his claim for deduction in respect of the five miles. His appeal to the courts against this assessment was successful. Since he had two places where his duties were performed, the hospital and his residence with the telephone, the expenses of travel between the two places were deductible.[23] Lord Wilberforce said that the job as actually constituted and the purpose for which he incurred the expenses differed greatly from *Ricketts* case.[24]

(3) *Taylor* v. *Provan*[25]

This case suggests that the personal qualifications of the taxpayer may sometimes supply the material to satisfy the objective test of necessity. The taxpayer (T) was a Canadian citizen living in Toronto. He was the acknowledged expert in the brewing world on successful expansion by means of amalgamation and merger. T did most of his work in connection with the English amalgamations in Canada and the Bahamas, but he made frequent visits to England. He had extensive Canadian interests for which he worked from his offices in Toronto and the Bahamas. He agreed to serve as director of brewing companies "for reasons of prestige", although this had the unfortunate effect of bringing him within what are now TA 1988, ss 153, 154. T received no fees for his services since he regarded it as a business recreation, but his travelling expenses were reimbursed. The House of Lords held unanimously that the reimbursements were sums spent on behalf of the company and were taxable under TA 1988, s. 153. The House held (by 3–2) that the expenses were deductible. Of the majority, Lord Morris[26] and Lord Salmon[27] held that the taxpayer's duties were performed both in the UK and in Canada so that there were at least two places of work. Travel to England could not therefore be dismissed as travel from home to a place of work.

Lord Reid, however, gave a rather different account of *Owen* v. *Pook*.[28] He considered that the distinguishing fact in *Owen* was that O had been in part-time employment, and that it had been impossible for the employer to fill the post otherwise than by appointing someone with commitments that could not be given up. It was therefore necessary that whoever was appointed should incur travelling expenses. This approach goes much wider than any pronouncement in recent years and undermines both the decision of the House of Lords in *Ricketts* v. *Colquhoun* and much of the practice of the Revenue. It followed that the expenses

[22] [1969] 2 All ER 1, 45 TC 571. *Owen* v. *Pook* was distinguished in *Bhadra* v. *Ellam* [1988] STC 239, *Parikh* v. *Sleeman* [1988] STC 580 (upheld on narrower grounds, [1990] STC 233, CA) and *Knapp* v. *Martin* [1999] STC (SCD) 13 (all cases concerning the medical profession).

[23] See Lord Guest, 45 TC 571, 590, Lord Pearc, 591 and Lord Wilberforce, 596.

[24] Ibid.; see Ward [1988] *BTR* 6, 14, 15.

[25] [1974] STC 168, [1974] 1 All ER 1201, 49 TC 579.

[26] Ibid., 177, 1210, 609.

[27] Ibid., 191, 1224, 623.

[28] Ibid., 174, 1207.

were deductible because T was the only person who could do this job which he was only willing to do from Canada, and that he did some of the work in Canada.

The question arises how far Lord Reid's approach undermines the earlier decision in *Ricketts* v. *Colquhoun.* No member of the majority in *Taylor* v. *Provan* wished to question the result of that earlier decision but Ricketts' post as Recorder of Portsmouth was part time and anyone appointed would, at that time, have had to be a member of the Bar. However, Ricketts was not the only member of the Bar who could have been appointed and it was possible that another appointee would have lived in Portsmouth. Another explanation supporting the older case could be that Rickett's home was not a place of work. This would conclude the matter, if as may well be the case,[29] Lord Reid's explanation of *Owen* v. *Pook* rested on the assumption that there were two places of work.

An alternative explanation—itinerants

The explanation of *Owen* v. *Pook* and *Taylor* v. *Provan* may not be that home was one of the places of work, but that in each case their employment was, in a sense, itinerant. In *Owen* v. *Pook* there was no reason why the employment should have been located in O's home. What mattered was that he assumed responsibility for the patient when he received the telephone message. If he was out with friends for the evening and had given their telephone number instead of his own, that should not make his friend's house one of his places of work. The point was *when* his duties commenced rather than *where.* In the same way, in *Taylor* v. *Provan* the House of Lords seemed to be concerned with the question "was he travelling in the performance of his duties" rather than "was his office a home and, if not, did he travel from his office or from his home". On this approach one can reconcile the earlier decision of *Nolder* v. *Walters*[30] where an airline pilot sought unsuccessfully to deduct the cost of travelling from his home to the airport. The fact that he was summoned by his employer made no difference. While travelling to the airport he was not under his employer's command. He was travelling to his office, not from one office to another. If this approach is right far more attention is being paid to the subjective circumstances of the parties to the contract than was apparent from the approach of Lord Blanesburgh in *Ricketts* v. *Colquhoun.*[31]

18.2.3 Amount

It is unclear whether the objective rule that the expenses must have been necessarily incurred limits the *amount* of expenditure that may be deducted. In *Marsden* v. *IRC*[32] the taxpayer, who was an investigator in the Audit Division of the Inland Revenue, used his car for travelling on official business. There was no evidence that he could not have travelled by public transport. His claim to deduct the difference between the allowance he received, which was based on car mileage, and what he actually spent, was rejected by his employers and by the courts. Pennycuick J. said that the scale of expenses must be a question of fact and degree, and that the answer must turn not only on the price of transport but also on such considerations as speed, convenience, the purpose of the journey, and the status of the

[29] This emerges from ibid., 174, 1207, 605.

[30] (1930) 15 TC 380.

[31] See, generally, Ward [1988] *BTR* 6.

[32] [1965] 2 All ER 364, 42 TC 326; see also *Perrons* v. *Spackman* [1981] STC 739 where it was held that a mileage allowance was an emolument of the taxpayer's employment, since it included a significant contribution to the overhead costs of putting a car, which was maintained for both private and official use, on the road and could not therefore be a mere reimbursement of expenses actually incurred.

officer, etc.[33] In *Owen* v. *Pook*[34] Lord Wilberforce rejected the idea that an expense was deductible only if precisely those expenses had to be incurred by each and every employee.

18.2.4 *Category (b): travel to or from a temporary workplace*

Category (b) establishes that expenses may be deducted where they are attributable to the necessary attendance at any place of the holder of the office or employment in the performance of the duties of the office or employment, provided these expenses are not expenses of (i) ordinary commuting or (ii) private travel.

The first words retain both the element of necessity and of the performance of duties and seem to be inspired by (and fit the facts of) the decisions in *Owen* v. *Pook* and *Taylor* v. *Provan;* however, the words also fit *Ricketts* v. *Colquhoun.* Their purpose is, subject to exclusions (i) and (ii), to allow the costs of travel from home or a *permanent* workplace, to a *temporary* workplace—and of the return travel. The rule allows the deduction of all costs so incurred and not, as was first enacted, only the additional costs. In computing additional costs it was initially proposed that there would be a deduction for any saving realised by not having to incur ordinary commuting costs; however, this proved unworkable.[35]

A workplace is permanent if it is one which the employee regularly attends in the performance of the duties of the employment provided it is not a temporary workplace.[36] The concept of the permanent workplace has to be extended for depots and bases and for area-based employees.[37] The key to the new rule is the temporary (non-permanent) workplace, defined as a place which the employee attends in the performance of the duties of the employment for the purpose of performing a task of limited duration or for some other temporary purpose. This clearly fits *Owen* v. *Pook* and *Taylor* v. *Provan,* but it also fits *Ricketts* v. *Colquhoun*; Haverfordwest, London and Portsmouth were all temporary. The concept of a temporary workplace is narrowed by the exclusion of a place where the employee is to work for 24 months or for all of a fixed term.[38]

Exclusion of ordinary commuting travel

Ordinary commuting travel means travel between the employee's home and permanent workplace; it also covers travel from a place that is not a workplace in relation to the employment, to that permanent workplace.[39] Commuting expenditure is therefore non-deductible whether it is on travel from home or from a friend's home or a hotel. Travel between any two places which is for practical purposes substantially ordinary commuting travel is treated as ordinary commuting travel.[40]

[33] [1965] 2 All ER 364, 367, 42 TC 326, 331. One may add that of these the status of the officer looks extremely odd and the Revenue's own scale of allowances made to Marsden, which gave, depending upon the type of business on which he was engaged, two quite distinct allowances, makes a nonsense of some of the arguments used by the Inland Revenue in these cases.

[34] [1969] 2 All ER 1, 12, 45 TC 571, 596.

[35] TA 1988, s. 198A, proposed to be added by FA 1997, s. 62 but repealed by FA 1998, s. 61 without having ever coming into effect. See Inland Revenue Press Release, 8 April 1998, (1998) *Simon's Tax Intelligence* 602.

[36] Ibid., Sch. 12A, para. 4.

[37] Ibid., Sch. 12A paras 6, 7.

[38] Ibid., Sch. 12A, paras 4, 5.

[39] TA 1988, Sch. 12A, para. 2(1).

[40] Ibid., Sch. 12A, para. 3.

Exclusion of private travel[41]

There can be no deduction for costs of travel between the employee's home and a place that is not a workplace[42] in relation to the employment (E1). If the place is one where the employee, E, works, but for a different employer (E2) or on E's own account, the costs are not deductible from the emoluments of E1. In addition, there can be no deduction for the costs of travel between two places if neither is a workplace in relation to the employment. The Recorder's travel to Portsmouth in *Ricketts* v. *Colquhoun* was private so far as the Lord Chancellor's Department was concerned. Travel between any two places which is, for practical purposes, substantially ordinary private travel is treated as private travel.[43]

Application of rule

The words requiring that the travel be required by the employment are presumably to be applied objectively. The Revenue has stated that it will not seek to disallow first class rail travel on the ground that only standard class was necessary.[44] However, this does not allow relief where the mode of transport is a form of reward as opposed to being attributable to business travel.[45]

Examples[46]

Alan has his permanent workplace in Bristol, where he is a lathe operator. One day he has to travel from home to Bath to look at a new machine. He is entitled to relief for the full cost of his return journey from home to Bath because it is a journey to a temporary workplace.

Betty lives in Cheltenham and each day drives to her permanent workplace in Swindon where she works as a trainee accountant. No relief is available for the journey from Cheltenham to Swindon as this is ordinary commuting.

Clive lives and works in Dagenham but goes to Devon for the weekend to stay with friends. He remains in Devon on the Monday, working on papers he has brought with him from the office. He is not entitled to relief for the cost of the journey from Dagenham to Devon as it is private travel.

Derek normally works at his employer's offices in Edinburgh, travelling each day from his home in East Kilbride. One day he has to visit Perth to undertake some work in Perth for his employer. The cost of the return journey from East Kilbride to Perth is £34. Derek is entitled to relief for £34, being the full cost of the business travel.

Emma is an engineer who works on installing machines at the premises of her employer's various clients throughout the UK. Emma has no permanent workplace and attends each temporary workplace for a short period only. One week she travels between her home in Folkestone to work at an employer's client's premises in Falkirk, where she stays in a hotel for four nights and then returns to Folkestone. The cost of the Folkestone to Falkirk return journey is £130. The cost of four nights in the hotel plus meals is £300. Emma is entitled to relief for £430, being the full cost of her business travel.

41 Ibid., Sch. 12A, para. 2.

42 I.e. a place at which the employee's attendance is necessary in the performance of the duties of the employment (ibid., Sch. 12A, para. 2(3)).

43 Ibid., Sch. 12A, para. 3.

44 IR booklet IR161, para. 5.14.

45 Ibid., para. 5.15.

46 Based on ibid., para. 1.11.

18.2.5 Other travel rules

Incidental overnight expenses

TA 1988, s. 200A provides a statutory exclusion for certain incidental overnight expenses. The broad effect is to exclude any charge on the expenses[47] where the overnight accommodation costs associated with them would be allowable deductions under the various travel rules.[48] A maximum of £5 per night is available for expenses in the UK and £10 elsewhere, but these limits may be varied by statutory instrument. The limits are spread over the period of absence rather than being applied to each night separately, but the effect of exceeding the maximum is that the whole sum becomes taxable.

An allowable, incidental, overnight expense is one paid wholly and exclusively for the purpose of defraying, or of being used for defraying, any expense which is incidental to being away from the usual place of abode during a qualifying absence from home. An absence from home qualifies if it is a continuous period throughout which the employee is obliged to stay away from his usual place of abode and during which he has at least one overnight stay away from his place of abode. In addition, there must be no overnight stay at a place other than a place the expenses of travelling to which are deductible expenses which would be deductible if they had been incurred.

Car parking

The provision of car parking facilities (s. 197A) is also excluded from various heads of charge. The reason for this apparently strict rule is that an earlier attempt to charge such benefits was found to be unworkable. (See §15.1.1)

Miscellaneous—official travel

The legislation contains exceptions for leave travel facilities for the armed forces (TA 1988, s. 197) and for incidental benefits to holders of certain public offices (s. 200AA). Special rules apply to allowances for MPs, which have now been extended to the costs of visits to EC institutions in Brussels, Luxembourg or Strasbourg.[49] The rules have also now been extended to members of the Scottish Parliament and Welsh Assembly.[50]

18.2.6 Employer assistance with travel to and during work

FA 1999 introduces five provisions to prevent the tax system interfering with environmentally sensible ideas on the part of employers. By giving relief for the costs of travel to work as well as during work these rules represent a major change of theory.

[47] Added by FA 1995, s. 93 The exclusion is effective for TA 1988, ss 141 (non-cash vouchers: s. 141(6C)), 142 (credit tokens: s. 142(3C)), s. 153, 155(1B), (1C) (charge under s. 154).

[48] Ibid., s. 200A(l)–(3), i.e. not only TA 1988, s. 198, but also ss 193, 194 (foreign travel), 195 (employees not domiciled in the UK) and 332 (minister of religion). However, some provisions allowing the deduction of travel expenses do not open the door to s. 200A: s. 193(4) (board and lodging) and ss 194(2), 195(6) (accompanying spouse or child).

[49] TA 1988, s. 200 amended by FA 1993, s. 124.

[50] FA 1999, s. 52.

Works bus service

TA 1988, s. 197AA removes any charge to tax under either s. 154 or the vouchers rules in s. 141 if an employer provides a works bus service.[51] The bus must have a seating capacity of 12 or more (so excluding minibuses).[52] The service must be one for conveying employees on qualifying journeys; the employees may belong to one or more employers.[53] Journeys qualify not only if they are between one workplace and another but also, and in complete contrast to the rules in s. 198A, between home and workplace.[54] In either case the journey must be in connection with the performance of the duties of the office or employment, and the service must be available to employees generally.[55]

In an unusual—and hideous—legislative form of words, the exemption is stated to be "subject to substantial compliance with the condition that the service must be used only by employees or their children".[56] This means that the exemption will not be lost just because the bus is used for some other occasional purpose. It is necessary, however, to distinguish the service from the bus itself. If the bus is used for qualifying journeys and for separate non-qualifying journeys there will be a charge for the latter; if, however, there are non-qualifying aspects to a single journey there will be a charge unless the substantial compliance condition is satisfied. The reference to children allows the bus to be used for getting children to school, but is not confined to that.[57]

Support for public transport

TA 1988, s. 197AB removes any charge under s. 154 where an employer provides financial or other support for a public transport bus service. Again, the employees may belong to one or more employers and the service must be for qualifying journeys.[58] The support must be provided directly to the operator, the terms on which the employees travel must not be more favourable than to other passengers, and the service must be available to employees generally; as before, the bus must be a large bus.[59] The substantial compliance condition is repeated here;[60] its effect is that the support should be only (or substantially only) for qualifying journeys.

Motor bikes and cycles

The various exemptions from tax for car parking spaces are extended to spaces for parking motor cycles and facilities for parking cycles.[61] Why cycles need "facilities" and motor cycles need only "spaces" is unclear. Presumably this wording is intended to cover facilities for locking bicycles up.

[51] TA 1988, s. 197AA(1), (2), added by FA 1999, s. 48.
[52] TA 1988, s. 197AA(3), (8).
[53] Ibid., s. 197AA(2).
[54] Ibid., s. 197AA(3), (7).
[55] Ibid., s. 197AA(4), (7).
[56] Ibid., s. 197AB(4).
[57] Children are defined in ibid., s. 197AA(5); they must not be over 17.
[58] Ibid., s. 197AB(1), (2), added by FA 1999, s. 49.
[59] TA 1988, s. 197AB(1), (3), (6).
[60] Ibid., s. 197AB(4).
[61] FA 1999, s. 50, extending TA 1988, ss 141(6A), 142(3A) 155(1A), 197A; cycle and motor cycle are defined by reference to the Road Traffic legislation (s. 46(3)) and include tricycles as well as bicycles.

Bikes (and trikes)

TA 1988, s. 197AC removes any charge under s. 154 or 141 where an employer lends an employee a cycle or a cyclist's safety equipment.[62] The benefit or facility must be available to employees generally. The employee must use it only for qualifying journeys, but this condition is subject to the same substantial compliance language as s. 197AB.[63] Safety equipment is not defined, but presumably includes lights, reflective strips and coats and safety helmet; it is unlikely to cover fancy gears (which will be part of the cycle) or a rain-cape or lock. Some softening of these boundaries may occur in practice.

Bicycle mileage

In addition, the Revenue has announced a tax-free business allowance of 12p per business mile. This allows an employer to pay an employee such a sum and for the employee to claim that allowance to the extent that the employer does not pay it. The employee may not claim both this allowance and the capital allowance.[64] Contrary to the terms of the capital allowance legislation, the Revenue intends to allow costs of travel to and from work under this head.

18.2.7 Motor mileage allowances

If R, the employer, pays E, the employee, a mileage allowance, any profit made by E is taxable under general principles. There is, however, a voluntary administrative arrangement known as the fixed-profit car scheme. The scheme is a safe harbour scheme; sums paid within the limits are safe. The scheme covers only sums paid for business travel—not sums paid for private travel.

Rates for 2000–01 are as follows:[65]

Up to 4,000 miles	*After 4,000 miles*	
Up to 1,000 c.c.	28p	17p
1,000–1,500 c.c.	35p	20p
1,501–2,000 c.c.	45p	25p
over 2,000 c.c.	63p	36p

As part of this adjustment the rules with regard to capital allowances and on loans to finance the purchase of cars are relaxed by the removal of the word "necessarily".[66]

Mileage allowances—the difference between the Revenue's conservative estimate of running costs and the higher figures paid by companies are considered to be remuneration and, as such, taxable. Figures published by motoring organisations often include the costs of breakdown recovery and of interest foregone on the value of the car—which are clearly liable to tax.

62 TA 1988, s. 197AC(1), (5), added by FA 1999, s. 47(1).
63 TA 1988, s. 197AC(4).
64 Inland Revenue Notes to Finance Bill 1999, cl. 47 (which became FA 1999, s. 50.
65 Inland Revenue Press Release, 14 December 1999, (2000) *Simon's Weekly Tax Intelligence* 7.
66 See amendments to CAA 1990, s. 27 and TA 1988, s. 359.

18.3 Expenses other than Travelling Expenses

Like travelling expenses, non-travelling expenses must be incurred in the performance of the duties of the office or employment and necessarily be so incurred. In addition, these other expenses must also be incurred wholly and exclusively in the performance of those duties. The words of TA 1988, s. 198 were described by Vaisey J.[67] as being "stringent and exacting; compliance with each and every one of them is obligatory if the benefit of the rule is to be claimed successfully. They are to my mind, deceptive words in the sense that when examined they are found to come to nearly nothing at all".

18.3.1 In the performance of duties

As with travelling expenses the cases draw a sharp distinction between expenditure incurred *in the performance of* the duties of an office, and expenditure incurred in order either to enable the employee to do the job initially[68] or to enable him to perform the duties of that office more efficiently. Thus, the cost of a housekeeper to look after one's family and so enable one to go out to work is not deductible,[69] a situation which will be radically changed in effect (but not in theory) by the working families tax credit.

Subscriptions

Under s. 198, subscriptions to professional bodies paid by a county medical officer of health were disallowed,[70] even though the journals received from those societies enabled him to keep himself properly qualified. This rule has subsequently been reversed by statute and subscriptions are now deductible—but only to listed societies and a very limited list of professional bodies[71] (the list does not cover trade unions). This does not usually extend to allow professional people to claim tax relief on their membership subscriptions to professional bodies while employed.[72] An actor is now allowed to deduct agent's fees, including payments to bona fide co operatives.[73]

Improvement not enough

A schoolteacher who attended a series of weekend lectures in history at a college for adult education for the purposes of improving his background knowledge could not deduct those expenses.[74] There is a distinction between qualifying to teach and getting background material, on the one hand, and preparing lectures for delivery, on the other hand.[75] Similarly a

[67] *Lomax* v. *Newton* (1953) 34 TC 558, 561–2.

[68] *Lupton* v. *Potts* [1969] 3 All ER 1083, 45 TC 643; *Elderkin* v. *Hindmarsh* [1988] STC 267, 60 TC 651.

[69] *Bowers* v. *Harding* [1891] 1 QB 560, 3 TC 22; *Halstead* v. *Condon* (1970) 46 TC 289.

[70] *Simpson* v. *Tate* [1925] 2 KB 214, 9 TC 314, Rowlatt J.

[71] TA 1988, s. 201; the list of professions does not include lawyers or accountants, but this does not prevent people in self-employment from deducting these costs. A list of approved societies is available from the Inland Revenue for £5; see (1998) *Simon's Tax Intelligence* 986. On fees for solicitor's practising certificates, see notice by the Law Society, 24 February 1993, (1993) *Simon's Tax Intelligence* 341.

[72] HC Written Answer, 30 March 1990, (1990) *Simon's Tax Intelligence* 317.

[73] TA 1988, s. 201A, added by FA 1990, s. 77, as amended by FA 1991, s. 69.

[74] *Humbles* v. *Brooks* (1962) 40 TC 500; but contrast ESC A64 and Individual Learning Accounts (above chapter 15).

[75] (1962) 40 TC 500, 504. Even if this distinction had been ignored the expenditure might have failed on the ground of necessity since it was possible that a properly qualified history teacher could have been appointed who would not have needed to attend the course.

clerk who was obliged to attend late meetings of the council and who bought himself a meal before the meeting was not allowed to deduct the cost of the meal; he had been instructed to work late, not to eat.[76] On similar grounds an employee was not allowed to deduct the costs of a record player and gramophone records which he had purchased for the purpose of providing a stimulus of good music while he worked especially late at night. As Cross J. drily observed, "it may well be that (he) was stimulated to work better by hearing good music, just as other people may be stimulated to work better by drink . . .".[77]

Newspapers

The House of Lords demands uniformity between Scotland and England. The distinction between expenditure incurred in the performance of the duties of the office and that which is incurred simply to prepare oneself to carry out those duties has been recent case-law. In *Smith* v. *Abbott*[78] four journalists claimed in respect of expenditure on newspapers and periodicals.[79] The Commissioners held in relation to each of them that the reading of the material was a necessary part of their duties as staff photographer, sports reporter, news sub-editor and picture editor; it was inherent in their jobs. They therefore concluded that the expenses were deductible. This was upheld by Warner J. and by the Court of Appeal, but reversed (by a majority) by the House of Lords. Lord Templeman pointed out that the reading was not done at their place of work but at home, while travelling to and from work and in the employee's own time;[80] the fact that there was no contractual obligation to buy and read these papers was irrelevant.[81] Under such circumstances the journalists did not purchase and read the newspapers in the performance of their duties but for the purpose of ensuring that they would carry out their duties efficiently.[82]

The first two reasons for Lord Templeman's conclusions are non-controversial: that any other decision would enable journalists to claim for a wide range of items entirely on their own discretion, including wining and dining;[83] and that the work of the journalists did not begin until they reached the office.[84]

The third reason is different: that on the almost identical facts in *Fitzpatrick* v. *IRC (No. 2)*, a Special Commissioner sitting in Scotland had reached a different decision from that of the General Commissioners in *Smith* v. *Abbott*, and they could not both be right.[85] This is fallacious since all depends upon the evidence, and two other members of the majority, Lord Jauncey and Lord Mustill, were much more circumspect in concluding that while there were differences in evidence, they were not in the end sufficient to justify a different decision.[86] The dissentient, Lord Browne-Wilkinson, concluded that the court had no power to overrule the findings of the Commissioners.[87] His points were dissected by Lord

[76] *Sanderson* v. *Durbidge* [1955] 3 All ER 154, 36 TC 239; nor could the recorder in *Ricketts* v. *Colquhoun* [1926] AC 1, 10 TC 118.

[77] *Newlin* v. *Woods* (1966) 42 TC 649, 658.

[78] [1994] STC 237, 66 TC 407, HL.

[79] Technically, they were claiming under s. 198 in order to escape from a charge under s. 153 in respect of an allowance to cover these items.

[80] [1994] STC 237, 245b, 244a, 247d; 66 TC 407, 524, 522 527 respectively.

[81] Ibid., 245j, 524.

[82] Ibid., 243b, 521.

[83] Ibid., 247a, 526.

[84] Ibid., 244a, 522.

[85] Ibid., 242e, 520.

[86] Ibid., 248 255, 528, 536; the fifth member of the Committee, Lord Keith, agreed with Lord Templeman.

[87] Ibid., 254, 535.

Templeman in a manner which was fraternal only in the sense that the best rows are within the family.[88]

18.3.2 *Necessarily*

The cases often fail to distinguish the requirement that the expense be incurred in the performance of the duties of the office from the requirement that it be necessarily so incurred. It is, however, clear from the cases on travel expenses that the test of necessity is objective.[89] Hence an employee with defective eyesight cannot recover the cost of his glasses.[90]

The fact that the employer requires the particular expenditure is not decisive.[91] As Donovan L.J. put it, "The test is not whether the employer imposes the expense but whether the duties do, in the sense that irrespective of what the employer may prescribe, the duties cannot be performed without incurring the particular outlay".[92] Therefore, a student assistant in the research laboratories of a company, who was required to attend classes in preparation for an external degree from the University of London, was not allowed to deduct his expenses,[93] any more than a soldier was obliged to share in the costs of the mess.[94]

In *Brown* v. *Bullock*[95] a bank manager was not allowed to deduct the cost of his subscription to a London club even though it was "virtually a condition of his employment". However, in *Elwood* v. *Utitz*[96] a director of a company in Northern Ireland who was obliged to travel to and stay in London frequently was allowed to deduct the costs of his subscription to a London club since he was buying accommodation and the fact that he chose to buy it at a club rather than a hotel was immaterial.

18.3.3 *Wholly and exclusively*

Many of these cases could as easily be explained on the ground that the expenditure was not incurred wholly and exclusively for the employment. Thus, in the mess cases there was some element of personal benefit,[97] while in *Brown* v. *Bullock* the bank manager derived personal benefit from the membership of the club. Unlike the test of necessity, the requirement of "wholly and exclusively" is not wholly objective.[98] Thus, the expenditure may satisfy this test

[88] Ibid., 247–8, 527.

[89] *Ricketts* v. *Colquhoun* [1926] AC 1, 10 (seen above at §18.2.1). But if the taxpayer is the only person capable of doing the job, different questions arise (*Taylor* v. *Provan* [1974] STC 168, [1974] 1 All ER 1201, 49 TC 579; see above at §18.2.2).

[90] *Roskams* v. *Bennett* (1950) 32 TC 129.

[91] But the fact that an employer has not sanctioned it greatly weakens the taxpayer's case; see *Owen* v. *Burden* [1972] 1 All ER 356, 358, 47 TC 476, 481 (county surveyor unable to deduct cost of journey to Japan to attend world road congress) and *Maclean* v. *Trembath* (1956) 36 TC 653, 666.

[92] *Brown* v. *Bullock* (1961) 40 TC 1, 10.

[93] *Blackwell* v. *Mills* [1945] 2 All ER 655, 26 TC 468. He was not performing his duties as a laboratory assistant when he was listening to the lecture (see p. 470).

[94] *Lomax* v. *Newton* [1953] 2 All ER 801, 34 TC 558; *Griffiths* v. *Mockler* [1953] 2 All ER 805, 35 TC 135. A major in the Royal Army Pay Corps would have been subject to disciplinary action if he had not paid, but mess membership was not necessarily in the performance of his duties as an officer.

[95] [1961] 1 All ER 206, 40 TC 1. Counsel for the bank manager conceded that his client could still perform the duties of a bank manager even though he had not been a member of the club.

[96] (1965) 42 TC 482.

[97] *Griffiths* v. *Mockler* (1953) 35 TC 135 at 137.

[98] *Elwood* v. *Utitz* (1965) 42 TC 482, 498, *per* Lord MacDermott C.J.

if its sole object is the performance of duties regardless of the fact that it may bring about some other incidental result or effect.[99]

Where a person wears ordinary clothes but of a standard required by the employer, no part of the cost is deductible.[100] However, where a car is being used sometimes for business purposes and sometimes for personal purposes, part of the costs are allowable. The distinction between the two cases is that when the car is being used for business purposes it is being used only for those purposes, whereas when the clothes are worn at work they have a dual purpose, part-business, part-personal.[101] Therefore, where a telephone is used partly for business calls the taxpayer can deduct the business calls but not the others; in theory, there is no deduction for any part of the telephone rental.[102]

18.3.4 Miscellaneous non-travel provisions

Entertainment expenses

TA 1988, s. 577 prohibits the deduction of relevant business entertainment expenses not only under Schedule D but also under Schedule E.[103] This could lead to a double non-deduction if the employee incurs an expense which the employer reimburses, or where the employee is given an allowance for the purpose. Not only is the employee taxable in respect of the reimbursment or allowance but the employer is unable to deduct the expense of reimbursement or allowance. Under these circumstances the employee is not taxable on the reimbursement or allowance.[104]

Security

Expenses on security assets and services are made expressly deductible.[105]

Retirement

Payments to pension schemes are deductible under the relevant legislation (see chapter 30 below).

Payroll giving

In a major departure from orthodox tax theory, an employee is allowed to deduct from his pre-tax pay contributions to charity under a payroll deduction scheme. There is now no maximum amount. The scheme has effect both for Schedule E and for PAYE.[106]

FA 2000 not only removes the limits on the amounts given by payroll giving (£1,200 in 1999–00) but also provides a temporary 10% enhancement of the benefit to the charity.[107]

[99] 42 TC 482, 497, relying on cases decided under ScheduleD, Case II—but before *Mallalieu* v. *Drumond* [1983] STC 665, 57 TC 330.

[100] By analogy with *Mallalieu* v. *Drummond*, ibid.,and subject to the same exceptions.

[101] *Hillyer* v. *Leaks* [1976] STC 490, 51 TC 590; *Woodcock* v. *IRC* [1977] STC 405, 51 TC 698; and *Ward* v. *Dunn* [1979] STC 178, 52 TC 517 .

[102] *Lucas* v. *Cattell* (1972) 48 TC 353.

[103] TA 1988, s. 577(1)(b).

[104] Ibid., s. 577(3).

[105] FA 1989, s. 50–52; apportionment is directed where there is dual purpose (s. 51); for the Revenue view on scope, see ICAEW Memorandum TR 759, (1989) *Simon's Tax Intelligence* 719.

[106] TA 1988, s. 202, as amended by FA 1996, s. 100 and FA 2000, s. 38. Payment can be made through an agency charity approved by the Revenue (TA 1988, s. 202(7)).

[107] FA 2000 s. 38.

Liability insurance premiums and uninsured liabilities

TA 1988, s. 201AA allows a deduction for money spent either on discharging a qualifying liability together with associated costs and expenses, or on a premium for a qualifying contract of insurance relating to an indemnity against a qualifying liability. The expense must be met out of the emoluments of the office or employment. The effect is to remove liability on the employee where these costs are met by the employer and to give relief for the employee's own expenditure—including expenditure up to six years after the year in which the employment ends.[108]

Post-employment

Post-employment deductions may be set against total income.[109] The relief may, like post-cessation business expenses, be set against CGT.[110] The burden must fall on the employee rather than the employer.

18.4 Reflections

The test of deductibility under TA 1988, s. 198 is strict, even severe. A particularly strong example of this is *Eagles* v. *Levy*[111] where the employee had to sue his employer to recover wages due to him and was not allowed to deduct the costs of the action. Such costs were not incurred in the course of the performance of his duties. The self-employed could presumably deduct the costs of pursuing a trade debtor.

The restrictive nature of the test of deductibility has often been commented upon, usually adversely,[112] and it remains true that the test appears to be much stricter than that laid down under Schedule D, Cases I and II where the requirement is that the expenditure be wholly and exclusively for the purposes of the business.[113]

A good example of the discrepancy is *Hamerton* v. *Overy*[114] where a full-time anaesthetist sought to deduct the cost of maintaining a telephone, a maid to take messages, a subscription to the Medical Defence Union and the excess of his car running expenses over his allowance received from his employers. All these items would have been deductible had he been in private practice under Schedule D, Case II; none were deductible under Schedule E. Had he succeeded in establishing two places of work as the taxpayer did in *Owen* v. *Pook*, the first and last expenses might well have been deductible.

The discrepancy creates tax planning problems. If Tom, a trader, incorporates his business, his allowable expenses will fall under Schedule E. Some who fall within Schedule E try

[108] TA 1988, s. 201AA, added by FA 1995, s. 91. For the Revenue interpretation of the provisions, see Revenue Interpretation RI 131.

[109] FA 1995, s. 92.

[110] Ibid., s. 92(6)–(8).

[111] (1934) 19 TC 23.

[112] Rowlatt J. in *Ricketts* v. *Colquhoun* (1924) 10 TC 118, 121; Croom Johnson J. in *Bolam* v. *Barlow* (1949) 31 TC 136, 129; Danckwerts J. in *Roskams* v. *Bennett* (1950) 32 TC 129, 132; Harman L.J. in *Mitchell and Edon* v. *Ross* [1960] Ch 498, 532,[1960] 2 All ER 218, 232, 40 TC 11, 51. But *cf.* Lord Radcliffe in *Mitchell and Edon* v. *Ross* [1962] AC 814, 841, [1961] 3 All ER 49, 56, 40 TC 11, 62; and Rowlatt J. in *Nolder* v. *Walters* (1930) 15 TC 380, 389.

[113] See Lord Evershed M.R. in *Brown* v. *Bullock* (1960) 40 TC 1, 9. However, note also Brodie, *Tax Line* (May 1995), 7 citing an instance where the Schedule E tax payer could deduct an expense where the Schedule D taxpayer could not, because the former came within a Revenue agreement.

[114] (1954) 35 TC 73.

to avoid the problem by forming a management company which employs them: their own expenses remain under Schedule E, but the company may, in computing its profits, deduct expenses not deductible by an individual employee. The essence of this distinction is that Schedule E requires that the expense be necessarily incurred in the performance of the duties, while Schedule D is satisfied with a purpose test.

However, the discrepancy can be exaggerated. First, many expenses disallowed under Schedule D are similarly disallowed under Schedule E. Thus, travelling expenses from home to work are disallowed under both Schedules,[115] as are other expenses of a personal nature, such as living expenses. Secondly, it must be noted that some expenses allowed under Schedule D may subsequently be recouped by the Revenue as, for example, where trading stock is bought and later sold or valued at market value on discontinuance.[116] Again, the cost of a home office which is allowed under Schedule E will not affect the exemption of the principal private residence from CGT, whereas the same allowance under Schedule D will result in a partial loss of that exemption. Thirdly, there remains the crucial difference between an employment and a profession or trade, and between being a servant and being an owner. If E, an employee, incurs expense for his employer, E's employer may reimburse the expense, whereas a trader has to bear the expense itself. Unfortunately, the reimbursement may be taxable, especially where TA 1988, s. 153 is in issue, as in *Smith* v. *Abbott*.[117] The parties have two solutions. One is for the employer to incur the expense, so excluding s. 153; the other is to increase the employee's wages sufficiently to cover the taxable reimbursement.

One legislative approach to the problem is to keep the present strict rule and provide exceptions for particular situations, such as the child-minding expenses disallowed in *Halstead* v. *Condon*[118] or the fees payable in *Lupton* v. *Potts*.[119] In practice the Revenue seem to allow[120] some expenses, such as the non-taxation of allowances for teachers or judges in respect of books, or the home study allowance.[121] Legislation has been passed to deal with relocation expenses §15.5. The present system appears to have regional differences; such erratic administration is unfair.

[115] See MacDonald [1978] *BTR* 75, commenting on *Sargent* v. *Barnes*.

[116] TA 1988, s. 100.

[117] [1998] STC 267.

[118] (1970) 46 TC 289.

[119] [1969] 3 All ER 1083, 45 TC 643.

[120] For some there is at least a published extra-statutory concession: see ESC Al (flat rate allowances for costs of tools and special clothing). Other reliefs depend on agreements between the Revenue and various trades unions, the results being made available to their members.

[121] This was thought to be outside s. 198 in *Roskams* v. *Bennett* (1950) 32 TC 129, but inside s. 198 in *Elwood* v. *Utitz* (1965) 42 TC 482, 495.

19

Business Income—Part I: Scope

19.1 Introduction

19.1.1 Trade

Schedule D, Case I taxes the profits of a trade carried on in the UK or elsewhere.[1] Case I charges only annual profits and is therefore not a capital gains tax,[2] although the width of the definition of trade may make it appear like one at times.

Trade is defined statutorily as including every trade, manufacture, adventure or concern in the nature of trade.[3] Judicial definitions of trade have been given sparingly. In *Ransom* v.

[1] TA 1988, s. 18. On "or elsewhere", see below at §19.1.3.

[2] On Revenue power to make alternative assessments, see e.g. *IRC* v. *Wilkinson* [1992] STC 454, 65 TC 28, CA. Presumably a taxpayer cannot make alternative self-assessments.

[3] TA 1988, ss 831, 832. On the relations between the last words and the nouns, see *Johnston* v. *Heath* [1970] 3 All ER 915, 46 TC 463.

Higgs[4] Lord Reid said that the word "is commonly used to denote operations of a commercial character by which the trader provides to customers for reward some kind of goods or services", and in the same case Lord Wilberforce said, "[T]rade normally involves the exchange of goods or services for reward . . . there must be something which the trade offers to provide by way of business. Trade moreover presupposes a customer". Therefore, where the British Olympic Association set about raising fund by sponsorship and donations a Special Commissioner held that the activities were not commercial and so did not amount to a trade.[5]

The question whether there is a trade, as defined, is one of fact. This means that it is for the Commissioners not only to determine the primary facts, such as what transactions were carried out, when, by whom and with what purpose, but also to conclude that the transaction was or was not a trade as defined.[6] Although this conclusion is an inference it is usually treated as one of fact.[7] Where the findings are inconsistent it is for the court to judge.[8]

It should be remembered that it is not always to the advantage of the Revenue to argue that a particular transaction is an adventure in the nature of trade, since losses resulting from an adventure will be eligible for loss relief.[9] In this connection one may note the old Australian rule which allowed a taxpayer to claim a loss only if the taxpayer reported that the asset was acquired for profit when making the first return after the acquisition.[10] UK tax advisers take the view that self-assessment only requires the reporting of income and not of a loss.

19.1.2 Who is trading?

Not me but my partner

If T is trading, then T, and only T, is liable to tax on the profits. Tax is levied on the traders and not on the transactions. Hence, if T carries out three transactions each with a different partner, it is possible to conclude that in view of the frequency of the transactions T was carrying on a trade, but that T's partners were not.[11] The boundary between enabling someone else to carry on a business and carrying it on oneself is a fine one.[12]

Not me but my company or trust

Where T is trading but the profit accrues to W, who is not carrying on the trade, no charge can be made on T. In *Ransom* v. *Higgs*[13] land was owned by a company owned by H and his wife. H agreed to a scheme by which the company developed the land and paid the profits to a discretionary trust. It was held that the trade of developing the land was not carried on

[4] [1974] 3 All ER 949, 955, *per* Lord Reid, 964, *per* Lord Wilberforce. An external Name at Lloyd's does not trade at all (*Koenigsberger* v. *Mellor* [1995] STC 547, 67 TC 280).

[5] *British Olympic Association* v. *Winter* [1995] STC (SCD) 85.

[6] *Leeming* v. *Jones* [1930] 1 KB 279, 15 TC 333, CA; affd. *sub nom. Jones* v. *Leeming* [1930] AC 415, 15 TC 333, HL; *Hillerns and Fowler* v. *Murray* (1932) 17 TC 77.

[7] See, e.g. Endicott (1998) 114 *LQR* 292 and above §4.4.2.

[8] *Simmons* v. *IRC* [1980] STC 350, [1980] 2 All ER 798, 53 TC 461; see Preece [1981] *BTR* 124 and Walters [1981] *BTR* 379.

[9] *Stott* v. *Hoddinott* (1916) 7 TC 85; but *cf. Lewis Emanuel & Son Ltd.* v. *White* (1965) 42 TC 369.

[10] Income Tax Act (Australia), s. 52, although the Commissioner had the power to grant relief if this was not observed (applies only to pre-1985 property because of the introduction of CGT in Australia in 1985).

[11] *Pickford* v. *Quirke* (1927) 13 TC 251; *Marshall's Executors* v. *Joly* [1936] 1 All ER 851, 20 TC 256.

[12] *Alongi* v. *IRC* [1991] STC 517.

[13] [1974] STC 539, [1974] 3 All ER 949, 50 TC 1; see Twitley [1974] *BTR* 335.

by H. As Lord Reid put it, "He did not deal with any person. He did not buy or sell anything. He did not provide anyone with goods or service for reward. He had no profits or gains".[14] There was no evidence that the trade carried on by the company was in fact carried on by H. H had not compelled but merely persuaded the company to conduct a trading operation and so could not be said to be the trader. In deciding who is trading the court looks to the facts. In *Smart* v. *Lowndes* [15] a half share in land owned by T's wife was held to be T's trading stock.

A rogue case

Where a trading operation is carried out by a company there is some authority for the view that the gain realised on the sale of shares in the company can be a trading receipt (*Associated London Properties Ltd* v. *Henriksen*[16]). Although the Court of Appeal was clear that the decision turned on its facts, it is not completely clear what these facts were. If the facts had been that the new company was simply the agent of its owners, so that in fact the trade was carried on by them and not by the company, the case could be treated as just a useful illustration of a general principle; however, the case appears to involve a fine disregard of the separate legal personality of the company. The decision has not been much used by the Revenue despite its potentialities to counter tax avoidance.

19.1.3 Where is the trade carried on?

Although Schedule D, Case I applies to a trade carried on in the UK or elsewhere,[17] case-law provides that a trade carried on wholly outside the UK is within Schedule D, Case V and not Case I.[18] A trade or profession carried on partly in the UK and partly outside is within Case I. These distinctions are still important; they used to be of even greater importance when the remittance basis applied to Case V but not to Case I.

Where a non-resident carries on a trade or profession in the UK, liability arises under Schedule D, Cases I and II. However the person is only chargeable on the profits arising in the UK.[19]

The question of where a person is carrying on a trade turns on the question where the activities take place from which the profits truly arise. This issue can be decided by looking at the place the contract is made (see below at §60.2).

19.1.4 Profession or vocation

Schedule D, Case II charges income tax on the profits of any profession or vocation. Neither term is defined by statute. Case-law establishes that a profession involves the idea of an occupation requiring either purely intellectual skill, or of manual skill controlled, as in painting and sculpture or surgery, by the intellectual skill of the operator. Such occupations are distinct from those which are substantially the production or sale, or arrangements for the production or sale of commodities. Therefore a journalist and editor carries on a

14 Ibid., 545, 955, 79.

15 [1978] STC 607, 52 TC 436, narrowing still further *Williams* v. *Davies* [1945] 1 All ER 304, 26 TC 371.

16 (1944) 26 TC 46; distinguished in *Fundfarms Development Ltd.* v. *Parsons* [1969] 3 All ER 1161, 45 TC 707.

17 TA 1988, s. 18(1)(a)(ii).

18 *Colquhoun* v. *Brooks* (1889) 14 Ap Cas 493, 2 TC 490.

19 TA 1988, s. 18(1)(a)(iii).

profession, but a newspaper reporter carries on a trade.[20] The question is one of fact and degree and the crux is the degree of intellectual skill involved. Where the Commissioners held that a person who ran a service for taxpayers seeking to recover overpaid tax or to reduce assessments was carrying on a trade, the Court of Appeal considered that there was no error of law.[21]

"Vocation" is a word which has fallen out of fashion—today one probably thinks of an actor as carrying on a profession rather than a vocation.[22] Tax case-law treats a vocation as analogous to a calling, a word of great signification meaning the way in which one passes one's life.[23] A dramatist,[24] racing tipster[25] and jockey[26] have all been held to be carrying on a vocation but not a perennial gambler,[27] nor a film producer.[28]

Where an individual is carrying on a profession the assessment under Schedule D, Case II on the profits of that profession will encompass profits on transcations closely linked with that professional activity even though they would, if taken on their own, be carrying on a trade. In *Wain* v. *Cameron*[29] Professor Wain had carried on his profession of writer for at least 30 years. He then sold his manuscripts and working papers to his university library, but retained the copyright. The court held that the gains made on the sale were chargeable under Schedule D, Case II as part of the profits of his profession.

A profession must be distinguished from a trade because:

(1) certain capital allowances, e.g. those for industrial buildings and research and development, are available only to traders;[30]
(2) whereas an isolated transaction may be an adventure in the nature of trade, an isolated service cannot fall within Case II but only within Case VI;
(3) the rule in *Sharkey* v. *Wernher* (see below at §23.5.1.3) may not apply to professions;
(4) exemption from CGT for certain damages is confined to profession and vocations;[31]
(5) there is some suggestion that the deduction rules are less fair for professions than for trades;[32]
(6) a company may not be able to carry on a profession; [33]
(7) until 1999–2000[34] cash accounts could be used for professions.

[20] *IRC* v. *Maxse* [1919] 1 KB 647 at 656, 12 TC 41 at 61.

[21] *Currie* v. *IRC* [1921] 2 KB 332, 12 TC 245. Other traders include a stockbroker (*Christopher Barker & Sons* v. *IRC* [1919] 2 KB 222), and a photographer (*Cecil* v. *IRC* (1919) 36 TLR 164).

[22] Laurence Olivier was held to be carrying on a vocation in *Higgs* v. *Olivier* (1952) 33 TC 133.

[23] *Partridge* v. *Mallandaine* (1886) 18 QBD 276, 278, 2 TC 179, 180, *per* Denman J.

[24] *Billam* v. *Griffith* (1941) 23 TC 757.

[25] *Graham* v. *Arnott* (1941) 24 TC 157.

[26] *Wing* v. *O'Connell* [1927] IR 84.

[27] *Graham* v. *Green* [1925] 2 KB 37, 9 TC 309.

[28] *Asher* v. *London Film Productions Ltd.* [1944] KB 133,[1944] 1 All ER 77.

[29] [1995] STC 555, 67 TC 324. Contrast *Satt* v. *Fernandez* [1997] STC (SCD) 271 where a Special Commissioner held that the profession of an author carried on by S was separate from a trade of publishing (also carried on by S); at that time cash accounts were acceptable for the profession but not for the trade.

[30] The other allowances not available to professions are those for industrial buildings, mineral extraction, agricultural buildings and dredging.

[31] TCGA 1992, s. 55.

[32] *Norman* v. *Golder* (1944) 26 TC 293, 297, *per* Lord Greene M.R.

[33] *William Esplen, Son and Swainston Ltd.* v. *IRC* [1919] 2 KB 731; but the point was left open by Browne Wilkinson J. in *Newstead* v. *Frost* [1978] STC 239, 249, 53 TC 525, 537.

[34] Statement of Practice SP A27; the change was made by FA 1998, s. 42.

19.1.5 Property income

Income from property is not trading income. Therefore, income from the exploitation of property rights by letting out residential property,[35] granting licences to use intellectual property is not within Schedule D, Case I or II. See also below at §19.7

19.2 Illegal trading[36]

The question whether the profits of an illegal trade are taxable has produced conflicting *dicta*, but the answer clearly ought to be, and on balance of authority now is, "yes". The difficulty with UK case law is finding decisions dealing with trading which is criminal, as opposed to contracts which are unenforceable for illegality.[37] However, in *Minister of Finance* v. *Smith*[38] the Privy Council held that the profits of illegal brewing during the prohibition era were taxable. Today, the true principle may be that taxpayers cannot set up the unlawful character of their acts against the Revenue.[39]

There have been some suggestions that the profits of burglary would not be taxable, because crime is not a trade.[40] It is, however, suggested that these cases should not be followed; any other conclusion may lead to distinctions between acts illegal *per se*, and acts which are merely incidental to the carrying-on of a trade. There may be difficulty in calculating profits in such cases since there is a civil obligation to restore the goods to their owner, and it should be remembered that a consistently unprofitable trade may not be a trade at all.

Fines are not deductible in computing trading profits.[41] On the rule barring the deduction of certain payments which amount to criminal offences, see above at §7.6

19.3 Adventures in the Nature of Trade—Scope

19.3.1 Principles, facts and examples

The question whether there is a trade or an adventure in the nature of trade is one of fact. What follows is an attempt to synthesise the many cases in this area and to indicate not only what factors the courts take into account but also the frail nature of those factors. However,

[35] TA 1988, s. 491(8).

[35] *Webb* v. *Conelee Properties Ltd.* [1982] STC 913.

[36] See Mulholland and Cockfield [1995] *BTR* 572; and Day [1971] *BTR* 104.

[37] For example, *IRC* v. *Aken* [1990] STC 497, CA (prostitution a trade but not criminal). See also *Partridge* v. *Mallandaine* (1886) 18 QBD 276, 2 TC 179 (bookmaker's profits were taxable even though wagering contracts were unlawful) and *Lindsay, Woodward and Hiscox* v. *IRC* (1933) 18 TC 43.

[38] [1927] AC 193.

[39] *Southern* v. *AB* [1933] 1 KB 713, 18 TC 59 (profits of bookmaker's street and postal betting were taxable); *Mann* v. *Nash* [1932] 1 KB 752, 16 TC 523 (profits of "fruit" and "diddler" automatic machines were taxable); contrast *Hayes* v. *Duggan* [1929] IR 406 (profits of illegal sweepstake were not taxable; the court should uphold the policy of a statute passed to prevent corruption of the public). It may need emphasising today that such activities were then actually criminal.

[40] For example, Lindsay v. *IRC* (1932) 18 TC 43, 56, *per* Lord Sands.

[41] Fines are not deductible expenses (*McKnight* v. *Sheppard* 1999 STC 669, 674, discussing *IRC* v. *Alexander von Glehn & Co. Ltd.* [1920] 2 KB 553, 12 TC 232); fines for excess axle loads on lorries were held deductible in *Day and Ross Ltd.* .v. *R.* [1976] CTC 707, but these would not now be followed in the UK. See discussion by Brooks (1977) 25 *Can. Tax Jo.* 16.

it is hard not to agree with the following comments of Sir Nicolas Browne Wilkinson V.-C. in 1986:[42]

> "Like the Commissioners I have been treated to an extensive survey of the authorities. But as far as I can see there is only one point which as a matter of law is clear, namely that a single one-off transaction can be an adventure in the nature of trade. Beyond that I have found it impossible to find any single statement of law which is applicable to all the cases in circumstances. I have been taken through the facts of the cases . . . I fear that the General Commissioners may become as confused by that process as I did. The purpose of authority is to find principle not to seek analogies to facts."

In 1904 the Lord Justice Clerk said that the question was whether the sum or gain which has been made was a mere enhancement of value by realising a security, or a gain made in an operation of business in carrying out a scheme for profit-making.[43] In 1955 the Royal Commission listed six "badges of trade":[44] (1) the subject-matter of the realisation; (2) the length of period of ownership; (3) the frequency or number of similar transactions by the same person; (4) supplementary work on or in connection with the property realised; (5) the circumstances responsible for the realisation; and finally (6) motive. A slightly different list of badges is used in this text.[45]

Two examples

(1) In *Wisdom* v. *Chamberlain*[46] the taxpayer (W) had assets worth between £150,000 and £200,000. Fearing that sterling might be devalued, W's accountant concluded that silver bullion would be a suitable hedge and tried to buy £200,000 worth for W. However, the brokers would sell only £100,000 worth, a transaction which was financed on a loan from the brokers of £90,000 at 3% above bank rate. Five months later the accountant managed to get £200,000 worth of bullion from the brokers on the basis that the original purchase would be repurchased by the brokers, at a loss to the taxpayer of £3,000. The new deal was financed by loans of £160,000 from a bank and £40,000 from the brokers, both for a maximum period of one year and at high rates of interest. The brokers were under an obligation to buy back for £210,000 within a certain period. Between October 1962 and January 1963 the bullion was disposed of at a profit of £48,000 after deducting interest of £7,000.

The Commissioners held that this was a transaction in the nature of trade, and the Court of Appeal held that they were amply justified in reaching that conclusion. For Harman LJ. .this was "a transaction entered into on a short term basis for the purpose of making a profit out of the purchase and sale of a commodity and if that is not an adventure in the nature of trade I do not really know what it is".[47] Salmon L.J. observed that if the taxpayer had realised his other assets and used the proceeds to finance the purchase of the silver the case might have been different. The facts of the case, however, presented a trading adventure—"and a very sensible and successful one. I for my part cannot see that it is any the less a trading adventure because [it is described] as something to offset the loss incurred by a fall in the value of sterling or as a hedge or insurance against devaluation".[48]

42 *Marson* v. *Morton* [1986] STC 466, 470.
43 Lord Macdonald in *California Copper Syndicate Ltd.* v. *Harris* (1904) 5 TC 159, 165.
44 Cmd 9474 (1955), para. 116.
45 For another list, see *Marson* v. *Morton* [1986] STC 46, 59 TC 381, discussed below.
46 [1969] 1 All ER 332, 45 TC 92.
47 Ibid., 336, 106.
48 Ibid., 339, 108.

(2) By contrast, in *Marson* v. *Morton*[49] T, who owned a company which traded as wholesale potato merchants, bought three or four acres of land—on the advice of an estate agent (L). He had no plan to use the land. He intended to make a capital profit and perhaps sell it in two years (L said that T might double his money). T had no idea as to the cost of the land and it was only when he was asked to sign documents that he realised that a third party was involved in lending the money. His trust in L was based on the fact that L had appeared in good company at a weekend gathering. Three months later L advised T to sell the land. L did not tell T that the purchaser was a company with which L was connected. T had not sought independent advice on the value or potential of the land. L had, correctly, told T that the land had planning permission. T had intended to keep the land as a medium-term investment, but by the time he had acquired it he was feeling "edgy" about L and was glad of the chance to sell. L did not quote any selling price and T did not seek independent advice. At that time the difference between income tax and CGT rates was very high. The General Commissioners held that as L had not been instructed to sell at any particular price or time the transaction was like an investment in stocks and shares. Sir Nicolas Browne Wilkinson V.-C. described the facts as highly unusual and the procedures adopted as "extremely unconventional, to say the least" and the case as one of those which fell into the no man's land. He refused to interfere with the the decision of the Commissioners that T was not trading.

19.3.2 Purpose of profit

An intention to make a profit is not a necessary ingredient of a trade but its presence helps to establish a trading transaction.[50] Operations of the same kind, and carried out in the same way, as those which characterise ordinary trading are not the less trading operations because they make a loss or there is no intention to make a profit.[51] However, a scheme which inevitably involves a loss may not be a trading transaction; [52] so losses on loan transactions with no commercial element in them have been disallowed.[53]

Looking beyond cases which have no commercial purpose, it is important to pay attention to actions rather than to words. In *Ensign Tankers (Leasing) Ltd.* v. *Stokes*[54] the House of Lords held that the investment of funds in the production of a film was a trading transaction even though much of the motivation was to obtain a tax advantage. The transaction was not a sham and could have resulted in either a profit or a loss; there was real expenditure of real money. In the Court of Appeal it had been held that there was an intention to gain a fiscal advantage. In such circumstances the Court of Appeal remitted the case to the Commissioners to weigh the fiscal elements against the non-fiscal elements to decide whether the transaction was entered into (a) for essentially commercial purposes but in a fiscally advantageous form, or (b) essentially for the purpose of obtaining a fiscal advantage

[49] [1986] STC 46, 59 TC 381.

[50] *Torbell Investments Ltd.* v. *Williams* [1986] STC 397, 59 TC 357.

[51] See Lord Reid in *J. P. Harrison (Watford) Ltd.* v. *Griffiths* [1962] 1 All ER 909, (1960) 40 TC 281, and cases there cited. See also *Building and Civil Engineering Holidays Scheme Management Ltd.* v. *Clark* (1960) 39 TC 12 (profit but not trading). A related issue is whether a particular transaction carried out by a person who is clearly trading forms part of the trade, even though a loss must result.

[52] *F.A. and A.B. Ltd.* v. *Lupton* [1971] 3 All ER 948, 47 TC 580.

[53] *Overseas Containers Finance Ltd.* v. *Stoker* [1989] STC 364, 61 TC 473, CA.

[54] [1992] STC 226, 243j, 64 TC 617, 749.

under the guise of a commercial transaction.[55] However, in the House of Lords Lord Templeman said, surely correctly, that neither the Commissioners nor the courts were competent or obliged to decide such issues.[56] In that case Lord Templeman said of *F.A. and A.B. Ltd.* v. *Lupton*[57] that there the tax avoidance scheme negatived trading because, on the true analysis of the transaction, the trader did not trade at all; there was neither profit nor loss. The House in that case had not addressed the problem of what was to happen where, as in *Ensign* itself, there was actual expenditure.

Mere charity

If there is an intention to make a profit but then to apply it in some worthy way, there is a trading activity. The tax system is concerned with the acquisition, not with the distribution of profit.[58] However, it is necessary to distinguish a trade from a merely charitable endeavour. In *Religious Tract and Book Society of Scotland* v. *Forbes*[59] the question was whether colportage, i.e. the sending out of colporteurs to sell Bibles and to act as cottage missionaries, was a trade. The Court of Exchequer (Scotland) ruled that the activity, which could not possibly be carried on at a profit, could not be a trade, with the result that the losses on colportage could not be set off against what were undoubtedly trading profits from the society's book shops. It would therefore appear that while the impossibility of profit will prevent the activity from being a trade, the absence of a profit motive will not.

19.3.3 Motive for acquisition

The motive attending the acquisition of an asset is a factor which, when there is doubt, is to be thrown into the balance.[60] An acquisition under a relative's last will and testament is clearly different from a purchase with a view to speedy resale.[61] If T embarks on an adventure which has the characteristics of trade, T's purpose or object cannot prevail over it. But if the acts are equivocal, T's purpose or object may be very material.[62] If a bank acquires the shares of a customer who was in difficulties, but not intending to hold the shares as circulating assets, the transaction will be on capital account.[63]

The acquisition of an asset with the hope of making a profit on the resale does not inevitably signify an adventure in the nature of trade since a good investment should generate some capital appreciation.[64] The time at which resale is foreseen is of greater importance.[65]

[55] [1991] STC 136, 147–9, 64 TC 617, 720–722, *per* Browne-Wilkinson V.-C. The Court of Appeal had reversed Millett J.

[56] [1992] STC 226, 241, 64 TC 617, 742.

[57] [1971] 3 All ER 948, 47 TC 580.

[58] *Mersey Docks and Harbour Board* v. *Lucas* (1883) 8 App Cas 891, 2 TC 25.

[59] (1896) 3 TC 415. On the need to take a broad view when many activities are intertwined, see *British Olympic Association* v. *Winter* [1995] STC (SCD) 85.

[60] As in *Lucy and Sunderland Ltd.* v. *Hunt* [1961] 3 All ER 1062, 40 TC 132 (Commissioners finding that there was a trade reversed) and *West* v. *Phillips* (1958) 38 TC 203 (houses built to let were investments); see Bates [1958] *BTR* 76.

[61] But distinguish *Pilkington* v. *Randall* (1965) 42 TC 662 where one beneficiary bought the interest of another and was held to be within Schedule D, Case I.

[62] *Iswera* v. *IRC* [1965] 1 WLR 663, 668, *per* Lord Reid.

[63] *Waylee Investment Ltd.* v. *Commrs of Inland Revenue* [1990] STC 780, PC; see also *Beautiland* v. *Commrs of Inland Revenue* [1991] STC 467, PC.

[64] *IRC* v. *Reinhold* (1953) 34 TC 389.

[65] With the emphasis on "foreseen" as opposed to when it actually took place (*Marson* v. *Morton* [1986] STC 46, 59 TC 381).

However, if taxpayers argue that it was not their intention to make a profit through resale, the onus is on them to produce some plausible explanation for the purchase, such as an intention to enjoy the income before reselling.[66] Further, taxpayers' assertions that they intended to buy an asset for investment purposes, whether as an investment fund for old age or as a hedge against devaluation,[67] have not been allowed to stand against other facts. The Revenue thus seems to get the best of both worlds: the taxpayer's state of mind can make up for equivocal acts, while unequivocal acts cannot be distorted by intent.[68]

In assessing these matters the case stated must be examined in the round.[69] A finding that the taxpayer had no predetermined intention to sell one property when buying another is only one finding.[70] If there is no prospect of immediate profit through resale this may suggest that the acquisition is not an adventure in the nature of trade. However, whatever the taxpayer's original intention may have been, that may change.

Companies

A separate question concerns companies which, as legal persons, have their capacity limited by their objects. The court, in deciding whether or not there is an adventure, may look at the objects of the company,[71] but a statement therein limiting the company's powers to investment is not conclusive against liability to tax on its income.[72] On the other hand, if a company is set up which has the power to purchase land and to turn it to account, such operations are likely to be regarded as trading operations,[73] and it has been suggested that the mere setting up-of a company points to a trading intention because of the implied continuity of the company.[74]

Pension fund trustees

The question of motive reappears in the important case of *Clarke* v. *British Telecom Pension Scheme Trustees*,[75] a major case on the taxation of pension schemes. The taxpayers were trustees administering pension schemes and, as such, were exempt from tax on various forms of investment income, including underwriting commissions charged under Case VI, but not if charged under Case I.[76] The Revenue made assessments on the basis that the commissions were chargeable under Case I. On the evidence, transactions were frequent and with relative lack of risk that the sub-underwriters would be left with the shares.[77] The Commissioners had described the trustees' entry into these arrangements as "habitual, organised, for reward, extensive and business-like" but that they came within Case VI. The

[66] *Reynold's Executors* v. *Bennett* (1943) 25 TC 401.

[67] *Wisdom* v. *Chamberlain* [1969] 1 All ER 332, 45 TC 92.

[68] For example *Mitchell Bros* v. *Tomlinson* (1957) 37 TC 224.

[69] For a good example, see *Kirkham* v. *Williams*, [1991] STC 343, 64 TC 253.

[70] Kirkby v. Hughes [1993] STC 76.

[71] *Cooksey and Bibbey* v. *Rednall* (1949) 30 TC 514, 521.

[72] *Eames* v. *Stepnell Properties Ltd.* 43 TC 678, CA; *Emro Investments Ltd.* v. *Aller* (1954) 35 TC 305.

[73] *IRC* v. *Reinhold* (1953) 34 TC 389; and see *IRC* v. *Korean Syndicate Ltd.* [1921] 3 KB 258, 12 TC 181; and *Ruhamuh Property Co. Ltd.* v. *FCT* (1928) 41 CLR 1648; see also *Lewis Emanuel & Son Ltd.* v. *White* (1965) 42 TC 369.

[74] *IRC* v. *Reinhold* (1953) 34 TC 389, *per* Lord Carmont.

[75]]2000] STC 222; see Kerridge [2000] *BTR* 397.

[76] TA 1988, s. 592(3)(c).

[77] It is true that the underwriting commissions all related to companies in which the trustees held shares, but the opportunity to earn those commissions did not appear to have come to them because they owned the shares, which may afford only a slender basis of distinction.

Court of Appeal, reversing Lightman J. and restoring the decision of the Commissioners, held that the transactions fell outside Case I and so were not taxable under Case I.

It is likely that if these transactions had been carried out by an ordinary individual liability would have arisen under Case I. However, ordinary individuals do not have the same overall investment responsibilities as trustees, and it is therefore necessary to wait and see what, if anything, the House of Lords may do in another case.[77a]

19.3.4 The individual

Existing trader

Where a single transaction is involved and is of a nature close to, but separate from, what is undoubtedly a trade carried on by an individual, it is likely that the courts will conclude that the transaction is an adventure in the nature of a trade.[78] In *T. Beynon & Co. Ltd.* v. *Ogg*,[79] where the company acted as agents for the purchase of wagons and bought some on their own account, the profits on the resale of those wagons were held taxable, as they were in *Cape Brandy Syndicate* v. *IRC*[80] where South African brandy was acquired for blending and resale in the UK by three persons who were members of firms engaged in the wine trade. In these cases, T was held assessable on the profits of the adventure in the nature of trade; however, the profits did not form part of the other trading activities, but did have a distinct taxable source.

Skills?

There is some authority to suggest that if a person has a skill and makes money by it, the profit is more likely to be taxable;[81] however, today the absence of a skill appears to be neutral.[82]

19.3.5 The subject matter

The courts take the view that certain commodities are more likely to be acquired as investments than as the subject of a deal. There are two main groups of examples. Objects recommended for investment in the light of these cases include wine, gold coins and reversionary interests. Antiques and works of art are similarly recommended, provided they are retained for some time and not sold by commercial methods.

Not income yielding?

If the object yields income, whether in the form of rent or dividends, that object was at one time more likely to be an investment than an object which yields no income.[83] Where the court can see some fruit, the source of the fruit is likely to be a tree. A subtle case is *Snell* v. *Rosser Thomas & Co. Ltd.*[84] where the taxpayer, a developer, bought a house and 5¾ acres of

[77a] Leave to appeal was refused by the CA.

[78] *Cayzer and Irvine & Co.* v. *IRC* (1942) 24 TC 491, 496, *per* Lord Normand.

[79] (1918) 7 TC 125.

[80] [1921] 2 KB 403, 12 TC 358.

[81] *Smith Barry* v. *Cordy* (1946) 28 TC 250, 260, *per* Scott L.J.; but doubts as to the correctness of this decision were raised in *Ransom* v. *Higgs* [1974] STC 539, [1974] 3 All ER 949.

[82] *Johnston* v. *Heath* [1970] 3 All ER 915, 921, *per* Goff J.

[83] *Salt* v. *Chamberlain* [1979] STC 750.

[84] [1968] 1 All ER 600, 44 TC 343; and consider the factory in *W. M. Robb Ltd.* v. *Page* (1971) 47 TC 465 (factory built to let or to sell; Commissioners' finding that there was a trade not disturbed).

land. The house produced rent from tenants but the land produced no income and was therefore stock in trade. In determining whether or not there is income the courts have looked not simply at the flow of money to the taxpayer, but also at any outflow. In *Wisdom* v. *Chamberlain*[85] the interest payments were of importance, while in *Cooke* v. *Haddock*[86] rent of £167 a year had to be set against the £320-a-year interest.

However, *Marson* v. *Morton*[87] stressed that it was no longer self-evident that land could not be an investment unless it produced income. While the legal principle could not change, life itself could. "Since the arrival of inflation and high rates of tax on income new approaches to investment have emerged putting the emphasis on the making of capital profits at the expense of income yield."[88] Commissioners should not treat new investments as falling within Schedule D, Case I just because those interests did not generate income (as conventionally understood), nor endeavour to put old types of investments into Schedule D, Case I for the same reason when other factors point in the other direction.

Profits on a sale of property which produces income may nonetheless be taxable under Schedule D, Case I; all depends on the individual circumstances of the case. Thus, stocks and shares bought by a bank in order to make good use of funds in hand and subsequently disposed of in order to finance repayments to depositors were treated as trading stock of the banking business.[89] Moreover, a company which in addition to building ships, ran a passenger service and bought and sold four ships for that service in rapid succession, was held taxable on the profits from the resales of the passenger ships as part of their general Schedule D, Case I profits.[90]

Aesthetics etc.

If the object does not yield income but can be enjoyed in kind, so that there is pleasure or even pride in its possession,[91] as where a person buys a picture for purposes of aesthetic enjoyment, any profit on resale will escape income tax. Conversely, the purchase of a commodity which gives no such pleasure and which cannot be turned to account except by a process of realisation, may well give rise to a taxable profit.[92] Examples of this turn not only on the nature of the commodity, such as the railway wagons in *Gloucester Railway Carriage and Wagon Co. Ltd.* v. *IRC*,[93] but also on the quantity, as in *Rutledge* v. *IRC*[94] which involved the resale of one million rolls of lavatory paper; however, as always, these are questions of fact and it was also important in *Rutledge* that T had no intention other than to resell the property at a profit.[95]

85 [1969] 1 All ER 332, 45 TC 92.

86 (1960) 39 TC 64.

87 [1986] STC 463, 59 TC 381.

88 Ibid., 472, 393, *per* Browne-Wilkinson V.-C.

89 *Punjab Co-operative Bank Ltd.* v. *Amritsar IT Comr Lahore* [1940] AC 1055, [1940] 4 All ER 87; a similar rule applies to insurance companies (*General Reinsurance Co. Ltd.* v. *Tomlinson* [1970] 2 All ER 436, 48 TC 81, discussed in *General Motors Acceptance Corpn* v. *IRC* [1985] STC 408, 59 TC 651).

90 *J. Bolson & Son Ltd.* v. *Farrelly* (1953) 34 TC 161.

91 See Lord Normand in *IRC* v. *Fraser* (1942) 24 TC 498; *quaere* how a trust can enjoy such an object—in which case one should consider the liability of pension funds which purchase works of art.

92 Consider the tax position of unit holders in trusts whose purpose is to make investments in commodities, as distinct from unit holders in companies producing commodities.

93 [1925] AC 469, 12 TC 720; see Ziegel [1961] *BTR* 155, 164.

94 (1929) 14 TC 490; and see also *Martin* v. *Lowry*, [1927] AC 312, 11 TC 297 (44 million yards of aeroplane linen).

95 *Mamor Sdn Bhd* v. *Director General of Inland Revenue* [1985] STC 801, 806, PC.

Land

Land is another asset which can easily yield taxable profits.[96] If the owner of a house actually lives in it, the house is unlikely to be trading stock. However, occupation is not conclusive and courts are reluctant to disturb a finding by the Commissioners that there was an adventure in the nature of trade. In *Page* v. *Pogson*[97] T built a house for himself and his wife and then sold it six months after completion. He then built another house nearby but had to sell it when his job was moved from the south to the east of England. He was held taxable on the profits of the sale of the second house, and Upjohn J. felt himself unable to reverse that finding although doubting whether he would have reached that decision himself.

19.3.6 Processing—supplementary work

The alteration of the asset by the taxpayer may suggest that there is an adventure in the nature of trade. If a purchaser carried through a manufacturing process which changed the character of the article, e.g. converting pig-iron into steel, there is likely to be a trade. However, merely to put the asset into a condition suitable for a favourable sale, such as cleaning a picture or giving a boat a general overhaul, would not suggest a trade. In *IRC* v. *Livingston*[98] the taxpayer, a ship repairer, together with a blacksmith and a fish salesman's employee, purchased a cargo vessel which they converted into a steam drifter and then sold without using it for fishing. The alterations took nearly four months and were carried out by two of the three for wages. The Court of Session held that the profit was taxable.

The mere enhancement of value, as by obtaining planning permission,[99] is not sufficient to create a trade, nor is the normal use of the asset. So, whereas the planting of rubber trees did not indicate a trade in *Tebrau (Johore) Rubber Syndicate Ltd.* v. *Farmer*,[100] the blending of brandy in the *Cape Brandy Syndicate* case did.[101]

Jenkinson v. *Freedland*[102] must be regarded as a most unusual case. There, the taxpayer bought two stills which were coated with a resinous substances and succeeded in removing it by a process of his own devising. It was held that there was no trade on these particular facts, but this turned largely on the eventual sale of the stills by the taxpayer to his own company.

19.3.7 Realisation

Reasons

"Some explanation, such as a sudden emergency or opportunity calling for ready money, negatives the idea that any plan of dealing prompted the original purchase."[103] There are few reported cases in which this point has been successfully made. In *Stott* v. *Hoddinott*[104] an

[96] See Crump [1961] *BTR* 95; Pearce [1962] *BTR* 144; and TA 1988, s. 776.
[97] (1954) 35 TC 545; *cf. Sharpless* v. *Rees* (1940) 23 TC 361; and *Shadford* v. *H. Fairweather & Co. Ltd.* (1966) 43 TC 291.
[98] [1927] SC 251, 11 TC 538.
[99] *Taylor* v. *Good* [1974] STC 148, [1974] 1 All ER 1137, 29 TC 277; see Nock [1974] *BTR* 184.
[100] (1910) 5 TC 658.
[101] [1921] 2 KB 403, 18 TC 358.
[102] (1961) 39 TC 636.
[103] Royal Commission 1955, Cmd 9474 (1955), §115.
[104] (1916) 7 TC 85; see also *Mitchell Bros* v. *Tomlinson* (1957) 37 TC 224; and *Page* v. *Pogson* (1954) 35 TC 545.

architect was obliged, as a term of a contract, to take up shares in the company granting him the contract. He subsequently sold those shares in order to provide funds to take up shares under later contracts with other companies. It was held that this was a capital transaction and, as such, he was not entitled to relief in respect of the loss he sustained.

Machinery

The presence of an organisation through which the disposal of the asset is carried out is one of the hallmarks of a trade, not least because the expenses of such an organisation will be deductible in computing the net profit on the deal.[105] Equally, another factor in deciding whether or not a trade has been discontinued is whether the trade organisation has ceased to exist in an identifiable form.[106] However, the presence or absence of an organisation is not conclusive in deciding whether or not there has been an adventure in the nature of trade. As Lord Wilberforce said in *Ransom* v. *Higgs*, "Organisation as such is not a principle of taxation, or many estimable ladies throughout this country would be imperilled".[107]

The number of steps

The number of steps taken to dispose of the asset is a fragile indicator of a trade.[108] The purchase of goods in bulk and their resale in smaller quantities is the essence of a wholesale–retail trading operation. In *Cape Brandy Syndicate* v. *IRC*[109] one of the factors in favour of a trade was that the brandy was disposed of in some 100 transactions spread over 18 months. On the other hand, the fact that a large number of disposals of land occurred did not make them trading transactions in *Hudsons Bay Co. Ltd.* v. *Stevens.*[110]

Conversely, a single disposal can nonetheless amount to an adventure in the nature of trade.[111]

19.3.8 Frequency of transactions

The frequency of transactions is only one factor in determining whether a trade exists; an investor is still an investor even though the investments are switched. As Harman J. once said, "A deal done once is probably not an activity in the nature of trade, though it may be. Done three or four times it usually is. Each case must depend on its own facts".[112]

However, while it is clear that repeated transactions may support the inference of a trade, and that an isolated transaction may nonetheless be an adventure in the nature of trade, there is also authority that where a transaction is repeated the court may use that fact to place the label of trade onto the original transaction. In *Leach* v. *Pogson*[113] T was a serial driving school incorporator. It was agreed that he was liable to income tax on the profits from subsequent transactions, but T argued that he was not liable in respect of the profit on the first. It was held that he was so liable and that the subsequent transactions could be used

[105] Lord Radcliffe in *Edwards* v. *Bairstow and Harrison* [1955] 3 All ER 48, 58, 36 TC 207, 230.
[106] *Andrew* v. *Taylor* (1965) 42 TC 557.
[107] [1974] 3 All ER 949, 966; note ESC C4.
[108] *IRC* v. *Reinhold* (1953) 34 TC 389, 395, *per* Lord Russell.
[109] [1921] 2 KB 403, 417, 12 TC 368, 376. For another example, see *Martin* v. *Lowry* (1926) 11 TC 297, 320.
[110] (1909) 5 TC 424.
[111] For example, *T. Beynon & Co. Ltd.* v. *Ogg* (1918) 7 TC 125.
[112] *Bolson* v. *Farrelly* (1953) 34 TC 161, 167; see also *Foulds* v. *Clayton* (1953) 34 TC 382, 388; *Pickford* v. *Quirke* (1927) 13 TC 251.
[113] (1962) 40 TC 585.

to support that conclusion. It is probably of great importance that in that case, while he had no intention of embarking upon the business of establishing and selling motoring schools when the first one was set up, T did have that intention before he sold it. The case would thus appear to be correctly decided, although perhaps more appropriately dealt with as a case of a change in the character of the transaction.

19.3.9 Duration of ownership

A "fast buck" is the essence of a deal. A long period between the acquisition of an asset and its disposal may corroborate an intention to hold it as an investment.[114] Conversely, a quick sale invites a scrutiny of the evidence to see whether the acquisition was made with that intent.[115] One element of an investment is that the acquirer intends to hold it for some time, with a view to obtaining either some benefit in the way of income in the meantime or obtaining some profit, but not an immediate profit by resale.[116] Where the asset can only be turned into profit by resale the court adopts a realistic approach.[117]

However, while an asset acquired on a short-term basis, as in *Wisdom* v. *Chamberlain* (above), will often be the subject of an adventure, it does not follow that a disposal within a short period amounts to a trade, as *Marson* v. *Morton* (above) shows. In *IRC* v. *Reinhold*[118] the taxpayer admitted that he acquired the property with the intention of reselling it and that he had instructed his agents to sell whenever a suitable opportunity arose. The land was sold after three years. This isolated transaction escaped income tax. Much more doubtful, however, is the decision of Danckwerts J. in *McLellan, Rawson & Co. Ltd.* v. *Newall*[119] in which the Commissioners' decision that there was a taxable profit was reversed, even though the taxpayer had entered into an arrangement to sell the woodlands while he was still negotiating for their purchase.

19.3.10 Timing

It is a question of fact not only whether there is an adventure in the nature of trade but also when it begins—and ends. It is also important to separate the question whether a trade has begun from the question whether any income has arisen from it.[120] Where an asset is acquired and subsequently disposed of, it is open to the court to conclude from the evidence that the whole transaction was an adventure in the nature of trade. It is, however, open to the court to conclude that an asset was acquired with the intention of retaining it as an investment but that trading subsequently commenced, so that the profit accruing on resale is taxable.[121] What is clear is that at any one time the asset must either be trading stock or a capital asset; it cannot be both at the same time.[122]

[114] *Harvey* v. *Caulcott* (1952) 33 TC 159, 164, *per* Donovan J.
[115] *Turner* v. *Last* (1965) 42 TC 517, 522–3, *per* Cross J.
[116] *Eames* v. *Stepnell Properties Ltd.* (1966) 43 TC 678, 692, *per* Buckley J.
[117] *Eames* v. *Stepnell Properties Ltd.* [1967] 1 All ER 785, (1966)43 TC 678 (Commissioners' finding there was no trade reversed); see Harman L.J., 794, 701.
[118] (1953) 34 TC 389.
[119] (1955) 36 TC 117.
[120] See *Eckel* v. *Board of Inland Revenue* [1989] STC 305, PC.
[121] *Taylor* v. *Good* [1973] 2 All ER 785, [1973] STC 383, 49 TC 277.
[122] *Simmons* v. *IRC* [1980] STC 350, [1980] 2 All ER 798, 53 TC 461; see Preece [1981] *BTR* 124; Walters [1981] *BTR* 379. It is also clear that a case stated must be examined in the round (*Kirkby* v. *Hughes* [1993] STC 76, 65 TC 532).

In computing the profit where the trade is begun after the asset is acquired, the asset must be brought into account at its market value at that time.[123]

19.4 Sales by Personal Representatives and Liquidators

19.4.1 The rule

Personal representatives (PRs) may be empowered to carry on the deceased's (D's) business by the terms of the will; however, their acts may amount to carrying on a trade for the purposes of Schedule D, Case I whether or not there is such power.[124] If they are held to be trading, the liability to tax is theirs personally—not *qua* executor.[125] The job of PRs is to realise the assets of the estate and distribute them among the beneficiaries. There is therefore a presumption that they were not carrying on a trade if all they did was realise the asset in a way advantageous to the estate.[126]

19.4.2 Farming

Whether the acts amount to carrying on a trade is a matter of degree and must depend on the nature of the trade, as two cases concerning farming show. In *Pattullo's Trustees* v. *IRC*[127] the taxpayers were the representatives of a tenant farmer (D) who also carried on the trades of cattle dealer and feeder. The farm and the cattle dealing business were bequeathed specifically, so that the only asset to be realised was the feeding business. D died in November, when the cattle were already on the land of other farms feeding from and manuring that land. The PRs considered they had to complete the contracts for economic reasons. They also bought more cattle in order to consume the remaining feedstuffs on the farms. The cattle were all sold by the following June. The Commissioners held that the PRs were carrying on the business of cattle feeding and were not simply preparing the estate assets for sale, even though this was their motive. The Court of Session held that there was evidence to support the Commissioners' finding of liability to tax through trading.

However, in *IRC* v. *Donaldson's Trustees*[128] the Commissioners held there was no trading; again, their conclusion was not reversed by the Court of Session. In this case D was a farmer whose sole interest was a pedigree herd of Aberdeen Angus cattle. D died in March 1955. The trustees were advised to sell the heifer calves in September 1955 and the bull calves in February 1956. They did this, but had to keep the cattle alive and well in the meantime. The manager was told that the cattle were to be sold and the farm was rearranged for preparing them for sale instead of grazing and breeding. It was held that the occupation of the farm was simply for the termination of husbandry and there was no trade.

[123] *Simmons* v. *IRC* [1980] STC 350, [1980] 2 All ER 798, 53 TC 461. This is the converse of *Sharkey* v. *Wernher* (see below at §23.5.3). See also TCGA 1992, s. 161 (and below at §42.3). Cases in which this rule should have been applied include *Leach* v. *Pogson* (1962) 40 TC 585 and *Mitchell Bros* v. *Tomlinson* (1957) 37 TC 224.

[124] *Weisberg's Executrices* v. *IRC* (1933) 17 TC 696.

[125] *Cohan's Executors* v. *IRC* (1924) 12 TC 602. Note Romer L.J. in *Hillerns and Fowler* v. *Murray* (1932) 17 TC 77, 92.

[126] *Cohan's Executors* v. *IRC* (1924) 12 TC 602, 620, *per* Sargant L.J.; approved by Greene M.R. in *Newbarns Syndicate* v. *Hay* (1939) 22 TC 461, 472.

[127] (1955) 36 TC 87.

[128] (1963) 41 TC 161.

It is thus a question of fact and degree whether the acts amount to the realisation of the asset or to trade.[129] However, if the acts are equally consistent both with the carrying-on of a trade and with mere realisation, the act will be mere realisation since to hold otherwise would deprive the executors of their right *vis-à-vis* the Revenue to realise their testator's assets in the ordinary way.[130] In *Donaldson's Trustees* the PRs were able to show a positive change from the normal pattern of farming. In *Pattullo's Trustees* the Revenue could show, by the purchase of extra cattle, a continuation or development of the trade.

19.4.3 Insisting against partners

Where D was carrying on a trade in partnership with others, the executors may insist that the assets should be realised on D's death so that they may administer the estate. Where assets are realised the court may hold that, as far as the estate is concerned, the process is one of mere realisation.[131] In the absence of a finding that the executors did not consent to the continuation of the trade, but insisted upon their share of the assets, the court will uphold a finding by the Commissioners that there was a continuation of the trade.[132]

19.4.4 Liquidation

The duty of a liquidator (L) is like that of the PRs—to realise the assets.[133] The courts may ask the question: what reason is there to suppose that the winding-up was done for any purpose other than the normal carrying-out of the duties of a liquidator?[134] There is a presumption that a mere disposal is not a trading operation.[135] On the other hand, the payment to the liquidator of sums in respect of trading contracts made before the date of liquidation will be trading receipts.[136]

19.5 Retirement—When Does Trading End?

19.5.1 Selling trading stock

To dispose of trading stock following retirement may well be trading, since the moment when trade ceases is a question of fact. Declarations by the trader are not, of themselves,

[129] *Wood* v. *Black's Executor* (1952) 33 TC 172.

[130] *Newbarns Syndicate* v. *Hay* (1939) 22 TC 461, 476, *per* Greene M.R.

[131] As in *Marshall's Executors, Hood's Executors and Rogers* v. *Joly* [1936] 1 All ER 851, 20 TC 256, where it was proved.

[132] As in *Newbarns Syndicate* v. *Hay* (1939) 22 TC 461 where the process of realisation took 10 years and the executor attended all partnership meetings as a voting participant, something he was not entitled to do as the mere executor of a deceased member.

[133] *IRC* v. *Burrell* [1924] 2 KB 52, 73, 9 TC 27, 42, *per* Atkin L.J. In these cases it is irrelevant that the assets were the trading stock of the company or represented undivided profit. The same principles apply to trustees holding on an assignment for the benefit of creditors (*Armitage* v. *Moore* [1900] 2 QB 363, 4 TC 199, supplying steam power is trading, not realising an asset) and to a receiver for debenture holders (*IRC* v. *Thompson* [1936] 2 All ER 651, 20 TC 422).

[134] *Wilson Box (Foreign Rights) Ltd.* v. *Brice* [1936] 3 All ER 728, 20 TC 736, esp. 742 *per* Lawrence J., and 747, *per* Slesser L.J.; and *John Mills Production Ltd.* v. *Mathias* (1964) 44 TC 441, 456, *per* Ungoed Thomas J.

[135] *Wilson Box (Foreign Rights) Ltd.* v. *Brice* [1936] 3 All ER 728, 20 TC 736.

[136] *IRC* v. *Oban Distillery Co. Ltd.* (1932) 18 TC 33.

decisive. In *J. and R. O'Kane Ltd.* v. *IRC*[137] the taxpayers had carried on the business of wine and spirit merchants. They announced their intention to retire in early 1916 but did not complete the disposal of their stock until late 1917, an operation which was carried out mostly in 1917 and which took the form of many small sales. The only purchases made for the business after the announcement of their retirement were under continuing contracts with distillers. The Special Commissioners held that the trade did not end in early 1916 and that the proceeds of the disposal sales were therefore taxable as the profits of the trade. The House of Lords held that there was abundant evidence for the Commissioners' findings.

On the other hand in, *IRC* v. *Nelson*[138] there was only a 12-day gap between the decision to retire and the disposal of the stock, and the whole stock was sold together with the rest of the business (the casks, the trade name and office furniture and fittings) in one sale to one customer. The Commissioners held that the disposal was not by way of trade and the Court of Session held that there was evidence to support the conclusion.

19.5.2 *Completing contracts*

Problems arise on the completion of executory contracts entered into before retirement. In *Hillerns and Fowler* v. *Murray*[139] the trade was run by a partnership which was dissolved by lapse of time under the terms of the partnership deed. At that time the partners held trading stock and subsequently acquired other stock under contracts entered into before the dissolution. The trading stock was used to fulfil orders placed by customers before the dissolution; no new contracts, whether for purchase or sale, were entered into after dissolution. The Commissioners held that there was evidence of trading after dissolution. Although Rowlatt J. reversed their decision, the Court of Appeal held that there was evidence to support the Commissioners' conclusion; the (alleged) presumption that a sale by an executor or liquidator was a realisation of an asset and not a trading activity, did not apply.

Where, however, it is clear that trading has ceased, subsequent disposals will escape income tax.[140] Therefore, a sale of slag heaps 18 years after a company's iron works had shut down was not a part of their trade; it was not argued that this was a new trade.

19.5.3 *Is purchaser trading?*

Where T sells a trade to another (P), T ceases to trade. Whether P, in selling T's former trading stock, commences to trade or simply realises assets is a matter of fact.[141] If P is a company which is under some obligation to hand over the whole or part of the profits of the trade to T, it may be concluded that P is simply T's agent, so that T does not cease to trade.[142] An alternative conclusion on the facts may be that the old trade has ceased but that T has commenced a new trade through the agency of P.[143] The choice between these two outcomes is not merely academic since, apart from the commencement and cessation provisions, there are such questions as unused loss relief which will be lost under the second outcome.

[137] (1922) 12 TC 303.
[138] [1939] SC 689, 22 TC 716.
[139] (1932) 17 TC 77.
[140] *Beams* v. *Weardale Steel Coal and Coke Co. Ltd.* (1937) 21 TC 204.
[141] *Lucy and Sunderland Ltd.* v. *Hunt* [1961] 3 All ER 1062, 1066, 40 TC 132, 139.
[142] *Baker* v. *Cook* [1937] 3 All ER 509, 21 TC 337.
[143] *Southern* v. *Watson* [1940] 3 All ER 439, 23 TC 566; see also *Parker* v. *Batty* (1941) 23 TC 739.

19.6 Mutual Business

19.6.1 The idea

It is necessary to distinguish a profit from a trade, from an excess of contribution over expenditure. If a person allows himself £60 a week for housekeeping, but spends only £50, no one would contend that the £10 saved was taxable profit. The immunity of the £10 from tax rests on two principles, either of which is sufficient: one is that a person cannot trade with himself; the other is that the sum does not represent a profit.

Example—clubs

This immunity has been applied to groups of people who combine for a purpose and contribute towards expenses, as in the case of a golf club whose members pay a club subscription. Here, any excess of income from subscriptions over expenses is free from tax.[144] Each member is entitled to a share of the surplus and it is irrelevant that there is only a limited liability to contribute to any deficiency.[145] Wherever, therefore the contributors to, and the recipients from, the fund are the same people[146] it is impossible to say that the contributors derive profits from the contributions made by themselves to a fund which could only be expended or returned to themselves.[147] Even if the club had a bar at which drinks were served at prices which yielded a profit, there is no liability to tax since the bar is merely a part of the club, and is open only to members, who thus make certain additional contributions to the fund. The situation is different where the bar is open to the public,[148] since the contributors to the fund are no longer the same as the recipients from it; profits from the bar would be taxable even if the rest of the club ran at a loss. Liability would also arise if the facts showed that the bar was a distinct trading venture separate from the rest of the club. The mutuality principle extends to mutual insurance companies and to institutions like the BBC[149] and members' clubs.

19.6.2 Mutual companies

The principle of mutuality applies even though the contributions are made to a separate legal entity[150]—such as a company—provided the company exists simply for the convenience of its members and as an instrument obedient to their mandate (e.g. a mutual insurance company).[151] Income from investments is taxable in the usual way. Any excess of premium income over liabilities will also be the income of the company. However, provided such income is returnable to the members either in the form of bonuses or by way of reduc-

[144] *Carlisle and Silloth Golf Club* v. *Smith* [1913] 3 KB 75, 6 TC 48 and 198; distinguished in *Carnoustie Golf Course Committee* v. *IRC [*1929] SC 419, 14 TC 498.

[145] *Faulconbridge* v. *National Employers Mutual General Insurance Association Ltd.* (1952) 33 TC 103.

[146] But identity does not mean absolute equality (*Municipal Mutual Insurance Ltd.* v. *Hills* (1932) 16 TC 430, 448, *per* Lord Macmillan); as long as the relationship is reasonable.

[147] See *English and Scottish Joint Co-operative Wholesale Society Ltd.* v. *Assam Agricultural IT Comr* [1948] AC 405, 419, [1948] 2 All ER 395, 400; *per* Lord Normand. *IRC* v. *Eccentric Club Ltd.* [1924] 1 KB 390, 12 TC 657; and Finlay J. in *National Association of Local Government Officers* v. *Watkins* (1934) 18 TC 499, 506.

[148] *Grove* v. *Young Men's Christian Association* (1903) 4 TC 613.

[149] *BBC* v. *Johns* [1964] 1 All ER 923, 41 TC 471.

[150] See Rowlatt J. in *Thomas* v. *Richard Evans & Co. Ltd.* [1927] 1 KB 33, 47, 11 TC 790, 823.

[151] For criticism, see Royal Commission, Cmd 9474 (1955), §22; and [1961] *BTR* 398 (JGM).

tion of premiums, that income is exempt from tax since, although the company is trading,[152] this sum is not a profit to its members.[153] A member who surrenders a policy loses any entitlement to future bonuses despite having contributed to them. Conversely, a person who becomes a member of the company by taking out a policy, may become entitled to a portion of the surplus contributed by someone else. Such possibilities do not prevent there being mutuality, since the excess of contributions must go back to the policy holders as a class even if not precisely in the proportions in which they have contributed to them.[154]

It is, however, essential that such companies should be mutual companies, i.e. where only the policy holders are the members of the company. If the company has shareholders who do not hold life policies but who are entitled to the profits of this business, the company is not a mutual company.[155] Today, a body corporate and an unincorporated association are subject to corporation tax. TA 1988, s. 490 ensures that distributions to members will be charged to Schedule F income tax; however, the charge applies only to distributions out of profits chargeable to corporation tax so that the principle of mutuality remains.

19.6.3 Limits of mutuality

(1) Dealings with non-members

The principle of immunity applies only to profits from mutual dealings between contributors. Mutual insurance companies are taxable on the ordinary income accruing from transactions with non-members. Thus, in *New York Life Insurance Co* .v. *Styles*[156] the House of Lords held that the company was not taxable on its profits from premium income from members' participating policies. It was agreed that the company was taxable on its profits from policies for fixed sums without profits and from its general annuity business with strangers, since they were not members of the company, just as it was taxable on its investment income. Exemption is afforded not to the profits from members, but to the non-profit of mutual dealings.

(2) Lack of genuine mutuality

In *Fletcher* v. *IT Comr*[157] a members' club owned a bathing beach in Jamaica. It permitted guests at certain hotels to use the beach on payment of an entrance fee. The club was clearly taxable on the profits of these fees since it was carrying on a trade with non-members. The club then altered its arrangements, abolishing the payment of a fee by the hotel guests and making the hotels voting members of the club.[158] However, each hotel member, like each individual, held only one share. The hotels, like the individual members, paid a sum by way of subscription, and, in addition, a sum which was based on the number of its guests using the beach. Gross receipts were £1,750. The Revenue sought to tax the club on the profit

[152] See Lord Cave in *IRC* v. *Cornish Mutual Assurance Co. Ltd.* [1926] AC 281, 286–7, 12 TC 841, 866–7, criticising Lord Watson in *New York Life Insurance Co.* v. *Styles* (1889) 14 App Cas 381, 2 TC 460.

[153] See, e.g. Lord Macmillan in *Municipal Mutual Insurance Ltd.* v. *Hills* (1932) 16 TC 430, 448.

[154] On position of newcomers, see Upjohn J. in *Faulconbridge* v. *National Employers Mutual General Insurance Association Ltd.* (1952) 33 TC 103, 121, 124–5.

[155] *Last* v. *London Assurance Group Coprn* (1885) 10 App Cas 438, 2 TC 100; but see now TA 1988, s. 433.

[156] (1889) 14 App Cas 381, 2 TC 460; see also *Municipal Mutual Insurance Ltd.* v. *Hills* (1932) 16 TC 430, HL.

[157] [1972] AC 414, [1971] 3 All ER 1185; distinguished in *Westbourne Supporters of Glentoran Club* v. *Brennan* [1995] STC (SCD) 137.

[158] An earlier scheme had made the hotels members but without voting rights, and it had been held that this scheme failed because the hotels were not truly members.

element in the relevant proportion of the hotel membership subscription. Lord Wilberforce said that although a uniform fee was not essential, nevertheless, if mutuality were to have any meaning:[159]

> "there must be a reasonable relationship, contemplated or in result, between what a member contributed and what, with due allowance for interim benefits of enjoyment, he may expect or be entitled to draw from the fund; between his liabilities and his rights."

The great use of the beach made by hotel guests was not sufficient allowance, and so the mutuality principle did not apply.

This decision provides the (uncited) basis for a Revenue interpretation on profits arising from green fees at a golf club. Clearly, the profit arising from fees paid by a member is not taxable, whereas profit from fees paid by a non-member is taxable. However, temporary membership will be enough to create mutuality only if the rights of temporary members are similar to those of full members.[160]

(3) Non-mutual business with members[161]

Not all business between a company and its members is mutual business. A business cannot escape tax on its profits for a year simply because, at the end of the year, it discovers that all its business has been with its members.

In *English and Scottish Joint Co-operative Wholesale Society Ltd.* v. *Assam Agricultural IT Comr*[162] a company was set up to own and manage a tea estate with the bulk of its produce going to its two shareholders who advanced money by way of loan to be set off against the price due for the tea supplied by the company to its shareholders. It was held that the company had earned profits from dealings with its shareholders and so was taxable. This conclusion could not have been avoided by restricting the company's business to sales to its members.[163] A different result might have been reached if the business had not been incorporated; a different practical result would have been reached if the price paid for the tea had been fixed so that no profit would have been earned.[164]

19.6.4 Emasculated legislation

An attempt was made in 1933[165] to tax the profits of mutual companies from dealings with members by directing that such profits or surplus should be treated as if those transactions were transactions with non-members. Since it was the mutuality of the transaction rather than the fact that it was with a member which gave immunity from taxation, the House of Lords, in a somewhat unimaginative construction of the statute, ruled that even if the transactions had been with non-members they would have been exempt from tax, thus depriving the statute of any force.[166] When such companies became the subject of profits tax, the

159 [1971] 3 All ER 1185,1191.

160 RI 84; see Harris [1998] *BTR* 24.

161 *Municipal Mutual Insurance* v. *Hills* (1932) 16 TC 430; see above at §0.00.

162 [1948] AC 405, [1948] 2 All ER 395.

163 Ibid., 417, 399.

164 Ibid., 421, 401 (perhaps by treating the application of profit as a discount reducing the price); see *Pope* v. *Beaumont* [1941] 3 All ER 9, 24 TC 78.

165 FA 1933, s. 31.

166 *Ayrshire Employers Mutual Insurance Association Ltd.* v. *IRC* [1946] 1 All ER 637, 640, 27 TC 331, 347; note the comments in *Fothergill* v. *Monarch Airlines Ltd.* [1981] AC 251. The section remained on the statute book unamended until the pre-consolidation changes of 1987.

legislature was more direct and simply taxed the profits of the trade of mutual companies. This more direct approach succeeded.[167]

19.6.5 Clawback of tax-deductible contribution

The exemption from tax afforded by mutual dealings does not operate to prevent certain contributions being claimed as deductions in computing the taxable income of the contributor.[168] Thus, a payment to a fire insurance scheme is deductible whether or not the scheme is mutual. If the mutual business then ceases there will be a repayment to the contributor (C) of any surplus—but without any charge to tax. C may recover more than has been paid.[169] If C made a contribution of £100 and has a marginal tax rate of 40%, the after-tax cost of the contribution would be £60; if, however, the business is wound up there will be a repayment of £100 free of tax. Without special legislation this device could be used to build up tax-free reserves. Hence, TA 1988, s. 491 provides that where a body corporate is being wound up or dissolved, and a non-taxable sum was paid to a person who was then allowed to deduct that payment in computing the profits, gains or losses of a trade, profession or vocation, the receipt is treated as a trading receipt of the trade or, if the trade has ceased, as a post-cessation receipt.

S. 491 applies only where the receipt is not otherwise taxable and where the receipt does not represent capital—a phrase which is very widely defined.[170] The section is confined to situations where the mutual business is carried on by a body corporate and not just a company as defined for corporation tax (the reasoning behind this restriction is not clear).

19.7 Occupation of Land or Trade

Schedule A income derived from the exploitation of property is property income under Schedule A, rather than trading income under Schedule D, Case I.[171] Income arising under the revised Schedule A, which is treated in many ways as if it were a trade, is nonetheless not trading income and remains taxable under Schedule A. Therefore, income from furnished lettings is taxable under Schedule A (if the land is in the UK) or Schedule D, Case V (if it is not).[172] See further below at §§25.3 and 25.7.

19.7.1 Farms

All farming and market gardening in the UK is taxed under Schedule D, Case I[173] and all farming carried on by any particular person or partnership or body of persons is treated as one trade.[174]

[167] See also Royal Commission, Cmd 9474 (1955), §593.

[168] *Thomas* v. *Richard Evans & Co. Ltd.* [1927] 1 KB 33, 11 TC 790.

[169] *Stafford Coal and Iron Co. Ltd.* v. *Brogan* [1963] 3 All ER 227, 41 TC 305, HL; see [1963] *BTR* 370 (JGM).

[170] TA 1988, s. 491(8).

[171] *Webb* v. *Conelee Properties Ltd.* [1982] STC 913.

[172] *Gittos* v. *Barclay* [1982] STC 390, 55 TC 633

[173] TA 1988, s. 53(1). On the scope of market gardening, see *Bomford* v. *Osborne* (1940) 23 TC 642, 660, esp. *per* Scott L.J. Originally, farmers came within Schedule B and remained there partly because of the difficulty farmers had in keeping accounts. When they were moved to Schedule A, the Chancellor, announcing the proposed change was misreported as saying that farmers should be treated like other "traitors" rather than "traders" (Sabine, *History of Income Tax*, 118).

[174] TA 1988, s. 53(2); hence, if X has farm A, with accrued losses and unused capital allowances, and buys farm

19.7.2 Other land

The occupation of land for purposes other than farming or market gardening managed on a commercial basis and with a view to realisation of profits is similarly within Schedule D, Case I.[175] Actual occupation is required; granting a licence to someone else to occupy is not enough. [176]

19.7.3 Woods

Until 1988, woodlands managed on a commercial basis were subject to a separate regime under Schedule B; the repeal of Schedule B means that such profits are now not taxed as income at all.[177] Actual occupation was required under this rule; simply having a licence to fell and remove timber or clear the land for replanting was not enough.[178] By statute the cultivation of short rotation coppice is regarded as farming not forestry.[179] See further below at §25.6

19.7.4 Mines. etc.

Profits from mines, quarries and other specified concerns including ferries and canals also fall within Schedule D, Case I.[180]

B, he may set those losses and allowances against the profits of farm B even if subsequently he sells farm A (*Bispham* v. *Eardiston Farming Co. (1919) Ltd.* [1962] 2 All ER 376, 40 TC 322; noted at [1962] *BTR* 255. This provision does not appear to apply to market gardening; see, generally, de Souza [1991] *BTR* 15.

175 TA 1988, s. 53(3). See *Sywell Aerodrome Ltd.* v. *Croft* [1942] 1 All ER 110, 24 TC 126. If the land is not managed on a commercial basis a charge may arise under Schedule D, Case VI (see above at §10.11).

176 *Webb* v. *Conelee Properties Ltd.* [1982] STC 913, 56 TC 149.

177 TA 1988, s. 54; repealed 1988. On boundary of Schedules B and DI, see below at §25.6.

178 TA 1988, s. 16(6) repealed in 1988.

179 FA 1995, s. 154; this is for the purposes of income tax and CGT, but not IHT.

180 TA 1988, s. 55.

20

Business Income—Part II: Basis of Assessment and Loss Relief

20.1 Current Year Basis

For many years, and for most of the years over which the case-law relevant to Schedule D, Cases I and II has been developed,[1] the profits of a trade or profession were taxed on a "preceding year" basis (see below at §20.5) After a transitional year in 1996–97 the new "current year" basis was applied to all such profits as from 1997–98; the new rules were already in force for trades and professions begun on or after 6 April 1994. The same years also saw the start of the new self-assessment regime. Introducing both changes at the same time attracted much criticism.

[1] The preceding basis has never been part of corporation tax (which was introduced in 1965).

20.1.1 Summary

The new system is designed to ensure that over the lifetime of the business the profits brought into tax are the same as the profits actually earned by that business—by the use of "basis periods". Usually the basis period will be the 12-month period used by the business for its own accounting process. The tax system also has a fall-back position to tax by reference to the profits accruing from 6 April to 5 April.

Special rules apply when a business starts, when there is a change of accounting date and when the business ends. When a business starts it is possible that some profits will be used in each of the two years; such doubly brought-in profits are called "overlap profits". The taxpayer will be given credit, called "overlap relief", for the doubly charged profits by being allowed to deduct an equivalent sum later on—either at the end (or "discontinuance") of the business, when all things can be brought into line, or on a prior change of accounting date ("change of basis"). The amount of overlap profit is not index linked and the tax on those profits is little better than a forced loan to the Government.

As under the previous law, if the taxpayer dies the personal representatives are liable in the place of the deceased and the tax is a debt due from and payable out of the estate.[2]

20.1.2 The normal rule

Normal 12-month accounting periods

Where there was a basis period for the immediately preceding year, and that basis period was not given by the "commencement" rules, and that period begins immediately after the end of that basis period and has lasted 12 months,[3] the profit of the accounting period is taken i.e. is the accounting period is the basis period. Therefore, if T's business has been running for some years using a calendar year basis and T makes £20,000 profit in the year ending 31 December 2000 and £30,000 in the year ending 31 December 2001, this rule will give £20,000 as the figure for 2000–01 and £30,000 for 2001–02.

20.1.3 The basic or fall-back rule

TA 1988, s. 60(1) requires T to be taxed on the profits of the year of assessment, apportioning profits of particular periods, on a daily basis, as necessary.[4] If a business makes £10,000 profit in the 12-month period ending on 5 October 2000 and £20,000 in the six months ending on 6 April 2001, the profits for the year 2000–01 will be £25,013, i.e. £5,013 (183/365ths of £10,000) plus £20,000. The basic rule is excluded where any of the other rules apply.[5]

[2] TA 1988, s. 60(4).
[3] Ibid., s. 60(3)(b).
[4] TA 1988, s. 72; the daily basis is required by s. 72(2), although the Revenue is said to allow other bases, e.g. monthly, provided they are used consistently.
[5] Ibid., s. 60(2), referring to ss 61–63.

20.1.4 *The commencement rules*

Year of commencement—tax year 1

When a trade is commenced, a charge arises in that first year and extends to the profits arising in the year.[6] Therefore, if T starts to trade on 1 January 2001 and makes up the first set accounts to the period ending 5 April 2001, the profit of that accounting period is taken for the year 2000–01. If the first set of accounts is made up to 31 December 2001, then the profit of that accounting period will be apportioned to 2000–01 on a daily basis (95/365ths); so, if the profit for the calendar year shown by the accounts is £365,000, the amount apportioned to 2000–01 will be £95,000.

Second tax year of business and the overlap profit

The treatment of the second year depends on how the accounts are made up, as follows.

12 month accounting period ending in second tax year: first accounts s. 60(3)(a). The 12-month period ending with T's accounting date is taken if the tax year is the first year of assessment in which the accounting date falls 12 months or more after the commencement date.[7] So, if T begins the business on 1 January 2001 and makes up the *first* accounts to 31 December 2001, the profits of that first period are taken for 2001–02; if those profits come to £365,000, tax is due on £365,000. The self-assessment must be made by 31 January 2003 and tax paid by then. Of the £365,000, £95,000 was also taken for 2000–01; this sum is treated as "overlap profit", i.e. the profit of the period overlapping the two tax years.

—not the first accounts: It is not actually necessary that these should be T's first set of accounts. TA 1988, s. 60(3)(a) also applies if T starts to trade on 1 January 2001 but makes up the first set of accounts to 28 February 2001 and the second set to 28 February 2002. The second set will be used since what is required for s. 60(3)(a) is a 12-month set of accounts ending in year 2. The year 2001–02 is still the first tax year in which the accounting date falls 12 months or more after the commencement date, and the 12-month accounting period is still relevant. This time it will be the profits from 1 March 2001 to 5 April 2001 which will provide the overlap profit.

Accounting period ending in year 2 less than 12 months. If, as before, T starts business on 1 January 2001 but makes up the *first* accounts to 30 September 2001, TA 1988, s. 60(3)(a) is not satisfied and another rule must apply—if necessary the basic rule in s. 60(1). If T's *second* set of accounts run to 30 September 2002 this rule will apply to make the accounting profits of the period ending 30 September 2002 the profits for 2002–03. The self-assessment for 2002–03 must be made by 31 January 2004.

Accounting period ending in year 2 greater than 12 months. T must take the profits of the 12 months ending with the accounting date (apportioning as necessary). Therefore if, once again, T starts business on 1 January 2001 but makes up the first set of accounts 14 months later (28 February 2002), the tax profits for year 2 will be an apportioned part of the figures for that 14-month period (365/424ths) will be used. It will be appreciated that in these circumstances the start of the basis period for year 2 will be later than the start of the business, and year 1 will tax the profits of the opening period down to 1 March 2001 only once.

No accounting period ending in second year. Here, the actual profits of year 2 are used, i.e. the basic rule in s. 60(1) applies.[8]

[6] Ibid., s. 61(1).
[7] Ibid., s. 60(3)(a).
[8] Ibid., s. 61(2).

20.2 Overlap Profits

Because of these complicated rules, the same accounting profits may appear in the taxable profits for both years 1 and 2. This is because the profit period for the second year overlaps that period for the first year, hence the expressions "overlap period" and "overlap profits". These rules fall short of the scheme adopted by most other countries and which the UK tax system was able to adopt for corporation tax in 1965—a simple current year basis. Quite what rational reason there is for having to wait until the end of one's trading life before being given credit for the double taxation, with no indexation for inflation and with no regard for the different rates of tax which may be in force in the different years, is hard to imagine. Overlap profits can also arise if there is a change of accounting date and the gap between the start and end of the period is less than 12 months.[9]

Taking the first three years together it can be seen that the new system brings about an alignment of the basis period with the annual accounting period either in the second or the third year. Once this has been done the basis period will change only if there is a discontinuance or an effective change of accounting date.

The simplest way to avoid the double charge is to have no taxable profits for the opening period. Another way is to have no overlap period, i.e. to have the business year end on 5 April (or, in practice, 31 March) profits. It may be that the real purpose of the overlap rules is to encourage taxpayers to take such a date.

In general, the earlier in the year the business starts the greater the amount of overlap period, and so potential overlap profit. If the business begins on 7 April 2001 and ends on 6 April 2002 the first year profit will virtually all be charged in year 2001–02 and again in 2002–03. By contrast the business beginning on 5 April will have, only one day of overlap profit.[10]

Overlap profits may also occur if they arose in 1996–1997 from a business begun before 6 April 1994.[11]

Relief for the double tax is give when the business ceases (see below at §20.3) or there is a change of accounting date to a date *later* in the year (see below at §20.4).

Although a 31 March or 5 April year end will avoid an overlap profit, it does not follow that this must be the date to choose. If a business will have a modest or very low profit in the first year and thereafter a significant rise, it may be worth having a 7 April or 30 April year end: the amount of overlap profit will be modest and the deferral of tax liability significant.[12] However, whatever date is chosen, the more the tax is deferred the greater is the need to ensure that there is enough money with which to pay the tax which eventually accrues.

20.3 Discontinuance—The Final Year

Where a trade is discontinued, the basis period for the year of discontinuance will generally be the period beginning immediately after the end of the basis period for the preceding year

[9] TA 1988, s. 62 below § 20.4.2 (and under certain transitional rules).
[10] See below at n. 12.
[11] FA 1994, Sch. 20, para. 2(4), as amended (1995); for details, see Tiley and Collison, *UK Tax Guide* (Butterworths, 1998–1999), para. 7.44.
[12] Hill in Tolley, *Tax Planning 1999–2000*, 239, 243.

of assessment and ending with the date of discontinuance.[13] While this means that the basis period may be longer than 12 months, it also ensures that there will be no gap between the basis periods and that, over the life of the business, all the profits will have been brought into charge to tax. Termination is not usually treated as a change of accounting date. [14]

Example

T has been making up his accounts on a yearly basis ending on 30 June. T ceases to trade on 31 December 2001. The last year that will have been taxed is the year ending 30 June 2000, the figures being used for 2000–01. For 2001–02, the year of "discontinuance",the basis period covers all the remaining days i.e. 1 July 2000 to 31 December 2001 (549 days).

The only exception to this rule is where the trade ceases in the second year, but this is a matter of formulation not of policy. The basis period begins on 6 April of that second year and ends with the date of discontinuance.[15] Here, too, there is no gap between the two periods nor, incidentally, is there any overlap.

The significance of discontinuance is that it may bring about a claim for overlap relief and the deduction from the final profits of any remaining overlap profits figure.[16] Assuming no changes of accounting date and a constant 12-month cycle, the overlap profit will be that which arose for the 279 days from 1 July to 5 April of the business' first year. Subtracting 279 from 549 leaves 270, which is precisely the number of days from 6 April to 31 December 2001.

If the relief causes a loss, the excess is given loss relief in the usual way against general income of that year and the previous year under TA 1988, s. 380 (or in an appropriate case under TA 1988, s. 381); however, it may also be treated as a terminal loss and carried back three years under s. 388 (see below §20.10).

Terminal loss relief which cannot be absorbed within this three-year period is lost, so that the profits which will have been assessed to the business will be greater than the profits actually earned.[17] Where this is a risk, the presence of overlap profits from the opening year may exacerbate the problem since the relief for overlap profits take the form of a simple deduction from trading profits; at the very least, taxpayers ought to have the right to repayment of the overlap profit regardless of the loss position. The present position encourages taxpayers to close their business before they might otherwise do so; the presence of overlap profits increases that risk.

20.4 Change of Basis Period

Taxpayers may change their accounting dates, whether because accounts are not made up to the old date, or are made up to a new date, or both. This freedom is unlimited during the first three years. However, later changes must meet three conditions:[18] (1) that the first

[13] TA 1988, s. 63(b).

[14] Inland Revenue booklet SAT 1 (1994), §§1.75–1.77 pointing out that while s. 63 overrides s. 62 for the year of cessation itself, s. 62(5) may cause a change in the year before the year of assessment, but adding that the change will be ignored if it is not notified.

[15] TA 1988, s. 63(a).

[16] Ibid., s. 63A(3).

[17] Fuller, Simons (2000) 7 *Tax Briefing Issue* 5.

[18] TA 1988, s. 62A.

accounting period ending with the new date must not exceed 18 months; (2) that notice is given to the inspector no later than 31 January following the year of assessment; and (3) that either (a) no accounting change has been made in any of the preceding five years of assessment or (b) T can satisfy the Inland Revenue that the change is being made for bona fide commercial reasons—an expression which does not extend to the obtaining of a tax advantage.[19] An Inland Revenue officer who is not satisfied of this must give notice within 60 days; an appeal lies to the Commissioners.[20]

20.4.1 New period

One of the statutory terms is the "relevant period", which is defined as the period beginning immediately after the end of the basis period for the previous year of assessment and ending with the new date.[21] Where these conditions are satisfied, the relevant period begins immediately after the end of the previous accounting period and ends on the new accounting date—whether it is more or less than 12 months.

20.4.2 New overlap profit

Where the relevant period is less than 12 months, the basis period is the period of 12 months ending on the new date;[22] this means that there will be an overlap period in which profits will be taken more than once. Suppose that T has operated on a year basis from 1 July 2000 to 30 June 2001, but subsequently changes to a calendar year ending on 31 December 2001. The profit from 1 January to 31 December 2001 will be taken for 2001–02, even though part of that period has already been taken for the 2000–01, six-month accounting period.

20.4.3 Overlap relief

If, on the other hand, the relevant period is more than 12 months, the basis period is the relevant period itself.[23] This will, in turn, give rise to immediate overlap relief for any overlap profits remaining unrelieved. So, if the accounting period is 18 months, overlap relief will be available for six months. If the overlap period was nine months, this will means that approximately[24] two-thirds of the original overlap profit will now be available for deduction. It will be seen that the two-thirds fraction is applied to the original, unindexed overlap profit—not to the equivalent proportion of the current profits.

It may be worth making a change of accounting date earlier rather than later, especially if this means reducing profits below the higher rate threshold. Perhaps it is for such reasons that changes of accounting date are permitted without preconditions in the first three years.

19 Ibid., s. 62A(5), (9).
20 If T's application fails, a new attempt may be made the following year—or T may revert to the original date.
21 TA 1988, s. 62(2).
22 Ibid., s. 62(2)(a).
23 Ibid., s. 62(2)(b).
24 Because the sums are calculated on a daily, not a monthly, basis.

20.4.4 Failure to satisfy rules

Where the above conditions are not satisfied, but the change of accounting period occurs in the second or third year of assessment, the rules outlined above apply nonetheless. In other years, if these conditions are not satisfied the basis period will continue to be the period of 12 months ending on the old accounting date and making any apportionments between actual accounts as may be necessary.[25] This can have perverse effects where the new accounting date fails because the period exceeds 18 months.[26] i.e. Condition (1) above at 20.4.

20.4.5 Strict formula for overlap profits and relief on change of accounting date

The formula used to determine the amount of overlap profits which can be used on a change of accounting date is: $(O \times (B - C))/D$ where O is the overlap profit less any amount already relieved in this way, B is the number of days in the basis period and C is the number of days in the year of assessment (365 or 366). D is more complex, being the aggregate of the number of days in the period (or periods) which have been taken into account twice but with a deduction for the number of days given by the variable $B - C$ in any previous applications of the section.

Example
A started business on 1 July 1997. The first year's profits came to £12,000. As already seen, the effect of TA 1988, s. 61 is that A's taxable profits for 1997–1998 will be 279/365 × £12,000, or £9,172, and for the second year £12,000. A's overlap profits from this are agreed at £9,172. In 2001, A decides to change the accounting date to 31 December 2001. The basis period for 2001–02 is 1 July 2000 to 31 December 2001 (549 days).

Applying the above formula, B will be 549 days; C will be 366 (2,000 is a leap year) and D will be 279. The resulting fraction is applied to O, £9,172, and means that £6,016 will be available for set-off against the profits for the 18-month period for 1999–2000 and that only £3,156 will be left for relief on a subsequent change of accounting date or on cessation of the business.

It remains to be seen to what extent the Revenue will insist on a strict day-based calculation as opposed to the broader month basis, which would have given a figure of £6,000, with £3,000 left over for later relief.

20.5 Historical note: The Preceding Year Basis

Before 1997–1998 income tax was levied on the profits and gains of the trade, profession or vocation on a preceding year basis, i.e. on the profits of the year preceding the year of assessment. As has been seen, if a business makes up its accounts on a calendar year basis, the profits for the year from 1 January to 31 December 2000 will—under present rules—be the profits or gains to be charged in the tax year 2000–01. Under the preceding year basis, the tax year 2000–01 would take the profits of the business period ending in the year *before*

[25] TA 1988, s. 62(1)(b), (3), (4).

[26] While the 12-month cycle will be followed from the new date, the basis period under s. 60 will still be the old date.

2000–01, i.e. the profits of the period 1 January to 31 December 1999. This enabled the precise liability for the tax year 1999–00 to be fixed before 1 January 2000, the date on which one half of the tax fell due, the second half being due on 1 July. The present system achieves the same objective by making the tax payable on 31 January 2001, and echoes the old system by demanding payments on account on 1 January and 1 July 2000.

There were two main problems with the preceding year basis. The first was that the Revenue thought, correctly, that ordinary taxpayers could not understand it and so could not be expected to apply it properly under the new self-assessment system. The second problem was that the system contained overlaps in the early years of assessment (on a scale much greater than under the current year system) and compensated for this by having gaps at the end of the life of the business. Therefore, while the profits of some periods were taxed more than once at the beginning of the business, there were periods at the end of the business where the profits were not taxed at all. This meant not only that the total profits subjected to tax were not the same as those earned by the business over the lifetimes of that business, but also that taxpayers could exploit these gaps.[27]

20.6 Starting (Commencement)

20.6.1 When does trade commence?

Importance

It is important to determine when a trade commenced in order to apply TA 1988, ss 61 and 62 correctly, and to fulfil the obligations arising from self-assessment.

At one time this was important because pre-commencement expenditure was deductible only as a result of specific statutory provisions.[28] Today, an expense incurred in the seven years before trading is treated simply as an expense incurred on the day of commencement.[29] This relief is not, however, without its traps. A pre-commencement expense is deductible only if incurred by the trader, not by someone else; therefore, the benefit of the expense will be lost if the business is incorporated when trading begins. Similarly, if company A in a group incurs the expense, while company B, in the same group, carries on the trade, neither can deduct—A never trades, while B does not incur the expense.[30]

Preparing to commence a trade is not the same as commencing a trade

Neither the formation of an intention to commence trading nor the incurring of capital expenditure for the purpose of preparing to trade prove that the trade has begun.

In *Birmingham and District Cattle By-Products Co. Ltd.* v. *IRC*[31] the appellant company was incorporated on 20 June 1913. Its directors then arranged for the installation of plant and machinery and entered into agreements for the purchase of raw materials and the sale of its products. The raw materials were received on 6 October. The company's trade was held to begin on 6 October, when it started to use the raw materials to manufacture its product.

[27] For example, *Reed* v. *Clark* [1986] Ch 1, [1985] STC 323, 58 TC 528; and legislative counter in TA 1988, s. 110A treating a change of residence as a cessation and commencement.

[28] *City of London Contract Corpn Ltd.* v. *Styles* (1887) 2 TC 239.

[29] TA 1988, s. 401.

[30] RI 32.

[31] (1919) 12 TC 92 (an excess profits duty case).

However, in *Cannop Coal Co. Ltd.* v. *IRC*,[32] where the trade was to be the mining of coal by sinking pits in the Forest of Dean, the company had, since 1909, extracted a certain amount of coal from a drift nearby for use in its machines and, finding that it had extracted more than it needed, sold the excess to the public. The company was held to have commenced trading when it sold the excess coal to the public, and not in 1912 when coal began to emerge from the pits. That the coal company was engaged in a trade in those three years seems beyond argument and it was too fine a point to say that the trade was different from the mining of coal from the pits.

A difficult question concerns the use of small-scale pilot projects involving resale to the public in deciding precisely what product to make. It was important in *Cannop Coal Co. Ltd.* v. *IRC* that the sales were substantial,[33] and it may therefore be that pilot projects are not trading.

20.6.2 Commencement—developing existing trade or starting new trade?[34]

If A carries on a business and starts a new line of activity, it is a question of fact and degree[35] whether A is developing an existing activity or starting a second (parallel) business. There is no rule of law that a person, whether or not a company, cannot carry on more than one business, and it is immaterial that there is one consolidated balance sheet. As Rowlatt J. put it in a case where the two activities had both been bought from another company, "the real question is, was there any inter-connection, any interlacing, any interdependence, any unity at all embracing those two businesses?".[36] Therefore, if a trader commences a new trade alongside his established trade, the two trades are treated separately,[37] even for purposes of loss relief and capital allowances; the sources are distinct. Conversely, the amalgamation of two trades may be treated as the cessation of both and the commencement of one new trade.[38]

A relatively modern example is *Seaman* v. *Tucketts Ltd.*[39] In 1956 control of the company was acquired by a new group. The company carried on the trade of manufacture and sale of confectionery; this included the purchase and resale of such goods from other manufacturers, which ended early in 1958. In September 1958 the two retail shops were closed and in November 1958 manufacture ceased. By April 1959 the existing stocks and the factory had been sold. The company which had previously bought sugar and cellophane for its own business now bought these for resale to the new parent company at cost plus 10%. Two years later it began to supply confectionery again. Reversing the Commissioners, Pennycuick J held that the only true and reasonable conclusion was that, at the end of 1958 when the manufacture had ceased, a new trade of sugar merchants, including the buying and selling of cellophane paper, had been commenced. The case was remitted to the Commissioners to determine whether the confectionery trade had been discontinued or had been merely quiescent.

[32] (1918) 12 TC 31 (another excess profits duty case). In both instances the Revenue won.

[33] In one year 68% of the coal was resold, and in another, 84%.

[34] See also Revenue Bulletin (February 1996), 285.

[35] *Howden Boiler and Armaments Co. Ltd.* v. *Stewart* (1924) 9 TC 205; and *Cannon Industries Ltd.* v. *Edwards* (1965) 42 TC 151.

[36] *Scales* v. *George Thompson & Co. Ltd.* (1927) 13 TC 83, 89.

[37] *Fullwood Foundry Ltd.* v. *IRC* (1924) 9 TC 101.

[38] *George Humphries & Co.* v. *Cook* (1934) 19 TC 121.

[39] (1963) 41 TC 422.

Seaman v. *Tucketts Ltd.* shows that not only may there be a termination of one trade and the commencement of another but there may also be a contraction of one trade and the commencement of another, even though the second trade deals with a commodity employed in the original trade. There is also authority that a substantial change in management policy can lead to a discontinuance and a new commencement.[40] However a barrister does not, on taking silk, start a new profession.[41]

A partnership example

TA 1988, s. 113 applies where there is a change in the person running the trade, and assumes that the trade carried on by the previous owner is continued under the new partnership. If the new owner does not carry on the existing business but starts a new one, there will be a discontinuance. In *Maidment* v. *Kibby*[42] the taxpayer partners ran a fish and chip shop in P; they then bought a shop in Q and ran the new shop in their own style, under their own name, with a single system for buying materials and with one set of accounts. The Revenue argued that the Q shop had retained its identity, that there had therefore been a change of persons running the trade and so a discontinuance. The Commissioners rejected the argument; the High Court held that it was open to them to do so.

20.7 Stopping (Discontinuance)

20.7.1 Is there a discontinuance?

A discontinuance occurs where T, a trader, ceases to carry on the trade or, in appropriate circumstances, changes the manner of trading. It is a question of fact whether the particular change is the ceasing of one trade and the commencement of another, or is simply a normal development of the previous trade.

Where a taxpayer has, for example, two offices, and closes one down the question is whether the continuing office is continuing the trade. Clearly, this will be so if the original business was not one, but two separate businesses each run from its own office, in which case the continuing office continues its trade as before.[43] As with commencement, these are matters of fact and degree. In *Rolls Royce Motors Ltd.* v. *Bamford*[44] the original Rolls Royce Ltd., RRL, had developed and built motor cars since 1906; since 1915 it had also been involved in the manufacture of aero engines. In 1971 a large project, the RB211 engine, went seriously wrong; the aero engine business was put into the hands of a new company, and the motor company business was put into the hands of the (separate) taxpayer company, RRM. The Commissioners' decided that RRM had not been carrying on the same trade as RRL; the court held that this was the only rational conclusion and so RRM could not use the losses incurred by RRL on the RB211 project.

[40] See Rowlatt J. in *Kirk and Randall Ltd.* v. *Dunn* (1924) 8 TC 663, 670.
[41] *Seldon* v. *Croom-Johnson* [1932] 1 KB 759, 16 TC 740.
[42] [1993] STC 494, 66 TC 137.
[43] *C. Connelly & Co.* v. *Wilbey* [1992] STC 783, 65 TC 208.
[44] [1976] STC 162, 51 TC 319.

Resting not dead

A trade does not cease if it is merely in abeyance. There is therefore no discontinuance just because of a mere interruption in production[45] or disposal of assets,[46] nor even the appointment of a receiver.[47] Business is not the same as "being busy" and long periods of inactivity may occur.[48] It is, however, a question of fact whether a particular trade has lapsed into a period of quiescence or has ceased. A trade may be treated as permanently discontinued notwithstanding that the former trader later commences a new trade which is in all respects identical with the previous ceased trade.

Contrasting cases

In *Kirk and Randall Ltd.* v. *Dunn*[49] the new owners of a trading company obtained no new contracts and tried to sell the premises; they then had their works and plant requisitioned during the First World War. However, the managing director tried to obtain contracts overseas. Rowlatt J., reversing the Commissioners, held that the company was still trading since there was evidence of business activity resulting in expenditure and loss. However, in *J. G. Ingram & Son Ltd.* v. *Callaghan*,[50] where the period was much shorter, the Court of Appeal upheld the Commissioners' finding that there was not just unprofitability but inactivity, and so a discontinuance. In this case the company had, by May 1961, ceased to produce rubber goods, sold off its stock and dismissed its staff, the plan being to switch to plastics. From September 1961 to June 1962 products were manufactured by another subsidiary of the owner and sold over the company's name. In this way the goodwill was kept alive, but the operations of the company were confined to little more than bookkeeping and debt collecting. It was held that the trade was not kept alive between those dates. A similar conclusion was reached in *Rolls Royce Motors Ltd.* v. *Bamford*[51] where there was a discontinuance, even though the company was actually reverting to its former, narrow trade. This may have been because the reversion was due to a sudden crisis which the company solved by disposing of many of its activities.

20.7.2 Effects of discontinuance

When a trade, profession or vocation is permanently discontinued, the basis of assessment is determined by TA 1988, s. 63. However, special rules relating to relief for losses and capital allowances which may, contrary to the usual rule, be carried back on discontinuance. In so far as these losses or capital allowances exceed the income of the period over which they are taken back, they are lost (save for post-cessation receipts) and cannot be used by anyone else, even a successor to the trade. S. 100 directs the valuation of trading stock.

At one time sums paid just before discontinuance would be non-deductible because they were not spent in order to keep the business alive.[52] A statutory exception was made for

[45] *Merchiston Steamship Co. Ltd.* v. *Turner* [1910] 2 KB 923, 5 TC 520.

[46] *Aviation and Shipping Co. Ltd.* v. *Murray* [1961] 2 All ER 805, 39 TC 595; see also *Watts* v. *Hart* [1984] STC 548, 58 TC 209.

[47] *Wadsworth Morton Ltd.* v. *Jenkinson* [1966] 3 All ER 702, 43 TC 479.

[48] *South Behar Rly Co. Ltd.* v. *IRC* [1925] AC 476, 12 TC 657; *cf. Morning Post Ltd.* v. *George* (1941) 23 TC 514.

[49] (1924) 8 TC 663. See also *Robroyston Brickworks Ltd.* v. *IRC* (1976) 51 TC 230.

[50] [1969] 1 All ER 433, 45 TC 151, CA. The same conclusion was reached in *Tryka Ltd.* v. *Newall* (1963) 41 TC 146, ChD, noted in [1964] *BTR* 286, and *Goff* v. *Osborne & Co. (Sheffield) Ltd.* (1953) 34 TC 441.

[51] [1976] STC 162, 51 TC 319.

[52] *Gooden* v. *A. Wilson's Stores Holdings Ltd.* (1961) 40 TC 161.

certain redundancy payments,[53] but the principle itself is now doubtful as it has been held that a sum paid in order to close a business down is still incurred for the purpose of producing profits.[54]

20.8 Succession or Buying Assets[55]

20.8.1 The concept

A succession arises where a business which was owned by A is transferred to B, who carries it on. The question whether the trade has been transferred by A to B, or whether A has disposed of the business, is relevant in various parts of the tax legislation.[56] Thus, TA 1988, s. 343 allows a loss to be transferred from company P to company S if S takes over the trade from which the loss has arisen (and S is P's subsidiary). This also has implications for commencement and discontinuance since if B simply buys assets, the matter can be treated as yet another activity of B's existing trade; if, however, B succeeds to A's trade, A will cease to carry on the trade (discontinuance) and B will start the trade (commencement), alongside B's existing trade. Where a succession to a trade occurs, neither losses nor unused capital allowances incurred by A can be used by B[57]—unless express authority can be found.

The origin of the concept of succession lay in the application of the rule that profits were measured not on the preceding year basis but on the average of three previous years' business. The original concept of succession allowed B to continue to use the three years' average which A had started. It was necessary, therefore, that there existed a "very close identity" between the business in A's ownership and the business in B's. The reform of Schedule D in 1926 ended the three-year moving average and directed that there was a discontinuance by A and a commencement by B even though there was a succession.

Effects on B—the acquirer

If B succeeds to A's trade, B will be taxed in the opening years in accordance with the rules for commencement,[58] even though B absorbs the acquired trade into an existing one and that it is, in reality, one business.[59] However, once TA 1988, s. 61 is spent, the figures for the trade acquired will form part of the general profit of the trade into which it has merged. Again, these sections are applicable whether in their new or old form. If the new trade is not absorbed into, the old but is a distinct entity, the commencement provisions will apply and there will be no merging once those provisions are spent.

[53] TA 1988, s. 90, see RI 103.

[54] *IRC* v. *Cosmotron Manufacturing Co. Ltd.* [1997] STC 1134; see also Lord Clyde in *IRC* v. *Patrick Thomson Ltd.* (1956) 37 TC 145, 157; noted in Baker [1958] *BTR* 89.

[55] See Graham [1959] *BTR* 193.

[56] See also CAA 1990, s. 152 below §25.2.2 and TCGA 1992, s. 164 (retirement relief) below §42.5.2.

[57] For example *Rolls Royce Motors Ltd.* v. *Bamford* [1976] STC 162.

[58] TA 1988, s. 113.

[59] *Bell* v. *National Provincial Bank* [1904] 1 KB 149, 5 TC 1; *Briton Ferry Steel Co. Ltd.* v. *Barry* [1939] 4 All ER 541, 23 TC 414; if it is a separate trade it must be treated separately (*Scales* v. *George Thomson & Co. Ltd.* (1927) 13 TC 83).

20.8.2 *Rules on whether there has been a succession*

The question for the Commissioners is "whether it is true and fair to say that the business in respect of which the successor is said to be making profits is the business to which [the successor] succeeded".[60]

(1) Purchase of assets of trade is not a succession

The issues are similar to the question of whether there has been a disposal of the business for CGT retirement relief,[61] but the cases have proceeded independently. Thus, where a company which ran a tramp shipping business bought a ship second hand from another trader, there was no succession to that person's trade, but only the purchase of a ship.[62] This is, however, a question of fact, and it was important in that case that the purchaser acquired no list of customers along with the ship, that the ship had no special route along which only she plied her trade, and that no goodwill came with the ship.

Since the origin of the concept of succession lay in the application of the rule that profits were measured by the average of three previous years' business, there had to be a "very close identity" between the business in the former proprietorship and the business in the new proprietorship.[63] A very close identity is, however, not the same as a complete identity. Thus, a successor to a business with, e.g. 50 shops, may choose to close some of them in order to make alterations in the goods sold, to change suppliers or to cut out a particular class of customer or particular area.[64] The question whether such changes prevent there being a succession to the business is one of fact.

There may be a succession even though there is no purchase of the entire assets.[65] In one case a circular was distributed to the former trader's customers that the new owners had acquired the "trading connection" of the former traders. The Commissioners held that there was no succession, and the courts felt unable to reverse that conclusion. Conversely, in another case, a circular distributed to the public described the new firm as "successors", even though they new firm took over no merchandise, no lists of customers and none of the staff, except a few work people. However, they were held to be successors by the Commissioners and the courts, again, declined to intervene.[66]

(2) No succession to a *part* of a trade

In *James Shipstone & Son Ltd.* v. *Morris*[67] Rowlatt J. stated

> "Another point Mr. Latter laid some stress on was this. he said you cannot be successor to a part of a trade. He cited Mr. Justice Bray's remarks in a case in the 'Law Times', the name of which I forget for the moment. I think that is quite sound when you get two parts of a trade, as an omnibus business separate from a tramway business, as it may very well be, but I do not think it means that if

[60] *Laycock* v. *Freeman, Hardy and Willis Ltd.* [1938] 4 All ER 609, 614, 22 TC 288, 298, *per* Sir Wilfrid Greene M.R.

[61] See below at §42.5.2.

[62] *Watson Bros* v. *Lothian* (1902) 4 TC 441. Compare *Bell* v. *National Provincial Bank of England* [1904] 1 KB 149, 5 TC 1.

[63] *Reynolds, Sons & Co. Ltd.* v. *Ogston* (1930) 15 TC 501, 524, *per* Rowlatt J.; approved by Lord Hanworth M.R. at 527.

[64] *Laycock* v. *Freeman, Hardy and Willis Ltd.* (1938) 22 TC 288, 297, *per* Sir Wilfrid Greene M.R.

[65] *Reynolds, Sons & Co. Ltd.* v. *Ogston* (1930) 15 TC, 524.

[66] *Thomson and Balfour* v. *Le Page* (1923) 8 TC 541.

[67] *James Shipstone & Son Ltd.* v. *Morris* (1929) 14 TC 413, 421; and see *Stockham* v. *Wallasey Urban District Council* (1906) 95 LT 834.

what is succeeded to is not the same extent of trade or even does not include a particular line of customers, it necessarily follows that there cannot be a successor to the trade, looking at it broadly. There must be two businesses, one left and the other taken. It does not mean to say you have only taken part of the business in the sense that what you have got is not quite so extensive as what went before."

(3) No succession by accident

No succession occurs through the accidental acquisition by B, who continues in business, of custom left by A, who goes out of business. For there to be a succession there must be a transfer by one trader to another of the right to that benefit which arises from connection and reputation.[68]

(4) Succession only to existing trade

No succession occurs where the trade has ceased before being acquired by B, its new owner, nor where B closes down the business immediately after acquiring it. Thus, if a business went bankrupt and remained in the hands of the trustee in bankruptcy for 12 months before the assets were sold, it is likely that such a sale would be treated as a sale of assets rather than of the business.[69] Indeed, there is authority that where a business has had to sell to recoup heavy losses, it is likely that there is no succession.[70] However, where a business suffered extensive fire damage and ceased to trade with the public, but kept together its employees and various pieces of equipment, a delay of 17 months between the fire and the acquisition of the business by a new owner did not prevent there being a succession.[71]

20.8.3 Applying the rules

The leading modern case on TA 1988, s. 343 and the transfer of losses to a new company in the same ownership is *Falmer Jeans* v. *Rodin.* A manufactured jeans for B, which B sold. B supplied the materials to A and B paid for A's services on a cost plus basis. When A began making losses it stopped trading and transferred its trade and assets to B. Thereafter, manufacturing appeared as a separate cost-centre in B's accounts. Millett J., allowing B's appeal from the Commissioners, held that B was carrying on A's trade, i.e. there was a succession (s. 343 applied and B could use A's losses).

Apart from *Falmer Jeans* the case-law is dominated by two old cases. In *Laycock* v. *Freeman, Hardy and Willis Ltd.*[72] the respondent company (B) bought shoes from wholesalers and resold them to the public. Some 20% to 30% of its supplies came from two subsidiary companies which it controlled. In 1935 the subsidiary companies went into voluntary liquidation and the liquidator assigned all the assets and goodwill to B, which also took on all the staff. B then sold all the products of the factories previously owned by the subsidiary companies in its shops.

The Court of Appeal held that there was no succession. The business of the subsidiary companies was that of wholesale manufacturing concerns; that business had ceased. Manufacturing was still carried on but the business of wholesale manufacturing was not.

[68] *Thomson and Balfour* v. *Le Page* (1923) 8 TC 541, 548.
[69] *Reynolds, Sons & Co. Ltd.* v. *Ogston* (1930) 15 TC 501 at 528, *per* Greer L.J.
[70] *Wilson and Barlow* v. *Chibbett* (1929) 14 TC 407 at 413, *per* Rowlatt J.
[71] *Wild* v. *Madam Tussauds (1926) Ltd.* (1932) 17 TC 127.
[72] *Laycock* v. *Freeman, Hardy and Willis Ltd.* [1938] 4 All ER 609, 614, 22 TC 288, 298, *per* Sir Wilfrid Greene M.R.

There was no provision allowing the profits realised by the retail sales to be dissected and split up into a wholesaler's profit and a retailer's profit, and then deeming the wholesale part to have been taken over by B.

This is inconsistent with *Falmer Jeans* and it is therefore not surprising that Millett J. criticised the older case's distinction between manufacturing for sale wholesale and manufacturing goods for sale retail, as false: "It is impossible to discern any sensible fiscal policy for differentiating, for the purpose of applying the opening year provisions, between the acquisition of a manufacturing business by a wholesaler and the acquisition of a similar business by a retailer. They are both examples of vertical integration".[73]

Laycock v. *Freeman, Hardy and Willis* was distinguished in *Briton Ferry Steel Co. Ltd.* v. *Barry*,[74] where the appellant company produced steel bars which were then supplied to six wholly owned subsidiary companies. These companies, in turn, converted the bars into blackplate and tinplate. Sales were handled by another wholly owned subsidiary. In 1934 the six subsidiary companies were wound up and the conversion of the bars into blackplate and tinplate was carried on by the appellant company using the plant and workforce of the former companies. The Commissioners held that there was a succession to the trades carried on by the subsidiaries. The fact that the company, through its shares, already controlled them was irrelevant, as was the fact that another subsidiary company controlled their sales.[75] The Court of Appeal refused to interfere with that decision.

In *Laycock* v. *Freeman, Hardy and Willis* the business of the subsidiaries—making profits by wholesale sales—had ceased, and the business of retail manufacturing had begun. In *Briton Ferry* the business of the subsidiary companies—making profits by the conversion of steel bars into blackplate and tinplate and resale—still existed, but was being carried on by someone else,[76] with the retail side being handled by a separate legal entity. The fact that someone had previously supplied the steel bars was irrelevant.

The approach of Millett J. in *Falmer Jeans* is based on a more flexible view of business. Suppose that the old cases were taken at face value and there was a manufacturing concern with five distinct stages involved in the manufacturing process, each stage carried out by a separate company. The old cases would suggest that if one company takes over its neighbour, there would be a succession if the acquiring company was at an earlier stage in the process but not if it was at a later stage. As Millet J. said, any vertical integration should suffice.

A further problem concerns the calculation of the profit of the trade acquired. In *Laycock* v. *Freeman, Hardy and Willis* the Court of Appeal held that it was "wholly illegitimate" to invent a notional sale from the wholesale stage of the enterprise to the retail stage at a price which would yield a notional "wholesale profit".[77] But in *Briton Ferry* the same court, having again rejected a notional sale, directed that the transfer of the steel bars from one artificial side of the trade to the other should be treated as carried out at the actual cost of production. This ensured that the profit from the whole operation would be attributable to the newly acquired sector of the trade.[78] It is submitted that the court was perhaps being a little ingenuous.

[73] [1990] STC 270, 279–80, 63 TC 55, 68.
[74] [1939] 4 All ER 541, 23 TC 414; applied *IRC* v. *Spirax Manufacturing Co. Ltd.* (1946) 29 TC 187.
[75] [1938] 4 All ER 429, 434–5, 23 TC 414, 431–2, *per* Macnaghten J.
[76] [1939] 4 All ER 541, 547, 23 TC 414, 431, *per* Sir Wilfrid Greene M.R.
[77] [1938] 4 All ER 609, 616, 22 TC 288, 300, *per* Sir Wilfrid Greene M.R.
[78] [1939] 4 All ER 541, 550, 23 TC 414, 434, *per* Sir Wilfrid Greene M.R.

20.9 Partnerships

20.9.1 Is there a partnership?

It is a question of fact whether a particular person (P) is a partner in an enterprise or merely a senior employee. However, in so far as this involves construing a document, it will raise questions of law. Although the receipt by P of a share of the profits is prima facie evidence that P is a partner, further evidence may be needed to establish exactly when the partnership begins to trade.[79]

In *Fenston* v. *Johnstone*[80] the appellant wished to buy some land but lacked finance. He therefore agreed with another person to share the profits and losses and to assist in the development of the land. The written agreement stated that there was no partnership, and described the appellant's share of the profits as a fee for introducing the other person to the vendor. The court held that there was a partnership. However, in *Pratt* v. *Strick*[81] the court held that there was no partnership where a doctor sold his practice to another but agreed, as part of the sale, to stay in his house with the purchaser for some three months introducing the purchaser to the patients and sharing receipts and expenses over that period. In both the above cases the courts reversed the Commissioners.

20.9.2 Taxation of partnerships

For partnerships not controlled from abroad, the application of the current year basis meant a complete rewriting of the basic rules (TA 1988, s. 111).[82] A partnership is not treated for the purposes of the Tax Acts as an entity which is separate and distinct from its partners. Instead, profits are computed as if the partnership were an individual, and a partner's share in the profits for a period are to be determined according to the interests of the partners during that period.[83]

TA 1988, s. 111 deems each partner (P) to carry on a separate own trade commenced on becoming a partner.[84] If the actual trade was previously carried on, the deemed trade is taken to begin when the actual trade began.[85] Proceeding symmetrically, the law states that the deemed trade ends when P ceases to be a partner or, where the actual trade is subsequently carried on by P alone, the time when the actual trade or profession is permanently discontinued.[86] These rules apply to trades, professions and businesses[87] and to claims for losses,[88] as well as to tax on profits and to non-trading income of the partnership.[89]

These changes mean that partners are individually liable for tax on their own shares of the profits and that the taxable share is related to the actual share and not the profit-sharing ratio in force in a subsequent year. Moreover, once the trade has begun there will be

[79] *Saywell* v. *Pope* [1979] STC 824, 53 TC 40.
[80] (1940) 23 TC 29.
[81] (1932) 17 TC 459; see also *Bulloch* v. *IRC* [1976] STC 514, 51 TC 563.
[82] FA 1994, s. 215(4), (5); the reference to control from abroad is to TA 1988, s. 112(3).
[83] TA 1988, s. 111(1), (2), (3).
[84] Ibid., s. 111(3)(a).
[85] Ibid., s. 111(3)(b).
[86] Ibid., s. 111(3)(c).
[87] Ibid., s. 111(5).
[88] Ibid., s. 111(2).
[89] Ibid., s. 111(4).

no deemed discontinuance by reason of a change in the partners so far as the continuing partners are concerned (since the deemed separate trade has not ended).[90]

In the days of the old regime, when there was only one trade carried on by all the partners, a change of partners led to a discontinuance with a commencement of the same trade by different people. The consequences of this rule (including an opt-out election from some of the rules) were laid down by TA 1988, s. 113. This section has been rewritten for the new regime. There is now no discontinuance for the person continuing to carry on the business; of course, there is a discontinuance for those who leave.

20.9.3 Mixed partnerships[91]

Where a partnership includes a company, the profits of the trade are computed as if the partnership were a company and the member company's shares ascertained and subjected to corporation tax. Income tax is chargeable on the share of individual partners.[92] There is no transfer of a trade on a change of a corporate partner. These provisions do not apply to chargeable gains.[93]

20.10 Trading Losses

20.10.1 Set-off against general income of that and previous year of assessment

If a trade, profession or vocation sustains a loss, the correct figure for the profits chargeable to income tax for the year is nil. Under TA 1988, s. 380, a person who sustains trading losses may claim relief from tax[94] on an amount of income for that year equal to the amount of the loss; as such, where the income exceeds the loss the taxpayer is relieved of all liability to tax.[95] This formula means that loss relief is computed on an accounts basis, i.e. by reference to the same periods as income from the same source. It also means that the income can be from any source and of any type, whether earned or unearned, or savings.

The deadline for the notice is 31 January following the year when the loss arises.[96] It appears that a claim must be for the *whole* of the loss which can be set against the income—one cannot make a claim just a part e.g. for such part of the income as reduces one's income to the amount of one's personal reliefs. So if one has income of £10,000, the personal relief of £4,385 and a loss of £8,000, one has to use the whole loss of £8,000, so "wasting" £2,385 of the personal relief. Alternatively one may choose not to use the relief at all and hope to get better value for it under another rule in another year. If a loss arises in two fiscal years, e.g. on commencement or a change of accounting date, the loss belongs to the first year.[97]

Unused loss relief can be carried back one year and set off against general income of that year.[98] Therefore, in the cases of the loss of £8,000 above, if one has personal reliefs of £4,385

[90] Ibid., s. 113(2).
[91] Ibid., s. 114.
[92] Ibid., s. 114(3). The section fails to deal with a trust or estate which is a partner.
[93] Ibid., s. 115(7).
[94] On relief for a Lloyd's name, see *Holliday* v. *De Brunner* [1996] STC (SCD) 85.
[95] TA 1988, s. 380(1)(a).
[96] Ibid., s. 380(1).
[97] Ibid., s. 382(3).
[98] Ibid., s. 380(l)(b).

for the previous year, also and income of £14,000 for that year, one can use whole loss of £8,000 for that year. If one has losses for more than one year, relief claimed on the current year basis will be given priority over relief carried back one year,[99] but there is no obligation to claim relief on the current year if one prefers instead to carry it back. Needless to say, the relief cannot be claimed twice.

20.10.2 Set-off against future profits of that trade

To the extent that relief for the allowable loss has not been given against general income, whether under TA 1988, s. 380 or some other provision, TA 1988, s. 385 allows the loss to be carried forward and set off against the future profits (if any) of the trade.[100] This period is not limited to a certain number of years.[101] The relief must be given against the earliest profits available,[102] and a claim must be made.[103]

Where the trade has received income taxed by deduction at source, such as interest or dividends, the loss carried forward under s. 385 can be set off against that taxed income, and a repayment claim made in the case of interest.[104] However, this applies only when the payment received under deduction would have been treated as trading profits but for the fact that tax had already been deducted.[105]

The right to roll losses forward is available provided only that the taxpayer carries on the particular trade; it is lost, therefore, on discontinuance of the trade.

Incorporation of business

If the business is transferred to a company, and the sole or main consideration is the transfer of shares of the company to an individual (or nominees), an accumulated loss may be carried forward by the previous owner.[106] This provision applies whether the business is incorporated or taken over by an existing company. S. 386 does not allow the company to claim relief against the future profits of the trade, but allows T, the individual, to claim relief against income derived by T from the company, whether by dividend or otherwise, for example under a service agreement; however, the loss must be set off against earned income before being set off against distributions. In this way the trading loss can be set against income from the company no matter how the company makes its profits, e.g. from other trades. It is not necessary that T or T's nominees own all the shares in the company. The relief may be claimed provided only that the company carries on that business and the individual pays tax.

In addition, T, the individual, must be beneficially entitled to the shares throughout the tax year for which relief is claimed.[107] Curiously, there seems to be no requirement that the beneficial ownership be unbroken, only that it last throughout the year of assessment in question. If, therefore, T sells the shares in January 2000 but then buys them back in June 2000, T should be able to resume the loss claim in 2001–02.

[99] TA 1988, s. 380(2).
[100] Ibid., s. 385(1); see *Gordon and Blair Ltd.* v. *IRC* (1962) 40 TC 358.
[101] For comparative (corporation tax) limits, see OECD Report (1991), Table 3. 8.
[102] TA 1988, s. 385(1)(b).
[103] On importance of claim, see *Richardson* v. *Jenkins* [1995] STC 95, 67 TC 246.
[104] TA 1988, s. 385(4).
[105] On which, see *Nuclear Electric plc* v. *Bradley* [1996] STC 405, 68 TC 670, HL; and below at §47.5.1 n. 57.
[106] TA 1988, s. 386.
[107] Ibid., s. 386(3).

20.10.3 Losses in early years of trading

A carry-back of a trading loss is permitted under s. 381 where the loss arises in the year of assessment in which the trade is first carried on, or the next three years of assessment;[108] it thus applies to losses arising in the first four years of business. The loss may be carried back and set off against *general* income for the three years before that in which the loss is sustained. Income of an earlier year is taken first, so a loss incurred in 2001–02 can be carried back to 1998–99. When the accounting period of the business goes past the end of the year of assessment in which the trade begins, the loss in that period is apportioned. Partial claims for loss relief are not permitted. It should also be noted that since relief is given by reference to the basis period and not to the fiscal period, the choice of accounting date will determine how far back one can go.

Example

Ann starts a business on 1 January 2001. Her income for the years of assessment from 1996–97 is as follows:

Salary	1998–99	£5,500
	1999–00	£6,700
	2000–01	£17,000
	2001–02	£3,500
Trading loss: year to 31.12.02		(£6,000)
Year to 31.12.03		(£12,000)

Assume that Ann' s personal allowance in 2003–04 is £5,000. Her losses are

2001–02	¼ × (£6,000)		(£1,500)
2002–03	¾ × (£6,000)	(£4,500)	
and	¼ × £(12,000)	(£3,000)	
			(£7,500)
2002–03	¾ × (£12,000)	(£9,000)	

Ann will not make a claim under s. 380 for 2001–02 since her income (£3,500) was covered by personal reliefs. She could claim under s. 381 in respect of the losses in both 2001–02 and 2002–03. The relief given will be as follows:

1998–99

Income	£5,500	
Less claim under s. 381 for 1999–2000		(£1,500)
Taxable	£4,000	

1999–00

Income	£6,700
Less claim under s. 381 for 2000–01	(£6,700)
Taxable	nil

2000–01 Income £17,000

Less claim under s. 381 for 2000–01 (£7,500 − £6,700) + 2001–02 (£9,000) (£9,800)

Taxable £7,200

[108] It is the loss that arises in the fiscal year which is relievable (see *Gascoine* v. *Wharton* [1996] STC 1481, 69 TC 147 where a taxpayer unsuccessfully argued that reliefs should be given for a loss arising in an accounting period, part of which was not incurred during the year of assessment).

Although s. 381 applies both to trades and professions, it applies only to individuals. If a trade is acquired from a spouse, the four tax years run from the date the spouse began to trade.[109] However, this restriction applies only when T, the claimant, acquired the trade from a spouse to whom T was then married and with whom T was then living; it follows that this restriction does not apply where T succeeds to a trade on the death of the other spouse.

Although relief may be claimed under both TA 1988, ss 380 and 381, and the claimant may decide in which order to apply the reliefs, the loss cannot be apportioned between them.[110]

20.10.4 Terminal losses

A terminal loss is a loss sustained in the year of assessment in which the trade is permanently discontinued and in that part of the preceding year of assessment beginning 12 months before the date of discontinuance.[111]

Once a trade, profession or vocation has been permanently discontinued, there can *ex hypothesis* be no carry-forward of a loss under TA 1988, s. 385. A terminal loss may, however, be carried back and set off against the profits charged under Schedule D in respect of the trade for the year in which the trade ends and the three preceding years of assessment. Relief is given as far as possible from the assessment of a later rather than earlier year.[112] Assessments may thus have to be reopened. The reference to the year of discontinuance is needed for the following situation. If the trading year ends in June 2001 and discontinuance occurs in December 2001, a loss in the final period of trading can be set against the income until June under s. 388 as well as against general income under s. 380.

Example

Tom, a trader retires on 30 September 2001. Tom's results for the four years to 31 March 2001 and for the final six months were as follows:

Year ended	31.3.98	£12,000
	31.3.99	£11,000
	31.3.00	£12,000
	31.3.01	£4,000
Period to	30.9.01	(£14,000)

No tax will be due in 2001–02 and the £14,000 loss will set off against the 2000–01 profit of £4,000, reducing it to nil; the balance of £10,000 will be sat against the 1999–00 figure of £12,000, leaving £2,000 taxable for that year.

As with TA 1988, s. 385, dividends or interest on investments arising during any relevant period but which are excluded from the computation of profits because taxed at source may be used as profits against which the terminal loss may be set.[113] Special rules apply to payments made under deduction of tax, e.g. under TA 1988, s. 350; the profits are treated as reduced (and so the terminal loss increased) by the gross amount of such payments.[114] An

[109] TA 1988, s. 381(5).
[110] *Butt* v. *Haxby* [1983] STC 239, 56 TC 547.
[111] TA 1988, s. 388(6).
[112] Ibid., s. 388(3).
[113] Ibid., s. 388(4).
[114] Ibid., s. 388(5).

exception is made in computing the terminal loss if the payment made under deduction of tax is treated as a loss item by s. 387.

Where a partner (P) retires, a discontinuance occurs under s. 113 and a terminal loss is calculated for the retiring partner only. This loss is set off against that part of the partnership income which was included in P's total income for each relevant year. P's share of the loss is governed by his share of the profits at the date of discontinuance. If a continuance election is made, no terminal loss relief is permitted for any of the partners.[115]

20.10.5 What is a trading loss?

Schedule D rules

Loss relief is important not only to the genuine trader but also to others who have used it as the basis of schemes. To claim relief the trader must have been carrying on a trade, and allowable expenses must exceed trading receipts.[116]

S. 384

S. 384 provides that a trading loss qualifies for relief only if the trade was carried on on a commercial basis and with a view to the realisation of profit.[117] Further, the trade must have been carried on in a commercial way for the whole of the year of assessment, whether or not there has been a change in the manner in which the trade was being carried on and whether or not there has been a change in the persons running the trade, if at least one person was running it for the year. If the trade was set up or discontinued (or both) in a year of assessment, the test is applied to those parts of the year in which the trade was in being. By concession, relief can be claimed in respect of maintenance expenses of owner-occupied farms not carried on on a commercial basis,[118] a concession that also applies to ss 387 and 390.

With a view to profit

The loss is not relievable unless the trade was being carried on on a commercial basis and with a view to the realisation of profits. In *Walls* v. *Livesey*,[119] the Special Commissioner considered that relief under s. 381 was available where profits may have been expected a reasonable time after the four-year period provided for claims. The Revenue seems to take a narrower view.[120] Given that the question whether a particular activity constitutes a trade and the question whether this trade is carried on with a view to profit are both questions of fact and, hence, solely within the jurisdiction of the Commissioners, one may note with interest the Revenue view that it would expect a written business plan to be prepared at the outset—with credible figures.

Expenses treated as losses

Loss relief is restricted to trading losses as just defined. However, certain expenses which do not enter into the computation of profits and losses of the trade are treated as loss items, e.g.

[115] Ibid., s. 389(4).

[116] See *Ensign Tankers Leasing Ltd.* v. *Stokes* [1992] STC 226, 64 TC 617. HL; and *FA and AB Ltd.* v. *Lupton* [1971) 3 All ER 948, 47 TC 580; see above at §19.3.1 as to what is a trading transaction.

[117] TA 1988, s. 384; *Walls* v. *Livesey* [1995] STC (SCD) 12; *Wannell* v. *Rothwell* [1996] STC 450, 68 TC 519; and *Delian Enterprises* v. *Ellis* [1999] STC (SCD) 103. On genesis of the legislation, see Stopforth [1999] *BTR* 106.

[118] ESC B5.

[119] [1995] STC (SCD) 12.

[120] Inland Revenue Tax Bulletin (October 1997), 473.

annual payments made by the trader wholly and exclusively for the purposes of the trade and which fall within TA 1988, s. 349,[121] and interest payments made for the same purposes and being payments eligible for relief under s. 353.[122]

20.10.6 Restrictions on reliefs for certain trading losses

(1) Limited partnerships

In a limited partnership the limited partner's capital contribution (and so the amount of risk borne) is limited. The agreement may nonetheless provide that the trading loss of the partnership should be attributed to the limited partners in full. In *Reed* v. *Young*[123] the House of Lords held that relief could be claimed under TA 1988, s. 380 even where the loss so attributed exceeded the amount of capital at risk. TA 1988, s. 117(1)(a) now limits the relief given under s. 380. The restrictions apply both to limited partnerships registered as such and to similar arrangements limiting liability.[124] Relief is limited to "the relevant sum", which is the amount of the capital contribution at "the appropriate time" (broadly, the end of the relevant year of assessment). In essence, these reliefs are available only to the extent that the taxpayers' capital is actually at risk. Losses caught by s. 117 may still be carried forward for relief under TA 1988, s. 385.

(2) Commodity futures

Losses on dealings in commodity futures are restricted where partnerships are involved.[125]

(3) Hobby farming

Where losses are sustained in a trade of farming or market gardening, relief is not available under s. 380 or 385 if, despite satisfying the test in s. 384, a loss was incurred in each of the five prior years.[126] It should be remembered that all farming, but not market gardening, is treated as one trade, so that a loss on one farm may be set off against the profits of another. Special provision is made for the genuine farmer who has a reasonable expectation of profit, but whose business will take longer than six years to come right.

20.10.7 Partnership losses

Loss relief is always granted to a "person". Thus, where a partnership produces a loss, the loss is apportioned among the partners and each individual partner may choose to make whatever claim is appropriate for his individual circumstances. (This treatment is afforded to Scottish partnerships as well as English partnerships.[127]) Thus, partner A may wish to set his share of the trading loss against his investment income; partner B may choose to carry forward his loss against trading profits of a later year.

[121] TA 1988, s. 387.
[122] Ibid., s. 390.
[123] [1986] STC 285, 59 TC 196.
[124] TA 1988, s. 117(2); the Budget press release refers to persons participating in joint venture arrangements when liability is limited (see (1985) *Simon's Tax Intelligence* 147); the phraseology covers, e.g. non-recourse loans.
[125] TA 1988, s. 399(2).
[126] Ibid., s. 397.
[127] Ibid., s. 111(1).

21

Business Income—Part III: Principles and Receipts

21.1 The Measure of Income: The Role of Accounting Principles

21.1.1 Current principles

TA 1988, s. 18 charges tax on the annual profits or gains arising or accruing from the trade, profession or vocation, while TA 1988, s. 60 adds (unhelpfully) that the measure is "the full amount of such profits".[1]

In some countries, and particularly in continental Europe, the starting point is the set of accounts prepared by the firm's accountants.[2] A change to an accounts system is often

[1] The original version of TA 1988, s. 18 referred to "profits or gains", but this was changed by FA 1998. For a discussion of a fundamentally different scheme based on economic rent see

[2] See, e.g. material in Ault *et al.*, Part 1; Sandler *History's Legacy*, (Institute of Taxation, London 1993); and *Fiscal v. Commercial Profit Accounting in Netherlands, France and Germany* (IBFD, 1998). See also McCourt and Radcliffe [1995] *BTR* 461.

suggested as part of a process of tax reform, either as a step in its own right or as part of tax simplification. The current relationship between accounting practice and UK tax law is shown by case-law and especially a decision of the Court of Appeal in 1993 and, for accounting periods beginning on or after 6 April 1999, by FA 1998, s. 42.

FA 1998, s. 42 requires that the profit must be computed on an accounting basis which gives a true and fair view, subject to any adjustments required or authorised by law in computing profits for those purposes. So capital expenditure, which may be allowed by accounting practice but not by law must be removed from the list of deductible expenditure as an adjustment required by law while capital allowances may then be substituted as an adjustment authorised by law if the taxpayer wishes to claim them. (FA 1998 also contains rules governing the transition from the old case-law basis to the new "true and fair" view; the rules impose a "catch-up" charge but also provide an income spreading relief.[3]) The problem of when an adjustment is required or authorised by law will have to be addressed by the courts. In 1999 the Revenue announced its acceptance of a new accounting code, Financial Reporting Standard 12 (FRS 12), for matters relating to future repairs and to provisions for future rent.[4] As will be seen, it may be that FRS 12 is in some ways stricter than the rules which the courts had just developed in these areas.

The introduction of s. 42 has been highly controversial.[5] It is unclear what difference it will make, and it is even less clear whether the changes it may make are desirable. In any event, even accountants have no clear idea what is meant by a "true and fair view".[6] What accountants have done is to set up mechanisms for advising on issues as they arise.[7] Further, as recently as 1982, accountants argued against the use of current cost accounting as a way of addressing inflation issues because it involved too much subjective judgment.[8] These anxieties have been reinforced by books and press stories showing that accountants' professional activities on behalf of their clients can be very creative.[9] However. it is clear that s. 42 is not intended as a one-way street in favour of the Revenue; it is open to the taxpayer to rely on a return made on the basis of an accounting practice which gives a true and fair view as required by s. 42.[10]

Case-law

Before FA 1998 there were two distinct approaches to the relationship between questions of law and principles of accountancy: one asserted that the court should first look to see what accountancy prescribed, and then see whether any rule of law contradicted it;[11] the other asserted that the court should first determine the question as a matter of law, see whether accountancy gave a different answer, and then determine which should prevail. It will be appreciated that the first approach gives much greater weight to accountancy practice than

[3] FA 1998, s. 44, Sch. 6.

[4] Inland Revenue Press Release, 20 July 1999, (1999) *Simons Weekly Tax Intelligence* 1302.

[5] On the relationship in general, see [1995] *BTR* 433–520 (special edition). From an accounting perspective, see also Davies, *Generally Accepted Accounting Practice in the United Kingdom*, ch. 3. On FA 1998 changes, see Hole [1998] *BTR* 405, 410 *et seq.*

[6] See (1992) *Accountancy Age* 19 March. For a lawyer's view of "true and fair view", see McGee [1991] *MLR* 874.

[7] This is the function of the Accounting Standards Board and the Urgent Issues Task Force.

[8] 1982 Green Paper on Corporation Tax, Cmnd 8456. Chapter 9.

[9] See, e.g. the celebrated book by Terry Smith, *Accounting for Growth* (Century Business, London, 1992).

[10] The court might now reach a different conclusion from the outcomes in *Meat Traders* v. *Cushing* [1997] STC (SCD) 245, and *Robertson* v. *IRC* [1997] STC (SCD) 282.

[11] For example Salmon J. in *Odeon Associated Theatres Ltd.* v. *Jones* [1972] 1 All ER 681, 689, 48 TC 257, 283A; Lord Haldane in *Sun Insurance Office Ltd.* v. *Clark* [1912] AC 443, 455, 6 TC 59, 78; and Lord Clyde in *Lothian Chemical Co. Ltd.* v. *Rogers* (1926) 11 TC 508, 520; see also *Report of the Committee on the Taxation of Trading Profits* Cmd 8189 (1951) §135 (the Tucker Report).

the second. The former approach has, in effect, been enshrined by FA 1998, s. 42 for accounting periods beginning on or after 6 April 1999.

The former approach was accepted by the Court of Appeal in *Gallagher* v. *Jones*[12] when it doubted whether any judge-made rule could override a generally accepted rule of commercial accountancy which (a) applied to the situation in question, (b) was not one of two or more rules applicable to that situation, and (c) was not shown to be inconsistent with the true facts or otherwise inapt to determine the true profits or losses of the business. This new approach has been followed in later cases.[13] For periods before FA 1998 took effect, this decision still applies. However, the decision has not been universally welcomed; as Freedman scathingly noted, "The arguments for the taxpayer were too stark and left important issues unexplored. These issues were not explored because of the weight given to SSAP 21. To accept a standard without investigation of its objectives and effects is . . . an abdication of responsibility by the court".[14] It will be necessary to wait and see whether later courts addressing issues from these years will take any note of such criticisms, but this is doubtful. In 1999 the Revenue announced, when dealing with a year before FA 1998, s. 42 applied, that it was abandoning long held views about what the law requires in the area of provisions for future rent and repairs. (Surprisingly the Revenue abandoned these views after a High Court decision, and did not wait for the decision of the House of Lords.)

A decision in which the courts made a ruling in an area where there was no, one, single recognised practice was *Willingale* v. *International Commercial Bank Ltd.*[15] The taxpayer bank held a number of bills of exchange issued by borrowers all over the world and maturing over periods from one to 10 years. The issue was whether the bank could bring the proceeds of such bills into the account only when the bills matured (or were disposed of), or whether, following the practice applied to the clearing banks, it could bring in a part of the expected profit each year. The House, upholding all the lower tribunals, held that the bank, although having made up its accounts on the basis of this clearing bank practice, was entitled to insist that, for tax purposes, the other basis should be taken since this would be in conformity with a fundamental principle that profits should not be taxed until ascertained. The decision was by a bare majority and has been heavily criticised. The statement by Lord Fraser that the accounts which excluded the accrued discounts would have given a true and fair view of the state of the bank's business and would have been just as satisfactory for commercial purposes as accounts which included them, is almost certainly wrong.[16]

21.1.2 Problems in the relationship between tax and accounting

Possible relationships

It is clear that the aim of accountants is in some senses the same as that of the Revenue: both seek to measure the income of a precise, and so artificial, period.[17] The balance of the

[12] [1993] STC 537, esp. 555–6, *per* Sir Thomas Bingham M.R.

[13] *Johnston* v. *Britannia Airways Ltd.* [1994] STC 763; on which, see Park, Cook and Oliver [1995] *BTR* 499. Following this case, ICAEW wrote to the Inland Revenue for clarification of the Revenue's interpretation of this decision. The correspondence is published in ICAEW Press Release, 12 April 1995, *Guidance Note TAX 10/95*, (1995) *Simon's Weekly Tax Intelligence* 703. See also *Sycamore plc and Maple Ltd.* v. *Fir* [1997] STC (SCD) 1.

[14] [1993] *BTR* 468, 477.

[15] [1978] 1 All ER 754, [1978] STC 75, 52 TC 242; on which, see Pagan [1992] *BTR* 75; see also Vinelott J. in *Pattison* v. *Marine Midland Ltd.* [1981] STC 540.

[16] See [1978] STC 75, 80, 52 TC 242, 272; and White [1987] *BTR* 292, 295.

[17] See Walton J. in *Willingale* v. *International Commercial Bank Ltd.* [1976] STC 188, 194–5.

relationship may take many forms, among which the system could be said (a) simply to accept the accounting treatment at face value, (b) follow the accounting treatment while reserving to itself a power to depart from it for some good reason of its own, (c) explicitly adopt the accounting treatment for certain items only [18] or (d) refuse to follow the accounting treatment at all.

What is accounting practice?

Where the parties seek to rely on accounting practice, evidence must be put before the Commissioners. The evidence may show that there is one generally accepted way of doing some thing or that there are several ways of doing it. In the UK, accounting practice has developed since the establishment of the Accounting Standards Committee in 1970, superceded by the Accounting Standards Board (ASB) in 1970[19]; the ASB was set up under powers in the Companies Act 1989. Comments by judges, and even academic criticisms relating to years before 1970, should not be given much weight.[20] It should be noted that accounting developments have been taken over into company law. The ASB issues, among other things, statements of standard accounting practice (SSAPs), which are statements of practice and not of principle, and financial reporting standards (FRSs). The Financial Reporting Council, a body on which the professional accounting bodies are joined by other city institutions, guides the ASB and acts as a proactive voice in public debate on these matters.[21]

SSAPs and FRSs are clearly relevant to establishing a true and fair view for the purposes of FA 1998, s. 42. They are also within the approach adopted by the courts in 1993. In *A Firm v. Honour*,[22] by contrast, there was no SSAP available to the court. Although the court in *Symons* v *Weeks*[23] had adopted the timing treatment in SSAP9 for receipts, the Revenue at first refused to accept claims made under SSAP9 for losses on long-term contracts. SSAP9 states that these losses must be recognised as soon as they can reasonably be foreseen. The High Court, agreeing with the Special Commissioner, rejected the Revenue's argument. The Revenue conceded defeat.[24]

General principles of accounting practice

Although accounting practice has developed SSAPs for some areas, there are many areas which are unexplored. It is certainly much easier to conclude that a certain rule of tax accounting is contrary to generally recognised accounting principles, than it is to define such principles.[25] In these areas more general principles apply, including prudence and materiality.

Prudence demands that losses be written off as soon as they are recognised. This is inconsistent with a principle of tax law, which states that neither profit nor loss should be anticipated.[26] However, that principle of tax law has now been repudiated by the Revenue;[27] prudence, therefore, rules.

The concept of *materiality* means that accountants may disregard items in making up

[18] E.g. corporation tax rules for foreign exchange gains and losses and loan relationships.
[19] See White [1987] *BTR* 292.
[20] For example, Lord Denning's dismissive reference in *Heather* v. *PE Consulting Group* 48 TC 293, 322F.
[21] Thomas, *Introduction to Financial Accounting* (McGraw-Hill, 1999), 11
[22] [1997] STC (SCD) 293; noted by Freedman [1998] *BTR* 186 *et seq.*
[23] [1983] STC 195.
[24] Inland Revenue Press Release, 20 July 1999, (1999) *Simons Weekly tax Intelligence* 1302.
[25] Seghers (1948) *National Tax Jo.* 341.
[26] Freedman [1998] *BTR* 186.
[27] Inland Revenue Press Release, above at n. 24.

accounts if those items would not be material, i.e material to those users of the data who could expected to be influenced by them in their economic decisions.[28] This unquantifiable approach approves broad brush treatment at a level which may be regarded as highly material by the Inland Revenue.

Economic effect[29]Accountants may take a broad view where the same economic effect can be achieved by different forms of legal relationships. Thus, legal differences, which are not relevant for financial reporting purposes, are ignored for financial reporting; whether they should be ignored for tax purposes depends on what the tax rule is. Legal differences which are not relevant for financial reporting may still be relevant for tax purposes.[30] Tax officials may instead insist that each transaction be analysed strictly; they will certainly insist that each of the two parties to a transaction treats it the same way.

For whom are accounts prepared?

Accounts are written for those who want to use accounts; tax computations are prepared for the Inland Revenue. Accounts are used by managers for purposes of internal management, and by those outside a company when deciding whether to invest in that company through share equity, or to make a loan to the company. The interests of such groups are not the same as those of the Inland Revenue. For example, French supermarket companies are owned by families or other large shareholders and use accelerated depreciation to minimise taxes on profits; most British supermarkets depend on the stock market for capital and depreciate their assets slowly in order to boost profits.[31]

Why not let accounting practice rule?

Despite judicial and parliamentary (and even, now, Inland Revenue) enthusiasm for incorporating accounting practices into tax law, this approach remains controversial. Although, at first sight, accepting accounting treatment at face value would avoid the need for a second set of accounts for tax purposes, this is very naïve, as continental experience shows:

(1) In countries where accounts are used as the tax base, one result has been very conservative accounting policies. Revaluations of assets in balance sheets may a disposal for CGT, and so a charge to tax; to avoid this, revaluations do not take place. This strictness is not what financial markets need, and some countries have developed a pattern by which individual companies adopt the strict approach, while group accounts are constructed on a less conservative and more subjective approach. Once the company wants to be quoted on the New York Stock Exchange, the need for more transparent accounts can cause unpleasant tax liabilities.
(2) Generally Accepted Accounting Principles or GAAPs should be seen as a developing body of principles rather than a precise set of rules; to make tax follow GAAPs may inhibit the development of those principles. In continental Europe very strict accounting rules have developed (to reduce subjectivity).
(3) There is no reason to assume that accounting practice should necessarily adapt to the Revenue's view, and may develop differently over time. Rejecting the idea that legisla-

[28] ICAEW Technical Release 32/96, para. 4.
[29] See Macdonald (1991) 54 *MLR* 830, 837–46.
[30] See *Klockner Ina* v. *Bryan* 63 TC 1, 26–7.
[31] Cortejns, Cortejns and Lal INSEAD paper, cited in *The Economist*, 29 April 1995.

tion may require the tax system to follow whatever system of Current Cost Accounting was in force at that time, the Revenue's 1982 Green Paper on Corporation Tax stated, "If this were the case, the effect would be that the ultimate decision about the level of taxation for business profits would to a significant degree be delegated to the accounting profession. It is difficult to see that this would be acceptable to Parliament".[32] One solution suggested in 1982 was to avoid the problems of change by sticking to the practice in force at the time and require government agreement to any change. This would, however, quickly lead to a re-emergence of divergence between companies wanting to adopt the newer practices for their own purposes and other companies.

(4) Many practices are now applied only to certain taxpayers. UK GAAPs have been developed by and for the UK corporate sector; small businesses are meant to have administrative costs alleviated and are not expected to adopt all of them. Thus, SSAP9, which was used in *Symons* v. *Weeks* (above), was not meant to apply to small businesses.

21.1.3 Remaining differences between UK tax law and accounting—current issues

Given the qualification in s. 42 and in *Gallagher* v. *Jones* (above), ordinary principles of commercial accounting must sometimes yield to tax law.[33] Examples are as follows:

(1) The courts have consistently held that the question whether an expenditure is on capital or revenue account is one of law—whatever the accounting view.[34] By treating these issues as questions of law the courts have enabled themselves to keep complete residual control.
(2) It is an elementary accountancy principle that capital expenditure on a depreciating asset must be written off over the lifetime of the asset. However, tax law allows the deduction of capital expenditure only if that expenditure falls within the capital allowances system (see chapter 24 below).
(3) Prudent accountancy practice writes off abortive expenditure as a revenue expense, but there is tax law authority that abortive capital expenditure is not deductible.[35]
(4) Certain expenditure, which is clearly revenue rather than capital, is nonetheless not deductible because barred it is by TA 1988, s. 74, e.g. as not incurred "wholly and exclusively" for the purpose of earning a profit or because it is not directed to the earning of profits.
(5) Certain items of expenditure will be deducted by the accountants in ascertaining the income for the year, but disallowed by some other express provision such as business entertainment expenses.[36]
(6) The courts have not confined their decisions on points of accountancy to those situations where an express statutory provision is in point. In the past, the courts have also ruled on such questions as the correct method of assessing work in progress,[37] and of

[32] Cmnd 8456, para. 10.26.
[33] Viscount Simonds in *Ostime* v. *Duple Motor Bodies Ltd.* [1961] 2 All ER 167, 169, 39 TC 537, 566.
[34] *Beauchamp* v. *F. W. Woolworth plc* [1989] STC 510, 61 TC 542, where the tax treatment coincided with the accountancy treatment. See also *Associated Portland Cement Manufacturers Ltd.* v. *Kerr* [1946] 1 All ER 68, 27 TC 103 (decision against accounting evidence); and *Heather* v. *P.E. Consulting Group* [1973] 1 All ER 8, 48 TC 320 (decision consistent with accounting evidence).
[35] *Southwell* v. *Savill* [1901] 2 KB 349, 4 TC 430.
[36] TA 1988, s. 577(see below at §22.3.6).
[37] *Ostime* v. *Duple Motor Bodies Ltd.* (see below at §23.5.4).
[38] For example the prohibition of LIFO (see below at §23.5.2).

valuing stock in trade[38]—matters where there is no express provision, and, in the last case, the courts have ruled that there is such a thing as the "correct" method even though accountancy knows of many methods. The extent to which the courts will treat these as valid legal principles circumscribing s. 42 is unclear, as is the Revenue's willingness to stand by some of them. One should note that previously the Revenue was not swayed by arguments based on consistency from year to year, nor inhibited about seeking to change the basis from year to year, e.g. cash-to-earnings basis. The Revenue has also challenged accounts on bases which it has previously accepted over a period of many years.[39]

(7) Bona fide commercial payments and receipts sometimes fall outside the tax system, whereas they cannot fall outside the accounting system, e.g. exchange differences on a liability, as in *Beauchamp* v. *Woolworth*.[40]

Tailpiece

In the 1980s the position of accountants was well summarised, as follows:[41]

> "Accountants have in the game of business aspired to be players, or at least umpires, but over the years have been relegated to the humble office of score keeper. Their revenge for this ignominy was to keep the score in such a way that neither the players nor the umpire could ascertain the true state of the game."

Today, it may be concluded that the players and umpire have become so bemused by the facts with which they are presented that the score keeper has become the rule maker.

21.2 Trading Stock

A payment arising from the disposal of trading stock in the normal course of business is normally a trading receipt. Trading stock is not defined[42] but means (a) raw materials, (b) finished products and (c) work in progress. It does not extend to plant, mere utensils (as distinct from raw materials) or a source of trading stock.

It follows that the question whether an item is trading stock must depend on the nature of the trade. In *Abbott* v. *Albion Greyhounds (Salford) Ltd.*[43] a greyhound racing company argued that the dogs used in their races were trading stock and so should be valued at the end of each year. This was rejected by Wrottesly J. on the ground that the saleable value of the kennel was at no time a commercial picture of the company's success or failure. Had the company bought and sold dogs by way of trade the answer would have been different. Similarly, working sheepdogs would not be regarded as trading stock of a farm. This is separate from the question whether a profit on sale would be a capital or an income receipt.

Special rules relating to farm animals are contained in TA 1988, Schedule 5.

[39] For example *BSC Footwear Ltd.* v. *Ridgway* [1970] 1 All ER 932, 47 TC 511 (practice accepted for 30 years); and *Ostime* v. *Duple Motor Bodies Ltd.* [1961] 2 All ER 167, 39 TC 537 (practice accepted for 28 years).

[40] [1989] STC 510, 61 TC 542.

[41] White Addington Society Address.

[42] Except in TA 1988, s. 100. In *Willingale* v. *International Commercial Bank Ltd.* [1978] STC 88 an argument that the bills of exchange were trading stock was not pursued.

[43] [1945] 1 All ER 308, 26 TC 390; see also *General Motors Acceptance Corpn* v. *IRC* [1985] STC 408.

21.3 Capital Receipts

A sum arising from the disposal of the business itself or of a business asset is normally a capital receipt. In *British Borneo Petroleum Syndicate Ltd.* v. *Cropper*[44] a sum received in return for the surrender of a royalty agreement was held to be a capital receipt. The terms on which an asset is sold may, however, give rise to a taxable profit. In *Lamport and Holt Line Ltd.* v. *Langwell*,[45] A, a shipowner, sold shares in B, a company trading as fuel suppliers, to C, another company of fuel suppliers. The contract provided that A should receive part of the commission which C received for supplying oil to A. These part-commissions were held to be trading receipts of A.

21.4 Receipts for Non-Trade Purposes

While a payment in return for goods or services supplied in the course of trade will be a trading receipt, a payment made for reasons other than trade will not. This is because a sum received otherwise than in return for trading activities is simply a windfall in the nature of a gift; it is a by-product of a trade rather than an operation in the carrying-out of the trade.[46] Therefore, a solicitor or doctor does not have to bring into professional accounts a legacy from a grateful client, even though the legacy is expressed to be in gratitude for professional services to the testator or the testator's late spouse.[47]

The courts look at the reason for the payment—not whether there was an obligation to pay it. However, the payment of an extra sum for work already paid for will usually be a trading receipt even though the payment was voluntary.[48] A testimonial or solatium after the trading connection has ceased will escape tax because the payment in made in *recognition* of past services, not in respect of past services (e.g. settling an unpaid bill), nor for future services.[49] The question turns on the nature of the payment rather than the motive of the payer. The fact that the payer chooses a measure related to previous services, e.g. a sum equivalent to five years' commission is similarly irrelevant.

In *Murray* v. *Goodhews*[50] a brewing company terminated a number of tenancy agreements with the taxpayer and chose to make voluntary payments of some £81,000 over two years. These payments were held not to be trading receipts. Three factors pointing this were: (1) that, although an *ex gratia* payment had been mentioned early in the negotiations, there was no disclosure of the basis on which the payment was calculated, (2) there had been no subsequent negotiations between the parties on this point; and (3) the amount had not been calculated by reference to profit earned.

[44] [1969] 1 All ER 104, 45 TC 201.

[45] (1958) 38 TC 193; see also *Orchard Wine and Spirit Co.* v. *Loynes* (1952) 33 TC 97.

[46] *Simpson* v. *John Reynolds & Co. (Insurances) Ltd.* [1974] STC 271, 290, 49 TC 693, *per* Pennycuick V.-C.

[47] *Simpson* v. *John Reynolds* [1975] STC 271, 273 *per* Russell L.J.

[48] *Temperley* v. *Smith* [1956] 3 All ER 92, 37 TC 18; *Isaac Holden & Sons Ltd.* v. *IRC* (1924) 12 TC 768, (see below at §23.4.3.3); *Australia (Commonwealth) Taxation Commr* v. *Squatting Investment Co. Ltd.* [1954] AC 182, [1954] 1 All ER 349.

[49] *Murray* v. *Goodhews* [1978] STC 207, 213, [1978] 2 All ER 40, 46, 52 TC 86, 109, *per* Buckley L.J. See Eyre [1978] *BTR* 65; and Davies [1979] *BTR* 212.

[50] [1978] STC 207, [1978] 2 All ER 40, 52 TC 86. On deduction by the brewers, see *Watney Combe Reid & Co. Ltd.* v. *Pike* [1982] STC 733, 57 TC 372.

Payments escaping tax on this basis have included a payment to a firm of accountants on not being reappointed to act as auditors to a company which had changed ownership, the sum being equivalent to one year's salary,[51] and a payment to an insurance broker on the ending of a relationship with a client when that client, was taken over by another company.[52] In practice, a prize awarded to an author for his literary work is not treated as taxable.[53]

On the other hand, a payment to assist a taxpayer club to improve its curling facilities was held to be a trading receipt since the purpose of the payment was to enable the club to remain in business.[54] Similarly, in *McGowan* v. *Brown and Cousins*[55] a payment to compensate an estate agent for the loss of a fee-earning opportunity was held to be a trading receipt.

The issue is one of fact. In *Murray* v. *Goodhews* the payment escaped tax despite the continued trading relationship between the parties, whereas in *McGowan* v. *Brown and Cousins* the payment was taxable even though the trading relationship had ended. The latter point is reinforced by the decision in *Rolfe* v. *Nagel*.[56] Here a payment made by one diamond broker to another, because a client had transferred his business, was held taxable. The facts were unusual in that the broker was unable to earn commission from a client until the client had been accepted as "an active client", a process taking a number of years. Other facts supported this conclusion; thus, the two brokers agreed to accept whatever a third broker would think suitable and the sum, £15,000, was not paid until the client became "active".

The fact that these testimonial payments escape tax is consistent with the case-law under Schedule E. The payment may, as a capital receipt, be liable to CGT. In practice the Revenue has treated treated such payments, as payments for goodwill and so as potentially eligible for the obsolescent retirement relief. These payments ought, therefore, to be treated as business assets for CGT tapering relief.

21.5 Incidental Payments

A payment arising incidentally in the course of a trade may be a trading receipt even though it is not for the supply of stock in which the trader actually trades; the recurrence of such transactions will make this conclusion more likely. The cases concern items which are used (or used up) in the running of the trade without being clearly either capital or trading stock. They arise in the course of the conduct of the business and, by and large, from that business being carried on in the ordinary way. Cases where payments for compensation have been treated as trading receipts (see §21.7) may be seen as further examples.

[51] *Walker* v. *Carnaby, Harrower, Barham and Pykett* [1970] 1 All ER 502, 46 TC 461.
[52] *Simpson* v. *John Reynolds & Co. (Insurances) Ltd.* [1975] STC 271, 49 TC 693, CA.
[53] (1979) *Simon's Tax Intelligence* 76.
[54] *IRC* v. *Falkirk Ice Rink Ltd.* [1977] STC 342, [1977] 3 All ER 844, 51 TC 42.
[55] [1975] STC 434, 52 TC 8.
[56] [1982] STC 53, 55 TC 585.

21.5.1 Investments of spare cash

Where a bank or insurance company invests spare cash in securities or shares on a short-term basis, profits on resale may be trading receipts of the bank or company.[57] However, such profits were held to be part of a separate trade when realised by another type of company.[58]

21.5.2 Foreign exchange[59]

Today, a special regime applies to foreign exchange transactions by most companies subject to corporation tax;[60] this regime does not apply to the remaining companies or to those subject to income tax. This special regime ignores the distinction between income and capital but still asks whether a foreign exchange transaction is made in the course of trade. Most of the income tax case-law concerns the distinction between income and capital.

Suppose that a trader (T) invests in foreign exchange which is later realised at a gain (or loss). Foreign exchange profits arising on capital account are capital and so not trading receipts.[61] However in *Imperial Tobacco Co. Ltd.* v. *Kelly*[62] the company bought tobacco leaf in America and, to this end, bought dollars over the year. With the outbreak of the Second World War the company, at the request of the Treasury, stopped buying American leaf and thereafter its dollars were acquired by the Treasury at a profit to the company. The Court of Appeal held this to be profit of the trade. It did not matter that the company did not carry on the trade of dealing in foreign exchange; what mattered was that the dollars had been bought as the first step in an intended commercial transaction. One can thus view the dollars as equivalent to raw materials.

The court left open the correctness of the earlier case of *McKinlay* v. *H. T. Jenkins & Son Ltd.*[65] A firm of builders who intended to buy marble in Italy had bought lire for £16,500. The lira then rose in value against the pound and the holding was sold in order that a profit might be realised on the exchange. The sale price was £21,870, a net profit of approximately £6,700. The value of the lira then fell and the firm bought the required currency needed £19,386, which sum was allowed as a deduction in computing the profits. Rowlatt J. upheld the Commissioners' decision that the £6,700 was not taxable as a profit of the trade. Today, it seems likely that the profit would be taxable, either because the case cannot stand with the later decision of the Court of Appeal in *Imperial Tobacco* or because the decision to withdraw the lire holding from the ambit of the trade may cause the rule in *Sharkey* v. *Wernher*[64] to operate.

A trading profit is only taxable if it has arisen; in foreign exchange transactions the courts have distinguished conversion, which may cause a profit to arise, from mere translation, which does not. In *Pattison* v. *Marine Midland Ltd.*[65] a bank raised a fund of dollars by way of loan and proceeded to lend dollars in the course of its banking business. When the orig-

[57] *General Reinsurance Co. Ltd.* v. *Tomlinson* (1970) 48 TC 81; see also *Nuclear Electric plc* v. *Bradley* [1996] STC 405, 68 TC 670.

[58] *Cooper* v. *C. and J. Clark Ltd.* [1982] STC 335, 54 TC 670.

[59] On treatment of financial futures and options, see Statement of Practice SP 14/91. (obsolete)

[60] See below at §48.3.

[61] *Davies* v. *Shell Co. of China Ltd.* (1951) 32 TC 133.

[62] [1943] 2 All ER 119, 25 TC 292; see also *Landes Bros* v. *Simpson* (1934) 19 TC 62; and *O'Sullivan* v. *O'Connor* [1947] IR 416.

[63] (1926) 10 TC 372.

[64] See below at §22.5.1.

[65] [1984] STC 10, 57 TC 219, HL; see Pagan [1984] *BTR* 161.

inal funding loan was repaid, the dollar had strengthened against sterling. The House of Lords held that the bank was not taxable on the sterling profit that arose on the withdrawal of the money from the bank's lending fund since the fund had never been converted into sterling and had been translated into sterling only for balance sheet (as distinct from profit and loss account) purposes. As the fund had never been converted into sterling, the money was like an asset held by the company, generating income by being hired out. The asset might be specific or, as in *Pattison* v. *Marine Midland Ltd.*, fungible.

The 1993 corporation tax regime on foreign exchange also permits a company to carry on its trade, compute its profits and express them for corporation tax in a currency other than sterling (in defined circumstances).[66] These changes do not apply to income tax and are discussed elsewhere (see below at §48.2). *Pattison* v. *Marine Midland* and the subsequent statement of practice on matching transactions remain applicable for income tax.[67]

21.5.3 *Contracts for supply of trading stock*

A profit arising on the disposal of a contract for supply of trading stock may be a trading receipt—provided it takes revenue form. In *George Thompson & Co. Ltd.* v. *IRC*[68] certain ships belonging to a shipping company had been requisitioned by the Australian Government. The company was left with contracts for the supply of coal in excess of its needs. It therefore transferred the benefit of the contract to another company—not by assignment, but by a transfer of the right to take delivery at a premium first of 6s a ton and then of 10s a ton. Although the company had only rarely sold coal previously, Rowlatt J. had no difficulty in holding that this was a revenue receipt of the trade. The coal had not been bought as capital on capital account, but as a thing which the company needed to buy and use as consumable stores. The purchase of the coal had been arranged as a part of the company's business, so that it could not be treated as a separate business.

21.5.4 *Know-how*

Old law

The old cases on know-how distinguished payment for the *use* of know-how[69] from payment for *disposing* of know-how (e.g. when the know-how was disposed of along with other assets of the trade in a foreign country).[70] Where, however, the company had to supply know-how as a condition of entering into a trading arrangement in a country with which there had been no previous trade, the receipt was one on revenue account since the transaction did not materially affect the company's profit making structure.[71]

[66] FA 1993, ss 92–94, now superseded by FA 2000, s. 106.

[67] For criticism, see Henbrey [1986] *BTR* 1.

[68] (1927) 12 TC 1091.

[69] *Rolls Royce Ltd.* v. *Jeffrey* [1962] 1 All ER 801, 40 TC 443 (noted at [1961] *BTR* 263); *Musker* v. *English Electric Co. Ltd.* (1964) 41 TC 556 (noted at [1963] *BTR* 306) (see below at §24.11); and *IRC* v. *Desoutter Bros Ltd.* (1945) 29 TC 155, 162; but *cf. IRC* v. *Iles* (1945) 29 TC 225. On patent royalties as deductions, see below at §22.3.6.

[70] *Evans Medical Supplies Ltd.* v. *Moriarty* [1957] 3 All ER 718, 37 TC 540.

[71] *Coalite and Chemical Products Ltd.* v. *Treeby* (1971) 48 TC 171; followed in *John and E. Sturge Ltd.* v. *Hessel* [1975] STC 127 at 148 Walton J. upheld 1975 STC 573 (CA);, 51 TC 183, 208.

Current law

Statute now provides that all payments in return for know-how are trading receipts if the know-how has been used in the trade and the trade is still carried on.[72] Where a person *disposes* of a trade or part of a trade, any consideration for know-how is generally dealt with as a payment for goodwill. However, this does not apply where the parties jointly elect otherwise, or if the trade was carried on wholly outside the UK (in which circumstances the old case-law will apply).[73]

21.6 Payments for Restriction of Activities or Sterilisation of Assets

A payment received as the price for a substantial restriction on a business or as compensation for the sterilisation of a capital asset is either not a trading receipt at all or is a capital receipt. However (as will be seen below at §21.7), a payment received as a surrogatum for trading profit is itself a trading receipt. The boundary between the two is easier to state than to apply.

In applying the two principles the court's task is complicated by the fact that a payment may come within this head even though the measure used by the parties to determine the level of payment is loss of profit—the measure does not determine the quality of the payment. The leading modern authority is *Higgs* v. *Olivier*.[74] Mr Laurence Olivier (as he then was), a well-known actor, had entered into a covenant that he would not, for a period of 18 months, appear as an actor in, or producer or director of, any film to be made anywhere by any other company. In return he received £15,000 from the company which had just made the film *Henry V*, in which he had starred. The reason for this deal appears from the case stated: "He was quite a popular film actor, appearing in quite the ordinary kind of films, and the company thought that if he made a more ordinary film than Henry V, the public would go to that instead". The covenant was made after the film had been completed and released in England, where it did not make much money; the film was hailed a success only after its release in New York. Thus, the covenant was separate from the original contract to make the film. The Special Commissioners held that the sum was paid to Mr Olivier for refraining from carrying on his vocation, and was therefore a capital receipt. The Court of Appeal held that the payment was for a restriction extending to a substantial portion of professional activities open to him, and so was not a trading receipt; it may thus be seen as analogous to the solatium cases (see above at §21.3). The court also stressed that the covenant could not possibly be regarded as being in the ordinary run of the vocation of actors.

By contrast, in *White* v. *G. and M. Davies (a firm)*[75] the receipt of a premium payment by a farmer under an EEC scheme was held to be a trading receipt. In return for the payment the farmer undertook not to sell milk products for four years and to ensure that dairy cattle accounted for no more than 20% of his herd. Browne-Wilkinson J. distinguished *Higgs* v. *Olivier* on the basis that the current restrictions controlled the way in which the taxpayer

[72] TA 1988, s. 531(1).

[73] Ibid., s. 531(3).

[74] [1952] 1 Ch 311, 33 TC 136. *The Times*, 23 November 1944 wrote: "A great play has been made into a great film . . . his white horse and his armour become him wonderfully . . . [the film] is a test case to see whether there is a future in the cinema for Shakespeare and others of his cast and mould".

[75] [1979] STC 415, 52 TC 597; the judge noted the unfairness of treating the payment as income of one year. Today, the farmer would be able to use the averaging regime (explained above at §12. 5) and would also benefit from the reduced rates of income tax in 1988.

carried on his business, whereas this had not been so in the earlier case. A similar result was reached in *IRC* v. *Biggar*.[76] Another way of distinguishing these cases is to stress that the covenant in *Higgs* v. *Olivier* was most unususal.

The rule was applied in *Murray* v. *Imperial Chemical Industries Ltd*.[77] where the company received a capital sum in return for agreeing not to trade in a certain country; this "keep-out" payment was made under an agreement whereby the company allowed another firm to use its patent in that country. However, the was not applied in *Thompson* v. *Magnesium Elektron Ltd*.[78] where a company producing magnesium, and therefore needing chlorine, agreed to buy chlorine from another company and agreed not to manufacture chlorine or caustic soda (a by-product of the manufacture of chlorine) beyond its own needs. The company was to receive payments calculated on the amount of caustic soda it would have produced. It was held that the payments simply affected the price the company was paying for its chlorine. It would appear that if the payment had been a lump sum it would not have been a trading receipt,[79] since the form of the payment would have suggested that it was made for not making caustic soda, rather than of for receiving chlorine.

21.7 Surrogata for Trading Profits—Compensation Payments

21.7.1 Basic rule

A sum received in respect of trading stock is income whether it is the proceeds of sale, damages for breach of contract or for tort, or compensation on compulsory acquisition. The occasion for the receipt is immaterial. Lord Clyde illustrated this in *Burmah Steamship Co. Ltd.* v. *IRC*:[80]

> "Suppose someone who chartered one of the Appellant's vessels breached the charter and exposed himself to a claim of damages . . . there could, I imagine, be no doubt that the damages recovered would properly enter the Appellant's profit and loss account for the year. The reason would be that the breach of the charter was an injury inflicted on the Appellant's trading, making (so to speak) a hole in the Appellant's profits, and damages recovered could not be reasonably or appropriately put . . . to any other purpose than to fill that hole. Suppose on the other hand, that one of the taxpayer's vessels was negligently run down and sunk by a vessel belonging to some other shipowner, and the Appellant recovered as damages the value of the sunken vessel, I imagine that there could be no doubt that the damages so recovered could not enter the Appellant's profit and loss account because the destruction of the vessel would be an injury inflicted, not on the Appellant's trading, but on the capital assets of the Appellant's trade, making (so to speak) a hole in them, and the damages could therefore . . . only be used to fill that hole."

The appellants had bought a ship which required extensive repairs before it could put to sea. The repairer was in breach of contract in that he did not complete the repairs until some five months after the due date. The appellant recovered £1,500 damages for late delivery, the sum being an estimate of the loss of profit. The sum was held to be income. The purchase

76 [1982] STC 677, 56 TC 254.

77 [1967] 2 All ER 980, 44 TC 175. For Revenue practice, see note RI 52.

78 [1944] 1 All ER 126, 26 TC 1.

79 As in *Margerison* v. *Tyresoles Ltd.* (1942) 25 TC 59; see Hannan and Farnsworth, *The Principles of Income Taxation* (Stevens, 1952), 138

80 (1930) 16 TC 67, 71, 72.

price of the ship would, however, have been a capital item; it should follow, therefore, that had the purchaser arranged for a reduction in price, that reduction would have meant a lower capital price, and so would have been a taxable income receipt.[81] A payment for the use of a capital asset is a revenue receipt, but one for its realisation is a capital receipt.[82]

21.7.2 Examples

The rule that a surrogatum for loss of profit is an income receipt has been applied consistently in the following circumstances: where a company which had acquired a licence to take Noel Coward's *Cavalcade* on tour in the UK received damages because a film of that show was released to the detriment of the profits of the tour,[83] where a firm who made steamships received damages from a purchaser in return for the cancellation of an agreement to buy ships;[84] where timber which was the trading stock of a company was destroyed by fire and sums were received from an insurance company equal to the replacement value of the timber;[85] and, similarly, where sums were payable under an insurance policy against loss of profit.[86] Payments by the state for loss of profit to an individual while serving on a jury or local authority are considered to be taxable receipts.[87]

Slightly less obviously, the rule has been applied where a company received a large sum under a life policy it held on one of its key employees,[88] the services of the employees being regarded as being as much part of the trading activities of the business as the goods which were its trading stock. The court had noted that sums paid to induce the resignation of a director had been held to be income expenditure.[89]

Tankers

A company whose jetty was damaged by the negligent navigation of a tanker was held taxable on the damages received in so far as they represented damages for loss of the use of the jetty during repairs, but not on the much larger sum needed to repair the jetty.[90] It is unclear what would have happened had there been no clear apportionment of the damages.

Related points

When the payment is a capital receipt, it may well give rise to CGT.[91]

[81] Ibid., 73, *per* Lord Sands. See also *Crabb* v. *Blue Star Line Ltd.* [1961] 2 All ER 424, 39 TC 482 (proceeds of insurance policy against late delivery held to be capital). On treatment of compensation payments for compulsory slaughter of farm animals, see ESC B11.

[82] *Greyhound Racing Association (Liverpool) Ltd.* v. *Cooper* [1936] 2 All ER 742, 20 TC 373.

[83] *Vaughan* v. *Archie Parnell and Alfred Zeitlin Ltd.* (1940) 23 TC 505; criticised by Hannan and Farnsworth, above at n. 80, 263–4. It follows that no deduction for tax can be made in assessing the damages (*Diamond* v. *Campbell-Jones* [1961] Ch 22, [1960] 1 All ER 583.

[84] *Short Bros Ltd.* v. *IRC* (1927) 12 TC 955.

[85] *J. Gliksten & Son Ltd.* v. *Green* [1929] AC 381, 14 TC 364.

[86] *R.* v. *British Columbia Fir and Cedar Lumber Co. Ltd.* [1932] AC 441; see also *Mallandain Investments Ltd.* v. *Shadbolt* (1940) 23 TC 367.

[87] RI 18.

[88] *Williams Executors* v. *IRC* [1942] 2 All ER 266, 26 TC 23. It appears that in general it is Revenue practice not to treat lump sum proceeds as trading receipts if no claim was made to deduct the premiums as trading expenses. But it does not follow that the company can opt to have the proceeds treated as capital by not claiming relief for the premiums; the proper tax treatment of the proceeds must be considered on its own merits.

[89] *B. W. Noble Ltd.* v. *Mitchell* (1926) 11 TC 372.

[90] *London and Thames Haven Oil Wharves Ltd,* v. *Attwooll* [1967] 2 All ER 124, 43 TC 491.

[91] Under TCGA 1992, s. 22; see *Lang* v. *Rice* [1984] STC 172, CA.

The rule that a surrogatum for loss of profit is an income receipt has also been applied to compensation for increased revenue expenditure.[92]

Where both the lost profits and the damages are taxable, no account is taken of the tax situation in assessing the damages, save for the exceptional case where justice demands it.[93] Where damages are received for loss of profit, the fact that the damages are used to write down certain capital expenditure incurred during the contract is irrelevant; the payment is nonetheless an income receipt.[94]

21.7.3 Basis of measure does not determine quality of payment

There is no relation between the measure used for the purpose of calculating a particular result and the quality of the figure arrived at by means of the application of that test. In *Glenboig Union Fireclay Co. Ltd.* v. *IRC*[95] the taxpayer company (G) held leasehold rights in certain fireclay seams with the right to remove minerals. The seam ran under the railway track of the Caledonian Railway Company (CalR). CalR obtained an interdict to prevent G from removing fireclay from the seam pending the hearing of its case against G, in which it claimed that although the lease granted the right to remove minerals, fireclay was not a mineral. CalR lost its case and then exercised its powers compulsorily to prevent G from exercising its rights. Eventually it was agreed that a large sum should be paid to G for loss of the fireclay. The House of Lords held that the sum was a capital receipt. The case concerned excess profits duty and it was the Revenue who argued that the receipt was capital.[96] The company argued that as that seam would have been fully worked out in two-and-a-half years the sum paid was nothing but a surrogatum for profits lost. Lord Buckmaster regarded that argument as fallacious:[97]

> "In truth the sum of money is the sum paid to prevent the Fireclay Company obtaining the full benefit of the capital value of that part of the mines which they are prevented from working by the railway company. It appears to me to make no difference whether it be regarded as the sale of the asset out and out, or whether it be treated merely as a means of preventing the acquisition of profit which would otherwise be gained. In either case the capital asset of the company to that extent has been sterilised and destroyed, and it is in respect of that action that the sum . . . was paid. . . . It is now well settled that the compensation payable in such circumstances is the full value of the minerals that are left unworked, less the cost of working, and that is of course the profit that would have been obtained were they in fact worked. But there is no relation between the measure that is used for the purpose of calculating a particular result and the quality of the figure that is arrived at by means of the application of that test."

Glenboig—fine points

Compensation for the sterilisation of a capital asset is a capital payment but this leaves the question, what is a capital asset?[98] In *Glenboig* an item of fixed capital was sterilised. This must be distinguished from the prevention of the acquisition of profit.[99]

[92] *Donald Fisher (Ealing) Ltd.* v. *Spencer* [1989] STC 256, 63 TC 168, CA.

[93] *Deeny* v. *Gooda Walker Ltd.* [1995] STC 439, 453; Potter J. affirmed in the House of Lords on other grounds at [1996] STC 299.

[94] *IRC* v. *Northfleet Coal and Ballast Co. Ltd.* (1927) 12 TC 1102.

[95] (1922) 12 TC 427, 464, HL, *per* Lord Buckmaster.

[96] The higher the company's profits before 1914, the lower the excess profits duty.

[97] (1922) 12 TC 427, 464.

[98] On goodwill as capital asset, see Lord Evershed M.R. in *Wiseburgh* v. *Domville* [1956] 1 All ER 754, 758, 36 TC 527, 539.

[99] For example *Waterloo Main Colliery Co. Ltd.* v. *IRC* (1947) 29 TC 235.

Extraction industries have always been odd for tax purposes since the process of their trade turns fixed capital into circulating capital.[100] Thus, in *Glenboig*, had CalR accidentally destroyed the fireclay after it had been extracted it would appear that the sums payable by way of damages would have been a trading receipt.

The House of Lords did not have to consider the correct tax treatment of the damages for wrongous interdict.[101] The Court of Session held that the sum was a capital receipt on the ground that it was the reimbursement of expenditure of a capital nature because it proved to be totally fruitless owing to the expropriation proceedings.[102] The parties settled this aspect of their liability before going to the House of Lords. If this payment had been held to be a revenue receipt[103] the droll result would have been that: (a) the payment computed by reference to loss of profit was a capital payment, while the payment in this case, not so computed, but which was for loss of profit, is a trading receipt; and (b) a payment relating to a period of three years would be an income payment, whereas the payment in this case, relating to the two-and-a-half years it would have taken to exhaust the fireclay, was a capital payment.

21.7.4 Contracts relating to structure of business

Damages paid for breach of a contract to make good the loss of profit from that contract will usually be treated as income. It makes no difference what the importance of the contract is to the trade. However, it is necessary to distinguish profit-earning contracts from those relating to the whole structure of the profit-earning apparatus of the trade. In *Van den Berghs Ltd.* v. *Clark*[104] the appellant company entered into an agreement with a competing Dutch company in 1912. The agreement provided for the sharing of profits, the bringing-in of any other margarine concerns they might acquire and the setting-up of a joint committee to make arrangements with outside firms as to prices and limitation of areas of supply of margarine. The agreement was intended to last until 1926 at the earliest, with later variations extending that to 1940. The outbreak of the First World War upset the arrangements of the Dutch company and eventually that company agreed, in 1927, to pay the appellant company £450,000 for cancellation of the agreement. The House of Lords held that the sum was paid for loss of future rights under the agreement, which was a capital asset and therefore was a capital receipt. Lord Macmillan said:[105]

> "The . . . agreements which the Appellants consented to cancel were not ordinary commercial contracts made in the course of carrying on their trade; they were not contracts for the disposal of their products or for the engagement of agents or other employees necessary for the conduct of their business; nor were they merely agreements as to how their trading profits when earned should be distributed between the contracting parties. On the contrary the cancelled agreements related to the whole structure of the Appellants profit making apparatus. They regulated the Appellants' activities, defined what they might and what they might not do, and affected the whole conduct of

[100] *Taxes Comr* v. *Nchanga Consolidated Copper Mines Ltd.* [1964] AC 948, 964, [1964] 1 All ER 208, 212, *per* Lord Radcliffe.

[101] The amount payable to the fireclay company in respect of expenses of keeping the seam open but unused while the interdict prevented them from working it.

[102] *British Insulated and Helsby Cables Ltd.* v. *Atherton* [1926] AC 205, 211, *per* Viscount Cave L.C.; *Southern* v. *Borax Consolidated Ltd.* [1940] 4 All ER 412, 23 TC 597.

[103] As suggested by Lord Clyde in *Burmah Steamship Co. Ltd.* v. *IRC* (1930) 16 TC 67, 72; although in the *Glenboig* case Lord Clyde had thought it a capital receipt (1922) 12 TC 427, 450).

[104] (1935) 19 TC 390, HL.

[105] Ibid., 431, 432.

their business. The agreements formed part of the fixed framework within which their circulating capital operated; they were not incidental to the working of their profit making machine but were essential parts of the mechanism itself. They provided the means of making profits, but they themselves did not yield profits."

Structure

Sums paid on the *variation* of an agreement which relates to the whole structure of the profit-making apparatus are capital. In *Sabine* v. *Lockers Ltd.*[106] the taxpayers held the main distributorship for the Austin motor company in the Manchester area; they were not allowed to enter into any agreement with any other manufacturer. Sums paid for variation of that contract were held to be capital receipts. The distributorship lasted only for one year, with a right of renewal for a further year, but there was reasonable prospect of further yearly renewals.

Disposal contract as structure?

In both *Van den Bergh's Ltd.* v. *Clark* and *Sabine* v. *Lockers Ltd.* the agreements related to the framework of the company's business, rather than to the disposal of the company's products. It is less easy, but apparently not impossible,[107] for a contract of the latter type to be treated as a capital asset. However, the mere fact that traders arrange their work on the basis of a particular contract is insufficient to make that contract one relating to the structure of their business. Thus, a shipbuilding company may make only a few ships a year, but an order for a ship is a profit-yielding contract; damages for breach will therefore be an income receipt.[108]

21.7.5 Agency contracts

The restriction, even though temporary, of profit-making apparatus is very different from the mere loss of trading opportunity which occurs when an agency contract on commission ends and a lump sum is received for the cancellation. At first sight it would seem that such contracts, producing income, must be capital assets,[109] but they are usually treated as revenue assets since their acquisition and replacement is one of the normal incidents of the business. They are disposal contracts in that the company is disposing of services. Such contracts are not a capital assets, and the sums received will be taxed as mere trading receipts. In *Shove* v. *Dura Manufacturing Co. Ltd.*[110] Lawrence J. gave three reasons why there was nothing of a capital nature about these contracts: "No money was spent to secure it; no capital asset was acquired to carry it out; its cancellation was only an ordinary method of modifying and realising the profit to be derived from it".

In *Kelsall Parsons & Co.* v. *IRC*[111] the appellants commenced business in Scotland as manufacturer's agents and engineers in 1914 when one of their two agencies was for a firm in Birmingham making electric switch gear. A series of agency agreements was made with the

[106] (1958) 38 TC 120.

[107] Note Ungoed Thomas J. in *John Mills Productions Ltd.* v. *Mathias* (1964) 44 TC 441, 453.

[107] *Short Bros Ltd.* v. *IRC* (1927) 12 TC 955; for a similar result for a film star see *John Mills Productions Ltd.* v. *Mathias* (1964) 44 TC 441.

[109] *Anglo-French Exploration Co. Ltd.* v. *Clayson* [1956] 1 All ER 762, 766, 36 TC 545, 557, *per* Lord Evershed M.R.

[110] (1941) 23 TC 779, 783.

[111] (1938) 21 TC 608; applied in *Creed* v. *H. and M. Levinson Ltd.* [1981] STC 486, 54 TC 477; see also *Croydon Hotel and Lesure* v. *Bowen* [1996] STC (SCD) 466.

firm the last of which was for three years from 30 September 1932, but this was terminated by agreement on 30 September 1934, the firm agreeing to pay £1,500 compensation to the appellants. The Court of Session held that the sum was a trading receipt. It was true that the appellants had built up a considerable technical organisation to handle this particular agency agreement,[112] but that was insufficient to bring the facts within the principle in *Van den Berghs Ltd.* v. *Clark.* In reaching this conclusion it was important to Lord Normand and Lord Fleming that the agreement had only one year to run. As Lord Normand put it, this was not a case where "a benefit extending over a tract of future years is renounced for a payment made once and for all".[113]

Exception

In *Barr Crombie & Co. Ltd.* v. *IRC*[114] the appellants managed ships; 98% of its business came from an agreement with another company for a period of 15 years from 1936, which was terminated in 1942 when the shipping company went into liquidation. A large sum paid in respect of the eight years left of the agreement was held to be a capital receipt. Taking all the facts into account, Lord Normand considered that the effect on the company's structure and character was such as to bring the facts within *Van den Berghs Ltd.* v. *Clark.*

Although Millett L.J. noted subsequently[115] that the effect of the cancellation was to leave the company with practically nothing left of its business, the difficulty remains that *Barr Crombie* illustrates that the distinction between a contract which is merely one created in the ordinary life of the business and one which relates to its profit-making structure can be a matter of degree rather than kind. It is possible to use dramatic language to show the importance of that degree, as Lord Russell did in *IRC* v. *Fleming & Co. (Machinery) Ltd.*,[116] where he distinguished the situation in which the rights and advantages surrendered on cancellation were such as to destroy or materially cripple the whole structure of the recipient's profit-making apparatus, involving the serious dislocation of the normal commercial organisation and resulting, perhaps, in the cutting-down of staff previously required, from that in which the benefit surrendered was not an enduring asset and where the structure of the recipient's business was so fashioned as to absorb the shock as one of the normal incidents to be expected and where it appears that the compensation received is no more than a surrogatum for future profits surrendered.[117] These are, however, only explanations and illustrations. There was no reduction in the staff employed as a result of the cancellation of the agreement in *Van den Berghs Ltd.* v. *Clark*; but the fact that the workforce had to be reduced after the cancellation was insufficient to turn the compensation into a capital receipt in *Elson* v. *James G. Johnston Ltd.*[118] In *Barr Crombie* itself Lord Normand stressed that none of the factors which distinguished the case from *Kelsall, Parsons & Co.* v. *IRC* were of themselves conclusive. but the combination was.[119]

What *Barr Crombie* establishes is that compensation may be a capital receipt even though the contract is a disposal contract. However, there is also authority for the proposition that

[112] 21 TC 608, 615.
[113] Ibid., 620.
[114] (1945) 26 TC 406. See also *California Oil Products Ltd.* v. *FCT* (1934) 52 CLR 28 (company formed to operate one agency and liquidated following its cancellation; compensation on cancellation was held to be a capital receipt).
[115] *Vodafone Cellular Ltd.* v. *Shaw* [1997] STC 734, 740 CA.
[116] (1951) 33 TC 57, 63.
[117] Ibid., *per* Lord Russell.
[118] (1965) 42 TC 545.
[119] (1945) 26 TC 406, 412.

a pure disposal contract will not be a capital asset, no matter how big it is.[120] Therefore, it must be concluded that in *Barr Crombie* the contract was a capital asset primarily by reason of its duration and, because the business had been built around that contract, it was not a mere disposal contract.[121] The agency had been the company's principal asset since the trade commenced so that it could not be said that its loss was a normal incident of the business. Further, the loss of the agency necessitated the complete reorganisation of the taxpayers' business, a reduction in staff and the taking of newer and smaller premises. Such a case must therefore be distinguished from one in which the taxpayer can, in fact, continue in exactly the same line of business as before, notwithstanding that his one source of income has ceased.[122]

21.7.6 Subsidies

Subsidies are treated on the same principles as compensation payments. The court looks to the business nature of the payments and treats them as trading receipts at the time of payment, if they were intended to be used in the business. Where a subsidy is paid in advance and may therefore have to be repaid, in whole or in part, the question is whether the payment is a loan or a receipt.

Payments in the nature of a subsidy from public funds made to an entrepreneur to assist in the carrying-on of the trade or business are trading receipts.[123] A subsidy which takes the form of a payment to bring the receipt for an item of trading stock product up to a certain level is clearly a trading receipt.[124] Similarly, payments to enable the trader to meet trading obligations are trading receipts when made; however, payments of unemployment grants to assist with a specific project of a capital nature have been held not to be trading receipts.[125] In general a payment to maintain employment is neither clearly capital nor revenue.[126]

The subsidy may come from another company. In *British Commonwealth International Newsfilm Agency Ltd.* v. *Mahany*[127] a payment to a subsidiary company as a supplement to its trading revenue and in order to preserve its trading stability was held to be a trading receipt.

21.8 Money Not Yet Belonging to Trader

Where a trader receives sums of money from customers on their behalf, the receipt is not a trading receipt and so is not to be brought into account. This is the case even though the

[120] *John Mills Productions Ltd.* v. *Mathias* (1964) 44 TC 441, 456,*per* Ungoed Thomas J.

[121] *Cf.* ibid., 455, *per* Ungoed Thomas J.

[122] *A Consultant* v. *Inspector of Taxes* [1999] STC (SCD) 64.

[123] *Pontypridd and Rhondda Joint Water Board* v. *Ostime* [1946] AC 477, 489, 28 TC 261, 278, *per* Viscount Simon; see also *Poulter* v. *Gayjon Processes Ltd.* [1985] STC 174. TA 1988, s. 93 expressly makes grants under the Industrial and Development Act 1984 and similar Acts trading receipts unless clearly capital.

[124] *Lincolnshire Sugar Co. Ltd.* v. *Smart* (1935) 20 TC 643, 667. See also *Higgs* v. *Wrightson* (1944) 26 TC 73 (ploughing subsidies held to be trading receipts); *Burman* v. *Thorn Domestic Appliances (Electrical) Ltd.* [1982] STC 179, 55 TC 493.

[125] *Seaham Harbour Dock Co.* v. *Crook* (1930) 16 TC 333; as explained in *Poulter* v. *Gayjon Processes Ltd.* [1985] STC 174, 58 TC 350.

[126] *Ryan* v. *Crabtree Denims Ltd.* [1987] STC 402, 60 TC 183; although the judgment in this case focuses on the purpose for which the payment is applied, it is to be assumed that one looks first at the purpose for which the payment was made

[127] [1963] 1 All ER 88, 40 TC 550, HL. *Cf. Moss' Empires Ltd.* v. *IRC* [1973] AC 785, 21 TC 264.

trade is carried on by a partnership and the sums held for the customers are allocated to the partners as a domestic arrangement for book-keeping purposes.[128] If, however, the sums originally repayable to the customers cease to be so by reason of the Limitation Act 1980, they become trading receipts of the period when the claims are barred.[129] In such cases the quality and nature of the receipt are fixed when the money is received, but the timing issue is different.[130] It remains to be seen whether accounting standards will be developed to change these rules, and whether the courts will accept such standards as overriding these legal principles.

The question whether the money belongs to the customers or to the trader must depend on the facts. Where a sum is paid to a trader by way of part payment, it is still the customer's money; whereas if the money is paid by way of deposit, it is irrecoverable by a purchaser in default and so becomes the property of the trader immediately on payment. A deposit is therefore a trading receipt.[131]

21.9 Payment Falling Within Different Schedule or Case

Income correctly taxed under another Schedule should not be taxed under Schedule D, Case I and so cannot enter into the computation. Thus, rental income in respect of land in the UK is assessable under Schedule A,[132] and income from an employment is taxed under Schedule E. A line must also be drawn between trading receipts and payments falling within Schedule D, Case III; a payment which forms part of the trading activities of the recipient cannot be pure income profit in his hands and so cannot fall within Case III. A payment incorrectly received under deduction of tax[133] must form part of the profits, while one that was correctly so received cannot be a trading receipt.[134]

If, however, a particular receipt can be taxed under both Case I and another Case, it cannot be assessed to tax twice. The Revenue may override the taxpayer's choice.[135]

Where dividends are received by a trader dealing in investments, those dividends should be taxable under Schedule F and only under that Schedule. However, statute provides that they are to be taxed only under Schedule D, Case I—this was introduced so as to prevent any right to claim repayment, or make any other use, of any tax credit.[136]

On boundary with Schedule A see §25.2.

[128] *Morley* v. *Tattersall* [1938] 3 All ER 296, 22 TC 51 (the limitation period did not begin to run in this case in respect of any of the payments: 29 TC 274, 284).

[129] *IRC* v. *Jay's the Jewellers Ltd.* [1947] 2 All ER 762, 29 TC 274.

[130] *Tapemaze Ltd.* v. *Melluish* [1999] STC (SCD) 260.

[131] *Elson* v. *Price's Tailors Ltd.* [1963] 1 All ER 231, 40 TC 671.

[132] See below at §25.1; see also *Lowe* v. *J. W. Ashmore Ltd.* [1971] 1 All ER 1057, 46 TC 597 (sales of turf by farmer taxable under Case I not Schedule A); noted at [1970] *BTR* 416.

[133] Under TA 1988, ss 348–50; see below at §27.5.

[134] *British Commonwealth International Newsfilm Agency Ltd.* v. *Mahany* [1963] 1 All ER 88, 40 TC 550.

[135] *Liverpool and London and Globe Insurance Co.* v. *Bennett* [1913] AC 610, 6 TC 327; for Revenue powers under self-assessment, see TMA 1970, s. 28A(7A) and FA 1998, Sch. 18, para. 84.

[136] TA 1988, s. 95, as amended in 1997 (see below at §24.11). On previous law, see speech of Viscount Simonds in *Cenlon Finance Ltd.* v. *Ellwood* [1962] 1 All ER 854, 40 TC 176; criticised at [1962] *BTR* 320 and [1963] *BTR* 133; and *F. S. Securities Ltd.* v. *IRC* [1964] 2 All ER 691, 41 TC 666, HL; noted at [1964] *BTR* 53 and [1964] *BTR* 281.

21.10 Valuing the Receipt: Market Value

In deciding the amount to be included as a trading receipt, regard must be had to the rules substituting market value for any price agreed between the parties, especially TA 1988, s. 770A (see below at §61.3) and the rule in *Sharkey* v. *Wernher* (see below at §23.5.1).

21.11 Mining

Special rules provide that where a person resident or ordinarily resident in the UK is entitled to receive mineral royalties under a mineral lease or agreement, one half of the proceeds are to be treated as income and one half as capital gains.[137] The land concerned may be in the UK or overseas.

21.12 Reverse Premiums[138]

Reverse premiums, known in Canada by the more appropriate name of "lease inducement payments",[139] were held to be capital receipts, and so non-taxable, in the 1998 Privy Council's decision in *CIR* v. *Wattie*.[140] This decision produced a lack of symmetry in that such payments would often be made by property developers so that the sums paid would be deductible, while the sum received would not be taxable. However, there were many instances in which this lack of symmetry did not arise.[141] The decision has now been superseded by FA 1999, Schedule 6 which applies to premiums received on or after 9 March 1999.[142] Such payments are now taxable—regardless of their treatment in the hands of the person making the payment. The rule catches payments and other benefits. Examples of other benefits, which must be paid to X, are contributions to X's costs in fitting out the building or relocating a business, and taking over X's liabilities under an old lease of the premises.[143]

The payment must be made by way of inducement in connection with a "relevant transaction", i.e. one under which X, or a person connected to X, becomes entitled to an estate or interest in, or a right in or over, land. The payment must come from G, the grantor of the estate, interest or right, or other persons connected with G.[144] The purpose is to catch the reverse premium paid when the lease is granted; it is not intended to catch a payment by a lessee to someone to persuade them to take over a lease when the lease subsequently becomes onerous.[145] However, the Revenue view is that Schedule 6 catches a premium

[137] TA 1988, s. 122.

[138] See Challoner [1999] *BTR* 350.

[139] See, generally, Carr (1998) 46 *Can. Tax Jo.* 953.

[140] [1998] STC 1160. The decision is equally applicable to UK tax (see ibid., 1169j, 1170e, *per* Lord Nolan). See Coull [1999] *BTR* 117.

[141] For example *Southern Counties Agricultural Society* v. *Blackler* [1999] STC (SCD) 200.

[142] FA 1999, s. 54(2); the treatment doe not apply if the person was entitled to the payment immediately before that date. See also ibid., s. 54(3)

[143] Inland Revenue Notes to Finance Bill 1999, para. 31.

[144] FA 1999, Sch. 6, para. 1; on connected person status, seeibid., Sch. 6, para. 7, referring to TA 1988, s. 839.

[145] Inland Revenue Notes to Finance Bill 1999, para. 33. The Revenue view is that a rent-free period is another reverse premium, but that no notional charge arises.

payable to an assignee where it is, in substance, an inducement to take a grant of a lease dressed up as an assignment.[146]

The tax treatment of X depends on X's tax status. If a trading purpose exists, the reverse premium enters the profits of that trade, profession or vocation under Schedule D, Case I or II.[147] In any other circumstances, it may come within Schedule A or Schedule D, Case V.[148] In any event, the sum is treated as a revenue receipt.[149]

Timing

Under the principles of commercial accounting which apply to business profits, and to Schedule A, the receipt will be spread over the period of the lease or, if shorter, until the first rent review.[150] However, if the arrangements are not at arm's length, i.e. some or all of the parties to the relevant arrangements are connected persons and the terms of those arrangements are not such as would reasonably have been expected if those persons had been dealing at arm's length,[151] the whole sum must be taxed at once or, as the statute more precisely puts it, in the first relevant period of account.[152] Therefore, if the trade has not yet begun it will be treated as taxable in the first period of account of that trade.

Capital allowances

Where the premium has been taken into account in calculating the allowable expenditure for capital allowance purposes, by reducing the allowable expenditure, it is not chargeable under these rules. This is to prevent what would, in effect, be a double charge.[153]

Special rules

Taxability is excluded if the transaction relates to an individual's only or main residence,[154] or if the matter already falls within TA, 1988 s. 779 or 780 as a sale and leaseback.[155] Special rules apply to insurance companies.[156]

[146] Ibid.
[147] FA 1999, Sch. 6, para. 2(2)
[148] Ibid., Sch. 6, para. 2(3).
[149] Ibid., Sch. 6, para. 2(2).
[150] Inland Revenue Notes to Finance Bill 1999, para. 32.
[151] Defined in FA 1999, Sch. 6, para. 4.
[152] FA 1999, Sch. 6, para. 3.
[153] Ibid., Sch. 6, para. 5; see also Inland Revenue Press Release 19 May 1999, (1999) *Simon's Weekly Tax Intelligence* 934.
[154] FA 1999, Sch. 6, para. 6.
[155] Ibid., Sch. 6, para. 7 (see below at §22.8).
[156] Ibid., Sch. 6, para. 4.

22

Business Income—Part IV: Trading Expenses

22.1 Basics

Right

The right to deduct expenses in computing taxable profit rests not on any express statutory provision, but on the absence of any express prohibition; the right to deduct is inferred from the fact that it is the profit, not the receipts, of a trade that are taxed.[1] UK tax law has proceeded on its usual pragmatic basis.[2]

Incurred

An expense cannot be deducted if it can be recalled at will or recouped from another person.[3] In *Rutter* v. *Charles Sharpe & Co. Ltd.*[4] the company made payments to trustees of a

[1] TA 1988, s. 817 prohibits all deductions save those expressly authorised; TA 1988, s. 74 does not authorise deductions but forbids them. On the difficulties in this formulation, see Romer L.J. in *Anglo Persian Oil Co. Ltd.* v. *Dale* [1932] 1 KB 124, 144, 16 TC 253, 272.

[2] For a discusison of the relationship between the deductibility of expenses and consumption, see Edgar in Krever (ed.), *Tax Conversations* (1997), 309–27.

[3] *Bolton* v. *Halpern and Woolf* [1979] STC 761, 770; reversed for other reasons at [1981] STC 1453, 53 TC 445.

[4] [1979] STC 711, 53 TC 163.

fund held for the benefit of its employees. It was held that the company could not deduct these payments since as it could, at any time, wind up the scheme and then enforce the return of the payments. The mutuality principle may lead to the same conclusion where a payment is made to a trade association—as opposed to a company.[5]

Another problem arises where the trader purchases supplies from a subsidiary or related company and a part of the profit accruing to the other company will be returned to the trader. In *IRC* v. *Europa Oil (NZ) Ltd.*[6] the profit accruing would return to the trader as tax-free dividend and the price was fixed in advance to ensure the exact return to the trader. The Privy Council held that the expenditure was not incurred exclusively in the purchase of trading stock and, under the (sensible) tax system prevailing in the country, an apportionment was allowed. However, all depends on the facts. In a later case[7] the Privy Council held that the relations between the trader and the supplier were such that the former had no legal right to the profit, and so the whole sum was allowed to be deducted.

The right to deduct is limited by a number of case-law rules developed from the statute and/or the courts' notion of the meaning of profit:

(1) the expense must have been incurred for business purposes—the principle of remoteness (§22.2);
(2) it must have been incurred only for business purposes—the principle of duality (§22.2);
(3) it must have been incurred for the purpose of earning profit—the rule in *Strong & Co. of Romsey Ltd.* v. *Woodifield* (§22.3.1);
(4) it must be an expense of earning profit and not a division of profit (§22.3.2);
(5) it must be of an income nature as opposed to a capital nature, i.e. it must be a revenue expense (§22.4);
(6) it must not be barred on grounds of public policy (§22.5); and
(7) it must not be expressly barred by some statutory provision (§22.6).

Previously, the courts stated that, in answering all these questions, regard must be had to established commercial accounting principles.[8] Today, the role of accounting practice is less clear since many of these rules are now treated as matters of law rather than of fact and so potentially outside s. 42 and Lord Bingham's *dictum* in *Gallagher* v. *Jones* (above §21.1). However, evidence of accounting practice is no doubt admissible.

22.2 Wholly and Exclusively—Remoteness and Duality

In a relatively recent exchange of views one leading writer showed that the rules were obscure, inconsistent and generally inequitable, while another thought that the law was clear-cut, uniform and generally inequitable.[9] Case-law before (or since) has not improved matters. Rules (1) and (2) are derived from TA 1988, s. 74(a) which prohibits the deduction

[5] The Revenue will grant a complete deduction in return, taxing the association; see *Simons Taxes*, B.3.1441.
[6] [1971] AC 760.
[7] *IRC* v. *Europa Oil (NZ) Ltd.* [1976] STC 37.
[8] *Usher's Wiltshire Brewery Ltd.* v. *Bruce* [1915] AC 433, 468, 6 TC 399, 436, *per* Lord Sumner.
[9] See the exchange between Kerridge [1986] *BTR* 36 and Ward [1987] *BTR* 141. See also Klein (1966) 18 *Stan LR* and Halperin 122 *University of Pennsylvania LR* 859 for traditional perspectives; and Griffith (1994) 41 *UCLA LR* 1769 for quasi-optimal analysis. For a discussion of Griffith and similar authors, see Edgar, in Krever (ed.), above at n. 2, 293 at 351–7.

of expenses not being money wholly and exclusively laid "for the purposes of the trade". Rule (1) states that an expense which is not for the purposes of the trade is not deductible; rule (2) states that an expense which is partly for the purposes of the trade and partly for other purposes similarly is not deductible. Rule (2) is thus little more than an *a fortiori* example of rule (1). Where the liability is non-deductible for duality, a payment to be rid of the liability will be similarly non-deductible. In *Alexander Howard & Co. Ltd.* v. *Bentley*[10] the taxpayer company paid a lump sum to be rid of a contingent liability to pay an annuity to the widow of its governing director; the annuity payments would not have been deductible since not paid wholly and exclusively for trade purposes but rather as an adjunct to shares; it followed that the lump sum payment was similarly not deductible.

A *dictum* based on a concession in a case suggests that the word "wholly" may refer to the quantum of the money expended, while the word "exclusively" refers to the motive or object accompanying it.[11] However, taken literally, this would mean that the purchase of two different items at one time and by one payment would not be deductible at all even though the bill clearly listed the two items and gave separate prices. This cannot be (and is not) correct and it is doubtful, therefore, whether the concession should have been given even this degree of credence.[12]

22.2.1 Four rules from three cases

The case-law is dominated by three modern decisions: *Mallalieu* v. *Drummond*,[13] *Vodafone Cellular Ltd.* v. *Shaw*[14]and *McKnight* v. *Sheppard*.[15] *Mallalieu* v. *Drummond*, a House of Lords' decision, is the leading authority in this area, the main speech being by Lord Brightman; it suggests three rules. *Vodafone Cellular Ltd.* v. *Shaw*,[16] a Court of Appeal decision with the main judgment by Millett L.J., glosses all three rules and adds a fourth. *McKnight* v. *Sheppard*, a House of Lords' decision, appears, like *Vodafone*, to confine some of the possibilities aroused by *Mallalieu* v. *Drummond*.

The rules which emerge seem to be as follows: (a) those laid down by the House of Lords in *Mallalieu* v. *Drummond*; and (b) the *Vodafone* glosses.

(1) (a) Whether the expenditure was incurred exclusively to serve the purposes of the trade is a question of fact; (b) the purpose must be to benefit the trade rather than the trader.
(2) (a) In deciding the taxpayer's purpose, the court is not confined to conscious purposes; (b) save in obvious cases which speak for themselves, the court must determine the taxpayer's subjective intentions at the time of the payment, but the court must also have regard to those consequences which are so inevitably and inextricably involved in the payment that, unless merely incidental, they must be taken to be a purpose for which the payment was made.[17] It is clear that (b) places significant limits round the potential scope of (a); these limits were reinforced in *McKnight* v. *Sheppard*.

[10] (1948) 30 TC 334.
[11] Romer L.J. in *Bentleys, Stokes and Lowless* v. *Beeson* [1952] 2 All ER 82, 85, (1952) 33 TC 491, 503. Romer L.J. pointed out that this was conceded, not argued.
[12] See Kerridge [1986] *BTR* 36.
[13] [1983] 2 AC 861, [1983] STC 665, HL. For Australian development, see *Magna Alloys and Research Pty Ltd.* (1980) 80 ATC 4542; and Parsons, *Income Taxation in Australia* (Lawbook Co., 1985), 6.2–6.16.
[14] [1997] STC 734, CA.
[15] [1999] STC 669.
[16] [1997] STC 734, CA.
[17] Some of these phrases derive from the speech by Lord Oliver in *MacKinlay* v. *Arthur Young* [1986] STC 491, 504, 62 TC 704, 757.

(3) (a) One must distinguish a second "purpose" behind the expenditure, which will disqualify the deduction, from an "effect" of that expenditure, which will not disqualify the expenditure even though some benefit accrues to the taxpayer, T; (b) the benefit to T will be an "effect" rather than a purpose if it is "a consequential and incidental effect".

(4) *Vodafone* only: the question does not involve an inquiry of T whether T consciously intended to benefit a trade or personal advantage by the payment. The primary inquiry is to ascertain what was the particular object of T in making the payment; it is then for the Commissioners to classify that purpose as business or personal.

The following text will relate these rules to the facts

Mallalieu v. *Drummond*

The facts. In this case a barrister sought to deduct revenue expenses incurred in connection with dark clothes she had bought for wear in court, such clothes being required by court etiquette. The undisputed evidence was that her expenditure was motivated solely by thoughts of court etiquette and not at all by mere human thoughts of warmth and decency. Counsel for the taxpayer disclaimed any reliance on his client's dislike of black clothing, so the question was reduced to this: if clothing is purchased for use only on business occasions and such clothes are only so used (or for proceeding to and from work) is the expense deductible? The House of Lords said "no".

Rule (1) and (2). In addition to the business purpose there were the other purposes of warmth and decency. As Lord Brightman said, "I reject that notion that the object of a taxpayer is inevitably limited to the particular conscious motive in mind at the moment of expenditure".[18]

Rule (3). Earlier cases had decided that the courts could ignore an incidental benefit to the taxpayer. This was, in effect, reformulated by Lord Brightman in his distinction between the object of the taxpayer in incurring the expenditure and the effect of the expenditure:[19] "An expenditure may be made exclusively to serve the purposes of the business, but it may have a private advantage. The existence of that private advantage does not necessarily preclude the exclusivity of the business purpose".[20] His Lordship gave an example of a medical consultant flying to the south of France to see a patient; if a stay in the south of France was a reason, however subordinate, no deduction could be claimed whereas if it were not a reason, but an unavoidable effect, the deduction could be made.

While there may be substance in what the House of Lords said, there are uncomfortable questions of degree to be resolved. Thus, Lord Brightman would have allowed expenditure by a self-employed nurse on clothing dictated by the practical requirements of the act of nursing and the maintenance of hygiene, and even that by a self-employed waiter on the provision of "tails", this being the particular design of clothing required in order to obtain engagements.[21] For similar reasons, presumably, the Revenue was disposed to concede expenditure on wig, gown and bands in the instant case. While the borderline nature of these cases may be clear, the reasoning behind that status is not. Lord Brightman could not have meant that the nurse's uniform has no purpose of warmth or, at least, decency. What

[18] [1983] STC 665, 673b, 57 TC 330, 370.

[19] For early worries, see [1983] *BTR* 199.

[20] [1983] STC 665, 669f, 57 TC 330, 366.

[21] Ibid., 673e, 370.

he probably meant was that the warmth/decency purpose is so incidental as to qualify as an effect rather than a purpose.

Vodafone Cellular Ltd. v. *Shaw*

The taxpayer company, T, was part of a group of companies. An expense was incurred by T which benefited two other companies in the group. The Commissioners decided that the directors wanted to benefit the trading entity which the three companies represented, and had given no thought to the position of the two subsidiaries. However, the purpose of the directors was to benefit the trading position of the whole group; the interest of all three companies were considered together.[22] Under the absurd and unjust rules stemming from the duality principle, an expense incurred by one group company to benefit its own trade only is deductible in full; by contrast, an expense incurred for the trade of itself and of two sibling companies is not deductible at all. The Commissioners, and Jacob J., concluded that the purpose was to benefit all three companies and not just T, so that none of the expenditure was deductible. This was reversed by the Court of Appeal on the ground that the real purpose was to benefit only its own trade, and that the Commissioners had drawn the wrong conclusions from their own findings.

In *Vodafone*, T was one of three companies which ran a mobile phone business, the split of this corporate structure being required by the Department of Trade. T had acquired rights to certain American know-how in return for a regular series of payments; T incurred the expense in issue in the case by paying a lump sum to be rid of the liability. The regular payments had been made by T alone; there was no obligation on the other companies to contribute to these payments, although T could look for some reimbursement in some circumstances. The payment of the lump sum by T clearly benefited all three companies.

McKnight v. *Sheppard*

The most recent decision, *McKnight* v. *Sheppard*,[23] accepts the *Vodafone* approach to *Mallalieu* v. *Drummond*. A taxpayer, S, incurred legal expenditure in proceedings before his professional body (the Stock Exchange). If found guilty he could have been suspended from carrying on his profession, or expelled altogether. The Commissioner found that the sole purpose was the preservation of his trade, and that considerations of personal reputation were effects rather than purposes. The House of Lords agreed and held that the legal expenditure was deductible because the expenditure was for the purpose of enabling S to carry on business. The question whether there was secondary purpose of protecting S's name and reputation was classified by Lord Hoffmann as an effect and not as a purpose, the basis for which was the finding by the Commissioner.

As Lord Hoffmann put it, after referring to Lord Brightman's example of the medical consultant:[24]

> "If Lord Brightman's consultant had said that he had given no thought at all to the pleasures of sitting on the terrace with his friend and a bottle of Côtes de Provence, his evidence might well not have been credited. But that would not be inconsistent with a finding that the only object of the journey was to attend upon his patient and that personal pleasures, however welcome, were only the effects of a journey made for an exclusively professional purpose. This is the distinction which

[22] Case stated, paras 12.30–12.35.

[23] [1999] STC 669 agreeing with CA [1997] STC 684.

[24] Ibid., 673f.

the commissioner was making and in my opinion there is no inconsistency between his conclusion of law and his findings of fact."

The case depends crucially on the findings of fact. Had the commissioner found that concern for personal reputation had been a purpose and not an effect, it is unlikely that the appeal by S would have succeeded. Why decency and clothing should be subsconcious purposes in *Mallalieu* v. *Drummond*, while personal reputation was here only an effect, is unclear; this lack of clarity is institutionalised by treating it as a matter of fact. Since *Mallalieu* v. *Drummond* there seems to be only one reported case in which a subconscious purpose has prevented a deduction.[25]

22.2.2 Dissection (permissible) contrasted with apportionment (not permissible)

The duality rule does not permit the apportionment of expenses incurred for dual purposes. However, it does not prevent the dissection of expenditure to discover parts which are wholly and exclusively for business purposes, which are deductible. If a professional person (P) uses a room at home as an office, the expenses of that office are deductible, and this will be so even though the electricity, council tax and other bills apply to the house as a whole and have to be dissected in order to discover the part attributable to the office.[26] In these cases, the sum is dissected in order to discover that part which is wholly for business purposes, wholly being a matter of quantum; the test of exclusive business purpose is then applied to that part. Therefore, a telephone bill can be dissected to see which calls were business; however, the limits of the dissection rule were shown by a Schedule E case in which the courts refused to allow the deduction of part of the three-month rental payment.[27]

Examples of Dissection

Dissection received its most generous application in *Copeman* v. *William J. Flood & Sons Ltd.*[28] An unreasonable amount of remuneration had been paid to an employee but the court allowed the employer to deduct that part which would have been reasonable. There could have been no dissection in *Bowden* v. *Russell and Russell* where T had a dual purpose in crossing the Atlantic, since the precise point in mid-Atlantic at which the solicitor ceased to be travelling for personal reasons and began to travel for business reasons could not be identified.

22.2.3 Commentary

The present position is unsatisfactory since there is clear evidence from the 1950s that the Revenue did, in practice, allow an apportionment in a situation similar to *Bowden* v. *Russell and Russell* (above) provided there was a genuine business element, as would be the case with the running and garage expenses of a car used partly for personal and partly for busi-

[25] *Taylor* v. *Clatworthy* [1996] STC (SCD) 506 (lending money on terms which were very attractive to the lender, e.g. 33.3% interest, not just to secure appointment but also to make good investment). See also *Executive Network* v. *O'Connor* [1996] STC (SCD) 29, 35 (even if not a conscious motive it was inescapably an object for incurring the expense).

[26] *Gazelle* v. *Servini* [1995] STC (SCD) 324.

[27] *Lucas* v. *Cattell* 48 TC 353.

[28] [1941] 1 KB 202, 24 TC 53. Other excessive remuneration case include *Scott and Ingham* v. *Treharne* 9 TC 69 and *Horton* v. *Young* 47 TC 60; but contrast *Earlspring Properties Ltd.* v. *Guest* [1993] STC 473. On whether tax systems can/should police levels of remuneration by limiting deductions, see Stabile, 72 *St Johns Law Review* 81.

ness purposes.[29] Whether the Revenue practice, backed by the courts, has become more severe since then is unclear.[30]

The problem of devising an acceptable way to distinguish business expense from other expenditure is not unique to the United Kingdom.[31] Moreover, the literature shows that the problem is a difficult one.[32]The harshness of the UK rule can be softened by allowing apportionment, as in Australia,[33] but this still leaves the decision on which basis the apportionment should be made.[34] Another problem is devising a system of rules which are efficient in the economic sense, i.e. rules which encourage efficient mixed expenditures, and discourage those which are inefficient.[35]

A solution may be to separate personal benefit from work benefit. However, Kerridge shows that benefit is a slippery concept. Thus, lunch with a client may yield three types of benefit to the taxpayer: a work benefit (how much they would have spent if they had only professional purposes in mind); a pleasure benefit (how much they would have been willing to spend if they had only been looking after themselves); and a necessity benefit (how much extra they had to spend over the normal cost of sandwiches). Adding these together may give a total figure greater than the actual cost. Thus, if the lunch cost £20, the three benefits might be worth £24, £4 and £2 respectively. Of these, the necessity benefit is the easiest to measure, the others being significantly more subjective. Rules could be devised which allowed T to deduct the amount by which the expenditure (£20) exceeded the non-work benefit (£4 + £2), i.e. £14, sums up to the equivalent of the work benefit (£20) or a proportion which the work benefit (20) bore to the total benefit (30), i.e. 13.67.

These three rules allow apportionment. However, Kerridge suggests other possible rules. Thus, a) any deduction of spending with mixed purposes could be forbidden (the UK rule), b) the deduction of the entire expense if the work benefit alone (£24) would justify the expense (£20) could be permitted, as here, or c) a deduction in full could be allowed whenever the work benefit (£24) exceeded the non-work benefit (£6). These rules avoid apportionment problems at the expense of sharp distinctions at the margins.

Efficient taxation analysis begins by stating that a mixed expenditure is efficient if, in a non-tax world, the cost of the expenditure is less than the sums of its business and personal values. In a world with taxes, it is necessary to examine after-tax costs and after-tax values. Under an ideal tax structure only expenditures which are efficient under a pre-tax basis would be made. Inefficient expenditures could be made unless the system taxes the elements of personal consumption. This approach has been explored by Griffith[36] in ways which are initially similar to Kerridge. Under this approach, full deductibility of the expense is permitted, but tax is then charged on the basis of personal consumption, or the excess, if any,

[29] See *Report of the Committee on the Taxation of Trading Profits*, Cmd 8189 (1951), 157 and 161 and Royal Commission Cmd 9474 (1955), paras 123, 129, 133.

[30] See Kerridge [1986] *BTR* 36, 43. See also the discussion of *McLaren* v. *Mumford* [1996] STC 1134 by Grierson [1996] *BTR* 627 and Freedman [1996] *BTR* 634.

[31] On the United States see Andrews (1972) 86 *HLR* 309; Halperin (1974) 122 *Univ. Penn LR* 859; Klein (1966) 18 *Stan LR* 1099; and the immensely enjoyable "Life is a Beech" by Newman (1988) 38 *Tax Notes* 501; see also Ault *et al.*, 204–19.

[32] Kerridge [1986] *BTR* 36 and Ward [1987] *BTR* 141.

[33] Income Tax Act 19??, s. 51(1); the leading case is still *Ronpibon Tin NL* v. *FCT* (1949) 79 CLR 47; but see also *Ure* v. *FCT* (1981) 11 ATR 484. For detailed discussion of older cases, see Parsons, *Income Taxation in Australia*, ch. 9. The *Ure* case concerned interest; on interest deduction under this rule in Australia, see discussion in Parsons ibid., 6.86–6.141.

[34] For example *Fletcher* v. *FCT* (1991) 22 ATR 613.

[35] Griffith (1994) 41 *UCLA LR* 1769.

[36] Ibid.

of cost (£20) over business value (£24) or proportion which the business (£24) bears to personal values (£6). Griffith then looks at the differences between the methods with regard to (a) information requirements and (b) distribution effects, before turning, in a highly sophisticated analysis, to ask which may be the most efficient. The Griffith solutions make better sense in the context of the US tax system, with its global concept of income. The UK has to try to achieve efficient results by forbidding or apportioning deductions. So far it has not shown much interest in trying.

2.2.4 *Examples*

Food, drink and conferences

The subconscious purpose test causes problems with residential conference expenses. The costs of food and lodging must be incurred at least partly because one has to eat and sleep[37] (or are these just unavoidable effects of the initial decision to attend the conference?). *Watkis* v. *Ashford Sparkes & Harwood*[38] was the first case on this issue after *Mallalieu* v. *Drummond.* Nourse J. held that the cost of overnight accommodation at the annual conference of a firm was deductible and that no distinction could be drawn between the costs of accommodation and the costs of food and drink consumed. This was despite the fact that in the same case expenditure on meals taken at a time when the taxpayers would normally have eaten was held to be incapable of being incurred exclusively for business purposes. The moral seems to be that if a taxpayer wishes to secure deduction of meal expenditure, he must also have accommodation expenses. The test in such cases is whether the expense is incurred as a business person or as a human being. In reliance on this approach, Nourse J. also held that the cost of modest lunches eaten by solicitors during office meetings was not deductible.

Nourse J. specifically held that certain older cases (*Edwards* v. *Warmsley, Henshall & Co.*[39] and *Bowden* v. *Russell and Russell*[40]) were unaffected by *Mallalieu* v. *Drummond.* In *Edwards* a partner in a firm of chartered accountants was allowed to deduct costs of travel, accommodation and a conference fee when representing the firm at the International Congress of Accountants in New York. In *Bowden* the sole partner of a firm of solicitors was not allowed to deduct the cost of attending meetings of the American Bar Association in Washington and the Empire Law Conference in Ottawa. The evidence against him was so overwhelming that the Revenue argued it both on the basis of remoteness and on duality.[41]

Groups of companies

As the *Vodafone* case above shows, the duality rule has been invoked by the Revenue not only to prevent a deduction incurred for a personal purpose, but also where the other purpose is the trading purpose of another trade, even where the trade is carried on by another group

[37] See also *Caillebotte* v. *Quinn* [1975] STC 265, [1975] 2 All ER 412, 50 TC 222 (the extra cost incurred because the taxpayer had to eat while on business away from home was not deductible). See also Shaller 24 *Duqesne LR* 1129

[38] [1985] STC 451, 58 TC 468; followed in *Prior* v. *Saunders* [1993] STC 562, 66 TC 210. On acceptance of this decision and practice for lorry drivers see RI 51.

[39] [1968] 1 All ER 1089, 44 TC 431.

[40] [1965] 2 All ER 258, 42 TC 301.

[41] He went in an unofficial capacity and was accompanied by his wife, although no claim was made in respect of those expenses attributable to her. He admitted that there were also holiday and social purposes. for the trip He argued that his attendance was in order to maintain the firm's efficiency, to obtain new clients and to improve the office organisation. See, further, Kerridge [1986] BTR at 52.

member.[42] This means that a company will be unable to deduct expenditure incurred partly for its own purposes and partly for the trading purposes of another group member. This unfortunate result can be avoided by establishing that, while the expenditure benefits both companies, nonetheless the purpose was to benefit only one.[43] This was achieved in *Vodafone* where the expense was incurred for the trading entity as a whole without giving conscious thought to the position of individual companies.[44] It can also be avoided by sharing the costs with the other companies so that each pays its own share; however the basis on which that division should be made is not clear.

Expenditure for the purpose of two separate trades of one person is, in theory, deductible from neither,[45] but it is unlikely that this absurd result would be applied by the Revenue or by the courts.

Where one company in a group takes over trading stock from another company in the group the costs of the acquisition are deductible even though the group or the other company may have motives of its own; what is important is the motive of the company making the expenditure.[46]

Charity not business

Expenditure in the form of subscriptions to charity are the generous acts of good citizens. There is, therefore, a duality of capacity about the payment—part as trader, part as citizen.[47] However, whether the explanation is remoteness or duality, such expenditure is rarely deductible.[48] The same reasoning bars payments for political purposes.[49] Gifts other than to charity also fall within TA 1988, s. 577 (see below at §22.6.3).

Trade associations

Subscriptions to trade associations are, according to case-law, deductible to the extent that the expenditure by the association would have been deductible if incurred directly by the subscriber.[50] In practice, however, the Revenue grants complete deduction for the subscription in return for the taxability of the association.[51] Contributions to approved local enterprise agencies are deductible by express provision.[52]

[42] [1995] STC 353; see also *Garforth* v. *Tankard Carpets Ltd.* [1980] STC 251, 53 TC 342; the same point arose in *Lawson* v. *Johson Matthey plc* [1990] STC 149, 158–9, 65 TC 39, 52–3, but was not argued on appeal; see also *Watney Combe Reid and Co.* v. *Pike* [1982] STC 733, 57 TC 372. For an exceptional case the other way, see *Robinson* v. *Scott Bader Co. Ltd.* [1980] STC 241, [1980] 2 All ER 780, 54 TC 757.

[43] As in *Robinson* v. *Scott Bader Co. Ltd.*, ibid.

[44] For a perhaps optimistic view of the case, see Saunders [1997] *BTR* 404.

[45] See Walton J. in *Olin Energy Systems Ltd.* v. *Scorer* [1982] STC 800 at 820, 58 TC 592 at 612.

[46] *Torbell Investments Ltd.* v. *Williams* [1986] STC 397.

[47] See Romer L.J. in *Bentleys, Stokes and Lowless* v. *Beeson* [1952] 2 All ER 82, 85, 33 TC 491, 505. For another reason, see below at §22.0.

[48] *Bourne and Hollingsworth Ltd.* v. *Ogden* (1929) 14 TC 349 (annual subscription to hospital used by employees deductible in practice, but two, special, large subscriptions not deductible); *Hutchinson & Co. (Publishers) Ltd.* v. *Turner* [1950] 2 All ER 633, 31 TC 495. See ESC B7 (1994) *Simon's Direct Tax Service*, Division H4.2 and ESC B32 (1994) on expenses of running a payroll-giving scheme.

[49] *Joseph L. Thompson Ltd.* v. *Chamberlain* (1962) 40 TC 657; *cf. Morgan* v. *Tate and Lyle Ltd.* [1954] 2 All ER 413, 35 TC 368 (discussed below at §22.5.3).

[50] *Lochgelly Iron and Coal Co. Ltd.* v. *Crawford* (1913) 6 TC 267.

[51] See *Simon's Direct Tax Service*, above at n. 48, B3.1441. On the non-taxability of the association, see *Joseph Adamson & Co.* v. *Collins* [1938] 1 KB 477, 21 TC 400.

[52] TA 1988, s. 79.

Medical expenditure

At first sight medical expenditure is incurred to put right that which is medically wrong, and so not for business purposes; the subconscious medical purpose cannot be ignored. In *Murgatroyd* v. *Evans-Jackson*[53] the taxpayer, a trademark agent, fell ill and was treated in a private nursing home for five weeks, his reason for selecting private care being that he required a separate room from which to conduct his business, a facility not available under the National Health Service. He claimed only 60% of the cost, a matter which admitted duality of expenditure, but Plowman J. also held that had the taxpayer claimed the whole of his costs he would still not have been able to deduct the expense since one reason for going into the nursing home was to receive treatment. However, it could be argued that since the choice was not between a greater and a lesser expense but between no expense at all under the National Health Service and this expense as a private patient, the whole expense was in fact for business purposes. Moreover, the decision does cause some fine distinctions. Thus, if the agent had had a bed in a room with other patients but had also rented another room as an office, the rent of that other room would have been deductible. *Murgatroyd* v. *Evans-Jackson* must be distinguished from a case where the operation itself is for business purposes.[54]

Travelling and commuting expenses

Travelling expenses provide further examples of the general rule.[55] Travel from home to one's main place of work is not deductible, even though one works at home. Expenses incurred by a barrister in travelling from home to chambers were not deductible, even though the Revenue had granted a "study allowance".[56] The reason for the distinction is that, although the barrister works in both places, it is clear that the profession is carried on in chambers; chambers, not home, provide the base of operations and so travel from chambers to home in the evening is not motivated wholly and exclusively by the desire to do more work. The expense is thus, at least in part, a personal living expense and not a business expense.[57] Similarly, solicitors are not able to deduct the cost of travelling from home to office. However, if a solicitor had two offices, and went to the nearer office first, then to the further office and then back to the nearer office, he would be allowed to deduct both journeys between the offices.[58]

Such a conclusion rests on the fact that the office is a place where the profession is carried on. Where a dental surgeon visited his laboratory (L) on his way through from his home (H) to his surgery (S), he was not allowed to deduct the cost of travel from L to S.[59] The purpose of the expenditure was to get from H to S; the fact that it also enabled him to stop at L could not affect that purpose.

A person's home may be a base of operations. If so the costs of travel from the base of

[53] [1967] 1 All ER 881, 43 TC 581; noted by Wallace [1967] 285; and see *Norman* v. *Golder* [1945] 1 All ER 352, 26 TC 293; see also Kerridge [1986] *BTR* 41.

[54] See Pennycuick J. in *Prince* v. *Mapp* [1970] 1 All ER 519, 525, 46 TC 169, 176.

[55] *Sargent* v. *Eayrs* [1973] STC 50, [1973] 1 All ER 277, 48 TC 573; see Macdonald [1978] *BTR* 75, 83. The matter is also discussed by Smith [1977] *BTR* 290, [1978] *BTR* 203 and [1981] *BTR* 211.

[56] *Newsom* v. *Robertson* [1952] 2 All ER 728, 33 TC 452; the allowance would have been granted under TA 1988, s. 74(c).

[57] [1952] 2 All ER 728, 730, 33 TC 452, 462, *per* Somervell L.J.

[58] Ibid.,731, 464, *per* Denning L.J.

[59] *Sargent* v. *Barnes* [1978] STC 322, [1978] 2 All ER 737, 52 TC 335.

operations to places of work are deductible, as in the case of an independent contracting bricklayer.[60] However, when the occupation is itinerant only within a certain area but the taxpayer lives outside that area, the costs of travel, at least as far as the border of that area, would not be deductible.[61]

Miscellaneous personal (non-deductible) expenses

These include, for example, the revenue costs of a *pied à terre* over the office[62] and sums paid to children in the nature of pocket money rather than payments for services on the taxpayer's farm.[63] Expenditure on a child's nanny is not deductible; expenditure for secretarial services is deductible. Payments to a nanny for secretarial services are therefore deductible, where the facts are established.[64]

There have, as yet, been no cases on the deduction of educational expenses.[65]

Cases have been decided primarily under TA 1988, s. 74(a), although many have been argued under s. 74(b) in the alternative. There is no reported case of an expense being deductible under s. 74(a) but not under s. 74(b).

22.2.5 Purposes and partnerships

Since, in English tax law, a partnership is not a taxable entity, it follows that the purposes to be investigated are those of the partners. This can seem unreal where a firm has, for example, 98 partners, and it is therefore tempting to equate such partnerships with companies, which have separate legal personality. Provided that temptation is resisted it will follow that expenditure incurred to reimburse a partner for the costs of removing personal belongings, when moving the place of work from one part of the country to another at the request of the other partners, will not be deductible. The House of Lords so held in *MacKinlay* v. *Arthur Young McClelland Moores & Co.*[66]

Logic does not require the non-deductibility of payments in return for goods or services supplied by the partner to the partnership. So, where P, the partner, has granted the partnership a lease of property owned by P, there is no reason why the rental payments should not be incurred wholly and exclusively for business purposes;[67] they will, of course, be taxed in the hands of P, the partner/landlord, under Schedule A.

[60] *Horton* v. *Young* [1971] 3 All ER 412, 47 TC 60; see Paterson [1971] *BTR* 376.

[61] [1971] 2 All ER 351, 356, *per* Brightman J.

[62] *Mason* v. *Tyson* [1980] STC 284, 53 TC 333.

[63] *Dollar* v. *Lyon* [1981] STC 333, 54 TC 549; see also *Earlspring Properties Ltd.* v. *Guest* [1993] STC 473, 67 TC 259.

[64] RI 82. On child care costs, see also Heen (1995) 13 *Yale Law and Policy Review* 173.

[65] See Davenport (1992) 42 *Case W. Res. LR* 793 and McNulty (1973) 61 *California LR* 1.

[66] [1989] STC 898, HL; reversing [1988] STC 116, 62 TC 704, CA; see below p. 401.

[67] *Heastie* v. *Veitch & Co. Ltd.* [1934] 1 KB 535, 18 TC 305; see also Lord Oliver in *MacKinlay* v. *Arthur Young* [1989] STC 898, 905, 62 TC 704, 755.

22.3 Expenditure Must Be Incurred for Purpose of Earning Profits (the Davey *Dictum*)

In *Strong & Co. of Romsey Ltd.* v. *Woodifield*[68] Lord Davey said, "It is not enough that the disbursement is made in the course of or arises out of or is connected with the trade or is made out of the profits of the trade. It must be made for the purpose of earning profits". This famous gloss on the statute seems to have little effect in the practice of the Revenue, but enables the Revenue to grant, by concession, that which ought to be deducted as of right.

The taxpayer company's business included both brewing and innkeeping. A chimney at one of its inns fell and injured a guest. The guest sued and recovered damages of £1,490, which the company sought to deduct in computing its profits. Today the case is remembered principally for Lord Davey's *dictum*. However, for Lord Loreburn and the other members of the House (but not for Lord Davey) the critical provision was what is now TA 1988, s. 74(e) which prohibits the deduction of any loss not connected with the trade, profession or vocation. Whether the expense is barred by s. 74(a) or (e) is, in one sense, immaterial: the expense may not be deducted. It has been pointed out that there is no case in which it has been distinctly held that an expenditure which satisfies s. 74(a) has not passed s. 74(e).[69]

In an unhappily apt phrase, Lord Loreburn said that losses could not be deducted "if they fall on the trader in some character other than that of trader". He considered that the loss fell on the trader in its character as householder, not as trader. It may be supposed that one reason why this decision has not been reversed is that businesses now insure their premises, such premiums being deductible.[70] The fineness of the distinction inherent in the House of Lords' approach may be seen from two examples given by Lord Loreburn:[71]

> "losses sustained by a railway company in compensating passengers for accident in travelling might be deducted. On the other hand if a man kept a grocer's shop, for keeping which a house is necessary, and one of the window shutters fell upon and injured a man walking in the street the loss arising thereby ought not to be deducted."

Not only were these examples unclear, but they could be made to suggest that deduction should have been allowed in that case. First, it is not clear what point was being made. On the one hand, the example of the grocer's house was reasonably clear: if the house was separate from the shop then there is a distinction between trading expenses and personal expenses, and the same might be true if the premises were all in one and the shutter fell off the residential part of the premises. If, however, the point was the distinction between trading and personal expenses, then surely the expense should have been deductible in the instant case.

However, if the distinction was between trading and householding (between, at that time, Schedule D, Case I and Schedule A), that suggests a very restricted scope to be given to the example of the railway company, and could mean that the company could deduct expendi-

[68] [1906] AC 448, 453, 5 TC 215, 220. This decision was based largely on what is now TA 1988, s. 74(e) (see below at §23.6.1), but is generally treated as an authority on TA 1988, s. 74(a) (e.g. *Morgan* v. *Tate and Lyle Ltd.* [1954] 2 All ER 413, 35 TC 367; see below at §22.5.3). For another case exploring the relationship between s. 74(a) and (e), see the judgment of Lightman J. in *McKnight* v. *Sheppard* [1996] STC 627, but note reversal for other reasons in [1997] STC 846 and [1999] STC 669.

[69] *McKnight* v. *Sheppard* [1997] STC 846, 851, *per* Nourse L.J.

[70] *Usher's Wiltshire Brewery Ltd.* v. *Bruce* [1915] AC 433, 6 TC 399.

[71] Ibid., 452, 419.

ture for damages where the engine was driven negligently with a resulting accident, but not if injury occurred by a piece of station platform giving way. What would happen if there were a defect in a piece of static equipment, such as a signal is, again, unclear. Lord James expressed doubts about the application of the principle to the inn customer but would have had no doubts about the non-deductibility of an injury to a stranger walking down the street outside the inn. Such a distinction seems quite incredible today.

22.3.1 Examples of sums satisfying test

The test is relatively easy to satisfy: sums spent for the purpose of earning profit will be deductible even though no profit is expected that year;[72] moreover, since the test is one of purpose, the sums will be deductible even though no profits accrue at all.[73] Losses incurred which are incidental to the carrying-out of the business are similarly deductible.[74] Damages for libel can be deductible when the libel is published in the course of a newspaper business; such damages must be distinguished from those payable for a libel not incidental to the business[75] and from penalties imposed by a court or professional tribunal.[76] Penalties, fines and interest charges in respect of the VAT legislation are expressly non-deductible.[77] In Australia, sums lost in an armed robbery were deductible because the banking of takings was part of the operations of the business.[78]

Damages for wrongful dismissal of employees are, in practice, allowed, although this is hard to reconcile with Lord Davey's *dictum*. Legal expenses are also deductible even though not for the direct purpose of earning profits, provided they are incurred in the running of the business.[79] Advertising expenses, although originally in doubt,[80] are now clearly deductible,[81] as are sponsorship costs, provided, in practice, that the sole purpose is to provide the sponsor with a benefit commensurate with the expenditure.[82]

Dictum applied

In *Knight* v. *Parry*[83] a solicitor was not allowed to deduct the costs of defending (successfully) an action in which professional misconduct and breach of a former contract of employment were alleged. The court held that the sums were spent, at least in part, to ensure that the solicitor was not precluded from carrying on his practice, and this was not the same

[72] *Vallambrosa Rubber Co. Ltd.* v. *Farmer* (1910) 5 TC 529; *James Snook & Co. Ltd.* v. *Blasdale* (1952) 33 TC 244. On timing, see below at §23.3.2.

[73] *Lunt* v. *Wellesley* (1945) 27 TC 78.

[74] *Golder* v. *Great Boulder Proprietary Gold Mines Ltd.* (1951) 33 TC 75. A sum paid in settlement of a civil claim in connection with the formation of a company was held to be deductible because it was not paid for any proven infraction of the law. On losses resulting from the collapse of BCCI see Inland Revenue interpretation RI 57.

[75] *Fairrie* v. *Hall* (1947) 28 TC 200.

[76] *IRC* v. *Von Glehn & Co. Ltd.* [1920] 2 KB 553, 12 TC 232. *McKnight* v. *Sheppard* [1999] STC 6769; the taxpayer did not appeal against this part of the judgment of Lightman J. ([1996] STC 627). On Canadian experience, see Krasa (1990) 38 *Can. Tax Jo.* 1399; see also below at §22.6.

[77] TA 1988, s. 827(1).

[78] *Charles Moore and Co. (WA) Pty* v. *FCT* (1956) 95 CLR 344.

[79] See *Spofforth and Prince* v. *Golder* [1945] 1 All ER 363, 26 TC 310; see also the judgment of Lightman J. in *McKnight* v. *Sheppard* [1996] STC 627, but note reversal for other reasons at [1997] STC 846 and [1999] STC 669.

[80] See Kelly C.B. in *Watney & Co.* v. *Musgrave* (1880) 1 TC 272, 277.

[81] *Morley* v. *Lawford & Co.* (1928) 14 TC 229.

[82] HL Written Answer, 26 October 1987, Vol. 489, col. 405. If the taxpayer enjoys ballooning, does this enable his company to deduct the sponsorship costs of a balloon journey across the Atlantic? What if he is a sole trader?

[83] [1973] STC 56, 48 TC 580.

as expenditure referable to the carrying-on of that practice. This was criticised by Lightman J. in *McKnight* v. *Sheppard.*[84]

Comment

The principle of deductibility has become so wide that the *dictum* in *Strong & Co. of Romsey Ltd.* v. *Woodifield* should either be repealed or be regarded as having force only in the light of the frequently quoted statement of Viscount Cave L.C.:

> "a sum of money expended, not of necessity and with a view to a direct and immediate benefit to the trade, but voluntarily and on the grounds of commercial expediency, and in order indirectly to facilitate the carrying on of the business, may yet be expended wholly and exclusively for the purposes of the trade."[85]

The Davey gloss on the statue seems to have relatively little overall effect, but is still capable of biting at times. Its repeal was recommended by the Tucker Committee and the Royal Commission.[86] However, Lord Radcliffe once said that he did not know of a wider criterion that would not be vulnerable in other ways and that the phrase had become part of our income tax language;[87] he could have added that it had also become part of some Commonwealth statutes.[88]

22.3.2 Expenditure not division of profits

A sum paid in the course of earning a profit is clearly distinct from a distribution of the profit made. A dividend by a company or a payment under a profit-sharing arrangement is a distribution of profit made and not an expense of earning it;[89] by contrast, a payment of interest will usually be a deductible expense. The question whether a payment is one of interest or a distribution of profits is one of substance.[90]

The rule has been applied to render certain payments by a company purporting to be by way of remuneration to directors or employees non-deductible. Therefore, remuneration based on a percentage of profits (deductible) must be distinguished from a distribution of profits (non-deductible). While a resolution at an annual meeting to pay a bonus as an appropriation of profit will be conclusive that it is just that (and so no-deductible),[91] the absence of such a resolution does not make it deductible.[92] Excessive remuneration has generally been dealt with under the "wholly and exclusively" rule, but this rule could have been applied instead. This rule also bars a deduction for reserves for future expenditure.[93]

[84] [1996] STC 627, 675. This issue was not addressed by the Court of Appeal [1997] STC 846 or House of Lords [1999] STC 665.

[85] *British Insulated and Helsby Cables Ltd.* v. *Atherton* [1926] AC 205, 211.

[86] *Report of the Committee on the Taxation of Trading Profits*, Cmd 8189 (1951), §§151–154; and *Royal Commission on the Taxation of Profits and Income, Final Report*, Cmd 9474 (1955), §128, the latter stating that "it is extremely difficult to give it any concrete meaning".

[87] *IRC* v. *Dowdall O'Mahoney and Co. Ltd.* [1952] 1 All ER 531, 542 and 33 TC 259, 285.

[88] For example Canada: see *Royal Trust* v. *MNR* [1957] DTC 1055; and Australia: *Charles Moore and Co. (WA) Pty* v. *FCT* (1956) 95 CLR 344.

[89] See *Eyres* v. *Finnieston Engineering Co. Ltd.* (1916) 7 TC 74; *Utol Ltd.* v. *IRC* [1944] 1 All ER 190; see ch. 46 below on meaning of distribution under Schedule F.

[90] *Walker* v. *IRC* [1920] 3 KB 648.

[91] As in *Pegg and Ellam Jones Ltd.* v. *IRC* (1919) 12 TC 82.

[92] See Lord Maughan in *Indian Radio and Cable Communications Co. Ltd.* v. *IT Commr Bombay* [1937] 3 All ER 709, 713–14; and *British Sugar Manufacturers Ltd.* v. *Harris* [1938] 2 KB 220, 21 TC 528. See also *Union Cold Storage Co. Ltd.* v. *Adamson* (1931) 16 TC 293; *Overy* v. *Ashford Dunn & Co. Ltd.* (1933) 17 TC 497.

Partnerships

Payments by a partnership to its employees will be treated as deductions, but the division of profits between partners must be just that, and no payment to a partner in return for services can qualify as a deductible emolument.[94] A partnership can deduct the cost of the salary of an employee, but not the share of profits accruing to a partner. However, rent paid by the partnership to a partner is deductible, unless excessive.[95] A payment towards a partner's personal removal costs, being personal in nature, cannot be deducted.[96]

Profit-sharing

A payment by a company to an approved profit-sharing scheme is an allowable deduction,[97] and it is understood that, in practice, the Revenue will allow the deduction of a sum equal to 5% of profits to a non-approved scheme.

The TOTE

The present rule was applied to prevent the deduction of sums paid out of the totalisator fund (TOTE) to racecourse owners to assist in improving amenities at racecourses and to provide subsidies to owners and trainers.[98] The distinction inherent in the rule is a fine one, but turns on the precise definition of the trade. The trade was that of running totalisators at racecourses and the expenditure in question was not incurred for the purpose of that trade.

Taxes

The rule has also been applied to prevent the deduction of taxes on profits, whether imposed by the UK[99] or some foreign government.[100] However, other taxes may be deductible. Thus, business rates[101] may be deductible, as may road licences and stamp duty,[102] in all instances depending upon the actual circumstance of the case. In *Harrods (Buenos Aires) Ltd.* v. *Taylor-Gooby*[103] the taxpayer company operated in Argentina and was liable to an annual local tax levied on the capital of the company. The court held that the tax was deductible since it was not a tax that depended upon the company having earned any profits, but was simply an essential cost of trading in that country. The actual circumstances may show that the particular tax is a capital expense, in which case it will not be deductible.[104]

[93] *Edward Collins & Sons Ltd.* v. *IRC* (1925) 12 TC 773.

[94] Salaried partners are, in practice, treated as employees, not partners.

[95] *Heastie* v. *Veitch & Co.* [1934] 1 KB 535, 18 TC 305.

[96] *MacKinlay* v. *Arthur Young McClelland Moores & Co.* [1989] STC 898, 62 TC 704.

[97] TA 1988, s. 85; for similar payments to other schemes infra 22.8(7).

[98] *Young* v. *Racecourse Betting Control Board* [1959] 3 All ER 215, 38 TC 426.

[99] Lord Halsbury in *Ashton Gas Co.* v. *A.-G.* [1906] AC 10, 12.

[100] *IRC* v. *Dowdall O'Mahoney & Co. Ltd.* [1952] 1 All ER 531, 33 TC 259. On deduction of overseas tax, see now TA 1988, s. 811 (TA 1970, s. 516) and below at §64.2.

[101] *Smith* v. *Lion Brewery Co. Ltd.* [1911] AC 150, 5 TC 568.

[102] *Harrods (Buenos Aires) Ltd.* v. *Taylor-Gooby* (1963) 41 TC 450 *per* Buckley J.

[103] (1963) 41 TC 450.

[104] For example stamp duty on conveyance of land forming part of the fixed capital of the trade or if the payment in *Harrods (Buenos Aires) Ltd.* v. *Taylor-Gooby* had been a once-only payment for the right to trade in Argentina.

Costs of tax appeals

More controversially, the rule has been applied to prevent the deduction of expenses incurred by a company in appealing, successfully, against an assessment to tax on profits. The expense of preparing the documents needed to be filed under the Companies Acts would clearly be deductible, as would the preparation of accounts for internal management.[105] However, as Lord Simonds put it in *Smith's Potato Estates Ltd.* v. *Bolland*:[106]

> "What profit he has earned he has earned before ever the voice of the tax-gatherer is heard. He would have earned no more and no less if there was no such thing as Income Tax. His profit is no more affected by the exigibility of tax than is a man's temperature altered by the price of a thermometer, even though he starts by haggling about the price of it."

As a matter of practice, the Revenue does allow the costs of preparing the income tax return, but not additional accountancy expenses incurred as a result of an investigation revealing discrepancies where negligent or fraudulent conduct is involved.[107] In *McKnight* v. *Sheppard*[108] Lord Hoffmann gave a resounding defence of *Smith's Potato Estates*. The costs were not an element in the computation of profit but were logically and temporarily subsequent to the profits being earned.

22.4 Expenditure Must Be Revenue, not Capital

22.4.1 Introduction

Capital expenditure is not deductible in computing profits even though incurred wholly and exclusively for business purposes;[109] such expenditure may qualify for relief under the capital allowance system (see chapter 24 below). The task of distinguishing revenue from capital expenditure is not easy, and the problem has been made difficult by the inevitable fact that words or formulae that have been found useful in one set of facts may be neither relevant nor significant in another.[110] No test is paramount.[111] There is no rule whereby the treatment of the expenditure in the hands of the payer predetermines its character in the hands of the payee; so, an item can be a revenue expense for the payer and a capital receipt for the recipient or, conversely, a capital expense and a revenue receipt.[112]

In deciding these difficult questions the court's task is to determine the true profits of the business. However, the court is hampered by the fact that a deductible expense must be

[105] *Worsley Brewery Co. Ltd.* v. *IRC* (1932) 17 TC 349, esp. 360, *per* Romer L.J.

[106] [1948] 2 All ER 367, 374, 30 TC 267, 293. One criticism is that expenditure in order to preserve the company's assets is deductible (see *Morgan* v. *Tate and Lyle*, below at §22.5.3). However, the expense must still avoid 22.3.2; the motive for the payment cannot turn a profit into an expense. This reasoning seems to be contrary to that of the Court of Appeal in *Heather* v. *P.E. Consulting Group Ltd.* [1973] 1 All ER 8, 48 TC 320. The position cannot therefore be clearly stated.

[107] Statement of Practice SP A28, as modified by Statement of Practice SP 16/91 and amended for self-assessment by RI 192.

[108] [1999] STC 669, 674e.

[109] On history, see Edwards [1976] *BTR* 300.

[110] *Taxes Commr* v. *Nchanga Consolidated Copper Mines Ltd.* [1964] AC 948, 959, [1964] 1 All ER 202, 212, *per* Lord Radcliffe.

[111] See *Caledonian Paper plc* v. *IRC* [1998] STC (SCD) 129, 134; citing *Regent Oil Co. Ltd.* v. *Strick* [1966] AC 295, 43 TC 1.

[112] *Regent Oil Co. Ltd.* v. *Strick*, ibid.

entered when the expense is incurred and therefore cannot be spread over a number of years. It follows that to allow a major item of expenditure as a deduction in one year, when its benefits will be spread over many, will necessarily give a distorted picture of the profitability of the company.[113] This accounting-based approach suggests that accounting principles could have a role to play in deciding whether a particular expense is capital or revenue in nature; however, such principles cannot make any part of a capital expense deductible.

22.4.2. Concepts/tests

(a) Fixed and circulating capital[114]

Expenditure on the fixed capital of a business is capital expenditure, not revenue. Fixed capital is retained in the shape of assets which either produce income without further action, e.g. shares held by an investment company, or are made use of to produce income, e.g. machinery in a factory. Circulating capital is that which the company intends should be used by being temporarily parted with and circulated in the business only to return with, it is hoped, profit, e.g. money spent on trading stock.[115] The difficulty with this test is that it sometimes begs the very question at issue.[116]

(b) Enduring asset or advantage: the *Atherton* test

The second test was enunciated by Viscount Cave in *Atherton* v. *British Insulated and Helsby Cables Ltd.*[117] and became known as the enduring benefit test. Viscount Cave stated:

> "When an expenditure is made not only once for all, but with a view to bringing into existence an asset or advantage for the enduring benefit of a trade, I think there is very good reason (in the absence of special circumstances leading to an opposite conclusion) for treating such an expenditure as properly attributable not to revenue but to capital."

The principal difficulty with this test is that many types of expenditure have an enduring effect, and not all of them are of a capital nature. Thus, a payment to be rid of an unsatisfactory employee or agent is a revenue expense,[118] but one to be rid of a term of a lease is a capital expense.[119] A payment to a trust for the benefit of certain employees where the amount and duration of the fund were uncertain and the whole fund could have been distributed at any time was held to be a revenue expense.[120] A payment to persuade an institution to buy the worthless shares of a subsidiary was similarly held to be revenue since the expenditure did not bring any asset into existence or procure any advantage for the enduring benefit of the trade but was, instead, to remove the threat to the taxpayer's whole trade resulting from the subsidiary's insolvency.[121] It may therefore be as well remember that the

[113] See Lord Reid in 316, ibid., 31.

[114] The dual reference to capital is unfortunate, but it refers to the capital of the company and so the source from which the expenditure is funded. Relatively recent instances of judges using the concept include *Pattison* v. *Marine Midland*, [1981] STC 540, 555, Vinelott J., and [1984] STC 10, 11, Lord Fraser; see also Reynolds [1982] *BTR* 238.

[115] See Swinfen Eady L.J. in *Ammonia Soda Co.* v. *Chamberlain* [1918] 1 Ch 266; Romer L.J. in *Golden Horseshoe (New) Ltd.* v. *Thurgood* [1934] 1 KB 548, 18 TC 280; and *Pattison* v. *Marine Midland Ltd.* [1981] STC 540. This is not a question of pure fact (*Pyrah* v. *Annis & Co. Ltd.* (1956) 37 TC 163, 173 *per* per Lord Evershed M.R.).

[116] See Lord Macmillan in *Van den Berghs Ltd.* v. *Clark* (1934) 19 TC 390, 432.

[117] [1926] AC 205, 213, 10 TC 155, 192.

[118] See *Anglo Persian Oil Co. Ltd.* v. *Dale* (1931) 16 TC 253.

[119] *Tucker* v. *Granada Motorway Services Ltd.* [1979] STC 393, [1979] 2 All ER 801.

[120] *Jeffs* v. *Ringtons Ltd.* [1985] STC 809, [1986] 1 All ER 144.

[121] *Lawson* v. *Johnson Matthey plc* [1992] STC 466, 470, HL; distinguished in *Stone & Temple Ltd.* v. *Waters* [1995] STC 1.

purpose of Lord Cave's remarks was not to provide an infallible guide in all circumstances, but to explain how to approach one-off payments.

(c) Identifiable asset

In *Tucker* v. *Granada Motorway Services Ltd.*[122] it was held that it is necessary first to identify the asset on which the sum has been spent, and then classify the sum spent. Sums spent on an asset of a non-capital nature cannot be capital; sums spent on capital assets may be. If the asset is of a capital nature, the nature of the particular expense must be considered. Therefore, sums spent on acquiring the capital asset will be capital, while sums spent maintaining or repairing it will be revenue. At this point the earlier tests may reappear, as in *Walker* v. *Joint Credit Card Co. Ltd.*[123] and *Whitehead* v. *Tubbs (Elastics) Ltd.*[124]

This test has been used in connection with liabilities. If the liability is on capital account, a loss, e.g. an exchange loss, incurred on repayment of the loan will be a capital loss, whereas it would have been a revenue loss if the loan had been a revenue transaction.[125]

The test is not without difficulties. The place of the asset within the business is not usually too difficult to determine; indeed, it is similar to the old distinction between fixed and circulating capital. However, problems arise where the asset is not discernible as part of the assets of the business, as with trading arrangements with other traders or the modification of a company's charter or articles of association. Money spent in removing restrictions on a company's business has been held to be a revenue expense.[126]

Care must also be taken in defining the asset accurately.[127] Thus, if T borrows money for a period, does T simply receive cash or a furtherance of the trade for the period of the loan?[128] It would, however, be foolish to reject the asset test simply because it does not provide an answer to all cases; the danger is that it will be applied, as have its predecessors, without regard to the variety of facts or the disclaimer of universality uttered by its formulators.

(d) Once for all

In *Vallambrosa Rubber Co. Ltd.* v. *Farmer*[129] Lord Dunedin said that capital expenditure was something which would be spent once and for all, and income expenditure was something which would recur every year. In *Ounsworth* v. *Vickers Ltd.*[130] Rowlatt J. refined the point by saying that the distinction was between expenditure to meet a continuous demand and expenditure made once and for all. The case-law shows that one-off expenditure can be revenue, as in *IRC* v. *Carron*,[131] and regular payment can be capital, as in *Ramsay* v. *IRC*.[132]

[122] [1979] STC 393, [1979] 2 All ER 801.

[123] [1982] STC 427, 437 (court had to decide whether apayment to a business rival to close its business was made to secure an enduring benefit to trade or was made in relation to short-term advantages; the court held the payment to be capital (in the absence of evidence that the rival's trade was withering away within a reasonable space of time).

[124] [1984] STC 1, CA (payment for release from terms of loan agreement lasting nine years was held to be a capital payment for a capital asset).

[125] *Beauchamp* v. *F. W. Woolworth plc* [1988] STC 714, 721c; reversed on appeal at [1989] STC 510, 61 TC 542, HL.

[126] Held to be a revenue expense in *IRC* v. *Carron Co.* [1968] SC 47, 45 TC 18, HL.

[127] *Bolton* v. *International Drilling Co. Ltd.* [1983] STC 70, 56 TC 949.

[128] See *Beauchamp* v. *F. W. Woolworth plc* [1989] STC 510, 61 TC 542.

[129] (1910) 5 TC 529, 536.

[130] (1915) 6 TC 671, 675.

[131] [1968] STC 47, 45 TC 18, HL.

[132] (1938) 23 TC 153 (see below at §27.4.5).

(e) Capital structures

In *Taxes Comrs* v. *N'Changa Consolidated Copper Mines Ltd.*[133] Lord Radcliffe said that there was a demarcation between the cost of creating, acquiring or enlarging the permanent (which does not mean perpetual) structure of which the income is to be the produce or fruit, and the cost of earning that income itself or performing the income-earning operations. He added that this was probably as illuminating a line of distinction as the law by itself is likely to achieve. This approach is used in the explanation which follows.

22.4.3 Examples

(1) Acquisition of a business (capital) or running a business (revenue)

The costs of acquiring a business are capital expenses. Expenses incurred shortly after acquiring a business may be treated as part of the acquisition cost and so non-deductible.[134] The matter is, however, one of fact.[135]

Emoluments

The costs of running a business are clearly revenue expenses and, as such, payments to employees for their services are deductible.[136] To allow such payments to be taxable in the hands of the employee, but not deductible by the employer, would amount to double taxation. There is, however, no correlation between the two and it is possible for a payment to be deductible by the employer and not taxable to the employee,[137] as in the case of certain benefits in kind. Deductible sums include not only salaries proper, but also pensions[138] and retirement gratuities. There is no rule that to be deductible the payment must relate to services rendered in that year.[139] However, lump sum payments to fund future payments tend to be capital payments.[140]

FA 1989 introduced an important timing rule for the deduction of emoluments which was, broadly, that these are not to be deductible for Schedule D, Case I or II until the sum is brought into charge on the employee under Schedule E.[141]

(2) Facilities for and reorganisation of the business (capital)

Facilities for the reorganisation of the business are clearly capital of the business, so expenditure on them may be capital. Thus, building a factory is a capital expense, as is ancillary

[133] [1964] AC 948, 960, [1964] 1 All ER 208.

[134] *Royal Insurance Co.* v. *Watson* [1897] AC 1, 3 TC 500; *Bassett Enterprises Ltd.* v. *Petty* (1938) 21 TC 730.

[135] *IRC* v. *Patrick Thomson Ltd.* (1956) 37 TC 145.

[136] But not sums paid to the Revenue in respect of tax not deducted under the PAYE scheme (*Bamford* v. *ATA Advertising Ltd.* [1972] 3 All ER 535, 48 TC 359). Incentive payments are deductible even if they are to enable the workforce to buy control of the employer (*Heather* v. *P.E. Consulting Group Ltd.* [1973] 1 All ER 8, 48 TC 320; see the discussion of this case in *E. Bott Ltd.* v. *Price* [1987] STC 100, 106).

[137] See above at §14.1.2. Conversely, employers cannot deduct the costs of share options (since there is no "cost" this does not prevent the employee from being taxable in appropriate circumstances, as in *Weight* v. *Salmon* (1935) 19 TC 174 (see above at §16.1).

[138] *Smith* v. *Incorporated Council of Law Reporting for England and Wales* (1914) 6 TC 477.

[139] *Hancock* v. *General Reversionary Society and Investment Co. Ltd.* [1919] 1 KB 25, 7 TC 358.

[140] *Rowntree & Co. Ltd.* v. *Curtis* (1924) 8 TC 678; *British Insulated and Helsby Cables Ltd.* v. *Atherton* [1926] AC 205, 10 TC 155. But see TA 1988, s. 592(4) (FA 1970, s. 21(3)). See also *Hancock* v. *General Reversionary Society and Investment Co. Ltd.* [1919] 1 KB 25, 7 TC 358; and *Jeffs* v. *Ringtons Ltd.* [1985] STC 809, [1986] 1 All ER 144, 58 TC 680.

[141] FA 1989, s. 43.

work, such as the provision of a water supply, drainage and roads.[142] Similarly the cost of sinking a mine shaft is a capital expense,[143] as is the cost of reconverting an oil rig at the end of its lease period,[144] or the cost of acquiring a waste tipping site,[145] although legislation now permits the deduction of both restoration payments and preparation expenditure in closely defined circumstances.[146] Capital allowances may be available for such expenditure, but the availability of capital allowances excludes the revenue deduction for restoration payments and preparation expenditure on waste disposal projects.

The expense of moving from one set of business premises to another is a capital expense,[147] although the costs of removing trading stock are not so regarded. In practice, removal costs which are forced on the trader, as on the expiration of a lease, are allowed. Where, however, the general rule applies, it prevents the deduction of ancillary costs such as conveyancing expenses.

Once-for-all expenditure on a reorganisation may be capital. This was so in *Watney Combe Reid & Co. Ltd.* v. *Pike*[148] where a brewery made *ex gratia* payments to tenants under a scheme by which separate management companies were substituted for tenants. The purpose was to make the assets more profitable, but it was important that the scheme involved a new corporate structure and a new way of doing business.

Facilities may be financial as well as physical. In *Whitehead* v. *Tubbs (Elastics) Ltd.*[149] a payment was made to secure the release of a term in a loan agreement which had significantly limited the company's power to borrow money. This payment was held to be capital. By contrast, in the earlier case of *IRC* v. *Carron*[150] the court held that a payment to secure the alteration of a company's constitution was a revenue expense. *Carron* was distinguished in *Whitehead, inter alia* on the ground that in *Carron* no asset was brought into existence, nor was there any expenditure on any asset or liability of the company.

Costs of loan capital. The distinction between income and capital corporation tax for the purposes of loan relationships and foreign exchange transactions has been abolished. The distinction, however, remains central for income tax. Statute permits the deduction of incidental costs of loan finance,[151] and interest is the subject of a special set of rules (see below at §22.6.2). In *Beauchamp* v. *F. W. Woolworth plc*[152] the taxpayer, with an annual turnover of some £300 m, borrowed 50 m Swiss francs for a five-year period; the loan was immediately converted into sterling. The following year the taxpayer incurred a second such loan, which was also converted. In due course the loans were repaid but, owing to the decline of sterling against the Swiss franc, at a large loss. The House of Lords held that the loan was an accretion to capital and not a revenue transaction and therefore the loss was not allowable. The precise *ratio* is not easy to determine. At one point Lord Templeman spoke of the loan having to be temporary and fluctuating, and incurred in meeting the ordinary running

[142] *Boyce* v. *Whitwick Colliery Co. Ltd.* (1934) 18 TC 655; *Bean* v. *Doncaster Amalgmated Collieries Ltd.* [1944] 1 All ER 621, 27 TC 296; *Pitt* v. *Castle Hill Warehousing Co. Ltd.* [1974] STC 420, [1974] 3 All ER 146. See also *Ounsworth* v. *Vickers Ltd.* [1915] 3 KB 267, 6 TC 671.

[143] *Bonner* v. *Basset Mines Ltd.* (1912) 6 TC 146.

[144] *RTZ Oil and Gas Ltd.* v. *Elliss* [1987] STC 512, 61 TC 132.

[145] *Rolfe* v. *Wimpey Waste Management Ltd.* [1989] STC 454, CA (Special Commissioner reversed, 62 TC 399).

[146] TA 1988, ss 91A, 91B.

[147] *Granite Supply Association Ltd.* v. *Kitton* (1905) 5 TC 168.

[148] [1982] STC 733.

[149] [1984] STC 1, CA; 57 TC 472.

[150] (1968) 45 TC 18, HL.

[151] TA 1988, s. 77.

[152] [1988] STC 714; this marks the case off from *Pattison* v. *Marine Midland Ltd.* [1984] STC 10, 57 TC 219.

expenses of the business.[153] However, this was said in the context of distinguishing *Regent Oil Co. Ltd.* v. *Strick*[154] and stress was laid on the question whether the petrol tie or loan could be said to be an ordinary incident of marketing. A more abstract statement by Lord Templeman was that the loan would be on revenue account only if it were part of the ordinary day-to-day incidence of carrying on a business.[155] This seems to be the more promising starting point.

(3) Expansion of a business (capital) or maintenance of a business (revenue)

The expense of an application for planning permission over land is generally capital since the land is a capital asset and this expense is more than mere maintenance.[156] Similarly, the premises are capital assets, so that, for example, where a brewer applies for a licence for new premises the legal cost of applying for the new licence is not deductible.[157] In *Pyrah* v. *Annis*[158] it was held that the costs of an unsuccessful application to vary an existing public carrier's licence by increasing the number of vehicles from four to seven was capital expenditure because the licence was an asset retained by the trader which produced income. This must be distinguished from *IRC* v. *Carron*[159] where the company was entitled to deduct the legal costs of altering its charter so as to remove restrictions on ordinary business operations.

Sums spent on software to ensure that an existing computer system can cope with the millennium are regarded as revenue expenditure. However, such sums will be capital expenditure if they are part of a major new project instituting other changes, and that project is itself capital in nature.[160]

(4) Preservation of capital (revenue)

Sums paid to preserve the capital or capital assets of the business are revenue expenses. The capital preserved may include the goodwill and the ability to trade. In *Cooke* v. *Quick Shoe Repair Service*[161] the firm had bought a business and arranged for the vendor (V) to settle outstanding liabilities to suppliers and employees. When V failed to do so the firm paid off the creditors and was held entitled to deduct the sums so paid because they were paid to preserve the goodwill of the business, not to buy it.

Sums paid to protect title to capital assets have been held to be revenue expenses. The reason for this is that the expenses are incurred in maintaining the company's capital and so are just as deductible as expenses of repair and maintenance on the fixed assets of the

153 [1989] STC 510, 518, 61 TC 542, 581.

154 [1966] AC 295, 43 TC 1. This test was also applied in *Tanfield Ltd.* v. *Carr* [1999] STC (SCD) 213.

155 [1989] STC 510, 517, 61 TC 542, 581.

156 *ECC Quarries Ltd.* v. *Watkis* [1975] STC 578, [1975] 3 All ER 843, 51 TC 153 . A land developer can deduct such expenses since the land is not capital for such a trader.

157 *Morse* v. *Stedeford* (1934) 18 TC 457.

158 [1956] 2 All ER 858, 37 TC 163.

159 (1968) 45 TC 18.

160 Revenue Interpretation (April 1998), (1998) *Simons Tax Intelligence* 690.

161 (1949) 30 TC 460; described as "an odd case" by Walton J. in *Garforth* v. *Tankard Carpets Ltd.* [1980] STC 251, 259, 260, 53 TC 342, 351. See also *Walker* v. *Cater Securities Ltd.* [1974] STC 390, [1974] 3 All ER 63, 49 TC 625 (the taxpayer owned shares in a customer-company. X had an option to buy these shares. The sum paid by taxpayer to X for release of the option was held to be a revenue expense. This conclusion is supported by Revenue evidence). In *Bolton* v. *International Drilling Co. Ltd.* [1983] STC 70, 92, 56 TC 449, 475, a payment was considered in substance to be to keep an important customer, not just to acquire a capital asset.

company.[162] Such expenditure does not result in either the improvement or the acquisition of a fixed capital asset.[163]

Sums spent to protect the good name of the business by resisting an unfounded allegation of misrepresentation have been held deductible, as have sums paid by way of settlement of a civil claim against the trade.[164]

The importance of correctly identifying the asset being protected was shown in *Bolton* v. *International Drilling Co. Ltd.*[165] Here, a company's sole income-earning asset was originally acquired subject to another person's option to reacquire it. A sum paid for release of the option was held to be capital expenditure because until that time the trade's right in the asset was not one of complete ownership; the payment did not preserve the original title but improved it.

Mr Cube. A controversial application of the above principle occurred in *Morgan* v. *Tate and Lyle Ltd.*[166] where the company successfully claimed to be entitled to deduct expenses incurred in a publicity campaign to defeat the proposed nationalisation of the company which was to take the form not of the compulsory acquisition of its shares, but the compulsory acquisition of its assets. On this basis the House of Lords held that the costs of the campaign were deductible. If the company had been faced with a takeover of its business by a group of persons anxious to acquire control through the purchase of its shares, it was clear that the costs of resisting such a takeover would not have been deductible, the threat in such a case being to the existing management rather than to the assets or trade of the company. Those who, like the author, read the advertisements did not always appreciate that the company was resisting not nationalisation in general, but merely one form of nationalisation on terms thought disadvantageous to the shareholders.

Preserving trade by what means? In *Lawson* v. *Johnson Matthey plc*[167] it was held that where an expense had been incurred to preserve the company's trade, the court could ignore the means by which it was done (by the disposal of worthless shares in a subsidiary company). The House of Lords held that, on the facts, that money was paid, and paid solely, to enable the taxpayer company to continue in business; the test was objective.[168]

(5) Ending onerous contractual obligations and restrictions (either)

A payment for disposing of a permanent disadvantage or onerous burden may be an enduring benefit and so a capital expense. This will usually be the case where the expenditure replaces the source of disadvantage with a new asset.

One starting point is to ask whether the payments made under the liability being disposed of would themselves be revenue expenses.[169] A payment to settle a capital liability is clearly a capital payment. Therefore, where a company had agreed to buy a ship to use in its trade, a payment made on cancellation of the contract was a capital expense.[170]

[162] Distinguish *Pitt* v. *Castle Hill Warehousing Co. Ltd.* [1974] STC 420, [1974] 3 All ER 146 where a sum paid to exchange one capital asset (a strip of land) for another (an easement over another strip) was held to be capital.

[163] *Southern* v. *Borax Consolidated Ltd.* [1940] 4 All ER 412, 23 TC 597.

[164] *IT Comr Bihar and Orissa* v. *Singh* [1942] 1 All ER 362.

[165] [1983] STC 70, 56 TC 449. In *Walker* v. *Joint Credit Card Co. Ltd.* [1982] STC 427, 55 TC 617 sums paid not just to preserve goodwill, but to improve it, were held to be capital expenditure.

[166] [1954] 2 All ER 413, 35 TC 367. *Cf. Hammond Engineering Co. Ltd.* v. *IRC* [1975] STC 334. On deductibility of expenditure on 1975 Common Market Referendum, see Lustgarten [1976] *BTR* 337.

[167] [1992] STC 466, HL; reversing [1991] STC 259, 65 TC 39, CA.

[168] See Saunders [1992] *BTR* 150.

[169] *Bean* v. *Doncaster Amalgamated Collieries Ltd.* (1944) 27 TC 296, 312, *per* Simon L.J.

[170] *Countess Warwick Steamship Co. Ltd.* v. *Ogg* [1924] 2 KB 292, 8 TC 652.

Contracts. Conversely, an expense incurred to dispose of a revenue expense ought to be deductible; if a surrogatum for loss of profit is a trading receipt, a commutation of deductible outlay should be a revenue expense. In *Mitchell* v. *Noble*[171] a payment to be rid of a director whose continuance in office would have been detrimental to the company was held to be a revenue expense because: the company received no enduring advantage; no asset of the company was enhanced; an employee is not a permanency; and the satisfactory state of the workforce is not regarded as part of the capital of the business. In *Anglo-Persian Oil Co. Ltd.* v. *Dale*[172] this was extended to allow deduction of substantial payments to agents to terminate an agency agreement which still had 11 years to run. This decision equated an agency with a contract of employment and rested on the statement by Lawrence L.J. in the Court of Appeal that the cancellation "merely effected a change in the company business methods and internal organisation leaving its fixed capital untouched".

However, while it appears that payments to dispose of liabilities which are capital in nature will not be deductible, it does not follow that payments to dispose of or replace revenue expenses are necessarily deductible. It is necessary to distinguish disposing of a charge on revenue, from acquiring a capital asset which enables disposal of such a charge. The purchase of labour-saving machinery is a capital expense and cannot be converted into a revenue expense simply because it can be shown to reduce the wage bill.[173] In addition, if a channel is continually being silted up and the trader decides to replace the silting channel with a concrete one, that is capital expenditure even though the costs of clearing the silt would have been a revenue expense.[174]

Leases. Where the lease is a capital asset of the business, a payment for the surrender of the lease in commutation of the liability to pay rent is a capital expense and not deductible.[175] Similarly, a payment to vary the terms of the lease will be a capital expense because the payment rendering the lease either more advantageous or less disadvantageous improves the lease. In *Tucker* v. *Granada Motorway Services Ltd.* the landlord (the Minister of Transport) was entitled to rent from the lessees of a motorway service station together with an additional rent based on takings, the latter to include an element for tobacco duty. As tobacco duty rose the lessees found it difficult to make a profit and so it was agreed to exclude the tobacco duty from the calculation in return for a lump sum. The House of Lords held that the lump sum was a capital expense; it was irrelevant that the purpose of the expenditure was to increase profit.[176]

Payments of rent under the lease are revenue expenses, whereas the payment of a premium is capital[177]—even if paid by instalments—provided the lease itself formed part of the capital structure of the business.[178] Therefore, where a company had a lease of a shop for five years and the company ceased to use that shop after two years, the rent was

[171] *Mitchell* v. *B. W. Noble Ltd.* [1927] 1 KB 719, 11 TC 372.

[172] [1932] 1 KB 124, 141, 16 TC 253, 272.

[173] *Anglo-Persian Oil Co. Ltd.* v. *Dale* (1931) 16 TC 253, 261, *per* Rowlatt J.

[174] *Mitchell* v. *B. W. Noble Ltd.* [1927] 1 KB 719, 728, 11 TC 372, 415, *per* Rowlatt J.

[175] *Cowcher* v. *Richard Mills & Co. Ltd.* (1927) 13 TC 216; *Mallett* v. *Staveley Coal and Iron Co. Ltd.* [1928] 2 KB 405, 13 TC 772; see also *IRC* v. *William Sharp & Son* (1959) 38 TC 341.

[176] [1979] STC 393, [1979] 2 All ER 801, 53 TC 92. See also *Southern Counties Agricultural Society* v. *Blackler* [1999] STC (SCD) 200 (payment of reverse premium capital).

[177] On adjustment where part of premium is treated as income, see TA 1988, s. 87.

[178] *IRC* v. *Adam* (1928) 14 TC 34; see *Report of the Committee on the Taxation of Trading Profits*, Cmnd 8189 (1951), §247. On adjustment where part of premium is treated as income, see TA 1988, s. 87.

deductible in computing its profits assuming, as was the case, that the trade itself was still conducted from other premises.[179]

(6) Repairs (revenue) or improvements (capital)[180]

TA 1988, s. 74(1)(d) expressly disqualifies "any sums expended for repairs of premises occupied . . . for the purposes of the trade beyond the sum actually expended for the purpose", a provision which restricts deductions to sums actually spent and therefore prohibits the deduction of sums set aside by way of reserve for future expenditure. S. 74(1)(g) prohibits the deduction of any capital employed in improvements of premises occupied for the purposes of the trade, profession or vocation. At first sight, paragraph (g) seems to be directed to the source from which the trader chooses to finance the improvements; however, it is generally taken to mean that sums spent on improvements are capital payments and therefore not deductible, while sums spent on the repair of capital assets are deductible. The question whether work is a repair or an improvement is one of fact.[181]

Trains and chimneys. Money spent on the replacement of one kind of rail by a superior kind is not deductible, since it increases the value of the railway line.[182] Expense incurred in increasing the number of sleepers under each rail was admitted to be capital expense in *Rhodesia Railways Ltd.* v. *Bechuanaland Protectorate IT Collector*,[183] but the railway company was allowed to deduct as repairs the cost of works in renewing 74 miles of railway track by replacing rails and sleepers. This was not an improvement since it only restored the worn track to its normal condition and did not increase the capacity of the line in any way. Money spent on pulling down a chimney and building a new, bigger and better chimney,[184] or on renovating a factory with a higher roof line and so more space, is not deductible.[185]

Improvements pre-empting repairs. No deduction may be claimed for such part of the expenditure on improvements as would have been needed to pay for mere repair.[186] As Danckwerts J. commented, "it seems . . . to be a hardship and something which is calculated to discourage manufacturers from making the best use of their property".[187] On the other hand, if the work consists of a number of separate jobs it may be possible to distinguish between the different items, thus allowing some of the expense. In *Conn* v. *Robins Bros Ltd.*[188] the construction of a lavatory was held to be an improvement, but the insertion of steel joists was held to be a repair.

These rules are not confined to physical assets. Sums spent on training courses for proprietors are regarded as capital if they are intended to provide new expertise, knowledge or skill, as distinct from mere updating.[189]

[179] *IRC* v. *Falkirk Iron Co. Ltd.* (1933) 17 TC 625.

[180] There is much comparative interest to be derived from Durnford (1997) 45 *Can. Tax Jo.* 395.

[181] *Conn* v. *Robins Bros Ltd.* (1966) 43 TC 266, 274.

[182] *Highland Rly Co.* v. *Balderston* (1889) 2 TC 485; and see *LCC* v. *Edwards* (1909) 5 TC 383.

[183] [1933] AC 368, 372; but see Lord Cooper in *Lawrie* v. *IRC* (1952) 34 TC 20. 25.

[184] *O'Grady* v. *Bullcroft Main Collieries Ltd.* (1932) 17 TC 93.

[185] *Thomas Wilson (Keighley) Ltd.* v. *Emmerson* (1960) 39 TC 360; *Lawrie* v. *IRC* (1952) 34 TC 20; *Mann Crossman and Paulin Ltd.* v. *IRC* [1947] 1 All ER 742, 28 TC 410.

[186] For reasons which are no longer rational, a different rule applies to Schedule A: IR 150, paras 147 *et seq.*

[187] *Thomas Wilson (Keighley) Ltd.* v. *Emmerson* (1960) 39 TC 360, 366.

[188] (1966) 43 TC 266.

[189] Inland Revenue interpretation RI 1.

(7) Renewals (capital) or repairs (revenue)?[190]

This is another version of (6) above. The replacement of a slate on a roof would be a repair, but the rebuilding of a retort house in a gas works would be a renewal.[191] As Buckley L.J. said in *Lurcott* v. *Wakely and Wheeler*[192] (not a revenue case):

> " 'repair' and 'renew' are not words expressive of clear contrast . . . repair is restoration by renewal or replacement of subsidiary parts of a whole. Renewal, as distinguished from repair, is reconstruction of the entirety, meaning by the entirety not necessarily the whole but substantially the whole subject matter under discussion."

Baxter has suggested that "repairs" are the opposite of "improvements", but that some expenditure on repairs can be on capital account.[193] Using this approach, expenditure on reinstating the capital value of business assets is capital expenditure. It is clear that the scope of repairs is treated as a question of law—and so within the court's jurisdiction.

This test presupposes a satisfactory definition of the unit repaired or renewed. In *O'Grady* v. *Bullcroft Main Collieries Ltd.*[194] a chimney used to carry away fumes from a furnace had become unsafe, and so the company built a new one. Rowlatt J. said that in his view the chimney was not a part of the factory, but an entirety, and so capital. Similarly, in *Wynne-Jones* v. *Bedale Auction Ltd.*[195] it was held that the relevant unit was the cattle ring, not the whole auction complex, so that the expenditure was capital. On the other hand, in *Samuel Jones & Co. (Devonvale) Ltd.* v. *IRC*[196] the costs of replacing an unsafe chimney at a factory were held deductible. In the Court of Session, which reversed the Special Commissioners, Lord Cooper said that the factory was the entirety, the chimney, therefore, was only part of the entirety. The court also stressed the low cost of the replacement of the chimney relatively to the insured value of the factory, a point not taken in *O'Grady* v. *Bullcroft Main Collieries Ltd.* The distinction between "a part" and "the entirety" appears to be a convenient method of describing a conclusion rather than a helpful test, but it contains the words by reference to which the evidence is assembled and assessed.

The question seems to be one of the size and importance of the work. One big job may be capital, whereas a combination of small jobs may be revenue. In *Phillips* v. *Whieldon Sanitary Potteries Ltd.*[197] the replacement of a barrier protecting a factory from water in a canal was held to be a renewal and so capital expenditure, the court taking into account the extent of the work, the permanent nature of the new barrier and the enduring benefit it would confer on the business by preserving a part of the fixed capital. In that case Donovan J, followed the *Bullcroft* case and reversed the Commissioners.

An expenditure may be in respect of a repair as opposed to a renewal, even though it is carried out some time after the need for the repair first arose. Thus, the costs of keeping a

[190] See Smith [1982] *BTR* 360, 366 *et seq.*

[191] See Rowlatt J. in *O'Grady* v. *Bullcroft Main Collieries Ltd.* (1932) 17 TC 93, 101 and Donovan J. in *Phillips* v. *Whieldon Sanitary Potteries Ltd.* (1952) 33 TC 213, 219.

[192] [1911] 1 KB 905, 923, 924; cited, e.g. by Lord MacMillan in *Rhodesia Railways Ltd.* v. *Bechuanaland Protectorate IT Collector* [1933] AC 368, 374. The case concerned the construction of a lessee's covenant to keep in thorough repair and good condition.

[193] [1977] *BTR* 184.

[194] (1932) 17 TC 93; the *ratio* was that the chimney was an addition, there being no evidence that the old one was pulled down.

[195] [1977] STC 50, 51 TC 426; the whole case is severely criticised by Baxter [1977] *BTR* 184. See also *Margrett* v. *Lowestoft Water and Gas Co.* (1935) 19 TC 481 (replacement of reservoir capital).

[196] (1951) 32 TC 513.

[197] (1952) 33 TC 213; contrast *Conn* v. *Robins Bros Ltd.* (1966) 43 TC 266.

channel dredged would be income expenditure even though the dredging was done only once every three years or so.[198]

(8) The initial repair problem[199]

Where a trader acquires an asset which requires extensive repairs before it is in a usable condition, the expenses of those repairs are not deductible since they are as much capital expenditure as the costs of acquiring the asset itself. Were the rule otherwise a trader could convert at least a part of the prospective capital expense into a revenue item by buying the asset in an incomplete state and finishing the work himself, perhaps by employing the person who had worked on it before its acquisition.

In *Law Shipping Co. Ltd.* v. *IRC*[200] a shipping company bought a ship which was at that date ready to sail with freight booked. The Lloyd's survey was then overdue but, with the consent of the insurers, the ship was allowed to complete the voyage. The ship cost £97,000 and the company had to spend an extra £51,558 on repairs in order for the vessel to pass the survey. Of that sum, some £12,000 was in respect of repairs caused by deterioration during the voyage and was allowed by the Revenue; the balance of £39,500 was not. The Court agreed.

In *Law Shipping* the expenditure was required to make the asset commercially viable; a different rule applies where the asset is already so viable. In *Odeon Associated Theatres Ltd.* v. *Jones*[201] the company bought a cinema in 1945. Only small sums had been permitted to be spent in the previous five years, and restrictions on repair work lasted for some time after the war. The cinema was open to the public and was a profit-earning asset. The Court of Appeal held that sums spent subsequently to the acquisition in respect of the deferred repairs were deductible. The primary reason was that such would be in accordance with the normal principles of commercial accountancy, as the Commissioners had made a finding not made in the *Law Shipping* case. However, there were other differences. Although in the *Law Shipping* case the ship had been permitted to complete one voyage, it was clear that subsequently a full insurance survey would be needed and the price showed that substantial expenditure would be needed before the ship would again be a profit-earning asset. By contrast, the cinema was an immediate income-earning asset and it appeared that the price had not been affected by the fact of disrepair. Two other facts are material. First, even if the vendors had wished to carry out the repair work before the sale they would have been unable to do so because of the restrictions. Secondly, there was no indication that the taxpayer had in fact been put to greater expense by reason of the deferred repairs.

(9) Allowable capital expenditure—the renewals basis

The distinction between repair and renewal is blurred by the Revenue practice of allowing the cost of replacing machinery and plant as a revenue expense. This practice is distinct from the capital allowances system. There appear to be two distinct legal bases for this practice (which, confusingly, is called a renewals allowance). One is the general theory of profit which would equate a renewal with a repair and would regard both as maintaining intact

198 *Ounsworth* v. *Vickers Ltd,* (1915) 6 TC 671, *per* Rowlatt J.

199 See Smith [1982] *BTR* 360, 361.

200 [1924] SC 74, 12 TC 621; see also *IRC* v. *Granite City Steamship Co. Ltd.* [1927] SC 705, 13 TC 1, and the expenditure on the branch line in *Highland Rly Co.* v. *Balderston* (1889) 2 TC 485.

201 [1972] 1 All ER 681, 48 TC 257, CA. This decision must cast doubt on *Jackson* v. *Laskers Home Furnishers Ltd.* [1956] 3 All ER 891, 37 TC 69; on which, see Silberrad [1957] *BTR* 73.

the capital originally invested in the physical assets of the business.[202] The disadvantage of this basis is that it is inconsistent with the cases considered above and would presumably apply to a range of expenditures other than those on machinery and plant.

The second basis rests on TA 1988, s. 74)(1)(d) which disallows sums spent on the "supply, repairs or alterations of any implements, utensils or articles employed, for the purposes of a trade, profession or vocation, beyond the sum actually expended for those purposes". As drafted, this simply prohibits the deduction of reserves for future expenditure and so may be taken to allow actual expenditure; further, it draws no distinction between initial and replacement utensils. Moreover, it would confine the allowance to implements, utensils and articles and thus would not necessarily cover all types of machinery and plant.[203] It seems best to regard this as an extra-statutory concession dating from the days when there were no capital allowances. This not only avoids the above problems, but also justifies the Revenue's insistence that some renewals allowances are to be made only over a period of two or three years.

Where the renewals basis is adopted, the allowance given is the cost of the new article (excluding additions or improvements), less the scrap or realised value of the replaced article. The cost of the new article may be greater or less than that of the old. Claiming the renewals allowance when the replacement is bought does not to prevent a later switch to the capital allowance system. The two systems of relief are alternatives, although, since the renewals allowance usually gives an immediate write off of all the expenditure, it is usually advantageous.[204]

(10) Trading stock—the tree (capital) or the fruit (revenue)

The purchase of trading stock is generally a deductible revenue expense. However, care is needed to distinguish the purchase of trading stock from the purchase of an asset bearing trading stock. Thus, the purchase of a mine for extraction purposes is an item of capital expenditure and not the purchase of trading stock.[205] In *IRC* v. *Pilcher*[206] a fruit grower was not allowed to deduct the cost of purchasing a cherry orchard, not even that part which represented the value of the nearly ripe crop. The contract had expressly included "this year's crop" but that meant only that the vendor was not to be entitled to pick the crop ripening between contract and completion. The grower had purchased an income-earning asset and not two separate items namely the trees and the crop.

In these cases, trading stock is distinguished from capital. As such, considerable care is needed in defining the trade. In one case sums spent by a timber merchant on the purchase of standing timber were not deductible,[207] whereas in another case the costs of standing timber bought by a dealer in standing timber were deductible.[208]

The purchase of a business and the purchase of trading stock as part of that business are both capital expenditure. Normally, separate entries will take care of trading stock *stricto sensu*, but this will not cover incidental profit-making sources. In *John Smith & Son* v.

[202] See 114th Report of Commissioners of Inland Revenue, § 40.

[203] See *IRC* v. *Great Wigston Gas Co.* (1946) 29 TC 197. An item may be capital expenditure even though on utensils: see *Hinton* v. *Maden and Ireland Ltd.* [1959] 3 All ER 356, 38 TC 391.

[204] See ESC B1.

[205] *Alianza Co. Ltd.* v. *Bell* [1906] AC 18, 5 TC 172; *Stratford* v. *Mole and Lea* (1941) 24 TC 20.

[206] [1949] 2 All ER 1097, 31 TC 314. It is unclear how far the case turns on the distinction between *fructus naturales* and *fructus industriales* (see Tucker Report, above at n. 178; and criticism by Crump [1960] *BTR* 366).

[207] *Hood Barrs* v. *IRC (No. 2)* [1957] 1 All ER 832, 37 TC 188; noted by Silberrad [1957] *BTR* 174; see also *Kauri Timber Co. Ltd.* v. *IT Commr* [1913] AC 771.

[208] *Murray* v. *IRC* (1951) 32 TC 238.

Moore[209] the taxpayer had inherited his father's business in return for a sum which included a figure of £30,000 for specific unexpired contracts for the supply of coal. The son was not allowed to deduct the £30,000. Viscount Haldane held that the contracts formed part of his fixed capital, so that it was the coal which was the circulating capital; Lord Sumner held that the business was not that of buying and selling contracts but buying and selling coal, and that the price paid was the price of acquiring the business.[210]

The decision clearly needs some explanation since contracts for the supply of trading stock can lead to trading profits in ways other than taking delivery of trading stock.[211] In *Taxes Comr* v. *N'Changa Consolidated Copper Mines Ltd.*[212] Viscount Radcliffe explained the decision as resting on two important elements in the facts of the case: one element was that an aggregate price had been paid for the entire business as it stood; the other was that the son did not acquire stock in trade. However, the facts suggest that the son was not carrying on business on his own account before his father's death, in which case it was a simple case of pre-trading expenses. This leaves the court free to dissect the price paid where the business is taken over by a person already trading.

(11) Trading arrangements

General sums paid to regulate the structure of a business tend to be capital, although the duration of the arrangement is of importance.[213] A sum paid in instalments to secure a customer for 10 years was held to be capital,[214] as was a payment to a trade association to prevent the sale of the business of a member of the association to a non-member.[215]

A payment to a retiring employee for a covenant not to compete was held to be capital and so deductible.[216] It can be argued both that such payment was made in order to preserve the business and so was deductible, but that a significant advantage was also gained, and so the payment was of capital.[217] On balance, it would seem that since the expense of buying up a rival business in order to suppress it is capital, the same should apply to a long-term agreement to the same effect. Such arrangements relate to the commercial structure of the business. The question is, however, one of fact and degree.

Petrol ties.[218] After 1945 the petrol trade was arranged at retail level on the basis that a garage would sell several brands of petrol. However, after 1950 oil companies began to secure exclusive agreements with garage owners under which X Co. would provide the owners with benefits if the owners agreed, through contractual ties, to sell only X Co.'s petrol.[218a] Some payments were held to be revenue expenditure of the oil companies, even in cases of contractual ties which were to last five years.[219]

[209] [1921] 2 AC 13, 12 TC 266.

[210] Ibid., 20, 282, 283.

[211] *Thompson* v. *IRC* (1927) 12 TC 1091.

[212] [1964] 1 All ER 208, [1964] AC 948. See also *Whimster & Co.* v. *IRC* (1925) 12 TC 813; and Lord Reid in *Regent Oil Co. Ltd.* v. *Strick* [1965] 3 All ER 174, 185, 43 TC 1, 36.

[213] See *Taxes Commr* v. *N'Changa Consolidated Copper Mines Ltd.* [1964] AC 948, [1964] 1 All ER 208 (one year—revenue expense).

[214] *United Steel Companies Ltd.* v. *Cullington* (1939) 23 TC 71.

[215] *Collins* v. *Joseph Adamson & Co.* [1937] 4 All ER 236, 21 TC 400.

[216] *Associated Portland Cement Manufacturers Ltd.* v. *Kerr* [1946] 1 All ER 68, 27 TC 103.

[217] Note Lord Reid in *Regent Oil Co. Ltd.* v. *Strick* [1965] 3 All ER 174, 183, 43 TC 1, 35.

[218] For a general discussion of the cases, see Whiteman [1966] *BTR* 115; the leading cases were cited in *Rolfe* v. *Wimpey Waste Management Ltd.* [1988] STC 329, 62 TC 399.

[218a] *BI Australia Ltd.* v. *Taxation Commr*[1966] AC 224, [1965] 3 All ER 209.

[219] *Bolam* v. *Regent Oil Co.* (1956) 37 TC 56.

The garage owner's tax liability was different. In so far as the payments were for reimbursement of capital expenditure, they were capital receipts,[220] as where the petrol company paid for substantial new buildings. However, in so far as the payments were reimbursements of revenue expenditure, for example sales promotion, they were revenue receipts.[221] Further, if the amounts were related to gallonage they were treated as rebates on trading stock and so revenue payments.[222] On the other hand, the garage owner could successfully invoke the principle in *Glenboig Union Fireclay Co. Ltd.* v. *IRC* by arguing that the payment was in return for the restriction of his trading opportunities, an argument that succeeded in a case involving a 10-year tie.[223]

The exclusivity war was not confined to the UK. In *BP (Australia) Ltd.* v. *Taxation Commr*[224] the Privy Council considered sums paid by an oil company by way of a "development allowance" to garage owners in return for a five-year tie (the amount being related to the estimated gallonage), to be revenue expenditure.

Lease and leaseback. In order to ensure that the sums received were capital receipts, a system of the lease and lease back was adopted. The garage owner would grant a lease to the oil company which would promise to pay a nominal rent and a large premium. The company would then sub-lease the garage to the owner, who would covenant to sell only the company's products, on breach of which the sub-lease would end. The premium would be a capital receipt by the garage owner (although now subject to tax in part by TA 1988, s. 34).

This scheme was considered by the House of Lords in *Regent Oil Co.* v. *Strick*,[225] its judgment being given on the same day as the Privy Council in *BP (Australia) Ltd.* v. *Taxation Commr*, with identical judges but no mention of the one case in the other. Payments under the scheme by Regent Oil were based upon estimated gallonage and the period ranged from five years to 21 years. It was stated that the company had 5,000 agreements in the UK, mostly of the older variety without a lease.

The House of Lords unanimously held that the payments in respect of the lease arrangements were capital expenditure and so not deductible. The distinction between a five-year tie of the old type, the expenditure on which was a revenue item, and a five-year lease, the premium on which was a capital item, meant that the distinction had to be sought in the nature of the asset acquired by the company. Under the lease scheme not only did the company acquire an interest in the land, but also a better security since if the owner broke the covenant it could terminate the sub-lease and take possession under the lease. The commercial needs of the company in a changing market, which had affected the Privy Council, were ignored by the House of Lords. An argument that the ties were payable out of circulating capital because they were to secure orders and would therefore come circulating back, which had impressed the Privy Council, was trounced by the House of Lords.

The present position is, to say the least, uncertain. A tie accompanied by a lease would seem to be capital; but Lord Reid in *Regent Oil Co.* v. *Strick* considered that payments for very short leases, e.g. two or three years, might be revenue.[226] A tie unaccompanied by a

220 *IRC* v. *Coia* (1959) 38 TC 334.

221 *Evans* v. *Wheatley* (1958) 38 TC 216; *Tanfield Ltd.* v. *Carr* [1999] STC (SCD) 213.

222 In *Regent Oil* v. *Strick* [1965] 3 All ER 174, 191, 43 TC 1, 43 Lord Morris approved *Bolam* v. *Regent Oil* only on this ground.

223 *IRC* v. *Coia* (1959) 38 TC 334.

224 [1965] 3 All ER 209, [1966] AC 224.

225 [1965] 3 All ER 174, 43 TC 1.

226 See 43 TC 1 at 38; note also the Revenue view that a lump sum spent on computer software will be treated as revenue expenditure if the software has a useful economic life of less than two years (Inland Revenue interpretation RI 56).

lease will usually be a revenue expense, even if it lasts for five years. There is authority that such a tie for 20 years will not be a revenue expense since it lacks the element of recurrence, but where the line is to be drawn between five and 20 years remains to be seen (although in *Bolam* v. *Regent Oil* a six-year tie was classified as revenue). The stress in the House of Lords on the nature of the asset acquired suggested that a premium payment in respect of a lease would be a capital item. One reason for this was that the payment would be capital in the hands of the recipient, an erroneous reason made the more absurd by the subsequent decision by the legislature to tax part of the premium as income of the recipient. Whether a premium in respect of a short lease would be treated as a revenue item remains to be seen.

In *Beauchamp* v. *F. W. Woolworth plc*[227] Lord Templeman, in explaining these cases, stated that where the expenditure had been held to be a revenue account it was because the petrol tie had become an integral method of trading and an ordinary incident of marketing. These cases were therefore immaterial in considering the status of a five-year loan.

22.5 Public Policy

The court may refuse to allow the deduction of expenses on grounds of public policy. This is the basis for the view of the House of Lords in *McKnight* v. *Sheppard*[228] disallowing the deduction of a fine imposed by a professional body. The purpose of the fine was to punish the taxpayer and that purpose would be diluted if he were allowed to share the cost with the rest of the community by being allowed to deduct it for tax purposes. However, legal fees incurred in connection with the hearing were deductible since the rule of public policy did not extend this far.[229]

22.6 Statutory Prohibitions

22.6.1 General

TA 1988, s. 74 contains many prohibitions in addition to s. 74(1)(a). Many of these deductions are clearly not allowable on normal accountancy principles. The list antedates those principles; in 1951 its retention was recommended in order that Inspectors of Taxes might have something in black and white to show small shopkeepers who are "among the class of persons most apt to suppose that they might charge some of their domestic expenses against their business receipts".[230]

S. 74(1)(b) prohibits the deduction of sums for the maintenance of the parties, their families in establishments or any sum expended for other domestic or private purposes distinct from the trade, profession or vocation. Whether the first limb prescribes a purely objective test is not yet settled. It has been held that the expression "maintenance", while not restricted to domestic maintenance, is confined to the ordinary necessities of life.[231]

227 [1989] STC 510, 518, 61 TC 542, 581.

228 [1999] STC 669, esp. 674f, 675c, *per* Lord Hoffmann.

229 On the similar US rule, see Tyler 2 *Tax Law Review* 665.

230 *Report of the Committee on the Taxation of Trading Profits*, Cmd. 8189 (1951), §137.

231 *Watkis* v. *Ashford Sparkes & Harwood* [1985] STC 451; s. 74(1)(b) was also considered briefly in *Prince* v. *Mapp* (1970) 46 TC 169.

S. 74(1)(c) prohibits the rent of domestic office and dwellinghouses.

S. 74(1)(d) concerns the repair of premises and the supply, repair and alteration of articles and utensils and limits the deductions to sums actually so expended [232](see above at §22.4.3).

S. 74(1)(e) prevents the deduction of any loss not connected with or arising out of the trade, profession or vocation. This provision provided the *ratio* for the majority of the House of Lords in *Strong* v. *Woodifield* (see above at §22.3.1). A loss is different from an expense in that it comes from outside the trader's pocket, not within. Thus, petty pilfering by an employee is a loss, but money spent on legal advice is an expense or disbursement.[233] The provision also means that a loss sustained in a transaction not forming part of the trade cannot be deducted.[234] S. 74(1)(e) has been said to involve substantially the same test as s. 74(1)(a);[235] however, the boundary is not yet finally settled.[236]

S. 74(1)(f) prohibits the deduction of any capital withdrawn from, or any sum employed or intended to be employed as, capital in the trade, but with an express allowance for interest.[237] The prohibition of sums spent as capital is statutory authority for the non-deduction of capital expenses. The opening words refer particularly to capital losses in connection with loans and guarantees financing the trade. There is, however, a distinction between a capital loss and a revenue loss. Losses on money advanced by a consortium to a colliery company were held to be capital,[238] but losses incurred when a solicitor guaranteed a client's overdraft were held to be revenue, the distinction being that the guarantee was a normal incident of the profession.[239] Today, the section operates to prohibit the deduction of a premium due on the redemption of preference shares or the repayment of loan capital. The section does not appear to apply to an exchange loss incurred on repayment of a loan in foreign currency; this section applies only to the loans themselves.[240]

S. 74(1)(g) prohibits the deduction of capital employed on improvements of business premises (see above at §22.4).

S. 74(1)(h) prohibits any deduction for interest which might have been made if any of the sums mentioned in s. 74(f), (g) had been laid out as interest. This bars notional interest, but not actual interest.

S.74(1)(j) concerns debts not shown to be bad (see below at §23.3).

232 In *Jenners Princes Street Edinburgh Ltd.* v. *IRC* [1998] STC (SCD) 166 this was held to mean expended in an accounting sense, and so permitted the deduction of the full cost of repairs when the contract had been put out to tender. The effect of the change from "premises occupied for the purposes of a trade" to "premises occupied for a Schedule A business" is unclear: see Gammie and de Souza, Vol. 1, para. A.5.107; and *Taxation of Rents* (IR 150), para. 157.

233 *Allen* v. *Farquharson Bros & Co.* (1932) 17 TC 59, 64, *per* Finlay J. See also *Roebank Printing Co. Ltd.* v. *IRC* (1928) 13 TC 864; and *Bamford* v. *ATA Advertising Ltd.* [1972] 3 All ER 535, 48 TC 359.

234 For example *FA and AB Ltd.* v. *Lupton* (see above at §19.1).

235 *Sheppard* v. *McKnight* [1997] STC 846, 851, *per* Nourse L.J.; however, see above at §22.3.

236 See the interesting discussion in *Sycamore and Maple* v. *Fir* 1997 STC (SCD) 1, 91 *et seq.*

237 This reverses *European Investment Trust Co. Ltd.* v. *Jackson* (1932) 18 TC 1.

238 *James Waldie & Sons* v. *IRC* (1919) 12 TC 113; for a fuller example, see *Beauchamp* v. *F. W. Woolworth plc* [1987] STC 279.

239 *Hagart and Burn-Murdoch* v. *IRC* [1929] AC 386, 14 TC 433, HL; *Jennings* v. *Barfield and Barfield* [1962] 2 All ER 957, 40 TC 365.

240 *Beauchamp* v. *F. W. Woolworth plc* [1988] STC 714, 718c, 61 TC 542, 568; it follows from this decision that the earlier decision in *European Investment Trust Co. Ltd.* v. *Jackson* (1932) 18 TC 1, which disallowed interest under this provision, was to be explained solely on the ground that a concession as to the meaning of the statute was disregarded (see [1988] STC 714, 718a, 61 TC 542, 568). In other words the decision should be disregarded. This issue was not touched on by Lord Templeman in the House of Lords ([1989] STC 510, 61 TC 542).

S. 74(1)(k) bars any average loss beyond the actual amount of loss after adjustment, and concerns insurers.

S 74(1)(l) prohibits the deduction of any sums recoverable under an insurance or indemnity. This is surprisingly limited and does not prohibit the deduction of sums recoverable, for example, in tort, although any sums actually recovered will be taken into account.

Under s. 74(1)(m)–(p) the rule that business expenses are deductible must be adjusted when it conflicts with the delicate system of deduction of tax at source, which applies to annuities or other annual payments payable out of profits or gains, any royalty[241] or other sum paid in respect of the use of a patent.[242] The adjustment is made by providing that no deduction may be made on account of such payments when the profits are computed. This leaves the trader with the right to deduct tax when making the payment and, if the facts fall within TA 1988, s. 348, to retain the tax and so recover the tax relief in respect of the expenditure. Each category of payments must, however, be considered. It will be noted that payments for bona fide commercial reasons in connection with an individual's trade, profession or vocation are not affected by the changes made to the scope of Schedule D, Case III in 1988.[243]

Interaction with ss 348 and 349

Annuities or other annual payments are not deductible as a business expense if, in addition to satisfying all the usual tests of such payments, they are payable out of profits or gains. This has been taken to mean that they must form a charge on the profits as opposed to being an element in computing those profits, so that sums are a deductible expense if deductible in computing those profits.[244] Where the business consists of the grant of annuities, those annuities are not payable out of profits or gains, so that the payments will be deductible in computing the profits or gains.[245] On the other hand, an annuity payable to the widow of a deceased partner would be payable out of profits or gains. The phrase "any royalty or other sum paid in respect of the user of a patent" is misleadingly wide. Since the reason for the prohibition of deduction is because of the relationship with TA 1988, ss 348 and 349, an expense will fall within this prohibition only if it has the quality of income in the hands of the recipient. Further, the expense must be for the use, as distinct from the acquisition, of a patent, so that, for example, a right to restrain the patent holder from exercising his patent in a particular area is more than a mere right of user.[246]

Under s. 827, payments of penalties, interest and surcharges under the VAT legislation are non-deductible.

22.6.2 Interest

A person carrying on a trade can, in computing the profits, deduct the interest payments incurred in that trade. Such payments will be deductible on general accounting principles, so that deductibility is distinct from the special rules discussed above at §10.1. However, certain special provisions exist.

241 TA 1988, ss 74(1)(l), 348, 349.

242 Ibid., ss 74(1)(p), 348, 349. Mining rents were removed in 1995 and 1997.

243 Ibid., s. 347A(2).

244 *Paterson Engineering Co. Ltd.* v. *Duff* (1943) 25 TC 43.

245 *Gresham Life Assurance Society* v. *Styles* [1892] AC 309, 3 TC 185.

246 *Gresham Life Assurance Society* v. *Styles* [1892] AC 309, 320, 3 TC 185, 192, *per* Lord Watson; *British Salmson Aero Engines Ltd.* v. *IRC* [1938] 2 KB 482, 22 TC 29.

TA 1988, s. 74(m) prohibits the deduction of any interest paid to a non-resident if, and so far as, the interest is charged at more than a reasonable commercial rate. This allows the deduction to the extent that it is reasonable, only prohibiting the deduction of the excess.

TA 1988, s. 82 concerns *annual* interest paid to non-residents; short interest (see below at §27.3) may be ignored. The section provides that no deduction for the interest paid may be claimed unless the person making the payment has deducted income tax at the lower rate (under TA 1988, s. 349(2)) and has accounted for the tax to the Revenue. The gross amount paid is deductible in computing profits.

Foreign interest

However, interest may still be deductible, even if paid gross, by a trader resident in the UK, where the interest is both payable and paid outside the UK under an obligation incurred exclusively for purposes of the trade.[247] In addition, the liability must have been incurred for a trade carried on outside the UK or the interest must be payable in foreign currency. The purpose is to assist foreign trade or to encourage traders to borrow overseas, a policy much encouraged in the late 1960s. This exception does not apply if the borrower controls the lender, or *vice versa*, or both are under common control.

22.6.3 Business gifts and entertainment expenses

The general rule that expenses incurred wholly and exclusively for the business were deductible led to particular problems in the area of business entertainment expenses, such expenses being deductible even though paid on a lavish scale. A famous example was the modest firm which, in the 1960s, deducted £3,600 in computing its profits, of which £1,700 was on account of the purchase of a grouse moor. While such expenditure may have been justified by a business purpose, there was also the chance that the hospitality was offered purely in the hope that it would be reciprocated, which meant that the leisure activities of senior businessmen were being subsidised by the Revenue. Even today lavish entertainment is available. A day out at the British Grand Prix complete with helicopter ride costs £1,000.[248]

Prohibition

TA 1988, s. 577 now prohibits the deduction of expenses—including incidental expenses—incurred in providing business entertainment—a phrase defined to include hospitality of any kind.[249] S. 577 also extends to the provision of gifts,[250] subject to the *de minimis* exception of £10 p.a. The disallowance turns on the facts, not the purpose of the trader.[251] Normally, this disallowance affects computation under Schedule D or Schedule A. Where an asset is used for business entertainment purposes, any capital allowance otherwise claimable is disallowed.[252]

S. 577 also extends to Schedule E. If the employer pays an employee an allowance purely for entertainment purposes, the employer may not deduct the allowance in computing his profits; the employee is taxable on the allowance but may deduct all expenditure satisfying

247 TA 1988, s. 82(2).
248 *The Economist*, 10 June 2000, 39.
249 TA 1988, s. 577(5).
250 Ibid., s. 577(8).
251 *Fleming* v. *Associated Newspapers Ltd.* [1972] 2 All ER 574, 46 TC 401 (see below).
252 TA 1988, s. 577(6)(c).

the rule in TA 1988, s. 198 whether or not it would satisfy TA 1988, s. 577. If, however, the employer pays the employee a general allowance to cover terms which include entertainment, the position is reversed. The employer may deduct the cost of the allowance, assuming that it also satisfies the other rules (e.g. TA 1988, s. 74(a)), but the employee may deduct only such entertainment costs as satisfy both ss 198 and 577.[253]

Permitted entertainment expenses rules are as follows:

(1) Expenses incurred in the entertainment of bona fide members of staff are deductible. Curiously, the requirement of reasonableness is absent here.[254] The exception does not apply when the entertainment is incidental to the provision of entertainment for outsiders.

(2) The costs of small gifts are deductible if they carry conspicuous advertisements, such as calendars and diaries.[255]

(3) Expenses are deductible if they are (a) incurred in the provision of that which it is a person's trade to provide, if it is provided by him in the course of his trade for payment, or (b) gratuitously if it is provided with the object of advertising to the public generally.[256] Examples of expenses within group (a) would be the provision of food by a restaurateur or of theatre tickets by a theatre owner, and examples of those within group (b) are free samples of products or complimentary theatre tickets for the press, although not for friends.

The exception is limited to the provision of "anything which it is his trade to provide". "Anything" has been construed to mean business entertainment, so that it must be a person's trade to supply such entertainment. Hence, a journalist providing drinks for potential sources of information, or meals for the softening-up of contributors, does not fall within the exception.[257] It was a person's trade to produce newspapers not refreshment; it would follow that if that person offered not drinks but a copy of his paper, that expense might be deductible.

Another problem is whether the person must supply the entertainment himself. Thus, if the owner of a fried chicken shop provides business entertainment in his own shop, with his own fried chicken, he can clearly deduct his costs, but it is not clear whether he could deduct the costs of entertaining the same people at the Ritz. In this latter instance he is supplying that which it is his trade to supply, but the sums would probably not be deductible merely because of the coincidence of the entertainment provided with his own trade. It is probable that the expense is deductible only if his trade supplies the entertainment.

(4) Expenses incurred in making a gift to a charity, including the Historic Buildings Commission and the National Heritage Memorial Fund, are excluded from s. 577.[258] This leaves the taxpayer with the task of ensuring that the gift also escapes s. 74(1)(a).

253 TA 1988, s. 577(3). This reverses the normal process under s. 153, which charges the employee but allows the employer to deduct (see above §18.4.3).

254 Ibid., s. 577(5).

255 Ibid., s. 577(7). The cost to the donor must not exceed £10 per donee per year (s. 577(8)(b)).

256 Ibid., s. 577(10).

257 *Fleming* v. *Associated Newspapers Ltd.* [1972] 2 All ER 574, 46 TC 401.

258 TA 1988, s. 577(9).

22.7 Sale and Leaseback; Disallowance of Excess Rent

22.7.1 Leasebacks of land

Where rents in excess of the commercial rent are paid under a leaseback arrangement, the excess is not deductible.[259] Where the asset sold is a lease for a term not exceeding 50 years and it is leased back for a term not exceeding 15 years, a part of the sale consideration which would otherwise be capital is taxed as income.[260] That part is 16 − n/15 where n is the term of the new lease. Therefore if the leaseback is for six years, two-thirds of the capital element of the sale consideration is treated as income and can only deduct two-thirds.

22.7.2 Leased assets other than land

Where, before the sale and leaseback, the asset was used in the trade, the allowable deduction is limited to the commercial rent.[261] Disallowed rental payments may, however, be rolled forward and used in later periods when the rent paid is below the commercial rent. Where the asset was not so used, and the payer, having received a tax deduction for his rent, then receives a capital sum under the lease, the deduction is clawed back to the extent of that sum;[262] the clawback is reduced when part of the rent has been disallowed. This rule also applies where the lessor's interest belongs to an associate of the payer and the associate receives a capital sum, in which case the charge is on the associate.

22.8 Expressly Permitted Expenditure

Certain types of expenditure are made deductible by statute. These are mostly items which would otherwise be non-deductible under s. 74(1)(a) or are capital expenditure. They include:

(1) incidental costs incurred by a company in obtaining the acceptance of certain bills of exchange (s. 78);
(2) incidental costs of loan finance (s. 77);
(3) contributions to approved local enterprise agencies (s. 79), local enterprise companies, training and enterprise councils (TECs) and business-link organisations (s. 79A); the sunset provision was removed by FA 2000, s. 88;
(4) applications for patents (ss 83 and 526);
(5) gifts in kind to charities (s. 83A) (added by FA 1999, s. 55);
(6) gifts to educational establishments (s. 84) (rewritten by FA 1991, s. 68); RI 151 extends this to gifts of trading stock to other charities;
(7) sums spent in establishing share option schemes, profit-sharing schemes or ESOPs, as well as payments into approved share schemes or ESOPs for employees, even though representing a division of profits (ss 84A, 85 and 85B);

259 Ibid., s. 779. Top-slicing relief used to be available, but was repealed for 1989–1990 and subsequent years.
260 Ibid., s. 780.
261 Ibid., s. 782.
262 Ibid., s. 781; "capital sum" includes insurance proceeds.

(8) the costs of seconding employees to charities (s. 86);
(9) the costs of employees seconded to various educational bodies or sent away for training s.86(3)) (as widened by FA 1999) and s. 588, ESC A63 and A64;
(10) contributions to agent's expenses paid in connection with the payroll deduction scheme for charitable gifts by employees (s. 86A);
(11) premiums in connection with leases payable in respect of business premises when the landlord is chargeable under Schedule A (s. 87);
(12) certain capital expenditure by a cemetery or cremation authority (s. 91);
(13) rents paid for tied premises (s. 98);
(14) certain sums in connection with post-cessation receipts (s. 105);
(15) payments to an employee under a restrictive covenant under TA 1988, s. 31 (s. 323);
(16) payments by market boards to reserve funds (s. 509);
(17) certain payments under schemes for rationalising industry (s. 568);
(18) payments under certified and statutory redundancy schemes (ss 568 and 572), employer's redundancy payments (s. 579(2)) and costs of providing counselling services to employees in connection with the termination of their employment (s. 589A(8));
(19) payments to superannuation funds (s 592 (4));
(20) payments to personal pension schemes (s. 643);
(21) most sums permitted under the capital allowance system (CAA 1990);
(22) revenue expenditure on scientific research (CAA 1990, s. 136);
(23) payments by football pool companies to certain trusts (FA 1991, s. 121(2)).

Of the above, (2) is worth noting. The expenditure must be incurred wholly and exclusively for the purpose of obtaining finance or repaying it. It has been held that expenses incurred in repaying a loan, the effect of which will be to enable the business to borrow new money for expansion, is not within s. 77 since the expansion purpose prevents it.[263]

22.9 Enhanced Expenditure; FA 2000 Tax Credit for Revenue Expenditure

The concept of a tax credit for revenue expenditure is in some ways similar to the old investment allowance (see chapter 24.1 below). However it is a brand new device of the sort of which the current chancellor is so fond; it is targeted (i.e. cheap in exchequer terms), it is confined to expenditure on research and development enterprise by small and medium sized enterprises. It is nonetheless interesting especially as the company may claim a tax credit even where there are insufficient profits. The IFS estimates that it may increase research and development spending by £200 m or 2% but this is only on the most optimistic assumptions. As it is confined to companies it is considered in the section on corporation tax (see below §47.2.2).

[263] *Focus Dynamics* v. *Turner* [1999] STC (SCD) 1.

23

Business Income—Part V: Timing and Trading Stock (Inventory)

23.1 Accounting Bases, Earnings Basis and Cash Basis

23.1.1 Current status

The tax system measures the profits of a business for a particular period. Today, FA 1998, s. 42 provides that the profit must be measured on accounting bases which give a true and fair view—subject to any adjustment required or authorised by law. The 1993 decision of the Court of Appeal in *Gallagher* v. *Jones* (above at §21.1) also refers to the role of accounting practice in measuring profits, unless it is "otherwise inapt to determine the true profits or losses of the business". These two formulae give courts considerable flexibility in preferring a rule of law to accounting practice, but so far the courts have shown few signs of wanting to do so, and the Revenue has shown little enthusiasm in inviting the courts to do so.

The various accounting bases may conveniently be called earnings bases—to distinguish them from the cash basis. FA 1998, s. 43 abolished the cash basis, subject to transitional relief for new barristers and advocates (see below at §23.1.3).[1] Where the new rules mean a change in the way work in progress is treated a special catch-up charge prevents too much income arising in one year (see below at §23.5.3).

[1] FA 1998, ss 42, 43.

Under the earnings bases the actual dates of payment are ignored; sums due but not yet paid, whether debits or credits, are brought into account.[2] This is now subject to a special statutory rule for the payment of remuneration chargeable in the hands of the payee under Schedule E.[3] The cash basis took into account only sums of money actually spent or received, regardless of when they became due.

One consequence of the cash basis was that post-cessation receipts escaped all income tax. Therefore if a barrister retired from practice because he was appointed to the Bench or to government office (such as Lord Chancellor), all sums paid after the day of retirement would be tax free. There was no obligation to enter the unpaid sums as a debt due to the barrister since this obligation arose only when an earnings basis was used. This immunity from taxation arose from the doctrine of the source; when the sums were paid there was no source and so they could not be taxable income. This anomaly was criticised by the Royal Commission in 1955,[4] and was changed by FA 1960 (now TA 1988, s. 104). It is reasonable to suppose that Lord Simon, who served as Lord Chancellor in two administrations, took advantage of this pre-1960 gap in the law on each occasion it arose before him; his remarks in some of the tax avoidance cases should, perhaps, be read in the light of this good fortune.

23.1.2 Finality of accounts; reopening

A recurring issue is whether the tax system will allow an account to be reopened. The two UK rules are as follows:

(1) an account can be reopened to include figures which do not appear in the accounts at all or are shown to be wrong; however
(2) the account cannot be reopened if the amount of the liability stated in the accounts was correctly stated as the finally agreed amount of the liability.

The leading case on (2) is *British Mexican Petroleum Co. Ltd.* v. *Jackson.*[5] The taxpayer company had incurred a large liability in year 1; in year 3 the creditor released part of that liability The House of Lords held, first, that the release could not alter the amount of the liability entered for the year 1 and, secondly, that the sum released could not be treated as a trading receipt in year 3.[6]

Release of debts

Legislation reversed the second part of the *British Mexican* decision. The release is now to be treated as a trading receipt in the period of release.[7] This suggests that the legislature accepted the first part of the decision in *British Mexican.* The Revenue view is that a release is a release whether it is gratuitous or for value; however, the extent of any value received would have to be brought into account to reduce the sum taxable.[8] Statute provides that a

[2] See also TA 1988, s. 110(3).
[3] FA 1989, s. 43 (but note adjustment permitted by s. 43(5), (8)).
[4] Royal Commission on the Taxation of Profits and Income, *Final Report*, Cmnd 9474 (1955), 12.
[5] (1932) 16 TC 570; and see Atkinson J. in *Jays the Jewellers Ltd.* v. *IRC* [1947] 2 All ER 762, at 768, 29 TC 274, 284.
[6] The UK has no "recapture of tax benefit" doctrine, as does the United States—see the *Kirby Lumber* case ((1931) 284 US 1); on cancellation of debt in the United States see Bittker and Thompson (1978) 66 *California LR* 1159.
[7] TA 1988, ss 94, 87(4).
[8] Inland Revenue interpretation RI 50. The Revenue view is based on cases decided under TA 1988, s. 421.

release forming part of a voluntary arrangement under the Insolvency Act 1986 does not give rise to a trading receipt.[9]

Illustration—*Symons* v. *Weeks*

Under rule (1) above, the figure originally entered can be adjusted if it has not yet been finally agreed between the Revenue and the taxpayer as a final figure,[10] and *a fortiori* where no figure appeared in the accounts at all.[11] In such instances the courts favour the use of hindsight. In *Symons* v. *Weeks*[12] Warner J. reasserted the authority of rule (2) above. Staged payments to architects involved a substantial element of payment in advance, but the exact whole fee would not be known until the work was completed. In accordance with accounts which had been properly drawn up, only a portion of the sum received in a year was shown as a trading receipt. Warner J. said that *Simpson* v. *Jones*,[13] which had given us rule 1, could not apply to a case where accounts had been drawn up correctly, and that it was therefore not open to the Revenue to amend the figures retrospectively. The taxpayer was right in seeking to be taxed on the figures in the accounts.

23.1.3 Transitional relief for barristers and advocates

FA 1998, s. 43 gives special relief to barristers and advocates, who are in actual practice for a period of account ending no more than seven years after starting to practice, i.e. when they first hold themselves out as available for fee earning work. Once they move to a basis within s. 42 they may not move back.[14] The s. 43 basis allows barristers and advocates to compute profits on (a) the old cash basis or (b) by reference to fees earned, whose amount has been agreed and in respect of which a fee note has been delivered. While (b) looks like the earnings basis, it fall short of a basis within s. 42 because it requires no calculation for work in progress or any other refinement sought by accounting principles. Whether this should be seen as a tribute to the lobbying powers of the legal profession or a comment on the problems solicitors have in extracting money from clients is unclear. The chosen basis must be applied consistently.[15] Barristers and advocates may choose at any time during the seven years to switch to the general rule in s. 42.

23.2 Receipts

Three general principles have been developed by the courts (but, as always, these are now subject to accounting principles): the first is a realisation principle based on the time when the profits are ascertained or realised; the second is a matching principle which will override the first principle when it is appropriate to do so and shift the receipt back to the period when the receipt was earned;[16] the third principle is that the courts will give effect to

[9] Ibid., s. 94 as amended by FA 1994, s. 144(2) for releases on or after 30 November 1993.

[10] *Bernhard* v. *Gahan* (1928) 13 TC 723.

[11] *Simpson* v. *Jones* [1968] 2 All ER 929, 44 TC 599.

[12] [1983] STC 195, 56 TC 630 (Warner J. pointed out that if the Revenue had not insisted on a change from cash basis to earnings basis it could have got what it wanted).

[13] [1968] 2 All ER 929, 44 TC 599.

[14] Ibid., s. 43(4).

[15] FA 1998, s. 43(3).

[16] See the speeches of Lord Fraser and Lord Keith in *Willingale* v. *International Commercial Bank* [1978] STC 75, 52 TC 242. See also Freedman [1987] *BTR* 61 and 104; and White [1987] *BTR* 292.

accounting evidence to move a payment which has been received forward to a later accounting period. The three principles are now discussed in turn.

23.2.1 Profits ascertained or realised

This principle is a rule against anticipation of profits.[17] The accounting principle of prudence is another basis for the rule; FRS 12 forbids the recognition of a contingent asset, i.e. a possible asset arising from past events whose existence will be confirmed only by the occurrence of one or more future events not wholly within the entity's control.

Sums due whether to or from the trade must be entered when, and only when, all the conditions precedent to earning or paying it have been fulfilled; this is a question of construction of the particular contract.[18] The leading case is *J. P. Hall & Co. Ltd.* v. *IRC.*[19] In March 1914 the company made a contract to supply certain electric motors, deliveries to begin in June 1914 and end in September 1915, with payment within one month of delivery. The final delivery did not take place until July 1916. The company argued that the receipts should have been taken as earned when the contract was made—in March 1914. Lord Sterndale M.R., put the matter simply, "These profits were neither ascertained nor made at the time these two contracts were concluded".[20] The profits therefore could not have been anticipated.

As Baxter shows,[21] such analysis is on the simple side. In the real world of commerce: (1) the trader (T) glimpses the far-off possibility of gain; (2) T starts to deploy assets, e.g by buying raw materials; (3) the assets mature, e.g become finished goods; (4) the trader becomes entitled to payment; (5) T receives payment; and (6) any risk of claims in respect of the contract, e.g. for faulty goods, passes away.

In such cases everything turns on the construction of the agreement or statute giving rise to the payment. In *Johnson* v. *W. S. Try Ltd.*[22] a payment for compensation for refusal of planning consent was held to date from the date of the final agreement with the council, it being open to the council until that time to change its mind and grant the consent. FRS 12 dictates a similar result. In *Willingale* v. *International Commercial Bank Ltd.*[23] the House of Lords held that bills of exchange owned by the bank gave rise to profit only when they were realised, whether by sale or on maturity. FRS 12 does not dictate this result, which was probably wrong in 1977 and is certainly wrong now.[24]

23.2.2 Matching principle: relating back to time profit earned

Under this principle legal rules and accounting principles also converge; both wish to match the receipts with the relevant expenditure. Payments have been related back to the moment of the service even though there was no legal right to payment at the time of that service, as

[17] For example Lord Reid in *Duple Motor Bodies* v. *Ostime* (1961) 39 TC 537, 569. For an efficiency analysis of rules from a US perspective see Shaiviro (1992) 48 *Tax Law Review* 1.

[18] *Johnson* v. *W. S. Try Ltd.* (1946) 27 TC 167 at 185, *per* Lord Greene M.R.

[19] [1921] 3 KB 152, 12 TC 382.

[20] Ibid., 155 389. The company's case was not strengthened by the fact that its accounts showed the receipts as brought in only after delivery.

[21] [1978] *BTR* 65, 67.

[22] [1946] 1 All ER 532, 27 TC 167.

[23] [1978] STC 75, [1978] 1 All ER 754, 52 TC 242.

[24] For guidance on the timing of the receipt of income in the form of agricultural subsidies see Inland Revenue interpretation IRI 94.

in *Isaac Holden & Sons Ltd.* v. *IRC* (see below); moreover, payments have been related back even though the trade has since been discontinued.[25]

The general principle was stated by Viscount Simon L.C. in *IRC* v. *Gardner, Mountain and D'Ambrumenil Ltd.*:[26]

> "services completely rendered or goods supplied, which are not to be paid for till a subsequent year, cannot generally be dealt with by treating the taxpayer's outlay as pure loss in the year in which it was incurred and bringing in the remuneration as pure profit in the subsequent year in which it is paid or due to be paid. In making an assessment . . . the net result of the transaction, setting expenses on the one side and a figure for remuneration on the other side, ought to appear . . . in the same year's profit and loss account and that year will be the year when the service was rendered or the goods delivered . . . This may involve . . . an estimate of what the future remuneration will amount to . . . (but this provisional estimate) could be corrected when the precise figure was known, by additional assessment. . ."

The matching principle matches receipts with the moment the services are rendered or the goods supplied, not with the moment a legally enforceable right to payment arose. This has three consequences:

(1) Where the goods have been delivered, so that the contract has been executed, but payment will not become due until some later time, that payment must be related back to the time of the delivery; in the meantime a provisional figure may have to be put into the accounts. In *IRC* v. *Gardner, Mountain and D'Ambrumenil Ltd.* sums due to be paid and so paid only in 1938 in respect of underwriting services performed in 1936 were attributed to 1936.[27]

(2) A payment cannot be related back to a time before the services were completed or the goods delivered.[28]

(3) A payment cannot be related back if it is not directly in return for goods supplied or services rendered.[29] So in *Gray* v. *Lord Penrhyn*[30] a firm of auditors had been negligent in failing to spot defalcations by the taxpayer's employees. The firm subsequently made good the loss but the sums were not related back to the years of the defalcations or the negligence. Instead, the sums were treated as trading receipts in the year of payment which was also the year in which the liability was agreed. This may also be one of the factors behind the decision of the House of Lords in *Willingale* (above).[31]

Apart from *Gardener, Mountain*, the leading case is *Isaac Holden & Sons Ltd.* v. *IRC*.[32] The company was a member of a federation of companies engaged in combing wool for the Government. In July 1918 a provisional price increase of 10% was agreed between the federation and the Government to operate from 1 January 1918, and in 1919 a total increase of 20% with effect from 1 January 1918 was agreed. The company's trading account ending 30 June 1918 had included the 10% increase, but Rowlatt J. directed that it should take account

[25] *Severne* v. *Dadswell* [1954] 3 All ER 243, 35 TC 649.
[26] (1947) 29 TC 69, 93.
[27] For modern law of taxation of Lloyd's underwriters, see FA 1993, ss 171–84.
[28] *John and E. Sturge Ltd.* v. *Hessel* [1975] STC 127, 51 TC 183; *J. P. Hall & Co. Ltd.* v. *IRC* [1921] 3 KB 152, 12 TC 382 (see above at §7.00).
[29] *Severne* v. *Dadswell* [1954] 3 All ER 243, 248; 35 TC 649, 659, *per* Roxburgh J.
[30] [1937] 3 All ER 468, 21 TC 252.
[31] [1978] STC 75, 87, *per* Lord Keith.
[32] (1924) 12 TC 768.

of the 20% increase. The accounts were reopened because no provision for this possibility had been made in the original accounts.

Receipts have been adjusted to take account of subsequent payments not only where services have been rendered, as in the previous cases, but also where the Government requisitioned trading stock,[33] and a ship,[34] where payments wrongfully extracted by a government official were reimbursed[35] and where a ministry agreed to modify an agreement so as to make good a loss sustained by the taxpayer, but took a long time paying the sum.[36]

In *Harrison* v. *John Cronk & Sons Ltd.*[37] the House of Lords held that there could be no relating back where, at the end of the trading period, only a guess could be made as to the correct measure of the eventual receipts. The case has since been described in the House of Lords as exceptional and as laying down no such general principle.[38] The decision may also be per incuriam since none of the cases on relating back were cited.

23.2.3 Special rules for default of debtor

An adjustment for the default of a debtor is made when the default occurs, and is not related back. This is implemented by TA 1988, s. 74(j) which was rewritten in 1994 to take account of developments in insolvency law.[39] No deduction may be made for any debts except: (a) a bad debt proved to be such;[40] (b) a debt or part of a debt released by the creditor wholly and exclusively for the purposes of his trade, profession or vocation as part of a voluntary arrangement which has taken effect under or by virtue of the insolvency legislation; (c) a doubtful debt to the extent estimated to be bad, meaning, in the case of the bankruptcy or insolvency of the debtor, the debt, except to the extent that any amount may reasonably be expected to be received on the debt. Of these, (b) was new and (c) rewritten. The reason for the introduction of (b) was that the previous version allowed debts to be deducted only when and to the extent that they were proved to be bad, i.e. irrecoverable. This did not allow the deduction of debts released as part of the new insolvency practice. For similar reasons (b) now provides that a deduction may be taken where the debt is a doubtful debt to the extent that it is estimated bad.[41] This should enable creditors to obtain relief even though they could be expected to have recovered more of the debt by putting the debtor into liquidation or bankruptcy.

The test for (a) can be severe. A distant prospect that a company's debt may have been paid by the former chairman under a personal guarantee prevented a claim for relief from being established.[42] Meanwhile the value of the potential right to deduct declines year by year.

33 *IRC* v. *Newcastle Breweries Ltd.* (1927) 12 TC 927.

34 *Ensign Shipping Co. Ltd.* v. *IRC* (1928) 12 TC 1169.

35 *English Dairies Ltd.* v. *Phillips* (1927) 11 TC 597.

36 *Rownson, Drew and Clydesdale Ltd.* v. *IRC* (1931) 16 TC 595. In each of the above four cases the effect was to increase the taxpayers' liability to excess profits duty.

37 [1936] 3 All ER 747, 20 TC 612.

38 *IRC* v. *Gardner, Mountain and D'Ambrumenil Ltd.* (1947) 29 TC 69, 106, *per* Lord Porter, 94, *per* Viscount Simon; see also at 111, *per* Lord Simonds.

39 Insolvency Act 1986; or the Insolvency (Northern Ireland) Order 1989 (SI 1989/000). See RI 81.

40 For an example, see *Sycamore and Maple* v. *Fir* [1997] STC (SCD) 1, 67 *et seq.*

41 TA 1988, s. 74(1)(j) replaced by FA 1994, s. 144(1); see also Inland Revenue Press Release, 30 November 1993, (1993) *Simon's Tax Intelligence* 1514, and RI 81.

42 *Taylor* v. *Clatworthy* [1996] STC (SCD) 506.

Reserves

TA 1988, s. 74(j)also has the effect of disallowing a tax deduction for a general reserve set up for bad debts. Each debt must be separately justified.[43] The practice of the Revenue is that if a debt becomes bad in a year after it first accrues, an allowance can be made in that later year with no relating back.[44] *A fortiori* where a debt is brought in, no allowance can be made for the expense of collecting it in a later year—such expenses belonging to the later year.[45] Accounting practice may allow for general reserves. Presumably s. 74(j) will override such practice unless *Absalom* v. *Talbot*[46] applies.

Unremittable debt

A debt which has been paid in a foreign country but in circumstances in which exchange control restrictions in that country do not allow the debt to be remitted is not technically a bad debt. However, the debt will, by concession, be treated as a bad debt if reasonable steps have been taken to remit the debt, the amount is still unremittable one year after the end of the accounting period in which it arose, and the debt cannot be used to cover expenditure in the foreign country. In addition, the debt must not be covered by insurance. The assessment must not have become final and conclusive.[47]

Valuation of debt: *Absalom* v. *Talbot*

TA 1988, s. 74(j) deals only with deductions and does not state what debts are to be brought into account, nor at what value. The value of a debt is a matter of fact and is not necessarily its face value, even if it is not proved to be a bad debt. In *Absalom* v. *Talbot*[48] the taxpayer was a speculative builder. His purchasers had the option, after payment of a deposit and a sum borrowed from a building society, of leaving the balance outstanding on granting the taxpayer a second mortgage on the house, the sum to be repaid with interest over a period of 20 years. The Revenue insisted on the face value of the debts being incorporated into the accounts until such time as it was proved to be bad, seeing no difference between the present circumstances and those in which the builder, having received the amount outstanding, chose to lend it out at interest. This was rejected by a bare majority in the House of Lords.

Once it was accepted that the value of debts was not their face value, considerable problems of implementation arise. One solution would have been to bring in the payments as they were made. The objection to that in 1944 was that payments after a discontinuance would have escaped tax even though the earnings basis was employed, an objection no longer valid.[49] Another solution would have been to value the debts, but here it would not have been possible to make adjustments to take account of actual returns. Therefore,

[43] On special rules for bank debts to overseas governments, see TA 1988, ss 88A, 88B, 88C, inserted by FA 1990, s. 74. See also the Debts of Overseas Governments (Determination of Relevant Percentage) Regulations 1990 (SI 1990/2529), as amended by SI 1993/1623; *Simon's Direct Tax Service*, Pt. H2.

[44] *Absalom* v. *Talbot* [1944] 1 All ER 642, 26 TC 166. This Revenue practice was approved by Lord Atkin and by the two dissentients, Lord Simon and Lord Porter. Lord Russell of Killowen and Lord Thankerton expressed no opinion. The practice was accepted by Macnaghten J. and the Court of Appeal in *Bristow* v. *William Dickinson & Co. Ltd.* [1946] KB 321, 27 TC 157.

[45] *Monthly Salaries Loan Co. Ltd.* v. *Furlong* (1962) 40 TC 313. In 1961 the Revenue made special arrangements for credit traders: see *Simon's Direct Tax Service* above at n. 43, Pt. B3, 1151 *ff.*

[46] [1944] 1 All ER 642, 26 TC 1669.

[47] ESC B38; Inland Revenue Press Release, 11 April 1991, (1991) *Simon's Tax Intelligence* 395.

[48] [1944] 1 All ER 642, 26 TC 166.

[49] Because of TA 1988, s. 103.

Lord Atkin, in *Absalom* v. *Talbot*, preferred the inclusion of the debts at their face value on one side of the account, and a reserve on the other which would be calculated on the ordinary risk of bad debts, but adjusted annually to take account of actual payments made or not made. Such a reserve would not be prohibited by s. 74(j) because that section applies only to debts correctly brought in at face value.

23.2.3 Payment in advance—relating forward?

It ought to follow from the matching principle that where a payment is received in advance that sum should enter the account only when the service has been rendered or the goods supplied. A case supporting this is *Symons* v. *Weeks*,[50] but that decision may best be seen as one based on strong accounting evidence. Case-law on expenses[51] also recognises spreading forward on the basis of a possible accounting method. In the United States this spreading forward of a prepayment has been denounced as bad economics, bad accounting and bad tax.[52]

Older authority[53] holds that money belonging to the trader will be treated as a trading receipt when received (or due); this overrides the matching principle at least where the sum received is final and is a trading receipt, and may be taken as applying in the absence of accounting evidence. In *Elson* v. *Price's Tailors Ltd.*[54] customers ordering a made-to-measure garment would be asked for a deposit. These deposits were, as a matter of practice, returned to customers who did not like the finished goods but some clients did not return to claim their deposits. Before the Commissioners the taxpayer argued that the deposits should have become trading receipts only when the customer took delivery. The Crown argued for the date the deposits became forfeitable or, alternatively, when they were transferred to head office. Ungoed-Thomas J. held that the payments were truly deposits and not part payments and so were security for the completion of the purchase; the money therefore belonged to the taxpayer and the payments were trading receipts when received.

However, the judge went on to reject the argument that the relating back doctrine applied where the payment preceded the performance of the contract. This seems illogical. He applied the decision of the House of Lords in *Smart* v. *Lincolnshire Sugar Co. Ltd.*[55] where subsidies were paid by the Government to farmers subject to the proviso that these were to be reduced retrospectively if the market price rose. The House held that these were receipts in the year of receipt and not the year when the contingency of repayment ceased. Although the House was clearly right to hold that these were trading receipts, and it was open to the House to hold that the payments should be assigned to the year of receipt,[56] it does not follow that subsidies should be treated in the same way as payments for service. Moreover, in *Elson* v. *Price's Tailors* the Crown did not apparently argue for the year of receipt but only for the date the deposits were forfeitable. The point should therefore be regarded as open, espe-

[50] [1983] STC 195, 56 TC 630; see also *Arthur Murray (NSW) Pty Ltd.* v. *FCT* (1965) 114 CLR 314. On history of the Murray Dance Studios, see *The Economist*, 14 August 1999, 76.

[51] For example *Johnston* v. *Britannia Airways* [1994] STC 763, 67 TC 99.

[52] Johnson (1995) 50 *Tax Law Review* 373; note also Halperin (1985) 95 *Yale Law Journal* 516 arguing that the customer making the prepayment should be taxable on the interest that could be attributed to such a prepayment; and Klein (1994) 41 *UCLA LR* 1686.

[53] *Elson* v. *Price's Tailors Ltd.* [1963] 1 All ER 231, 40 TC 671.

[54] See above §21.8.

[55] [1937] 1 All ER 413, 20 TC 643.

[56] *Cf. Short Bros* v. *IRC* (1927) 12 TC 955, where payments for the cancellation of a shipbuilding contract were attributed to the year of cancellation and not the (later) years when the ships would have been built.

cially as far as part payments are concerned. This view is strengthened by the decision of the House of Lords in *Sun Insurance Office* v. *Clark*,[57] not cited by Ungoed-Thomas J. in *Elson* v. *Price's Tailors*, where premiums paid in advance for a year were not treated as income only of the year of receipt, but a proportion was to be carried forward to the following year.

23.2.4 Receipts in kind: timing governs quantum

The only difference between a payment in money and a payment in kind is that the value of the former is more obvious. Where, therefore, a trading receipt is received otherwise than in sterling, whether in foreign currency or in kind, a value must be put on the receipt at the time it becomes a trading receipt, i.e. when it is delivered or, if earlier, when it is due. Subsequent changes in value should be ignored.[58]

It is no objection to such valuation that the benefit in kind cannot, in fact, be converted into cash. In *Gold Coast Selection Trusts Ltd.* v. *Humphrey*[59] the trust had sold certain rights in a gold mine concession in exchange for shares in a company and was held taxable on the value of the shares so received, even though it would have been impossible to obtain a reasonable price for them if they had all been sold in one go on the Stock Exchange.

Where a dealing company receives shares, such shares will be valued as trading receipts only when they represent the end of a trading transaction, as opposed to a step in the course of a transaction.[60] There must, however, be some sort of realisation. In *Varty* v. *British South Africa Co.*,[61] by contrast, a company had an option to subscribe for shares in company C at par and decided to exercise that option. The court held that there was no realisation and so no taxable profit at the time. The question in all cases is one of fact and substance, but the *Varty* case appears to be the only reported instance involving securities where the court has held that there was no realisation. Therefore, even an exchange of shares under a company amalgamation scheme has constituted a realisation, as has the exchange of mortgage bonds against one company for debenture stock in a new one when the first company's finances were being restructured.[62] Even the exercise of an option in a government savings scheme to convert the holding into a new government stock was held to be a realisation.[63]

On this basis, where securities—the original holding—are held as circulating capital, trading receipts arise when they are disposed of and allowable expense on their reinvestment in the new holding. If, however, they are held as fixed capital, a form of rollover relief may apply, so postponing liability in respect of the resulting capital gain (see below at §42.4). To further the policy behind CGT relief, TA 1988, s. 473 provides that where that relief would apply if the assets were such that the proceeds of sale would not be trading receipts, then the original holding is not treated as disposed of and the new holding is treated as the same asset.

[57] [1912] AC 443, 6 TC 59.

[58] *Greig* v. *Ashton* [1956] 3 All ER 123, 36 TC 581.

[59] [1948] 2 All ER 379, 30 TC 209. See [1970] *BTR* 150.

[60] In *Royal Insurance Co. Ltd.* v. *Stephen* (1928) 14 TC 22, 28.

[61] [1965] 2 All ER 395, 42 TC 406.

[62] *Royal Insurance Co. Ltd.* v. *Stephen* (1928) 14 TC 22; *Scottish and Canadian General Investment Co. Ltd.* v. *Easson* (1922) 8 TC 265.

[63] *Westminster Bank Ltd.* v. *Osler* [1933] AC 139, 17 TC 381.

23.3 Expenses

In relation to expenses two sets of issues arise: the first is what to do with a liability which is not yet certain; the second is how to deal with a liability which has arisen but which needs to be entered into the accounts over more than one period of account (i.e. spread).

23.3.1 Contingent liabilities[64]

The question whether a deduction can be made for a contingent liability must be answered first by reference to sound principles of accountancy practice. Such evidence was not forthcoming in *Peter Merchant Ltd.* v. *Stedeford.*[65] The taxpayer ran a canteen for a factory owner and was under a contractual obligation to replace utensils. Owing to wartime scarcities, however, it was not possible to replace the utensils. The accountant recommended that the amounts owing under the liability to replace be deducted each year. However, he had committed an error of law by construing the contract to mean that there was a liability to replace the stock each year rather than at the end of the contract; it followed that deduction could not be allowed each year.

Accounting practice, as set out in FRS 12 and, therefore, applicable to tax law under FA 1998, s. 42, distinguishes liabilities for which provision must be made in the accounts (so giving rise to the deduction for tax purposes) from liabilities for which a note to the account suffices (for which no deduction will be made.) Provision *must* be made (a) if the entity has a present obligation as a result of a past event, (b) it is probable that a transfer or economic benefit will be required to settle the obligation and (c) a reliable estimate can be made of the amount of the obligation. Contingent liabilities, for which a mere note suffices and so have no tax consequences (as yet), are possible obligations arising from past events whose existence will be confirmed only by the occurrence of one or more uncertain future events not wholly within the entity's control, or present obligations arising from past events which are not recognised because it is not probable that a transfer of economic benefit will be required to settle it or the amounts cannot be measured with sufficient reliability. No provision should be made for merely contingent assets, i.e. a possible asset where the inflow of economic benefit is probable but not virtually certain. FRS 12 is a change in accounting practice, and certain cases in which evidence of old accounting practices led the courts to allow a deduction would now be decided differently.

Pre-1998 case where the court ruled against the deduction of a future liability—no change

Expenses are not deductible simply because the events giving rise to the need for that work have occurred. In *Naval Colliery Co. Ltd.* v. IRC[66] a company's mines were damaged during a strike which ended on 2 July 1921; no element for the costs of reconditioning the mine could be included for the period ending 30 June 1921. The same decision would be reached under FRS 12.

[64] See Thomas, *An Introduction to Financial Accounting* (McGraw Hill, 3rd ed. 1999), 366–8.
[65] (1948) 30 TC 496.
[66] (1928) 12 TC 1017.

Pre-1998 cases where the court allowed a deduction and where the same result follows under FRS 12

In *Herbert Smith* v. *Honour*[67] a firm of solicitors moved to a new office block which it leased. The firm was still liable to pay rent in respect of premises it no longer occupied, but the market was weak. The firm sought to deduct a sum in the year of the move to cover the expected shortfall between the sums it was still liable to pay and the sums it was liable to get back in rent on subleases. The 1990 forecast proved to be over-optimistic and further provisions had to be made in later years. The Revenue disputed the company's right to deduct the sum in 1990 insisting instead that only the actual shortfall accruing in 1990 should be deducted, on the basis that liabilities could not be anticipated. The Commissioners agreed with the Revenue, noting that the firm's method was not the only one which accountants could use. In the High Court the firm's appeal was allowed. The court held that the commercial principle of accounting should be accepted, and there was no rule of law against anticipating liabilities which prevented the court from accepting it. The Revenue accepted the decision and announced its acceptance of FRS 12 for future years.[68] The facts come within FRS 12 since the liability to pay the rent on the lease of the vacated premises had accrued.

Pre-1998 cases where the court allowed a deduction, but where FRS 12 may prohibit it

In *IRC* v. *Titaghur Jute Factory Co. Ltd.*[69] a foreign statute imposed an obligation on employers to pay gratuities to employees on leaving the company service. The amount depended on the final salary and the length of service, including years of service before the statute came into force. However, the statute did not require the company to set aside sums to meet this obligation. Taken literally, FRS 12 would disallow this deduction in that there was no present obligation arising out of a past event. Such an interpretation of FRS 12 would seem unduly restrictive; alternatively, FRS12 is itself perversely restrictive.

Similar problems arose in *Johnston* v. *Britannia Airways Ltd.*[70] Here the court allowed a company's major overhaul costs in respect of aero engines to be spread over the period of three or four years leading up to the overhaul. This decision depended on the recognition of the treatment as being in accordance with the then accepted principles of commercial accountancy, and followed the general approach to such questions taken in *Gallagher* v. *Jones.*[71] However, it is hard to see that there was any present obligation to overhaul the engines until the four-year period had expired.

Jenners Princes Street Edinburgh Ltd. v. *IRC*[72] was a decision before FRS 12, but following *Gallagher* v. *Jones.* The company was faced with a large repair expense. It had completed a feasibility study in year 1, and in year 2 had entered into a contract for the works to be carried out over a period covering years 2 and 3. The company sought to deduct the entire

[67] [1999] STC 173.

[68] Inland Revenue Press Release, 20 July 1999, *Simons Weekly Tax Intelligence* 1302.

[69] [1978] STC 166, 53 TC 675; see Edey [1956] *BTR* 1172 and Phillips [1957] *BTR* 351. See also the decision of Lush J., allowing the deduction of future expenses of maintaining graves, in *London Cemetery Co.* v. *Barnes* [1917] 2 KB 496, 7 TC 92.

[70] [1994] STC 763, 66 TC 77; for view that the case was explicable under the matching principle, see Macdonald [1995] *BTR* 484, dissented from by McMahon and Wheetman [1997] *BTR* 6.

[71] [1993] STC 537, 67 TC 99, CA; discussed in the two articles mentioned in ibid.

[72] [1997] STC (SCD) 196. On Revenue acceptance, see Inland Revenue Press Release, 20 July 1999, (1999) *Simon's Weekly Tax Intelligence* 1302.

expenditure costs in year 1 on the basis of established accounting principles. Surprisingly, the appeal succeeded; even more surprisingly, the Revenue acquiesced in this. The decision is inconsistent with old case-law, such as the *Naval Colliery* case (above). FRS 12 seems to prevent the company in such circumstances from any right to deduct the sum until year 2.

A case which may be relevant to condition (c) of FRS 12 (above) is *Southern Railway of Peru Ltd.* v. *Owen.*[73] This case also involved setting aside sums for future payments to employees on redundancy, retirement or death. The payments were to be of one month's salary for each completed year of service, the salary being computed according to the rates in force at the time of redundancy or other cause, with certain protection for employees whose salaries declined. No payments were due, however, if an employee on a fixed-term contract resigned before the term had expired, nor where an employee was dismissed for just cause.

The company argued that it should charge against each year's receipts the cost of making provision for the retirement benefits that it would ultimately have to pay, and conceded that, as a corollary, it would not be able to deduct the actual payments made each year. These figures were rejected by the House of Lords. It held, first, that the figures failed to take account of the length of time that would pass before the payments would become due (a factor which could be met by a discounting process), secondly that the company failed to recognise that the legislation which had created the present pension system could also vary it and, thirdly, that there was the possibility that a certain number of employees would forfeit their rights to payments. For these reasons the figure which the company was trying to deduct, although correctly deducted in order to give a "true and fair" view of the profits, and necessarily so for the purposes of the Companies Acts, was not sufficiently precise for the Income Tax Acts and so would not be allowed by FRS 12.

Many cases involve provisions under foreign legislation. Payments to UK-approved pension schemes are deductible under TA 1988 when they are made, i.e. when paid by the company to the pension scheme managers or trustees.[74] This is an example of a rule of law overriding an accounting principle.

23.3.2 Payments attributable to more than one year: spreading

In relation to payments attributable to more than one year, the question is the opposite of that governing contingent liabilities. The question is whether a payment which has been made can be taken as a deduction, or whether it must be spread forward. In 1993 the Court of Appeal, in *Gallagher* v. *Jones,*[75] held that the expenses must indeed be spread forward if accounting practice required it, and concluded that SSAP 21 did so require it. It followed that no rule of law could prevent the application of SSAP 21. The same result would now follow under FA 1998, s. 42. In *Gallagher* v. *Jones* the hirer had to make an initial payment of £14,561 and then 17 monthly payments of £2,080; thereafter, the rent was £35 a year for 21 years.

Before the introduction of FRS 12, SSAP 21 applied to finance leases, which were to be contrasted with operating leases. Under an operating lease the non-cancellable period was usually much less than the economic life of the asset and the lessor was at risk with regard

[73] [1956] 2 All ER 728, 36 TC 602; see [1986] *BTR* 4; and the decision of Lush J., allowing the deduction of future expenses of maintaining graves in *London Cemetery Co.* v. *Barnes* [1917] 2 KB 496, 7 TC 92.

[74] TA 1988, s. 592(4).

[75] [1993] STC 537, 66 TC 77, CA. For criticism see §21.1.

to the market value of the asset at the end of the lease. Under a finance lease these risks are shifted to the lessee; payment under the lease are much more closely related to the economic life of the asset.[76]

These developments left the earlier decision in *Vallambrosa Rubber Co. Ltd.* v. *Farmer*[77] in an uncertain state. In that case the company sought to deduct the costs of superintendence, weeding, and control of pests and similar expenditure on a rubber estate even though rubber trees take seven years to start producing rubber, and so only one in seven of the rubber trees was actually in production. The claim succeeded. The case itself was concerned mainly with the distinction between capital and revenue. It does not appear that the Crown argued that the expenses should have been allowed only when the trees began to produce. In *Gallagher* v. *Jones* the Court of Appeal said that the case did not lay down a broad principle.[78] Today it would seem that the accounting principle of prudence would require the deduction of such sums when they are incurred.

In *Gallagher* v. *Jones* the position concerned finance lease and SSAP 21. The Revenue had indicated in 1991 that they accepted SSAP 21 and that payments under finance leases were deductible for tax purposes as they were allocated under SSAP 21, and not simply by reference to the date they fell due.[79] The company failed in its claim to deduct sums paid under a finance lease as they were made. The lease provided for payments, during an initial period of 24 months, of a large initial payment, followed by 17 monthly instalments; in the secondary period which began after 24 months a nominal rent was due. The Revenue argued that the initial payment and the 17 monthly instalments should be spread evenly over the 24-month period as suggested in SSAP 21. Reversing Harman J., the Court of Appeal held that SSAP 21 should be followed. The uncontradicted evidence before the Commissioner given by an eminent accountant was that the taxpayers' simple approach would give a completely misleading picture of their trading results.

23.4 Post-Cessation Receipts and Expenses

23.4.1 Receipts[80]

Sums received after a discontinuance by a person who had previously carried on a trade, profession or vocation and relating to that trade were at one time not taxable. This was because they were received when the source no longer existed.

The problems: films and debts

Such (tax free) sums could arise even when the earnings basis had been properly applied at the discontinuance. Under the earnings basis any sum due appeared as a credit item in the final account so that at first sight no loss to the Revenue accrued. However, two problems arose. The first problem related to certain types of earnings which, because of their uncertain nature, could not be included in the profits figures until they took the shape of payments. One case concerned a percentage of film receipts paid to a film actor; and another

[76] On taxation of leasing, see Mainwaring, *Tolley's Leasing in the UK.*
[77] (1910) 5 TC 529.
[78] [1993] STC 537, 547f. 66 TC, 113, CA.
[79] Statement of Practice SP 3/91 (for leases entered into on or after 11 April 1991).
[80] See Heaton [1960] *BTR* 268; Monroe [1961] *BTR* 284.

royalty payments in respect of books.[81] The Revenue could not reopen the accounts since a best estimate of earnings had been made.

The second problem related to debts. A sum owed to a trader could, in the final account, have been written off as irrecoverable; a subsequent, unexpected payment would therefore escape tax.[82] Conversely, the final account might have included a debt the trader owed in respect of the trade, but the creditor might have released the debt after the discontinuance. These matters could not lead to the reopening of the accounts since the accounts were correct when submitted.

The legislative solution

Originally introduced in 1960, TA 1988, s. 103 made two changes to the earnings basis (and analogous amendments to the cash basis[83]). First, all sums received after[84] the discontinuance and arising from the carrying-on of the trade are chargeable provided their value was not brought into computing the profits of any period before the discontinuance. The charge arises under Schedule D, Case VI.[85]

Secondly, where a debt has been allowed in the computation of the profits of a trade since it was discontinued, and the whole or any part of the debt is later released, the amount released is treated as a sum received.[86] A covenant by the creditor not to sue, being analytically distinct from a release, might not cause a charge to tax, but decisions such as *McGuckian* suggest that too much reliance should not be placed on this. A release forming part of a voluntary arrangement under the Insolvency Act 1986 does not give rise to a trading receipt.[87]

Three exclusions

S. 103 does not apply to sums received by a person beneficially entitled to them who is not resident in the UK, provided the sums represent income arising from a country or territory outside the UK.[88] Also excluded are lump sums paid to the personal representatives of authors—but not the author themselves—of a work as consideration for the assignment by them of the copyright or public lending rights, wholly or in part.[89] Finally, sums received on the transfer of trading stock or work in progress are excluded to prevent an overlap with TA 1988, ss 100 and 101 and to avoid depriving the exceptions in those sections from any effect.

Cash basis

Cash basis taxpayers were also caught by s. 103. Subsequently, a more general provision under s.104 taxed all other post-cessation receipts except two of the payments also excluded

[81] *Stainers Executors* v. *Purchase* [1951] 2 All ER 1071, 32 TC 367; and *Carson* v. *Cheyney's Executors* [1958] 3 All ER 573, 38 TC 240; noted by Stanford [1959] *BTR* 72. If not originally received in the course of trade, the receipts would be, and would continue to be, taxable under Case III: *Mitchell* v. *Rosay* (1954) 35 TC 496, 502; the source would be the obligation, not the trade.

[82] The UK has no general doctrine that the cancellation of a debt gives rise to income; this is in part due to the Schedular system.

[83] TA 1988, s. 103(2)(b).

[84] Contrast *Symons* v. *Weeks* [1983] STC 195, 56 TC 630 where the sum was received before the discontinuance, but was not recognised as a trading receipt for accounting purposes until after the discontinuance.

[85] TA 1988, s. 103(1), (2)(a).

[86] Ibid., s. 103(4). This provision is not well drafted; it refers to the amount released when it presumably ought to refer to the release in respect of a debt "so far as allowed as a deduction (*Simpson* v. *Jones* [1968] 2 All ER 929, 936, 44 TC 599, 609, *per* Megarry J.).

[87] TA 1988, s. 103(4A), to TA 1988, s. 74(j).

[88] Ibid., s. 103(3).

[89] Thus preserving the immunity from tax in the *Haig* case (see below at §28.5).

from s. 103, i.e. sums paid to a non-resident representing income from outside the UK and lump sums paid to the personal representatives of an author in respect of copyright or public lending right.

Tax treatment

Any sum caught under s. 103 or 104 is treated as earned income.[90] The sum will usually be taxed by reference to the year of receipt but it may, at the option of the taxpayer or T's personal representative, be carried back to the date on which the discontinuance occurred.[91] The price for backdating is the loss of the right to claim any allowance or loss under s. 105.[92]

There is nothing in s. 103 or 104 requiring that the payment be made to the former trader. It is, however, provided by s. 106 that if the right to receive the payments caught by these sections is transferred, the sale proceeds are chargeable under Schedule D, Case VI. Where a trade is transferred and the transferee acquires the right to collect what would otherwise be post-cessation receipts of the former trader, no charge arises and the sums paid to the transferee are treated as the receipts of his trade as they are received.[93] Where the right to receive the payments is given away, it would appear that no tax can be charged under Schedule D, Case VI even if the payments are then made to a person connected with the former trader. Although ss 103 and 104 might leave this point open, it is suggested that s. 106 is needed only if there is, in general, no liability on the transferee.

23.4.2 Expenses and unused capital allowances

In calculating the sum to be charged, any expenses that could have been claimed if the trade had continued are deductible; a claim may also be made for any capital allowance to which T was entitled immediately before the discontinuance.[94] Further provisions allocate these sums where charges arise under TA 1988, ss 103 and 104 and for preventing double relief.

The above rules were limited to the extent that relief relief could be given only if provision had been made for expenses in the final accounts or there were chargeable post-cessation receipts against which they could be set.[95] The rules were relaxed by the addition of s. 109A by FA 1995:[96] the payment must be made within seven years of the discontinuance; relief is given not by being taken back to the final year of trading or by being set against post-cessation receipts only, but by being set against income of that year equal to the amount of the payment.

S. 109A relief related only to certain types of expenditure. The payments must have been made wholly and exclusively for the purposes specified and various related receipts must be brought into account. The categories include expenditure to remedy defective work done in the course of the former trade or profession by way of damages, (whether awarded by a court or agreed in negotiation on a claim), and legal or other professional expenses incurred in connection with claims for such expenditure, or insurance against the risk.

[90] TA 1988, s. 107.
[91] Ibid., s. 108.
[92] Ibid., s. 109.
[93] Ibid., s. 106(2). A (so far) unsucesful attempt to bring facts within s. 106(2) was made in *Brewin* v. *McVittie* [1999] STC (SCD) 5 where the Revenue used the *Ramsay* principle to argue that there had been no real change in the person carrying on the business.
[94] TA 1988, s. 105.
[95] See Inland Revenue interpretation RI 25.
[96] For expenses incurred after 29 November 1994 (FA 1995, s. 90).

Any sum received in meeting the costs incurred in collecting a debt already taken into account in computing the profits or gains of the former trade or profession must be set off. S. 109A also deals with the converse case of business debts due at the time of the discontinuance but which subsequently prove to be uncollectable. Although these now satisfy the terms of TA 1988, s. 74(j), no adjustment can be made to the final year's profits and the business is left nursing the unexpected loss. Under s. 109A a deduction can be made for the bad debt.[97]

23.5 Trading Stock (or Inventory) and Work in Progress

23.5.1 Disposal of trading stock: substitution of market value

In general, where trading stock is disposed of, the sum to be entered into the accounts will be the actual price realised on the disposal. If the goods have been given away, perhaps for reasons of advertisement, there will be no sum to be entered. Neither the Revenue nor the taxpayer is, in general, allowed to substitute a fair market price for that in fact obtained.[98] There are three exceptions to this rule: transfer pricing; *Watson* v. *Hornby*; and *Sharkey* v. *Wernher*. The third may simply be a development of the second.

Exception (1) Transfer-pricing

The first exception arises where one of the parties to a transaction was directly or indirectly participating in the management and control of capital of the other party, and the terms of the contract or other provision are not those which would have been made between independent persons.[99] This 1998 provision is discussed further at §61.3 below. This rule applies only if the "provision" would generate an advantage in relation to UK tax.[100] The definition of such an advantage excludes the provision where both parties are subject to UK tax in relation to it. The UK tax must be effective tax and so not prevented by an exemption from UK tax or the availability of a foreign tax credit or deduction.[101]

Exception (2) *Watson Bros* v. *Hornby*[102]

Where one trader has two distinct trades and transfers goods from one trade to the other, the transfer must be treated as a sale and purchase, not at cost, but at a reasonable price.[103] In *Watson Bros* v. *Hornby* the trader transferred stock from a trade taxed under Schedule D, Case I—that of chicken breeder and hatcher—to a farm which at that time was taxed under Schedule B. The court held that the sale should be at a reasonable price; as the market value was less than the cost of production the taxpayer succeeded in establishing a trading loss.

[97] TA 1988, s. 109A(5)—but with rules to protect the Revenue.

[98] *Craddock* v. *Zevo Finance Co. Ltd.* [1946] 1 All ER 523, 27 TC 267, 288.

[99] TA 1988, Sch. 28AA, para. 1. This superseded TA 1988, s. 770 which had originally appeared as FA 1951, s. 37, replacing General Rule 7 of ITA 1918 which had been confined to dealings between a resident and non-resident. See White [1979] *BTR* 35.

[100] TA 1988, Sch. 28AA, para. 1(2)(b).

[101] Ibid., Sch. 28AA, para. 5; see Inland Revenue Press Release, 2 July 1998, (1998) *Simons Tax Intelligence* 990.

[102] [1942] 2 All ER 506, 24 TC 506; see also *Long* v. *Belfield Poultry Products Ltd.* (1937) 21 TC 221.

[103] Sale of Goods Act 1893, s. 8. TA 1988, s. 770A, like s. 770 before it, applies only where there are two traders.

Exception (3) *Sharkey* v. *Wernher*[104]

The same principle of transfer at a reasonable price applies more broadly, i.e.when a trader disposes of trading stock otherwise than in the course of trade, for example when trading stock is withdrawn for personal consumption or use by the trader or any other person, unless the disposal is a genuine commercial transaction. The value entered in the books of the transferor is also entered in the books of any trader acquiring the stock.[105] A system which provided for no figure to be entered into the accounts by way of credit on the occasion of a self-supply would give the self-supplier a great tax advantage. In reading the cases it should be recalled that most of these transactions took place when there was no CGT.

In *Sharkey* v. *Wernher* Lady Zia Wernher carried on the business of a stud farm; she also rode horses for pleasure. She transferred a horse reared at the farm to her personal use and entered the costs incurred in respect of the horse until the date of its transfer as a credit item in the account of the stud farm; there was therefore no attempt to take tax advantage of the deductions she had already been allowed. The Revenue thus turned its defeat in *Watson Bros* v. *Hornby* to good use; she had to enter the horse at market value.

Objections

Exception (3) is subject to three technical objections,

(a) The profit alleged to be made comes from a course of dealing with oneself; it is precisely because this is alleged to be impossible that no charge to tax arises from mutual dealings. In reply, Viscount Simonds said that "the true proposition is not that a man cannot make a profit out of himself but that he cannot trade with himself",[106] a principle which was not to apply where trading stock was removed from the trade for a man's own use and enjoyment. However, this is not consistent with other formulations of the mutuality principle.

(b) The decision appears to conflict with the fundamental principle that a person is taxed on what is actually earned and not on what he might have earned. However, in *Sharkey* v. *Wernher* the taxpayer received value; the question therefore is the figure to be entered in the accounts. Lord Radcliffe rejected the idea of taking the cost figure on the grounds that market value "gives a fairer measure of assessable trading profit" and was "better economics".[107] A trader concerned with the profitability of the trade would find that "better book-keeping" would use market value. However, the issue is not what is good book-keeping but the correct basis for taxation. In this regard it may be noted that the cost figure was in conformity with then accepted accountancy practice[108] and the views of the Royal Commission.[109]

(c) It is said that if *Sharkey* v. *Wernher* was correctly decided there is no need for TA 1988, s. 770A or its predecessor, s. 770. There is little substance to this objection. It is now clear that *Sharkey* v. *Wernher* applies to transactions between different persons whether or

[104] [1955] 3 All ER 493, 36 TC 275.

[105] *Ridge Securities Ltd.* v. *IRC* [1964] 1 All ER 275, 44 TC 373. See Crump [1964] *BTR* 168. This means that the transferee gets the whole profit free of tax, but a double charge to tax is avoided; contrast *Skinner* v. *Berry Head Lands Ltd.* [1971] 1 All ER 222, 46 TC 377 when the transferee was fixed with the whole gain; noted by Nock [1971] *BTR* 189.

[106] [1955] 3 All ER 493, 496, 36 TC 275, 296.

[107] Ibid., 506, 307.

[108] See Lord Oaksey (dissenting); and Edey [1956] *BTR* 23, 34.

[109] Above at n. 4, §§489–90.

not one controls the other, so that its ambit is wider than these sections; further, it is also clear that a transaction may be at an undervalue and still outside *Sharkey* v. *Wernher*, so that s. 770A may apply. In addition, s. 770A applies to assets other than trading stock; it is not yet clear whether *Sharkey* v. *Wernher* does. To make matters better still for the Revenue, it appears that *Sharkey* v. *Wernher* can be used even though s. 770A is excluded.

The limits of the rule in *Sharkey* v. *Wernher*

The most serious criticism of the decision of the House of Lords is simply that of the uncertainty as to the scope of the notional income.

(a) It would appear first that the rule is confined to Schedule D. Thus, landlords who allow themselves to occupy one of their houses would not be treated as owing themselves an economic rent for the property chargeable under Schedule A. At one time this could be stated with some confidence. Since the reformulation of Schedule A, and its use of Schedule D principles in determining profit, this may, however, be less certain.

(b) It is not clear whether the rule applies to professions. In *Mason* v. *Innes*[110] the author, Hammond Innes, wrote a book called *The Doomed Oasis*. Shortly before completing the manuscript he assigned the copyright to his father by way of gift. It was agreed that the market value of the copyright at that date was £15,425. The rule in *Sharkey* v. *Wernher* was not applied. The effect in *Mason* v. *Innes* was that not only did the Revenue see its share of the copyright vanish, but it was still left bearing the loss of tax resulting from the deduction of expenses incurred by the author in the creation of the copyright. Lord Denning M.R., said that a professional man was different from a trader, and suggested that a picture painted by an artist was different from a horse produced on a stud farm. His Lordship's second reason was that this professional man was taxed on a cash basis, whereas a trader was taxed on an earnings basis, a distinction which ought to be irrelevant since it goes to calculating liability to tax rather than deciding what items should be taxable.[111] His Lordship's third reason was the set of anomalies that would result, notably in contrast with the rules which permitted spreading of copyright income and the taxation of post-cessation receipts, both of which provisions must have been passed on the basis that notional sales could not arise from the transfer of the copyright.[112] On the other hand, the area is full of anomalies anyway. A more convincing reason for the decision of the Court of Appeal is given by Potter:[113]

> "the whole point of *Sharkey* v. *Wernher* was that some figure had to be entered in the trading account because an item of trading stock that stood in that account at cost was taken out. An author does not however enter his copyrights in his professional account. He does not deal in copyrights. His earnings are in essence fees for services, not proceeds of sale of assets. He pays tax on what he receives or is entitled to receive, no account being taken of opening or closing stock."

On this basis *Mason* v. *Innes* was correctly decided, but it may mean a closer examination of the boundary between a profession and a trade. Thus, an artist who sells his

[110] [1967] 2 All ER 926, 44 TC 326; criticised by Pickering [1967] *BTR* 76 and 209. Assignments of copyright may fall within TA 1988, s. 775 (see below at §57.7) and may also be subject to CGT and IHT.

[111] See, however, Russell L.J. in *Mason* v. *Innes* 44 TC 326, 341.

[112] TA 1988, ss 534, 104.

[113] [1964] *BTR* 438, 442.

own pictures might be regarded as carrying on the profession of an artist and the trade of a picture dealer. In this event the value of the paintings will be entered into his trading account at their then market value. However while Potter's suggestion is convincing, it may also be obsolete. As a result of FA 1998, s. 42, professional persons are required to bring the value of work in progress into their accounts; work in progress leads to copyrights.

(c) *Mason* v. *Innes* may mean that the rule applies only to dispositions of trading stock[114] and so does not extend to other items in the trade. Thus, the disposal of an agency at an undervalue would not be a disposal of trading stock nor would the private papers transferred in *Wain* v. *Cameron.*[114a] If this is correct, there will be analogous exclusions for the assets of a profession.

(d) The rule does not apply to a sale at a fairly negotiated price. In *Jacgilden (Weston Hall) Ltd.* v. *Castle*[115] a property developer acquired the right to buy a hotel for £72,000. He later transferred that right to a company for £72,000, although at the time the hotel was worth £150,000. The company then sold the hotel for £155,000. The company sought to have the hotel entered into the books of the company at its market price as opposed to the actual cost price—and failed. There was no question of the contract for sale being an illusory, colourable or fraudulent transaction; it was a perfectly straightforward and honest bargain between the developer and the company.

(e) The rule may not apply to a transfer on discontinuance to one carrying on a trade in the UK and in whose accounts the cost of the stock transferred will appear as a revenue deduction.[116] The statutory rule in TA 1988, s. 100 may here exclude *Sharkey* v. *Wernher.*

23.5.2 End of year valuations

The value of trading stock unsold at the end of one period is entered into the account of that period as a receipt and into the account of the next period as an expense; it is thus sold from one year to the next. The figure entered is cost or market value—whichever is the lower.[117] The effect is that losses may be anticipated, but not profit—an example of the sound conservative accounting principle of prudence.

Income tax is charged on the profit of the trade over a particular period, usually the accounting year of the business. The true profit for the period—ignoring overheads—is not simply sums for goods sold received minus sums spent, but sums received for goods sold minus sums spent on those goods. Thus, suppose that R, a retailer, sells shoes. In the first year R spends £100,000 on shoes, and sells half of them for £100,000. In the second year R sells the other half for £100,000, but buys no more stock. On a naive view the profit for the first year was nil, but for the second year £100,000; this would give a very distorted view of the profitability of R's business. Hence, the rule takes £50,000 (the cost of the unsold trading stock) as a receipt for the first year and an expense of the second. Over the two-year

[114] See Russell L.J. in *Mason* v. *Innes* 44 TC 326, 341.

[114a] [1995] STC 555. See above §19.1.4.

[115] [1969] 3 All ER 1110, 45 TC 685. In *Julius Bendit Ltd.* v. *IRC* (1945) 27 TC 44 the test seems to have been whether the deal was a bona fide trading transaction (which it was); the same result was reached in *Craddock* v. *Zevo Finance Co. Ltd.* [1944] 1 All ER 566, 27 TC 267. These cases might be decided differently today, but the principle which they represent is probably sound.

[116] *Moore* v. *R. J. MacKenzie & Sons Ltd.* [1972] 2 All ER 549, 48 TC 196; noted by Nelson [1972] BTR 118.

[117] *Whimster & Co.* v. *IRC* (1926) 12 TC 813.

period the naive view and the correct view produce the same total profit. They differ in the methods of determining the profit of a particular artificial period during the life of the business. This rule can also be seen in the context of matching; it ensures that the receipts from the second year sales are matched with the purchase costs of the shoes then sold.

In valuing stock the taxpayer may use any method which gives a true and fair view on an accounting basis subject to any adujstment required or authorised by law. Earlier Revenue practice was similar.[118]

Trading stock

The first problem is to decide the range of assets to which the valuation should apply. In the case of manufacturing the term "trading stock" covers raw materials, finished stock and work in progress (on which see below at §23.5.3); therefore it does not cover capital assets. Stock not yet delivered is not yet trading stock.[119] Similarly, a loss on the hiring of ships on time charter could not be anticipated by the invocation of this rule,[120] since such charters are not trading stock. Whether losses other than on trading stock can be anticipated is another matter; today, the new reliance on FRS 12 may allow the deduction of such losses.

Which stock is it?

The next problem is to determine what trading stock is to be valued. While a small shoe shop may be able to determine precisely which shoes were sold at the end of the year, it is less practicable to expect an oil distributor to be able to say how many litres of oil it has in stock at the end of work on the last day of the accounting period, and there is in fact no obligation on it to measure the stock at the end of that day before resuming business. The Revenue appears content to rely on an annual stocktaking, with any necessary adjustments.

The cost of the goods is complicated if the goods are fungibles, and prices alter in the course of the trading period. Three principal types of formulae are used by accountants. The first, which is the one generally accepted for tax purposes, is "first in, first out" (FIFO), i.e. last in, still there. If prices are rising this means using the cheaper stock first, so that the cost of the goods sold is low. The stock remaining at the end of the year, a plus item in the accounts, will therefore be the more expensive items. The FIFO system has the advantage that the closing stock will be valued at the more recent prices so that, depending on the rapidity of turnover and the rate of price change, it will be valued at a figure more or less close to replacement cost. FIFO has, however, the converse disadvantage that it matches past costs with current receipts and thus, in an era of inflation, an over-optimistic picture of profitability. This led to the introduction of stock relief, which applied from 1975 to 1984.

The second formula, which was rejected for tax purposes by the Privy Council in *Minister of National Revenue* v. *Anaconda American Brass Ltd.*[121] is the opposite of the first, i.e. last

[118] Statement of Practice SP 3/90. See also Inland Revenue interpretation RI 98 On change of method, see below p. 445. Statement of Practice SP 3/90 has now been superseded by Inland Revenue Press Release, 20 July 1999, (1999) *Simons Weekly Tax Intelligence* 1302.

[119] *Edwards Collins & Sons Ltd.* v. *IRC* (1925) 12 TC 773. In *Willingale* v. *International Commercial Bank Ltd.* there was no suggestion that the bills were trading stock; otherwise, the Revenue would have won.

[120] *Whimster & Co.* v. *IRC* (1926) 12 TC 813; and see *Scottish Investment Trust Co.* v. *Forbes* (1893) 3 TC 231; and *Lions Ltd.* v. *Gosford Furnishing Co. and IRC* (1961) 40 TC 256 (future hiring receipts not stock in trade); on which, see Silberrad[1962] *BTR* 119.

[121] [1956] AC 85, [1956] 1 All ER 20; see criticism by Edey [1956] *BTR* 23 and Harris, April Conference of Canadian Tax Foundation (1967), 93, 95. See also Eldridge (1953) 6 *National Tax Jo.* 52; Barron (1959) 12 *National Tax Jo.* 367; and Phillips (1960) 13 *National Tax Jo.* 383. The company made cogent, if self-interested, submissions to the Canadian Royal Commission (on file at the Canadian Tax Foundation in Toronto).

in, first out (LIFO). LIFO is common practice in the United States and is permitted under the Companies Act;[122] however, its use is discouraged by SSAP 9 and by the Revenue.

The third formula —the weighted average—is a compromise. This looks at the different prices paid for the stock over the period and weights the price according to the quantity of stock bought at each price.

The different methods of determining the stock to be valued yield different results and so different profit figures for each accounting period. However, over the lifetime of the business all three methods will give the same figure of profits if applied consistently, since the same total amount will have been spent on stock and received on sales, and any remaining stock is valued under TA 1988, ss 100 and 102. Aberrations will occur where there is a change in the method of valuing stock during the lifetime of the trade. For tax purposes, there will also be the same total profit to be taxed, although different tax rates and, for individuals, the complexities of overlap profits and overlap relief mean that the total tax charged may vary according to the method chosen.

Cost

The cost is that at the original acquisition. Expenses incurred in keeping the goods in good condition are ignored;[123] these expenses properly belong to the time they were incurred since their value will not be recouped subsequently.

Market value

Market value means net realisable value, and not replacement cost. Thus, where a retail shoe shop values trading stock, the correct figure for market value should be the normal retail price, rather than the price the shop would have to pay wholesale to replace that stock. On the other hand, if the trade were that of a wholesale supplier of shoes, the figure would be that which the trader would receive on a wholesale disposal.

In *BSC Footwear Ltd.* v. *Ridgway*[124] the House of Lords held that a retail shoe shop should value unsold stock by reference to the value to be expected in a sale and with a deduction for the salesperson's commission, but without any allowance for the general expenses of the business for later periods of account. Therefore, no deduction could be made for the normal retail mark-up. As Lord Pearson put it:[125]

> "The correct principle is that goods should not be written down below cost price unless there really is a loss actual or prospective. So long as the fall in prevailing prices is only such as to reduce the prospective profit the initial valuation at cost should be retained."

The formula applied

In applying the formula—cost or market value, whichever is the lower—each item may be treated separately so that one may be valued at cost and another at market value.[126] This is consistent with the idea of anticipating losses but not profits. Where stock is acquired by gift the receipt is treated as being at market value.[127] When the transfer falls within the rule in

122 Thomas, *An Introduction to Financial Accounting* (McGraw Hill, 1999), 166.

123 *Ryan* v. *Asia Mill Ltd.* (1951) 32 TC 275, 298, *per* Lord Reid.

124 [1971] 2 All ER 534, 47 TC 511; noted by Clarke [1970] *BTR* 65 (CA) and [1971] *BTR* 318 (HL) See also criticism by Cope 4 *Journal of Business Finance* 98.

125 [1971] 2 All ER 534, 550, 47 TC 511, 540.

126 *IRC* v. *Cock Russell & Co. Ltd.* [1949] 2 All ER 889, 29 TC 387.

127 See per Lord Greene M.R. in *Craddock* v. *Zevo Finance Co. Ltd.* [1944] 1 All ER 566, 27 TC 267.

Sharkey v. *Wernher*, the value at which the transferor is taken to dispose of it is taken as the acquisition cost to the transferee.

Change of method

The same method must be used at the end of the year as was used at the beginning.[128] However, the method used at the opening of the second period need not be the same as that used at the closing of the first period. Where such change occurs there will be either a double charge or no charge at all on the difference between the closing stock of the first period and the opening stock of the second.[129]

Land developer: ground rents and rentcharges

Where a builder (X) grants a house purchaser a long lease but charges both a premium and a ground rent, there is no outright disposal of X's interest in the land.[130] X's previous freehold interest is now subject to the lease. It follows that the reversion is still part of X's stock and must be entered at cost or market value, whichever is the lower.[131] The cost of the reversion must include that part of the cost which is the building cost. The formula to ascertain that part is A/A+B, where A is the market value of the reversion (traditionally a multiple of the rental) and B is the premium.[132]

A very different situation arises if X reserves a rentcharge,[133] chief rent or, in Scotland, a ground annual.[134] The House of Lords has held that there is a realisation of the interest in land for money (the price) and money's worth (the rent). The market value of the rentcharge must therefore be entered as a trading receipt in the year of sale; the rent is also treated as a trading receipt when it falls due. On the other hand, the eventual disposal of the land will not give rise to a trading receipt unless the court holds that there is a trade of dealing in rentcharges.

23.5.3 Work in progress

Where the trader is a manufacturer and there is work in progress at the end of the accounting period, the value of that work in progress must be brought into account . Under current accounting practice, SSAP 9 directs that the costs should cover the employees' time up to the balance sheet date, plus attributable overheads. If the contract is a long-term contract, the provisions of SSAP 22, which was applied in *Symons* v. *Weeks* or any superseding accounting principles, should be observed.

It is often difficult to determine cost. In *Duple Motor Bodies* v. *Ostime*[135] the company made motor bodies and had, since 1924, used the "direct cost" of ascertaining the cost of the work in progress, meaning that only the cost of materials used and labour directly employed

[128] *Steel Barrel Co. Ltd.* v. *Osborne No. 2* (1948) 30 TC 387.

[129] Although the Revenue will not agree to a change without good reason, it does not seem to insist upon consistency in its own conduct: see, e.g. *Ostime* v. *Duple Motor Bodies Ltd.*, n. 135 below, and *BSC Footwear Ltd.* v. *Ridgway* [1971] 2 All ER 534, 47 TC 511.

[130] *B. G. Utting & Co. Ltd.* v. *Hughes* [1940] 2 All ER 76, 23 TC 174.

[131] *Heather* v. *G. and A. Redfern and Sons* (1944) 26 TC 119.

[132] See case stated in *J. Emery & Sons Ltd.* v. IRC [1937] AC 91, 20 TC 213, 219.

[133] *Broadbridge* v. *Beattie* (1944) 26 TC 63.

[134] *J Emery & Sons Ltd.* v. *IRC* [1937] AC 91, 20 TC 213.

[135] [1961] 2 All ER 167, 39 TC 537.

in the manufacture were included. This gave a loss of £2,000. The Revenue argued that the cost should have been computed on the "on-cost basis", meaning that there should also have been included the proportion of overhead expenditure, with the effect that the profits for the year would have increased, since the deductible expenses would have been offset by the extra item on the credit side of the balance sheet. This gave an extra profit figure of £14,000. This would have the odd result that if work were slack, so that the same quantity of overheads would have to be spread over fewer items, the "cost" of the work in progress would be increased, so that while the company's receipts dropped, its taxable profits in respect of work in progress would be increased. The accountancy profession was divided on the issue of which method should be adopted. The House of Lords held that the Revenue had failed to show that the "direct cost" was wrong, especially in this case where it had been used for so long, and dismissed the Revenue's appeal. It declined to lay down any general principle—the real question was what method best fitted the circumstances of the particular business.

A question the courts have found difficult is whether the trader can anticipate a loss in respect of work in progress. The market value of work in progress is difficult to assess since the work, as such, is unsaleable, a point agreed on the facts in *Duple Motor Bodies* v. *Ostime*. Where, however, it is clear that a loss will be incurred when the work is completed, there seems to be no way in which that loss can be anticipated, although in *Duple Motor* Lord Reid said that there must be some way of doing it.[136] SSAP 9 now allows the deduction of provisions for irrecoverable charges.

Change of valuation basis

Where a firm changes its basis of valuation the strict position is that this may result in an extra profit which would have accrued during earlier years if the new system had been in operation. Such extra profits are taxable in the year in which they accrue, which is the year in which they are revealed, and are not backdated.[137] However, Revenue practice now distinguishes valid bases of valuation, i.e. bases accepted by the accountancy profession, from invalid bases. Where a change is made from one valid basis to another the opening stock figure must remain the same as the closing figure for the previous period. Therefore, whether the change results in a higher or lower opening figure, the Revenue will neither allow a tax-free uplift nor seek to tax the business arguing that the opening and closing figures in the year of change must be on the same basis.[138] A change from a non-valid basis to a valid basis is also likely to receive indulgent treatment—provided there is no question of fraud or negligence.

Catch up charge on change of accounting basis

FA1998, s. 42 requires all taxpayers under Schedule D, Cases I and II to report their income on an accounting basis which gives a true and fair view of the profits. Certain professions taxable under Schedule D, Case II have previously adopted different bases. Any relevant accounting rules, such as SSAP 9 and SSAP 22, must therefore be observed.

Accounts for 1999–00 will have been drawn up in line with the new accounting principles. However, accounts for 1998–99 will have been drawn up on the old-fashioned basis,

[136] Ibid., 572. This valuation would have avoided the problem in the case since the market value of a half-finished coach is probably less than the cost.

[137] *Pearce* v. *Woodall-Durkhon Ltd.* [1978] STC 372, [1978] 2 All ER 793; criticised by Chopin [1978] *BTR* 313. See also Statement of Practice SP 3/91, para. 3; see also paras 7–9 on long-term contracts. On "repeal" see above n. 118.

[138] Statement of Practice SP 3/91, para. 4.

e.g. cash basis. This means that while no figure will have been entered in 1998–99 for work in progress, etc., a very large figure may have been entered for 1999–00 because the closing figure for 1998–99 will also have been the opening figure for 1999–00. In order to give relief the difference between the two is not taxed at once in 1999–00. Instead, the adjustment charge[139] is spread over 10 years. In each of the nine years beginning with 1999–00 taxable profits are increased by 1/10 of the adjustment charge or, if less, 1/10 of the total profits of that year. In the tenth year, any remaining adjustment is brought into charge.[140] If the business ends before the end of year 10, any remaining charge is brought in immediately.

The taxpayer may elect to bring forward any part of the amount to be brought into charge.[141] This may be advantageous if the taxpayer had a loss in that year, or if the extra could be used in some other way, such as increasing allowable contributions to a personal pension scheme.

23.5.4 Valuation of trading stock on discontinuance

Three rules

When a trade has been discontinued the general rule, rule (a), is that stock is entered at market value.[142] However, under rule (b), the sale price is preferred where the stock is sold, etc., to a person who carries on, or intends to carry on, a trade in the UK provided the cost will enter that person's trading income.[143] However, rule (b) could lead to manipulation, so that, if the parties are connected, the price to be taken is that which would have been obtained in a transaction between independent persons dealing at arm's length; this is rule (c).[144]

Exceptions to rule (c)

Rule (b) is preferred to rule (c) if the stock consists of debts of overseas governments or parts of a production herd.[145] Probably of greater importance is the provision under which rule (b) may also still apply by election of the parties if the figure given under rule (c) exceeds both the price paid by the purchaser and the "acquisition value" of the stock.[146] The acquisition value is the most that would be taken into account for the purposes of assessing its cost if there had been an open market sale.[147] The point of this exception is to allow the parties to avoid the charge on unrealised profits which would otherwise arise.[148] Whatever figure emerges from these rules is then taken as the cost of the stock to the purchaser.[149]

The purpose of TA 1988, s. 100 is to prevent a person from discontinuing business, bringing trading stock into account at cost value and then reselling it at the higher market value, so securing a large gain free of income tax, as nearly happened in *J. & R. O'Kane & Co. Ltd.*

[139] Defined in FA 1998, Sch. 6, para. 3.

[140] Ibid., Sch. 6, para. 4.

[141] Ibid., Sch. 6, para. 5.

[142] TA 1988, s. 100(l)(b).

[143] Ibid., s. 100(IA), added by FA 1995, s. 140; see [1995] *BTR* 254. See *Moore* v. *R. J. Mackenzie & Sons Ltd.* [1972] 2 All ER 549, 48 TC 196 (above at n. 116). Trading stock is defined in s. 137(4).

[144] TA 1988, s. 100(lA)(b), added by FA 1995, s. 140 for discontinuance after 25 November 1994; for definition of connected persons, see s. 100(IF).

[145] TA 1988, s. 100(IB).

[146] Ibid., s. 100(IC).

[147] TA 1988, s. 100(ID).

[148] Inland Revenue Press Release, 29 November 1994, (1994) *Simon's Tax Intelligence* 1479.

[149] TA 1988, s. 100(IE).

v. *IRC.*[150] S. 100 applies whenever a trade is discontinued. However, perhaps because it is an anti-avoidance provision it does not apply where a trade carried on by a single individual is discontinued by reason of death.[151] The market value will, however, be taken for IHT.

Similar rules apply to work in progress at the discontinuance of a profession. The phrase "the amount that would have been paid for a transfer as between parties at arm's length" is substituted for "market value". Where this amount exceeds the actual cost of the work, the taxpayer may elect to pay no tax now but have any sums actually received later taxed as post-cessation receipts under TA 1988, s. 103.[152]

[150] (1922) 12 TC 303.
[151] TA 1988, s. 102(2).
[152] Ibid., s. 101(2); on post-cessation receipts, see above §23.4.

24

Capital Allowances

24.1 Introduction

24.1.1 The problem

Expenses incurred in the acquisition of a capital asset are not deductible in computing the profits of a trade.[1] If the asset has a limited life, its value to the business will decline. The causes of this decline may be physical, such as wear and tear on plant and machinery, or economic, such as obsolescence or a change in trading policy. The decline causes the cost of the asset to become an expense to the company for accounting purposes; the capital has been

[1] See above §22.5 and *Coltness Iron Co.* v. *Black* (1881) 6 App Cas 315, 1 TC 311.

consumed. Depreciation is deductible for accounting purposes, but no provision was originally made for tax purposes, perhaps because income tax was thought to be only temporary.

The UK tax system has relaxed this strict approach by making allowances for certain capital expenditure, including the capital allowance system. When claimed, capital allowances displace the deductibility of expenditure on renewals.[2] The structure of the present system goes back to the Income Tax Act 1945, which defined certain types of capital expenditure qualifying for allowances, and specified different rates of allowance. Broadly speaking, the list is the same today, although there have been changes in the way in which the allowances are made. The legislation is now consolidated in the Capital Allowances Act 1990.

24.1.2 History[3]

The first statutory allowance was granted in 1878 "as representing the diminished value by reason of wear and tear during the year" of plant and machinery used in a trade. This allowance was held not to extend to obsolescence, a matter changed by concession in 1897 and by statute in 1918. Also in 1918 special depreciation allowances were made to mills, factories and other similar premises,[4] on the basis that the vibrations from the machinery might weaken the building. The Royal Commission of 1920 considered, but rejected, any general scheme of capital allowances.

The Income Tax Act 1945 took a wider view; the basic structure remains in place today. It defined those types of capital expenditure which qualified for allowances; many did not—and still do not—qualify. Apart from allowances for plant and machinery, all allowances were confined to income taxable under Schedule D, Case I (some clearly to particular trades), and did not extend to Schedule D, Case II or Schedule E. A few allowances applied to Schedule A, which were widened by FA 1997.[5]

24.1.3 Accelerated allowances

For many years the tax system enshrined the belief that tax allowances encouraged investment. Hence, elaborate allowances were given to allow the writing-off of capital expenditure far ahead of any real depreciation or obsolescence. However, legislation in 1984 and 1985 reduced the rates of allowances, making them closer to actual depreciation, and compensated for this by reducing the rate of corporation tax. This has not prevented Parliament from reviving specially enhanced allowances from time to time. Those who believe that adjusting allowance affects the overall level of investment point to the fact that capital investment by UK businesses is a lower percentage of GNP than spending by either consumers or governments; it is also much more volatile.[6]

[2] See above at §22.4(9) (p. 412).

[3] On history, see Royal Commission on the Taxation of Profits and Income, *Final Report*, Cmnd 9474 (1955), §§308–26; Richardson Committee on Turnover Taxation, Cmnd. 2300 (1964) ch. 6; and Edwards [1976] *BTR* 300.

[4] Still to be found in CAA 1990, s. 18(1)(a).

[5] See below at §25.2.3 (CAA 1990, s. 28A); see also ibid., s. 29 (furnished holiday lettings).

[6] See below at §24.12.2.

24.2 Elements

24.2.1 *Three types of allowance*

The UK system uses three types of allowance:[7]

(1) an initial or first year allowance[8] of a substantial percentage of the capital expenditure, only a few of which are currently available;
(2) a writing down allowance during the life of the asset, which clearly does not apply if the 100% initial allowance has been used.
(3) a balancing allowance or charge at the end of the trade or the life of the asset.

The third technique is designed to bring the allowances into line with actual expense. If the amount so far allowed is less than the amount spent, an extra or "balancing" allowance is permitted. If, however, the allowance exceeds the expense, a sum is imposed by way of "balancing charge" to recapture that part of the allowance which was not needed. The charge recovers only the amount that has been allowed, any excess being a matter for CGT. There is no provision whereby the balancing charge may be spread over the number of years for which the allowance was claimed. Therefore, the tax charged may exceed the tax saved through the allowance. Today, a balancing charge is treated as a trading receipt.[9]

Example

A buys an asset for £1,000 and has claimed £500 allowances when selling it for (a) £600; (b) £450; (c) £1,200. In (a) there is a balancing charge of £100; in (b) there is a balancing allowance of £50; and in (c) there is a balancing charge of £500 the remaining £200 being left to CGT.

The current rates of allowance are set out in the table, over.

24.2.2 *Incurring capital expenditure*

Capital expenditure excludes any sums allowable as deductions in computing the profits or gains of the trade, profession or employment carried on by the person incurring the expense.[10] This boundary is not precise.[11] No allowance can be claimed for sums reimbursed by others if those others can obtain capital allowances or a deduction in computing profits[12] or for subsidies from public or local authorities, save for certain grants under the

[7] In 1954 an investment allowance was introduced, which was, in effect, a tax-free subsidy. It did not reduce the depreciable cost of the asset for other allowances, nor was it taken into account for the purpose of any balancing allowance or charge. See, further, Cmnd 9667. It was abolished in 1966, FA 1966, s. 35.

[8] The difference is that an initial allowance and a writing down allowance can be claimed in the first year; however a first year allowance and a writing down allowance cannot both be claimed in the first year.

[9] CAA 1990, s. 140(2) added by FA 1994. In *IRC* v. *Wood Bros (Birkenhead) Ltd.* [1959] AC 487, 38 TC 275 the House of Lords held that the balancing charge was not income of the company for the purpose of the then surtax direction. This was reversed for the apportionment of the income of close companies under the 1965 scheme.

[10] CAA 1990, s. 159(1).

[11] For example *Rose & Co. (Wallpaper and Paints)* v. *Campbell* [1968] 1 All ER 405, 44 TC 500 (pattern books of current wallpaper stock not capital expenditure).

[12] CAA 1990, s. 153(2), (3).

	First year	Initial	Writing down
Industrial buildings	—	20%(T1)	4% SL
Hotels	—	20%(T1)	4% SL
Assured tenancies	—	—	4%(O) SL
Industrial and commercial buildings in enterprise zones			
	—	100%	25% SL
Machinery and plant	40%(T)	—	25% RB
long life	—	—	6% RB
Mines/oil wells	—	—	25% or 10% RB
Dredging	—	—	4% SL
Agriculture, forestry buildings and works	20%(T)		4% SL
Research and development			
(ex Scientific research)	100%	—	—
Patents	—	—	25% RB
Knowhow	—	—	25% RB
Ships	Free depreciation (a)		
ICT (small enterprise)	40% (T2)	—	25% RB

T1 = temporary (1992–1993). T2 = temporary (2000–03). (O) = obsolete, not applicable to expenditure after March 1992.
SL = straight line reduction of percentage of initial expenditure. RB = Reducing balance reduction of percentage of previous balance.

Industry Acts and the Industrial Development Act 1982.[13] Provision is, however, made for allowances for contributions to the capital expenditure of others.[14]

Not finance

The capital expenditure must have been incurred on the construction of the building or the provision of the machinery and plant, etc; sums spent on the provision of finance do not qualify. In *Ben-Odeco Ltd.* v. *Powlson*[15] the taxpayer was going to carry on a trade of hiring out an oil rig. In order to finance the construction of the rig, it had to borrow money, and for this had to pay commitment fees (£59,002) and interest (£435,988). These sums were charged to capital (correctly) in the company's accounts. However, the House of Lords held that the sums were spent not on the provision of machinery and plant but on the provision of money and so did not qualify for capital allowances. This case was distinguished in *Van Arkadie* v. *Sterling Coated Materials Ltd.*[16] where the extra (sterling) cost of a price to be paid by instalments but in foreign currency was treated as allowable expenditure. It was critical in this case that the contract provided for payment to be made by instalments; a different conclusion would have been reached if the contract had provided for a single payment which had been made with the aid of a loan from a bank which the purchaser then paid off in instalments.

When incurred?

Two rules apply. The first looks at the date on which the obligation to pay becomes unconditional.[17] Where the purchaser acquires title before the obligation becomes unconditional,

[13] CAA 1990, ss 153, 154, amended by FA 1990, Sch. 13, para. 5; and see *Birmingham Corpn* v. *Barnes* [1935] AC 292, 19 TC 195. For an exception to s. 153, see FA 1990, s. 126(4) (payments to football clubs out of reduced betting duty). See also ESC B 49 for repayment of grant by taxpayer.
[14] CAA 1990, s. 154; see also s. 155.
[15] [1978] STC 460, [1978] 2 All ER 1111.
[16] [1983] STC 95.
[17] CAA 1990, s. 159(3); see also Inland Revenue interpretation RI 54.

the expenditure will be treated as incurred in the period in which title passed, provided the obligation becomes unconditional not more than one month after the end of that period.[18] This rule is excluded if an expenditure is deemed to be delayed; for example, capital expenditure incurred before a trade is commenced is deemed incurred on the day of commencement.[19]

The second rule applies the date to the date on which the expenditure became payable.[20] It applies where the due date for payment is more than four months after the obligation to pay has become unconditional.

The first rule is a recent relatively change; previously only the second rule applied. The reason behind this change was to bring the capital allowance rules into line with accountancy practice (which takes this date as the one on which title normally passes). The difference is that an obligation to pay may have become unconditional even though the sum does not have to be paid until a later date,[21] here the due date for payment is taken. The rules on timing also include an anti-avoidance rule which applies where the obligation to pay becomes unconditional on a date earlier than that which accords with normal commercial usage, and the sole or main benefit to be derived is the obtaining of the allowance.[22]

A special case—non-recourse finance

Under a non-recourse finance arrangement the lender does not seek repayment from the borrower personally but is content with some other source, e.g. from the stream of income from the asset. Such loans are common in extraction industries, where the bank is content to be repaid from the stream of money flowing from the ore extracted. However, such arrangements have also been used in tax avoidance schemes. The present status of expenditure financed by non-recourse loans is unclear following the opaque speech of Lord Templeman in *Ensign Tankers (Leasing) Ltd.* v. *Stokes*.[23] In principle, as Millett J. had held at first instance, the fact that a borrower who obtains a non-recourse loan incurs no personal liability to repay the lender ought to be irrelevant; the capital allowance legislation is concerned with the taxpayer's ability to spend it in acquiring the asset, not with the taxpayer's liability to repay the lender.[24] In the House of Lords Lord Goff explained that the non-recourse nature of the loan was only one of the elements which enabled him to conclude that this expenditure had not been incurred by the taxpayer; other factors included the fact that the lender was L, the US film producer company, that the money was paid into a special bank account opened at a bank nominated by L, and that when the money was paid in by L an identical sum was repaid by the taxpayer to L out of the same account on the same day. On such facts Lord Goff found it impossible to conclude that the money paid into the account by L was in any meaningful sense a loan; the payment was simply money paid in as the first step in a tax avoidance scheme.[25] Lord Templeman, however, with whom all the other judges agreed, stated that:[26]

18 CAA 1990, s. 159(4).
19 Ibid., s. 159(8).
20 Ibid., s. 82(3).
21 Ibid., s. 159(5).
22 Ibid., s.159(6).
23 [1992] STC 226, 64 TC 617, HL (see above at §5.6.4); on US experience, see Shaviro (1989) 43 *Tax Law Review* 401.
24 [1989] STC 705, 769, 64 TC 617, 705.
25 [1992] STC 226, 246, 64 TC 617, 747–8.
26 Ibid., 233, 733.

"by reason of the non-recourse provision of the loan agreement the loan was not repayable by [the taxpayer] or anyone else. A creditor who receives a participation in profits in addition to the repayment of his loan is of course a creditor. But a creditor who receives a participation in profits instead of the repayment of his loan is not a creditor. The language of the document in the latter case does not accurately describe the true legal effect of the transaction which is a capital investment by the "creditor" in return for a participation in profits."

After mentioning the views of Millett J., Lord Templeman went on to set out the type of facts which Lord Goff had stressed. The result is that it is unclear whether non-recourse finance never works, or whether it fails only in circumstances such as those in *Ensign Tankers.*[27]

24.2.3 Giving effect to allowance

Capital allowances are given effect either in taxing the trade or by discharge or remission of tax.[28]

Taxing the trade—expenses

Where the allowance is given effect in taxing the trade, it is treated as a trading expense for the period of account to which it relates; similarly, a balancing charge is treated as a trading receipt.[29] Therefore, the correct profits figure will be profit less capital allowances, and any excess allowances will automatically generate a trading loss. Claims for allowances are made in the tax return.[30] Any Schedule A business is taxed in the same way.[31]

The allowance is "treated as" a trading expense rather than being an expense. Hence, a taxpayer is under no obligation to take allowances available but has a discretion whether or not to take them.[32] In relation to non-resident companies, rules direct the separation of sources subject to income tax from those subject to corporation tax.[33]

Allowances are computed by reference to qualifying expenditure and disposals in each period of account.[34] Since allowances are given on an annual basis they will be increased or reduced if the chargeable period is greater or less than 12 months. The concept of the chargeable period has replaced the old concept of the basis period.[35]

The "chargeable period" is the accounting period of a company or the period of account of someone liable to income tax.[36] Where the allowance is made in taxing the trade, the period of account is usually any period for which accounts are made up for the purposes of the trade.[37] Where, as in the opening two years, two periods of account overlap, the period common to both is deemed to fall in the first period of account only. If there is an interval

[27] For Revenue treatment of "security" arrangements in relation to the special allowances for films, see Statement of Practice SP 1/98, paras 66–68.

[28] I.e. under CAA 1990, s. 140(2) or 141. Difficult problems arose in the days of the preceding year of assessment where an allowance was at risk of being given twice or not at all except under special rules.

[29] CAA 1990, s. 140(2), substituted by FA 1994, s. 211. For scientific research allowances, see s. 140(5); on widening definition of trade to include toll road undertaking, see s. 140(6).

[30] CAA 1990, s. 140(3), substituted by FA 1994, s. 211; so TMA 1970, s. 42 does not apply. For self-assessment and corporation tax, see FA 1998, Sch. 18, Pt. IX.

[31] CAA 1990, ss 9(1A), (1B) and 28A, as amended and added by FA 1995, Sch. 6, paras 8, 29. See below at §25.2.

[32] *Elliss* v. *BP Oil Northern Ireland Refinery Ltd.* [1987] STC 52, 59 TC 474, CA.

[33] CAA 1990, s. 149.

[34] Defined in ibid., s. 160, as amended FA 1994.

[35] See CAA 1990, s. 160 original version.

[36] Ibid., s. 161(2), as amended by FA 1994.

[37] CAA 1990, s. 160(2), substituted by FA 1994, s. 212.

between two periods of account, the interval is deemed to be part of the first period of account.[38] In this way the allowance—or charge—is given only once. Any period of account greater than 18 months is subdivided; the first subdivision begins with the commencement date of the original period, and later subdivisions are set at 12-month intervals.[39] Any net loss is given effect as an ordinary trading loss and so set off against general income under TA 1988, s. 380 or 381, or rolled forward against future profits under s. 385 (see above at §20.10)

Allowances given by repayment

Other allowances, where there is no available trade, e.g. for agricultural buildings, are given effect by discharge or repayment of tax on the appropriate income.[40] Other examples are allowances for investment and insurance companies.[41] Any excess is carried forward to the income of the same class in succeeding years. Any balancing charge is made under Schedule D, Case VI.[42] Where the allowance does not fall to be given for the trade, profession, vocation or employment, the period of account is the year of assessment.[43]

Capital allowance or revenue expense—distinctions

It is worth setting out the ways in which a capital allowance differs from a deductible expense as follows:

(1) the allowance must be an item of capital expenditure as distinct from revenue;
(2) whereas a revenue expense is deductible unless statute otherwise directs, a capital allowance is only made if the statute permits;
(3) whereas an allowance may be claimed in respect of expenditure incurred before a trade commences (although only when the trading begins[44]), an expense so incurred is deductible only if it is incurred within seven years of the trade beginning (see above §20.6);
(4) an expense incurred partly for trade and partly for other purposes is not deductible, whereas such duality results in an apportionment of capital expenditure;[45]
(5) a revenue expense is deductible at once and in full, whereas allowances are made only at specified rates and often over several years;
(6) a revenue expense must be taken into account at the proper time, whereas there is no obligation to claim a capital allowance

24.2.4 Amounts: Price or market value?

Sales between connected persons?

The amount of a balancing charge or allowance clearly depends upon the amount received. Normally, the actual sale price is taken. However, market value is taken if the buyer is a body

[38] CAA 1990, s. 160(3), (6), substituted by FA 1994.
[39] CAA 1990, s. 160(4), substituted by FA 1994.
[40] CAA 1990, s. 141; on the trade of leasing, see below at §24.4.4. S. 141 was simplified when self-assessment was introduced. On agricultural buildings see s. 132(2).
[41] TA 1988, ss 75, 76; see CAA 1990, s. 28.
[42] For example CAA 1990, ss 9(6), 15(2).
[43] Ibid., s. 160(5) substituted by FA 1994.
[44] CAA 1990, s. 1(10).
[45] For example *G. H. Chambers (Northiam Farms) Ltd.* v. *Watmough* [1956] 3 All ER 485, 36 TC 711 where an extravagant choice of motor car for personal reasons led to a reduction in the allowance.

of persons[46] over whom the seller has control,[47] or vice versa, or both buyer and seller are under the control of some other person.[48] This is to allow the transfer of the property between such connected persons in such a way that no balancing adjustment is necessary. This election is available only when capital allowances and charges can be made on both parties.[49] The election must be made within two years of the sale.[50] The election is not open to a dual resident investment company.[51] The election cannot be made if it appears that the sole or main benefit which might have been expected to accrue was the obtaining of an allowance or deduction.

Market value is also taken whenever it appears that the sole or main benefit which might have been expected to accrue was the obtaining of an allowance or deduction.[52] No election is possible here.

Machinery and plant have their own more complex regime.[53] Know how has its own provision.[54]

Apportionment of proceeds

Special rules apply when the sale involves an asset in respect of which allowances have been claimed and another asset. The net proceeds of sale are apportioned and the Commissioners are not bound by any apportionment made by the parties.[55]

Discontinuance and Deferrals: succession to trades

In general, where a trader (T1) discontinues a trade, a balancing charge or allowance is made. Any capital allowances still unused cannot be carried forward if one trade ends and another one begins.[56] If the trade is transferred to another (T2), T2 may be able to claim allowances in respect of its own capital expenditure including that in respect of items bought from T1; that expenditure may give rise to balancing charges or allowances to T1. Machinery and plant have their own rules. [57] The rules do not apply to hotels or assured tenancies.

A similar deferral election on the transfer of a trade is made where one party is resident in one member state of the EC and the other in another member state.[58]

Market value is also used on certain deemed discontinuances under TA 1988, ss 113 and 337. The new traders are entitled to allowances as if they had acquired the assets at market price,[59] although they are not entitled to initial, as opposed to writing down and first year allowances. Curiously, perhaps, these rules do not apply to research and development allowances.[60]

46 Defined in TA 1988, s. 832(1).
47 Defined in CAA 1990, s. 161(2).
48 Defined in ibid., ss 157, 158, and TA 1988, s. 839. Allowances under CAA 1990, Pt. V are excluded (s.158(5)).
49 Ibid., s. 158(3)(a), as amended by FA 1993.
50 CAA 1990, s. 158(4).
51 Ibid., s.158(3)(b).(See below at §58.6).
52 Ibid., s. 157(1)(b); see *Barclays Mercantile Industrial Finance Ltd.* v. *Melluish* [1990] STC 314, 63 TC 95.
53 CAA 1990, ss 75–76B (see below at §24.4.7) and s. 157(5).
54 TA 1988, ss 531(7), 532(5)(b).
55 CAA 1990, s. 150; e.g. *Fitton* v. *Gilders and Heaton* (1955) 36 TC 233; *A. Wood & Co. Ltd.* v. *Provan* (1968) 44 TC 701.
56 See above at §20.8 and below at §47.2.
57 CAA 1990, ss 77, 78.
58 Ibid., s. 152B, added by F (No. 2) A 1992, s. 67.
59 CAA 1990, s. 152.
60 Ibid., s. 152(1), (3) excludes Part VII.

24.2.5 *Choice of allowances*

A capital expense may fall within more than one category of allowance. In the absence of any express provision the taxpayer can choose the most favourable category.[61]

24.3 Industrial Buildings

24.3.1 *General*

Structure of allowances

Initial allowances may be claimed where a person incurs capital expenditure on the construction of an industrial building or structure which is to be occupied for the purposes of a trade.[62] If the building is to be occupied by a lessee or licensee it is the occupier's trade that is relevant. [63] The conditions for the (much more important) writing down allowance require that the person is entitled to an interest in the building or structure, that that interest is a "relevant" interest and that the building is an industrial building at the end of the relevant period.[64]

Allowances are confined to the expenses of construction; the cost of the land is excluded.[65] The costs of certain preliminary works, such as cutting, levelling and tunnelling, may be claimed only if the works are carried out in order to prepare the land for the installation of machinery or plant.[66] The costs of repairs are allowed as if they were construction costs unless they are deductible as revenue expenses. If a building is improved or altered, the costs of that work are treated as a separate subject for allowances.[67]

24.3.2 *Definition of industrial buildings*

The allowance may only be claimed if the building is an industrial building or structure, which is elaborately defined in CAA 1990, s. 18 and increasingly litigated. It is fair to say that the courts, taking their lead from some narrow legislation, have taken a consistently restrictive view of what can come within s. 18. The general effect of the definition is to confine allowances to productive, as opposed to distributive, industries. It is not necessary that the building be constructed in this country, and foreign plantations are expressly mentioned and defined; however, the profits or gains of the foreign trade must be assessable under Schedule D, Case I and not Case V.[68]

[61] Ibid., s. 147

[62] Ibid., s. 1.

[63] Ibid., s. 1(4) and see Statement of Practice SP 4/80 (separate lettings of workshops for small businesses).

[64] Ibid., s. 3.

[65] Ibid., s. 21; on VAT note ss 1(A) and 3 (2A)–(2C), added by FA 1991.

[66] Ibid., s. 13. "Cutting" received a narrow construction in *McIntosh* v. *Manchester Corpn* [1952] 2 All ER 444, 33 TC 428.

[67] CAA 1990, s. 12.

[68] Ibid., s.18(13).

Certain trades

A building in use for the purposes of a trade carried on in a mill, factory or other similar premises is an industrial building, as is a building for the purposes of a trade which consists in the taking and catching of fish or shellfish.[69] Various other trades are specified.[70] A building is a factory only if something is made there; as such, a repair depot normally cannot qualify.[71]

Manufacturing or processing

The building will also qualify if it used for the manufacturing or processing of goods or materials, or subjecting goods or materials to any process.[72] "Goods" means merchandise, rather than simply chattels. In *Buckingham* v. *Securitas Properties Ltd.*[73] a security firm constructed a special area in which bulk coins and notes were broken down into individual wage packets. The court held that the notes and coins were not "goods"; if they had been goods the court would have held that they were not being "subjected to any process". A similar approach was adopted in *Girobank plc* v. *Clarke*[74] where a document or data processing centre did not qualify. In *Bestway Holdings Ltd.* v. *Luff*[75] the court held that goods were not subjected to a process where they were checked and packaged as part of a cash and carry warehouse operation. A building used for the maintenance or repair of goods will qualify if the goods or materials are employed in a trade or undertaking which itself qualifies.[76]

Storage etc.

The building will also qualify as an industrial building if it is used for the storage[77] of goods which are to be used for manufacturing or processing or which having been manufactured or processed awaits delivery to a customer. It will also qualify for the storage of goods on arrival by any means of transport in any part of this country from outside. The word "storage" has been held to indicate that the category was confined to buildings in the vicinity of an airport or seaport and to facilities needed in the ordinary process of physically transporting goods (so not extending to quarantine kennels).[78] Stockists can claim allowances provided they carry on the trade of storing goods.[79] The test is whether the building is used

[69] CAA 1990, s.18(1)(a), (f); a private road built on industrial estate may also qualify (s. 18(8)).

[70] Ibid., s. 18(1) generally.

[71] *Vibroplant Ltd.* v. *Holland* [1982] STC 164, 54 TC 658.

[72] CAA 1990, s. 18(1)(e), (3). For a macabre case, see *Bourne* v. *Norwich Crematorium Ltd.* [1967] 2 All ER 576, 44 TC 164; this expenditure would seem now to qualify as plant (*IRC* v. *Barclay, Curle & Co. Ltd.*[1969] 1 All ER 732, 45 TC 221 (see below at §24.4.4)).

[73] [1980] STC 166, 53 TC 292.

[74] [1998] STC 182, CA. It is unclear whether the Court of Appeal thought that the assets were "subjected to a process"; Nourse L.J. expressed no opinion.

[75] [1998] STC 357; see Salter [1999] *BTR* 189; see also Revenue Bulletin December 1999 and Tiley and Collison §8.13.

[76] CAA 1990, s. 18(3). This would not have helped in the *Vibroplant* case (see note 71 above) since the trade of plant hire would not qualify under CAA 1990, s. 18(1).

[77] See *Dale* v. *Johnson Bros* (1951) 32 TC 487.

[78] *Copol Clothing Co. Ltd.* v. *Hindmarch* [1984] STC 33, [1984] 1 WLR 411, CA; see Marsh [1984] *BTR* 124; and *Carr* v. *Sayer* [1992] STC 396where the provision was confined to facilities needed in the ordinary process of physically transporting goods and so did not extend to quarantine kennels.

[79] This will be the case even where the stockist does not subject the materials to the industrial process himself; see *Crusabridge Investments Ltd.* v. *Casings International Ltd.* (1979) 54 TC 246 (a case concerning an action for breach of a covenant in a lease in which the term "industrial building" was held to cover a warehouse used for the storage of tyres before they were sold for remoulding); and Inland Revenue Press Release, 26 March 1982, (1982) *Simon's Tax Intelligence* 145.

for the purposes of a trade which consists in the storage of qualifying goods, and not whether the building is used for the storage of such goods. An allowance can therefore be claimed for a building even though it is also used in part for the storage of other goods.[80]

Exclusions

S. 18 specifically excludes any building used as, or as part of, a dwelling-house, retail shop, showroom, hotel or office and of any building ancillary to the purposes of those excluded.[81] In determining what is an office, the courts have not been blinded by terminology. Thus, a drawing office is no more an office than a machine shop is a shop.[82] A commissioner's finding that a document and data processing centre was not an office was held by the Court of Appeal to be one which he was entitled to reach.[83] In this context, "ancillary" means "subservient" or "subordinate". Buildings which are warehouses used exclusively to receive and store goods, and then distribute those goods for retail sales in a group's retail shops, clearly come within that subordinate role and so cannot attract allowances.[84] However, the result may be different if the building is used to serve not only the taxpayers' retail shops, but also a wholesale business for other customers.[85]

Extensions

An office built in a designated enterprise zone qualifies for special 100% initial allowances, together with 25% writing down allowances as appropriate.[86] The allowance is extended to the provision of sports pavilions[87] whether or not the trade falls within the qualifying list. Expenditure on safety at sports grounds may qualify for the more generous machinery and plant allowance.[88]

Parts of buildings

If only part of a building qualifies for an allowance, an apportionment is made. However, the whole cost is allowed where the cost of the qualifying part is 75% or more of the total cost.[89] This raises the difficult problem of defining a building. If a building includes an office, the cost of which is less than 25%, an allowance is made in respect of the whole cost. If, however, the office is a separate building, no allowance can be made even though its cost is 25% or less of the total cost of the building. Separate blocks which are not physically integrated do not form one building.[90]

Example

30% of the area of a factory building is used as a showroom, and the capital expenditure on the showroom area is 20% of the total. The expenditure on the showroom is less than 25% of the total cost, so no apportionment is necessary.

[80] *Saxone Lilley and Skinner (Holdings) Ltd.* v. *IRC* [1967] 1 All ER 756, 44 TC 122.

[81] CAA 1990, s. 18(4).

[82] *IRC* v. *Lambhill Ironworks Ltd.* (1950) 31 TC 393 (where the office qualified because of its essentially industrial character).

[83] *Girobank plc* v. *Clarke* [1998] STC 182; see Morgan [1998] *BTR* 517.

[84] *Sarsfield* v. *Dixons Group plc* [1998] STC 938.

[85] *Kilmarnock Equitable Cooperate Society Ltd.* v. *IRC* (1966) 42 TC 675; distinguished in the *Dixon* case. See Hughes [1980] *BTR* 459.

[86] CAA 1990, s. 1; on entreprise zones in general, see Watson, *Tolleys Tax Planning 1999–2000*, 497.

[87] CAA 1990, s. 14; and see *Simon's Direct Tax Service*, Pt. B2.310

[88] See CAA 1990, s. 70.

[89] Ibid., s. 18(7); this raises nice questions if the building contains machinery which is affixed to the floor.

[90] *Abbott Laboratories Ltd.* v. *Carmody* [1968] 2 All ER 879, 44 TC 569.

24.3.3 *The relevant interest—who can claim the allowances?*

The concept of "relevant interest" is central to almost all aspects of buildings allowance. Although not relevant to the initial allowance—which is claimed by the person who incurs the cost of the building—writing down and balancing allowances may be claimed only by the person with the relevant interest.[91] On a sale of the relevant interest the purchaser may be entitled to further allowances and the vendor to a balancing charge.[92]

The "relevant interest" means the interest in that building to which the person, O, who incurred the expenditure, was entitled when it was incurred.[93] So, if a lessee, L, spends money improving property, L can claim the allowance—but L's landlord cannot. If O, the owner of the freehold, incurs the expense and later leases the building to someone else, O may use the allowances as part of his Schedule A business;[94] it is, however, essential that the lessee use the building for qualifying purposes.[95] A person entitled to a highway concession in respect of a toll road is treated as having an interest in the road and that interest can be a relevant interest.[96]

Election

The rigid insistence on tying the right to the allowance to the relevant interest would be inefficient in circumstances where, for example, a pension fund (which pays no tax and which therefore cannot make use of the allowances) wishes to finance the construction of a building which would then be used by a tenant under a long lease. Therefore, where a long lease is granted, and both lessor and lessee so elect, the lessee may claim the allowances even though the expenditure was incurred by the lessor. The mechanism for this change is that the newly created lease is designated the relevant interest in place of the reversionary interest.[97] The same applies where a long sub-lease is created out of a lease. Any capital sum paid by the lessee (or sub-lessee) becomes the sum in respect of which the allowance can be claimed. It follows that the grant of such a lease may cause a balancing allowance or charge to accrue to the lessor. A long lease is defined as one exceeding 50 years.[98]

No election

The election may not be made where lessor and lessee are connected persons.[99] The election is also excluded if it appears that the sole or main benefit which might be expected to accrue is the obtaining of a balancing *allowance*.[100] It appears that the sole object of obtaining a balancing *charge*, perhaps to soak up other reliefs, does not prevent the rule from operating.

Initial allowance

If the building has not been used before the lease is granted, the lessee may claim not only the writing down allowance but also any initial allowance. This is of particular importance

91 CAA 1990, s. 3(1)(c). On the situation where the expense is shared, see CAA 1990, s. 154.
92 Ibid., s. 10.
93 Ibid., s. 20.
94 Under ibid., ss 9, 141, 145 (corporation tax).
95 Ibid., ss 1, 3.
96 Ibid., ss 3(5), 20(5), (6); on definition, see s. 21(5AA) added by FA 1995.
97 CAA 1990, s. 11. Claims must be made within two years of the date the lease takes effect (s. 11(3)).
98 The rules in TA 1988, s. 34 are used (see below at §25.5.1); CAA 1990, s. 16(5) is ignored (s. 11(4)).
99 Ibid., s. 11(6)(a); TA 1988, s. 839.
100 CAA 1990, s. 11(6)(b), TA 1988, s. 839. See *Barclays Mercantile Industrial Finance Ltd.* v. *Melluish* [1990] STC 314, 63 TC 95.

where the lessor is an exempt person, such as a local authority or charity, since it is only the lessee who will have taxable income against which to set the allowance.

Lease ends: allowance continues

If the relevant interest is a lease, the holder of that interest may still claim the allowance even after the lease has ended, if there is a holding over with the consent of the landlord, or a new lease is taken in pursuance of an option in the first lease.[101] Where the lease is surrendered and so becomes merged in another interest, that other interest becomes the relevant interest so that the right to the allowance is not lost[102]—similarly if the lessee acquires the reversionary interest. This scheme does not apply where the new lease is granted to the original lessee otherwise than under a right in the original lease. In such circumstances a balancing allowance or charge cannot be avoided.

If the relevant interest is a lease and the lease ends but the landlord pays the lessee a sum, e.g. for improvements carried out by the lessee, the lease is treated as if it had been surrendered.[103] If the landlord grants a new lease to a different person and the new lessee pays a sum to the first lessee, the leases are treated as one and the same so that the new lessee has the "relevant interest".[104]

Licence not lease

A licence is particularly useful for those starting up small workshops and businesses, since the obligations of a licensee are normally less onerous than those of a lessee—an important consideration if cash problems are an issue. Previously, where industrial property was only occupied by someone (S) for the purposes of S's trade under a licence, S had no property interest and could not therefore claim any industrial buildings allowances. The legislation was therefore extended to cover licensees. Today, where an owner, O, or a lessee, L, grants a licence to S, S's interest is treated as if it is subject to a lease, thus allowing S to claim the allowances.[105] Claims for allowances can also be made where the premises are occupied by more than one licensee provided the licensees are carrying on industrial businesses.[106]

24.3.4 Initial allowances

Initial allowances have been repealed, save for expenditure incurred where the site of the building is in an enterprise zone, provided it was incurred not more than 10 years after the site was first included.[107] The rate of allowance is 100%, reduces to 75% for certain regional development expenditure.[108] Since the enterprise zone rules are designed to stimulate development in these zones, they apply only to expenditure incurred during the first 10 years of the zone's life. Allowances are available not only for industrial buildings and hotels,[109] but also for all other commercial buildings used for trading or professional purposes—other than dwelling houses.

[101] CAA 1990, s. 16(4), (5).
[102] Ibid., s. 20(3).
[103] Ibid., s. 16(6).
[104] Ibid., s. 16(7).
[105] Ibid., s. 1(4).
[106] Ibid., s. 18(6).
[107] Ibid., s. 1(1).
[108] Ibid., s. 2.
[109] Qualifying hotels in enterprise zones are still entitled to the enterprise zone allowance (FA 1990, Sch. 13, para. 1); on entreprise zones generally, see Watson, *Tolleys Tax Planning 1999–2000*, 497.

Further provisions are designed to ensure that the purchaser of a building buying it after the expiry of the 10-year period but before the building is brought into use is entitled to the initial allowance.[110] Similarly, where buildings are sold once within two years of being brought into use there is a balancing charge or allowance on the seller.[111] These allowances are available only for expenditure incurred within the first 10-year period.[112] If expenditure is contracted for while the building is in the enterprise zone, provided it is incurred within 10 years of that expiry, i.e. 20 years after the site first became part of an enterprise zone,[113] CAA 1990, s. 158 applies[114] to allow for a temporary reintroduction of initial allowances for capital expenditure on industrial buildings for a period of one year beginning 1 November 1992. CAA 1990, s. 1, the general provision for initial allowances, was modified by a new CAA 1990, s.2A.[115] The rate of allowance was 20%.

24.3.5 The writing down allowance

Writing down allowances are available to the person entitled to the relevant interest in the building, provided the building was used as "an industrial building" at the end of the chargeable period.[116] The allowance is 4% of the cost for a full year but this is to be reduced or increased if the chargeable period is less or more than 12 months.[117] Allowances are available during periods of temporary disuse.[118] In a straightforward case, without any such breaks, the expense will have been written off after 25 years.

24.3.6 Balancing allowance and charge

A balancing allowance or charge arises if, within 25 years of the building being first used, the relevant interest is sold, or the building is demolished, destroyed or ceases to be used altogether.[119] No allowance or charge arises merely because the building ceases to be used for the purpose of a qualifying trade, although an adjustment will be made on a subsequent sale or demolition, etc.[120] In the meantime the writing down allowance ceases unless the cessation of use is purely temporary.[121]

A balance is also struck if, within 25 years of the building being first used, the relevant interest ends and is not deemed to continue[122]—as where the interest merges in the reversionary interest—or where the relevant interest depends upon a foreign concession which ends.

[110] CAA 1990, s. 10A added by F (No. 2) A 1992. See Inland Revenue Press Release, 16 December 1991, (1992) *Simon's Tax Intelligence* 5.

[111] CAA 1990, s. 10B, added by F (No. 2) A 1992.

[112] CAA 1990, ss. 10A(1)(b), 10B(1)(b).

[113] Ibid., s. 17A, added by F (No. 2) A 1992; on entreprise zones generally, see Watson, above at n. 109, 497.

[114] CAA 1990, s. 158(2)(a), as amended by FA 1993.

[115] Added by FA 1993, s. 113; other modifications were the exclusion of CAA 1990, s. 17A (which bars expenditure incurred more than 20 years after designation of an enterprise zone).

[116] CAA 1990, s. 3(1).

[117] Ibid., s. 3(2), amended by FA 1994.

[118] CAA 1990, s. 15.

[119] Ibid., s. 4(2). On balancing charge after cessation of trade, see ESC B19 (1994).

[120] Ibid., s. 4(5)–(9).

[121] Ibid., s. 8(7).

[122] Ibid., s. 4(1).

The residue of expenditure

The charge or allowance depends upon the "residue of expenditure" which is the original cost minus the allowances made[123] (whether initial or writing down). It is seen more simply, but less precisely, as the residue of unrelieved expenditure. This residue is set against any sale, insurance compensation or salvage monies.[124] Where the residue is greater than those sums, the difference is the subject of the balancing allowance; where it is less, the difference is the subject of the balancing charge, subject to the rule that the charge may not exceed the allowances made.[125] In making these calculations any periods during which the relevant interest was held by the Crown, or by someone outside the charge to UK tax, are treated as if any allowances that could have been claimed by an ordinary taxpayer had been claimed.[126]

Example 1

V's building cost £100,000 in year 1, but is destroyed in year 13. The total allowances will be £52,000 (13 years at 4%), making a residue of expenditure of £48,000. If compensation amounts to £40,000, there will be a balancing allowance of £8,000 to bring the total allowances in line with total expenditure. If the compensation is £60,000, there will be a balancing charge of £12,000.

If the building was not used for a qualifying trade throughout the period, the balancing adjustment must reflect this fact. Allowances or charges are made by reference to the adjusted net cost of the building, which is the excess of capital expenditure over the proceeds, reduced in the proportion that the period of qualifying use bears to the whole period.

Example 2

An industrial building was constructed for £25,000. It was used for a qualifying purpose for two years, then as an office (a non-qualifying purpose) for one year and then reverted to a qualifying use for the fourth year. The building is sold at the end of year 5 for £17,000. The balancing adjustment is calculated as follows: (1) calculate the net cost of the building to the taxpayer (£8,000) then the proportion of that figure which is attributable to qualifying use (£6,400, i.e. 4/5 × £8,000); (2) Calculate the allowances given (£5,000, or 5 years at £1,000 a year) and deduct the net cost applicable to the qualifying use (£6,400). This gives a balancing allowance of 1,400 (£6,400 − £5,000).

The purchaser

The purchaser, P, is entitled to an allowance provided the building is used by P for a qualifying purpose. P is entitled to a writing down allowance based on the residue of expenditure, i.e. the remaining unrelieved expenditure of P's vendor, *plus* any balancing charge (or minus a balancing allowance).[127] This sum is spread evenly over the remaining 25-year period, and is in no way tied to a 4% figure. Therefore, if, in Example 1 above, the building

[123] Ibid., s. 8; scientific research allowances are taken into account (FA 1990, Sch. 13, para. 2). Any initial allowance for the additional VAT liability under the capital goods scheme is treated as written off when the liability is incurred (CAA 1990, s. 8(2), as substituted by FA 1991). On rebates, see CAA 1990, s. 8(12A). S. 8 was amended for the new system of allowances for income tax by FA 1994.

[124] Defined in CAA 1990, s. 156.

[125] Ibid., s. 9.

[126] Ibid., ss 15, 16, and note amendment of s. 8(13)(d) by FA 1994.

[127] Ibid., s. 3(3). On relief when vendor's expense was on revenue account, see s. 10(4), (5).

had been sold for £40,000, V would have been given a balancing allowance of £8,000. P could then have spread the £40,000 over the 12 years of the 25 years remaining. This means that P's £40,000 would be written off at the rate of £3,333 p.a., as opposed to V's £4,000 . If the building had been sold for £100,000, V would have had a balancing charge of £52,000 and P would have written off the £100,000 over 12 years making £8,333 a year.

It also follows that if the sale took place after the 25 years had expired, V would get no balancing charge and P would get no allowance at all. The sharp contrasts for both parties—between a disposal after 24 years and 364 days and one three days later—are striking; whether they are sensible is a very different matter.[128]

Minor matters

The residue of expenditure is calculated by taking account of any reliefs that could have been claimed, but were not because the relevant interest was held by the Crown or by an exempt person.[129] This is important whenever the building is sold for less than its original cost. On a sale between connected persons who elect for the building to be transferred at its written down value, the residue of expenditure is carried through to the purchaser, save where there is a tax avoidance motive, in which case market value is taken.[130]

Building not land

Special rules clarify the sum paid on the sale of a relevant interest.[131] Since the allowance is intended to cover the element of the price paid for the building, the value of the land must be deducted, and any value attributable to elements over and above those which would feature in a normal commercial lease must be negotiated in the open market. This is achieved by describing any of the elements as arrangements having an artificial effect on pricing, and then directing that the amount of the price paid which is attributable to such arrangements be deducted.[132]

24.3.7 Other buildings

Hotel buildings and extensions

Hotels do not qualify for the general industrial buildings allowances since they do not come within the list of trades permitted. However, an annual writing down allowance of 4% is available, calculated on a straight line basis.[133] Subsequent holders of the relevant interest may write off the residue of the expenditure over the balance of the 25-year period.[134] A person buying a qualifying hotel unused is treated as having incurred expenditure on its construction when the purchase price becomes payable.[135] The hotel must be a "qualifying hotel", a concept which is elaborately defined.[136] The hotel may be outside the UK but the

[128] Thus, if the parties try to avoid a sale within the period by the device of a lease plus an option to buy after the 25-year period has expired, they run the risk of any premium for the lease being treated in part as income.

[129] CAA 1990, s. 8(14).

[130] Ibid., ss 157, 158.

[131] Ibid., s. 10D, added by FA 1995, s. 100; this applies also to a person who is deemed to have incurred expenditure under ss 10–10C in respect of compensation and salvage monies, etc. See Inland Revenue Press Release, 29 November 1994, (1994) *Simon's Tax Intelligence* 1482.

[132] CAA 1990, s. 10D(2)–(4), added by FA 1995.

[133] CAA 1990, s. 7; the previous 20% initial allowance was repealed by FA 1985, s. 66 as from 1 April 1986.

[134] Under CAA 1990, s. 3(3).

[135] Ibid., s. 10(1)(b).

[136] Ibid., s. 19(1); on the requirement to offer breakfast and dinner, see Statement of Practice SP 9/87.

trade must be taxed under Schedule D, Case I. The costs of dwelling accommodation for the owner are not allowable, but such costs would be allowable if the trade were incorporated and the accommodation were for a director or employee.

Dwelling houses—assured tenancies

Allowances may also be given for the cost incurred before 1st April 1992 in the construction of "qualifying dwelling houses" which, broadly speaking, must be let on assured tenancies within the meaning of the Housing Act 1980, s. 56 or its successor in Part I of the Housing Act 1988.[137] Although it is not necessary for the landlord to be a company for the purposes of the assured tenancy scheme, the landlord must be a company if capital allowances are claimed under these provisions.

A writing down allowance of 4% per annum is given, and balancing allowances and charges apply as appropriate.[138] Expenditure for which capital allowances have been given under these provisions is not deductible when computing any allowable loss for CGT purposes on the disposal of the building.[139]

24.4 Machinery and Plant

24.4.1 Elements

Outline

The present scheme of capital allowances for machinery and plant was first enacted by FA 1971; the Act has been much amended. The basic structure consists of first year allowances[140] and annual writing down allowances.[141] For some time up to 1984, first year allowances were given at a rate of 100%. These were abolished by FA 1984, but were revived at a lower rate on a temporary basis subsequently because the economy was in recession (1992–1993)[142] or out of a wish to help small enterprises (each year since 1997). The rate of these revived first year allowances has varied.

First year allowances are also available under transitional relief for certain regional projects in development areas.[143] Writing down allowances are given at a rate of 25% on the value of qualifying expenditure; expenditure on (and receipts on the disposal of) different items of machinery and plant are usually pooled. Special rules apply to short life assets, long life assets, leased assets, ships, motor vehicles, computers and films, etc.

Apportionment

The expenditure on machinery and plant must be incurred wholly and exclusively for the purposes of the trade.[144] However, unlike the rules for deductible revenue expenditure, there is a system of apportionment where expenditure is incurred for dual

[137] Ibid., ss 84, 86. An initial allowance was phased out by 1986.

[138] Ibid., ss 85, 87–89.

[139] TCGA 1992, s. 41(4).

[140] CAA 1990, s. 22. It was not possible to claim both the first year allowance and the writing down allowance for the same period—which is why the allowance is called a first year allowance rather than an initial allowance.

[141] CAA 1990, s. 24.

[142] Ibid., s. 22(3B).

[143] Ibid., s. 22(2); for history and avoiding Hybrid Bill status, see Lawson, *Memoirs*, 354.

[144] CAA 1990, ss 22 (1), 24(1)(a).

purposes.[145] Expenditure on a part of machinery or plant or on a share in such assets qualifies for an allowance.[146]

Three restrictions on first year allowance

Special rules apply to restrict first year allowances where (1) there is a sale between connected persons, (2) the machinery or plant continues to be used for the purposes of a trade carried on by the *seller*, or (3) it appears that the sole or main benefit which might otherwise have been expected to accrue to the parties was the obtaining of the allowance. The first year allowance is withdrawn and writing down allowances are given to the purchaser by reference to the disposal value brought into account by the vendor.[147] This also applies to agreements for sale, sale and leaseback etc.[148]

Price or market value?

The amount of expenditure for which the taxpayer, T, is entitled to claim is not usually a problem where the asset is bought outright. If T brings machinery or plant into use in the trade and had originally bought the asset for other purposes, or if the asset is acquired by way of gift, it used to be the market value of the asset when it was brought into the use of the trade which was taken as the amount of expenditure incurred.[149]

However where the relevant event occurs on or after 21 March 2000 the allowance will be based on the lower of that market value and the (unindexed) original cost.[150] So if a world class violinist buys a Stradivarius for his collection and later decides to use it for public performance, the allowance will be given by reference to the original cost; of course the term cost has to be taken in its CAA context so that if the violinist inherited the violin the market value at the time of the inheritance would be used rather than cost.

Non Residents—The precise treatment of non-residents with taxable activities in the UK through a branch or agency has been clarified by FA 2000 with effect from 21 March 2000.[151] Entitlement to the allowance now depends on liability to UK tax. So where only a part of the trade is subject to UK tax only an equivalent part of the allowance may be claimed; to achieve this the UK part of the trade is treated as a separate trade. Consequential rules have to apply to changes in the amount of UK trade so that there is a reduction in the allowance if the portion of the trade attributable to the UK part declines.[152]

Similar reliefs

Equivalent relief is given under CAA 1990 for expenditure on thermal insulation (s. 67), fire safety, provided this is required by a fire authority under Fire Precautions Act 1971, s. 5(4) or s. 10 (s. 69), safety at sports grounds (s. 70) and on personal security measures (ss 71 and

[145] CAA 1990, s. 79.

[146] Ibid., ss 161 (7), 83(4).

[147] Ibid., s. 75, as extended by CAA 1990, s. 76, covers not only the situation in which the machinery or plant continues to be used in the seller's trade but also that when it is used in the trade of a person connected with the seller without having been used in any other trade in the interim (except the trade of leasing). On s. 75, see *Barclays Mercantile Industrial Finance Ltd.* v. *Melluish* [1990] STC 314, 63 TC 95.

[148] CAA 1990, s. 75(2), (3).

[149] Ibid., s. 81; the gift is treated as a purchase from the donor for this amount for the purposes of s. 75.

[150] CAA 1990, s. 81(2AA) and (2AB) added by FA 2000 s. 75.

[151] CAA 1990, s. 83(2A) added by FA 2000 s. 75; naturally s. 82(2A) does not apply to those parts of the CAA which already refer to activities outside the UK—i.e. Chapter V (39–50), s. 64A, 75–78.

[152] CAA s. 79A added by FA 2000 s. 75.

72).[153] While these expenditures attract capital allowances they do not give rise to balancing charges.

Partners

Where the plant is used by a partnership for a trade carried on by the partnership, allowances will be given to the partners in the usual way. Special provision is made where a partner owns the asset but allows the partnership to use it for its trade. Here, the allowance will be given to the partnership, and any sale or gift by the partner to the partners will be ignored. This provision does not apply where the plant is leased to the partnership for payment.[154]

Scope

Plant and machinery allowances apply to commercial trades[155] and to professions or vocations.[156] They are adapted for Schedule A businesses,[157] furnished holiday lettings[158] and for insurance companies.[159]

Employees

An employee can obtain capital allowances to set against Schedule E income in respect of "machinery and plant necessarily provided by the employee for use in his employment".[160] The term "necessarily" means that a finding that another holder of the office could have performed the duties without incurring the expense is fatal to the claim.[161] For most employments, it is not possible for E, the employee, to claim a capital allowance for a computer/word processor purchased by E for use in E's employment since it is usually possible to perform the duties of that employment equally by pen, paper and brain.[162] Moreover, the Revenue often argues that the very fact that E purchases the equipment rather than his employer is proof that the purchase is not "necessary" for the employment. This test is relaxed in relation to purchases of motor vehicles or bicycles. Where a car, etc., is provided partly for use in the employment and partly for private use,[163] the capital allowance is computed under the normal rules, as if it were entirely for use in the employment. The resultant allowance is usually scaled down by the proportion to which the car is used for employment against its total use. E does not have to show that the provision of the motor car is necessary for the performance of the duties of the employment,[164] only that it is actually used. A capital allowance is available, even though another individual may have chosen to perform the duties of that particular employment on, for example, a bicycle or on horse. Since the figures issued by the Revenue for the fixed-profit car scheme include an allowance for the capital cost of the vehicle, no capital allowance claim can be made if the employee receives a mileage allowance at the FPCS rate (see above at §18.2.7).

153 See also ESC B16 concerning expenditure on fire safety in Northern Ireland and by lessors.
154 CAA 1990, s. 65.
155 Ibid., ss 22(1) and 24(1).
156 Ibid., s. 27(1)(a).
157 Ibid., s. 28A, added by FA 1997.
158 CAA 1990, s. 29.
159 Ibid., s. 28.
160 Ibid., s. 27.
161 *White* v. *Higginbotham* [1983] STC 143, 57 TC 2839 (no allowance for audio visal aids for clergyman).
162 On the absence of a tax charge where a computer was provided by the employer, see above at §17.5.
163 CAA 1990, s. 27(2A), (2B), added by FA 1996.
164 This partly mirrors the distinction between travelling and other expenses in TA 1988, s. 198.

Claims and backdating

It used to be that notification of the claim had to be made no later than 12 months from the 31 January after the year of assessment. Therefore claims for 2000–01 must be made by 31 January 2003.[165] This oddly drafted provision was introduced to limit the extent to which taxpayers could backdate claims for allowances when assets were reclassified as plant.[166] In 1994 new rules on the boundary between setting and plant were introduced (see below); however, there is nothing in the remainder of s. 118 to confine the ambit of this rule to such situations. The rule, having had its intended effect, has been repealed.[167]

24.4.2 "Belong to"

The asset must "belong to" the person incurring the expense in consequence of the payment.[168] In *Stokes* v. *Costain Property Investments Ltd.*[169] a tenant had installed a lift in a leased building. Since the lifts immediately became the property of the landlord under general land law principles, they could not be said to "belong to" the tenant and so the tenant was not entitled to the allowance.[170] Further, in *Melluish* v. *BMI (No. 3)*,[171] the House of Lords held that a lessee has no right to an allowance where he has a right to remove the fixture at some future time, e.g. at the end of the lease, but which fixture has become the property of the landlord in the meantime. This is because the concept of a fixture which remains personal property is a contradiction in terms and an impossibility in law;[172] and because the argument would make it uncertain whether an asset belonged to—or ceased to belong to—the lessee according to whether he had or had not got a right to remove the asset (e.g. where the landlord committed a breach of the lease which the tenant then foregave). It follows that a contractual right to remove the fixture cannot prevent it becoming part of the land and so ceasing to belong to the installer.

The words "in consequence of" were held to be satisfied where a payment was made by the taxpayer to induce the holder of an option to reacquire the property to release that option.[173]

In *Melluish* the taxpayer leased central heating, boilers, lifts and similar equipment to local authorities. The items were installed in buildings owned by the local authorities. In so far as *Melhuish* decided that equipment-lessors could obtain allowances under the special rules introduced to reverse *Costain* (see p. 469), where plant was leased to non-taxpayers such as charities or local authorities, the decision was reversed by FA 1997—save where the *lessor* had an interest in the land.[174]

[165] FA 1994, s. 118(3). The Board is given a discretion to extend this period by FA 1994, s. 118(5) and Statement of Practice SP 6/94.

[166] See, generally, Inland Revenue Press Release, 30 November 1993, (1993) *Simon's Tax Intelligence* 1539.

[167] FA 2000 s. 73.

[168] CAA 1990, ss 22(1)(b), 24 (1)(b).

[169] [1984] STC 204, [1984] 1 All ER 849, CA; see Scott [1985] *BTR* 46. Contrast the "relevant interest" rules for industrial buildings (above at §24.3.3). See also *Melluish* v. *BMI (No. 3) Ltd.* [1995] STC 964, 68 TC 1.

[170] The landlord (to whom the lifts did belong) could not claim an allowance because it had not incurred the expenditure.

[171] [1995] STC 964, 68 TC 1.

[172] Ibid., 971, 974, 71–72, 75, *per* Lord Browne-Wilkinson.

[173] *Bolton* v. *International Drilling Ltd.* [1983] STC 70, 56 TC 449.

[174] CAA 1990, s. 53(1A)–(1C) added by FA 1997, Sch. 16, para. 3.

Reversing *Costain*

The situation resulting from *Stokes* v. *Costain* was unjust and a new scheme was introduced for expenditure incurred in 1984.[175] A fixture is treated as belonging to the lessee (L) (or similar person) who incurred the expenditure in providing the machinery or plant for the purposes of a trade carried on by L (or for leasing otherwise than in the course of a trade) if (i) the machinery or plant becomes in law a part of the land and (ii) at that time L has an interest in the relevant land.[176] The rules also apply where the plant becomes a fixture before the capital expenditure is incurred. The lessee's allowance excludes the lessor's allowance, but a lessor who contributes to the expenditure is not excluded.[177] Naturally, (i) and (ii) above turn on land law principles. Tax courts have had to consider whether automatic public conveniences (APCs) and bus shelters were part of the land (they were) and whether a right to enter to clean, maintain and repair was enough for (ii) (it was not).[178]

Special provisions govern disputes over whether the item is a fixture,[179] expenditure (and disposals) by equipment lessors[180] and the transfer to a lessee of the right to an allowance.[181] Rules also apply where an interest in the land is sold and the price is referable to the fixture,[182] and when the fixture ceases to belong to a particular person.[183] These rules are to be taken at face value; the allowances are not confined to cases where the user is liable to tax.[184] As a result of 1997 changes, the rules limit the amount qualifying for allowances to the original cost of the fixtures and prevent multiple claims.[185] Rules also prevent the acceleration of allowances.[186] On a more helpful note, the 1997 legislation allows the vendor and purchaser of property to allocate part of the purchase price to fixtures.[187]

FA 2000 widens the definition for qualifying expenditure by an equipment lessor to cover leased assets under the Affordable Warmth programme.[188] The same Act amends the definition of fixture so as to include boilers and radiators even though these are (relatively) easy to remove; as this was always thought to be the law, the change has retroactive effect.[189]

24.4.3 What is machinery and plant?

General

Neither machinery nor plant is defined in CA 1990, and the question whether an item is plant or machinery depends on the facts of the case. Where an item qualifies both for plant

175 Before 1984 matters were dealt with by concesssion; the taxpayers in *Stokes* v. *Costain* were apparently not willing to agree to one of the conditions in that concession.

176 Defined in CAA 1990, s. 51(2)–(5).

177 Under ibid., ss 51(8), 154.

178 *Decaux* v. *Francis* [1996] STC (SCD) 281.

179 CAA 1990, s. 51(4). On disposal value, see ibid., s. 59.

180 Ibid., ss 53, 58.

181 Ibid., s. 55; and where the lessee would be entitled to the allowance, but the lessor would not (s. 56).

182 Ibid., s. 54: no balance is struck just because of a rebate of VAT under the capital goods scheme (s. 54(1)(c), added by FA 1991, Sch. 14, para. 10).

183 CAA 1990, s. 57.

184 *Melluish* v. *BMI (No. 3) Ltd.* [1995] STC 964, 980b, 68 TC 1, 82I, HL, *per* Lord Browne-Wilkinson.

185 CAA 1990, ss 56A–56D, added by FA 1997, Sch. 16, para. 4.

186 CAA 1990, s. 59A, added by FA 1997, Sch. 16, para. 5.

187 CAA 1990, s. 59B, added by FA 1997, Sch. 16, para. 6.

188 FA 2000 s. 79 amending CAA s. 53.

189 FA 2000 s. 78 amending CAA s. 51.

and machinery allowance and industrial building allowance,[190] it is likely that the former, usually more generous, relief will be claimed.[191] Parliament has attempted to provide some clarification on the boundary between plant and its setting but with what success remains to be seen (see below at §24.4.5).

Different definitions have been suggested for specific instances. In *Yarmouth* v. *France*[192] a claim was brought by a workman under the Employers' Liability Act 1880 for damages for injuries sustained due to a defect in his employer's plant, in that case a vicious horse. Lindley L.J. stated:[193]

> "in its ordinary sense (plant) includes whatever apparatus is used by a business man for carrying on his business—not his stock-in-trade, which he buys or makes for sale; but all goods and chattels, fixed or movable, live or dead, which he keeps for permanent employment in his business."

This test has been helpful but not exclusive[194] in capital allowance cases. The test clearly covers fixtures and fittings of a durable nature. Therefore, railway locomotives and carriages[195] and tramway rails[196] have been held to be plant, as have knives and lasts used in the manufacture of shoes,[197] but not the bed of a harbour,[198] nor stallions for stud purposes.[199]

It is now clear that machinery and plant is not confined to things used physically,[200] but extends also to the intellectual storehouse of the trade or profession, e.g. the purchase of law books by a barrister.[201] However, rights to exploit plant are not plant—a matter of great concern in the area of intellectual property.[202] It is not necessary that the object be active, although a passive object may be less obviously plant.[203]

It has been suggested, e.g. by the Revenue, that a thing which lacks physical manifestation cannot be plant. If this is true, it leads to a substantial and regrettable lack of clarity with regard to many items of intellectual property. The piecemeal provisions for copyright, know how and certain types of scientific research are no substitute for a modern and coherent law. Special legislation now applies to computer software (see below).

Computer software

Where capital expenditure is incurred on the outright acquisition of computer software the normal plant and machinery allowance is available.[204] However, problems arise where a capital sum is paid for a licence to use the software, or for the provision of software by electronic means. In the first instance, it cannot be said that the software belongs to the taxpayer

190 *IRC* v. *Barclay Curle & Co. Ltd.* [1969] 1 All ER 732, 45 TC 221 (see above at §24.4.4); the area of overlap has been reduced by the new rules on when settling is plant.

191 Double allowances are excluded by CAA 1990, s. 147.

192 (1887) 19 QBD 647.

193 Ibid., 658.

194 Lord Donovan in *IRC* v. *Barclay Curle & Co. Ltd.* [1969] 1 All ER 732, 751, 45 TC 221, 249.

195 *Caledonian Rly Co.* v. *Banks* (1880) 1 TC 487.

196 *LCC* v. *Edwards* (1909) 5 TC 383.

197 *Hinton* v. *Maden and Ireland Ltd.* [1959] 3 All ER 356, 38 TC 391 (expected to last only three years); noted at [1959] *BTR* 454.

198 *Dumbarton Harbour Board* v. *Cox* (1918) 7 TC 147.

199 *Earl of Derby* v. *Aylmer* [1915] 3 KB 374, 6 TC 665

200 *McVeigh* v. *Arthur Sanderson & Sons Ltd.* [1969] 2 All ER 771, 775, *per* Cross J.; noted at [1969] *BTR* 130.

201 *Munby* v. *Furlong* [1977] STC 232, [1977] 2 All ER 953.

202 *Barclays Mercantile Industrial Finance Ltd.* v. *Melluish* [1990] STC 314, 63 TC 93, 122.

203 *Jarrold* v. *John Good & Sons Ltd.* [1963] 1 All ER 141, 40 TC 681.

204 On boundary between capital and revenue, note Inland Revenue interpretation RI 56; *Simon's Direct Tax Service*, Pt. H5.4.

while, in the second, it may lack the degree of tangibility necessary for plant to exist.[205] Today, software acquired under a licence is treated as belonging to the trader (T) as long as T is entitled to the right, while computer software is treated as being machinery or plant.[206] The meaning of "computer software" is to be determined by the courts.[207]

24.4.4 Plant or setting

Statutory prescription of settings[208]

Since 1994, CAA 1990, Schedule AA1 has governed the boundary between machinery and plant and settings. This elaboration does not affect a number of special provisions which treat specified expenditure as if it were machinery or plant—e.g. thermal insulation, fire safety, sports grounds and security.[209] Further, nothing in the Schedule affects the question whether expenditure on the provision of any glasshouse which is constructed so that the required environment (i.e. air, heat, light, irrigation and temperature) for growing plants is provided automatically by means of devices which are an integral part of its structure, is, for the purposes of this Act, expenditure on the provision of machinery or plant.[210] The stated purpose of this change is that buildings and structures cannot qualify as plant (although it is also stated that the broad aim is that expenditure on buildings and structures which already qualify as plant should continue to do so).[211] However, for the most part the list reflects what the courts have achieved. The effect of the change is partly to provide detailed guidance and partly to prevent judges from changing the law themselves.

(a) Buildings. Schedule AA1 deals first with buildings, and excludes from the category of "machinery or plant" any expenditure on the provision of a building. It defines "building" as including any asset in the building which is incorporated into the building, or which, by reason of being moveable or otherwise, is not so incorporated, but is of a kind normally incorporated into buildings.[212] This abstract statement is supplemented by Table 1 which has two columns of items; all items are then swept into the definition of buildings. Items in the first column cannot be machinery or plant; items in the second column may.[213] Examples of items in column 1 are walls, floors, ceilings, doors, gates, shutters, windows and stairs; examples of items in column 2 are electrical, cold water, gas and sewerage systems provided mainly to meet the particular requirements of the trade, or provided mainly to serve particular machinery or plant used for the purposes of the trade. Cold stores, caravans provided mainly for holiday lettings and any moveable building intended to be moved in the course of the trade may also be plant. The legislation leaves it to the taxpayer to establish that these items are plant under existing law case law. To make things clearer it is provided that an asset cannot come within column 2 if its principal purpose is to insulate or enclose the interior of the building or provide an interior wall, a floor or a ceiling which (in each case) is intended to remain permanently in place.[214]

205 *Barclays Mercantile Industrial Finance Ltd.* v. *Melluish* [1990] STC 314, 63 TC 93, 122.

206 CAA 1990, s. 67A(1), (2), added by F (No. 2) A 1992, s. 68.

207 HC Official Report, Standing Committee B, col. 351, 25 June 1992. *Quaere* whether the courts will use the definition in the Copyright, Designs and Patents Act 1988.

208 Added by FA 1994, s. 117.

209 CAA 1990, Sch. AA1, para. 4, added by FA 1994, s. 117, and referring to CAA 1990, ss 67–71.

210 Ibid., Sch. AA1, para. 5(2).

211 Inland Revenue Press Release, 30 November 1993, (1993) *Simon's Tax Intelligence* 1539.

212 CAA 1990, Sch. AA1, para. 1(2).

213 Ibid., Sch. AA1, para. 1(3).

214 Ibid., Sch. AA1, para. 1(4).

(b) Structures, assets and works. A "structure" is defined as a fixed structure of any kind, other than a building. Again, the legislation begins with a prohibition—expenditure on the provision of machinery or plant does not include any expenditure on the provision of structures or other specified assets or any works involving the alteration of land.[215] Table 2 has two columns, and items in column 1 cannot qualify, whereas items in column 2 may do so. Examples from column 1 include any dam, reservoir or barrage (including any sluices, gates, generators and other equipment associated with it), any dock and any dike, sea wall, weir or drainage ditch; the column ends ominously with any structure not within any other item in this column. The second column includes expenditure on the provision of towers used to support floodlights, of any reservoir incorporated into a water treatment works, of silos used for temporary storage or on the provision of storage tanks, of swimming pools, including diving boards, slides and any structure supporting them and of fish tanks or fish ponds. Column 2 was substantially widened in the course of debate.[216]

(c) Land Finally, Schedule AA1 provides that expenditure on the acquisition of any interest in land cannot qualify as plant. This bar also extends to any asset which is so installed or otherwise fixed in or to any description of land as to become, in law, part of that land.[217]

Plant or setting: case-law principles

Plant does not include the place where the business is carried on; "plant" is that with which the trade is carried on as opposed to the "setting or premises" in which it is carried on.[218] Plant carries with it a connotation of equipment or apparatus, either fixed or unfixed. It does not convey a meaning wide enough to cover buildings in general. It may cover equipment of any size. Equipment does not cease to be plant merely because it discharges an additional function, such as providing the place in which the business is carried on, e.g. a dry dock,[219] but these categories are not necessarily mutually exclusive and the different scope of the allowances makes correct classification of great practical importance. It has been held that special partitioning used by shipping agents to subdivide floor space to accommodate fluctuating office accommodation requirements was plant, some stress being laid on the fact that office flexibility was needed.[220] Something which becomes part of the premises, as opposed to merely embellishing them, is not plant save where the premises are themselves plant,[221] as in *IRC* v. *Barclay, Curle & Co. Ltd.* (see below).

Defining the unit

It is often a crucial question whether various items are taken separately or treated as one installation. This is a question of fact, and so for the Commissioners to decide, subject to the tests in *Edwards* v. *Bairstow and Harrison.* In *Cole Brothers Ltd.* v. *Phillips*[222] the taxpayer, T, had spent money on electrical installations in a large department store (John Lewis at the

[215] On which, see *Family Golf Centres Ltd.* v. *Thorne* [1998] STC (SCD) 106.

[216] See Inland Revenue Press Release, 9 March 1994, (1994) *Simon's Tax Intelligence* 339.

[217] CAA 1990, Sch. AA1, para. 3, added by FA 1994, s. 117; the definition of "land" in the Interpretation Act 1978 is modified (CAA 1990, Sch. AA1, para. 5).

[218] *Jarrold* v. *John Good & Sons Ltd.* [1963] 1 All ER 141, 40 TC 681, 696. *per* Pearson L.J.

[219] See Sir Donald Nicholls V.-C. in *Carr* v. *Sayer* [1992] STC 396, 402, 65 TC 15, 22.

[220] *Jarrold* v. *John Good & Sons Ltd.* [1963] 1 All ER 141, 40 TC 681. The decision of the Commissioners was left intact.

[221] *Wimpy International Ltd.* v. *Warland* [1989] STC 273, 279e, 61 TC 51, 96, CA, *per* Fox L.J.

[222] [1982] STC 307 HL; [1981] STC 671, 55 TC 188, CA.

Brent Cross shopping centre). One argument advanced by T was that the whole electrical installation was one item. This was rejected by the Commissioners; the appellate courts treated the issue as a matter of fact for the Commissioners, but the discomfort shown by the speeches in the House of Lords is marked.[223] The issue arose more recently in *Attwood* v. *Anduff Carwash Ltd.*[224] where the question was whether a car wash site was a single plant. The Commissioners held that it was, but the appellate courts held that neither the whole site nor the wash hall alone could be treated as a single unit.

(a) Dry dock

While there is a clear distinction between the shell of a building and the machinery currently used in it, there are considerable difficulties where a large and durable structure is created for a specific purpose. This occurred in the leading case of *IRC* v. *Barclay, Curle & Co. Ltd.*[225] The taxpayer had constructed a dry dock, a process requiring the excavation of the site and the construction of a concrete lining. The Revenue agreed that such expenditure incurred on the dock gate and operating gear, the cast iron keel blocks and the electrical and pumping installations related to plant, but argued that while the expenses of excavation and concreting might relate to industrial building, they did not relate to plant and machinery. The Revenue lost. It will be noted that while a dock is now classified in Schedule AA1 as a structure, and so not capable of qualifying for allowances as plant, a dry dock is classified differently. The expenditure on the concrete lining was held to be in respect of plant because it could not be regarded as the mere setting in which the trade was carried on, but was an integral part of the means required for the trading operation. Lord Reid said that a structure which fulfils the function of plant was, prima facie, plant.[226] However, later cases show that this "business" or "function" test must yield to the "premises" test (see (b) below).

Where capital expenditure is incurred on alterations to an existing building incidental to the installation of machinery or plant for the purposes of trade, allowances may be claimed in respect of such expenditure just as if the works formed part of the machinery or plant.[227]

(b) Fast food restaurant

The mere fact that an item has a business use (the business test) does not make it plant; an item cannot be plant if its use is as the premises or place on which the business is conducted (the premises test).[228] In *Wimpy* v. *Warland*[229] the taxpayer sought (unsucessfully) to claim allowances for expenditure on shop fronts, wall panels, suspended ceilings, mezzanine floor, decorative brickwork, wall finishes a trapdoor and ladder. As Fox L.J. stated:

> "There is a well established distinction, in general terms, between the premises in which the business is carried on and the plant with which the business is carried on. The premises are not plant. In its simplest form that is illustrated by [the] example of the creation of atmosphere in a hotel by beautiful buildings and gardens on the one hand and fine china, glass and other tableware on the other. The latter are plant; the former are not. The former are simply the premises in which the business is conducted."

[223] See [1982] STC 307, 312–13, *per* Lord Hailsham, 314f, *per* Lord Wilberforce, and 316a, *per* Edmund Davies.
[224] [1997] STC 1167, CA.
[225] [1969] 1 All ER 732, 45 TC 221.
[226] Ibid., 740, 239.
[227] CAA 1990, s. 60.
[228] *Wimpy International* v. *Warland* [1988] STC 149, 171b, 61 TC 51, 82d, *per* Hofmann J.
[229] [1989] STC 273, 279, 61 TC 51, 96, CA.

(c) Planteria

Gray v. *Seymour's*[230] involved what might loosely be called a high-tech glasshouse used in a garden centre. As Nourse LJ stated:

> "While the cold frames which formerly provided a similar function to that of the planteria might well have been plant, the same cannot be said of the planteria itself. It is a structure to which plants are brought already in a saleable condition, albeit that some of them tend to be in there for quite considerable periods and others require special treatment . . . The fact that the planteria provides the function of nurturing and preserving the plants while they are there cannot transform it into something other than part of the premises in which the business is carried on. The highest it can be put is that it functions as a purpose-built structure. But . . . that is not enough to make the structure plant."

Defining setting

The distinction between setting and plant depends in part upon the degree of sophistication to be employed in the concept of a setting.[231] The problem is acute when electrical apparatus and wiring are concerned.[232] The matter must be resolved by the use of the functional test so that, for example, while lighting will not usually be plant it will become so if it is of a specialised nature, as where it is designed to provide a particular atmosphere in a hotel; this must be judged by reference to the intended market.[233] The Revenue has consistently refused to treat wiring leading to such apparatus as plant. The statutory list in Schedule AAI places mains services and systems of electricity generally in the category of assets which cannot qualify as plant, while allowing electrical systems provided mainly to meet the particular requirements of the trade or to serve particular machinery or plant used for the purposes of the trade.[234]

Case-law survey

The case-law distinction between buildings and apparatus is, perhaps inevitably, indistinct. Relatively recent cases have shown that items which cannot be plant under the case-law test include a prefabricated building at a school used to accommodate a chemical laboratory,[235] a canopy over a petrol station[236] (although this has since been doubted[237]), an inflatable

[230] [1995] STC 706, 711b, 67 TC 401, 413. For a general Revenue view on glasshouses, see Inland Revenue interpretation RI 33, updated by RI 185.

[231] *Imperial Chemical Industries of Australia and New Zealand* v. *Taxation Commr of the Commonwealth of Australia* (1970) 120 CLR 396.

[232] In *Cole Brothers* v. *Phillips* [1982] STC 307, HL; [1981] STC 671, 55 TC 188, CA, the Revenue agreed that wiring to certain items such as alarms and clocks was plant, but said that (a) transformers, switchgear and the main switchboard and (b) specially designed lighting fittings, were not plant. The Commissioners held that the transformers were plant, but not the other items under (a) or any of (b). The Court of Appeal held that the switchboard was plant because of the fact that some of the wiring had been agreed to be plant. The House of Lords agreed with the Court of Appeal in treating the remaining items as matters for the Commissioner's decision as matters of fact.

[233] *Cole Bros Ltd.* v. *Phillips* [1982] STC 307, 55 TC 188, HL; *Hunt* v. *Henry Quick Ltd.* [1992] STC 633, 65 TC 108; *IRC* v. *Scottish and Newcastle Breweries Ltd.* [1982] STC 296, 55 TC 252 (note that the light fitting was allowed in *Wimpy International Ltd.* v. *Warland* [1988] STC 149, 176, 61 TC 51, 88). On the 1982 House of Lords' decisions, see [1983] *BTR* 54.

[234] The Revenue relies strongly on *J. Lyons & Co. Ltd.* v. *A.-G.* [1944] Ch 281, [1944] 1 All ER 477; on Sch. AA1, see para. 1, Table 1, head B, but note also head 1 in col. 2.

[235] *St John's School* v. *Ward* [1975] STC 7, 49 TC 524 (note the astonishingly harsh refusal by Templeman J. to allow an apportionment between the building and the equipment).

[236] *Dixon* v. *Fitch's Garage Ltd.* [1975] STC 480, [1975] 3 All ER 455, 50 TC 509.

[237] *Cole Bros Ltd.* v. *Phillips* [1982] STC 307, 311, 55 TC, 223, *per* Lord Hailsham; but see the pointed comment of Walton J. in *Thomas* v. *Reynolds* [1987] STC 135, 140, 59 TC 502, 508.

cover over a tennis court,[238] and a floating ship used as a restaurant.[239] These failed the business test since they performed no function in the trade. Many of these cases now appear in the statutory list of assets which cannot qualify as plant. Permanent quarantine kennels,[240] putting greens at a nine-hole golf course[241] and a car-washing facility operated on a conveyor belt system[242] probably met the business test, but certainly failed the premises test.

On the other hand, it has been held that a silo used in the trade of grain importing was not simply part of the setting and had to be considered together with the machinery and other equipment within it.[243] Similarly, a swimming pool at a caravan site was held to be plant since it was part of the apparatus of the business.[244] Also held to be plant were decorative screens placed in the windows of a building society's offices (since the screens were not the structure within which the business was carried on),[245] and, perhaps surprisingly, mezzanine platforms installed by a wholesale merchant to increase storage space.[246] In the celebrated House of Lords' case of *IRC* v. *Scottish and Newcastle Breweries Ltd.*[241] murals designed to attract customers were held to be plant, as was a metal seagull sculpture and other items designed to create "ambience".

These cases prove the old adage that an ounce of evidence (before the Commissioners) is worth a ton of law. Of the 12 cases reported between 1975 and 1997, seven were cases in which the Revenue successfully appealed against a commissioner's determination that the items were plant, one was a successful appeal by a taxpayer against a commissioner's decision in favour of the Revenue, in two the court agreed with the Commissioners that the items were plant, and in two the Commissioners had originally decided that *some* items were plant, but the court subsequently decided that *more* items were plant.

Of the items which the courts have decided are plant, one or two have now been set out in the non-plant category by the statutory list.[248]

24.4.5 *First year allowances*

First year allowances[249] were abolished by FA 1984, with a saving for transitional relief for certain regional projects in development areas.[250] Today, they also apply, at the rate of 40%; long life assets do not qualify.[251] First year allowances apply only to small or medium-sized enterprises. These were solemnly re-enacted each year since 1997–1998, but not necessarily with the same rates, but have now been made permanent.[252] First year allowances do not

238 *Thomas* v. *Reynolds* [1987] STC 135, 59 TC 502.

239 *Benson* v. *Yard Arm Club Ltd.* [1979] STC 266, [1979] 2 All ER 336, 53 TC 607.

240 *Carr* v. *Sayer* [1992] STC 396, 65 TC 15.

241 *Family Golf Centres Ltd.* v. *Thorne* [1998] STC (SCD) 106.

242 *Attwood* v. *Anduff Car Wash Ltd.* [1997] STC 1167, CA.

243 *Schofield* v. *R. and H. Hall Ltd.* [1975] STC 353, 49 TC 538.

244 *Cooke* v. *Beach Station Caravans Ltd.* [1974] STC 402, [1974] 3 All ER 159, 49 TC 514.

245 *Leeds Permanent Building Society* v. *Procter* [1982] STC 821, 56 TC 293.

246 *Hunt* v. *Henry Quick Ltd.* [1992] STC 633, 643–4, 65 TC 108, 124 (note the doubts of Vinelott J.).

247 [1982] STC 296, 55 TC 252, HL.

248 For example the windows in *Leeds Permanent Building Society* v. *Procter* [1982] STC 821; whether the dock in *Barclay Curle* itself is redesignated depends on whether "any dock" includes a dry dock.

249 CAA 1990, s. 22. It was not possible to claim both the first year allowance and the writing down allowance for the same period, which is why the allowance is called a first year allowance rather than an initial allowance.

250 CAA 1990, s. 22 (2); for history and avoiding hybrid Bill status, see Lawson, *Memoirs*, 354.

251 CAA 1990, s. 22(3D). For 1997–1998, see CAA 1990, s. 22(1AA), (3C).

252 FA 2000, s. 70. For the 1997–1998 period the rate was 50%, but 12% for long life assets; from 1 November 1992 to 31 October 1993 the rate was 40% and applied to most assets and all sizes of business (CAA 1990, s. 22 (3B)).

apply to machinery and plant for leasing, motor cars, sea-going ships or assets used for a railway.[253] If the base period is less than one year, an appropriate proportion of the allowance is given.

A special 100% rate also applies for expenditure on assets to be used in Northern Ireland.[254] The rate applies only to small or medium-sized businesses for expenditure from 12 May 1998 to 11 May 2002, and had to be modified to meet EC rules on state aids.

Small and medium-sized

The Companies Act definition of "small and medium-sized" is used. If it is an unincorporated business, it must satisfy these conditions as if it were a company.[255] A company is a medium-sized company (and *a fortiori* a small company) if its business satisfies any two of the following three conditions: a turnover of not more than £11.2 m; assets of not more than £5.6 m; and no more than 250 employees. Where the business is carried on by a company which is a member of a group, the group must not be a large group. In deciding whether the group is medium-sized or a large group, the numbers used for the single company are applied to the group as a whole.[256] The cost of this relief for 1998–1999 is put at £300 m.

First not last

No allowance may be claimed for the period during which permanent discontinuance takes place; only a balancing allowance (or charge) is made.[257]

Small enterprises and Temporary ICT allowance

Enterprises are small if they satisfy two of the three tests—turnover £2.8 m, assets £1.4 m and 50 employees. This subset of small and mexium sized enterprises matters because FA 2000 provides a 100% first year allowance for expenditure by small enterprises on information and communications technology (ICT); the expenditure must be incurred between 1 April 2000 and 31 March 2003.[258] The main qualifying assets are computers. The elements of ICT are computers and associated equipment, internet-enabled mobile phones and computer software;[259] the list may be redefined or added to by Treasury order.[260]

24.4.6 Writing down allowances, balances and the pool

The writing down allowance, which is given on a 25% reducing balance basis, applies where the taxpayer, T, incurs capital expenditure on the provision of machinery and plant wholly and exclusively for the purposes of the trade. In addition, the asset must belong to T in consequence of the expenditure. It is not necessary that the asset should have been brought into use in the trade. If the chargeable period is greater or less than 12 months the figure of 25% is increased or reduced accordingly.[261]

[253] CAA 1990, s. 22 (4).
[254] Ibid., s. 22(3CA).
[255] Ibid., s. 22A.
[256] Ibid., s. 22A(1)(b) and (4).
[257] Ibid., s. 22(4)(a).
[258] CAA 1990, s. 22(3E)–(3H) added by FA 2000, s. 71 for expenditure on or after 28 July 2000.
[259] CAA 1990, s. 22(3F), (3G).
[260] CAA 1990, s.22(3H).
[261] Ibid., s. 24(2)(a)(ii), as amended by FA 1994.

Pooling

Generally, all plant and machinery used in the trade is placed in one pool and the writing down allowance is applied to the value of the pool.[262] However, certain items *must* be pooled separately. These are:

(1) assets used partly for non-business purposes;[263]
(2) assets the wear and tear on which is subsidised;[264]
(3) "expensive" road vehicles;[265]
(4) ships[266] (here the law allows deferments of writing down allowances at will);
(5) long life assets;[267]
(6) any asset held for the purpose of a different trade—each trade has its own pool. Where statute deems a separate trade to be carried on, the asset will be pooled separately.[268] This affects private road vehicles which are not expensive,[269] assets for leasing outside the UK where a restricted rate of writing down allowance applies,[270] and each lease otherwise than in the course of the trade of leasing.[271]

The reasoning behind separate pools for (1) and (2) was that these assets were not entitled to first year allowances; with the reduction in the scope of FYAs it became less sensible to maintain these rules and so, 16 years after Nigel Lawson's decision to remove most of the FYAs, FA 2000 provides that with effect from 6 April 2000 (1 April for corporation tax) the requirement of a separate pool is removed; the balance of the separate pool is merged with the general pool. However the legislation allows the taxpayer to defer the change for a year.[272]

Certain short-life assets *may* be pooled separately if the taxpayer so elects.[273]

Where a first year allowance is taken, T may *not* also claim a writing down allowance for that first year.[274] When the 40% allowance was taken, the allowance in the second year is 25% of the 60% of the expenditure remaining.[275]

No writing down allowance may be claimed for the period during which permanent discontinuance takes place; only a balancing allowance (or charge) is made.[276]

A balancing adjustment may be made where a non-resident trades through a branch or agency in the UK and the proportion of the total trade represented by the UK branch or agency changes—downwards (i.e. is reduced).[277]

[262] Ibid., s. 24(2).
[263] Ibid., s. 79.
[264] Ibid., s. 80(5).
[265] Ibid., ss 34, 41.
[266] Ibid., s. 31.
[267] Ibid., ss 38E, 38F.
[268] Ibid., s. 61(1).
[269] Ibid., s. 42(1).
[270] Ibid., ss 36, 41.
[271] Ibid., s. 61(1).
[272] CAA s. 41 as amended by FA 2000 s. 74.
[273] Ibid., s. 37.
[274] Ibid., s. 66. This is what marks a "first year" allowance off from an "initial" allowance.
[275] Ibid., s. 62.
[276] Ibid., s. 24(2)(b).
[277] Ibid., s. 79A added by FA 2000 s. 74.

Examples

If an asset cost £1,000, and it was the only asset in the pool, the allowance would be £250 in the first year, but 25% of (£1,000 − £250), i.e. £187.50 in the second.

Suppose that an asset was bought in year 1 for £1,000, a second asset was bought in year 2 for £9,250, and in year 3 the first asset was sold for £1,000. The allowances would be year 1, £250 and year 2, £2,500. At the start of year 3 the qualifying expenditure would be £10,250 − (£250 + £2,500) or £7,500. This must be reduced by the £1,000 disposal so that in year 3 the allowance will be 25% of (£7,500 − £1,000) = £1,625.

Where more items come into the pool, the writing down allowance is 25% of the excess of sums spent over sums so far allowed whether under a first year allowance or a writing down allowance plus disposal value.

24.4.7 Disposal value[278]

Disposal value is relevant when:[279]

(1) the asset ceases to belong to T, the claimant;[280]
(2) T loses possession of the asset in circumstances in which it is reasonable to assume that the loss is permanent;
(3) the asset ceases to exist as such (as a result of destruction, dismantling or otherwise);
(4) the asset begins to be used wholly or partly[281] for purposes other than those of the trade; or
(5) the trade is permanently discontinued.

Balancing effects

If the qualifying expenditure exceeds the disposal value, the writing down allowance of 25% of the excess may be claimed. If the disposal value exceeds the qualifying expenditure, a balancing charge equal to that excess is made; however, a balancing allowance will be given only when the trade ceases.

Amounts

The disposal value to be brought into account depends upon the event by reason of which it is taken into account,[282] but it cannot exceed the capital expenditure incurred on that item, any excess being subject to capital gains legislation. The disposal value to be deducted from the pool must not exceed the cost of the plant to the person disposing of it.

Market value. Where the plant was acquired as a result of a transaction or series of transactions between connected persons, the greatest acquisition expenditure incurred in any of the transactions concerned is the maximum disposal value.[283] This rule applies not only on a disposal to a connected person, or to an acquisition from a connected person but extends to an acquisition as a result of a transaction between connected persons, with whom the dis-

278 Defined in CAA 1990, s. 26 (see abvove at §24.2.4).
279 See ibid., s. 24(6) and, in relation to computer software, s. 24(6A), added by F (No. 2) A 1992.
280 CAA 1990, s. 60(2).
281 Or partly ceasing to be so used (ibid., s. 79).
282 Ibid., s. 26.
283 Ibid., s. 26(3).

poser need not be connected.[284] If the asset has been sold,[285] the proceeds of sale are taken, and if that sale has been affected by some event, for example if the asset has been damaged, account is also taken of any insurance or compensation money received.

Where the market value is greater than the proceeds of sale, market value will be taken unless there is a charge to tax under Schedule E or the buyer can, in turn, claim a capital allowance in respect of machinery or plant or a scientific research allowance.[286] The reason for this is presumably because the low sale price will give rise, in turn, to low allowances. There is also a bar on taking an undervalue if the buyer is a dual resident investment company connected with the seller—introduced as part of the general drive against such companies.[287]

End of asset. If the event is the demolition or destruction of the asset, the disposal value is the sum received for the remains, together with any insurance or compensation. In other instances of permanent loss, for example theft, the disposal value is simply any insurance or compensation. In all other cases, market value is taken.

End of trade. If the event is the permanent discontinuance of the trade, which is followed by the sale, demolition, destruction or permanent loss of the asset, the disposal value on discontinuance is that specified for the event. A special election may apply if there is a succession to a trade by a connected person,[288] in which case the predecessor's written down value will override other provisions referring to market value.[289] No election may be made if the buyer is a dual resident investment company.[290] The right to elect is restricted to cases where both parties are within the charge to UK tax on the profits of the trade, and is subject to a time limit of two years starting with the date of the transaction.[291] The election can be made by a partnership.[292] In all other cases market value is taken.[293] For the period in which permanent discontinuance occurs neither first year nor writing down allowances are given, everything being settled by the balancing allowance or charge.

In appropriate cases the disposal proceeds may be apportioned.[294]

Where the disposal comprises certain qualifying gifts, e.g. to an educational establishment within TA 1988, s. 84, there is a nil disposal value.

24.4.8 Short life assets—the non-pooling option

The effect of the 25% writing down allowance is that, thanks to its reducing balance basis, approximately 90% of the cost will be written off over eight years. Because some assets have a shorter life expectancy, rules allow such assets to be kept out of the general pool.[295] If the asset is disposed of, any balancing allowance is given immediately instead of waiting for the overall effect on a pool—but only if it is disposed of within, approximately, five years.

284 Ibid.
285 See *IRC* v. *West* (1950) 31 TC 402.
286 CAA 1990, s. 26(1)(b); on time of sale, see s. 161(10), as amended by FA 1990, Sch. 13, para. 6.
287 CAA 1990, s. 26(1)(b).
288 Ibid., s. 77.
289 Ibid., s. 77(3), (4), (8). The provisions overridden are ss 41(5), 78(1).
290 Ibid., s. 77(2).
291 Ibid., s. 77(3)(b).
292 Ibid., s. 77(6).
293 Ibid., s. 78; on succession on death, note s. 78(2A), added by FA 1990.
294 CAA 1990, ss 150, 151.
295 Ibid., s. 37. On practice, see Statement of Practice SP 1/86.

The asset will be kept in a pool of its own and the normal 25% writing down allowance applied on a reducing basis.[296] The (irrevocable) election to treat the asset as a short life asset must be made within two years of the year of acquisition.[297] The election is not available in relation to assets which are required to be pooled separately in any case.[298] The election may be made even though the asset qualifies for the temporary first year allowances.[299]

In practice assets which have an expected useful life of less than two years are depreciated over the life span, and are not pooled.[300]

2.4.9 *Long life assets*

The writing down allowance for plant and machinery is reduced to 6% per annum, calculated on a reducing balance, where it is reasonable to expect that the plant and machinery will have an economic life of at least 25 years.[301] This is because of the substantial disparity between the rapid rate at which capital allowances are given and the slow rate at which plant, such as reservoirs and power stations, are written down in the financial accounts of newly privatised companies. Assets excluded from this rule include fixtures in a dwelling house, retail shop, showroom, hotel or office, and any mechanically propelled road vehicle.[302]

Where this treatment is applied, the long life asset is treated as creating a pool separate from other assets. Other provisions apportion composite expenditure between a long life asset and an asset with a shorter life.[303]

24.4.10 *Motor vehicles*

Full allowances

Expenditure on certain types of road vehicle can be treated as ordinary expenditure on machinery and plant. The favoured vehicles are:[304]

(1) goods vehicles of a construction primarily suited to the carriage of goods or burden of any description;
(2) vehicles of a type not commonly used as private vehicles and unsuitable to be so used, for example works buses and minivans;[305] and
(3) vehicles provided wholly or mainly for hire to, or for carriage of, members of the public in the ordinary course of a trade.[306] Shooting brakes are thought to fall outside this favoured group. Rules distinguish the ordinary car rental business from the increasingly common leasing arrangement whereby a (new) car is leased to a person for two or three years; however, cars leased to persons receiving mobility allowance are treated favourably.[307]

296 CAA 1990, s. 37(3).
297 Ibid., s. 37(2).
298 The list is in ibid., s. 38
299 Ibid., s. 38(m) does not mention s. 22(3B) (3C) or (3D).
300 *Tax Bulletin* (November 1993).
301 CAA 1990, s. 38C, added by FA 1997; see Gammie [1997] *BTR* 241.
302 CAA 1990, s. 38B, added by FA 1997.
303 CAA 1990, s. 38A, added by FA 1997.
304 CAA 1990, s. 36.
305 *Roberts* v. *Granada TV Rental Ltd.* [1970] 2 All ER 764, 46 TC 295.
306 CAA 1990, s. 36(2).
307 A category defined by ibid., s. 36(4).

Restricted allowances

Expenditure on cars outside the above categories and costing less than £12,000 is pooled separately from other assets, but forms one single pool.[308]

Where the capital expenditure on a car exceeds £12,000, each car is treated as a separate asset and the allowance is limited to a maximum of £3,000 (i.e. 25% of £12,000). The effect of the £3,000 limit is to defer the benefit of the relief. The figures of £3,000 and £12,000 are reduced or increased proportionately if the chargeable period is less or greater than 12 months.[309]

When a car costing more than £12,000 is *leased*, further special rules apply to restrict the relief normally given in computing profit for hiring charges.[310] These special rules do not apply where the car is subject to a hire purchase agreement under which the hirer has an option to buy the car for an amount equivalent to 1% (or less) of the retail price of the car when new.[311] The amount paid by way of rent is reduced in the proportion which the £12,000, plus half the amount by which the retail price of the vehicle when new exceeds £12,000, bears to that retail price. Thus, if a car cost £18,000 new and the rent is £5,600, the amount claimable for tax is (£12,000 + (£18,000 − 12,000)/2)/£18,000 or 5/6 × £5,600 = £4,666. The missing 1/6 will never qualify for relief.

24.4.11 Hire purchase

Where machinery or plant is purchased by the taxpayer, T, on hire purchase or conditional sale contracts, first year and writing down allowances may be claimed in respect of the capital element.[312] The machinery or plant is treated as belonging to T and to no one else provided as T is entitled to the benefit of the contract. Capital expenditure to be incurred by T under the contract after the machinery or plant has been brought into use in the trade is treated as incurred at that time. T is thus treated as incurring the full capital cost at that time. Special provisions apply where the option under the contract is not exercised.[313]

The actual words of this provision go wider than merely hire purchase. The Revenue has pointed out that the words of the provision are apt to cover situations in which capital expenditure is incurred on goods which are never owned, e.g. a deposit paid for goods which are then not supplied.[314]

Where this rule deems the asset to belong to X but the special rules for fixtures deemed it to belong to Y, the fixtures rule prevails;[315] although this was introduced by FA 2000 it is deemed always to have had effect. Where the hire purchase rule deems the asset to be X's and it then becomes a fixture and so as belonging to Y, X is treated as selling the asset to Y. This rule is not retroactive and does not apply to assets becoming fixtures before Royal Assent (28 July 2000); FA 2000 does not specify the price at which the sale is treated as taking place.

[308] Ibid., s. 34(2) as amended by F (No. 2) A 1992.

[309] CAA 1990, s. 34, as amended by FA 1994.

[310] CAA 1990, s. 35(2); on effect of rebate of hire charge, see ESC B28.

[311] CAA 1990, s. 35(3), added by FA 1991.

[312] CAA 1990, s. 60. A hirer under such an agreement is very different from a mere lessee; see Inland Revenue Press Release, 27 October 1986, (1986) *Simon's Tax Intelligence* 680.

[313] CAA 1990, s. 60(2).

[314] Inland Revenue interpretation RI 10.

[315] CAA s. 60A added by FA 2000, s. 80.

24.4.12 Leasing—special rules

Trade of leasing qualifies

If T leases out an asset in the course of a trade, capital allowances will be available in the usual way. T is entitled, as owner of the goods leased, to the allowances, whether these are first year or writing down allowances. However, in relation to first year allowances it is expressly provided that these are available only if it appears that the machinery or plant will be used for a qualifying purpose in the requisite period and will at no time in that period be used for a non-qualifying purpose.[316] There may be difficulties in showing that the asset "belongs to" T if the lessee has been given an option to purchase the asset but this issue remains unexplored.[317]

Not in course of trade—restriction of first year allowance

Where T leases out an asset otherwise than in the course of trade, capital allowances may be available whether or not the asset is used for the purpose of a trade carried on by the lessee.[318] The lessor is treated as carrying on a notional but separate trade (and therefore pooled separately from any other assets for the writing down allowance).[319] The restriction on first year allowances, which applies where the lessor carried on a trade of leasing, also applies here.[320] It is also provided that where an allowance is made, it cannot be set off against the general profits of the lessor, but only against the income from the notional separate trade of leasing.[321] The question whether the asset is provided wholly and exclusively for the notional trade is determined according to the facts.[322]

Qualifying purpose—role

The concept of a qualifying purpose is significant in several respects:

(1) it may disqualify the asset from giving rise to a first year allowance;
(2) it may cause the asset to be pooled separately for the writing down allowance;
(3) rules direct the reduction of the writing down allowance from 25% to 10% in cases of overseas leasing, but even that reduced allowance is not available if the asset is used for a non-qualifying purpose and certain other conditions are satisfied.

The point of these further conditions is to ensure that the lease generates an adequate flow of income.[323] The restriction to 10% does not apply if the person is using the asset exclusively for the purposes of earning profits which are chargeable to tax in the UK. However, "profits or gains chargeable to UK tax" do not include those arising to a person who can claim relief under a double taxation agreement, e.g. the UK branch of a foreign

[316] CAA 1990, s. 22(4)(c); on the meaning of "qualifying purpose" and "requisite period", see ss 39, 40.
[317] The effect of an option needs close attention; in practice, the lessee can be given much the same economic benefit by reducing the leasing charge or extending the period of the lease.
[318] CAA 1990, s. 61(1); on cessation of leasing, see s. 61(1)(b); on meaning of lease (to include an agreement for a lease but not a mortgage), see s. 61(8).
[319] Ibid., s. 61(1).
[320] Ibid., s. 22(4)(c).
[321] Ibid., s. 61(5) s. 145(3); group relief is excluded by s. 61(7).
[322] Ibid., s. 61(3); however, s. 61(1) does not apply to machinery or plant let for use in a domestic house (s. 61(2)).
[323] Ibid., s. 42(3); the 25% rate was kept for certain ships and aircraft leased on charter (s. 39(6)–(8)).

company.[324] The restriction to 10% does not apply to short-term leasing or the leasing of a ship, aircraft or transport container used for a qualifying purpose.[325]

What is a qualifying purpose?

The concept of qualifying purpose covers a number of situations in which (1) the buyer uses the asset for short-term leasing, or (2) the lessee uses the asset for short-term leasing and either is resident in the UK or uses it in a trade carried on here, or (3) the buyer uses it for the purposes of a trade other than leasing.[326] However, the principal circumstance is where the asset is leased to lessees who use it for purposes other than leasing, *but* the lessees would have been entitled to capital allowances in respect of the asset if they had incurred the expenditure themselves.[327] The purpose of these rules is to exclude the situation in which the lessee uses the asset for personal consumption.

Restrictions on use of losses against general income

In relation to income tax (but not to corporation tax), losses arising from leasing, whether from first year or writing down allowances, can be set against general (i.e. non-leasing) income only if the lessor carries on a trade of leasing for at least six months, and substantially whole time.[328] The effect of this is to make equipment leasing an unattractive proposition, except when it is a full-time business.

Restrictions apply to leasing partnerships. For example X, Y and Z Ltd. are partners who buy plant and claim allowances. X and Y then withdraw from the partnership leaving Z to face the balancing charge, but Z is a non-resident company. Relief under TA 1988, ss 380 and 381 is denied where the scheme has been entered into with a company partner in prospect.[329]

Lessee's expenditure

Where the lessee (L) incurs capital expenditure on the provision of machinery or plant for the purposes of L's trade under the terms of L's lease, the asset is treated as belonging to L provided the trade continues.[330] The asset in fact belongs to the owner-lessor (O). When the lease ends the rules as to disposal value and balancing charges are applied as if the original expenditure had been incurred by O. Thus, the allowance is given to L, but any balancing charge may be levied on O. As a result of the rules reversing *Stokes* v. *Costain Property Investments Ltd.*[331] this does not now apply to machinery and plant which becomes part of a building on other land.

Finance leases[332]

Finance leases have attracted special attention in recent years. As have already seen, *Gallagher* v. *Jones* required the lessee to spread the actual payment over an appropriate period. The lessor will be taxed on the gross rentals received, but with a reduction for

324 Ibid., s. 50(2), added by FA 1993.
325 CAA 1990, s. 42(1).
326 Ibid., s. 39(3)–(5).
327 Ibid., s. 39(2).
328 TA 1988, s. 384(6)–(8); on "substantial" in a related CGT context, see *Palmer* v. *Maloney* [1999] STC 890.
329 CAA 1990, s. 142.
330 Ibid., s. 61(4).
331 [1984] STC 204, [1984] 1 All ER 849, CA; CAA 1990, s. 61(4)(b) (see above at §24.4.2).
332 Note definition in ibid., s. 82A, added by F (No. 2) A 1997, s. 47.

capital allowances. Both these elements have now been affected by recent legislation.[333] On the income side, FA 1997 requires that where the lessor's accounting profit is greater than the taxable profit, the accounting profit is to be preferred, so accelerating the taxable profit.[334] On the capital allowance side, a full year's allowance is available in the first year only if the asset was bought on the first day of the accounting period; if it was bought halfway through, only one half of the allowance is available.[335] Allowances may now only be used by the finance lessor where plant is sold to, and leased back by, a finance lessor to the original vendor;[336] this is to stop unused allowances being passed back to the vendor. As from the Royal Assent to FA 2000 this allowance is limited to the lower of cost price to the lessor and cost price to the lessee.[337] Further, allowances will not be available to the finance lessor if there are arrangements in the lease which remove the risk of loss if the terms of the contract are broken.[338] Finally, restrictions are imposed where a finance lessor acquires the asset on hire purchase by a combination of hire purchase contracts and finance leases.[339]

24.5 Ships

Ships have, for many years been treated specially for capital allowance purposes. In effect, free depreciation is allowed.[340] Expenditure on ships is not pooled. There is no statutory definition of a ship, but there have been many decisions on its meaning under the Merchant Shipping Acts. A hopper barge without engine or sail was held to be a ship,[341] but a floating gas container without power and not fitted for navigation was not.[342] A statutory definition of qualifying ships is, however, provideds for the purpose of the 1995 rules on deferment of balancing charges.[343]

Balancing charges arising on the disposal of qualifying ships[344] may be rolled over for a period of up to three years to be set off against subsequent expenditure[345] on new ships within that period. The ship may have been owned by the taxpayer previously, but there must be a six-year gap between ownership.[346]

FA 2000 introduces an alternative basis of taxation of shipping under which corporation tax would be based, in part, on tonnage.[346a]

333 i.e. F(No .2)A 1997 and FA 2000.

334 FA 1997, Sch. 12, para. 5; on Sch. 12, see Higginbotham [1997] *BTR* 236.

335 CAA 1990, s. 25 (5A)–(5C), added by F(No .2)A 1997, s. 44.

336 CAA 1990, s. 76A, added by F (No. 2) A 1997, s. 46.

337 CAA 1990, s. 76, added by FA 2000, s. 77.

338 CAA 1990, s. 76A(7).

339 Ibid., s. 60(2A) added by FA 1997, s. 45.

340 Ibid., s. 30(1).

341 *The Mac* (1882) 7 PD 126, CA.

342 *Wells* v. *Gas Float Whitton No. 2 (Owners)* [1897] AC 337, HL; see also *Wirth Ltd.* v. *SS Acadia Forest* [1974] 2 Lloyd's Rep 563.

343 This limit does not apply if the ship is lost at sea or is irreparably damaged (CAA 1990, s. 33E(1), (2) added by FA 1995, s. 96).

344 Defined by CAA 1990, s. 33E, added by FA 1995. See Inland Revenue Press Release, 20 July 1994, (1994) *Simon's Tax Intelligence* 882.

345 Defined by CAA 1990, s. 33D.

346 Ibid., s. 33D(4).

346a FA 2000 s. 82 and Sch. 22. There is much useful background in *Independent Inquiry into a Tonnage Tax*, published by H. M. Treasury on 12 August 1999.

24.6 Films Tapes and Disks

Previously, investment in master copies qualified for 100% first year allowances,[347] but this was stopped in 1982. Today CAA 1990, s. 68 treats certain expenditure as revenue expense; this means that capital allowances are not available but all allowable expenses are deductible. Preliminary expenditure is allowed immediately[348] and production or acquisition expenditure is written off over three years.[349] However, full and immediate write-off is allowed for certain British films costing £15 m or less to make; this provision has a sunset clause in that it does not apply to expenditure after 1 July 2002.[350] The film must be certified by the Secretary of State under the Films Act 1985, Schedule 1 as a qualifying film, i.e. it must meet certain criteria with regard to the EC content of a film and residence of the "filmer" and others, but may take the physical form of a disk, negative or tape.[351] The provisions do not apply to audio tapes, disks or non-qualifying films.

The essence of these reliefs is to recognise the long time gap between the incurring of expenditure on a film and the film's release. The rules bring forward the date at which relief can be given, but this is a matter of election.[352] Relief for preliminary expenditure of a revenue nature is also given, as is relief for abortive expenditure.[353] Relief for production expenditure of a revenue nature, so far as not already written off as preliminary expenditure, is written off over a three-year period at a flat rate. Producers wishing to remain within the existing capital allowances rules may opt out of these rules; a formal election is necessary.[354]

FA 2000 contains a number of tidying-up provisions.

24.7 Mining

UK companies operating abroad usually derive their money from mining metals and petroleum. Companies operating within the UK mine building materials, notably sand and gravel, china clay and slate. The history of capital allowances has been erratic to say the least and different rules apply according to the place being mined. The current rules were introduced by FA 1986.[355]

24.7.1 Qualifying expenditure

"Qualifying expenditure" is defined both by inclusion[356] and exclusion.[357] Thus, the expense incurred in an abortive application for planning permission is allowed,[358] but expense incurred on the acquisition of a site on which further expense will be incurred

[347] As in *Ensign Tankers (Leasing) Ltd.* v. *Stokes* [1992] STC 226, 64 TC 617, HL.
[348] Subject to a cap; the expenditure must not exceed 20% of total shooting as at the first day of shooting.
[349] F (No. 2) A 1992, ss. 41, 42.
[350] CAA 1990, s. 68(9); F (No. 2) A 1997, s. 48.
[351] F (No. 2) A 1992, s. 43. See Inland Revenue Press Release, 23 June 1992, (1992) *Simon's Tax Intelligence* 638.
[352] CAA 1990, s. 68(6A), (9A)–(9C), added by F (No. 2) A 1992.
[353] CAA 1990, s. 68(10), added by F (No. 2) A 1992 and F (No. 2) A 1992, s. 41.
[354] CAA 1990, s. 68(6A), (6B), (9A)–(9C), added by F (No. 2) A 1992.
[355] On transition, see CAA 1990, s. 119.
[356] Ibid., s. 105(1).
[357] Ibid., s. 105(5).
[358] Ibid., s. 105(6).

which will qualify for relief, is not.[359] Expenditure on machinery and plant is usually left to the machinery and plant system of allowances, but this will not apply where the expense is a pre-trading expense and the asset is disposed of before the trade begins; such expense may, therefore be qualifying expenditure.[360] A similar rule applies to pre-trading exploration expenditure.[361] Also included are certain payments by mining concerns for site comfort and development outside the UK.[362] Expenditure on restoring a site at the end of the operation also qualifies.[363] A source of mineral deposits includes a source of geothermal energy.[364]

When qualifying expenditure is incurred for the purposes of mineral extraction, a writing down allowance is given by reference to the amount by which the qualifying expenditure exceeds any disposal proceeds received during the period. The scheme is a simple reducing balance, so that previous allowances reduce the qualifying expenditure. For pre-trading expenditure on machinery and plant disposed of before the trade begins, and pre-trading exploration expenditure, the figure is 10%; for other qualifying expenditure, the figure is 25%.[365] The allowance is given in taxing the trade.[366] The cost of the land is not qualifying expenditure; a valuation is carried out by assuming that there is no source of mineral deposits, and that only existing or authorised use is allowed.[367]

24.8 Dredging

Allowances are given for capital expenditure incurred in dredging. The trade must consist of maintaining or improving the navigation of a harbour, estuary or waterway; alternatively, the dredging must be for the benefit of vessels using a dock occupied for the purpose of the trade, as where a trader incurs it own expense for its own dock.[368] Dredging refers only to acts done in the interests of navigation.[369] In general, the allowance is similar to that for industrial buildings. The straight line writing down allowance is 4%.[370] If the trade is permanently discontinued before the expenditure has been written off, there is an immediate write-off of the balance.[371] There is no balancing charge.

24.9 Agricultural Land

An allowance may be claimed by a person with a major interest in agricultural land who incurs capital expenditure on the construction of farmhouses, farm buildings, cottages,

359 CAA 1990, s. 105(5)(a).
360 Ibid., s. 106; otherwise the machinery and plant rules apply (s. 105(4)).
361 Ibid., s. 107.
362 Ibid., s. 108; where the building is in the UK the industrial buildings allowance may apply (e.g. s. 18(5)).
363 Ibid., s. 109 (but only if the work is carried out within three years of the termination; the cost is treated as incurred when the trade ends).
364 Ibid., s. 121(1).
365 Ibid., s. 98.
366 Ibid., s. 104.
367 Ibid., s. 110; a similar valuation is used for calculating the disposal proceeds (s. 102).
368 Ibid., s. 134(1), undoing *Dumbarton Harbour Board* v. *Cox* (1918) 7 TC 147. Note amendment by FA 1994, s. 213.
369 CAA 1990, s. 135(3).
370 Ibid., s. 134(2).
371 Ibid., s. 134(2).

fences and other works, e.g. drainage.[372] The allowance is a writing down allowance over 25 years, i.e. 4% p.a.[373]

For expenditure incurred before 1 April 1987 under a contract entered into before 14 March 1984 the allowances comprised an initial allowance of 20%, followed by a straight line writing down allowance of the remaining 80% over the next eight years. The 20% initial allowance was revived for expenditure incurred between 1 November 1992 and 31 October 1993,[374] but not since.

The allowance is set primarily against agricultural income.[375] The separate industrial buildings allowance may sometimes be available.

The expenditure must have been incurred for the purposes of husbandry[376] on the agricultural land, but an apportionment is made where the expenditure is only partly for that purpose.[377] Where the expenditure is on a farmhouse, only one-third is allowable and a smaller proportion is taken if the accommodation and amenities of the farmhouse are "out of due relation to the nature and extent of the farm". A farmhouse is a building used by the person running the farm as a farmhouse.[378] In *Lindsay* v. *IRC*[379] the only house on a sheep farm was occupied by a shepherd and the owner resided in the United States, but the house was held to be a farmhouse. In *IRC* v. *John M. Whiteford & Son*[380] the fact that the occupier was one of the partners running the farm did not mean that his house was necessarily a farmhouse; rather, it could be an agricultural cottage and so entitled to the full allowance. The proper criterion is not the status of the occupant but the purpose of the occupation of the premises.[381] In that case there was evidence that the farm was run from the house of the other partner. In both cases the decision of the Commissioners was upheld. If the farmhouse is of a scale extravagantly large for the purpose for which it is being used, it may be entitled to no allowance whatsoever.[382]

The details of the allowance are similar to those for industrial buildings. There are also rules for balancing allowances or charges on the happening of a "balancing event", which is defined as arising when the relevant interest is transferred and where the building is demolished, destroyed or otherwise ceases to exist.[383] This is a matter of election if the relevant interest is sold; both vendor and purchaser must elect.[384] Under the pre-1986 system, balances were not struck so there were neither balancing allowances nor balancing charges.

Where one party has control over the other, the parties are under common control or are connected persons, or the object of the disposal is to obtain a deduction or allowance, the

[372] Ibid., ss 123, 122 (pre-1986 expenditure). "Major interest" is defined in s. 125 and includes an owner in fee simple, a lessee and the Scottish equivalent; the mortgagor holds the major interest rather than the mortgagee. CAA 1990, s. 154, concerning contributions, applies to agricultural allowances as from 27 July 1989 (s.155(8)). Allowances for forestry land were abolished for chargeable periods beginning on or after 20 June 1989 (FA 1989, s. 120).

[373] More generous rules applied to expenditure incurred before 1 April 1987 under a contract entered into before 14 March 1984.

[374] CAA 1990, s. 124A, added by FA 1993, Sch. 12.

[375] CAA 1990, s. 132.

[376] Defined in ibid., s. 133(1) to include intensive rearing of livestock or fish.

[377] Ibid., s. 124.

[378] *Lindsay* v. *IRC* (1952) 34 TC 289, 292, *per* Lord Carmont.

[379] Ibid.

[380] (1962) 40 TC 379.

[381] Ibid., 384, *per* Lord Clyde.

[382] Ibid.

[383] CAA 1990, ss 128, 129.

[384] Ibid., s. 129; the election also applies to certain accidents (see s. 129(1)(b)).

anti-avoidance provisions with regard to sales are adopted for this allowance, but without the right to elect to substitute market value for the price agreed by the parties.[385] A separate rule directs the adjustment of the proceeds of sale where the relevant interest is disposed of subject to a subordinate interest; the value of the subordinate interest may not be ignored.[386]

24.10 Research and Development Allowances

FA 2000 makes two important changes in this area. First, it provides some new definitions and procedures for the long established scientific research allowance, now renamed Research and Development allowances. Secondly, it provides a new tax credit for expenditure on research and development by small and medium sized companies (and not other forms of enterprise). These new credit rules give a credit for 150% of the expenditure incurred by companies but do not apply if the expenditure is capital in nature;[387] see below §47.2.2. It is worth noting however that the definition of small and medium sized follows European lines and not those for FYAs for machinery and plant.

Research and Development allowances, previously called scientific research allowances are available for capital expenditure on research and development, provided it is related to the trade carried on (or to be carried on).[388] The research may be carried on by someone other than the trader provided it is on behalf of the trader, an expression which requires something close to agency.[389] The allowance does not extend to the costs of creating a training centre since research is confined to natural or applied science for the advancement of knowledge.[390] Whether activities are research and development is now decided by reference to accounting concepts.[391] Costs in acquiring rights in scientific research are not allowed. Apportionment of expenditure is permitted.[392]

The allowance is 100% of the cost. The rate of allowance was not reduced as from 1 April 1986. Balancing allowances and charges apply only if the asset ceases to be used for scientific research and is then (or later) sold (or destroyed).[393] The relevant chargeable period is that in which the expenditure was incurred, save that for pre-trading expenditure the chargeable period beginning with the commencement is taken.[394]

For expenditure incurred after 31 March 1985 these allowances and charges arise when the asset ceases to belong to the person whether through sale, destruction or any other

[385] CAA 1990, s. 133(8), s. 157.

[386] Ibid., s. 130.

[387] FA 2000, Sch. 21, para. 3(2); Appeal on whether now lie within the ordinary tax appeal structure and not as previously the Secretary of State for Trade and Industry; CAA 1990, s. 82A as added by FA 2000 clause 67 and Sch. 19.

[388] Ibid., s. 137; revenue expense may be deductible under s. 136 and TA 1988, s. 521. On "relating to", see *Salt* v. *Young* [1999] STC (SCD) 213 where the Special Commissioner said that one should not trace causality back too far. T's trade was in publishing books but that did not mean that expenditure on a computer used in carrying out research in writing the book was deductible under this head. On meaning of research and development see TA 1988 s. 837 (referred to by CAA 1990, s. 139).

[389] CAA 1990, s. 137; *Gaspet Ltd.* v. *Elliss* [1985] STC 572.

[390] CAA 1990, s. 139. On meaning of when an asset is sold, see s. 139(4).

[391] TA 1988, s. 837A(2)–(5); this brings in SSAP 13.

[392] CAA 1990, s. 137(4).

[393] Ibid., s. 138.

[394] Ibid., s. 137(5), as amended by FA 1994.

event.[395] Sums paid to approved research associations, universities and institutions may be deductible as if they were revenue expenditure.[396]

Transfers after 16 March 1993 may now fall within CAA 1990, s. 158 (see above at §24.2.4). Where the taxpayer elects for that provision to apply the amount to be taken is either nil (where the 100% allowance has been claimed under s. 137) or in other cases the full amount of the expenditure.[397]

24.11 Patents and Know How

Since 1945 a special regime treats sums derived from the disposal of patents as income, and conversely, allows expenditure on acquiring patent rights. Today, there is an annual writing down allowance of 25% (reducing balance basis);[398] this regime also applies to the costs of acquiring know how,[399] a term defined as information likely to assist in the manufacture or processing of goods or materials.[400] Balancing allowances and charges apply if the rights come to an end or are disposed of.[401] Royalties payable under a patent agreement to a non-resident are subject to deduction at source under TA 1988, s. 349. Before 1986 the capital cost of purchasing patent rights was, broadly speaking, allowed by equal annual instalments over 17 years.[402]

Capital payments received for the disposal of patent rights are taxed as income and spread over six years. If the individual dies before the six-year period ends, any remaining instalments may be spread back; similar rules apply on discontinuance or on the winding-up of a company.[403]

24.12 Commentary: Policy and History

24.12.1 Policy

The need for tax rules for capital allowance arises from the initial decision to deny any deduction for capital expenditure. As was seen at the beginning of this chapter, the background problem arises from the need to recognise that there is a cost to the business because of the decline in the value of the assets due to physical deterioration or obsolescence. The declining value could be recognised by annual valuations, but this would be too subjective and/or expensive in practice; as such, accountants use a cost recovery or writing off system.

[395] On values to be taken see CAA 1990, s. 138(4). On meaning of relevant event, see s. 138(1). On change, see FA 1985, s. 63; the old rules remain for expenditure incurred before that date and for expenditure incurred after that date but before 1 April 1987 under a contract entered into before 13 March 1984.

[396] Under CAA 1990, s. 136(b); on meaning of research for a class of trade, see s. 139(1)(d).

[397] Ibid., s. 158(2)(d), added by FA 1993, s. 117 and amended by FA 1994, s. 119.

[398] TA 1988, s. 520.

[399] Ibid., s. 530.

[400] Ibid., s. 533(7); and see Inland Revenue interpretation RI 46.

[401] Ibid., s. 523.

[402] Ibid., s. 522.

[403] Ibid., s. 524.

24.12.2 Grander theories

Depreciation rules would also be needed under a comprehensive income tax, unless an accounting definition of income was adopted so that full depreciation was made over an appropriate period. Such rules would not be needed under an expenditure tax since all investment would be deductible immediately.

A price is paid if such alternatives are rejected. Theorists complain that systems such as the UK's begin by discriminating against capital spending and in favour of employment costs; these systems then adjust by giving allowances, and over-compensate by also allowing a deduction for interest on the money used to buy the asset. Theorists have further enjoyment with the idea of an economic rent which would take capital expenditure into account.[404] The big question whether allowances can affect investment decisions must be seen as part of a wider view of the effects of taxes on business behaviour.[405] Those who believe that adjusting allowance affects the overall level of investment, point to the fact that capital investment by businesses is a lower percentage of GNP than spending by either consumers or governments; also, it is much more volatile.[406]

24.12.3 The UK system—scope and rates[407]

As has been seen, the UK tax system of allowances is as haphazard and history-driven as other parts of the system. The UK system is unusually strict (i.e. mean) in relation to assets for which it allows deductions, notably by the exclusion of non-industrial buildings, the curious rules under which the industrial buildings allowance works for only the first 25 years of this building's life and, at least until 2000, the shamefully slow refusal to do much more than the minimum to adapt the system to take account of the development of intellectual property rights.

The UK's policy on the actual rate of depreciation has shifted dramatically over the years. This is because although the current view is that the tax system should recognise the need to write off the cost of depreciating assets, another view would argue that the stimulation of investment demands tax incentives (which view dominated in the period before1984).[408] This older idea can be traced back to 1932—the middle of the depression—when allowances were first made available at a rate faster than the commercial rate of depreciation.[409] The decision to revive, even if on a temporary basis, the first year allowance, in 1992, was also attributable to the need to give relief for the recession.[410] In 1954 investment allowances were added to the rights under the writing-off process. The weakening of the depreciation basis was also seen in the rules for machinery and plant which, apart from the

[404] The idea of rent is associated particularly with the great economist Ricardo, see his collected works (ed.) Saffra, CUP. A rent resource tax for oil and gas is discussed by Garnaut and Ross 85, Economic Journal 272; on North Sea Oil taxation see Devereux and Morris IFS Report Series No. 6 (1983).

[405] See Mintz (1996) 16(3) *Fiscal Studies* 23, 46–9.

[406] For example Ford and Poret, *OECD Economic Studies No. 16*; cited in *The Economist*, 14 May 1991.

[407] See *Corporation Tax*, Cmnd 8456, ch. 15. For comparative material, see *OECD Taxing Profits in a Global Economy*, ch. 3, tables 3.5, 3.9–3.12.

[408] See Prest and Barr, *Public Finance in Theory and Practice*, 16.4 and, Hendershott and Cheng, *How Taxes Affect Economic Behaviour* (Brookings, 1981), 85, both stressing other factors affecting investment decisions such as interest rates and inflation. See also the review of older literature by Sumner, IFS Lecture Series (No. 4) (1976).

[409] Accountancy depreciation can consider the individual asset; a tax system must accommodate many kinds of assets in one rate, unless it opts for free depreciation.

[410] On effects, see Bond, Denney and Devereux (1993) 14(2) *Fiscal Studies* 1. Other alleviating rules, e.g. extending relief for corporate losses, were introduced at the same time by FA 1992.

first year allowance, applied a single rate of depreciation (25%) whatever the life of the asset, to any remaining expenditure and to a general pool of such expenditure. Today, special rules for short or long life assets modify this criticism in part. However, the palliatives for small and medium-sized enterprises can be seen as some crude offset for other regulatory burdens imposed upon them. Meanwhile, the combination of the rules on rates and scope mean that very different rates of return can be made from different investments. Those who like the present system argue that there is little evidence of underinvestment. There is a significant need for helpful empirical work here.

It was perhaps ironic that the tax system abandoned depreciation as the rational basis of its allowances system just as such evidence as there was suggested that the incentive effects of the allowances were limited and related more to the timing of investment than to its volume. When 100% allowances were given the question could be asked what further incentives remained, other than outright cash grants,[411] and where it would all stop. Was the effect of the system simply to maintain marginally profitable businesses and to exempt manufacturing industries from liability to corporation tax?

The current scheme, which has been in place since 1984, reduced corporation tax rates by reducing capital allowances; the overall result was to reduce the incentives to invest but with very marked, short-term opportunities as the new rates came in.[412] This was coupled with the further irony of a rapidly contracting manufacturing base, the very area of the economy most favoured by the 1970's approach, and sharply rising real tax burdens for the corporate sector.[413]

24.12.4 Further problems

Other issues remain.[414] Why should the allowances be on a historic cost basis with no allowance for inflation?[415] In a period without inflation there is no problem since the replacement cost will equal the allowed cost—for an exactly equivalent asset. The issue is whether the purpose is to find the correct balance if the trade were to cease that day, or to tackle the problem of financing a continuing trade. However, such raising of the cost base would also require adjustments to the balancing charges,[416] which is at present levied on purely paper gains. Again, why should the balancing charge be limited to recapturing the allowance already made, and why not extend it to the capital gain arising on disposal? Why should there be such different allowances for such different assets? At present, pooling is confined to machinery and plant and its effect is close to permitting rollover relief, as in CGT. Why should there be no allowance for the depreciation of what, for many, is their most important capital asset—their own earning power?[417] Why should one not be able to write

[411] Allowances are also given in the form of relief for interest payments. Grants were introduced between 1966 and 1970: see, *inter alia*, Lazar [1966] *BTR* 179, Cmnd. 4516, §2; and, in a wider context, Sharpe 95 LQR 206. On discretionary element, see *British Oxygen Co. Ltd.* v. *Minister of Technology* [1971] AC 610, [1970] 3 All ER 165.

[412] Devereux (1988) 9(1) *Fiscal Studies* 62.

[413] Feldstein and Summers (1979) *National Tax Jo.* 4.

[414] See ideas discussed in *Corporation Tax*, above at n. 392, chs 11, 15.

[415] For a comparison of accelerated depreciation with inflation adjustments, see Feldstein (1981) 34 *National Tax Jo.* 29.

[416] See Tucker, Cmd 8189 (1951), §§102–115; Royal Commission on the Taxation of Profits and Income, *Final Report*, Cmnd 9474 (1955), §§350–62. Morley, *Fiscal Implications of Inflation Accounting*, cha. 1.

[417] In 1915 excess profits duty was applied to trades but not to professions. McKenna, the Chancellor of the Exchequer, justified this on the ground that it would be impossible to devise a satisfactory datum line in the case of members of a profession who made their profits by the excessive expenditure of their capital, that is their energy, brain power and health.

off the costs of one's training for a profession?[418] Again, why should the system take the form of a deferral of tax? In such form it is a long-term credit and therefore has no effect on reported profits; an immediate tax credit might be preferable.[419] To all these proposals there is one short reply, namely that they make the mistake of supposing that the system has something to do with justice, equity and depreciation; it has not. Such proposals are best seen as (possibly expensive) tools of economic planning.

418 On human capital, see Beer [1987] *BTR* 392; and other articles cited above at §7.1.

419 See discussions by Lindholm (1951) 4 *National Tax Jo.* 180; Wiseman (1963) 16 *National Tax Jo.* 36; and Bird (1963) 16 *National Tax Jo.* 41.

25

Income from Land in the United Kingdom: Schedule A

25.1 Basic Structure

Income arising under Schedule A was rationalised for income tax in 1995[1] and for corporation tax in 1998;[2] the income tax rules were amended in 1998. The rationalisation was needed because of the advent of self-assessment: not even the Revenue thought that the old rules, which had existed since 1963, were intelligible.

Schedule A income is taxed on a current income basis using most of the Schedule D, Case I rules for the calculation of income, including the requirement of an acceptable accounting basis subject to any adjustments required or authorised by law. However, the Schedules remain distinct.[3] Income under Schedule A is not trading income; therefore it cannot be earned income under TA 1988, s. 833 and so cannot be relevant earnings for pension

[1] FA 1995, s. 39, Sch. 6; on transition, see HC Official Report, Standing Committee D (Sixth sitting), col. 166, 9 February 1995, and Inland Revenue Press Release, 20 February 1995, (1995) *Simon's Weekly Tax Intelligence* 250.

[2] FA 1998, s. 38, Sch. 5. Interest paid remains within the loan relationship rules. Losses are given relief in the same ways as excess management charges of an investment company (TA 1988, s. 392A); group relief is governed by TA 1988, ss 403–403AE, 494A, with a separate anti-avoidance rule for changes of ownership (s. 768D). These rules are modified for non-resident companies and insurance companies (s. 15, para. 1(3), referring to ss 15(1A), 432AA, 441B(2A) respectively); however, this is principally to ensure that the Schedule A business of such companies is kept separate from their other businesses.

[3] The boundary between trade and property is explored in the Canadian context by Durnford (1991) 39 *Can. Tax Jo.* 1131.

contribution rules. Moreover, separate legislative provision must be made for losses and capital allowances; CGT reliefs applicable to trading do not apply automatically.

The corporation tax rules were changed later. This was because the old system gave companies a certain flexibility with regard to interest payments and, in the case of investment companies, management expenses.[4]

25.2 Basis of Charge and Calculation of Income

25.2.1 Elements of Schedule A

Tax is charged on the annual profits or gains arising from any business carried on for the exploitation—as a source of rents or other receipts—of any estate, interest or rights in or over any land in the UK.[5] The idea of estate or interest in land in the UK is widened to cover the right to use a caravan or houseboat at a single location in the UK.[6] Income from land outside the UK continues to be taxed under Schedule D, Case V, but such income is calculated in the same way as for Schedule A.[7] Schedule A does *not* apply to profits arising from the occupation of land (see below at §25.7).

Lest the term business be considered too restrictive, Schedule A has a second limb, which covers transactions entered into for such exploitation, the transaction being deemed to have been entered into in the course of such a business.[8]

Annual profits

The use of the words "annual profits" underlines the point that capital sums are not caught by Schedule A—unless some other provision so provides. Payments for wayleaves are brought in where they are for an easement over land within a Schedule A business.[9]

Business A

"Schedule A business" is defined as any business, the profits or gains of which are chargeable to income tax under Schedule A, including the business treated as arising under the second limb.[10] The words "exploitation as a source of rents or other receipts" replace the idea of receipts "arising by virtue of ownership". It is as yet unclear whether this is simply a modernisation of language (for a more managerial age). The words "as a source of rents or other receipts" are expressed to include payments in respect of a licence to occupy or otherwise use land or the exercise of any other rights over land, rentcharges, ground annuals, feu duties, and other annual payments reserved in respect of, or charged on, or issuing out of, land.[11]

Rent

Rent under a lease, which includes the use of furniture, was at one time chargeable wholly under Schedule D, Case VI unless the landlord elected to be taxed in part under Schedule A.

[4] HC Official Report, Standing Committee D (Sixth sitting), col. 166, 9 February 1995.
[5] TA 1988, s. 15, para.1(1).
[6] TA 1988, s. 15, para. 3. By concession, rental income from caravan sites may be amalgamated with associated trading income—ESC B29.
[7] TA 1988, s. 65A, added by FA 1995, s. 41.
[8] TA 1988, s. 15, para. 1(2).
[9] FA 1997, s. 60.
[10] TA 1988, s. 832 (1), as amended by FA 1995, Sch. 6, para. 28.
[11] TA 1988, s. 15, para. 1(4).

Since 1998 such rent is taxed entirely under Schedule A—unless it has already been taxed under Schedule D, Case I as the profits of a trade which makes the furniture available for use in premises.[12]

Liability

The income tax charge applies to the person receiving, or entitled to, the income, a formula which is the same as for Schedule D.[13] The income is charged on the full amount of the profits or gains arising in the year of assessment—a current year basis.[14] The tax is due, like all other parts of income tax under the self-assessment regime, on 31 January after the end of the year of assessment. The payment on account rules in TMA 1970 s. 59A apply to this as to other types of income.

Rent

Rent is not defined for tax purposes. Its general meaning[15] is a payment due from tenant to (land)lord by reason of tenure; it must be reserved as rent. However, it has been held that a payment can be rent even though there is no right to distrain for it.[16] The rent is a sum payable for the lease, and the obligation to pay passes to an assignee. The payment of a premium in instalments is not rent.[17]

Other receipts

"Other receipts" which may arise from the exploitation of land are stated to include payments in respect of a licence to occupy or otherwise use land, or exercise any other right over land. Examples include such items as licence fees for advertisement hoardings, parking fees and service charges which are not reserved as rent, provided they are not in respect of services constituting a trade. Thus, a separate charge for meals would fall within Schedule D, Case I, whereas if a lease provides for the provision of a service for which no separate payment is made, e.g. heating, the whole rent comes within Schedule A and the cost of heating is an allowable expense. In *Beecham Group Ltd.* v. *Fair*[18] payments made by an employer to an employee for the use of the employee's garage to store samples and stock for use in the employee's work were held to fall within Schedule E, not Schedule A. The Revenue allows a trader, who lets a part of the building in which it carried on a business, to treat the rents as trading income.[19]

Some situations are impossible to classify. Where a farmer sold turf from his land he was held taxable under Schedule A but also, in the alternative, under Schedule D, Case I.[20] It is unclear what effect this breach of the Schedular system may have.

Damages

Damages for trespass to land and loss of rent are not liable to income tax as rent.[21] However, damages to a landlord in respect of a tenant overstaying the end of a lease were held to be

[12] Ibid., s. 15, para. 4.
[13] Ibid., s. 21(1); old rules in ibid., s. 23 for collecting tax from agents and lessees were abolished in 1995.
[14] Ibid., s. 21(2).
[15] On general meaning, see Gray, *Elements of Land Law* (2nd ed, Butterworths), 701–706.
[16] *T. and E. Homes Ltd.* v. *Robinson* [1979] STC 351, 52 TC 267.
[17] But it may be taxed as if it were rent (TA 1988, s. 35).
[18] [1984] STC 15, 65 TC 219.
[19] Inland Revenue Booklet 150, *Taxation of Rents*, §§501 *et seq.* On apportionment between Schedule A and Schedule D, Case I when the election is not made, see ibid., §522.
[20] *Lowe* v. *Ashmore Ltd.* (1970) 46 TC 597; see also above at §19.7.
[21] *Hall & Co.* v. *Pearlberg* [1956] 1 All ER 297n, [1956] 1 WLR 244.

income in later Privy Council case,[22] so the matter may be less clear. If the payments are not taxable at all, it follows that in assessing damages the court should take account of the tax which the plaintiff has not had to pay and grant only the net sum under the rule in *British Transport Commission* v. *Gourley*.[23] This situation must be distinguished from that where an action is brought for arrears of rent, since such sums are clearly within Schedule A.

25.2.2 Exclusions from Schedule A

Specifically excluded from Schedule A are:[24]

(1) profits arising from the occupation of land see below §25.7;
(2) any profits or gains charged to tax under Schedule D, Case I, by TA 1988, s. 53(1) (farming and market gardening), s. 55 (mines, quarries, sand and gravel), or s. 98 (profits of tied premises);
(3) any sums charged to tax under Schedule D, Case III by TA 1988, s. 119 or 120 (mining and other royalties);
(4) in the case of a company, any debits and credits brought into account under the loan relationship rules of FA 1996, exchange gains and losses under the foreign exchange rules of FA 1993, or the qualifying payment rules of FA 1994 (interest rate and currency contracts).

Capital

Tax under Schedule A is still a tax on income and not on capital gains.[25] A premium accruing on the grant of a lease giving possession of premises would, but for special legislation in TA 1988, ss 34–36, fall outside Schedule A. However, a gain accruing from the assignment, as distinct from the grant of a lease,[26] or the grant of a lease of shooting rights, is a matter for CGT, not Schedule A. Similarly a sum payable in return for the grant or release of an easement would normally escape Schedule A, as would a one-off payment for allowing a motorway contractor to tip sub-soil onto a taxpayer's land.[27]

25.2.3 Basis of charge and calculation of income

Schedule D, Case I rules

In computing Schedule A income the principles of Schedule D, Case I apply.[28] Various Case I computational rules in TA 1988[29] or later legislation apply.[30] These include rules relating

[22] *Raja's Commercial College* v. *Gian Singh & Co. Ltd.* [1976] STC 282, [1976] 2 All ER 801, PC (damages for almost six years; occupation after end of lease; damages equal to excess of market rent over rent under former lease).

[23] [1956] AC 185, [1955] 3 All ER 796. In *Hall* v. *Pearlberg*, above at n. 21,the rate of tax used was that at the time of the judgment, but this appears to be wrong since the rates of tax for the years in issue were known.

[24] TA 1988, s. 15, para. 2.

[25] See, for example, the arguments raised (unsuccessfully) in *Jeffries* v. *Stevens* [1982] STC 639 and *Lowe* v. *J. W. Ashmore Ltd.* (1970) 46 TC 597.

[26] Unless the original lease is granted at an undervalue (TA 1988, s. 35; see below at §25.5.4).

[27] *McClure* v. *Petre* [1988] STC 749, 61 TC 226.

[28] TA 1988, s. 21A(1).

[29] Ibid., s. 72 (apportionment) and most of ss 74–99, i.e. all the provisions of Chapter V of Part IV (computational provisions relating to the Schedule D charge).

[30] TA 1988, Sch. 21A (2); FA 1988, s. 73(2) (consideration for restrictive undertakings); FA 1989, s. 76 (expenses in connection with non-approved retirement benefit schemes); ibid., ss 112, 113 (expenditure in connection with the provision of a security asset or service).

to business entertainment expenses, expenditure involving crime and redundancy payments,[31] and the Schedule D timing rule for deducting emoluments.[32] More crucially, they include the "true and fair view" provisions in FA 1998, ss 42 and 46(1), (2) (provisions as to computation of profits and losses).

The provisions of TA 1988 which are excluded, are:[33] s. 82 (interest paid to non-residents); s. 87 (treatment of premiums taxed as rent); s. 96 (farming and market gardening: relief for fluctuating profits); and s. 98 (tied premises: receipts and expenses treated as those of trade). The first two sections contain rules which are superseded by other rules in Schedule A, while the two latter sections refer to matters which are excluded from Schedule A.

Non-computational rules in TA 1988, which are made to apply to Schedule A,[34] are most of the post-cessation rules,[35] i.e. ss 103–106, 108, 109A, 110, 113 (effect for income tax purposes of change in the persons engaged on trade), s. 337(1) (effect of company beginning or ceasing to carry on trade) and 401(1) (pre-trading expenditure). In addition, the FA 1998 rules on change of accounting basis in s. 44 and Schedule 6 apply.

Timing—receipts

Given the application of the true and fair view provisions in FA 1998, tax computations must be prepared on an acceptable accounting basis—subject to any adjustment required or authorised by law. This generally means that incomings are recognised on a matching basis and not simply by reference to when they were due or, still less, to when they were received. Therefore, rent payable in advance or arrears must be attributed to the use of the property for the period for which the tenant is paying—making such apportionments as may be needed. However sums which cannot be attributed to a period should probably be taxed by reference to the time they were received; this receives indirect support from the 1998 rule that a receipts basis is applied to the various sums caught under ss 34–36.

Receipts will also include service charge contributions from tenants. However, if the property is residential the landlord's duty to keep the money in a separate account may prevent this.[36] Whether a stand-alone maintenance trust is a good planning idea is uncertain.[37]

Expenses

The correct treatment of expenditure also depends on accounting principles. A premium on an insurance policy may properly be split between tax years and related to the period for which the insurance cover was provided. In *Jenners Princes Street Edinburgh Ltd.* v. *IRC*[38] the Special Commissioners held that in accordance with accounting practice it was permissible for the company to make provision for the full cost of repairs when the contract was put out to tender and that this was not barred by TA 1988, s. 74(d).

[31] TA 1988, ss 577, 577A, 579, 580; others are ss 588–589B.

[32] FA 1989, s. 43.

[33] TA 1988, s. 21A(4)

[34] [1956] AC 185, Sch. 21B.

[35] The exceptions are ibid., s. 107 which treats the post-cessation receipt as earned income, and s. 109 which provides a special relief for persons born before 6 April 1917.

[36] Landlord and Tenant Act 1987, s. 43 (2)(b); see de Souza (1998) *Private Client Business* 267, 270.

[37] See de Souza, ibid., 271.

[38] (1998) STC (SCD) 166; s. 74(d) restricts certain deductions to sums actually expended, but this was held to mean expended in an accounting sense. On Revnue acceptance of this decision, see Inland Revenue Press Release, 20 July 1999, (1999) *Simons Weekly Tax Intelligence* 1302.

Pooling

Since the source is the business of exploiting land it is no longer necessary, as it was under the old law, to treat different properties as different sources; expenses incurred on different properties will be pooled regardless of whether they are still owned. However, it should not be forgotten that expenditure incurred in whole or in part for non-commercial reasons should not now be allowable at all. It is likely that the new system for Schedule A will highlight problems with the duality principle.

25.2.4 Partnerships

Where a trading partnership receives income from various sources, the basis period for determining income which accrues to the partnership, and which is then treated as income of the individual partners, is the Schedule D, Case I or II basis period for the relevant year of assessment.[39] This applies overlap profits rules for all income—including Schedule A income. Overlap relief is given under those rules at a subsequent change of accounting date or on the early retirement of the partner. However, joint ownership of property does not, of itself, create a partnership. Where there is no partnership the partnership return is not required and there is no overlap problem. It is very important therefore to be able to determine whether income is from partnership property or joint property.[40]

25.2.5 Deductions

Special deductions

Certain situations attract special rules for deductions, as follows: land managed as one estate (s. 26), maintenance funds for historic buildings (s. 27) and expenditure on sea walls (s.30). Each has both an income tax version and a corporation tax version. S. 26 is to be repealed as from 6 April 2001;[41] the possible effects of this change on heritage estates have been controversial.[41]

Capital allowance

Capital allowances are given for machinery and plant used in the Schedule A business as if it had been set up on or after 6 April 1995.[42] Expenditure on plant to be used in a dwelling house is excluded.[43] Allowances may also be claimed for industrial buildings and agricultural buildings.[44]

Interest

The calculation of income by reference to Schedule D, Case I means that interest will be deductible, or not, according to the rules in TA 1988, ss 74, 349, etc. The change may also means that interest will be deductible by reference to the date on which it falls due rather than the date of payment. This also means not only that there is a duty to withhold lower[45]

[39] TA 1988, s. 111(4), (7), (8).

[40] For a discussion of five different situations, see see Tiley and Collison, *UK Tax Guide 1999–2000* (Butterworths), para. 9.06.

[41] FA 1998, s. 39.

[42] CAA 1990, s. 28A, added by FA 1997.

[43] CAA 1988 s. 28A(3); apportionment for part such use is directed by s. 28(4).

[44] CAA 1990, ss. 9 and 132.

[45] TA 1988, s. 4A.

rate tax in the circumstances prescribed, but also that the duality rules in TA 1988, s. 74(a) will become relevant—a matter of particular importance if the property is not let at a commercial rent. If property is let at a commercial rent for part of the year, and at a non-commercial rent for the rest of the year, apportionment of the interest would seem to be possible. The change also meant that it was no longer necessary to retain the special interest relief rule in TA 1988, s. 355(1)(b) for property available for letting for 52 weeks in any period and actually let at a commercial rent for at least 26 weeks.[46]

25.2.6 Payments to non-residents

Where the Schedule A income accrues to a person whose usual place of abode is outside the UK, (the "non-resident"),[47] there has long been an obligation on the person making the payment, and on a person who is the agent of a non-resident agent, to deduct tax at basic rate.[48] The tax must be accounted for quarterly;[49] there is an obligation to make an annual return.[50] The present rules give the Revenue power to allow the payment to be made gross if it approves an application by the non-resident;[51] that approval may be withdrawn.[52] The withholding rule does not apply where the income is paid to the UK branch of a non-resident company and which is chargeable to corporation tax.[53]

This procedure does not require notice by either the landlord or the Revenue to the tenant, on whom is cast therefore a duty to know the landlord's usual place of abode. Under established case-law, the right to deduct tax is lost as soon as the payment is made gross.[54] There is no right to make good the failure to deduct by making a deduction from a subsequent payment, even one falling within the same tax year.[55] The cases may have to be reconsidered in the light of the restitution decision of the House of Lords in *Kleinwort Benson Ltd. v. Lincoln City Council*.[56]

25.3 Furnished Lettings

25.3.1 General rules

Rent for the occupation of the property charged under Schedule A now also extends to situations where the rent includes the use of furniture.[57] Further rules apply if the rent fulfils the conditions for furnished holiday lettings.

[46] It was necessary to have a further new provision for corporation tax (ibid., s. 338A) but this was swept away when the new corporation tax rules for loan relationships came into force in 1996.

[47] On problems with this formulation see §26.5.

[48] TA 1988, s. 42A, added by FA 1995, and SI 1995/2902, reg. 8(2) and 9(1). The earlier rule, TA 1988, s. 43, used the machinery in ss 349, 350.

[49] SI 1995/2902, reg. 10.

[50] Ibid., reg. 11.

[51] The conditions are set out in SI 1995/2902, reg. 17; among other things, the non-resident must show that he has complied with any requirements of the Tax Acts or Management Acts or that he does not expect to be liable to pay any UK tax.

[52] SI 1995/2902, reg. 19.

[53] Ibid., reg. 8(3).

[54] *Tenbry Investments Ltd. v. Peugeot Talbot Motor Co. Ltd.* [1992] STC 791.

[55] Ibid.

[56] See below at §27.5.5.

[57] TA 1988, s. 15, para. 4. The Law Commission rejected a proposal to move rent from furnished lettings into

The capital allowance rules applicable where machinery and plant are let by a person do not apply where the letting is for use as a dwelling house.[58] Concessionary relief is therefore given for wear and tear on furniture in furnished lettings. Broadly, T may elect to choose between the actual costs of replacement on the "renewals" basis, or take a 10% deduction from the rent received less any council tax or water rates which the landlord pays.[59] Taking the 10% deduction does not prevent T from claiming renewals allowance for renewing fixtures which are an integral part of the building.

However, no deduction has been permitted for the landlords' costs of obtaining alternative accommodation for themselves, since these are in the nature of personal expenditure.[60]

Example

Furnished Lettings Assessment 2000–01 (not furnished holiday lettings)

Year ended 5 April 2001

Rent received		£3,500
Less allowable expenses		
Council tax	£560	
Water rates	£80	
Wear and tear (10% of rent received net of deductions)	£286	
Insurance	£300	
Repairs to property	£500	
Accountancy fees	£600	£2,326
Profit		£1,174

25.3.2 Furnished holiday lettings

TA 1988, ss 503 and 504 treat the income as arising under a Schedule A business—the income is not moved to Schedule D. The following rules (otherwise applicable only to trades) apply:

(1) the income is to be treated as earned income and so as relevant earnings for personal pension arrangements and retirement annuity contracts;
(2) loss relief rules as for trades (see above at §10);
(3) capital allowances (see above at §24.3);
(4) rollover relief for CGT (see below at §42.4);
(5) retirement relief for CGT (see below at §42.5);
(6) CGT relief for gifts of business assets (see below at §36.3);
(7) bad debt CGT relief for loans to traders (see below at §34.4); and
(8) relief for pre-trading expenditure(see above at §20.6).

Schedule A partly because the variable amounts from such furnished lettings make the Schedule A machinery less appropriate (Cmnd 4654 (1971) §61). The advent of self-assessment removes this problem.

58 CAA 1990, s. 61(2).

59 ESC B47; T must also deduct any payments for services normally borne by a tenant.

60 *Wylie* v. *Eccott* (1913) 6 TC 128.

The three-year carry back rule for losses in the first three years of a trade (TA 1988, s. 381) is adapted.[61] However, the relief allowing trading losses to be set against capital gains does not extend to losses from furnished holiday lettings.

Expenditure is deductible as if the letting were a trade.[62] The CGT rules in (4)–(7) above apply as if the "trade" were carried on throughout the year and the property used only for such purposes, save where the accommodation is neither let commercially nor available to be so let (unless prevented by works of construction or repair).[63] The purpose of this rule is to withhold the relief if there is any period of owner-occupation. Provision is also made where the house being replaced was eligible for exemption as an only or main residence.[64]

The rules are intended to bring a measure of certainty to these areas. Where the taxpayer does not fulfil the stringent conditions laid down it may still be possible to argue that a trade is being carried on and so come within Schedule D, Case I, rather than Schedule A. The rules may be seen as a recognition of the artificial nature of the division between property income and trading income; it remains to be seen whether other instances of this artificiality will also be amended.

Stringent conditions must be satisfied before a letting is treated as a furnished holiday letting. The property must be in the UK, the letting must be on a commercial basis and with a view to the realisation of profit, and the tenant must be entitled to the use of the furniture. The property must be available for letting to the general public during the season and available for not less than 140 days, it must be let for at least 70 days and, for a period of at least seven months, it must not normally be in the same occupation for continuous periods exceeding 31 days. Where these conditions are fulfilled in relation to one property but not another, the taxpayer may elect to have the properties averaged. Thus, if property 1 is let for 80 days and property 2 for 68 days, an averaging election will make both properties let for 74 days, so that both qualify.

These conditions must be satisfied by reference to periods of 12 months, being the year of assessment for an individual and the accounting period of a company. Special rules apply where the accommodation was not within these rules in the previous year: the 12-month period runs from the date of the first letting; in the converse situation, the period begins on the last date of letting.

25.4 Rent a Room Exemption

The purpose behind this complicated relief is to provide an incentive to those who have spare rooms in their homes and wish to let them out.[65] A "qualifying individual" who receives relevant sums in respect of a "qualifying residence", may elect to be exempt from income tax on the relevant sums up to a limit—currently a gross rent of £4,250, although this figure may be varied by Treasury order.[66] Sums are relevant if they are in respect of the use of furnished accommodation in the residence (or residences), or any relevant goods or

[61] TA 1988, s. 503(2)–(4).
[62] Ibid., s. 503(5).
[63] TCGA 1992, s. 241(4), (5).
[64] Ibid., s. 241(6).
[65] Inland Revenue Press Release, 18 June 1992, (1992) *Simon's Tax Intelligence* 617.
[66] F (No. 2) A 1992, s.59, Sch. 10, paras 1,6, 9; and SI 1996/2953. It should be noted that the figure may be reduced by the Order.

services.[67] Goods and services are relevant if they are, or are similar in nature to, meals, cleaning and laundry.[68] If the individual has any non-relevant sums from the same residences, relief is not available.[69]

The Revenue view is that this relief does not extend to income from uses other than as furnished living accommodation.[70]

A residence is a qualifying residence if it is the individual's only or main residence at any time in the basis period.[71] In this, and in the definition of a residence, the rules are similar to those for the old deduction of mortgage interest.[72] Because the relief is from Schedule D, Case I, with its various basis period rules, reference must be made to the basis period, i.e. a period in which profits or gains income tax falls finally to be computed in respect of the source.[73]

The exemption is given in respect of relevant sums, which are, as already seen, defined in terms of sums accruing, and so do not take account of any allowable deductions. The exemption is given up to a basic amount, currently £4,250. This applies to the basis period and subsequent 12-month periods.[74] This amount is reduced by 50% (to £2,125) if, at any time during the year, sums accrue to any other person (or persons) in respect of the residential accommodation or relevant goods or services, and at that time the residence is the individual's only or main residence.[75] This rule applies where, for example, A and B share a house and jointly let a room to C or A lets a room to D, and B lets a room to E. However, this rule applies only where A and B receive money; if A and B arrange affairs so that all the income accrues to A or to B, the limit will be £4,250; if the money is shared, the limit will be £2,125. In determining the gross sums received, account must be taken of any balancing charge falling due in respect of machinery and plant by including that amount as part of the gross receipt.[76]

The relief is in respect of sums accruing, and account is not generally taken of any capital allowances or balancing charges, or of any other expenses.[77] Two sets of elections flow from this. First, the taxpayer may elect that the relief should not apply;[78] this will be valuable if, for example, the allowable expenses and other deductions give rise to a loss. Secondly, the taxpayer may choose between being taxed on the whole profit in the usual way, or elect[79] to be taxed on the gross receipts so far as they exceed £4,250,[80] provided receipts exceed that amount only by a small amount.

67 F (No. 2) A 1992, s. 59, Sch. 10, para. 2(2).
68 Ibid., s. 59, Sch. 10, para. 8.
69 Ibid., s. 59, Sch. 10, para. 2(3), (4).
70 RI 80.
71 F (No. 2) A 1992, s. 59, Sch. 10, para. 4.
72 Ibid., s. 59, Sch. 10, para. 7; there is no relief for job-related accommodation.
73 Ibid., s. 59. Sch. 10, para. 3.
74 Ibid., s. 59, Sch. 10, para. 5(3).
75 Ibid., s. 59, Sch. 10, para. 5(4).
76 Ibid., s. 59, Sch. 10, para. 9(4)–(6).
77 Ibid., s. 59, Sch. 10, para. 9(3)–(6).
78 Ibid., s. 59, Sch. 10, para. 10.
79 Ibid., s. 59, Sch. 10, para. 11.
80 On form of election, see ibid., s. 59, Sch. 10, para. 12.

25.5 Taxation of Premiums as Income

25.5.1 Elements

Since Schedule A taxes only the annual profits and not the capital gains arising from land, the payment of a premium by a tenant to his landlord escapes Schedule A[81] even though it results in a lower rent and so a lower income for the landlord. Premiums on leases not exceeding 50 years are now taxed, but in a special way, by TA 1988, ss 34–39 (most of which have both income tax and corporation tax versions). On similar legislation introduced by FA 2000 to counter "rent factoring" see below §25.8.

Premium

A premium is defined[82] as including "any like sum whether payable to the immediate or superior landlord or to a person connected[83] with such landlord". Thus, a payment required by a landlord on the grant of a lease to a tenant, and a payment exacted by the tenant on the grant of a sub-lease would both fall within this rule; a payment required by the tenant on the assignment of the lease, however, would not. Case-law provides a further definition of premium as any sum of money paid by the tenant to the landlord in consideration of the grant of a lease.[84] It is unclear whether a payment of the lessor's costs by the lessee will be a premium.[85] The sum need not be mentioned in the lease document. A sum paid in or in connection with the granting of a lease, e.g. key money, is presumed to be a premium, but it is open to the taxpayer to show some reason for the payment other than the grant.[86]

Duration of lease

The rules apply only where the duration of the lease does not exceed 50 years.[87] The definition of a 50-year lease takes full account of the commercial realities. Thus, if a tenant has a 40-year lease with an option to extend it for a further 20 years, account may be taken of the circumstances making it likely that the lease will be so extended. Similarly, if a tenant, or a person connected with him, has the right to a further lease of the same premises or part of them, rather than a right to extend the existing lease, the term may be treated as not expiring before the end of the further lease. Both these provisions, by lengthening the lease, favour the landlord. However, if any of the terms of the lease (whether relating to forfeiture or to any other matter) or any other circumstances render it unlikely that the lease will continue beyond a date falling short of the expiry of the term of the lease, the lease will be treated as if it ended not later than that date, provided the premium would not have been substantially greater had the lease been expected to run its full term.[88] Thus, a 51-year lease with an option to the landlord to terminate it after five years would be treated as a

[81] *O'Connor* v. *Hume* [1954] 2 All ER 301, [1954] 1 WLR 824. Conversely, payment of the premium by the lessee was held to be a capital expense in *Green* v. *Favourite Cinemas Ltd.* (1930) 15 TC 390.

[82] TA 1988, s. 24(1). On pre-1963 leases, see ibid., s. 39(1).

[83] Defined in ibid., s. 839. A payment to a third party other than a connected person is a probably a premium; such a payment is a premium for the purposes of Landlord and Tenant (Rent Control) Act 1949 (*Elmdene Estates Ltd.* v. *White* [1960] AC 528, [1960] 1 All ER 306). A premium in non-monetary form is caught (TA 1988, s. 24(4)).

[84] *Clarke* v. *United Real (Moorgate) Ltd.* [1988] STC 273, 299, 61 TC 353, 387, *per* Walton J. (a CGT case).

[85] See Beattie [1963] *BTR* 245.

[86] TA 1988, s. 24(2).

[87] Ibid., s. 34(1).

[88] Ibid., s. 38.

five-year lease, as would one which provided that after five years the rent, originally a full commercial rent, should be quintupled. The question of what is "unlikely" is judged at the time the lease is granted.[89] The rule, by focussing on what is likely or unlikely, means that a lease for lives can fall within these rules if the life is unlikely to last more than 50 years despite the imposition of a 99-year lease under the Law of Property Act 1925, s. 149.

25.5.2 *Taxing the premium*

A premium payable in respect of a lease not exceeding 50 years is treated as payable by way of rent and falls within Schedule A;[90] if it is payable to someone other than the landlord the recipient is treated as carrying on a separate Schedule A business and is taxed on that income.[91] The landlord or other person is treated as becoming entitled when the lease is granted however it is brought into account for tax purposes when received.[92]

Without modification, this rule could cause two problems. The first is a sharp distinction between a 49-year lease and a 51-year lease. The second is that it could result in a substantial sum—which is really attributable to the number of years the lease is expected to run—being treated as the income of one year.

The first problem is solved by the fractional reduction of the premium, that fraction being related to the duration of the lease, as defined; the longer the lease, the less the chargeable sum.[93] The premium is reduced by 1/50 for each complete period of 12 months (other than the first) comprised in the duration of the lease.[94] Only complete years are taken into account, so that a premium on a lease for two years less a day would be chargeable in full. The sum by which the premium is reduced is not taxable in any subsequent year.[95] The second problem is regarded as no longer causing any difficulty in view of the sharp reduction in income tax rates in 1988; the earlier top-slicing relief provisions were therefore repealed.[96] If the premium is payable by instalments, the taxpayer (T) can spread the taxable fraction of the premiums over a period permitted by the Revenue; this period must not exceed eight years.[97]

25.5.3 *Widening the net*

Improvements—payments in kind

TA 1988, s. 34(2) provides that if the terms subject to which the lease is granted impose on the tenant an obligation to carry out any work on the premises,[98] then the amount by which

[89] TA 1988, s. 38(2).

[90] Ibid., s. 34(1).

[91] Ibid., s. 34(6). S. 392(4) states that there can be no loss relief, but the failure to repeal this in 1998 may have been an oversight.

[92] Ibid., s. 34(1) and (7A). *Quaere* how one "grants" an agreement for a lease; see further *City Permanent Building Society* v. *Miller* [1952] Ch 840, 853, [1952] 2 All ER 621, 628.

[93] Ibid., s. 34(1).

[94] This could have been more elegantly expressed by stating that the fraction chargeable shall be (50, minus the number of years of the lease, plus one) over 50.

[95] The part not taxed as a premium may nonetheless be liable to income tax under Schedule D, Case I, if the lessor deals in land, or to CGT.

[96] FA 1988, s. 75, repealing TA 1988, Sch. 2.

[97] TA 1988, s. 34(8).

[98] This premium does not extend to work on other property belonging to the landlord; nor does it apply when the tenant does work under an obligation outside the lease.

the value of the landlord's estate immediately after the commencement of the lease exceeds the value which it would have had if no such obligation had been imposed on the tenant, is treated as a premium. The measure of liability is the benefit received by the landlord, not the cost incurred. Since the provision applies whenever there is an obligation to carry out work, there is a specific exclusion where the works are such that the costs would be deductible by the landlord as an expense of his Schedule A business if he had to carry out those works, e.g. works of maintenance.[99]

Commutation of rent or surrender of lease

TA 1988, s. 34(4) treats as a premium any sums which become payable by the tenant in lieu of rent or as consideration for the surrender of the lease, but only if those sums are payable under the terms of the lease. A payment in lieu of rent is attributed to the period covered by the payment. Therefore, if, under a 10-year lease, the tenant pays rent of £7,000 p.a., but with the right at any time after the first year to pay £50,000 and a rent of only £2,000 p.a., and that right is exercised, the £50,000 is treated as a premium.

In calculating the charge to tax on sums in lieu of rent the duration of the lease is the period for which the payment is being made. Thus, if the right in the above example is exercised when there are eight years of the lease remaining, the calculations assume an eight-year lease.

Variations and waivers

A sum payable by a tenant on the surrender of a lease, where that sum is not stipulated in the original lease, does not fall within TA 1988, s. 34(4).[100] However, such sum may come within s. 34(5), which catches payments payable by the tenant as consideration for the variation or waiver of any terms of the lease. A "waiver" means the abandonment of a right in such a way that the other party is entitled to plead the abandonment by way of confession and avoidance if the right is later asserted; it is not confined to total abandonment of the right. Therefore where a tenant's option to renew a lease had lapsed, a sum paid to the landlord for the reinstatement of the option was a payment for the variation or waiver of a term of the lease,[101] whether or not such sums were stipulated in the lease. Payments within s. 34(5) are treated as becoming due when the contract of variation is entered into[102] and not, as under s. 34(1) or (4), when it becomes payable by the tenant.[103] However, in all three cases the payment is taken into account only when received.[104] Further, payments within s. 34(5), if paid to someone other than the landlord are chargeable only if paid to a person connected with the landlord, there being no such restriction for payments within s. 34(4).[105] Pre-1963 leases are also caught.[106]

[99] TA 1988, s. 34(3).

[100] Nor does s. 34(4) apply to payments due on expiration of the term of forfeiture. *Quaere* a clause which allows the tenant to break the lease on payment.

[101] *Banning* v. *Wright* [1972] 2 All ER 987, 48 TC 421, HL, where the option lapsed owing to a breach of covenant by the lessee.

[102] TA 1988, s. 34(5)(b).

[103] Ibid., s. 34(4)(b).

[104] Ibid., s. 34(7A).

[105] Ibid., s. 34(7).

[106] Ibid., s. 39(2).

25.5.4 Assignment of lease granted at an undervalue

Although, in general, payments by an assignee of the lease to the assignor escape tax, this will not be the case if the lease was granted to the assignor or some predecessor in title at an undervalue.[107] If A grants a lease to B at a rent plus a premium, the provisions discussed above will charge the premium to income tax. If A grants the lease to X, who assigns it to B, and X is obliged to pay A money for the privilege of assignment, the sum will be taxed to A under TA 1988, s. 34(4) or (5). If X is not obliged to pay A money for the privilege, the economic benefit may still accrue to A if, for example, X is a connected person or a family company. S. 35 therefore provides that (a) if the original[108] grant of the lease was at an undervalue, so that a sum could have been charged by way of premium—"the amount foregone"—that sum shall be computed, and (b) if the lessee subsequently assigns the lease, any consideration payable on the assignment can be taxed to X the assignor under Schedule A as if it had been a premium[109] under the lease, but only to the extent of the amount forgone.[110]

This rule cannot be avoided by X assigning to Y without permission, who then assigns to B at a premium, since s. 35 applies to any assignment of the lease. Therefore Y would be liable to tax under Schedule A on the excess of the premium paid to him by B over any premium paid by him to X. This process continues until the amount that has been rendered chargeable equals the amount forgone.

The amount chargeable is that before the percentage reduction; the reduction is calculated by reference to the initial duration of the lease and so remains constant.

Example

In 1996 A granted B a lease for 26 years at a premium of £1,000 and a peppercorn rent; the lease is worth £80,000. A is chargeable under Schedule A on £1,000 less 50% = £500.

In 1998 B assigned the lease to C for £10,000. B is chargeable under Schedule D, Case VI on £10,000 less £1,000 already charged, less 50% = £4,500.

In 2000 C assigns the lease to D for £9,000. C is not chargeable as the premium C receives is less than the one he paid.

In 2002 D assigns the lease to E for £200,000, its current market value. D is chargeable on £80,000 original value less £1,000 charged to A and £9,000 charged to B, less 50% = £35,000.

It can be seen that the charge is on the assignor, not the grantor, and that it applies whenever the original grant was at an undervalue; it is not confined to situations where the lessee is a person connected with the grantor. S. 35 applies when the sum is payable to a person other than the assignor, although the charge will still fall on the assignor.

25.5.5 Sale with right of reconveyance

Despite TA 1988, ss 34, 35, it is possible to exact the equivalent of a premium from a "tenant" by conveying to him the entire interest of the vendor while reserving to the vendor a right to reacquire the property at some future date. Thus, instead of giving B a seven-year

[107] Nor if the landlord takes a short lease back (ibid., s. 34).

[108] If the original grant was for full value the fact that a subsequent assignment was not for full value does not create a potential charge under TA 1988, s. 35.

[109] The fractional reduction rules apply; the Schedule A charge arises under TA 1988, s. 15, para. 1(2).

[110] Any excess may be liable to CGT.

lease for £4,000, A could convey the land to B for £6,000 and reserve a right to buy it back from B for £2,000 after seven years. TA 1988, s. 36 is designed to correct such a situation. It applies when the terms subject to which an estate or interest is sold provide that it will or may be required to be reconveyed to the grantor (A) or to a person connected with A.[111] The amount by which the sale price exceeds the repurchase price is charged to the vendor—not the connected person—under Schedule A,[112] the amount being assessed at the time of the sale and not of the repurchase. The sum so charged is not described as a premium, but the fractional reduction for the length of the "lease" will apply, thus reducing the amount chargeable by 1/50 for each complete year after the first year between the sale and the reconveyance.[113] If the sale does not fix the date of the reconveyance, but fixes the price, it is assumed that the reconveyance will occur at the earliest possible date. [114] If the sale does not fix the date of the reconveyance and the price varies with the date, the sum to be taxed will be computed on the assumption that the price on reconveyance will be the lowest obtainable.[115]

A notional premium may also arise if the terms of the sale provide that the purchaser is to lease, rather than reconvey, the property back to the vendort. If the lease is to be later than that, the grant of the lease back is treated as a conveyance of the property at a price equivalent to the sum of (a) the amount of the premium (if any) for the lease back and (b) the value, at the date of the sale, of the right to receive a conveyance of the reversion immediately after the lease begins to run. Thus, deducted from the original sale price is the value of the reversion on the lease and any premium paid.[116]

No notional premium arises if the lease is granted and begins to run within one month after the sale; this protects the normal commercial transactions of lease and lease back.

25.5.6 Reliefs

Franking the premium on a sub-lease

If a charge to tax has arisen on a payment under TA 1988, s. 34 or 35, but not s. 36, that payment can be used to frank, in whole or in part, a similar charge arising from a dealing with the interest granted. This is designed to prevent a double charge to tax. Thus, if A grants a lease for 46 years to X, and X pays a premium of, e.g., £10,000, that premium will be subject to tax under s.34(1), the amount chargeable being £1,000. If X assigns the lease to Y, normally[117] no charge will arise, but if X grants Y a sub-lease for, e.g., nine years and exacts a premium of, e.g., £1,200, he is liable to be taxed on £1,008 under s. 34(1). Relief is given for the sub-lease premium.[118] The amount chargeable on the grant by A to X (£1,000), is "the amount chargeable on the superior interest", and the amount chargeable on the grant by X to Y (£1,008), is "the later chargeable amount". The amount to be charged to X on the grant of the sub-lease is the excess, if any, of "the later chargeable amount" over the appropriate

[111] Defined in TA 1988, s. 839.

[112] The Schedule A charge arises under TA 1988, s. 15, para. 1(2).

[113] Ibid., s. 36(1). This provision causes difficulty in the common case where a landowner sells mineral rights but with an option to buy back at the land's agricultural value.

[114] Ibid., s. 36(1).

[115] Ibid., s. 36(2)(a).

[116] Ibid., s. 36(3).

[117] Ibid., s. 35 (lease at undervalue) (see above at §25.5.4).

[118] Ibid., s. 37(2).

fraction of the amount chargeable on the superior interest.[119] The numerator of the appropriate fraction is the period in respect of which the later chargeable amount arose (nine years), and the denominator is the period in respect of which the earlier amount arose (46 years),[120] so that the fraction will be 9/46 of £1,000 = £196. The excess of the later chargeable amount is therefore £1,008 − 196 = £812, and X's chargeable amount is reduced to £812.

If the second sum, i.e. that payable by Y to X, is payable by instalments, X's relief will be to treat those instalments as rent.

The purpose of the relief is not only to avoid a double charge to tax but also preserve the tax neutrality between an assignment of a lease and the grant of a sub-lease. Thus, the longer the sub-lease is, the greater the appropriate fraction of the first sum chargeable which can be set off against the new charge.

Relief is not available for sums charged under s. 36. Previously, schemes were entered into specifically so as to create large sums deductible under s. 37 or 87. An interest in land would be sold off with a provision for reconveyance at a reduced price. Today, where a vendor is assessed under s. 36 on the notional extra rent, the purchaser can no longer set that rent off against any tax due on the grant of a sub-lease (s. 37), nor may the notional rent be deducted under s. 87.

Set-off of premium against rent

If a tenant (T) grants a sub-lease, the rent received under that sub-lease is taxable, but T may deduct the rent paid under his own lease. Similarly, if T pays a premium charged under TA 1988, s. 34 or 35, but not s.36, there is a deduction of part of that premium from the rent derived from the sub-lease.[121]

Example

If A grants B a lease for 25 years, paying a premium of £10,000, and B sublets to C for £600 a year, B is allowed to deduct from his receipts the sum of 1/25 × £10,000 × (50 − 24)/50 = £5,200/25 or £208 plus any rent paid to A. The set-off is thus limited to that part which is taxable in A's hands. If B assigns the lease to X, X may also set off the £208 each year. Where the sub-lease is also at a premium, B may deduct the taxable element of the premium paid to A from the taxable element of the premium he receives from C. Where the sub-lease is at a premium and a rent, the part of the premium paid to A is set off against the taxable element of the premium in priority to the rent.

25.5.7 Interaction of Schedule A premium rules with Schedule D, Case I

Where the tenant (T) can deduct the rent paid in computing the profits of the Schedule D, Case I business, whether because the lease is of business premises or trading stock, T may similarly deduct the proportion of any premium charged under TA 1988, s. 34 or 35.[122] That proportion is spread over the duration of the lease.

Rental income accruing to a dealer in land should be charged under Schedule A. However, if the income is small in relation to other income, it is treated as part of the computation under Schedule D, Case I.[123]

119 TA 1988, s. 37(5).
120 Ibid., s. 37(7).
121 Ibid., s. 37(4).
122 Ibid., s. 87.
123 Law Commission, Cmnd 4654 (1971), §69.

Where a dealer in land receives a payment which is taxable as a premium under s. 34(1), (4) or (5) or s. 35 or 36 and a part is chargeable under those sections,[124] that part is so charged and only the excess is treated as trading income.

25.6 Occupation Of Woodlands

Woodlands occupied on a commercial basis are not taxed either under Schedule A (which specifically excludes profits arising from the occupation of land), nor under Schedule D, Case I. Previously, woodlands were taxed under Schedule B, but this was abolished in 1988.[125] The transitional rules expired in 1993.

Schedule B is of interest as an example of imputed income. The charge was on the value of land used for commercial forestry, which worked out at about 15p per acre. The basis was applied throughout the period of occupation of the land by the taxpayer.

25.7 Exclusion—Occupation of Land

There is no liability to tax under Schedule A[126] (or Schedule B) on an occupier (O) in respect of the value of O's occupation of land. Profits arising otherwise may be taxable under some other Schedule.[127]

It follows the case-law on Schedule B is of interest here. If the occupier cuts the timber and turns it into furniture, profits from the furniture trade will be taxed under Schedule D, Case I.[128] In *Collins* v. *Fraser*[129] it was held that the payment under Schedule B extended provided all that was done to the timber was in order to make the produce of the soil marketable in some shape or form. This may go as far as turning timber into planks, At which point trade would take over and the timber would be entered into the accounts of the trade at the then market value, thus ensuring that all "profits" up to that time would be outside the charge to income tax. Profits derived after that point from the making of crates were held to be taxable. Parliament has declared that short rotation coppice is an activity of farming and not woodlands.[130]

[124] TA 1988, s. 99(2), (3); but note the qualification on s. 36(2)(b) in s. 99(3).

[125] For history, see *Simon's Direct Tax Service*, A5.101; and Scott L-.J. in *Bamford* v. *Osborne* [1940] 1 All ER 91, 94, 23 TC 642, 651.

[126] TA 1988, s. 15, para. 2 (1).

[127] For example Schedule D, Case I, as in *Jaggers* v. *Ellis* [1996] STC (SCD) 440 (profits from Christmas tree operations were held taxable under Schedule D, Case I since the source was a Christmas tree plantation not a woodland).

[128] *IRC* v. *Williamson Bros* (1949) 31 TC 370, 377. The boundary between trade and property is explored in the Canadian context by Durnford (1991) 39 *Can. Tax Jo.* 1131.

[129] [1969] 3 All ER 524, 46 TC 143, Megarry J. Similar problems arose over the extent of farming when that fell within Schedule B: see e.g. *Back* v. *Daniels* [1925] 1 KB 526, 544, 9 TC 183, 203, *per* Scrotton L.J. (a cheese factory would be outside Schedule B); *Long* v. *Belfield Poultry Products Ltd.* (1937) 21 TC 221 (profits from hatching out eggs were not profits from the occupation of land, so falling outside Schedule B).

[130] FA 1995, s. 154.

25.8 Rent Factoring TA 1988 Sections 43A–43G

TA 1988 sections 43A–43G were added by FA 2000 and apply to transactions entered into on or after 21 March 2000.[131] Like the premium rules just described these rules are aimed at attempts to turn what would have been an income payment into a capital payment; these attempts involve selling (or factoring) a right to receive a stream of income payments, such as rent, for a single sum.[132] The sections provide back-up not only for TA 1988, s. 36 but also for TA 1988 s. 780. The legislation is framed in terms of companies and their accounts.

The key concept of a finance agreement is defined in s. 43A. This arises if, in accordance with normal accounting practice, the accounts of a company receiving money under a transaction would "record a financial obligation" (in relation to that receipt; it does not matter whether it recorded as a lease creditor or otherwise).[133]

S. 43B deals with finance agreements which transfer rent or, more formally, a right to receive rent in respect of land in the United Kingdom from one person to another. However s. 43B does not apply to the simple grant of a lease of such land since this is already covered by s. 34. The sum received is called a finance amount and is made taxable in full as income under Schedule A; it is taxes as income for the period in which the finance agreement is made.

S. 43C provides a number of exceptions to 43B. These exceptions are of two sorts. The first sort is policy driven. S. 43B does not apply if the new period over which the sums will be paid exceeds 15 years; so only rent transfer agreements with an economic life of less than 15 years will be caught. Similarly s. 43B is not to apply where the arrangements for the reduction of the financial obligation substantially depend on a person's entitlement to an allowance under the Capital Allowances Acts. This exception only applies if the parties are not connected; its purpose is to protect sales and leasebacks which are driven by capital allowance considerations.[134]

The second group of exceptions arise from the interaction of s. 43B with the anti-avoidance provisions in s. 36 and s. 780 and also prevents double charges.[135]

The basic structure in s. 43B is then applied to the situation of the interposed lease, i.e. where there is a finance agreement under which a lease is granted in respect of land in the United Kingdom, a premium is payable in respect of the lease, and the receipt of the premium falls within the fefinition of a finance agreement.[136] The premium is brought within the Schedule A business for the chargeable period in which the agreement is made.

S. 43E mirrors s. 43C. So s. 43D is excluded if the term over which the financial obligation is to be reduced exceeds 15 years. In order to encourage long term investment it is also excluded if the length of the lease does not exceed 15 years or the length of the lease is not significantly different from the term over which the financial obligation is to be reduced. It is also excluded if the matter is with an unconnected person, and driven by the same capital allowance considerations. It is also excluded if all or part of the premium is brought into account in computing the profits of a trade for the purposes of Case I of Schedule D.[137] Where s. 43D(2) applies it will exclude any charge under s. 34.

Special rules apply to insurance companies.[138]

[131] FA 2000 s. 110(2).

[132] Inland Revenue Notes to Finance Bill 2000, clause 109.

[133] TA 1988, s. 43A(1); 43A(2)–(3) deals with normal accounting practice and group accounts while (4) tells one when a company is treated as receiving money. S. 43G is the interpretation provision.

[134] TA 1988 s. 43C(1) and (2).

[135] TA 1988, s. 43C(3) and (4).

[136] TA 1988 s. 43D(1).

[137] TA 1988 s. 34E.

[138] TA 1988, s. 43F; see also s. 43C(6) and 43E(4).

26

Interest and Premium, Bond and Discount: Schedule D, Case III

26.1 Taxation of Interest: Introduction[1]

Today, interest received is charged to income tax under Schedule D, Case III if the source arises in the UK, and under Schedule D, Case IV (or, possibly, Case V) if the source is outside the UK.[2] Before 1996, interest payable out of any public revenue, whether of the UK or another state, was charged under Schedule C. Schedule C was abolished both for income tax and corporation tax in 1996 and its operation transferred to Schedule D, Case III.[3]

26.1.1 The scope of Schedule D, Case III

TA 1988, s. 18[4] directs that the tax is payable on:

"(1) interest on money, whether yearly or otherwise, . . . whether such payment is payable within or outside the UK,[5] either as a charge on property of the person paying the same by virtue of any

[1] For comparative treatment, see IFA Cahiers 1994 Conference, Vol. LXXIXa, especially the general report by Arnold at 491–540 (and Bibliography). While this Cahier concentrates on interest as a deduction, there is much of importance on the definition of interest. On the Canadian definition of interest, see Edgar (1996) 40 *Can. Tax Jo.* 277, which also discusses reform on the lines of the accruals system adopted in New Zealand (subsequently also adopted for corporation tax in the UK). For an account of the very interesting New Zealand Accrual rules, see Smith (1998) 46 *Can. Tax Jo.* 819. For theoretical discussions of ways of tackling the time value of money, see Halperin (1986) 95 *Yale LJ* 506; and Lokken (1986) 42 *Tax Law Review* 1.

[2] For corporation tax, interest is charged under Schedule D, Case III only; Case IV and any relevant application of Case V were abolished in 1996.

[3] TA 1998, s. 17, repealed by FA 1996, Sch. 7.

[4] Other provisions cause income to be taxed under Schedule D, Case III; e.g. TA 1988, ss 119, 554. For list, see *Simon's Direct Tax Service*, Pt. B5.103.

[5] These words focus on where the sum is payable.

deed or will or otherwise, or as a reservation out of it, or as a personal debt or obligation by virtue of any contract, or whether the same is received and payable half yearly or at any shorter or more distant periods but not including any payment chargeable under Schedule A;

(2) all discounts [see below at §26.6]; and

(3) income from securities payable out of the public revenue of the United Kingdom or Northern Ireland."

With the single exception of a "relevant discounted security" (see below at §26.6.3) no deductions can be made—a rule which applies with equal ferocity to Schedule F (dividends).[6] This means that interest paid on a loan to buy securities cannot be set directly[7] against the interest received. Before 1969 a general relief was available against income for interest paid on loans so that, while it could not be set directly against the interest received, it could, nonetheless benefit from the relief in a different way. Since 1969 relief for interest paid has been restricted (see above at §10.1). The rule against deduction of expenses associated with the receipt of interest and dividends gives this charge something of the air of a gross receipts tax, a matter of importance when other countries are considering whether to grant credit relief for the UK tax paid. Other costs incurred, e.g. legal fees on making the loan, are matters for CGT, if at all.[8]

The recipients of these income payments are liable to income tax, generally by self-assessment under Schedule D, Case III. The deduction at source rules in TA 1988, ss 348 and 349(1) do not apply to interest. However, s. 349 (2) does apply (see below at §26.5.2); so that certain types of interest attract an obligation on the payer to withhold at the 20% savings rate (with varying degrees of sanction).

26.1.2 Basis of assessment

Since 1996–1997 assessments under Schedule D, Case III have been made on a strict current year basis.[9] This means that a person is taxed on the full amount of interest arising in the period 6 April to 5 April. An exception arises where a trading partnership receives income outside Schedule D, Case I, e.g. interest, where the income of the basis period for the partnership is taken instead to determine the income of the partnership. which income is then apportioned to the individual partners.

For periods before 1996 the preceding year basis was used unless statute otherwise provided (as it did for bank and building society interest).[10] Under the preceding year basis special rules applied for opening and closing years.[11]

When does income arise?

Generally, income arises only when it is received or enures for a person's benefit.[12] For this purpose it has been held that payment by cheque is not income when the cheque is received

[6] TA 1988, s. 64; and see *Soul* v. *Caillebotte* (1964) 43 TC 657. For Schedule F, see TA 1988, s. 20.

[7] A right to deduct may arise under the corporation tax loan relationship rules where the taxpayer is carrying on an investment trading business and so can deduct under Schedule D, Case I, or where the interest, while falling outside the loan relationship rules, qualifies as a management expense of an investment or insurance company.

[8] Most debts are not assets for the purposes of CGT anyway (TCGA 1992, s. 251).

[9] TA 1988, s. 64, added by FA 1994, s. 206.

[10] TA 1988, s. 64 (original version).

[11] TA 1988, ss 66, 67 (repealed with effect from 1996 by FA 1994).

[12] *Dunmore* v. *McGowan* [1978] STC 217, [1978] 2 All ER 85, 52 TC 307; see also *Whitworth Park Coal Co. Ltd.* v. *IRC* [1961] AC 31, [1959] 3 All ER 703, 38 TC 531.

but, probably, only when the proceeds of the cheque are received, whether as cash or on being credited to the account of the payee.[13]

The question when a payment enures to the advantage of a taxpayer has been explored in cases concerning banks, where the payment of interest is deferred or diverted. Simple deferral of the bank's liability to pay interest to the lender means that the interest has not been received and so is not yet taxable; it does not matter whether this deferral is forced, voluntary or by agreement. This must be contrasted with cases where the lender, L, has done something in respect of the interest and the interest has been appropriated to L's use in some way, it deposited at L's directions or is lying under L's name at the bank.[14]

In *Dunmore* v. *McGowan*[15] the interest not paid to L was held by the bank in accordance with an agreement under which neither interest nor the balance of the account could be withdrawn while the taxpayer was under a liability to the bank in respect of a guarantee. The Court of Appeal held that the interest income was taxable to the taxpayer as it arose each year. This case, which at first sight seems to be wrong in that a promise by a debtor to pay is not usually regarded as a receipt of income, can be justified on the basis that it was not a case of non-receipt by the taxpayer, but of positive appropriation by him. This was followed in *Peracha* v. *Miley*[16] where interest credited to the taxpayer, but retained by the bank as security under a guarantee, was held taxable when so credited, even though it was highly unlikely in that case that the taxpayer would ever see any of his interest.

Earlier, *Dunmore* v. *McGowan* had been distinguished in *Macpherson* v. *Bond.*[17] Here the taxpayer had charged money in a bank account to a bank to secure the debts of a third party. Vinelott J. held that on the facts the crediting of the money to the taxpayer's account did not reduce any personal liability on the part of the taxpayer to the bank under a guarantee to the bank, because no guarantee had been given.

26.2 Meaning of Interest

There is no statutory definition of "interest".[18] Case-law, however, provides four elements in establishing "interest". First, as Rowlatt J. put it in *Bennett* v. *Ogston*,[19] interest is "payment by time for the use of money". Therefore, a payment on a loan may be interest, but a dividend on a share is not. Secondly, the payment must not be excessive, a rule which may be based on Scots, i.e. civil, law origins.[20] Thirdly, the use of the word "interest" is not

[13] *Parkside Leasing Ltd.* v. *Smith* [1985] STC 63, 69d (if the crediting is conditional, it is assumed that income is not received until the crediting has become unconditional). Contrast the rule for the payment of tax in TMA 1970, s. 70A; and for PAYE payments, SI 1993/744, reg. 43(7A).

[14] Neuberger J. in *Girvan* v. *Orange Personal Communication Services Ltd.* [1998] STC 567, 588e

[15] [1978] STC 217, [1978] 2 All ER 85, 52 TC 307. The court rejected an argument that the arrangement amounted to a trust since there was no evidence to support it. Had a trust been established the income could not have been said to have accrued to the taxpayer even though he would have gained some incidental advantage from it.

[16] [1990] STC 512, 63 TC 444, CA. *Macpherson* v. *Bond* [1985] STC 678, 58 TC 579 (see below) was, in turn, distinguished on the basis that in *Peracha* v. *Miley* there was an immediate reduction in the amount of the taxpayer's personal liability.

[17] [1985] STC 678, 58 TC 579; whether Vinelott J. was right to distinguish *Dunmore* v. *McGowan* in this way was deliberately not commented upon by Dillon L.J. in *Peracha* v. *Miley* [1990] STC 512, 518 63 TC 444, 464.

[18] See Beer [1986] *BTR* 271.

[19] (1930) 15 TC 374, 379.

[20] *Cairns* v. *MacDiarmid* [1982] STC 226; but, on appeal Sir John Donaldson M.R. thought that, on the facts, the payment might be just ([1983] STC 178).

conclusive. Therefore, where the "interest" was due shortly after the loan and exceeded the principal sum, the court had little difficulty in holding that the payment was not interest.[21] Fourthly, in the UK, unlike some other countries, there has to be some underlying debt or other obligation to pay money to which the interest relates. These four basic principles have been embroidered in the cases.

Compensation for delay in payment must be distinguished from compensation for delay in performing some other obligation. Payments by time for the use of money are distinct from payments by time for non-performance of obligations; the fact that time is used to measure a payment is not enough to make the payment interest when there is no principal debt.[22] Suppose that A has just bought a lot of whisky and then gives B an option to buy that whisky at any time within six months at a price of £100, plus "interest" at the rate of 12% per annum from that time A bought the whisky until B exercises the option. If B exercises the option after three months and pays £103, this would be a simple purchase for £103 and not a purchase for £100 plus £3 interest.[23] This is because until B exercises the option there is no underlying contract for purchase in respect of which the interest can accrue. The situation is therefore distinct from that in which B had agreed to buy in the first month and had also agreed to pay an extra 1% a month for each month until the payment was made. In such cases one must not assume that a sum which is an ingredient in determining an interest payment is itself a payment of interest; the question is whether it is payment by time for the use of money.[24]

It is unclear whether a payment by a guarantor in respect of interest due from the principal debtor is itself interest.[25] However, a payment under a contract of indemnity has been held to be interest where the guarantor expressly guaranteed payment of this interest by being party to a promissory note "as primary obligor", as distinct from accepting a general obligation to make good the general contractual defaults of the principal.[26]

26.2.1 Premiums and discounts

If A lends B money for a fixed period, A may insist not only on the current general rate of interest but also on some extra payment. A may charge extra interest or ask for a larger sum to be paid back than was lent, i.e. a premium. A premium will be treated as an interest payment unless it can shown that it is a payment on some other account, e.g. to cover the risk of foreign exchange fluctuation or the risk of non-payment. If it is a payment on some other account it may be income under Schedule D, Case VI, or even a capital receipt.

Premium and interest

Where A borrows £90 from B on the basis that A will not only pay a reasonable commercial rate of interest for the loan for the year, but will also repay £100 in 12 months, the extra £10

[21] *Ridge Securities Ltd.* v. *IRC* [1964] 1 All ER 275, 44 TC 373; *cf. Chevron Petroleum (UK) Ltd.* v. *BP Development Ltd.* [1981] STC 689.

[22] *Re Euro Hotel (Belgravia) Ltd.* [1975] STC 682, [1975] 3 All ER 1075. See discussion by Edgar (1996) 44 *Can. Tax Jo.* 327.

[23] Sir Robert Megarry V.C. in *Chevron Petroleum (UK) Ltd.* v. *BP Development Ltd.* [1981] STC 689, 695j.

[24] See also *Cooker* v. *Foss* [1998] STC (SCD) 189.

[25] See *Westminster Bank Executor and Trustee Co. (Channel Islands) Ltd.* v. *National Bank of Greece SA* (1970) 46 TC 472, 485 (Court of Appeal saying that it was); but *cf.* 494 (point left open by the House of Lords). This is different from the question whether the guarantee payment is interest "on a loan", a matter of importance for deduction under TA 1988, s. 353 (see ch. 10 above).

[26] *Re Hawkins, Hawkins* v. *Hawkins* [1972] Ch 714, [1972] 3 All ER 386.

is a premium and is not treated as interest for tax purposes.[27] A different result would be reached if A had not agreed to pay any interest at all; here the £10 would be treated as interest since it was clearly payment by time for the use of money. Similarly, if interest is charged at an unreasonably low rate and the extra sum is geared to the length of the loan, the courts have held the extra sum to be interest, even though the parties called it a premium.[28] This does not breach the "form versus substance" rule, since the description given by the parties is not conclusive of its legal form and the test is whether £10 or the extra sum represents payment by time for the use of money. Extrinsic evidence is admissible.

Discount, interest and premium

A may issue promissory notes at £90 with a promise to redeem at £100 in one year's time. Despite the economic similarity with the premium, the legal position here is different; the £10 is treated as a discount, not as a premium. Profits arising from discounts are not interest (see below at §26.6),[29] although they are taxed as income under Schedule D, Case III. Although these distinctions are easy to put into words and, once grasped, generate a certain satisfaction, they are unreal in economic or commercial terms.[30] Both discounts and premiums are payments by time for the use of money and should be treated alike—as they are now for corporation tax and generally for income tax. However, whereas corporation tax has created a whole, new, statutory scheme and language under which income (and expenses) accrue year by year so that distinctions between income and capital have (almost) been abolished, income tax has continued to be considered under the old concepts.

Cases

In *Davies* v. *Premier Investment Co. Ltd.*[31] a company issued unsecured promissory notes at par without interest, but offered to redeem them at a premium of 30% after six years, with the alternative of a premium calculated at 5% p.a. should the company redeem the notes or go into voluntary liquidation before six years. The premium was held to be interest. This conclusion might not have been reached had the premium been 30% regardless of when the notes were redeemed.

Where normal commercial rates of interest are charged the question whether any "premium" or discount is taxed as interest is determined according to the following rules laid down in *Lomax* v. *Peter Dixon*:[32]

(1) if interest is charged at a rate that would be reasonably commercial on a reasonably sound security there is no presumption that a "discount" or a "premium" is interest;
(2) the true nature of the payment is a matter of fact rather than of law;
(3) among the factors relevant will be the contract itself, the term of the loan, the rate of interest expressly stipulated for, the nature of the capital risk and the extent to which, if at all, the parties expressly took or may reasonably be expected to have taken the capital risk into account in fixing the terms of the contract.

[27] *Lomax* v. *Peter Dixon* [1943] 2 All ER 255, 259, 25 TC 353, 363.
[28] *IRC* v. *Thomas Nelson & Sons Ltd.* (1938) 22 TC 175.
[29] See also *Lomax* v. *Peter Dixon* [1943] 2 All ER 255, 259, 25 TC 353, 363, *per* Lord Greene M.R.
[30] See Warren (1993) 107 *HLR* 460.
[31] [1945] 2 All ER 681, 27 TC 27.
[32] [1943] 2 All ER 255, 262, 25 TC 353, 367.

It should also be noted that in *Lomax* the payments were made by a foreign company, and under the foreign law the payments probably were interest (and so deductible under that law).

26.2.2 Interest and damages

The notion that interest is a type of service charge for the use of money may explain the initial reluctance of judges to treat as interest for income tax purposes sums awarded as interest when calculating damages—such sums originally being treated as extra damages.[33] In *Riches* v. *Westminster Bank Ltd.*,[34] however, this approach was held to be wrong. The taxpayer successfully sued a business partner for his share of the profit on a transaction (£36,255) which the partner had concealed. The judge also awarded him £10,028 as interest at 4% since the original deception, exercising his discretion under the Law Reform (Miscellaneous Provisions) Act 1934, s. 3. It was held by the House of Lords that the £10,028 was interest. As Lord Simon put it, "It is not capital. It is rather the accumulated fruit of a tree which the tree produces regularly until payment".[35]

26.3 Yearly Interest

It is sometimes necessary (usually when considering deductions rather than receipts) to distinguish yearly or annual interest from other interest.[36] The basic rule is that interest payable on loans or other sums which are expressed or intended to last 12 months or longer is yearly interest, while interest on loans both expressed and intended to last less than 12 months is not. In applying this test the courts have regard to the business realities of the situation.[37]

Yearly interest, which presumably means the same as annual interest, is not defined by statute. The distinction between yearly and short interest depends on the intention of the parties.[38] If a banker makes a loan to a customer, to be repaid at the end of three months, the interest payable is not annual.[39] If, on the other hand, a mortgagor executes the usual form of mortgage, under which he becomes liable at law to pay the amount borrowed at the end of six months, the interest payable is, nonetheless, annual.[40] A technical explanation for this distinction is that in the case of a bank loan, the contract specifies that the repayment of capital with interest is to be on a fixed day, and there is no law, without a new contract by the parties, which states that interest is payable thereafter as a matter of right.[41] A more simple explanation is commercial reality: mortgages are not usually repaid at the end of six months; both parties envisage that the mortgage may last longer than 12 months and thus

[33] For example *IRC* v. *Ballantine* (1924) 8 TC 595.
[34] [1947] 1 All ER 469, (1947) 28 TC 159.
[35] Ibid., 471, 188.
[36] See, e.g. TA 1988, ss 82, 349(2).
[37] *Minsham Properties Ltd.* v. *Price* [1990] STC 718, where a loan replacing a short-term overdraft was held to be a long-term loan generating yearly interest.
[38] *Cairns* v. *MacDiarmid* [1983] STC 178, 181, CA.
[39] *Goslings and Sharpe* v. *Blake* (1889) 23 QBD 324, 2 TC 450.
[40] *Re Craven's Mortgage, Davies* v. *Craven* [1907] 2 Ch 448.
[41] *Goslings and Sharpe* v. *Blake* (1889) 23 QBD 324, 328, 2 TC 450, 454, *per* Lord Esher.

the loan is in the nature of an investment, as opposed to a short loan on moneys presently payable but held over.[42]

In determining whether interest is yearly, the courts have regard to substance, so that a three-month loan does not carry yearly interest merely because the rate is expressed in annual terms.[43] A loan of no fixed term carries yearly interest even though that interest is payable half yearly, quarterly or weekly.[44] Following the same approach, interest may be yearly even though the principal is payable after less than a year[45] or even on demand.[46] Interest may be yearly even though the amount borrowed and the rate of interest both fluctuate.[47] Interest will also be yearly if the period of the loan is expressed and intended to be one year only.[48]

It is hard to see why, given the above approach, interest awarded on damages[49] or interest payable by a purchaser on an outstanding contract[50] should be yearly, at least in the absence of some positive intention on the part of the vendor to treat the outstanding amount as an investment rather than a nuisance. These are both, however, situations in which the courts have held the interest to be yearly interest.

26.4 Accrued Interest

26.4.1 General position

Few areas better show the difficulties encountered by the UK tax system in clinging to the distinction between income and capital than this.[51] The FA 1996 loan relationship rules for corporation tax have enabled these rules to be abolished—but only for corporation tax (see below §48.1).

As a matter of general law, interest accrues from day to day even if it is payable only at intervals and is therefore apportionable in point of time between persons entitled in succession to the principal.[52] However, if a person owning a security sells that security with the right to any accrued interest, the price received for the security is just that, and cannot be dissected into one element representing the principal, and another representing the unpaid but accrued interest.[53] It follows that the *purchaser* is liable to tax on the whole of the interest paid.[54] This starting point may still apply (for income tax) when the accrued interest scheme (see below at §26.4.2) does not apply; the starting point cannot apply for corporation tax since the 1996 loan relationship rules supersede it.

42 *Garston Overseers* v. *Carlisle* [1915] 3 KB 381, 6 TC 659, *per* Rowlatt J.
43 *Goslings and Sharpe* v. *Blake* (above). See also *Cairns* v. *MacDiarmid* [1982] STC 226.
44 *Re Janes' Settlement, Wasmuth* v. *Janes* [1918] 2 Ch 54.
45 As in a mortgage.
46 *Corinthian Securities Ltd.* v. *Cato* [1969] 3 All ER 1168, 46 TC 93; noted at [1970] *BTR* 144.
47 *IRC* v. *Hay* (1924) 8 TC 636.
48 *Ward* v. *Anglo-American Oil Co. Ltd.* (1934) 19 TC 94 (*quaere* if repayable in 365 days).
49 *Jefford* v. *Gee* [1970] 2 QB 130, 149, [1970] 1 All ER 1202, 1210; the facts were unusual in that the sale was deferred for more than 12 months.
50 *Bebb* v. *Bunny* (1854) 1 K & J 216. On practical problems, e.g. under TA 1988, s. 349(2)(c), see [1971] *BTR* 333.
51 For a view that the trouble stemmed from an unsophisticated view of ownership, see Cunningham and Schenk (1992) 47 *Tax Law Review* 725.
52 *Halsbury's Laws of England* (4th ed.), Vol. 32, para. 106.
53 *Wigmore* v. *Thomas Summerson & Sons Ltd.* [1926] 1 KB 131, 9 TC 577.
54 *Schaffer* v. *Cattermole* [1980] STC 650.

These general rules gave rise to the sale of gilts before the stocks went ex-div, and the consequent conversion of income into capital gain for the seller. Of course, the buyer would be subject to tax on the whole of the income of the period, even though ownership had persisted only for a part of it, but the difficulties inherent in this could be avoided if the buyer was a charity or pension fund, or some other entity exempt from tax. One risk for the buyer would be greed; if the sales occurred sufficiently often, they could attract a Revenue argument that this was an adventure in the nature of trade. If the seller were held liable under Schedule D, Case I this could not affect the tax position of the buyer if that person was subject to tax under Schedule D, Case III.

The theoretical analysis devised by the courts was carried further when the courts held that the right to the interest could be sold separately from the securities themselves and the purchase price would be for the sale of a right and not an interest payment, even though the date for payment had arrived before the sale.[55] Legislation to counter these decisions in certain tax saving situations is considered below at §57.2.

26.4.2 Accrued interest scheme

The provisions outlined below at §57.2 were not effective to counter the practice of bond washing. For a long time the Treasury, presumably anxious to do nothing to inhibit the sale of gilts, was content with the large revenue loss which stemmed from the freedom to convert accrued income into capital gain, even though the purchaser may have been a tax-free pension fund, and the vendor safe from CGT by reason of the annual exemption, or holding the securities for at least 12 months. This changed in 1986: presumably the Treasury was then confident about its ability to sell gilts and therefore more able to proclaim its belief in tax neutrality. When the scheme is excluded, the rules described at §26.4.1 above still apply.

In essence, the scheme is simple. Where securities bearing interest are disposed of, the tax system will treat the interest as accruing from day to day. Therefore, on the sale of such securities cum-div, the vendor (V) must pay tax on the interest accruing to that date, and the purchaser (P) will deduct that amount from the interest payment V receives, so that only the interest accruing after the purchase will be charged to tax. When the purchase is made ex-div, the converse rules apply. Since the scheme, in effect, treats what had been capital gain as income, it is interesting to note the convergence of rules under this scheme and CGT rules.[56]

Assets

"Securities" are defined[57] widely and include any loan stock at a fixed or variable rate of interest,[58] whether issued by a public body, company or any other body. Specific exclusions apply to ordinary or preference shares, national and war savings certificates, bills of exchange and other bills and certificates of deposit.

[55] *IRC* v. *Paget* [1938] 1 All ER 392, 21 TC 677; see below at §57.2.

[56] For example TA 1988, s. 727 on stock lending explicitly referring to CGT rules, and the final amendment of the provisions dealing with death (s. 721) to bring it into line with a CGT change made 25 years earlier.

[57] Ibid., ss 710, 713.

[58] The term "interest" is defined in ibid., s. 711(9).

Transfer with accrued interest

On a transfer[59] with accrued interest the transferor is treated as entitled to a sum equal to the "accrued amount", which is a time-apportioned part of the later interest payment, although this will be overridden by the actual payment when the transferee accounts separately for the interest and capital.[60] For the purposes of the time apportionment, the transferor (V) is treated as entitled to interest accruing for the number of days up to and including the date of settlement.[61] An interest period must not exceed 12 months.[62]

Sums

The accrued proportion of the interest on the securities payable for the period is A ÷ B, where A is the number of days in the interest period up to and including settlement day and B is the number of days in the interest period.

Example

A security has interest payment dates of 15 January and 15 July. It is quoted ex-div on 28 December and 27 June. The six monthly interest payment is £500.

If V sells the security cum-div in a period ending with settlement day on 15 December, V will not actually receive the interest payment due on 15 January, but, for tax purposes, is treated as receiving (153/184) × £500 = £415.76.

The figures conform to the words of the legislation, but not to Stock Exchange practice which is to take the number of days from the last interest payment to the date of the settlement date and divide it by 365 (366 in a leap year). This factor is then applied to the year as a whole. It is understood that these figures, which are shown on contract notes, are accepted by the Revenue.

If, in the example above, V had sold ex-div with a settlement day on 2 January, he would have received the whole interest payment on 15 January but would be entitled to treat a fraction of it as capital; the fraction would have been (184 − 171)/184 which, applied to £500, gives a rebate of £35.33.

Converse—without accrued interest

On a transfer without accrued interest V is treated as entitled to relief on the "rebate amount" and the transferee is treated as entitled to that amount.[63] The rebate amount is calculated in a similar way to the accrued amount but is, of course, the converse figure.[64]

Tranches

Where securities are issued in tranches the rules, as originally framed, failed to catch a device in which the size of an existing issue was increased by the issue of further securities of the same stock without distinguishing between the original issue and the new issue. The

[59] Defined in ibid., s. 710(5) as including sale, exchange and gift. Where a person exchanges a gilt for a gilt strip there is a deemed transfer (s. 722A).

[60] Ibid., s. 713.

[61] Defined in ibid., s. 712.

[62] See ibid., s. 711(4).

[63] Ibid., s. 713(3).

[64] Ibid., s. 713(5).

price of the new securities would include a sum representing interest on the existing securities. That sum is now subject to the apportionment system.[65]

Timing

Where, under these rules, V is treated as entitled to a sum, the sum is treated as received on the last day of the interest period.[66] The charge is under Schedule D, Case VI.[67] An interest period is a period ending with an interest payment day,[68] but any period in excess of 12 months is divided, so that no period can exceed 12 months; [69] in this way an interest period can end without an interest payment day.

Relief for P

It is central to the scheme that P, the party not treated as receiving income, is granted relief. The relief is set against any sums P is treated as receiving under these rules[70] and is then set against the sums actually received by way of interest during the interest period.[71] Where the interest period does not end with an interest payment day and there is no deemed income under these rules, the relief may be rolled forward to the next interest period.[72]

Exclusions

The abovee rules are excluded in a number of situations, in which case there will be no deemed income for one party. The exceptions are:[73]

(1) where V (the transferor) is trading and the transfer is taken into account in computing V's profits;
(2) where V is an individual[74] and on no day in the year of assessment in which the interest period ends (or the previous year) does the nominal[75] value of securities held by V exceed £5,000 (when income from the securities is deemed to be the income of another person, the securities are treated as belonging to both[76]);
(3) a *de minimis* provision similar to (2) for an estate in administration;[77]
(4) a *de minimis* provision similar to (2) for a trust for a disabled person;[78]
(5) where V is not resident in the UK for any part of the chargeable period, nor ordinarily resident for that period and is not a non-resident UK trader;[79]
(6) where the transferor is an individual entitled to the remittance,[80] basis and any interest in the year of transfer would be taxed on that basis under Schedule D, Case IV or V;

[65] TA 1988, s.726A, added by FA 1991.
[66] Ibid., s. 714(1).
[67] Ibid., s. 714(2).
[68] Ibid., s. 711(3).
[69] Ibid., s. 711(4); the tax treatment is governed by s. 711(8).
[70] Ibid., s. 714(3).
[71] Ibid., s. 714(5).
[72] Ibid., s. 714(6).
[73] Ibid., s. 715.
[74] Husband and wife living together are treated as one person.
[75] Defined in TA 1988, s. 710(11) as the value by reference to which the interest is calculated, or the original issue price.
[76] Ibid., s. 710(9).
[77] Ibid., s. 715(1)(c).
[78] Defined by reference to TCGA 1992, Sch. 1.
[79] Defined by TA 1988, s. 715(4), (5).
[80] See below at §60.3.

(7) where the interest arises from stock lending transactions;[81]
(8) where the interest arises from on-cash collateral provided in connection with approved stock lending arrangements.[82]
(9) securities which are exempt while held by non-residents.[83]

Reliefs

The relief provisions are similarly drafted but separate.[84] It follows that the exclusion of the transferor from tax on an accrued amount in respect of a sale cum-div does not, in itself, deny the transferee relief for that amount.

Special transactions

Special rules apply to nominees and trusts,[85] situations where foreign currency is involved,[86] delayed remittances,[87] appropriations to and from trading stock,[88] conversion of securities,[89] transfers which carry a right to receive the interest on a payment day falling before the settlement day (such interest is called "unrealised interest"),[90] variable rate securities[91] and situations in which the interest is in default.[92]

Companies

The abolition of the accrued income scheme for corporation tax meant that special exemptions for insurance companies[93] could be repealed; the earlier adoption of similar revaluation rules for Lloyd's underwriters in 1993 meant the repeal of special rules in relation to them.[94] Special rules for building societies[95] were repealed in 1991 when the tax treatment of societies was aligned with that of banks.

Exempt entities

Transfers by charities[96] are exempt, but special rules apply if the property ceases to be held for charitable trusts. Transfers by retirement schemes are also exempt from TA 1988, s. 713 if the interest would have been exempt.[97]

[81] TA 1988, ss 129 (as amended by FA 1991, s. 57), 727, 828, Sch. 29, and the Income Tax (Stock Lending) Regulations 1989 (SI 1989/1299) as amended by SI 1990/2552, SI 1992/572, SI 1993/2003; for an explanation of the final SI, see (1993) *Simon's Tax Intelligence* 1161.
[82] TA 1988, s. 129A, Sch. 5A, added by FA 1995.
[83] FA 1996, s. 154, superseding TA 1988, s. 715(g), (h) (repealed by FA 1996).
[84] TA 1988, s. 715(2).
[85] Ibid., ss 711(6), 720. On common investment fund, note ibid., s. 382(2)–(4).
[86] For example, in calculating the amount of interest or the nominal value under ibid., s. 713.
[87] Ibid., s. 723.
[88] Ibid., s. 722.
[89] Ibid., ss 710(13), 711(6).
[90] Ibid., s. 716.
[91] Ibid., s. 717.
[92] Ibid., s. 718; for unrealised interest in default, see s. 719.
[93] Ibid., s. 724.
[94] Ibid., ss 710(14), 721(5), (6), 725, 452(9), repealed FA 1993.
[95] TA 1988, s. 726.
[96] Ibid., s. 715(1)(d)–(3).
[97] Ibid., s. 715(1)(k), (2).

Option

The accrued income scheme does not apply to a transfer of securities if there is an obligation in that or some related agreement to buy the same or similar securities back, or if there is an option to reacquire the securities and that option is subsequently exercised.[98]

Other tax rules

Certain rules concern the effect of charges on CGT and double taxation relief. On a sale cum-div where an accrued amount is treated as a person's income, the disposal consideration is reduced by an equal amount to avoid a dual charge. Similarly, the effect of a relief is to increase the consideration to avoid a double loss.[99] If the accrued income scheme is excluded (e.g. by reason of exemption), there is no adjustment for that party for CGT purposes. Double tax relief for any foreign tax may be given by way of credit if the income falls or would have fallen within Schedule D, Cases IV and V. When an actual payment of interest is reduced for tax purposes by a relief under these rules any foreign tax credit may also be reduced.[100] Provision is made for the interaction of the new scheme with TA 1988, s. 739.[101]

Death

At one time there was a deemed transfer of securities, with accrued interest, to the personal representatives.[102] However, since 1996 no such transfer takes place if the securities are passed on to a legatee. In this way the accrued income scheme finally took the CGT approach adopted in 1971. Where the securities are not transferred to a legatee but disposed of by the personal representatives, the scheme will apply in the usual way. If the securities were disposed of by V (the now deceased) in V's lifetime, the scheme will apply in the usual way, but the personal representatives may have to settle V's tax liability in respect of the transfer.

26.5 Deduction of Tax at Source

26.5.1 Relevant deposits

Deduction of tax at the lower rate (20%) applies to interest on "relevant deposits" made with a "deposit-taker".[103] "Deposit-taker" is, broadly, any bank, but can also be a local authority.[104] A deposit is "relevant" if the person beneficially entitled to it is an individual (provision is made for concurrent interests), a personal representative as such, or to trustees of a discretionary or accumulation trust.[105] Thus, the scheme does not apply to payments

[98] TA 1988, s. 727A, added by FA 1995, s. 79. On Treasury power to modify by regulation following the introduction of a gilt repo market, see TA 1988, s. 737E, added by FA 1995, s. 83. On scope of s. 727A, note HC Official Report, Standing Committee D (Twelfth Sitting), cols 365, 366; (1995) *Simon's Weekly Tax Intelligence* 359.

[99] TA 1988, Sch. 29.

[100] Ibid., s. 807.

[101] Ibid., s. 742(4)–(7).

[102] Ibid., s. 716, repealed in 1996.

[103] Ibid., s. 480A; the savings (20%) rate is directed by ibid., ss 1A, 4(1A).

[104] The list is set out in ibid., s. 481(2) but s. 482(6) contains exceptionally wide powers enabling the Treasury to designate persons as deposit-takers (see also s. 481(2)(d)).

[105] Ibid., s. 481(4), (4A); on Scottish partnerships, see s.481(4)(b).

to companies or trusts (at least when no individual is entitled to the current income; see below at §29.2.4). The current year basis applies.[106]

Among deposits not considered "relevant"[107] are qualifying certificates of deposit, general client account deposits, premium trust funds of Lloyd's underwriters, debts on securities listed on a recognised stock exchange, debentures, foreign accounts for non-residents and certain large deposits (£50,000) for a minimum period of 28 days.[108] Also excluded are certain payments on the disposal or exercise of certain rights connected with deposits.[109] The Revenue has powers to make exceptions[110] and to give the necessary authority for alternative audit arrangements for non-UK residents.[111]

Building society accounts

Income tax at the lower rate (20%) is withheld from interest arriving on building society accounts under regulations made under TA 1988, s. 477A. However, income tax will be deducted under the "relevant deposit" rules if the building society becomes a bank.

26.5.2 Other payments of interest

Payments of yearly interest falling within TA 1988, s. 349(2) are made subject to withholding at the 20% lower rate.[112] Payments fall within s. 349(2) if they are made (a) by a company[113] or local authority otherwise than in a fiduciary or representative capacity, or (b) by or on behalf of a partnership of which a company is a member. Further, tax must be deducted by any person if yearly interest is paid to another person whose usual place of abode is outside the UK (a form of withholding tax).[114]

Even if the payment satisfies the above criteria, it must be paid gross if it is interest payable in the UK[115] on an advance from a bank carrying on a bona fide banking business[116] in the UK,[117] or the interest is paid by such a bank in the ordinary course of its business, a question answered by reference to ordinary UK banking practice at the time. Yearly interest paid by a bank where the borrowings relate to the capital structure of the bank do not qualify.[118]

Where the interest payment is subject to deduction, the payer must account for the tax to the Revenue (the procedure in s. 349(2) being adopted) and provide a certificate of deduction. A further sanction is provided by TA 1988, s. 82(1)–(5), which restricts a trader's right

[106] Ibid., s. 480C, added in 1990 but now superfluous.

[107] Ibid., s. 481(5).

[108] On building societies, see (1987) *Simon's Tax Intelligence* 335.

[109] I.e payments within TA 1988, s. 56A—see s. 481(5A).

[110] Ibid., s. 480B, added FA 1990.

[111] TA 1988, s .482A, added by FA 1991, s. 75.

[112] TA 1988, s. 349 (2); until 1968 payments of yearly interest, as opposed to short interest, came within the full scheme of deduction at source (now ss 348, 349). Short (i.e. not yearly) interest payments have always been free of withholding—and were not deductible under s. 835 (*IRC* v. *Frere* [1964] 1 All ER 73, 42 TC 125). On early history, see Stebbings [1989] *BTR* 348.

[113] On what the company does with the tax deducted, see TA 1988, Sch. 16, especially paras 5, 6 (see below at §47.4). A company is defined in ibid., s. 831.

[114] Although exceptions are made here also (see ibid., s. 349(3) and note s. 349(3)(g), added by FA 1993, s. 59, for deposit-takers).

[115] See Statement of Practice SP1/95. See also Inland Revenue Press Releases, 30 January 1995, 22 February 1995, (1995) *Simon's Weekly Tax Intelligence* 184, 345.

[116] See *United Dominions Trust Ltd.* v. *Kirkwood* [1966] 1 QB 783, [1965] 2 All ER 992

[117] *Hafton Properties Ltd.* v. *McHugh* [1987] STC 16.

[118] See *Royal Bank of Canada* v. *IRC* (1971) 47 TC 565; and Statement of Practice SP 12/91.

to deduct interest paid to a non-resident where the payment of yearly interest[119] by a person carrying on a trade or profession such a payment to a person not resident in the UK[120] is only deductible if tax has been withheld under s. 349(2).

As from 2001 there will be new deduction rules for public revenue dividends and Eurobonds, FA 2000 s. 111 and 112.

26.6 Discounts

26.1.1 What are discounts?

When the Government (or a company) borrows money for a certain period, e.g. seven years, by means of a bond or bill, the bill is issued at, e.g., £60 with a promise that the Government or company will pay a larger sum, say e.g. £100, at the end of the period. The bond may—or may not—also carry interest. The £40 profit made by the holder, X, at the end of seven years is a profit or a discount and is taxable under Schedule D, Case III on receipt.[121] In the UK[122] it is not taxable as interest.[123] If a regular business of discounting exists, the assessment is made instead under Case I—if the Revenue so chooses.[124] The £40 discount looks very like an interest payment. The distinction between a debt of £100 with a discount of £40, and a debt of £60 with a premium of £40, is a fine one; in each case the total sum eventually paid is £100. However, the distinction is real in law:

> "In the interest account, interest upon the amount is charged upon each bill until it is actually paid; but when a bill is discounted, the interest to be deducted is calculated up to the time when it becomes due and for no longer period."[125]

26.6.2 Traditional viewpoint—liability on maturity

Liability arises when the income promised by the issuer is realised, i.e. when the bill reaches maturity.[126] In *Ditchfield* v. *Sharp*[127] trustees bought an interest-free promissory note with a guarantee from the vendor that they would receive not less than 75% of the face value. The profit accruing on maturity was held liable to tax under Schedule D, Case III as this was an income receipt from a discounting transaction. The Court of Appeal also held that if the whole gain could be liable to tax as arising from a discount then the whole gain should be so taxed, notwithstanding that, on another analysis, at least part of the gain could be said to be interest.

Companies

The traditional way in which discounts are taxed is not immediately obvious. Where a company, for example, issued bonds at £60 and promised to redeem them in seven years' time

[119] TA 1988, s. 82 uses the word "annual".

[120] Confusingly, s. 82 is couched in terms of "residence", while s. 349 refers to "abode".

[121] *Brown* v. *National Provident Institution* [1921] 2 AC 222, 232, 8 TC 80, 83, *per* Lord Haldane; and *Lomax* v. *Peter Dixon* [1943] 1 KB 671, 27 TC 353, 364, *per* Lord Greene M.R.

[122] These give rise to problems in many tax systems; see Ault *et al.*, 260.

[123] *Ditchfield* v. *Sharp* [1983] STC 590, 57 TC 555, CA.

[124] As in *Willingale* v. *International Commercial Bank Ltd.* [1978] STC 75, 52 TC 242.

[125] *Thompson* v. *Giles* (1824) 2 B & C 422, 432, *per* Holroyd J.; and see *Torrens* v. *IRC* (1933) 18 TC 262.

[126] See Hembrey [1982] *BTR* 74.

[127] [1983] STC 590, 57 TC 555, CA; the taxpayers were not allowed to argue that, since the notes were long term, the profit could be capital; such a point should have been taken before the Commissioners.

at £100, there was a loss to the company of £40. The tax system, while allowing the company to claim that loss, did so only when the loss was realised—i.e. when the bonds were redeemed for £100. However, since 1996 the loan relationship rules for companies means that the loss will now be spread over the years on an accrual basis.

Bond holders

Bond holders were treated symmetrically. Therefore, if X bought the bond on issue at £60 and received £100 on maturity three years later, there would be liability of the profit of £40 on maturity—and not before. However what if towards the end of year 5 X sold the bond to Y for, say, £92? On the traditional analysis, X's gain of £32 was not treated as an income profit of £32 but as a capital gain of that amount. When at the end of the seventh year, Y received £100 there would be an income receipt not of £8 but of the whole £40 profit which was due to the holder on maturity. Whether Y would also be treated as suffering a capital loss of £32 would depend on other rules. Needless to say, Y would either be a complete idiot to enter into such a transaction or would have reliefs available to absorb the income of £40 or be exempt from tax. Such a system lasted until 1984 only because the structure of the tax system ensured that there were always knowledgeable vendors and purchasers with widely differing tax circumstances. Since 1984 there have been special rules for deep discount bonds but the old rules remain for what one might call "shallow" discount bonds. The rules from 1984 to 1996 are now obsolete—except for transitional effects; as just explained, the traditional analysis is not obsolete.[128]

26.6.3 1996 onwards—"relevant discounted security"

Definition

When the corporation tax rules for loan relationships were introduced by FA 1996 the income tax rules were simplified. There is now only one category which receives special treatment—the relevant discounted security (RDS). To see whether a security comes within this category the amount paid on issue must be compared with the amount payable on redemption (the result is the discount). The amount paid on issue excludes certain allowable costs.[129] The amount payable on redemption excludes any payment by way of interest on that occasion.[130] The discount is relevant if it represents more than 15% of the amount payable on redemption, or if it is 15% or less but exceeds ½Y%, when Y is the number of years between issue and redemption; months and part months may be taken into account as fractions of years.[131] Therefore a discount of 5% is deep if the life of this security is less than 10 years. Gilt strips are specifically included in this regime.[132]

The 1996 rules did not, however, cover circumstances where the holder became entitled to payment on redemption.[133] In seeing whether the gain was "deep", the amount payable on redemption was compared with the amount payable on the earliest possible redemption date. If the holder had an option to redeem at par or at a very small discount, the security

[128] On the effect of the 1984 changes, see Hills 5(3) *Fiscal Studies* 62

[129] FA 1996, Sch. 13, para. 3(4), referring to para. 1(4).

[130] Ibid., Sch. 13, para. 3(6).

[131] Ibid., Sch. 13, para. 3(4).

[132] Ibid., Sch. 13, para. 14.

[133] Ibid., Sch. 13, para. 3, as rewritten by FA 1999, s. 65; see Lindsay [1999] *BTR* 351; see also Inland Revenue Press Release 15 February 1999, (1999) *Simons Weekly Tax Intelligence* 253. On timing, see FA 1996, Sch. 13, para. 3(3).

would not be "relevant" since it would not be deep enough. In turn, this enabled the holder to defer any tax until redemption as opposed to intermediate transfer (i.e. under the old, pre-1984 rules), while the issuing company could get a deduction year by year because of the corporation tax loan relationship rules.

To correct this lack of symmetry, FA 1999 provides that every possible occasion must be examined, not just the earliest; if the gain is, would or might be deep on any one of those occasions the security is "relevant"[134] and so comes within the rules. An exception is made where the holder's option to redeem arises because of a default by the issuer—provided a redemption is unlikely. [135] This applies only to redemptions which were at the option of the holder.[136]

Issue

However, there are no special rules to determine the date of issue. Case-law suggests that shares are issued when an application has been followed by allotment and notification—and completed by entry on the register. In the case of securities, allotment and notification should suffice.[137] The presence of an enforceable contract to issue is not enough.

Special rules apply to issues in tranches.[138]

Redemption

The date of redemption is important under these rules. The redemption date is the earliest date on which the holder has an absolute right to require redemption.[139] The concept of redemption is also important as an occasion on which a charge arises under the rules. Conversion is equated with redemption—whether the conversion is into share capital or any other securities—provided the conversion is made under rights conferred by the securities.[140]

Exclusions

The following securities cannot be RDSs:[141]

(1) shares in a company;
(2) gilt-edged securities which are not strips;[142]
(3) excluded indexed securities, i.e. where the amount payable on redemption is linked to the value of a chargeable asset;[143]
(4) life assurance policies;
(5) capital redemption policies;[144] and

[134] FA 1996, Sch. 13, para. 3(1) (1999 version).

[135] Ibid., Sch. 13, para. 3(1A) (1999 version).

[136] FA 1999, s. 59(1A)(a); further rules apply if the issuer and holder are connected or the main or one of the main benefits of the redemption is to obtain a tax advantage(s. 59(1C), (1D).

[137] This was the conclusion reached by the House of Lords in connection with BES schemes, see *National Westminster Bank* v. *IRC* [1994] STC 580, 67 TC 1; contrast TA 1988, Sch. 4, para. 1(3) (old law) where shares were contained in letters of allotment.

[138] FA 1996, Sch. 13, para. 10.

[139] FA 1996, Sch. 13, para. 3(5).

[140] Ibid., Sch. 13, para. 5.

[141] Ibid., Sch. 13, para. 3(2).

[142] On which, see FA 1996, Sch. 13, para. 14; "strip" means anything which, within the meaning of s. 47 of the Finance Act 1942, is a strip of a gilt-edged security (Sch. 13, para. 15).

[143] Defined in FA 1996, Sch. 13, para. 13. See also *Investor* v. *IRC* [1998] STC (SCD) 244.

[144] Within the meaning of TA 1988, Pt. XIII, ch. II (i.e. ss 539–54).

(6) subject to special rules, securities issued under the same prospectus as other securities which have been issued previously and which are not themselves RDSs.

Charge on transfer of RDS

Schedule D, Case III charges the profits arising on a transfer of a RDS. Unlike the traditional approach and the rules from 1984 to 1996 (and even the remainder of Schedule D, Case III), these rules allow the taxpayer (T) to set certain expenses against gains and even to end up with a loss. This is of great importance in theory since the income tax charge under Schedule D, Case III is aligning itself with CGT rules and so reducing the difference between the two taxes; any difference would be unreal in this area.

A profit may arise where T transfers the RDS or becomes entitled, as the person holding the security, to a sum on its redemption. To see whether there is a profit, the amount payable to T on the transfer or redemption is compared with the amount T paid to acquire the RDS. The excess (the statute does not use the simple word "gain") is reduced by allowable costs to give the profit. The profit arises in the year of the transfer or redemption and not when the sum is received. Allowable costs, which the statute calls "relevant costs", are broadly the costs incurred by T in connection with the acquisition, transfer or redemption. The sum paid for the asset itself is not a cost incurred in connection with the acquisition—and vice versa.[145] If these calculations yield a loss, relief may be claimed by setting the loss against general income of the year of the transfer or redemption.[146] Where these rules apply the accrued income scheme is excluded.[147] TA 1988, ss 739 and 740 (dealing with the transfer of assets abroad) are made expressly applicable.[148]

Exemptions

Exemptions exist for profits accruing to charities and pension fund schemes.[149] Conversely, there is no relief for losses.

Market value

Echoing CGT rules, a transfer is treated as made at market value if it is between connected persons for a consideration which is not in money or money's worth or otherwise than by way of bargain at arm's length.[150]

Transfer

"Transfer" means any transfer of the security by way of sale, exchange, gift or otherwise.[151] Like the CGT rules, there are express provisions[152] for conditional agreements—which only become transfers when they become unconditional—and for treating a transfer under an agreement as taking place when the agreement is made provided the transferee becomes entitled to the security at that time. However, unlike the CGT rules, there is no express provision for mortgages, bankruptcy or hire purchase. The Revenue may be hoping that the use

[145] FA 1996, Sch. 13, para. 1(4).

[146] Ibid., Sch. 13, para. 2—the claim must be made within a period ending 12 months after 31 January following the end of the year of assessment.

[147] Ibid., Sch. 13, para. 11.

[148] Ibid., Sch. 13, para. 12.

[149] Ibid., Sch. 13, para. 7.

[150] Ibid., Sch. 13, paras 8, 9; on connected persons, see TA 1988, s. 839.

[151] FA 1996, Sch. 13, para. 4(1).

[152] Ibid., Sch. 13, para. 4(3), (4).

of the word "transfer" as opposed to "disposal" may prevent problems such as the scope of part disposals.

Death

Where T dies, there is a deemed transfer of the security immediately before death at market value. T's personal representatives are treated as acquiring the security for that amount on T's death.[153] On a transfer of the RDS by personal representatives to a legatee, the personal representatives are treated as obtaining, in respect of the transfer, an amount equal to the market value of the security at the time of the transfer. There is nothing akin to the CGT rules which treat the legatee's succession as dating back to the death.[154] It appears that basic rate income tax will apply to any profits realised by the personal representatives in the course of administering the estate; the oddity is that since 1998 capital gains realised by the personal representatives are charged at the "rate applicable to trusts", which is higher.

Trustees

Where the security is held by trustees, the profit is calculated in accordance with the rules already outlined. If income arising from the trust would be treated as that of the settlor, the same treatment applies to this profit. If the trustees pay at "the rate applicable to trusts", that rate applies to the trustees. Trustees of other trusts and personal representatives pay at the basic rate only. If the trustees sustain a loss, the loss can be set only against profits arising under these rules and not against general income.[155] The rules do not apply to non-resident trustees or to unauthorised unit trusts.[156]

26.6.4 History: 1984–1996

From 1984 to 1996 much more complicated rules applied. In 1984 special rules for "deep discount securities" were introduced.[157] The rules were amended in 1989 to include a new category of "relevant deep discount securities". FA 1989 also introduced rules for a new category of asset, "deep gain securities". The purpose of the 1989 changes was to extend the 1984 rules to new types of security which will become possible following the abolition of the new issues queue.[158]

The 1984 rules for deep discount securities meant that if, as in our previous example (see above at §26.6.2), X sold the bonds in the course of its life, the income tax liability would be shared between X and Y, instead of all falling on Y. However, the income accruing to X was calculated not on the basis of the actual price received from Y, but on an even attribution of the income over the life of the bond under a mathematical formula.[159] If that formula gave X income of £91 rather than £92, the extra £1 was dealt with under the CGT regime. In its turn, Y was treated as acquiring at £91 and so as having an income of £9 on maturity, not £8. The 1989 rules for deep gain securities were simpler in that there was no mathematical

[153] FA 1996, Sch. 13, para. 4(2).
[154] Ibid., Sch. 13, para. 6 (7), (8).
[155] Ibid., Sch. 13, para. 6(4).
[156] Ibid., Sch. 13, para. 6(2), (3); para. 6(3) is subject to para. 12 which explains how TA 1988, ss 739, 740 are to apply.
[157] Consolidated as TA 1988, Sch. 4.
[158] Inland Revenue Press Release, 14 March 1989, (1989) *Simon's Tax Intelligence* 193.
[159] TA 1988, Sch. 4, para. 4 (repealed 1996); the fraction attributable to each year was deductible by the company year by year as a charge on income—ibid., Sch. 4, para. 5 (also repealed 1996).

formula. In consequence, X would be treated as realising income of £22, while Y would be treated a receiving income of £8.[160]

26.6.5 *Free of tax for non-residents*

The Treasury has power to issue securities on condition that they would be free of tax in the hands of non-residents.[161] In *Hughes* v. *Bank of New Zealand*[162] it was held that the Revenue could not get round this rule by charging tax under Schedule D, Case I. The case also held that the non-resident could deduct the cost of obtaining capital invested in this way; but, by FA 1940, s. 60, the Treasury was given power to issue securities on terms which overrode that aspect of the decision.

26.7 Certificate of Deposit

The tax treatment of profit arising from a certificate of deposit (CD) is an example of the statutory use of Schedule D, Case VI to catch certain profits which fall through the tax net. Under general tax law, any profit from the sale of a certificate was previously exempt from CGT,[163] while no income tax charge could arise unless the holder was a dealer and so liable under Schedule D, Case I. There was no liability under Schedule D, Case III since the gain was not in the nature of interest, and the profit on a discount was charged to the person holding the certificate on maturity.[164] Statute therefore intervened and provided that the profit should be charged under Schedule D, Case VI.[165] The effect is that now all profit will be charged to tax whether it is interest or capital gain on disposal or maturity. Interest on CDs of £50,000 or more may be paid without deduction of tax at source.[166]

This is now supplemented where there is a right under an arrangement to receive an amount (with or without interest) in pursuance of a deposit of money. When the right comes into existence there is no CD in respect of that right, but the person for the time being entitled to the right is entitled to call for a CD.[167] This is presented as a kindness to enable paperless CDs to be treated in the same way as paper CDs, to the benefit of the Central Moneymarkets Office of the Bank of England.[168]

160 FA 1989, Sch. 11, para. 5—the company was unable to deduct anything until maturity. FA 1989, Sch. 11 was repealed by FA 1996.

161 See now FA 1996, s. 154 and FA 1998, s. 161; on exemption from accrued income schemes, see TA 1988, s. 715(1)(f).

162 [1938] 1 All ER 778, 21 TC 472.

163 By TCGA 1992, s. 251.

164 See above at §26.2.

165 TA 1988, s. 56; "certificate of deposit" hass a wide definition under ibid., s. 56(5).

166 Ibid., s. 710(3)(da).

167 Ibid., s. 56A, added by F (No. 2) A 1992, Sch. 8.

168 Inland Revenue Press Release, 10 March 1992, (1992) *Simon's Tax Intelligence* 322.

27

Annuities and Other Annual Payments: Schedule D, Case III

27.1 Brief History

Annuities and annual payments (AAPs) used to be of great importance in personal tax planning since they provided the basic means of transferring income between taxpayers. AAPs also made use of a system of deduction at source (see below at §27.5), which was not only an elegant device in the nineteenth century system which used a single rate of tax, but also the product of a great deal of history;[1] the system was also a delight for examiners. The system of deduction at source did not fit with the system as easily once higher rates of tax were introduced. Nonetheless, the system of assigning income (and income tax liability) survived[2] until well into the 1980s, when it was used by grandparents to pay grandchildren's school fees and by parents to support their adult children at university;[3] such covenants were examples of tax mitigation rather than avoidance.[4] Finally, in 1988 the scope of the system of deduction at source was greatly reduced by excluding from Schedule D, Case III all but a few types of income paid by individuals. The concepts remain important, however, for the taxation of trusts and companies.[5] The 1988 reforms, while succeeding in reducing its scope, failed to reduce the conceptual junkheap of the tax system.

[1] See, generally, Soos, *The Origins of Taxation at Source* (IBFD, 1998); the early part of the story is also told in [1995] *BTR* 49. For 1980s criticism, see [1982] *BTR* 263.

[2] The practice was also defended in Royal Commission on the Taxation of Profits and income, *Final Report*, Cmnd 9474 (1955) §§144–61 (especially §§149 *et seq.*).

[3] The Inland Revenue supplied a do-it-yourself kit in IR 74.

[4] Lord Templeman in *IRC* v. *Challenge Corporation* [1986] STC 548, 554.

[5] See TA 1988, s. 347(A)(2); the scheme for the taxation of annual payments is used for distribution by unauthorised unit trusts (ibid., s. 469(3),(4)).

In this chapter, §§27.2–27.4 deal with the scope of Schedule D, Case III in relation to AAPs, while §27.5 deals with the machinery for deduction at source under TA 1988, ss 348 and 349.

27.2 Schedule D, Case III

27.2.1 Today's scope

Today, the scope of Schedule D, Case III, although greatly reduced for individuals, still applies to certain situations in which AAPs made by individuals are income of the recipient; in turn, such AAPs are also deductible by the assignor. Naturally, these rules do not apply if the special settlement rules decree the income to be that of the assignor after all.

Payments by individuals

Annual payments which remain chargeable under Schedule D, Case III now that covenanted payments to charity have been removed by FA 2000,[6] are payments made for bona fide commercial reasons in connection with the individual's trade, profession or vocation, e.g. partnership retirement annuities[7] and certain earn-out arrangements.[8] The legislation also includes payment of interest (but these are not subject to the full system of deduction at source) and payments within TA 1988, s. 125(1) (but this apparent latitude is to enable the anti-avoidance aspect of s. 125 to work). Payments outside Schedule D, Case III are neither deductible as an allowable charge on the income of the payer, nor taxable income of the payee.[9]

The legislation further provides that in computing foreign income, no deduction may be made on account of an annuity which would not have come within Schedule D, Case III if it had arisen in the UK.[10]

AAPs (unless excluded under the rules outlined above) come within Schedule D, Case III. If they have a foreign source they will come within Schedule D Case IV or V. The system of deduction at source applies only to Case III and cannot apply to Cases IV and V. TA 1988, s. 18[11] directs that tax is imposed on the annuity or other annual payment, whether payable within or outside the UK,[12] and whether charged on property or a personal debt; sums within Schedule A cannot come within Schedule D, Case III.

No deductions for expenses can be claimed so that, as with interest and dividends, this charge has something of the air of a gross receipts tax.[13]

[6] Defined in ibid., s. 347A(7), (8), added in 1995 but repealed by FA 2000 s. 41.
[7] On Scottish partnerships, see TA 1988, s. 347(6).
[8] *IRC* v. *Hogarth* (1940) 23 TC 491; distinguishing *Ramsay* v. *IRC* (1935) 20 TC 79.
[9] TA 1988, s. 347A(1).
[10] See ibid., s. 347A(5).
[11] Other provisions cause income to be taxed under Schedule D, Case III, e.g. TA 1988, ss 119, 554. For list, see *Simon's Direct Tax Service*, Pt. B5.103.
[12] These words focus on where the sum is payable; if the *source* of the interest is a foreign source, then the income falls under Schedule D, Case IV (see below at §60.2) and not Case III.
[13] A matter of importance when other countries are wondering whether to grant credit relief for the UK tax paid.

27.2.2 Basis of assessment

Since 1996–1997 almost all assessments under Schedule D, Case III have been made on a strict current year basis,[14] i.e the full amount of income arising in the period 6 April to 5 April.[15] Before 1996 the preceding year basis was used unless statute otherwise provided.[16]

When does income arise?

The meaning of this expression was discussed in the context of the pre-1996 rules. Generally, income under AAPs arises only when it is received, not when it is due. The concept of "enuring to one's advantage"[17] developed in the interest cases, has not been explored in the context of AAPs; this may be because of the dominating influence of the system of deduction at source which naturally highlights actual payment. Following the interest treatment, it is likely that a payment by cheque will not be income when the cheque is received but, probably only when the proceeds of the cheque are received, whether as cash or credited to the payee's account.[18]

27.3 Annuity

An annuity arises "where an income is purchased with a sum of money and the capital has gone and has ceased to exist, the principal having been converted into an annuity".[19]

An annuity must be distinguished from the payments of a debt by instalments.[20] In an annuity the capital has gone and, in a normal life annuity contract, payments will continue provided the annuitant lives; an annuity is thus an insurance against outliving capital. On the other hand, where a debt is paid by instalments, the debt remains, and liability is not usually affected by the death of either party.

Advances

If T buys an annuity from an annuity with cash it is clear that what is received is an annuity, and tax is due on the payments received. Several cases have been concerned with attempts to get payments of the same economic value as an annuity out of an annuity company, while making sure that the payments are not themselves annuities. The two principal cases [21] have been described as very special, and the reasoning of one as hard to follow.[22]

[14] TA 1988, s. 64, as replaced by FA 1994, s. 206.

[15] If a trading partnership receives income outside Schedule D, Case I, the basis period for the partnership is taken instead.

[16] TA 1988, ss 66, 67 (repealed with effect from 1996 by FA 1994).

[17] *Dunmore* v. *McGowan* [1978] STC 217, [1978] 2 All ER 85 (see above at §26.1.2); see also *Whitworth Park Coal Co. Ltd.* v. *IRC* [1959] 3 All ER 703.

[18] *Parkside Leasing Ltd.* v. *Smith* [1985] STC 63, 69d (if the crediting is conditional it is assumed that income is not received until the crediting has become unconditional).

[19] *Foley* v. *Fletcher and Rose* (1858) 3 H & N 769, 784, *per* Watson B. Purchased annuities are now dissected (TA 1988, s. 656); see below at §54.7.

[20] See above at §26.4.5.

[21] Principally, *Perrin* v. *Dickson* [1930] 1 KB 107, 14 TC 608 (deposit not annuity); distinguished in *Sothern-Smith* v. *Clancy* [1941] 1 All ER 111, 24 TC 1 (annuity).

[22] By Lord Greene M.R. in *IRC* v. *Wesleyan and General Assurance Society* [1948] 1 All ER 555, 30 TC 11.

Another decision treating sums borrowed as loans not annuities[23] has now been reversed by narrow legislation.[24] All that can be said is that every case must be determined on its own facts. Many advances by insurance companies are now taxed (see below at §55.2.5).

27.4 Other Annual Payments[25]

"Annual payment" is construed *eiusdem generis* with annuities[26] or yearly interest of money;[27] a rent of land is not an annual payment.[28] Although the legislation talks of "payments", payments in kind fall within Schedule D, Case III.[29] Case-law establishes that a payment is an annual payment if (1) there is some legal obligation to pay the sum, (2) it possesses the essential quality of recurrence implied by the description annual, (3) it is "pure income profit" in the payee's hands, (4) it belongs to the payee and (5) it is part of the payee's income of the payee as opposed to being a capital payment. There may be a sixth rule, i.e. that the payment must be a "division of the profits of the payer". An annual payment may be removed from this category by statute, as has been done with personal injury damages in the form of periodical payments and similar compensation under statutory or other schemes.[30]

27.4.1 The obligation

The question whether there is an obligation to pay an annual payment is distinct from whether the obligation is created for valuable and sufficient consideration,[31] and has been satisfied on relatively flimsy facts.[32] The obligation may be involuntary, e.g. under a court order or a statute.[33]

A series of voluntary gifts or *ultra vires* payments by a company cannot be annual payments.[34] Dividend payments by companies are not annual paymentss since a company is under no obligation to pay a dividend.[35]

Where trustees have an express discretion to make payments to an object of the trust,[36] sums paid under that discretion are not regarded as voluntary;[37] (see below at §29.2.5).

Payments by trusts are not affected by FA 1988 and so remain Schedule D, Case III income of the recipient.[38]

[23] *IRC* v. *Wesleyan and General Assurance Society*, ibid.
[24] TA 1988, s. 554.
[25] By concession, sickness benefit payments arranged by an individual, as distinct from his employer, are taxed only if they continue for at least a year before the year of assessment (ESC A26).
[26] The 1988 legislation assumes that an annuity payable by an individual is an annual payment.
[27] *IRC* v. *Whitworth Park Coal Co. Ltd.* [1958] 2 All ER 91, 102, 38 TC 531, 548, *per* Jenkins L.J.
[28] *Hill* v. *Gregory* [1912] 2 KB 61, 6 TC 39; see now TA 1988, s. 18.
[29] Presumably the machinery in ibid., ss. 348, 349 does not apply.
[30] Ibid., ss 329AA, 329AB; for another example, see FA 1991, s.121 (payments by pools promoters to support games, etc.).
[31] *Smith* v. *Smith* [1923] P 191, 197, *per* Lord Sterndale, and 202, *per* Warrington L.J.
[32] For example *Dealler* v. *Bruce* (1934) 19 TC 1.
[33] See above at n. 30.
[34] *Ridge Securities Ltd.* v. *IRC* [1964] 1 All ER 275, 44 TC 373.
[35] *Canadian Eagle Oil Co. Ltd.* v. *R* [1945] 2 All ER 499, 504, (1945) 27 TC 205, 245.
[36] A payment by a charitable trust would, however, be regarded as voluntary since the beneficiary under the trusts is a charity and not the person benefited (*Stedeford* v. *Beloe* [1931] 2 KB 610, 626, *per* Romer L.J.).
[37] *Drummond* v. *Collins* [1915] AC 1011, 6 TC 525 (a decision on Schedule D, Case V).
[38] TA 1988, s. 347A(2) is confined to individuals.

27.4.2 Recurrence

It is the word "annual" which indicates that a payment falling within Schedule D, Case III must, like interest on money or an annuity, have the quality of being recurrent or capable of recurrence.[39] For this reason an obligation which cannot last longer than 12 months cannot create an annual payment.[40] On the other hand, if the obligation can endure that long, it is irrelevant that the payment is payable weekly[41] or monthly. It is irrelevant that the sum paid may vary; so, payment of such a sum that, after tax at the basic rate in force in the year of payment, equals £50, is an "annual payment". It is also irrelevant that the obligation is contingent, so that no sum may be payable under the obligation at all, as under a guarantee. The purpose of the rule seems to be to exclude payments which are casual and temporary and therefore fall more easily into Schedule D, Case VI (which has no requirement of recurrence) than Case III.[42]

Weekly payments are "annual". The annual payment in such cases is the weekly sum multiplied by the number of weeks in the year, which may be 52 or 53 depending upon the day of the week on which the obligation falls.

27.4.3 Pure income profit[43]

It is inconsistent with the scheme of deduction at source that Schedule D, Case III should contain payments which are likely to be gross receipts of the payee against which expenses can be set, and so not pure income.[44] Hence, a trading receipt cannot be an annual payment. Scrutton L.J. provided a famous example in *Howe* v. *IRC*:[45]

> "If a man agrees to pay a motor garage £500 a year for five years for the hire and upkeep of a car, no one suggests the person paying can deduct income tax from each yearly payment. So if he contracted with a butcher for an annual sum to supply all his meat for a year, the annual instalment would not be subject to tax as a whole in the hands of the payee, but only that part of it which was profits."

The same principle applies to receipts of the payee's profession. Where a solicitor trustee was entitled to charge for his services under a charging clause, such payments were not within Schedule D, Case III even though, by agreement with the beneficiaries and other trustees, they took the form of a percentage of the trust income.[46] On the other hand, an annuity of £100 paid to a trustee for acting as trustee was held to be an annual payment.[47] Since a trustee has no right to charge for his time and trouble, but only for his expenses, both payments are acts of bounty on the part of the settlor; however, the former is a receipt of the firm for services rendered, whereas the latter is not.[48] This throws doubt upon the annuity's status as an annual payment, although the point was expressly left open and the Revenue

39 *Moss Empires Ltd.* v. *IRC* [1937] AC 785, 795, 21 TC 264, 299, *per* Lord Maugham.

40 *Smith* v. *Smith* [1923] P 191, 196, *per* Lord Sterndale.

41 TA 1988, s. 18; see also *Re Jane's Settlement* [1918] 2 Ch 54.

42 *Whitworth Park Coal Co. Ltd.* v. *IRC* [1959] 3 All ER 703, 716, 38 TC 531, 575, *per* Lord Radcliffe.

43 In *IRC* v. *London Corpn (as Conservators of Epping Forest)* [1953] 1 All ER 1075, 1081, 34 TC 293 at 320 Lord Normand said that the formula would lose nothing by the omissions of the words "pure" and "profit".

44 *Whitworth Park Coal Co. Ltd.* v. *IRC* [1959] 3 All ER 703, 715, 38 TC 531, 575, *per* Lord Radcliffe.

45 [1919] 2 KB 336, 352, 7 TC 296, 303; see also *Re Hanbury, Comiskey* v. *Hanbury* (1939) 38 TC 588.

46 *Jones* v. *Wright* (1927) 13 TC 221.

47 *Baxendale* v. *Murphy* [1924] 2 KB 494, 9 TC 76.

48 In *Dale* v. *IRC* [1953] 2 All ER 671, 676, 34 TC 468, 493 it was held that such an annuity is earned income, a conclusion which may be inconsistent with its annual payment status.

does not appear to have pressed it. Similarly, any annuities or annual profits and gains which are charged under Schedule A or E fall outside Schedule D, Case III.[49]

Other payments; the non-fatal effect of counter-stipulations

The presence of some counter-stipulation may deprive payment to a non-trading body of its character of pure income benefit. The difficulty is to know where precisely this line is to be drawn. At one time it was thought that the presence of *any* counter-stipulation or condition would be fatal,[50] but this view was rejected by the House of Lords in *Campbell* v. *IRC*.[51] Today, a counter-stipulation will deprive the payment of a quality of pure bounty, but not necessarily of its character as pure income profit. In *Campbell*, Lord Donovan pointed out that in *Westminster* v. *IRC*[52] Lord Macmillan said that if, in return for the annuity, the employee had promised to work for lower wages, the payments would still be within Schedule D, Case III, a view with which Lord Wright agreed.

In *Campbell* v. *IRC*, A had a business which T, a charitable trust, wished to acquire. Under a scheme, A covenanted with T that A would pay a sum equal to 80%[53] of net profits toT; T would then pay the money over to C, a company in which the owners of A had an interest. The scheme failed because the legally enforceable obligation on T to use the same amount of money to pay for the goodwill deprived the payment of the character of pure income profit.[54] Lord Hodson and Lord Upjohn expressly left open the question of what would have happened if the obligation had not been legally enforceable.[55] Today, it would seem that the same result would apply if there had been no legally enforceable obligation, but simply a *Craven* v. *White* inevitability.[56]

Charities and pure income profit

The above problems were discussed in connection with covenants in favour of charities, which may offer inducements in order to obtain those covenants. In *IRC* v. *National Book League*[57] the charity provided a central lending library, arranged exhibitions, ran a book information service and made available to members various rooms at its headquarters such as sitting rooms, a restaurant and a cocktail bar. Payments under covenants in its favour were held not to be pure income profit. The correct basis of the decision is that the covenants were simply a club subscription in return for the annual provisions of goods and services.[58] The question of what inducements can be offered remains, therefore, a matter of doubt.

[49] TA 1988, s. 18.

[50] For example the judgments of the Court of Appeal in *IRC* v. *National Book League* [1957] 2 All ER 644, 37 TC 455; and *Campbell* v. *IRC* [1967] 2 All ER 625, 45 TC 427.

[51] Ibid.

[52] [1968] 3 All ER 588, 606, 45 TC 427, 474.

[53] The figure of 80% was chosen because the covenant was not deductible for profits tax, and 20% was needed to pay that tax.

[54] [1970] AC 77, 108, [1968] 3 All ER 588, 603, 45 TC 427, 472, *per* Lord Upjohn; ibid., 99, 595, 463, *per* Lord Dilhorne; 110, 604, 473, *per* Lord Donovan; ibid., 102, 598, 466, *per* Lord Hodson; and ibid., 104, 600, 468, *per* Lord Guest. A subsidiary point was whether the income of T has been applied to charitable purposes only; the House of Lords held that it had been so applied, reversing the Court of Appeal and reinstating Buckley J.

[55] 45 TC 427, 466D, 470A.

[56] See above §5.6.4. However, not every payment by a subsiary to a parent falls foul of *IRC* v. *Campbell* (see *Nightingale Ltd.* v. *Price* [1996] STC (SCD) 116).

[57] [1957] 2 All ER 644, 37 TC 455.

[58] *Campbell* v. *IRC* [1968] 3 All ER 588, 594, 45 TC 427, 462; and *IRC* v. *National Book League* [1957] 2 All ER 644, 652, 37 TC 455, 475, *per* Morris L.J.

The provision of such facilities as private viewing days for friends of a particular museum, or priority booking for certain performances by a theatre or opera company, is probably not sufficient to prevent payments from being the pure income profit of the charity. The offer of seats at reduced prices was fatal in one first instance decision[59] decided before, and not commented upon in, *Campbell* v. *IRC*. The effect of the very common practice of third parties offering discounts has not been determined; since these have no cost for the charity it is hard to see why they affect the question whether a payment is pure income profit.

From 1988 to 2000, covenants in favour of charities were only effective gifts to charity if they were "covenanted payments to charity". This definition[60] did not refer to Schedule D, Case III, so ignored the concept of pure income profit; instead, it excluded from the favoured category any payment for consideration in money or money's worth.[61] The scope of this last phrase has been clarified in part by FA 1989, s. 59, but only in relation to charities for the preservation of property or the conservation of wildlife for the public benefit,[62] for which charities the right of free admission is ignored.[63] The provision is aimed mostly to protect the National Trust and the RSPB but, of course, must be phrased objectively. One question will be to see how some of the benefits commonly offered can be valued (e.g dis-counts provided by third parties) and whether "money's worth" extends to such discounts.

On benefits and the gift aid scheme see below §31.6.2.

27.4.4 Income of the payee

The payment must be income of the payee (T) and not that of someone else; it will not be T's income if there is a legally enforceable obligation requiring T to hand it on to someone else. This is another explanation of *Campbell* v. *IRC*.[64]

27.4.5 Capital or income? The dissection problem

The issue

An annual payment is taxable within Schedule D, Case III only if it is income. Where, therefore, a series of payments is made, the law must decide whether the payments are the income of the recipient or merely a payment of capital by instalments: if the former, each payment is an annual payment; if the latter, each is capital and so not an annual payment. The answer may be that the payment is partly income and partly capital. However, in this instance the income element is not an annual payment, but instead one of interest. The question for the court is the true legal nature of the transaction which the parties have entered into.[65] In answering this question, extrinsic evidence is admissible.[66]

[59] *Taw and Torridge Festival Society Ltd.* v. *IRC* (1959) 38 TC 603, [1960] BTR 61.

[60] TA 1988, s. 347A(7); gift aid has its own 2.5% limit (FA 1989, s. 25(2)(e)).

[61] See ch. 00 below; and Robson [1988] *BTR* 231.

[62] Bodies listed in TA 1988, s. 507 qualify; see Ghosh and Robson [1993] *BTR* 496.

[63] FA 1989, s. 59(3).

[64] For example [1970] AC 77, 108, [1968] 3 All ER 588, 603, 45 TC 427, 472, *per* Lord Upjohn.

[65] *IRC* v. *Church Commrs for England* [1976] STC 339, [1976] 2 All ER 1037. An agreement may contain two different types of payment, as in *IRC* v. *British Salmson Aero Engines Ltd.* [1938] 3 All ER 283, 22 TC 29.

[66] *IRC* v. *Church Commrs for England* [1976] 2 All ER 1037, 1044, *per* Lord Wilberforce.

The test

The test is whether, as a matter of substance, the payments are instalments of the purchase price or pure income payments.[67] This is not regarded as destroying the principle laid down in *Duke of Westminster* v. *IRC* (above §5.6.1) because the test does not involve putting upon a transaction between parties a character which in law it does not possess, but instead discovering what is the true character in law of the transaction which was entered into.[68]

Four preliminary points

Four matters are clear, although they tend to add to the confusion. First, the fact that a payment is made out of capital in no way affects the question whether the payment is income of the recipient. Therefore, annuity payments are taxable even though under the terms of the will or settlement giving rise to it the trustees are empowered to have recourse to capital in order to pay the sum, and the trustees exercise that power.[69] Secondly, the label which the parties choose to give to the payment is not conclusive; thus, an "annuity" payment has been held to be capital.[70] Thirdly, the courts have stressed that the question in every case is one of the true legal nature of the transaction[71] and that every case is to be decided on its own facts. A particular fact may have been the dominating factor in a case but that is not the same as a conclusive test.[72] Fourthly, the courts have stated that they cannot regard the conduct of the parties as conclusive, but that they may draw comfort from the fact that the decision of the court corresponds with that conduct.[73]

Four principles

(1) Where a definite sum of money is due and the payment of that sum in one lump would be a capital receipt of the payee, as where it is made in return for an asset, the same quality attaches to the payment even though it is paid by instalments. Such payments will not be annual payments.[74]

This principle is best illustrated by contrasting two cases on sales of businesses. In *Ramsay* v. *IRC*[75] T agreed to buy a dental practice. A primary price of £15,000 was agreed, but T agreed to pay it in the form of £5,000 immediately and subsequently to pay each year for 10 years a sum equal to 25% of the net profits of that year. These were described as capital payments and no interest was payable. It was held that the payments were not annual payments but capital instalments so that the taxpayer could not deduct income tax when making each payment; this conclusion coincided with what the parties had actually done.

In *IRC* v. *Hogarth*[76] partners in a business agreed to pay one of the non-retiring partners not only his share of the capital account and assets of the firm, but also a sum equal

[67] *Brodie's Will Trustees* v. *IRC* (1933) 17 TC 432, 440.
[68] *Mallaby-Deeley* v. *IRC* [1938] 4 All ER 818, 825, 23 TC 153, 167, *per* Sir Wilfrid Greene M.R.
[69] See below at §29.3.5.
[70] *Secretary of State in Council of India* v. *Scoble* [1903] AC 299, 4 TC 618.
[71] *IRC* v. *Church Commrs for England* [1976] STC 339, [1976] 2 All ER 1037.
[72] *Dott* v. *Brown* [1936] 1 All ER 543.
[73] *IRC* v. *Hogarth* (1940) 23 TC 491, 500, *per* Lord Normand.
[74] There is very little to be gleaned from *Foley* v. *Fletcher and Rose* (1853) 3 H and N 769 other than an inconclusive survey of a wide variety of solutions.
[75] (1935) 20 TC 79; see also *Mallaby-Deeley* v. *IRC* [1938] 4 All ER 818, 23 TC 153.
[76] (1940) 23 TC 491; see also *Jones* v. *IRC* [1920] 1 KB 711, 7 TC 310; doubted by Scott L.J. in *Dott* v. *Brown* [1936] 1 All ER 543.

to one-fourteenth part of the net profits of the business for the three years ending 31 December 1937, 1938 and 1939, under deduction of tax. The partners making this payment sought to deduct these sums from their income for surtax purposes, something they could do only if the payments were income of the recipient. The Court of Session held that they were income, first because a statement that the payments were to be made under deduction of tax indicated that fact and, secondly, because the payments were in satisfaction of a claim to annual profits or gains.

(2) However, where a bargain was always considered to be in income terms, and was concluded in income terms, and there was nothing in the documents to give the transaction a capital character, the payments will be pure income. This is even more likely to the payments are expressed in terms strongly suggestive of income, such as a rentcharge.

In *IRC* v. *Church Commrs for England*[77] a charity sold a reversion on a lease to the tenant in consideration of rentcharges, payable annually for 10 years and amounting in aggregate to £96,000 each year. It was clear that at no time was the purchaser willing to purchase for a single lump sum. The House of Lords held that these payments were pure income and could not be dissected into capital and interest payments.

(3) Where, despite principle (1) above, a series of payments are made in exchange for a right to income payments, the payments are likely to be pure income.

This is the basis of the decision in *IRC* v. *Hogarth* (above).[78] Another example is *Chadwick* v. *Pearl Life Insurance Co.*[79] The plaintiff (P) owned a lease which had 10 years to run. The total income from the sub-lease was £1,925 p.a. and the rent payable under the lease was £300, leaving a rental income of £1,625. P sold his interest to the defendant (D) for £1,000 and a covenant by D to pay £1,625 p.a. for 10 years. No sum was fixed as the total amount due on the sale, although that total sum could clearly have been ascertained (£17,250). Since the intention of the transaction was that P should continue to receive as income to the end of the term the same amount he had previously received as rent, Walton J. concluded that the payments were income, although he observed that the distinction was a fine one.

(4) If the payment is not pure income, it may be dissected into capital and interest where the parties, who are buying and selling a capital asset, having agreed on a price, then make provision for payment of that price by instalments, the amount of which is so calculated, and shown to be so calculated, as to include an interest element.[80] In *Secretary of State in Council of India* v. *Scoble*[81] the East India Company bought a railway from a company and was empowered to pay outright or in instalments over a period of 46 years; the instalments, although called an annuity, were dissected.

Where no lump sum purchase price has been agreed, the question is decided after consideringt the transaction as a whole. This may explain the most extreme example of dissection: *Vestey* v. *IRC*.[82] The taxpayer sold shares worth £2 m for £5.5 m, the sum to be paid in 125 yearly instalments of £44,000. The agreement stated that the price of

[77] [1976] STC 339, [1976] 2 All ER 1037. This case may be taken as an *a fortiori* example of principle (3) since the calculation of the sum involved a wish to maintain an income equivalent to the rent for the remainder of the lease and to establish a fund which could then yield that sum in perpetuity.

[78] (1940) 23 TC 491.

[79] [1905] 2 KB 507.

[80] *IRC* v. *Church Commrs for England* [1976] STC 339, 345, [1976] 2 All ER 1037, 1043, *per* Lord Wilberforce.

[81] [1903] AC 299, 4 TC 623.

[82] [1961] 3 All ER 978, (1961) 40 TC 112; Phillips [1962] *BTR* 32.

£5.5 m was to be without interest. The Revenue sought to charge the taxpayer to surtax either on the whole payment as an annuity or on a part of it as interest. Cross J. upheld the second claim.

The enthusiasm with which Cross J. preferred the second approach to the first is not to be found in the later decision of the House of Lords in *IRC* v. *Church Commrs for England*.[83] The facts of that case fell on the other side of the line principally because the transaction was thought of throughout in income tax terms (see principle (2)), and because there was no evidence that the parties had ever settled on a firm lump sum price. Lord Wilberforce accepted the *Vestey* decision as correct despite the fact that the only figure agreed on by the parties was the overall price of £5.5 m.[84]

Today it is likely that, when the parties have agreed on a fixed sum, the sum will be dissected and will not be pure capital unless the period is short and the contract is in a common form. Dissection into interest and principal was directed in *Vestey* where the period was 125 years, but not in *Ramsay* where the period was 10 years and the contract was for the disposal of a business, the price being ascertained on a common and reasonable basis.

27.4.6 Doubtful rule: division of profits

This unilluminating rule, which asserts that the payment must be a division of profits as opposed to spending profits, concentrates on the payer; assignments of income must be distinguished from a mere spending of profits.[85] This concentration on the payer seems out of place when the issue is whether certain payments are income of the payee and gives a disproportionate effect to TA 1988, s. 348.

27.5 Machinery: Deduction at Source

27.5.1 The scheme

Under TA 1988, s. 348 where P makes a payment to T out of P's income which has been brought into charge to income tax and the payment is an annuity or annual payment, so that T's income comes within Schedule D, Case III, P has a right to deduct basic rate tax. Therefore, if P is due to pay T £100, P will deduct £22 and pay only £78.

Basic rate of tax

It had long been the law that P will deduct at the basic rate of tax. The introduction of the lower rate of tax on savings income, however, led to a change in 1996.[86] Deduction at basic rate continues to apply to (1) annuities and annual payments other than interest and (2) payments in respect of patent royalties. All other payments within the scheme in TA 1988,

[83] [1976] STC 339, 345, [1976] 2 All ER 1037, 1043, *per* Lord Wilberforce.

[84] Actuarial report made to the trustees referred to in the case stated in *Vestey* v. *IRC* (1961) 40 TC 112, 115.

[85] *Jones* v. *Wright* (1927) 13 TC 221, 226, *per* Rowlatt J.; and see Lord Hanworth M.R. in *Westminster* v. *IRC* (1935) 19 TC 490, 505.

[86] The change was not required by the introduction of the lower rate itself in 1991 or the reduction in the liability of basic rate taxpayers in respect of dividends in 1994.

s. 348 and 349 now suffer deduction at 20%.[87] The following account deals with an annuity or other annual payment, so that the rate at which tax is withheld is basic rate.

Taxed income

The deduction of £22 in the above example is treated as income tax paid by T.[88] It follows that if T's marginal rate of tax is 22% there is nothing more to be done. If, however, T's rate is 0%, he may recover the £22 by making a repayment claim to the Revenue (not P). If T's rate is 10%, he may make a claim for 12%. If T's rate is 40% he must pay a further £18. Anomalously, while there is a duty on P to supply a certificate to show that tax has been deducted,[89] there is no penalty for non-compliance, a matter of considerable practical importance.

S. 348 not only allows P to act as tax collector for T, but also allows P to keep the £22. This is the mechanism whereby P's payment to T is treated as an assignment of P's income to T, with the result that it is deductible—or not taxable—in P's hands. The scheme thus has two functions. The first is to make a provisional assessment on T by allowing P to deduct basic rate tax at source: this may be called the withholding function. The second is to give effect to P's right to deduct the payment in computing total income by first making P pay tax at basic rate on this part of his income and then permitting him to recoup that tax on making the payment:[90] this may be called the relief function.

The scheme applies where payment is made out of income which has been brought into charge to income tax. TA 1988, s. 3 ensures that tax will be paid if P has enough income; s. 3 also directs that, subject to other provisions of the Act, the rate of tax paid by P will be basic rate only. This means that P is not liable to higher rate tax. P is not entitled to personal reliefs on the slice of his income assigned to T;[91] it follows that P must pay tax at 22% on that slice and then recoup that amount under s. 348. If P only has savings income taxed at 20%, an extra 2% must be paid.[91a]

Untaxed income

If P's total income is less than £100, TA 1988, s. 348 does not apply. Originally, P was expected to make the payment in full, but this was not always convenient since P may not have known what his final tax liability would be when making the payment. Therefore, s. 349 makes P deduct the £22, as under s. 348, but this time to account for it to the Revenue.

Examples

In each case P is to make an annual payment to T of £100.

(1) P's total income is £10,000—s. 348 applies. P pays T £78.

(2) P's total income is £100,000—s. 348 applies. P pays T £78. S. 348 only authorises deduction at basic rate. If P can deduct this payment in computing his total income, any deduction in respect of higher rates, i.e. for excess liability, will be given effect when the higher rate liability is calculated. This is usually achieved by lengthening the band of P's income subject to basic rate and so reducing the amount subject to higher rates (as with X's covenant of £1,000 in the example above at §12.4).

[87] TA 1988, ss 1A, 4(1), (1A), added by FA 1996.
[88] TA 1988, s. 348(1)(d).
[89] TMA 1970, s. 106(1).
[90] TA 1988, s. 3.
[91] Ibid., s. 276.
[91a] See JFAJ [1996] *BTR* 342.

(3) P's total income is £1,000—s. 348 applies. P would normally pay no tax since his total income is more than offset by the personal relief. However, P must pay basic rate tax on £100 of income under s. 3 and may then recoup that tax by withholding under s. 348.

(4) P's total income is nil—s. 349 applies. P pays T £78 and the Revenue £22.

(5) P's total income is £60—s. 349(1) applies. This section requires P to pay T £78; P is liable to basic rate tax of £13.20 on £60 and to account to the Revenue for basic rate tax of 8.80 on £40.

27.5.2 Payments within the scheme

Annuities and other annual payments come within the scheme provided they are taxable as T's income under Schedule D, Case III. In addition to annuities and annual payments, the scheme also covers any royalty or other sum paid in respect of the use of a patent.[92] Annuities and other annual payments which would otherwise be within the scheme after 1988 are nonetheless excluded if they are (a) charged on land—chargeable under Schedule A,[93] (b) made under a source sited outside the UK—chargeable under Schedule D, Case IV, or (c) from a source sited inside the UK but in favour of a non-resident and exempt under a double tax treaty.[94]

The scheme of deduction at source originally applied not only to most annuities and annual payments but also to payments of yearly interest and, in effect, to dividends.[95] Today, most interest payments are outside the scheme[96] and dividends are the subject of a special regime under Schedule F; attempts to convert interest payments into annuities are meant to be frustrated by TA 1988, s. 786.[97]

27.5.3 Payer's right to deduct

Under s. 348, P, who makes the payment, is entitled to deduct income tax when making the payment,[98] but only at the basic rate.[99] If the payments are made late, the rate of tax to be deducted is that in force when the payment falls due.[100] It is unclear whether this, in turn, makes T liable in the year the payment fell due even though the payment is received in a later year. Under s. 348, P is entitled—not obliged—to deduct tax; an obligation may, however, arise in some other way. In *Re Sharp*[101] trustees of a settlement failed to deduct tax when paying certain annuities. This was a breach of trust because they had overpaid the annuitant at the expense of the other beneficiaries and were therefore compelled to make good the loss.

Under s. 349(1), P is obliged to deduct "a sum representing the amount of income tax on the payment"[102] and is accountable to the Revenue for tax at the basic rate[103] on the whole

92 Ibid., s. 348(2); the deduction is at basic rate.

93 Ibid., ss 15, 18.

94 For example royalty payments under Art. 12 of the US–UK Treaty.

95 Income Tax Act 1918, All Schedules Rule 20.

96 But see TA 1988, s. 350 (see above at §26.5 andbelow at §47.4).

97 However, its neighbour, s. 787, was given a relatively narrow interpretation in *Westmoreland Investments* v. *Macniven* [1998] STC 1131, CA.

98 TA 1988, s. 348(1)(b).

99 Ibid., s. 4 (or the lower rate under s. 4(1A) applies).

100 *IRC* v. *Crawley* [1987] STC 147, 59 TC 728.

101 [1906] 1 Ch 793.

102 TA 1988, s. 349(1).

103 Ibid., s. 4.

sum. Where the payment is partly from taxed income, P is accountable for tax at the appropriate rate on that part not paid from taxed income; P may thus keep the balance of the deduction. P is accountable whether or not that deduction is made.[104]

Under s. 349(1) the duty to deduct is imposed on the person "by or through whom" it is made. Where, therefore, solicitors held funds for a person obliged to make a payment falling within s. 349(1), the solicitors were held accountable.[105] The words "through whom" are apt to cover any agent, even a bank.

27.5.4 Tax deducted—T's immunity from basic rate liability

Under TA 1988, s. 348, T, the payee, is treated as having paid the amount of income tax which has been deducted.[106] Under s. 349(1), if P, the payer, has deducted tax, T, the payee, is regarded as having paid basic rate income tax and so is safe from direct assessment, whether or not the payer accounts for the tax to the Revenue.[107]

27.5.5 Failure to deduct

The Revenue and the parties

Under s. 348 the deduction is treated as income tax paid by T, the payee.[108] Therefore, if no deduction is made, no tax can be treated as having been paid. It seems to follow that if tax is not deducted, T must make a self-assessment under Schedule D, Case III.[109] The Revenue view is that no repayment claim can be made by T if no deduction has been made.[110]

If s. 349(1) applies and tax is not deducted, T, the payee, must pay tax through the self-assessment process.[111] However, since P is obliged, not entitled, under s. 349(1) to deduct tax, and to account for it to the Revenue, P is also liable.[112] The amount on which T is assessable is the amount payable. If P makes a covenanted payment of £100 but fails to deduct the £22 tax, the Revenue may charge P with the tax of £22. There is no rule which treats P as having paid the £100 net of tax so as to cause that figure actually paid to be grossed up to £128.20.[113]

The parties *inter se*

If P fails to deduct tax under s. 348, and so pays more than necessary, he will be able to recover the overpayment from T whether the mistake is one of fact or law. Until 1998 only sums paid under mistake of fact could be recovered. However, in *Kleinwort Benson Ltd.* v. *Lincoln City Council*[114] the House of Lords held that restitution for unjust enrichment is not

[104] Ibid., s. 350(1).

[105] *Rye and Eyre* v. *IRC* [1935] AC 274, 19 TC 164; and see *Howells* v. *IRC* [1939] 3 All ER 144, 22 TC 501.

[106] TA 1988, s. 348(1)(d).

[107] *Stokes* v. *Bennett* [1953] 2 All ER 313, 34 TC 337.

[108] TA 1988, s. 348(1)(d).

[109] TA 1970, s. 52(1)(a) precluded any direct assessment on the payee but in 1973 this was replaced by what is now s. 348(1)(d). Direct assessment on P is now possible and is common where T is subject to higher rate liability, whether or not P deducts basic rate tax under s. 348.

[110] This was subject to concessionary relief for maintenance payments which took the odd form of allowing the payer to deduct the payment in computing his income (ESC A52); for a critical comment, see [1985] *BTR* 329.

[111] *Grosvenor Place Estates Ltd.* v. *Roberts* [1961] 1 All ER 341, 39 TC 433.

[112] TA 1988, s. 349 (2); *Lord Advocate* v. *Edinburgh Corpn* (1905) 7 F (Ct of Sess) 1972.

[113] *IRC* v. *Watson* (1943) 25 TC 25.

[114] [1999] 2 AC 349.

excluded by mistake of law. The House also held that the new rule applied to payments made before 1998 even though at the time of payment the older rule was firmly established. The new principles of restitution contain a number of defences which will have to be worked out. Under the pre-1988 understanding of the law, P was treated as making a gift which, being complete, could not be undone. It followed that in general no action would lie against the overpaid T for recovery of the sum, and P had no right to withhold later payments to secure reimbursement.[115] This rules was subject to a number of exceptions[116] and it is necessary to wait to see how those old exceptions will be made to fit in with the new principles of restitution.

27.5.6 Which section?

A number of situations test the boundary between ss 348 and 349.

Delayed payment

A payment due in year 1 in which P had sufficient taxable income for the payment to fall within s. 348, is paid[117] in year 2 when there is not sufficient income. Since the right to deduct under s. 348 arises only on "making" the payment, and since, in general, the income is treated as taxable to the recipient under Schedule D, Case III only in the year in which it is received, it would appear that the date, upon which the question of which section should apply depends, should be determined by reference to the date of the payment. This is the Revenue view. However, by concession P may take a credit for the sum which could have been deducted under s. 348, and set that against the liability under s. 349(1).[118] If the Revenue view is right, problems arise when the years are reversed. If year 1 is the s. 349(1) year and year 2 is the s. 348 year, no liability appears to arise at all. The Revenue view seems doubtful. Moreover, the general gearing of s. 348 to the date the payment becomes due, the repetition of that in s. 835, and the provision that tax is to be deducted at the rate in force when the payment became due,[119] suggest that s. 348 should apply on such facts.

Tax paid in year of payment

Since TA 1988, s. 348 requires that the payment is wholly payable out of taxed profits, tax must be borne in the year of the payment. If there is insufficient income in that year, P cannot come within s. 348 by pointing to excess income from previous years[120] any more than if he is forced to make the payment out of capital.[121] Similarly, P falls within s. 349(1), and not s. 348, if he is exempt from income tax[122] or if the profits of that year escape income tax because losses from previous years are rolled forward so as to relieve those profits from tax.[123]

115 *Re Hatch* [1919] 1 Ch 351.
116 *Revenue Law* (3rd ed.), para. 13.63.
117 On "payment", note *Minsham Properties Ltd.* v. *Price* [1990] STC 718.
118 ESC A16.
119 TA 1988, s. 4; applied in *IRC* v. *Crawley* [1987] STC 147. If the payment is not made at all there is no liability to tax (*Woodhouse* v. *IRC* [1936] 20 TC 673).
120 *Luipaard's Vlei Estate and Gold Mining Co. Ltd.* v. *IRC* [1930] 1 KB 593, 15 TC 573.
121 *Brodie's Trustees* v. *IRC* (1933) 17 TC 432.
122 *Duncan's Executors* v. *Farmer* (1909) 5 TC 417; as where the payer is subject to corporation tax.
123 *Trinidad Petroleum Development Co. Ltd.* v. *IRC* [1937] 1 KB 408, 21 TC 1.

Irrelevance of actual source

In general, the question of which cash resources are used to make the payment is irrelevant. As Lord Wilberforce said in *IRC* v. *Plummer*:[124]

> "What is significant . . . is not the actual source out of which the money is paid, nor even the way in which the taxpayer for his own purposes keeps his accounts, if indeed he keeps any, but the status of a notional account between himself and the Revenue. He is entitled, in respect of any tax year, to set down on one side his taxed income and on the other the amount of the annual payments he has made and if the latter is equal to or less than the former, to claim the benefit of the section."

Charging payment to capital

If P makes a deliberate decision to charge the payment to capital and that payment has some practical effect, such as entitling the taxpayer to a larger subsidy as in *Birmingham Corpn* v. *IRC*,[125] the payment is governed by TA 1988, s. 349, not s. 348. However, in *Chancery Lane Safe Deposit Co. Ltd.* v. *IRC*[126] the House of Lords held that s. 348 would not apply where a particular payment had been charged to capital, not as a matter of mere domestic accounting but as the result of a deliberate decision, even though the company had ample funds out of which to meet both the interest payments and dividends. The practical effect of creating a fund out of which larger or later dividends could be paid was sufficient to exclude s. 348.

There is much to be said for the dissenting views trenchantly expressed by Lord Reid and Lord Upjohn in *Chancery Lane*. First, there was no previous authority compelling the House to that conclusion. One early case had been found to be similar on the facts but, as Lord Upjohn memorably observed, "We are not bound to follow a case merely because it is indistinguishable upon the facts. A decision even in your Lordships' House is binding on your Lordships only because it lays down some principle of law or for reasoning on some particular facts".[127] Secondly, it would not be easy to distinguish mere domestic accounting from a deliberate decision. Thirdly, in this case the decision led to effective double taxation.[128] Today, the issue is not a live one for companies subject to corporation tax since statute expressly prevents the deductibility of charges on income where a payment is charged to capital.[129] Outside the corporate sphere it is hard to see what effect it may have on income tax save, perhaps, where a trader has eccentric taste.[130]

27.5.7 Commentary

The scope of the scheme contained in TA 1988, ss 348 and 349 has been greatly reduced (see above at §27.2.1) but outright abolition might have been better.[131] The same result could be achieved by scrapping the deduction at source and simply allowing P to deduct these items

[124] [1979] STC 793, esp. 799, *per* Lord Wilberforce. See also Lord Morris in *Chancery Lane Safe Deposit Co. Ltd.* v. *IRC* [1966] 1 All ER 1, 12, 43 TC 83, 112. This is the *ratio* of the case (*Moodie* v. *IRC* [1990] STC 475, 496, *per* hoffmann J.; see also [1991] STC 433, CA).

[125] [1930] AC 307, 15 TC 172; see also *BW Nobes and Co. Ltd.* v. *IRC* [1964] 2 All ER 140, 43 TC 133.

[126] [1966] 1 All ER 1, 43 TC 83. The decision was reaffirmed in *Fitzleet Estates Ltd.* v. *Cherry* [1977] STC 397, [1977] 3 All ER 996, 51 TC 708, HL, showing that if the House of Lords is to be persuaded that it has made a mistake, it is best to show that the erroneous case is not recent.

[127] [1996] 1 All ER 1, 128, 43 TC 83, 122.

[128] The company paid tax on its profits but could not recoup that tax by withholding under s. 348.

[129] TA 1988, s. 338(6) (see below at §47.4.3).

[130] See Lord Wilberforce in *IRC* v. *Plummer* [1979] STC 793, 799.

[131] See generally [1981] *BTR* 263.

in computing total income. The disadvantages of the present scheme are many: it is complex in itself, is responsible for other complexities and opens the door to odd devices giving rise to planning and anomalies. The complexities of the system include not only the border between the two provisions and problems of timing, but also the problem of the relationship between s. 348 and the charging provisions in Schedule D. Therefore, does deductibility under s. 348 determine whether a payment falls within Schedule D, Case III, or is it the other way round?[132] Among the legislative complexities for which the scheme is responsible are: the many rules which need to state whether or not a particular piece of specially taxed income is to be treated as taxed for s. 348; the case-law rule that income within Schedule D, Case III cannot be a trading receipt;[133] some of the tortuous provisions in the now superseded ss 660–685; and the decision in *Ang* v. *Parrish*.[134] The planning opportunities were revealed by the *Church Commissioners* case and the anomalies by the boundary between an obligation to pay cash (within s. 348 and so deductible in computing income) and one to deliver in kind (not within s. 348 and so not deductible).

27.6 "Free of Tax"

27.6.1 Effect of agreements

TMA 1970, s. 106(2) provides that any agreement for the payment of interest, rent or other annual payment in full, without allowing the deduction of income tax, is void; in other words the part relating to non-deduction is of no effect..[135] If P agrees to pay T £100 a year without deduction, P is nonetheless entitled to deduct tax under s. 348, or bound to do so under s. 349. S. 106(2) applies only to agreements,[136] and not to wills or orders of the court.[137] In appropriate cases the court will rectify an agreement to avoid s. 106(2).[138]

Where there is an agreement that P shall pay T £100 "free of tax", the House of Lords held in *Ferguson* v. *IRC*,[139] overriding a long line of authority, that such agreement does not fall foul of s. 106(2); by construing the agreement to mean that P must pay T such sum as, after deduction of income tax, leaves £100. On the facts, T's relevant marginal rate was basic rate; it is unclear what would happen if T's marginal rate were 40% or 0%.

27.6.2 The rule in Re Pettit

Where P is to pay T £100 "free of tax", P will make a payment of £100; if T's marginal rate is 22%, this is equivalent to £128.20 gross and T's income is therefore taken to include not £100 but £128.20. If T has no other income, he may reclaim £28.20 from the Revenue on account of his personal reliefs. If T were allowed to keep the sum, he would benefit by

[132] See *IRC* v. *Frere* [1964] 3 All ER 796, 42 TC 125; *IRC* v. *Whitworth Park Coal Co. Ltd.* [1959] 3 All ER 703, 38 TC 531; and *McBurnie* v. *Tacey* [1984] STC 347.

[133] For example TA 1988, ss 313, 421, 476, 547, 233, 426(1)(d).

[134] See below at §31.1.

[135] *Booth* v. *Booth* [1922] 1 KB 66.

[136] *Re Goodson's Settlement, Goodson* v. *Goodson* [1943] Ch 101, [1943] 1 All ER 201.

[137] An agreement to carry out an order of the court is subject to s. 106(2) (*Blount* v. *Blount* [1916] 1 KB 230).

[138] *Burroughes* v. *Abbott* [1922] 1 Ch 86; distinguished in *Whiteside* v. *Whiteside* [1950] Ch 65, [1949] 2 All ER 913; on rectification, see also below at §68.5

[139] [1969] 1 All ER 1025, 46 TC 15.

£128.20, and not £100 as undertaken by P. T is therefore directed by the rule in *Re Pettit*[140] to hold the sum recovered from the Revenue on trust for P—and T is under an obligation to make the repayment claim.[141] If T has other income, the value of the personal reliefs must be shared between the annuity and the other income; the rule in *Re Pettit* will apply to that proportion of the reliefs which the gross amount of the annuity bears to T's total income. It should be noted that in every reported case T has been entitled to a repayment of tax. However, the principle should apply wherever T is entitled to set a relief from tax against annuity income in whole or in part—and not simply when a repayment claim is made to the Revenue. T is obliged to account for relief from tax not only in respect of personal allowances but also for loss relief claimed under TA 1988, s. 380.[142] Although he is under a duty to make the claim for a repayment when it is due, T would appear not to be obliged to claim relief under s. 380 rather than under s. 385. The obligation to account causes problems in adjusting the total income of P and T. Revenue practice is to treat P as entitled to additional income equivalent to the grossed-up sum repaid.

In practice there is a clear distinction between £100 "free of tax", to which the rule in *Re Pettit* applies, and "such sum as after deducting tax at the current rate shall leave £100"—known as a formula deduction covenant—to which the rule does not apply; the former indicates the extent to which T is to benefit, while the latter does not. Where the annuity is "free of tax", the annuitant is assured of a constant net sum and the payer of a constantly fluctuating liability; where the deduction formula applies, the payer is assured of a constant net outflow and the payee of constantly fluctuating net receipts. In addition, where the annuity is "free of tax", the liability of the payer will vary according to the financial position of the payee; where the deduction formula is used, the benefit to the payee varies with his financial position. The rule in *Re Pettit* does not apply to a deduction formula covenant.

The rule in *Re Pettitt* applies to agreements, estates and trusts. However, its status in Scotland is unclear. Illogically, the rule does not apply to court orders,[143] with the result that the same words will have one effect in an agreement and a different effect in an order.[144]

27.6.3 Construction of court orders

Since TMA 1970, s. 106(2) does not apply to court orders, the courts have long felt able to construe an order to pay £x "free of tax" as an order to pay such sum as, after deduction of income tax at the basic rate, leaves £x.[145] If the order is to pay "£x less tax", it is construed as an order to deduct basic rate tax on £x under TA 1988, s. 348 or 349 and to pay the balance. The words "less tax" are taken simply to show that tax must be deducted by the payer from the amount specified.

[140] [1922] 2 Ch 765.

[141] *Re Kingcome, Hickley* v. *Kingcome* [1936] Ch 566, [1936] 1 All ER 173. On the position of non-residents, see *Re Jubb, Neilson* (1941) 20 ATC 297. In *Re Batty, Public Trustee* v. *Bell* [1952] Ch 280, [1952] All ER 425. Vaisey J. held that a wife could be made to elect for separate assessment so as to be compelled to make the repayment claim. On appeal it was held that the rule in *Re Pettit* did not apply, so this issue was not discussed. However, if the husband holds any repayment on trust for the wife (*Re Cameron, Kingsley* v. *IRC* [1965] 3 All ER 474, 42 TC 539) it ought to follow that the payer can compel the wife to compel the husband to make the claim. See also *Re Tatham, National Bank Ltd. and Mathews* v. *Mackenzie* [1945] Ch 34, [1945] 1 All ER 29.

[142] *Re Lyons, Barclays Bank Ltd.* v. *Jones* [1952] Ch 129, [1952] 1 All ER 34.

[143] *Jefferson* v. *Jefferson* [1956] 1 All ER 31, [1956] P 136.

[144] See cases cited below at §67.5

[145] *Spilsbury* v. *Spofforth* [1937] 4 All ER 487, 21 TC 247.

28

Schedule D, Case VI

28.1 Principles

Income tax is charged under Schedule D, Case VI on any annual profits or gains not falling under any other Case of Schedule D and not charged by virtue of Schedules A, E and F. It is thus the residual Case in the residual Schedule. In addition, the Taxes Acts often direct that a particular type of payment which is brought into charge to income tax is to be charged under Schedule D, Case VI, e.g. liability under TA 1988 s. 660C, the settlement provisions in that Act and under s. 761 on offshore income gains.

Four principles may be stated: (a) the profit must be annual; (b) it must be of an income nature; (c) it must not be gratuitous; and (d) it must be analogous to some other head of Schedule D. In relation to (a), it has been held that annual does not mean recurrent.[1] Casual profits may therefore be caught but only if they are of an income, as opposed to a capital, nature.[2] As Rowlatt J observed, "Annual can only mean calculated in any one year and . . . 'annual profits or gains' means 'profits or gains in any year as the succession of years comes round' ".[3] The word "annual" does not therefore add very much by way of definition, which is not surprising since all the other Cases of Schedule D also tax annual profits or gains, and Case VI is analogous to them.

A profit derived from the sale of an asset will either be income from an adventure in the nature of trade, and so taxable under Schedule D, Case I, or be of a capital nature, and so outside both Case I and Case VI.[4]

[1] *Jones* v. *Leeming* [1930] AC 415, 422, (1930) 15 TC 333, 359, *per* Viscount Dunedin; see also Rowlatt J. in *Townsend* v. *Grundy* (1933) 18 TC 140, 148.

[2] *Jones* v. *Leeming* [1930] AC 415, (1930) STC 333; for a complex example, see *Black Nominees Ltd.* v. *Nicol* [1975] STC 372.

[3] In *Ryall* v. Hoare [1923] 2 KB 447, 455; see also "the plant is not annual—it is the sowing that is annual" (at p. 454). See also Lord Inglis in *Scottish Provident Institution* v. *Farmer* (1912) 6 TC 34, 38: "There is nothing said in the Act about a gain being necessarily within the year of assessment".

[4] *Jones* v. *Leeming* [1930] AC 415, (1930) 15 TC 333.

To be of the nature of income a receipt must have a source and be distinct from that source. Hence, a mere gift, the finding of a thing or mere gambling winnings (see below at §28.2) do not fall to be taxed as income under Schedule D, Case VI[5] any more than does a capital gain. On the other hand, a receipt in return for services rendered will be caught by Case VI if not by some other Case. In such circumstances, the effort made in rendering the service is regarded as the source.

28.2 Gambling and Distinguishable Transactions

28.2.1 Punter and bookmaker

Profits arising from gambling transactions do not fall within Schedule D, Case VI;[6] such transactions are merely irrational agreements. The events which entitle gamblers to their winnings do not, of themsleves, produce the profit; there is no increment and no service, only an acquisition.[7] This must be distinguished from an organised seeking of profits, which may create a trade and so give rise to profits or gains. Even where, as in *Graham* v. *Green*, gambling is the taxpayer's sole means of livelihood, it is not a trade and so any winnings escape Schedule D, Cases I, II[8] and VI. However, this does not prevent courts from holding that a bookmaker is carrying on a vocation and is therefore taxable under Schedule D, Case II, the distinction being that a bookmaker has an organisation.[9]

28.2.2 Gambling incidental to other activities

Mere gambling winnings are distinct from winnings incidental to a taxable activity. Thus, in *Norman* v. *Evans*[10] the taxpayer leased horses bred at his stud to other persons to be raced by them, and received half of all of the horses' winnings. The sums paid were held to be taxable under Schedule D, Case VI as being sums due under the lease. However, where a bet is made on professional skill, it is still only a bet and therefore not taxable.In *Down* v. *Compston*[11] a golf professional, taxable under what is now Schedule E, was held not taxable in respect of money won on bets with other persons with whom he played golf. This decision should be contrasted with certain Commonwealth cases where gains from betting associated with other taxable horse racing activity have been subjected to income tax as part of that other activity—by a horse owner,[12] horse trainer,[13] registered bookmaker[14] and even by a horse owner who leased racehorses from his stud farm.[15] The question must be one of fact. *Down* v. *Compston* was distinguished in *Burdge* v. *Pyne*[16] when the proprietor of a gam-

5 See *Graham* v. *Green* [1925] 2 KB 37, 39 and 9 TC 309, 312, *per* Rowlatt J.
6 *Graham* v. *Green*, ibid.
7 See ibid., 139, 312, *per* Rowlatt J., who draws a parallel with finding and gift.
8 The Revenue argued in favour of liability under Schedule D,Case II in *Graham* v. *Green*, ibid.
9 *Partridge* v. *Mallandaine* (1886) 18 QBD 276; and *Graham* v. *Green* [1925] 2 KB 37, 42, (1925) 7 TC 309, 314.
10 [1965] 1 All ER 372, (1965) 42 TC 188, *per* Buckley J.
11 [1937] 2 All ER 475, (1937) 21 TC 60, *per* Lawrence J.
12 *Knight* v. *Taxation Commr* (1928) 28 SR NSW 523.
13 *Holt* v. *Federal Taxation Commr* (1929) 3 ALJ 68.
14 *Vandenberg* v. *Taxation Commr New South Wales* (1933) 2 ATD 343.
15 *Trautwein* v. *Federal Taxation Commr* (1936) 56 CLR 196.
16 [1969] 1 All ER, (1969) 45 TC 320.

bling club was held taxable on the profits of his own gambling at the club under Schedule D, Case I.

28.2.3 *Futures etc.*

Also to be distinguished from mere gambling is speculation. A person who, for example, buys shares on the stock exchange for cotton futures[17] in the hope of an increase in capital value is a speculator and not a gambler. The distinction is that the contract to buy or sell the cotton is a very real one from the point of view of the vendor and gives rise to very real contractual rights, whereas in a gambling transaction both parties regard the matter as a mere wager. The profits of speculation in commodity futures will be taxable under Schedule D, Case I if there is a sufficient substratum of activity to give rise to the finding that there is a trade.[18]

28.2.4 *Services*

Also to be distinguished from mere gambling are payments for the provision of services. So a professional tipster is taxed under Schedule D, Case II.[19] An occasional tipster may fall into Schedule D, Case VI since Case II contains no concept analogous to an adventure in the nature of trade.

28.3 Profits Analogous to Trading Profits

Given the width of the judicial definition of trade and the statutory notion of an adventure in the nature of trade,[20] it might appear that there is little scope for Schedule D, Case VI. Indeed, as already seen,[21] it is clear that in relation to an isolated transaction where a profit arises on resale of an object, there is no scope for Case VI. Where, however, there are regular as opposed to isolated transactions,[22] there is some authority for a charge under Case VI. Case-law shows that profits from stud fees for serving mares of other owners are taxed under Case VI rather than under Case I[23] provided the matter is simply incidental to the business. The legislative decision to charge farmers under Schedule D, Case I rather than under Schedule B removed most, but not all, of the tax advantages derived by the taxpayer from not being charged under Case VI. It seems likely, in the light of the cases on income derived from property and services, that even very occasional fees will be taxable.

Liability under Schedule D, Case I differs from that under Case VI in a number of respects:

(1) generally liability under Case I is on a business year basis, with the problems of the profits of any overlap period, while liability under Case VI is simply on a current year basis;[24]

17 *Cooper* v. *Stubbs* [1925] 2 KB 753, (1925) 10 TC 29; followed in *Townsend* v. *Grundy* (1933) 18 TC 140.

18 See Pollock M.R. in *Cooper* v. *Stubbs* [1925] 2 KB 753, 765, (1925) 10 RC 29, 48.

19 *Graham* v. *Arnott* (1941) 24 TC 157.

20 TA 1988, s. 832(1).

21 *Jones* v. *Leeming* [1930] AC 415, 420, (1930) 15 TC 333, 357, *per* Lord Buckmaster.

22 *Earl of Derby* v. *Bassom* (1926) 10 TC 357, 371, *per* Rowlatt J.

23 At that time farming was taxed under Schedule B and not, as now, Schedule D, Case I (TA 1988, s. 53(1)). Assessments in stud fees under Case VI were upheld in *Malcolm* v. *Lockhart* [1919] AC 463, (1919) 7 TC 99.

24 TA 1988, ss 60, 69.

(2) capital allowances may be available under Case I but not under Case VI;
(3) income under Case I may be earned and so be relevant earnings for pension provision; not all income under Case VI will be so treated;[25]
(4) losses suffered under Case I may be set off against general income of that and the next year, but only against later profits of the same trade; losses under Case VI may only be set off against other Case VI income, but can be rolled forward against all such income of later years;[26]
(5) profits under Case I are computed on an approved accounting basis; those under Case VI are computed on a receipts basis;[27]
(6) the income of a charity under Case I is exempt from tax if certain conditions are met; there is no exemption for the income of a charity under Case VI;[28]
(7) while income from investments is exempt in the hands of the trustee of a pension fund, there is also an express exemption for income from underwriting commissions taxable under Case VI; the exemption does not extend to Case I.[29]

The differences may be illustrated by the plight of owners of stately homes who open their homes to visitors. If this is done on a commercial basis, liability arises under Case I; if it is not, liability arises under Case VI. Under Case VI the only costs allowable will be those involved in showing the house, such as wages of guides, additional cleaning, advertising and the purchase of souvenirs. If, however, the matter comes within Case I, also deductible are the costs of upkeep of the building and its gardens, wages of caretakers and gardeners, heating, lighting and insurance. Allowances may also be claimed for expenditure on car parks, plumbing, refreshment rooms and access roads.

28.4 Activities Analogous to a Profession or Vocation

There is no concept in Schedule D, Case II equivalent to an adventure in the nature of trade under Case I. Therefore, a taxpayer receiving profits in return for services which are not sufficiently regular to amount to a vocation will not be taxed under Schedule D, Case II but only under Case VI. Again, however, care must be taken to distinguish income in return for services from capital receipts for the disposal of property.

28.4.1 Casual authorship

In *Hobbs* v. *Hussey*[30] T, a solicitor's clerk, who had not previously carried on the profession of author, agreed to write his memoirs and assign the copyright in return for payment. T was held taxable on the proceeds under Case VI. In *Earl Haig's Trustees* v. *IRC*,[31] however,

[25] See definition section in ibid., s. 833(4)(c); and see above at §7.8.2. In *Hale* v. *Shea* [1965] 1 All ER 155, (1965) 42 TC 260. Buckley J. appears to have thought that the question of whether income was earned was independent of the question of whether liability arose under Case VI.

[26] TA 1988, ss 380, 383, 392.

[27] *Pearn* v. *Miller* (1927) 11 TC 610, 614; *Grey* v. *Tiley* (1932) 16 TC 414.

[28] TA 1988, s. 505. However, where a provision charges tax under Case VI it may grant exemption from tax to a charity; see, generally, *Tax Bulletin* (December 1995); and Knox [1996] *Private Client Business* 260.

[29] TA 1988, s. 592 (3); considered in *Clarke* v. *British Telecom Pension Fund Trustee Ltd.* [2000] STC 222 CA.

[30] [1942] 1 All ER 445, (1942) 24 TC 153.

[31] [1939] SC 656, (1939) 22 TC 725.

trustees who held the copyright in certain diaries and who allowed an author to use the materials in those diaries "so far as the public interest permitted" in return for a half share in the profits of the book, were held not taxable. The Court of Session held that the sums were capital payments in return for the partial realisation of assets and so escaped income tax and not, as the Special Commissioner had held, remuneration for the use of and access to the diaries by the author, and so taxable under Case VI as being income derived from property.

The question is whether the transaction is really a sale of property, or the performance of services. A transaction may be one for the performance of services even though it involves some subsidiary sale of property, e.g. dentures supplied by a dentist. Therefore, in *Hobbs* v. *Hussey* the payments were held to be income even though, as part of the contract, the taxpayer transferred his copyright in the articles.[32] In *Alloway* v. *Phillips*,[33] where memoirs were ghosted, the fact that the author promised not to write for any other publisher was not sufficient to fall outside of Case VI since this restriction was simply an adjunct of the main contract.

It has not been easy for taxpayers to place themselves on the *Haig* side of the line, which is of course inherently vague. Thus, in *Housden* v. *Marshall*[34] where a jockey agreed to make available to a reporter his reminiscences and supporting documents together with the right to use a facsimile of his signature, payments to the jockey were held taxable.

The situation is complicated by two further factors. First, the test of what is income as opposed to capital seems to be different under Case VI from that under Case II where sums received for the sale of copyright have been held to be income receipts.[35] Secondly, the Solicitor-General commented in *Hobbs* v. *Hussey* that he was not to be taken as admitting that the *Haig* case was rightly decided.[36] However, it would appear to follow from the present authorities that had Hobbs and Marshall written their reminiscences first and then allowed them to be published, sums received in return for the sale would have escaped tax under Schedule D, Case VI but would, in such circumstances, now be liable to capital gains tax. What was fatal to their case was that under the contract they agreed to perform services, in the one case to write memoirs and in the other to supply information. Thus, where there has been a discontinuance of a profession so that Case II is inapplicable, a subsequent sale will not be caught by Case VI if there have been no activities analogous to a profession after discontinuance.[37]

28.4.2 *Introduction fees*

A person who introduces a potential purchaser to a vendor may expect some appreciation in pecuniary form. An introducer having a right to sue for these sums is taxable under

[32] See Lawrence J. in *Hobbs* v. *Hussey* [1942] 1 All ER 445, 446, (1942) 24 TC 153, 156. For the converse case where the court disregarded a trifling service, see *Bradbury* v. *Arnold* (1957) 37 TC 665; and the *Earl Haig* case (1939) 22 TC 725.

[33] [1980] STC 490, [1980] 3 All ER 138, (1980) 53 TC 372 (see below at §28.6).

[34] [1958] 3 All ER 639, (1958) 38 TC 233, where Harman J. reversed the Special Commissioners.

[35] *Howson* v. *Monsell* [1950] 2 All ER 1239, (1950) 31 TC 529 (Schedule D, Case II). *Cf. Beare* v. *Carter* [1940] 2 KB 187, (1940) 23 TC 353 (Schedule D, Case VI).

[36] [1942] 1 KB 491, 495, (1942) 24 TC 153, 155.

[37] *Withers* v. *Nethersole* (1948) 28 TC 501, HL. See also *Beare* v. *Carter* [1940] 2 KB 187, (1940) 23 TC 353 where the advance to an author for a new edition of a work published many years previously was held to be a capital sum which was not assessable.

Schedule D, Case VI.[38] In the absence of such a right there is no liability under Case VI;[39] such sums escape tax just like any other gifts, the law not concerning itself with the motive of a donor. An introducer content to rely on faith rather than law will escape tax. This principle was extended in *Scott* v. *Ricketts*,[40] where an estate agent was paid £39,000 in consideration of withdrawing any claim he might have to participate in a development scheme. The Court of Appeal held that although the payment was made under a contract there was no liability under Case VI: (a) because the original scheme was not a legally enforceable agreement; and (b) because the payment was made in settlement of a moral claim or for the sale of an asset, and neither gave rise to a profit within Schedule D, Case VI. It is highly questionable whether the sum was paid under a contract since a moral claim does not amount to good consideration.

28.4.3 Miscellaneous

Commission payments received by a director for guaranteeing the company's bank overdraft have were taxable under Schedule D, Case VI because they were received by virtue of services which had been rendered.[41] The same result followed when a solicitor guaranteed an overdraft of a third party, since the commission was earned by the pledging of credit.[42] In each case there was a contractual right to the payment. Whether such sums should be taxed under Case II or Case VI is one of fact. Such receipts are held taxable and are not treated as capital payments because the source from which the income flows is not the service, but the individual's efforts and those efforts are capable of recurring.[43]

There was some doubt whether a prostitute was taxable under Case II or Case VI, or not at all. It appears that where the Revenue is aware of the source of income, a charge has been made under Case VI. However, a charge under Case I has now been upheld. [44]

28.5 Analogy of Income from Property

Schedule D, in addition to taxing the annual profits of a trade, profession or vocation, also taxes the annual profits or gains arising or accruing from any type of property whatsoever. Although the cases under Schedule D, Case VI have not always been decided expressly on this analogy, it would appear that many of the cases can be so rationalised and, indeed, that much of the talk of a "source" is an implicit recognition of the analogy. Thus, stud fees received for the services of a stallion[45] could be caught using this analogy. However, where sums derived from the sale of a right to nominate a particular dam for whom the stallion should stand were taxed, the analogy of the sale of property was specifically rejected.[46]

[38] *Brocklesbry* v. *Merricks* (1934) 18 TC 576. The possibility of a charge under Schedule D, Case II was reserved by the Crown. See also *Bloom* v. *Kinder* (1958) 38 TC 77.

[39] *Dickinson* v. *Abel* [1969] 1 All ER 484, (1969) 45 TC 353.

[40] [1967] 2 All ER 1009, (1967) 44 TC 303.

[41] *Ryall* v. *Hoare* [1923] 2 KB 447, (1923) 8 TC 521.

[42] *Sherwin* v. *Barnes* (1931) 16 TC 278; but *cf. Trenchard* v. *Bennet* (1933) 17 TC 420 where in reality shares received were not for the guarantee but in order to gain control of a company—a capital asset—and so were not taxable.

[43] *Whyte* v. *Clancy* [1936] 2 All ER 735, (1936) 20 TC 679.

[44] *IRC* v. *Aken* [1990] 1 WLR 1374, [1990] STC 497, (1990) 63 TC 395, CA.

[45] As in *Earl of Derby* v. *Bassom* (1926) 10 TC 357.

[46] *Benson* v. *Counsell* [1942] 1 All ER 435, (1942) 24 TC 178.

Again, sums received for the use, as distinct from the disposal, of information,[47] for the display of property such as Earl Haig's diaries,[48] for the pledging of credit,[49] or for the leasing of a horse[50] could all fall intelligibly within this analogy, which has the further advantage of focusing attention on the sums earned by the property, which would be income, as distinct from the sums received on the disposal of the property, which would be capital.

Where the property is land, income received is usually taxable under Schedule A, especially in the new form of Schedule A now applicable to both income tax and corporation tax. Previously, income outside Schedule A and so caught by Schedule D, Case VI included sums received for car parking, or visitors' green fees at a golf club.[51] Income derived from the furnished letting of a house,[52] being in return for the use of the furniture as well as for the use of the land, previously fell within Schedule D, Case VI but is now all within Schedule A.[53]

Income derived from commodity and financial futures and traded options was removed to CGT by FA 1985.[54] This change does not affect income arising from dealing in assets in such a way as to give rise to liability under Schedule D, Case I.[55]

28.6 Foreign Questions

In accordance with the general principles of the tax system, gains accruing to non-residents which would be taxable under Schedule D, Case VI, are presumably so taxable where the source of income is in the UK.[56] In *Alloway* v. *Phillips*[57] a person resident in Canada who agreed to provide information in Canada about her life as the wife of one of the Great Train Robbers was held taxable under Case VI because the contract was made, enforceable and provided for payment in England, by a company resident in England. On this basis a different result would have been reached if the contract had been with the company's Canadian subsidiary.

Where the source of income is outside the UK but the income arises in favour of a UK resident, the charge will presumably arise under Case V rather than under Case VI.[58] Any other conclusion would remove the remittance basis[59] from any income within Case VI, while leaving it intact for income within other Cases.

47 As in *Housden* v. *Marshall* [1958] 3 All ER 639, (1958) 38 TC 233.

48 See Lord Normand in *Earl Haig's Trustees* v. *IRC* [1939] SC 676, 682, (1939) 22 TC 725, 732.

49 For example *Wilson* v. *Mannooch* [1937] 3 All ER 120, (1937) 21 TC 178.

50 For example *Norman* v. *Evans* [1965] 1 All ER 372, TC 188, 42.

51 *Coman* v. *Rotunda Hospital (Governor) Dublin* [1921] 1 AC 1, esp. 12–14, (1921) 7 TC 517, 559, 560. See also *Forth Conservancy Board* v. *IRC* [1931] AC 540, (1931) 16 TC 103.

52 Furnished letting is not usually a trade: see *Gittos* v. *Barclay* [1982] STC 390; on the boundary between trade and property in the Canadian context, see Durnford (1991) 39 *Can. Tax Jo.* 1131.

53 TA 1988, s. 15(4).

54 Now TA 1988, s. 128.

55 Ibid.

56 As in *Curtis-Brown Ltd.* v. *Jarvis* (1929) 14 TC 744.

57 [1980] STC 490, [1980] 3 All ER 138, (1980) 53 TC 372.

58 *Colquhoun* v. *Brooks* (1889) 14 App Cas 493, (1889) 2 TC 490, HL (see below at §60.2) and note *Lilley* v. *Harrison* (1952) 33 TC 344, CA.

59 TA 1988, s. 65(4),

28.7 Computation

Tax is chargeable under Schedule D, Case VI in respect of annual profits and gains, and not simply on receipts. Sums spent in earning the receipts may therefore be deducted in computing the taxable profits or losses. Tax is charged under Case VI on a current year basis.[60] Any necessary apportionments of income are carried out on the basis of days.[61]

Any loss under a transaction[62] falling within Case VI may be set off against income from any other transaction within Case VI of that or any later year, [63] subject, however, to express statutory direction, e.g. transactions involving lease premiums before 1998.[64] Case VI losses may not be set off against income under another Case of the same year.

Income is chargeable under Case VI when it is received. This emerges from the unsatisfactory case of *Grey* v. *Tiley*[65] where counsel for the Crown conceded that the taxpayer could not be taxed in respect of the year when the money became due to him.

[60] TA 1988, s. 69. Before 1996–1997 an inspector could direct that another period be taken.
[61] Ibid., s. 72 as amended by FA 1995, s. 121—and not months, as previously.
[62] On meaning of transaction, see *Barron* v. *Littman* [1951] 2 All ER 393, (1951) 33 TC 373.
[63] TA 1988, s. 392.
[64] Ibid., ss 40(5), 392(4).
[65] (1932) 16 TC 414, where the court felt bound by *Leigh* v. *IRC* [1928] 1 KB 73, (1928) 11 TC 590 (Case IV).

29

Trusts

29.1 General

UK rules on the taxation of trust are a mixture of judge-made law and statutes. The judge-made rules are sensible efforts to adapt the tax system to the trust;[1] the statutory additions are concerned generally to prevent taxpayers taking advantage of the trust regime through discretionary trusts.

The problem of the relationship between the taxation of trustees and the taxation of beneficiaries resembles that of companies. One can devise various models. What we shall call Model 1 would levy no tax at trustee level, but simply allow income to flow through to the beneficiary; this could be supplemented by a rule collecting provisional tax at trustee level on behalf of the beneficiary (Model 1A). Model 2 , the opposite of Model 1, would treat the trustees as a legitimate object of taxation, and not tax the beneficiary at all. Models 3 and 4 would mitigate the severity of Model 2. Model 3 would tax the trustees first, but then allow the beneficiary a credit for the tax paid at trustee level. Model 4 would tax the trustees but would allow them to deduct those parts of income passed on to the beneficiary. If the income tax were a flat rate tax with no personal deductions, it might not make much difference which model were adopted. Given the existence of a progressive tax, however, choices must be made. The UK system uses Model 3 for most type of trusts but Model 4 for certain discretionary trusts (but see §29.3.4).

The need for separate rules for discretionary trusts is to prevent a trust being used as a device in which income is taxed at rates below the individual top rate of 40% and then accumulated; this point is all the more relevant when it is recalled that as late as 1978–1979 the top rate of income tax for individuals was 98%.

In the UK, where trustees act on behalf of an incapacitated person, they are treated as the agents of the beneficiary and tax is assessed on the trustees on behalf of (and by reference to the circumstances of) the beneficiary.[2]

[1] This chapter deals with express trusts. On constructive trusts and the tax system, see Glover, in Oakley (ed.), *Trends in Contemporary Trust Law* (OUP, 1996), 315–31; and Brown and Rajan (1997) 45 *Can. Tax Jo.* 659.

[2] TMA 1970, s. 72; *IRC* v. *McIntosh* (1955) 36 TC 334.

A consultative document on the reform of this area of income tax was issued in 1991. It included a proposal to integrate income tax and CGT treatments. but this was abandoned.[3] For FA 2000 rules on certain gifts to charity by trusts see below p. 587.

29.2 Trustee

29.2.1 The trustee's liability

The basis for liability to income tax of a trustee under the UK system must be sought in the present legislation and in history. Income tax under Schedules A and D is charged on the person "receiving or entitled to" the income charged.[4] Under Schedule F, a tax credit is available to a person "receiving" a distribution,[5] who pays tax at the appropriate rate, with the amount of tax credit reflecting that fact.[6] Trustees come within each of these rules even though they are not entitled to the income beneficially; they are "entitled" to the income in that they can sue for it and they may be said to receive it.

As trustees

Trustees are assessable to income tax regardless of the personal tax circumstances of the beneficiary or of themselves. They are assessable and chargeable not as agents for the beneficiary, nor as trustees per se, but simply because they receive income.[7] This is so even if there is only one beneficiary who is of full legal capacity.[8]

Trustees cannot be taxed if their circumstances (or the circumstances of those of them whom it is sought to tax) are such as to prevent them from being within the charge to tax. In *Dawson* v. *IRC*[9] there was a discretionary trust and no beneficiary was entitled to the income. The administration of the trust was carried on outside the UK, the principal beneficiaries were resident outside the UK, and no income was remitted to the UK. There were three trustees, only one of whom was resident in the UK. The Revenue's attempt to tax the single UK resident trustee failed since it could not show that the trustee had sufficient control [10] over the income so that the income had accrued to him. This decision rejected an established Revenue practice and was reversed by legislation.[11]

In calculating the total income of trustees for the purposes of tax liability, the trust income is not added to their personal incomes; conversely, trustees' personal incomes are ignored in computing their liability as trustees.

[3] See Inland Revenue Press Rrelease, 18 March 1993, (1993) *Simon's Tax Intelligence* 516. For reviews, see Kerridge 110 LQR 84; Venables (1992) 13 *Fiscal Studies* 106; and Venables, *Comments on the Trusts Consultative Document* (Key Haven, 1991).

[4] TA 1988, ss 21(1), 59; see also *Dawson* v. *IRC* [1989] STC 473, (1989) 62 TC 301, HL; and *Reid's Trustees* v. *IRC* [1929] SC 439, (1929) 14 TC 512.

[5] TA 1988, s. 44.

[6] Ibid., ss 1A, 1B

[7] *Williams* v. *Singer* [1921] 1 AC 65, 71, 7 TC 387, 411, *per* Viscount Cave.

[8] *Hamilton Russell's Executors* v. *IRC* (1943) 25 TC 200.

[9] [1989] STC 473, (1989) 62 TC 301, HL; in the Court of Appeal ([1988] STC 684) considerable emphasis was placed on the joint nature of the title and responsibility of trustees; see [1989] *BTR* 249.

[10] There was negative control in that the trustee's consent was needed before the discretions could be exercised, but this was held not to be sufficient.

[11] FA 1989, s. 110. It should be noted that none of the income accrued to trustees in that case from sources in the UK; the decision insists on finding a basis for liability in the words of the taxing statutes (i.e. TA 1988, ss 18, 59) rather than on established practice.

Reliefs

A trust may not claim any personal reliefs of the trustees, nor, since it is not an "individual",[12] may the trust claim any personal reliefs for itself. On the other hand, a trust may be entitled to various reliefs which are available to "persons", such as loss relief or deductions on account of interest. Similarly, a trust may deduct and retain income tax on making a payment falling within TA 1988, s. 348. The trustees may be guilty of a breach of trust if they fail to so deduct.[13]

Expenses

In computing the taxable income of a trust outside TA 1988 s. 686,[14] no deduction may be made for trust expenses incurred in the administration of the trust, any more than individuals with investment income can deduct associated expenses.[15] If a trustee has £1,000 net rental income, and £100 trust expenses, income tax for 2000–01 will be 22% of £1,000, i.e. £220. This bar is directed at trust expenses, not expenses which are deductible in computing particular income from a particular source. Where a trust carries on a trade, it is taxable only on the profits of that trade; any expenses incurred in earning those profits may be deducted according to normal principles. Such profits are not earned income of the trust.[16]

Most trust income will be investment income arising under Schedule D, Case III, or Schedule F, and so is usually subject to taxation by deduction at source. In other instances, for example where the trustees receive rent or carry on a trade, they must make a self-assessment.[17]

29.2.2 Exceptions to general liability

Income accruing to beneficiary not to trustees

Since trustees are liable to tax simply because income accrues to them, it follows that they are not liable where income accrues only to the beneficiary. In *Williams* v. *Singer*[18] income from investments held in the United States was, at the direction of the trustees, who were resident in the UK, paid directly to the beneficiary, who was domiciled and resident outside the UK. The beneficiary, if taxable at all, would only have been taxed on a remittance basis and, since no income was remitted to this country, no tax was due from her. The Revenue's attempt to charge tax on the trustees failed.[19] The trustees had not been "in actual receipt and control" themselves and so were not liable.

TMA 1970, s. 76. A trustee who has authorised the receipt of profits by the person entitled thereto, or his agent, is only required to make a return of the name, address and the profits of that person, i.e. the beneficiary. This was relied on in the House of Lords in *Williams* v. *Singer* as negativing any further liability on the trustees,[20] but is completely immaterial since

12 It is very difficult to find authority for this rule, but it is generally accepted: see Farrand [1977] *Conv (NS)* 5.

13 *Re Sharp*, [1906] 1 Ch 793.

14 On s. 686, see above at §11.2.4.

15 *Aikin* v. *Macdonald's Trustees* (1894) 3 TC 306.

16 *Fry* v. *Shiel's Trustees* [1915] SC 159, (1915) 6 TC 583 (see above at §7.9.2).

17 TMA 1970, ss 8A, 9.

18 [1921] 1 AC 65, (1921) 7 TC 387. See also *Dawson* v. *IRC* [1988] STC 684, (1988) 62 TC 301 CA.

19 Conversely, in *Drummond* v. *Collins* [1915] AC 1011, (1915) 6 TC 525, where foreign income accrued to a non-resident trustee, by whom it was accumulated, there was no liability on a resident beneficiary who was chargeable only on a remittance basis, since it was not his income.

20 [1921] 1 AC 65, 71, (1921) 7 TC 387, 411.

it is concerned only with the trustee's duty to supply information with regard to the assessment of the beneficiary.

Beneficiary not liable to income tax

Where trustees receive income, they may not be assessed if the income accrues to a beneficiary in whose hands it is not liable to income tax.[21] This is a second explanation of *Williams* v. *Singer*.[22] This applies only where the link between the income and the beneficiary is established; it cannot apply to absolve trustees when, for example, income is accumulated contingently for a beneficiary.[23]

This exception cannot be said to be firmly grounded since it blurs the nature of the trustees' liability with that of the beneficiary.[24] It comes close to saying that the trustee is not liable to income tax when there is a beneficiary with a vested life interest[25] (see below).

If the exception is sound, it is very limited, applying only where the income is not liable to income tax in the hands of the beneficiary (as where he is non-resident), not where the income is liable to tax but no income tax will be due (e.g. by reason of personal allowances due to the beneficiary).

29.2.3 Rates of tax

Non-discretionary trusts

Generally, neither the starting rate[26] nor the higher rate of tax applies to trustees since they are not "an individual"; income tax is therefore charged at the rate appropriate to the type of income. If the income is not savings income, e.g. rents or trading profits, the basic rate of 22% is applied. For savings income other than Schedule F income, the lower rate of 20% applies. Schedule F income will usually be taxed at the Schedule F ordinary rate of 10%, but with a 10% credit.

Certain types of Schedule F income will be taxed at 25%—"the Schedule F trust rate"[27]—usually applicable only to trusts within TA 1988, s. 686. These are the distributions listed in s. 686A and are the purchase or redemption by the company of its own shares or rights to acquire shares.[28] The 25% rate does not apply to certain types of trust (e.g. unit trusts, pensions and charities), to income treated as the settlor's[29] or to purchases falling within TA 1988, s. 219 (subject to capital gains treatment).

Discretionary and similar trusts

Trustees are liable to tax at a special rate—"the rate applicable to trusts"—where the income is to be accumulated or is payable at the discretion of the trustees or any other person

[21] Lord Clyde in *Reid's Trustees* v. *IRC* [1929] SC 439, 449, (1929) 14 TC 512, 525.

[22] [1921] 1 AC 65, 00, (1921) 7 TC 387, 412.

[23] Such income does not "belong to" the beneficiary (*Stanley* v. *IRC* [1944] 1 All ER 230, (1944) 26 TC 12). *Sed quaere* if the beneficiaries are non-resident; see *Kelly* v. *Rogers* [1935] 2 KB 446, 468, (1935) 19 TC 692, 714.

[24] The position is further complicated by the rule that a trustee may be liable for tax due from a non-resident beneficiary under TMA 1970, s. 78 (non-residents).

[25] It is clear that the beneficiary is liable (*IRC* v. *Hamilton Russell's Executors* [1943] 1 All ER 474, (1943) 25 TC 200), as are the trustees (see above, n. 8).

[26] TA 1988, s. 1(2)(aa), added by FA 1992, s. 9.

[27] TA 1988, s. 686(1A). See, generally, Revenue Interpretation, February 1999, (1999) *Simons Weekly Tax Intelligence* 254.

[28] TA 1988, s. 686A(1)(2).

[29] Ibid., s. 686A(1)(4).

(whether or not there is a power to accumulate).[30] This definition focuses on the trust definition of income, not the tax definition. If trustees develop land and the proceeds are treated as capital for trust purposes, a charge to basic rate income tax may nonetheless arise under TA 1988, s. 776. However, no charge will arise under s. 686 since this section applies only to sums which are income "to be accumulated or payable at" the trustee's discretion; as the sums are trust capital they do not come within this definition.[31]

The rate of tax was previously equal to the sum of the basic and additional rates, but is now set at 34%,[32] thus falling between corporation tax and higher income tax rates. This means a surcharge of 12% on most types of income, but 14% on income from savings other than dividends. Schedule F income is taxed at the special Schedule F trust rate of 25%.[33] This is 9% lower than the normal rate applicable to trusts and reflects the reduction in the tax credit for individual shareholders. The tax is due under a self-assessment on 31 January following the end of the year of assessment in which it arose.[34]

The rules in s. 686 are not confined to discretionary trusts as such, but also apply where beneficiaries have contingent interests and the Trustee Act 1925, s. 31 empowers the trustees to apply income for their maintenance. The rules also apply to income which the trustees have power to withhold, e.g. when they exercise a power to accumulate under a protective trust where the discretionary trust has arisen.[35]

Non-resident trustees may be liable to additional rates under s. 686 even though they are not liable to basic rate tax on that income.[36]

Exceptions. S. 686 does not apply to sums which, before being distributed, are income of any person other than the trustees, e.g. a beneficiary with a vested interest in the income or of an annuitant; sums which are treated as income of the settlor are also excluded.[37] Exceptions also exist for charities and pension funds.[38]

Expenses. In relation to expenses, a two-pronged rule applies. First, expenses properly chargeable to income are excluded from s. 686. The question whether an expense is properly chargeable to income is determined according to general trust law, any express provision in the instrument permitting the charge of the expense against income being ignored.[39]

Secondly, however, such expenses are to be charged at the rate that would have applied if they had not been subject to s. 686.[40] This formula continues the effect of the old rule under which s. 686 took the form of an additional rate. Where the discretionary trust is not resident in the UK, the expenses which can be relieved in this way are limited to the fraction equivalent to the proportion of the trust's total income which is subject to UK tax. For this

30 Ibid., s. 686(1)

31 Potter and Monroe, *Tax Planning*, §3-07; for a similar problem where sums are paid to trustees by a company buying it own shares in circumstances not coming within TA 1988, s. 219, see ibid., §3-08.

32 TA 1988, s. 686(1A).

33 Ibid., s. 686(1AA); the types of income are listed in s. 686(5A) and include Schedule F income, equivalent foreign income, stock dividends within s. 249, sums released under s. 421 and certain sums paid on redemption or purchase of shares by a company of its own shares.

34 TMA 1970, s. 59B(4).

35 *IRC* v. *Berrill* [1981] STC 784, (1981) 55 TC 429.

36 *IRC* v. *Regent Trust Co. Ltd.* [1980] STC 140; this is despite the fact that the credit for s. 686 tax against s. 687 liability is not available on a literal interpretation of s. 687(3)(a).

37 TA 1988, s. 686(2)(b).

38 Ibid., s. 686(2)(c).

39 In *Carver* v. *Duncan* [1985] AC 1082, [1985] STC 356, (1985) 59 TC 125, HL, life insurance premiums and fees for investment advice were held to be non-deductible; it was not clear whether they were "expenses" anyway.

40 TA 1988, s. 686(2AA).

purpose, trust income which escapes UK tax because the trustees are non-resident or are able to use double taxation relief is not "subject to UK tax".[41] Expenses are disallowed if the income is payable to a non-resident beneficiary in whose hands it is not liable to UK tax.[42]

Rate order. Since there are now so many different rates of tax applicable to different types of income, rules are needed to direct the order in which deductions are made.[43] The order is: (a) Schedule F income, widened to cover some related corporate distributions; (b) foreign savings income; (c) other savings income; and (d) income chargeable at basic rate.

29.3 Beneficiary

29.3.1 Beneficiary's credit for tax paid by trustees

Where trustees have paid the tax and administration expenses and the balance belongs to a beneficiary (B) as income, as where B has a vested life interest in the income, that balance is liable to income tax as B's income. The amount received is grossed up at the relevant rate to take account of the basic or lower rate tax paid by the trustees; in turn, B can use that tax as a credit. Therefore, a net receipt of rental income of £702 will be grossed up at 22% to £900. If B's rate of tax is nil, he will recover £198 from the Revenue. A receipt of interest of £720 will be grossed up 20% and B will recover £180. If B is liable to tax on the interest at 40%, he must pay an extra £180 to make a total of £360.

Schedule F income of £810 is grossed up to £900 by adding back the credit of £90 at 10%. In accordance with the new regime for dividend taxation, however, the £90 cannot be recovered from the Revenue. If B is liable to tax at the Schedule F upper rate of 32.5%, tax of £292.50 will be due, against which the £90 credit can be set, making a net payment of £202.50.

While the credit process is clear, the underlying theory is not. Where B is currently entitled to the income under the trust, the result of the decision of the House of Lords in *Baker* v. *Archer-Shee*[44] is that B is entitled to—and so taxable on—the income as and when it arises in the hands of the trustee.[45] This means that B will be taxable under the Schedule and Case appropriate to the income as it arises. Different principles apply where there is an annuity under the trust, since the annuitant is liable under Schedule D, Case III (and the rules in TA 1988, ss 348 and 349).

[41] TA 1988, s. 686(2A), (2B).

[42] Ibid., ss 686 (2A), 689A (non-residence).

[43] Ibid., s. 689B.

[44] [1927] AC 844, (1927) 11 TC 749. For facts, see below at §60.2. The facts of this case were favourable to the Revenue's contentions. Not only was the beneficiary sole life tenant, she had also been given the power to nominate trustees and was herself involved with the management of the fund to the extent that her consent was needed for any change of investments. The majority decision may be criticised for failing to distinguish between an active and a passive trust; it can be argued that the decision does not apply to an active trust. See also the explanations in *Reid's Trustees* v. *IRC* [1929] SC 439, (1929) 14 TC 512.

[45] However, in determining whether the income is earned or investment income, the question is whether it was earned by the beneficiary and not whether it was earned by the trustees (see above at §7.9.2).

29.3.2 *Vested rights in income*

When do vested rights exist?

A beneficiary is currently entitled to the trust income if the trustees are under a duty to pay the income to the beneficiary who is then absolutely entitled to it—or to have it applied at his direction.[46] Benefits in kind are caught; the question whether the benefit is convertible into money is irrelevant.[47] If the beneficiary's title to the income is contingent, or vested subject to being divested,[48] it is not taxable as his income. Where a trustee receives income from investments held for a tenant for life, each sum received is the income of the tenant for life as soon as it is received and regardless of the date on which it is paid over to the beneficiary. This is because the income is immediately under the beneficiary's control.[49]

Rights arising under a Scottish interest in possession trust are technically annual payments under Schedule D, Case III; but it is provided that where English law would treat the beneficiary as having an equitable right in possession, the rights of the beneficiary are to be treated in the same way—despite the general Scottish position.[50] This decree does not apply if the trustees are not resident in the UK.

Expenses

Sums received by the beneficiary are grossed up to reflect the tax rate paid by the trustees. However, this grossed-up income will not necessarily be the same as the trustees' income. *Macfarlane* v. *IRC*[51] decided that trust expenses, although non-deductible in computing the trustees' income, are deductible in computing the income of the beneficiary. Suppose that a trust has gross rental income of £1,000, and expenses of £100. For 2000–01 income tax on the trustees will be £220, i.e. 22% of £1,000. The beneficiary will receive £680; £680 grossed up at 22% gives income of £871.80 (not £900). The beneficiary thus gets credit only for the 22% tax paid by the trustees on £871.80 (£191.80), and not the whole £220 tax paid by them.

Is this rule correct? Certainly its basis is suspect. *Macfarlane* v. *IRC* rests on an earlier case[52] in 1926 in which the Court of Session held further that the beneficiary's income was the sum received net of tax paid by the trustees and then minus expenses, making a sum of £580 in the above example. The reasoning on this point was destroyed by the decision of the House of Lords in *Baker* v. *Archer-Shee* but was reaffirmed on the main point by *Macfarlane* v. *IRC*.[53] The reason given for the deduction was that the expenses were incurred before the beneficiary received the money, not by anyone she employed but by the trustees appointed by the settlor.[54] This is inconsistent with the notion that the income is the beneficiary's as soon as it is received by the trustees.[55] The anomaly may be the prohibition on allowing the trustees to deduct their expenses.[56]

[46] *Tollemache* v. *IRC* (1926) 11 TC 277; *Miller* v. *IRC* [1930] AC 222, (1930) 15 TC 25.
[47] *Lindus and Hortin* v. *IRC* (1933) 17 TC 442.
[48] *Stanley* v. *IRC* [1944] 1 All ER 230, (1944) 26 TC 12; *Brotherton* v. *IRC* [1977] STC 73, (1977) 52 TC 137.
[49] *Spens* v. *IRC* [1970] 3 All ER 295, 299, 46 TC 276, 285, *per* Megarry J.
[50] This is because of the intricacies of the taxation of dividends and is probably obsolete (FA 1993, s. 118); for explanation, see Inland Revenue Press Release, 9 July 1993, (1993) *Simon's Tax Intelligence* 1048.
[51] [1929] SC 453, (1929) 14 TC 532.
[52] *Murray* v. *IRC* (1926) 11 TC 133.
[53] Cited with approval by Lord Blanesburgh in *Baker* v. *Archer-Shee* (1926) 11 TC 749, 786.
[54] (1926) 11 TC 133, 138, *per* Lord Sands.
[55] *Cf.* Lord Sands in ibid., 540.
[56] These expenses are deductible in computing the trust's liability to the applicable rate for discretionary and accumulation trusts (TA 1988, s. 686(2A)).

Other deductions and reliefs

Other concerns arise over the difference between trust income under trust law and the beneficiary's income for tax purposes. Thus, trust law is not concerned with capital allowances (or balancing charges), nor relief for losses from earlier years still less with the now obsolete preceding year basis. A trust may be able to charge depreciation or other expenses expressly prohibited for tax purposes in its trust accounts. These do not usually cause a difference between the income of the trustees and the income of the beneficiary for tax purposes, except in relation to expenses. The position with regard to capital allowances is not clear.[57]

Stock dividends

An enhanced stock dividend may be income or capital of the trust, or may give rise to an obligation on the trustees to take the payment as capital but to compensate the life tenant for the loss of the dividend. Revenue practice is to accept the treatment decided upon by the trustees—provided it is supportable on the facts.[58] In *Sinclair* v. *Lee*[59] an allocation of shares to a trust on a demerger gave rise to no tax liability on the trustee because of an express provision; it was only prevented from being taxable income of the income-beneficiary by being classified by the court as capital. This decision has been criticised for creating a wholly unsatisfactory distinction between shares received (as in this case) on an indirect demerger, and those received in a direct demerger (which would belong to the tenant for life).[60] Others view the decision as a welcome limitation on the rights of the income beneficiary in a modern commercial context.

29.3.3 No vested right in income

Accumulations

A beneficiary may have a vested and indefeasible interest in income, but a different set of rights in capital. In *Stanley* v. *IRC*[61] the appellant had a vested life interest in certain property, but the trustees had a power under Trustee Act 1925, s. 31 to accumulate the income during his minority. This power was exercised until the appellant reached the age of majority, when he became entitled to the accumulated income. When the appellant reached that age, the Revenue sought to levy additional assessments to cover the years in which the income had been accumulated. Trustee Act 1925, s. 31 provided that when a person died before reaching the age of majority, the accumulated income was to be paid not to that person's estate, as would be the case if his title to that income were absolute, but instead added to capital. It followed that although the infant beneficiary had a vested life interest, he had only a contingent right to the income or, at best, a right that was vested subject to being divested if he failed to reach the age of majority. It could not be said that the income was his in the years as it arose since there would be no guarantee that he would reach that age and so no certainty that he would be entitled to the income.

[57] On the question of whether the tenant for life is entitled to capital allowances, see Venables, *Tax Planning Through Trusts*, §20:20 and Venables, *Comments on the Consultative Document*, above at n. 3, App. C. On allocation of tax burdens more generally, see Goodman (1983) 31 *Can. Tax Jo.* 169–82.

[58] See Statement of Practice SP 4/94; and discussion by Hutton in *Tolley's Tax Planning 1999–2000*, 1707 1715–1721.

[59] [1993] Ch 497, [1993] 3 All ER 926.

[60] Hitchmough [1993] *BTR* 406, 408.

[61] [1944] 1 All ER 230, (1944) 26 TC 12.

The case also illustrates that when the beneficiary under an accumulation trust reaches the age of majority, or whatever event is specified in the trust, and so becomes entitled to the accumulated income, that income cannot be taxed as his in the year of receipt because it is then a capital payment to him and not the income of that year.

Today, the tax liability of the beneficiary under an accumulation trust depends on the nature of the right in the income. If B's interest is vested, B will be taxed like any other beneficiary with such an interest. The income—less trust expenses—is taxed as B's income, even though it is, in fact, accumulating in the hands of the trustees. Moreover, the fact that B has such a right will mean that the trustees do not have to pay at the special rate applicable to trusts.[62] This will occur when a contingent beneficiary reaches the age of majority since s. 31 gives him a right to subsequent income, even though his interest in capital remains contingent.

If, however, B's interest is contingent, as when he is still under 18, the income cannot be treated as B's unless and until it is actually made his e.g. under a power.[63]

TA 1988, s. 687

Basic Rule. Where trustees make any payment to the beneficiary in the exercise of a discretion[64] and the payment is income of the person to whom it is paid,[65] TA 1988, s. 687 requires the trustees to gross up the payment at the applicable rate.[66] Therefore, if the trustees make a payment of £1,980 in 2000–01, this will be grossed up at 34% to £3,000 (i.e. £1,980 + £1,020). This is so whether or not there is trust income available—TA 1988, ss 348 and 349 are excluded—in that year. The tax of £1,020 can be collected from the trustees.[67] This tax is due on 31 January following the end of the year in which it arose.[68] It follows that the beneficiary, B, is then treated as receiving £3,000 which has been taxed at 34%; any further tax liability (if B is a higher rate taxpayer) or repayment (if B is not) will be calculated on that basis.

Is it income? S. 687 applies only if B receives income. Once income has been accumulated it becomes capital for trust purposes, so that any later payment will be capital and outside s. 687. No part of s. 687 treats a payment of capital as income if it could have been paid out of income if it had not been accumulated; such a device is part of the anti-avoidance rules in ss 660A *et seq.*

Credit for taxes paid. The trustees' liability to the Revenue under s. 687 can be reduced by various payments. The first and principal deduction will be any tax under s. 686. This set off is available even if the s. 686 tax was paid in a previous year of assessment.

Complications arise when the rates change. Thus, if the trust accumulates income in year 1 when the rate is, say, 34%, but makes the distribution in year 2 when the rate is 50%, the trust will have to pay at 34% in year 1 under s. 686, but can use that tax only against the tax due at 50% under s. 687 in year 2, so causing an extra 16% to be due. The beneficiary's income is grossed up at the rates for year 2. If, on the other hand, the rate drops from 50%

[62] Because it belongs to the beneficiary before it is distributed (TA 1988, s. 686(2)(b)).
[63] *Drummond* v. *Collins* [1915] AC 1011, (1915) 6 TC 525.
[64] The same words as in TA 1988, s. 686.
[65] Or is treated as income of the settlor.
[66] TA 1988, s. 687 (1), (2).
[67] Ibid., s. 687(2). Note ESC B18 where income would escape UK tax if paid direct to the beneficiary instead of through a trust. On concession for employee trusts, see ESC A68.
[68] TMA 1970, s. 8A(1A).

to 34%, it appears that the extra 16% already paid is lost. Further, if the liability under s. 687 is in a year previous to that in which the liability arises under s. 686, it seems that no relief can be given. This is where Model 4 (p. 557) is not applied precisely.

Credit for tax on Schedule F income. The second deduction comprises a group of taxes paid on types of Schedule F income.[69] These are listed separately because the rate of credit which can be used has been reduced following the 1999 changes to the tax credit on dividends. The full effect of these changes was not appreciated since it was assumed that trusts would fund must of these payment out of accumulated pre-1999 income; however, it has become a real problem for new trusts and for those which have exhausted pre-1999 income.

The effect of the changes is that the tax available for credit against s. 687 liability is restricted to the difference between the trust Schedule F rate of 25% and the ordinary Schedule F rate of 10%. This restriction increases the tax cost of a distribution out of such income over costs out of other income, such as interest or rent. Thus, suppose that the trust has a dividend of £1,000 gross (£900 net); tax under s. 686 at 25% will be £150 (i.e. £250 less £100 credit), leaving the trustees with £750. If they wish to distribute the entire £750 they must gross up that £750 at 34%, making a gross sum of £1,136. This means that the trustees must actually pay not only the £150, but also the £236.36 to gross up the payment to £1,136, making a total of £386.36. This sum is 42.93% of the net dividend of £900 and means that other trust income must be raised to fund the tax liability. If the trustees wish to ensure that all the tax comes out of the net dividend received, they will pay out only £594; this sum, when grossed up at 34%, make the necessary gross payment of £900.[70] Other examples have produced a 48.63% rate.[71] The figures mean that trustees may be advised not to invest in equities, a classic breach of the principle of neutrality.

One solution to this problem is to prevent the income from being trust income in the first place (see above §29.2.2). However, the Revenue does not regard a mere dividend mandate directing payment to the beneficiary instead of to the trust as sufficient for this purpose.

Credit for other taxes. Further rules apply to allow tax paid on (1) undistributed income on hand when the new regime was introduced in 1973,[72] and, subsequently,[73] (2) a stream of receipts which show how complicated the tax system has become. The list includes sums charged under overseas bonds (s. 761), the accrued income scheme (s. 714 or 716), development gains and the old and new rules for discounted securities.

29.3.4 Discretionary trust and annual payments

TA 1988, s. 687(1) refers to payments[74] of income, thereby excluding payments of capital. S. 687(1) rules apply in lieu of ss 348 and 349. S. 687 thereby assumes that such payments fit into the general scheme of income as annual payments taxable to the beneficiary under Schedule D, Case III. Three points arise.

69 TA 1988, s. 687(a1)–(bc).
70 These figures come from RI 199, *Tax Bulletin* 39 (February 1999).
71 Bickerdike [1998] *Private Client Business* 88, 92; see also Thompson [1999] *Private Client Business* 44.
72 FA 1973, s. 17(3) (proviso).
73 TA 1988, s. 687(3)(d)–(k).
74 Widened by ibid., s. 687(5) to cover payments in money or money's worth.

(1) Capital or income—loans

The rules apply only where the receipt by the beneficiary properly falls to be treated as his income, and so not where it is a capital payment. Where, therefore, trustees make a loan to the beneficiary eligible for the receipt of income, the receipt cannot be treated as his income, and no tax will be due. However, the courts have treated such payments as income where the trustees have no power to make the loan.[75] Further, whether a payment is a loan or income is a question of fact.[76]

(2) Non-resident beneficiary

A non-resident beneficiary receiving income under a discretionary trust is not generally entitled to repayment of the tax borne by the trustees. However, in practice the Revenue "looks through" to the underlying income and may grant any relief, including double taxation relief under the applicable agreement, which could have been available if the income had been paid direct.[77] The question whether the Revenue should "look through" more frequently is an interesting one.

(3) Capital as income

Where trustees hold property on trust but have to pay an annuity, or other annual payment, the annuitant's liability falls to be determined under Schedule D, Case III. This liability survives the 1988 changes to Case III since those changes apply only to annual payments made by individuals.[78]

Whether the payments are to be regarded as an annuity or as a series of payments of capital depends upon the rights of the recipient, and not on the source of the payments. In *Brodie's Will Trustees* v. *IRC*[79] the annuity was charged on both income and capital so that the trustees were under a duty to have recourse to capital. The payments were held to be annuities and so wholly taxable as income of the recipient. In *Lindus and Hortin* v. *IRC*[80] trustees had a discretion to use capital to make good any shortfall in the trust income; the payments were held to be annuities. This principle was applied in *Cunard's Trustees* v. *IRC*[81] where the trustees had power to use capital to supplement the income of the tenant for life.

In all the above cases there was a series of recurrent payments over a substantial period of time. The cases were taken by the Revenue to justify the position that any payment out of the capital of a trust fund which was intended to be used by a beneficiary for an income purpose (e.g. payment of school fees) was income of the beneficiary.[82] However, this approach was rejected by the Court of Appeal in *Stevenson* v. *Wishart*,[83] where payments made in exercise of a power over capital[84] were not payments of income and could not be

[75] *Esdaile* v. *IRC* (1936) 20 TC 700; the lack of power could not be cured by agreement between the trustees and only some of the beneficiaries.

[76] *Williamson* v. *Ough* [1936] AC 384, (1936) 20 TC 194. *Cf. Peirse-Duncombe Trustees* v. *IRC* (1940) 23 TC 199.

[77] Statement of Practice SP 3/86; for Revenue practice where there is a discretionary trust of the residue of an estate of a deceased person, see above at §30.7.

[78] TA 1988, s. 347A(2).

[79] (1933) 17 TC 432.

[80] (1933) 17 TC 432.

[81] [1946] 1 All ER 159, (1946) 27 TC 122.

[82] See Venables, *Tax Planning Through Trusts*, above at n. 57, §20:19.

[83] [1987] STC 266, [1987] 2 All ER 428; on which, see Wiggin and Rawlinson [1986] *BTR* 124; and Potter and Monroe, *Tax Planning*, above at n. 31, §3-09.

[84] This is an important case since the beneficiary was also an income beneficiary.

turned into income simply because they were applied to an income purpose. Where trustees have a discretion to resort to capital, the effect of exercising that discretion may be to cause the payment to fall within TA 1988, s. 687, since the sum is received by A, the annuitant, as income even though it was not A's income before the discretion was exercised.

The Revenue approach was also rejected in the earlier case of *Lawson* v. *Rolfe*,[85] where a tenant for life was entitled, under the law applicable to the settlement, to all bonus shares issued by corporations in which the trust held shares. Issues of such shares were frequent and the Revenue argued that the frequency of the payments meant that they should be treated as income payments and so taxable in the hands of the beneficiary. This argument was rejected. There was all the difference in the world between a series of payment by the trustees under the terms of the will, and the distributions by the companies in this case which, as far as the trust was concerned, were purely fortuitous and unplanned.

Whether it is advantageous to convert capital into income depends on the tax circumstances of those concerned.[86] If the beneficiary is not a higher rate tax payer and the trust has surplus s. 686 income accumulated from previous years, creating Schedule D, Case III income will enable the difference between 34% and the beneficiary's rate to be repaid. Nor should it be forgotten that income payments are excluded when considering exit charges for IHT, thanks to IHTA 1984, s. 65(5)(b) see below §72.4.

85 [1970] 1 All ER 761, (1970) 46 TC 199; see [1970] 1970 *BTR* 142.

86 Potter and Monroe, above at n. 31, §3-10.

30

Death and Estates

30.1 General

Estates must settle the liability of a deceased person (D) to income tax on the income that accrued during D's lifetime.[1] The time limit for making assessments (even for negligence) is three years from 31 January following the end of the year of assessment in which the death occured.[2] Therefore, if D died in November 1999, the three-year period expires on 31 January 2004. The Revenue may, within that period go back six years to collect tax due to D's fraud or negligence, i.e. back to the year 1993–1994.[3] In computing this liability the personal reliefs of D before the year of death are permitted in full; there is no reduction where D died before 5 April. If the deceased was carrying on a trade, his death will involve a discontinuance and so possible use of overlaps profits.[4] The personal representatives (PRs) may obtain a tax return immediately.[5]

Income becoming due after, but in respect of a period before, the death of D is treated as that of the estate, not of D, for the purposes of income tax.[6] However, for the purposes of IHT, income is apportioned. This means that a part of the payment may be charged both to IHT as the D's asset and to income tax as the income of the estate (and so perhaps of the beneficiary). In computing the beneficiary's income for excess liability, the residuary income of the estate is therefore reduced by the amount of IHT payable in respect of that income.[7]

[1] TMA 1970, s. 74, and note s. 40(1).
[2] Ibid., s. 40(1); the normal period is five years.
[3] Ibid., s. 40(2).
[4] On PRs' liability see TA 1988, s. 60(4).
[5] Inland Revenue Press Release, 4 April 1996, (1996) *Simon's Weekly Tax Intelligence* 663.
[6] *IRC* v. *Henderson's Executors* (1931) 16 TC 282; the situation may be distinguished from that in which the dividend becomes due before, but is paid after, the death (*Potel* v. *IRC* [1971] 2 All ER 504, (1971) 46 TC 658).
[7] TA 1988, s. 699; excess liability is defined in s. 699(2).

30.2 Liability of the Personal Representatives

Like trustees, PRs are assessable to income tax on the income of the estate at the lower (savings) rate on savings income, the ordinary Schedule F rate on dividend income and basic rate on other income. Gains accruing on certain life policies are treated as income of the PRs.[8] Like trustees, PRs are not liable to tax at the higher rate, nor can they use the starting rate.[9] They are not liable to the 34% rate applicable to trusts, which is, however, used for capital gains, making this one of the every few areas in which the CGT rate is higher than the income tax rate.[10]

PRs may not use any of D's personal allowances remaining unabsorbed by D's income. They may, however, claim relief in respect of interest payments or in respect of any loss which *they* incur in running a business. Interest in respect of unpaid IHT is not deductible,[11] but interest on a loan to pay IHT is deductible if the loan is made to the PRs and relates to tax payable on personalty before the grant of representation. Only interest on the first year of the loan is deductible; excess interest can be carried back and then forward.[12]

On liability to tax on trading income, see above at §19.6.

30.3 Liability of the Beneficiary

30.3.1 General

Until the administration is complete no beneficiary has any rights in the property of the estate or to the income from it.[13] It follows that no beneficiary is liable to income tax on the income of the estate[14] as such; liability may arise when an income distribution is made to a beneficiary.

The question whether administration is complete is a matter of fact, the issue being whether the residue has been ascertained.[15] A prolonged administration may mean a fund administered with expertise and not taxed at higher or Schedule F upper rates of income tax; conversely, if the prospective beneficiaries had low incomes and so unused personal allowances, the administration might be expedited.

UK and foreign estates

The rules for taxing the beneficiaries vary according to whether the estate is a UK estate or a foreign estate. A UK estate is defined as one where the income of which comprises only income which has borne UK tax or for which the PRs are directly assessable. However, an

[8] TA 1988, ss 547(1)(c), (7A), 553(7A).

[9] *IRC* v. *Countess of Longford* [1927] 1 KB 594, (1927) 13 TC 573. There is no liability at the rate applicable to trusts (TA 1988, s. 686(6)).

[10] TCGA 1992, s. 4(1AA).

[11] *Lord Inverclyde's Trustees* v. *Millar* (1924) 9 TC 14.

[12] TA 1988, s. 364.

[13] *Stamp Duties Comr (Queensland)* v. *Livingston* [1965] AC 694, [1964] 3 All ER 692.

[14] *R* v. *IT Special Purposes Comrs, ex parte Dr Barnardo's Homes National Incorporated Association* [1920] 1 KB 26, (1920) 7 TC 646; *Corbett* v. *IRC* [1937] 4 All ER 700, (1937) 21 TC 449; see also *Prest* v. *Bettinson* [1980] STC 607, (1980) 53 TC 437.

[15] *George Attenborough & Son* v. *Solomon* [1913] AC 76.

estate is not a UK estate if the PRs are exempt from UK tax by reason of residence outside the UK.[16] It follows that if a foreign estate only has income which is neither taxed by deduction nor assessable on the PRs, there is no liability to UK income tax.[16a] An estate which is not a UK estate is a foreign estate.[17] In applying these rules certain amounts are ignored, i.e. are stock dividends, the release of a loan from a close company and certain gains on life policies.[18]

Specific legacies

Where the PRs vest a specific legacy in the legatee (L), intermediate income accruing during the administration is related back and so assessed on L at the time income accrued to the property.[19]

Interest

Where a legacy carries interest, L is liable to tax on that interest under Schedule D, Case III if it has become L's income. An attempt to disclaim the interest failed where a sum had been set aside to pay the legacy.[20] From this it should follow that where no sums have been set aside, L may have a right to interest but will not be taxable in respect of it yet. Where L receives the legacy with interest, it is an open question whether the payment relates back.

30.3.2 Residue

Grossing up at the applicable rate

Any sums which are actually paid[21] during the administration period, whether in respect of a limited or absolute interest, are grossed up[22] at the applicable rate. They are then treated as the beneficiary's income for the year of assessment in which the sum was paid or, if the interest has ceased, as income for the year of assessment in which it ceased.[23] Income from a foreign estate is not subject to UK tax; if UK tax has nonetheless been charged, e.g. by deduction at source, the gross income is apportioned, so that the income must be grossed up to reflect the UK tax paid.[24]

The applicable rate does not mean the rate applicable to trusts under s. 686; it means the rate applicable to the type of income in the residuary estate out of which the amount is paid, i.e. Schedule F (10%), other savings (20%)[25] or basic rate (22%).[26] Where dividend income is treated as having borne tax at the special rate for dividends, the normal dividend rules apply. The beneficiaries may then use the tax charged at the applicable rate as a credit against their own tax liability. As from 1999–2000 ,and in conformity with the new treatment of dividends, the beneficiary cannot make a repayment claim in respect of any Schedule F income, but may use such income to frank payments falling within TA 1988, s. 348 or 349.[27]

[16] TA 1988, s. 701(9) on residence see below §58.9.
[16a] *Simons Taxes* §C.4.104.
[17] Ibid., s. 701(10).
[18] Ibid., s. 701(10A).
[19] *IRC* v. *Hawley* [1928] 1 KB 578, (1928) 13 TC 327.
[20] *Spens* v. *IRC* [1970] 3 All ER 295, (1970) 46 TC 276; *cf. Dewar* v. *IRC* [1935] 2 KB 351, (1935) 19 TC 561.
[21] Widely defined in TA 1988, s. 701(12).
[22] Ibid., s. 695(2), (4), 696(3), (4); benefits in kind must be grossed up (*IRC* v. *Mardon* (1956) 36 TC 565).
[23] Ibid., s. 695(2).
[24] Ibid., s. 695(5).
[25] Ibid., s. 698A, referring to ss 1A and 1B.
[26] Ibid., s. 701(3A).
[27] Ibid., s. 699A(1A), (6), as amended by F (No. 2) A 1997, s. 33.

Source

Rules are needed to determine the source of any income distributed. Therefore, distributions are treated as coming first from income taxed at basic rate, then income taxed at lower rate and, finally, from "relevant amounts"—principally Schedule F income.[28]

Income untaxed in hands of PRs

Special rules apply to certain types of income which are not directly assessable to UK tax in the hands of the PRs. These are stock dividends, release of loans made to a participator in a close company, certain gains on life policies[29] and, since 1999, all Schedule F income.[30] Such income is referred to as "relevant amounts".[31] When amounts are allocated to individual beneficiaries, these types of income are allocated last.[32] Relevant amounts are treated as having borne tax at the Schedule F rate, except life policy gains which are treated as having borne tax at the basic rate.[33] No repayment of tax may be made and the tax may only be treated as franking payments within TA 1988, ss 348 and 349(1) if it is Schedule F income. The tax is available as a credit against the beneficiary's own tax liability in respect of the limited interest arising from a foreign estate; it is this credit which represents the change from earlier rules. The rules also specify the rate of UK tax, which is the applicable rate for such payments out of UK estates. Schedule F income was brought into the list of relevant amounts in 1999 so as to prevent any right to repayment of tax.[34]

Trusts as beneficiaries

The applicable rate rules are different if the income is distributed to a discretionary or other trust subject to the special rate of tax applicable to trusts,[35] in which case the 34% rate is used.

30.4 Residuary Beneficiary

30.4.1 Limited Interest

Beneficiaries have a limited interest if they do not have an absolute interest but would have a right to income if administration were complete.[36] It is an open question whether a person whose interest is vested subject to being divested is entitled to the income.[37]

Any sums which are actually paid[38] during the administration period in respect of a limited interest are grossed up[39] at the applicable rate under the rules explained at §30.3.2 above. They are then treated as the beneficiary's income for the year of assessment in which

28 TA 1988, s. 701 (3A)(b), as amended
29 Ibid., s. 699A(1)(a) refers to ss 249(5), 421(2), 547(1)(c).
30 Ibid., s. 699A(1)(b), (1A) refer to Schedule F and a distribution within s. 233(1).
31 Ibid., s. 699A(1).
32 Ibid., s. 699A(2)(b), referring to TA 1988, s. 701(3)(A).
33 TA 1988, s. 699A(3), (4).
34 Ibid., s. 699A (1A), (6), as amended by F (No. 2) A 1997, s. 33.
35 TA 1988, s. 698A(3), as amended by F (No. 2) A 1997 s. 33, excluding s. 698 (1), (2).
36 TA 1988, s. 701(3).
37 The doubts stem from *Stanley* v. *IRC* (see above at §29.3.3).
38 Widely defined in TA 1988, s. 701(12).
39 Benefits in kind must be grossed up (*IRC* v. *Mardon* (1956) 36 TC 565).

the sum was paid or, if the interest has ceased, as income for the year of assessment in which it ceased.[40] Income from a foreign estate is grossed up to reflect the UK tax paid.[41]

Completion of administration

Where the administration of an estate is complete the beneficiaries bring in income that has accrued to the PRs during the administration as and when it is received by them,[42] as part of their self-assessment.

Any sums in the estate remaining payable to the beneficiary are income of the year in which the administration is completed. This is subject to one minor qualification; if the beneficiary's interest ended before the year in which administration was completed, e.g. where he dies, it is instead treated as income of the year in which the interest ceased.[43] For estates where the administration was completed before 6 April 1995, a much more complex system required a spreading-back of the remaining sums over the period of administration.[44] The new rule is simpler to apply (and more appropriate to self-assessment), but means that income will be concentrated in one year.

The income on which the beneficiary is taxed will almost certainly bear little relation to the actual income of the estate in respect of which the PRs are chargeable. This is partly because administration expenses are deductible in computing the beneficiary's income, not in computing the estate income, but also because the fluctuation in rates of tax and the variation in the estate income mean that the estate income may arise at times different from the dates of payment.

Source

Income of a legatee who is not resident or not ordinarily resident in the UK may, by concession, be treated as if it arose directly from the various sources, even though the estate is a UK estate (e.g. where sole assets are UK government securities).[45] This a famous example of "looking through" to the underlying income; legislative action to decide when the law should look through and when it should not is needed urgently.

Information

The PRs have a duty to provide the beneficiary with information on the amount of tax at the applicable rate which the income is deemed to have borne.[46]

30.4.2 Absolute interest

A beneficiary (B) has an absolute interest in residue if, on the hypothesis that the administration were then complete, he would be entitled to the capital or part of it in his own right.[47] It is unclear whether a person entitled to capital but subject to the payment of an annuity is entitled to it "in his own right".[48]

40 TA 1988, s. 695(2).
41 Ibid., s. 695(5).
42 FA 1995, Sch. 18.
43 TA 1988, s. 695(3) (1995 version).
44 Ibid., s. 695(3) (original version).
45 ESC A14.
46 TA 1988, s.700(5), (6), added by FA 1995.
47 Ibid., s. 701(2).
48 See *Simon's Direct Tax Service*, Pt. C4.107.

Sums actually paid[49]

Payments during the administration period are grossed up at the applicable rate and treated as the beneficiary's income of the year of payment.[50] The various rules as to applicable rates and sources of payments are explained above at §30.3.

Payments in excess of aggregate income entitlement

Since B is also entitled to the capital, rules separate income payments from capital payments. Income treatment applies only to the extent of the B's "aggregate income entitlement" for that year; any excess is treated as capital. "Aggregate income entitlement" is the amount which would be the aggregate of the amounts received for that year of assessment and all previous years of assessment in respect of the interest if that person had a right in each year to receive those amounts, and had received the amounts in the case of a UK estate; these sums must be grossed up to reflect income tax at the applicable rate for that year.[51] In the case of a foreign estate this calculation assumes that B has received only the residuary income for that year, without grossing up.[52]

Residuary income

Residuary income is defined as the aggregate of income received but with a deduction for interest, annuities or other annual payments charged on the residue. Also deducted are the management expenses of the PRs in so far as they are properly chargeable to income.[53] If deductions exceed the sums paid as income the deficit may be carried forward.[54]

Completion of administration

When the administration is completed the amount paid out during administration is compared with the aggregate income entitlement down to and including that year. If the amount paid is less than the entitlement, the balance is treated as income paid immediately before the end of the period of administration.[55] This balance must be grossed up as necessary. Adjustments are also necessary if the benefits received are less than the aggregate residuary income, for example if debts payable out of residue are discovered late in the administration period. Any reduction is carried out first against the income of the year of the completion of administration, with any remaining reductions taking effect against the income of earlier years.[56]

Exempt beneficiary

If the residuary beneficiary is exempt from income tax, a repayment may be due. In the days of composite rates a repayment could be obtained if the residuary income included building society income since the Revenue did not look through to the underlying source.[57]

[49] Widely defined in TA 1988, s. 701(12).
[50] Ibid., s. 696(3), as replaced by FA 1995.
[51] TA 1988, s. 699A, added by FA 1995.
[52] TA 1988, s. 696(3B).
[53] Ibid., s. 697(1).
[54] Ibid., s. 697(1A), added by FA 1995, Sch. 18, para. 4(1) and ESC A13 (1994).
[55] TA 1988, s. 696(5) substituted version; a different rule applied before 1995.
[56] Ibid., s. 697 (1995, Sch.1 8, para. 4(2)). On power to make assessments, see ibid., s. 700(2).
[57] Statement of Practice, SP 7/80 (obsolete).

However, look-through was permitted by concession, and to the taxpayer's advantage, in certain instances, e.g. where B was a non-resident.[58]

Information

The PRs are under an obligation, enforceable at the suit of the person making the request, to respond to a request in writing of details of the deemed income.[59]

30.5 Residue Held on Discretionary Trusts

If the residue is held on discretionary trusts, the provisions so far considered do not apply, since there exist neither absolute nor limited interests. Therefore, the scheme used for limited interests applies instead.[60] Where income is paid indirectly through a trustee, any payment to the trustee is treated, for the purpose of the rules, as income paid of the trustee.[61]

30.6 Successive Interests in Residue

30.6.1 Death of beneficiary before administration complete

Provision is made for the possibility that the beneficiary dies before administration is complete. If the beneficiary had an absolute interest, that interest passes to his PRs and the income of the first estate will form part of the beneficiary's estate. The PRs are treated as succeeding to the absolute interest despite their representative status.[62]

30.6.2 Successive limited interests

Where successive interests in the residue arise for some other cause, such as assignment or disclaimer, different rules apply.[63] Where successive limited interests follow each other, they are treated as being one and the same.[64] While this means that the whole residuary income will be divided between successive holders, allowance will be made for sums due to the first holder which are paid to that holder after the assignment, such sums being treated as income of the first holder.

30.6.3 Limited then absolute

If a limited interest is followed by an absolute interest, the absolute interest is treated as having always existed. TA 1988, s. 696 is then applied as if the payment made to the holder of the limited interest had been made to the holder of the absolute interest. This does not undo

[58] ESC A14.
[59] TA 1988, s. 700(5), (6).
[60] Ibid., s. 698(3), applied also to payments made via discretionary trusts (Statement of Practice, SP 4/93).
[61] TA 1988, s. 698A(2), added by FA 1993.
[62] TA 1988, s. 698(1).
[63] Ibid., s. 698(1A), added by FA 1995.
[64] TA 1988, s. 698(1B), added by FA 1995.

the liability of the holder of the limited interest, but ensures that all the income is properly taxed to one or other of them and that each is taxed on what he actually receives.

30.6.4 Successive absolute interests

Successive absolute interests may arise as by assignment. Here, the change in beneficiary is ignored. The aggregate income entitlement is calculated in the usual way. The effect is that each beneficiary is taxed on what he received. If any adjustment has to be made at the end of the administration period, this will fall primarily on the second holder of the interest.[65]

[65] TA 1988, s. 698(2), substituted by FA 1995.

31

Income Splitting: Arrangements and Settlements

31.1 Introduction

TA 1988, Part XV[1] contains a series of provisions designed for three purposes. The first is to restrict the use of other taxable entities (such as trusts) as piggy banks, in which income can be taxed at the rates appropriate to that entity, rather than at the settlor's (S's)marginal rates, and so grow more rapidly before being passed back for the settlor or S's spouse to enjoy. This is clearly of less importance now that tax rates on income do not exceed 40%; the difference between the maximum trust rates (34%) and the top individual rate of 40% is still significant if large amounts of money are involved.

The second purpose is to restrict the income splitting opportunities within the family between spouses and between parents and minor children. The third purpose was to restrict the income assignment possibilities created by the system for taxing covenants (see above at §27.5), which system remains in place despite the abolition of the general right of individuals to deduct sums paid under covenants.

These provisions were comprehensively rewritten and simplified with effect from the beginning of 1995–1996, a reform which was most welcome. Separate and unchanged rules apply to funds for the maintenance of heritage property.[2] The 1995 reforms originally

[1] On early history, see articles by Stopforth [1987] *BTR* 417, [1990] *BTR* 225, [1991] *BTR* 86, [1992] *BTR* 88, [1994] *BTR* 234, [1997] *BTR* 276 and, on charitable covenants, [1986] *BTR* 101.

[2] TA 1988, s. 691.

contained two provisions which would have recast the treatment of loans between settlors and settlements. These were later withdrawn for reconsideration but with the consequence that some old provisions (TA 1988, ss 677, 678, 682) linger on (see below at §31.4).

Under the current rules the offending income is treated as that of the settlor (S) for all income tax purposes;[3] S is given a right to recover the tax from the entity concerned.[4] The previous rules had a halfway stage—treating the income as income of S for excess liability only. The new rule draws no distinction between income which is accumulated and that which arises; unfortunately, this distinction remains important for the retained provisions (see below at §31.4).

When income is treated as that of S under one of these rules, the correct legal analysis is that the income arises first in the hands of the settlement and then is transferred to, or back to, S by parliamentary transfer. This can have surprising results, especially if the disposition which is treated as a settlement is the creation of a right to annual payments by a covenant. In *Ang* v. *Parrish*[5] the taxpayer made a covenant in favour of his parents-in-law which fell foul of the now repealed TA 1988, s. 683. The taxpayer only had earned income out of which to make the payments. Walton J. held that the payment came back to him as investment income and so was subject to income tax at the additional rate, even though the payment was originally made out of earned income. This decision left the taxpayer's final state worse than the first. It is one more example of the folly of the system of deduction at source now, thankfully, greatly reduced. A rational system of taxation would have prescribed deductions, e.g. payments under covenants, and then listed the circumstances in which deduction was not permitted. We do not yet have that rational system.

A study of these rules might leave one with the impression that a trust is never effective for tax purposes. This is untrue. Provided one avoids settlements in favour of a spouse or unmarried minor children, and has taken all steps to exclude oneself, income may be accumulated or distributed without any adverse income tax consequences under these rules. Even settlements in favour of unmarried minor children may work provided the income is accumulated while they have that status. One may even be a trustee and thus control the selection of beneficiaries, again other than one's spouse or unmarried minor children, under a discretionary trust or a power of appointment.

The principle in *IRC* v. *Ramsay* and *Furniss* v. *Dawson* can apply in this area,[6] and has already been applied to reverse one earlier House of Lords' decision.[7]

31.2 Arrangements and Settlements

It is unfortunate that TA 1988, Part XV is formally entitled "Settlements", rather than some longer but more accurate title such as "ineffective dispositions of income". The law does not take the view that income splitting should be countered only where it takes place behind devices akin to the strict settlement. The term "settlement" "includes any "disposition, trust, covenant, agreement, arrangement or transfer of assets".[8] The essence of a settlor is as the source of the funds from which the income derives.

[3] TA 1988, s. 660A.
[4] Ibid., s. 660F.
[5] [1980] STC 341, [1980] 2 All ER 790, (1980) 53 TC 304.
[6] *Ewart* v. *Taylor* [1983] STC 721.
[7] *Moodie* v. *IRC* [1993] STC 188; reversing *IRC* v. *Plummer* [1979] STC 793, [1979] 3 All ER 775, (1979) 54 TC 1.
[8] TA 1988, s. 660I(1).

The word "settlement" is not a dominating word which colours the others; the word "arrangement" is not a term of art.[9] Acts which have been held to be settlements include the setting-up of corporate structures (arrangement) and the disclaimer of an interest by a beneficiary (disposition). The limiting factor is that a transaction can be a settlement only if it contains an element of bounty (see below at §31.2.2). The Revenue view is that bringing a spouse into partnership is an arrangement. Therefore, if a wife brings her husband into partnership and he does not truly earn his share of the profits, the income accruing to him will be treated as accruing to her; bounty is shown by the fact that he did not earn his share.[10]

31.2.1 Cases

Pollyanna and *Tiger Bay*

In *IRC* v. *Mills*[11] the taxpayer was Hayley Mills (H) who, as a child film star, appeared in many films. In order to make sure that her earnings were "legally protected", her father, John Mills, formed a company and settled the shares of that company on trust for H with various contingent remainders over. H then signed a service contract with the company giving the company the right to her exclusive services for a period of five years at a salary of £400 a year. The company received large sums for the films H made (including Polyanna and Tiger Bay), and distributed those sums in the form of dividend to the trustees. Since the trustees did not distribute the income, the question arose whether the income accumulated by the trust could be treated as H's. The House of Lords held that there was a settlement, that H was the settlor and that the source of the dividends was the money paid for her work so that she had by her work provided the settlement with income indirectly. The result was that income accumulated by the trustees was deemed to be H's.[12]

Disclaimer as disposition

In *IRC* v. *Buchanan*[13] property was settled by X on A for life, with remainder to B for life on protective trusts and remainder to B's children. The settlement also provided that if B should disclaim her life interest, the property should be administered at the moment when B's interest would have fallen into possession as if B were dead, thus avoiding the discretionary trusts that would otherwise have arisen on A's death following the disclaimer. B disclaimed her interest and the next day A released his interest. The Court of Appeal held that the destruction of an interest was a disposition. B had a disposable interest in that she had the right to income after A's death and could end that entitlement or not as she chose. The result was that the disclaimer was a settlement, and so income arising in favour of B's infant children was deemed to be B's.[14]

[9] Greene M.R. in *IRC* v. *Payne* (1940) 23 TC 610, 626. Cf. *Shop and Store Developments Ltd.* v. *IRC* [1967] 1 AC 472, [1967] 1 All ER 42 (stamp duty).

[10] Potter and Monroe, *Tax Planning*, §2-03, adding that because the matter is an "arrangement" and not an outright gift, s. 660A (6) cannot apply.

[11] [1974] 1 All ER 722, [1974] STC 130. Note TA 1988, s. 775 (below at §57.6). Where a stranger provides trustees with advice as a result of which the income of the fund is increased, it appears that this section cannot apply since the stranger provides advice not funds (see *Mills* v. *IRC* 49 TC 367, 408, *per* Viscount Dilhorne.

[12] Under what was then TA 1988, s. 673; the income would now be caught by ibid., s. 660A.

[13] [1957] 2 All ER 400, (1957) 37 TC 365.

[14] Under what was then TA 1988, s. 663; the income would now be caught by ibid., s. 660B.

31.2.2 No bounty, no settlement

If there is no element of bounty the transaction is not a settlement; this follows even if the transaction is not carried out for commercial reasons. In *IRC* v. *Levy*[15] an interest-free loan by a taxpayer to a company wholly owned by him—a transaction which the Commissioners had found to contain no element of bounty—was not a settlement.

In *IRC* v. *Plummer*[16] a charity paid £2,480 to the taxpayer (T) who covenanted to pay the charity a sum which, net of tax at basic rate, would amount to £500 each year for five years. The purpose of the scheme was to enable T to reduce his liability to surtax. The payments were annual payments, being income of the charity under Schedule D, Case III and, in consequence, deductible under TA 1988, s. 835. The difference between £500 grossed up at basic rate and £500 was thus relieved from surtax, enabling T to keep the benefit of the tax relief himself. Despite the fact that the arrangement was made solely to obtain the tax advantage the House of Lords held that as there was no bounty since, between the parties, it was not a settlement. Today the scheme would fail either because the House has since held that the payments were not "annual payments" after all[17] or because such schemes were stopped (prospectively) by statute in 1977 (see below at §31.6.3). However, this still leaves *Plummer* as an example of the no-bounty test.

The validity of the bounty test has been questioned. Suppose that X settles property for two years upon trust for X absolutely if X survives the period and, if not, for Y, and that Y provides full consideration for his interest. *Plummer* seems to say that there is no settlement and yet this is the very type of avoidance at which provisions like the old TA 1988, s. 673 were aimed.[18]

In applying the test the courts look at the transaction as a whole. In *Chinn* v. *Collins*[19] trustees exercised a power of appointment in favour of a beneficiary who later assigned his contingent interest under that exercise as part of a scheme to avoid tax. The House of Lords held that there was as settlement. The settlor's bounty in creating the settlement remained incomplete until the appointment was made and the trustees then conferred bounty on the beneficiary.

The test of bounty was applied in *Butler* v. *Wildin.*[20] Parents who were architects had worked for a company without fee. They had arranged for shares to be held by their infant children. It was held that there was a settlement—the parents were being bounteous to their children.

31.2.3 Property comprised in settlement

The term "settlement" is so widely defined that the more crucial question[21] is to determine what property is comprised in the settlement. The key statutory concept is that property is settled by S if it originates from S. References to property comprised in the settlement refer

[15] [1982] STC 442, (1982) 56 TC 68.

[16] [1979] STC 793, [1979] 3 All ER 775. For an interesting analysis of the speeches, see Murphy and Rawlings (1981) 44 MLR 617, 643 *et seq.*

[17] *Moodie* v. *IRC* [1993] STC 188; see, generally, Gillard, *In the Name of Charity* (1987).

[18] Venables, *Tax Planning Through Trusts* (Chatto & Windus, 1987), §20:26.

[19] [1981] STC 1, [1981] 1 All ER 189, (1981) 54 TC 311; see discussion in *IRC* v. *Levy* [1982] STC 442, (1982) 56 TC 68.

[20] [1989] STC 22, (1989) 61 TC 666.

[21] *Chamberlain* v. *IRC* [1943] 2 All ER 200, 203, (1943)25 TC 317, 329, *per* Lord Thankerton.

only to property originating from S;[22] references to income arising include only income originating from S.[23] References to property originating from a settlor refer to (a) property which S has supplied directly or indirectly for the purposes of the settlement, (b) property representing that property and (c) so much of any property as represents both property so provided and other property as, on a just apportionment, represents the property so provided.[24] It is expressly provided that property representing accumulated income is caught.[25]

In *Chamberlain* v. *IRC*[26] S transferred assets to a company which he controlled, and trustees acquired ordinary shares issued by the company. The trustees paid for the shares with money given to them by S. S later gave them more money with which to buy further shares. It was held that the property comprised in the settlement was the money given by S and the shares purchased with that money—but not the assets of the company itself.

31.3 Settlor

31.3.1 Settling property

Direct and indirect provision

The term "settlor" is widened to cover not only any person by whom the settlement was made,[27] but also a person who has made or entered into a settlement directly or indirectly. This phrase is then made the subject of a non-exclusive example, "by having provided or undertaken to provide funds, directly or indirectly for the purposes of the settlement".[28] In *IRC* v. *Buchanan* (above) B made the settlement, and was therefore a settlor, when she disclaimed her interest. Similarly, there was an indirect provision of funds in the case of the film star in *IRC* v. *Mills*[29] where it was said that purpose connotes neither a mental element nor a motivating intention.

Any steps

S makes a settlement by carrying out any steps of that settlement. Where the taxpayer had carried out one step, and later a scheme was devised and carried out by his solicitors and accountants, the scheme was held to be part of his settlement even though he was not consulted or present at any meetings.[30] An infant can make a settlement—as in *IRC* v. *Mills*.[31]

Reciprocal deals

The notion of a settlor is widened to include one who has made a reciprocal arrangement with another person for that other person to make or enter into the settlement. The purpose here is to catch the obvious device whereby A makes a settlement on B's children, and in

[22] TA 1988, s. 660E(2)(a).
[23] Ibid., s. 660E(2)(b).
[24] Ibid., s. 660E(5).
[25] Ibid., s. 660E(7)(b).
[26] *Chamberlain* v. *IRC* [1943] 2 All ER 200, (1943) 25 TC 317.
[27] TA 1988, ss 660G I, 682A(1).
[28] Ibid., s. 660 I(2).
[29] [1974] 1 All ER 722, 727, [1974] STC 130, 135, *per* Viscount Dilhorne.
[30] *Crossland* v. *Hawkins* [1961] 2 All ER 812, (1961) 39 TC 493.
[31] No argument was raised that Hayley Mills could have the arrangement set aside on the grounds of its invalidity by reason of her infancy.

return, B makes a settlement on A's children; however, there must be a reciprocal arrangement.[32] If X gives property to Y who transfers it to a settlement, Y is the settlor and X is not—unless there is some conscious association between X and the proposed settlement.[33]

Presumption

Where funds are provided for a settlement a very strong inference is drawn that those funds are provided for the purpose of the settlement,[34] an inference which will be rebutted if it is established that they were provided for another purpose. In *IRC* v. *Mills* the infant provided funds for the purposes of a settlement, even if unconsciously.

31.3.2 Multiple settlors: whose income?

The breadth of the definition of "settlement" and "settlor" means that more than one person may be a settlor in relation to a particular settlement.[35] Two issues arise: (a) are there two settlors? and (b) if so, what are the consequences?

More than one settlor?

Where there is more than one settlor the rules apply to each settlor as if each were the only settlor.[36] Given the definition of settlement, it follows that there are two or more settlors if income arising under the settlement originates from two or more persons. References to property comprised in the settlement refer only to property originating from that settlor, and references to income arising include only income originating from that settlor.[37]

Consequences

Where the property originating from the settlor is not the only property in the settlement, an apportionment is made.[38]

Cases

In *IRC* v. *Mills* it was held that while the father was clearly a settlor, so also was his daughter, H, and, since it was H's services which supplied the company with funds from which to pay dividends to the trust, she indirectly provided the income for the settlement; hence, all the income originated from her. The problem of the two settlors did not therefore arise in relation to the taxpayer and her father, and what would happen in such a case was left undecided by the House of Lords.[39]

In *IRC* v. *Buchanan*[40] the Revenue argued that the income accrued to B's children in consequence of her disposition. Yet if A had not released his interest no income would actually have accrued to the children. The Revenue won but did not make any assessment for any

[32] For example *Hood Barrs* v. *IRC* [1946] 2 All ER 768, (1946) 27 TC 385.
[33] *Fitzwilliam* v. *IRC* [1993] STC 502, 516, *per* Lord Keith.
[34] *IRC* v. *Mills* [1974] 1 All ER 722, 727, [1974] STC 130, 135.
[35] Defined in TA 1988, s. 660G.
[36] Ibid., s. 660E (1).
[37] Ibid., s. 660E (2).
[38] Ibid., s. 660E (5); on accumulated income, see ibid., s. 660E(7)(b).
[39] In the Court of Appeal, Orr L.J. suggested that this was simply a case in which it is left to the Revenue authorities to act reasonably ([1973] STC 1, 22, [1972] 3 All ER 977, 998).
[40] [1957] 2 All ER 400, (1957) 37 TC 365.

year before that in which A died. In the Court of Appeal X was regarded as not being a settlor for this purpose, a conclusion difficult to reconcile with *Chinn* v. *Colllins*.[41]

In *D'Abreu* v. *IRC*[42] in simplified terms, property had been settled by P on his daughters J and A; each half was held for life with remainders over to children in default of appointment and, in default of children, the half was to pass to the other. In 1959 J, who never married, released her power to appoint in favour of any husband she might marry; A then released and assigned her contingent interest in J's half to the trustees of her half and then exercised the power of appointment in favour of her children. The result was that when J died in 1963 the income from her half accrued to A's children who were still infants. Oliver J. held that, as in *Buchanan*, the whole of the income accruing to A's children did so in consequence of A's acts and so fell within what is now TA 1988, s. 660B. However, he went on to say that even if J were also a settlor, the provisions directed that the section was to apply to each settlor as if each were the only settlor; all the income therefore originated from A and apportionment could not be made on the basis of an actuarial valuation of their interests in 1959.

Two comments may be made. First, the decision draws a sharp and unfortunate distinction between successive and other interests. Thus, if A and J had, under the Variation of Trusts Act 1958, extracted capital sums which they had then jointly settled on A's children, it is at least arguable that the income from J's fund would not have fallen within the section. Secondly, difficulties remain. Suppose that there are successive life interests for H and W and they both release their interests in favour of their infant children; it seems unlikely that a court would say that they were both settlors and so tax the income twice. The appropriate answer would be to apportion on the basis of actuarial valuation of their interests, but this was rejected in *D'Abreu* v. *IRC* (above). To treat the matter as turning on the reasonableness of the Revenue is to make liability turn on administrative discretion, the very view rejected by the House of Lords in *Vestey* v. *IRC*.[43] It is therefore to be hoped that *D'Abreu* v. *IRC* is not the last word.[44]

31.4 Charge on Income Arising

31.4.1 What is income arising?

The provisions charge S on income arising under the settlement. Income arising under a settlement includes any income chargeable to income tax, whether by deduction or otherwise; it thus makes no allowance for any trust management expenses.[45] It also includes any income which would have been so chargeable if it had been received in the UK by a person domiciled, resident and ordinarily resident in the UK. This creates a hypothetical remittance to a hypothetical resident and so catches all income wherever it arises.[46] An exception must therefore be made to deal with a settlor who is not domiciled or resident or ordinarily

[41] [1981] STC 1, [1981] 1 All ER 189.
[42] [1978] STC 538.
[43] [1980] AC 1148, [1980] STC 10.
[44] However the approach of Chadwick J. in the IHT case of *Hatton* v. *IRC* [1992] STC 140 (see below at §70.4) clearly contemplates two persons being settlors of the same property.
[45] TA 1988, s. 660I(3).
[46] Reversing *Astor* v. *Perry* [1935] AC 398, (1935) 19 TC 255.

resident in the UK and so would not be chargeable to UK tax on that income.[47] This exception is then qualified to deal with the situation in which the income is remitted. Such remitted income is treated as arising in the year of remittance if S would have been taxable in the UK by reason of his residence.[48]

31.4.2 First charging provision: settlor retaining interest

TA 1988, s. 660A begins by deeming all income arising under a settlement to be income of the settlor for all purposes of the Income Tax Acts and not as the income of any other person. It then goes on to exclude this deeming treatment where the income arises from property in which S has no interest.[49] In deciding whether this exclusion is satisfied, S is to be regarded as having an interest in property if that property or any derived property is, or will or may become, payable to or applicable for the benefit of S or S's spouse in any circumstances whatsoever.[50] "Derived property" means income from that property or any other property directly or indirectly representing proceeds of, or of income from, that property or income.[51]

Illustration of the first general provision—revocable settlements

If a settlement can be revoked and, on that revocation, the property reverts to the S or S's spouse, the terms of s. 660A will be satisfied and income arising is treated as that of S.[52] If, on revocation, only a part of the property will so revert, only that part of the trust income arising is treated as S's income. Powers caught include a power to advance the whole of the settled capital to S [53] and a power to diminish the property comprised in the settlement or the income which people other than S or S's spouse might receive from it.[54] If, in such circumstances the rights of S or S's spouse are increased, s. 660A will apply. These illustrations come from decisions on the pre-1995 rules.

Other examples of s. 673 (and so s. 660A) applying include the failure to transfer S's entire beneficial interest with a consequent resulting trust,[55] or S retaining a general power of appointment or a special power of which he was one of the objects. This was carried further in *Glyn* v. *IRC*[56] where the power was to be exercised jointly by S and his son. Although the Revenue admitted that s. 673 would not have applied if the power had been vested in the son alone, the court held that S was caught by the section. This conclusion seems surprising in view of the fact that the son's concurrence was needed for the exercise of the power, but it may be regarded as having been realistic since s. 673, unlike s. 660A, was concerned only to charge income which was accumulated. If no appointment could be made without S's consent he could thereby determine whether or not the income was accumulated. It is unclear whether the fact that the settlement itself was brought about by a joint arrangement with the son forms part of the *ratio* of the case; it certainly provides a means of distinction.

[47] TA 1988, s. 660I(4).
[48] Ibid., s. 660G(4).
[49] Ibid., s. 660A(1).
[50] Ibid., s. 660A(2).
[51] Ibid., s. 660A(10).
[52] A supplemental deed is not retroactive (*Taylor* v. *IRC* [1946] 1 All ER 488n, (1946)27 TC 93).
[53] *Kenmare* v. *IRC* [1957] 3 All ER 33, (1957) 37 TC 383.
[54] Legislation overruling *IRC* v. *Saunders* [1957] 3 All ER 43, (1957) 37 TC 416; see [1957] *BTR* 392.
[55] *Hannay's Executors* v. *IRC* (1956) 37 TC 217; as nearly happened in *IRC* v. *Bernstein* [1961] 1 All ER 320, (1961) 39 TC 391; and *Pilkington* v. *IRC* [1962] 3 All ER 622, (1962) 40 TC 416.
[56] [1948] 2 All ER 419, (1948) 30 TC 321.

However, not every chance of the reduction in the trust assets gave rise to an application of the old provision—only a power to be found in the settlement and derived directly therefrom. In *IRC* v. *Wolfson*[57] the settlement was of shares in a company which was controlled by S. S was thus in a position to deprive the trust of its income. This was held not to amount to a power of revocation. However, a different result might have followed if the company had been set up as part of the scheme of settlement; it would then have been permissible to look at the structure of the company to determine whether there was a power of revocation.[58] Therefore, if a settlement is expressed to endure only as long as the company exists, and S has the power to cause the company to go into liquidation, s. 660A may apply.[59]

Limits of "in any circumstances whatsoever"—case law from earlier provisions

The language of TA 1988, s. 660A(2) is based on that found in the now repealed TA 1988, s. 673.[60] Limits placed on the scope of the phrase "in any circumstances whatsoever" are as follows:

(a) No interest is retained if S's power over the assets is fiduciary rather than beneficial. In *Lord Vestey's Executors* v. *IRC*[61] a power to direct investments granted to S and another and not to the trustees did not cause s. 673 to operate. Similarly, the possibility that S might become a trustee of another settlement to which the first settlement transfers funds should not have that effect.
(b) The section did not apply if the property may only come back to S only through the independent act of a third party.[62] In *Muir* v. *IRC*[63] Pennycuick J. stated that the section must be confined to cases where income or property will or might become payable to or applicable for the benefit of S either under the trusts of the settlement itself or under some collateral arrangement having legal force. Therefore, the possibility that a beneficiary to whom funds are properly paid might then decide to make a gift to S should not be taken into account. The same would hold good if a beneficiary chose to leave his property to S by will. However, where S's position as heir gave him the right to succeed not as beneficiary under the beneficiary's will or intestacy but because the remainder was given by the settlement to those falling within the class, s. 673 did apply.[64] S. 660A will, as such, also apply.
(c) The possibility that the property will come back to S's estate after death and not during S's lifetime is too remote.[65]
(d) The mere fact that there is some doubt about the validity of the trust does not cause the section to apply.[66] Eventually the doubt would be resolved one way or another and then

[57] [1949] 1 All ER 865, (1949) 31 TC 158.

[58] Ibid., 868, 169, *per* Lord Simonds.

[59] By analogy with *IRC* v. *Payne* (1940) 23 TC 610. Cf. *Chamberlain* v. *IRC* [1943] 2 All ER 200, (1943) 25 TC 317.

[60] This provision also stated that S retained an interest if, "in any circumstances whatsoever, any income or property which may at any time arise under or be comprised in that settlement is, or will or may become, payable to or applicable for the benefit of [S] or [the spouse] of [S]".

[61] [1949] 1 All ER 1108, (1949) 31 TC 1.

[62] *Fitzwilliam* v. *IRC* [1993] STC 502, 516, *per* Lord Keith, on an analogous provision.

[63] [1966] 1 All ER 295, 305, (1966) 43 TC 367, 381.

[64] *Barr's Trustees* v. *IRC* (1943) 25 TC 72.

[65] *IRC* v. *Gaunt* [1941] 2 All ER 82, (1941) 24 TC 69. It is unclear whether S's spouse must also predecease the return of the asset to his estate; since the spouse will benefit, if at all, only through S's generosity in leaving her an interest in his estate, it seems that the section should not apply.

[66] *Muir* v. *IRC* [1949] 1 All ER 1108, (1949) 31 TC 1; *Barr's Trustees* v. *IRC* (1943) 25 TC 72.

the issue could be determined. Unfortunately, this could have caused a problem for the Revenue since by the time the doubt was resolved it might be too late to make an assessment. Under the self-assessment regime this problem is shifted to taxpayers. A different problem might arise under the wait-and-see rule for perpetuities since the validity of the remainder will not be resolved until some future date. It is presumed that the statutory direction[67] that the gift will fail only when it becomes clear that vesting cannot occur within the perpetuity period, and that the gift is to be treated as valid until that time, is effective for tax purposes, thus excluding s. 673.

(e) The possibility that S may derive some incidental benefit in the course of a commercial transaction should be ignored.[68] This gives rise to many difficulties, not the least of which is distinguishing circumstances where the benefit of the interest is incidental to the commercial transaction of the loan from those where the commercial rate of interest is incidental to the benefit of obtaining a loan.

(f) Presumably, the possibility of subsequent legislation or the migration of the trust to a country which would regard the trust (or part of it) as invalid should be ignored.[69]

The Revenue originally took the view that S retained an interest if the trustees could, or had the power to, pay the CTT (now IHT) due on the transfer since the property in the settlement could be used to meet a liability that was S's—even though jointly with the trustees. This view was later abandoned.[70]

Statutory limits—when is a spouse not a spouse?

The new rules state that a "spouse" of the settlor does not include: (a) a person to whom S is not for the time being married but may later marry; or (b) a spouse from whom S is separated under an order of a court, or under a separation agreement or in such circumstances that the separation is likely to be permanent; or (c) S's widow or widower.[71] Of these, (a) is an enactment of previous Revenue practice; (b) is a recognition of the fact that the marriage is at an end; and (c) is in line with earlier case-law, since an ex-spouse is not a spouse.[72]

Inter-spousal gifts

The new general rule as stated in TA 1988, s. 660A(1) would deprive gifts between spouses of any effect for income tax. Not wishing to inhibit such generosity, but anxious to prevent the undue exploitation of the separate taxation of spouses, the legislation directs that an outright gift of property by one spouse to the other will not be treated as a settlement unless either (a) the gift does not carry a right to the whole of that income, or (b) the property is wholly or substantially a right to income.[73] A gift is stated not to be an outright gift if it is subject to conditions, or if the property given or any derived property is or will or may become, in any circumstances whatsoever, payable to or applicable for the benefit of the

[67] Perpetuities and Accumulations Act 1964, s. 3(1).

[68] See *Wachtel* v. *IRC* [1971] 1 All ER 271, 280, (1971) 46 TC 367, 381; see Burgess [1971] *BTR* 278 and note Lord Morton in *Lord Vestey's Executors* v. *IRC* (1949) 31 TC 1, 114, who said that while a loan at a commercial rate of interest might benefit a person by tiding him over a difficult period, it was not money lent "for the benefit of" the debtor within TA 1970, s. 447.

[69] *Quaere* whether the trust contained an express power to migrate to a country with such a rule.

[70] Statement of Practice SP 1/82 (for years 1981–1982 *et seq.*).

[71] TA 1988, s. 660A(3).

[72] Statement of Practice SP A30; severely restricting *IRC* v. *Tennant* (1942) 24 TC 215. Point (c) comes from *Lord Vestey's Executors* v. *IRC* [1949] 1 All ER 1108, (1949) 31 TC 1.

[73] TA 1988, s. 660A(6).

donor.[74] Also outside s. 660A is an irrevocable allocation of pension rights by one spouse to the other in accordance with the terms of a relevant statutory scheme[75] (see further above at §8.2).

Payments on family breakdown are also outside these provisions. More formally, s. 660A(1) does not apply to income arising: under a settlement made by one party to a marriage by way of provision for the other after the dissolution or annulment of the marriage, or while they are separated under an order of a court; under a separation agreement; or in such circumstances that the separation is likely to be permanent.[76] This applies only to the extent that the income arising is payable to or applicable for the benefit of that other party.

Gifts to charity FA 2000

(See also Chapter 53.) Thanks to FA 2000 new rules allow a trust to make gifts to charity without triggering any liability under the provisions discussed in this chapter.[77] The new rules apply to "qualifying income" accruing to the trust after 5 April 2000; income qualifies if it is to be accumulated, is payable at the discretion of the trustees or any other person (whether or not there is a power to accumulate) or which before being distributed belongs to any person other than the trustees. The former phrase covers discretionary trusts, the latter interest in possession trusts; in the former case the charity is an object of the discretion and in the latter it is entitled to income under the terms of the trust. The trustees must be resident in the UK and this condition must be satisfied when the income arises.

The effect of the new rules is that the rules in this chapter are excluded if the income belongs to the charity under the trust or is given by the trustees to the charity during the year. However, this does not mean that there are no income tax issues. What it means is that the qualifying income is treated as that of the trust as opposed to the settlor. This opens the way for the liability of the trustee and beneficiary to be determined in the normal way under the rules in chapter 29.

If the trust is bare trust, the rules in the present chapter do not apply anyway; any gift by the trust in these circumstances is treated as a gift by the individual beneficiary under the normal gift aid rules.

Where the trust is an interest in possession trust and the charity is entitled to the income, the trustees pay the income tax in the usual way qua trustees and then hand the sum net of tax income to the charity. The charity can then reclaim the tax already paid by the trustee under the rule in chapter 29—and so not if the source is a dividend.

Where the trust is not an interest in possession trust but e.g. a discretionary trust, the trustee will have to settle the trust liability under s. 686 (at 34%). So if the trust income is £1,000 the trustees will have £660 to pay to the charity and the charity will recover £340 from the Revenue in respect of the credit arising under s. 687.

A source problem arises if the qualifying income given away to charity is less than the income arising. Where this occurs the charity's income is drawn rateably from the different types of income e.g. dividend income taxed at 10%, savings income at 20% and rental income taxed at 22%.[78] Naturally this yields to any express provision in the settlement. It will be interesting to see whether it will become normal practice to include clauses

[74] Ibid., s. 660A(6).

[75] Ibid., s. 660A(7). This is due to be repealed for 2001–2002 and later years and replaced by the wider s. 660(A)(9)(c).

[76] Ibid., s.660A(8).

[77] FA 2000, s. 44(1).

[78] Ibid., s. 44(2).

directing where charitable payments should be made from—and how quickly the fiscal assumptions underlying those clauses will change.[79] S. 44(3) simply refers to a "requirement" that a particular source be used.

Relief is to be given for management expenses to the extent that the gift to charity is treated as coming from qualifying income.[80] Suppose that a charitable interest-in-possession trust, from which the settlor is not entirely excluded, has £1,000 of qualifying savings income and £100 of management expenses so that £900 is left over. The trustees pay £200 in income tax, leaving them with £700. If they give £350 to charity the charity will be able to reclaim £100 from the Revenue, i.e. will be able to reclaim the credit not only on the £350 received but also on the £50 spent on management expenses.

Loans

FA 2000 also contains rules excluding the rules in this chapter where an individual makes interest free, or low interest, loans of money to a charity. The FA 2000 rules, which are self standing and not interpolated into s. 660A, apply to all income arising on or after 6 April 2000; this means that they apply whether the loan was made before, on or after 6 April 2000.[81]

But for the new rule, s. 660A would apply to the income from such a loan since the loan capital will come back to the settlor, i.e. the lender, when the loan is repaid. It appears that not only had charities found ways round this problem but the Inland Revenue had been generous (or lax) in deciding whether or not to apply the letter of s. 660A to such loans. The purpose of the change is to encourage the making of such loans.

Pension funds

FA 2000 also provides that as from 2001–02 benefits under any approved pension scheme are not income to which s. 660A can apply (TA 1988, s. 660(9)(c)).

Permitted interests

Certain types of interest may be retained by S without causing a charge under TA 1988, s. 660A(1), which are not quite identical to the old exceptions.

No charge arises if S only has rights or a hope in the event of: (a) the bankruptcy of someone who is or may become beneficially entitled to the property or any derived property; or (b) an assignment of or charge on the property or any derived property being made or given by some such person; or (c) in the case of a marriage settlement, the death of both the parties to the marriage and of all or any of the children of the marriage; or (d) the death at any age of a child of S who had become beneficially entitled to the property or any derived property at any age not exceeding 25.[82] It will be seen that (d) refers to death at any age, whereas the earlier law had referred to death under 25.

It will be seen that these conditions are alternatives, so that s. 660A is avoided if any one of them is satisfied. However, the legislation goes on to say that s. 660A is also avoided if and so long as some person is alive and under the age of 25 during whose life that property, or any derived property, cannot become payable or applicable as mentioned in that subsection

[79] FA 2000, s. 44(3).
[80] Ibid., s. 44(4).
[81] Ibid., s. 45.
[82] TA 1988, s. 660A(4).

except in the event of that person becoming bankrupt or assigning or charging his interest in the property or any derived property.[83]

The difference between the first group of provisions and the longer provision is that the four events listed in the first paragraph above are alternatives, but those in the second paragraph are not. Thus, a settlement on trust to accumulate the income until X reaches the age of 25 and then for X for life determinable on X's bankruptcy and then to revert to the settlor, will not satisfy the conditions in the first paragraph, but will satisfy the conditions in the second. Had the accumulations been directed to end at 28, not 25, the accumulated income would have been treated as that of the settlor only in the years after X reached 25.

Effects of charge

The tax due from S is charged under Schedule D, Case VI.[84] The deductions and reliefs allowed are the same as would have been allowed if the income had actually been received by S,[85] and the income is deemed to be the highest part of S's income.[86]

S is given a right of indemnity for the amount of the tax paid against any trustee, or any other person to whom the income is payable by virtue or in consequence of the settlement.[87] S may obtain a certificate with relevant details from the Revenue. Nothing in these rules excludes a charge to tax on the trustees as persons by whom any income is received.[88]

S can make a claim for any personal reliefs that would otherwise be unused; any repayment of a sum which could not have been claimed back had the trust income not been deemed to be S's must be handed over to the trust.[89]

Example

Suppose that Simon, a settlor, has personal allowances of £4,385, but that his income is only £2,000. In 2000–01 the trustees receive income of £6,000 gross which is required to be treated as that of S. The trustees will pay tax at 22% on £6,000 = £1,320. Under these rules S's total income is now £2,000 + £6,000 = £8,000. Deducting personal allowances of £4,385 leaves him with taxable income of £3,615. So tax is due from him at 10% on £1,520 and 22% on £2,095 = £612.90. He can recover from the Revenue the tax already paid by the trustees on all the income which is deemed to be his. The correct tax is £612.90 so he recovers £1,320 – £612.90 (i.e. £707.10), which he must pay over to the trustees.

Although S will, usually, have a marginal rate higher than that of the beneficiary, it may happen that the reverse is the case and, in that event, TA 1988, s. 660A, which treats the income as S's, may actually reduce the amount of tax otherwise payable. However, there are limits. In *Becker* v. *Wright*[90] the payee was resident in the UK but her father-in-law, the payer, was resident in Trinidad. A covenant was to last only three years and the payee's husband was assessed to tax under Schedule D, Case V. He argued that the effect of s. 660 was to deem the income to belong to the payer (i.e. the payee's father in law "for all the purposes of the Income Tax Acts") and so was not his. Stamp J., however, held that this would mean

[83] Ibid., s. 660A(5).
[84] Ibid., s. 660C(1).
[85] Ibid., s. 660C(2).
[86] Ibid., s. 660C(3).
[87] Ibid., s. 660D(1).
[88] Ibid., s. 660D(3).
[89] Ibid., s. 660D(2).
[90] [1966] 1 All ER 565, (1966) 42 TC 591.

a charge on income of a non-resident arising outside the UK, which was contrary to the general principles of the UK tax system.

31.4.3 Income arising under an accumulation settlement—parental settlements on unmarried minor children[91]

The UK income tax system does not aggregate the income of a child with that of the parent. Since 1936 an exception has been made to prevent income splitting when the income is derived from the parent. Such income is attributed to the parent, but only provided the child is unmarried and under the age of majority, i.e. 18, so that income arising in favour of adult children escapes this rule.[92]

The rule contained in TA 1988, s. 660B is that any income arising under a settlement as previously defined, and which does not fall within the general rule in s. 660A, but which is paid during the life of the settlor to or for the benefit of S's unmarried minor child, is treated as that of S.[93] There is a *de minimis* exception of £100 from all sources within s. 660B (both, i.e. income distributed, which is caught, and income accumulated which does not cause a charge).[94] The rule applies whenever the settlement was made—whether before or after 1995.

The definition of settlement includes a transfer of assets; s. 660B therefore catches payments even though the settlor does not retain an interest. So an outright gift of money by a father where money was paid into a savings bank account was held to be a settlement.[95] It is important to remember that in such circumstances it is only the income derived from the gift which is treated as the father's income, not the sum given by him.

S. 660B also applies whether the income arises under an ordinary trust or a bare trust.[96] Before FA 1999 the rule did not apply where income arose under a bare trust created by the parent for the child, i.e. where the capital and income were held on trust for the child absolutely, and the income arising was simply retained by the trustee, i.e. not formally accumulated.[97] S. 660B would have applied if the income had been paid out while the child was under 18 but not if it had been simply stored.[98]

"Child" is defined as "including a stepchild and an illegitimate child".[99] The 1995 definition, unlike its predecessor, does not mention an adopted child, presumably because an adopted child is to be treated as the child of the adoptive parents.[100] Whether this includes a foster child remains to be seen, although this seems unlikely since the two examples in the statutory definition are precise legal relationships. If payments are made to or for a child who has, since the date of the settlement, been adopted by someone else, the correct construction of s. 660B would suggest that the beneficiary must be a child of the settlor in the year of assessment; being a child of the settlor at the date of the settlement is not enough.

91 See Kerridge 110 *LQR* 84, 97 *et seq.*

92 TA 1988, s. 660B(6)(b).

93 Ibid., s. 660B(1); references to payments include payments in money or money's worth (s. 660B(6)(c)).

94 Ibid., s. 660B(5), as amended by FA 1999, s. 64(1); pre-1999 trusts remain subject to the old rule: see s. 64(5).

95 *Thomas* v. *Marshall* [1953] 1 All ER 1102, (1953) 34 TC 178.

96 TA 1988, s. 660B(1)(b), added by FA 1999, s. 64; Inland Revenue Press Release, 9 March 1999, (1999) *Simon's Weekly Tax Intelligence* 459.

97 This applies to settlements made or on or after 9 March 1999 and for income arising from property added on or after that date (FA 1999, s. 64 (5)); apportionments are to be made on a just and reasonable basis.

98 See Miller [1999] *BTR* 350.

99 TA 1988, s. 660B(6)(a).

100 Adoption Act 1976, s. 39.

Where a settlor is assessable to tax under s. 660B, any tax paid by the trustees at the rate applicable to trusts in respect of income distributed is available to the settlor as a credit.[101] By concession, this extends to non-resident trusts.[102]

Accumulations and s. 660B

No charge arises under s. 660B if income arising under a settlement is retained or accumulated by the trustees. Similarly, no charge arises if income has not been retained or accumulated and a capital payment is made.[103] However, once income has been retained or accumulated, any subsequent payment made by virtue or in consequence of the settlement (or any relevant enactment) to or for the benefit of an unmarried minor child of the settlor falls within s. 660B income if or to the extent that there is available retained or accumulated income.[104]

In deciding whether there is retained or accumulated income available, it is necessary first to calculate the aggregate income which has arisen under the settlement since it was begun and then deduct four categories of payment:[105]

(1) income which has already been treated as income (whether of S or of a beneficiary);
(2) income which has been paid (whether as income or capital) to or for the benefit of a beneficiary other than an unmarried minor child of S. It will be seen that only actual payments are taken into account—and only payments out of income;
(3) income arising under a bare trust in 1995–1996 and the next two years and which has slipped through the tax net but only to the extent that the income was subject to tax (i.e. not exempt by reason of allowances to be set against total income—e.g. personal allowances).[106] The effect of this change is that where income has arisen in favour of the child before 9 March 1999 and has escaped tax at that time because of the child's personal allowances, it will be caught if it is distributed on or after that date;
(4) income properly spent on trust expenses or, more formally, income applied in defraying trust expenses of the trustees which were properly chargeable to income (or would have been so chargeable but for any express provisions of the trust). The definition of this category is the same as for s.686 (on which, see above at §29.2.4).

The legislation also makes express provision for an offshore income gain[107] accruing in respect of a disposal of assets made by a trustee holding them for a person who would be absolutely entitled as against the trustee but for being minor. In such circumstances the income treated as arising by reference to that gain is deemed to be paid to that person.[108]

The absence of the previous requirement of irrevocability is illusory since revocability will cause the settlement to fall within s. 660A.

S. 660B and pre-1999 bare trusts[109]

It should be noted that the 1999 change to the tax treatment of bare trusts does not affect existing trusts and applies only where s. 660B applies, i.e. where the settlor is the parent

[101] TA 1988, s. 687.
[102] ESC A93.
[103] S. 660B does not apply to a payment of capital.
[104] TA 1988, s. 660B(2).
[105] Ibid., s. 660B(3).
[106] Ibid., s. 660B(3)(bb), (3A) added by FA 1999, s. 64(2), (3); on commencement date, see s. 660B(6).
[107] TA 1988, s. 660B(4), i.e a gain within Part XVIII, ch. 5.
[108] The reference to income is to that arising under ibid., s. 761(1).
[109] See Miller [1999] *BTR* 350.

and not, for example, a grandparent. There are still CGT advantages to a bare trust for a minor.

31.5 Capital Sums Paid to the Settlor

31.5.1 Basics—capital sums

The text that follows outlines rules which were resurrected in the course of the 1995 Finance Bill debates. The rules have two advantages. The first is that they are tolerably well known; the second is that they are significantly better than the rules proposed in the Finance Bill. However, while these rules are well known they are still riddled with traps: "loans and repayments of loans between settlor and settlement should be avoided at all costs".[110]

If income has been accumulated and a capital sum is paid by the trustees directly or indirectly[111] to S, TA 1988, s. 677 treats that sum as S's income unless it was not paid for full consideration in money or money's worth.[112] This applies whenever there is "available income"[113] in the trust, i.e. both where accumulated income exists in the fund when the sum is paid and, subject to limits, even when the accumulation arises subsequently.

In one instance, however, even sums paid for full consideration cause a charge. If the trustees lend money to S or S's spouse there is a promise to repay—and so full consideration—and yet also the risk that the repayment terms might not be enforced, at least as long as S is alive. In this way S could create a fund which would be taxed only at trust rates and yet enjoy what was once S's own money at the same time. S. 677 therefore defines capital sum as any sum paid by way of a loan, and goes on to extend this to any sum paid (by the trustees to S or S's spouse) by way of repayment of a loan.[114]

A capital sum does not cause s. 677 to apply if it could only be payable to S in one of the events specified in ss.660A(4), (5).[115]

At first, s. 677 did not catch payments to third parties to whom S owed money.[116] However, this and other loopholes are now sealed; the term "capital" sum extends to: (1) any sum paid to S (or to S's spouse) jointly with another person; (2) any sum paid to a third party at S's direction; (3) any sum paid to a third party by virtue of the assignment by S of the right to receive it; and (4) any sum otherwise paid or applied by the trustees for the benefit of S.[117]

31.5.2 Loans and repayments

Loan

The concept of "loan" is central to TA 1988, s. 677, yet the term is not further defined. Case-law shows that the term is not confined to the common law relationship of debtor and

[110] Potter and Monroe, *Tax Planning*, §3-05.

[111] TA 1988, s. 677(1); it is unclear whether these words add anything (*IRC* v. *Wachtel* [1971] 1 All ER 271, (1971) 46 TC 543).

[112] TA 1988, s. 677(9).

[113] Defined in ibid., s. 677(2).

[114] Ibid., s. 677(9), as amended in 1995.

[115] See above at §31.4.1.

[116] *IRC* v. *Potts* [1951] 1 All ER 76, (1951) 32 TC 211.

[117] TA 1988, s. 677(10).

creditor, and applies equally where there is an equitable right to reimbursement.[118] A loan need not be in cash, and a secured loan is still a loan. A loan is a loan even though the person giving it may view the transaction as an investment.[119]

Repayment of loan as relief

Once the loan is repaid it ceases to be subject to s. 677 for the years subsequent to that in which the repayment takes place.[120] Therefore, if a loan was made in 1990–1991, was repaid in 1999–2000 and income is accumulated for the first time in 2000–2001, s. 677 will have no effect. Furthermore, if S receives a loan of £5,000 which is then repaid, and a new loan of £5,000 is taken out, S will be liable to a charge on £5,000, not £10,000

Repayment of loan as charge

S. 677 applies also where a loan by S to the trustees is repaid.[121] Analogous mitigating rules apply. Where the loan has been repaid but S then makes a further loan of an amount not less than the original loan, s. 677 does not apply.[122] This provision is curious in that it applies only where the original loan has been completely repaid; there is no proportionate relief for a partial repayment. However, while the rule requires complete repayment, this does not necessarily mean repayment in full; an agreement by S to accept a lesser sum in complete discharge of the original loan may suffice.

Fine distinctions—loans and guarantees

The capricious nature of s. 677 has caused much adverse comment, especially when innocent transactions are caught. In *De Vigier* v. *IRC*[123] trustees held property for two infant children contingently upon their attaining the age of 25, with a power to accumulate and maintain. The trustees had wished to take advantage of a rights issue by a company whose shares they held, but they had no money and no power to borrow. The trustees were S's wife and a solicitor. S's wife therefore paid £7,000 into the trust bank account to pay for the shares and, within nine months, that sum had been repaid in two equal instalments. S was held taxable on the grossed-up equivalent of £7,000 (£12,174 at that time). The sum was paid by way of repayment of a loan. The fact that her right to the repayment arose from the equitable right of an indemnity given to a trustee who incurs expenses on behalf of the trust, rather than the common law claim on a contract of loan, made no difference. Yet, had the trust had the power to borrow, and had S's wife merely guaranteed that loan, no charge would have arisen.[124] In this case an advance of money was made to the trust upon the terms that it was to be repaid out of the trust fund. This was held to be a loan.

31.5.3 The charge from income

The whole purpose of the legislation is to prevent settlors deriving benefit for themselves from property, the income of which may be taxed at a lower rate than if it were still theirs. TA 1988, s. 677 therefore applies only to the extent that the payment could have been made

[118] *De Vigier* v. *IRC* [1964] 2 All ER 907, (1964) 42 TC 24.
[119] *McCrone* v. *IRC* (1967) 44 TC 142.
[120] TA 1988, s. 677(4).
[121] See *Piratin* v. *IRC* [1981] STC 441.
[122] TA 1988, s. 677(5).
[123] [1964] 2 All ER 907, (1964) 42 TC 24.
[124] Ibid., 33, *per* Russell L.J.

from income, i.e. to the extent that the income arising under the trust since it was created,[125] is greater than the sums distributed or which, although not distributed, have already been treated as S's, together with the tax on these payments.[126] Perhaps because the payment is made to S, he is given no statutory right to be reimbursed out of the trust funds in respect of the tax; for the same reason, any repayment of tax by reason of S's personal reliefs may be retained by S.[127] These acts of apparent generosity are, however, more than offset by the fact that there is no way of refunding the tax when S, or S'estate, repays the loan.[128]

Eleven-year rule

Where the capital sum paid exceeds the undistributed income, the excess is carried forward and charged to S in the next year to the extent that there is undistributed income available up to the end of that year, and so on for succeeding years subject to a maximum of 11 years. There is no 11-year maximum to the carry-back rule where the income has been accumulated before the capital sum is paid. An allowance is made for sums already charged under s. 677.[129] Once the 11-year limit has passed it falls out of account for s. 677 but it cannot then reduce the amount of available income which may be matched against a subsequent capital payment.

The charge

The sum charged on S under Schedule D, Case VI is the undistributed income grossed up at the rate applicable to trusts (34%).[130] Credit is given for such tax as has been charged on the trust.[131] Trustees who have made payments to S, and which fall within s. 677, must therefore distribute all the trust income each year until S dies, or the 11-year period expires.

If S emigrates it would appear that, the source being within the UK, the charge to tax remains although if S has little other UK income the tax bill may be reduced.

Risks

A further problem is that the sum is treated as S's income in the year of payment notwithstanding that it may have been accumulated over many years. It is small wonder that most trusts now contain a clause making it a breach of trust to pay any capital sum to S or S's spouse. Such clauses are simply a reminder to trustees, since payments actually made can fall within s. 677 even though in breach of trust.

31.5.4 Sums from connected bodies

S. 677 applies with equal vigour to capital sums received by S from a body corporate connected with the settlement, e.g. a loan from the company.[132] A body corporate is connected with a settlement if it is at any time in the year either (a) a close company (or not a close

[125] Or since the year 1937–1938 if shorter!

[126] TA 1988, s. 677(1), (2).

[127] *Cf.* ibid., s. 677(8).

[128] *Cf.* ibid., s. 419(4); see below at §51.4.

[129] On previous law, see Lord Reid in *Bates* v. *IRC* [1967] 1 All ER 84, 90, (1967) 44 TC 225, 261.

[130] TA 1988, s. 677(6), (7).

[131] Ibid., s. 677(7).

[132] Ibid., s. 678. For reason, see Lord Reid in Bates v. *IRC* [1967] 1 All ER 84, 90, (1967) 44 TC 225, 261.

company only because it is not resident in the UK) and the participators then include the trustees of the settlement, or (b) controlled by such a company.[133]

Associated payment—five-year period

Partly because of the habit of using accumulation trusts to receive dividend income from private companies, which income was not needed by the family owners, TA 1988, s. 677 was a lethal trap whenever S considered making a loan to the company, or vice versa. In order, therefore, to limit the operation of s. 677 to those situations in which it could fairly be said that S was deriving some benefit from the accumulation, s. 678 provides that s. 677 shall apply only where there has been an "associated payment", i.e. a payment by the trustees to the company in a period of five years ending or beginning with the date on which the payment is made to S. Further, s. 677 doess not apply where the loan is repaid within 12 months and the period for which loans are outstanding in any five-year period does not exceed 12 months.

Timing

The 1995 legislation makes one minor change to the application of s. 678. By repealing s. 678(7) it has endeavoured to ensure that when a capital payment is made by the company to S, and that payment precedes the making of an associated payment from the trustees to the company, S is not taxed until that associated payment is made.[134]

31.6 Settlements of Income—Covenants and Other Annual Payments

31.6.1 General

Covenants and other obligations under which annual payments arise are clearly settlements and so potentially within these rules. TA 1988, s. 347A deprives most annuities or other annual payments by individuals of any income tax effect. Such payments are neither deductible as a charge on the income of the payer, nor income of the payee arising under Schedule D, Case III.[135] The effect of this is that since no income arises under the disposition giving rise to the legal obligation to make the payments, there is nothing for s. 660A to bite on.

However, some payments fall within Case III and are not removed by s. 347A. For these, the income arising will be treated as that of S under s. 660A, unless S can show that the income arises from property in which he has no interest, or a statutory exclusion applies.

The 1995 legislation directs that two groups of annual payments are excluded from ss 660A, etc. The first group is maintenance payments. Income does not fall within s. 660A if the settlement was made by one party to a marriage by way of provision for the other party either after the dissolution or annulment of the marriage, or while they are separated under an order of a court or under a separation agreement, or in such circumstances that

[133] TA 1988, s. 682A, added by FA 1995, Sch. 17, para. 11, but repeating the formula in the repealed TA 1988, s. 681(5). This means that whenever a trust has shares in a family company S must beware whenever he takes or makes a loan (ss 677, 419; and see below at §5.1.4).

[134] Inland Revenue Press Release, 28 March 1995, para.4, (1996) *Simon's Weekly Tax Intelligence* 549.

[135] TA 1988, s. 347A(1).

the separation is likely to be permanent. This income must be payable to or applicable for the benefit of that other party.[136]

The second group consists of annual payments made by an individual for bona fide commercial reasons in connection with his trade, profession or vocation, and, until 2000–2001, covenanted payments to charity.[137]

31.6.2 Covenanted payments to charity

A "covenanted payment to charity" is defined as a payment made under a covenant otherwise than for consideration in money or money's worth.[138] The payment must be in favour of a body of persons or trust established only for charitable purposes. In addition, the payments must be payable for a period, which may exceed three years. but must be incapable of earlier termination under any power exercisable without the consent of the persons for the time being entitled to the payments. These rules have ceased to apply as a result are not affected by the extension of gift aid relief under FA 2000 (see Chapter 53 below).

As we have seen, above §27.4.3, the 1988 rules required that the covenant should be made otherwise than for a consideration in money or money's worth.[139] The gift aid rules into which such covenants, even existing covenants, have now been moved require that neither the donor nor any person connected with him may receive a benefit in consequence of making it.[140] These rules as revised for 2000–01 provide that the benefit in consequence must not exceed 2.5% of the amount of the gift subject to a maximum of £250 (which is 2.5% of £10,000.[141] There are also new rules for annualising the value of certain benefits and donations e.g. where the right to receive benefits extends over a period of less than 12 months.[142] Like the 1988 rules before them there is also an express exclusion for the right to free admission to view property or wildlife where the preservation of property or conservation of wildlife is the sole or main purpose of the charity.[143]

31.6.3 Reverse annuities

TA 1988, s. 347A does not affect the operation of s. 125,[144] which was introduced in 1977 to deal with "reverse annuities".[145] Under s. 125, where the annuity or annual payment is made under a liability incurred for money or money's worth, not all of which is required to be brought into account in computing the income of the person making the payment, the payment is not deductible in computing total income. TA 1988, ss 348 and 349 are also excluded.

The rule applies whenever the payment is made under a liability incurred for money or money's worth. It does not therefore affect purely voluntary covenants; nor does it affect the purchase of annuities from insurance companies since the sums paid by the individual will enter into the profits of the company. There are a number of other exceptions.[146]

[136] TA 1988, s. 660A(8).
[137] Ibid., s. 660A(9). See FA 2000 s. 41.
[138] Ibid., s. 347A(7), added by FA 1995, Sch. 17, para. 4. The definition was extended to the bodies mentioned in s. 507 by s. 347A(8); for discussion, see Robson [1998] *BTR* 231.
[139] TA 1988, s. 348(7) repealed by FA 2000.
[140] FA 1990, s. 25(2)(e); on mechanics see above at §10.6.2.
[141] FA 1990, s. 25(5) and 5A.
[142] FA 1990, s. 25(5B)–(5D).
[143] FA 1990, s. 25(5E)–(5G); on earlier law see FA 1989 s. 53.
[144] TA 1988, s. 347A(2)(d).
[145] Ibid., s. 125, reversing *IRC* v. *Plummer* [1979] STC 793, [1979] 3 All ER 775 (see above at §31.2.2).
[146] TA 1988, s. 125(3).

PART III

Capital Gains Tax

32

Introduction and Policy

32.1 Outline

In the UK tax is charged on capital gains realised—or deemed to be realised—when assets are disposed of and the resulting computation shows a net gain. The key concepts are asset, disposal and gain. For individuals the rates are tied to the income tax rates for savings income—10%, 20% or 40%. The tax is complicated because practical and policy reasons make it fall short of the Haig-Simons theoretical ideal concept of income discussed in Chapter 1. In 1966 Muteen observed that the idea behind the tax was not to collect money for the fisc—that could be done more simply—but to bring more equity into the system.[1] In 1995 Muteen concluded that a CGT simple enough to be easily administered may tolerate inequities of a degree many experts would find intolerable.[2]

Using provisional figures, *Inland Revenue Statistics 1999* (chapter 14) show that in 1997–1998, 144,000 individuals paid £1.6 bn in CGT on gains of £5.47 bn, while 28,000 trusts paid £374 m in CGT on gains of 1.59 bn. While many gains are realised by individuals at the top end of the income scale, figures for 1996–1997, show that £340 m of gains were realised by those with taxable incomes below £3,900 and £660 m by those below £25,500. In 1996–1997, £4.7 bn of gains were realised, of which £3.8 bn was from financial assets, £706 m from land and buildings and £172 m from antiques, jewellery, paintings, etc.

32.2 Why Tax Capital Gains?

The main reason for taxing capital gains is that capital gains, whether or not realised, are just as much relevant to ability to pay as income liable to income tax and therefore should be

[1] [1966] *BTR* 138, 139.
[2] In Sandford (ed.), *More Key Issues in Tax Reform*, 34, 47.

taxed on grounds of equity, both vertical and horizontal.[3] Indeed for economists,[4] capital gains are just as much income as profits of a trade or a salary. Thus, an increase in wealth due to the sale of shares in a company, the increase being due to the retention and reinvestment of profits by the company, is hard to distinguish from an increase due to the receipt of a dividend. Nor, to theoreticians, is there any need for a realisation; there is an increase in wealth whether or not that increase is realised. The same is true where the increase in share value is due to the market deciding to capitalise an expected increase in company income.[5] The development of new financial instruments have made this simple truth even clearer. If capital gains were taxed as income this would avoid the problems of distinguishing between income and capital receipts[6] and reduce the erosion of the tax base through taking income benefits in capital form. However while everyone (or nearly everyone) in the world of theory agrees with such an approach, no tax system taxes capital gains in this way.[7] Some countries, including the UK, tax on a realisation basis and may even tax some accrued gains whether or not they have been realised. However, many systems which tax realised gains do not do so on the same basis as income and many tax gains only partially. There seems to be an atavistic impulse which prevents the full taxation of gains; this leads to a lack of principle, with gaps in the tax base and inconsistent changes in legislation.[8] Whether that impulse is soundly based, and whether capital gains should, in the jargon, enjoy some "preference", is still unresolved.[9] Some regard the whole idea of a CGT as flawed.[10]

32.3 Design Problems

32.3.1 Accruals or realisation[11]

Most tax systems, including that in the UK, tax gains only on a realisation basis. This means that although tax is deferred until such time as the gain is realised, by the same token no relief is given for the sum invested in the purchase of the asset until realisation. To tax accrued but unrealised gains would require annual valuations, a matter of particular diffi-

[3] The majority report of the UK Royal Commission of 1955 was against capital gains taxation—see Royal Commission on the Taxation of Profits and Income, *Final Report*, Cmnd 9474 (1955), 94–108. Their views are dissected and rejected in the Minority Report (pp. 34–84). The case for CGT is also considered (enthusiastically) in Krever and Brooks, *A Capital Gains Tax for New Zealand* (Institute of Policy Studies, Wellington, 1990), where a valuable bibliography is buried in the footnotes. A CGT was advocated for New Zealand in a consultative document issued in 1989, but not implemented. For a wide-ranging survey of US literature, see the "Report of a Colloquium on Capital Gains" 48 *Tax Law Review* 315. Among older sources, see David, A*lternative Approaches to Capital Gains Taxation* (Brookings, 1968); Report of the Royal Commission on Taxation (Ottawa, 1996) (Carter Report), Vol. 3, 325–87; Seltzer, *The Nature and Tax Treatment of Capital Gains and Losses* (New York, National Bureau of Economic Research, 1951); Simons, *Personal Income Taxation*, ch. 7; Ilersic, *The Taxation of Capital Gains* (1962); Australian Taxation Review Committee Preliminary Report, ch. 9; Australian Tax Forum, Vol. 1, Issue No 2; Blum (1957) 35 *Taxes* 247; and Kaldor, *An Expenditure Tax* (Unwin, 1955), 54–87.

[4] For example Simons, above at n. 3, 9; Miller (1950) 59 *Yale Law Jo.* 837, 1057; and Sandford, *Taxing Personal Wealth* (George Allen & Unwin, 1971), ch. 7.

[5] But see Royal Commission Minority Report, above at n. 3, §110.

[6] See especially Break, (1952) 7 *Journal of Finance* 214.

[7] For the position in OECD countries in 1990, see T*axing Profits in a Global Economy* (OCED, 1991), Table 3.4 (corporate gains) and Table 3.21 (investors in shares); and Messere, above at n. 0, 312–22.

[8] See Evans and Sandford [1999] *BTR* 387.

[9] See Cunningham and Schenk "Tax Law Review Symposium" 48 *Tax Law Review* 319, and comments by Halperin (p. 381) and Shaviro (p. 393).

[10] For a vigorous denunciation of the tax, see *A Discredited Tax: The CGT Problem and its Solution* (IEA, 1992).

[11] For an analysis in efficiency terms, see Zodrow (1993) 48 *Tax Law Review* 419, 467 *et seq.*

culty for non-financial assets.[12] Taxing accruals also raises the question whether it is desirable to compel a person to sell in order to raise the money needed to pay the tax. Further, such a system requires equitable relief for losses.

However, to tax gains only as they are realised, as is the system in the UK, gives rise to the so-called lock-in effect[13]—the taxpayer is reluctant to realise the gain for fear of the consequent tax liability, a prospect rendered even less attractive by the fact that the system may provide, as in the UK and the United States, that gains accrued but unrealised on death escape CGT altogether. The incentive to defer disposal of an asset arises because of the costs of switching investments rather than retaining them. Thus, suppose I have an asset with £100 base cost; the current value is £160. If I sell it and pay CGT of £24 (40% of the gain) I shall only have £136 to reinvest. This means that if I was getting 10% on my previous investment (£16 p.a.) I must now look for a return for 11.76% to maintain that £16 return. These figures ignore both indexation and tapering reliefs.

There are two contrary legislative solutions to this. One is to allow a deferral of tax whenever there is a change of investment. This is axiomatic under an expenditure tax (ET) and also achieved under the suggested capital disposal tax (CDT). Its adoption, using either an ET or a CDT, would drive a big wedge between the treatment of capital gains and ordinary income. An alternative solution is sporadically to direct deemed realisations—particularly on death.

32.3.2 Losses

The issue of losses probably most restrains tax designers. Full adoption of a CGT should mean full relief for losses—including not only setting capital losses off against ordinary income but even rolling losses back.[14] Under an ET (below §32.5) or a CDT (below §32.6) this problem would not arise since relief for the purchase price will have been given earlier.

32.3.3 Inflation

To make no allowance and so simply to tax on a paper gain is to turn CGT into a form of wealth tax,[15] and to provide a further disincentive to investment or saving. It also gives government a vested interest in inflation. Yet to make an allowance for inflation in CGT while making no such allowance for those living on fixed incomes is to create an inequity.[16] One answer is to align the rate of tax on capital gains with that on income, as is now done in the UK. The raising of the income tax threshold in approximate line with inflation may then be seen as a sufficient protection for those living on fixed incomes and those living on capital gains. The UK was, comparatively, very generous in granting both a large annual exemption and indexation relief.

[12] See Sandford, Willis and Ironside, *Wealth Tax* (Heinemann, 1975), ch. 10. The taxation of unrealised gains was dismissed as "incapable of satisfactory solution" by the Carter Report, above at n. 3, Vol. 3, 50. Today an accruals basis of taxation is used in the UK for foreign exchange transactions and various financial instruments, but only for corporation tax and for certain assets held by insurance companies (TCGA 1992, s. 212). An accruals basis is also used in New Zealand for many financial assets.

[13] A variant form of lock-in arises if the rate of tax fluctuates—as where a part of the gain is treated as income.

[14] As was done in the United States until the 1930s; see Ilersic, above at n. 3.

[15] See Sandford, above at n. 4, 238–40; Royal Commission Canada Study 19, 73–82. On computation issues, see Morley, *Fiscal Implications of Inflation Accounting* (IFS, 1974), 24–7.

[16] Ilersic, above at n. 3, 22–5.

If inflation is taken into account, various techniques are available. One would be simply to raise the acquisition and allowable deductions each year by a certain amount—the solution adopted in the UK from 1982–1998 for CGT and still in place for corporation tax.[17] Another technique would be to lower the rate of tax according to the number of years over which the asset had been held.[18] This is now done in the UK, but only in part, through the tapering relief for years after 1998.

32.3.4 Attribution to a particular year

One of the objections to a CGT is the inherent unfairness of taxing very occasional gains as income of one year, a matter of greater moment in the 1960s and 1970s when the rates of income tax were more progressive than now. Systems with a general averaging scheme can integrate the gains tax with the income tax by treating the whole or part of the gains as income.[19]

32.3.5 Private residence

Typical of the holes in the tax base for CGT is the exemption for residences (see below §34.7). This exemption is very expensive and must be seen primarily as a political decision.[20] There are no technical reasons for the exemption, which could be viewed as further encouragement for individuals to invest their wealth into that privileged asset, the family home. Until 1998 the United States used a rollover rule which allowed owners to postpone their liability to tax until death or until they bought a lower cost house combined with a limited exemption ($125,000) for people over 55.[21] In 1997 the United States moved to a cash limited exemption of $500,000 for joint filers.[22]

32.4 Criticisms of a CGT[23]

32.4.1 Economic risks

A CGT is not necessarily free of economic risks. It might, in the absence of generous rollover relief, reduce saving.[24] This is of concern in the corporate sector where such an effect would run counter to the policy of encouraging firms to retain profits to finance investment. This, however, raises issues not only of the relationship between the taxation of company profits

[17] On complicated calculation where many different items of expenditure have occurred, e.g. in assembling a holding of shares in a company at different times and at different prices, see Chapter 41 below.

[18] See Sandford, above at n. 4, 240.

[19] In the UK between 1962 and 1971 gains realised within six months (subsequently one year) were treated as income under Schedule D, Case VII.

[20] See McGregor (1973) 21 *Can. Tax Jo.* 116; Clayton (1974) 22 *Can. Tax Jo.* 295, Ilersic, above at n. 3, 44; the rule is defended by Willis and Hardwick, *Tax Expenditure in the United Kingdom* (1978), 49–51.

[21] IRC sx 1031 (the rollover) and 121 (for the over-55s); see Bittker op cit. sx.44.5

[22] Non-joint filers were allowed $250,000; the exemption was not meant to be used more than once very two years: Auten and Seschovsky (1997) *National Tax Journal Conference Proceedings* 223; Carter Report, above at n. 3, Vol. 3, 358 recommended an exemption for gains up to a limit ($25,000) but the Act simply exempted them.

[23] See, e.g. *A Discredited Tax: The CGT Problem and its Solution* (IEA, 1992) and below n. 36.

[24] *Quaere* whether this has led to the huge increase in the percentage of saving channelled through privileged savings media. For an analysis, see Zodrow (1993) 48 *Tax Law Review* 419, 469 *et seq.*

and the taxation of dividends, but also the use by the Government of capital allowances and investment grants. Further, a CGT may discourage risky investments.[25] These fears do not appear to have been borne out[26] and, in any case, must be set against the distortions which result from a system which exempts capital gains completely. The extent to which CGT has assisted in raising the cost of capital since 1965 is uncertain.

32.4.2 *Yield*

The yield from CGT is not substantial,[27] and may fluctuate unpredictably; the legislation is necessarily complicated, and the extent of avoidance and evasion is uncertain.[28] Compliance costs incurred by taxpayers[29] and the cost to the Revenue are not negligible. The UK tax, with its exclusion of pre-1982 gains realised after March 1988, its generous annual exemption and its many other exemptions, whether on grounds of practicality (such as chattels disposed of for less than £6,000) or expediency (such as gambling winnings and the principal private residence) shows all the characteristics of the compromise needed to provide a tax that is politically acceptable while being neither too inequitable nor too unworkable. It may be concluded that the present position reflects the view that the justification for a CGT is simply that the inequities of having one are less than the inequities of not having one.[30]

32.4.3 *Other countries*

The treatment of business assets and corporate gains raises other issues. A 1991 survey of corporate capital gains rules showed that of the 24 OECD countries, only New Zealand and Denmark exempted these receipts.[31] Most countries taxed such gains at the normal corporate rate, but many did so only if they were recognised in the balance sheet for the business at end of the year. Belgium, France, Greece and Ireland provided some special rates (of which only Ireland gave relief for inflation). There were adjustments for inflation in only five countries—Australia, Iceland, Ireland, Portugal (but only for depreciable assets and land) and the UK. Tax was deferred if reinvested in 13 countries (including the UK).[32] It remains to be seen whether competitive pressures or EU harmonisation will erode the UK's position.

[25] On risk, see Bankman and Griffith (1992) 47 *Tax Law Review* 377; (1992) 48 *Tax Law Review* 163; Zodrow, above at n. 24, 478 suggests that a cut in the CGT rate would make business people less risk-averse.

[26] "The taxation of property gains has had very little effect on the level of investment in the United States": Carter Report, above at n. 3, vol. 3, 339 and Vol. 6, ch. 37; but contrast Wallich (1965) 18 *National Tax Jo.* 133, 437; see Blum, (1965) 18 *National Tax Jo.* 430: Zodrow, above at n. 24, 466, notes the decline in the importance of the individual as a source on investment funds.

[27] The yield from income tax may increase since it is no longer worth converting income into capital.

[28] Substantial avoidance was checked by *Ramsay* v. *IRC* [1982] AC 300, [1981] STC 174, (1981) 54 TC 101 (see above at §5.6.4) and various pieces of legislation, especially TCGA 1992, ss 30, 137.

[29] See, generally, Sandford, *Hidden Costs and Tax Compliance Costs* (Fiscal Publications, 1995), ch. 7.

[30] Sandford, above at n. 4, 24.

[31] For a more modern analysis of five countries, see Evans and Sandford [1999] *BTR* 387.

[32] *Taxing Profits in a Global Economy* (OECD, 1991), Table 3.4.

32.5 Capital Gains and an Expenditure Tax

Although part of the attraction of an expenditure tax (ET) is the proper and consistent treatment of capital expenditure and receipts, the Meade Committee thought it necessary to retain a CGT for some assets.[33] Under its main proposals the purchase price of a registered asset would be a deductible expense in the year of purchase, and the proceeds would be a taxable receipt in the year of receipt. There would thus be no difference in the tax treatment of the proceeds of the asset and the income from it. Conversely sums spent on an unregistered asset would be ignored—as would the proceeds on disposal. The Committee classified most durable goods used for personal consumption, e.g. clothes and furniture, as unregistered assets. Problems would arise, however, if potentially valuable assets, for example a painting by Rembrandt, could be treated as being unregistered assets. The Committee therefore favoured the retention of a CGT for such assets, such a tax being properly indexed and containing generous rollover provisions.

32.6 Capital Disposals Tax

Under a capital disposals tax (CDT) tax would be levied on the difference between the amount received on the disposal of qualifying assets (broadly the same assets as are now subject to CGT) and the amount spent on the acquisition of such assets in each tax year. The similarity to the expenditure tax is obvious, i.e. tax would be payable on the amount by which dissaving exceeds saving in any one year. CDT reduces the fiscal discrimination between savings in different forms and financed in different ways. For example, under CDT it makes no difference whether a given investment is reinvestment or is financed out of income. Since tax crystallises only when the disposal proceeds are spent, there is no lock-in problem and there would be no tax discrimination in switching investments. Finally, by abandoning the matching concept, CDT eliminates many of the complexities of CGT at a stroke—complex indexation provisions become superfluous, as do rules for matching share transactions, part disposals and so forth.[34]

32.7 Brief History of CGT

Not one year has gone by without some tinkering or more drastic reform of CGT. What follows is a brief outline of the key dates.

1965–1970: CGT is and always has been a highly political tax. It was introduced into the UK by the Labour Government in 1965 as tax separate from income tax and with its top rate at 30%. Before then a number of capital receipts had been drawn into the income tax net, e.g. premiums on leases and certain bond washing proceeds. In 1962 a more general tax on capital gains was introduced by the Conservative Government in partial response to a boom in land and share prices but only for short-term gains (short term initially meant six

[33] At 179–80.

[34] IFS Commentary No. 8, *Reforming Capital Gains Tax*, §1.24.

months, but this was extended to 12 months in 1965). The short-term tax took the form of Schedule D, Case VII and, naturally, charged income tax rates. Case VII continued in 1965 alongside the CGT which was charged at much lower rates—for most taxpayers. The 1965 Act was in some ways a purist's dream, with countless deemed disposals (especially for settled property) and a pure system for taxing gains on death, under which death gave rise to a disposal at market value by the deceased. Unfortunately, the Act was not well drafted.

1970–1974: The return of the Conservative Government in 1970 meant extensive revision of the legislation. The deemed disposal on death was replaced by the present rule under which there is an acquisition by the personal representatives at market value but no disposal by the deceased. This meant that estate duty (later to be superseded by CTT and IHT) became the sole tax on death, and the concept of charging all gains during an individual's lifetime was dropped. Other changes included the abolition of Schedule D, Case VII and several of the deemed disposals for settled property.

1974–1979: Under another Labour Government various experiments were tried out in relation to the tax threshold. Anti-avoidance provisions were introduced, the most spectacular of which dealt with the facts of *Ramsay* before that case reached the courts (now TCGA 1992, s. 30).

1979–1997: This was a period of Conservative Government. The two most notable dates were 1982, which saw the introduction of indexation relief for inflation (but only for periods after 1982, so requiring much valuation of assets by reference to 1982) and 1988, when the rate of CGT was aligned with that of income tax by treating the gain as being the top slice of income. This increase in the effective rate of tax from 30% to 40% was offset by the removal of any, still unrealised, pre-1982 gains from any liability to CGT. Reliefs were introduced or expanded, e.g. reinvestment relief (1993), but there were also many anti-avoidance provisions.

1997: This year saw the advent of a Labour Government committed to reducing short term-ism. As part of this drive, so-called tapering relief replaced indexation relief but only for periods after March 1998. Tapering relief is a common feature of other systems, but most such systems allow the taper to continue until no charge is levied once an asset has been held for more than a certain number of years. Spain moved away from this taper system to the system the UK was abandoning. Other changes have included the phasing-out of retirement relief and the abolition of the reinvestment relief. In 1999 the rate structure was changed yet again and the UK had only two rates of CGT for individuals—20% and 40%—by analogy with income from savings. FA 2000 made the 10% rate available for capital gains, but did not back date it.[35] Over the years, the gap between corporate taxation of gain and CGT has widened. Typical of this is the fact that tapering relief was not applied to corporate gains in 1998 and has not been extended to them since.

The future of CGT is unclear. It is a major problem for certain types of taxpayer, but the combination of the annual exempt amount with indexation and tapering reliefs means that there is not a very large constituency of voters demanding reliefs. There is probably little political will to make further substantial structural changes following the unpopularity of tapering relief.

It is surely significant that the Inland Revenue's June 2000 Consultation Document on allowing companies subject to corporation tax to defer liability arising on the disposal of substantial shareholdings if the proceeds are reinvested in appropriate companies or assets

[35] FA 2000 s. 37.

begins its explanation in terms of the world economy. Similarly a recent Canadian Study,[36] while making many interesting theoretical points in favour of a tax preference for capital gains, also emphasises the need to be competitive with the United Stataes, which also has a large tax preference for capital gains.

[36] Mintz, CD Howe Institute Commentary No. 137, February 2000 (available on www.cdhowe.org.)

33

Structure and Elements

33.1 Legislation

CGT is paid by individuals, partners, trusts and estates. The CGT legislation was first introduced in 1965, and was then consolidated in the Capital Gains Tax Act 1979. Because companies pay corporation tax on their capital gains rather than CGT, certain parts of the legislation dealing with companies formed part of TA 1970 and so also of the next consolidation of income and corporation taxes in 1988. These parts were united with the rest of the capital gains legislation in the 1992 consolidation; because it covers both CGT and corporation tax the Act is entitled the Taxation of Chargeable Gains Act 1992 (TCGA 1992).

33.1.1 Concessions

The CGT legislation is backed up by the usual array of concessions, statements of practice, Revenue interpretations and a very detailed Inland Revenue *Manual.* These informal arrangements sometimes allow taxpayers to defer a charge. Naturally, the Revenue assumes that the taxpayer will declare and pay the deferred tax in due course, but the fact that the deferral was given on the basis of a concession rather than strict law meant that there was often no legal obligation on the taxpayer to do so. It says much for UK taxpayers that most made their proper returns in due course. However, some did not and so rules provide that, where a person has taken advantage of such a concession, there is now a legal obligation to pay the deferred tax in due course; a charge is imposed on the amount of the gain relieved for the earlier period. The charge is a reserve power in that it is imposed only if the taxpayer fails to observe the terms of the concession. The charge cannot be for less than the gain deferred by way of concession; it is unclear whether, due to the tapering relief rules, it may sometimes be for more.[1]

33.1.2 Interpretation

The capital gains legislation is interpreted in much the same way as other tax legislation; a number of the leading avoidance cases have been CGT cases. However, CGT is still a relatively new tax and the courts have not yet decided whether "gain" is to develop the same degree of nuance as the term "income", which has quite clearly developed a meaning of its own. While the courts have mixed imaginative constructions in cases like *Marren* v. *Ingles*[2] and principled arguments rooted in a clear view of the structure of the Act in cases like *Kirby* v. *Thorn EMI*,[3] they have also given us the notorious case of *Smith* v. *Schofield*[4] where the judges were sharply divided over whether the word "gain" took its meaning from its context or whether it has a meaning independent of the context, the latter view prevailing in the House of Lords.

In *Aberdeen Construction Group* v. *IRC*[5] Lord Wilberforce stated that any interpretation of the statutory provisons must have a "guiding principle", and that the purpose of the legislation is to tax capital gains and make allowance for capital losses "each of which ought to be arrived at on normal business principles. To paraphrase a famous cliché, the capital gains tax is a tax upon gains: it is not a tax upon arithmetical differences ". Insofar as this statement is intended to mean that a court should hesitate before accepting results which are paradoxical and contrary to business sense (as Lord Wilberforce also stated), the statement is welcome, but courts have not always heeded this advice.

33.1.3 Scheme of the Act

The scheme of the CGT legislation is that for there to be a charge to tax there must be: (a) a "disposal"—of a type relevant to CGT (which may be real or deemed); (b) of an "asset" of a type relevant to CGT; (c) by a person chargeable to the tax; on which (d) a chargeable gain computed under the Act arises. As is clear from (d), only "chargeable" gains are subject to tax. Tax is charged on chargeable gains accruing to (i.e. realised by) a person, other than a company, during a year of assessment.[6] The Act does not specify how a gain should be computed but simply directs that one must first determine the consideration, i.e. the value received from the disposal, whether real or market value, of the asset and then deduct the allowable costs associated with the asset. This can encourage judges to see CGT as a simple

[1] TCGA 1992, ss 284A, 284B added by FA 1999, s. 76; see Shipwright [1999] *BTR* 357; see also Inland Revenue Bulletin No. 43 and *CGT Manual*, paras 13650–62.

[2] [1980] 1 WLR 93, [1980] STC 500, (1980) 54 TC 76.

[3] [1987] STC 621, (1987) 60 TC 519, CA.

[4] 65 TC 669. Here Charles Potter Q.C. and a unanimous Court of Appeal ([1992] STC 249) disagreed with Hoffman J. ([1990] STC 602) and a unanimous House of Lords ([1993] STC 268 [1993] 1 WLR 398).

[5] [1978] AC 885, 893, [1978] STC 127, 131, (1978) 52 TC 281, 296F.

[6] TCGA 1992, s. 1.

tax on arithmetic differences rather than one with its own principles.[7] The allowable costs may, in turn, attract an indexation allowance or the gain may attract tapering relief. Accountancy practice has nothing to contribute in identifying what is a "disposal" and, unfortunately, little to say when measuring the sum charged. The rules contained in the legislation can be far removed from sums which could be identified as a gain in constructing financial accounts.

33.1.4 CGT and income tax

CGT is a tax separate from income tax, although a number of the machinery provisions relating to assessments, appeals, etc. are common. Any gain liable to income tax is excluded from CGT.[8] Losses available for set-off against income are not allowable losses for CGT, although some relief has been provided for trading losses to be set against capital gains.[9] Conversely, an excess of capital losses cannot be set off against income liable to income tax. Further, deductions that are or would be allowable for income tax are not generally allowable for CGT.[10]

Although sound theory would try to reduce the differences between the taxation of ordinary income and that of capital gains, the UK tax system still contains many substantial differences in addition to those described above. Whereas income tax requires that income should have arisen from a source within the Schedular system, CGT requires the presence of a particular asset; whereas income tax requires a receipt or accrual, CGT requires a disposal; income tax has nothing equivalent to the indexation and tapering reliefs which are part of CGT; the income tax personal reliefs have at best a distant counterpart in the annual exempt amount; exemption of particular items from income tax or CGT sometimes overlap but usually diverge; finally, the rules on international scope are much wider for income tax than for CGT, since a non-resident is rarely subject to CGT but is potentially liable to income tax on income from any UK source. These differences usually stem from the fact that the UK's CGT is little more than a pragmatically constrained tax bolted on to the income tax system to catch gains from particular assets.

Rates of income tax and CGT are usually the same in that the same rate structure is used, but with the capital gains added to the top slice of income (see below at §33.3). However there are some situations in which the CGT rate is higher than the income tax rate. These are: (a) where a gain arises in the course of administration of an estate (capital gains are charged at 34%, whereas income is charged at 22%); (b) on a capital distribution from a foreign trust where the supplementary charge means a top rate of 64% as opposed to the top income tax charge of 40%; and (c) where the effect of the tax credit accompanying a dividend can lower the effective rate of tax in contrast with a capital transaction where no credit is available.

Much tax legislation is premised on a wish to prevent people converting income into capital gains. In view of the many differences which have now arisen there are frequently situations in which it is better to come within income tax than within CGT. The CGT legislation has not yet countered such planning devices. This may be sound policy, but it reinforces the view of CGT as a device designed primarily to protect the income tax base.

[7] However, the arithmetical differences must relate to the particular assets in issue (*Whittles* v. *Uniholdings (No. 3)* [1996] STC 914, 924, *per* Nourse L.J.).

[8] TCGA 1992, s. 37.

[9] FA 1991, s. 72. See below §33.10.5.

[10] TCGA 1997, s. 39.

33.1.5 Scope

Some reliefs are exemptions from liability—by declaring that the disposal or the asset is not a chargeable disposal or asset. Other reliefs postpone or defer a liability until a later disposal; the latter is usually effected by adjusting the cost base.

Before 6 April 1998 CGT gave indexation relief for inflation; for later periods tapering relief applies. If an asset acquired in 1996 is sold in 2000, each relief applies to its own period, i.e. 1996–1998 and 1998–2000; tapering relief does not apply for corporation tax and so indexation relief still applies in full. The extent of the tapering relief depends on whether the asset is a business asset or a non-business asset. For a non-business asset the effect of full tapering relief is that the percentage of the gain taxed drops from 100% to 60% over a 10-year period (with no reduction for first three years, but subsequently 5% per year); for business assets the percentage droped originally from 100% to 25% over the 10-year period (with no reduction in the first year, but then a steady 7.5% per year). However, FA 2000 makes the taper steeper; the 25% is now reduced after four complete years, and there is a 17.5% reduction after one year. See further below §§43.3 and 43.4.

CGT does not apply to gains accruing before 1965. The rebasing of the tax to 1982 provides further reliefs for asset acquired before 1982 but subject to restrictions which may involve the pre-1988 law. See further below §§43.5 and 43.6.

33.1.6 Deferral of CGT

TCGA 1992 contains a number of rules deferring liability to tax; these rules are of two types. One type is sometimes called "rollover" relief and applies where the gain is rolled over from one asset to another by being removed from the sale figure for the first asset and added to the purchase price of the second. For example, A buys at 40 and disposes to B at 100; B later sells the asset at 150. A has a gain of 60 and B of 50. If the tax system imposes a rollover, A is treated as selling to B at 40; B will have to pay tax on the whole 110. This result is achieved where the A–B disposal is directed to be at such figure that neither gain nor loss accrues to A. The introduction of taper relief has produced the odd result that it applies only to B's period of ownership; B cannot use A's and A's taper releif is lost. Sometimes these deferrals are a matter of election; the taper relief rule makes the election decision less obvious.

The same reduction in the value of the asset may be directed where A disposes of one asset and acquires another. Here A can also only use taper relief for the new period of ownership. If the postponement represents sound tax policy it is unfortunate that the taper relief undermines that policy.

The second type of deferral rule is called "holdover" relief and arises where the tax system allows A to defer liability to pay tax on the 60 gain until some later event. The gain is not rolled into the base cost of another asset. Here only one taxpayer is involved.

Although these two techniques are used extensively in the legislation, they are not always consistently referred to as rollover and holdover.

33.2 Persons Chargeable

CGT is charged on chargeable gains accruing to a person in a year of assessment during any part of which he is resident in the UK, or during which he is ordinarily resident in the UK.[11] A non-resident is subject to CGT only in respect of UK assets used for the purposes of a trade carried on in the UK through a branch, or UK assets held for the purposes of the branch.[12]

Partners are each liable for the tax on their share of gains realised by the partnership. A European Economic Interest Grouping (EEIG) is treated in broadly the same way as a partnership for the purpose of charging tax on capital gains.[13]

Trustees and personal representatives are chargeable in respect of gains realised on a disposal, whether actual or deemed, in the course of administration. Personal representatives may also be liable for tax due in respect of gains realised by the deceased in his lifetime.

A body subject to corporation tax has its gains charged to that tax and not to CGT. Shareholders are liable to CGT on the disposal of their shares, assuming that they are not corporations. Corporation tax paid by a corporation is not imputed to the shareholder even though it be shown that the latter's gain is attributable entirely to the gain already taxed in the company. This can lead to double taxation of gains—and double relief for losses. However, if a capital gain is distributed by the company to the shareholder, the corporation tax paid may be partially imputed by virtue of the tax credit attaching to the distribution. Undistributed capital gains of a non-resident close company may be attributed to the participators.[14]

Authorised unit trusts, venture capital trusts and investment trusts are exempt from tax on capital gains.[15] For other savings vehicles, see Chapter 54.

33.3 Rates of Tax

Since 1988–1989 CGT has been charged at income tax rates. From 1965–1988 CGT was a flat rate tax at 30%. Today, an individual's net chargeable gains for the year of assessment are treated as the top slice of income in computing the CGT liability.[16] Tax is payable at the starting rate of 10%, the lower rate of 20% or the higher rate of 40%.[17] The 20% rate applies to the extent that the net chargeable capital gains plus taxable income fall below the basic rate limit (£28,400). The income starting rate of 10% was extended to CGT by FA 2000. The 20% rate will apply whatever the nature of the asset, i.e. whether or not the income from the asset qualifies for the savings rate of 20%. Personal reliefs (or other income tax deductions, except trading losses) may not be used to offset chargeable gains.[18] The tax charged remains CGT, not income tax.

[11] TCGA 1992, s. 2(1). In *R* v. *IRC, ex parte Fulford-Dobson* [1987] STC 344 an attempt by a taxpayer to get round this rule by a scheme using ESC D2 failed (see above at §3.3.1).

[12] TCGA 1992, s. 10.

[13] Ibid., s. 510A(6) see below at §42.7.7.

[14] Ibid., s. 13.

[15] Ibid., s. 100(1).

[16] Ibid., s. 4, as amended by FA 1999, s. 26.

[17] TCGA 1992, s. 4(1AA) and 4(1AB); contrast Ireland where only the higher (40%) rate was applied when CGT was first introduced.

[18] Although by reducing the rate of tax on income they may reduce the rate of tax on the gains.

As from 1998–1999 all trusts pay at the special trust rate of 34%, as do estates.[19] Before 1998–1999 only discretionary trusts paid at the special rate, with other trusts and all estates paying at the basic rate of income tax.

33.4 Annual Exempt Amount

There is a simple annual exemption for gains accruing to individuals;[20] for 2000–2001 the figure is £7,200, which contrasts with £4,385 personal relief for income tax.[21] This annual exemption is index linked, unless Parliament decides otherwise. Husband and wife are each entitled to the annual exemption. On annual exemptions for trusts and estates see §39.6.1 and §40.1.2.

33.5 Payment of CGT

CGT is due on the same day as income tax, i.e. 31 January following the end of the year of assessment in which the gain is realised. No payment on account is required and capital gains do not affect the calculation of the sum required on account for income tax. The problems of valuation inherent in the CGT regime are relevant to surcharges and penalties, but not to interest.[22] For administration of CGT see Tiley and Collison §§14.01 et seq.

33.6 Payment by Instalments

CGT may be paid by instalments in three situations:

(1) Where the consideration is payable in instalments and the taxpayer, T, so chooses (TCGA 1992, s. 280). Payments must be spread over a period starting on (or after) the date of disposal and extending at least 18 months. CGT may then be paid in instalments extending over a maximum period of eight years; instalment relief also ends once the last instalment of consideration is received if this is earlier. Before self-assessment this relief was available only if T could satisfy the Board that "he would otherwise suffer undue hardship"; today, this restrictive condition no longer applies. Payment by instalments does not apply where the sale agreement operates so that the full sum is paid at the time of the sale, but some or all of the sale consideration is then lent back to the purchaser. In *Coren* v. *Keighley*,[23] land was sold for £3,750 with a loan back to the purchaser of £2,250 repayable by monthly instalments; CGT was due on the entire £3,750 at the normal due date. A separate rule provides an adjustment where the consideration is later shown to be irrecoverable.[24]

[19] FA 1998, s. 120; more fully the rate applicable under TA 1988, s. 686.
[20] TCGA 1992, s. 3.
[21] CGT (Annual Exempt Amount) Order 2000 (SI 2000/808); (2000) *Simon's Weekly Tax Intelligence* 517. See also below §33.11.
[22] A "best estimate" of figures must be marked as such and will then not prevent the return from being a completed return: see Rev Booklet SAT2 (1995).
[23] (1972) 48 TC 370.
[24] TCGA 1992, s. 48.

(2) For gifts of certain assets (s. 281). The asset must be land, share or securities giving the donor a controlling interest, or unquoted shares or securities .[25] This relief is not available if there is a holdover election available under s. 165 (gift of business asset) or 260 (gift subject to IHT).
(3) Under TCGA 1992, Schedule 7, paragraphs 4–7. The instalment option is also available where an election to hold over the gain is available, but the gain that can be held over under the terms of that election is less than the chargeable gain that arises. This will commonly be the case where shares are given away and the company whose shares are transferred has chargeable assets that are not chargeable business assets.[26] If the donee sells the asset, all instalments of tax that have not been paid at that date become immediately payable, with interest.[27]

33.7 Tax Base Exemptions and Reliefs[28]

The following assets are exempt assets in that no chargeable gain arises on the disposal of them—and so no relief is given for any loss arising:

(a) debts other than the debt on a security (s. 251);
(b) covenants (s. 237);
(c) certain wasting assets (ss 45);
(d) private residence (s. 222) (cost in 1998–1999 £1,000 m);
(e) government stock (s. 115);
(f) qualifying corporate bonds (s. 115);
(g) EIS shares and certain BES shares s. 150 and 150A;
(h) woodlands (s. 250);
(i) passenger vehicles (s. 263);
(j) certain chattels (s. 262).

Certain events or disposals are treated as not giving rise to a chargeable gain as follows:

(a) death s. 62 (cost in 1997–1998 £675 m);
(b) gifts to charity (s. 256);
(c) share for share exchanges (s. 135) or other company reconstructions (s. 127);
(d) inter-spouse transfers (s. 58);
(e) transfers of assets within a group (s. 171);
(f) transfers by certain special taxpayers (ss 215–221 and 264–267);
(g) transfers of shares to an employee share ownership trust (s. 229);
(h) transfer to the Treasury in settlement of an inheritance tax liability of a work of art (s. 257);
(i) shares within a personal equity plan or ISA (s. 151);
(j) decorations for valorous conduct (s. 268);
(k) foreign currency for personal use (s. 269).

Of these (c)–(e) may in effect simply defer tax but the others are genuine exemptions. We shall come across other deferrals of tax in the course of Part III.

[25] Ibid., s. 281 see below §41.3.5.
[26] Ibid., s. 281(1)(b)(ii).
[27] Ibid., s. 281(7)(b).
[28] *Inland Revenue Statistics 1999*, Tables 1.6 and B.1; for reliefs for which no cost can be given, see ibid., B.2.

Other genuine exemptions include the retirement relief (s. 163) which is now being phased out (see below §42.5). In 1997–98 this cost £180m. Reinvestment relief (s. 164A), which was a form of deferral was repealed in 1998 but almost immediately replaced by other deferral rules for investment in companies with qualifying trades (see further below §41.8 and chapter 54).

33.8 The Market Value Rule

Under TCGA 1992, s. 17 an acquisition or disposal of an asset is treated as taking place at market value if it takes place otherwise than by way of a bargain made at arm's length. The legislation states that this applies in particular where the acquisition or disposal is by way of gift or on a transfer into settlement by a settlor or by way of distribution from a company in respect of shares in the company.

S. 17 also states that the market value rule applies where

> "the acquisition or disposal is wholly or partly (a) for a consideration that cannot be valued, or (b) in connection with an individual's own or another's loss of office or employment or diminution of emoluments, or otherwise in consideration for or recognition of his or another's services[29] or past services in any office or employment or of any other service rendered or to be rendered by him or another."

S. 17 is excluded if there is an acquisition of an asset without a disposal and the consideration is either non-existent or is less than the market value.[30] In these circumstances the acquisition consideration will be nil, or the actual value, as appropriate. The purpose of this rule is to defeat schemes known as "reverse *Nairn Williamson* schemes", under which shares were issued to shareholders (so being acquired by them without being disposed of by the issuing company). Although a relatively small amount might be subscribed (especially if the issued share capital was not substantial), the shares acquired were valued at market value thus giving the shareholders a substantial uplift in the base cost of their holding. Such schemes would now probably fall foul of the *Ramsay* principle.[31]

33.9 Connected Persons

Many CGT rules turn on connected person status,[32] e.g. the market value rule.[33] Connected persons for the purposes of CGT are those within the following five categories:

33.9.1 Relatives

A taxpayer is connected with his/her spouse, brother, sister, ancestor or lineal descendant. A taxpayer is also connected with the spouse of any one of those individuals and with those

[29] For example *Director* v. *Inspector of Taxes* [1998] STC (SCD) 172.
[30] TCGA 1992, s. 17(2).
[31] [1982] *BTR* 13, 16.
[32] For example restriction of loss relief (s. 18(3) and loans s. 251(4)).
[33] TCGA 1992, s. 18(2) deems transfer to be not by way of bargain at arm's length.

relations of the spouse.[34] An individual's uncle, aunt, nephew and niece are not connected persons for CGT purposes, although they are for IHT purposes.[35] A spouse is a spouse, whether living with the other spouse or separated. A spouse, thus, ceases to be a connected person, and the spouse's relatives cease to be connected, only at decree absolute.

33.9.2 Trusts

A trustee (X) is connected with the settlor (S) of the settlement of which X is trustee and with any person who is connected with S—so long as S is alive.[36] The income tax meaning of the word "settlor" applies,[37] thus including any person who has "provided or undertaken to provide funds directly or indirectly for the purpose of the settlement, or has made with any other person a reciprocal arrangement for that other person to make or enter into the settlement".

X is also connected with any close company of which the trustees of the settlement are participators, with any company controlled by such a company and with any company that fulfils this definition, but is not close solely by virtue of not being resident in the UK.[38]

A person's network of connections as trustee is separate from that as himself. X, as trustee, will be treated as connected with S's daughter, P, so far as trust matters are concerned. If X sells his personal property to P, this is not necessarily a transaction between connected persons.

A connection can only be made through an individual while still living. Thus, after the death of S, X is not connected with any individuals under these provisions.

33.9.3 Partners

Partners are connected with persons with whom they are in partnership, with the spouse of any partner and with the brother, sister, ancestor or lineal descendant of any partner. However, this connection does not apply "in relation to acquisitions or disposals of partnership assets pursuant to bona fide commercial arrangements".[39] Any transaction between an incoming partner and the existing partners is in practice treated as a bona fide commercial arrangement made otherwise than between connected persons.[40]

The scope of the bona fide arrangement rule is uncertain.[41] Where the partnership contracts with an individual partner to sell to that partner, for a commercial consideration, an asset that has previously been on the partnership balance sheet, it is clear that the subsection operates so that the transaction is not treated as being made between connected persons. However, it is less clear where the asset in question has not been on the partnership balance sheet, as is commonly the case with goodwill.

[34] Ibid., s. 286(2).
[35] IHTA 1984, s. 272.
[36] TCGA 1982, s. 286(3).
[37] I.e. from TA 1988, s. 660G.
[38] TCGA 1992, s. 286(3A).
[39] Ibid., s. 286(4); see Goldberg [1975] *BTR* 91 and Ray [1975] *BTR* 198..
[40] Statement of Practice SP D12.
[41] See Tiley and Collison, *UK Tax Guide*, 16.51. Probably the better view of such a transaction is that a distinction has to be drawn between: (i) an asset owned by the partnership, which is a "partnership asset" within the meaning of s. 286(4); and (ii) an individual's interest in the partnership, which is not a "partnership asset" within the meaning of s. 286(4).

33.9.4 Companies and other companies

A company is connected with another company if the same person has control of both, or a person has control of one and persons connected with him, or he and persons connected with him, have control of the other. The same applies if a group of two or more persons has control of each company, and the groups either consist of the same persons or could be regarded as consisting of the same persons by treating (in one or more cases) a member of either group as replaced by a person with whom he is connected.[42]

33.9.3 Companies and controlling individuals

A company is connected with an individual if that individual has control of it or where a group of individuals who are connected persons have control of the company.[43] Further, any two or more persons acting together to secure and exercise control of a company are treated in relation to that company as connected with each other.[44]

33.10 Losses

Relief for Losses in Same Year as Gains. CGT is charged on the balance of chargeable gains less allowable losses realised in a year of assessment.[45] Allowable losses[46] thus attract automatic relief by set-off against total chargeable gains for that year. This is not a matter of election, and so applies whether or not the effect is to waste the annual exempt amount. Thus if A has £7,000 of chargeable gains and £7,000 of allowable losses in the same year A has no liability to CGT but also no losses to use in another year

33.10.1 Computation

Computation of Losses. Losses are computed in the same way as gains. If the disposal can give rise to a chargeable gain, it can also give rise to an allowable loss; whereas if it gives rise to a non-chargeable gain, it cannot give rise to an allowable loss.[47]

Unused Loss —Carry Forward not Back. Any allowable loss not relieved by offset against other gains in the year in which it arises is carried forward and set against chargeable gains accruing in the next subsequent year in which they arise.[48] Whereas the automatic offset of an available loss against gains of the same year is made before considering the annual exempt amount, losses brought forward from a previous year are only relieved insofar as they bring the net gains down to the amount specified as the annual exempt amount.[49] Where the loss brought forward exceeds the excess of gain over the annual exempt amount,

[42] TCGA 1992, s. 286(5).
[43] Ibid., s. 286(2).
[44] Ibid., s. 286(3); on the meaning of a similar income tax expression, note *Steele* v. *European Vinyls Group* [1996] STC 785.
[45] TCGA 1992, s. 2(2a).
[46] For an example of the difficulties some taxpayers have in understanding how losses may (and may not) arise, see *Neely* v. *Ward* [1991] STC 656.
[47] TCGA 1992, s. 16(2).
[48] Ibid., s. 2(2)(b).
[49] Ibid., s. 3(5)(b).

the still unrelieved loss is carried forward to a later year. So if A has £7,000 of allowable losses in year 1 and £7,000 of chargeable gains in year 2, A is not obliged to put the losses against the gain in year 2 but can roll them forward to a later year.

It will be seen that the loss is carried forward not back. If B has £7,000 of chargeable gains in year 1 after taking account of the annual exemption (i.e. £14,200 of gains altogether) and £7,000 of allowable losses in year 2, B is not allowed to carry the loss back to year 1—but may still carry the loss forward to year 3 and later years. The refusal of the system to allow losses to be carried back encourages taxpayers to dispose of assets in good time so as to use a loss.

33.10.2 Carry back on death

Where the deceased (D) made disposals prior to his death and has losses arising from disposals in the fiscal year in which D dies, the losses are set first against chargeable gains for that year and then against any chargeable gains in the previous three years, later years being counted before earlier years.[50]

Where, at death, the market value of an asset is less than the deceased's acquisition cost, no allowable loss arises. This is because the asset is deemed to have been acquired by the personal representatives without the deceased having made a disposal. This is the disadvantage of the rule that also excludes unrealised capital gains from CGT on D's death.

33.10.3 Taper and indexation reliefs

Losses arising on the disposal of assets are calculated in the usual way. Since taper relief only reduces a gain it cannot create a loss. To see how loss relief ties in with taper relief it is necessary to proceed in stages.

The starting point is that taper relief applies to the balance of gains and losses for the year.[51] Where there is one disposal which produces a gain, taper relief reduces that gain; the annual exemption is applied after that. Where there are two disposals, each producing a gain, each gain is given its own taper relief; the annual exemption is applied after that. See further below §43.3.3.

Where there is more than one gain in the fiscal year, any losses are deducted from the separate gains in the order that gives the lowest charge to tax.[52] The point of this rule is to make it clear that if the taxpayer realises two gains in a year, and one had a higher tapering relief than the other, losses must first be set against the gain on the asset with the lower relief, i.e. the higher amount of tax. This may occur where the assets have been held for different lengths of time or for the same length of time but one is a business asset and the other a non-business asset.

Indexation and Loss Relief. Indexation as reformed in 1995 does not allow the creation of a loss but only the reduction of a gain to zero. This restriction is contrary to principle (see below §43.4). It may also have an unfortunate effect where an asset is split into two parts which are disposed of separately. Whereas indexation relief would apply in the normal way to an outright disposal of the asset in one transaction, the splitting of the asset may give rise

50 Ibid., s. 62(1)(b).
51 Ibid., s. 2A(2).
52 Ibid., s. 2A(6).

to a gain on one part of the asset, reduced to a lower level by indexation, and a gain on another part which is more than offset by indexation relief. The situation is even worse if the net result of the sale of the second part is a loss before any indexation relief is applied.

33.10.4 Restrictions on loss relief

Disposal to a connected person

The tax system is very suspicious of losses arising on a disposal of an asset to a connected person. Relief is permitted only against a chargeable gain arising from a disposal to that same connected person. The gain may arise in that or in some later year (as long as connected person status continues) but not an earlier year.[53]

International elements

No relief is permitted for a non-resident on assets outside charge. A person who is neither resident nor ordinarily resident in the year of assessment is subject to CGT only on assets used for the carrying-on of a trade of a branch in the UK.[54] It follows that relief for losses is available only in respect of such assets. [55]

No relief is permitted for losses of a non-domiciled person. An individual who is not domiciled within the UK is subject to CGT on an asset situated overseas only on a remittance basis.[56] Since a remittance cannot include a loss, no relief is available for losses on such (foreign) assets.[57]

33.10.5 Assets of negligible value[58]

Where A invests money in an asset which later become valueless, it is clear that A has suffered a commercial loss. Since there is no actual disposal, relief is provided by allowing A to make a claim, the effect of which is to treat the claim as a disposal.[59] A must be able to show that there has been an "entire loss, destruction, dissipation or extinction of an asset". A claim may be made whether or not any capital sum has been received by way of compensation or otherwise. The claim may be part of the self-assessment, or free standing.[60] The effect of a claim is that the asset is treated as having been sold and immediately reacquired at the date of the claim for an amount equal to the value specified in the claim.

Backdating

A claim may be made so that the date of disposal is treated as having been made on any date specified during the period from 24 months before the beginning of the fiscal year in which the claim is actually made.[61] Thus, a claim made on 31 January 2001 can be backdated to 6 April 1998. In order to backdate in this manner, the asset must be of negligible value at both the date of claim and the earlier date. Indexation can only be claimed in accordance with the legislation in force at the date of claim.

53 TCGA 1992, s. 18(2), but with an exception in subs. (3) for certain trusts for the public good.
54 Ibid., s. 10(1).
55 Ibid., ss 10, 16(3).
56 Ibid., s. 12.
57 Ibid., s. 16(4).
58 On partnership interests becoming of negligible value, see Eastaway [1984] *BTR* 207.
59 TCGA 1992, s. 24.
60 FA 1996, Sch. 17, para. 2(2).
61 Ibid., Sch. 35, para. 4.

Negligible

"Negligible" is less than "small" and so should be considerably less than the 5% Revenue yardstick used for the word "small".[62] The Revenue usually accepts that such a claim arises where the loss is less than £10,000, where the company is registered in the UK, is not a plc and is in liquidation or has ceased trading.[63] If an asset has been stolen the Revenue will accept a claim despite the fact that the asset is still in existence with its value unchanged.

Indexation allowance and negligible value claim

Since one is dealing with a loss there is no room for indexation relief after April 1995.[64] Even where the claim is backdated to a date before 6 April 1995, indexation allowance is excluded.[65]

Land and buildings: separate assets

For the purpose of a negligible value claim, a building may be treated as a separate asset from the land on which it is situated.[66] Where there is a claim that a building has become of negligible value, the effect of the claim is to establish a loss on the building but, at the same time, to treat the site as having been sold and immediately reacquired for an amount equal to its market value. If this yields a gain on the land that gain will automatically offset (and so reduce) the loss.

Recovery

An asset may have a negligible value at one date and then regain value. Such an outcome does not undo the negligible value claim—it simply lands one with a potential CGT liability based on the gain as compared with the value accepted at the time of the claim.[67]

33.10.6 Set-off of trading losses

Income losses are not, in general, a permitted deduction from chargeable gains in the case of persons other than companies. However, trading losses under Schedule D, Case I may be set off against chargeable gains.[68] The amount of the loss for which relief may be claimed is the balance after set-off against income for the year of loss or any other year. The loss is treated as an allowable capital loss for that year, and is therefore set off against chargeable gains before taking account of the annual exemption. Therefore, if D has £10,000 of chargeable gains and £9,000 of trading loss, the relief will reduce the chargeable gains to £1,000 which will be covered by the annual exemption. There is no provision for claiming only part of the trading loss which would otherwise be available. If the trading loss exceeds the chargeable gains for the year, the excess is not treated as an allowable capital loss but is carried forward as a trading loss, not a capital loss.[69] Because a claim for set-off of trading

[62] The Revenue release lists of quoted securities which it accepts have become of negligible value for the purposes of TCGA 1992, s. 24.

[63] Revenue Internal Guidance, *Capital Gains Manual*, CG 13139–46.

[64] FA 1994, s. 93.

[65] TCGA 1992. s. 24(2)(c).

[66] Ibid., s. 24(3).

[67] Ibid., s. 24(2)(a). For recent list see (2000) *Simons Weekly Tax Intelligence* p. 966.

[68] FA 1991, s. 72; see Stopforth [1992] *BTR* 384 emphasisimng reasons for procedural complexities.

[69] FA 1991, s. 72(3).

losses against general income can be made for the year following the year of loss,[70] a CGT claim may also be made for that year—provided the trade continues in that year.[71]

33.11 Spouses

33.11.1 Separate taxation

Since 1990 CGT, like income tax, has generally ignored the conjugal relationship. Spouses pay their own CGT arising on the disposal of their own assets.[72] As individual taxpayers, each is entitled to claim a full annual exempt amount each year—currently £7,200.[73] In 1988 the annual exempt amount was reduced from what would have been £6,900 to £5,000 in anticipation of the separate taxation of spouses; it remained at £5,000 for the next three years.

It has always been the case that the gains and losses arising to one party to a marriage have been *computed* separately from those arising to the other party. Prior to 1990–1991 CGT tax was levied on the husband for gains made both by him and by his wife, unless they were living apart.[74]

Where there is a disposal of property which has been held jointly by husband and wife, the split of proceeds and acquisition costs follow the division of the equitable interest between husband and wife. Where no division is specified, Revenue practice is to regard the split as being into two equal halves.[75] The special income tax treatment is not applied, except that where the couple declare an unequal split of income, the Revenue will presume that this also holds for CGT.[76]

The rate of CGT on each spouse's net gains is calculated by treating the gains as the top slice of their income. Neither the exempt amount nor any allowable losses are transferable between the spouses.

33.11.2 Transfers between spouses living together

Transfers between spouses who are living together are treated at taking effect at such value that neither gain nor loss accrues to the disposing spouse.[77] This gives the married couple an advantage in that it enables one spouse to switch the potential liability on an, as yet unrealised, gain (or entitlement to an allowable loss) to the other spouse, so that the other spouse can dispose of the asset and so realise the gain or loss.[78] However, it prevents the spouses

70 TA 1988, s. 380(2).

71 FA 1991, s. 72(6).

72 TCGA 1992. s. 279(7).

73 Ibid., s. 3.

74 CGTA 1979, s. 45; see *Aspden* v. *Hildersley* [1982] STC 206 (an election was available to charge tax on the wife for her gains; the tax was calculated by splitting the single annual exempt amount between the spouses; for discussion of Revenue view that *Aspden* was wrong, see Potter and Monroe, §2.25).

75 Inland Revenue Press Release, 21 November 1990, (1990) *Simon's Tax Intelligence* 985.

76 On joint holdings, see Thexton, *Taxation*, Vol. 143, 170.

77 TCGA 1992, s. 58; on use of this to avoid tax, see *Gubay* v. *Kington* [1984] STC 99 and notes by Goodhart and Dolby at [1984] *BTR* 117 and 124, the latter arguing whether Lord Templeman failed to spot a case of tax avoidance.

78 Potter and Monroe, above at n. 74, §2-21 suggest that if the recipient spouse sells the asset on, the transfer to that spouse should take place before finding a purchaser to avoid *Furniss* v. *Dawson* problems.

further manipulating their entitlements to reliefs, etc., by passing the asset back and forth at current market values. S. 58 applies if the spouses are living together at any point in the year of assessment; it probably follows that s. 59 applies if the spouses separate during the year and the transfer is made after the separation but before the end of the year.[79]

The no gain/no loss rule does not apply to appropriations to or from trading stock; in such circumstances market value is instead taken to preserve the integrity of the rules on the interaction of income and CGT. Nor does the rule apply to *donatio mortis causa*, the purpose here being consistency with the exception from CGT of assets passing on death.

Indexation and tapering reliefs

Where ta transfer takes place between spouses who are living together, any indexation allowance available to the disposer is taken into account in computing the acquirer's cost of acquisition, subject to the general rule since 1993 that its effect is only to reduce a gain.[80] For similar reasons, any period of ownership by the transferring spouse is available to the transferee.[81]

33.11.3 Separation

If the spouses separate, the no gain no loss rule continues to apply until the end of the tax year in which they separate. However, they are still connected persons until decree absolute of divorce (and may continue to be connected persons under some other rule, e.g. business partners). A transfer which takes place as part of the financial settlement on divorce is normally regarded as being for a consideration which cannot be valued, and so takes place at market value.[82] The choice of assets to be transferred is naturally a matter to which much thought must be given. In *Aspden* v. *Hildesley*[83] a husband transferred property to his wife; the property comprised a house which was not his only or main residence. The husband was held taxable on the increase in value of the house since he had acquired it.

The precise timing on transfers is thus a matter of some importance. Where the parties reach agreement on the terms of their settlement and the agreement then becomes part of a court order the usual view is that the transfer takes place at the time of the consent order—and not that of the prior agreement—or, if different, the decree absolute.[84]

Main residence problems

Once the spouses are no longer living together they may each have an exempt only or main residence. However, this exemption is tied to ownership. If, therefore, H owns the property, but W occupies it, the relief may be lost; in practice this is not a problem if the transfer is made within three years of the parties separating (not divorcing). While there is a Revenue concession[85] allowing the exemption if W is occupying the property, the concession does

[79] Potter and Monroe, above at n. 74, §2.25.

[80] TCGA 1992, s. 56(2), (3); on pre-1993 indexation, see ibid., s. 55(7); on preservation of pre-1982 basing, see ibid., Sch. 3, para. 1.

[81] Ibid., Sch. A1, para. 15.

[82] TCGA 1992, s. 17(1)(b) and *Inland Revenue CGT Manual*, para. 22509. Timing transfers so that they take place after connected party status ceases may be advantageous if TCGA 1992, ss 29 and 30 (value shifting) provisions are potentially applicable.

[83] [1982] STC 206.

[84] See discussion in (1996) 138 *Taxation* 324.

[85] ESC D6.

not apply if H is living in another property and claiming that as his only or main residence. The concession applies only where H transfers the house to W—and not if the house is sold to a third party. Since the concession encourages the spouses to rearrange their interests before separation it may precipitate hostile acts; this runs counter to recent family law legislation and contrasts with the IHT exemption for transfers between spouses.

The courts may order that one spouse be allowed to occupy the property with the children while they are growing up and then order a sale when the property is no longer needed, with the proceeds being then divided between the spouses (the *Mesher* order).[86] The effect of this order is to retain the exemption while the arrangement lasts. There is some uncertainty about the effect of a clause that the occupying spouse should pay "rent" to the other; if it is truly rent then it will be chargeable income of the recipient (and not deductible by the payer) and will endanger the entitlement to the CGT exemption.[87] Another form of order creates a deferred charge, under which H will receive either a specified sum of money or a specified proportion of the proceeds when the property is sold. Unfortunately, because of the CGT rules on debts, the above two orders may produce different results. If H is entitled to a specified proportion of the proceeds, he may be treated as realising a gain when the charge is realised.[88] Problems also arise if the spouses have joint interests in land and exchange those interests on separating. There is some relief if the value of the interests exchanged is identical, but this will rarely be achieved.[89]

The court may order secured maintenance. This may involve the transfer of property by one spouse (H) to trustees; W then looks to the trustees and not to H for payment. When W ceases to be entitled to payments the trust ends and the property is transferred back to H. The transfer to the trustees will be a disposal for CGT purposes at current market value (since the trustees and the spouses are connected persons). If the trustees dispose of the assets during the trust, a CGT charge on those assets will arise (for which H may be made accountable).[90]

[86] See *Mesher* v. *Mesher* [1980] 2 All ER 126.
[87] See Wylie, *ICAEW Digest No. 200* (December 1999), para. 1.8.
[88] Ibid., para. 1.9.
[89] Ibid., para. 1.10, using s. 152 (assets qualifying for business relief) and ESC D26.
[90] Ibid., para. 1.11.

34

Assets

CGT applies only to a gain realised on the disposal of an asset. This has two major consequences: first, if there is no asset there can be no chargeable gain—or allowable loss;[1] and secondly, qualifying expenditure can be deducted only when the asset to which it relates is disposed of.

34.1 What is an Asset?

TCGA 1992, s. 21(1) states that all forms of property are assets whether or not situated in the UK. Property is not further defined. Assets are, however, stated to include (a) options, debts and incorporeal property generally, (b) any currency other than sterling,[2] and (c) any form of property created by the person disposing of it, or otherwise coming to be owned without being acquired. Property "owned without being acquired" covers items such as goodwill[3] and property which is simply found. Property "created" includes items such as paintings, copyrights, patents and crops.

This definition leaves uncertain the scope of many shadowy rights which might be called incorporeal property. The statutory words do not confine the definition to interests in or

[1] For example a loss arising on a liability (*Beauchamp* v. *Woolworth* [1989] STC 510, (1989) 61 TC 510).

[2] Distinguish a holding of foreign currency from a debt expressed in foreign currency which will generally be an exempt asset below §34.4.1 (for a limited exception, see TCGA 1992, Sch. 11, paras 13, 14).

over other property. Hence, rights under contractual licences may equally be "property" and sums received on the redemption of a rent-charge, the release of a covenant and the release of a right to occupy the matrimonial home may all give rise to CGT (TCGA 1992, s. 22).

These are, however, actual or potential legal rights of action and capable of being owned in the normal legal sense. "Rights" which may underly such rights of action but which cannot be owned in this sense are not assets. In *Kirby* v. *Thorn EMI*[4] the Court of Appeal held that a company's right to trade and compete in the market place is not an "asset", but held that a payment which could be related to the goodwill of the company, as distinct from the goodwill of one of its subsidiaries, was taxable.

The meaning of "asset" had been considered in the earlier House of Lords' decision in *O'Brien* v. *Benson's Hosiery (Holdings) Ltd.*[5] There the House held that the bundle of rights of an employer under a service agreement was an asset for CGT so that a sum received by the employer to secure the release of the employee was derived from that asset and so liable to CGT. The fact that the rights could not be assigned by the employer was irrelevant. It was sufficient that they could be "turned to account". *Kirby* v. *Thorn EMI* provides a necessary check on some of the arguments in *O'Brien* which had come close to saying that if a sum was received then it must have been derived from property. It must also be remembered that in *O'Brien* the right was, like the others already mentioned, legally enforceable in some way or other. However, in view of the approach in *O'Brien* it would follow that an unenforceable promise is probably an asset despite an old estate duty case[6] in which the proceeds of a void insurance policy were held not to be part of the deceased's estate. The same applies to rights barred by statute especially as such rights can be enforced indirectly and the acknowledgement of a claim can revive a right that would otherwise be statute barred.

34.2 Identifying the Asset

CGT is charged on a gain; the gain is the consideration received for the asset less the cost (or deemed cost) of the asset. The correct identification of the asset is therefore important. Further, where CGT is charged under TCGA 1992, s. 22 on a capital sum derived from an asset, the gain is computed by taking from the capital sum received the cost (in whole or in part) of the asset that has directly caused the receipt of the capital sum. It is, therefore, critical to identify correctly the asset from which the consideration or capital sum is derived.[7] This causes particular problems where a compensation claim arises in connection with a contract relating to an asset and that asset receives special treatment under the CGT rules.

A precise and almost unworkable view of the matching process was taken in *Zim Properties Ltd.* v. *Procter*;[8] the law is made less rigid in practice by ESC D33. In *Zim*, Warner J. held that a right of action for damages relating to a conveyance of property was an asset

[3] See TA 1988, s. 531(2).

[4] [1987] STC 621, (1987) 60 TC 519; on this basis amateur status is not an asset and so the sum received in *Jarrold* v. *Boustead* (see above at §14.4.4) would not be subject to CGT. *Quaere* the sums received in *Higgs* v. *Olivier* (1952) 33 TC 136.

[5] [1980] AC 562, [1979] STC 735, [1979] 3 All ER 652, but cf. *Cleveleys Investment Trust Co.* v. *IRC* [1975] STC 457, (1975) 51 TC 26 (rights acquired by a guarantor against the debtor company on discharge of a debt to a third party were not assets for CGT).

[6] *A-G* v. *Murray* [1904] 1 KB 165.

[7] See, e.g. Sparkes [1987] *BTR* 323; and [1988] *BTR* 29.

[8] [1985] STC 90, (1985) 58 TC 371.

separate from the property conveyed. The taxpayer (T) had contracted to sell property, but the purchaser repudiated the contract alleging that T's solicitors had failed to demonstrate good title to the property. T then sued its solicitors for negligence; the action was settled out of court by the solicitors paying T damages of £69,000.

T claimed that the £69,000 was compensation for the depreciation in value of the property caused by the solicitors' action (or inaction). Rejecting this view, Warner J. said that:

> "assuming . . . that it was proper to describe the £69,000 as 'compensation' for something, it could only be described as compensation for the consequences of the firm's alleged negligence. The depreciation in the value of the properties was not a consequence of that negligence. It was something which, if it happened, happened as a result of the forces affecting the property market in Manchester, independently of that negligence."

The effect of this decision would be to deny a deductible acquisition cost in many circumstances. In relation to underlying assets, ESC D33 states:

> "Where the right of action arises by reason of the total or partial loss or destruction of or damage to a form of property which is an asset for capital gains tax purposes, or because the claimant suffered some loss or disadvantage in connection with such a form of property, any gain or loss on the disposal of the right of action may by concession be computed as if the compensation derived from that asset, and not from the right of action. As a result a proportion of the cost of the asset, determined in accordance with normal part-disposal rules . . . may be deducted in computing the gain. For example, if compensation is paid by an estate agent because his negligence led to the sale of a building falling through, an appropriate part of the cost of the building may be deducted in computing any gain on the disposal of the right of action . . .
>
> *Other reliefs and exemptions.* If the relief was or would have been available on the disposal of the relevant underlying asset, it will be available on the disposal of the right of action. For example, if compensation is derived from a cause of action in respect of damage to a building suffered by reason of professional negligence, and the compensation is applied in restoring the building, deferment relief under [TCGA 1992, s. 23] will be available as if the compensation derives from the building itself and not from the right of action.
>
> Other reliefs which may become available in this way include private residence relief, retirement relief and roll-over relief. The Board . . . will be prepared to consider extending time limits in cases where because of a delay in obtaining a capital sum in compensation, the normal time limit allowed for a relief has elapsed. If the right of action relates to an asset which is specifically exempt from capital gains tax, such as a motor car, any gain on the disposal of the right of action may be treated as exempt."

34.3 Pooled Assets—Securities

In general, each asset is treated as a distinct item so that tax arises only on the disposal of that asset, and is then computed in the light of the expenditure on that asset. Shares or securities of a company being of the same class and held by one person in one capacity are regarded as indistinguishable parts of a single asset—a holding—so that the sale of a part of the holding is treated as a part disposal[9] (see further below at §41.2). At one time this applied to any fungible assets but this is no longer the case.[10]

9 TCGA 1992, s. 104.
10 CGTA 1979, s. 65(7)(b); not re-enacted in TCGA 1992.

34.4 Loans, Debts and Covenants

Loans and debts give rise to several problems. The basic rule is that neither chargeable gain nor allowable loss arises from a debt. This is subject to exceptions for (a) a debt on a security, (b) certain foreign bank accounts for private use and (c) the assignee of the debt. Relief is given for losses on certain loans to traders and for guarantors of such loans. There are also special rules for covenants, government stock and qualifying corporate bonds.

34.4.1 Exclusion for debts

No chargeable gain arises on the disposal of a debt, other than a debt on a security.[11] The assumption behind the exemption from CGT is, no doubt, that an ordinary commercial debt does not normally produce a gain but only the risk of a loss, and so it would be inappropriate to provide tax relief for losses arising from such risks. This assumption must give ground in a number of circumstances. From 1985 until 1993, when a fixed sum debt would always create a loss by virtue of indexation being available, there was considerable activity in attempting to identify a debt as a debt on security[12] and, hence, able to trigger an allowable loss.

The general exemption rule applies to debts in foreign currencies. Thus, if $100,000 is lent when the exchange rate is $1.50 to the pound and then repaid some years later when the exchange rate is $2 to the pound, the gain is not subjected to CGT. This contrasts with the treatment of a bank deposit.[13] If £50,000 is converted at £1—$2 and put on the dollar denominated bank deposit, and then the $100,000 is withdrawn once the exchange rate has moved to £1—$1.50, the gain of £16,667 is subject to CGT (unless the deposit is for personal expenditure outside the UK of the taxpayer or his family or dependants).[14]

Loss and connected person

A further restriction on allowable losses is imposed when a debt is assigned to a connected person. No allowable loss can arise on the disposal of a debt (whether or not it is a debt on a security) by a person connected with the original creditor (or with his personal representative or legatee) and they acquired the debt directly from the creditor, or indirectly through other connected persons.[15]

Satisfaction as disposal

The satisfaction of a debt is treated as a disposal of the debt by the creditor.[16] This rule is subject to exceptions for certain company reconstructions and amalgamations.[17] It applies to all debts, including debts on a security. The disposal occurs when the debt is satisfied. Satisfaction of part of the debt mean a part disposal.

Provision is made for the situation in which the debt is satisfied not by a payment but by the transfer of an asset.[18] Assuming that the satisfaction is not a chargeable disposal within s. 251(1), rules are needed to protect the creditor should the asset be later disposed of. In cal-

[11] TCGA 1992, s. 251(1).
[12] As in *Taylor Clark International* v. *Lewis* [1998] STC 1259.
[13] TCGA 1992, s. 252.
[14] Ibid., s. 252.
[15] Ibid., s. 251(4).
[16] Ibid., s. 251(2).
[17] Ibid., s. 251(2), subject to ss 132, 135.
[18] Ibid., s. 251(3).

culating the gain on such a disposal the creditor's acquisition cost is the higher of a) the market value of the asset and b) the amount of the debt.[19] So if an asset worth £8,000 is transferred in satisfaction of a debt for £10,000 and later sold by the creditor for £13,000, there is a gain of £3,000 not £5,000. In this way the creditor does not have to pay tax on the first £2,000 gain of the gain which is actually his loss on the debt. Any indexation allowance is calculated on the £8,000 not the £10,000. Naturally if the value of the property acquired is greater than the amount of the debt the higher value is taken; so if the asset is worth £11,000 and is later sold for £13,000 the gain is only £11,000; the point of this rule is less obvious.

Where property is sold, but the price is left outstanding by way of a loan and the purchaser defaults so that the vendor takes back the property, ESC D18 may enable the erstwhile vendor to choose to treat the transaction, for CGT purposes, as if it had not occurred.

34.4.2 Loans to traders

Relief is available for losses on certain loans to traders. The money must be used by the borrower (B) wholly for the purposes of a trade carried on by B, not being a trade which consists of or includes the lending of money. B must be resident in the UK. The debt must not be a debt on a security.[20]

Conditions for relief

The loan must be wholly or partially irrecoverable[21] and the lender (L) must not have assigned the right to recover the irrecoverable amount. L and B must not be either spouses living together or group companies when the loan was made or at any subsequent time.[22] The "subsequent time" is up to the time at which the claim for relief is made.

As originally enacted, the relief was given on a claim being made, and the loss accrued at the date of making the claim, even though the loan may have been irrecoverable at an earlier date. However, there is now legislative provision for backdating the claim to the time it became irrecoverable, subject to a maximum of two years.[23] Neither indexation nor tapering relief is available.

Clawback

The relief is clawed back if L later receives any repayment of the loan, or other consideration in respect of it. L is treated as having made a gain equal to "so much of the allowable loss as corresponds to the amount recovered".[24]

Guarantors

Where a payment is made by a guarantor (G) guaranteeing a qualifying loan to a trader, G may claim a loss equal to the amount he pays under the guarantee.[25] Neither indexation nor tapering relief is available. G may not claim relief if L and B were companies in the same group of, either when the loan was made or at any subsequent time. Relief is also denied

19 On which see *Stanton* v. *Drayton Commercial Investments Ltd* [1982] STC 585, 55 TC 286.
20 TCGA 1992, s. 253(1); debt on a security is defined in s. 132.
21 Defined by ibid., s. 253(9); see also *Cann* v. *Woods* [1999] STC (SCD) 77.
22 TCGA 1992, s. 253(1).
23 Ibid., s. 253(3A), added in 1996 enacting previous ESC D36.
24 TCGA 1992, s. 253(5).
25 Ibid., s. 253(4); on timing see s. 253(4A) added by FA 1996.

where the guarantor and lender are both companies in the same group at the time the guarantee was given, or at a subsequent time.[26] Relief is available where the guarantor and the borrower are companies in the same group.

34.4.3 Debt on a security

Debt

The traditional meaning of a "debt" is a liability to pay a certain sum of money. In *Marren* v. *Ingles*,[27] the taxpayer argued that an obligation to pay a sum of money in the future, the sum to be related to the future profits of the business being sold, was a debt and so outside CGT. The House of Lords rejected this plea. The meaning of the word "debt" depended very much on its context. It was capable of including a contingent debt which might never be payable. It was also capable of including a sum of which the amount was not ascertained. However, it did not apply to "a possible liability to pay an unidentifiable sum at an unascertainable date". This conclusion did not prevent the contract from creating an asset within the scope of the CGT legislation, and a gain arose. Planning measures usually involve ensuring that a debt is created.[28]

"On a security"

The expression "a debt on a security" is not defined in the legislation. Lord Wilberforce in *Ramsay* v. *IRC*,[29] said that many learned judges have found it baffling both on the statutory wording and as to the underlying policy. It should be noted that the taxpayer lost in all five cases mentioned in this section.

S. 132(2)(b) defines "security" as "includ[ing] any loan stock or similar security whether of the Government of the United Kingdom or any other government, or of any public or local authority in the United Kingdom or elsewhere, or of any company, whether secured or unsecured". The term is made expressly applicable in other parts of the Act including s. 251. The Revenue view is that the reference to loan *stock* implies a class of debt, the holdings in which are transferable by purchase and sale, and the words "whether secured or unsecured" in the definition make the existence of a charge immaterial.[30]

Judicial view—investment and market

The principal judicial view is that such a debt is be something in the nature of an investment, and refers to those securities which are or can be subject to a conversion.[31] Stress has also been laid on embodiment of the obligation in a certificate which is evidence of the ownership of the share or stock and of the right to receive payment. A debt on a security is a debt evidenced in a document as a security. As such it is different from a letter of acceptance or a bill of exchange or an unsecured debenture.[32] The same emphasis on a document or certificate creating a marketable security can be seen in *Aberdeen Construction Group Ltd.* v. *IRC*,[33] where the taxpayer company had contracted to sell a loss-making subsidiary in the

26 TCGA 1992, s. 253(4)(d).
27 [1980] STC 500, 506, (1980) 54 TC 76, 100, *per* Lord Fraser.
28 See [1984] *BTR* 259.
29 [1982] AC 300, 329 [1981] STC 174, 184, (1981) 54 TC 101, 189.
30 Statement of Practice SP D25.
31 *Cleveleys Investment Trust Co.* v. *IRC* (1971) 47 TC 300, 315, *per* Lord Cameron.
32 Ibid., 315, *per* Lord Migdale (dissenting).
33 [1978] AC 755, [1978] STC 127, (1978) 52 TC 281.

days before relief for losses to qualifying traders was available. The terms of sale allowed the sale of the share capital for £250,000 on condition that the company wrote off loans totalling £500,000 made to its subsidiary. The parent tried to get relief for the loans thus written as being a "debt on a security". The claim failed.

Unusual debts

Different considerations apply to unusual debts. T's claim failed in *Ramsay* v. *IRC*[34] where T tried to establish that the debt was not a debt on a security and so not subject to any chargeable gain. Lord Wilberforce stressed that the debt was very different from ordinary debts. In his opinion, Parliament had been trying to distinguish mere debts, which normally (although there were exceptions) did not increase but could decrease in value, from debts with added characteristics such as could enable them to be realised or dealt with at a profit. It was important to contrast debts simpliciter, which could arise from trading and a multitude of other situations, commercial or private, and loans, which were certainly a narrower class, and which presupposed some kind of contractual structure. Lord Wilberforce considered that this debt was a debt on a security. It was created by contract, the terms of which were recorded in writing; it was designed, from the beginning, to be capable of being sold, and, indeed, to be sold at a profit.[35]

In a later case, *Taylor Clark International Ltd.* v. *Lewis*,[36] a loss arose on a promissory note. Holding that the debt was not a debt on a security, the court stressed the lack of a "structure of permanence"; the debt has no fixed term, and repayment could have been demanded by the creditor, or effected (without penalty) by the debtor, at any time". The key to that case was that a debt on a security had to be marketable in realistic sense.[37]

34.4.4 Covenants

No chargeable gain accrues on the disposal of a right to, or to a part of, annual payments due under a covenant made by any person and which was not secured on any property.[38] This is presumably because the annual payments are themselves taxable in full as income.

In *Rank Xerox Ltd.* v. *Lane*,[39] the House of Lords held that this rule was confined to situations where there was a gratuitous promise to make the payments and the promise was enforceable only because of its form. In that case the taxpayer was held liable on the gain arising from the disposal to its shareholders of a right to receive royalty payments.

34.5 Tangible Movable Property

The appropriate treatment of movable property[40] gives rise to some difficulty. For example, the tax system would tax an individual on gains realised if he sells his Louis XV bed at a gain,

[34] [1982] AC 300, [1981] STC 174, (1981) 54 TC 101.
[35] Ibid., 329, 184, 189.
[36] [1997] STC 499, 522d, *per* Robert Walker J. at first instance.
[37] [1998]STC 1259, 1272, *per* Peter Gibson L.J.; see also *Tarmac Roadstone Holdings Ltd.* v. *Williams* [1996] STC (SCD) 409.
[38] TCGA 1992, s. 237(c).
[39] [1979] STC 740, (1979) 53 TC 185. For an interesting analysis of the speeches, see Murphy and Rawlings (1981) 44 *MLR* 617, 632 *et seq.*
[40] Rules which apply only to tangible movable property will not cover fixtures before severance.

while not allowing him any relief if he throws away his worn out sheets and duvets. Some systems allow segregate assets into different classes, e.g. into "personal use" assets and others, and allow losses on personal use assets to be set only against gains on such assets. The UK adopts a more Draconian approach. Some assets simply do not give rise to chargeable gains and so do not give rise to allowable losses. This occurs if the movable property is (a) a wasting asset or (b) sold for £6,000 or less or (c) a road vehicle .

34.5.1 Wasting assets

No chargeable gain accrues on the disposal of tangible movable property or an interest in such property in which the property is also a wasting asset.[41] A wasting asset is defined as an asset having a predictable life of 50 years or less.[42] Plant and machinery is always assumed to have a life of less than 50 years.[43] However, the exemption for wasting chattels does not apply to assets in respect of which capital allowances were or could have been claimed, or to commodities dealt with on a terminal market.[44] See further below §42.1.

34.5.2 Disposal for £6,000 or less

If an asset which is tangible movable property is disposed of and the amount or value of the consideration does not exceed £6,000, there is no chargeable gain.[45] The consideration taken into account is the gross amount, before any expenses of disposal, although full effect must be given to any indexation relief. Therefore, the sale of an asset bought for £800 in 1999, but sold for £6,000 in 2001, attracts no CGT.

If the asset is sold for more than £6,000, any gain is computed in full in the normal way. This could lead to ludicrous differences in treatment once the consideration passes £6,000 sharp. Marginal relief therefore applies under which the gain is limited to five-thirds of the difference between the consideration and £6,000 if this would give a lower figure.[46] If the asset is sold for £6,400, the gain would have been £5,600, but this is restricted to £400 × 5/3 (i.e. £667).

Losses

Where a chattel is disposed of for less than £6,000 the allowable loss is computed on the assumption that the consideration was £6,000. If A acquires an antique object for £7,000 but sells it, in a falling market, for £5,200, the loss will be limited to £1,000. The system rightly sees no need for marginal rules for losses.

Anti-avoidance provisions

1) Part disposal

Provisions exist to counter exploitation of the chattel exemption by successive disposals of part-interests in a chattel worth more than £6,000. Where there is a disposal of a right or

[41] TCGA 1992, s. 45(1).

[42] Ibid., s. 44, applied by s. 45(5).

[43] Ibid., s. 44(l)(c). The Revenue considers that the definition of "machinery" includes antique clocks and watches, as well as custom-made vehicles such as racing cars, commercial vehicles and locomotives, etc. (Inland Revenue interpretation RI 88). Such items are consequently exempt if used for private purposes.

[44] TCGA 1992, s. 45(2)–(4).

[45] Ibid., s. 262(1). For disposals before 6 April 1989 the limit was £3,000.

[46] Ibid., s. 262(2).

interest in or over tangible movable property, the consideration for the disposal is treated as the aggregate of the sum received for the interest disposed of and the market value of the remainder.[47] Any marginal relief is calculated as already described by reference to the deemed consideration for the disposal, and the relief is then allocated *pro rata* to the actual disposal consideration.

Suppose that in 2001 Q sells a one-third share in a watercolour for £2,500. He had bought the water colour two years before for £900. The value of his remaining two-thirds interest is £5,000. The disposal consideration is deemed to be £7,500 and so the chattel exemption is not available. The gain is then calculated under the normal part disposal rules: Q is allowed to deduct one-third of the acquisition costs (£300) from the receipt of £2,500 giving a gain of £2,200. The five-thirds marginal relief alternative gives a figure of 5/3 × (7,500 − 6,000) or £2,500 as opposed to £6,400 (7,500 − 900), and so is applicable. When the £2,500 is allocated *pro rata* the gain of £2,500 on the one-third interest is reduced by £833 to £1,667.

This principle is also applied to the loss restriction. If, in the above example, Q had purchased the picture for £8,400, and had sold a share for £1,500 (value of remainder £3,000), the position would be as follows. The allowable loss without restriction is £1,300, i.e. £1,500 (proceeds) less allowable costs (£2,800). However, if the proceeds are deemed to be £6,000 against allowable costs of £8,400 there is a loss of £2,400 of which Q's share will be one-third, or £800.

These rules do not require that several part disposals are treated as taking place at one time. It follows that there may still be an advantage in making a series of part disposals in order to take advantage of the annual exemption or some other personal circumstance.

2) Sets

Different provisions apply to a set of articles where the owner can make a disposition of one of the items in the set rather than, in the case of a single object, making a part disposal of it. The disposal of one item of the set is not treated as a part disposal of the set. However, special rules apply if there is a disposal of more than one item (a) to the same person, (b) to persons who are acting in concert, or (c) to persons who are connected with each other (but not necessarily connected with the disposer).

Whether the disposals take place on the same or different occasions, the two or more transactions are treated as a single transaction disposing of a single asset with any necessary apportionments of marginal relief and in restriction of losses.[48] The apportionment is made by reference to the consideration received for each of the items concerned. If disposals of parts of a set are made over a period of years, it appears that marginal relief or loss restriction for earlier years may be affected, although there is no extension of the normal six-year time limit for assessment or repayment claims. The following example illustrates the use of these rules to deny s. 262 relief.

Example

Geoff purchases a set of six antique dining chairs for £5,400 (£900 each) in October 1998. In December 2000, he sells three of the chairs to a dealer for £4,200 (£1,400 each). He sells the remaining three chairs to the same dealer also for £4,200 a year later in September 2001.

[47] Ibid., s. 262(5).

[48] Ibid., s. 262(4). *Quaere* when the recipients must be acting in concert or connected persons; is it the time of the first disposal or the subsequent one, or both?

Disposal proceeds per chair come to £1,400, with allowable cost of £900, so G has a chargeable gain of £500. Applying s. 262(4) the consideration (£8,400) exceeds £6,000, so the only question is whether marginal relief applies. The effect of marginal relief would be to limit the chargeable gain limited to 5/3 × (£8,400 − £6,000) = £4,000, or £667 per chair As this sum exceeds the actual gain of £500 it is ignored.

There is no definition of a set, although the Revenue used to take the view that only two items cannot constitute a set.[49] The statute requires that items of a set should all have been owned at one time by one person and that they are disposed of by that person. The provisions do not apply where the set is owned by connected persons.

34.5.3 Motor vehicles

Motor vehicles are not chargeable assets if adapted or constructed for the carriage of passengers; the exemption does not apply to a vehicle of a type not commonly used as a private vehicle and unsuitable to be so used.[50] The Revenue will not agree to exemption for single-seater sports cars or motor cycles[51]—presumably because it considers that a driver is not a passenger. This unimaginative construction is probably wrong, but a literal-minded court might uphold the Revenue. One consequence of the Revenue's position is that an expensive motor cycle bought for £10,000 and sold for £6,000 will give rise to a loss claim for £4,000—unless regarded as a wasting asset.

34.6 Land

34.6.1 General

Land is responsible for a substantial portion of the yield from CGT. In 1994–1995, i.e. before the stock market boom, 24% of the net gains came from land, as opposed to 71% from financial assets; in 1996–1997 the figures were 15% and 81% respectively.[52]

Land attracts a number of special rules modifying or illustrating the basic principles of CGT. Because of its capacity to generate substantial increases in wealth through development, CGT has attracted special legislation in the past. TA 1988, s. 776, introduced in 1969 when CGT rates were lower than income tax rates, is still in force; since s. 776 charges certain profits to income tax it will exclude any charge to CGT. Development land tax was in force from 1976–1985;[53] and existed alongside both CGT and the charge under s. 776.

Definition of land

The definition of land includes buildings of any tenure"[54] and any "right in or over land".[55] The CGT rules do not usually refer to "land" but to "an interest in land;" this includes an interest in a building, even though the land beneath may be in separate ownership. As a result of the wide definition of "land", the Revenue considers that rollover relief is poten-

[49] However, in *Tax Bulletin*, Issue 45 (January 2000), the Revenue discusses whether a pair of guns may be treated as a set.

[50] TCGA 1992, s. 263.

[51] *Manual CG*, para. 76907.

[52] *Inland Revenue Statistics 1998 and 1999*, Table 14.4.

[53] For a general review see Grant [1986] *JPL* 453. On abolition see Lawson, *Memoirs*, 363.

[54] TCGA 1992, s. 288(1).

[55] Interpretation Act 1978, Sch. I.

tially available on the grant of an option over land, despite the treatment in TCGA 1992, s. 144 where an option is regarded as separate from the asset to which it relates.[56]

Location

In determining whether an asset is located in the UK or elsewhere, any interest in land will be treated as situated where the land is situated, except where the interest is solely in the land acting as security.[57] A debt secured on land is located where the creditor is resident.[58]

Wasting asset

Freehold land is never a wasting asset, whatever its nature and whatever the nature of the buildings and works on it. A lease with 50 or fewer years to run is a wasting asset.[59]

Effect of exchange of joint interests

If A and B are joint beneficial owners of a piece of land and they exchange their interests so that each becomes sole owner of part, a strict analysis says that A has made a disposal of A's interest in the part now owned solely by B—and vice versa—so giving rise to a disposal by each of them.[60] To avoid this result concessionary rollover relief applies.[61] Where the property is a dwelling house, so that the only or main residence exemption may apply, the concession will be given only if all individuals accept that they acquire the other person's interest at its original base cost and on the original date of acquisition.

34.6.2 Furnished holiday lettings

Furnished holiday lettings are treated as a trade for CGT; all individual lettings made by one person (or one partnership) are treated as one single trade.[62] CGT reliefs are available in respect of (1) rollover relief under TCGA 1992, ss 152–157, (2) retirement relief under ss 163, 164 and Sch. 6 (where still available), (3) holdover relief under s. 165 and (4) relief for loans to traders under s. 253.

The property must have been let commercially, or available to have been so let or prevented from being let commercially by works of construction or repair. At least one of these conditions must have been satisfied at some time during the chargeable period.[63]

The treatment afforded to furnished holiday accommodation is not dependent on profits being made.[64]

34.7 Exemption for Only or Main Residence

34.7.1 Basic rules

A gain is wholly or partly exempt if it is attributable to the disposal of, or of an interest in,[65] a dwelling house which is or has been the owner's only or main residence. The house does

56 Revenue interpretation RI 11.

57 TCGA 1992, s. 275(1).

58 Ibid., s. 275(1), (2).

59 Ibid., s. 44(1)(a).

60 Doubt may have been cast on this analysis by the judgment in *Jenkins* v. *Brown* [1989] STC 577, where a disposal was held not to have occurred on a distribution of land holdings out of a pool held by trustees. It was held that the measure of the beneficial interests of the settlors was unaffected by the trust.

61 ESC D26; the concession is based on the analogy of TCGA 1992, ss 247, 248.

62 Ibid., s. 241(3).

63 Ibid., s. 245(1). For an individual, the chargeable period is the fiscal year; for a company the chargeable period is the accounting period.

64 *Walls* v. *Livesey* [1995] STC (SCD) 12.

65 TCGA 1992, s. 222. The Revenue accepts that an "interest" does not extend to a residence occupied under licence: see Inland Revenue interpretation RI 89.

not have to be such a residence at the time of disposal, provided it was such at some time during the period of ownership.[66]

Interest in the house

Because the exemption is confined to interests in the house, disposals of assets other than such interests are not exempt. The Revenue, rightly, treats an interest in the proceeds of sale of land as an interest in land, but does not grant relief where the house is owned through a housing association; this view is certainly harsh and possibly wrong. Since a leasehold interest is an interest in land, a sum paid by a landlord to the lessee of such a property to secure the surrender of the lease is exempt.[67] By concession, the Revenue also extends relief to profits realised by employees who, under relocation arrangements set up by their employer, sell their house to a relocation company (or to the employer) at market value and share in any subsequent profits on the sale of the house.[68] There is no requirement that the residence should be in the UK.

Dwelling house

The residence must be a dwelling house; this is a question of fact. The term "dwelling house" is not defined; the equivalent income tax relief for mortgage interest was extended to caravans and house boats,[69] and a caravan has qualified for CGT.[70] The courts also look at the degree of residence—temporary residence does not suffice, as was made clear when a taxpayer unsuccessfully argued that one month's stay while purchasing a permanent home should qualify.[71]

Purpose of gain

The exemption is lost if the acquisition of the house was wholly or partly for the purpose of making a gain from its disposal.[72] Similarly, where expenditure is incurred in carrying out improvements or in acquiring additional land with the purpose of gain, there will be a charge on the proportion of the gain attributable to that expenditure. A mere hope of making a gain is probably insufficient to lose the exemption.

34.7.2 Residence[73]

Associated buildings

The courts have had much difficulty with buildings related to the home. In one case it was held that a separate bungalow adjacent to but within the curtilage of a dwelling house was part of the dwelling house even though the bungalow was occupied by a part-time care-

[66] TCGA 1992, s. 222.

[67] *Quaere*, however if he receives compensation for agreeing not to seek a new lease since the interest is disposed of.

[68] ESC D37.

[69] TA 1988, s. 354(7) (now repealed).

[70] See *Makins* v. *Elson* [1977] STC 46, (1977) 51 TC 437 on the degree of residence required.

[71] *Goodwin* v. *Curtis* [1998] STC 475; see also *Moore* v. *Thompson* [1986] STC 170, (1986) 61 TC 15.

[72] TCGA 1992, s. 224(3); see *Jones* v. *Wilcock* [1996] STC (SCD) 389 (taxpayer unsuccesfully argued that he was caught by s. 224(3) so as to be able to claim loss relief; those who believe that property values always go up should study the figures in this case).

[73] See Lee [1988] *Conveyancer* 143; and Wilde [1993] *Conveyancer* 222.

taker.[74] However, this approach was rejected by the Court of Appeal in *Lewis* v. *Lady Rook*.[75] Adopting an "entity" approach, with the dwelling house as the "entity", the court was not concerned by the fact that the other building was separate from the main building, but asked whether it was part of the dwelling house. This was to be answered by asking whether it was "within the curtilage of and appurtenant to" the main house. In that case the exemption did not apply to a gain realised on the sale of a cottage occupied by a gardener even though she could summon help from the gardener by ringing a large ship's bell or flashing a flashlight. She was also held chargeable for an earlier period during which the cottage had been occupied rent free by the widow of a previous gardener; the effect was to penalise a person for acting in a benevolent capacity towards a person to whom she felt a moral obligation.[76]

Grounds of the main residence

As well as the actual site of the dwelling house, land is included in the exemption if the owner has it as the garden or grounds of the dwelling house, for his own occupation and enjoyment. There is no express requirement that the house and garden be adjacent. If the garden or grounds exceed 0.5 hectare, the exemption applies only if the Commissioners are satisfied that the larger area was, having regard to the size and character of the house, required for the reasonable enjoyment as a residence.

The sale of a garden separate from the rest of the house causes difficulties. To be exempt the garden must be occupied as such, with the house, at the time of the disposal. Where the house is sold with part of the garden and the remainder of the garden is sold later, the subsequent sale is not entitled to the exemption.[77] If the order of sales were reversed both sales would qualify.[78] The point is taken by the Revenue only where the garden has development value.[79] A separate sale of the garden may, where the garden is in excess of 0.5 hectare, weaken the plea that the garden was required for the reasonable enjoyment of the house.

The garden does not have to be adjacent to the house. In *Wakeling* v. *Pearce*[80] the Special Commissioners applied the exemption on the sale of a plot physically separate from the taxpayer's residence by a distance of some 25–30 feet. The Commissioners found, as a fact, that the land in question had been used as the garden or grounds of the house by the taxpayer for many years and this use continued up to the time of sale.[81]

Several flats or one home?

A no less intriguing problem arose in *Honour* v. *Norris*[82] where five flats in separate buildings in a London square were used to create a single home. If outhouses or separated

[74] *Batey* v. *Wakefield* [1981] STC 521, (1981) 55 TC 550; distinguished on its facts in *Green* v. *IRC* [1982] STC 485, (1982) 56 TC 10. See also *Markey* v. *Sanders* [1987] STC 256, (1987) 60 TC 245 (staff bungalow within grounds and separated by ha-ha was taxable—Commissioners reversed); and *Williams* v. *Merrylees* [1987] STC 445, (1987) 60 TC 297 (staff lodge exempt—Commissioners not reversed but doubted).

[75] [1992] STC 171, (1992) 64 TC 567. As to the Inland Revenue interpretation of "curtilage", see Inland Revenue interpretation RI 75.

[76] Sparkes [1990] *BTR* 260, commenting on the decision of the Chancery Division at [1990] STC 23.

[77] *Varty* v. *Lynes* [1976] STC 508, (1976) 51 TC 419.

[78] The position where the sales are simultaneous is unclear.

[79] CCAB, June 1976.

[80] [1995] STC (SCD) 96.

[81] For Revenue practice, see RI 119 which treats gains as taxable if they arise from land used for agriculture, commercial woodlands, trade or business, or which has been fenced off from the residence to be sold for development. The exemption will however apply to land which has traditionally been part of the grounds of the residence but which, at the date of sale, is unused or overgrown, and to paddocks or orchards—provided there is no significant business use.

[82] [1992] STC 304.

gardens can be part of a residence it seems odd that different accommodation should not be found in adjacent buildings. However, Vinelott J. rejected out of hand a submission that these flats could form one residence; declining to lay down any general principles he described the submission as "an affront to common sense".[83]

34.7.3 Periods when not used as the main residence

Full exemption applies where the dwelling house has been occupied throughout the period of ownership as the owner's main residence.[84] Where the period of ownership contains other periods, the starting point is to apportion—on a simple fractional bases. If a house has been sold realising a gain of £100,000 and was used for letting for the first seven years and as a residence for the last seven years, one half of the gain will be exempt under s. 222. A similar result may be reached if the division was by space and not by time.[85] The legislation contain several rules designed to provide further relief

Last 36 months

The last 36 months of ownership are treated as a period of owner occupation, whether or not so occupied, provided the house has at some time been the only or main residence.[86]

Apportionment—time

As already seen, where the house was used as main residence for only part of the period of ownership, partial exemption applies, and is given by apportionment of the overall gain rateably to the period of owner occupation as a main residence.[87] Where the individual has held different interests in the property, the period of ownership is treated as commencing with the acquisition of the first interest in respect of which allowable expenditure was incurred.[88] The apportionment rule is mandatory; there is no for market valuation on a change of use.

Example

Jim purchased a house as his main residence for £20,000 in March 1973 and occupied it as such until 31 May 1982. From then until its sale in September 2001, the house was occupied rent-free by J's son and daughter in law. The net proceeds of sale are £250,000. (Value at 31 March 1982: £80,000.)

[83] See angry criticisms by Norris (the taxpayer) in [1993] *BTR* 24, 40: "It may reasonably be expected that a High Court judge will have a greater knowledge of the law than a body of lay Commissioners but it is by no means necessarily to be expected that he has been blessed with a greater ration of common sense. If the courts are to abandon law in favour of common sense then different sources will have to be found for the selection of judges". See also Pearce Crump [1993] *BTR* 12.

[84] TCGA 1992, s. 222. The legislation does not say that the ownership must be of the land, and it is therefore arguable that the period of ownership is that of the dwelling house, a matter of importance where land is bought and a house is subsequently built on it.

[85] TCGA 1992, s. 222(10).

[86] Ibid., s. 223(1), (2). The period was extended to 36 months in relation to disposals on or after 19 March 1991 (previously 24 months). The period may, however, be further amended by Treasury order. The length of the period is intended to take account of the prevailing level of activity in the housing market.

[87] TCGA 1992, s. 223(2); only periods of ownership after 31 March 1982 are relevant in making the time apportionment. (s. 223(7)).

[88] Ibid., s. 222(7).

Disposal consideration	£250,000	
MV (31 March 1982)	£80,000	
Indexation allowance:	£82,800	£162,800
Taper relief: Gain × 90%		£87,200
		£78,480

The exempt period is the last three years and first two months = 38 months. Total period of ownership is 234 months, so the exempt part of the gain is 38/234 (£12,745) and the chargeable part is 196/234 (£65,735).

Space

Apportionment will also take place if a part of the house has been used exclusively for business purposes, e.g. a surgery attached to a doctor's residence.[89]

Letting—£40,000 Exemption

Gains attributable to a period of letting as residential accommodation are partially or wholly exempt; this additional relief is available on a letting either of the whole dwelling house or of part of it.[90] In *Owen* v. *Elliott*[91] the Court of Appeal gave a generous interpretation of this exemption holding that accommodation could be regarded as let "as residential accommodation" even though the occupants did not use it as residential accommodation. The case involved a family run hotel partially occupied by the family as their home; the hotel was held to have been let as residential accommodation.

The gain which becomes chargeable as a result of the letting is reduced by the smaller of (a) the gain attributable to owner-occupation, and (b) £40,000.[92] It seems that in a case where chargeable gains arise as a result of letting and also for some other reason, e.g. the house is left unoccupied or is used partially for business, the gain resulting from the letting must be identified separately. However, there are no provisions setting out how this is to be done.

Suppose that T sells his house at a net gain of £51,000, and that one-third of the gain comes within this rule. The rule states that the chargeable gain (£17,000) attributable to this one-third is to be chargeable only to the extent that it exceeds (a) £34,000 and (b) £40,000; it is therefore exempt from tax. If the gain is increased by 50% to £76,500, the chargeable gain goes up to £25,500; the figure for (a) is now £51,000 and (b) 40,000; (b) ensures that the gain is still exempt. However, if we the gain is increased by 75%—to £133,875—the chargeable gain is now £44,625, (a) is now £89,250 and (b) is still £40,000; (b) is the critical lower figure and T has a potential CGT liability on £4,625 (potential in that it may be covered by T's annual exemption).

34.7.4 Periods of deemed residence

The rules deem periods of non-occupation as periods of residence.

[89] Ibid., s. 224(1); no relief is lost if a room is used exclusively for employment purposes or partly for business purposes and partly for personal use (RI 80).

[90] Ibid., s. 223(4). Distinguish a lodger living as a member of the owner's family (see Statement of Practice SP 14/80). The letting must be as residential occupation, i.e. the persons to whom the accommodation is let must use it as their home.

[91] [1990] STC 469, (1990) 63 TC 319 CA; see Sparkes [1990] *BTR* 385.

[92] TCGA 1992, s. 223(4)(b).

First, as already seen, the period of 36 months immediately before disposal is treated as a period of owner occupation.[93] In practice, a 12-month period before occupation is also treated as owner occupation if the owner cannot take up residence because the house is being built or repaired.[94] Only the excess is then treated as a chargeable gain.[95]

Secondly, certain other periods are treated as periods of residence, provided they are both preceded and followed by periods of occupation[96] and no other residence is eligible for relief during the period of absence. These periods, which may all be claimed in aggregate, are:

(1) any period of up to three years;
(2) any period of overseas employment;[97]and
(3) any period not exceeding four years during which the owner could not occupy the house by reason of place of work or a reasonable condition imposed by an employer that he should reside elsewhere.[98]

Where the period of absence under (1) or (2) is exceeded, only the excess (not the whole period) is treated as giving rise to a chargeable gain.[99]

Third, job-related accommodation. The insistence on actual occupation of the dwelling house was harsh on those who had to live in accommodation provided by their employers. The legislation therefore treats the period of ownership as a period of occupation,[100] where a person, E, resides elsewhere in accommodation which is job-related. That other accommodation is job-related if it fulfils criteria identical with those for exemption from TA 1988, s. 145.[101] The exemption applies to the ownership of a dwelling house provided E intends to use it in due course as E's only or main residence; it is not clear whether the land must be in the UK or the Republic of Ireland.[102] Similar relief is provided in the case of self-employed persons where they are required to occupy the dwelling house for the purposes of carrying on their trade under the terms of a contract entered into at arm's length.[103] The reliefs are withheld if E has a material interest in the company unless the employment is as a full-time working director or the company is non-profit-making or established for charitable purposes only;[104] there is an analogous restriction for the self-employed.[105]

34.7.5 Election for main residence

An individual may only have one exempt residence. If T has more than one residence, there must be an election to decide which is to be exempt.[106]

[93] TCGA 1992, s. 223(1).

[94] ESC D49.

[95] (1983) *Simon's Tax Intelligence* 116.

[96] Periods of occupation need not immediately precede and follow the period of absence, but they must be periods of actual occupation, not other qualifying periods of absence. Where on a person's return, he is not able to resume occupation because the terms of his employment require him to live elsewhere, this condition is treated as satisfied (ESC D4).

[97] Where the house belongs to one spouse and the other is required to go overseas, the condition is treated as satisfied (ESC D3).

[98] TCGA 1992, s. 223(3), (7).

[99] (1983) *Simon's Tax Intelligence* 116, para. 13; and confirmed by the Inland Revenue Technical Division.

[100] TCGA 1992, s. 222(8).

[101] TA 1988, s. 356(3)(a), applied by TCGA 1992, s. 222(8)(a).

[102] As was required by the equivalent relief for mortgage interest (TA 1988, s.354(1)).

[103] TA 1988, s. 356(3)(b), (5); as from 1983, see TCGA 1992, s. 222(9).

[104] TA 1988, s. 356(4); on definitions see s. 356(6) and above at §17.1.

[105] TA 1988, s. 356(5).

[106] Under TCGA 1992, s. 222(5).

An individual may only elect between dwelling houses. T could not select a house which was always let to tenants, although an occasional letting is probably not inconsistent with residence. Any such election can take effect for a period beginning up to two years before the election is made.[107] However, the election must be made within two years of the taxpayer having more than one residence, even though it may be varied thereafter. [108] Thus, suppose that X buys house 1 in January 2001; buys house 2 in May 2002, so giving rise to a right to elect between houses 1 and 2—until May 2004. X then disposes of house 1 in June 2003 and buys house 3 in November 2003, so having two houses once more. X can elect, but can an election in favour of house 2 be backdated to May 2002 or only from November 2003? The answer is that it can be backdated only to November 2003. This decision has been criticised as being odd in practical terms.[109]

If a taxpayer has more than one residence then, if his interest in each of them, except one, is such as to have no more than a negligible capital value on the open market (e.g. a weekly rented flat or accommodation provided by an employer), the two-year time limit for nominating one of those residences as the individual's main residence for capital gains purposes will be extended where the individual was unaware that such a nomination could be made.[110] The late election will be deemed effective from the date on which the individual first had more than one residence.

Where a husband and wife live together they are entitled to only one private residence exemption between them and they must jointly make any election.[111] Whether or not the spouses have more than one house, a spouse may take advantage of any period during which the house was the main residence of the other.[112] Thus, if the husband dies and leaves the main residence to his wife, who does not occupy the house but sells it four years later, she will not be taxed in full on the whole gain since the death, but only on a proportion which takes account of her husband's period of occupation—whether or not she was also in occupation.

34.7.6 Dwelling house held by trustees

An exemption may be claimed by trustees if the dwelling house is owned by them and has been the main private residence of someone entitled to occupy it under the terms of the trust, or who is allowed by the trustees to occupy it and would be entitled to the income from the house or from the proceeds of sale.[113] When trustees of a discretionary trust in exercise of their discretion allow an object of the trust to occupy the house, the object is entitled to occupy the house under the terms of the trust since there is a right to remain in occupation until asked to leave by the trustees.[114]

[107] Ibid., s. 222(5)(a).

[108] *Griffin* v. *Craig-Harvey* [1994] STC 54, 66 TC 396.

[109] See Norris [1994] *BTR* 534, drawing attention to the difficulties a taxpayer would have faced if the court had looked at *Hansard*; for another comment, see Hutton (1994) *Private Client Business* 146.

[110] ESC D21.

[111] TCGA 1992, s. 222(6). As to the position where one spouse has interests in more than one residence, and the other spouse has none, see RI 75. The position is unaffected by the independent taxation of married couples. On separated couples, see ESC D6 (1994), and above at §33.10.

[112] TCGA 1992, s. 222(7).

[113] Ibid., s. 225.

[114] *Sansom* v. *Peay* [1976] STC 494, [1976] 3 All ER 375.

By concession, the relief applies also to property held by personal representatives but occupied both before and after the death by an individual entitled to an absolute or a limited interest in the proceeds of sale.[115]

34.7.7 Residence of dependent relative—5 April 1988 position preserved

Before 1988 an individual, or a married couple living together, could also claim exemption in respect of one private residence which was provided for a dependent relative rent-free and without any consideration of any sort.[116] Although this relief has been withdrawn it may still apply if the property is disposed of today, but was the sole residence of a qualifying dependent relative on 5 April 1988 or at some earlier time. Occupation after April 1988 may qualify if it has been continuous and existed on that date. However, a break in occupation after 1988 followed by a resumed occupation is not enough for later periods to qualify for the exemption.

34.8 Works of Art

Three special rules apply to works of art: (a) exemption for disposals to the right people; and (b) conditional exemption for CGT by analogy with the IHT treatment and c) holdover relief.

34.8.1 Exempt disposals

A gain is exempt from CGT if the disposal is (i) of property accepted by the Treasury in satisfaction of a liability to inheritance tax [117] or (ii) to a museum, etc., and where the disposal is "otherwise than by sale", [118]

34.8.2 Conditional exemption

Where IHTA 1984, s. 30 gives conditional exemption from inheritance tax on a transfer, there is an equivalent exemption from CGT.[119] However, this exemption is confined to gifts and certain deemed disposals by trustees. The conditional exemption takes the form of holdover relief; the disposal is treated as having been made for a consideration such that it is made at no gain/no loss. CGT may arise on a later sale if IHT also becomes chargeable.[120]

34.8.3 Holdover relief

There is also a holdover relief when assets are transferred to a fund established for the maintenance of historic buildings etc.[121]

[115] ESC D5.
[116] TCGA 1992, s. 226
[117] Ibid., s. 258(2)(b); IHTA 1984, s. 230.
[118] TCGA 1992, s. 258(2)(a); IHTA 1984, Sch. 3.
[119] Ibid., s. 258(3).
[120] Ibid., s. 258(5).
[121] TCGA 1992, s. 260(2)(b)–(f).

34.9 Woodlands: Timber

No CGT charge arises on the disposal of trees or saleable underwood in respect of woodlands managed by the occupier on a commercial basis and with a view to the realisation of profits.[122] Land on which short rotation coppice is cultivated is treated as agricultural land, not woodland.[123]

On a disposal of any woodland, such part of the acquisition cost—or the disposal consideration—as is attributable to the trees and underwood is disregarded for CGT. This exclusion prevents a taxpayer from buying land, cutting the timber and then claiming a loss for the decline in value due to the felling.

[122] Ibid., s. 250 Before 6 April 1988 the exemption for the disposal of standing timber was applied to woodlands within Schedule B for income tax purposes.

[123] FA 1995, s. 154. The provision is deemed to have come into force on 29 November 1994.

35

Disposals: (1) General

35.1 Meaning of Disposal

In the world of tax planning, disposals may be made either to realise a gain or to trigger a loss; in the real world they are made because owners want to rearrange their assets or simply need some cash. The central concept of disposal is not defined,[1] but nor has it yet caused much reported litigation. It seems to cover any form of transfer or alienation of the beneficial title to an asset (whether legal or equitable) from one person to another, involving a disposal by one and an acquisition by the other. A disposal by trustees of shares in the course of administration is clearly a disposal on this definition since beneficial title passes to the purchaser; the fact that the disposers are not beneficially entitled is irrelevant. An exchange of assets is a disposal of each asset involved. An involuntary disposal can still be a disposal;[2] however a disclaimer does not constitute a disposal.[3]

The Act extends the concept of disposal by treating certain shifts of economic value as disposals even though no asset is disposed of (see below at §35.5). In looking at these and other deemed disposals the courts have been reluctant to treat a disposal as occurring at a time when the alleged disposer might not have been aware of it, for example through losing the capacity to have children.[4]

[1] Definitions are available in other Acts, e.g. TA 1988, ss 776(4), 777(2), (3). In *Turner* v. *Follet* [1973] STC 148, (1973) 48 TC 614, the Court of Appeal made extremely heavy weather of the point whether the definition in the text is right. A loan is not a disposal, but a loan must be distinguished from a gift: see *Dewar* v. *Dewar* [1975] 2 All ER 728. On switching between different unit trusts in a multi-portfolio, see TCGA 1992, s. 102.

[2] But this effect may be undone by legislation (TCGA 1992, s. 66 (bankruptcy), ss 245, 246 (compulsory purchase)).

[3] Ibid., s. 62(8)(a); see *Re Paradise Motor Co. Ltd.* [1968] 2 All ER 625.

[4] *Figg* v. *Clark* [1997] STC 247; for an example of such reluctance in the context of capital allowances see Lord Browne Wilkinson in *Melhuish* v. *BMI (No 3)* [1995] STC 964, 974b, (1995) 68 TC 1, 75.

35.2 Timing of Disposal

Just as there is no general definition of a disposal, so there is no general rule for the timing of a disposal (or acquisition). While there are some specific rules, general matters are left as questions of general law. Therefore, the gift of a chattel takes effect when there has been delivery of the chattel with the requisite intention. Similarly, the transfer of shares other than bearer shares requires the registration of the transfer by the company. Transfers of other types of property, such as land or copyright, require certain formalities, such as a deed or writing.[5]

A transfer which falls short of these formalities may nonetheless be an effective transfer in equity and so qualify as a disposal for CGT. Thus, in *Re Rose*[6] a gift of shares was held to be effective in equity for estate duty purposes when the transferor/settlor had done all in his power to complete the transfer and all that remained was registration by the company; this would have continued even if the directors had refused to register the transfer, By contrast, in *Re Fry*[7] the transferor still had to complete certain exchange control forms and so equity could not intervene to make the gift effective. *Re Rose* had distinguished the earlier decision in *Macedo* v. *Stroud*[8] where it was held that a gift of shares became effective only when registration took place because the registration was undertaken by the donor himself and not some third party.

35.2.1 Disposal under contract: when the contract is made

Where an asset is disposed of and acquired under a contract, the time at which the disposal and acquisition take place is the time the contract is made and not, if different, the date of conveyance.[9] Thus, the usual time will be that at which the acceptance reaches the offeror, subject to the rules on postal acceptance.

Variations: is there a disposal under the contract?

The general rule applies only when the disposal takes place "under the contract"; whether this is so is a question of fact. The question can be particularly difficult if a contract is later varied and the issue arises whether the disposal is under the original contract as varied, or under a new contract. In *Magnavox Electronics Co. Ltd.* v. *Hall*[10] X made a contract to sell property to A in 1978; A later defaulted and a new purchaser, B, was found who was willing to buy, but at a lower price. In July 1979 X acquired a company, S; S took an assignment of the contractual rights from A. X and A then varied the original contract so as to reflect the new lower price agreed with B; S made a separate contract to sell the property to B. The Court of Appeal held that these arrangements did not enable X to argue that the disposal took place under the 1978 contract—and so in 1978. The agreement between X and S did not vary the 1978 contract since A was not a party to it. The court invoked *Furniss* v. *Dawson*[11] to disregard the interposition of S.

[5] For example the Law of Property Act 1925, s. 52 or the Copyright Designs and Patents Act 1988, s. 90(3).
[6] [1949] Ch 78.
[7] [1946] Ch 312.
[8] [1922] 2 AC 330.
[9] TCGA 1992 s. 28(1).
[10] [1986] STC 561, (1986) 59 TC 610.
[11] [1984] AC 474, [1984] STC 153, (1984) 55 TC 324.

Contract *un*enforceable

However, if the disposal is under the contract it will be treated as made when the contract is made even though the contract itself is unenforceable.[12]

Conditional contract

If the contract is conditional, the disposal occurs when the condition is satisfied; condition here means something on which the existence of the contract depends, rather than a major contractual term.[13] The courts have taken a pragmatic rather than legalistic line.[14]

Condition precedent

An example of a condition which will defer the time of the disposal is a condition precedent. In *Pym* v. *Campbell*[15] a sale of a patent was subject to the invention being approved by a third party; the third party did not approve and so the purchaser was not liable for refusing to complete the purchase. Another example would be an agreement to sell land subject to the grant of planning permission for the construction of a building on the land; this would be conditional until planning permission was obtained.[16]

Condition subsequent

As is clear from *Pym* v. *Campbell*, a contract which is subject to a condition precedent to its formation is not strictly a conditional contract since there can be no contract at all until the condition is satisfied. The phraseology cannot apply to a condition subsequent. Hence, it is considered that a contract with a condition subsequent would give rise to a disposal only when it is clear that the condition cannot occur.

Contractual conditions

The fact that a contract to dispose of an asset is expressed to be subject to performance by X, the transferee, of obligations imposed on X by the contract (promissory conditions precedent to performance) does not make the contract a conditional contract. Thus, an agreement to grant a lease of land subject to the construction of a building on the land by the intending lessee was held to be unconditional in *Eastham* v. *Leigh London and Provincial Properties Ltd.*[17] Similarly, a condition under which the contract terminates on the failure by one of the parties to perform his obligations under the contract (a promissory condition subsequent) would not make the contract a conditional contract.

Disposals under a consent order

Normally, the terms of a consent order made by agreement between the parties to court proceedings derive their force and effect from the parties' agreement and so take effect when the agreement is made. In matrimonial proceedings, however, the terms embodied in the order derive their effect from the order itself and not from the agreement.[18] In *Aspden* v. *Hildesley*[19] the agreed terms were embodied in an order made before decree absolute. This

[12] *Thompson* v. *Salah* (1972) 47 TC 559 (a case concerning Schedule D, Case VII).
[13] *Hatt* v. *Newman* [1999] STC (SCD) 171.
[14] *Eastham* v. *Leigh London and Provincial Properties Ltd.* (1971) 46 TC 687, CA.
[15] (1856) 6 E&B 370.
[16] As in *Hatt* v. *Newman* [1999] STC (SCD) 171.
[17] (1971) 46 TC 687, CA.
[18] *De Lasala* v. *De Lasala* [1979] 2 All ER 1146, PC.
[19] [1982] STC 206, (1982) 55 TC 608.

was not a full consent order, but an order that the agreed terms be filed "and made a rule of court". Nevertheless, it was argued that the terms had effect only by virtue of the order and that, as the order was made before decree absolute, it was conditional upon the decree nisi being made absolute in due course; this was to make the disposal under the terms in the order take effect on decree absolute.[20] However, the court held that this was not made out on the facts; the agreement provided for the immediate transfer of the taxpayer's interest in the property and could not have been set aside if the decree had not been made absolute.

35.2.2 *Is a contract a disposal?*

S. 28 deals with the timing of the disposal when an asset is transferred under a contract and does not answer the question whether the contract itself is the disposal. This question is or has been of importance for several reasons. First there is the basic obligation on a taxpayer under the self-assessment regime to report a disposal; if the disposal has not yet occurred there is no obligation to report it. Secondly, there is as more sophisticated problem. S. 28 applies only when the asset is conveyed or transferred and so does not expressly deal with a contract which is not completed. Where a deposit is forfeited, the forfeiture is not treated as the disposal of an asset,[21] but the contract itself will be treated as a part disposal of the asset if it creates an interest in or right over the asset,[22] a matter which presumably turns on whether equity could order specific performance of the contract. If, however, the specifically enforceable contract is itself the disposal, then the Revenue may be able to ignore the subsequent ending of the contract and so charge CGT both on the original part disposal and the subsequent ending of the equitable interest. This, however, is unlikely.

In view of the practical difficulties raised it seems preferable to reject the notion that the contract is itself a disposal, and to do so whether or not the contract is specifically enforceable. It follows that when property is disposed of under an unconditional contract of sale, the disposition takes place under the contract, and that when the contract is not followed by a disposal it is not open to anyone to treat the contract itself as a part disposal.[23]

35.2.3 *Asset lost or destroyed*

Where an asset is deemed to be disposed of by reason of its entire loss or destruction, the time of the deemed disposal is the time at which the loss or destruction occurs.[24] Where the owner of the asset later receives compensation for the loss, the date of receipt is the time of disposal.[25] These statements may be reconciled by treating the right to receive compensation as a separate asset arising at the time of the loss, or at the time the claim is proved, so that the receipt of compensation is the disposal of that right, not the disposal of the original asset. However, this conclusion is inelegant.

[20] Matrimonial Causes Act 1973, ss 23(5), 24(3).
[21] TCGA 1992, s. 144(7).
[22] Ibid., s. 21(2).
[23] By analogy with the forfeiture of deposit rule in TCGA 1992, s. 144(7).
[24] Ibid., s. 24(1).
[25] Ibid., s. 22(2).

35.3 Disposals Which Are Not disposals: Mortgages, Bankruptcy and Hire Purchase

Certain disposals are removed from giving rise to a potential CGT charge because the reality of the situation persuaded the legislature that there was no underlying disposal. This reality is all the clearer because while in mortgages everyone expects the property to pass to the mortgagor at the end of the period expectations, exactly the opposite is the case for hire purchase. Under hire purchase transactions there is a disposal at the beginning of the period of use. If, for any reason, the property does not pass to the hirer, the tax is "adjusted".[26]

35.3.1 Mortgages

A mortgage is, in essence, a security for a debt; as such neither a conveyance or transfer by way of security nor a retransfer on redemption of the security is treated as involving any acquisition or disposal.[27] Any dealing with the asset by the mortgagee for the purpose of giving effect to the security is treated as an act by a nominee of the mortgagor. So a sale will be a disposal by the mortgagor.[28]

An asset is treated as passing free of the security. When an asset is acquired subject to a security, the value of any liability taken over by the acquirer is treated as part of the consideration; a converse rule applies on disposal.[29] If an asset is bought for £3,000, subject to a mortgage of £7,000, the buyer is treated as buying it for £10,000; and if the asset is then sold for £5,000, still subject to the mortgage and not having reduced that mortgage, there will be a gain of £2,000 since the consideration on disposal will be £12,000.

When a vendor disposes of land, grants a mortgage to the purchaser and later recovers possession on default by the purchaser, the original disposal is, by concession, undone.[30]

35.3.2 Bankruptcy

Just as the mortgagee's acts are treated as those of the mortgagor, so the acts of a trustee in bankruptcy are treated as those of the bankrupt.[31] However, the trustee in bankruptcy is assessable for the tax.[32]

35.3.3 Hire purchase

Where a person, P, acquires an asset under a contract of hire purchase, the transaction is treated as if it amounted to an entire disposal of the asset to P at the beginning.[33] If the

[26] Ibid., s. 27.

[27] Ibid., s. 26(1). On what is a mortgage, see *Beattie* v. *Jenkinson* [1971] 3 All ER 495, (1971) 47 TC 121 (a decision on Schedule D, Case VII). Since 1925 a mortgage of freehold land does not end by retransfer but by cesser of the mortgagee's leasehold interest. One must presume that the draftsman's apparent oversight would be corrected by any court.

[28] TCGA 1992, s. 26(2).

[29] Ibid., s. 26(3). This rule is stated to apply where the liability is assumed by the acquirer; however an assignee of a mortgagor does not *assume* the liability (*Waring* v. *Ward* (1802) 7 Ves 332); technical arguments have not found great favour with the courts.

[30] ESC D18.

[31] TCGA 1992, s. 66.

[32] *Re McMeekin* [1974] STC 429, (1974) 48 TC 725, QBD (NI).

[33] TCGA 1992, s. 27.

period terminates, but the property in the asset does not pass to P, all necessary adjustments are made. The implication appears to be that the disposal and acquisition deemed to have occurred at the outset are then treated as not having taken place, so that the hirer is not treated as disposing of the asset when the interest terminates. However, P may be treated as having disposed of his rights under the contract, depending upon the circumstances.

The legislation does not state how the disposal consideration is to be valued. However, the Revenue practice in hire purchase cases is to divide the total of the rent and purchase price into capital and interest elements, and tax only the latter as income. If this is followed, the capital element will be the purchase price rather than the sum payable under the option. In practice the asset will probably be a car (as in *Lyon* v. *Pettigrew*[34] where the vehicle was a taxi but a chargeable gain arose in respect of consideration paid for the licence), a wasting chattel or a chattel whose cost is less than £6,000, so that the problem may not arise often.

35.4 Disposal Without Acquisition

35.4.1 Capital sums derived from assets

A disposal of assets by their owner may occur even though no asset is acquired by anyone else, for example if the owner of the assets receives a capital sum which is derived from the assets.[35] This last, simple-looking phrase has caused many problems.[36] S. 22 applies only to a capital sum; if a receipt is held to be income rather than capital, it cannot apply.[37]

S. 22 applies "in particular" to four types (see below at §35.4.2) of capital sum. It follows that facts may come within the general words even if not within the four categories. However, facts apparently within one or other of the four categories cannot be brought within the section if they do not come within the general words;[38] moreover, the four categories can be looked at as aids to the interpretation of the general words. The rule requires that the asset should have been owned by the person treated as disposing of them. A mere hope or expectation cannot be owned, and so, presumably, cannot be an asset. However, the wide scope of the term and the willingness of the courts to infer the existence of an asset from the receipt of a sum should not be overlooked.

In *Marren* v. *Ingles*[39] shares were sold for a cash sum plus the right to receive a further sum to be computed by reference to future, unpredictable events. The right to receive the future sum was held to be an asset.[40] When the events occurred and the further sum was paid, that sum was "derived from" the right to receive the sum and so there was a disposal of that asset. This is so whether or not the person paying the capital sum acquires any asset.[41]

34 [1985] STC 369, (1985) 58 TC 452.

35 TCGA 1992, s. 22.

36 See Sparkes [1987] *BTR* 323.

37 *Lang* v. *Rice* [1984] STC 172 where a sum paid as compensation for loss of trading profit was held to be an income receipt and so outside s. 22.

38 *Zim Properties Ltd.* v. *Procter* [1985] STC 90, 106, (1985) 58 TC 371, 390 relying on what, in effect, Lord Wilberforce and Lord Fraser both said in *Marren* (*Inspector of Taxes*) v. *Ingles* [1980] 3 All ER 95, [1980] STC 500, (1980) 54 TC 76 to overrule the contrary view expressed by Nourse J. in *Davenport* (*Inspector of Taxes*) v. *Chilver* [1983] STC 426, 439, (1983) 57 TC 661, 677.

39 [1980] 3 All ER 95, [1980] STC 500, (1980) 54 TC 76.

40 *Marren* v. *Ingles*, ibid.

41 Reversing *IRC* v. *Montgomery* [1975] STC 182, 189, (1975) 49 TC 679. As to "earn-out" sales where the deferred consideration takes the form of shares, see TCGA 1992, s. 138A.

The requirement that the capital sum must be derived from an asset applies to each of the four categories; a sum derived from some other source is not caught by these rules. Sums payable under the Agricultural Holdings Act 1986 to an agricultural tenant for disturbance on the surrender of his tenancy[42] or under the Landlord and Tenant Act 1954 to a business tenant for like loss are not subject to CGT. The sums are payable under the Acts by way of compensation for various types of loss and expense and so are not sums derived from the lease.[43] Compensation under an order in Council for expropriation of an asset by a foreign government has been held liable to CGT because, *inter alia*, the right to compensation in that case was an independent property right.[44]

Where a person received a capital sum in settlement of an action for negligence against solicitors in relation to a conveyancing matter concerning particular properties, it was held that the charge to CGT stemmed from the right to sue and not from the properties concerned and thus was not a part disposal of those properties.[45] A sum received for entering into a restrictive covenant, in connection with the sale of shares in subsidiary companies, has been held not to be a capital sum derived from an asset, because the freedom to engage in the activities concerned was not an asset. However, the sums were held to have been received in part for agreeing not to exploit the goodwill attaching to the group and so were taxable anyway.[46]

Compensation for the release of an option to participate in a development has been held taxable under this head.[47] The fact that another provision stated that the abandonment of an option is not the disposal of an asset was irrelevant.[48]

35.4.2 The four categories

Categories (1) and (2)—compensation and insurance payments

If capital sums are received by way of compensation for any kind of damage or injury to or loss of or depreciation of assets, there is a disposal of those assets, and a consequent gain or loss by reference to the acquisition cost of those assets. These words are of wide effect and are not limited to physical damage A similar rule applies to sums received under a policy of insurance of the risk of any kind of damage or injury to, or the loss or depreciation of, assets Thus, if a trader loses a capital asset by fire and recovers under his insurance policy, there is a disposal of the asset even though the insurance company does not acquire it

Compensation or damages received as the result of a court action, or by negotiated settlement of such an action, is a disposal of the right of action and is subject to CGT. In most cases, the base cost of the rights will be nil where they came into being on or after 10 March

[42] *Davies* v. *Powell* [1977] 1 All ER 471, [1977] STC 32, (1977) 51 TC 492. One must distinguish the statutory exclusion in TCGA 1992, s. 249 for certain grants to vacate uncommercial agricultural land under the Agriculture Act 1967 s. 27.

[43] *Drummond* v. *Austin Brown* [1984] STC 321, 325, (1984) 58 TC 67, 86, which distinguished a sum paid by a landlord in return for the surrender of the "fag end" of a lease. It was also important that the landlord was entitled to possession. On distinction between surrender and notice to quit see *Barrett* v. *Morgan* [2000] 1 All ER 481.

[44] *Davenport* v. *Chilver* [1983] STC 426, (1983) 57 TC 661, although in this case liability was virtually removed because the new right was deemed to have been acquired for market value. The position would now be different as a result of TCGA 1992, s. 17(2).

[45] *Zim Properties Ltd.* v. *Procter* [1985] STC 90, (1985) 58 TC 371; but see ESC D33. For a more fundamental argument that CGT is not payable on damages at all, see Wilde [1991] *BTR* 5.

[46] *Kirby* v. *Thorn EMI* [1987] STC 621, (1987) 60 TC 519

[47] *Powlson* v. *Welbeck Securities Ltd.* [1987] STC 468, CA, (1987) 60 TC 268.

[48] TCGA 1992, s. 144(4) see below §38.3.

1981. This is so even if the compensation or damages relate to an underlying asset. However, Revenue Concession D11 may relate the damages to the underlying asset where the right of action arises because of total or partial loss of, or damage to, the asset. Thus, the base cost of the asset will be available to compute any chargeable gain, and the various replacement and reinstatement reliefs may be claimed. Where there is no underlying asset, e.g. in a case involving damages for professional negligence resulting in expense to the plaintiff, any gain is, by concession, treated as exempt. Payments made under a contractual warranty or indemnity are not regarded as affected by the *Zim Properties* case[49] and will reduce the purchaser's acquisition cost.

Sums obtained by way of compensation or damages for any wrong or injury suffered by an individual on their person or in their profession or vocation are not chargeable gains.

Reliefs

Restoration. In the absence of special provisions, compensation or insurance payments for damage to assets would be treated for CGT as part disposals. However, under s. 23(1) if the sum is wholly (or all but a small sum which is not needed for the purpose) applied in restoring the asset, the receipt is not to be treated as a disposal. If the restored asset is later disposed of, the sums received are deducted from the allowable expenditure. If only a part of the sum is so used that part will be deducted from allowable expenditure on a subsequent disposal, but the remainder will be treated as consideration for a part disposal of the asset.[50]

Example

Alf's picture cost £6,000 in 1977. In 1994 the picture, then worth £120,000, was damaged in a fire. Alf incurred £20,000 in restoration costs but received £20,000 under his insurance policy. This receipt can be treated as a disposal under s. 22 for £20,000. However, A may instead claim that it should not be so treated, in which case the allowable expenditure on the picture (which includes the cost of restoration) will be reduced by £20,000 if he later sells the picture or otherwise disposes of it. If, however, he recovers £25,000, the part spent in restoration (£20,000) will be treated as outlined above, while the balance of £5,000 will be taxed immediately.

Replacement. If the asset is not damaged, lost or destroyed, there is relief from CGT on replacement. The compensation or insurance payment received must be applied in acquiring a replacement asset within one year of the receipt or such longer period as the inspector may allow.[51] The consideration for the disposal is then treated as such that neither gain nor loss accrues. The acquisition cost of the new asset is reduced by the excess of the compensation (plus scrap value, if any) over the deemed consideration for disposal of the old asset.[52] The reduction can be greater than the chargeable gain where not all of the gain would have been chargeable.

Example

A acquired an asset for £10,000, spending a further £2,000 on it. The asset was destroyed in an accident caused by B's negligence and has a scrap value of £500. B pays £15,000 damages.

[49] *Zim Properties Ltd.* v. *Procter* [1985] STC 90, (1985) 58 TC 371.
[50] TCGA 1992, s. 23(3).
[51] Ibid., s. 23(4).
[52] Ibid., s. 23(5).

The replacement asset costs £16,000. The disposal is treated as taking place at £12,000 (ignoring indexation). The new asset is treated as being acquired at £16,000 less £15,000 – (£10,000 + £2,000), i.e. £3,000 and less the scrap value, giving a revised cost of £12,500, not £16,000.

If the asset is lost and only part of the sum is used to replace it, there is some relief, provided the part unspent is less than the amount of the gain. In other words, postponement of tax liability is available only to the extent that it is necessary to make use of the gain in the replacement.

There are three limitations under this rule. First, this relief, in effect, allows taxpayers to postpone their tax liability, not escape it, unless perhaps they can later take advantage of an exemption such as that on death. Secondly, these rules do not apply to wasting assets.[53] Thirdly, the relief is expressed to be limited to an owner of property.[54]

When a building is destroyed or irreparably damaged, and compensation received is spent on constructing a replacement building on a separate site, both the original and the replacement buildings may, by concession, be treated as an asset separate from the land, in order to claim the replacement relief.[55]

Category (3)—forfeiture or surrender of rights

Capital sums received by a person in return for forfeiture or surrender of rights, e.g. the surrender of a lease, or for refraining from exercising rights, are taxable. Thus, a sum received for the release of a restrictive covenant or for an agreement not to sue on a contract would be chargeable events. As has been seen, it is not possible to use TCGA 1992, s. 22 to widen the scope of the term "assets".[56] No charge arises, therefore, when a sum is received for the surrender of something which is not an asset (e.g. the right to play amateur rugby, as in *Jarrold* v. *Boustead*[57]). Nor does a charge arise when the asset surrendered is an exempt asset (e.g. a life interest under a settlement) or a debt. If the owner of a right over an asset releases it, there is a disposal even though no consideration in received.[58]

Category (4)—use of assets

Capital sums received for the use or exploitation of assets are also caught. Thus, a sum received in return for the right to exploit a copyright or to use the goodwill created by that person would be caught, including, perhaps, the part disposal resulting from a restriction on trading activities as in *Higgs* v. *Olivier* (see above at §21.6).

35.5 Gratuitous Value Shifting: Disposals of Value Without Disposal of Asset

TCGA 1992 contains unusual and sometimes complex rules relating to value shifting. Principal examples include TCGA 1992, s. 29 (see below at §36.6) and ss 30–34 (see below at §50.8).

[53] Ibid., s. 23(6).

[54] Insurance proceeds received by the lessee of land are, by concession, exempt if accepted by the lessee in discharging an obligation to restore damage to property (TCGA 1992, s. 23(8), replacing ESC D1).

[55] ESC D19.

[56] *O'Brien* v. *Benson's Hosiery (Holdings) Ltd.* [1978] 3 All ER 1057, [1978] STC 549, CA.

[57] (1964) 41 TC 701 above §14.4.4.

[58] The disposal will be treated as taking place at market value if done gratuitously (TCGA 1992, s. 17(2)).

35.6 Part Disposals

35.6.1 *The A/(A + B) formula*

Where there is a part disposal, the proportion of the acquisition cost attributable to the part disposal is A/(A + B), where A is the consideration for the disposal and B is the market value of the remainder.[59] Assume that some years ago X bought a house and grounds asset for £90,000. Part of the grounds is sold for development, for which X received £100,000. The market value of the house and land following the sale is £250,000. The consideration received is £100,000. The proportion of the £90,000 which can be deducted is 100,000/(100,000 + 250,000) (or 2/7) which gives £25,714. Indexation relief will be applied to the £25,714 consideration; taper relief will be applied to the gain of £64,286.

This apportionment process applies only to the costs common to the part disposed of and the part retained. There is no appointment of expenditure which, on the facts, is wholly attributable to either the part disposed of or that retained.[60] The incidental costs of the part disposal therefore are attributable solely to the part disposed and are not apportioned. In practice the formula is not strictly applied on the disposal of quoted shares in a pool, the costs being apportioned simply *pro rata* to the number of shares disposed of.

The cost of the part of the land disposed of can be calculated on an alternative basis, under which the part disposed of will be treated as a separate asset and any fair and reasonable method of apportioning part of the total cost to it will be accepted, e.g. a reasonable valuation of that part at the acquisition date.[61]

35.6.2 *What is a part disposal?*

Under TCGA 1992, a part disposal arises where "an interest or right in or over the asset is created by the disposal, as well as where it subsists before the disposal, and generally, there is a part disposal of an asset where, on a person making a disposal, any description of property derived from the asset remains undisposed of".[62] This very wide definition presumably refers only to beneficial property, so that a declaration of trust over an asset gives rise to a total rather than a part disposal. There is therefore a part disposal when either (a) there is a disposal of a physical part of an asset, as in the example above of selling a part of grounds, or (b) rights are created out of an asset, as where a lease is granted by the freeholder or an easement over land. From (b) it follows that an agreement which has purely contractual effect is not of itself a part disposal.[63]

The boundary between the disposal of an entire asset or a part disposal of a larger asset is difficult to draw and is best seen as a question of fact. It is, however, of great importance because of the different methods of calculation. In relation to a piece of land with distinguishable elements, such as a house, garden and farm buildings, etc., the Revenue approach is that a single acquisition bought in one go is best treated as a single asset. The approach of

59 Ibid., s. 42. For provisions where there was a part disposal before 6 April 1988 of an asset owned on 31 March 1982, see ibid., Sch. 3, para. 4.

60 S. 42 (4).

61 Statement of Practice SP D1.

62 TCGA 1992, s. 21(2)(a). See generally Whiteman op. cit., §§7.21 et seq.

63 *Anders Utkilens Rederi A/S* v. *OIY Lovisa Stevedoring Co. A/B and Keller Bryan: Transport Co. Ltd.* [1985] STC 301.

the Revenue is different, however, if the correspondence surrounding the acquisition shows that different units were looked at separately, or if it is otherwise possible to make a satisfactory apportionment of the price.

There is some direct authority. In *Cottle* v. *Coldicott*[64] the Revenue successfully argued that the sale of a milk quota without any land was the sale of a separate asset and not a part disposal of the land—a conclusion which may have turned on matters of EC law rather than traditional English law. *Anders Utkilens Rederi A/S* v. *OIY Lovisa Stevedoring Co. A/B and Keller Bryan: Transport Co. Ltd.*[65] was a more complex case. The taxpayer (T) was a defendant in litigation. The plaintiff and T settled an appeal. Under the terms of the compromise T agreed to sell its premises, plant and machinery (the property) and to divide the proceeds with the plaintiff. T subsequently went into creditor's voluntary liquidation; the property was sold a year later. In a dispute between the plaintiff and T as to the burden of tax, the court held that the compromise was a part disposal by T to the plaintiff—and so T had to pay the tax then arising. T argued unsuccessfully that the terms were merely contractual and that the plaintiff received no proprietary interest until the proceeds were received. In *Berry* v. *Warnett*[66] S transferred shares to a nominee trustee and a few weeks later assigned his beneficial interest to a Jersey company in return for money and a life interest. The House of Lords held that the sale was a disposal of S's entire beneficial interest in the shares and not a part disposal of the holding. The life interest could not be said to be property "derived from" an asset remained undisposed of. In the *Zim* case (see above) the court held that a sum received on the settlement of a negligence action against solicitors arose from the right to sue, which was an asset separate from the property to which the claim related.

In order to solve these issues it is worth remembering that the actual question is whether TCGA 1992 s. 42 applies, and that both ss 21(1)(b) and 42(2) refer to "property remaining undisposed of". Whiteman points out that there can be an entire disposal even though the person disposing of the asset is left with a chargeable asset related in some way to the original. He cites situations in which an asset is transferred to a company in return for new shares issued by the company and where there is a sale of a business for unascertained consideration.[67] These must be contrasted with other situations which are unquestionably examples of part disposals, such as the grant of a lease out of a freehold and the sale of shares forming part of a pool. A possible test is that in the first two cases the person making the disposal is left with an item of property which did not exist before the disposal; whereas in the last two there is an asset which can be identified as being undisposed of throughout. However, the legislation talks of there being a part disposal when T holds "any description of property derived from the asset remaining undisposed of."[68] This suggests that some disposals are part disposals even where there is not an asset remaining in the vendor's ownership throughout the transaction. Thus, a sale of land subject to a leaseback is generally treated as a part disposal, even though there is an instant during the transaction at which the person making the disposal has no interest in the land at all.[69] Whiteman concludes that this may leave *Berry* v. *Warnett* as an isolated case.

[64] [1995] STC (SCD) 239.
[65] [1985] STC 301.
[66] [1982] STC 396, (1982) 55 TC 92.
[67] Whiteman op. cit. §§7-27 and 7-28.
[68] TCGA 1992, s. 22(1)(b).
[69] On dangers of such arguments, see Lord Hoffmann in *Ingram* v. *IRC* [1999] STC 37, at 44.

35.6.3 Relief from A/A 1 B for certain "small" part disposals

The practical disadvantage of the A/A + B formula is the need to calculate B, the market value of the part remaining—a process which may be expensive. To solve this, the TCGA 1992 provides a different treatment in four circumstances. There is no immediate charge to tax, but the consideration received is treated as reducing the acquisition cost which is set against the ultimate disposal of the asset concerned. This treatment is not available if the consideration received for the part disposed of exceeds the expenditure allowable in respect of the entire asset; here, there is an immediate charge to CGT.[70] The four circumstances are (1) a capital distribution,[71] (2) cash received on a share reorganisation,[72] (3) a premium on conversion of securities[73] and (4) cash received on compulsory acquisition of land.[74]

In addition, the sum received must be "small". It was not immediately clear whether "small" meant small in absolute terms or only in proportion to the purchase price. In *O'Rourke* v. *Binks*[75] the latter view was rejected. T received £246,000 on a reorganisation. This amounted to 15.58% of the acquisition cost of the original holding, but less than 5% of the value of the original holding immediately before reorganisation. The Court of Appeal held that this was not "small", holding that what was "small" was a question of fact and degree and had to be considered in the light of the circumstances in any particular case. The court stated that the purpose of the legislation was the need to avoid assessments in trivial cases; this was not such a case. However, there is no evidence for the court's view that this was the purpose of the legislation. Subsequently the Revenue stated that it would continue its long-standing approach of accepting as "small" 5% or less than the value of the shares/land, but would also accept as "small" any receipt of £3,000 or less. A taxpayer may, however, argue that the particular circumstances of a case justify an amount in excess of these limits to be regarded as "small" or, alternatively, an amount below these limits should not be so regarded.[76]

Where there is a part disposal of land, the consideration received is treated as reducing the base cost, in the same way, if the consideration does not exceed the lower of £20,000 or one-fifth of the market value of the land holding immediately prior to the part disposal.[77]

[70] For example TCGA 1992, s. 244.
[71] Ibid., s.122(2).
[72] Ibid., s. 116(13).
[73] Ibid., s. 133(2).
[74] Ibid., s.243(1)(a).
[75] [1992] STC 703, 65 TC 165.
[76] RI 164.
[77] TCGA 1992, s. 242(1)(a), (3)(a).

36

Disposals: (2) Gifts, Bargains Not at Arm's Length and Other Gratuitous Transactions

36.1 Gift As Disposal[1]

Some jurisdictions think it inappropriate to charge tax where no value is being realised. Others, like the UK, treat the passing of an asset from one person's tax regime to another's as an occasion of charge. Under FA 1981 the donor could have elected for a deferral of tax on a gift, but this was repealed by FA 1989.[2] The gain is computed on the basis that the asset is disposed of at its market value at the time it is given.[3] In *Turner* v. *Follett*[4] the taxpayer argued that in giving the shares away he had suffered a capital loss and it was contrary to natural justice to treat him as having made a gain. The Court of Appeal rejected his appeal.

A gift may be exempt under one of the general exempt disposal rules. In addition, there are express exemptions for a *donatio mortis causa*[5] and a gift of land to a housing association[6]

36.1.1 When does a gift take place?

There are no special CGT rules to determine when a gift takes place. Under the general property law rules[7] a gift becomes effective when the donor either makes an effective transfer of the asset to the donee with the intention of making a gift, or makes an effective

[1] See, generally, Venables [1989] *BTR* 333.
[2] FA 1981, s. 78, extended by FA 1982, s. 82, but repealed by FA 1989, s. 124.
[3] TCGA 1992 s. 17(1).
[4] 1973] STC 148.
[5] TCGA 1992, s. 62(5).
[6] Ibid., s. 259
[7] *Milroy* v. *Lord* (1862) 4 De GF & J 264.

declaration of trust. An example of the latter is *Berry* v. *Warnett*.[8] The taxpayer, T, settled shares on trust on 4 April 1972 giving himself a life interest, and sold the life interest two days later for £130,753. The House of Lords held that the settlement on 4 April 1972 constituted a disposal of the shares for CGT; T was assessed by reference to the market value of the shares on that date.

36.1.2 Donee's CGT liability

Although the primary CGT liability is with the donor, D, if the D fails to pay the tax within 12 months of the date from which it becomes payable, the Revenue may assess the donee, E.[9] The liability is still D's; as such, if D is a higher rate taxpayer and has used his annual exempt amount on other disposals, the Revenue can collect tax equal to 40% of the gain from E, even though E may be impecunious. E is given a right of reimbursement from D.[10] The assessment must be raised within two years of the tax having been due and payable by the donor. Thus, for a gift made in 1997–1998, the Revenue is only able to collect tax from the donee by raising an assessment between 1 February 2000 and 31 January 2001.

36.2 Connected Persons

Many CGT rules turn on connected person status.[11] For definition of connected person, see above at §33.8.

TCGA 1992, s. 18(2) applies the market value rules in s. 17 to any disposal between connected persons.[12] This treatment applies irrespective of the motive of the parties or the price paid. It also entails that holdover relief under s. 165 may be available.[13] However, s. 18(2) is excluded if s. 17 is also excluded; it will not apply, therefore, where there is an acquisition but no disposal, e.g. an issue of shares by a company to a controlling shareholder, or a disposal but no acquisition, e.g. on the repurchase or redemption of shares by a company.[14]

Loss relief is restricted where a loss arises on a disposal to a connected person. See above at §33.9

36.2.1 Market value where assets disposed of in a series of transactions: connected persons

In estimating the market value of an asset for CGT, regard is normally had only to that asset in isolation. However, the value may be increased by s. 19 where a disposal forms one of a series of linked transactions.

[8] [1982] STC 396, 55 TC 92, [1982] 2 All ER 630.
[9] TCGA 1992, s. 282(1).
[10] Ibid., s. 282(2).
[11] For example loans (s. 251(4)).
[12] TCGA 1992, s. 18(2) deems the transfer not to be by way of bargain at arm's length.
[13] This can be useful where a commercial bargain is entered into, but the parties cannot be certain that the value placed on the asset by the Revenue will equate to their own view of the value. The availability of a holdover election is also potentially of assistance where there are a number of transactions and one of the transactions, viewed alone, could be held to trigger a gain in excess of the gain computed by reference to the consideration actually passed.
[14] TCGA 1992, s. 17(2).

S. 19 applies where, by two or more transactions, A disposes of assets to another person, B, with whom A is connected—or to two or more persons with each of whom A is connected. Connected person status is vital and there must be connection with a common disponor (not necessarily between each disponee).[15]

S. 19 is an anti-avoidance rule, and applies only if the original market value[16] of the assets transferred is less than the appropriate portion of the aggregate market value of the assets disposed of by all the transactions in the series.[17] The original market value is simply the market value determined without regard to the linked transactions rule. The aggregate market value used to determine the uplifted transaction value is the value of the transferred assets in aggregate, determined as at the time of the transaction in question.

However, it is in some ways a weak anti-avoidance rule. It applies to linked transactions (transactions which take place within a six-year period).[18]

Suppose that A has a 60% holding in A Co. On 1 January 2000 A transfers a 20% holdings to B. This is repeated on 1 January 2001 and 2002. The 2001 and 2002 transactions are linked with the 2000 transaction and with each other. Assuming (as is usually the case) that the value of the 60% holding is greater than the value of three 20% holdings, s. 19 makes each subject to CGT on the basis that the value given away is one-third of a 60% holding. If the value of a 40% holding is greater than that of two 20% holdings, s. 19 will apply in 2001 to adjust the figures for the first two transfers. It will then be adjusted in 2002.

The linked transactions rule does not override the normal rule as to valuation on a disposal between spouses living together.[19] Special provisions apply to assets passed down chains, which include intra-group transfers.[20]

In contrast to the rule in *Furniss* v. *Dawson*, it is generally considered that this rule is solely a valuation rule and does not change the timing of the disposal.

36.3 Holdover Relief: Disposal of Asset Within Specified Categories

36.3.1 How holdover relief operates

Holdover relief is available on gifts and whenever there is "a disposal otherwise than under a bargain at arm's length".[21] The gain that would otherwise be chargeable to tax is held over so that the gain crystallised by the donor, D, is reduced to nil. The donee's, E's, acquisition cost is also reduced. Full tapering relief is given at the time of the gift; E's own tapering relief period begins at the time of the gift. E cannot use D's periods. For indexation relief periods, E's indexation allowance is given on the basis of the reduced figure. The gain held over is after taking account of any retirement relief available to D.

A partial holdover claim is not permitted. The holdover relief claim must be for the whole of the gain (subject only to the statutory reduction given by virtue of actual consideration or by chargeable non-business assets). Suppose that D's acquisition cost of the business asset was £40,000 and that D gives the asset to E when it is worth £100,000 after four years'

15 Ibid., s. 19(1).
16 Ibid., s. 20(3).
17 Ibid., s. 20(4), (6)–(9).
18 Ibid., s. 20(3).
19 Ibid., s. 19(2).
20 Ibid., s. 19(5)–(6)
21 Ibid., ss 1651 (1)(a). It also extends to settled property, see ibid. Sch 7, para 2. See generally Whiteman op. cit. §§18.51A et seq.

ownership. The gain of £60,000 is subject to full taper relief of 25% reducing the gain from £60,000 to £15,000. Assuming they elect to holdover, the chargeable gain is reduced from £15,000 to nil. Now assume that E sells the asset for £150,000 after a further five years. The sale proceeds (£150,000) are reduced by the base cost; this is £100,000, but has to be reduced by £15,000 on account of the gain held over. This makes deductible costs of £85,000 and the gain £65,000.

Taper relief at 25% reduces the gain from £65,000 to £16,200. Thus, the whole £110,000 gain becomes taxable but all on E's disposal—not part on D's and part on E's. Since the asset has been held for 9 years altogether, tapering relief is more valuable than if D has simply held the asset throughout the 12-year period.

Non-residence—and emigration

The relief is available only if E is resident in the UK, so as to ensure that the deferred tax will eventually be paid. If E is a UK resident company, it must not be controlled by a person or persons who are neither resident nor ordinarily resident in the UK, and the person who controls the company must not be connected with the donor.[21a] Gifts to dual resident trusts are also outside the relief.[22]

Where the donee becomes non-resident, the gain held over becomes subject to CGT, and the deferral ends.[23]

Restrictions

The right to hold over is subject to various restrictions where the gain is otherwise chargeable or wholly relieved.[24] However, in addition, holdover is not permitted for disposals on or after 9 November 1999 where the transfer is of shares and securities and the transferee is a company.[25] The reason for this change was that the holdover was being widely abused.[26] This abuse arose where the purpose was not to defer the liability on a bona fide gift but to avoid a CGT liability on an anticipated sale. This could be achieved if the company could use some tax exemption or other tax shelter. Other changes with effect from the same date prevent holdover relief on a disposal to a dual resident trust.[27]

Forms

Unless the gain is made on a disposal to trustee, both D and E must sign the claim,[28] which must be made within six years of the end of the fiscal year in which the disposal is made.[29] Procedures exist under which the election for relief may be made without a valuation of the asset being agreed with the Revenue.[30]

21a TCGA 1992, ss 166 and 167.
22 TCGA 1992, s. 169.
23 Ibid., s. 168.
24 Ibid., s. 165(3), referring to Sch. 6, esp. para. 7(2) or 8(2) but also to s. 116(10b) and s. 260(3).
25 TCGA 1992, s. 165(3)(b), as amended by FA 2000, s. 90.
26 IR Notes to Finance Bill 2000, s. 90.
27 By adding s. 169 to list in s. 165(1).
28 TCGA 1992, s. 165(1).
29 TMA 1970, s. 43.
30 Statement of Practice SP 8/92.

36.3 2 Qualifying assets

The asset must be

(a) an asset used for the purposes of a trade carried on by the transferor or by his personal company;[31] or
(b) unquoted shares or securities in a trading company,[32] or
(c) shares or securities in a trading company which is the transferor's personal company;[33] or
(d) property that qualifies for agricultural property relief for inheritance tax purposes.[34]

Category (a) includes an asset used for the purpose of a trade carried on by D in partnership; the size of D's interest in the partnership is not relevant. For (c), an individual's personal company is one in which the individual is able to exercise not less than 5% of the voting rights in the company.[35] The legislation takes a relaxed view of (d), which applies whether D is entitled to relief at 50% or at 100%. The claim is not limited to the value on which agricultural property relief is available. If farmland is given away and the majority of the value of the land is a reflection of its potential development value, rather than its agricultural value, holdover relief may nevertheless be claimed on the entire gain.

Sale at undervalue

Where consideration passes on a transfer, but the consideration is less than the market value of the asset transferred, holdover relief can be claimed provided the other conditions for relief are fulfilled. In such a case, the gain held over is reduced by the amount by which the sale consideration exceeds the sums allowable as acquisition costs.[36] Suppose that the land cost £50,000 and is worth £110,000 when it is sold for £65,000. The £60,000 gain which would otherwise be held over must be reduced by £15,000 to £45,000.

The effect of claiming relief on the sale undervalue is to leave in charge the gross gain without any deduction for tapering relief. The benefit of the taper will be enjoyed by E when ultimately disposing of the asset; E can include D's years of ownership for the taper period.

Partial reliefs

Apart from sales at undervalue, relief is available on an apportioned basis if :

(a) the asset was not used for the purpose of a trade throughout the period of ownership;[37]
(b) the disposal is of a building and part of the building was not used for the purpose of the trade;[38]
(c) the disposal is of shares in a company and the company has nonbusiness chargeable assets at the time when a disposal is made of its shares.[39]

[31] TCGA 1992, s. 165(2)(a).
[32] Ibid., s. 165(2)(b)(i).
[33] Ibid., s. 165(2)(b)(ii).
[34] Ibid., Sch. 7, para. 1(1).
[35] Ibid., s. 165 (8)(a); before 1993 the test was whether it was D's family company.
[36] Ibid., s. 165(7).
[37] Ibid., Sch. 7, para. 5.
[38] Ibid., Sch. 7, para. 6.
[39] Ibid., Sch. 7, para. 7.

An asset used for the purpose of trade, etc., must be so used at the time of disposal.[40] Point (a) applies if the asset was so used at the time of disposal, but there were periods of other use earlier; a time apportionment takes place.[41] For (b) a "just and reasonable" apportionment is made.[42] No apportionment is necessary, however, in the case of land and buildings qualifying for agricultural property relief.[43]

36.3.3 Other rules[44]

Holdover relief is computed on the gain before retirement relief.[45] However, the gain held over can never exceed the gain arising after retirement relief.[46]

36.4 Holdover Relief: Gains Subject to Inheritance Tax

There is no restriction on the type of asset for which a claim may be made under s. 260 which allows a holding over of a gain arising on any transfer which is chargeable to IHT. "Chargeable" means immediately chargeable (as opposed to a Potentially Exempt Transfer). It is not necessary for IHT actually to be payable as the requirement is satisfied where the transfer is covered by the IHT annual exempt amount or by the IHT nil rate band. Relief is not available for a PET, even if it becomes chargeable by virtue of the death of the donor within the seven-year period.[47] However, the relief can be claimed in respect of certain transfers which are exempt from IHT.[48]

A claim for holdover relief under s. 260 cannot be made in respect of a transfer between spouses living together. Hence, where spouses have separated, the transfer of an asset from one spouse to the other after the end of the fiscal year in which they separate crystallises a capital gain on which tax is potentially payable, unless the conditions of s. 165 are fulfilled.

It is also excluded if the transfer is to a dual resident trust.[49] This applies as from 9 November 1999.

There is some uncertainty over the scope of the holdover relief where the IHT transfer relates to property subject to an A and M trust. Holdover relief is available where the disposal is an occasion on which IHT tax would be chargeable but for IHTA 1994, s. 71(4). S. 71(4) is a relief from IHT where the beneficiary of such a trust acquires an interest in possession. However, the beneficiary will usually be treated as having already acquired an interest in possession at age 18[50] even if the property remains in the settlement. S. 71 will apply only if that normal rule is excluded.

40 The Revenue take a strict view of this rule (CG 66952).

41 TCGA 1992, Sch. 7, para. 5(1).

42 TCGA 1992, Sch. 7, para. 6(1).

43 Ibid., Sch. 7, paras 5(2), 6 (2).

44 On holdover relief and 1982 rebasing, see ibid., Sch. 4, para. 5.

45 Ibid., s. 165(6).

46 Ibid., Sch. 7, para. 8.

47 IHTA 1992, s. 260(2)(a).

44 Ibid., s. 30 or 78(1) (designated property or work of art); ss 27, 57A or Sch. 4 (maintenance funds for historic buildings), s 24 (transfer to a political party) and s. 71 (accumulation and maintenance trust).

49 TCGA 1992, s. 260(1) as amended by FA 2000, clause 89.

50 As in *Begg-MacBrearty* v. *Stilwell* [1996] STC 413.

Where, as often happens, the vesting of capital has been preceded by the vesting of the interest in possession, the conditions for holdover relief do not, strictly, apply. This is because the occasion on which the IHT relief has applied is not the occasion on which the asset "passes to" the beneficiary. It is not clear is what happens if the trustees exercise a power of advancement on the beneficiary's eighteenth birthday, so that the CGT disposal occurs on the same day but not from the same cause.

36.5 Holdover Relief and Property in Trust

The vesting of property in a beneficiary is a disposal by trustees and is made "otherwise than under a contract at arm's length".[51] Hence, an election for holdover relief can be made where either s. 260 is satisfied and the transfer is chargeable to IHT (which will always be the case where there is a transfer in or out of a discretionary settlement), or s. 165 applies because the asset is a qualifying asset. The settling of property and the passing of an asset to a beneficiary by virtue of the exercise of the trustees' discretion are also "otherwise than under a contract at arm's length" and so holdover relief may be available.

An election to hold over a gain arising on the transfer into trust is made unilaterally by the settlor.[52] An election on the transfer of an asset out of trust is made by the trustees and the recipient beneficiary jointly.

Holdover relief can be claimed by trustees where an asset is used for the purposes of a trade carried on by a beneficiary who has an interest in possession in the settled property.[53]

Where trustees transfer shares to a beneficiary and wish to claim holdover relief under s. 165, it is necessary for the shares to be either unquoted shares in a trading company or for the trustees to be entitled to exercise 25% or more of the voting rights in the company immediately prior to the disposal.[54]

36.5.1 Death crystallises charge

Where an election for holdover relief is made on the transfer of an asset into trust, whether under s. 165 or 260, the gain held over is brought into charge on the death of any life tenant of the trust.[55] The gain brought into charge is normally the gain which was held over; however, the gain brought into charge cannot exceed the gain measured by reference to the market value of the asset at the time of the death of the life tenant. This gain may, in turn, be held over under s. 260 as the death of the life tenant is an occasion of charge to inheritance tax. There is, however, one exception to the availability of the further claim to holdover relief where, at the death the property passes to the surviving spouse of the deceased life tenant or into trust in which the surviving spouse has a life interest.[56]

Where the gain is crystallised, an immediate charge to CGT arises, unless a deferral may be claimed because the asset comes within s. 165(2).

[51] TCGA 1992, s. 165(1)(a).
[52] Ibid., s. 165(1)(b).
[53] Ibid., Sch. 7, para. 2(2)(a)(ii).
[54] Ibid., Sch. 7, para. 2(2)(b).
[55] Ibid., s. 74.
[56] IHTA 1984, s. 18(1) then operates so that the transfer is not chargeable to inheritance tax; hence, the condition for a holdover relief claim under TCGA 1992, s. 260 is not satisfied.

36.6 Gratuitous Value Shifting; Disposal of Value Without Disposal of Asset

The term "disposal" is widened to catch three types of transaction. In all three, the market value which would be payable by the acquirer under a bargain at arm's length is taken as the consideration; any consideration given for the disposal is taken into account. TCGA 1992, s. 29 is discussed here (rather than in the general chapter on disposals) because it is an unusual provision. A charge arises whether or not there is any consideration, so that potentially it applies whether the disposal is gratuitous or for value.[57] However, it follows from this that, unlike normal disposals, there is no charge to CGT where the consideration given equals (or exceeds) that full market value.

The first type of transaction is where "a person" has control of a company and exercises that control so that value passes out of shares in the company owned by him, or by a person with whom he is connected, and passes into other shares in, or rights over, the company.[58] A controlling shareholder using his voting power to pass a resolution increasing the rights of a particular type of share at the expense of his own is clearly shifting value to the other shareholders, although no particular piece of property has been disposed of.[59] The controlling shareholder cannot claim holdover relief on the deemed disposal since no shares have actually been transferred—even though holdover relief could have been claimed on a gift of the shares themselves. Despite the fact that the singular "person" is referred to, it has been held that the section applies where two or more persons control the company.[60] It has also been held that control was exercised when, under a pre-arranged scheme, a winding-up resolution was passed even though the taxpayer himself did not vote on the motion.[61] Outside the context of a scheme, the taxpayer must presumably vote in order to "exercise" control.

The second type of transaction is where, after a transaction whereby the owner of any property has become the lessee of the property, there is an adjustment of the rights and liabilities of the lease which is as a whole more favourable to the lessor.[62]

The third type of transaction is where an asset is subject to a right or restriction and a transaction takes place whereby that right or restriction is extinguished or abrogated in whole or in part. The figure taken is the value accruing to the owner of the property from which the restriction falls.[63]

The unusual nature of this rule is mirrored by the rule for losses;[64] where value has passed out of shares in this way loss relief may not be claimed. A literal reading would suggest that this no-loss rule applies only to shares and not to the second or third type of transaction.

[57] TCGA 1992, s. 29(1)(a).

[58] Ibid., s. 29(2).

[59] The legislation does not, however, limit itself to value shifting into shares held by others, and could apply where value is shifted between different classes of shares held by the same person This is understood to be the Revenue view.

[60] *Floor* v. *Davis* [1979] STC 379,52 TC 609 [1979] 2 All ER 677.

[61] In the light of the decision in *W T Ramsay Ltd.* v. *IRC*, see above §5.6.4, it would appear that the same result would have been reached if, as part of the scheme, they had voted against the resolution.

[62] TCGA 1992, s. 29(4).

[63] Ibid., s. 29(5).

[64] TCGA 1992, s. 29(3).

37

Leases

37.1 General

The CGT rules governing leases are complex. In part, this simply reflects the complexity of the transactions with which the law is dealing; however, it also reflects the complexity of neighbouring areas of tax law, especially income tax. The provisions deal with two main issues: (a) the determination of gains or losses on the disposal of the lease by the lessee; (b) the circumstances in which the grant of a lease is a disposal or part disposal by the landlord—and how any gains should be computed. These rules apply generally to leases of movable and immovable property.

37.2 Wasting Asset Rules

Special computational rules apply on the disposal of a lease which has 50 years or less to run at the time of the disposal. Such a lease is a wasting asset.[1] The wasting asset writing down rules apply as soon as the lease becomes a wasting asset;[2] subsequently, however, they apply regardless of the original length of the lease.

Three rules apply to determine the duration of a lease; these are to prevent short leases appearing as long leases.[3] The rules are applied by reference to the facts which were known or ascertainable at the time when the lease was created (or acquired by the disposer)[4] and are as follows:

(1) *notice*: where the lease can be ended by notice given by the landlord it is treated as ending at the earliest date on which it could be ended.[5] A lease for 50 years which the

[1] TCGA 1992, s. 44.
[2] Ibid., Sch. 8, para. 1(5).
[3] They are similar, but not identical, to the Schedule A rules in TA 1988, s. 38.
[4] TCGA 1992, Sch. 8, para. 8(6).
[5] Ibid., Sch. 8, para. 8(2).

landlord may terminate by notice after five years is treated as a five-year lease—even after the five-year period has passed;

(2) *commercial reality*: where any of the terms of the lease render it unlikely that the lease will continue beyond a certain date, the lease is treated as ending on that date.[6] A lease which specifies a date on which rent is to be increased is treated as a lease expiring on that date;[7]

(3) *extension*: where the terms of the lease include provision for the extension of the lease beyond a given date by notice given by the tenant, these provisions apply as if the term of the lease extended for as long as it could be extended by the tenant, but subject to any right of the landlord by notice to determine the lease.[8]

A lease of movable property which is a wasting asset is deemed to terminate not later than the end of the life of the wasting asset.[9]

A lease with less than 50 years to run is not treated as a wasting asset in two situations. The first is where, at the beginning of the ownership of a lease, it is subject to a sub-lease not at a rack rent, and it is estimated at that time that the value of the lease, when the sub-lease falls in, will exceed the lessee's acquisition cost; such a lease is not a wasting asset until the sub-lease falls in.[10] The second exception is where the lease qualifies for capital allowances, e.g. on a lease of an industrial building; this is the normal rule for all assets qualifying for capital allowances.[11]

37.3 Writing Down the Expenditure

A lease of land becomes a wasting asset only when it has less than 50 years to run.[12] When a lease has no more than 50 years to run, the expenditure attributable to its acquisition is deemed to waste away over the balance of its duration. TCGA 1992, s. 46 directing a straight line basis does not apply. Instead, a special curved basis applies to a lease of land, with less depreciation in the early years of the lease and more depreciation towards its end. This curved basis was thought to give the true commercial measure. Despite this, the straight line basis was selected for other parts of CGT, notably pre-1965 assets and wasting assets other than land.

Any applicable indexation relief[13] is given only on the expenditure not yet written off.

So suppose that A block of flats was leased for 99 years from 1 January 1936 and that the leasehold interest was acquired by A on 31 May 1997 for £105,000 and sold on 1 March 2001 for £500,000. The unexpired term on acquisition in 1997 was 37 years and 7 months and on disposal was 33 years 10 months. The table gives the relevant percentages as 93.901 (P1) and 91.010 (P3). The statute directs that A may not take account of a fraction of the expenditure of £105,000; that fraction is (P1 – P3)/P1. The fraction works out at 0.031 so 3.1% of the acquisition cost (£3,255) is disallowed. This reduces the allowable acquisition cost from £105,000 to £101,745 and increases the gain (before indexation or other reliefs) from £395,000 to £398.225.

[6] TCGA 1992, Sch. 8, para. 8(3).
[7] Ibid., Sch. 8, para. 8(4).
[8] Ibid., Sch. 8, para. 8(5).
[9] Ibid., Sch. 8, para. 9(3).
[10] The Act contains various formulae; it is not clear whether, when the lease does become a wasting asset, the amount P(l) is 100.00 (the normal rule for leases which become wasting assets by passing the 50-year point), or the percentage applicable to the actual duration left. The latter seems more sensible.
[11] TCGA 1992, Sch. 8, para. 1(6).
[12] Ibid., Sch. 8, para. 8(1).
[13] TCGA 1992, s. 53(3).

The reason why the fraction refers to P3 rather than P2 is that P2 is reserved for any allowable costs of improvement etc. since the asset was acquired.

37.3.1 Situations attracting special treatment

Landlord and Tenant Act 1954

A new lease granted as the result of an application under the Landlord and Tenant Act 1954 is a new asset—separate from the original lease and so not derived from it.[14] None of the expenditure in respect of the original lease is available to be taken into account in relation to a disposal of the new lease.

Leasehold Reform Act 1967

A new lease under the Leasehold Reform Act is not an extension of the old lease.[15] This is because the CGT legislation requires the extension to be included in the terms of the lease; the statutory right arises under the Act, not under the lease.

Surrender and regrant

By concession, no CGT charge is treated as arising if the old lease is surrendered in return for the grant of a new, longer lease of the same property to the same lessee.[16] The transaction must be between unconnected parties bargaining at arm's length, and not connected with a larger scheme or series of transactions. The lessee must not receive a capital sum and the terms of the new lease must not differ from those of the old lease in any respect other than its duration and the amount of rent payable.

Merger

Where the lessee acquires a superior lease or the freehold reversion, the interests in the two assets are merged and the original lease is extinguished.[17] By concession, the expenditure allowable on a disposal of the merged interest will include the costs of the superior interest and of the first lease (written down if the duration was less than 50 years) to the date of the acquisition of the superior interest. If the superior interest is itself a lease with a duration of less than 50 years, the total of these amounts is written down to the date of disposal of the merged lease.[18]

37.4 Granting a Lease: Premium

The CGT rules on the grant of a lease refer frequently to the concept of a "premium". A "premium" is defined as includings any sum (other than rent) paid on or in connection with the grant of a tenancy, except in so far as other sufficient consideration for the payment is shown to have been given. A premium also includes "any like sum, whether payable to an intermediate or a superior landlord"[19]—presumably meaning a sum paid by the tenant to the landlord for the lease. See also above §25.5.1 on premium for Schedule A.

14 *Bayley* v. *Rogers* [1980] STC 544, (1980) 53 TC 420.
15 *Lewis* v. *Walters* [1992] STC 97, (1992) 64 TC 489.
16 ESC D39.
17 TCGA 1992, s. 43; on taper relief see ibid., Sch. A1, para. 14.
18 ESC D42.
19 TCGA 1992, Sch. 8, para. 10(2).

In *Clarke* v. *United Real (Moorgate) Ltd.*[20] counsel tried to gloss over these words by arguing that the sum had to be paid to the landlord "as landlord". The judge agreed that sums paid for plumbing work were not a premium partly because, on counsel's definition, they were not paid to the landlord as landlord, and partly because, as the judge pointed out, they were not paid to the landlord in consideration for the grant of the lease. However, sums agreed to be paid to the landlord under the terms of a construction lease did amount to a premium, even though the sums were equal to the costs of construction.

Statute treats certain sums as lease premiums, e.g. payment in lieu of rent, consideration for the surrender of a lease and consideration for the variation of a lease.[21]

In relation to Scotland, a premium includes, in particular, a grassum payable to any landlord or intermediate landlord on the creation of a sub-lease.[22]

Gifts and connected persons. Where there is a variation or waiver of any of the terms of a lease and, had the transaction been at arm's length, a sum would have been expected to have been paid as consideration for the variation or waiver, this sum is treated as a lease premium if the landlord and tenant are connected persons, or the transaction was entered into gratuitously.[23]

When does the premium arise? The time at which the lease premium is deemed to have arisen depends on the event. Where an actual premium is paid, the time is the date of the grant of the lease.[24] A payment in lieu of rent or a variation or waiver is treated as arising when the sum is payable.[25] Where the premium is imputed by the relationship between the parties, the operative date is the date on which the sum would have been payable had the parties acted at arm's length.[26]

37.5 Granting a Lease as a Part Disposal: Computational Problems

Where the payment of a premium is required under a lease there is a part disposal of the freehold or other asset out of which the lease is granted.[27] This is in accordance with general principles, but is expressly articulated. Where a lease is granted for a full rent but without a premium there is a part disposal but no chargeable gain will arise; this is because the only consideration received is the right to the rent, and that is not relevant consideration.[28] Where the lease granted is a bargain at arm's length, or if the lessee is a person connected with the lessor, the amount of the premium deemed to have been given is the market value of the lease.[29]

[20] [1988] STC 273, (1988) 61 TC 353. This test comes from the judgment of Lord Goddard in *R.* v. *Birmingham (West) Rent Tribunal* [1951] 2 KB 54, 57, [1951] 1 All ER 198 at 201: "The whole conception of the term is a sum of money paid to a landlord as consideration for the grant of a lease".
[21] TCGA 1992, Sch. 8, para. 3, amended by FA 1996.
[22] Ibid., Sch. 8, para. 10(3).
[23] Ibid., Sch. 8, para. 3(7).
[24] Ibid., s. 28(1), Sch. 8, para. 3.
[25] Ibid., Sch. 8, para. 3(2)(a), (3)(a).
[26] Ibid., Sch. 8, para. 3(4).
[27] Ibid., Sch. 8, para. 2(1).
[28] Ibid., s. 37(1).
[29] Ibid., s. 17(1).

Where there is a part disposal, the A/A + B formula in TCGA 1992, s. 42 is applied. In valuing B (the property remaining undisposed of), it should be noted that B includes the right to the rent or other payment. [30]

Example

T bought a freehold factory for £180,000 in May 1994. After occupying it for the purposes of his own business, he grants a 15-year lease to a company for £50,000 with effect from 1 December 2001. The capitalised value of rentals under the lease is £150,000 and the freehold reversion is worth £200,000. This means that A = 50,000 and B = (200,000 + 150,000); so A/A + B = 50,000/50,000 + 350,000, or 1/8. This means that the allowable expenditure is restricted to 1/8 × £180,000, i.e. £22,500. The indexation allowance is also applied to £22,250 (giving) £2,633. Total allowable expenditure of £25,133 is set against the disposal consideration of £50,000 to give a net gain of £24,867; assuming that taper relief reduces the gain from 100% to 50%, the final figure for the chargeable gain is £12,433.

Sublease out of short lease. The A/A + B formula in s. 42 does not apply in the case of a lease granted out of a lease which is a wasting asset under the rules just described.[31] Rules restrict the part of the expenditure on the short head lease which can be deducted. That part is the part that may be written off, using the curved line basis for land and the straight line basis for other assets.[32] These rules apply not only to acquisition costs but also to expenditure on improvements.[33]

Low Premium. If the premium is less than the sums which would be obtainable if the rent receivable under the sub-lease were the same as the rent payable under the head lease, (e.g. if the rent charged on the sub-lease is double that charged under the lease out of which the sub-lease is created), a further adjustment takes place. If the premium is one half of the amount so obtainable only one half of the expenditure attributable to the sub-lease is taken.[34]

Sub lease of part. Further provisions deal with the grant of a sub-lease of *part* of the land comprised in the head lease.[35] The proportion of the expenditure is taken by comparing the value of the property covered by the sub-lease with the value of all the property comprised in the head lease; the remainder of the expenditure is apportioned to the part not disposed of.

Income Tax. Where income tax has been paid in respect of the premium by the sub-lessor, rules exist to prevent double charging. If the lease has been granted out of a freehold or long lease, the premium subject to CGT is reduced by the amount subject to income tax.[36] However, the reduced premium is substituted only in the numerator, not in the denominator, of the A/A + B formula for apportioning allowable expenditure. In the case of a short lease granted out of a short lease, the CGT computation follows the normal

[30] Ibid., Sch. 8, para. 2(2), applying s. 42.
[31] Ibid., Sch. 8, para. 4.
[32] Ibid., Sch 8 para. 4(2)(a). If the lease is granted out of a short lease, the allowable expenditure is the amount which will have wasted over the term of the sub-lease, given by the fraction P(4) − P(5)/P(l)I, where: P(l) = the percentage applicable to the unexpired term of the head lease at the date of acquisition; P(4) = the percentage applicable to the unexpired term of the head lease at the date the sub-lease is granted; P(5) = the percentage applicable to the unexpired term of the head lease at the date the sub-lease expires.
[33] TCGA 1992, Sch. 8, para. 4(2).
[34] Ibid., Sch. 8, para. 4(2)(b).
[35] Ibid., Sch. 8, para. 4(3).
[36] Ibid., Sch. 8, para. 5(1).

format and the amount of the premium subject to income tax is then deducted from the chargeable gain.[37] This deduction may reduce a gain but may not create an allowable loss.

37.6 Reverse Premiums

Reverse premiums, better described as lease inducement payments, are paid by the landlord to the tenant to persuade the tenant to take up the lease on the terms offered. Such premiums are now treated as revenue receipts,[38] and so cannot give rise to CGT for the tenant; even before 1999 there were no CGT implications for the tenant since the tenant was not disposing of an asset. The landlord is usually carrying on a trade so that these expenses would be deductible under Schedule D, Case I; where the landlord in not carrying on a trade the statutory hypothesis of the trade will prevent any CGT deduction. Further, any expenditure would at best be to enhance the value of the landlord's interest and, since this will cease to be reflected in the state of the asset[39] once the lease has expired, it is yet again not deductible.

37.7 Mineral Royalties

Where mineral royalties are received under a mineral lease or agreement, one half of the royalties received are treated as income and one half as capital.[40] The capital element is then a capital sum derived from an asset.[41] Where the royalty relates not only to the winning and working of the minerals but also to other matters an aportionment mah be needed.[42]

[37] TCGA 1992, Sch. 8, para. 5(2).
[38] FA 1999, s. 54, Sch. 6 (see above at §21.12).
[39] As required by TCGA 1992, s. 38(l)(b).
[40] Ibid., s. 201(1).
[41] Ibid., s. 22(l)(d). See Inland Revenue, *Capital Gains Manual*, CG 12960–6.
[42] The Mineral Royalties (Tax) Regulations 1971 (SI 1971/1035).

38

Options

38.1 Outline

The real world provides many instances of options, ranging from an agreement to buy a specific piece of property, to contracts bought and sold on international exchanges. CGT begins by stating that an option is an asset for CGT,[1] but then provides many other rules. Special rules are required to charge any sums paid on the grant of an option (by treating the grant of an option as a self-standing disposal) and to deal with the effects of both the exercise and abandonment of an option. In addition, there are a number of special computation rules and rules for special types of option. These provisions deal with "call" options, options under which X has a right to buy an asset, and "put" options, where X has a right to sell. It is not necessary that the intended vendor in either of these options should already be the owner of the property.

38.1.1 Definitions

Quoted options are those which are quoted on a recognised stock exchange at the time of the disposal.[2] *Traded options* are those which are quoted on a recognised stock exchange or a recognised futures exchange at the time of the disposal.[3] *Financial options* are those other than traded options, relating to financial matters such as currency, shares, securities or interest rates.[4]

1 TCGA 1992, s. 21(1)(a); see Baxter (1975) *Conv* 240.
2 TCGA 1988, s. 288(1).
3 For "recognised stock exchange" and "futures exchange", see ibid., s. 288(1), (6).
4 Defined ibid.,s. 144(8); the Treasury may expand the financial option category by order (s. 144(9)).

38.2 Grant of Option

The grant of an option is treated as the disposal of an asset, *viz.* the option.[4a] This treatment is provisional; later events may cause the grant to be charged as part of a larger transaction, e.g. where the option is exercised. The Revenue often waits to see whether the option is exercised before making an assessment under this rule, particularly where the sum paid for the option is small and the option period is short. This treatment is specified as to apply in particular, but not (by inference) exclusively, where grantors bind themselves to sell what they do not own, and, because the option is abandoned, never have occasion to own, and where grantors bind themselves to buy what, because the option is abandoned, they do not acquire.[5]

In *Randall* v. *Plumb*[6] the taxpayer received £25,000 for the grant of the option but this sum was repayable in certain circumstances; the court decided that, in the circumstances, the contingent obligation to repay had to be taken into account notwithstanding the option rules. So the Revenue could not simply charge the whole £25,000.

Any part disposal, which might otherwise arise if the option was granted over property in which the grantor had an interest and the option were specifically enforceable, is excluded.[7] The exclusion of the part disposal appears to be applied by the Revenue only for the purpose of computing gains on the grant of the options. If, on general principles the option is an interest in the underlying asset (as in the case of an option to acquire an estate in land), the gain may qualify for reliefs such as replacement of business assets, provided the requisite conditions are satisfied in relation to the underlying asset.[8]

Since the grant of an option is considered to be a disposal of a separate asset, and not a part disposal of the grantor's interest in the asset, there is no allowable expenditure other than incidental costs of disposal and the full net amount of any consideration received for the grant of the option is taxable. Neither indexation nor tapering relief applies.

The grant of an option to acquire an asset can be a disposal even though the grantor will not dispose of any asset when the option is exercised; for example, if a company issues options to subscribe for its own shares, the exercise of the options would not involve any disposal by the company.

38.3 Simple Disposal of Option

Where a person entitled to exercise an option disposes of it, e.g. by sale, exchange or gift, the gain or loss is computed according to normal CGT principles, including, where appropriate, the wasting asset rules. Special rules apply only where the disposal is by the abandonment of the option or by its exercise.

The disposal of a *traded* option by the grantor is disregarded for CGT if it arises because the option is closed out by acquisition of a second traded option of the same description.

4a Ibid., s. 144(1).
5 Ibid., s. 144(1).
6 [1975] STC 191, (1975) 50 TC 392; criticised by Baxter [175] *Conv* 240, 243, 247. See also above at §37.5
7 *Randall* v. *Plumb*, ibid.; and *Strange* v. *Openshaw* [1983] STC 416, (1983) 57 TC 544.
8 Revenue interpretation RI 11.

The costs of closing out, including the cost of the second option plus incidental costs of acquisition, are deducted in computing the gain on grant of the original option.[9]

38.3.1 *Abandonment of option*

General rule

The abandonment of the option by the person entitled to exercise is not normally a disposal.[10] The effect is to prevent any argument that any money lost by the grantee should give rise to an allowable loss.

Deemed disposal due to receipt of capital sum on abandonment

Case-law holds that there will however be a disposal by the grantee if a capital sum is received for abandoning the option. This disposal is taken to arise under TCGA 1992, s. 22 as the receipt of a capital sum derived from an asset.[11] The receipt of a sum for the "release and abandonment" of an option was treated in the same way;[12] it follows that an agreement to release the option may also amount to an abandonment and the sum received taxed in full. It is more than likely that the draftsmen did not consider abandonment for consideration.[13]

Losses and certain types of option

An allowable loss may be treated as arising if the option is a quoted option to subscribe for shares, a traded option, a financial option, or an option to acquire business assets. This is because in relation to these assets, TCGA 1992, s. 144(4) directs that there is to be a disposal on abandonment. In computing the losses the wasting asset rules in s. 46 do not apply.[14]

Forfeiture of deposit as abandonment of option

The forfeiture of a deposit paid in contemplation of a proposed purchase or in respect of any other transaction is treated as if it were the abandonment of an option binding the grantor to sell.[15] Hence, there is no loss relief for the person losing the deposit. However, there is a disposal of an asset (the option) by the party who received the deposit; the amount forfeited is treated as the consideration received. Since the "option" is a chargeable asset in its own right these consequences ensue even though the asset to which it relates may have been exempt, e.g. a private residence.

[9] TCGA 1992, s. 148.

[10] Ibid., s. 144(4).

[11] *Golding* v. *Kaufman* [1985] STC 152, (1985) 58 TC 296. The decision of Vinelott J. has been criticised for giving an unduly wide meaning to the term "abandonment" when the same result could have been reached by a simpler route: see Marsh [1985] *BTR* 124. On this basis, "abandonment" should be narrowly construed, so leaving releases and surrenders of options within the CGT net.

[12] *Welbeck Securities Ltd.* v. *Powlson* [1987] STC 468, (1987) 60 TC 269, CA; criticised by JFAJ [1987] *BTR* 304.

[13] JFAJ [1987] *BTR* 304, 307 arguing that such sums are not within CGT.

[14] TCGA 1992, s. 146.

[15] Ibid., s. 144(7).

38.4 Exercise of Option

On exercise of the option, the grant and the exercise are treated as one transaction;[16] the disposal is treated as taking place when the option is exercised.[17] One effect of this rule is to prevent a sale from being carried out in two stages by option and exercise so as to take double advantage of the annual exemption. However, for the purposes of the indexation allowance, the cost of the option is treated as an expense separate from the price paid for the option. Taper relief applies as from the exercise of the option.[18]

38.4.1 Treatment of grantor

Call options

In the case of a "call" option, i.e. one binding the grantor to sell an asset, the consideration received for grant of the option is treated as part of the consideration for the sale.[19] From this, it may be inferred that the single transaction referred to is the sale of the asset. Hence, there is no longer any liability under s. 144(1) on the grant of the option.

Non-chargeable gains

Where the exercise of the option involves a transaction which is not a disposal, e.g. an option followed by the issue of shares by a company, no chargeable gain arises either under s. 144(1) on grant of the option or under s. 144(2) on the subsequent transaction. A similar non-chargeable result would occur if the option were one to purchase an asset where the disposal of the asset would be exempt, e.g. the grantor's principal private residence.

Cash settlements

A special rule applies where the grantor pays the option holder cash in full settlement of all obligations under the option. The grant and exercise are treated as a single transaction in which the money paid for the option is the consideration for the option and the sum paid in settlement is an item of incidental expenditure incurred.[20] Apportionments are applied where a payment is made in partial settlement.

Put options

In the case of a "put" option, i.e. one binding the grantor to buy, the consideration for the option is deducted from the grantor's allowable costs in respect of the asset when that asset is subsequently disposed of.[21]

Indexation

Although the allowable costs are reduced, it does not follow that indexation relief will be available only in respect of the expenditure as reduced. This relief continues to be available in respect of the sum paid for the option as from the time it was paid.[22]

16 TCGA 1992, s. 144(2).
17 Ibid., s. 28(2).
18 Ibid., Sch. A1, para. 13.
19 Ibid., s. 1444(2)(a).
20 Ibid., s. 144A, added FA 1994.
21 TCGA 1992, s. 144(2)(b).
22 Ibid., s. 57(2), (3).

38.4.2 Treatment of grantee

The exercise of an option is not a disposal of any asset by the grantee.[23] Whether the option is exercised as between the original parties or assignees, the acquisition and the exercise of the option are treated as a single transaction.

Call options

Where the option binds the grantor to sell, the grantee's costs in acquiring the option are added to the costs of acquiring the asset. Although the option would have been a wasting asset in relation to a disposal of the option, there is no reduction in the cost of the option. Indexation relief is applied to the two sums separately.[24]

Connected persons

Different rules apply on disposal of an asset acquired by the exercise of an option in situations involving connected persons. Where the grantor and the grantee are connected persons, a loss accruing to the grantee will be an allowable loss only if it accrues on the disposal of the option at arm's length to a person not connected with him.[25] It follows that in the case of a call option, the disposal of any asset acquired by exercise of the option cannot give rise to an allowable loss.

Cash settlements

Where the grantor pays the option holder cash in full settlement of all obligations under the option, the grant and exercise are treated as a single transaction in which the sum paid is the consideration for the disposal of the option and the settlement money is treated as an item of incidental expenditure incurred.[26] Apportionments are made where a payment is made in partial settlement.

Put options

Where the option binds the grantor to buy, the cost of the option to the grantee (or to his assignees) is treated as an incidental cost in relation to the grantee's disposal of an asset on exercising the option.[27] It follows that there will be no indexation relief in respect of the cost of the option. If the grantor and the grantee are connected persons, no allowable loss can arise to the grantee on exercise of the option.[28]

38.5 Options Binding Grantor to Transactions other than Sale or Purchase

References to options include options binding the grantor to grant a lease for a premium or to enter into any other transaction which is not a sale; references to buying and selling in pursuance of an option are construed accordingly.[29] If X grants Y a binding option to grant

23 Ibid., s. 144(3).
24 Ibid., s. 145.
25 Ibid., s. 18(5).
26 Ibid., s. 144A, added FA 1994.
27 TCGA 1992, s. 144(3)(b).
28 Ibid., s. 18(4).
29 Ibid., s. 144(6).

a lease and the option is exercised, the grant of the option plus the grant of the lease for a premium are treated as a single transaction. The consideration received by X for the option will be added to the premium on the lease; the sum will be treated as received by X for the grant of the lease. If the option is not exercised, X is treated as having disposed of the option[30] and so is chargeable.

Since neither the abandonment nor the exercise of the option by Y is a disposal of any asset by Y, a forfeited deposit is not an allowable loss.[31]

Where Y exercises the option, the acquisition of the option and the transaction resulting from its exercise are treated as a single transaction. Y's acquisition costs for the lease will be the sum paid for the option and the premium.

Just as with an option to buy or sell, so the option may relate to a transaction which is not a disposal for CGT, e.g. an option binding a company to issue shares to the holder of the option. Where, on the exercise of the option, the grant of the option and the issue of the shares are treated as a single transaction,[32] no chargeable gain arises. Chargeable gains could, however, arise if the option was abandoned and never exercised, as the grant of the option is treated as a disposal.

38.6 Application of Wasting Asset Rules

An option having a predictable life of 50 years or less is a wasting asset; the rules[33] restricting the deduction of expenditure therefore apply. The costs are written off over the life of the option on a straight-line basis.

If there is a transfer of an option to buy or sell quoted shares or securities, the option is regarded as a wasting asset, the life of which ends when the right to exercise it ends or, if earlier, when it becomes valueless.[34]

If the option is exercised, the full amount paid for the grant is added to (or deducted from) the amount payable on exercise, without writing off any amount up to the date of exercise.

These wasting rules do not, however, apply to options to acquire assets to be used for the purposes of a trade carried on by the person acquiring the assets. In addition, the rules do not apply to a quoted option to subscribe for shares in a company,[35] traded options or financial options.

38.7 Further Rules

Gains accruing on the disposal by any person of any option or contract to acquire or dispose of gilt-edged securities or qualifying corporate bonds are not chargeable gains.[36] This is because chargeable gains do not arise on the disposal of either of these assets.

Further rules apply to options over rights to acquire qualifying shares in a building society, various employee share option and incentive schemes.[37]

[30] Under TA 1988, s. 144(1).
[31] TCGA 1992, s. 144(7).
[32] Ibid., s. 144(2).
[33] Ibid., s. 46.
[34] Ibid., s. 146(2), (4)(b).
[35] Ibid.
[36] S. 115. The concept of disposing of the contract is widened by s. 115(3) to cover the closing-out of the contract by entering into a contract with reciprocal obligations, i.e. a matched transaction.
[37] TCGA 1992, ss 149–149B.

Printed in the United Kingdom
by Lightning Source UK Ltd.
102507UKS00001B/40-99

9 787770 041327